Adobe® Creative Suite Bible

Adobe® Creative Suite Bible

Ted Padova
Kelly Murdock
Wendy Halderman

Wiley Publishing, Inc.

Adobe® Creative Suite Bible

Published by
Wiley Publishing, Inc.
111 River Street
Hoboken, N.J. 07030-5774
www.wiley.com

Copyright © 2004 by Wiley Publishing, Inc., Indianapolis, Indiana

Published by Wiley Publishing, Inc., Indianapolis, Indiana

Published simultaneously in Canada

ISBN: 0-7645-7155-9

Manufactured in the United States of America

10 9 8 7 6 5 4 3 2 1

1B/QR/QZ/QU/IN

For general information on our other products and services or to obtain technical support, please contact our Customer Care Department within the U.S. at (800) 762-2974, outside the U.S. at (317) 572-3993 or fax (317) 572-4002.

Wiley also publishes its books in a variety of electronic formats. Some content that appears in print may not be available in electronic books.

Library of Congress Control Number: 2004111951

Trademarks: Wiley and the Wiley logo are trademarks or registered trademarks of John Wiley and Sons, Inc. and/or its affiliates. Adobe is a registered trademark of Adobe Systems Incorporated. All other trademarks are the property of their respective owners. Wiley Publishing, Inc. is not associated with any product or vendor mentioned in this book.

WILEY

About the Authors

Ted Padova is the author of more than a dozen computer books, the most recent include: *Adobe Acrobat PDF Bible* (John Wiley & Sons) versions 4, 5, & 6; *Adobe Acrobat 6 Complete Course*; *Creating Adobe Acrobat Forms*; and *Teach Yourself Visually Acrobat 5*. He is the host for Total Training Systems Total Acrobat 6 series of seven videos on Acrobat Standard and Acrobat Professional.

Ted has been involved in PostScript imaging for over a decade and started a computer service bureau in 1990 in Ventura, California. He is the CEO and managing partner of The Image Source Digital Imaging and Photo Finishing Centers of Thousand Oaks and Ventura California.

For sixteen years, he has been a university instructor, teaching classes in Adobe Photoshop; Adobe InDesign; Adobe Illustrator; Adobe PageMaker; QuarkXPress; HTML and Web page design, Scanning and Calibrations; and Adobe Acrobat at the University of California, Santa Barbara and UCLA. He is an internationally recognized expert on Adobe Acrobat, PDF, and digital imaging, speaking nationally and abroad at many computer conferences.

Kelly Murdock has been authoring computer books for several years now and still gets immense enjoyment from the completed work. His book credits include various Web, graphics, and multimedia titles, including four previous editions of the book, *3ds max 6 Bible*. Other major accomplishments include *Master VISUALLY HTML and XHTML, JavaScript Visual Blueprint, Adobe Atmosphere Bible*, and co-authoring duties on two editions of the *Illustrator Bible* (for versions 9 and 10).

With a background in engineering and computer graphics, Kelly has had many opportunities to flex his design muscles from Web site creation and design to freelance 3D design projects. In his spare time, Kelly enjoys the outdoors and loves rock climbing, mountain biking or skiing. He has recently formed a design company with his brother, Chris, called Logical Paradox Design.

Wendy Halderman is an award-winning typographer, graphic designer, and fine artist. As both a staff and freelance designer, she has produced a wide variety of marketing communication materials for clients in the financial, retail, IT, media, educational, and non-profit industries. Her 14-year-old company, Halderman Graphic Design, is based in Ventura, California, and serves clients nationwide.

Credits

Acquisitions Editor
Tom Heine

Project Editor
Maureen Spears

Technical Editor
Adam Pratt

Copy Editor
Elizabeth Kuball

Editorial Manager
Robyn Siesky

Vice President & Group Executive Publisher
Richard Swadley

Vice President & Executive Publisher
Bob Ipsen

Vice President and Executive Publisher
Barry Pruett

Project Coordinator
Maridee Ennis

Graphics and Production Specialists
Beth Brooks
Jonelle Burns
Amanda Carter
Lauren Goddard
Denny Hager
Joyce Haughey
Jennifer Heleine
Barbara Moore
Lynsey Osborn
Ron Terry
Mary Gillot Virgin

Quality Control Technician
John Greenough

Proofreading and Indexing
TECHBOOKS Production Services

Acknowledgments

The authors want to thank the production crew and staff at Wiley Publishing for all their support and assistance in producing this work and our Acquisition Editor, Tom Heine for his continued support throughout the project.

Additionally, we want to extend a big thank you to our Technical Editor Adam Pratt, Application Engineer at Adobe Systems for the Creative Pro Products. Thank you Adam for all your support and assistance.

We extend our appreciation to many fine people, too numerous to mention, at Adobe Systems who are always readily available to answer questions and the entire development teams for the Creative Suite products.

Ted Padova

Above all I want to thank my colleague and best friend Wendy Halderman for jumping in to rescue the project and help us get the book out on time. With a schedule that had no room for taking on additional projects, Wendy graciously added her expertise in writing chapters on design and typography. Thank you Wendy for doing such a great job.

I'd also like to thank our other co-author Kelly Murdock who took on a rigorous schedule completing his assignment within an impossible time frame. Thank you Kelly for all your great contributions.

Kelly Murdock

The first person, I'd like to thank would be Ted for inviting me to be a part of this project. Ted has been the steady hand that has guided this project with his vision and direction. I could always count on him to provide the honest feedback that pushed me to do my best.

I'd also like to extend thanks to Tom Heine, the editor at Wiley who invited me to join Ted in the project, and all the other editors and personnel at Wiley for their consistent excellent work, especially Maureen Spears, who played a key role in the development of this title.

As always, I'd like to extend a warm thanks to my dear wife and children who have sacrificed much in letting me take on yet another book project. To Angie, I'd like to apologize for letting the "honey do" list get so long, to Eric, thanks for not playing any network games on my main computer while I've been writing and to Thomas, how about a long bike ride (I guess we should get your bike fixed first) and a game of football.

I'd also like to thank the fine individuals at Adobe and Extensis who were quick to get me the latest versions of the software that I needed for this project and for creating such great solid products that have been a joy to work with.

Wendy Halderman

My heartfelt appreciation goes to Ted Padova, whose unwavering support and enthusiasm made my contribution to this book possible. Without his superior guidance, I never would have made it through the storm. I also want to thank my three wonderful sons, Cody, Dillon and Warren, who always find a way to make me laugh when I need it most. You are truly my life's greatest gifts.

Contents at a Glance

Contents

Part I: Getting to Know the Creative Suite   1

Part II: Getting Started with Design Workflows   173

Chapter 5: Creating Production Workflows 175

Chapter 6: Creating Color-Managed Workflows 185

Chapter 7: Using Version Cue 201

Part III: Working with Objects and Images   221

Chapter 8: Creating, Selecting, and Editing Objects and Images 223

Part IV: Working with Type   481

Chapter 13: Working with Fonts 483

Chapter 14: Working with Styles 497

Chapter 15: Working with Text Frames 535

Part VII: Document Repurposing   779

Part IX: Printing and Digital Prepress   1031

Chapter 34: Choosing Print Setups 1033

Chapter 35: Commercial Printing 1067

Appendix: Keyboard Shortcuts in the Adobe CS Programs 1097

Introduction

Welcome to the Adobe Creative Suite Bible — your comprehensive guide to working with the complete suite of Adobe's imaging programs. In this book, we make an effort to help you understand design and productivity features available from all the Creative Suite (CS) programs and how the documents you create from the individual applications work together to help you create and publish content for print, Web hosting, and CD-ROM replication.

So why would we spend time covering subjects that are individually treated in other Wiley Bible publications? This is a good question and the answer should be clear to you before you walk out of your local bookstore with this sizeable volume. It's true that there is a Wiley Bible covering each of the individual programs mentioned in this book. These other works are comprehensive and teach you just about every tool and feature related to the specific programs.

This book is much different than the other Bibles. Our primary focus is to cover workflow solutions for independent designers and members of design teams working in agencies, publication houses, and any firm related to publishing for screen, print, and Web. Therefore, we won't go into minute detail on each program, and often we point you to one of the other fine Wiley publications to amplify your learning.

We assume you have some experience in at least one of the programs covered in this book. You may be a designer who works religiously with Adobe Photoshop, QuarkXPress, and Macromedia FreeHand. Or you may work with Adobe Illustrator and Adobe Photoshop, but know little about page-layout programs. What you need to know are essential methods for integrating application documents among the CS programs. Perhaps you don't need to know every aspect of Adobe InDesign, but you want to create sophisticated layouts using many outstanding type features and want to know how to import images in your designs.

If you're switching from another program or you want to add one of the CS applications to your design toolbox, this book helps you understand the relationships among programs and how to seamlessly integrate files among the most sophisticated suite of software applications ever developed for creative professionals.

As we said, the focus is on workflow solutions. In this book, you learn how to set up the CS applications for workflow environments, step through the creative workflow process, and get to productivity without having to master every feature in a program. The tools and tasks related to office workers and business professionals have been left out. Rather, the emphasis is on a complete coverage of tools and workflows to help creative professionals get up to speed fast.

How to Read This Book

The *Adobe Creative Suite Bible* is made up of 35 chapters in 9 parts. Unlike other comprehensive computer publications that target beginning users, reading this volume assumes you have some basic knowledge of at least one imaging program like Photoshop, an illustration program, or a layout program. We further assume you know something about user interfaces common to imaging programs that use palettes, menus, and tools. And, we make the assumption you know some aspects of the professional printing market for commercial prepress and printing.

Because you have some knowledge of computer programs similar to those found in the Creative Suite, you can jump in anywhere and learn about any feature set. In most chapters, we include a discussion concerning the integration of the CS programs. Therefore, a chapter dealing with text includes text handling not only in InDesign, but Illustrator, Photoshop, GoLive, and Acrobat. Rather than think of the programs you want to learn about, search more for the techniques and features you want to learn.

To give you a broad idea of how the programs work together, we recommend you look over Chapter 2, where we provide steps you can replicate to produce a design piece using the CS programs. Chapter 2 helps you understand the interoperability of the CS programs.

Apart from Chapter 2 and the specific features you want to learn, keep in mind that this book, like other Wiley Bible publications, is a reference work. Keep it handy as you work in the CS applications, and refer to the index and contents when you need help working on a task or trying to further understand one of the programs.

Icons

What would a Bible be without icons? The use of icons throughout the book offer you an at-a-glance hint of what content is being addressed. You can jump to the text adjacent to these symbols to help you get a little more information, warn you of a potential problem or amplify the concept being addressed in the text. In this book you'll find the following icons:

A caution icon alerts you to a potential problem in using one of the CS applications, any tools or menus, or any issues related to exchanging files between programs. Pay close attention to these caution messages to avoid some problems.

A note icon signifies a message that may add more clarity or help you deal with a feature more effectively.

Tips help you find shortcuts to produce results or work through a series of steps to complete a task. Some tips provide you with information that may not be documented in the Help files accompanying each of the CS programs.

Walking you through steps and techniques in a linear fashion is almost impossible for a suite of programs. The applications have so many interrelated features that covering all aspects of a single feature in one part of a book just doesn't work. Therefore some common features for commands, tools, actions, or tasks may be spread out and discussed in different chapters. When the information is divided between different parts of the book, you'll find a Cross-Reference icon that refers you to another part of the book covering related information.

The Book Contents

To simplify your journey through the Creative Suite applications, the book is broken up into nine separate parts. There are a total of 35 chapters that address features common to creative production workflows. These parts are covered in the following sections.

Part I: Getting to Know the Creative Suite

To start off, we offer some basic information related to the Creative Suite Premium Edition. You're given a tour of the programs in the form of steps to produce design pieces and learn how these applications work together to help you publish your content. You learn how to set up the work environments in all the programs and set preference options for standardizing workflows.

Part II: Getting Started with Design Workflows

Design workflow is a broad term and may mean different things to different people. This part clarifies the meaning of workflow solutions as they apply to creative professionals and the CS applications, as well as introduces you to new tools for versioning documents and creating consistent color across the CS programs.

Part III: Working with Objects and Images

You have basically three elements used to communicate messages in artwork. Images, objects, and type constitute the content of your products. In this part, we focus on objects you might create in Illustrator, InDesign, and Photoshop, as well as images that are edited in Photoshop and imported into other CS programs.

Part IV: Working with Type

Setting type and working with type as text and objects are standard design practices everyone uses. With many new features for setting type in the CS applications, this part offers you a glimpse into how you can use the programs to implement these impressive new features.

Part V: Using Creative Suite and Microsoft

Whether Microsoft Office is part of your design toolbox or you acquire files from clients who provide you with Office documents, it's hard to talk about layout and design without introducing Office files. This part covers working with files that originate in Office programs and end up in one or more of the CS applications.

Part VI: Working in Creative Design Workflows

The CS applications offer you more than tools to create artwork. You can set up review sessions where you and your colleagues or clients mark up documents in a review session for collaboration. By using templates and models for design pieces, you can minimize duplication and learn to work faster. This part covers aspects of both collaboration and working efficiently.

Part VII: Document Repurposing

When you create documents for one output purpose and need to modify files for other output results, you're engaged in document repurposing. Rather than start anew each time a modification needs to be made for delivering files for alternative content, you can save time by reworking existing documents suited for a variety of purposes. This part covers various aspects of document repurposing.

Part VIII: Creative Suite Document Delivery Workflows

Issues related to Digital Rights Management, archiving documents, delivering files for Web hosting, and replicating CD-ROMs are but some of the delivery workflows you're likely to experience. This part covers preparing files for delivery in various forms.

Part IX: Printing and Digital Prepress

Printing files is still a major function of every creative professional's workflow. This part covers printing to composite printers and preparing files for commercial printing.

Appendices

Appendix A contains an extensive list of tables describing keyboard shortcuts for all the CS programs. As you work with customizing keyboard shortcuts as described in Chapter 3 or you want to expand your knowledge of using shortcuts, refer to Appendix A.

Staying Connected

About every five minutes, new products and new upgrades are distributed. If you purchase a software product, you can often find an updated revision not too long after release. Manufacturers are relying more and more on Internet distribution and less on postal delivery. You should plan on making routine visits to Adobe's Web site as well as the Web sites of manufacturers of third-party products. Anyone who has a Web site will offer a product revision for downloading or offer you details on acquiring the update.

Internet connection

With newer releases of computer software, it's almost essential that you have an Internet connection. The CS programs routinely prompt you to check for updates over the Internet. To optimize your performance with all the programs, you should run the software on a computer that has an Internet connection.

Contact Adobe Systems

Adobe Systems maintains a comprehensive Web site where you can find information on product upgrades, conferences and seminars, aftermarket books, help and technical support, as well as tips and techniques. Visit Adobe's Web site at www.adobe.com for the latest news related to all the CS applications.

Registration

Regardless of whether you purchase the Creative Suite or individual applications, Adobe Systems has made it possible to register the product. You can register on the World Wide Web or mail a registration form to Adobe. You'll find great advantages in being a registered user. First, update information will be sent to you, so you'll know when a product revision occurs. Secondly, information can be distributed to help you achieve the most out of using all the Creative Suite programs. By all means, complete the registration. It will be to your benefit.

Contacting Us

If, after reviewing this publication, you feel some important information was overlooked or you have any questions concerning the Creative Suite programs, you can contact us and let us know your views, opinions, hoorahs, complaints, or provide information that might get included in the next revision. If it's good enough, you might even get a credit line in the acknowledgments. By all means, send a note. E-mail inquiries can be sent to:

Ted at ted@west.net

Wendy at whalderman@earthlink.com

Kelly at kmurdock@sfcn.org

If you happen to have some problems with any of the CS programs, keep in mind, we did not engineer the programs. Inquiries for technical support should be directed to the software manufacturer(s) of any products you use. This is one more good reason to complete your registration form.

Getting to Know the Creative Suite

Introducing the Adobe Creative Suite

The Adobe Premium Creative Suite is composed of several programs designed to work together to accomplish all your publishing needs for output to print, screen viewing, and Web hosting. Instead of marketing the individual program components of the Creative Suite, Adobe Systems has spent much of its marketing effort targeting the entire Creative Suite to design professionals.

This chapter offers a description of the Creative Suite programs and gives you an idea for how they work together. In this chapter, you learn about the purpose of each program and the relationship each program has with other members of the Creative Suite team. Also, you receive a brief summary of new features contained in the latest releases of the individual programs.

Why Creative Suite?

For the most part, each program in the Creative Suite is an upgrade from a previous version, and each is available for upgrades individually. So, why is Adobe Systems spending so much marketing effort informing users about the benefits of the Creative Suite? And why talk about the Creative Suite as a single entity when users are likely to upgrade the individual software programs in their design studios? Or, you may think that you have one program developed by another software manufacturer that satisfies your design needs and fully supports document integration with many of the programs found in the Creative Suite. For example, you may use Adobe Photoshop and Adobe Illustrator along with QuarkXPress, or perhaps you use Adobe Photoshop and create layouts in Macromedia FreeHand. Possibly, these are the first questions on your mind as you see the advertising for Adobe imaging product upgrades.

The answer is that Creative Suite is a single design solution where the whole is greater than its parts. For years, Adobe Systems built applications on programs like Adobe Illustrator and Adobe InDesign as the core PDF technology. These programs evolved with common elements so that you, the creative professional, could easily exchange files among Adobe programs.

Rather than rely on a single program to perform tasks such as illustration, layout, and printing, Adobe offers you several applications, each a tool designed for a specific purpose to help you become more efficient in your creative process. These tools seamlessly integrate into the greater toolbox called Adobe Creative Suite. After working in individual programs, you can collect the creative elements together using Adobe InDesign CS as the tool to perform layout assembly. You can then travel to output by exporting files to PDF documents in Adobe Acrobat, or you can host parts of your layout on a Web site using Adobe GoLive CS.

As stand-alone programs, Adobe Creative Suite offers many new marvelous tools with enhanced features to create, design, and express your ideas. Individually, the CS applications are among the most impressive upgrades offered by any software manufacturer. Collectively, these tools are no less than amazing.

Native file support

The strongest argument for using Adobe Photoshop CS, Adobe Illustrator CS, Adobe InDesign CS, and Adobe GoLive CS together is that native file formats are easily transported between the CS programs. You no longer need to decide about saving Photoshop files as TIFF, EPS, GIF, PNG, or JPEG. Rather, you can import a native Photoshop PSD or Illustrator AI file into Adobe InDesign CS complete with layers and transparency. You can also import native Illustrator and Photoshop files directly in Adobe GoLive CS. The native file format import feature alone can save you space on your hard drive, because you need to save only a single file. Additionally, you save time in importing the correct file because only a single file is saved from the host application and used in your page layout or Web design. You can also directly open native Illustrator CS files in any Adobe Acrobat viewer, and you can open PDF documents in Illustrator and import them into InDesign and GoLive.

Cross-Reference   For information on importing native file formats across programs, see Part III.

Consistent user interface

Programs that creative professionals use today are sophisticated and complicated. One of the major problems facing many designers is the long learning curve necessary to become productive in a computer program. When you use several programs from several different computer-software manufacturers, your learning curve increases. Application-software companies develop software according to standards each company sets forth in the design of the user interface. One company may make extensive use of context-sensitive menus, while another company may avoid them. One company may use palettes and panes liberally, while another company relies on menu commands and dialog boxes. Add to these differences the extended use of keyboard shortcuts; program differences require you to spend a lot of time learning shortcuts. Additionally, the confusion of remembering one key sequence in one program invokes a different command than the same key sequence in another program.

In workflow environments, consistency is crucial. Time is money, and the time required to train your staff cuts into your productivity and your profits. When you use tools all developed by a single software manufacturer, you become more consistent in the design of the user interface and the keyboard shortcuts that access menus, tools, and commands. Adobe has taken the user interface design one step further by offering customizable keyboard shortcuts and custom workspaces in several CS programs.

Having a consistent look and feel in the user interface enables you to develop an intuitive sense for how to use a particular program to create a design project. The more intuitive the sense you develop about a manufacturer's products, the faster you can become productive. In some cases, you can jump into a new program, poke around, and understand many features without reading exhaustive manuals and books.

Cross-Reference For information on customizing workspaces and keyboard shortcuts, see Chapter 4.

Versioning tools

How many times have you created a tight comp and had a client tell you that he likes another version of the layout? You may create duotone images in Photoshop, offer a proof print to your client, and have the client tell you he wants another spot color in the Photoshop images. You offer a second proof and the client informs you the first proof print is really the one that best fits his campaign. You're back at your design studio scrambling through your hard drive looking for the first versions, locating the files and importing or relinking them back into the layout.

The Creative Suite lets you easily revisit earlier versions of illustrations, photo images, and layouts. Along with the standalone programs in the Creative Suite, you also receive Version Cue, a marvelous utility that permits you to save multiple versions of a design in the same file. You decide what version to promote to the current look, and the linked file in your InDesign CS document dynamically update. In workflow environments, nothing could more easily track the current version of a design and get you to final output swiftly with the correct version.

Cross-Reference For more information on installing and using Version Cue, see Part II.

Consistent color management

Have you ever created an illustration, dropped it into a layout program, and seen a completely different color rendered in the layout? How about scanned images appearing with one color in Adobe Photoshop and different color values in the layout program? With the Adobe Creative Suite, you can access the same color engine and color-management policies among the design programs and Adobe Acrobat. More than ever before, color management is true between programs and helps you produce files containing colors you expect to be replicated.

Cross-Reference For more information on managing color across the Creative Suite programs, see Chapter 6.

Dynamic object and image editing

Ever have last-minute changes that you need to make before the last FedEx pickup of the day? A layout is complete, but you need to quickly change an illustration or a photo image. In programs like Adobe InDesign CS, or even with embedded objects and images in PDF files, a double-click of the mouse button or the selection of a menu command launches the editing program that created the object or image and opens the file in a document window. You make your edits, save the file, and the edited version is dynamically updated in InDesign CS or Acrobat Professional. This kind of quick editing keeps you from having to find the original object or image, make edits, save back to another file format, update the link, and re-create a PDF file.

Cross-Reference For more information on dynamic object and image editing, see Chapter 24.

Visual file exchanges

Let's face it; creative people are more visual and often work best in situations where they can first see a document before importing it in another program. More than ever before, Adobe has created a visually friendly workplace for you. You can easily drag and drop objects and images between document windows from one program to another, drag files from the desktop to open document windows, and copy and paste objects and images between documents.

Cross-Reference

For more information on importing and exchanging documents among programs, see Part III.

Support for PDF

With InDesign CS as the central core of your Creative Suite programs for design purposes, PDF is the central file format for file exchanges and printing. All the Adobe CS programs support PDF imports and exports. InDesign CS supports exports to PDF/X format, which creates reliable documents for commercial printing. Photoshop CS supports the creation of PDF slideshows; Illustrator CS and InDesign CS support PDF creation with Adobe PDF Layers; and GoLive CS supports PDF imports as smart objects, PDF previews, and PDF exports. You can import media such as movie clips and sound files in InDesign CS and export them to PDF. Because PDF is the reliable standard for on-screen document viewing and output to professional printing devices, the CS programs take advantage of core PDF architecture.

Cross-Reference

For more information on PDF/X and commercial printing, see Chapter 35. For more information on PDFs and multimedia, see Chapter 29.

Understanding the Creative Suite

There are two versions of the Adobe Creative Suite. The Adobe Standard Creative Suite includes Adobe Photoshop CS, Adobe Illustrator CS, Adobe InDesign CS, and Version Cue. The Adobe Premium Creative Suite includes the same programs with the addition of Adobe Acrobat Professional and Adobe GoLive CS. We cover all the premium edition programs in the other chapters in this book. In addition to the programs, you also get more than 100 OpenType faces with the Creative Suite editions.

Note

Although the programs typically referred to as the CS applications include those mentioned in the preceding paragraph, you also find the addition of Adobe ImageReady CS. The CS version is also a new upgrade to ImageReady 7, which shipped with Photoshop 7.

Each of the programs is an upgrade from previous versions of the software, and Adobe Systems intends to upgrade the products in tandem for all future versions. Therefore, you can be confident that the next upgrade of a program like Photoshop will also include upgrades to Illustrator, InDesign, and GoLive.

Adobe Photoshop CS

If you're a creative professional, chances are you're no stranger to Adobe Photoshop. Adobe's flagship image-editing program is now in version 8 with the CS upgrade. However, the re-branding of the products refers to this version simply as Photoshop CS — the CS obviously standing for *Creative Suite*. As a stand-alone product, Photoshop has some very nice additions to an already feature-rich program. New enhancements to Photoshop add tools and options specific to interests by graphic designers, photographers, and Web designers. Among some of the more impressive additions to the program you'll find:

✦ **Enhanced File Browser:** The File Browser has been greatly improved in Photoshop CS. The new File Browser enables you to set custom thumbnail views, to flag files for viewing, and to set workspaces with different File Browser options for viewing and editing document metadata such as author, copyright information, modification date, keywords. You can search within the File Browser for files by keywords and view the search results in the File Browser window.

The File Browser enables you to select files in a contiguous or noncontiguous group and apply batch procedures to the selected files. From the Automate menu in the File Browser, you can perform actions like using Contact Sheet II with selected files and/or folders; export images to PDF that open in Full Screen mode in Acrobat complete with auto page flips with transitions; set up Web galleries; and execute batch sequences. Particularly helpful in workflows are the new features for saving work histories to a log file. You can save all the edits to a given image in the history file so other members of your design team can review them.

If you haven't used the File Browser much in previous versions of Photoshop, spending a little time learning the many new options offered by Photoshop CS (shown in Figure 1-1) may convince you to use it as your central digital imaging hub. Instead of using the Open command and browsing to folder locations, the File Browser along with the enhanced search features enables you to find files faster than ever.

Figure 1-1: The Photoshop CS File Browser

✦ **Customize keyboard shortcuts:** Ask yourself how many times you invert an image compared to the number of times you visit the Image Size dialog box. Shouldn't you use Ctrl/⌘+I to open the Image Size dialog box instead of converting a positive image to a negative image? If you agree, you can remap this keyboard shortcut along with any other keyboard shortcuts to execute commands to your liking. Photoshop CS enables you to customize your environment to suit your own preferences.

Caution   If you work in studios where you participate in workflows with other designers, be certain to plan your CS application preferences with members of your design team, especially if other workers use your computer. Individual users setting different environment preferences defeats the purpose of the Creative Suite. Remember, consistency across software and the machines used in your workflows reduces time to train new employees and helps set a consistent standard in your company. For more information on setting up work environments among the CS programs, see Chapter 3.

✦ **Convert Camera Raw files:** No longer do you need a $99 plug-in to open Camera Raw files in Photoshop. The new CS version supports opening many common digital cameras using native Camera Raw formats. When opening Camera Raw image files, you have an abundant set of features for adjusting calibration, lighting, exposure, brightness, temperature, noise, sharpening, and more.

✦ **New brightness adjustments:** Two nifty new features are in the Image ⇨ Adjustments menu.

   • **Match Color:** Enables you to apply luminosity values from one image to another image. You may have a portrait taken in a studio with excellent lighting and another of the same subject with poor lighting. Or you may have two completely different images, as shown in Figure 1-2, and want to map the brightness values of the better image to the image requiring adjustment. You can handle this without visiting the Levels dialog box, by accessing the Match Color command. You select the open document containing the luminosity values you want to apply from the Source pull-down menu. One click and — presto! — you remap the image, often with startling results.

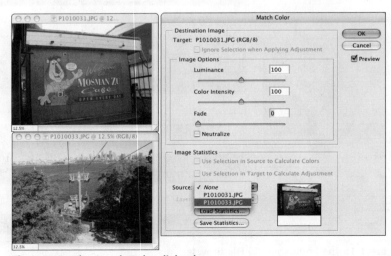

Figure 1-2: The Match Color dialog box

- **Shadow/Highlight adjustment**: You can easily correct foreground images with strong backlights and unintended silhouettes in the Shadow/Highlight dialog box. When you move the control sliders, only shadow and highlight brightness are adjusted, leaving all the midtones unaffected.

✦ **Crop and straighten photos:** If you're gang-scanning images for FPOs (for position only) or for final images, you'll find the Crop and Straighten Photos command in the Automate submenu a wonderful time-saver. Lay two or three photo prints on your scanner plate and scan in Photoshop. Select the Crop and Straighten Photos command and Photoshop automatically duplicates the image, crops out a photo, and repeats the process, eventually ending up with individual images cropped and straightened.

✦ **Filter Gallery:** The dialog box (Figure 1-3) enables you to preview and apply multiple filters, rearrange the order of filters, and preview results when you apply or turn off filters in combinations — all before actually applying the filter to the target image. If you have difficulty retracing your steps when you add multiple filters to create special effects, this feature is something you'll like.

Figure 1-3: The Filter Gallery dialog box enables you to add multiple filters in a dialog box and preview results before applying the filters to the active document.

✦ **Comprehensive 16-bit support:** In Photoshop 7, the Photoshop user community was delighted to see more support for applying many edits to 16-bit images. Now, in Photoshop CS, the editing possibilities in 16-bit files is expanded, offering you options for creating layers, adding type, adding vector shapes, and more.

✦ **Layer comps:** One of our favorite features is the addition of the Layer Comps palette. You can create different layer views in Photoshop and save the layer view as a layer comp. Turn on or off other layers and save as another layer comp. When you want to return to a given layers view, simply click on the respective eye icon in the Layer Comps palette.

✦ **Layer sets:** You can group multiple layers in layer sets much like you group objects you find nested in Adobe Illustrator layers. Create new sets and add layers to individual sets. You can turn on and off views of layer sets and save the different views as layer comps (described in the preceding bullet).

✦ **Add text to paths:** Use the Pen tool to create a path and add text to the path much like you add text to paths in Adobe Illustrator CS and Adobe InDesign CS.

✦ **Photomerge:** Take photos in a panoramic view and let Photoshop assemble the images automatically into a single panoramic image.

✦ **Pixel aspect ratio:** Photoshop introduces previews for images that will be seen on other screen formats such as NTSC monitors and wide screens.

There are many other new additions to Photoshop CS. You can view live histograms as you work, add a lens blur to change the depth of field on images, replace colors in much easier steps, create picture packages, create huge documents supporting 300,000 pixels square with as many as 56 different channels, add special action and title-safe guides for video editing, and much more. As a single program upgrade, Photoshop CS introduces many new features. As part of the CS library of programs, you'll find integration of your photo images with the other CS programs to be a breeze.

Adobe Illustrator CS

Tried and true Adobe Illustrator is the premier illustration program for designers and artists. Many people still use Macromedia Freehand because they know the program well and because they enjoy having multiple pages with different page sizes together in the same document. However, the advantages for using illustration programs together with other applications in the Creative Suite are significantly in favor of Adobe Illustrator. In the current version of Illustrator CS, you can import layered Illustrator files in Adobe InDesign, export layered Illustrator files to Adobe Acrobat while retaining layers in the destination PDF, dynamically edit objects from Acrobat layered PDFs in Illustrator, and take advantage of some new impressive features available in the CS version of Illustrator.

Cross-Reference   For more information on using Adobe Illustrator CS and some of its new features, see Part III.

Adobe Illustrator CS is version 11 of the program and boasts some new features as well as improvements in several areas. Among the best of these updates are an overall improvement in speed and performance, new features for the treatment of type, and a worthwhile Print dialog box. These and other Illustrator CS features include:

✦ **3D Effects:** An impressive 3D rendering function developed from Adobe Dimensions code. This feature is easier and faster than entry-level tools for creating 3D objects. You can revolve and extrude objects with previews as the objects are rendered, adjust lighting effects, and map artwork from objects in your Symbols palette. Target surface areas for mapping artwork are brilliantly shown in the Map Art dialog box selected from within the 3D Revolve Options or 3D Extrude and Bevel Options dialog boxes. As you map artwork to 3D objects, the preview shows a rendered version on the selected object, as shown in Figure 1-4.

✦ **Faster performance:** Just about every object you create or modify in Illustrator CS is rendered in the program much faster than some of the painfully slow operations in earlier versions of the program. The 3D object rendering will dazzle you on computers with moderate speeds and ample RAM.

✦ **Graphic styles:** Think about the object rendering tools discussed earlier in this section and working through a series of dialog boxes to apply rotations and lighting effects, mapping artwork on several sides, and then having to apply the same edits to other objects. Fortunately, Illustrator CS simplifies this process through graphic styles much like you would create styles when using text.

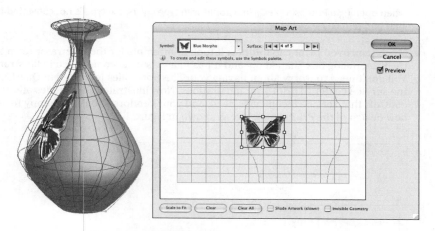

Figure 1-4: Artwork mapped from the Symbols palette

✦ **Scribble effects:** If you are an old-school graphic designer and you like the feel of creating thumbnails and roughs with a little less of the computer-generated artwork appearance and perhaps a softer, friendlier look to your illustrations, the Scribble effect is for you. Create any object and apply Scribble to it much like you would apply a filter.

✦ **New type control:** Illustrator CS has had a major upgrade to type features, including the addition of character and paragraph style sheets. For single-page ads and designs, the addition of style sheets enables you to perform tasks similar to setting type in layout programs.

✦ **Save files as templates:** Illustrator CS introduces saving files as templates, which makes your design workflows much easier when sharing common color swatches, character and paragraph styles, and graphic styles. Create all the style sheets, add colors to your Swatches palette, and save the file as a template. All users in your workflow open the templates and use the same styles and color palettes.

✦ **Enhanced Adobe PDF support:** Illustrator CS includes more Adobe PDF settings (formerly called job options) than previous saves to the PDF format. One great advantage in this new version is saving crop and bleed marks for previewing files designed for print from Adobe Acrobat. You have more consistency with transparency flattening and can save presets to control the attributes associated with saving as PDF. And, of course, Illustrator CS writes to the Acrobat 6 compatibility format, thus supporting Adobe PDF Layers when layered PDF exports are opened in Acrobat.

✦ **Tighter integration with layered Adobe Photoshop files:** Some features are not always obvious when you start using a new upgrade. Take editing text between Illustrator CS files and Photoshop CS files as an example. This version of Illustrator now shares the same text composition technology as Photoshop CS, thereby enabling you to edit text in files imported to and from Photoshop when the vector layers are preserved. When you export files that contain type in vector layers in native Photoshop format, the type is editable. When you save the same file as a Photoshop PDF and then open it in Illustrator CS, the type remains a vector object but converts to outlines.

Note
When opening a Photoshop PDF in Acrobat with type layers, the type is not converted to outlines and remains searchable.

✦ **Much-improved print capabilities:** It took 11 attempts for the Illustrator team to get the Print dialog box shaped up, and it has finally been accomplished in Illustrator CS. You don't need to worry about having your Illustrator files imported in QuarkXPress at the service center to print your illustrations. Now Illustrator CS includes all the print controls that service technicians need, and your vendors should be happy to see the new design of the Print dialog box as shown in Figure 1-5.

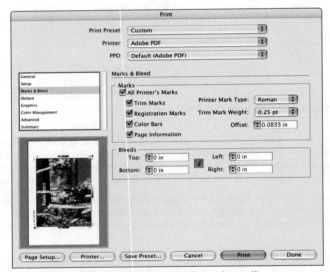

Figure 1-5: The new Illustrator CS dialog box offers much-improved options

✦ **Support for Microsoft Office:** A tighter integration with Microsoft Office files has been implemented in Adobe Illustrator CS. You can export files for importing in Microsoft Word, Excel, and PowerPoint. The artwork generated in Illustrator CS prints and displays with integrity from the Office applications.

✦ **Support for XMP metadata:** XMP (eXtensible Metadata Platform) is an Adobe-developed XML framework that standardizes the creation, processing, and interchange of *metadata*. You can use metadata for searching files and creating templates for importing and exchanging data elements much like a database structure. In a large company where many artists labor to produce content, using XML-based structures eases data through complicated workflows.

Cross-Reference
You may have heard much about XML (eXtensible Markup Language), but you may not know how to create XML documents or what to do with them. In Chapter 27, we cover examples for real-world uses of XML and how you can integrate XMP support from the CS programs in your workflows.

Adobe InDesign CS

Had we written this book in 2003, we would have been divided about choosing Adobe InDesign as the first program to use as a layout application. After the introduction of Adobe InDesign CS, we're unanimous in our belief that this program is, hands down, the best page-layout application ever developed for a microcomputer. No exceptions — Adobe InDesign CS is one of the more significant achievements among the CS programs. Typesetting in InDesign rivaling typesetting composers of yesterday and features you perhaps have wished for but may have concluded were impossible. Better integration with the other CS applications, better printing support, customizable workspaces, an abundance of new tools, enhanced color control, and more make Adobe InDesign CS the premier page-layout application for creative professionals.

InDesign is the central hub of your creative workflow. You bring together the images and objects created in Adobe Photoshop CS and Adobe Illustrator CS. You either import type created in a word-processing program, import from Adobe's new product InCopy, or you set type in the new InDesign Story Editor. With InDesign's free-form ease of page layout, you lay out a design for publication. You then export the InDesign document as a PDF file suited for print, Web hosting, electronic file exchanges, or CD-ROM replication. If you want to include your design as HTML files for Web hosting, you package the document for GoLive CS. As you can see, InDesign's role among the Creative Suite programs is the anchor where files are imported to assemble a design and ultimately exported for final packaging.

InDesign CS is a major upgrade now in version 3 of the program, and the host of new features is more than we can identify here. Among the more significant new additions include:

✦ **New Story Editor:** InDesign CS includes a Story Editor similar to what has appeared in Adobe PageMaker for several years. This story editor is more sophisticated, offering you many controls for the display of type as you create or edit copy in a separate window and the ability to apply styles; find and replace searched words, styles, fonts, indents, paragraph formatting, character colors, and OpenType features; fit copy to the layout; perform spell checks on one or multiple stories; provide an interactive preview for edited text in the Story Editor and in the page layout; apply XML tags; and more.

✦ **Separations and transparency previews:** InDesign CS offers soft proofing options for previewing colors, ink percentages, separations (individually and in combination with each other), as well as a preview for how objects are affected when transparency flattening occurs. If you've ever unintentionally introduced a spot color in a layout, InDesign CS shows you all colors — process and spot — that will print on separations. You can use the previews to preflight files before packaging them as PDFs for your printer.

✦ **Bleeds and slugs:** You can set up files with customizable bleed areas and an area for adding slugs. If you're designing work for newspapers, magazines, or any client and you want to add notes and descriptions in a slug, InDesign CS supports setting up slugs specific to each page in a file where you can set slugs to different sizes and positions. You can quickly preview your documents to show the trimmed page, a page with bleeds, and a page with the bleeds and slug.

✦ **Nested styles:** This feature is one of the more impressive additions to InDesign CS. Paragraph formatting may include a drop cap, the first two words in the first sentence bolded with a specific color, the remaining words set in a different font, and the following body copy in yet another font. Formatting multiple paragraphs with these attributes used to be very time-consuming and easily resulted in errors. Now, with InDesign CS, you can capture all attributes as a single style and, with one click, apply that style to one or more paragraphs within your document. To edit a font or color, simply return to the Paragraph Style Options dialog box shown in Figure 1-6, make your edits, and the copy is edited for all paragraphs identified with the respective style.

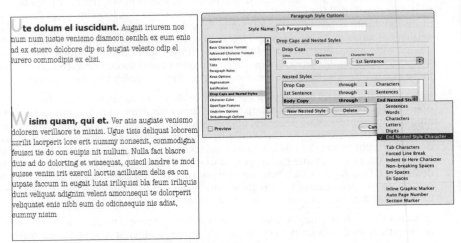

Figure 1-6: The Paragraph Style Options dialog box

✦ **Improved text-editing features:** A host of new features simplifies your text editing in InDesign CS. Switching from the Selection tool or the Direct Selection tool to the Type tool is easily handled by double-clicking in a body of text. You can use keyboard short-cuts (Option/Alt double-click with either selection tool) to quickly access the Text Frame Options dialog box where column attributes, inset spacing, baseline spacing, and vertical justification are handled. Preview real-time text reflows, text wraps, text frame scaling, and sizing. Scale text without adjusting type sizes using the transformation tools, align text to grids, set optical kerning to text for more visually attractive type formatting, and apply or suppress text wraps on hidden layers.

✦ **Running headers and footers for tables:** Import text probably should be tab-delimited data files, import Microsoft Excel files, or set type and convert to a table. You can then break up table text in several separate frames spread across a page or multiple pages, much like you would flow a body of text in columns or across multiple pages. Add a header or footer or both to the first table and all subsequent table links automatically update with the same headers and footers.

✦ **Info palette:** InDesign CS supports a new Info palette similar to the same palette in Adobe Illustrator CS and Adobe Photoshop CS. The InDesign CS Info palette shows you at-a-glance information related to a selected body of copy such as the number of words and characters contained in a text frame. This information is helpful where tight copy fitting is needed in your design.

✦ **Integration with Adobe InCopy:** Adobe InCopy is a stand-alone copy editor that you can purchase separately from the Creative Suite. InCopy is designed to handle the needs of copy editors in editorial workflows. Copy created or modified in InCopy is designed to work on the same InDesign file as the layout artist simultaneously without disturbing each other's edits. InDesign CS offers you complete integration with InCopy where editing is dynamic and immediately reflected in a document from edits made by members of your workflow team.

✦ **Enhanced support for native Illustrator and Photoshop file imports:** InDesign supports direct import of native file formats from Illustrator CS and Photoshop CS, including layers and transparency. New features added to native-file-format support include the ability to import files containing spot colors, spot channels, and DCS (Desktop Color Separation) file support when interacting with transparency.

Note　Because of so many improvements in all the authoring programs in the Creative Suite and much-improved color management across the programs, there is much less need today to save files from Photoshop as DCS 2.0. If you don't know what it means, don't worry about it—we won't spend much time talking about DCS files.

✦ **Workspace management:** Your InDesign CS workspace and user interface have been changed to a more flexible customizable environment. You can tuck away palettes on either the left or right side of the document window and dock them. Click on a tab and the palette springs open horizontally. After docking palettes and organizing your environment, you can save your workspace and return to your custom defaults. You can save multiple workspaces and switch between them from the selection of a simple menu command. A redesigned Control palette adds quick access to editing tools selected in the toolbox. You can display the toolbox in single or double columns and dock it at the top of the document window. You can customize keyboard shortcuts and you have options for using keyboard shortcuts consistent with or Adobe PageMaker.

✦ **Pathfinder palette:** The same options for combining vector objects with the Pathfinder tools found in Adobe Illustrator CS are also now available in InDesign CS.

✦ **New ink-mixing support:** In InDesign CS you can create custom ink sets well beyond specifying process and spot colors. The New Mixed Ink Group dialog box enables you to mix process colors with a spot color, add a spot color and a varnish together as a mixed ink, create a new mixed-ink group, apply the group to a range of colors, and automatically update all objects to reflect changes made in the mixed-ink group.

✦ **Transparency blending mode support:** Photoshop CS and Illustrator CS users will recognize blending modes such as multiply, screen, hard light, soft light, luminosity, and so on. These blending modes are in InDesign CS, where you can create the same effects you also apply in the other CS programs supporting blending modes.

In Figure 1-7, notice the Photoshop image containing transparency. The file was imported without clipping paths from a native Photoshop file. In the Transparency palette, Multiply was used to darken the image. The Photoshop image rests atop a vector object created in Adobe Illustrator CS. The only way you can create the same look using any other page-layout program is to rasterize the Illustrator file and create a composite image in Photoshop where the blending mode is used. Doing so prevents you from moving objects in the page-layout program or adjusting transparency to different levels, thereby adding more time and additional steps to your design-creation process if changes are needed.

✦ **New PDF export capabilities:** Export to PDF with Acrobat 6 compatibility and you can retain layers that you can individually view in any Acrobat 6 viewer. Export to PDF/X-1a or PDF/X3 formats for files destined for professional printing. Export rich media introduced in InDesign such as movie and sound clips to PDF for viewing in Acrobat viewers. Add bookmarks and buttons for creating interactive PDF documents.

Cross-Reference

To learn more about PDF/X formats, see Chapter 35. For more information on exporting InDesign documents to PDF with Adobe PDF layers, see Chapter 12.

Figure 1-7: InDesign CS blends raster and vector objects using transparency blending modes.

✦ **Package for GoLive:** To complete the integration between the CS programs, InDesign also supports exporting your content as XML for easy repurposing in Adobe GoLive. A much tighter integration between a layout in InDesign CS and exporting stories, images, and multimedia files to repurpose documents offer you impressive results.

Cross-Reference

For information on packaging InDesign files for Adobe GoLive CS, see Chapter 25. For more information on exporting XML, see Chapter 27.

✦ **Improved printing features:** Some of the clumsiness in the Print dialog box has been removed, and InDesign CS now offers printing controls that should be well accepted at service centers and print shops. Easier access to custom page sizes, autofitting printers' marks on output, and easy access to only one dialog box when printing files are all available in InDesign CS.

InDesign CS has more new features than the ones described here. A new measuring tool has been introduced; impressive support for XML and XMP is integrated in the program; new preferences for a host of new features have been added; type-on paths are supported, and much more.

Cross-Reference For more information on using new features in InDesign CS, look over the chapters in Part III.

Adobe GoLive CS

Adobe GoLive CS, now in version 7, is a Web authoring and site management program. As a stand-alone product, GoLive has suffered in sales because many Web designers favor other applications by several competing vendors. Because GoLive has had a major upgrade in the CS version, you should consider it for your Web design needs if you use the other CS applications. As a participant in the Creative Suite, GoLive CS has many benefits for handling file imports and exports similar to options in other CS programs. As a stand-alone editor, GoLive has been redesigned and has reached a level of sophistication equal to or greater than other HTML editing programs competing for the same market.

Cross-Reference For more information on using new features in GoLive CS, see Chapter 25.

Among some of the features available in GoLive CS are the ability to import native file formats from other CS applications much like you have available in InDesign CS including Photoshop layered files, smart objects, and smart tracing made from cutouts in other CS native files; complete integration with InDesign CS where paragraph, character, and inline text styles are translated in GoLive documents; consistent color management using the Adobe Color Engine; PDF previews of Web pages; visual CSS (Cascading Style Sheets) authoring and previewing; and a completely new source code. Some of these and other new feature highlights include:

✦ **Working with Smart Objects:** You can open, edit, and place Adobe Photoshop CS, Adobe Illustrator CS, and Adobe PDF documents within GoLive CS.

✦ **CSS packaging for GoLive:** You can package Cascading Style Sheets (CSS) from InDesign for GoLive complete with style sheets converted into internal and external CSS files.

✦ **Create rollovers from layered Photoshop files:** As native Photoshop PSD layered files can be imported in GoLive, you can easily create rollover effects using layers.

✦ **Import Photoshop swatches:** You can convert custom color from Photoshop's Color Swatches palette to GoLive color swatches. This enables you to maintain a consistent color scheme for a given client's print and Web graphics.

✦ **Consistent workspace management with InDesign CS:** The workspace architecture used in InDesign CS was originally derived from the GoLive architecture bringing both programs together with a similar user interface and workspace environment. You can dock and nest palettes on either side of the document window (as shown in Figure 1-8), save custom workspaces, and load them from a simple menu command much the same as you do in InDesign.

✦ **Image cropping:** GoLive CS supports cropping features consistent with cropping images in other CS applications. When working with native Adobe CS file formats such as Photoshop, Illustrator, and PDF, you can crop images directly in GoLive.

✦ **Advanced PDF support:** Create, view, and add links to PDF files directly from within GoLive CS. You can edit bookmarks and links in Adobe PDF documents without having to open files in Acrobat. You can create PDF previews of your Web designs before exporting to PDF.

✦ **Site diagram exports:** A site diagram can be exported from GoLive CS in PDF or SVG formats to assist you in collaborating with colleagues and clients.

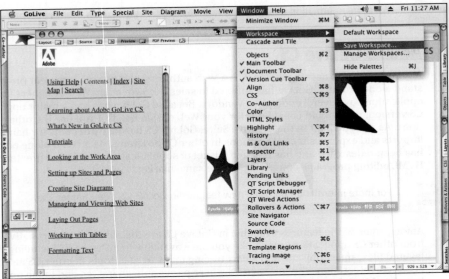

Figure 1-8: The GoLive CS user interface lets you dock and nest palettes.

✦ **Split views:** You can split views between Source view and Layout view for faster editing and toggling between the graphic user interface and editing source code.

✦ **Co-Author Editor:** Web site contributors can easily update Web sites using the Adobe Co-Author Editor. Rather than launch GoLive where the tools and environment is more intimidating, co-authors use a more simplified editor containing only the tools required to make edits. As the Web site designer, you specify co-author editing sections in your site design and permit access to the sections requiring ongoing edits with Adobe Co-Author Editor.

GoLive supports a long list of new features and is a major improvement over pervious versions of the program. If you're a graphic designer focused on print, perhaps the exports to GoLive from within InDesign CS is where you'll spend most of your time. If your work is Web site design, you'll want to spend a lot of time learning all the features GoLive offers you.

Cross-Reference

In this book, we offer you a starting point in Chapter 25, where you can glean some knowledge for using GoLive to create a Web site. In other chapters, we cover the integration of GoLive with the other CS programs. However, our treatment of GoLive is light and you'll need to acquire some other guides and publications in order to become proficient in using the program. In addition Total Training has released a CD called GoLive CS Essentials that we highly recommend.

Adobe Acrobat Professional

Whereas Adobe InDesign CS is the hub on your creative satellite, PDF is at the center of the file-format universe. All the CS programs export and import PDF documents, and the expansion for PDF support is found in all the new product upgrades. For design workflows, Adobe Acrobat Professional in version 6 offers you many tools to facilitate collaboration with colleagues, clients, and prepress technicians. You can

✦ Set up e-mail–based reviews for markup and approval of design concepts and proofs

✦ Export comments and corrections directly to Microsoft Word text documents (on Windows XP with Office XP only)

✦ Prepare files for electronic exchanges, Web hosting, and screen viewing complete with embedded graphics and fonts

✦ Prepare files for digital prepress and printing

✦ Authenticate and secure documents

✦ Develop media shows and slide presentations for kiosks, meetings, and presentations

✦ Design forms for point-of-sale purchases hosted on Web sites or distributed on CD-ROMs

✦ Organize your design environment and catalog design campaigns embedding native files in PDFs for an organized storage system

✦ Search for content contained on CDs, DVDs, network servers, and Web sites

✦ Create accessible documents for clients needing compliance with U.S. Federal law governing document accessibility

All in all, Acrobat Professional has a significant place in your design workflow.

Acrobat Professional was released several months earlier than the other CS programs and the re-branding of the program does not imply a part of the Creative Suite. Part of the reason for the early release of Acrobat was the necessity to develop the PDF 1.5 specifications used by all the other CS programs. With PDF version 1.5 and Acrobat 6 compatibility, you can enjoy features like creating Adobe PDF layers from the CS program exports to PDF and the creation of PDF/X files used for printing and prepress.

Adobe Acrobat is unlike the other CS programs in that the application is designed to serve many different office professionals. Acrobat might be used by engineers, legal professionals, business office workers, government workers, school districts, and just about anyone in any industry working on a computer today. Therefore, there are a number of tools you, as a creative professional, may not use when working in Acrobat just because those tools may not serve your needs. The following are among the additions to the new version of Acrobat that are most suited for design and publishing workflows:

✦ **E-mail–based reviews:** For design concepts routed through committees, offices, and remote locations, you can set up an e-mail–based review where a PDF document originating from sketches or electronic tight comps created in InDesign CS is sent to members of a creative team. People comment and return the comment data back to the PDF author, where comments are integrated back to the original PDF document. You can sort comments, set comment status, summarize comments, export comments to Word documents (on Windows XP with Office XP installed), invite additional reviewers, track reviews, and solicit client sign-offs on final proofs.

Note

E-mail–based reviews are accessible to either Mac or Windows users. Acrobat also supports another review process called browser-based reviews. At the introduction of Acrobat 6 Professional, and as of this writing, browser-based reviews are not available on the Mac. To address cross-platform performance more effectively, discussions on reviews in this book refer only to e-mail–based reviews.

✦ **New viewing tools:** Acrobat Professional introduces new viewing tools created with design professionals and engineers in mind. The Loupe tool is used to show a zoomed view in an area on a document page without the need to zoom in on the page. Artists creating large trade show panels can easily examine areas for proper design and potential printing problems. The Pan and Zoom window introduced in Acrobat 6 functions similarly to the Navigator palette in other Adobe CS applications where a thumbnail of a page is seen in its entirety while the page is zoomed in on the Document pane. In addition, you can split a view to show different pages in the same document in a split screen like the example shown in Figure 1-9.

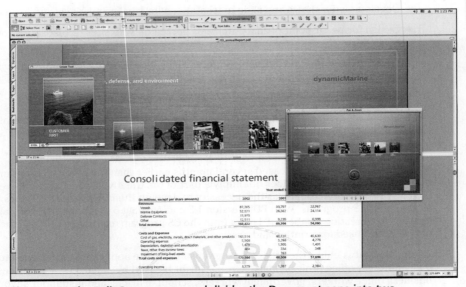

Figure 1-9: The Split Screen command divides the Document pane into two.

✦ **Soft proofing color:** Acrobat goes further than InDesign CS in offering you tools for proofing color. You can view separations like those described earlier in the InDesign CS new features, preview transparency, preview overprints, and preview color changes when changing color profiles.

✦ **Preflighting files:** Acrobat offers you an elaborate set of tools to *preflight* files before sending them to your printer. The Preflight command assesses your file for potential printing problems and reports back to you any problems found in the document. Custom Preflight profiles can be created in Acrobat, profiles can be exported and shared in your workflow, and profiles can be loaded from sets created by your printer. Job ticketing and reporting can be embedded in a PDF document as a result of preflighting the file.

✦ **Comprehensive print controls:** This version of Acrobat is the first version that supports professional printing without the need for acquiring an expensive third-party plug-in. Print options such as specifying halftone frequency, printing crop marks and bleed marks, printing separations, emulsion control, transparency flattening, and similar features found in layout programs are supported.

✦ **Search PDFs without index files:** You can search PDFs saved to a hard drive, a network server, a CD-ROM, or a DVD without the need for creating a search index file.

✦ **PDF/X compliance:** Built into Acrobat Distiller in the Acrobat Professional version, you can distill PostScript with PDF/X compliance. PDF/X is a subset of the PDF format more suitable for printing and prepress. You can create PDF/X-compliant files from within the Preflight: Profiles dialog box for PDF documents not distilled with PDF/X compliance.

✦ **View and manage Adobe PDF layers:** You can create layered files from Illustrator CS and InDesign CS. You can then view the resultant PDF containing layers in any Acrobat viewer version 6 and above. Creating layered PDFs offers you options for client previewing different designs for a campaign, design pieces with multiple languages, scientific and electrical drawings, and similar designs. You can merge layers, flatten layers, and change layer properties in Acrobat Professional.

Adobe Acrobat provides you with additional design opportunities for a variety of different output needs. New features for an elaborate set of multimedia support have been introduced in Acrobat Professional. You can secure files with Acrobat Security or with security handlers marketed by third-party vendors; create search index files to search collections of PDFs faster; create custom Adobe PDF settings (formerly known as job options) and distribute them to all your InDesign CS users for consistent PDF creation; certify documents with digital signatures; create PDF documents from any program; and import the PDF as a graphic image that can be sized and transformed in other CS programs. Use Acrobat as a file-format translator to port foreign file formats to all the other CS programs, and much more.

Version Cue

Along with the CS applications, with either the Standard or Premium edition, you also get a marvelous tool saves versions of your designs created in Adobe Photoshop CS, Adobe Illustrator CS, Adobe InDesign CS, and Adobe GoLive CS. Note that Version Cue support is not available in either Adobe Acrobat Professional or Adobe ImageReady CS.

Cross-Reference For more information on how to set up the Version Cue environment and how to save files with different versions, see Chapter 7.

After you install Version Cue and enable it in your System Preferences (Mac) or your Control Panel (Windows), an icon appears in the lower-left corner of the Save and Save As dialog boxes. You begin using Version Cue by saving a version of your design to a Version Cue-monitored folder, similar to what's shown in Figure 1-10. If you change the design — for example, changing a color in a duotone image in Adobe Photoshop CS — you can save the change as a separate version.

When you open an InDesign CS or GoLive CS file containing several versions or you place a file in InDesign CS, the version promoted to the top level is either the version you open or the file you see imported.

The advantage of using Version Cue is having easier tracking of your files and the current version used in a design project. Using the example of the Photoshop CS image imported into InDesign CS, if your client wants you to return to a previous version, you simply select the Versions menu command and promote the desired version to the top level. The Photoshop CS file imported in InDesign CS is dynamically updated in the InDesign CS document without your intervention.

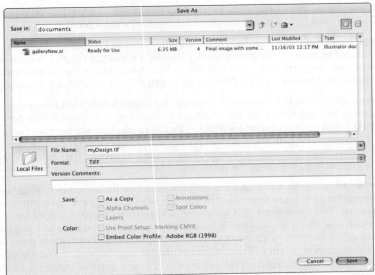

Figure 1-10: Version Cue helps you manage different versions of your project.

OpenType fonts

In addition to the programs contained in the Creative Suite, you also find more than 100 OpenType fonts installed after completing your CS applications installation. OpenType fonts are a new font technology developed by Adobe Systems and Microsoft. OpenType fonts offer you new type-handling features among many of the CS applications; starting to convert your type library to OpenType fonts as soon as possible is a good idea. The kind of benefits you derive from using OpenType fonts include:

✦ **Cross-platform support:** OpenType fonts are completely cross-platform. You can copy the same font to either Mac OS or Windows. Obviously, licensing restrictions do apply, so be certain to check these restrictions when installing fonts on multiple computers.

✦ **Reliability:** If you experience font problems at the time of printing, be certain to first reevaluate your font sets. Off-brand fonts, especially many of a TrueType nature, can prevent embedding problems. Furthermore, some quality fonts carry licensing restrictions that prevent font embedding. If you create PDF files with font embedding, be certain to review the licensing restrictions on your fonts and check to see if font embedding is prohibited. Many quality fonts offer you complete embedding permissions that help prevent problems when it comes time to print your creations. Among good-quality fonts that permit font embedding are those found in the Adobe type library of OpenType fonts.

✦ **More glyphs:** A *glyph* is an individual font character. TrueType fonts and all earlier PostScript fonts contain a maximum 256 glyphs. The new OpenType fonts can contain more than 65,000 glyphs. These additional characters offer you many discretionary options for kerning pairs and expanded ligatures as well as special characters, precisely proportioned fractions, and foreign-language character alternatives. A portion of a glyph set for an OpenType font installed with the Creative Suite is shown in Figure 1-11.

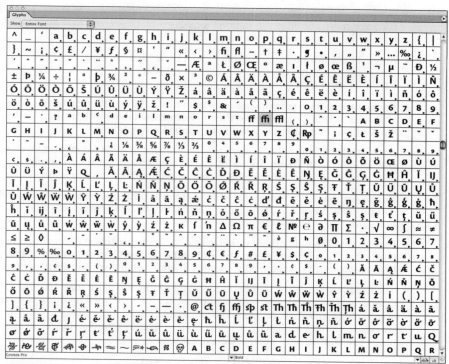

Figure 1-11: OpenType fonts offer you more than 65,000 characters.

✦ **Multi-language support:** All the OpenType Pro fonts contain characters needed for multiple-language typesetting.

✦ **Easier font management:** OpenType fonts contain only a single file for font viewing on-screen and fonts used for printing. Unlike PostScript fonts containing separate files for screen views and each face in a font set contained in a separate file, OpenType fonts are built in a single file, thereby providing you more ease in keeping track of fonts, installing them, and locating them.

Several CS applications support a Glyphs palette where you can view an entire font in a scrollable window. You can insert a character at the insertion point by double-clicking on a glyph in the palette. You no longer need to open a utility to view all characters in a given font set when using programs like Adobe InDesign CS and Adobe Illustrator CS.

Summary

✦ The Creative Suite is a collection of imaging applications offering professional designers complete integration for print, Web hosting, and screen viewing.

✦ Programs from a single software vendor provide consistent user interfaces and similar menu and tool functions, which reduce learning curves for new hires.

✦ Adobe Photoshop CS version offers new tools for brightness controls, a new File Browser, more automated functions, new layer management, new filter tools, and customizable keyboard shortcuts.

✦ Adobe Illustrator CS version 11offers new tools for creating 3D objects, character and paragraph style sheets, faster performance, tighter integration with Adobe Photoshop CS, enhanced PDF support, and improved print capabilities.

✦ Adobe InDesign CS version 3 offers sophisticated typesetting features, including optical character kerning, nested style sheets, formatting tables with headers and footers, a Story Editor, and integration with the Adobe InCopy Editor.

✦ Adobe GoLive CS version 7 offers new sophisticated tools for creating Web pages and Web sites. Together with Adobe InDesign CS and the other CS programs, GoLive CS supports file imports from native formats and direct exports to Adobe PDF.

✦ Adobe Acrobat 6 Professional offers the creative professional tools for reviewing comps, soft proofing color, preflighting documents, PDF/X compliance, and a new Print dialog box suited for professional printing.

✦ Version Cue is a utility that supports saving files from Adobe Photoshop CS, Adobe Illustrator CS, Adobe InDesign CS, and Adobe GoLive CS in different document versions. Changing versions dynamically updates linked files in the other CS programs.

✦ The Creative Suite Premium Edition provides you with more than 100 OpenType fonts. OpenType fonts are a new font technology jointly developed by Adobe Systems and Microsoft Corporation. An OpenType font can contain more than 65,000 glyphs, offering you more choices for ligatures, discretionary ligatures, foreign-language characters, proportional fractions, and special characters.

✦   ✦   ✦

Taking a Tour of the Creative Suite

The best way to understand the possibilities that the various Creative Suite applications offer is to walk through an example workflow that takes a project through each of the various applications. This tour starts out with Acrobat, where you can create a PDF file of an initial sketch that you can e-mail to all members of the creative team for review. The reviewers' feedback return is in the form of comments compiled within a single PDF file. This cycle continues until all members of the creative team approve the design.

With an approved design, you can use Photoshop and Illustrator to create and edit images and objects for the project. You can then import all this content into InDesign, where you lay them out with text. The final layout is then exported back to Acrobat, where it may be printed or repurposed for use on the Web using GoLive.

Starting with a Sketch in Acrobat

When a project first starts, you typically want to get input from several individuals on the creative team before the design is approved. Calling a meeting where all members of the creative team meet to discuss the design would accomplish the goal, but Acrobat makes another solution possible.

Using Acrobat, you can scan a rough design sketch into Acrobat where it is converted to a PDF file. Then, you can e-mail this PDF file to members of the creative team. Each member of the team makes his comments into the PDF file and e-mails the document back to its owner. All the comments are then compiled into a single PDF document that provides feedback. This cycle can then be iterated until all involved approve the design.

Cross-Reference   Complete coverage on e-mail review sessions is found in Chapter 22.

Scanning a sketch into Acrobat

Projects always start with an idea, but to share these ideas with others, they are usually sketched out roughly. These rough sketches may be scanned into a digital format where they are more easily distributed. Using a scanner or a digital camera, sketches or images may be directly scanned into Acrobat.

STEPS: Scanning a Sketch into Acrobat

1. **Initiate a scan in Acrobat.** Within Acrobat, choose File ➪ Create PDF ➪ From Scanner. This command opens the Create PDF From Scanner dialog box, shown in Figure 2-1. In the Device drop-down list, select the attached scanner and enable the Adapt Compression to Page Content check box. In the Compatible With drop-down list, select Acrobat 6.0 and Later, and click the Scan button.

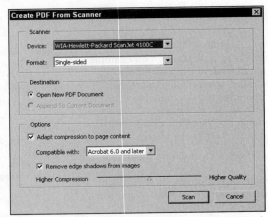

Figure 2-1: The Create PDF From Scanner dialog box

2. **Set the scanner preferences.** After click the Scan button, a dialog box for your scanner appears, like the one shown in Figure 2-2. Select the options appropriate for your sketched image and click the Preview button to check the scanning options. If you're comfortable with the preview, click the Scan button.

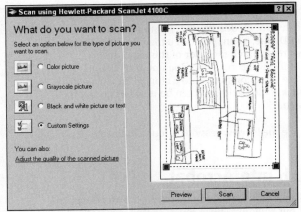

Figure 2-2: Each scanner has a similar dialog box to set scanning options.

3. **Rotate the page.** After the scan is complete, the rough sketch is visible in Acrobat, but the page is displayed using a Portrait orientation and the sketch was drawn using a Landscape orientation. To rotate the page, choose Document ➪ Pages ➪ Rotate. In the Rotate Pages dialog box that appears, select the option that rotates the page correctly. Figure 2-3 shows the rotated sketched page in Acrobat.

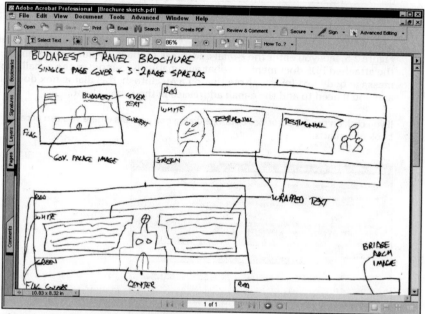

Figure 2-3: A scanned and rotated image in Acrobat

4. **Save the PDF file.** After the scanned file is loaded into Acrobat, the file needs to be saved before it's redistributed. To save the scanned image, choose File ➪ Save As. This command opens a file dialog box where you can name the file and specify a folder where you want to save the file.

Submitting a sketch for e-mail review

With a sketch scanned into Acrobat, you can send the PDF file out for review using e-mail or using a browser. These steps walk you through an e-mail review cycle. In actual projects, this review cycle may be repeated many times as needed.

STEPS: Submitting a Sketch for E-mail Review

1. **Send a PDF file for e-mail review.** To send the selected PDF file out for e-mail review, choose File ➪ Send by Email for Review. The Send by Email for Review dialog box, shown in Figure 2-4, opens. Here, you enter the e-mail address where you want the comments to come back to. You can edit this e-mail address at a future time using the Identity panel of the Preferences dialog box (Acrobat/Edit ➪ Preferences).

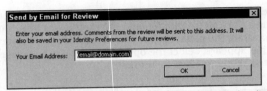

Figure 2-4: The Send by Email for Review dialog box

2. **Specify the reviewers' e-mail addresses.** The next dialog box to appear, shown in Figure 2-5, lets you enter the e-mail addresses of the individuals you want to review the attached PDF document. Acrobat automatically composes the e-mail subject and message body text for you. Note that on a Macintosh, this dialog box doesn't appear and you'll need to add the e-mail addresses in the e-mail client.

Tip   If you click on the To, Cc, or Bcc button, a dialog box appears where you can access an address book of contacts.

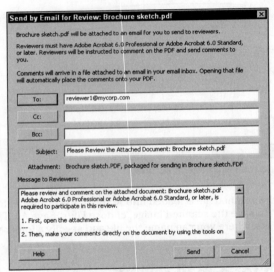

Figure 2-5: Sending your review of a PDF file by e-mail

3. **Send out e-mails.** When the e-mail addresses and message are completed, click Send. Acrobat delivers the e-mail message to your system's default e-mail application. If your e-mail system is set to automatically send out e-mails, the e-mail is sent automatically. But if not, you need to manually send out the e-mails.

Adding comments to the PDF

When a reviewer receives an e-mail requesting feedback, he can double-click on the attached file to open it in Acrobat. Within Acrobat, the Commenting toolbar may be used to add notes and comments to the sketch.

STEPS: Adding Comments to an E-mail PDF File

1. **Receiving a review e-mail.** Using your system e-mail client, the review request is sent out with the PDF file attached. Figure 2-6 shows what the resulting e-mail looks like.

Note

E-mail reviews can mix comments from Macintosh and Window platforms without any issues.

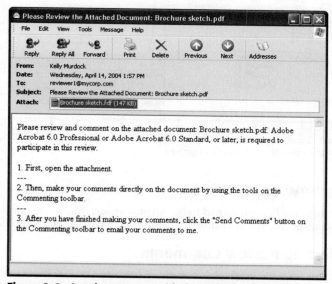

Figure 2-6: A review request with the PDF file attached

2. **Open the attached PDF in Acrobat.** If you double-click the attached PDF file, it opens within Acrobat. Comments are added to the document using the Commenting toolbar, which you may open by choosing Tools ➪ Commenting ➪ Show Commenting Toolbar.

3. **Add review comments to the PDF.** Click on the Note Tool button in the Commenting Toolbar. Click in the document where you want the note to be positioned. A note text area appears where you can type your message. Figure 2-7 shows the sketch document with some review comments added.

4. **Return comments.** After you've finished making comments, choose File ➪ Send Comments to Review Initiator. The PDF with its comments is sent back to the original sender.

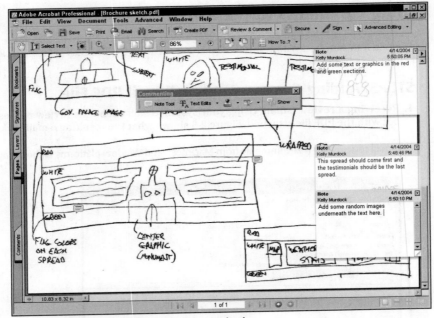

Figure 2-7: A sketch with comments attached

Collecting review comments

When the reviewed documents are returned to the original sender, the comments are merged into the original document. These comments may then be summarized and printed.

STEPS: Collecting Review Comments

1. **Merge comments with the original document.** When a review PDF file is returned, it can also be double-clicked within the e-mail message to open it within Acrobat. Acrobat recognizes the document as one that was sent out for review and incorporates the comments into the original document. When this happens, a message dialog box appears, as shown in Figure 2-8.

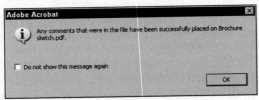

Figure 2-8: A message box appears when the comments from a reviewed PDF file are imported into the original document.

2. View and print a list of comments. After a reviewed document is merged into the original PDF file, you open the list of comments by clicking on the Comments tab to the left. All comments in the PDF file appear at the bottom of the document (Figure 2-9).

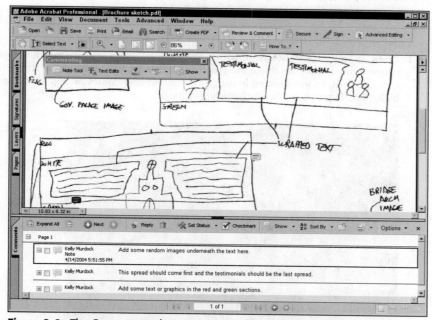

Figure 2-9: The Comments tab opens comments on the document.

3. Sort comments. The button along the top of the comments list lets you set the status of comments and sort them by type, page, author, date, color, or check mark status.

4. Print comments. To print the comments, click the Print button at the top of the Comments list or choose File ➪ Print with Comments.

Editing Images in Photoshop

When you have a good idea of the content that needs to be in the final document, you can use Photoshop to edit and prepare the images to be included. These edits can include altering the image properties to adjust the image levels, color balance, brightness, and contrast. Another common way to edit images is to crop the image to the relevant portion. For images that aren't rectangular, you may need to extract a portion of an image. For images that appear on top of other page elements, you'll want to add transparency. All these tasks may be completed in Photoshop.

Cross-Reference   Many Photoshop editing features are covered in Chapter 8.

Adjusting image properties

After all the images for the project have been identified, Photoshop's image adjustment features may be used to change the image levels or its brightness and contrast. Adequate contrast is essential for objects that are to be combined with text.

STEPS: Adjusting Image Levels and Contrast

1. **Open an image in Photoshop.** Within Photoshop, choose File ➪ Open and select an image to load. Because these images are to be used within a brochure, the levels and contrast need to be adjusted in order for the text that comes on top of the images to be legible. Figure 2-10 shows the original image.

Figure 2-10: This figure shows the original image before any adjustments.

2. **Auto-adjust the image levels.** With the image selected, choose Image ➪ Adjustments ➪ Levels. The Levels dialog box, shown in Figure 2-11, opens. This dialog box shows the Shadows, Midtones, and Highlights of the image. To auto-correct the balance of these levels, click the Auto button. The levels are evenly spaced and the image is adjusted.

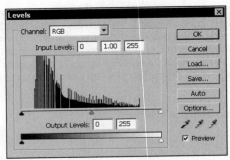

Figure 2-11: The Levels dialog box

3. **Adjust the brightness and contrast.** To change the brightness and contrast of the image, choose Image ➪ Adjustments ➪ Brightness/Contrast. This opens a simple dialog box with sliders for the Brightness and Contrast values. Set the Brightness value to –5 and the Contrast value to 25; then enable the Preview option to see the changes in the original image. This provides ample contrast for the text that is to appear on top of the image. Click OK to close the dialog box. Figure 2-12 shows the resulting image.

Figure 2-12: The image has sufficient contrast to make the text readable.

4. **Save the image.** Choose File ➪ Save to save the image with its changes.

Cropping images

Although the levels and the contrast of the image look good, there is still a strong light flare on the right side of the image that is casting some unwanted color into the image. This anomaly is easily removed using Photoshop's Crop tool.

STEPS: Cropping an Image

1. **Open an image in Photoshop.** Within Photoshop, choose File ➪ Open and select an image that you want to crop.

2. **Use the Crop tool.** Click on the Crop tool in the toolbar and drag within the interior of the image. This places a marquee with handles on each edge and corner. Click and drag the handles to precisely position the cropping marquee, as shown in Figure 2-13. Double-click within the cropping marquee to complete the crop.

3. **Save the image.** Choose File ➪ Save to save the image with its changes.

Figure 2-13: The marquee shows where the image is to be cropped.

Extracting images

Not all images included in a design need to be rectangular. Using Photoshop's Extract filter, you can separate objects from their background, replacing the background with a transparent area. These images can later be used to wrap text in a layout.

Cross-Reference

Extracting image objects using the Extract filter is covered in Chapter 10.

STEPS: Extracting an Object from an Image

1. **Open an image in Photoshop.** Within Photoshop, choose File ➪ Open and select an image that includes an object that you want to extract, such as the one in Figure 2-14.

2. **Increase the contrast between the object and its background.** Objects that have a clear contrast between the object and the background are much easier to extract. To increase the contrast for this image, choose Image ➪ Adjustments ➪ Auto Contrast.

3. **Open the Extract interface.** Choose Filter ➪ Extract to open the Extract filter interface, as shown in Figure 2-15.

4. **Highlight the object edges.** Click on the Edge Highlighting tool to the left, increase the Brush Size to 80, and enable the Smart Highlighting option on the right. Then drag over the edges of the object. Be sure to overlap the background.

Figure 2-14: This object should be easy to extract because the line between the object and its background has a high contrast.

Figure 2-15: The Extract interface has all its tools along the left edge.

5. **Fill the areas to keep.** Select the Fill tool and click within the object to mark it as the object to keep. The filled area is shaded with a blue highlight (Figure 2-16). If you have some gaps in the highlighted edge, the blue fill leaks into the background area. If this happens, select the Edge Highlighter tool again, close the gap, and refill the area you want to keep.

Figure 2-16: Use the Fill tool to mark the object that you want to keep.

6. **Preview the extraction.** With the object to keep marked, the Preview button becomes active. Click on the Preview button to see the extracted object. The resulting extracted object is shown in Figure 2-17.

Figure 2-17: The extraction is shown in the Preview pane.

7. **Clean up the edges.** Click on the Edge Touchup tool and drag on the edges that aren't extracted correctly. To erase part of the background that remains, use the Cleanup tool. Click OK when you're finished. Figure 2-18 shows the final extracted object.

Figure 2-18: An extracted image has a transparent background.

8. **Save the image.** Choose File ➪ Save to save the image with its changes.

Adding transparency

Adding transparency to an object makes the objects underneath it visible. Transparency is added to an image using the Opacity value found in the Layers palette.

Note   You can also use InDesign to adjust the transparency of placed objects.

STEPS: Making an Image Transparent

1. **Open an image in Photoshop.** Within Photoshop, choose File ➪ Open and select an image that you want to make transparent.

2. **Set the layer's Opacity value.** With the layer selected, set the Opacity value in the Layers palette to 90%. This value allows the colors underneath to be seen. You can also change the blending mode, but leave it set to Normal. Figure 2-19 shows the semi-transparent object.

3. **Save the image.** Choose File ➪ Save to save the image with its changes.

Figure 2-19: Changing the layer's Opacity value to a value less than 100% causes an image to be semitransparent.

Creating Illustrator Objects

Images included in a design are best edited in Photoshop, but your design might also call for vector-based objects such as logos, maps, and shapes. These objects are easiest to create in Illustrator. For this example, we create and warp a flag object. There is also a 3D filmstrip icon that is easily created in Illustrator.

Cross-Reference   Many Illustrator editing features are covered in Chapter 8.

Creating and filling objects

Illustrator's Toolbox includes many tools for creating objects. These objects may be freehand lines drawn with the Pen, Pencil, or Paintbrush tools; straight lines; text; or various shapes, including rectangles, ellipses, polygons, stars, arcs, spirals, and grids.

After you create an object by dragging it in the art board, you can select a fill color or define the width and color of its outline, called a *stroke*.

STEPS: Creating a Simple Flag Object

1. **Open Illustrator.** Within Illustrator, choose File ➪ New and create a new image.

2. **Create aligned rectangles.** Click on the Rectangle tool and drag in the art board to create a long thin rectangle to act as a flag stripe. Hold down the Option/Alt key and drag the rectangle downward. While dragging, press and hold the Shift key to constrain the movement in the vertical direction. Position the second rectangle under the first so that its top edge touches the bottom edge of the first rectangle. With the second rectangle

selected, choose Object ➪ Transform ➪ Transform Again to copy a third rectangle under the second, as shown in Figure 2-20.

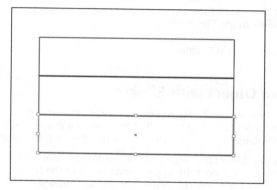

Figure 2-20: The aligned rectangles are ready for coloring.

3. **Add fill and stroke colors.** Select the top rectangle and click on the Fill box in the Toolbox. Then select the Red swatch in the Swatches palette to color this stripe red. Select the third rectangle and change the Fill box color to green. The middle stripe should remain white. Select all three rectangles and click on the Stroke box in the Toolbox; then select the None color to remove the stroke color.

4. **Add a flagpole.** Click on the Line Segment tool and drag from the top-left corner of the flag to a position underneath the flag with the Shift key held down to force the line to be straight. Click on the Default Fill and Stroke button under the Fill box for the line to make it appear black. The flag should now look like Figure 2-21.

5. **Save the file.** Choose File ➪ Save to save the file.

Figure 2-21: Filling separate rectangles with different fill colors.

Using effects

One common way to distort objects in Illustrator is with effects. Effects are applied to objects in memory allowing you to edit or remove them at any time using the Appearance palette. A large variety of effects are available in the Effect menu.

Cross-Reference   Applying Illustrator effects is covered in Chapter 10.

STEPS: Enhancing an Object with Effects

1. **Group the rectangles.** Before we can apply an effect to three separate rectangles, you'll need to group them together so the effect is applied to them as a group. With all three rectangles selected, choose Object ➪ Group. This groups the stripes into a single object.

2. **Distort the flag.** With the grouped object selected, choose Filter ➪ Distort ➪ Free Distort. The object opens in a dialog box. Select the upper-right corner of the bounding box and drag it downward; then select the lower-right corner and drag it upward to give the flag a slight taper, as shown in Figure 2-22.

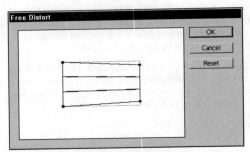

Figure 2-22: The Free Distort filter is used to give this flag a slight taper.

3. **Apply a Warp effect.** As a final step, choose Effect ➪ Warp ➪ Flag. In the Warp Options dialog box, set the Bend amount to 25% and click OK. The warped flag is shown in Figure 2-23.

4. **Add a Drop Shadow.** Select all objects and choose Effect ➪ Stylize ➪ Drop Shadow. Set Mode to Multiply, Opacity to 75%, X and Y Offsets to 7 pt, Blur to 5 pt, and Color to Black. Click OK. The final flag is shown in Figure 2-24.

5. **Save the file.** Choose File ➪ Save to save the file.

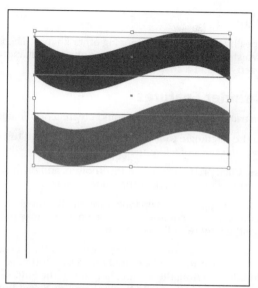

Figure 2-23: The Flag warp effect causes the flag to wave as if in the wind.

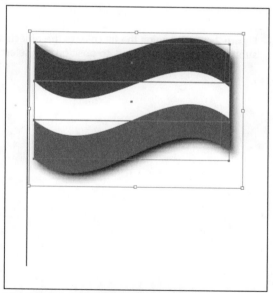

Figure 2-24: The Drop Shadow adds a much-needed element of depth.

Cutting holes in an object

You can create some complex shapes by combining or removing other shapes. The Pathfinder palette includes features to add two shapes together, subtract one shape from another, or compute the intersection of excluded areas in a shape.

STEPS: Using the Pathfinder Features

1. **Open Illustrator.** Within Illustrator, choose File ➪ New and create a new image.

2. **Create a rectangle.** Click on the Rectangle tool and drag in the art board to create a long thin rectangle to be several frames of a film reel.

3. **Set the fill and stroke colors.** Click on the Fill box in the Toolbox and change the color to orange. Then click on the Stroke box and select the None option.

4. **Create objects to subtract.** To create the filmstrip look, drag the Rectangle tool with the Shift key held down to create a small square to form one of the tracks that runs alongside the frames. Change the square's fill color to gray.

5. **Position the objects to subtract.** Position this square so it overlaps the top edge of the large thin rectangle. Click on the Selection tool and hold down the Option/Alt key while dragging the square to the left. As you drag the square, hold down the Shift key to move it in a straight line. Position it on the side opposite the first square. Select both square objects and drag them downward with the Option/Alt key held down. As you begin to drag them, hold down the Shift key to constrain their horizontal movement. Release the mouse when a small gap exists between the first and second row of squares, as shown in Figure 2-25.

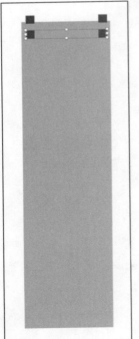

Figure 2-25: Changing the fill color of the objects to be subtracted makes them easy to position and select.

6. **Repeat the transformation.** With both transformed squares selected, choose Object ➪ Transform ➪ Transform Again. This duplicates the selected squares and moves the duplicates the same distance downward again. Continue selecting this command (or use its keyboard shortcut of ⌘/Ctrl+D) until the squares run the entire length of the filmstrip, as shown in Figure 2-26.

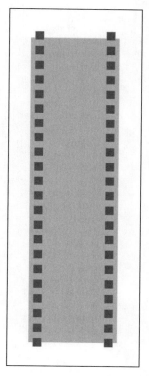

Figure 2-26: The Transform Again menu command is very convenient for creating a row of perfectly aligned objects.

7. **Create the center frames.** Select the Rounded Rectangle tool and drag to create an object that may be subtracted from the center frames of the filmstrip. With the Selection tool, drag the frame object so it overlaps the top edge of the filmstrip. Then hold down the Option/Alt key and drag the frame object downward. While dragging, hold down the Shift key to align the new object under the original one. Then use the Transform Again menu command to duplicate the frames down the entire strip, as shown in Figure 2-27.

8. **Use the Pathfinder subtract feature.** Drag over all the objects with the Selection tool and open the Pathfinder palette by choosing Window ➪ Pathfinder. Then click on the Subtract from Shape Area button in the Pathfinder palette. All gray objects are removed from the underlying filmstrip objects, as shown in Figure 2-28.

Figure 2-27: With all objects in their correct positions, the objects on the top and bottom of the filmstrip object are ready to be subtracted.

9. **Save the file.** Choose File ➪ Save to save the file.

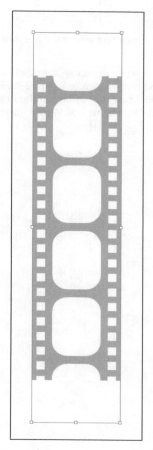

Figure 2-28: The Subtract Pathfinder feature makes cutting holes easy.

Extruding an object

Within the Effect ⇨ 3D menu are several effects that may be used to make simple shapes three-dimensional. These 3D shapes may be shaded and even have lights positioned to show highlights.

Cross-Reference

Using the 3D effects found in Illustrator is covered in Chapter 10.

STEPS: Using a 3D Effect

1. **Open Illustrator.** Within Illustrator, choose File ➪ Open and select the file that you want to make 3D.

2. **Apply the 3D Extrude & Bevel effect.** With the filmstrip object selected, choose Effect ➪ 3D ➪ Extrude & Bevel. This opens a dialog box, shown in Figure 2-29. In the 3D Extrude & Bevel Options dialog box, select the Off-Axis Front option in the Position field and set the Extrude Depth to 5 pt. Then click OK. Figure 2-30 shows the extruded filmstrip object.

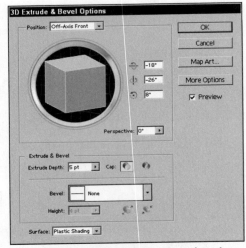

Figure 2-29: The 3D Extrude & Bevel Options dialog box

3. **Save the file.** Choose File ➪ Save to save the file.

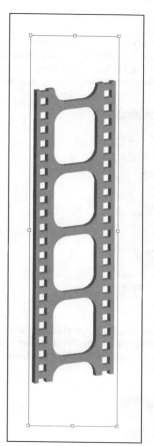

Figure 2-30: Extruding the filmstrip object gives it a sense of depth.

Versioning Files in Version Cue

As you make changes to project content, the Version Cue features are helpful in maintaining versions. To use Version Cue, you need to enable it for each application, which is typically done using a setting in the File Handling section of the Preferences dialog box. Once enabled, the Version Cue interface may be accessed using any of the standard file dialog boxes.

Cross-Reference Version Cue is covered in more detail in Chapter 7.

STEPS: Versioning Illustrator Files

1. **Enable Version Cue.** Within Illustrator, choose Illustrator ➪ Preferences ➪ File Handling & Clipboard (on the Mac) or Edit ➪ Preferences ➪ File Handling & Clipboard (on Windows). This opens the File Handling & Clipboard panel in the Preferences dialog box, shown in Figure 2-31. Click on the check box to enable the Enable Version Cue option, and click OK.

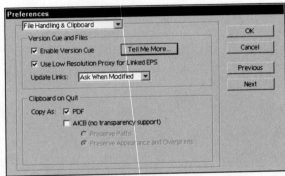

Figure 2-31: Use the Preferences dialog box to enable Version Cue.

2. **Turning on Version Cue.** After Version Cue is enabled for a specific application, you need to turn on the Version Cue client. Double-clicking on the Version Cue icon opens the dialog box, shown in Figure 2-32. In the Version Cue field, select the On option and click OK. This starts Version Cue.

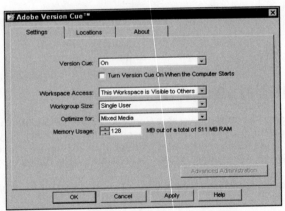

Figure 2-32: You must also turn on the Version Cue client.

3. **Access Version Cue while saving a file.** With a file that you want to save into the Version Cue workspace open in Illustrator, choose File ➪ Save As. In the Save As dialog box, shown in Figure 2-33, click on the Version Cue button.

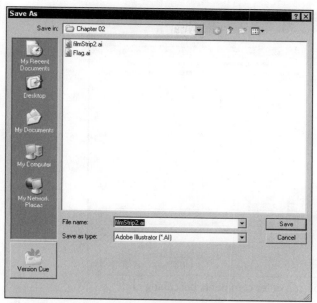

Figure 2-33: The Version Cue button in the file dialog box

4. **Create a new project.** In the Version Cue window that opens, click on the Project Tools button at the top of the dialog box and select the New Project menu command. This command causes a simple dialog box, shown in Figure 2-34, to appear, in which you can name the new project and type some project information. You can also opt to share this project with others.

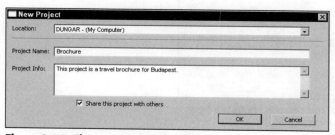

Figure 2-34: The New Project dialog box

5. **Save the file in Version Cue.** Double-click on the new project folder to view the contents of the folder. Then double-click on the documents folder and enter a name for the file to be saved. Figure 2-35 shows the Save As dialog box where a new file is being added to the Version Cue repository. For each file in the active directory, the number of available versions is listed along with the comments for the latest version. These sentences need to be rewritten because they totally miss the point of using Version Cue's versioning features.

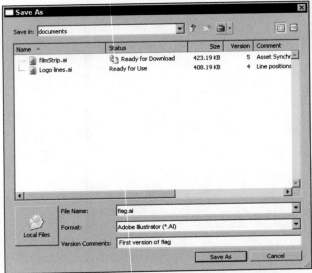

Figure 2-35: You can enter comments describing each saved version.

6. **Save a version.** To update the last saved file, choose File ➪ Save a Version. A dialog box, shown in Figure 2-36, appears, in which you can enter a comment for this version.

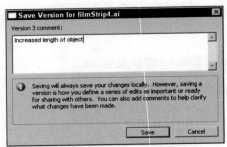

Figure 2-36: You can quickly save a new version of the current file.

Creating a Layout in InDesign

After you create all the content for the project using Photoshop and Illustrator, you can use InDesign to lay out the project in preparation for printing. Each object within InDesign is contained within a frame. These frames are easily moved and resized.

Images and objects placed within frames in a layout aren't embedded within the layout but instead are only links to the actual image and object files. This allows the representative images to be updated quickly. When the layout is exported or printed, InDesign looks at content that are referenced as links and loads the actual linked files into the exported or printed document.

Cross-Reference   Creating a layout and using master pages are covered in Chapter 23.

Creating a layout

Before the content is placed on the pages, creating a document lets you create all the pages and spreads contained in the project. You can also specify the number of pages as well as the page dimensions, margins, and columns.

STEPS: Creating an InDesign Layout

1. **Create a new InDesign document.** Within InDesign, choose File ➪ New ➪ Document. In the New Document dialog box, shown in Figure 2-37, set the number of pages to 7 and enable the Facing Pages option. Set the Width to 10 inches, the Height to 7 inches, and click on the Landscape Orientation button. Then set all the margins to 0.5 inches and the columns to 1, with a gutter of 0.

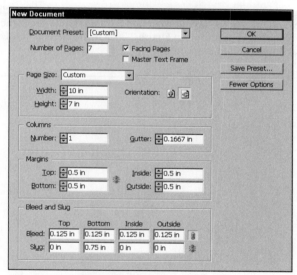

Figure 2-37: The New Document dialog box

2. **Set the bleed and slug dimensions.** While you're still in the New Document dialog box, click on the More Options button to reveal the fields for setting the bleed and slug dimensions. Set the Top Bleed value to 0.125 inches and click the Make All Settings the Same button to the right of the Bleed fields. Then set the Bottom Slug value to 0.75 inches and click OK.

3. **View the layout pages.** To see the layout pages, open the Pages palette by choosing Window ➪ Pages. The Pages palette is shown in Figure 2-38.

Figure 2-38: The Pages palette lets you view and select pages in a layout.

4. **Save the file.** Choose File ➪ Save to save the layout.

Importing content into InDesign

With a layout created, you can begin to import content into the InDesign layout by choosing File ➪ Place. Imported objects appear within frames that allow them to be easily moved about the layout.

STEPS: Importing Content into InDesign

1. **Create a layout frame.** Before importing an image into the InDesign layout, click on the Rectangle Frame tool and drag in the layout to create a frame that is the same size as the page marked by black lines, as shown in Figure 2-39. The frame you create is marked with diagonal lines through its center.

Figure 2-39: Two diagonal lines denote frames.

2. **Place images from Photoshop.** With the image frame created, choose File ⇨ Place. The Place dialog box (shown in Figure 2-40) looks like the Open file dialog box, except it lets you select a much large number of file types. Select the image file to place in the layout and click the Open button. The image is automatically loaded and sized to fit the frame.

Figure 2-40: The Place dialog box opens a variety of different file formats.

3. **Place objects from Illustrator.** The File ⇨ Place menu command may also be used to place objects created in Illustrator. For Illustrator objects, enable the Show Import Options check box in the Place dialog box. This causes the Place PDF dialog box, shown in Figure 2-41, to appear. In the Crop To drop-down list, select the Bounding Box option; enable the Transparent Background check box. Then click OK. The object to be placed appears on the cursor. Click in the upper-left section of the image to place the object.

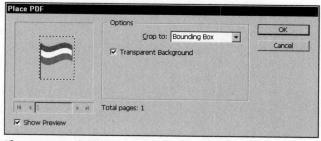

Figure 2-41: The Place PDF dialog box defines how objects are cropped.

4. **Resize the placed object.** The placed object appears within a frame. By dragging the handles, you can resize the frame, but the placed object's size doesn't change until you choose Object ➪ Fitting ➪ Fit Content to Frame.

5. **Enhance with InDesign objects.** The pole on the imported flag object is black, and it doesn't show up against the black background. Instead of creating a new object, you can simply add the flagpole using InDesign's Line tool. Select the Line tool and drag to replace the line. With the line object selected, change the stroke color to white. Figure 2-42 shows the flag object positioned and resized on the cover page.

Figure 2-42: Using the Fit Content to Frame menu command, you can make the placed content fit the frame.

6. **Save the file.** Choose File ➪ Save to save the layout.

Creating Master pages in InDesign

Using Master pages, you can place objects such as page numbers that appear on every page of the document. Master pages are created and accessed using the Pages palette.

STEPS: Using Master Pages

1. **Create a new Master spread.** Master pages are defined using the Pages palette. Using the palette menu, select the New Master palette menu command. In the New Master dialog box, shown in Figure 2-43, enter a prefix and a name for the master. Then enter **2** as the number of pages and click OK. The Master appears in the top of the Pages palette.

Figure 2-43: The New Master dialog box

2. **Apply the Master to pages.** With the new Master spread selected in the Pages palette, select the Apply Master to Pages palette menu command. In the Apply Master dialog box that appears, type the page numbers to which you want to apply the Master spread. The Pages palette is updated with the Prefix for the Master spread, as shown in Figure 2-44.

Figure 2-44: Master pages are displayed at the top of the Pages palette.

3. **Add content to the Master spread.** Double-click on the Master spread in the Pages palette to open the Master spread pages in InDesign. Create or place the content on these pages that should appear on all pages that the Master is assigned to, as shown in Figure 2-45.

4. **Add page numbers to the Master spread.** Select the Type tool and drag within the Master pages where you want the page numbers to appear. With the text cursor blinking in the text object, choose Type ➪ Insert Special Character ➪ Auto Page Number. The Prefix for the Master spread is listed in the text object, as shown in Figure 2-46. However, when you view a page that uses the Master page, the correct page number displays.

5. **Save the file.** Choose File ➪ Save to save the layout.

Figure 2-45: Content to the Master pages appears on all pages.

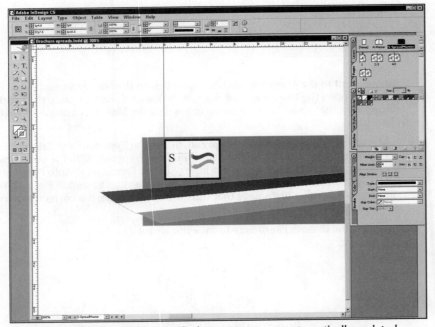

Figure 2-46: Page numbers specified on a Master are automatically updated whenever the page numbering changes.

Reshaping and wrapping text

Text is added to a layout by creating text frames with the Type tool. These text frames may be distorted by dragging on their corner and edge handles. By choosing Window ⇨ Type & Tables ⇨ Text Wrap, you can make the text wrap around objects and images in the layout.

Cross-Reference More details on working with text frames are presented in Chapter 15.

STEPS: Wrapping Text around Objects

1. **Create a text frame.** Text frames hold text. Using the In and Out ports, you can specify how text threads between multiple frames. To create a text frame, click on the Type tool and drag in the layout where you want the frame to be located, as shown in Figure 2-47.

Figure 2-47: The Type tool is used to create a text frame.

2. **Add text to the text frame.** With the text cursor blinking in the text frame, type the text into the text frame. (Or you can select the text that you want to paste from another application like a Word Processor and copy it to the Clipboard. Then, within InDesign, choose Edit ⇨ Paste.) The text appears, as shown in Figure 2-48, using the font and size specified in the Type menu.

Figure 2-48: You can add text to a text frame by copying and pasting.

3. **Reshape the text object.** With the text object selected, click on the Direct Selection tool in the Toolbox and, with the Shift key held down, drag the lower-left corner handle up to the top-left corner. Then drag the lower-right corner to the left until it forms a triangle shape, as shown in Figure 2-49. The text within the text object flows as needed to fit within the text object.

4. **Create a Clipping Path.** Another way to change the placement of text it to have it wrap around the borders of an imported image. A Clipping Path defines the area where the text can exist. InDesign lets you select to create a Clipping Path based on the image's Alpha Channel or a Photoshop Path, or it can detect the image edges to create a Clipping Path. With the image selected, choose Object ➪ Clipping Path. In the Clipping Path dialog box, shown in Figure 2-50, set the Type drop-down list to Detect Edges, the Threshold to 25, and the Tolerance to 2. Then click OK.

Figure 2-49: Changing text-frame shape changes how the text frame looks.

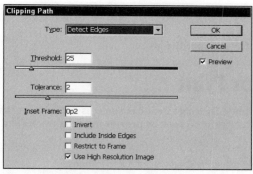

Figure 2-50: The Clipping Path dialog box.

5. **Specify how to wrap text.** Click on the image to select it. Then choose Window ➪ Type & Tables ➪ Text Wrap to open the Text Wrap palette. Click the Wrap Around Object Shape button, and the text wraps around the image using its Clipping Path as a border, as shown in Figure 2-51.

Figure 2-51: Using Clipping Paths, text wraps around an imported image.

6. **Save the file.** Choose File ➪ Save to save the layout.

Preparing a Layout for Print

When the document layout is complete, InDesign includes some useful features that are helpful as you prepare the document to be printed such as previewing separations and exporting the document to the PDF format.

Cross-Reference   See Part IX for more on printing using the Creative Suite applications.

Previewing separations

Often, previewing a document's separations prior to printing can help identify potential problems, allowing you to fix these problems before a costly print run. Separations for the current document may be viewed using the Separations Preview palette.

STEPS: Previewing Separations

1. **Open the Separations Preview palette.** To open the Separations Preview palette, shown in Figure 2-52, choose Output Preview ➪ Separations. Select the Separations option in the View field to see a list of each of the separations.

Figure 2-52: The Separations Preview lists a document's separations.

2. **View a separation.** To see a separation in the layout, click on the Visibility icon for the separations that you want to see, and the document is updated to show those selected separations, as shown in Figure 2-53.

Figure 2-53: The Visibility icons let you select which separations are displayed in the layout.

Exporting to PDF for printing

When exporting the layout to PDF, InDesign includes several export presets that you can use to configure the document for a specific destination. One of these presets is for print.

STEPS: Exporting to PDF

1. **Export to PDF using the Print preset.** Choose File ➪ PDF Export Presets ➪ Print. This opens a file dialog box where you can name the file to be exported. After you click the Save button, the Export PDF dialog box, shown in Figure 2-54, opens.

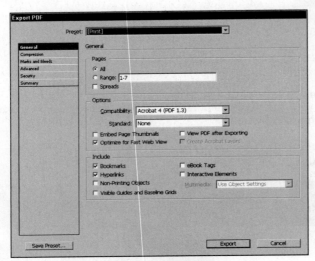

Figure 2-54: The Export PDF dialog box

2. **Open the PDF within Acrobat.** In the General panel of the Export PDF dialog box, enable the View PDF after Exporting option to have the document open in Acrobat after it's exported. Then click the Export button.

Repurposing a Document for Web Hosting

Completed print projects may be easily repurposed and used on the pages of a Web site. By doing this, you won't have to re-create designs specific to the Web. But Web pages require that the elements be optimized to reduce their file sizes.

Creative Suite offers two ways to repurpose designs for delivery on the Web. Acrobat files may be posted online and viewed using an Acrobat Reader plug-in, but before posting existing PDF files, Acrobat's PDF Optimizer feature may be used to reduce the size of the PDF file before posting it online.

In addition to PDF files, InDesign includes a feature that packages all content elements included in a layout and delivers it to GoLive where the elements may be reused in a Web page.

Using PDF Optimizer

The PDF Optimizer interface in Acrobat includes many settings to downsample images, unembed fonts and provide several cleanup options.

Cross-Reference

The PDF Optimizer is covered in Chapter 26.

STEPS: Using the PDF Optimizer

1. **Open the PDF Optimizer.** With the file that you want to optimize open in Acrobat, choose Advanced ⇨ PDF Optimizer. The PDF Optimizer interface, shown in Figure 2-55, includes three panels.

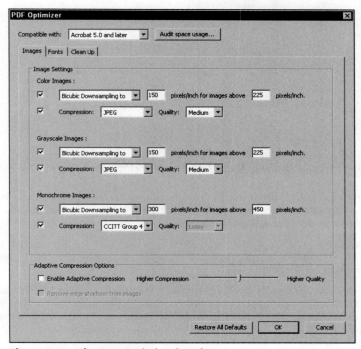

Figure 2-55: The PDF Optimizer interface

2. **Audit space usage.** Before changing any of the options, click the Audit Space Usage button at the top of the dialog box. Acrobat computes the size of all the various objects found in the PDF file and reports them in a Space Audit dialog box, shown in Figure 2-56.

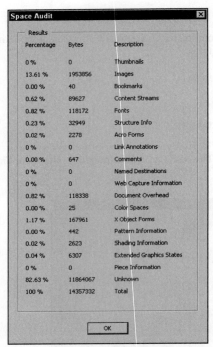

Figure 2-56: The Space Audit dialog box

3. **Configure image downsampling.** In the Images panel, select the Bicubic Downsampling option of 72 pixels/inch for all image above 72 pixels/inch. Then enable JPEG Compression with a Medium quality setting.

4. **Unembed fonts.** In the Fonts panel, select all the embedded fonts listed that you don't want to be included in the optimized PDF on the left and move them to the Fonts to Unembed pane on the right.

5. **Specify cleanup options.** Select the Clean Up panel, shown in Figure 2-57, and enable all the Remove and Discard options, making sure the Optimize the PDF for Fast Web View check box is enabled. Then click OK. In the file dialog box that opens, give the file a name and click OK.

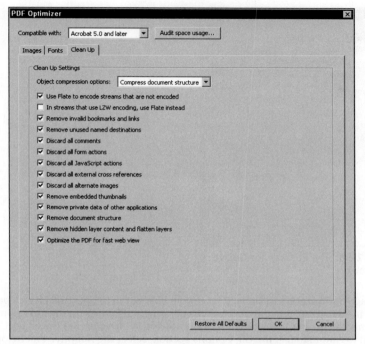

Figure 2-57: The Clean Up panel of the PDF Optimize dialog box

Packaging for GoLive

InDesign documents may be packaged and delivered for use in GoLive. This can make all images and objects in the design be downsampled and compressed and moved into a folder where GoLive can reference them. How the images are optimized is customizable.

Cross-Reference   More details on packaging for GoLive are covered in Chapter 25.

STEPS: Packaging an InDesign Layout for GoLive

1. **Open an InDesign document.** Choose File ➪ Open and locate the file that you want to package.

2. **Specify a package folder.** Choose File ➪ Package for GoLive. This command opens a file dialog box where you can name the folder where the packaged layout is placed.

3. **Set packaging options.** After a folder is selected, the Package for GoLive dialog box, shown in Figure 2-58, appears. This dialog box includes two panels. In the General panel, enable the View Package when Complete check box and set the View With drop-down list to GoLive.

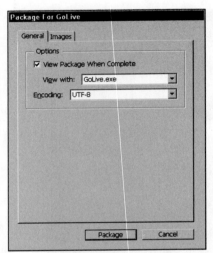

Figure 2-58: The Package for GoLive
dialog box

4. **Set image-optimization options.** Click on the Images tab to open the Images panel, shown in Figure 2-59. Enable the Optimized Formatted Images options to optimize and copy only the images using the formatting applied in InDesign. Set the Image Conversion method to Automatic. In the GIF Options section, select the Adaptive Palette option. In the JPEG Options section, set the Image Quality to Medium and the Format Method to Baseline. Then click the Package button.

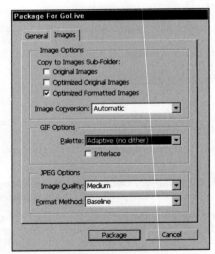

Figure 2-59: The Images panel in the
Package for GoLive dialog box

5. View the package in GoLive. After you click the Package button, all the elements used in the layout are copied to the designated package folder and the packaged PDF is opened within GoLive, as shown in Figure 2-60.

Figure 2-60: Once the packaged InDesign file is opened in GoLive, elements can be dragged to a Web page from the packaged window.

Summary

✦ Sketched ideas may be scanned directly into Acrobat and saved as a PDF file.

✦ PDF files may be submitted to reviewers by using e-mail. Reviewers can use Acrobat to enter comments into the PDF file and those comments are returned to the original sender.

✦ Photoshop is useful for editing images including adjusting image properties, cropping and extracting images and making images semi-transparent.

✦ Illustrator objects are also useful for enhancing a design. Using Illustrator's features such as effects, subtraction and 3D extruding, many interesting objects may be created.

✦ Version Cue enables Creative Suite users to save multiple versions of a file. It also enables workgroups of users to share and work on a project without interfering with one another.

✦ Content from multiple sources may be compiled and laid out in InDesign in preparation for printing and exporting.

✦ InDesign's Master pages let you place common elements that appear on multiple pages.

✦ Using the PDF Optimizer found in Acrobat, complex PDF files may be significantly reduced in size.

✦ InDesign files may be packaged for use in GoLive making it possible to repurpose layouts for use on the web.

✦   ✦   ✦

Setting Preferences

◆ ◆ ◆ ◆

In This Chapter

Understanding
preference settings

Setting individual
program preferences

◆ ◆ ◆ ◆

In your Creative Suite production workflow, you have seven different programs to work with: Illustrator CS, Photoshop CS, ImageReady CS, InDesign CS, Acrobat Professional, GoLive CS, and Version Cue. Fortunately, a single software publisher developed the programs, and the publisher uses a similar user interface among the programs. This alone helps you to develop an intuitive feel for how a program works and how to easily access commands that open tools and menus.

Taking the common user interface a step further, many of the CS programs offer you options for customizing your workplace and saving settings for preferences, creating custom workplace environments, and defining your own custom keyboard shortcuts to open menus and tools. In this chapter, you learn how to simplify your workflow by integrating common settings between programs that reduce confusion and the learning curve to master the program environments. All the CS programs are covered in this chapter; Version Cue is covered later, in Part II.

Getting to Know Common Preference Attributes

As stated in Chapter 1, this information is intended for people who have at least some experience with one of the CS applications in an earlier version. If you have such experience, you no doubt are familiar with preferences choices and options settings you make in preferences dialog boxes to help you customize a program to suit your work habits.

When creating a workflow either for yourself or for a group of production artists, you'll want to make preference choices in each of the programs to help you work effectively in a given program and, where possible, to help bring preference choices in parity between the programs.

If your workflow includes several other workers, and in particular if other workers use your computer in different shifts or at times when you're away from your desk, spend a little time talking with the people in your organization about the choices you'll make not only for preferences but also for the other items discussed in this chapter related to workspaces and keyboard shortcuts.

To begin our coverage on preferences, we start by addressing each application and offer a description of choices available respective to each program. The following is not intended to be exhaustive as far as preference options are concerned, but it does highlight some of the key points related to making adjustments for a Creative Suite workflow.

Opening the Preferences dialog box in all the CS programs can be handled with a keyboard shortcut. Fortunately, the shortcut is identical for all programs. Your first keyboard shortcut to commit to memory is ⌘/Ctrl+K. This shortcut opens the Preferences dialog box no mater what CS program you use. If you elect to use a menu command, Preferences are located under the application menu on the Mac (for example, the Illustrator menu to the right of the Apple logo/menu when using Adobe Illustrator CS) and under the Edit menu on Windows.

In all the programs, when you open the Preferences dialog box, a series of tabs or a list is made available for selecting categorical areas where specific options choices are found. In Illustrator CS and Photoshop CS, the categories are selected by opening a pull-down menu or clicking the Next/Previous buttons to change categories. InDesign, GoLive, and Acrobat use a list in the left pane of the Preferences dialog box to address specific categories. InDesign CS and Photoshop CS have a common function in that you can press ⌘/Ctrl+1, 2, 3, and so on, to toggle between the categories. When you first access a Preferences dialog box, General Preferences are selected in each program. If you select a category other than the General category in either GoLive CS or Acrobat Professional, the next time you return to the Preferences dialog box, the category remains selected. The other programs default back to showing the options for the General Preferences.

Setting application-specific preferences

You can open the Preferences dialog box with or without a document open in the application window. If you open preferences and make choices for some settings in some of the programs before you open a document, the preference options you enable or disable apply to all new documents you create. Some examples of application-specific preferences include setting the default page size in Adobe InDesign CS each time you create a new document. If your work most often involves a portrait U.S. letter–size page, you can set the preferences in InDesign CS to a standard portrait-size page. The same holds true for many other options like the units of measurement (inches, millimeters, picas, and so on).

In GoLive CS, you have options for viewing your document pages in a Layout mode, a Preview mode, a PDF preview, and several other choices. If you make a preference choice in GoLive before opening any document, the preferences apply to all subsequent files you view in GoLive CS.

In programs like Adobe Acrobat, almost all the preference choices you make are application-specific preferences and apply to all documents you subsequently open in Acrobat. Photoshop CS treats preferences similarly to Acrobat — preferences apply to all documents and most of the preferences you make in Illustrator CS behave similarly.

Setting document-specific preferences

In some cases, you can make a preference choice that applies only to an open document. This feature applies most often to InDesign CS. In InDesign, you can make a choice for the display performance of an open document or change the units of measure that apply to the open document. If you create a new document, you return to your default preferences. If you want to override defaults, close all open files and make your preference changes.

Tip

At times, you may be confused as to whether a preference setting is applied to a document or to the application. If you're not certain, make a preference choice with a document open in the application window. Save the file and close it. Create a new document and test the results. For example, check a font selection or a unit of measure in your new document if either choice was adjusted in your preferences. If the new document registers the same option as your old document, you'll know that the preference selection has been made as an application preference setting and will remain in effect until you change it.

Returning to default preferences

All the CS programs save preference changes to a file on your hard disk. If you want to return to the original preference settings (the ones in place when your CS programs were first installed), you can delete preference files from your hard disk. Preferences are much more complex in many CS programs and, often, you find many different preference settings that affect the behavior of a program. If you do intend to delete preferences, make a note for the location of a preference file and copy the file to another location on your hard disk. If you trash a file and the preferences are rebuilt or appear different than you expected, you can replace the new file with your copy. For specific locations of the preference files, use the online help in each CS program found under the Help menu. Follow the directions detailed in the help files to remove preferences manually.

In Illustrator CS, Photoshop CS, and InDesign CS, you can use a keyboard shortcut to delete preference files. In any of these programs, double-click on the program icon or click on a program alias in the Dock (Mac) or Start menu (Windows) and immediately press Shift+⌘+Option+Control (Mac) or Shift+Ctrl+Alt (Windows). A dialog box relative to the program you open asks you to confirm deletion of the preference file, as shown in Figure 3-1, when the keyboard shortcut is used. In this example, the key modifiers were used while opening Photoshop CS.

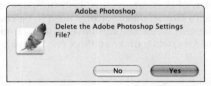

Figure 3-1: Click Yes in the dialog box to delete your preference file.

Making dynamic preference adjustments

When you change a preference setting, the change is dynamically applied to the application or a document for most settings in all the CS programs. You don't need to quit the program and relaunch it in order for the preference setting to be active. In a few cases, however, you need to restart a program in order to have new preference choices take effect. In Illustrator CS and Photoshop CS, changing the preferences for the plug-ins and scratch-disk locations requires you to restart the program before new locations for these items can be used.

Typically, you change the scratch partitions in these programs to a hard-disk hierarchy you want to use. For example, if you have two hard disks attached to your computer, you can set the primary scratch partition to the hard disk not containing your operating system and program files. The secondary partition is set to the drive containing your operating system and program files. When a choice like this is made, Illustrator and Photoshop first use the drive in the primary order as an extension of memory when a program eats up your available RAM. If more memory is needed, the partition in the second order is used, and so on. GoLive also has a scratch volume setting for QuickTime video editing, but I'm not sure it's worth mentioning.

With all other preferences, you can continue working in your program without relaunching it. The preferences remain in effect until you make another change in the Preferences dialog box. However, if you experience a program crash after making a new preference choice, the setting is not reflected when you relaunch the program, because preference settings are saved when quitting a program.

Tip   If you have many preference settings to change, make all your changes in the Preferences dialog box and then quit the program. Relaunch the program and all your preferences are intact. If you experience a program crash after relaunching the program, you won't have to reset the preference items you changed.

Setting the Program Preferences

Each of the CS applications has individual dialog boxes where preference choices are made. In some cases, preference options are identical between two or more programs; other choices are unique to each specific program. Some of the common options choices you'll want to understand are listed in the following sections, where preferences are covered for each individual program.

Illustrator CS preferences

When you press ⌘/Ctrl+K to bring up the Preferences dialog box in Adobe Illustrator CS, the default panel shows you the General Preferences, as shown in Figure 3-2. In the General panel, you'll find a number of options that change the view of elements on the Illustrator page and some settings that related to the behavior of objects. Not all these settings need to be coordinated and agreed upon by members of your workgroup. Some settings have an impact on your workflow with other artists and service providers, while other settings can be made according to users' personal preferences.

	Preferences
General	

Keyboard Increment: 0.0139
Constrain Angle: 0 °
Corner Radius: 0.17 in

☐ Object Selection by Path Only   ☐ Disable Auto Add/Delete
☐ Use Precise Cursors   ☐ Use Japanese Crop Marks
☑ Show Tool Tips   ☐ Transform Pattern Tiles
☑ Anti-aliased Artwork   ☐ Scale Strokes & Effects
☐ Select Same Tint %   ☐ Use Preview Bounds
☑ Append [Converted] Upon Opening Legacy Files

(Reset All Warning Dialogs)

OK
Cancel
Previous
Next

Figure 3-2: The Preferences dialog box

General Preferences

Among preferences choices that affect workflows are the following:

✦ **Show Tool Tips:** If other users work on your machine and they're not up to speed in Illustrator CS, showing tool tips can be a big help. A tool tip opens in a yellow rectangle when you place the cursor over a tool in Illustrator's toolbox.

Tip

At the top of the General Preferences is a setting for Keyboard Increment. This setting is a personal preference and not significant to workflows with other users. However, it is a personal choice you'll want to adjust from time to time. The setting in the adjacent field box relates to the amount an object moves when you strike an arrow key to nudge objects. If you work with a unit of measure like inches, setting the field box to a fraction of an inch is merely guesswork. A better adjustment might be to make these increments adjustable in points. If you want to quickly change the distance to a half a point for example, type **0p.5** (translating to 0 picas 0.5 points). This unit of measure works the same as when adjusting type sizes and leading distances.

✦ **Anti-Aliased Artwork:** The display of your vector objects is improved on-screen and may be helpful to other users to ensure they know the images are likely to print without jagged edges. Turning off this option has no effect on the printing of the image or porting it to other CS programs.

✦ **Append [Converted] Upon Opening Legacy Files:** This setting can have an impact on other users in your workflow. If the checkbox is enabled (checked or turned on) and you open an earlier version of an Illustrator document, the word *[Converted]* along with the brackets appears in the filename. If you save a converted file without changing the filename, the file appears with *[Converted]* contained in the name. If other users disable the checkbox, their converted files are saved with a default *not* including *[Converted]* in the filename. For the sake of consistency, be certain to agree upon how to set this option with your workflow colleagues.

✦ **Use Japanese Crop Marks:** This option is important for studios producing files that are printed in Japan. Japanese crop marks appear similar to crop marks printed from Adobe PageMaker. When you choose Filter ➪ Create ➪ Crop Marks with this option enabled, Japanese crop marks are created.

Other settings in the General Preferences help you work with Illustrator objects and views. You should become familiar with all the preference settings to help advance your knowledge of Illustrator CS, but the other settings have less impact on workflows in production studios. Therefore, we'll leave the remaining descriptions to what you can find in the *Adobe Illustrator CS Bible* by Ted and Jen Alspach (published by Wiley).

Converting legacy files in Illustrator CS

When you open a *legacy* Illustrator file (any file created in any version of Illustrator prior to the CS version), a dialog box opens, as shown in the following figure, informing you that the file was created in a previous version of Illustrator and asking you if you want to update the file.

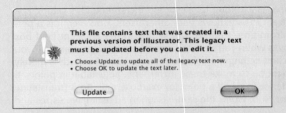

This dialog box opens because the type engine in Illustrator CS has been completely revamped, and all the type in the document needs to be updated. This dialog box also opens if no type exists in your legacy files.

To dismiss the dialog box, you have two choices. Click Update, in which case all type is updated in the document, or click OK. The default selection is OK, which is what happens if you press the Return/Enter key on your keyboard. The reason the default is set to OK is because your type may float on the page and lose many different paragraph attributes if you update the type in your document. Often, you'll find it better to *not* update all the type when you open a legacy file, particularly if you want to try to preserve the look of the original file.

Updating does occur when you click the Type tool in a block of text. Therefore, you can open the legacy file without performing a global update to the type and individually update different text blocks as you work on the document. You may find this option to be a better choice when working on legacy files with a lot of type.

Type and Auto Tracing

Click on the Next button in the Preferences dialog box, and you arrive at the Type and Auto Tracing preferences, as shown in Figure 3-3. Notice also that you can select the Type and Auto Tracing preferences by opening the pull-down menu and selecting Type and Auto Tracing. Most of these preference options are made for individual personal choices. Some attention should be paid to the following:

✦ **Size/Leading:** The Size/Leading adjustment can be performed using keyboard equivalents. To raise a point size in type, you press Shift+⌘+> (Mac) or Shift+Ctrl+> (Windows). Conversely, to lower point sizes, you press Shift+⌘+< (Mac) or Shift+Ctrl+< (Windows). For leading changes, you can use keyboard shortcuts Option/Alt+Down Arrow to increase leading and Option/Alt+Up Arrow to decrease leading. If you change the amount of the jump in points specified in the Size/Leading field box, users sharing your computer may immediately see unexpected results. If you want to change this option in multiple-user workflows, discussing it with your colleagues is best.

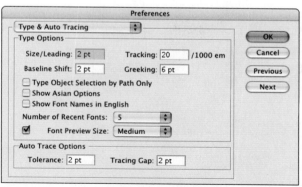

Figure 3-3: The Type and Auto Tracing dialog box

✦ **Baseline Shift:** The Baseline Shift setting is also accessible with keyboard shortcuts (Shift+Option/Alt+Up Arrow moves the baseline one increment up and Shift+Option/Alt+Down Arrow moves the baseline one increment down). Likewise, you may want to leave the Baseline Shift at default values.

✦ **Tracking:** Tracking affects the amount of space between characters. This type option can also be adjusted by using keyboard shortcuts (⌘/Ctrl+Right Arrow increases text tracking, and ⌘/Ctrl+Left Arrow tracks text more tightly). Once again, to prevent unexpected results from users, you may find the defaults to be adequate.

✦ **Type Object Selection by Path Only:** This preference option is important if InDesign users are sharing your computer. Essentially, when the check box is enabled, text can be selected only when you click either the Selection tool or the Direct Selection tool on the path (usually at the baseline of a line of text). A handy feature in both InDesign CS and Illustrator CS is when you double-click the Selection tool or the Direct Selection tool anywhere on a text block, the tool changes to the Type tool, where you can edit text in the block. If you enable this preference, InDesign CS users who know less about Illustrator will likely become confused. In multiple-user workflow environments, leaving the check box disabled is best.

Units and Display Performance

Click the Next button or select the pull-down menu and choose Units and Display Performance. The options choices for Units and Display Performance are shown in Figure 3-4.

✦ **General:** If you consistently design pieces in a unit of measure such as millimeters or inches, you should make the appropriate adjustment from choices you make in the General pull-down menu. This setting affects your personal workflow and your work in design production workgroups. The other settings for strokes and type are almost universally set to points, so leave these at their defaults.

✦ **Identify Objects By:** The default is set to Object Name, which is okay unless your workflow involves working with XML objects. If you do work with XML, you'll want to periodically change this preference setting. To understand completely how this option works, open the Window menu and click on Variables.

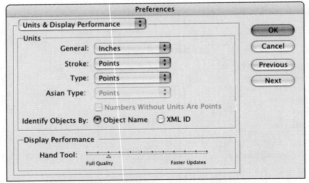

Figure 3-4: The Units & Display Performance preferences dialog box

Cross-Reference

For more information on XML, see Chapter 27.

Using XML objects requires you to adhere to strict naming conventions. If you save an Illustrator CS document as SVG (Scalable Vector Graphics) format for use with other Adobe CS programs, the names must conform to naming conventions permitted by XML. For example, you must begin an object name with a letter, an underscore, or a colon. Filenames with spaces are not permitted. When you change the preference setting in the Units and Display Performance to view XML IDs, Illustrator shows the ID that will be exported when the file is saved. You can view the names in the Visibility palette and edit the names as long as you adhere to conventions acceptable to XML. In Figure 3-5, you can see the Visibility palette as it is shown when objects are viewed by Object Name in the left palette and by XML ID in the right palette.

Figure 3-5: The Variables palette with the Units and Display Performance preferences enabled for Identify Objects by Object Name (left). On the right, the preference for Identify Objects By is changed to XML ID.

Guides and Grid

At first glance, the Guides and Grid may not seem important to you. However, the preference choices you make here can impact your work in the other Adobe CS applications or in workflows with multiple users. If you work with a grid, it will be beneficial to bring the grid size and style to identical views across all the CS programs supporting grids. Click the Next button or open the pull-down menu and choose Guides and Grid from the menu options to open the Guides & Grid preference options. A few key points to address in the dialog box shown in Figure 3-6 include the following:

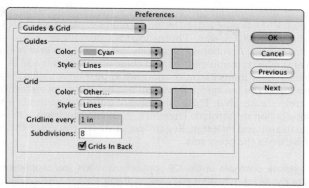

Figure 3-6: The Guides & Grid preference options dialog box

✦ **Guide Color:** Guides are drawn from the ruler wells, while grids are created on the pasteboard from attributes you set in the Guide and Grid preferences dialog box. The default Guides color is cyan in Illustrator CS and the same color value is used in Photoshop CS. In Acrobat, the Guides color is light blue. InDesign goes much farther in offering you options for individually changing guide attributes for margins, columns, bleeds, slugs, and background; none of the default colors match the other programs (see "InDesign preferences" later in this chapter). GoLive CS does not support a grid and guide preference option; however the layout grid added to a GoLive page is also light blue. Illustrator CS makes the only distinction between the colors of Guides and Grids in the default settings. While Guides are cyan, the Grid color defaults to a light gray. To avoid confusion when working between programs, you may want to change all grids and guides in all programs to the same value. Either a light blue or a cyan color intuitively suggests to users that the lines belong to either a grid or a guide.

✦ **Guide Style:** Illustrator CS and Photoshop CS offer you options between using lines or dots (Illustrator) and dashed lines (Photoshop). Because the other programs support lines only, you can leave the Style option set to the default Lines value.

✦ **Grid Color:** Illustrator CS and InDesign CS use a light gray as the default Grid color while Photoshop users a darker gray color. Acrobat and GoLive CS use blue for grid colors.

✦ **Grid Style:** The Style is the same as noted in the preceding bullet for Guide Style. Photoshop CS offers three options for lines, dashed lines, and dots. As a general rule, you might want to leave the Lines style at the default.

✦ **Gridline Every:** This unit is the major gridline measurement. If you are coordinating grids between programs, you'll want to set the same value in the other CS applications.

✦ **Subdivisions:** This item is the minor gridlines. Again, set this value the same across all programs. Both the major and minor gridlines are volatile and are likely to change according to your designs. You may want to decide on a color to be consistent across applications for guides and grid, but you're likely to make frequent changes to the major and minor divisions. Keep in mind that if you do so, you should review these settings when starting new designs. If you want to coordinate a grid between Illustrator or InDesign and Adobe Acrobat for creating a PDF form and you decide to use a layout grid, it will be best to check the grid settings before beginning your work. At times, you may also want to change the grid color if you need to see the grid while working on a background color similar to the grid color. This condition may also vary between projects, so you'll want to revisit these preferences often.

✦ **Grids in Back:** Illustrator CS offers you an option to position the grid behind all objects when the Grids In Back check box is enabled. InDesign CS offers separate settings for positioning the grids and guides in back while Photoshop CS automatically keeps all grids and guides in front of images. Acrobat is completely different — the grid is automatically placed on top of the background content and some elements you add in Acrobat such as form fields. Other items like note windows appear on top of grids and guides. Guides appear on top of the background content but behind some elements such as form fields you create in Acrobat. The positioning of grids and guides is not customizable in either Photoshop or Acrobat. Therefore, your only decision is to adjust grids in back between Illustrator and InDesign. Regardless of where you place the grid, try to keep it consistent between the programs.

Tip

Setting major and minor gridline distances in the CS applications offers you proportional spacing without the ability to create more custom grid designs. If you want to create a design grid not achievable in the Preferences dialog box, draw lines in Illustrator CS and use the Blend tool to set up spacing equidistant between the lines. Save the file as PDF. You can import the PDF document in InDesign and place the file on a background layer to use as your custom grid. You can open the PDF document in Acrobat and position elements created in Acrobat, such as form fields, and copy/paste them to your form design.

Smart Guides and Slices

The most important thing to remember when using Smart Guides is the keyboard shortcut to turn them on and off. ⌘/Ctrl+U toggles the on/off switch for Smart Guides. When the guides are turned on with all the default display options checked, as shown in Figure 3-7, you see temporary guidelines at 90-degree and 45-degree angles. These guidelines can get in the way when users want to draw freeform objects. Accessing a keyboard shortcut to turn them off is the best solution for hiding the guides. In workflow situations where many users work with Illustrator, they expect to have the guides turned off when striking the default keyboard shortcut. Be certain not to change this key sequence when assigning new keyboard shortcuts.

Cross-Reference

For more information on customizing keyboard shortcuts, see Chapter 4.

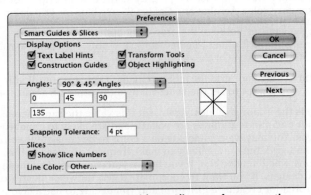

Figure 3-7: The Smart Guides & Slices preference options dialog box

Adding custom colors to the Preference dialog box on the Mac

If you want to change colors to a custom color for preference options in any of the CS programs where you see a color swatch like the one shown in Figure 3-7, double click on the color swatch. On Windows, you can make color choices from the Windows color palette and add custom colors by adjusting RGB values. However, on the Mac, with OS X Panther, you have many more capabilities for defining custom colors.

After double clicking on the color swatch, the Colors palette opens as shown in the following figure. In GoLive you must option-click. Click on the Color Palettes icon positioned third from the top-left in the Colors dialog box. From the List pull-down menu, you have menu choices for selecting different color palettes, and you also have an option for creating your own custom color palette. Select New from the pull-down menu and name your palette. In the following figure, we created a palette and named it CustomColors.

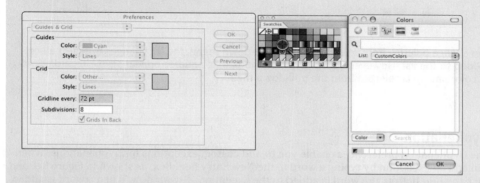

At this point you can select any color on your document page or pick a color from the Swatches palette to add to your custom color palette. Click the magnifying glass icon in the palette and position it over a color on a document page or position the magnifying glass over a color in the Swatches palette. Click the mouse button, and the color is added to the color bar adjacent to the magnifying glass in the Colors dialog box.

When you see a color in the color bar, you can click in the color bar and drag the color to the list window. The color is listed with a default name that includes your palette name (in this example, CustomColors–1) as shown in the following figure. Adding a second color creates a name CustomColor-2, and so on. You can also add the color to the swatches at the bottom of the dialog box and add colors from different palettes. Click in the color bar and drag to one of the squares at the bottom of the dialog box to add the color to the swatches.

Continued

Continued

As you change palettes from selections in the pull-down menu, the list changes to reflect all colors added to the list. However, colors added to the palette squares appear visible regardless of what color palette is selected from the pull-down menu.

Hyphenation

The Hyphenation preferences enable you to add custom exceptions for hyphenations. When you add an exception by typing a word in the New Entry field box, as shown in Figure 3-8, and click the Add button, the word is added to the Exceptions list window. When a word is added to the list, Illustrator won't hyphenate the word.

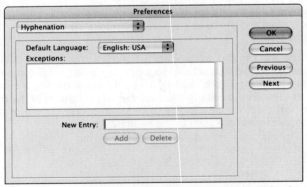

Figure 3-8: The Hyphenation preference options dialog box

If you create multiple-language documents, you'll want to change the Default Language option in the Preferences dialog box's Hyphenation sheet. Be certain to make the appropriate language choice from the options available in the pull-down menu when laying out a design in a specific language. Be certain to change the defaults back to the most commonly used language in your workflow before quitting Illustrator.

Note   InDesign has an impressive means for handling words for spelling and hyphenation. However, the dictionary and hyphenation editing occurs in a separate dialog box instead of the preference settings. To integrate hyphenation exceptions between the programs, you need to address preferences in Illustrator and separately address hyphenation exceptions in the Dictionary dialog box in InDesign.

Plug-Ins and Scratch

The Plug-Ins & Scratch preferences work the same in Photoshop and Illustrator. GoLive also supports one scratch disk for QuickTime editing. Scratch disks are used to store temporary files and the extension of memory when your physical RAM runs out. Ideally, scratch partitions are best used on secondary hard disks for primary scratch disk locations. For example, if you have a second hard drive attached to your computer, use the drive not containing your operating system and application files as the primary scratch disk. Your secondary scratch disk would be your boot drive containing your operating system.

As shown in Figure 3-9, Illustrator supports assigning two scratch disks. Photoshop supports up to four scratch disks. All hard disks and partitions connected to your computer appear from pull-down menus.

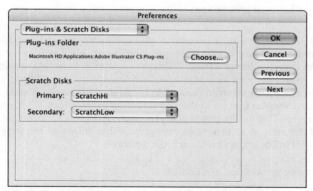

Figure 3-9: Illustrator supports up to two selections for scratch disks.

In workflow environments, one of the first tasks to perform after installing the CS programs is to visit the Plug-ins & Scratch preferences and identify what disks are used for primary and secondary scratch partitions. When you make choices for these preferences in either Illustrator or Photoshop, you need to quit the program and relaunch it before the preferences take effect.

Caution   When assigning scratch disk locations, be certain not to use slow devices such as USB hard disks, external Zip drives, memory cartridges, and so on. You can use external Firewire drives with satisfaction; however, the slower drives actually decrease performance when working with programs supporting scratch disks.

File Handling and Clipboard

There are two important considerations to make in the File Handling & Clipboard preferences dialog box, shown in Figure 3-10, with regard to workflow situations. These include handling Version Cue and the way you want to copy and paste Illustrator data.

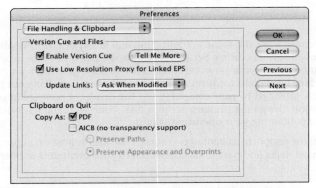

Figure 3-10: File Handling and Clipboard preferences

   ✦ **Enable Version Cue:** All the Creative Suite programs with the exception of Acrobat support Version Cue. In order to activate Version Cue, you need to enable it in your System Preferences (Mac) or Version Cue Control Panel (Windows). After activating Version Cue at the system level, you then need to activate Version Cue for individual programs. Version Cue is automatically activated from GoLive. In Illustrator, Photoshop, and InDesign, you need to turn Version Cue on in the File Handling preferences. Click on the check box for Enable Version Cue in Illustrator and you're ready to use Version Cue. Enabling Version Cue is dynamic in all programs except InDesign. InDesign requires you to enable Version Cue, quit InDesign, and relaunch the program.

Cross-Reference   For more information on using Version Cue, see Chapter 7.

   ✦ **Clipboard on Quit:** The description in this section of the File Handling and Clipboard dialog box is a bit misleading, because it implies that selections you make are handled when quitting Illustrator. In reality, you have to make your choice regardless of whether Clipboard data are converted upon quitting Illustrator or when copying and pasting data between Illustrator and InDesign. If you enable PDF as an option, the data pasted from Illustrator to an InDesign page is imported as a grouped object and uneditable. If you disable the PDF option and click on AICB (no transparency support), all pasted objects are individually selectable and editable in Adobe InDesign. You need to make a choice as to whether you want to have InDesign users edit objects in InDesign or restrict the object editing to Illustrator. For independent artists creating your own workflows, it's a good idea to enable the option for AICB so you can quickly access individual objects where you may want to change an object's color, move an individual object, or reshape an object.

Note   *AICB* stands for Adobe Illustrator Clip Board.

Photoshop CS preferences

Adobe Photoshop preference settings are accessed by pressing ⌘/Ctrl+K or by choosing Preferences from the Application menu (Mac) or from the Edit menu (Windows). The Preferences dialog box has nine panes that are accessed by opening the pull-down menu or by pressing the ⌘/Ctrl+1 through 9 keys when the Preferences dialog box is open. All the settings you make in Photoshop relate to tool and menu features apart from color settings options. For Color Settings, you need to access a different dialog box.

Cross-Reference   For color preference settings, see Chapter 6.

Among the preference options most applicable to workflow environments are those covered in the following sections.

General Preferences

Most of the options in the General Preferences are the same as Photoshop 7. The History Log item in the dialog box shown in Figure 3-11, however, is new to Photoshop CS and quite helpful in workflow environments. The History log file is a recorded history of a Photoshop session that can be reported in a text file or as XML metadata. The difference between the two files is that a text file records your steps in a Photoshop session and saves the steps to a text file apart from the edited image. When using metadata, the history steps are included in the file and can be viewed either in the File Info dialog box (File ➪ File Info) or in the File Browser window.

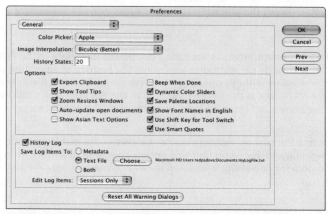
Figure 3-11: In the General Preferences, you can enable the radio button for recording history information.

To record your steps in an editing session, click the radio button for Metadata to include the history in the document or click the radio button for Text File to record steps in a separate ASCII file. You can click the Choose button and navigate your hard disk to choose a directory where you want to save your external file if Text File is selected as the option for the file history.

If using the Metadata option, open a file after setting your preferences to record your editing history. After completing your editing, choose File ➪ File Info; a dialog box opens showing you a panel of items on the left side and information about the selected item on the right. Click the History item as shown in Figure 3-12, and you see the document editing history in the right pane. All the steps performed in your editing session appear in a scrollable window.

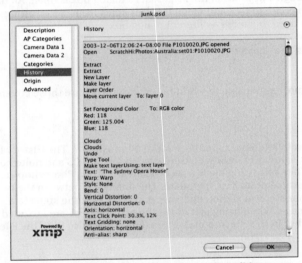

Figure 3-12: The History option shows the editing history steps.

What's very helpful in workflow environments is accessing document metadata in the File Browser window. You can view various file attributes and show the history of an editing session right in the File Browser window without opening the document. Click on a file in the File Browser and click the tab for Metadata in the lower-right side of the File Browser window. Scroll the Metadata scroll bar shown in Figure 3-13, and you can view the editing steps in the File Browser window.

If you need to retrace steps in a Photoshop editing session, be certain to enable an option for recording your history. In workflows where you find this option an essential feature for a production task, be certain the preference setting is enabled on all computers using Photoshop before beginning a project.

File Handling

Among the most important preference settings in a workflow is the new setting for enabling Version Cue. The traditional settings for File Saving Options are included in the File Handling preferences as well as the option for enabling Version Cue, as shown in Figure 3-14.

Figure 3-13: When viewing a document's editing history in the File Browser, you can see the editing steps without opening the file in Photoshop.

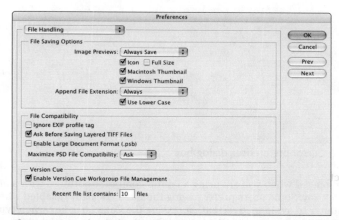

Figure 3-14: Check the box for Enable Version Cue Workgroup File Management to save different versions of a Photoshop file.

Version Cue offers you options for saving different file edits that are not available through creating different layers. For example, if you want to change the color mode of an image, you can't create a layer to accept a different color mode while maintaining other layers in another color mode. However, with Version Cue, you can convert modes and save different versions of the same file.

As a matter of practice, you'll want to enable Version Cue for all Photoshop work in your personal workflow or when working among groups of production artists.

Cross-Reference   For more information on Version Cue, see Chapter 7.

Display and Cursors

Display & Cursors offer you options for different channel displays, pixel dithering, cursor shapes for painting tools, and cursor displays for the non-painting tools, as shown in Figure 3-15. About the most important preference setting is to use the default Painting Cursor shape for a Brush Size, because most Photoshop users expect this cursor behavior when working in Photoshop. Another option common to many users is to leave the default for other Cursors at the Standard option that displays the tool icon for a selected tool in the Photoshop toolbox and to let users activate Precise cursors by pressing the Caps Lock key. In workflow situations, you'll want to keep these defaults intact if the behavior is familiar to the workgroup members.

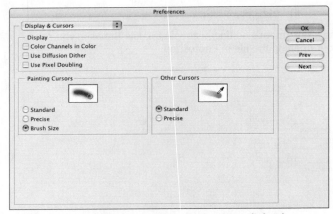

Figure 3-15: The Display & Cursor preferences dialog box

These defaults might be changed when you are using a laptop computer outfitted with a utility to disable the Caps Lock key. Some users prefer having the Caps Lock key disabled when working on a laptop computer to avoid inadvertently pressing the Caps Lock key when typing. If this is the case for individual users, the Display and Cursor preferences might be changed per individual users.

Transparency and Gamut

Users are accustomed to viewing transparency displayed as a grid with alternating white and gray squares. If you change the preferences in Photoshop, InDesign users may become confused. As a rule, keep intact the default settings shown in Figure 3-16.

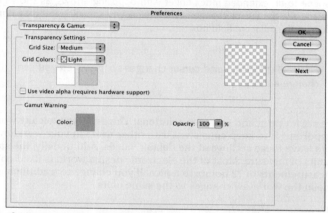

Figure 3-16: The Transparency & Gamut preferences dialog box

Units and Ruler

Units of measurement are specified in the Units & Rulers preferences. When you show rulers in Photoshop (press ⌘/Ctrl+R), the ruler units are derived from the dialog box shown in Figure 3-17. If your workflow consistently uses a particular unit of measure, you'll want to change the ruler units by accessing the desired unit of measurement from pull-down menu choices for Rulers. The default unit is inches.

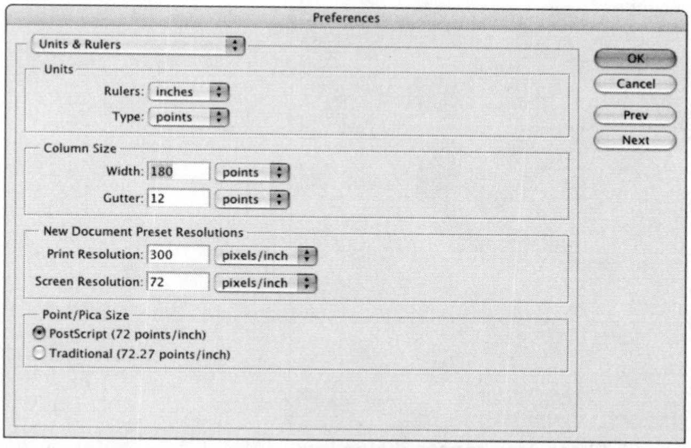

Figure 3-17: The Units and Rulers preferences dialog box

Columns and gutter sizes apply specifically to the file you are editing. Because users change column sizes according to an editing job, you don't have to worry about setting any particular default value.

Tip

When adjusting some options where values are changed in field boxes, you'll notice the hand cursor change shape to an extended index finger with opposing arrows, as shown in Figure 3-18. Whenever you see the cursor change to this shape, you can click and drag horizontally to change values in the adjacent field box.

Figure 3-18: The hand cursor changes shape when you can change a value.

New Document Presets are set for print and screen resolutions. The defaults typically work in most workflows. What's important is to keep consistent with other users in your workflow and be certain that all users leave these settings at the default values. Additionally, the same holds true for Point/Pica units of measure. Most of the electronic design world is fixed on PostScript point-to-pica measurements of 72 points to a pica. If you change to traditional values, be certain everyone in the workflow changes to the same units.

Guides, Grid, and Slices

The Guides and Grid options for colors and units of measure should match the other CS programs supporting Guides and Grid preference options. As mentioned earlier in this chapter when Guides and Grid was discussed with Adobe Illustrator CS, you'll want to bring the guide colors to the same values across the CS programs especially in multiple-user workflows. Although not a major problem, the grid color in Photoshop is a darker gray than the grid color used in Illustrator and InDesign. You change grid colors in Photoshop CS the same way you do in Illustrator CS. You have options for major gridlines (Gridline Every) and minor gridlines (Subdivisions), as shown in Figure 3-19.

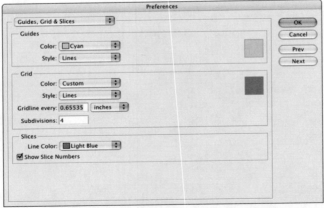

Figure 3-19: The Grids, Guides & Slices preferences dialog box

Cross-Reference   For information on changing guide colors and grid values, see the "Guides and Grid" section for Adobe Illustrator CS earlier in this chapter.

Slices are used when creating graphics for Web pages where an image may be divided in parts to optimize download speeds. When slicing images and objects, the sliced parts are represented with a keyline border. You have choices for the display of the keyline border colors in Photoshop CS, Illustrator CS, and ImageReady CS. Borders default to black in GoLive, and ImageReady slices default to a dark blue. Illustrator and Photoshop default to a light blue. You may find it unnecessary to bring the slice colors consistent between the CS programs, because each slice is also represented with a small icon in the top left corner denoting the number of the slice. This visual representation of slices may be enough to clearly show you when an image or object has been sliced. If you change default colors, again, the most important thing to do is keep consistent among other designers in your workflow.

Plug-Ins and Scratch Disks

Figure 3-20 shows that you have as many as four different scratch disks that can be identified in Photoshop CS. Because Photoshop is the most memory-hungry application in the Creative Suite, Scratch Disks options enable you to extend memory to multiple disk drives and partitions.

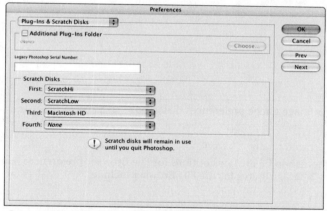

Figure 3-20: Photoshop CS supports up to four disk drives.

Additionally, Photoshop enables you to identify a second Plug-Ins folder where third-party plug-ins can be stored in a folder apart from the application plug-ins. If you use custom plug-ins to extend Photoshop features, keep your third-party plug-ins in a separate folder. To identify a second Plug-Ins folder, check the box for Additional Plug-Ins Folder. The Choose an Additional Plug-Ins Folder dialog box opens immediately the first time you check the box. Navigate your hard drive and select the folder containing your plug-ins. If you want to change the locations of plug-ins, click the Choose button and the same dialog box opens where you can locate another folder.

Memory and Image Cache

The preference options shown in Figure 3-21 are more individual and don't necessarily require consistency among other users in your workflow. Adjusting these settings depends on the physical attributes of the machine where Photoshop CS is installed. If memory is limited, try to reduce the cache level from the default value of 4 to a lower number. If all your work is performed in Photoshop, you can change the Maximum Used by Photoshop percentage of total memory allocated to Photoshop to a higher value than the default 50-percent figure. If using InDesign CS, Illustrator CS, and Adobe Acrobat and/or GoLive, leave the default maximum memory allocated to Photoshop at 50 percent to provide sufficient memory to the other programs.

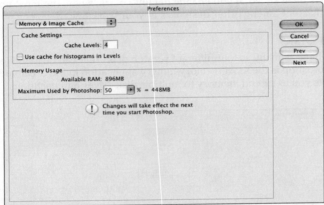

Figure 3-21: The Memory & Image Cache preferences dialog box

File Browser

The new File Browser in Photoshop CS includes options for File Browser preferences in a dialog box, as shown in Figure 3-22. Attributes for the File Browser include:

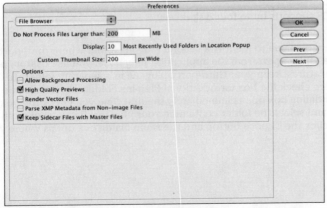

Figure 3-22: File Browser preferences are new in Photoshop CS.

✦ **Do Not Process Files Larger Than:** This setting can be important in your workflow. The default setting is 200MB. If a file is larger than 200MB, users expecting to see all files in the File Browser won't see an image preview for files above the setting in the field box. If you need to show image previews for larger files, change the setting according to the preferences of your workflow members.

✦ **Display:** The Location window appears in the top-left corner of the File Browser where you see a tab for Folder or your hard drive(s) locations. You can supply a value between 0 and 30 to view the most recently viewed folders in the File Browser. When you quit Photoshop or close the File Browser, the default location shown in the Location bar is derived from your last view.

✦ **Custom Thumbnail Size:** The View menu in the File Browser offers options for fixed thumbnail views of Small, Medium, and Large. You also have an option for a custom thumbnail view. The custom view for thumbnail images shown in the File Browser is determined from this preference setting. You can set the custom size from 128 pixels to 1024 pixels.

✦ **Allow Background Processing:** Image previews and metadata take some time to process and ultimately display in the File Browser window. You can choose to let your computer pre-generate the views in a memory cache in the background while you're working in the File Browser.

✦ **High-Quality Previews:** Image quality is improved when this option is enabled. Like everything else in Photoshop, as you improve views and use memory caches, the performance of the program slows down, especially on older computers with slower processors and less memory.

✦ **Render Vector Files:** The File Browser can display vector images you create in programs like Adobe Illustrator CS. If you want to see thumbnail views for vector images, they need to be rendered, which also slows performance. Check this box to see your Illustrator CS files as image previews.

✦ **Parse XMP Metadata from Non-Image Files:** Metadata can be supplied for many different file types, including non-image files such as text files. If you want to view or add metadata for these file types, select this option.

✦ **Keep Sidecar Files with Master Files:** *Sidecar files* are used to process metadata in other applications. The sidecar file is a separate file apart from your master file from which the XML data were extracted. If you want to edit the metadata or move, copy, delete, or rename XMP sidecar files along with a master file, leave the default option enabled.

For more information on XML data, see Chapter 27.

InDesign CS preferences

Adobe InDesign supports an elaborate set of preferences as well as options settings in a vast number of dialog boxes. On some occasions, you may expect to see a control in the Preferences dialog box and not find the option choice you want. If this is the case, poke around the dialog boxes and palettes and you're most likely to find a setting suited for a particular task. The first order of business when you begin using InDesign is to become familiar with all the preference choices.

One thing to keep in mind when you use Adobe InDesign CS is that preference choices can be enabled or disabled with or without a document open in the InDesign window. In many cases, changing a preference setting when no document is in view in the InDesign window changes the preference for all subsequent documents you create. If preferences are changed when a document is in view, often the preference change applies to only the open document. Therefore, you have a choice between setting application-level preferences and document-level preferences. Try to keep this in mind when you make changes in the Preferences dialog box as you customize the InDesign environment for your workflow.

General

The General preferences are shown each time you choose InDesign ➪ Preferences (Mac) or Edit ➪ Preferences (Windows) or press ⌘/Ctrl+K. General preferences, as shown in Figure 3-23, offer you options for page displays, handling the InDesign toolbar, printing options, and handling Clipboard data. Among the more important preference options for you to consider in workflow environments include the following:

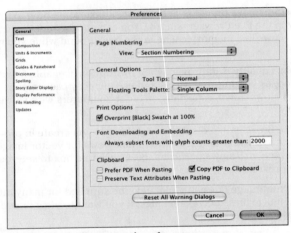

Figure 3-23: The General preference pane.

General Options

Choices in the General Options relate to the display of the InDesign toolbar that can be changed to view the palette as a single column, a two-column display, or an option for displaying the toolbar as a row for easy placement below the control palette at the top of the InDesign window. This personal preference affects single-user workflows but should be a standard you employ when multiple users access your machine. Other users working on the same machine should agree upon whatever display you choose.

Print Options

The default is selected for overprinting all objects specified with the Black Swatch at 100%. InDesign contains a Black Swatch in the color palette that you'll want to use for type; by default, all type using this color overprints when your files are printed.

Caution What's important is to be certain to create another Black Swatch for objects you don't want to overprint if you leave this preference setting unchanged. It's also critical in workflow environments to be certain the preferences and overprinting are consistent among all users.

For more information on overprints, see Part IX.

Font Downloading and Embedding

The default is set to subset fonts with *glyphs* (the number of characters in a font set) fewer than 2,000. This default applies to OpenType fonts where the number of glyphs can be more than 65,000. PostScript fonts contain a maximum of 256 glyphs. Instead of embedding fonts in files exported to PDF with all 65,000 characters in an OpenType font, the default is set to subset the fonts and embed only the characters used in the document if the glyph count is greater than 2,000. By default, you can leave this setting alone and readjust it for special circumstances if an entire OpenType font needs to be embedded in a PDF document.

Clipboard

Options for the Clipboard preferences related to copying data in InDesign and then pasting it into other CS programs or pasting other CS application data into InDesign offer choices for file format while copying and pasting and whether text attributes are preserved. Settings you make here are important when exchanging data between CS applications and when sending your InDesign files or other CS application files containing pasted InDesign data to other users. Essentially, you have two considerations: the file format used when you copy InDesign data and the attributes assigned when you paste data from other CS applications into an InDesign document.

✦ **Copying InDesign data:** The Copy PDF to Clipboard option has no effect on copying and pasting data from an InDesign page back into the same or a different InDesign file. Regardless of whether this option is selected, the copy/paste feature within InDesign behaves as you would expect in any program. When the Copy PDF to Clipboard option is disabled and you copy data from InDesign and then paste it into another CS application, the data are not pasted. You must enable the check box for Copy PDF to Clipboard in order to copy/paste or drag and drop data between InDesign and Photoshop and Illustrator.

Text can be copied and pasted between InDesign and GoLive and Acrobat, but you can't drag and drop text between the applications. A text insertion cursor needs to be present in GoLive or an insertion cursor created with Acrobat's TouchUp Text tool unless pasting in objects like form fields or comment pop-up note windows.

When copying data from InDesign to Photoshop CS, all type copied from a frame selection using the Selection or Direct Selection tool is pasted in Photoshop as a vector object and is rasterized when you press the Enter key to accept the data. If you want to paste editable text in Photoshop, first click the Type Tool in a document window, then choose Edit ➪ Paste. Type pasted in Illustrator CS is recognized as type regardless of whether the text is selected with the Type tool or with the Selection tool or Direct Selection tool.

✦ **Pasting data into InDesign:** There are two option choices that control pasting data from CS applications into InDesign. If you enable the option to Prefer PDF when Pasting, data copied from Illustrator preserves transparency, blends, patterns, and similar effects applied in Illustrator. If you elect not to use pasting PDF data, many of these effects are lost. The second option handles type integrity. If you disable the Preserve Text Attributes when Pasting option, type copied from Illustrator and pasted into InDesign loses text-editing capabilities and comes into InDesign as a grouped object. To preserve text editing, be certain this option is enabled.

Copying and pasting text on a path

InDesign CS supports creating type on a path. To create type on a path, use the Pen tool to draw a path. Click the Type tool in the InDesign Toolbox and hold the mouse button down until you see the Type on a Path tool. Select the tool and click on the path. The insertion point defaults to the left side of the line for left-justified text. Type a sentence and you can see the type following the path.

If you decide to copy type on a path from InDesign and paste the data into an Illustrator or Photoshop document, the type is broken up in Illustrator into single-character text blocks. Type pasted in Photoshop is pasted as an object and rasterized losing the type editing attributes. If you create an insertion cursor in either program, the type can be pasted at the insertion point but follows a straight horizontal line losing the path attributes. You can create a path in either Illustrator or Photoshop and paste type on a path, but this requires you to precisely draw the same path in Illustrator or Photoshop as you draw in InDesign.

For copying and pasting type on a path from InDesign to Illustrator while preserving the original path, you do have a workaround. Create a path in InDesign and add type similar to what's shown in the following figure. Be certain the preference option is enabled for Copy PDF to Clipboard, and copy the text and path.

text on a path created in Adobe InDesign CS

In Adobe Illustrator, paste the data and you'll notice the text block is broken up. As shown in the following figure, you can see small anchor points adjacent to each character indicating the line of text is broken. Selecting all the text in the line immediately demonstrates that only individual characters are selectable with the Type tool.

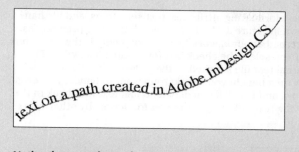

Notice the pasted text also contains a bounding box, as shown in the preceding figure by the lines at all sides around the text. To reform the paragraph, you need to delete the bounding box and either hide the path or lock it. With the Selection tool, select only the text characters—selecting only text should be easy after the bounding box is deleted and the path is either hidden or locked.

Choose Edit ⇨ Cut to cut the text and either unhide the path or unlock it so it's selectable. With the Type tool, click on the path to create an insertion point. Choose Edit ⇨ Paste and the text is reformed into a single body of type, as shown in the following figure.

Text

The Text preferences handle some text formatting attributes, text selections, and file handling. Most of the Type Options shown in Figure 3-24 relate to individual user preferences. The one option you need to be concerned about in workflow environments is the check box in the Links area of the dialog box. If you select the check box for Create Links When Placing Text and Spreadsheet Files, the external text file is linked to the InDesign file. For consistency's sake, you should decide how members in your workgroup want to handle text originating in programs like Microsoft Word and Excel. If you decide to link text files back to the original text file, you'll want to copy the text links to your server for access by other users editing the InDesign file.

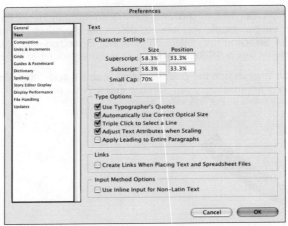

Figure 3-24: Text preferences handle various options for text display, selections, and file handling.

Composition

Composition preferences relate to text formatting issues and how text is wrapped around objects. How text is composed in InDesign might be a good topic for discussion among members of your workflow, because the behavior of text varies as you change the options. For example, changing an item as simple as Text Wrap Only Affects Text Beneath (shown in Figure 3-25) may present problems for other users if they expect the text wrap around images to be applied to objects behind text blocks. Some of the settings here affect the layout composition tasks, so changes from defaults should be shared with all users in a workflow.

Units and Increments

Similar settings are available in Adobe Illustrator for ruler units, and some of these option settings relate to individual user preferences. One important set of options to change is the Ruler Units items (see Figure 3-26). If most of your work is, for example, in millimeters, you should make a change for the Horizontal and Vertical ruler units by clicking the respective pull-down menu and selecting millimeters. This is one setting you may want to address before opening a document or creating a new document, because any preference change to units is reflected on all new documents you create.

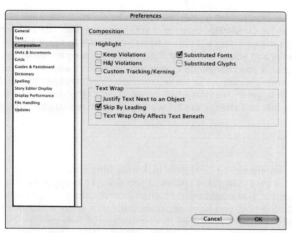

Figure 3-25: Text Composition preferences affect the appearance and manageability of text.

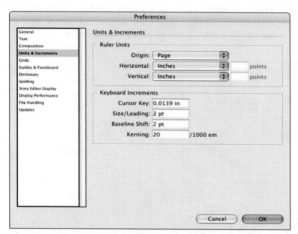

Figure 3-26: Units & Increments preferences enable you to globally change the unit of measure in your design layout.

Another setting, one that's more of a personal preference, is the Cursor Key distance. The default is 1 point. When an object is selected and you press an arrow key on your keyboard, the object moves in the direction of the arrow key the distance specified in this field box. If a 1-point increment is too much when you nudge objects, you may want to change the value to 0.5 (one-half point) or a unit you can comfortably use.

Tip

Nudging objects with the arrow keys moves a selected object the distance specified in the Units & Increments preferences for Cursor Key distance. If you press the Shift key and press an arrow key, the object moves the preference distance times ten. That is to say, if 1 point is used for the Cursor Key distance and you press the Shift key while pressing an arrow key, a selected object moves 10 points. If you change the Cursor Key distance to something like 2 points, pressing the Shift key while pressing an arrow key moves a selected object 20 points. If you need to nudge objects in larger increments upon occasion, you can open the Units & Increments preferences dialog box and change the Cursor Key distance repeatedly throughout a design session.

Grids

Changes for grids are the same as changing the Grid item in Adobe Illustrator. InDesign and Illustrator have consistent views for grid and guide colors. If you want to bring the other CS application grid appearances together, you might want to change grid colors in Photoshop and Acrobat. In the preferences dialog box, you have separate panes for grids and guides. Because InDesign is more elaborate with guide settings, it segregates the two categories into two separate preference dialog boxes.

An important item to note in the preference dialog box shown in Figure 3-27 is the last check box for Grids in Back. When the check box is enabled, a visible grid appears behind all text and objects. As a default, it's a good idea to leave this setting alone. Grids in front of your artwork can appear distracting. During an editing session, you may toggle the views, but at the end of a session in workflow environments you may want to return to defaults.

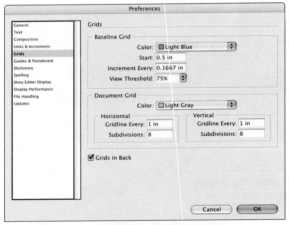

Figure 3-27: Grids preferences offer options for changing the grid appearances.

Guides and Pasteboard

InDesign offers you more options for viewing different types of guides than any of the other CS applications; understandably, the attribute choices offer more options. In Figure 3-28, you can see the default colors assigned to items like Margins, Columns, Bleed Area, and Slug Area. Colors are changed for any item by selecting from preset color values in the pull-down menus adjacent to the guide names or by selecting Custom from the bottom of the preset color list in the menu.

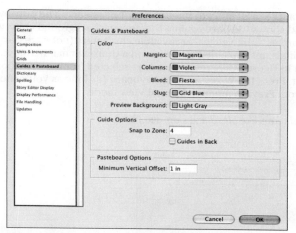

Figure 3-28: Guides & Pasteboard preferences offer several options for changing colors for the many different guides that can be displayed in a layout.

At first glance, you may wonder what the guides represent on the InDesign layout. In Figure 3-29, you can see the different guides assigned to a layout. Although the image in this figure is grayscale, the guide colors use the default color values shown in Figure 3-28.

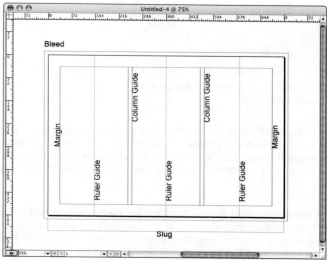

Figure 3-29: Guides are set for margins, bleeds, columns, ruler guides, and slug area.

You'll notice another setting denoted as Preview Background for the Color options. The default color is a neutral gray that appears around the layout page when you show a document preview. A nice feature in InDesign is the ability to preview a layout much like you would see a document trimmed at the print shop to the document page edge. The preview hides the slug and bleed area and shows the page against the preview background color without any visible guides, grids, margins, frame edges, or invisible characters (not necessary to include this exhaustive list, but if it's not explained elsewhere in a thorough manner now would be a good time) as shown in Figure 3-30. Preview mode is selected from the Toolbox or you can use a keyboard shortcut. Press the W key on your keyboard (as long as you're not already editing type) to toggle from Preview mode to Normal View mode.

Cross-Reference   For a better understanding of terms like *bleed* and *slug,* see Part 6.

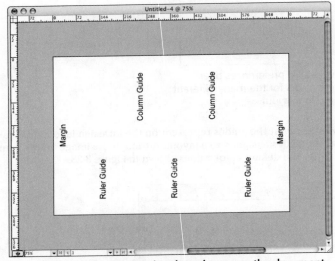

Figure 3-30: When Preview is selected, you see the document page against the preview background color.

Notice that the Guides and Pasteboard preferences also include an option for showing ruler guides in back. The default is set to show the guides in front of text and objects, because you're more likely to work with guides appearing in the foreground. If you need to temporarily change the position of ruler guides, check the box to display the guides in the background.

Dictionary

The Dictionary preferences enable you to choose a language for spell-checking and hyphenation exceptions as well as typographic symbols such as quotes you may want to use as defaults. Figure 3-31 shows a language choice from the Language pull-down menu for the language dictionary used for spell-checking. If you work with layouts in several languages, you'll want to revisit this dialog box and make changes as you check spelling and use hyphenation exceptions. As a default in your workflow, be certain to choose the language dictionary for the language used most often in your designs.

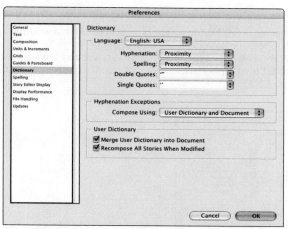

Figure 3-31: The Dictionary preferences specify the language dictionary.

Below the language dictionary, you find options for special character assignments. The default is set to use smart quotes for single and double quote characters. You also have choices from pull-down menu options for several quote characters including straight quotes and chevron symbols. You might change the quote symbols when typing programming code in a body of text. However, in most cases you'll want to use smart quotes for better-looking typography.

Spelling

Spelling preferences offer options for either including or excluding word instances, as shown in Figure 3-32. By default, all options are enabled. If you want to spell-check a document and exclude one of the items, uncheck the item to be excluded.

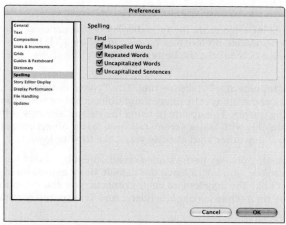

Figure 3-32: Spelling preferences offer four choices for items to be included or excluded in your spell check.

Story Editor Display

InDesign supports use of an impressive Story Editor where type is created in a window apart from the layout. Taking off from Adobe PageMaker's Story Editor, the InDesign Story Editor offers you a customizable display. You can view type in any color against any background color you want to use. In the Story Editor Display preferences, you make color choices from pull-down menus, as shown in Figure 3-33.

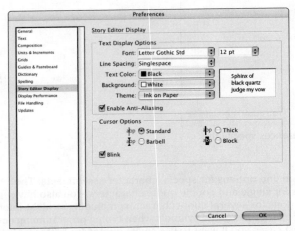

Figure 3-33: Story Editor Display preferences offer options settings for changing the display of the Story Editor.

Selecting the Enable Anti-Aliasing option smoothes text appearances, particularly at larger point sizes. Additional options offer you choices for cursor appearances while in Story Editor mode.

Display Performance

Perhaps nothing affects the speed of InDesign more than the display performance settings. You have choices in the Display Performance preferences (shown in Figure 3-34) for the quality appearances of objects and images. Obviously, the better the display, the slower the response you'll see from InDesign.

The default view is set to view all graphics at a Typical setting. The Typical option uses an image proxy of your placed artwork and displays the images and objects at low resolution with obvious degradation in viewing quality. The upside to using the default settings is that your editing session moves more quickly with faster screen redraws, faster object editing, faster text formatting, and just about any other kind of edits you make to your layout.

InDesign supports individually changing display performance on an object-by-object basis when working on a document. Therefore, you might leave the default views alone as a standard mode of operation. If you don't like the ugly look of vector objects, you can move the slider for Vector Graphics to the far right while leaving the Raster and Transparency settings at the default values.

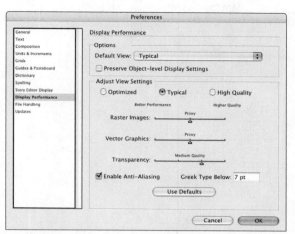

Figure 3-34: Display Performance preferences provide options for the quality of the displays for objects and images.

Another setting worth looking at is Greek Type Below. If you use a large display monitor, you might want to see text in smaller point sizes. When the text is *greeked,* it appears as gray bars in zoomed views when the point size falls below this setting. Change the value as needed for the kind of display you want to use.

Tip   If you create technical publications where screen shots are used to illustrate concepts using InDesign, set the Greek Type Below box to 0 (zero) points. When zoomed out of a view, you can see the type characters no matter what zoom level you use.

File Handling

The top Choose button in the File Handling preferences, shown in Figure 3-35, enables you to identify a folder where recovery files are created. If your InDesign program crashes during an editing session, you may be able to recover the file up to the last edits you made. If you're converting documents like QuarkXPress files and you suffer an application crash, you can often recover files that haven't been saved in InDesign format without going through document conversions all over again.

The Save Document Preview Image option is handy if you use a file-management tool to organize your files. If you don't use such a tool, you may want to enable the preference setting and save your files with image previews for later cataloging in a program supporting image previews. Even if you use no tool for organizing files, you can quickly see a thumbnail image of the first page in an InDesign file in the Open dialog box when you choose File ⇨ Open. The Open dialog box displays a thumbnail image of InDesign documents, as shown in Figure 3-36, when this preference setting is enabled. If the preference option is disabled, no appears in the Open dialog box.

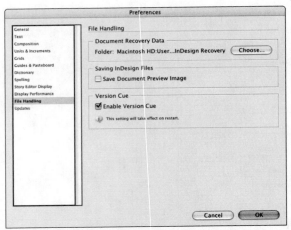

Figure 3-35: File Handling preferences offer options for recovering data, saving thumbnail previews, and enabling Version Cue.

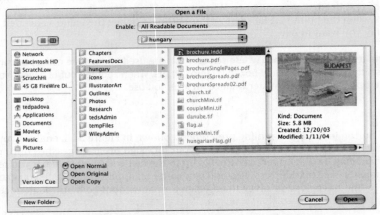

Figure 3-36: When saving files with Save Document Preview Image enabled, a thumbnail preview is displayed in the Open dialog box when you select the file.

The last option at the bottom of the File Handling Preferences dialog box is used for enabling Version Cue. Be certain this check box is enabled when you want to save document versions to the Version Cue workspace.

Cross-Reference   For information on using Version Cue, see Part II.

Updates

The Updates preferences shown in Figure 3-37 offers options for choosing the interval for updating your application file. File updates are checked via an online connection. When an update is posted on Adobe's Web site, the update check reports to you that an update is available and asks you to confirm a download and installation. What's important in workflow environments is to set the interval to the same timeframe on all computers. You won't want to have some designers using one version of InDesign while others are using a different version. Be certain to keep updates consistent throughout your workflow.

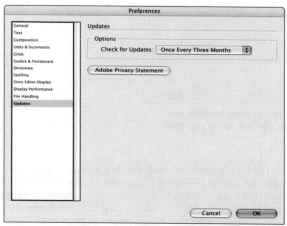

Figure 3-37: The Updates preference options offer different intervals for checking for updates to the InDesign program.

Acrobat Professional preferences

Adobe Acrobat is a unique application among the Creative Suite programs. Whereas all other programs are designed for a specific role in your design workflow, Acrobat is a program that can perform many different roles in a good number of different workflows. For example, Photoshop is known as an image-editing program, Illustrator is an illustration program, InDesign is a layout application, and GoLive is a Web construction application. Acrobat, on the other hand, cannot be identified as a tool for a specific role in the design process. Acrobat is an application that can be used by creative professionals; ebook authors; technical writers; prepress professionals; forms authors; content providers; multimedia specialists; Web designers; engineering professionals; legal professionals, and more.

Because Acrobat serves so many professionals in many different industries, all the tools and menu commands relate to more than what you use in a creative design workflow. Likewise, the extraordinary number of preference options relate to work other than you might perform as an artist.

Take a peek at the Preferences dialog box shown in Figure 3-38 by pressing ⌘/Ctrl+K, and you see options for Accessibility followed by a number of different category choices in the left pane continuing to the bottom where Web Capture is shown. Click on any one of the categories in the alphabetical list of preference categories and the options settings in the right pane change to reflect specific options for a selected category.

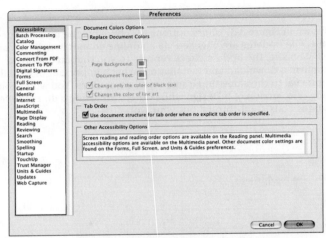

Figure 3-38: Acrobat Professional preference options are made by first selecting a category in the left pane and then changing settings in the right pane.

For your initial setup after installing the CS applications, you needn't be concerned with making changes to Acrobat's preferences. Unlike the other CS programs, Acrobat doesn't create new files from within the program. Files are created in the other CS applications and converted to PDF where the PDFs are opened in Acrobat. Therefore, coordinating preferences between Acrobat and the other CS programs during the design phase of your work is not relevant. Most often you'll use the commenting tools in your workflow, and you may at times visit the commenting preferences.

Cross-Reference   For more information on commenting in Acrobat, see Chapter 22.

Rather than discuss Commenting and other preferences specific to Adobe Acrobat now, we'll cover preference settings you'll want to make in chapters later in this book that deal with Acrobat and its role in the Creative Suite.

GoLive CS preferences

As with its other CS counterparts, the GoLive preference dialog box is accessed with the keystroke shortcut ⌘/Ctrl+K, or through the Application menu (Mac) or the Edit menu (Windows). Given that GoLive is designed for Web development rather than for the creation of print collateral, most of its preference settings are unique among the CS applications.

As shown in Figure 3-39, the preferences are listed by category on the left of the preferences window with a detail pane displayed to the right. When the preferences window is initially opened, you'll notice a plus sign displayed next to five of the preference categories. Click the plus sign to expose and expand a list of subcategory options, each having a corresponding detail pane on the right. Collapse the subcategory list again by clicking the minus sign. On the Macintosh platform, GoLive uses OS X style reveal triangles to show the subcategories of preferences.

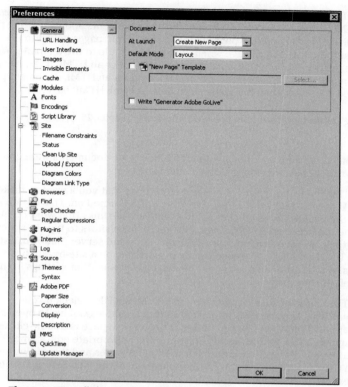

Figure 3-39: All the GoLive preference categories and subcategories

As noted in Chapter 1, this book deals with GoLive in a rather limited fashion and, therefore, this section focuses closely on the preferences most relevant to basic Web development while treating others in a more cursory fashion.

General Preferences

The General Preferences document settings allow you to determine whether GoLive will display a Welcome screen on opening, creating a new page, or doing nothing. The Welcome screen provides options to create a new document, browse for an existing document, or access a wizard that walks you through creation of a new site. Because each of these options is available from within GoLive, you may want to choose the Do Nothing option from the On Launch list menu.

Default Mode determines the initial view of a document when opened in GoLive. You'll spend most of your development time designing in Layout mode. Leave Layout as the Default Mode selection.

The "New Page" Template option allows you to designate an existing file as the starting point for your HTML documents. As an individual developer, and particularly as part of a workgroup, a standardized starting page can be a tremendous time-saver and a valuable tool in maintaining consistency within a site. You may choose to specify an actual template file rather than a simple HTML document as your New Page file. A template acts as a document master, from which HTML pages are generated. It contains page elements and formatting that you want included consistently on multiple pages within a site. HTML pages linked to the template are updated automatically by GoLive when changes are made to the template. When a New Page template is designated, whether an actual template file or an HTML page, using the File ➪ New Page command (⌘/Ctrl+N) from within GoLive opens an HTML document generated from the selected file rather than the application default blank HTML page.

Cross-Reference   For more on using GoLive templates to improve workflow, see Chapter 25.

If you want to make note in the source code of your HTML that your documents were created in GoLive, check the Write "Generator Adobe GoLive" check box.

✦ **URL Handling:** This is another group of preference settings that you'll want to make adjustments to. Leave the Make URLs Case-Sensitive option turned on. This option guarantees that the Web designer doesn't inadvertently create links that work on his or her local machine but break on a Web server. The ability for visitors to type in a mixed case file path in their browser is a function of the file name and server platform, not this setting. The URL Handling preference can be overwritten on a site-by-site basis from within the site window of an open site. The defaults for the other settings in this section can be left as they are.

✦ **User Interface:** The Launch Other Applications to Edit Media Files check box is selected by default. This preference is important in that it enables GoLive to open a specific editing application when a linked image or object on a page is double-clicked. Likewise, an image or media source file will appear in the appropriate editor when opened from the File tab of the site window. For a list of file types and the editing applications to which they are linked, see the File Mappings tab of the Web Settings dialog box. Web Settings can be accessed by going to GoLive ➪ Web Settings (Mac) or Edit ➪ Web Settings (Windows). The other settings in this section determine the size and appearance of selection handles and borders and are not critical in affecting workflow.

✦ **Images:** By default, a folder is created inside your GoLive folder for image files. The directory path is `Applications/Adobe GoLive CS/Import Images` (Mac) or `Program Files/Adobe GoLive CS/Import Images` (Windows). This folder holds image files as a default location for files such as imported Photoshop layers, low source images, and so on. If you want to designate another folder, click the Select button and the Select and Import Folder dialog box opens, where you can navigate your hard drive and select another folder to be used for image files.

✦ **Invisible Elements:** Invisible elements are separated into two categories: Hideable Document Markers and Global Settings. Hideable document markers are visual indicators of specific code-based formatting and functionality that otherwise have no identifiable visible representation when a page is viewed. Global settings are essentially visual design aids. To display invisible elements, with a Web page open and active, go to View ➪ Show Invisible Items (or press ⌘/Ctrl+Shift+I). Although these items do not appear in Preview mode or when the page is viewed in a browser, having the icons always visible can make it difficult, when designing in Layout mode, to get an accurate idea of page appearance. Go back to the View menu to make the invisible elements invisible once again.

The Invisible Elements preference dialog box allows you to customize and save selections of elements you want to be able to hide and conversely, those you want to be always visible. Deselect items in the Elements list to have them remain visible in Layout view. Perhaps for a team-based project, you might find it useful to always display document comments as well as Line Breaks and Anchor Boxes. Team members using the same shared element set will know what's going on in the HTML code by the element icons displayed on the page. To create a custom element set, click the Create New Set button near the foot of the Set pane, as shown in Figure 3-40. Enter a name to replace the default "New Set" and deselect the elements you would like to be visible in Layout mode.

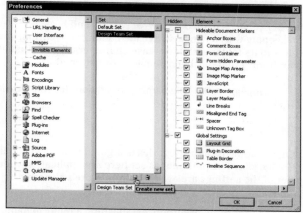

Figure 3-40: The Invisible Elements section of the General Preferences

✦ **Cache:** This cache setting allocates temporary storage space for Web pages being accessed via a WebDAV connection. It sounds like a really common feature, but it's actually for a really esoteric workflow.

Modules

GoLive incorporates a broad selection of modules, each designed to accomplish a specific task. The default settings here are fine; however, each enabled module adds to the memory requirements of the application, increasing launch time and affecting responsiveness. If you need to improve performance, you might consider disabling unnecessary modules. Click the Show Item Information arrow just beneath the list of modules to display an explanation of the purpose for each selected module. Click the arrow again to hide the description.

Fonts and Encoding

The Fonts preference settings allow you to set the default font faces for a variety of different languages. There is no need to change the existing settings.

The Encodings preference settings allow you to activate encodings for language scripts. Again, the default settings are fine.

Script Library

The Script Library options relate to the treatment of JavaScript in an HTML page. GoLive will either write the script directly into every page or generate an external JavaScript document that can be shared by multiple pages. The External Script Library document contains *all* the scripts included in GoLive, making for a rather lengthy file. It's a good practice to flatten the Script Library that you publish with your site.

Script Library settings can be designated as an application-level preference, a site-specific setting, or on a page-by-page basis. Script Library preferences do not affect preexisting documents, although document settings can be changed in the HTML tab of the Page Inspector. Document-level settings override site-specific Script Library preferences, which override the application-level settings.

By default, the external JavaScript file is named CSScriptLib.js and is saved to a site folder called GeneratedItems. In keeping with a conservative file-naming convention, you may want to rename both the file and its folder with lowercase characters. The Rebuild button is used to recreate a JavaScript library that has been damaged or flattened.

Cross-Reference For more about HTML file naming, see the "File-naming conventions for Web development" sidebar later in this chapter.

Site

The Site Preferences section, including its subcategories is arguably the most significant set of preferences affecting a GoLive site. The preferences set here are application-wide and affect all new sites. A number of the settings are available from a site's site window and, if reset there, override the application preferences for the active site.

When you're working alone or as part of a workgroup, establishing a uniform naming convention for your site pages is important. You'll want to set the defaults for the File Extension and Home Page Name as well as designate a name for the Folder for Generated Items.

Site Trash options are found in the same primary Site window. You have the option, when deleting files, to transfer them to a site trash folder instead of deleting them directly to the system trash. This is a failsafe-type option for the occasions where you hit the Delete key and then experience that terrible "What have I done?!" moment of horror. Not to worry—if you've selected Site Trash as a preference, you can restore whatever you may have inadvertently deleted. Site Trash can alternately function as a temporary storehouse for files not in current use within a site.

✦ **Filename Constraints:** This section of the Site preferences provides an assortment of Regular Expression definitions that constrain acceptable file names to defined parameters. Don't get overwhelmed by the unfamiliarity of these formulas. A description is provided in English for each option, and you should be able to find a rule that works well for you. It's recommended that you stick with GoLive Lowercase or some variation thereof. If you want to dive in and customize, the parameters can be refined to meet the specifications of your workgroup. When you're developing a site, it's important to have all members of your group maintain the same file-naming conventions and, consequently, share in the same filename constraints. Note that the filename constraints settings do not prohibit the user from creating a new file that violates the setting and it will not change the name of an existing file that violates the setting. It shows you the offending files in the Errors tab of the Site window.

File-naming conventions for Web development

Both .htm and .html are acceptable file extensions for HTML documents, although the industry seems to be leaning toward the .html extension as the standard. The home page file for any site is typically named index.html or indexindex.htm but other occasional possibilities might include a base filename of home or default. This is something you'll want to confirm with your hosting provider. The likelihood is that you'll be naming your home page index.html. You'll also want to check with your hosting provider, preferably before you begin your site development, about any particular file-naming conventions they might employ. To be safe that is, to ensure that your site files work equally as well on any server platform), you may choose to adhere to some rather conservative naming conventions. The basic rules are:

✦ Keep all filenames lowercase.

✦ Begin all filenames with either an underscore or a lowercase letter.

✦ Don't begin filenames with a number.

✦ Avoid all crazy characters, including spaces, /, &, . (period), and so on.

You'll also want to be conscious of keeping the length of your filenames to less than 32 characters to avoid having them truncated. The truly conservative approach, although no longer rigorously adhered to, would be to limit filenames to eight characters before the file extension. If you want to create a multiword filename, use an underscore to separate the words. As counterintuitive as it might be to establish such a naming convention up front, you can be assured that such precautions can save you untold aggravation on the back end. Take it from people who learned the hard way! Certainly, as part of a workgroup, it's important that all members of the group agree on a convention to employ.

✦ **Status:** The Status settings provide color-coding for files appearing in Navigation view and Links view when the display for these views is set to frames, ovals, or thumbnails. File status is set from the File tab of the Inspector palette.

✦ **Clean Up Site:** The Clean Up Site command is an essential site maintenance and pre-publication tool. Clean Up can be configured to remove orphaned files. Orphaned files are files that can be copied into the site folder and files in the site that are not referenced can be removed. or added to external references, colors, and font sets as determined by their use in the site. The Refresh button updates the contents of the site window.

✦ **Upload/Export:** Upload and Export are distinct from one another in that Export creates a copy of your site on your local machine, having modified its structure to comply with the requirements of a particular hosting server. Upload actually performs the file transfer to the remote hosting server. The settings available in this preference category apply to both Upload and Export. See Figure 3-41 for a clearer picture of the Upload/Export window.

Note

It's rare that a hosting service would require the export of a site prior to publishing, but the Export feature can be very handy if you need to deliver a functioning copy of a site on a CD-ROM for review, archiving, or offline presentation.

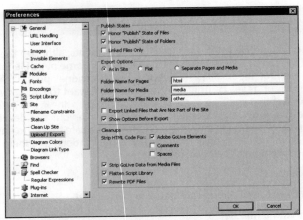

Figure 3-41: The Upload/Export window of the Site preference category

- **Publish States:** You have the opportunity from within GoLive to specify whether you want individual files and folders to be included in the site when it's published. The Published States preferences provide the option to honor your selection or bypass it by publishing only linked files within the site hierarchy.

- **Export Options:** These are relevant only when exporting a site rather than publishing it. The As in Site option maintains the hierarchy of files and folders, groups, and resources as they occur within your site and maps them accordingly to a newly created root folder. Flat exports all files into a root folder without any subfolders. Separate Pages and Media creates two subfolders within the root folder — one for HTML pages and the second for media files. If you've selected the Separate Pages and Media option, you can indicate your choice of names for the created folders. If you elect to export linked files that aren't part of the site, provide a name for the folder to which these files will be exported in the Folder Name for Files Not in Site text field. The Show Options Before Export check box allows you to review the options you've selected before exporting the site.

- **Cleanups:** This is another essential site-maintenance procedure, providing options to optimize your page code by removing elements extraneous to the appearance of your pages. The Stripping Adobe GoLive Elements and the GoLive Data from Media Files options removes proprietary GoLive code that enables many of the interactive editing capabilities of the application. The code is stripped only from the copies of the uploaded files leaving the originals on your local machine intact. A caution here: Removing unnecessary code will potentially improve the load time of your pages and there is really no downside *unless* you choose at a later date to retrieve pages from the server for further development. Perhaps you inadvertently deleted a file from your local machine and need to replace it. The file retrieved from the server will no longer have Smart Object links, layout grids, editable scripted actions, and so on. Measure the options carefully before choosing these two options. Stripping comments and spaces has a negligible effect on file size and page performance but makes your source code more difficult to read. The Flatten Script Library option is a recommended option as it scans all site documents that use the script library and retains only the code necessary to the site, often reducing the size of the script file dramatically. The Rewrite PDF Files option optimizes all PDF files within the site for quicker upload and faster viewing for visitors.

✦ **Diagram Colors:** This allows you to set color-coding for the variety of display panes and link references within GoLive. Within a workgroup, it would be important to have the settings remain consistent throughout the team.

✦ **Diagram Link Type:** Similar to Diagram Colors, this provides settings by which you can color-code the hierarchical relationships between linked files as they appear within a site diagram.

Browsers

This preference is fundamental to your work with GoLive, because it allows you to establish the browsers through which you'll be viewing and testing your pages. You can either add browsers manually or let GoLive scan your hard drive to find all available browsers for you. You can remove any unwanted browsers by pressing the Remove button at the bottom of the preference pane.

Find

The find and replace options available in this screen are straightforward and not unlike a standard find and replace dialog box. They allow you to set preferences to search text and HTML documents.

Test, test, and test again

In Web development, the importance of testing your site pages in multiple browsers and on multiple platforms cannot be stressed enough. Unlike print, Web design is a medium influenced by a number of variables outside the designer's control. The audience viewing your site will be doing so on a variety of browsers, have monitors of varying sizes set to various resolutions, and be running different platforms on their machines. Their machines will have different processing capabilities, their Internet connection speeds will vary, and their monitors will display colors with various levels of brightness, saturation, and spectrum. Not only that, but there is always the possibility that they have set their system or browser preferences to display fonts at a larger-than-standard size for ease of viewing. That said, as a Web developer, choosing your battles wisely is important. There are some factors that you just cannot control. You *can* however, and should, make design decisions with the demographics of your audience in mind. (For more on Web design fundamentals, see Chapter 25.)

The bottom line is that, at the very least, you'll want to test your site on multiple browsers (at least on Internet Explorer and Netscape), on multiple versions of those browsers if possible, and on different platforms (Windows and Mac at least). Why so much testing? The Web is an evolving technology and, as such, with each new browser release, changes (improvements?) have been made. In the beginning, back in the days of the browser wars, there was very limited standardization for the capabilities that a browser would support. Netscape and Internet Explorer were the primary players and each battled to offer better bells and whistles than the other. Their browsers are based on different fundamental models and, consequently, a number of elements needed to be coded one way for Netscape and another for Explorer — and that's only for the elements that were commonly supported. Also, due to the difference in the way the browsers interpret an HTML page, the same code often results in page elements appearing differently on-screen. Unfortunately, these differences were not always so subtle.

Although a great deal of standardization has been implemented since the "early days," there are still differences in how the same code appears on-screen from browser to browser and version to version, as well as differences in the supported features. Spare yourself and your clients unnecessary surprises by testing adequately before your formal site launch.

Spell Checker

Spell Checker displays a personal dictionary to which you can add entries manually by pressing the Add a New Word to Your Dictionary button at the bottom of the screen and entering the new word to replace the default "new word 1" text in the text field. Your new entry is added to the dictionary when you exit the preferences window entirely or switch to a different preference category.

Personal dictionary entries can be created for a wide variety of languages available from the Personal Dictionary For list menu. Remove entries from the personal dictionary by making a selection of the items you want to delete and pressing the trash can icon at the bottom of the screen.

Within a site, entries are added to your Personal Dictionary by pressing the Learn button from the within the GoLive spell checker. To access spell check when working in GoLive, go to Edit ➪ Check Spelling or use the keyboard shortcut ⌘/Ctrl+Shift+U.

Spell check should be considered an essential development tool. Nothing lowers the credibility of your message more quickly than misspelled words and typographical errors. The time it takes to run spell check on your site is *always* time well spent.

The Regular Expression section of the spell checker contains patterns that represent e-mail addresses and URLs (Uniform Resource Locators). The purpose of these expressions is to prevent the Spell Checker from identifying either e-mail or Web addresses as spelling errors.

Plug-ins

The Plug-ins preference window lists all the plug-ins installed in the GoLive application folder in addition to the file types to which each plug-in is mapped. The list is extensible with the option to add new plug-ins as needed or to add to the list of file extensions associated with any given plug-in.

Internet

If you're experiencing difficulty connecting to your hosting server, you may need to adjust the proxy settings in the Internet preference. You'll need to contact your server administrator to get the necessary host name and port number.

 Note For more information on proxy settings, check the support knowledge base on the Adobe Web site.

Log

The Log preference settings allow you to designate whether you want the Log window to track warnings and status messages along with the errors it tracks by default. You can also set the maximum number of items shown in the Log list.

Source

The Source preference and its subcategories provide a high level of customization for those who expect to do some serious work directly with the code of a page.

Adobe PDF

The compression options designated in the Adobe PDF dialog boxes are applied to PDF documents published to the hosting server when Rewrite PDF Files is selected in the Upload/Export subcategory of the Site preferences.

✦ **General:** "Save As" Optimizes for Fast Web View enables the PDF to be streamed over the Web, resulting in faster display than if the file were required to download in its entirety before viewing. This is the only setting out of all the PDF preferences that cannot be set on a case-by-case basis through the File Inspector when PDF Preview is the active document view.

✦ **Paper Size:** From within this window, you can choose from 26 preset paper sizes or create a custom paper size to which your PDFs are set to print. Select a paper size, and notice that the page dimensions are displayed based on the unit of measure you've chosen. Choose either landscape or portrait for your page orientation and decide whether you want the document contents to be shrunk to fit the printed page.

Don't underestimate the value of the Shrink Content to Paper Width option, particularly if you want to provide your viewing audience with a print-friendly version of a Web page. Certainly, you've experienced an occasion where you printed a page of a Web site from your browser, only to find that a good portion of the text from the right side of the page was simply cut off. Converting a Web page to PDF with the shrink option enabled will eliminate the problem entirely. See Figure 3-42 for clarification of the Paper Size preference options.

You can set page margins by entering your settings in the four text fields provided in the Margin section of the window. Checking the Open Action check box will set the PDF magnification to match the apparent size of the HTML text. This option is similar to using Document Properties in Acrobat and specifying a magnification level on the Initial View. Checking the Color Profile check box will embed the ICC profile in the PDF.

Cross-Reference

To understand more about ICC profiles and color management, refer to Chapter 6.

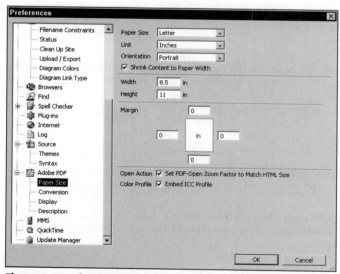

Figure 3-42: The Paper Size options allow you to define paper size, page margin, and display magnification for PDFs included in your published site.

Conversion

These settings relate to the conversion of an HTML page to PDF and the PDF version number used in the conversion. GoLive has a built-in PDF preview that employs the options chosen here as an application-wide default.

For more on setting page-specific PDF preferences, see Chapter 25.

✦ **Display:** Zoom Factor allows you to set the magnification percentage at which a page will be displayed upon opening. Display Mode determines whether to display a Single-page, Double-page or Multi-page view, and the Continuous Mode check box enables a viewer to scroll through a document without a jump from the end of one page to the beginning of another. The Smooth All options refine the view of text and images to eliminate jagged edges.

Show Annotations is useful if documents are being shared as part of a collaborative workflow and workgroup members have included notes and comments. This applies particularly to site diagrams that may be shared among members of the workgroup. Be aware that source code comments included in an HTML page do not convert to PDF comments, nor are they incorporated in any way into a PDF converted from a Web page.

The Page Background and Link Editing Color options allow you to apply custom colors to these elements. With the PDF Link Editor, from right within GoLive, you're able to modify, create, reposition, and delete link regions in an existing PDF.

For more on editing PDF link regions in GoLive, see Chapter 25.

✦ **Description:** This simply provides the opportunity to add metadata to the generated PDF including Title, Author, Subject, and Keywords.

MMS

MMS stands for Multimedia Messaging Service and is a protocol for use with MMS-enabled cell phones to send messages comprising a combination of text, sounds, images, and video.

For more information on MMS, check out www.mobileMMS.com.

QuickTime

The QuickTime preferences relate to the QuickTime editing capabilities built into GoLive.

Update Manager

As with the other CS applications, when participating in a workgroup, it's a good idea to coordinate the frequency of updates among team members to be sure that everyone has the same application features available.

Summary

✦ Preference settings are adjusted in the Preferences dialog box for each Creative Suite program. You can open the Preferences dialog box in each program through a menu command or by using the keyboard shortcut ⌘/Ctrl+K.

✦ Some preference settings apply to individual documents, while other preferences apply globally to an application's settings. You can usually make application-preferences changes while no document is open in the application window.

✦ Each of the Creative Suite programs has an elaborate set of preferences that help you customize your work environment to suit your personal choice for the way you want to work. When participating in production design workgroups, it's a good idea to discuss various preference settings and agree on choices with other members of your workgroup.

✦ You can return to default preferences by pressing Shift+⌘+Option+Control (Mac) or Shift+Ctrl+Alt (Windows) when launching Photoshop, Illustrator, and InDesign.

✦ Adobe Acrobat has an extensive set of preference options, many of which are not necessary to adjust in creative design workflows. Acrobat is the only CS application where new documents are normally not created in the program, therefore eliminating a need for many preference choices that pertain to new document designs.

✦ When initially setting up a new Web site in GoLive CS, several preference settings are critical. These settings can be set through the application Preferences window, in which case they apply to all newly created sites. Alternately, they can be set on a site-by-site basis in the Site Settings window of an open site. The relevant application-wide settings appear in the Preferences pane under the Site and Script Library categories.

✦   ✦   ✦

Understanding User Interfaces

Working with several programs developed by a single software manufacturer has great advantages: The programs support a common user interface, and access to tools, menus, palettes, and preferences is handled similarly among the programs. Even if you've never used a particular program in the Creative Suite (CS), you can explore a program that's new to you with an intuitive sense of knowing how to perform one function or another based on your experiences with other CS applications. The common user interface, knowing where to look for tools and commands to execute actions, and familiarity with the methods help shorten your learning curve.

Each of the Creative Suite programs obviously has unique aspects, but many aspects are exactly the same from one program to the next. In some cases, you can customize a program to suit your individual needs or a standard implemented for your workgroup. In this chapter, I cover tools, menus, commands, and customizing options to bring the programs close together.

Accessing Tools

Certainly anyone who opens one of the Creative Suite applications is aware of how to use tools nested in the Tools palettes. Illustrator, Photoshop, and InDesign have many tools in common. GoLive and Acrobat have fewer tools in common with these three programs.

Figures 4-1, 4-2, and 4-3 show the toolboxes from Illustrator, Photoshop, and InDesign, respectively. Tools listed in bold type are tools common among all three programs. Notice that the keyboard shortcuts used to access the tools are common, in most cases, among the programs (the shortcut you use to select the Pen tool in Photoshop is the same shortcut you use to select the Pen tool in InDesign, for example). The character in parentheses is used to select a tool in the toolbox.

Illustrator Toolbox

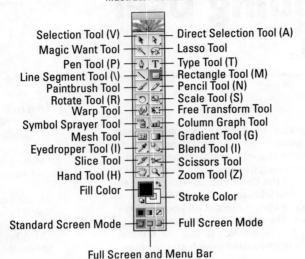

Selection Tool (V) — Direct Selection Tool (A)
Magic Want Tool — Lasso Tool
Pen Tool (P) — Type Tool (T)
Line Segment Tool (\) — Rectangle Tool (M)
Paintbrush Tool — Pencil Tool (N)
Rotate Tool (R) — Scale Tool (S)
Warp Tool — Free Transform Tool
Symbol Sprayer Tool — Column Graph Tool
Mesh Tool — Gradient Tool (G)
Eyedropper Tool (I) — Blend Tool (I)
Slice Tool — Scissors Tool
Hand Tool (H) — Zoom Tool (Z)

Fill Color — Stroke Color

Standard Screen Mode — Full Screen Mode

Full Screen and Menu Bar

Figure 4-1: Adobe Illustrator toolbox

Photoshop Toolbox

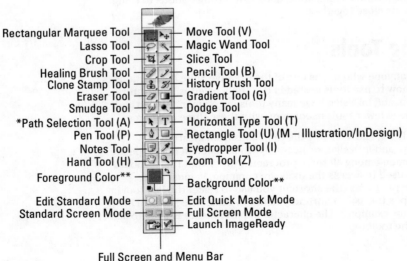

Rectangular Marquee Tool — Move Tool (V)
Lasso Tool — Magic Wand Tool
Crop Tool — Slice Tool
Healing Brush Tool — Pencil Tool (B)
Clone Stamp Tool — History Brush Tool
Eraser Tool — Gradient Tool (G)
Smudge Tool — Dodge Tool
*Path Selection Tool (A) — Horizontal Type Tool (T)
Pen Tool (P) — Rectangle Tool (U) (M – Illustration/InDesign)
Notes Tool — Eyedropper Tool (I)
Hand Tool (H) — Zoom Tool (Z)

Foreground Color** — Background Color**

Edit Standard Mode — Edit Quick Mask Mode
Standard Screen Mode — Full Screen Mode
— Launch ImageReady

Full Screen and Menu Bar

*Path Selection Tool (A); Direct Selection Tool (A) – Same in Photoshop
**Stroke and Fill Colors in InDesign and Illustrator

Figure 4-2: Adobe Photoshop toolbox

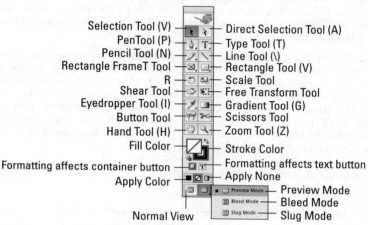

InDesign Toolbox

Selection Tool (V) — Direct Selection Tool (A)
PenTool (P) — Type Tool (T)
Pencil Tool (N) — Line Tool (\)
Rectangle FrameT Tool — Rectangle Tool (V)
R — Scale Tool
Shear Tool — Free Transform Tool
Eyedropper Tool (I) — Gradient Tool (G)
Button Tool — Scissors Tool
Hand Tool (H) — Zoom Tool (Z)
Fill Color — Stroke Color
Formatting affects container button — Formatting affects text button
Apply Color — Apply None
— Preview Mode
— Bleed Mode
— Slug Mode
Normal View

Figure 4-3: Adobe InDesign toolbox

Illustrator/InDesign/Photoshop common tools

The tools common to Illustrator, InDesign, and Photoshop include the following:

✦ **Selection tool (V):** Notice that the Move tool in Photoshop behaves like the Selection tool used in the other programs. The Move tool in Photoshop uses the same keyboard shortcut (V). Additionally, Photoshop has a Path Selection tool used for selecting vector objects. The Path Selection tool works similar to the selection tools in Illustrator and InDesign. In InDesign, you use the Selection tool to move objects and crop object and type frames.

✦ **Direct Selection tool (A):** The Direct Selection tool is used to reshape objects. In Photoshop, you access the Direct Selection tool by clicking on the Selection tool and holding down the mouse button. A pop-up toolbar opens from which you can select the Direct Selection tool.

When you click on an object with the Direct Selection tool, the anchor points are shown deselected. Clicking a single anchor point or a path segment moves just that point or segment, thereby reshaping the object. In all programs, you reshape paths using the Direct Selection tool. In InDesign, you also use the Direct Selection tool to move objects around a placeholder frame.

✦ **Pen tool (P):** The familiar Pen tool that originated in Adobe Illustrator is found in InDesign and Photoshop alike. The Pen tool is used to draw free-form paths in all the programs.

✦ **Type tool (T):** As the name implies, the Type tool is used for typing text. In each program, you find additional options for the Type tool by holding down the mouse button on the Type tool and selecting other type tools from the pop-up toolbars.

✦ **Line/Line Segment tool (\ in Illustrator and InDesign; U in Photoshop):** Drawing straight lines is handled with the Line tool (Photoshop and InDesign) or Line Segment tool (Illustrator). In Photoshop, you access the Line tool by clicking on the Rectangle tool and opening the pop-up toolbar or by pressing Shift+U several times until the Line tool appears in the toolbox.

✦ **Rectangle tool (M in Illustrator and InDesign; U in Photoshop):** The Rectangle tool appears at the top level in the toolbox. In each program, click and hold down the mouse button to open a pop-up toolbar where you can select other tools like the Ellipse tool, Polygon tools, and other special vector-shape tools. In Photoshop, the objects you draw with these tools remain vector shapes until they are *rasterized* (the process of converting vector objects to raster images). In InDesign, the tools are used for artwork where you apply fills and strokes; however, the shapes can take the same form as the Frame tools and act as containers for text and placed graphics.

For more information on rasterizing objects, see Part 3.

✦ **Pencil tool (N in Illustrator and InDesign; B in Photoshop):** Used for free-form drawing much like you would use a pencil for an analog drawing.

✦ **Eyedropper tool (I):** The Eyedropper Tool is used most often for color sampling in all three programs. In InDesign, the use broadens to sample certain styles such as type formatting.

✦ **Gradient tool (G):** Use the Gradient Tool for drawing linear and radial gradients applied to shapes and selections.

✦ **Hand tool (H):** The Hand Tool is used to move a document page around the monitor window.

✦ **Zoom tool (Z):** Click with the Zoom tool to zoom in on a document page. Press the Option/Alt key with the Zoom tool selected, and click to zoom out of the document page.

✦ **Fill/Stroke or Foreground/Background Color (D, X):** Press D to return colors to default values. Press X to switch between Foreground/Background and Stroke/Fill. In Illustrator and InDesign, the tools are used for assigning strokes and fills to objects. In Photoshop, the colors are used for foreground and background colors. A change of color from the Colors palette, the color wheel, or the Swatches palette is reflected in the tools in the toolbox.

Illustrator/InDesign common tools

Tools that are common to InDesign and Illustrator but that don't appear in the Photoshop toolbox include the following:

✦ **Rotate Tool (R):** Rotates objects by selecting and dragging or supplying numeric values in a dialog box.

✦ **Scale Tool (S):** Scales objects by selecting and dragging or supplying numeric values in a dialog box.

✦ **Shear Tool (O in InDesign; no equivalent in Illustrator):** Shears objects by dragging with the tool or entering numeric values in a dialog box. In Illustrator, the tool is accessed by holding down the mouse on the Scale tool and selecting the Shear tool from the pop-up toolbar.

✦ **Free Transform tool (E):** Transforms objects (scaling, rotating, distorting) by clicking and dragging a selected object.

✦ **Scissors Tool (C):** Used to cut a path drawn with the geometric tools or the Pen tool.

Illustrator/Photoshop common tools

Tools that are common to both Illustrator and Photoshop and not found in InDesign include the following:

✦ **Lasso Tool (L in Photoshop; Q in Illustrator):** Used to select pixels in Photoshop and objects in Illustrator.

✦ **Magic Wand tool (W):** In Photoshop, selects colors of common color values within a user-specified tolerance range. In Illustrator, selects objects of common color values.

✦ **Slice tool (K):** Used for slicing images/objects for Web hosting.

In addition to tools common between the programs, each application has a few unique tools. Photoshop has various tools for changing brightness values along with a Note Tool (also found in Acrobat), cloning tools, and the History Brush Tool. The Blend Tool, Mesh Tool, Graph Tools, Warp Tools, and Symbol Sprayer tools are unique to Illustrator. In InDesign, you find a Button Tool similar to the Button Form Field Tool in Acrobat.

Acrobat tools

Because the tools in Acrobat are so different from the tools in Illustrator, InDesign, and Photoshop, it makes more sense to list them apart from the other programs. Acrobat is a program serving many different business professionals, and some of the tools you find in Acrobat may not be used in your work as a creative professional. Nevertheless, it's a good idea to know what Acrobat offers in case you ever need to share PDF documents designed for other kinds of business uses.

Tools in Acrobat appear in separate toolbars. Unlike the other CS programs, the default position for the toolbars is horizontal across the top of the Acrobat window. Individual toolbars are docked in the Toolbar Well. You can open toolbars and dock them in the Toolbar Well or remove them from the Toolbar Well and place them anywhere in the Acrobat window as floating toolbars. Access toolbars by choosing View ➪ Toolbars and choosing the toolbar you want to see, or by opening a context menu on the Toolbar Well and selecting a toolbar to open as a floating toolbar. After a toolbar is opened in the Acrobat window, the toolbar can be docked in the Toolbar Well.

The individual toolbars include the following:

✦ **File toolbar (see Figure 4-4):** Includes tools used for opening, saving, printing, and e-mailing PDF files.

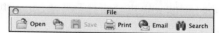

Figure 4-4: File toolbar

✦ **Tasks toolbar (see Figure 4-5):** This toolbar holds task buttons used to perform different tasks in Acrobat such as creating PDF files, securing files, commenting on files, and so on. The individual task buttons are shown or hidden from the Tasks toolbar by selecting View ➪ Task Buttons and choosing a button to show or hide.

Figure 4-5: Tasks toolbar

✦ **Advanced Editing toolbar (see Figure 4-6):** The Advanced Editing toolbar contains tools used for individual editing tasks in Acrobat, such as creating links, editing text, adding form fields, adding movies or sounds, and so on.

Figure 4-6: Advanced Editing toolbar

✦ **Commenting toolbar (see Figure 4-7):** Commenting tools are used for review and markup on PDF files where you might use strikethroughs, highlighting, and underlining, as well as mark text for insertion and other kinds of comments added to a PDF during a review session.

Figure 4-7: Commenting toolbar

✦ **Advanced Commenting toolbar (see Figure 4-8):** Additional comment tools such as the Drawing tools used frequently by engineers and planners are contained in the Advanced Commenting toolbar.

Figure 4-8: Advanced Commenting toolbar

✦ **Properties Bar (see Figure 4-9):** The Properties Bar changes according to the tool selected in other toolbars. In Figure 4-9, the Properties Bar shows options when a comment tool is selected.

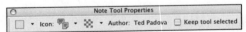

Figure 4-9: Properties Bar

✦ **Basic toolbar (see Figure 4-10):** The Hand tool similar to the Hand tool in other CS programs is contained in the Basic toolbar along with the Select Text and Snapshot tools.

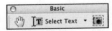

Figure 4-10: Basic toolbar

✦ **Navigation toolbar (see Figure 4-11):** Usually, this toolbar is one you won't need. The tools used for page navigation are identical to the tools you find in the status bar at the bottom of the Acrobat window.

 **Figure 4-11:** Navigation toolbar

✦ **Edit toolbar (see Figure 4-12):** Check Spelling is one of the tools contained in this toolbar, along with tools that execute commands for Undo, Redo, and Copy.

 Figure 4-12: Edit toolbar

✦ **Rotate toolbar (see Figure 4-13):** These tools are used to temporarily rotate pages as you view a PDF on-screen. After closing the document, the page orientation reverts to the original view, as when the file was initially created.

 Figure 4-13: Rotate toolbar

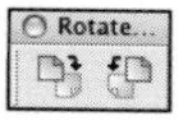

✦ **Zoom toolbar (see Figure 4-14):** A number of different tools are contained in the Zoom toolbar for zooming in and out of PDF pages.

 **Figure 4-14:** Zoom toolbar

✦ **Measuring toolbar (see Figure 4-15):** Engineers, planners, and scientists commonly use the measuring tools to measure distances and areas on drawings and architectural plans.

 Figure 4-15: Measuring toolbar

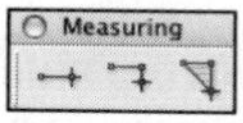

✦ **How To toolbar (see Figure 4-16):** Using this toolbar opens the How To pane, where help information related to using Acrobat is found.

 Figure 4-16: How To toolbar

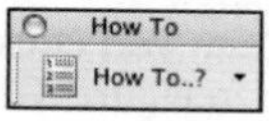

Opening toolbars in Acrobat

Toolbars are opened in Acrobat either from the View menu where you choose Toolbars and click on the toolbar you want to open or by opening a context menu on the Acrobat Toolbar Well. Control+click (Mac) or right-click (Windows) to open a context menu, as shown in Figure 4-17. When toolbars are opened from either the View menu or a context menu, they open as floating toolbars undocked in the Acrobat window.

Figure 4-17: By opening a context menu on the Acrobat Toolbar Well, you gain access to all toolbars.

Managing toolbars in Acrobat

Toolbars can be docked in the Acrobat window by manually dragging a toolbar to the Toolbar Well. An easy method for managing toolbars is to return to the context menu and make menu choices for organizing toolbars. At the bottom of the menu shown in Figure 4-17, you see Dock All Toolbars as a menu command. Choose this menu item, and all toolbars are docked in the Toolbar Well. When you want to return to default toolbars, select the menu command for Reset Toolbars.

GoLive tools

GoLive CS has a toolbox similar to other CS programs, but selecting tools is a little different in GoLive. The toolbox is divided vertically in two parts. The top half represents categorical groups of tools, while the lower half of the toolbox displays all tools within a selected category. Click on a tool in the top half of the toolbox and the tools change in the lower half of the toolbox. What looks like a toolbox in GoLive CS is actually called the Objects palette. Because all page building in GoLive is done via drag and drop, you don't actually use tools.

By default, there are nine categories of tools in the GoLive toolbox. When you click the first tool in the top-left corner (Basic tools), the toolbox appears as shown in Figure 4-18.

Figure 4-18: Click the Basic tools group in the top-left corner of the toolbox, and the tools change in the lower half of the toolbox to tools used in laying out a Web page.

The nine tool categories at the top of the GoLive toolbox are:

✦ **Basic:** Basic tools include items such as a layout grid, a frame tool, various tools for importing different forms of media, lines, anchors, line breaks, and other essential tools used for basic Web-page construction.

✦ **Smart Objects:** One of the improved and most impressive features in GoLive is the ability to work with Smart Objects. Smart Objects are native-application documents such as PDFs, Illustrator .ai files, and Photoshop .psd files. When importing a native file in GoLive, the document is sampled for Web hosting; however, and a smart link remains active with the native document. Changes made in the native source file are updated in the GoLive link.

Click on the Smart Objects tool in the GoLive toolbox, and the tools associated with Smart Objects appear in the toolbox as shown in Figure 4-19.

✦ **Forms:** The Forms tools are all the tools you need for creating HTML forms.

✦ **Head:** Header information such as metadata, keywords, links, commenting, scripts, and so on are part of the Head tools.

✦ **Frames:** Tools specific to working with frames and framesets are listed in the Frames tools.

✦ **Site:** Tools specific to editing site attributes such as fonts and colors are contained in the Site tools.

Figure 4-19: Smart Objects are used to import native documents created in other CS applications.

✦ **Diagram:** Tools specific to diagramming a site and creating site maps are contained in the Site tools.

✦ **QuickTime:** Tools used for editing media tracks are contained in the QuickTime tools.

✦ **SMIL:** Synchronized Multimedia Integration Language (SMIL) is used for multiple streaming and static media tracks in multimedia presentations for Multimedia Messaging Services (MMS) and MMS-compliant devices.

Nested tools

You'll notice in all CS programs except GoLive, the toolbox or toolbars contain pop-up toolbars or pull-down menus where other tools are selected. In Illustrator, Photoshop, InDesign, and Acrobat, the appearance of a tiny black triangle in the lower corner of a tool in the toolbox (Toolbar Well in Acrobat) alerts you to the fact that other tools reside below the tool in question. Click on a tool where you see a tiny rectangle within the tool's square in the toolbox, and hold down the mouse button. A pop-up toolbar opens, as shown in Figure 4-20.

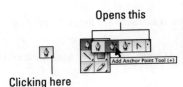

Figure 4-20: Click on a small rectangle appearing within a tool's square in a toolbox, and hold down the mouse button; a pop-up toolbar opens, displaying additional tools.

Accessing Tool Options

In Illustrator and InDesign, you have some option choices for certain tools that are controlled in accompanying dialog boxes. Not all tools have associated dialog boxes, so you need to either poke around or become familiar with tools offering these extended option choices. In Illustrator or InDesign, double-click the mouse button on tools in the toolbox, and you'll see a dialog box similar to Figure 4-21 for tools supporting further options in dialog boxes.

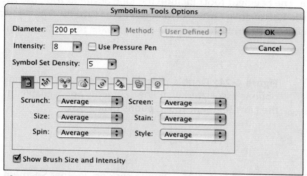

Figure 4-21: The Symbolism Tools Options dialog box

Illustrator tool options

Most often, double-clicking a tool opens an options dialog box typically not accessible other than by double-clicking a given tool. In some cases, double-clicking a tool opens a palette, a dialog box accessible through other commands, or a preference setting. Here's what happens when you double-click tools in Illustrator:

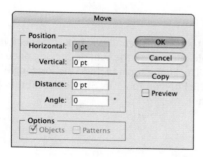 **Selection tools:** Opens the Move dialog box, shown in Figure 4-22. Objects should be selected in the document window before opening the dialog box. You can specify movement of objects for vertical and horizontal distances.

Figure 4-22: Double-click on either the Selection tool or the Direct Selection tool to open the Move dialog box.

 Magic Wand tool: Double-clicking the Magic Wand tool doesn't open a dialog box. Instead, the Magic Wand palette opens, as shown in Figure 4-23.

Figure 4-23: Double-click on the Magic Wand tool and the Magic Wand palette opens.

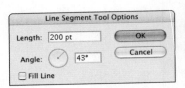**Segment tools:** A dialog box respective to the selected tool opens where you can make choices about options. You can also access the same dialog box by selecting a tool and clicking on the document page. The Segment tools include the Line Segment tool, the Arc Segment tool, the Spiral tool, the Rectangular Grid tool, and the Polar Grid tool. As shown in Figures 4-24 and 4-25, double-clicking different tools opens dialog boxes respective to the tool options.

Figure 4-24: Double-click the Line Segment tool, and options associated with line segments are available in the Line Segment Tool Options dialog box.

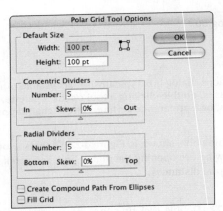

Figure 4-25: Double-click on another Segment tool, and options respective to that tool appear in another dialog box. In this example, I double-clicked on the Polar Grid tool.

Shape tools: These tools also open dialog boxes respective to the tool when double-clicking on the tool or clicking once in a document window. The Shape tools include the Rectangle tool, the Rounded Rectangle tool, the Ellipse tool, the Polygon tool, the Star tool, and the Flare tool. Figure 4-26 shows options for the Flare tool.

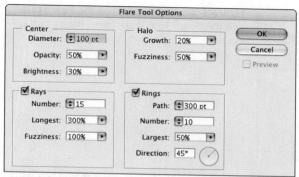

Figure 4-26: Double-click on another Segment tool, and options respective to that tool appear in another dialog box.

Paint Brush tool: A double-click on the tool opens the Paint Brush Tool Preferences dialog box, shown in Figure 4-27.

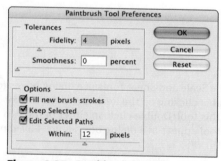

Figure 4-27: Double-click on the Paint Brush tool and the Paint Brush Tool Preferences dialog box opens.

Pencil tool/Smooth tool: Although the toolbar for the Pencil tool contains three tools (Pencil, Smooth, and Erase), only the Pencil tool and the Smooth tool use a dialog box where you can make options choices. Double-click on either tool, and a dialog box opens specific to the options for the selected tool. Figure 4-28 shows options choices for the Pencil tool.

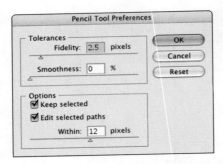

Figure 4-28: Double-click on the Pencil tool and the Pencil Tool Preferences dialog box opens.

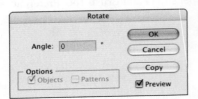**Rotate/Reflect tools**: Double-clicking on either tool opens a dialog box with options specific to the selected tool. In Figure 4-29, the Rotate dialog box opens after clicking on the Rotate tool.

Figure 4-29: Double-click on the Rotate tool to open the Rotate dialog box.

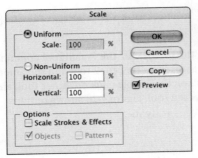**Scale/Shear/Reshape tools:** The Scale and Shear tools use dialog boxes for options settings. Note that double-clicking on the Reshape tool does not open a dialog box; no options are available for this tool. Double-click on either of the two other tools, and the options respective to that tool appear in a dialog box. Figure 4-30 shows the result of double clicking the Scale tool.

Figure 4-30: Double-click on the either the Scale or Shear tool to open a dialog box where you can make options choices.

Warp tools: The Warp tools include the Warp tool, the Twirl tool, the Pucker tool, the Bloat tool, the Scallop tool, the Crystallize tool, and the Wrinkle tool. Selecting a different tool and double-clicking on the selected tool opens a dialog box with options associated with that tool. In Figure 4-31, the Warp tool options are shown.

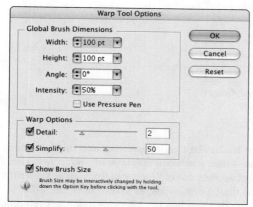

Figure 4-31: Double-click on the Warp tool and the Warp Tool Options dialog box opens.

Symbolism tools: The Symbolism tools — Symbol Sprayer, Symbol Shifter, Symbol Scruncher, Symbol Sizer, Symbol Spinner, Symbol Stainer, Symbol Screener, and Symbol Styler — have one advantage over other tools with respect to selecting tools and adjusting attributes: As was shown earlier in Figure 4-21, you can select any of the eight Symbolism tools directly in the Symbolism Tool Options dialog box. Therefore, you don't need to leave the dialog box, select another tool, and then reopen the dialog box to make adjustments respective to the selected tool. Double-clicking any of the Symbolism tools offers you options for selecting different tools and making options choices for a selected tool.

Graph tools: The Graph tools include the Column Graph tool, the Stacked Column Graph tool, the Bar Graph tool, the Stacked Bar Graph tool, the Line Graph tool, the Area Graph tool, the Scatter Graph tool, the Pie Graph tool, and the Radar Graph tool. Double-clicking on any tool in this group opens the Graph Type dialog box, shown in Figure 4-32. Like the Symbol tools, among the Graph tools options is the ability to select the tools in the Graph Type dialog box and make attribute changes for any one of the tools in the same dialog box. Double-click on any tool and you can make settings choices for the respective tool.

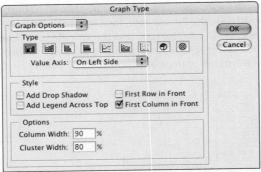

Figure 4-32: Double-click on any one of the Graph tools and you can make changes for options settings respective to that tool.

Eyedropper/Paint Bucket tools: The Eyedropper tool and the Paint Bucket tool perform similar tasks — they just work opposite of each other. The Eyedropper lifts color, and the Paint Bucket applies color. When you double-click on either tool, the Eyedropper/Paint Bucket Options dialog box opens, as shown in Figure 4-33. Nested among these tools is the Measure tool. If you double-click the Measure tool, the Preferences dialog box opens, which allows you to change Guide and Grid colors.

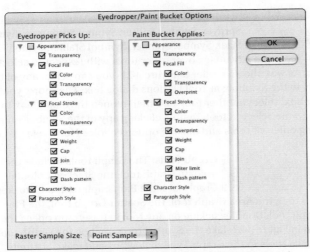

Figure 4-33: Double-click on either the Eyedropper tool or the Paint Bucket tool to open the Eyedropper/Paint Bucket Options dialog box.

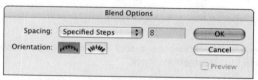 **Blend Tool/Auto Trace tool:** Double-click on the Blend tool to open the Blend Options dialog box, shown in Figure 4-34. Notice that you can also open the same dialog box by clicking the Blend tool on one option, then pressing the Option/Alt key when clicking on the second object to be included in the blend. Also contained in this tool group is the Auto Trace tool. No options are available by double-clicking the Auto Trace tool. Auto Trace attributes are set in the Type and Auto Tracing preferences.

Figure 4-34: Double-click on the Blend tool and the Blend Options dialog box opens.

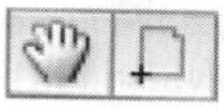

Hand tool: Double-clicking the Hand tool sets the page view to a fit-in-window view. This view is also acquired in all CS applications by pressing ⌘/Ctrl+0 (zero).

Zoom tool: Double-click the Zoom tool to show the document window in an actual-size view (100% view).

Fill/Stroke tools: Double-clicking the Fill or Stroke tool opens the system Color Picker, shown in Figure 4-35. Note that programs like Photoshop open the Color Picker with a single click, while Illustrator requires you to double-click either tool.

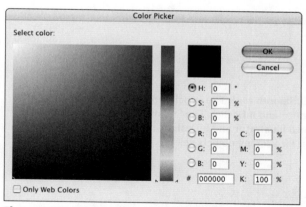

Figure 4-35: Double-click either the Fill or Stroke tool to open the Color Picker.

InDesign tool options

InDesign is like a mixture of the UI (user interface) between Illustrator and Photoshop. In Illustrator, most tools have associated options palettes accessed by double-clicking a tool in the toolbox. Likewise, some of InDesign's tools also have similar options dialog boxes accessed the same way as in Illustrator. In Photoshop, tools don't have pop-up dialog boxes opened by double-clicking a tool; Photoshop uses an options bar that changes options settings each time a different tool is accessed. Likewise, in InDesign, you have a Control palette where many options settings are made respective to the currently selected tool. Tools in InDesign that support dialog boxes for options settings include the following:

Note Accessing some dialog boxes when double-clicking on a tool in the InDesign Toolbox requires you first to select an object in the document window.

Selection/Direct Selection tools: The same Move dialog box opens in InDesign as you find in Illustrator when double-clicking on one of the Selection tools. Note that to open the Move dialog box, an object must be selected in the document window before you double-click on either tool. Notice that the options for the Move dialog box are almost always the same in the various programs, but the items that can be moved do vary a little. In Illustrator, either Objects or Patterns are targeted for movement. In InDesign, the only option is to move the content of the selected object, as shown in Figure 4-36.

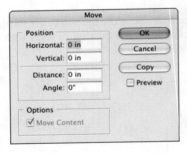

Figure 4-36: InDesign's Move dialog box is almost identical to Adobe Illustrator's Move dialog box with the exception of the Options choices.

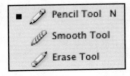

Pencil/Smooth tool: The Pencil tool options are identical in Illustrator and InDesign. The Smooth tool options vary slightly between Illustrator and InDesign. InDesign supports an additional option for keeping objects selected, as shown in Figure 4-37.

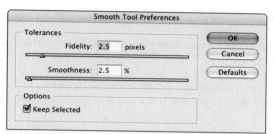

Figure 4-37: InDesign's Smooth Tool Preferences dialog box offers similar options to those in Illustrator.

Polygon tool: Double-click the Polygon tool to open the Polygon Settings dialog box, shown in Figure 4-38. A similar dialog box opens in Illustrator when you select the Polygon tool and click in the document window.

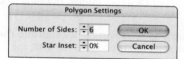

Figure 4-38: Double-click the Polygon tool to open the Polygon Settings dialog box.

Eyedropper tool: The Eyedropper tool in InDesign has similar options choices to those found in Illustrator. Because there is no Paint Bucket tool in InDesign, you see only options for the Eyedropper tool, as shown in Figure 4-39.

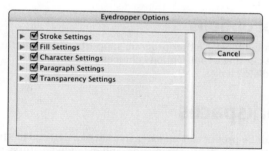

Figure 4-39: Double-click the Eyedropper tool to open the Eyedropper Options dialog box.

Rotate tool: The Rotate tool offers options settings in a dialog box similar to those found in Illustrator.

Scale tool: The Scale tool options are similar to those found in Illustrator.

 Shear tool: Rounding out the last of the transformation tools, the Shear tool also has options choices similar to Illustrator.

 Hand tool: The same effect takes place when you double-click the Hand tool in InDesign as you have in Illustrator. A Fit Page view is the result of double-clicking the tool in the toolbox.

 Zoom tool: Likewise, double-clicking the Zoom tool is the same as in Illustrator, where an Actual Size view is displayed in the document window.

Photoshop tool options

In Photoshop, double-clicking tools produces an effect with only the Hand tool and the Zoom tool. Double-click the Hand tool, and you see the active document window zoomed to a Fit on Screen view. This view is similar to Fit Window view in other CS applications. Double-click the Zoom tool, and the window zooms to Actual Size view.

Remaining options for tools are addressed in Photoshop's options bar. Click a tool and the options bar changes to reflect choices pertaining to the selected tool. In Figure 4-40, the Paint Bucket tool was selected.

Figure 4-40: When you click on a tool in the Photoshop toolbox, the options bar changes options respective to the active tool.

Acrobat and GoLive tool options

Acrobat and GoLive make use of extended tools. Neither program supports options settings in dialog boxes that open from double-clicking a tool. Options choices are contained in palettes, preferences, and properties dialog boxes.

Using Palettes and Workspaces

A common characteristic among all Adobe products is an extensive set of palettes. Palettes offer you options choices for various tool uses, menu commands, and extended features not available through the selection of a tool or menu command. For the most part, palettes are accessed and used in all the CS programs similarly.

To open a palette, click the Window menu and select the palette you want to open. If a palette name appears with a check mark in the Window menu, the palette is already open in the application window. In Figures 4-41 through 4-44, you can see the lists of palettes appearing in Illustrator, Photoshop, InDesign, and GoLive, respectively.

 Note Palettes are always listed alphabetically.

Figure 4-41: Illustrator palettes are accessed from the Window menu. Menu names with check marks indicate what palettes are currently open.

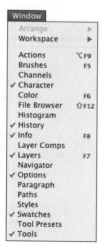

Figure 4-42: Photoshop palettes are accessed by selecting palette names from the Window menu.

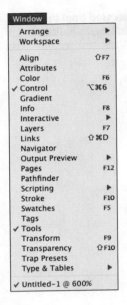

Figure 4-43: InDesign palettes are accessed from the Window menu.

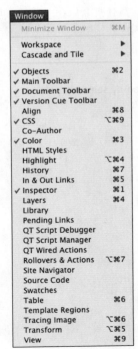

Figure 4-44: GoLive palettes are accessed from the Window menu.

Acrobat also makes use of palettes; however, accessing the palettes is handled from a different menu. To open palettes in Acrobat, select View ➪ Navigation Tabs and choose the palette to open from the submenu, as shown in Figure 4-45.

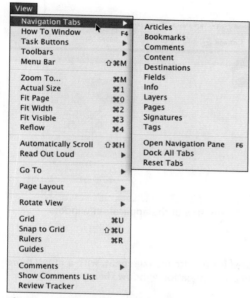

Figure 4-45: Acrobat palettes are accessed from a submenu by selecting View ➪ Navigation Tabs.

Managing palettes

The extraordinary use of palettes in all the CS applications requires you to spend a little time managing palettes, showing only the palettes you need for any given editing job. Opening all the palettes at once in any program reduces a lot of screen space that you'll need to work on your documents. Fortunately, the programs have methods for docking palettes in wells or beside the application window.

Illustrator palettes

Of the CS programs, Illustrator has the least impressive means for managing palettes. Illustrator palettes are placed along the right side of the document window by default, as shown in Figure 4-46. When you open a new palette by selecting the Window menu and then selecting a palette name appearing without a check mark, the palette opens in the application window as a *floating palette*. A palette is said to be floating when it is undocked in any CS program. To move a palette in Illustrator, drag the palette by the title bar (the topmost horizontal bar running across the top of a palette) to any side of the application window. When you drag to the edge of the application window in any direction, the palette snaps into position. If you're dragging to the right side of the application window, the palette snaps to the right side but moves freely up and down.

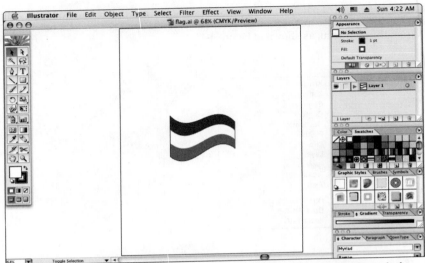

Figure 4-46: Illustrator palettes are docked to any side of the application window.

InDesign and GoLive palettes

InDesign and GoLive share the same features for palette management, with a much more impressive means for arranging palettes in the application window than any other CS program.

You access invisible palettes the same as you do in Illustrator: by opening the Window menu and selecting the palette you want to open. The palette opens as a floating palette. Collapsing the palette is where you see a big difference between InDesign/GoLive and Illustrator.

Each palette has a tab; when the palette is opened as a floating palette, you see a single tab denoting the palette name. Click the tab and drag to either the left or right side of the application window. The palette snaps when you move the palette to the edge of your screen. Unlike Illustrator, the palettes don't snap vertically to the top or bottom of your screen.

Note   GoLive does snap to top and bottom, but they do not snap top and bottom in InDesign.

When palettes are collapsed in InDesign or GoLive, the palette names and tabs rotate, providing you more screen real estate to work on your projects. When you need access to palette options, click the tab name, and the palette expands horizontally, providing you access to all the palette settings. In Figure 4-47, InDesign palettes are collapsed on the right side of the screen with the Swatches palette expanded.

Figure 4-47: Palettes docked to the right side of the application window where the tabs are rotated. Clicking a tab expands the palette to the left horizontally.

GoLive palettes are handled in the same manner as InDesign. Notice that in Figure 4-48 the Inspector palette is expanded to provide access to the attribute choices in that palette.

Tip Option/Alt-click on the tab of a collapsed palette to hide or reveal all collapsed palettes at the same time.

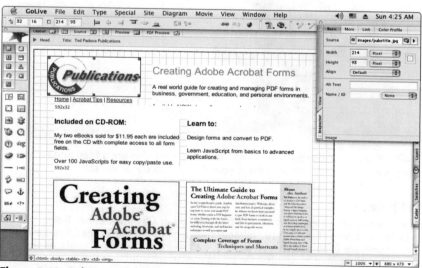

Figure 4-48: Palettes are docked in GoLive the same as they are in InDesign.

Photoshop palettes

Photoshop goes one step farther than Illustrator when it comes to docking options, but it's still not quite as good as the docking options in InDesign and GoLive. In Photoshop, by default, palettes are docked along the right side of the application window, much like you find in Illustrator. Photoshop also has a docking well where you can dock palettes and tuck them away, similar to the way InDesign and GoLive hide palette options. On the top-right of the options bar, you notice a horizontal gray bar, the Docking Well. Drag a palette tab to the gray bar, and release the mouse button. The palette is docked in the well. Drag additional palettes, and you can add them to the well. When you want to gain access to a palette's options settings, click on the tab, as shown in Figure 4-49.

Caution If you don't see the Docking Well in Photoshop, that's because your monitor resolution is not sufficient to show the Docking Well. The availability of the palette is dependent on a monitor resolution greater than 800 pixels wide.

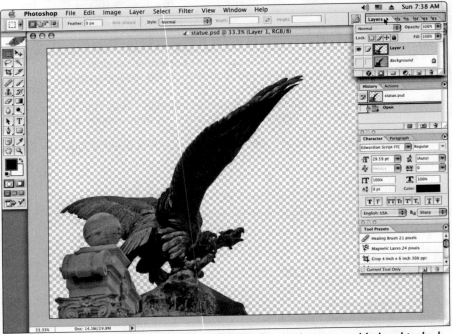

Figure 4-49: Photoshop also has a Docking Well where palettes are added and tucked away to provide you more room for editing your Photoshop documents.

Acrobat palettes

Acrobat uses a slightly different metaphor from the other CS applications. If you talk about palettes in Acrobat, you also need to consider toolbars. Unlike the other CS programs, not all of Acrobat's tools are visible when you launch the program. Therefore, tools, as well as palettes, need to be loaded in Acrobat for various different editing tasks.

When you launch Acrobat, the default tool set appears at the top of the application window, as shown in Figure 4-50. Individual tools are contained within toolbars that are docked in the Toolbar Well.

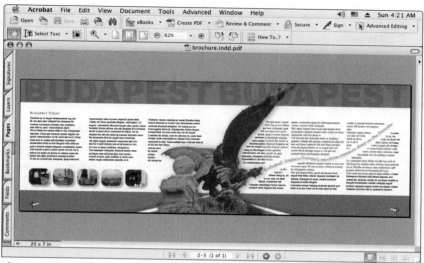

Figure 4-50: By default, a handful of tools appear docked in the Toolbar Well when you first launch Acrobat.

The default tools can be removed from the Toolbar Well and hidden from view or used as a floating toolbar, or additional tools can be added to the Toolbar Well. To gain access to additional toolbars, choose View ➪ Toolbars and select the toolbar you want to open from the submenu list. An easier method for accessing tools in Acrobat is to open a contextual menu. Control+click (Mac) or right-click (Windows) on the Acrobat Toolbar Well to open a context menu, as shown in Figure 4-51.

Figure 4-51: Open a context menu on the Toolbar Well, and select the toolbar you want to open.

If you want to return the Toolbar Well view to defaults, open a context menu and select Reset Toolbars. Also, when toolbars appear as floating toolbars in the Document pane, you can easily dock the toolbars by selecting Dock All Toolbars from the same context menu.

Note Acrobat's toolbars are undocked from the Toolbar Well by dragging the separator bar on the left side of the toolbar. Look for a vertical embossed line appearing to the left of some tools. Clicking and dragging on the separator bar is the only way to move toolbars around the Document pane.

In addition to toolbars, Acrobat also makes use of palettes, as described for all the other CS applications. To open a palette, you need to access the Navigation Tabs submenu (refer to Figure 4-45). When a palette is selected in the Navigation Tabs submenu, it opens as a floating palette. Docking palettes in Acrobat appears similar to GoLive and InDesign; however, the palettes need to be docked in one specific place called the Navigation pane. Notice that palettes in Acrobat are not docked on the left or right side of the application window, but rather within the Navigation pane appearing on the left side of the document window. To dock a palette in the Navigation pane, click on any tab in the pane to expand the window, or press the F6 key on your keyboard. Click on the tab in a floating palette and drag it to the Navigation pane, as shown in Figure 4-52.

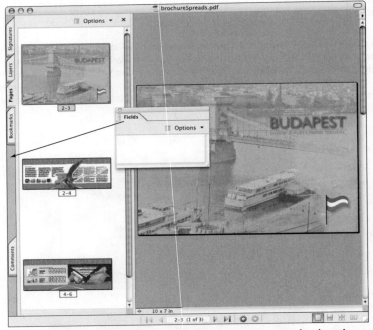

Figure 4-52: Dock a palette in Acrobat's Navigation pane by dragging a tab to the open pane and releasing the mouse button when the tab appears over the pane or area where the Navigation tabs appear.

Tip Palettes can also be dropped in the Navigation pane without expanding the pane. Just drag a tab to the left of the vertical bar separating the tabs from the Document pane or on top of any tab in the closed pane.

Nesting palettes

Palettes can be nested in groups in all the CS applications. When using floating palettes, you can nest palettes together that give the appearance of a single palette with multiple tabs. Open any palette, and drag the tab from another open palette to the destination palette. When the cursor appears over the tab area in the target palette, release the mouse button and the target palette accepts the new addition. In Figure 4-53, you can see the Layers palette in InDesign being moved to a palette containing several tabs.

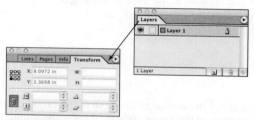

Figure 4-53: Palettes are nested together by dragging tabs from one palette to another.

To undock a tab from a palette, click and drag the tab away from the palette. When you release the mouse button, the tab appears in its own palette.

Grouping palettes also occurs at another level in InDesign and GoLive. In InDesign and GoLive, drag a palette tab to a collapsed palette at one of the vertical edges of the application window. When the palette tab snaps into position and appears rotated, you can drag another palette tab to the docked palette. Add as many tabs to a collapsed palette as you like, but keep in mind they need to be grouped and ungrouped one palette at a time. In Figure 4-54, you can see several palettes docked together in InDesign and another palette to be added to the group by dragging the tab to the collapsed palettes.

Figure 4-54: To add a palette to a docked group, drag the palette tab to the tab well in the docked palette group.

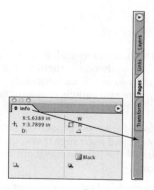

In Illustrator, Photoshop, and Acrobat, you don't have an option for nesting palettes in the docking well. Photoshop and Acrobat offer you the opportunity to dock individual palettes in the docking areas (referred to as the Palette Well in Photoshop and the Navigation pane in Acrobat). However, grouping palettes together is permitted only in InDesign and GoLive. Illustrator unfortunately provides no palette well for collapsed palettes.

Palettes can also be nested in a hierarchy in all CS programs except Acrobat. If you want palettes in view without docking them on the sides of the application window, you can group several palettes together and move them around the application window as a grouped object. In any CS program except Acrobat, drag one palette tab to the base of another palette, as shown in Figure 4-55.

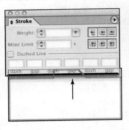

Figure 4-55: To add a palette below another palette, click on a palette tab and drag to the base of the target palette. When the horizontal black line appears at the base of the target palette, release the mouse button.

Be certain to drag a palette by the tab and move the cursor to the base of the target palette. When you see a horizontal black line at the base of the target palette, release the mouse button and the palettes are grouped as shown in Figure 5-56. When you drag the title bar on the top of the palette, both palettes move together as a group. If you need to undock a palette, click on the palette tab for the palette to be moved and dragged away from the group.

Figure 4-56: When palettes are grouped, you can move them together by dragging the palette title bar.

Saving workspaces

Palettes offer you many options for addressing features and techniques available in the CS applications. They're essential program components and you'll rarely edit without making use of options contained in at least one palette. Those palettes you use most frequently are ones you'll want to keep open and have accessible every time you launch your program of choice.

Fortunately, all the CS applications remember the organization of your workspace each time you quit a program and relaunch it. If you move palettes around and rearrange them, then quit the editing program, the next time you open the program all the palette views are displayed according to the last view from the last editing session.

In Acrobat, not only do the palettes in the Navigation pane keep their last position, but all the toolbars you loaded are also placed in position exactly the same as the last Acrobat editing session. The same holds true for Illustrator and Photoshop with respect to palette positions.

However, Photoshop, InDesign, and GoLive have an additional benefit not found in either Illustrator or Acrobat: options to save custom workspaces.

In workflow environments where computers may be shared, the ability to save workspaces is a true benefit. You can customize your work environment to suit your own personal choices for palette positions, and save the palette views as your personal workspace. Notice that in Figure 4-57 the InDesign workspace includes several palettes nested and docked along the right edge of the application window. To capture the position of the palettes, select Window ⇨ Workspace ⇨ Save Workspace. The Save Workspace dialog box opens prompting you for a workspace name. Type a name for your workspace and click the Save button. The new workspace is accessed in InDesign by selecting Window ⇨ Workspace ⇨ *workspace name* (where *workspace name* is the name you added). Each time you add a new workspace, the new workspace name is added to the Workspace submenu. Therefore, multiple users can save their own workspace preferences on the same computer.

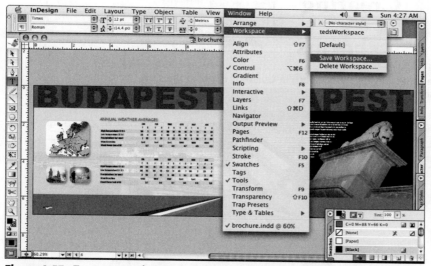

Figure 4-57: To save a workspace in InDesign, first arrange your palettes exactly as you want them to appear when you open the application.

GoLive's and Photoshop's treatment in regard to saving workspaces is the same as you find with InDesign. The menu command is identical and the same dialog box opens to prompt you for a workspace name. Figure 4-58 shows the workspace created for GoLive and the menu command accessed to save the workspace.

Inasmuch as saving a workspace in Photoshop uses the same menu command as InDesign and GoLive, the workspace includes the open palettes docked to the right of the application window and those tabs docked in the Docking Well. Since Photoshop does not support nested palettes in the Docking Well, you're limited to the view you can create in Photoshop and saving that view as a workspace, like the example shown in Figure 4-59.

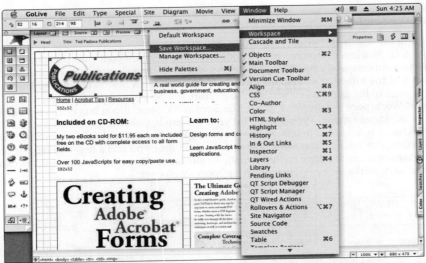

Figure 4-58: Saving a workspace in GoLive is handled the same as saving a workspace in InDesign.

Figure 4-59: Create the palette view you want in Photoshop and save the workspace. When you reopen the application and select your workspace, the palettes jump to position from the view you saved.

The one thing to remember when adjusting workspaces is that all CS programs remember the last view you had before quitting the program. Therefore, if you save a workspace, then move palettes out of their docked positions and rearrange them differently from the saved workspace, after quitting the program and relaunching it, the last view you created becomes the new default. To regain your workspace view, select Window ⇨ Workspace ⇨ *workspace name* (where *workspace name* is the name you used when you saved the workspace).

Some Common User-Interface Features

The inclusion of tools, palettes, and menus in all the CS programs makes for a common user interface where you can more easily discover new tools and editing techniques when first learning a program. Just as these features behave similarly across the CS programs, you also have some additional features consistent among programs that help reduce the learning curve when picking up a new Adobe CS program. Some of the most advantageous of the common user-interface items found in all CS programs include context menus and help documents.

Using context menus

If at any time you have difficulty finding a tool or menu command for a given task, first try to open a context menu. In all CS applications, context menus are used and the menu choices change according to the tool you select in the toolbox or toolbar. Context menus are opened by Control+clicking (Mac) or right-clicking (Windows). The context menu pops up at the cursor location, as shown in Figure 4-60.

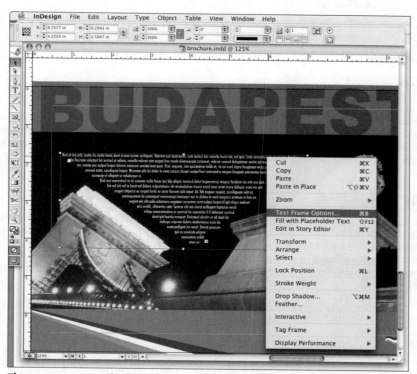

Figure 4-60: Control+click (Mac) or right-click (Windows) to open a context menu.

Context menus are not limited to document pages. You can also open context menus in some palettes in Photoshop, GoLive, and Acrobat. In Figures 4-61 through 4-63, you can see examples of context menus opened on palettes in Photoshop, GoLive, and Acrobat, respectively.

Figure 4-61: A context menu is opened on the Layer Comps palette in Photoshop.

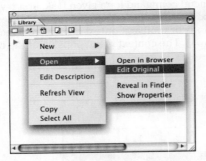

Figure 4-62: A context menu is opened on the Library palette in GoLive.

Tip

As you work in the CS applications, try to get in the habit of opening a context menu when you want to apply an edit to an object, page or function. The only way to determine whether a context menu offers a menu option is to poke around and try. As you become familiar with menu options, you'll begin to work much faster.

Getting help

You might think that with a purchase as substantial (both in terms of program features and the money you spent) as Creative Suite, you would get a hefty library of documentation. When you open the box for the CS installer CDs, you quickly learn that accompanying documentation is not offered in printed form. Instead of providing printed user manuals, Adobe created several different types of help information accessible as you work in the CS programs.

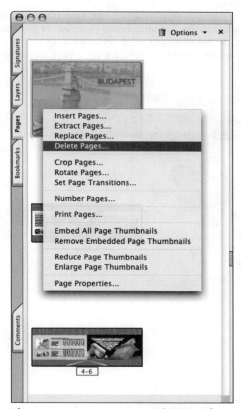

Figure 4-63: A context menu is opened on the Pages palette in Acrobat.

Help files

In terms of user guides and documentation, what Adobe CS offers is an elaborate form of help files that you access from the Help menu in all CS programs. While you're working in a program, and when you need to meet tight deadlines, the online help files should be a welcome addition to the CS features. In all programs but Acrobat the help files are HTML documents. In Acrobat, the help file is a PDF document with a custom user interface.

From any CS program, open the Help menu and select *program name* Help (where *program name* is the name of the program you're currently using). For example, in Adobe InDesign, select Help ➪ InDesign Help; in Photoshop, it's Help ➪ Photoshop Help; and so on.

After you access the Help command, the Help home page opens. In Illustrator, the Help home page looks like Figure 4-64. All the CS applications offer a similar home page where you can click on any of the contents items to take you to linked pages, click on Index to open the index page that is hyperlinked to pages, or click on Search to open a page where a search is performed.

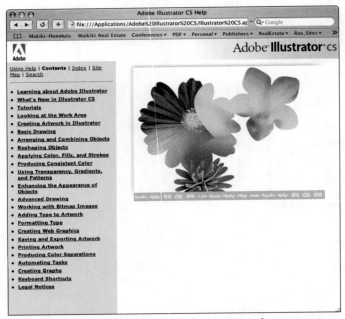

Figure 4-64: Help menus contain a home page where you can click on outline topics or use buttons for accessing an index or searching through the help files.

In Acrobat, you access a PDF file either by using the Help menu or by using the How To pane, shown in Figure 4-65. By default, the How To pane opens on the right side of the Document pane when you first install Acrobat. Click on any of the listed items in the How To pane and help information respective to the selected item appears. Adobe designed the Acrobat user interface to help users quickly find help information on selected topics commonly used by Acrobat users. Design professionals will find quick access to Print Production and Review & Comment (two How To topics) helpful when working in Acrobat.

Figure 4-65: Acrobat has a How To menu that enables you to find help information on selected topics when you first launch the program.

There's also a button in the Acrobat How To pane that allows you to access the Complete Acrobat 6.0 Help document. Click on this link in the How To pane and the Acrobat Help document opens, as shown in Figure 4-66. Although the file is a PDF document, you'll find items such as Contents, an Index, and a Search feature to be the same as the HTML help files.

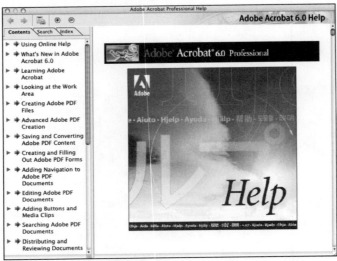

Figure 4-66: Unlike the other CS programs that use HTML documents for help files, Acrobat uses a PDF document with a custom user interface.

Tip   Regardless of what CS application you work in, be sure to frequent the Help menus when you can't find a solution for working with tools and menus.

Note   Although the Complete Acrobat 6.0 Help document is a PDF file, it was designed by Adobe engineers with a custom user interface and appears not quite the same as PDF files to which you may be accustomed. When the file opens, it appears on *top* of the Document pane, not contained *within* the Document pane as you would expect to view a PDF document. Furthermore, if a foreground PDF file appears in front of the Help document, you won't find it listed in the Window menu as you find with all open PDF files. Therefore, navigating the Help file can be a little awkward, and you might prefer using a standard PDF file that conforms more to the behavior you expect when viewing PDFs in Acrobat. If this is the case, open your Adobe Acrobat 6.0 Professional folder in your Applications folder (Mac) or Programs folder (Windows) and find the Help subfolder. Inside this subfolder, you'll find the ACROHELP.PDF file. Open the file and you find a comprehensive help document in standard PDF format.

Online help

The Adobe online help offers you help tips and techniques posted online at Adobe's Web site. You can find many useful tips and techniques hosted as Web pages, video downloads, and PDF documents. There are descriptions for new program features, plug-ins and add-ons for different CS programs, upgrade information, and links to customer-support pages.

You can access online help in all the CS programs under the Help menu and listed as *program name* Online, where *program name* is the name of the CS application you're currently using (for example, Help ➪ Photoshop Online).

Because these help files are hosted online, you obviously need an Internet connection to access them. Be sure your Web browser is operational, and click on the Online menu command in any CS program to open Web pages on Adobe's Web site.

Updates

All the CS programs have the Help ➪ Updates menu command. When you select Updates from the Help menu, the program from which the menu command was selected searches Adobe's Web site for update information. If an update exists, you're prompted for a download. Using the Updates menu command is an easy way to stay current with program upgrades and maintenance fixes. This is a command you should frequently use, because maintenance upgrades often repair bugs and programming errors in the applications. You can always expect an upgrade shortly after the release of each new program version.

Using Keyboard Shortcuts

Keyboard shortcuts are another item that could be listed as a common user-interface feature. We cover them here as a separate topic to elaborate a little bit more about the aspects of using keyboard shortcuts in the CS programs and customizing shortcuts for your personal workflow.

In Appendix A, you'll find a detailed list of keyboard shortcuts for all the CS programs and you can see how extensive the shortcuts are for all the CS programs. Many of the same notations can be found in the CS program's help files. Obviously, you don't want to spend a lot of time memorizing the shortcuts, but you'll want to take advantage of using shortcuts common among the CS programs to perform identical tasks. One great advantage of using the CS programs is that, because the applications are developed by a single software manufacturer, the keyboard shortcuts from one program to the next are often the same. In some cases, however, you also find inconsistency between the programs or perhaps some features that could use a keyboard shortcut where one doesn't exist. Fortunately, several CS programs offer you an option to edit and redefine keyboard shortcuts.

There are some differences between the CS applications in handling custom keyboard shortcuts and features available in one program versus another. So the following sections describe working with keyboard shortcuts and customizing them to suit your workflow according to each CS program.

Customizing keyboard shortcuts in Illustrator

Illustrator was the first of the CS programs developed by Adobe Systems and has a long tradition of assigned keyboard shortcuts to access tools and menu commands. As new programs have been developed, Adobe Systems has modified many keyboard shortcuts in Illustrator to match equivalent actions in other programs, such as Photoshop. If you want to return to a familiar keyboard shortcut in Illustrator, you can customize keyboard shortcuts.

Tip   If you work in a production environment and share your computer with others, it's a good idea to settle on agreed changes if they deviate from defaults used by other users. If you use your computer exclusively, you'll want to give a little thought to customizing keyboard shortcuts that are consistent between the CS programs. The more consistent you make your shortcuts, the less confusion you'll experience.

To customize a keyboard shortcut, choose Edit ➪ Keyboard Shortcuts. The Keyboard Shortcuts dialog box opens, as shown in Figure 4-67. In this dialog box, you can add a new keyboard shortcut for a menu command or tool selection, or change existing keyboard shortcuts to other keystrokes you want to use.

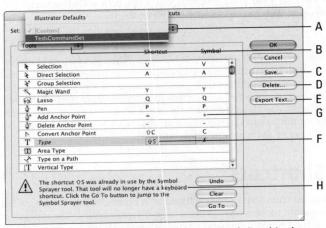

Figure 4-67: Custom keyboard shortcuts are defined in the Keyboard Shortcuts dialog box.

In the Keyboard Shortcuts dialog box, you have several options for creating a new shortcut or modifying an existing one. The options to understand in this dialog box include the following:

✦ **Set pull-down menu (A):** By default, the menu option is Illustrator Defaults. This menu choice remains listed in the pull-down menu so you can return to the Illustrator defaults at any time. When you assign a new keyboard shortcut or modify an existing one, the menu item changes to Custom. When you save your modified set, you're prompted to name the set. After saving, the name you use to identify your custom set is added to the pull-down menu.

✦ **Menu Commands/Tools (B):** Select from either Menu Commands or Tools to change shortcuts that invoke menu commands or select tools.

✦ **Save (C):** After changing the shortcuts to your personal liking, click the Save button to save your changes. The name you use for your set is added to the Set pull-down menu.

✦ **Delete (D):** The Delete button enables you to delete custom sets you add to the pull-down menu. To delete a set, first select the set to be deleted in the pull-down menu and then click the Delete button.

✦ **Export Text (E):** When you click on the Export Text button, all your keyboard shortcuts are identified in a text file. You can use the text file to share with other workgroup members. For more information on custom keystrokes in workgroup environments, see the "Custom shortcuts for workgroups" sidebar in this chapter.

✦ **Shortcut edits (F):** To change a shortcut, first click in the Shortcuts column in the row for the item you want to change. For example, if you want to reassign the keystroke for accessing the Type tool, click the cursor in the Shortcut column where the Type row appears.

✦ **Symbol (G):** The keyboard shortcut to access a tool or invoke an action is defined in the Shortcut column. Adjacent to the Shortcut column is the Symbol column. The characters you add here appear in a menu list and/or tool tip. Notice that when you view the menus in all CS programs, you see the menu name and often the keys used for the shortcut to access the menu item.

✦ **Warning (H):** If you define a tool or a menu command with a key combination that is already used to select a tool or invoke a command, a warning is displayed at the bottom of the dialog box. If you don't want to interfere with an existing shortcut, click the Undo button. If you're overriding a preexisting shortcut, you can edit the shortcut used by another tool or menu command. Click the Go To button and you're taken to the item using the shortcut you overrode. Add a new shortcut if you so desire.

Note

Mac OS X does not permit assigning ⌘+Option+8 as a menu command.

Custom shortcuts for workgroups

If you make changes with keyboard shortcuts and want to share your custom set with other users, you can easily copy your custom keyboard set to other computers. When you save a custom set, the new definitions are saved to a file. This file is stored in the user logon Library/Preferences/Adobe Illustrator CS Settings folder (Mac) or Documents and Settings\username\Application Data\Adobe\Adobe Illustrator Cs Settings folder on Windows. To find the files on Windows you need to turn on the ability to view hidden files and folders within the Tools ⇨ Folder Options ⇨ View ⇨ Advanced Settings ⇨ Files and Folders ⇨ Hidden Files and Folders ⇨ Show Hidden Files and Folders option. I know that's a mouthful, but that's where to find them and how to turn them on. WindowsCopy the file from one computer to the same folder on the other computers, and the keyboard-shortcuts set is added to the Illustrator Set pull-down menu.

If you make changes to the keyboard shortcuts either in an isolated environment or when working as part of a group, it's handy to have a template or guide that you can refer to in order to refresh your memory on changes made to the shortcut keys. When you create a custom set and click the Export Text button, all features that can accept keyboard shortcuts are exported along with all those features assigned a keyboard shortcut. The file is a text file with the items and keyboard shortcuts listed with tabs and carriage returns. You can easily convert the text file to a table in a program like Microsoft Word.

Tables are supported in Adobe InDesign; however, the text file exported from Illustrator cannot be imported directly into InDesign. In order to import the file in InDesign, you need to open it in Word and save the file from Word. Rather than performing two steps for saving from Word and creating the table in InDesign, you can create the table in Word and use the PDFMaker to create a PDF file.

When you open the exported file in Microsoft Word, the text appears as shown in the following figure. Tabs separate the item description from the keystroke used as the shortcut.

Continued

Continued

To convert the text to a table in Microsoft Word, select all the text in the document by pressing ⌘+A (Mac) or Ctrl+A (Windows). Choose Table ➪ Convert ➪ Text to Table. The Convert Text to Table dialog box opens, as shown in the following figure. Be certain to click the radio button for Tabs in the bottom-left corner of the dialog box. Word recognizes the columns to be created when you identify the separator.

Click OK and Word creates the table for you. With a Word document, you can host the file on a server or print the file and distribute it among users in your workgroup. For a more accessible document (for users who don't have Microsoft Word installed on their computers), use the PDFMaker Macro in Word and create a PDF document. The PDF file (shown in the following figure) can be viewed in any Acrobat viewer.

For more information on using the PDFMaker and converting Microsoft Word files to PDF, see Part V of this book.

Customizing keyboard shortcuts in Photoshop

Have you ever wondered why ⌘+I (Mac)/Ctrl+I (Windows) in Adobe Photoshop inverts an image when a much more functional use of the shortcut might be to open the Image Size dialog box? Well, the good news for Photoshop users is that Photoshop CS now supports creating custom keyboard shortcuts just like Illustrator CS. You can assign new keyboard shortcuts or remap existing keyboard shortcuts to menus and tools.

To change keyboard shortcuts, you start by opening the Keyboard Shortcuts dialog box by choosing Edit ⇨ Keyboard Shortcuts. The Keyboard Shortcuts dialog box opens, as shown in Figure 4-68.

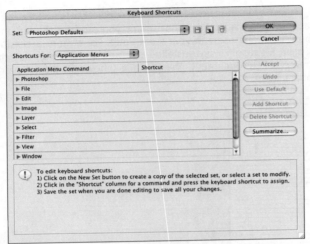

Figure 4-68: The Photoshop Keyboard Shortcuts dialog box offers very similar options to those found in the Illustrator Keyboard Shortcuts dialog box.

As you can see in Figure 4-68, the dialog box offers very similar options to the ones you find using the Illustrator Keyboard Shortcuts dialog box. The Set pull-down menu provides choices for using the default keyboard shortcuts or custom sets you create and save, much like those options discussed with Illustrator in the preceding section. From the Shortcuts For pull-down menu, you can choose to edit application menu commands, palette menus, or tools. When you select one of the categories from the Shortcuts For pull-down menu, the options change in the list below the pull-down menu. For Application Menus and Palette Menus, each menu is listed with a right-pointing arrow adjacent to the menu name. Click on the right-pointing arrow symbol, and the menu expands where each individual command is exposed. In Figure 4-69, you can see the Palette Menus selected from the Shortcuts For pull-down menu and the Layers palette expanded where all palette menu commands are listed. Notice that, by default, only three commands have shortcut-key equivalents.

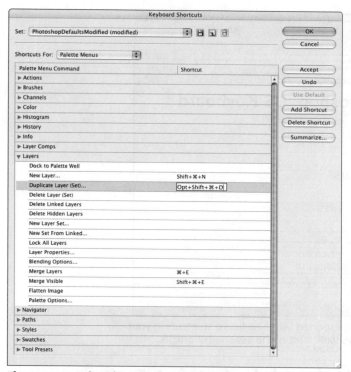

Figure 4-69: Select the category you want from the Shortcuts For pull-down menu and expand the menu or palette by clicking on the symbol adjacent to a palette name.

Most of the same options exist for creating, changing, and deleting keyboard shortcuts in Photoshop as you find in Illustrator. Photoshop enables you to export a list of all the assigned keyboard shortcuts; however, unlike the text-file export in Illustrator, Photoshop's export is in the form of an HTML file. Click on the Summarize button in the Keyboard Shortcuts dialog box, and the Save dialog box opens, allowing you to navigate your hard drive and locate a folder destination for your file. After saving the file, you can view the list of shortcuts in your Web browser, as shown in Figure 4-70.

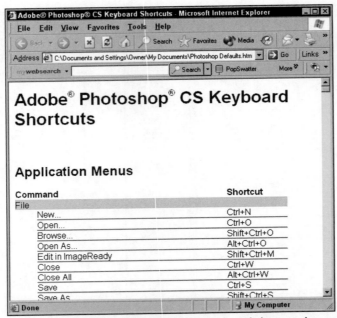

Figure 4-70: Open the exported list of keyboard shortcuts in your default Web browser to view a list of the assigned shortcuts.

Customizing keyboard shortcuts in InDesign

Fortunately, the Keyboard Shortcuts dialog box in all the CS applications that allow you to customize shortcuts is accessed with the same menu command. Select Edit ➪ Keyboard Shortcuts in InDesign, and the InDesign Keyboard Shortcuts dialog box opens. From a pull-down menu listed as Product Area, you see an extensive list of categories where keyboard shortcuts are assigned, as shown in Figure 4-71.

You select an option from the Product Area pull-down menu and click on a command in the Commands list box. From this point, you have another option where you can narrow the assignment of the keyboard shortcut to one of five categories listed in the Context pull-down menu. For example, if you wanted to assign a keyboard shortcut to convert a table to text, you would start by selecting Tables Menu in the Product Area. In the Commands list, you would select Convert Table to Text, and from the Context pull-down menu you would select Tables. Then you would click in the New Shortcut field box and press the keys to create the new shortcut. In Figure 4-72, you can see each of the selections that create this example for converting a table to text.

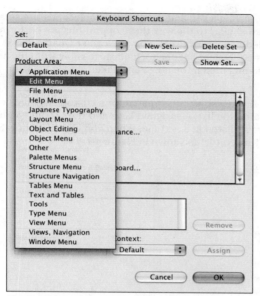

Figure 4-71: The Keyboard Shortcuts dialog box in InDesign contains an extensive set of categories from the Product Area pull-down menu.

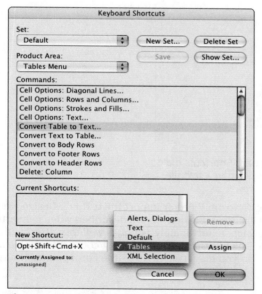

Figure 4-72: Keyboard Shortcuts dialog box shown with selections to convert a table to text

The basic options for creating new sets, saving a set, and being able to select custom sets from the Set pull-down menu are handled similar to the way these operations are performed in Illustrator and Photoshop. As an added benefit for users who are former QuarkXPress users, InDesign provides a QuarkXPress-equivalent set of shortcuts accessible from the Set pull-down menu. A PageMaker set is also included if the new PageMaker Plug-In Pack for InDesign CS is installed.

If you want to create a table describing the key shortcuts created for a custom set, click on the Show Set button. Like Adobe Illustrator, the list of assigned keys and those commands where no assignment has been made are all listed in a text file. When you click the Show Set button, the list appears in your default text editor, as shown in Figure 4-73.

Figure 4-73: Click Show Set in the Keyboard Shortcuts dialog box, and the list of keyboard shortcuts is listed in a text file.

You can save the text file and open it in Microsoft Word or import the text in InDesign where the text file can be converted to a table like the table conversion described when converting Illustrator text files. The text file for InDesign, unfortunately, is not as well formatted as the text file you have available in Illustrator. The InDesign text file doesn't convert to a table as cleanly as Illustrator's table conversion, so you may have to do a little editing to make a table guide for your workgroup.

Customizing keyboard shortcuts in GoLive

Keyboard shortcuts can also be assigned in GoLive. Choose GoLive ➪ Keyboard Shortcuts (Mac) or Edit ➪ Keyboard Shortcuts (Windows) to open the Keyboard Shortcuts dialog box, shown in Figure 4-74.

Note   Unlike the other CS programs, the Macintosh version of GoLive uses the application menu in Mac OS X rather than the Edit menu for opening the Keyboard Shortcuts dialog box.

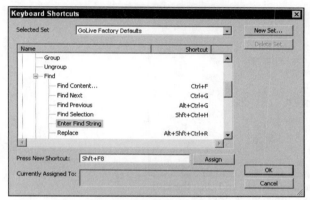

Figure 4-74: The Keyboard Shortcuts dialog box in GoLive

GoLive supports a list of commands in a list box that is expanded by clicking on a symbol adjacent to the menu name. On the Mac, a right-pointing arrow appears adjacent to the menu name; on Windows, the symbol is a plus sign. When expanded, the symbols change to a down-pointing arrow and minus sign, respectively.

As you scroll the list of commands in the list box, notice that the commands are nested in groups. Click on the symbol adjacent to a menu command and the list expands. In Figure 4-74, the Edit menu was expanded; then the Find command expanded to expand the nested group.

GoLive does not support saving a text file or creating an HTML file for a list of commands you can use as a guide.

Working with keyboard shortcuts in Acrobat

Acrobat is the only program in the Creative Suite that doesn't support creation of custom keystrokes for shortcuts. However, while discussing keyboard shortcuts, there is one thing important to point out when working in Acrobat: By default, accessing tools with keystrokes is not enabled. Users of earlier versions of Acrobat soon find that pressing the H key and expecting to select the Hand tool doesn't produce a result when they first launch Acrobat. In order to use key modifiers to access tools, you need to change a preference setting.

Open the Preferences dialog box by choosing Acrobat ➪ Preferences (Mac) or Edit ➪ Preferences (Windows). The Preferences dialog box opens by default to show the General preferences. If General is not selected in the left pane, as shown in Figure 4-75, click on General and the right pane changes to reflect the options available for the General preferences.

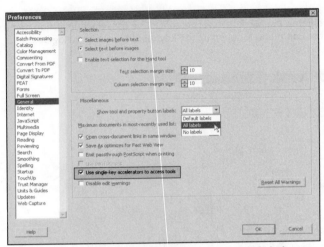

Figure 4-75: Open the General preferences and click the Use Single-Key Accelerators to Access Tools check box.

Be certain that Use Single-Key Accelerators to Access Tools is checked. If the check box is unchecked, pressing a key on your keyboard to access a tool won't work. By default, when you first load Acrobat, this check box is unchecked.

Unfortunately, you cannot change any keyboard shortcuts in Acrobat.

Assigning keyboard shortcuts

The vast number of options you have available and the number of different changes you can make to customize keyboard shortcuts in four out of the five CS programs is a bit mind-boggling. In workgroups, it's a good idea to sit down in committee and agree with partners and coworkers on what key assignments you want to make that change the default key combinations to access tools, menus, and palettes.

You can make a few changes to add new shortcuts without interfering with existing keyboard shortcuts by using the Function keys. For example, rather than use ⌘/Control + C, which interferes with an existing keyboard shortcut, you could use Shift + F8, which is a key combination unassigned to a command. By using the Shift key and a Function key, you can assign new shortcuts without disturbing assigned keystrokes. For a couple of preliminary recommendations, here are a few keystroke combinations you may want to assign in Photoshop and InDesign. Try to follow these steps to create your own custom keystrokes.

STEPS: Creating New Keyboard Shortcuts

1. **Open Adobe Photoshop.** One of the great new additions to Adobe Photoshop CS is the improved feature set in the File Browser. As a matter of default you'll want to use the File Browser as your central navigation hub whenever you work in Photoshop. By default, the File Browser is accessed by pressing Shift + Command + O (Mac) or Shift + Command + O (Windows). You can remap the shortcut keys to the same keyboard shortcuts using Function keys.

2. **Choose Edit ⇨ Keyboard Shortcuts.** The Keyboard Shortcuts dialog box opens.

3. **Open the Window menu.** In the list of Application Commands, scroll down to Window and click on the right-pointing arrow to expand the list.

4. **Scroll the window by dragging the elevator bar down or clicking on the down arrow in the list window.** You want to locate the File Browser command in the list, as shown in Figure 4-76.

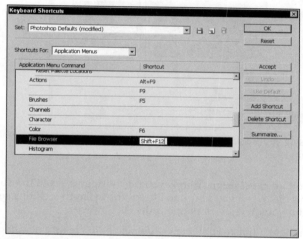

Figure 4-76: Expand the Window menu and click in the Shortcut column in the File Browser row.

5. **Click in the Shortcut column in the File Browser row.** When you click in the Shortcut column, a field box becomes active. Whatever you type in the field box becomes the new shortcut key.

6. **Press Shift+F12.** Pressing the Shift key and the F12 key assigns these keys to a shortcut that opens the File Browser.

7. **Click the Save icon.** To keep the shortcut as part of a modified set, you need to save your changes. The disk icon in the top row adjacent to the Set pull-down menu is used to save your changes. Click the disk icon and you're prompted in a Save dialog box to name your custom set. By default, the set is saved to the /Photoshop/Presets/ Keyboard Shortcuts directory.

8. **Name your file.** Supply a name in the Save dialog box, and leave the folder location at the default. Click Save to save the file.

9. **Test the keyboard shortcut.** If you followed all the steps, you should be able to open the File Browser using your new shortcut. Click OK in the Keyboard Shortcuts dialog box and press Shift+F12. The File Browser window should open, as shown in Figure 4-77.

Figure 4-77: By using your new keyboard shortcut, you can open the File Browser window.

10. **Quit Photoshop and open InDesign.** Your keyboard shortcut is saved to your custom Keyboard Shortcuts file. When you return to Photoshop in another editing session, pressing the keys for your new shortcut opens the File Browser.

11. **Create a new document.** Choose File ➪ New ➪ Document to create a new document window. Leave the defaults alone and click OK to create a new document with a blank page.

12. **Open the Keyboard Shortcuts dialog box.** Select Edit ➪ Keyboard Shortcuts to open the Keyboard Shortcuts dialog box.

13. **Select Type Menu in the Product Area.** Open the Product Area pull-down menu and select Type Menu.

Note   The menus listed in the Product Area are all listed in alphabetical order. The order in the menu does not follow the same list order as the top-level menu. By viewing the menu items in alphabetical order, you can easily find the menu you want.

14. **Select Fill with Placeholder Text.** This menu command is one you'll use many times when working in InDesign. When the cursor is placed in a text frame and you select the command, the text frame is filled with Greek type. No longer do you need to search your hard drive for a Lorem Ipsum file when creating comps in your layout program.

15. **Add the keyboard shortcut.** Click the cursor in the field box under New Shortcut, shown in Figure 4-78. Press Shift+F12 and the shortcut is added to the New Shortcut field box. Click the Assign button to assign the shortcut to the menu command. Click the Save button to save the new assignment.

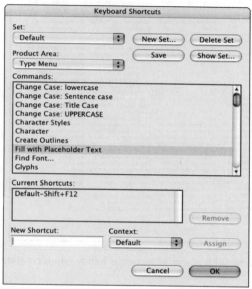

Figure 4-78: Click the field box and type your shortcut keys.

16. **Test the shortcut.** Click OK in the Keyboard Shortcuts dialog box. Click the cursor in a text frame or draw a frame with the Horizontal Type tool. Press Shift+F12. If you followed the steps, the type should fill the text frame. In Figure 4-79, I created an object and clicked the Horizontal Type tool in the frame. I pressed Shift+F12 and the object was filled with Greek text.

Obviously, in workflow environments where you want to bring all your workers together using common keyboard shortcuts, you'll want to get some feedback from your coworkers and come up with a paradigm for mapping custom keystrokes. By using the Function keys, you can assign keyboard shortcuts to unique features in all CS programs except Acrobat.

Figure 4-79: Filling a text frame with placeholder text is handy when creating comps in InDesign.

Summary

✦ Several CS programs have some common tools. The vast majority of common tools exist among Illustrator, Photoshop, and InDesign. The tools work similarly in the programs that use them. Accessing the tools using keystrokes is also common between the programs.

✦ Acrobat uses a variety of toolbars that can be opened and docked in the top-level Toolbar Well. Context menus help greatly in accessing tools in Acrobat.

✦ Some tool options are accessible in some CS programs by double-clicking a tool in the program's toolbox. Corresponding dialog boxes open where attributes are assigned for a given tool.

✦ Photoshop, InDesign, and GoLive offer options for saving workspaces. Workspaces involve arrangement of tools and palettes and the overall look of a program's editing environment.

✦ All the CS programs have some common user-interface features. Among the more popular are context menus and access to help documents.

✦ All CS programs with the exception of Acrobat offer you options for customizing keyboard shortcuts.

✦   ✦   ✦

Getting Started with Design Workflows

Creating Production Workflows

The Adobe Creative Suite is built around the concept of facilitating design production in workflow environments. Designers and production artists create workflows either as independent workers or as participants in workflow groups. A workflow helps you perform your work quickly and intelligently, often by streamlining redundant tasks. Workflows are designed to dramatically reduce the time you need to perform your work and reduce the time required to train new workers.

This chapter covers the initial development of production workflows as they relate to using the Adobe Creative Suite Premium Edition. With all the tools at hand, you'll gain an understanding of how to use the CS applications in workflows and how you can save time producing artwork.

Understanding Workflows

Workflows as they pertain to the Adobe Creative Suite can be divided into several groups. As a graphic designer, you may be primarily concerned with production workflows where artwork creations originate in programs like Adobe Illustrator CS and Adobe Photoshop CS. Document assembly may be performed in Adobe InDesign CS and from InDesign CS you may export files to Adobe PDF or package files for Adobe GoLive CS. Furthermore, you may integrate your native Illustrator and Photoshop files along with PDF in Adobe GoLive. From creation to final output, you have a workflow focused on production.

You may also be concerned with a color-management workflow to insure the color is consistent among all the applications you use to produce your artwork. This workflow might be a subset of your production workflow. The color-management workflow might extend beyond your office and continue to the print shop or service center. In this regard, you need to work together with service technicians working outside your environment.

Cross-Reference For information related to creating color-management workflows, see Chapter 6.

Yet another workflow that affects your final results when you prepare documents for print is the production center printing your jobs.

Printers and service bureaus develop workflows to run their production lines from digital file to final output. The bridge between you and the service center might include color management and file preparation to meet the standards set forth by your vendors. If you design files for print, you need to understand that the production center is part of your workflow and there is a great benefit to working together with your vendors to ensure your workflow is efficient and your product is delivered on time.

Cross-Reference   For more information on prepress and printing, see Chapter 35.

If you design files for Web hosting, you can include your Internet Service Provider (ISP) or your client's ISP in your workflow if your designs end up hosted on a site other than your own ISP. Working with ISP vendors is as important as working with print vendors. It is, therefore, equally important for you to include professionals at an ISP in your workflow.

Cross-Reference   For more information on Web hosting, see Chapter 30.

Regardless of whether you design files for print or for the Web, realize that you have two kinds of workflows with which you'll continually interact. Your internal workflow where you produce your artwork is something over which you have complete control. The workflows that extend to your print shop or ISP are something you over which you don't have complete control, so you need to negotiate standards with the vendors to develop consistent reliable output.

In this chapter, we look at workflows you create in your office for design production and understanding workflow concepts as they apply to the Adobe Creative Suite. In several later chapters in this book, we address how to set up the CS programs to suit your production workflow.

Workflows for Independent Artists

If you're an independent designer working in a one-person shop, you have some advantages in that you can customize and work with the Creative Suite applications as you see fit. You don't need to concern yourself with setting up your environment to suit the needs of multiple users. The advantage is having it all your way; the disadvantage is you have to do everything yourself — acting as the creative director, artist, image editor, layout artist, Web designer, and office manager.

As someone who works with all the CS programs, you'll want to take a little time to plan your workflow and take more time to become productive in using all the CS applications. An example of a workflow for an independent graphic designer is illustrated in Figure 5-1.

In the example workflow, you begin an assignment with a client meeting either personally or through e-mail or telephone calls. As you develop a concept and after interviewing your client, you prepare sketches or comps that are sent back to the client in an e-mail review using Adobe Acrobat Professional. If more than one person is part of a committee that ultimately approves your commission, each committee member receives your draft via e-mail for review. When the final comp is approved you begin your work on the project.

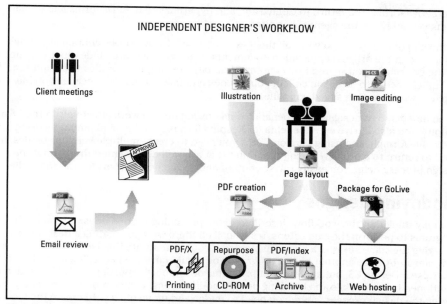

Figure 5-1: An example of a production workflow for an independent designer

If you need illustrated art as well as photo images, you may spend some time in Adobe Illustrator CS and Adobe Photoshop CS, where you create artwork. All layers are preserved in the documents, and you save your files in native formats.

If the copy is developed in a word processor foreign to you and not compatible with your text editors, you might ask your client to send you a PDF file, from which you extract the copy and import it into Adobe InDesign CS. You import the illustrations and images into Adobe InDesign, and fit the copy to the design.

You export the InDesign CS document as Adobe PDF and open the file in Adobe Acrobat Professional. You soft-proof the file to ensure all colors will print as you expect and then repurpose the file by reducing image resolution to create a smaller file. You may need to save this file as a copy with password security, which prevents your client from extracting data or printing the document. You e-mail the client, who signs off on the design with a digital signature in Adobe Acrobat Standard or Professional. When you receive approval from your client, you e-mail or FTP the high-resolution PDF document to your printer.

Cross-Reference For information on soft-proofing color, see Chapter 35. For information on repurposing files, see the section on document repurposing later in this chapter.

If Web design is part of your work, you return to Adobe InDesign CS and package the file for GoLive. You integrate the InDesign CS document in the Web site design and use repurposed PDFs designed for Web hosting and CD-ROM replication. If point-of-sale order forms are part of your commission, you create the form designs in InDesign CS or Adobe Illustrator CS and export/save to PDF. You use Acrobat Professional to add form fields and JavaScripts to create interactive forms. You return to GoLive and add hyperlinks to the PDF forms and upload the forms via GoLive to the client's Web site.

At the end of your job, you write all the files to a CD-ROM where PDFs contain attachments to quickly open the original application documents. You create a search index that you include on the CD to help you search PDF content. Metadata are supplied for files to permit searches and quick access to files. You collect your money and take a vacation, because you have an efficient workflow that saved you time.

As an independent designer, you benefit from knowing how to work effectively in the CS applications. You also derive extra benefits for keeping files reduced to a minimum by using only native file formats and using Version Cue if you need to create multiple versions of files. If you need to return to a project, having fewer files that are well documented throughout the design process helps you easily revise content and create new designs for the same client.

Modifying designs

You may think that the workflow described in the preceding section doesn't require all the CS programs to perform the same steps. It's true, if all there were to creating a design piece was following the same steps in a linear fashion, you could substitute the use of an illustration program and/or use another layout program. You would miss the packaging for GoLive if you don't use InDesign CS, but some layout programs do support exporting to HTML. What's not mentioned in the workflow is handling design modifications. Design modifications may occur during the design process where you need to nudge and move objects to create the look you want or when your client requests changes to objects, images, colors, type fonts, and so on.

The advantage of using the Creative Suite is more obvious when making changes to designs. As you change files, you can save different versions of the same file with Version Cue. If you need to change back to an earlier version, this tool alone will save you a lot of time. If you need to move or nudge objects, having files imported from native formats opens up your freedom for moving design elements without affecting underlying objects.

Cross-Reference   For information on using Version Cue, see Chapter 7.

Extending the workflow

Another advantage of using the Creative Suite is the easy portability of assets that can help you prepare files properly for vendors. When designing for print, you can acquire color profiles prepared by your vendor, designed for output on their devices.

Cross-Reference   For information on creating color-management workflows, see Chapter 6.

In addition to color management, you want to check your files for potential errors. When documents are *preflighted*, your files are analyzed for potential printing problems. Adobe Acrobat Professional contains a sophisticated preflight tool using built-in and/or custom preflight profiles. You can acquire preflight profiles from your service provider to use in Adobe Acrobat for checking files for proper printing. You can acquire profiles from vendor Web sites or have them e-mailed directly to you.

Cross-Reference   For understanding more about preflight and information on importing and exporting preflight profiles, see Chapter 35.

Workflows for Studios and Production Houses

If you work in a larger studio with coworkers participating in design projects, you need to be more concerned about the steps involved in your workflow and be consistent in all your tasks. Many studios that evolved with computer illustration and design often let employees determine what application software to use and what methods for creating designs to employ. The unknowing creative directors, who at times were computer illiterate, paid little attention to what tools were used and only focused on the final artwork. Today, some firms spend a lot of time updating documents from a variety of programs that their current staff no longer uses.

The first step in developing an efficient workflow is to begin with standards that all employees in a firm use. Deciding what application's software to use, setting standards for file naming conventions, determining what archiving methods to use, and developing policies for updating documents are all preliminary steps that you should integrate in a workflow schema before engaging in production tasks. The time spent on management is insignificant when you compare it to the time it takes to train current employees and hire new ones.

As an example of a studio or production-center workflow, Figure 5-2 shows how creative production personnel participate in a design project. After a project is approved, artists working in Adobe Illustrator CS and image editors working in Adobe Photoshop CS save files to a server. Copy editors save files to the server for the page layout artists to acquire. The page layout artists retrieve files, complete the designs, and save the completed designs back to the server. PDFs are exported from InDesign CS for print, Web hosting, CD-ROM replication, porting to handheld devices and tablets, and document archiving. Web designers retrieve InDesign files and package them for GoLive. PDFs are retrieved from the server for documents included on the Web site.

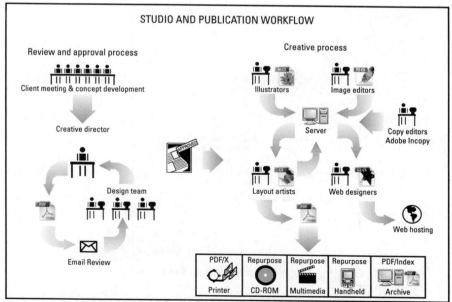

Figure 5-2: An example of a production workflow for a studio or production center

In this facility, it's easy to see how developing standards is critical for the workflow environment. When new employees are hired, they need to quickly fit into the workflow. Training new staff is a much easier task when following standards. If individual artists determine their own methods and use different programs to produce artwork, getting new employees up to speed is likely to take more time than you can afford.

Document Repurposing

Document repurposing is taking a file suited for one output purpose and optimizing it for another output purpose. In regard to the Adobe Creative Suite, Acrobat is the application best suited for document repurposing.

If you design a piece for print in InDesign CS, you have some options you can employ to repurpose a file. Because exporting to PDF is something you can do for printing, you can return to the InDesign file and export a second PDF document more suitable for Web hosting or screen displays. What goes on in InDesign CS is simply a matter of choosing the Adobe PDF settings most desirable for your output needs. To select the correct settings, follow these steps:

1. **Select File ➪ Export in Adobe InDesign CS.** The Export dialog box opens.

2. **From the Format pull-down menu, choose Adobe PDF.**

3. **Supply a name for the file in the Save As field and click Save.** A second dialog box opens where you set the attributes for the PDF file.

4. **From the top-level Preset pull-down menu, you make choices for the Adobe PDF settings you want to use, as shown in Figure 5-3.**

5. **Export to PDF. Click the Export button to complete the file export to PDF.**

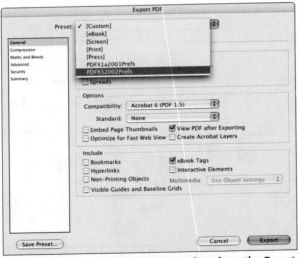

Figure 5-3: Choosing Adobe PDF settings from the Presets pull-down menu.

When you choose a setting that contains options for downsampling images, the resultant PDF document becomes a smaller file than when you create PDFs with settings where you apply no downsampling.

Cross-Reference To learn more about exporting to PDF from Adobe InDesign CS, see Chapter 35.

Another method you have for repurposing PDF documents lies in Adobe Acrobat Professional. You can open a PDF in Acrobat and select the Advanced ⇨ PDF Optimizer menu command. The PDF Optimizer provides you with options for downsampling images as well as any other options for reducing file sizes. In addition to using the PDF Optimizer, you can also set up a Batch Sequence to optimize a collection of PDF files together using the same amounts of downsampling and applying other attribute choices.

Cross-Reference To learn more about PDF Optimizer and creating Batch Sequences, see Chapter 26.

Repurposing documents is one of the true benefits of an efficient workflow. If you relied on other methods to repurpose a document from print to Web hosting, you must open files in Adobe Photoshop CS, downsample files, and save them as new files to disk. After downsampling the images, you must open your layout application and relink all the image links. Obviously, using PDF as your output format provides you with a much more efficient alternative when you need to repurpose documents.

Note Downsampling an image is the process of reducing file size by lowering the image's resolution (for example, taking a 300 ppi [pixels per inch] image and lowering the resolution to 72 ppi). You can downsample images in Adobe Photoshop and Adobe Acrobat, as well as use methods for downsampling from within Adobe GoLive.

Setting Workflow Standards

Whether you're an independent designer or you own or manage an agency, there are some considerations you should think about when designing your workflow. Too often, individuals or managers become subordinates to vendors, contracting professionals, or production personnel instead of taking control of their environment and encouraging others to fit within their workflow schema.

Instead of having others dictate or impose standards on you, try to give some thought to the way you want to work and how you want others to fit into your workflow. The following sections offer some suggestions you may want to consider.

Set standards for the tools used in your workflow

When hiring employees or working with contract artists, ask people to use the same tools you use in your workflow. If you use all the programs in the Adobe Creative Suite, be certain to hire employees skilled in these tools and make it a necessary condition for all your contracting artists and professionals to use the same tools. The time to train people who fit in your workflow is dramatically reduced if they're skilled in using the same tools.

Use vendors who support the tools you use

We often hear design professionals complain, "My print shop or vendor doesn't like to print from InDesign" (or another product). Having your vendor dictate what tools you use to perform your work is like the tail wagging the dog. After all, who is paying whom the money? If your vendor doesn't support one of the tools you use, and you produce even a moderate amount of work, tell your vendor that if they don't support your selection of software, you'll be forced to use their competitor across the street. Try this on for size and see how many vendors turn you down.

Devote time to ongoing training

Creative professionals today are in a category similar to other professionals like medical workers, legal workers, psychologists, educators, and people in all kinds of professions that deal with government regulations. All these professions require continuing education units (CEU) to sustain licensure or maintain compliance with changing laws. As a design professional, you work in an ever-changing world of high technology. The world of the creative professional in some ways changes more rapidly today than that of almost any other occupation. New software upgrades are occurring every 18 months. This rapid change related to the tools you use requires you and your staff to engage in ongoing training and education.

To help you work more effectively in your workflow, try to set up training sessions that you can provide in-house or with your vendors. You might approach a vendor and ask them to sponsor an evening session to introduce a new product upgrade. You can find many Adobe professionals working in cities throughout the world who are willing and able to make visits to communities for speaking sessions without charging any fees. You can also ask local community colleges and universities to sponsor similar events and hold workshops and classes on products you use in your workflow. In large agencies, you can employ policies and provide time off for production artists to take classes and workshops benefiting your workflow.

Develop a paradigm for managing your projects

Sometimes locating files and making file edits takes more time than designing a new piece from scratch. To avoid time lost due to searching for files, converting old files to newer versions, and locating fonts and assets contained in design projects, try to spend some time managing your artwork in an effective manner. With the CS programs, you can use Adobe Acrobat and create data sheets using form fields. When a form is created, you can use the form template to fill in new forms for each project. Try to complete a form for every project and supply all pertinent information on the data sheet related to personnel involved in the project and all related software used to create the project designs. Figure 5-4 illustrates a sample form created in Adobe Illustrator CS and opened in Adobe Acrobat where form fields were added.

Tip   Files saved from Adobe Illustrator CS as a native AI file with the Create PDF Compatible File option selected in the Illustrator Options dialog box can be opened directly in any Adobe Acrobat viewer including Adobe Reader.

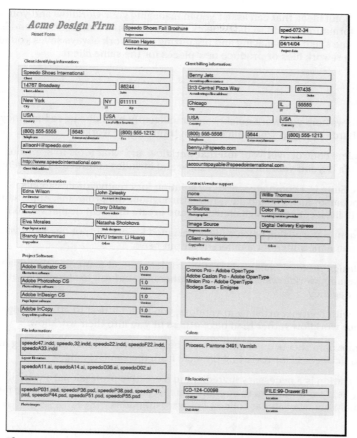

Figure 5-4: A sample form created in Adobe Illustrator CS and opened in Adobe Acrobat where form fields were added

As you can see in Figure 5-4, the agency personnel and contracting vendors are all listed by name. A separate document contains all the contact information for the contractors and vendors. The software and version numbers of the applications used in the project are listed, as well as design specifics such as fonts and colors. The fields in the lower-right corner describe the location of CD-ROMs and DVDs where the completed files are stored. You can store PDF forms like this on a network server and use Acrobat Search to search for them. In a matter of minutes, any employee in a company including new employees can locate the files for any given project.

Cross-Reference For more information on searching PDF documents, see Chapter 31.

You may find other helpful ideas that can assist you in managing your workflow and you may find other relevant information to add to data sheets. The most important issue at hand is realizing that a little time spent in managing and organizing your work always saves you more time when you need to rework files or produce new pieces for the same client.

Summary

✦ Efficient workflows help you work quickly and intelligently by reducing redundancy. Workflow standards can help you reduce time in training new workers.

✦ You have complete control over your internal workflow and what tools to use. Your workflow extends beyond your internal workflow and includes contractors and vendors.

✦ Adobe Creative Suite is a complete workflow solution for creative professionals, whereby all document files are fully integrated throughout the programs. Applications help you update files, change design elements, and create different design versions.

✦ You use document repurposing when a file is designed for one output need and you're reworking the same file suited for a different output need.

✦ Independent design professionals and creative art department managers are advantaged when planning workflows and attracting others to conform to standards set by an individual or agency.

✦ When working with contract artists and vendors, you'll find it best to attract people who fit into your workflow rather than have others fit you into their workflow.

✦ Keeping accurate data sheets on client projects helps you save time in relocating files and provides quick access for revisiting projects from the same clients.

✦ Continuing education is a necessary ingredient in a creative professional's work life. You can solicit help from vendors to support training sessions and utilize Adobe field specialists to help you stay abreast of new software upgrades.

✦　　✦　　✦

Creating Color-Managed Workflows

✦ ✦ ✦ ✦

In This Chapter

Getting familiar with
color profiles

Working with color in
CS applications

Using profiles

✦ ✦ ✦ ✦

Perhaps the greatest challenge to design professionals is getting color on printed output to look like the color displayed on computer monitors. Artists can easily overcome common design dilemmas such as working around font problems, learning functional aspects of applications software, avoiding pitfalls related to image handling, and a host of other nuisances that hinder progress. But when it comes to color-matching, the problems are more complicated and the solutions are often misunderstood and obscure.

Fortunately, Adobe has been working for several years on creating a common color engine that can be shared among imaging applications. The result of Adobe's efforts is exemplified in the CS applications. All the CS programs share the same Adobe Color Engine (ACE) that takes you one step closer to reliable color-matching among application documents, your computer monitor, and the output devices you use. In this chapter, we cover some fundamental information related to color management among the Adobe CS applications.

Color management is a complex topic. An accurate description for identifying all the variables related to rendering reliable color is well beyond the scope of this chapter. For more-sophisticated descriptions, look for books written specifically to help you understand and manage color on computers and output devices.

Cross-Reference For more information on managing color, see Deke McClelland's Wiley publication, Adobe Photoshop CS Bible."

Understanding Profiling

Color profiles provide the necessary information for the acquisition, display, and output of your images/documents. A color profile might be one you create through the use of calibration devices or ones you acquire from various equipment manufacturers. Color profiles interpret your images and documents in terms of display and output. Often, using a color profile can mean the difference between a printed image using the colors you expect on output and a rendered image with incorrect colors.

Profiles in workflows

The design of production pieces can make use of several different color profiles. You may have one profile developed for your scanner when acquiring an image through the scanning process. A calibrated profile converts the reflective artwork on your scanner platen to digital form, which captures and translates color the best it can, creating a digital file that is a close rendition of the print you scanned. When you open your scanned image in a program like Photoshop, you use a calibrated profile for your monitor. The scanned image color space is converted to the monitor working space. This conversion is a temporary condition and does not change the data in your image. When you finish your editing session, you convert the monitor color to the output color using yet another profile for your output device. The converted color ideally translates the color space from what you see on your monitor to the color space of your printer; the color range you see on your monitor fits as close as possible to within the color space of your output device. Throughout the color-management workflow, you're converting color from one space to another using color profiles.

Calibrating color

Software applications provide you with simplistic tools for calibrating color. You have tools such as Adobe Gamma installed on Windows to calibrate your monitor for white balance, gamma, black point, and so on. On Mac OS X, the operating system provides you with tools to calibrate your monitor. On a more sophisticated level, you can purchase calibration systems that create monitor color profiles and output profiles for you printing devices. Using hardware devices for calibrating color is much more sophisticated than relying on the software tools that Adobe and Apple provide.

In some circumstances, you can use profiles that come with the installation of the CS applications. Profiles designed for four-color process printing on coated stock are generic and often do a reasonable job matching color from screen to press. As the lowest cost option, you can use simple software monitor-calibration tools and get fairly close to the kind of output you want on four-color process printing. However, if you're particular about color, and if your output varies to a range of devices including composite color printers, then you may want to invest in calibration equipment suited to create profiles for your workflow.

"But I don't want to spend $3,000 for that kind of equipment!" is often the cry we hear from creative professionals. Here's an analogy to help drive home the point. Wendy wants a Mercedes. Kelly and Ted want Ferraris. However, none of us has enough in our bank accounts to purchase the vehicles. Hence, we don't get what we want. To bring this home to you, if you're struggling with color and you haven't purchased a calibration system, don't complain because you're not going to get what you want — it's just that simple!

Acquiring profiles

If the thought of spending thousands of dollars to calibrate your system doesn't sit well with you, you have some alternatives. In large production centers, you can use a single calibration system to calibrate all the hardware in your environment. With this method, you need only a single calibration tool to create profiles for all the monitors and in-house output devices. Calibration tools are not like software, where you need to license the tool for each user.

Independent graphic designers can solicit assistance from their service centers. Most print shops and service bureaus have calibration devices on hand. You can ask technicians to visit you to calibrate your monitor and provide you with the profiles they created for their equipment.

When you acquire profiles for output devices, you must install the profiles in the proper location on your hard drive. For Mac users, copy the profiles to `Hard Drive/<user name>/Library/Application Support/Adobe/Color/Profiles/Recommended`. On Windows XP and 2000, copy acquired profiles or profiles you create as a result of your calibration system to `C:\WinNT\System32\Spool\Drivers\Color`. When you install profiles in these locations, the profiles are accessible from all the CS programs. In Figure 6-1, you can see a profile accessed in the Photoshop CS Print dialog box.

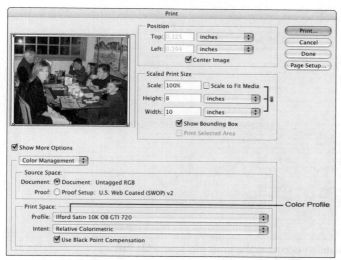

Figure 6-1: When placed in the proper location on your hard drive, the profile is accessible from all the CS applications.

Profile embedding

When you use a color workspace defined by selecting a color profile, you can embed the profile in your image or document. As a general rule, you should opt for profile embedding whenever possible. As a document prints, it assumes the profile of the printing device. When you embed a color profile in your documents, a color conversion takes place, translating the color within the embedded profile to the color within the output profile. In effect, this translation is a best effort to render all the color contained in your document with the closest matching color values in the output profile. If you elect not to embed a profile in your document, theoretically, the color monitor space on the system outputting your file converts to the output profile. If there is great disparity between your monitor workspace and the service center's monitor workspace, the color conversion could result in color shifts.

In Photoshop, profiles are embedded at the time you save your Photoshop document. A little bit of code is added to the Photoshop file containing the profile data. For RGB images, the amount of data added to the original file is minimal. With CMYK images, the file sizes can grow as much as a few megabytes. Be aware that profile embedding is only available for certain file formats. Photoshop native files are supported, as are TIFF, EPS, JPEG, PICT (Mac), and DCS files. If the check box is grayed out in the Save or Save As dialog box, you need to change the file format to one of the supported formats.

Choose File ➪ Save As and check the box for Embed Color Profile: *Name of Profile to Be Embedded.* In Figure 6-2, you can see that the Adobe RGB (1998) profile is used.

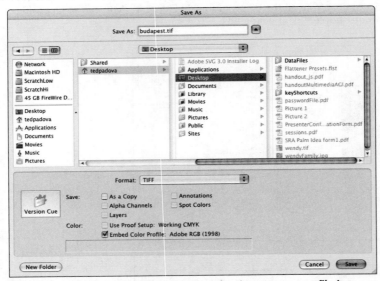

Figure 6-2: Profile embedding occurs at the time you save a file in Photoshop, EPS, JPEG, PICT, or DCS format.

In Illustrator and InDesign, you assign profiles from a menu command. In both programs, choose Edit ➪ Assign Profile(s), and the Assign Profile(s) dialog box opens. In Figure 6-3, you can see that, in Illustrator, the choices are limited to three options. Choose Don't Color Manage This Document when you want color management turned off for the current file. Choose Working CMYK to assign the monitor working space. Choose Profile to select one of the installed color profiles used by your output devices.

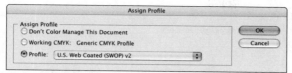

Figure 6-3: The Assign Profile dialog box, where profile assignment is made

In InDesign, you have more options for assigning profiles, as well as a preview check box where you can preview the results of profile assignment. Use the same Edit ⇨ Assign Profiles menu command, and the Assign Profiles dialog box, shown in Figure 6-4, opens.

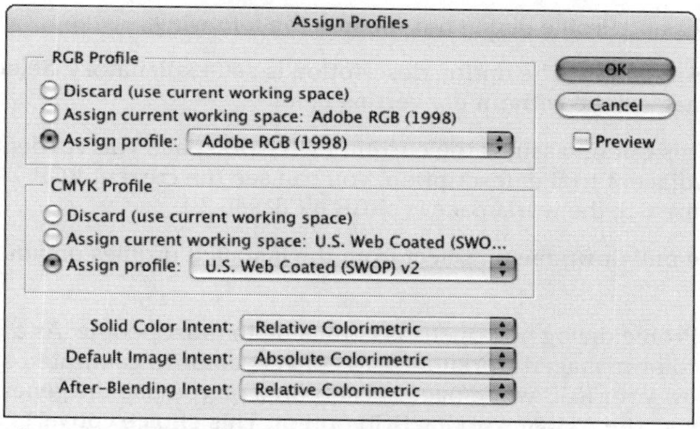

Figure 6-4: InDesign's Assign Profiles dialog box.

InDesign enables you to assign a working profile (RGB Profile) and an output Profile (CMYK Profile). In addition, you can also make choices for the rendering intent. Finally, check the Preview check box, and the document pages behind the dialog box dynamically reflect the color profile you select in the Assign Profiles dialog box.

In the case of both Illustrator and InDesign, when you save the documents the assigned profiles are saved with the file.

Profile mismatching

When you embed or assign a color profile to a document and your document is opened on a computer using another profile, there is a profile mismatch. When such mismatches occur, Illustrator, InDesign, and Photoshop all open dialog boxes to offer you some options on how to handle the mismatches. In Figure 6-5, you can see a file opening in Photoshop where a profile mismatch occurs.

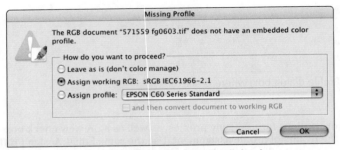

Figure 6-5: The Photoshop Missing Profile dialog box

The options available in the Missing Profile dialog box include the following:

✦ **Leave As Is (don't color manage):** The option description is self-explanatory. Selecting this option leaves the image alone without converting color.

✦ **Assign working RGB:** This option assigns the current RGB workspace you've identified in your color settings. Adjacent to the description, you can see the current RGB workspace listed. In Figure 6-5, the workspace is sRGB IEC61966-2.1.

✦ **Assign profile:** From the pull-down menu, select from the installed profiles on your system.

What to do when the Missing Profile dialog box opens is confusing to most people. As a general rule, the best option in a color-managed workflow is to convert color to calibrated systems. Therefore, when you know your RGB workspace is calibrated or you use the generic Adobe RGB (1998) profile, choose the Assign working RGB option. This choice converts the color embedded in the Photoshop image to the workspace you use. In essence, all the color potentially assigned in the original image converts to the best representation that your current monitor space can assume.

In Illustrator, a similar dialog box used for color-profile assignment opens as a warning dialog box, informing you of the color mismatch. In Figure 6-6, Illustrator's Missing Profile dialog box opens as a warning when a color mismatch is encountered. Notice the similarities between the Mismatch Profile and the Assign Profile dialog boxes. The options choices are self-explanatory.

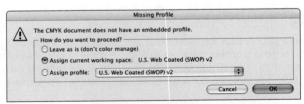

Figure 6-6: The Illustrator Missing Profile dialog box

In InDesign, you again have more options than when using Illustrator. The first of two dialog boxes used for profile mismatching is shown in Figure 6-7. The first of the two Embedded Profile Mismatch dialog boxes handles your monitor workspace if a mismatch occurs. Select from the same options as you have in Photoshop for discarding color profiles or converting color.

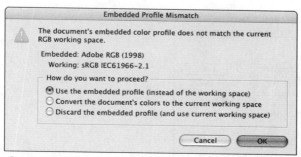

Figure 6-7: When a profile mismatch occurs in InDesign, the first warning dialog box addresses mismatches in RGB color.

After making a decision and clicking OK, the next dialog box, shown in Figure 6-8, almost identical to the previous dialog box, asks about the CMYK workspace. Make a choice, click OK, and the InDesign document opens, either discarding color profiles or converting color per your choices in the dialog boxes.

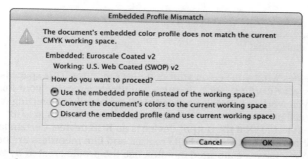

Figure 6-8: A second dialog box identical to the first Embedded Profile Mismatch dialog box opens. Here you make decisions about CMYK images.

Color Management in the CS Applications

When you want to manage color among the CS applications, you can benefit greatly from Adobe's Common Color Architecture. The profile management and assignment is similar among all the Adobe CS programs, and when you understand how to manage color in one program, you can easily apply the same settings across all the programs. Each of the applications begins by addressing the color settings via menu commands.

Managing color in Photoshop

You can address Photoshop color settings by choosing Photoshop ⇨ Color Settings (Mac) or Edit ⇨ Color Settings (Windows). The Color Settings dialog box, shown in Figure 6-9, opens. Check the box for Advanced Mode, and the dialog box expands to offer additional settings. The options choices you have for managing color in Photoshop include the following:

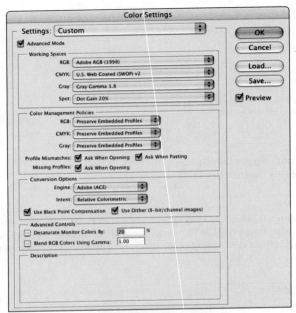

Figure 6-9: The Color Settings dialog box

✦ **RGB:** The RGB space defines what you see on your computer monitor. This space is commonly referred to as your *working space*. Because you perform most of your image editing on RGB images, you work in this color space before eventually converting to CMYK color for commercial printing. In some cases, you may leave images in RGB mode or not convert them to CMYK if the output device is an RGB device. Certain large-format inkjet printers, photo printers such as Fuji Frontier, and film recorders are best imaged from RGB files. If you have a calibrated monitor, use the profile created by your calibration equipment. If you plan on designing files for commercial output to imagesetters, platesetters, or press, use the Adobe RGB (1998) profile if your monitor is not calibrated. If your output is designed for screen and Web viewing, use sRGB IEC61966-2.1 as your monitor space.

✦ **CMYK:** This profile is used for the output device — typically a CMYK printing device for composite printing and press. If you are designing artwork for press, use the U.S. Web Coated (SWOP) v2 for printing in the U.S. If printing outside the U.S., use the model common to the area where you print your files. For example, use the Japan Color 2001 Coated when printing on coated stock in Japan. The settings you choose in this pull-down menu affect your color conversion when you convert color in Photoshop. If you prepare CMYK files for direct output or importing in other applications via the Image ➪ Mode ➪ CMYK Color menu command, Photoshop characterizes the color according to the output profile.

✦ **Gray:** The pull-down menu choices affect grayscale images only in terms of dot gain and gamma adjustments. The actual result of making changes among the available settings affects the dot gain on press. In simple terms, you can target grayscale images to print darker or lighter. By increasing the dot gain or the gamma, you darken the images. Decreasing the amounts has the opposite effects.

✦ **Spot:** The choices here are similar to the choices available for Gray, because the spot color separations are printed like gray plates. Making adjustments to the dot gain also results in darker and lighter images.

The next section in the Color Settings dialog box is Color-management policies. The choices here affect the profile management and mismatching behavior. You can instruct Photoshop to react to profile mismatches or ignore them according to the settings made from the pull-down menus:

✦ **RGB:** You have three options from the pull-down menu. This first item deals with the RGB workspace. If your workspace is the one we suggested earlier in this section in "the RGB section — Adobe RGB (1998) — then a file saved with embedded profiles using any other profile from the RGB workspace is a mismatch. Accordingly, you can instruct Photoshop to turn off color management for working spaces by selecting Off, choose Preserve Embedded Profiles to not affect a color conversion, or select Convert to Working RGB where the saved profile is converted to the current RGB working profile. Turning off color management ignores all color profiling. Preserving Embedded Profiles keeps the color the same as assigned in the profile. Convert to Working RGB converts the color to the current RGB working space.

✦ **CMYK:** The same options are available from pull-down menus as those found in the RGB pull-down menus.

✦ **Gray:** The same options are available from the same kinds of pull-down menus.

✦ **Profile Mismatches: Ask When Opening:** When you check the box, a dialog box prompts you when a mismatch occurs. For workflow environments, it's a good idea to check the box so you know when a color conversion is about to take place.

✦ **Profile Mismatches: Ask When Pasting:** If you copy data from one file and paste it into another file, you can copy an image with one embedded profile and paste the data into a document with another identified profile. Checking this box opens a dialog box alerting you to the color conversion.

✦ **Missing Profiles:** If you open legacy files or files that were not color-managed or have no profile assignment, you can instruct Photoshop to offer you an option for managing color in the opened files. A dialog box opens where you can assign profiles as the documents open in the Photoshop window.

✦ **Conversion Engine:** You have choices for using the Adobe Color Engine (ACE) or color engines that your operating system supplies. For handling color among the CS applications, use the Adobe Color Engine.

✦ **Intent:** There are four standard options related to color intent. *Intent* refers to what happens when color is converted, specifically in terms of white points and color equivalents. The options choices for intent include the following:

• **Perceptual:** Perceptual preserves the overall color appearance through the process of changing colors in the source color space so they fit inside the destination color space. This option is a particularly good choice when you have a number of colors that reside outside the destination color space. The color equivalents are matched as close as possible.

• **Saturation:** As the name implies, Saturation tries to preserve the most vivid colors from the source space to the destination space. You might select this option when you want to convert PowerPoint slides, Excel graphs and charts, and other documents where vivid colors are apparent.

- **Relative Colormetric:** This option tries to closely match the white point in the destination space with the same whites in the source space. After converting white, the other colors are matched as closely as possible. If you're pondering what space to use between Perceptual and Relative, use this option, because the whites are more likely to be reproduced accurately.

- **Absolute Colormetric:** This option is an effort to simulate the color including white point for one output device to a second device. If a white in the source document is a bluish white and the destination is a yellowish white, the conversion adds more cyan to simulate the cooler white, thus rendering a closer approximation of the original image.

✦ **Use Black Point Compensation:** As the intents take care of the whites in converting color from source images to destination images, the separate option for black point compensation takes care of black ink conversion. Without compensating for black when converting colors, you can end up with muddy non-rich blacks. As a matter of default, keep this check box checked.

✦ **Use Dither (8-bit/channel images):** 8-bit channel images are 24-bit color images (8-bits per channel for 3 channels). If color transitions are stepped or crude, you may need to smooth them out. This check box does just that. Keep the check box enabled for all color conversion.

✦ **Desaturate Monitor Colors By:** By default, some bright colors tend to appear somewhat flat on your computer monitor when using the Adobe RGB workspace. To render the images more true to appearance and prevent any misleading representations, keep this check box enabled.

✦ **Blend RGB Colors Using Gamma:** When colors are blended in Photoshop like image data appearing on one layer over another layer, the blending of the colors can show visible problems in shadows and on the edges of the layers. If you see visible problems like this, check this box.

Selecting settings

When you begin to edit the options in the color settings, the Custom name appears in the Settings pull-down menu. From the pull-down menu, you can select from all the settings files contained on your hard drive. If you make changes in the Color Settings, click on the Save button and you're prompted for a filename. Type a name for your settings file and click Save. By default, the file is saved to your Settings folder, where applications look for profiles to load in the Color Settings. On Windows the Settings folder is found at: Program Files//Common Files/Adobe/Color/Settings. On the Mac the files are saved to: Users/User Profile/Library/ Application Support/Adobe/Color/Settings. If you want to make color profiles accessible to all Adobe CS applications, Mac users should save the color settings to the system application support folder found at: Library/Application Support/Adobe/Color/Settings. Note that the latter Library folder is found at the root level of your hard drive.

Swapping profiles

If you create a settings file and click the Save button, the file is accessible to all the CS applications. If a settings file was developed in another CS application, click the Load button in the Color Settings, and the Load dialog box opens. The default directory is the Settings folder where your settings files are located. Select the file you want to load and click the Load button.

Managing color in Illustrator, InDesign, GoLive, and Acrobat

Quite simply, if you understand the options available in the Photoshop Color Settings dialog box, you can save a settings file and load that file in Illustrator. In Illustrator, choose Edit ➪ Color Settings. The dialog box shown in Figure 6-10 opens.

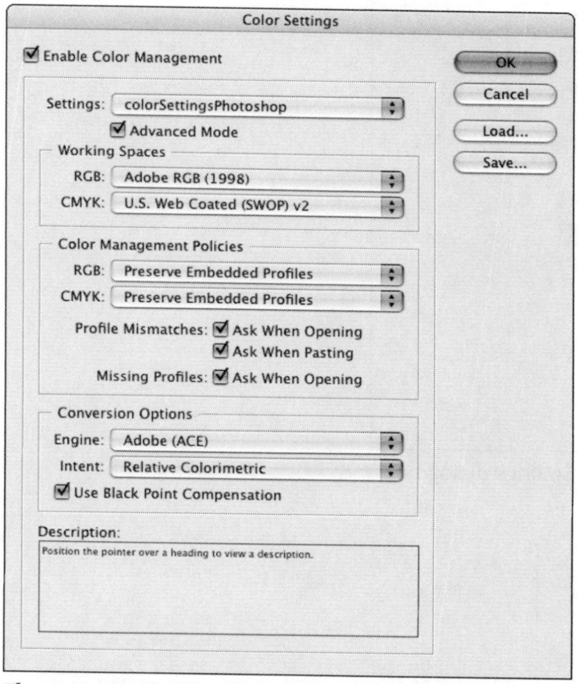

Figure 6-10: The Illustrator Color Settings dialog box.

As you can see, the options choices for profile management and working spaces are almost identical in Illustrator and Photoshop. From the Settings pull-down menu, select the profile you created in Photoshop and your color management is consistent between the two programs.

InDesign is identical to Illustrator in terms of opening the Color Settings dialog box and the options available to you for managing color. Choose Edit ➪ Color Settings, and the dialog box shown in Figure 6-11 opens. Notice that the options choices and the placement of the options in InDesign precisely match the settings in Illustrator.

Surprisingly, even GoLive uses the same color engine as the other CS applications, and the options choices in GoLive are identical to Illustrator and InDesign. GoLive's menu command to open the Color Settings dialog box is located in the same place as Photoshop. On the Mac, choose GoLive ➪ Color Settings. On Windows, choose Edit ➪ Color Settings. The GoLive Color Settings dialog box, shown in Figure 6-12, opens.

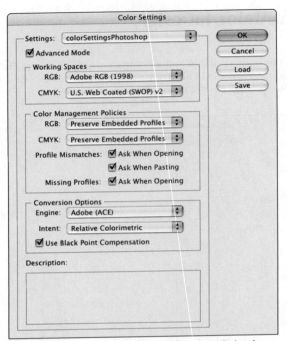

Figure 6-11: The InDesign Color Settings dialog box

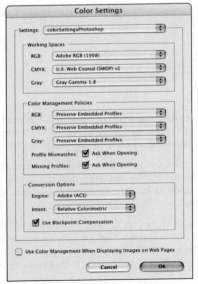

Figure 6-12: The Color Settings
dialog box in GoLive

GoLive has one additional option not found in the other CS applications — the check box at the bottom of the dialog box where you see Use Color Management When Displaying Images on Web Pages. Check this box when you want to apply color management on viewing Web pages. You'll note that the default for this option is unchecked. Because most Web browsers don't support color management, the check box is disabled.

Acrobat is the odd application for accessing the Color Settings dialog box, but the settings options are consistent in Acrobat with what you find in the other CS programs. To turn color management on, choose Acrobat ⇨ Preferences (Mac) or Edit ⇨ Preferences (Windows). In the Preferences dialog box, click Color Management in the left pane, and the color-management settings display, as shown in Figure 6-13. From the Settings pull-down menu, you can select the settings file you created in Photoshop, thus rounding your color-matching among all the CS programs.

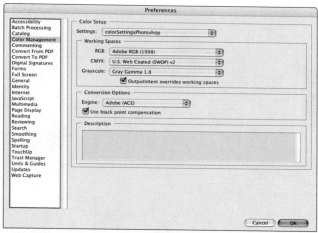

Figure 6-13: Open the Preferences dialog box in Acrobat and select Color Management in the left pane.

Printing with Profiles

All the information related to profiling and managing color is fine in a theoretical environment, but when it comes to the real world, you must implement all the work you do in setting up your environment and observe the results. Ideally, you would have a color-calibration device and calibrate your computer monitor and the output device for precise results.

When you use a color-calibration system, you calibrate your monitor and the output device and measure colors as they lay down on the substrate you use for your prints. You develop the profile for a given printer and a given paper. Once you develop the profiles, you edit your images according to the monitor working space so the color values on your monitor come within a predictable range on your output. In essence, the monitor and output device are in parity in terms of color.

To print an image from a program like Photoshop, you would follow these steps after calibrating your system:

Printing Composite Color Using Calibrated Profiles

1. **Adjust color settings.** Set up your color settings according to the calibrations you performed. Be certain to choose the monitor working space you used to calibrate your monitor.

2. **Print with Preview.** With your document open in Photoshop, choose File ➪ Print with Preview.

3. **Target the print for color management.** From the pull-down menu below the thumbnail image shown in Figure 6-14, select Color Management from the menu options.

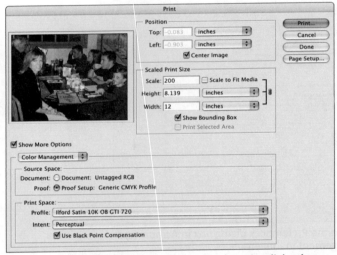

Figure 6-14: Select Color Management in the Print dialog box.

4. **Select the color profile created for the printer and paper.** In the Profile pull-down menu, select the profile created for the paper.

5. **Select the intent.** Select the intent from the menu options for Intent.

6. **Select print options for the target printer.** If you're printing to composite color devices, you have options for your printer via the print driver, as shown in Figure 6-15. Various color settings, paper types, speed for printing, and so on are options choices in the Print dialog box. Choose the options from the Print Settings (Mac) or Properties (Windows).

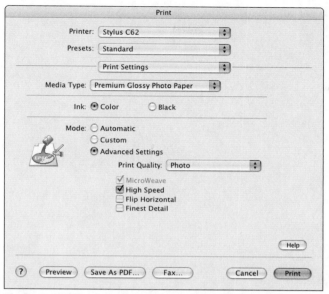

Figure 6-15: Set the print options from available settings defined by your print driver.

If you don't have a calibration system, you can run experiments using software tools to calibrate your monitor and test the output results. If you use this method, be ready to run tests many times before settling on a profile that works consistently for your printer.

Cross-Reference For more information on printing from Photoshop and the other CS applications, see Chapters 34 and 35.

Summary

✦ Color profiles are used to consistently reproduce color in your workflow among input devices, your viewing space, and your output equipment.

✦ Color calibration is optimum when using special tools to calibrate your computer monitor and output devices.

✦ Output profiles can be acquired from service providers and installed on your computer.

✦ When profiles don't match, it's best to convert color to your calibrated workspace.

✦ The Creative Suite applications use a common color engine developed by Adobe Systems.

✦ Color profiles developed in one CS application can be shared with all the other CS applications.

✦   ✦   ✦

Using Version Cue

Version Cue is a file-versioning system that is tightly integrated into all the CS version applications (because Acrobat 6 doesn't work with Version Cue, I think this is a better way to explain the compatibility). After Version Cue is enabled, you may access it from within all the standard file dialog boxes.

A key benefit of Version Cue is that it lets you set up projects that may be shared over a network. All files within these projects are version-controlled, allowing all members of the team to access the very latest versions of each file. The versioning features also ensure that team members don't accidentally save changes over the top of other changes.

Using the Version Cue Workspace Administration utility, you can control all aspects of Version Cue from an administration interface. This interface lets you create and edit the access and authentication for users, create and define project properties, and lock files.

Setting Up the Version Cue Workspace

Before you can use Version Cue, several steps are required to enable Version Cue for the various CS applications and to turn the Version Cue system on.

Note Version Cue comes only as part of Creative Suite. If you purchased only a single CS application, it won't include Version Cue, but the application can work with Version Cue if somebody else on your network has it installed.

Enabling Version Cue and setting preferences

When Creative Suite is installed, the Version Cue software (the CS apps are actually the clients) is also installed by default with the CS apps acting as clients. But even though Version Cue is installed, it isn't active until it's turned on.

To turn on Version Cue, double-click the Version Cue icon to open the Version Cue Preferences dialog box, shown in Figure 7-1. The Version Cue icon is found within the System Preferences (on the Mac) or in the Control Panel (in Windows). In the Version Cue Preferences dialog box, you can turn Version Cue on and off. You can also opt to turn Version Cue on when the computer starts.

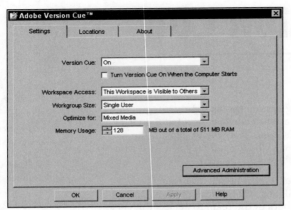

Figure 7-1: The Version Cue Preferences dialog box

The Workspace Access field lets you make the workspace shared or private. The two options are This Workspace Is Visible to Others and This Workspace Is Private.

The next three preferences are used to optimize the workspace and to specify the type of files that you'll be versioning. Workspace Size may be set to Single User, Small (2–4 People), Medium (5–10 People), or Large (10+ People). By specifying the workspace size, Version Cue can make more connections available so users don't have to wait as long to gain access to the files. The Optimize For field lets you select the type of media files you'll most often be saving. The options include Print Media (which are typically fewer in number, but much larger), Web Media (which includes a large number of smaller files), and Mixed Media.

The Memory Usage field lets you specify the amount of memory on your local machine or on the network that is available for Version Cue to use. Increasing this value enables you to retrieve files very quickly but leaves less memory available for the other applications.

Specifying workspace folders

When Version Cue is first enabled, two folders are created on your local system. The Version Cue folder is located in the Documents folder (on the Mac) or in the My Documents folder (in Windows). This folder holds temporary working copies of the files that you're currently editing.

The other folders are located by default in a folder where the Creative Suite applications were installed. These folders, consisting of folders named Adobe Version Cue\data and Adobe Version Cue\backups, hold the actual versioned files and are referenced in the Locations panel of the Version Cue Preferences dialog box, shown in Figure 7-2.

Caution   If you look at the files located in the data and backups folders, you won't be able to find any recognizable file formats. Do not manually move or edit any of these files; if you do, Version Cue won't work properly.

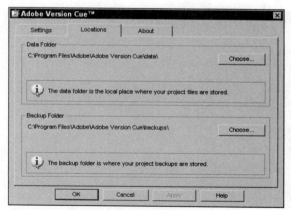

Figure 7-2: The Locations panel of the Version Cue Preferences dialog box includes a field where you can turn Version Cue on or off.

If you want to change the data and backups folder locations, you'll need to turn Version Cue off and click the Apply button before the Choose button in the Locations panel becomes active. After the Choose button is active, you can click it to select a new directory.

Enabling Version Cue within a CS application

For several of the CS applications, Version Cue isn't available (even if Version Cue is turned on) unless an option in the File Handling panel of the Preferences dialog box is enabled. To enable Version Cue for Photoshop, Illustrator, and InDesign, open the Preferences dialog box (found in the application-name menu on the Mac or in the Edit menu in Windows) and select the File Handling panel (within Illustrator, the option is located in the File Handling & Clipboard panel).

Within the File Handling panel of the Preferences dialog box, shown in Figure 7-3, is a Use Version Cue option. Enabling this option and restarting the application makes Version Cue available for that application. You might clarify that InDesign is the only CS application that needs to be relaunched before Version Cue works.

Note   GoLive doesn't need to be enabled using a preference and InDesign is the only application that needs to be restarted after the Version Cue preference is enabled.

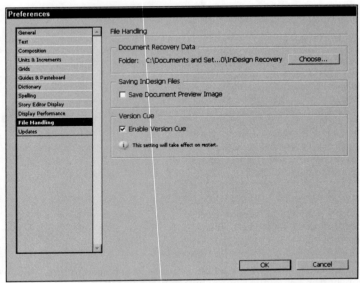

Figure 7-3: The File Handling panel of the Preferences dialog box for the various CS applications includes an Enable Version Cue option.

STEPS: Setting Up Version Cue

1. **Turn on Version Cue.** Open the System Preferences dialog box (on the Mac) or the Control Panel (in Windows) and double-click on the Version Cue icon. In the Version Cue Preferences dialog box, set the Version Cue option to On and click OK.

2. **Enable Version Cue for Photoshop.** Within Photoshop, choose Photoshop ➪ Preferences ➪ File Handling (on the Mac) or Edit ➪ Preferences ➪ File Handling (in Windows). In the dialog box that appears, check the Enable Version Cue Workgroup File Management option and click OK.

3. **Access the Version Cue interface.** Once it is enabled, you can access the Version Cue interface from within the file dialog boxes.

4. **Repeat these steps for the other CS applications.** Enabling the Version Cue preference within InDesign requires that the application be restarted before you can access the Version Cue interface.

Working with Version Cue Files

When Version Cue is turned on and enabled for the working application, you can access the Version Cue workspace by clicking on the Version Cue button that appears at the bottom of any file dialog box, as shown in Figure 7-4. File dialog boxes appear any time you choose File ➪ Open, File ➪ Save As, File ➪ Place, File ➪ Import, or File ➪ Export.

Note   The Version Cue button is not available for Photoshop's File ➪ Place menu command.

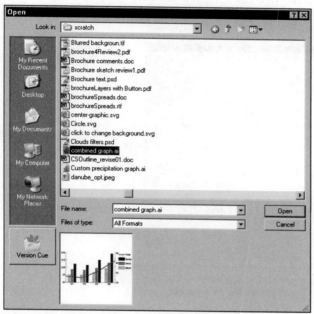

Figure 7-4: The Version Cue button located at the bottom of each file dialog box lets you access the Version Cue file interface.

The Version Cue file interface, shown for InDesign's File ➪ Open menu command in Figure 7-5, resembles a typical file dialog box with access to folders and files. If you double-click on a folder, all the subfolders and files contained within that folder are displayed. Clicking on the Up One Level button opens the folder above the current one.

Along the top of the file list are several information columns including Name, Status, Size, Version, Comment, Last Modified, and Type. Clicking on any of the columns in the Version Cue interface sorts the files by the selected column. For example, you can quickly see the largest file in a project by clicking on the Size column title. Clicking a second time on the column title reverses the sorting order.

The icon buttons in the upper-right corner let you toggle between List and Thumbnail views. Figure 7-6 shows the Thumbnail view of the Version Cue file interface for the File ➪ Open menu command in Illustrator.

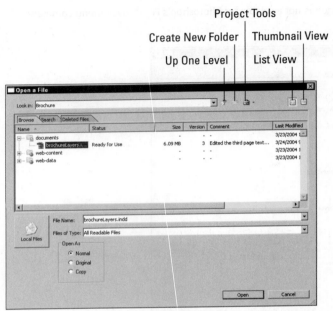

Figure 7-5: Double-clicking on a folder in the Version Cue file interface opens the folder and displays all the files within the folder.

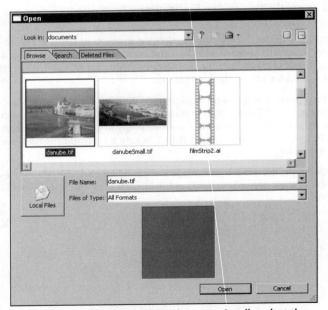

Figure 7-6: The Thumbnail view lets you visually select the file that you want to open.

Holding the mouse over a file displays a pop-up pane of information that includes the file's title, type, size, version number, last updated date, status, and project, as shown in Figure 7-7.

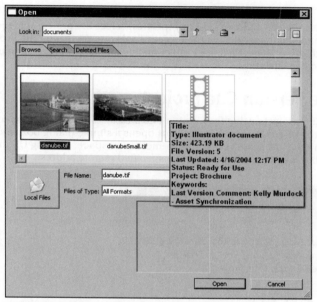

Figure 7-7: Holding the mouse cursor over a file in the Version Cue file interface displays a pop-up box of information.

If you need to access files that aren't part of the Version Cue project from the Version Cue file interface, you can revert to the standard file dialog box by clicking the Local Files button.

Creating a Version Cue project

To create a new project, select the top-level workspace folder, click on the Project Tools button in the Version Cue interface, and select the New Project menu command. This command opens a dialog box, shown in Figure 7-8, where you can name the project and enter a description for it. To make the project viewable to other users, enable the Share This Project with Others option.

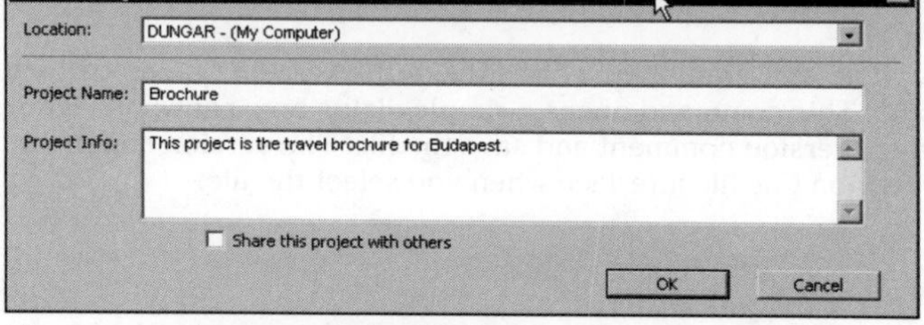

Figure 7-8: The New Project dialog box lets you name the project, type a description, and select to share this project with others.

After a Version Cue project is created, three folders appear by default under the project folder. These default folders are Documents, Web-Content, and Web-Data. The Documents folder holds all files created with Illustrator, InDesign, and Photoshop; the other two folders are used to save GoLive files.

If you ever need to change a project's name or other properties, select the project folder and choose the Edit Properties menu command from the Project Tools pop-up menu. The Project Tools pop-up menu also includes a Share/Unshare Project menu command that you can use to quickly change the project's share status.

Accessing remote Version Cue projects

To access remote Version Cue projects using the Version Cue interface, select the Connect To menu command from the Project Tools pop-up menu. This opens a simple dialog box, shown in Figure 7-9, where you can type in the address for the remote workspace. Clicking OK displays a dialog box of available remote workspaces at the specified remote address.

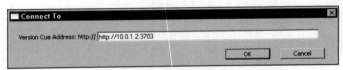

Figure 7-9: The Connect To dialog box lets you specify an address that includes remote Version Cue projects.

Opening Version Cue files

When a Version Cue file is opened, a copy of the latest version is copied to your local working directory found within the project folder in the Documents/Version Cue folder (on the Mac) or the My Documents/Version Cue folder (in Windows).

When you choose File ➪ Open in one of the CS applications, the Version Cue file interface includes three tabs at the top of the dialog box — Browse, Search, or Deleted Files.

The Browse tab lets you navigate the project folders. Clicking on the Search tab opens a panel, shown in Figure 7-10, where you can enter a keyword to search for. After you click Search, all files that match the search keyword are listed.

Saving Version Cue files

When you save Version Cue files by choosing File ➪ Save, the working copy is updated, but the actual versioned copy isn't updated until you choose File ➪ Save As or File ➪ Save a Version.

When you're ready to save a new version of the edited file to the Version Cue repository, choose File ➪ Save a Version. This command opens a simple dialog box, shown in Figure 7-11, where you can quickly type a version comment and save the file. The version comment that you enter appears in the Version Cue file interface when you select the file.

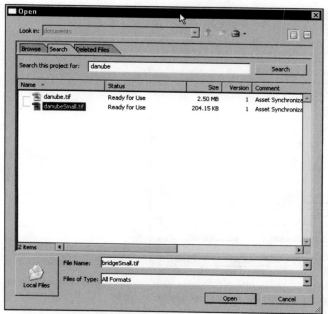

Figure 7-10: The Search panel of the Version Cue file interface is available when you choose File ➪ Open.

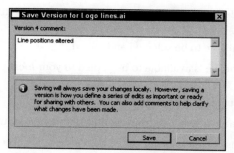

Figure 7-11: Choosing File ➪ Save a Version lets you enter comments for the file.

When you choose File ➪ Save As, the Version Cue file interface opens. The Version Cue file interface, shown in Figure 7-12, includes fields for naming the file, selecting a format, and entering version comments. If you choose to save the file using the same filename, a warning dialog box asks if you want to save these changes as a new version. If you select to save the file as a file with a new name, a whole new branch is created. This new branch has its own versions that are separate from the original file.

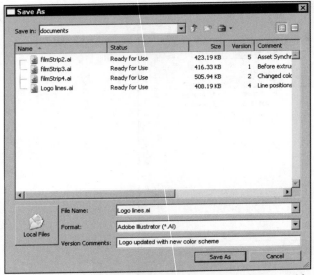

Figure 7-12: When the Version Cue file interface opens with the File ➪ Save As menu command, you may choose to save the file using a different name.

Understanding states

Each file that is saved is given a status that defines the state of the file. The available statuses include the following:

✦ **Available:** Indicates that the file is available to be selected and edited.

✦ **Ready for Download:** Indicates that the file is available to be copied to your local working file.

✦ **In Use By Me:** Indicates that you are currently editing this file.

✦ **In Use By Me Elsewhere:** Indicates that you're editing this file on a different computer.

✦ **In Use By User:** Indicates that the file is currently being edited by another user. The user's name is listed.

✦ **Offline:** Indicates that the file is unavailable because Version Cue has been turned off.

For files that are opened using the Version Cue interface, the status of the file is displayed in parenthesis in the title bar of the document, as shown in Figure 7-13.

Adding files to a Version Cue project

Choose File ➪ Save As or File ➪ Save a Version to add single files to a Version Cue project.

To add multiple files to a project, copy all the files into their correct folders of the working project file located in the Documents/Version Cue folder (on the Mac) or in the My Documents/Version Cue folder (in Windows). For example, design files created with

Photoshop, Illustrator, and InDesign should be put in the `Documents` folder under the project folder, and GoLive files should be placed in the `Web-Content` and `Web-Data` folders.

With the files added to the working directory, select the Synchronize menu command from the Project Tools pop-up menu. This command copies all the files added to the working directory to the Version Cue repository so they may be accessed by all users.

Version Cue status

Figure 7-13: When the Version Cue file is opened, the status of the file is displayed in the title bar for the document.

Working with versions

When a versioned file is opened within one of the CS applications, you can gain access to the various versions by choosing File ⇨ Versions. This command opens a dialog box, shown in Figure 7-14, where all the versions of the open file are listed along with their thumbnails, version numbers, and version comments.

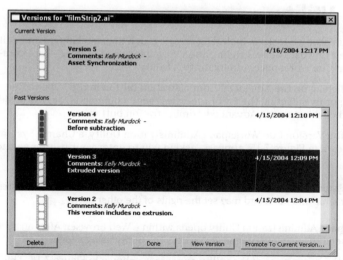

Figure 7-14: All the versions for an open file are accessible by choosing File ⇨ Versions.

Using this dialog box, you can select a version, delete a version, open a version, or promote a selected version to the current version.

Deleting Version Cue files

To delete a Version Cue-managed file, select the file in the Version Cue interface and choose the Delete menu command from the Project Tools pop-up menu. This moves the file to the Deleted Files tab.

To restore a deleted file that appears in the Deleted Files tab, select the file and choose the Restore menu command in the Project Tools pop-up menu. Selecting the Delete menu command for a file in the Deleted Files tab permanently deletes the file.

STEPS: Opening and Saving Files in Version Cue

1. **Verify Version Cue.** Open the Version Cue Preferences dialog box and make sure that Version Cue is turned on.

2. **Open a Version Cue file.** Within Photoshop, choose File ➪ Open. In the Open dialog box that appears, click the Version Cue button to access the Version Cue file interface. Double-click on the project folder and then on the Documents folder that includes the file you want to edit. Select the file and click Open.

3. **Edit the file.** Use the Photoshop tools to edit the file that you opened.

4. **Save a version.** When the edits are complete, choose File ➪ Save a Version. The Format Options dialog box appears for the file. Click OK and a Save Version dialog box opens where you can add a comment for the recent edits.

Using the Version Cue Workspace Administration Utility

Many Version Cue administrative tasks — including creating, deleting, backing up and editing projects, locking files, editing user access rights, and viewing logs and reports — are completed using the Version Cue Workspace Administration Utility.

Access this utility by clicking on the Advanced Administration button in the Version Cue Preferences dialog box, or by selecting the Edit Properties menu command from the Project Tools pop-up menu and clicking on the Advanced Administration button.

When you first access the Version Cue Workspace Administration Utility, a Change System Account dialog box, shown in Figure 7-15, appears, asking you to enter your username and password.

Note   All users on the system are given access to this utility, but only the user with the System Administrator username and password may set the rights of the other users.

The Version Cue Workspace Administration Utility opens within a Web browser. After an account has been created, you need to log in every time you access the utility using a login page.

After you've logged in, the home page of the utility appears, as shown in Figure 7-16. This home page includes four page links on the left — Home, Users, Projects, and Advanced. The home page also includes several common tasks that you may perform using this utility.

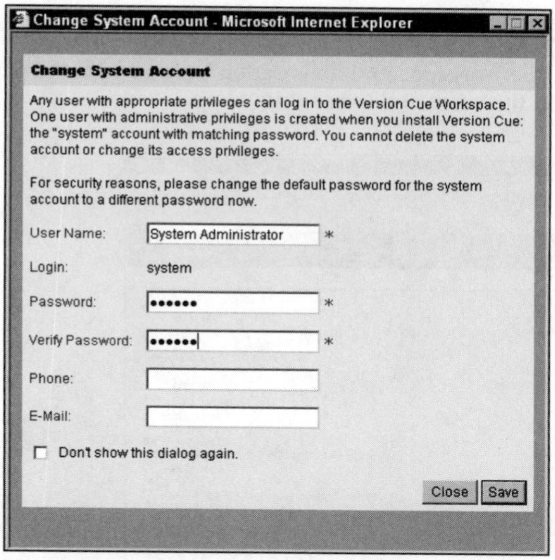

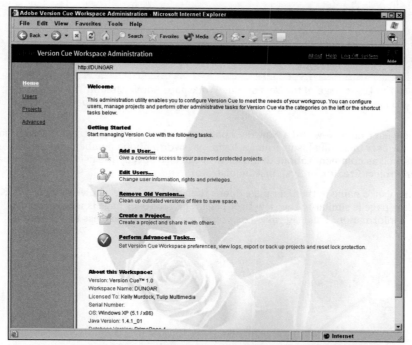

Figure 7-15: The Change System Account dialog box lets you enter a username and password for accessing the Version Cue Workspace Administration Utility.

Figure 7-16: The Version Cue Workspace Administration utility home page includes links to several different utility pages and several basic tasks.

Adding and editing users

Clicking the Users link in the Version Cue Workspace Administration Utility opens the page shown in Figure 7-17. This page lists all the users and their information.

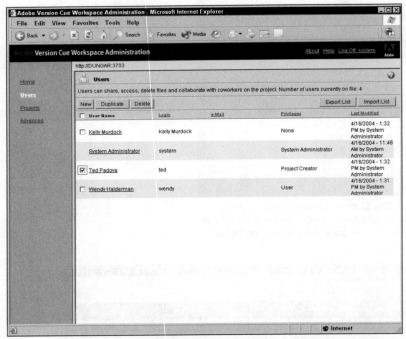

Figure 7-17: The Users page of the Version Cue Workspace Administration Utility lets you create, edit, and delete users who have access to the workspace.

To add a new user, click New and a New User page opens where you can enter the information for a new user including his username, login, password, phone number, and e-mail address, as well as comments about that user. You can also specify the user's privileges as None, User, Project Creator, or System Administrator.

Clicking on a user's name in the User page opens the Edit User page, shown in Figure 7-18. The Edit User page is similar to the New User page. The Edit User page is where you can edit a user's information. This page also lets you specify the user's access to the various projects.

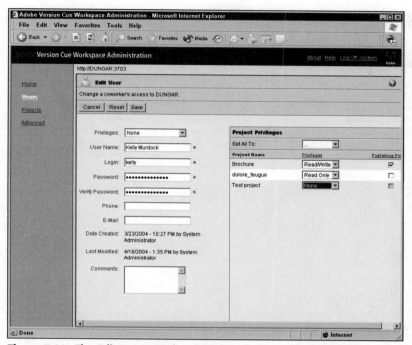

Figure 7-18: The Edit User page lets you change the user's rights to each project.

The User page also includes buttons to duplicate or delete the selected users. You can also import and export user lists to use with other workspaces.

Managing projects

The Projects page in the Version Cue Workspace Administration Utility opens a page, shown in Figure 7-19, that lists all the available projects. From within this page, you can click New to create a new project. Using the buttons, you can also duplicate, back up, export, and delete the selected projects.

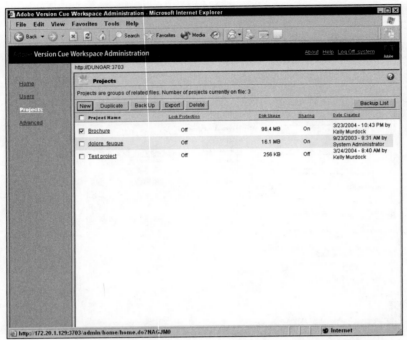

Figure 7-19: The Projects page of the Version Cue Workspace Administration Utility lets you manage projects in the current workspace.

Creating and editing projects

Clicking the New button in the Projects page opens the New Project page, shown in Figure 7-20. Here, you can select to create a blank project, import from a folder, import from an FTP server, or import from a WebDAV server. Each of these options walks you through the steps to create and define the properties for the project. Clicking the Next button moves to the next page.

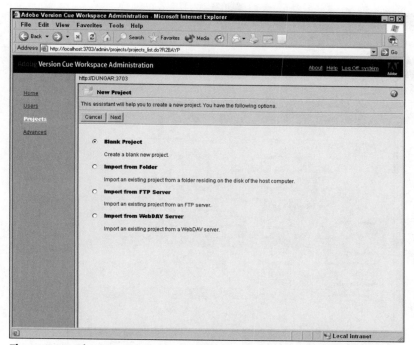

Figure 7-20: The New Project page lets you create new projects using several different options.

Clicking on a project name in the Projects page opens an editing page, shown in Figure 7-21, that lists the properties for this project, its assigned users, and any project backups. The properties for each project that you may set include Share the Project with Others, Require Assigned Users to Authenticate to This Project, and Enable Lock Protection for This Project.

If the Require Assigned Users to Authenticate to This Project option is selected, users need to log in with their usernames and passwords before they can access files in the Version Cue project.

If the Enable Lock Protection for This Project option is enabled, only one user can update the version of that file. Other users can open the file, but they're prevented from saving the file as a version of the original file. They may make changes and save the file with a different filename but not as a version of the original file.

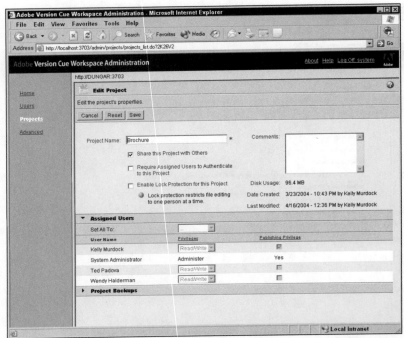

Figure 7-21: The Edit Project page lets you set properties for the project, such as sharing, authentication, and locking.

Backing up projects

If you click the Back Up button on the Projects page for a selected project, then a page, shown in Figure 7-22, appears where you can verify the name that is used for the backup. In this page, you can select which items are backed up. Clicking the Save button starts the backup process.

Back on the Projects page, the Backup List button opens a page that lists all the available backups. Selecting a backed-up project from the list opens a page with a Restore button that you may use to restore the backed up project.

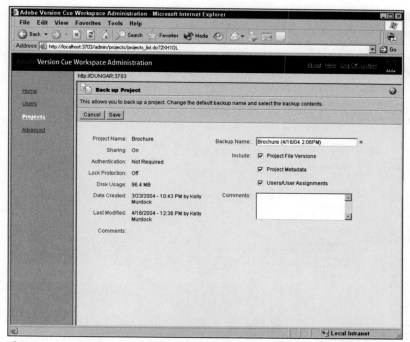

Figure 7-22: Clicking the Back Up button opens a page where you can select to backup the current project.

Using the Advanced features

The Advanced page in the Version Cue Workspace Administration Utility, shown in Figure 7-23, includes links to pages that let you set preferences, import Web workgroup backups, export projects, perform regular maintenance tasks, and view logs and reports.

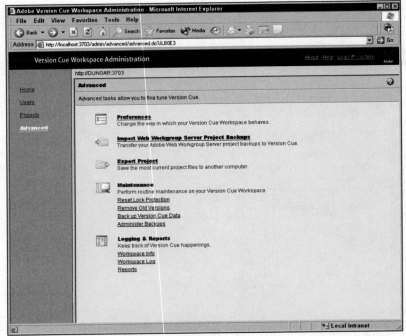

Figure 7-23: The Advanced page in the Version Cue Workspace Administration Utility includes several miscellaneous tasks.

Summary

✦ Before you may use the Version Cue features, the Version Cue client must be turned on using the Version Cue Preferences dialog box and Version Cue must be enabled for each CS application using their respective Preferences dialog boxes.

✦ You may access the Version Cue file interface by using any of the file dialog boxes used to open, save, place, import, and export files.

✦ The Version Cue file interface lets you create new projects, search for files, sort files, view thumbnails, and view deleted files.

✦ The Version Cue Workspace Administration Utility may be accessed from the Version Cue Preferences dialog box. This browser-based tool is used to create and edit users and projects, back up and restore projects, and view project reports.

✦   ✦   ✦

Working with Objects and Images

Creating, Selecting, and Editing Objects and Images

C reative Suite documents have two groups of items: *objects*, which are editable and which include paths, shapes, type, and even multimedia elements, and *images,* which are pictures composed of an array of colored pixels. Although you have some cross-over, you generally use Photoshop to work with images and Illustrator to work with objects. Most designs combine both of these items. Although all Creative Suite applications use both objects and images and have similar tools, this chapter focuses mainly on Illustrator and Photoshop. The other CS applications of InDesign, GoLive and Acrobat have features for working with objects and images that are the same as the features found in these two applications.

This chapter covers a lot of ground, including creating objects and images, the tools used to select them, and a sampling of the features used to edit them. The tools used to edit objects and images are as diverse as the tools and commands used to create and select them.

Creating objects in Illustrator

The most common Illustrator objects are created using the various Drawing tools. These tools are the second section of tools located in the Toolbox directly under the Selection tools, as shown in Figure 8-1. They consist of the Pen tool, the Type tool, the Line Segment tool, the Rectangle tool, the Paintbrush tool, and the Pencil tool. Each of these tools also has several additional fly-out tools that you can use to create objects.

Drawing in the workspace with any of these tools creates a line that Illustrator calls a *path*, which is identified as an object. When you select an object, its path and the points that make up its path are highlighted using the layer color.

In addition to the objects presented in this section, Illustrator includes some other tools that create objects, such as the Symbol and Graph tools.

Cross-Reference You can find information on Illustrator graphs in Chapter 20.

Figure 8-1: The Illustrator drawing tools

Using the Pen tool

You use the Pen tool to draw several connected lines by simply clicking once where you want the first anchor point and clicking again for each successive connected line.

But the power of the Pen tool isn't in creating straight lines. When you click with the Pen tool to place an anchor point, you can drag to extend a direction line that lies tangent to the curve. At the end of each direction line are direction points that may be moved to alter the curvature at the point. Figure 8-2 shows a path created with the Pen tool.

Tip   If you hold down the Shift key while dragging to create a direction line, the direction line is constrained to 45-degree increments.

Anchor point

Figure 8-2: The Pen tool can include straight and curved segments.

Direction point

Direction line

You can also use the Pen tool to do the following:

✦ **End a path:** Hold down the ⌘/Ctrl key when clicking to create the last anchor point. You can also end a path by selecting another tool.

✦ **Create a closed object:** Here, the first and last anchor points are the same. Position the last anchor point over the top of the first anchor point until a small circle appears as part of the cursor, then click.

✦ **Select individual points on a line:** Use the Pen tool with the Direct Selection or Lasso tools. If the point includes a direction line, then the direction line and its points appear. When a direction line and its points are visible, you can drag them to alter the curvature around the point.

✦ **Add or delete anchor points on a line.** You can perform these tasks by using the Add or Delete Anchor Point tools, which are Pen tool fly-out tools. Another fly-out tool, the Convert Anchor Point tool, changes points without any direction lines to a smooth curve point. You simply click on the point and drag out a direction line. This tool also changes smooth anchor points to hard points without a direction line when you click on the anchor points.

✦ **Add or delete point on a path:** With the Pen tool selected, move the cursor over the top of the selected path. A small plus sign appears as part of the cursor when you're over the path; a small minus sign appears as part of the cursor when you're over a point that you may want to delete. Holding down the Option/Alt key changes the cursor to the Convert Anchor Point tool.

Note

The Pen, Add Anchor Point, Delete Anchor Point, and Convert Anchor Point tools are found in Illustrator, Photoshop, and InDesign.

STEPS: Drawing with the Pen Tool

1. **Open an Illustrator document.** Choose File ➪ New to create a new document.

2. **Enable a snapping grid.** Choose View ➪ Show Grid to make a grid appear. Then choose View ➪ Snap to Grid. This enables snapping so all points snap to the visible grid.

3. **Draw straight lines.** Click on the Pen tool and click several times to create an anchor point every time you click.

4. **Close the shape.** To close the shape, move the cursor until it's on top of the first anchor point and click. A small circle appears as part of the cursor when it's over the first anchor point. Figure 8-3 shows the simple shape made from straight lines using the Pen tool.

5. **Draw curved segments.** With the Pen tool still selected, click to create the same shape beneath the first one, but after clicking each point, drag to pull a direction line out from the point. This line defines the curvature of the corner. Continue to click around the shape until the shape is closed.

6. **Edit the path points.** Select the Direct Selection tool, drag over each anchor point, and compare it to the anchor point across from it. Drag the direction points to make them similar to their opposite corner to make the object symmetrical. Figure 8-4 shows the resulting shapes.

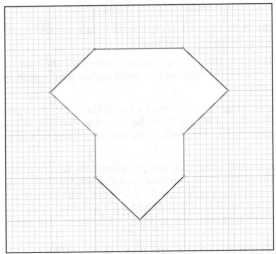

Figure 8-3: The Pen tool is used to create straight line shapes.

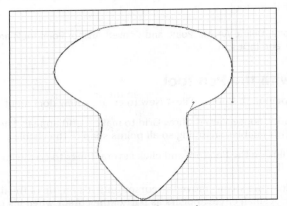

Figure 8-4: The Pen tool is also used to create curves.

Using the Type tool

You use the Type tool to create text objects. Clicking with the Type tool creates a Point text object, which you typically you use for a single line of text, such as a heading. You create a text-area object by dragging in the art board with the Type tool. All text that you type within a text object wraps to fit within the text object area.

Cross-Reference Type and all the type tools are covered in detail in Part IV.

Text objects aren't limited to a rectangular area created by dragging with the Type tool. Using the fly-out tools available under the Type tool, you can add text to a selected area or have text follow a path. There are also tools for creating text that runs vertically instead of horizontally.

Note   Type objects you create with the Type tool are a unique type of object. You edit them using the Type tool, you can select them in a similar manner as other objects by dragging over them with the Selection tool.

Creating lines and shapes

You use the Line Segment tool to create simple straight lines by clicking and dragging on the art board. If you double-click with the Line Segment tool, a dialog box, shown in Figure 8-5, opens where you can specify the line's length and angle. Holding down the Shift key while dragging constrains the line to 45-degree increments; holding down the Option/Alt key while dragging extends the line in both directions from the clicked first point; and holding down the Spacebar lets you move the line by dragging.

Figure 8-5: The Line Segment Tool Options dialog box

As fly-outs under the Line Segment tool, Illustrator includes tools for creating arcs, spirals, rectangular grids, and polar grids.

The Rectangle tool creates rectangle objects by dragging in the art board. Clicking without dragging opens a simple dialog box where you can enter precise Width and Height values. Holding down the Shift key creates a perfect square when you drag; holding down the Option/Alt key while dragging creates the rectangle from the center outward; and holding down the Spacebar lets you move and position the rectangle as you draw it out.

As fly-out tools under the Rectangle tool, you can find the Rounded Rectangle, Ellipse, and Polygon tools. Dragging the Ellipse tool with the Shift key held down creates a perfect circle. Clicking with the Polygon tool opens a dialog box where you can specify a radius and the number of sides to include in the polygon.

Note   Illustrator also includes tools for creating pointed stars and flares as fly-outs under the Rectangle tool.

Using the Paintbrush and Pencil tools

You can use both the Paintbrush and Pencil tools to draw freehand curves. The difference is that the Paintbrush tool applies a stroke to the resulting path. To draw with either the Paintbrush or Pencil tools, click and drag in the art board.

If you press the Option/Alt key and hold it down after starting a path, a small circle appears as part of the cursor, indicating that you're creating a closed path. When you release the mouse, regardless of where it's located, a line is drawn back to the first anchor point, creating a closed object.

If you double-click on either tool in the Toolbox, a dialog box of preferences for the selected tool appears, such as the Paintbrush Tool Preferences dialog box, shown in Figure 8-6. In this dialog box, you can set Fidelity and Smoothness values as well as other options:

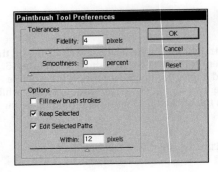

Figure 8-6: The Paintbrush Tool Preferences dialog box

✦ **Fidelity.** The Fidelity value determines how far the cursor can stray before a new anchor point is created. Increasing this value causes small changes in the path to be ignored. Figure 8-7 shows three curves drawn with the Paintbrush tool with different Fidelity settings. Notice how the curve with the lowest Fidelity value has the most anchor points.

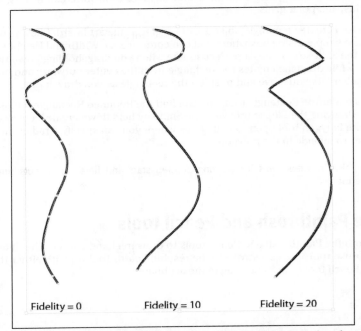

Fidelity = 0   Fidelity = 10   Fidelity = 20

Figure 8-7: Increasing Fidelity decreases the total number of anchor points.

✦ **Smoothness.** The Smoothness value can range from 0 to 100 and sets the smoothness of the resulting path.

✦ **Fill New Brush Strokes option.** Only available for the Paintbrush tool, this option allows you to apply a fill to the path. If the path isn't closed, an imaginary line is drawn between the first and endpoints of the path, and the interior portion is colored with the fill color.

✦ **Keep Selected option.** Causes the path to remain selected after you release the mouse button.

✦ **Edit Selected Paths option.** Enables you to redraw portions of the path using the selected tool when the cursor is within the specified number of pixels. With this option, you can move the tool over the top of the selected path. If a small x displays as part of the cursor, a new path is created; if the small x disappears, you can drag over the path and replace that portion of the path with the new dragged path.

The fly-out tools under the Pencil tool are the Smooth and Erase tools. You can drag the Smooth tool over the top of a selected path to reduce the number of anchor points and smooth the line. You can use the Erase tool to delete the path section that you drag over. You must select the path to use the Erase tool.

Tip   You can temporarily enable the Smooth tool when you have the Paintbrush or Pencil tool selected by holding down the Option/Alt key.

Creating objects in InDesign

InDesign, like Illustrator, relies heavily on the concept of objects. Almost everything placed in an InDesign document is an object. Objects are created in InDesign using the tools found in the second section of the Toolbox including the Pen tool, the Type tool, the Pencil tool, the Line tool, the Rectangle Frame tool, and the Rectangle tool along with the additional tools available as fly-outs.

All these tools include features that are similar to the Illustrator tools, but InDesign includes one additional object type created with the Frame tools. These frames offer a way to create an image placeholder.

Creating objects in Photoshop

Although Photoshop's forte is working with images, you can also use Photoshop to create *shapes*. The tools used to create objects in Photoshop are located in the third section of tools in the Toolbox, as shown in Figure 8-8. They include a Type tool, a Pen tool, and a Rectangle tool, along with several additional tools available as fly-outs.

When you select one of these drawing tools, the Options bar, shown in Figure 8-9, displays all the drawing tools. Selecting a drawing tool and clicking the arrow to the right of the tools opens a pop-up menu of settings for the selected tool. These pop-up menus of settings let you enter precise Width and Height values for the shapes.

Figure 8-8: The Photoshop drawing tools

Figure 8-9: The Options bar displays all the different drawing tools.

Photoshop also includes a Freeform Pen tool, as a fly-out under the Pen tool that acts like Illustrator's Pencil tool. It lets you draw freehand paths. If you enable the Magnetic option in the Options bar, the Freeform Pen tool detects areas of contrast and snaps the line to follow a pixel image behind it.

Specifying custom shapes

The Photoshop object tools (referred to in Photoshop as Drawing tools) also work just like their Illustrator counterparts. Among these tools is a unique tool called the Custom Shape tool, which is a fly-out under the Rectangle tool.

The Custom Shape tool lets you select a custom shape from a pop-up menu in the Options palette, shown in Figure 8-10. You add the selected shape to the document by dragging with the tool. Add new shapes to the pop-up menu by choosing Edit ➪ Define Custom Shape.

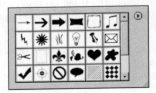

Figure 8-10: This pop-up palette lets you add Custom Shapes to the document.

Photoshop custom shapes are similar to Illustrator's symbols.

Cross-Reference Symbols are covered in the "Using Symbols, Styles, and Swatches," section later in this chapter.

Creating paths

If you select the Paths option in the Options bar, select a drawing tool, and then create a shape, Photoshop adds the shape to the Paths palette, shown in Figure 8-11. You can then use these paths to mask areas or define a clipping path. You can also convert them into a selection.

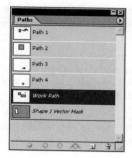

Figure 8-11: The Paths palette lets you store several different paths.

You can also export paths to Illustrator by choosing File ➪ Export ➪ Paths to Illustrator.

Cross-Reference   Using paths as clipping masks is covered in the "Creating a clipping mask in Illustrator," section later in this chapter.

Paths are temporary and appear as Work Paths in the Paths palette, but if you deselect the Work Path and draw another path, the first path disappears. Because paths placed in the Paths palette are temporary, you can save them using the Save Path palette menu command. This opens a simple dialog box where you can name the saved path. The saved path then appears permanently in the Paths palette.

Painting with shapes

All shapes drawn in Photoshop as objects are contained within special layers called *shape layers*. If a single shape layer includes multiple shapes, you can use the Pathfinder buttons to add, subtract, intersect, or exclude the overlapping areas.

Cross-Reference   More on the Pathfinder commands is covered in the section "Using Pathfinder features."

If you select the Fill Pixels option in the Options bar when drawing a shape in Photoshop, the shape becomes rasterized and becomes part of the pixel layer. For these painted shapes, you can select a blending mode and an opacity. You can also rasterize existing shapes by choosing Layer ➪ Rasterize ➪ Shape.

Creating and editing objects in Acrobat

All items in an Acrobat document are objects. Most of these objects are created from the original document when it's converted into a PDF file, but Acrobat also lets you create several objects that you can use to enhance the Acrobat document or to add review comments.

You select most Acrobat objects by choosing Tools ➪ Advanced Editing ➪ Select Object. When select, the object highlights and you can move it by dragging it to a new location. If you right-click on the object, a pop-up menu appears with commands to edit, align, center, distribute, and size the object. Most objects also include a pop-up menu option to access their Properties dialog box.

Adding document-enhancement objects

Objects used to enhance a PDF document — including the Article tool, the Movie tool, the Sound tool, the TouchUp Text and TouchUp Object tools, and several Form object tools — are located in the Tools ➪ Advanced Editing menu:

✦ **Article tool:** Use this to add several threaded text areas to the document. To create an article object, drag to create each of the threaded text areas and press the Enter key to complete the article. After the article is completed, a Properties dialog box appears, where you can enter the title, subject, author, and keywords for the article.

✦ **Movie and Sound tools**: Use these to add movie or sound files to an existing PDF document. After selecting either of these tools and dragging in the document, a dialog box opens where you can browse to the desired movie or sound file.

Cross-Reference
The details of using movie and sound files within an Acrobat document are covered in Chapter 32.

✦ **TouchUp Text tool:** Use this to add a new text object to the existing document. Selecting the Text TouchUp tool and clicking in the document with the ⌘/Ctrl key held down opens a dialog box where you can select the font and mode for the new text.

✦ **Form object tools:** The Tools ➪ Advanced Editing ➪ Forms menu includes several form objects that you can easily add to an Acrobat document by dragging its size. These form object tools include a Button tool, a Check Box tool, a Combo Box tool, a List Box tool, a Radio Button tool, a Text Field tool, and a Digital Signature tool. When you create a form object, a Properties dialog box (Figure 8-12) opens, where you can specify all the settings for the form object. The Properties dialog box includes four panels — General, Appearance, Actions, and Signed.

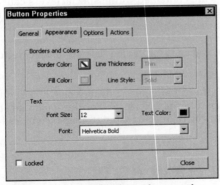

Figure 8-12: A dialog box of properties helps define the object's appearance.

Adding commenting objects

All the commenting objects for reviewing a document are included in the Tools ⇨ Commenting menu and Tools ⇨ Advanced Commenting menu. This menu includes the Note tool. Dragging with the Note tool in the document creates a Note object, which includes the name of the person making the comments, along with the date and time and a text area where the comments may be added.

The Commenting menu also includes the Stamp tool, which is used to add stamped image objects to the document. The Stamp tool menu includes many different default stamps choices, including stamps that say Approved, Confidential, Void, and so on. There is also a category of dynamic stamps that include the applier's name and date. Figure 8-13 shows several Acrobat objects including some note boxes and an Author stamp.

Figure 8-13: Commenting objects appear above the document.

To add more attention to a comment, you may select to use one of the tools found in the Tools ⇨ Advanced Commenting menu. These tools include a collection of drawing tools, including tools for creating rectangles, ovals, arrows, lines, clouds, polygons, and polygon line objects. The Advanced Commenting menu also includes a Text Box tool that creates highlighted text area objects, the Pencil tools, which lets you draw freehand objects, and the Pencil Eraser tool, which erases lines drawn with the Pencil tool. In addition, the Attach File tool opens a dialog box where you can select a file to attach to the document. After you've selected the file, the File Attachment Properties dialog box appears; here, you can define how the attachment looks in the PDF document. The Attach Sound tool opens a Sound Recorder, where you can record a simple audio message or select a sound file to attach to the document.

Creating objects in GoLive

GoLive, like InDesign, uses objects to lay out Web pages. All the objects that you can add to a Web page are available in different categories in the Objects palette. The various categories are listed at the top of the Toolbox, and selecting a category displays all the available objects as icons in the lower half of the Objects palette, as shown in Figure 8-14.

Figure 8-14: The GoLive Objects palette includes dozens of objects in several different categories.

Objects are added to a Web page by dragging its icon and dropping it on the Web page in the location where you want it to appear. The properties for the selected object are adjusted in the Inspector palette. You can also drag and drop object into the Source and Outline views. Double clicking on an object adds it to the page at the current location of the cursor.

Cross-Reference   You can learn more about working with GoLive objects in Chapter 25.

Painting Images

Unlike objects, which can be thought of as a group of items sitting on a shelf ready for you to placed in a document, you create images by drawing them on a canvas or by loading an existing image file. All the CS applications also support images, but the first place to look is obviously Photoshop.

Note   The process of creating objects within the CS applications is referred to as *drawing* and the process of creating images is called *painting*.

Painting images in Photoshop

The main tools used in Photoshop to paint images are the Paintbrush tool, the Pencil tool, and the Paint Bucket tool. All these tools apply the foreground color to the canvas.

Using the Paintbrush tool

The Paintbrush tool coupled with the Brushes palette offers unlimited flexibility and power in applying paint to the canvas. Selecting the Brush tool (B) in the Toolbox changes the cursor to match the shape of the selected brush. Dragging with this tool in the canvas paints a line using the properties set in the Brushes palette.

You may open the Brushes palette, shown in Figure 8-15, by choosing Window ➪ Brushes (F5) or by clicking on the Brushes tab on the right end of the Options bar. The Brushes palette includes many panels of properties that are opened by clicking on their panel name listed to the left of the palette. Most of these panels include a check box that lets you enable or disable the properties contained in the panel. The panels are as follows:

Note   The Brushes palette is active only when one of the painting tools is selected.

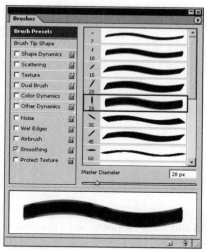

Figure 8-15: The Brushes palette includes many preset brushes to start with.

> ✦ **Brush Presets:** Lets you choose a brush from a long list of presets. To select a preset brush, just click on it and a preview of the selected brush appears at the bottom of the panel. You can also change the Master Diameter for the selected brush. In the Brush palette menu are several options for setting how the preset brushes are viewed, including Text Only, Small and Large Thumbnails, Small and Large Lists, and Stroke Thumbnail.
>
> The Brush palette menu also includes a New Brush Preset option that is used to add a new preset to the Brush Preset panel. A set of brush presets may be saved to the local

system using the Save Brushes palette menu command. The brush libraries are saved using an ABR file extension. Photoshop includes several brush libraries that may be loaded into the Brushes palette or selected from the bottom of the Brushes palette menu.

✦ **Brush Tip Shape panel**: Shown in Figure 8-16, this panel displays thumbnails of the brush tips for the respective brush presets listed in the Brush Presets panel. The brush tip properties let you change the tip's diameter and orientation using controls to flip the brush tip and set its angle and roundness. You can also alter its Angle and Roundness values by dragging in the diagram pane to the right of the Angle and Roundness values. The Hardness value sets the diameter of the brush's hard center, where no softening takes place. The Spacing value determines the distance between successive brush marks in a stroke. Low Spacing values causes the brush tip to overlap into a continuous path.

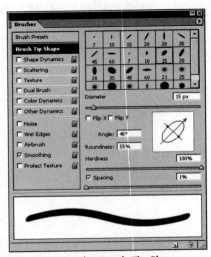

Figure 8-16: The Brush Tip Shape panel of the Brushes panel

✦ **Shape Dynamics panel**: Includes controls to add some randomness to the brush strokes, including the amount of jitter that is added. The Scattering panel is used to spread the brush tip over a given width with a specified density. The Texture panel lets you specify an underlying texture for the brush. The Dual Brush panel lets you select a secondary brush tip that is combined with the original brush tip to create a new unique pattern. The Color and Other Dynamics panels let you specify how the colors, transparency, and brightness change as the brush is painted.

The Noise, Wet Edges, Airbrush, Smoothing, and Protect Texture options don't open a panel of settings but may be enabled to change the characteristics of the selected brush.

When the Paintbrush tool is selected, the Options bar includes controls that let you select a tool preset or a brush tip. You can also select a blending mode to use and change the amount of opacity and flow that is applied to the brush.

STEPS: Painting with the Paintbrush Tool

1. **Open a Photoshop document.** With Photoshop open, choose File ➪ New to create a new document.

2. **Select a Brush.** Click on the Paintbrush tool to select it. In the Options bar, click on the Brushes tab to open the Brushes palette. Click on the palette menu and select the Special Effect Brushes command. A dialog box opens asking if you want to replace the brush sets. Click OK. The new brush set is displayed in the Brush Presets panel, as shown in Figure 8-17. In the Brush Presets panel of the Brushes palette, select the first brush preset, called the Azalea brush.

Figure 8-17: The brushes in the Brush Presets panel

3. **Set the brush properties.** In the Swatches palette, select an orange color. This color becomes the new foreground color. Click on the Color Dynamics panel in the Brushes palette and drag the Hue Jitter over to 50%.

4. **Paint with a Preset brush.** Drag with the Paintbrush tool in the canvas. The Azalea brush paints a random assortment of colored flowers in the canvas, as shown in Figure 8-18.

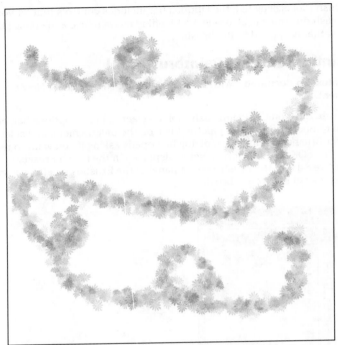

Figure 8-18: By altering the Hue Jitter in the Color Dynamics palette, the color of the flowers is changed as you paint with the brush.

Using the Pencil and Paint Bucket tool

The Pencil tool works just like the Paintbrush tool, except it produces a hard edge instead of a smooth, soft edge. The Pencil tool uses all the same controls found in the Brushes palette for specifying its shape and characteristics.

The Paint Bucket tool, located as a fly-out under the Gradient tool, applies the selected foreground color or pattern to an area where all the contiguous pixels are the same or within the specified Tolerance. You can select the properties of the Paint Bucket tool in the Options bar when the Paint Bucket tool is selected. You can also select a blending mode and an opacity.

Working with images in the other CS applications

All the other CS applications can work with images, but these images are confined to an object or frame. This lets you transform the images within the work area and place them relative to the other objects, but Illustrator and InDesign don't include any tools that alter the pixels by painting. You can load images into Illustrator and InDesign using the File ➪ Place menu command. These loaded images appear within an object or frame.

You can also convert certain text and vector objects to their bitmap equivalents through a process called *rasterizing*. Raster images may be moved back to Photoshop using the Clipboard. When pasted into Photoshop, the images are contained within a frame that allows you to move the object, but when you select a different tool, a confirm dialog box asks if you want to place the object. Choosing to place the object permanently places it in the current image.

Illustrator also includes an Auto Trace feature that works the opposite of rasterizing, allowing you to convert images into vectorized objects.

Caution   Rasterizing objects eliminates their resolution independence. Scaling a rasterized object reveals all the individual pixels.

Rasterizing objects

You can rasterize Illustrator objects by choosing Object ➪ Rasterize. This opens the Rasterize dialog box, shown in Figure 8-19, where you can select a color model, a resolution, a background, an antialiasing option, and a clipping mask, as well as specify whether space is added to the object:

Note   All objects that are saved using the Save for Web window are also rasterized.

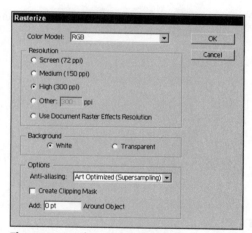

Figure 8-19: The Rasterize dialog box lets you specify a color model.

- ✦ **Color Model options:** Include RGB, CMYK, Grayscale, or Bitmap, depending on the color settings for the document.

- ✦ **Background options:** Define whether the object background are colored as white pixels or made transparent. Selecting the Transparent option causes an alpha channel to be saved with the document.

✦ **Anti-Aliasing options:** These include None, Art Optimized (which is used for graphics), and Type Optimized (which is used for text).

✦ **Create Clipping Mask:** Creates a clipping mask that hides all the background pixels. It isn't needed if the Transparent Background option is selected.

✦ **Add field:** Lets you specify a distance that is added to every edge of the rasterized object.

You can define all these settings for the document using the Document Raster Effects Settings dialog box, shown in Figure 8-20, which you open by choosing Effect ➪ Document Raster Effects Settings. You use these settings for any effects that need to rasterize the object as the effect is being applied.

Cross-Reference   More on using effects is covered in Chapter 10.

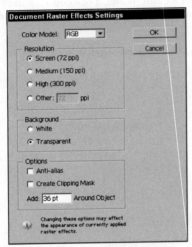

Figure 8-20: The Document Raster Effects Settings dialog box

STEPS: Rasterizing Objects

1. **Open an Illustrator document.** With Illustrator open, choose File ➪ New to create a new document.

2. **Drag a symbol from the Symbols palette.** For a quick object that may be rasterized, drag a symbol from the Symbols palette onto the art board.

3. **Resize the object.** Because the object loses its resolution independence when it's rasterized, drag on the bounding-box handles of the symbol with the Shift key held down to maintain its aspect ratio until it is the size you want to use, as shown in Figure 8-21.

Figure 8-21: Sizing the object in Illustrator before rasterizing.

4. **Rasterize the symbol.** With the symbol selected, choose Object ➪ Rasterize. The Rasterize dialog box appears. Select the RGB Color Mode, and change the Resolution depending on how the raster image intends to be used. Use Screen for images that are viewed on a computer monitor and High for raster images that are to be printed. Select Transparent as the Background and select the Art Optimized Anti-Aliasing option. Then click OK. Figure 8-22 shows the rasterized symbol.

Figure 8-22: The rasterized object appears the same as the object version, but if you were to scale the raster image, you would see the individual pixels.

5. **Copy the raster image to the Clipboard.** With the rasterized symbol still selected, choose Edit ➪ Copy. This copies the raster image to the Clipboard.

6. **Paste raster image into Photoshop.** With Photoshop open, choose File ➪ New. The New dialog box appears with the Clipboard preset selected. This preset has the exact dimensions of the raster image copied from Illustrator. Click OK to create a new canvas. Then choose Edit ➪ Paste. The raster image appears in the current open document within Photoshop inside a bounding box (see Figure 8-23). Drag the bounding box to the position where you want to place it, and click on the Selection tool. A simple confirmation dialog box appears, giving you the following options: Place, Cancel, or Don't Place. Click the Place button.

Figure 8-23: Raster images copied to Photoshop may be positioned before they're placed on the canvas.

Autotracing images

You can trace raster images and convert them into vector objects using the Auto Trace tool, which you find as a fly-out under the Blend tool. To trace an image, select it and click on a line within the image with the Auto Trace tool. The tool traces the line as best it can and creates a filled object that matches the traced line. If several lines exist, you need to click on each line. You can fill closed traced lines with the foreground color.

The settings for the Auto Trace tool are located in the Type & Auto Tracing panel of the Preferences dialog box, shown in Figure 8-24. The Tolerance value specifies how closely the image line is followed, and the Tracing Gap value sets the thickness of gaps that are ignored by the Auto Trace tool.

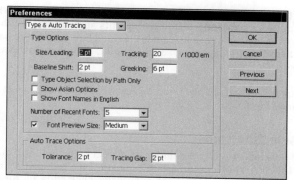

Figure 8-24: The Type & Auto Tracing panel of the Preferences dialog box

Selecting Objects

Before the properties of an object are displayed, you need to select the object that you want to change. Selecting an object is as easy as clicking on it with the Selection Tool. When selected, the object is surrounding with a bounding box. An object's bounding box may be used to transform the object.

Cross-Reference

Transforming objects is covered in Chapter 9.

The core Selection tools — including the Selection and Direct Selection tools found in Illustrator, Photoshop, and InDesign — all work the same.

Using Illustrator and InDesign's Toolbox selection tools

Both the Illustrator and InDesign's Toolboxes includes several tools for selecting objects and parts of objects. These tools are located at the top of the Toolbox, as shown in Figure 8-25 for Illustrator include the Selection tool, Direct Selection tool, the Magic Wand tool and the Lasso tool. InDesign includes the Selection and Direct Selection tools.

 Figure 8-25: The Illustrator selection tools

✦ **Selection tool:** The simplest way to select objects is to click on them with the Selection tool. You can also select multiple objects by dragging over them with the Selection tool. All objects that are at least partially included within the area that is dragged over are selected. You may also select several multiple objects by holding down the Shift key while clicking on each object.

Tip

You can access the Selection in Illustrator regardless of the current tool by holding down the ⌘/Ctrl key. This allows you to select an object quickly at any time. In Photoshop, the ⌘/Ctrl key accesses the Move tool; in InDesign, the ⌘/Ctrl key accesses the Direct Selection tool.

✦ **Direct Selection tool:** Use this to select individual points or segments on a path. When a path point is selected, it appears solid; unselected path points appear hollow. When the Direct Selection tool is over the top of a line segment, a small line appears as part of the cursor; if the Direct Selection tool is over an anchor point, a small hollow square appears as part of the cursor.

Note   Even if only a single path point is selected with the Direct Selection tool, the entire object is also selected and may be transformed.

Using Illustrator's other selection tools

Illustrator's Group Selection tool (available as a fly-out under the Direct Selection tool) may be used to select a single object that is part of a group. Double-clicking on a grouped set of objects selects the object and the group it belongs to. Each successive click adds another group level.

Illustrator's Magic Wand tool (Y) is used to select all objects that have a similar fill color, but using the Magic Wand palette, shown in Figure 8-26, you can choose to have the Magic Wand tool select all objects with a similar fill color, stroke color, stroke weight, opacity, and blending mode. For each of these (except for blending mode), you can specify a Tolerance value. The Tolerance value determines how loose the selected attribute may be while still being selected.

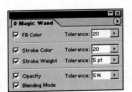

Figure 8-26: The Magic Wand palette lets you select which attributes to select.

Illustrator's Lasso tool (Q) may also be used to select multiple path points on multiple objects. Every object that has a point encircled by the Lasso tool is selected. Holding down the Shift key lets you add to the current selection; holding down the Option/Alt key subtracts from the current selection.

Note   You cannot select objects that are locked or hidden. To unlock all objects, choose Object ⇨ Unlock All (Alt+Ctrl+3 in Windows; Option+⌘+3 on the Mac). To show all hidden objects, choose Object ⇨ Show All (Alt+Ctrl+3 in Windows; Option+⌘+3 on the Mac).

Selecting by path only

By default, you can select objects by clicking on their fill, but this isn't your only option. If you have several overlapping objects, this option might lead to some frustration. The General panel of the Preferences dialog box (opened with the Illustrator/Edit ⇨ Preferences ⇨ General menu command) includes an Object Selection by Path Only option. With this option enabled, objects are only selected with the Selection tool when you click or drag over their path and not their fill.

Using Photoshop's other selection tools

Although you use most of Photoshop's selection tools to make pixel selections, Photoshop also includes Selection and Direct Selection tools specifically for selecting objects. When you select a layer containing images in the Layers palette, you can use Photoshop's Marquee, Lasso, or Magic Wand tools to select a pixel area. You move pixel selections using the Move tool, but the Move tool is also used to move objects when an object is selected.

When objects are created in Photoshop, each object resides on its own layer. This makes it so you can select only a single object at a time, but by linking layers together, you can move multiple objects simultaneously. With a single object selected and its layer selected in the Layers palette, click in the second column in the Layers palette of the layers that hold objects that you want to move with the selected object. This links the layers together so that moving one automatically moves the linked layers with it.

Selecting objects with Illustrator's Layers palette

You can use the Layers palette to select all objects contained on a layer or individual objects within that layer. To the right of the layer name in the Layers palette is a circle button used to target objects. Clicking on this target button for a given layer selects all objects on that layer. If you expand a layer, you can select the individual objects that make up the layer.

Cross-Reference   Layers are covered in detail in Chapter 11.

Using Illustrator's Select menu

In addition to the Toolbox tools, there are many selection-menu commands available in the Select menu. Choose Select ➪ All (⌘/Ctrl+A) to select all objects in the scene. Choose Select ➪ Deselect (Shift+⌘/Ctrl+A) to deselect all objects in the document so that no objects are selected. Choose Select ➪ Reselect to select again all objects that were previously selected.

Note   Photoshop also includes a Select menu, but all these menu commands apply to the pixel selection tools.

Choosing Select ➪ Inverse selects all objects that weren't selected and deselects all objects currently selected.

Objects can also be selected using their stacking order. Choosing Select ➪ Next Object Above (Alt+Ctrl+] in Windows; Option+⌘+] on the Mac) selects the object immediately above the current object in the stacking order. Choosing Select ➪ Next Object Below (Alt+Ctrl+[in Windows; Option+⌘+[on the Mac) selects the object immediately below the current object in the stacking order. If the topmost or bottommost objects are selected when these commands are used, the current object remains selected.

Note   The First Object Above, Next Object Above, Next Object Below, and Last Object Below menu commands are found in InDesign's Object ➪ Select menu.

The Select ➪ Same menu includes several options for choosing all objects that have similar properties. The options include Blending Mode, Fill & Stroke, Fill Color, Opacity, Stroke Color, Stroke Weight, Style, Symbol Instance, and Link Block Series.

The Select ➪ Object menu includes several subobjects that you may select for the selected object. These options include All on Same Layers, Direction Handles, Brush Strokes, Clipping Masks, Stray Points, and Text Objects.

The Select ➪ Save Selection menu command lets you name and save the current selection of objects. The Save selections may be recalled at any time by selecting the selection name from the bottom of the Select menu. Choosing Select ➪ Edit Selection opens a dialog box where you can rename or delete a selection.

Selecting Pixels in Photoshop

Just as Illustrator and InDesign include several tools that select objects, Photoshop includes several tools that select specific pixels. The Selection tools are located at the top of Photoshop's Toolbox and include several Marquee tools, several Lasso tools and the Magic Wand tool, as shown in Figure 8-27.

Figure 8-27: Photoshop's Toolbox includes several selection tools.

Using the Selection tools

When one of the Selection tools is selected, the Options bar displays four icon buttons that are used to create a new selection, add to the current selection, subtract from the current selection, and intersect with the current selection. These buttons let you continuously edit a selection until you have exactly what you want.

Holding down the Shift key while selecting an area adds to the current selection. Holding down the Option/Alt key subtracts from the current selection. Holding down the Shift+Option/Alt keys intersects the current selection.

The Options bar also lets you specify a feather amount and includes an option to enable antialiasing. Dragging with a selection tool in the canvas marks a selection with a blinking dashed line often called *marching ants*.

Note If a selection isn't visible, choose View ➪ Show ➪ Selection Edges.

You can only display one selection on the canvas at a time, but you may save and load selections by choosing Select ➪ Save Selection and Select ➪ Load Selection.

Using the Marquee selection tools

The Marquee selection tools included in Photoshop include the Rectangle Marquee tool, the Ellipse Marquee tool, the Single Row Marquee tool, and the Single Column Marquee tool. The difference among these tools is the shape of the selection they make.

In the Options bar, which appears directly under the menu at the top of the interface, shown in Figure 8-28, you can choose a selection Style as Normal, Fixed Aspect Ratio, and Fixed Size. If the Normal option is chosen, then a selection is made by clicking and dragging to specify the selection size. The Fixed Aspect Ratio option lets you specify Width and Height values.

Dragging with this option produces a selection that maintains the specified aspect ratio. The Fixed Size option also lets you specify Width and Height values. Clicking and dragging with this option drags a selection of the specified dimensions in the image.

Options bar

Figure 8-28: Selection tool options are displayed in the Options bar.

Holding down the Shift key while dragging with the Rectangle or Ellipse tools constrains the selection to a perfect square or circle. You can also hold down the Option/Alt key to drag from the center of the shape. Holding down the Spacebar lets you move the current selection as you make it. When you release the Spacebar, you can continue dragging to create the selection. The Single Row and Single Column Marquee tools let you click and drag to select a single row or column of pixels.

Using the Lasso selection tools

Photoshop actually includes three different Lasso tools:

✦ **Lasso tool:** You create a selection by drawing in the canvas. When you release the mouse, a straight line is drawn back to the point where you first clicked. If you hold down the Option/Alt key, you can click and drag to create straight lines. With the Option/Alt key held down, you can also press the Delete key to delete the last created straight line point or gradually delete the drawn path.

✦ **Polygonal Lasso tool:** This is the opposite of the Lasso tool. You create a selection by clicking at the endpoints of each successive straight line, but if you hold down the Option/Alt key, you can draw freehand. The Delete key also works to delete line segments. To close a selection created with the Polygonal Lasso tool, move the cursor near the starting point until a small circle appears as part of the cursor, and click or hold down the ⌘/Ctrl key and click or simply double-click and a straight line is created from the cursor's position to the starting point.

✦ **Magnetic Lasso tool:** This automatically creates selection anchor points based on the contrast of the image below. To use this tool, set the Width, Edge Contrast, and Frequency values in the Options bar. The Width value specifies how far around the cursor the Magnetic Lasso tool looks for contrasting pixels. The Edge Contrast value sets the amount of contrast required for an edge to be selected. The Frequency value determines the number of anchor points used to define the selection area.

Click on an image border that you want to trace with the Magnetic Lasso tool and drag along the image border. The tool places anchor points regularly along the path and connects them. If you click, you can manually place an anchor point as needed. The Delete key may be used to backtrack if needed and holding down the Option/Alt key changes the Magnetic Lasso tool to the normal Lasso tool for dragging or the Polygonal Lasso tool for clicking. Double-click or drag back to the first point again to close the selection.

Using the Magic Wand

The Magic Wand tool selects all areas with the same color or a color that is within the specified Tolerance value. The Tolerance value (found on the Options bar) can range between 0 and 255. Tolerance values of 0 require that the color values be exactly the same, and a Tolerance value of 255 is so forgiving that almost all colors are selected.

On the Options bar, the Contiguous option selects only those areas that are immediately con-nected to the selected color, but if the Contiguous option is deselected then all colors within the canvas that are within the Tolerance value are selected. The Use All Layers option makes selections from all layers, but only from the selected layer if disabled.

STEPS: Building a Selection

1. **Open a Photoshop document.** With Photoshop open, choose File ⇨ New to create a new document. Fill the entire image with a pattern by choosing Edit ⇨ Fill. In the Fill dialog box that appears, select the Pattern option and choose one of the default pat-terns; then click OK.

2. **Choose an initial selection.** Click on the Rectangle Marquee tool and drag in the can-vas to select a rectangular area.

3. **Subtract an interior section.** With the Rectangle Marquee tool still selected, click on the Subtract from Selection button in the Options bar. Then drag over an interior sec-tion of the current selection. The interior section is removed from the selection.

4. **Use the Ellipse Marquee tool.** Click and hold on the Rectangle Marquee tool to select the Ellipse Marquee tool from the fly-out menu. Click on the Add to Selection button in the Options bar. Then select the Fixed Size Style with Width and Height values of 64 pix-els. Click and drag the circular selection so it's positioned on top of each of the corners of the current selection.

5. **Save the selection.** With the selection completed, choose Select ⇨ Save Selection. In the Save Selection dialog box, give the selection a new name and click the OK.

6. **Fill the selection.** Choose Edit ⇨ Fill and, in the Fill dialog box, select to fill with the white color and click OK. The selection is now clearly visible, as shown in Figure 8-29.

Figure 8-29: Filling the selection with a color makes it easy to see.

Using the Selection menu

In addition to the Selection tools, Photoshop also includes a Select menu that holds many commands that are helpful for selecting pixels. Choose Select ⇨ All (⌘/Ctrl+A) to select all canvas pixels; choose Select ⇨ Deselect (⌘/Ctrl+D) to eliminate any selections. Choose

Select ⇨ Reselect (Shift+Ctrl+D in Windows; Shift+⌘+D on the Mac) to make the recent selection active again; choose Select ⇨ Inverse (Shift+Ctrl+I in Windows; Shift+⌘+I on the Mac) to deselect the current selection and select all pixels that weren't selected.

Selecting a color range

Choosing Select ⇨ Color Range opens a dialog box, shown in Figure 8-30, where you can select a range of colors in the image. With the dialog box open, the cursor changes to an eyedropper that you can use to click on the preview pane in the Color Range dialog box or within the actual canvas. The Preview pane is set to show the selection or the image, or you can use the ⌘/Ctrl key to switch between these two.

Note   If a selection exists in the canvas, opening Photoshop's Color Range dialog box displays the selected area only. If no selection exists, the entire image displays in the Color Range dialog box.

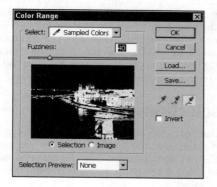

Figure 8-30: The Color Range dialog box

Increasing the Fuzziness value increases the color range included in the selection, much like the Tolerance value for the Magic Wand.

To add more colors to the selection, click on the Add to Sample eyedropper; to remove colors, click on the Subtract from Sample eyedropper. You can also select the Add to Sample eyedropper by holding down the Shift key and the Subtract from Sample eyedropper by holding down the Option/Alt key. The Invert option switches the colors used in the Preview pane.

The Select drop-down list at the top of the dialog box lets you select from several default colors, including reds, yellows, greens, cyans, blues, magentas, highlights, midtones, shadows, and out of gamut. The Out of Gamut selection in particular is useful as a color check prior to printing.

The Selection Preview options at the bottom of the dialog box project the selection back into the canvas using None, Grayscale, Black Matte, White Matte, or Quick Mask. Color Range selections may be saved using the AXT file extension and reloaded again.

Modifying a selection

The Select ⇨ Modify menu includes several commands that change the current selection. Each of these menu commands opens a simple dialog box, shown in Figure 8-31, where you can specify a pixel value. The Border menu command turns the selection into a border as wide as the specified Width value. The Smooth command eliminates any stray or jagged pixels by smoothing the entire selection. The Expand command increases the selection by the designated number of pixels. The Contract command reduces the selection by the designated number of pixels.

Figure 8-31: You can select a pixel value to add as a border.

Choosing Select ➪ Grow increases the selection step-by-step by gradually selecting similar adjoining colors. Choosing Select ➪ Similar increases a selection by selecting all colors similar to the selected color through the entire image.

Transforming selections

Choosing Select ➪ Transform Selection adds a bounding box to the current selection that lets you move, rotate, scale, shear, and change the perspective of the selection using the same bounding box controls used on objects. After all the transformations are made using the bounding box, confirm the transformation by selecting another tool. This action causes a confirmation dialog box appears letting you Apply, Cancel, or Not Apply all the transformations. The Cancel option removes the confirmation dialog box letting you transform the selection some more, but the Not Apply option returns the selection to its last transformation state.

Converting drawn paths into selections

Paths that are saved in the Paths palette may be turned into a selection using the Make Selection palette menu command. This opens the Make Selection dialog box where you can select a Feather Radius value and whether the selection is antialiased. You can also choose that the selection is a New Selection, added to the existing selection, subtracted from the existing selection, or intersected with the existing selection.

Organizing Objects

Illustrator and InDesign both include several ways to organize objects. The chief among these is the Layers palette, which lets you place objects on separate layers. Other organization features are contained within the Object menu; these features help in grouping and preventing unwanted edits by locking and hiding objects.

Cross-Reference The Object menu includes many other commands, such as commands to transform and arrange objects. These commands are covered in Chapter 9.

Adding objects to layers

All the CS applications, except for Acrobat, have layers accessed through a Layers palette. You create new layers by selecting the New Layer palette menu command or by clicking on the New Layer icon button at the bottom of the palette. All new objects are added to the selected layer, and objects may be moved between layers.

The first two columns of the Layers palette let you hide or lock layers by clicking in the column boxes. Locked and hidden layers cannot be selected or edited.

Cross-Reference Turn to Chapter 11 for much more information on layers.

Grouping objects

You may group together several selected objects by choosing Object ⇨ Group (⌘/Ctrl+G). Groups may also be nested. When a single object that is part of a group is selected with the Selection tool, the entire group is selected, but individual objects that are part of a group may be selected using the Group Selection tool in Illustrator. Choose Object ⇨ Ungroup (Shift+Ctrl+G in Windows; Shift+⌘+G on the Mac) to ungroup a grouped set of objects.

Hiding and locking objects

To prevent set objects from accidentally being selected or edited, you can lock and hide objects in Illustrator by choosing Object ⇨ Lock and by choosing Objects ⇨ Hide. Both of these menus let you lock (or hide) the current selection (⌘/Ctrl+2), all artwork above, or other layers. You cannot select objects you lock or hide. InDesign only includes the menu commands Object ⇨ Lock Position (⌘/Ctrl+L) and Object ⇨ Unlock Position (Alt+Ctrl+L in Windows; Option+⌘+L on the Mac).

Objects or layers that are locked have a small lock icon displayed in the second column of the Layers palette, as shown in Figure 8-32, and objects or layers that are hidden have no eye icon in the first column of the Layers palette. The Layers palette provides another way to quickly hide and lock objects by clicking on the palette's columns.

Note You can also lock or hide layers in Photoshop using the Layers palette: Select the layer and click the Lock Position or Lock All icons at the top of the Layers palette. When locked, a small lock icon appears to the right of the Layer name. You hide layers in Photoshop clicking the eye icon in the first column of the Layers palette.

Figure 8-32: The Layers palette allows you to lock or hide layer objects.

Filling and Stroking Objects

The two properties probably most common for objects are the object's fill and stroke. An object's *fill* is the color, gradient, or pattern that fills the interior portion of an object, and an object's *stroke* is the line or outline that makes up the object. Fills and strokes may be any color or they may be set to no color. Fills may also be added with a gradient or a pattern.

Applying fill and stroke colors to objects in Illustrator and InDesign

Fill and stroke colors are applied to objects using the colors for each that are identified in the Fill and Stroke boxes located at the bottom of the Toolbox, as shown in Figure 8-33. The Fill box looks like a filled colored square; the Stroke box looks like a thick outlined square. The Fill box is active by default, but you can click on the Stroke box to select it.

Tip The X key toggles between the Fill and Stroke color swatches in the Toolbox.

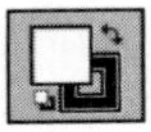

 Figure 8-33: The Fill and Stroke boxes appear at the bottom of the Toolbox.

With either the Fill or Stroke box in the Toolbox active, you can change the box's color by selecting a new color from the Color or Swatches palette or you can double-click on the box to access a Color Picker dialog box.

The double-headed arrow that appears above and to the right of the Fill and Stroke boxes swaps the colors, so the Fill color becomes the Stroke color and vice versa. The small icon to the lower left of the Fill and Stroke boxes set the Fill and Stroke colors to their defaults, which are a white fill and a black stroke.

Tip The keyboard shortcut to swap the Fill and Stroke colors is Shift+X; the keyboard shortcut for setting the fill and stroke colors to their defaults is D.

Below the Fill and Stroke boxes in the Toolbox are three simple icons, shown in Figure 8-34. These icons are used to set the active Fill or Stroke box to hold a Color (<), a Gradient (>), or None (/). When the None icon is clicked for either box, a red diagonal line appears in the box.

Caution Gradients may be applied only to a Fill, not to a Stroke, in Illustrator. If the Gradient button in Illustrator is clicked for a stroke, a gradient is added to the Fill box. InDesign can add gradients to strokes.

 Figure 8-34: The icons under the Fill and Stroke boxes can fill the selected object with a color, a gradient, or neither.

If the fill and stroke colors are changed without any objects selected, the selected colors are applied to the next objects that are created.

The Color palette also includes Fill and Stroke boxes that match those in the Toolbox, as shown in Figure 8-35.

 **Figure 8-35:** The Color palette also includes Fill and Stroke boxes.

One other place that may be used to change fill and stroke colors is the Attribute palette. Using the Attribute palette, shown in Figure 8-36, you can change the stacking order for fills and strokes. Attributes listed in the Appearance palette are applied to an object from front to back in the order that they appear in the Appearance palette.

Figure 8-36: The Appearance palette shows all an object's attributes.

By dragging the fill above the stroke, the fill appears above the stroke making any portion of the stroke that overlaps the fill hidden behind the fill.

Applying other stroke attributes

Although the only attribute that may be applied to a fill is a color, gradient, or pattern, strokes include several additional attributes. These attributes are applied using the Stroke palette, shown in Figure 8-37.

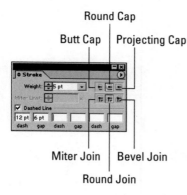

Figure 8-37: The Stroke palette includes additional stroke attributes.

The stroke weight defines how thick the stroke is. Half of the weight thickness appears on either side of the object path marked in the object's layer color when the object is selected. Stroke weights ranging from 0.25 points to 100 points may be selected from the pop-up menu to the right of the Weight field, or you may enter a custom weight value in the Weight field.

Note Entering a Weight value of 0 sets the stroke to None.

Selecting the Show Options palette menu command causes several additional stroke attributes to appear at the bottom of the Stroke palette.

The row of icons that appears to the right of the Weight field lets you select from three different cap styles that are applied to the end of the stroke. The three options are Butt Cap, Round Cap, and Projecting Cap. Butt Cap squares the ends of a stroke, Round Cap applies half a circle to the stroke ends, and Projecting Cap applies a square end that is extended half a line width beyond the end of the stroke.

Note   Selecting a cap style for a closed object such as a rectangle has no effect.

Beneath the three cap style buttons are three Join options. These buttons define how the corners of an object appear. The Join options are Miter Join, Round Join, and Bevel Join. Miter Join draws the corners as sharp squares, Round Join rounds the corners, and Bevel Join replaces the corners with diagonal lines. The Miter Limit sets a limit for the corner point as a number times the weight when Miter Joins are automatically switched to Bevel Joins.

If the Dashed Line option is selected, you can enter the Dash and Gap values for three separate dashes, enabling you to create many unique dashed lines. Not all the Dash and Gap values need to be filled in. Whatever values are entered are repeated around the entire object.

Figure 8-38 shows several stroke samples of various weights, cap types, and dashed lines.

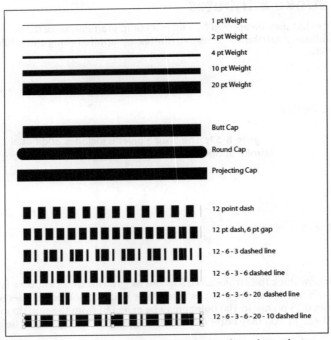

Figure 8-38: Altering the settings in the Stroke palette changes the attributes for the stroked path.

STEPS: Applying Fills and Strokes

1. **Open an Illustrator document.** With Illustrator open, choose File ⇨ New to create a new document. Choose Window ⇨ Symbol Libraries ⇨ Maps to open a palette of map symbols. Select and drag one of the symbols to the art board. The symbol is fairly small. Select a corner handle and drag it away from the symbol while holding down the Shift key uniformly scales the symbol.

2. **Expand and ungroup the symbol.** With the symbol selected, choose Object ⇨ Expand. In the Expand dialog box, select to expand both the Object and the Fill and click OK. Next choose Object ⇨ Ungroup three times to ungroup all the objects. The object now consists of two objects — a rounded black square and an airplane path — as shown in Figure 8-39.

Figure 8-39: You can select an object after expanding and ungrouping it.

3. **Select and apply a fill.** Click on the airplane path with the Selection tool. Notice that the Fill box is set to white and the Stroke box is set to None. With the Fill box selected, click on a blue color in the Swatches palette.

4. **Select and apply a stroke.** Click on the Stroke box at the bottom of the Toolbox to select it. Then choose a red color in the Swatches palette. In the Stroke palette, increase the Weight value to 10 pt and enable the Dashed Line option. Enter **20 pt** in the first dashed line field and **2 pt** in the second field. The stroke is updated as you change the Stroke settings in the Stroke palette. The resulting fill and stroke are shown in Figure 8-40.

5. **Copy the style to the Graphic Styles palette.** Choose Window ⇨ Appearance to open the Appearance palette, shown in Figure 8-41. Drag the Appearance icon to the left of the Path title in the Appearance palette to the Graphic Styles palette (or just drag the object itself to the Graphic Styles palette). This copies the created style to the Graphic Styles palette where it's applied to other objects.

Figure 8-40: After applying a stroke and fill to the interior shape, the design is altered dramatically with a few simple changes.

Figure 8-41: The Appearance palette shows all an object's attributes.

6. **Apply the copied style to the background object.** Select the background rounded square object and drag the copied style from the Graphic Styles palette to the background object. This applied the same fill and stroke attributes to the square object, as shown in Figure 8-42.

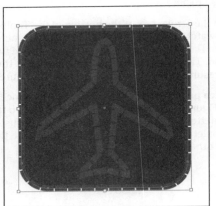

Figure 8-42: Styles copied to the Graphic Styles palette may be easily applied to other objects.

Filling and stroking a pixel selection

Although fills and strokes are mainly applied to objects, they may also be applied to a pixel selection in Photoshop using the Edit ⇨ Fill (Shift+F5) and Edit ⇨ Stroke menu commands. Both of these commands open a dialog box, shown in Figure 8-43, where you can select the color to use. The color options include Foreground Color, Background Color, Color (which opens a Color Picker), Pattern, History, Black, 50% Gray, and White. You can also select a blending mode, an opacity, and whether to preserve transparency.

Note   If the Edit ⇨ Fill menu command is used with no selection, the entire canvas is filled with the selected color.

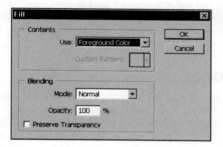

Figure 8-43: The Fill dialog box lets you select the color or pattern.

The Stroke dialog box, shown in Figure 8-44, also includes options to specify the width and color of the stroke and whether to place the stroke inside, in the center, or outside of the selection.

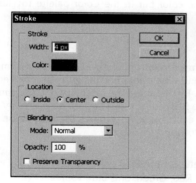

Figure 8-44: The Stroke dialog box lets you specify a width, a color, and whether the stroke appears inside, centered, or outside the selection.

Filling and stroking a Photoshop path

Paths in the Paths palette in Photoshop may also be filled and stroked using the Fill Path and Stroke Path palette menu commands. The Fill Path dialog box includes the same settings used to fill a selection along with a Feather Radius value and an Anti-aliased option.

The Stroke Path dialog box, on the other hand, includes a single option to select the Tool that is used to stroke the path, as shown in Figure 8-45. The options include all the various drawing and editing tools including Pencil, Brush, Eraser, Clone Stamp, Smudge, and so on.

Figure 8-45: The Stroke Path dialog box lets you select a tool to use to stroke the path.

Assigning Color

Color plays an important part in any design, and the color features found in the Creative Suite applications are amazingly diverse. Whether your documents are designed for print, CD-ROM, or a Web site, colors are easily selected and manipulated. You add colors to objects using fills and strokes, and you paint images using an assortment of tools.

Learning the various color modes

Color is a major part of any design, and in the CS applications, you can access several different color models, including RGB, Web Safe RGB, CMYK, HSB, and Grayscale. Which color model you use depends on where you intend the artwork to end up. For example, the RGB color mode works well if you intend your design to be viewed on a computer monitor via a CD-ROM. However, if the design is going to be placed on a Web site, you'll want to consider using the Web Safe RGB color mode. For designs that are to be printed, the CMYK color mode is appropriate. The good news is that you can switch between these different color modes at any time using the Color palette menu.

Tip Holding down the Shift key while clicking on the color bar in the Color palette toggles through the different color modes.

RGB color mode

This color mode is used to display colors on a computer monitor. Inside each computer monitor (or television) are thousands of tiny red, green, and blue phosphorous guns that project beams of red, green, or blue light, one for each pixel. By changing the intensity of each gun, you can control the resulting color of each pixel. The RGB color mode produces colors by mixing together red, green, and blue. The amount of each color determines the final color. Figure 8-46 shows the Color palette with the RGB color mode selected.

Figure 8-46: The Color palette for the RGB color mode includes separate sliders for Red, Green, and Blue values.

Note The RGB color system is *additive,* meaning that the colors combine to make white. This is different from the *subtractive* color system used by the CMYK color mode, in which the colors are created by mixing inks.

Common RGB colors

One of the easiest ways to learn how to use the RGB color values is to examine the relationships between the various RGB values and their resulting colors. Consider the following table of colors and RGB values.

Color	R value	G value	B value
Bright red	255	0	0
Medium red	192	0	0
Dark red	128	0	0
Bright green	0	255	0
Bright blue	0	0	255
White	255	255	255
Black	0	0	0
Light gray	192	192	192
Medium gray	128	128	128
Dark gray	64	64	64
Yellow	255	255	0
Cyan	0	255	255
Magenta	255	0	255

Within Photoshop and Illustrator, you can create colors by specifying the amount of each color to use. The values range from 0, which includes none of that color, to 255, which includes a full amount. A separate value is listed for red, green, and blue. By altering these color values, 16.7 million different colors are possible.

For example, a color that includes a value of 255 for red, 0 for green, and 0 for blue would be pure red. Amounts of 255 of each color produces white, and amounts of 0 of each color produces black. Equal amounts of each of the three colors produces gray. Mixing red and green produces yellow, mixing green and blue produces cyan, and mixing red and blue produces magenta.

Web Safe color mode

The Web Safe color mode is a subset of the RGB color mode that includes a limited palette of colors displayed more consistently without dithering on a browser regardless of the system used to view the design. Figure 8-47 shows the Color palette with the Web Safe color mode selected. Notice how the color values are displayed as hexadecimal numbers.

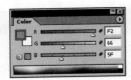

Figure 8-47: The Color palette for the Web Safe color mode.

Because of the difference between system color sets on Mac and Windows systems, some Web-page colors viewed on one system look dramatically different from the same Web page viewed on a different system. To fix this problem, a 216-color palette that includes colors that are common between Windows and Mac systems has been defined as a Web Safe palette. Using these colors ensures that the colors are consistent between different systems.

HTML code refers to Web colors using the hexadecimal (base-16) numbering system. The results are two-digit numbers instead of three, but the value is still the same. The hexadecimal equivalents to the RGB numbers are displayed in the Color Picker dialog box.

HSB color mode

The HSB color mode defines colors using the common physical properties of hue, saturation, and brightness. This color mode is useful if you need to change the brightness or a color without changing its hue. Hue is measured as a position on a circular color wheel, which ranges from 0 to 360 degrees. Red is found at 0 (and 360) degrees, yellow at 60 degrees, green at 120 degrees, cyan at 180 degrees, blue at 240 degrees, and magenta at 300 degrees. Figure 8-48 shows the Color palette with the HSB color mode selected.

Figure 8-48: The HSB color mode displays its values as percentages.

Colors found in between are a mixture of the primary colors. For example, orange is represented by 48 degrees between red and yellow. Colors on the opposite side of the color wheel are inverted pairs — red and cyan, yellow and blue, and green and magenta.

The Saturation value determines the purity of the color. This value can range from 0 to 100 percent. Reducing a color Saturation value is analogous to mixing the color with white. Colors with a 0 percent Saturation value are displayed as pure white, regardless of the Hue value.

Brightness is the opposite of saturation. It ranges from 0 to 100 percent and measures the amount of black that is mixed with the color. Reducing the brightness makes the color darker. HSB colors with a Brightness value of 0 are pure black.

Note   The Brightness value takes precedence over the Saturation value. A HSB color with a Saturation value of 0 still appears black if its Brightness value is 0.

Understanding hexadecimal numbers

Understanding the hexadecimal numbering system isn't that difficult. Our current numbering system is *base 10*, meaning that the numbers range from 0 to 9 before another digit is added. But the hexadecimal numbering system is *base 16*, meaning that the numbers range from 0 to 15 before adding another digit.

The characters used to represent the numbers 10 through 15 in the hexadecimal system are the letters A through F. So, counting in hexadecimal would be 00, 01, 02, 03, 04, 05, 06, 07, 08, 09, 0A, 0B, 0C, 0D, 0E, 0F, followed by 10.

For Web pages, the three hexadecimal values for red, green, and blue are combined into a single number that begins with a number sign such as #FF9910. If you know a few hexadecimal values, you'll be able to approximate color values listed in HTML code. Full color is denoted as FF, no color is 00, half color is 80, so #20FF31 is a green tint and #0C8091 is a darker-cyan color.

The advantage that hexadecimal numbers have for Web pages is that an RGB color is represented by 7 digits. If the base-10 numbering system was used, then 10 digits would be needed. Although saving three digits for each color doesn't seem like much, if you multiple that times the total number of pixels included in an image, the result makes a huge difference in the file size.

CMYK color mode

The CMYK color mode is based on cyan, magenta, and yellow inks that are mixed to create colors. The *K* stands for black. This color mode is used for designs that you print. Figure 8-49 shows the Color palette with the CMYK color mode selected.

Note

The letter *B* typically represents the color blue, so *K* represents black. Although you can create black by mixing full equal portions of cyan, magenta, and yellow inks, the actual result from mixing these inks is a muddy brown, so true black is printed using black ink.

Figure 8-49: When the CMYK color mode is selected, the out-of-gamut warning icon appears for all colors that are out of the CMYK gamut.

You specify CMYK colors by providing a percentage between 0 and 100 percent for each color. Digital printers typically print CMYK documents using a four-color process where the sheets are run once for each color.

Grayscale color mode

The Grayscale color mode converts all colors to grayscale values. This color mode is used for black and white images. Grayscale values are represented by a single brightness value that ranges from 0 to 100 percent with 0 percent being white and 100 percent being black. When colors are converted to grayscale, the color's luminosity value determines its grayscale value. Figure 8-50 shows the Color palette with the Grayscale color mode selected.

Understanding spot verses process colors

For colors saved to the Swatches palette, you can select the Color Type as a spot color or as a process color. These types correspond to different types of ink that are used to print the colors. Spot colors are printed using premixed inks, and process colors are mixed on the spot using CMYK values.

Spot colors require a separate printing plate for each spot color that is used in a document, but process colors can represent a wide range of colors using only four printing plates. So a document that has only one or two spot colors may be less expensive than a document with all process colors. Another advantage of spot colors is that they're used to print colors that are out-of-gamut for the CMYK color method.

Spot colors are identified in the Swatches palette by a small black dot that appears in the lower-right corner of the swatch. You can switch between spot and process colors in the Color palette by clicking on the spot or process color icons.

Figure 8-50: The Grayscale color mode includes a single value for brightness only.

Note Photoshop actually includes an additional color mode called the Lab color mode. The *L* stands for lightness, the *a* for the green-red color wheel axis, and the *b* for the blue-yellow color wheel axis. This color mode makes it intuitive to work with the luminance of an image.

Using the Color palette

Colors may be applied to an object's fill or stroke using the Fill and Stroke boxes in the Toolbox. Fill and Stroke boxes are also found in the Color palette (Figure 8-51) for convenience, which lets you specify specific colors using color values or select a color by simply clicking on the color bar.

Note To see the Fill and Stroke boxes and the color values for the selected color mode in the Color palette, select the Show Options palette menu command.

When the mouse is moved over the top of the color bar, the cursor changes to an eyedropper. Clicking on the color bar changes the color for either the Fill or Stroke box, whichever is active.

Tip If you drag one of the color value sliders with the Shift key held down, all color values scale along with the selected color. This works for all color modes except for the HSV and Grayscale.

Beneath the Fill and Stroke boxes in the Color palette are two icons that randomly appear as you drag about the color bar. The top icon is the Web Safe color warning. This icon looks like a simple cube and informs you that the current color is not a Web Safe color. The color swatch next to the icon displays the nearest Web Safe color and clicking on it changes the current color to the nearest Web Safe color.

Beneath the Web Safe color icon, another icon may appear that looks like a yellow triangle with an exclamation point inside it. This icon appears when the current color is out-of-gamut and is not available in the CMYK color mode. The color swatch next to it is the nearest color that is available in the CMYK color mode, which means it may be printed.

Web Safe color warning icon

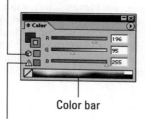

Figure 8-51: The Web Safe color warning icon and the Out-of-Gamut color warning icon both appear within the Color palette.

Color bar

Out-of-gamut color warning icon

The Color palette menu in Illustrator also includes two commands (Inverse and Complementary) for quickly locating the inverse or complementary color to the current color. An *inverse color* is opposite the current color in the color wheel for the current color model; a *complementary color* offers a decent amount of contrast to the original color.

Using the Color Picker

If you double-click on the Fill box in the Toolbox, a Color Picker, shown in Figure 8-52, appears. Using the Color Picker, you may select any color by manipulating the color values or by selecting a color from the color spectrum.

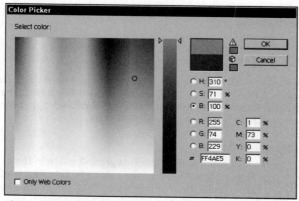

Figure 8-52: The Color Picker lets you select color, and it shows the color values.

Understanding gamut

Color models are based on theoretical values, but in real life all the colors that are defined mathematically aren't always possible. The actual range of colors that is possible for a certain color space or device is called its *gamut*. Any color that falls outside of its gamut is called *out-of-gamut* and may cause a problem for the device.

The color values for several color modes are displayed in the Color Picker. These values are linked to one another, so a change in one value impacts the other values. Toward the top of the Color Picker dialog box, the Web Safe and Out-of-Gamut icons randomly appear just like the Color palette along with color swatches that you can click to reset the color. The Only Web Colors option in the lower-left corner limits the colors in the color spectrum so only Web-safe colors are displayed. Figure 8-53 shows the Color Picker with this option enabled.

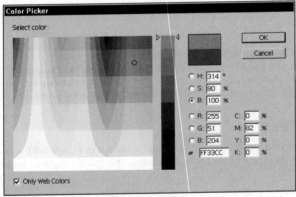

Figure 8-53: With the Only Web Colors option enabled, the total number of colors is severely limited.

Using the Eyedropper tool

In addition to using the Color Picker, you can select colors from within the image using the Eyedropper tool. The Eyedropper tool works differently in Photoshop and Illustrator. The tool in Photoshop is used to get only color. But in Illustrator and InDesign, the Eyedropper tool can retrieve appearance attributes, character style, and paragraph style.

Using Photoshop's Eyedropper tool

Dragging over an image with the Eyedropper tool changes the Foreground color. In the Options bar, you can use the color of the point directly under the tool or to sample a 3-x-3 or a 5-x-5 grid around the cursor. Holding down the Option/Alt key while dragging in the image with the Eyedropper tool changes the Background color.

Tip The Eyedropper tool may be temporarily selected while using one of the painting tools by holding down the Option/Alt key.

The Color Sampler tool is available as a fly-out under the Eyedropper tool. Using this tool, you can click on four different points in the image and the color values for those points are displayed in the Info palette. Only four color sample points may be placed in an image, but you can drag these points to new locations as needed or clear them all using the Clear button in the Options bar.

Using Illustrator's Eyedropper and Paint Bucket tools

You can use Illustrator's Eyedropper and Paint Bucket tools to gather property values from one object and apply them to another object. The specific properties that are gathered by the Eyedropper tool is set using the Eyedropper/Paint Bucket Options dialog box, shown in Figure 8-54, which is opened by double-clicking on the Eyedropper or Paint Bucket tools.

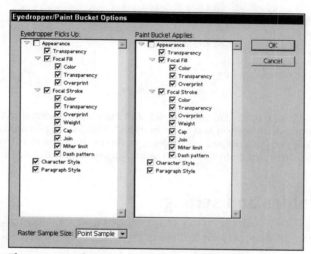

Figure 8-54: The Eyedropper/Paint Bucket Options dialog box

The attributes that are picked up by the Eyedropper tool and applied using the Paint Bucket tool may include Appearance attributes such as Transparency, Fill Color, Stroke Color, Stroke Weight, Cap and Join Type, and even Character and Paragraph Style. If you hold down the Shift key, then only the color attribute is gathered. You can also gather color from the computer's desktop using the Eyedropper tool by clicking and holding in the Illustrator document window and then dragging around the desktop.

The Eyedropper/Paint Bucket Options dialog box also lets you sample raster images using a point sample, a 3×3 pixel sample or a 5×5 pixel sample.

Note   The Option/Alt key lets you switch between the Eyedropper and Paint Bucket tools when one of them is selected.

Using InDesign's Eyedropper tool

The Eyedropper tool in InDesign works similar to the one in Illustrator, except it's used to both gather and apply the selected attributes. Double-clicking on the Eyedropper tool opens a dialog box of options, shown in Figure 8-55, that may be gathered using the Eyedropper tool.

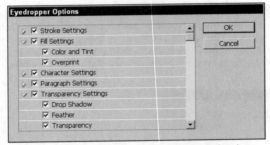

Figure 8-55: The Eyedropper Options dialog box in InDesign

Clicking on an object gathers all the attributes for that object, and the cursor changes so the eyedropper is pointing in the opposite direction and appears to be filled. Clicking on another object applies the attributes. You can click on multiple objects while the Eyedropper is filled. To fill the Eyedropper with new attributes, hold down the Option/Alt key while clicking on another object.

Managing color profiles and settings

Adobe understands all the issues surrounding color and has endowed the CS applications with color-management methods including a Color Settings dialog box accessed under the Edit menu.

This dialog box, shown for Photoshop in Figure 8-56, lets you select from several different color setting profiles. Using the same profile for all applications produces consistent color output regardless of the application or system. Some of these color setting profiles include North America General Purpose Defaults, U.S. Prepress Defaults, Web Graphics Defaults, as well as profiles for Europe and Japan.

The Color Settings dialog box also lets you define a custom color profile. Custom profiles may be saved and loaded for use across applications.

Cross-Reference   The Color Management features found in the various CS applications are covered in Chapter 6.

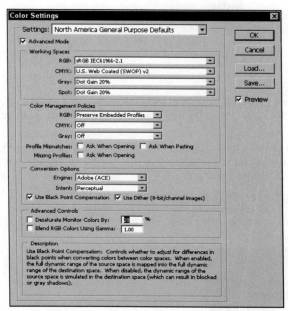

Figure 8-56: The Color Settings dialog box lets you select a default color profile.

Working with Gradients

When a light source shines on an object, the point closest to the light is usually the brightest and the light intensity gradually decreases the further you get away from the light. This decrease in light intensity over distance is called *attenuation,* and it's common for most light sources (the Sun being an exception to this principle).

Simple light attenuation may be simulated in Illustrator and Photoshop using gradients. Gradients let you specify two or more colors, and the gradient interpolates between these two colors by gradually changing between the specified colors.

Using the Gradient palette

In addition to color, gradients may be applied as an object fill by clicking on the Gradient button in the Toolbox or by clicking on the gradient in the Gradient palette. The Gradient palette, shown in Figure 8-57, includes controls for specifying gradient colors and behavior.

Figure 8-57: The Gradient palette lets you create custom gradients.

You can expand the Gradient palette in Illustrator and InDesign to show some additional controls including a Type drop-down list, which includes two gradient Types including Linear and Radial.

Linear gradients run in a straight line from the color specified at one end of the gradient to the color specified at the other end. For Linear gradients, you can specify an Angle value, which determines the direction that the gradient runs.

Radial gradients place the gradient color specified at one end of the Gradient palette at a specified point and the changing colors are displayed as concentric circles around this designated point. Figure 8-58 shows an example of a linear and a radial gradient.

Linear gradient

Radial gradient

Figure 8-58: Linear and radial gradients are uniquely different from each other.

The color bar at the bottom of the Gradient palette lets you specify gradient colors and the midpoints between those colors. The color stop icons appear below the gradient bar; the midpoint markers appear as diamond icons above the gradient bar. To change the position of either of these icons, drag them to the left or right. The position of the icon is displayed in the Location field as a percentage of the entire gradient.

To change the color of a color stop, select the color stop and choose a new color from the Color palette. When a color stop is selected, the small arrow above it turns black.

Note

You can select a color swatch to use in the gradient color stop by holding down the Option/Alt key while clicking on a color swatch, or you can drag swatch colors to the gradient color stops. But if you select a gradient color stop and click on a color swatch, the color in the swatch is selected and the gradient goes away.

To add new color stops to a gradient, click below the gradient bar where you want to position the new color stop, drag a color swatch from the Swatches palette to the gradient bar, or hold down the Option/Alt key and drag an existing color stop to the side. A new midpoint icon is added for each new color stop that is added.

Using the Gradient tool

Although the Angle may be specified for Linear gradients in the Gradient palette, the Gradient tool (found in the Toolbox) is useful for interactively specifying the gradient angle. With the gradient tool selected, click on a selected object where you want to position the leftmost gradient color and drag to where you want to place the rightmost gradient color. This lets you control precisely how the gradient runs across an object.

If the line that is dragged with the gradient tool lies at an angle, the Angle value is set accordingly. Holding down the Shift key while dragging constrains the angle to 45-degree increments.

The Gradient tool may also be used to cause a single gradient to span multiple objects. To do this, select all the objects and apply a gradient fill to them, then drag with the Gradient tool across the selected objects.

STEPS: Creating and Applying a Custom Gradient

1. **Open an Illustrator document.** With Illustrator open, choose File ⇨ New to create a new document. Select the Star tool and drag in the art board to create a star object.

2. **Apply a radial gradient.** With the star selected, click on the Gradient button at the bottom of the Toolbox. Then in the Gradient palette, select the Radial type. The star is filled with a radial gradient, as shown in Figure 8-59.

3. **Change the gradient colors.** With the Swatches palette and the Gradient palette opened at the same time, drag a bright yellow color swatch from the Swatches palette to the first color stop at the left end of the gradient bar in the Gradient palette. Then drag a red color swatch from the Swatches palette to the last color stop at the right end of the gradient bar in the Gradient palette. The colors are immediately applied to the star, as shown in Figure 8-60.

Figure 8-59: Selecting the Radial type applies a radial gradient to the object using its center as an endpoint for the gradient.

Figure 8-60: Dragging colors from the Swatches palette to the gradient bar color stops changes the colors applied to the gradient.

4. **Add a new gradient color stop.** Click under the middle of the gradient bar to create a new color stop. This new color stop uses the intermediate color from the gradient bar. Drag a black color swatch from the Swatches palette to the new color stop in the Gradient palette. The new color stop changes the color applied to the star dramatically, as shown in Figure 8-61.

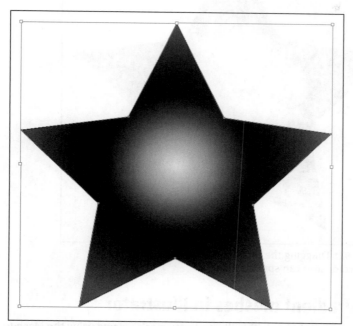

Figure 8-61: Clicking under the gradient bar adds a new color stop to the gradient bar.

5. **Reduce the black color stop spread.** To reduce the spreading color of the black color stop, select the midpoint icons above the gradient bar on either side of the black color stop and drag them toward the black color stop. This limits the spread of the black color within the gradient, as shown in Figure 8-62.

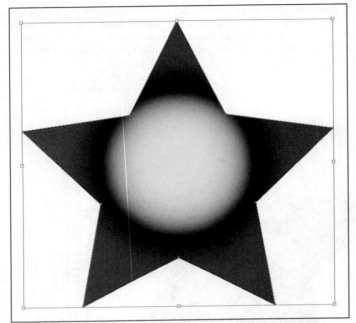

Figure 8-62: Dragging the midpoint icons changes how far a gradient color stop can spread its color.

Creating gradient meshes in Illustrator

You can change vector objects within Illustrator to mesh objects using the Mesh tool or the Object ➪ Create Gradient Mesh menu command. Mesh objects are divided into rows and columns with editable points located at each intersection. A gradient color stop may also be positioned at each intersecting point. Choosing Object ➪ Create Gradient Mesh opens a dialog box, shown in Figure 8-63, where you can specify the number of rows and columns to divide the object into.

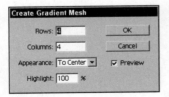

Figure 8-63: The Create Gradient Mesh dialog box

The Appearance drop-down list includes Flat, To Center, and To Edge options. The Flat option colors the entire object with a single fill color. The To Center option adds a white highlight at the center of the object that gradually changes to the fill color at the edges. The To Edge places a white highlight at the object's edges that gradually changes to the object's fill color at its center. The Highlight percentage sets how white the highlight color is.

Caution Mesh objects in Illustrator take up a lot of system resources and can greatly slow down your system if they're overly complex. It's best to keep mesh objects simple.

Figure 8-64 shows three simple rectangles that have been converted to meshes by choosing Object ➪ Create Gradient Mesh. The top mesh object uses the Flat appearance option, the middle one uses the To Center appearance option, and the bottom one uses the To Edges appearance option.

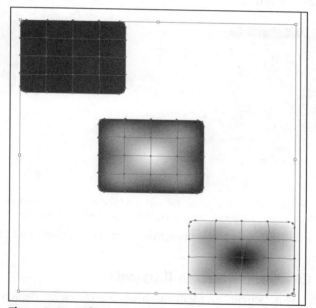

Figure 8-64: Selecting an Appearance option applies a highlight to a mesh.

The Mesh tool is used to place the intersecting mesh points within an object. After clicking to place an intersecting point on an object, you can choose a color from the Color palette to apply as a gradient color for the new intersecting point. Clicking again on the object with the Mesh tool creates another new intersecting mesh point. Holding down the Shift key while clicking on an object creates an intersecting mesh point without changing its fill color.

Objects that have a gradient fill applied to them may be expanded to a gradient mesh object with the Object ➪ Expand menu command. This opens a dialog box where you can select to expand the gradient to a Gradient Mesh object. Mesh object points may be selected and moved using the Direct Selection tool. You can change mesh point colors by dragging a color to a mesh point or apply a color using the Paint Bucket tool.

Working with Patterns

In addition to colors and gradients, Photoshop and Illustrator can use patterns to fill objects or paint onto images. Patterns are used differently in both these applications.

Using patterns in Illustrator

Patterns may be selected from the Swatches palette and applied as an object fill. Any artwork may be used as a new pattern by simply dragging the artwork to the Swatches palette or by selecting the artwork and choosing Edit ➪ Define Pattern. This opens a dialog box, shown in Figure 8-65, where you can name the pattern.

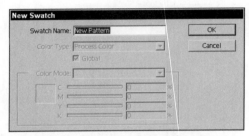

Figure 8-65: Choosing Edit ➪ Define Pattern creates a new swatch.

To add some spacing behind the pattern, drag a rectangle with its fill and stroke colors set to None, arrange this object as the backmost object, and include it as part of the pattern.

If the pattern fills an object that is larger than the pattern, then the pattern is tiled to fill the entire shape.

STEPS: Creating a Custom Pattern in Illustrator

1. **Open an Illustrator document.** With Illustrator open, choose File ➪ New to create a new document.

2. **Create a background area.** Select the Rectangle tool and drag in the art board to create a rectangle object that is the size of the pattern that you want to create. With the background object selected, set its Fill and Stroke to None.

3. **Add shapes to the pattern area.** Select the Ellipse tool and drag several small circles within the background square with the Shift key held down to make them perfect circles. Set each circle to have a different fill color, as shown in Figure 8-66.

4. **Resize the background square.** After creating all the pattern objects, select the background square object and resize it to fit all the objects within it.

5. **Define the pattern.** Drag over all the objects including the background square and all the colored circles, and choose Edit ➪ Define Pattern. In the New Swatch dialog box, name the new swatch and click OK. The new pattern is added to the Swatches palette.

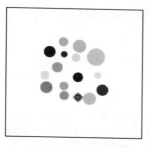

Figure 8-66: Patterns may be created using the Illustrator tools.

6. **Test the pattern.** Select the Rectangle tool and drag in the art board to create a rectangle that is larger than the pattern. Then click on the pattern swatch in the Swatches palette and the new pattern is applied to rectangle, as shown in Figure 8-67.

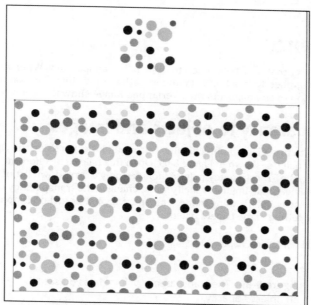

Figure 8-67: Apply new patterns to an object to see how the pattern tiles.

Using patterns in Photoshop

Patterns show up on the Options bar when the Paint Bucket, Pattern Stamp, Healing Brush, and Patch tools are selected. By clicking on the Pattern pop-up, you can access several default patterns, shown in Figure 8-68. The pop-up palette also includes a palette menu that you can use to create new patterns, load and save pattern sets, and access different pattern sets.

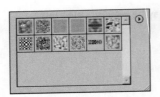

Figure 8-68: The Pattern pop-up palette displays a library of default patterns.

New patterns are created by selecting a portion of the image with the Rectangular Marquee tool and choosing Edit ➪ Define Pattern. This opens a dialog box where you can name the pattern. To apply a pattern to a selected area using the Edit, Fill menu command and select the Pattern option in the Fill dialog box or use the Pattern Overlay layer style.

Cross-Reference   Patterns may also be created in Photoshop by choosing Filter ➪ Pattern Maker. This opens a window where you can select and preview patterns. This window and the other filters are covered in Chapter 10.

Using Transparency

Another common property that may be applied to objects is transparency. When an object has some transparency applied to it, all objects underneath it are visible. For example, placing transparent text on top of an image lets the overlapped image show through the text.

Applying transparency to objects and images

Transparency is applied to the selected object in Illustrator and InDesign using the Opacity setting in the Transparency palette, shown in Figure 8-69. Open this palette by choosing Window ➪ Transparency. By default, the Transparency palette includes only a drop-down list of blending modes and an Opacity value. Changing the Opacity value changes the transparency of the selected object using the selected blending mode. Transparency in Photoshop is applied to layers using the Opacity setting in the Layers palette.

Cross-Reference   Layers are covered in detail in Chapter 11.

Figure 8-69: The Transparency palette lets you set an object's opacity.

Changing the Opacity value in the Transparency palette applies transparency to the selected object's fill and stroke. This value is then listed at the bottom of the Appearance palette, but you can apply different transparency values to the fill and stroke by selecting each in the Appearance palette prior to changing the Opacity value in the Transparency palette. The Opacity value for the fill or stroke is listed under each in the Appearance palette.

Selecting the Show Thumbnails palette menu command expands the palette to reveal a thumbnail of the selected object. The Show Options palette menu command reveals some additional options at the bottom of the palette.

Using blending modes

When you apply transparency to an object, the colors of the object positioned underneath the object blend together. Choosing a blending mode defines how the blend color and the base color are blended together. The *blend color* is the color of the overlaid object; the *base color* is the color of the underlying object.

The blending modes color object by:

✦ **Normal:** Using the blend color.

✦ **Darken:** Using either the base or blend color depending on which is darker. This is the opposite of the Lighten mode.

✦ **Multiply:** Multiplying the base and blend colors resulting in a darker color. Any color multiplied by white doesn't change the color and multiplying any color with black produces black. This is the opposite of the Screen mode.

✦ **Color Burn:** Darkening the base color. This is the opposite of the Color Dodge mode.

✦ **Lighten:** Using either the base or blend color depending on which is darker. This is the opposite of the Darken mode.

✦ **Screen:** Multiplying the inverse of both the base and blend colors resulting in a lighter color. Any color screened with black doesn't change the color, and screening any color with white produces white. This is the opposite of the Multiply mode.

✦ **Color Dodge:** Lightening the base color. This is the opposite of the Color Burn mode.

✦ **Overlay:** Mixing the base color with the blend color to lighten the highlights and darken the shadows.

✦ **Soft Light:** Lightening the light areas of the blend color and darkening the dark areas.

✦ **Hard Light:** Screening the light areas of the blend color and multiplying the dark areas of the base color.

✦ **Difference:** Subtracting the lighter of the base or blend colors from the other.

✦ **Exclusion:** Removing all the light value of the base or blend colors from the other.

✦ **Hue:** Colors the object using the luminance and saturation values of the base color and the hue of the blend color.

✦ **Saturation:** Colors the object using the luminance and hue values of the base color and the saturation of the blend color.

✦ **Color:** Using the luminance of the base color and the hue and saturation of the blend color. This is the opposite of the Luminosity mode.

✦ **Luminosity:** Using the hue and saturation values of the base color and the luminance of the blend color. This is the opposite of the Color mode.

Figure 8-70 shows examples of all the blending modes.

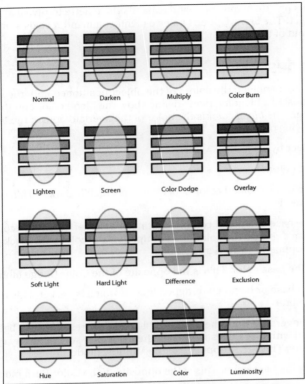

Figure 8-70: Side-by-side comparisons of all the different blending modes is helpful in understanding how they work.

Creating an opacity mask

An *opacity mask* is used to define how much transparency is applied to the objects on the linked layer. The white areas on the opacity mask have no transparency applied, but black areas are fully transparent. Gray areas are partially transparent.

To make an opacity mask, select two objects and choose the Make Opacity Mask palette menu command. The top object is used as the opacity mask, and the bottom objects are objects that are affected by the opacity mask.

In the thumbnail section of the Transparency palette, the objects that are affected by the opacity mask are displayed to the left, and the opacity mask is displayed to the right. The Clip option causes the opacity mask to act also as a clipping mask and the Invert Mask option inverts the opacity mask, making the transparent areas opaque and vice versa. Figure 8-71 shows an example of an opacity mask. The snapshots in the Transparency palette show the objects used to determine the transparency of the objects below.

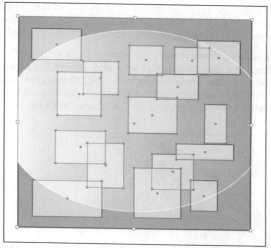

Figure 8-71: The colors in the opacity mask determine which objects are visible below.

STEPS: Creating an Opacity Mask

1. **Open an Illustrator document.** With Illustrator open, choose File ➪ New to create a new document.

2. **Create an object to mask.** Drag a symbol object on the art board from the Symbols palette and resize it to fit the art board. The resized object is shown in Figure 8-72.

Figure 8-72: This symbol is fully opaque with no transparency applied.

3. **Draw a mask object.** Select the Rectangle tool and drag it over the top of the symbol. With the fill box selected, choose the Gradient button in the Toolbox to apply a linear gradient to the rectangle. Make sure the rectangle is positioned above the symbol.

4. **Select all objects and create an opacity mask.** Drag over both objects with the Selection tool to select them. Open the Transparency palette and choose the Make Opacity Mask palette menu command. The symbol object and the gradient rectangle both show up as thumbnails in the Transparency palette; the black portions of the gradient mark where the underlying symbol is transparent, as shown in Figure 8-73.

Figure 8-73: Using the opacity mask, the butterfly gradually changes from transparent to opaque.

Using Symbols, Styles, and Swatches

All the CS applications make use of libraries. Open your favorite Creative Suite application, and you'll find libraries of symbols, styles, swatches, and brushes. Libraries are used to store any feature that has a lot of settings, allowing you to recall the settings at an instant without having to enter all the settings again. Across the various CS applications, creating and using library items are consistent whether you're dealing with brushes, styles, symbols, or swatches.

Many of the CS applications include many default libraries that you can open and use. For example, Illustrator's Window menu includes submenus of brushes, styles, swatches, and symbol libraries, and Photoshop includes default libraries of swatches, styles, and brushes that may be selected from the various palette menus.

Working with symbols in Illustrator

Symbols in Illustrator are a special type of object with a key advantage — reuse. If you add a symbol to a document and then reuse elsewhere in the same document, a new copy isn't required, because the symbol references the first object. This makes symbols very convenient to work with because adding hundreds of symbols to a single document doesn't dramatically increase the overall file size.

Cross-Reference Reference symbols are particularly useful for files viewed on the Web, such as SWF and SVG files. These file types are discussed in Chapter 32.

Accessing symbol libraries

Symbols are stored in libraries, and Illustrator includes several default symbol libraries that you may access by choosing Window ➪ Symbol Libraries or the Open Symbol Library palette menu command off the Symbols palette. Symbol libraries appear in their own custom palette when opened. Selecting the Persistent palette menu option causes the palette to open automatically when Illustrator starts.

In addition to the symbol libraries, the Symbols palette, shown in Figure 8-74, includes several default symbols. All symbols that are included in the current document are displayed in the Symbols palette. These symbols are associated with the current document and are saved as part of the document.

 Tip To remove all symbols that aren't used in the current document from the Symbols palette, choose the Select All Unused palette menu command and then choose the Delete Symbol palette menu command.

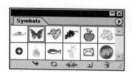 **Figure 8-74:** The Symbol palette holds symbol instances used in the document.

You add symbols to the Symbols palette by using the Add to Symbols palette menu command or by dragging the symbol to the Symbols palette. Also, any symbols selected from a symbol library are automatically added to the Symbols palette. You delete symbols in the Symbols palette with the Delete Symbol palette menu command or the trash can icon at the bottom of the palette. You can save all symbols in the Symbols palette to create a new symbol library using the Save Symbol Library palette menu command.

Inserting, editing, and creating symbols

From a symbol library or the Symbols palette, you can add a symbol to the current document by dragging it from the library to the art board, or by selecting the symbol and choosing the Place Symbol Instance palette menu command. Any symbols that are duplicated using the Option/Alt drag or the copy and paste methods are still symbol instances.

You can edit symbol instances by using the transform tools or by changing its color and style while still maintaining its symbol status. If more drastic editing is required, you can unlink a symbol using the Break Link to Symbol palette menu command. This command causes the symbol to be expanded.

You may add Illustrator artwork to the Symbols palette as a new symbol by simply dragging the selected object or group to the Symbols palette. You can also create a new symbol by selecting the artwork and choosing the New Symbol palette menu command or by clicking on the New Symbol icon at the bottom of the Symbols palette. Symbols may include vector, raster and type objects. To rename the new symbol, double-click on it in the Symbols palette. A Symbols Options dialog box appears, shown in Figure 8-75; here, you can type a new name for the symbol.

Figure 8-75: The Symbol Options
dialog box lets you rename symbols.

Using the Symbolism tools

You may use Illustrator's Symbolism tools to create a large number of symbols very quickly.
The various tools let you alter specific object properties such as size, rotation, color, and
style while creating a set of symbols.

The Symbolism tools include the following:

✦ **Symbol Sprayer:** Creates a set of symbols by dragging in the art board.

✦ **Symbol Shifter:** Moves symbols within a set relative to one another and to adjust the
stacking order.

✦ **Symbol Scruncher:** Changes the density of symbols within a set by pushing them
closer together or pushing them farther apart.

✦ **Symbol Sizer:** Increases or decreases the size of symbols within a set.

✦ **Symbol Spinner:** Rotates the symbols within a set.

✦ **Symbol Stainer:** Changes the colors of symbols within a set by adjusting their hue.

✦ **Symbol Screener:** Adjusts the transparency of symbols within a set.

✦ **Symbol Styler:** Applies a selected graphic style to symbols within a set.

With any of these tools selected, you can double-click on the tools to open the Symbolism
Tools Options dialog box, shown in Figure 8-76. Using this dialog box, you can set the diameter, intensity, and symbol set density. The Options dialog box also shows any shortcut keys
available for the various tools, such as holding down the Option/Alt key to reduce the size,
coloring, transparency, and style that is applied.

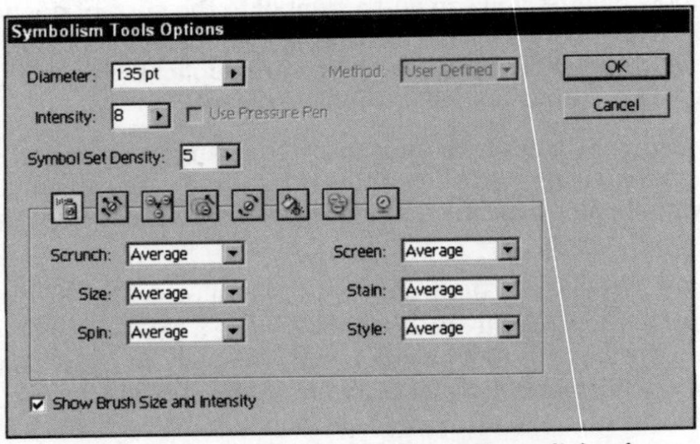

Figure 8-76: The Symbolism Tools Options dialog box

Figure 8-77 shows a simple example of the Symbol Sprayer tool created by selecting the fire symbol and dragging with the Symbol Sprayer over a path. After this set of symbols is created, you can use the other Symbolism tools to change the position, size, rotation, color, transparency, and style of the symbols in the set.

Figure 8-77: The Symbol Sprayer draws a path of symbol objects.

Working with styles in Illustrator

If you've tinkered with the appearance attributes applied to an object until it is perfect, you can save all these settings so they may be easily reapplied to other objects using styles. A *graphic style* is a collection of appearance settings stored within a library for easy recall.

Accessing style libraries

If you open Illustrator's Graphic Styles palette, shown in Figure 8-78, you'll see it contains several sample styles. To apply one of these styles to an object, just drag and drop it on the object.

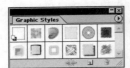

Figure 8-78: The Graphic Styles palette includes appearance attributes.

Illustrator includes, by default, several additional libraries of styles that you can access by choosing Window ➪ Graphic Style Libraries or by selecting the Open Graphic Style Library palette menu command in the Graphic Style palette. You may save the styles contained within the Graphic Styles palette as a new library using the Save Graphic Style Library palette menu command.

Photoshop also includes several default style libraries that are accessed from the Styles palette menu. To apply a style to the current canvas, simply click on the style in the Styles palette or drag it to the canvas. Opening a style library presents a dialog box where you can select to replace the current styles in the Styles palette with the new library or append them to the end of the palette.

Creating new styles

You add new styles to the Graphic Styles palette by selecting an object with a style that you want to add to the palette and choosing the New Graphic Style palette menu command or by clicking on the small New Graphic Style button at the bottom of the palette. Double-clicking on the style icon in the Graphic Style palette opens an Options dialog box where you can rename the selected style.

You can add custom styles to the Graphic Styles palette by dragging the Appearance icon at the top-left of the Appearance palette for the selected object to the Graphic Styles palette. Double-clicking on the style icon opens a dialog box where you can rename the style.

Working with swatches

If you've mixed and selected specific colors that you want to keep, you could write down the values for that color or you could add the color to the Swatches palette. Colors in the Swatches may be selected and applied to the Fill and Stroke boxes.

Using the Swatches palette

To add the current Fill or Stroke color to the Swatches palette, shown in Figure 8-79, simply drag the color from the Fill or Stroke box in the Toolbar to the Swatches palette or select the New Swatch palette menu command. If the New Swatch menu command is used, the New Swatch dialog box opens; here, you can name the new color swatch, specify the color type, and choose the color mode. The New Swatch dialog box also includes the values to specify a color depending on the selected color mode.

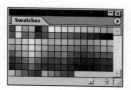

Figure 8-79: The Swatches palette holds colors, but in Illustrator it may also hold gradients and patterns.

Creating Custom Swatch libraries

Several default Swatch libraries are available by choosing Window ➪ Swatch Libraries; new swatch libraries may be created and saved. To create a new swatch library, choose the Save Swatch Library palette menu command. This opens a file dialog box where you can name the swatch library file. Swatch libraries use the AI file format just like standard Illustrator documents.

Note   Although the discussion of palettes in this section focuses on colors, you can also add and store gradients and patterns within swatch libraries. You use the buttons at the bottom of the Swatches palette to show only a single category of swatches.

You can also drag colors from the various swatch library palettes and dropped on the Swatches palette. Colors in the Swatches palette may be saved as a new swatch library using the Save Swatch Library palette menu command.

Using Photoshop's Preset Manager

Photoshop includes a clever way to manage all the various presets and libraries using a special dialog box called the Preset Manager, shown in Figure 8-80. This dialog box may be opened from most of the palette menus that include presets or libraries or by choosing Edit ➪ Preset Manager.

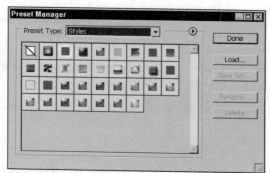

Figure 8-80: The Preset Manager dialog box in Photoshop

At the top of the dialog box is a drop-down list of the various preset types, including brushes, swatches, gradients, styles, patterns, contours, custom shapes, and tools. When a preset type is selected, its library of items is displayed. Using the palette menu, you can change how the items are displayed or choose one of the default libraries to open. The dialog box also includes buttons to load, save, rename, and delete the current sets.

Editing Objects

After you create objects, you have several ways to edit them. An object's position and orientation may be altered using the transformation tools, its properties may be changed using the various palettes such as Illustrator's Appearance palette, and filters and effects may be applied to change the object in many different ways.

Transformations are covered in Chapter 9. Applying filters and effects is covered in Chapter 10.

In addition to these editing methods, there are also several other ways to edit objects including joining, slicing, and cutting paths; blending objects; distorting objects; and using the Pathfinder features.

Editing paths in Illustrator

Paths are created by dragging with tools such as the Pen, Paintbrush, Pencil, and Line Segment tools, but there are also several tools that you may use to edit paths.

Using the Smooth and Erase tools

Drawing freehand paths with the Pencil tool often results in jagged lines, but these lines are easily smoothed over with the Smooth tool. The Smooth tool is a fly-out under the Pencil tool. Dragging over a freehand line with the Smooth tool gradually removes all the sharp changes in the line and smoothes it. Double-clicking on the Smooth tool opens a dialog box where you can set the Fidelity and Smoothness values for the tool. The Erase tool, a fly-out under the Pencil tool, may be used to delete a portion of the selected path. By dragging over the selected path with the Erase tool, the section that is dragged over is deleted.

Figure 8-81 shows a rough line drawn with the Pencil tool. The second line has been smoothed with the Smooth tool, and the portions of the last line were erased using the Erase tool.

You can select the Smooth tool by holding down the Option/Alt key when the Paintbrush or Pencil tool is selected.

Using the Reshape tool

The Reshape tool (located as a fly-out under the Scale tool) lets you select an anchor point, several anchor points, or a line segment as part of a path and drag it while maintaining the overall shape of the path. This causes the entire path to move along with the selected portion. By comparison, anchor points and line segments selected with the Direct Selection tool are moved independent of the entire path; the Scale tool moves all points equally in the scaled direction.

Figure 8-81: You use the Smooth and Erase tools to edit existing paths.

To select anchor points or line segments with the Reshape tool, simply click or drag over the portions of the path that you want to select. The relative distance between the selected points won't change as you drag the path; adjacent anchor points move in proportion to the distance from the selected points.

Figure 8-82 shows three duplicate paths. The left line was drawn with the Pencil tool. The middle path is a duplicate that was scaled horizontally, and the right path is a duplicate that was modified using the Reshape tool. Notice how the scaled path is distorted, while the reshaped path maintains its path details.

Figure 8-82: The Reshape tool can bend a path while maintaining its details.

Other methods to editing paths

The following is a list of other ways to edit paths:

✦ **Splitting paths:** You can use the Scissors tool to cut a path in two. You don't need the path to split it. The location where you click with the Scissors tool determines where the path is split.

✦ **Joining and averaging paths:** If the endpoints of two different paths are selected with the Direct Selection tool, you can make a straight line connect these two endpoints by choosing Object ➪ Path ➪ Join (⌘/Ctrl+J). The Object ➪ Path ➪ Average (Alt+Ctrl+J in Windows; Option+⌘+J on the Mac) menu command is also used to connect the endpoints of two paths, but instead of a straight line, this command opens a simple dialog box where you can select to move the endpoints to an average Horizontal, Vertical or Both position. After two paths are joined or averaged, they become a single closed shape.

✦ **Converting strokes to filled objects:** You can convert strokes into filled objects by choosing Object ➪ Path ➪ Outline Stroke.

✦ **Offsetting paths:** Choosing Object ➪ Path ➪ Offset Path opens a dialog box, shown in Figure 8-83, where you can specify an offset distance and a join type. The join types are the same as those in the Strokes palette, namely Miter (with a Miter Limit value), Round, and Bevel. This command may be used on open or closed paths. A positive Offset value offsets each point of the path outward; a negative Offset value offsets the path points for a closed shape inward.

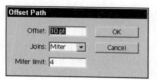

Figure 8-83: The Offset Path dialog box

Simplifying and cleaning up paths

Cleaning up a document reduces the file size. Choosing Object ➪ Path ➪ Simplify opens a dialog box, shown in Figure 8-84, where you can specify settings that reduce the path's complexity by eliminating unneeded anchor points. The Curve Precision value sets the amount that the path may change during the simplification process. A value of 100% requires that the original path be fully maintained.

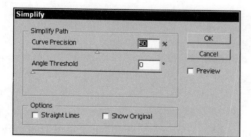

Figure 8-84: The Simplify dialog box lets you define how radically a path is simplified.

The Angle Threshold value determines the corner smoothness. If the angle of a corner point is less than the Angle Threshold value, the corner isn't smoothed.

Tip When you enable the Preview option, the total number of points in the original and simplified curves are displayed.

The Straight Lines option simplifies the curve using only straight lines; the Show Original option displays the original line in the art board.

Choosing Object ➪ Path ➪ Clean Up opens a dialog box, shown in Figure 8-85, where you can select to eliminate stray points, unpainted objects, and empty text paths. Stray points can appear by clicking once with the Pen tool, which typically happens when you click to select on object when the Pen tool is selected instead of the Selection tool. Unpainted objects are objects with None set for both the fill and stroke. Empty text paths are created by clicking on the art board with the Type tool.

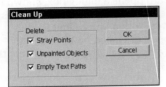

Figure 8-85: The Clean Up dialog box lets you select which cleanup objects to delete.

Splitting objects into grids

With a closed object selected, you can choose Object ➪ Path ➪ Split into Grids, which opens a dialog box, shown in Figure 8-86, where you can specify the number of rows and columns of a grid. You can also specify the height, width, gutter, and total dimensions of the grid cells. The Add Guides option creates guides for the top and bottom of each row and column, letting you change all the cells in a single row or column quickly.

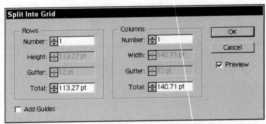

Figure 8-86: The Split into Grid dialog box divides a closed path into grid cells.

Cutting objects

Sometimes shape editing calls for removing or separating a portion of an object. There are several ways to split an object:

Note　You use the Slice tool to separate images and objects into slices. Each slice can hold vector or raster sections. By slicing documents, you can move them to the Web as separate files that work together.

✦ **Using the Knife tool:** The Knife tool (located as a fly-out tool under the Scissors tool) is a freehand tool that cuts through a selected object. Objects split where you drag the tool. Holding down the Option/Alt key drags a straight line.

✦ **Cutting holes in shapes:** You can use closed shapes as a cookie cutter to punch out the selected shape from all the objects beneath it. To do this, position the cutting object on top of the object that you want to cut, and choose Object ➪ Path ➪ Divide Object Below.

Creating compound paths and shapes in Illustrator

Compound objects are created when two or more selected paths or shapes are combined to create a single object. Compound objects are different from grouping objects. Objects within a group may have different attributes, but all the paths or shapes in a compound object share the same appearance attributes. Even though compound objects are combined to make a single object, the individual items may still be selected using the Direct Selection or Group Selection tools, just like groups. Compound objects may be restored to their original components using the Release menu command.

Creating compound paths

You can combine two or more paths into a compound path by choosing Object ➪ Compound Path ➪ Make (⌘/Ctrl+8). When paths are combined to create a compound path, the paths create a single path and a hole is left in the fill where the two paths were overlapped. Whenever paths are combined to create a compound path, the appearance attributes of the bottommost object are applied to the resulting path.

Using Pathfinder features

In addition to compound paths, Illustrator can create compound shapes using the Pathfinder palette, shown in Figure 8-87. Open this palette by choosing Window ➪ Pathfinder (Shift+F9). Selected objects are made into a compound shape using the Make Compound Shape palette menu command. This eliminates all the interior paths and combines all the shapes into a single compound shape.

Figure 8-87: The Pathfinder palette includes shape modes.

In addition to the palette menu command, you can also use the icon buttons found in the Pathfinder palette to add to the shape area, subtract from the shape area, intersect shape areas, or exclude overlapping shape areas. The Subtract button removes from the first object all shape areas that overlap the first object. The Intersect button leaves only those areas that are common to all selected shapes. The Exclude button removes all areas of the objects that overlap another shape.

After a compound shape is created, you can change the shape mode for any of the objects that make up the compound shape by selecting it with the Direct Selection tool and choosing a new button in the Pathfinder palette.

Whenever objects are combined to create a compound shape, the appearance attributes of the topmost object are applied to the compound object.

Note   Compound shapes use the appearance attributes of the topmost shape. Compound paths use the appearance attributes of the bottommost path.

Blending objects in Illustrator

The Blend tool (W) may be used to morph the shape, path, color, or style of one object to another. To use this tool, click on an object and then on a second object to blend to. Several intermediate objects appear between the two objects. Figure 8-88 shows a blend that moves between different shapes, strokes, and fills.

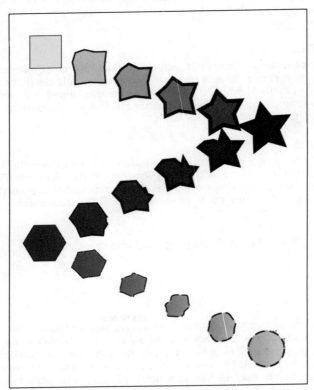

Figure 8-88: Blends can interpolate shapes, strokes, fills, and styles.

Blend objects are selected as a single object, but you may select individual objects that make up a blend object by using the Direct Selection tool. Changing a selected shape or color of either of the objects that make up the blend also updates the intermediate objects.

Double-clicking on the Blend tool opens the Blend Options dialog box, shown in Figure 8-89, where you can select a Spacing option of Smooth Color, Specified Steps, or Specified Distance. When the Smooth Color option is selected, Illustrator determines the number of steps needed to make a smooth color transition between the two blend objects. For the Specified Steps and Specified Distance options, you can enter the number of steps or the distance between each step.

The Blend Options dialog box also lets you set the Orientation to be either Align to Page or Align to Path. The Align to Page option orients all the blend objects relative to the art board; the Align to Path option orients the blend objects relative to the blend's spine path.

Figure 8-89: The Blend Options dialog box lets you define the number of steps between each blend object.

When a blend is made between two objects, a straight path connects the two objects. With the Direct Selection tool, you can select this path and add anchor points to it with the Add Anchor Point tool or by choosing Object ➪ Path ➪ Add Anchor Points. Dragging these new anchor points gives you control over how the path moves. As the path is altered, all the intermediate objects that are part of the blend follow the path.

In addition to the Blend tool, you can also blend two selected objects by choosing Object ➪ Blend ➪ Make (Alt+Ctrl+B in Windows; Option+⌘+B on the Mac). Blended objects may also be undone by choosing Object ➪ Blend ➪ Release (Alt+Shift+Ctrl+B in Windows; Option+Shift+⌘+B on the Mac). Choosing Object ➪ Blend ➪ Expand separates all the intermediate objects from the blend object and makes them independent, editable objects.

The line connecting two blend objects is called the *spine*. You may choose Object ➪ Blend ➪ Reverse Spine or choose Object ➪ Blend ➪ Reverse Front to Back to change the direction and stacking order of the blend objects. If a separate path is selected along with the blend, choosing Object ➪ Blend ➪ Replace Spine causes the blend to use the new selected path instead of the straight line spine.

Creating a clipping mask in Illustrator

A clipping mask is a closed object positioned over the top of objects that are to be clipped. With all these objects selected, choosing Object ➪ Clipping Mask ➪ Make (⌘/Ctrl+7) causes the top object to hide all the objects underneath. The clipping mask may be undone by choosing Object ➪ Clipping Mask ➪ Release (Alt+Ctrl+7 in Windows; Option+⌘+7 on the Mac).

Distorting objects in Illustrator

There are several different ways to distort objects with the Liquify tools and with Envelope Distort commands.

Using the Liquify tools

Illustrator includes several tools that you may use to distort selected objects. You use these tools by dragging over the selected objects with the selected tool. The longer you drag with the selected tool, the greater the effect. Figure 8-90 shows a simple circle that has been distorted using each of these Liquify tools. These tools collectively are called the Liquify tools and include the following:

✦ **Warp tool (Shift+R):** Stretches object paths by pushing or pulling them.

✦ **Twirl tool:** Causes paths to be twirled.

✦ **Pucker tool:** Sucks paths towards the cursor.

✦ **Bloat tool:** Pushes path edges away from the cursor.

✦ **Scallop tool:** Adds arcs and barbs to a path edge.

✦ **Crystallize tool:** Adds spikes to path edges.

✦ **Wrinkle tool:** Wrinkles the edge paths with details.

Cross-Reference   Most of the available Liquify tools may also be applied as filters and effects, which are covered in Chapter 10.

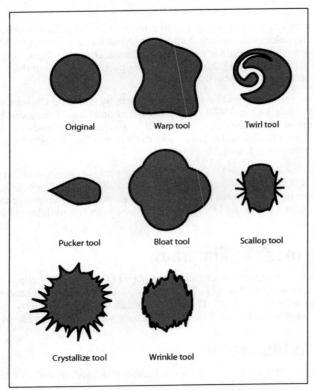

Figure 8-90: The Liquify tools provide several unique ways to distort objects.

Double-clicking on the tool opens a dialog box of options, like the Pucker Tool Options dialog box, shown in Figure 8-91. Using this dialog box, you can set the Width, Height, Angle, and Intensity of the tool's brush. You can also set the individual settings for the selected tool. The Show Brush Size option changes the cursor to an outline of the brush.

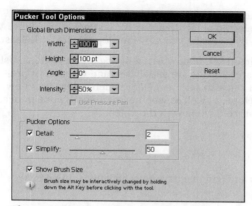

Figure 8-91: The settings for the various Liquify tools

Using the Envelope Distort command in Illustrator

Envelopes are preset or selected shapes into which object is distorted to fit inside. Choosing Object ⇨ Envelope Distort ⇨ Make with Warp (Alt+Shift+Ctrl+W in Windows; Option+Shift+⌘+W on the Mac) opens a dialog box of preset envelope shapes, shown in Figure 8-92, including Arc, Arc Lower, Arc Upper, Arch, Bulge, Shell Lower, Shell Upper, Flag, Wave, Fish, Rise, Fisheye, Inflate, Squeeze, and Twist.

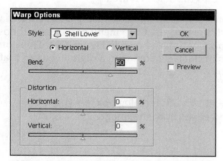

Figure 8-92: The Warp Options dialog box

Most of these preset envelope shapes are applied horizontally or vertically by a certain Bend amount. You can also specify the Horizontal and Vertical Distortion amounts.

You apply the envelope is as an editable mesh by moving its points with the Direct Selection tool. To apply a mesh to the selected object with a specified number of rows and columns, choose Object ⇨ Envelope Distort ⇨ Make with Mesh (Alt+Ctrl+M in Windows; Option+⌘+M on the Mac). This opens a dialog box where you can enter the number of mesh rows and columns.

Choosing Object ➪ Envelope Distort ➪ Make with Top Object (Alt+Ctrl+C in Windows; Option+⌘+C on the Mac) causes the top selected object to act as the distortion envelope. Any selected distortion envelopes are released by choosing Object ➪ Envelope Distort ➪ Release.

Choosing Object ➪ Envelope Distort ➪ Envelope Options opens a dialog box of options. Using these options, you can specify whether raster objects are antialiased and whether to preserve clipping masks or transparency. You can also set the *fidelity,* which determines how well the selected object fits within its envelope, as well as whether an object's appearance, linear gradients and/or pattern fills are distorted along with the object.

Editing Images

Just as when editing objects, several tools and commands are useful when editing images.

Cropping images in Photoshop

Image sizes are set when a document is first created or loaded into Photoshop, but you can cut out a portion of the image using the Crop tool or the Crop and Trim commands found in the Image menu.

✦ **Using the Crop tool:** With the Crop tool (C), you can drag on the portion of an image that you want to keep. This selected area is marked with a bounding box that is moved, scaled, and rotated by dragging on the handles at their edges and corners. When the crop area is correctly positioned and oriented, double-click with the Crop tool within the selected area, click the Commit button on the Options bar or press the Return/Enter key, and the image is cropped to the selected area.

✦ **Cropping and trimming an image:** You may also crop an image using a selection made with one of the default selection tools with the Image ➪ Crop menu command. Choosing Image ➪ Trim opens a dialog box of trimming options, shown in Figure 8-93. This command is useful for editing scanned images or images taken with a digital camera that include a border of color that you want to trim.

Figure 8-93: The Trim dialog box lets you trim unneeded edges from the image.

The Transparent Pixels option trims all the transparent pixels along the image edges. The Top Left Pixel Color and Bottom Right Pixel Color options trim all pixels that match the color of the top-left or bottom-right pixels. You can also select to trim just along the top, bottom, left, or right of an image.

Retouching images in Photoshop

Photoshop includes many tools to retouch an image. Most of these tools redistribute pixels by moving or copying pixels to other places within the same image. The tools used to retouch images include the Clone Stamp tool, the Pattern Stamp tool, the Healing Brush tool, the Patch tool, and the Color Replacement tool.

Using the Stamp tools

Two different Stamp tools are available in Photoshop, including the Clone Stamp tool and the Pattern Stamp tool.

The Clone Stamp tool allows you to paint pixels copied from a selected area to another area in the image. With the Clone Stamp tool selected, you can choose a brush tip and blending mode to use in the Options bar. Then hold down the Option/Alt key and click in the image to mark the area that you want to clone pixels from and paint in the area where you want to clone the pixels to.

If the Aligned option is selected, the pixels relative to the marked area are copied for every painted stroke. If the Aligned option is disabled, then every new stroke starts painting from the marked area.

The Pattern Stamp tool works just like the Clone Stamp tool, except it lets you paint with the pattern selected in the Options bar.

Using the Healing Brush and Patch tools

The Healing Brush tool, like the Clone Stamp tool, lets you select an area of pixels where the painted pixels are taken from using the Option/Alt key. But the Healing Brush tool matches the surrounding pixels where they're painted, making the pixels blend in with the image. This tool is great for removing small imperfections from a scanned image or a digital photo.

The Patch tool can also copy an area of pixels to another area in the image, and the moved pixels are blended into their new area matching the surrounding pixels. With the Patch tool, you can drag to select a freehand area like the Lasso tool. You can add to the selection by dragging with the Shift key held down or remove from the selection by dragging with the Option/Alt key held down. Holding down the Shift+Option/Alt keys while dragging over the selection keeps only the intersected selection. You can also change the selection area using the Add, Subtract, and Intersection buttons on the Options bar.

After a selection is made, you can choose the Source option in the Options bar and drag from within the selection. This projects the area under the cursor to the selected area, and if you release the mouse, the displayed pixels are copied to the selected area.

If the Destination option in the Options bar is enabled, then you can drag the selected area to the pixels that you want to cover. Each time the mouse is released, the dragged area is copied over the area that it's on top of. Dragging and releasing the mouse lets you replace many areas quickly.

Using the Color Replacement tool

The Color Replacement tool may be used to replace a selected color with the foreground color. The Mode options let you choose to replace pixels based on Hue, Saturation, Color, or Luminosity. The Sampling options let you replace the pixels continuously, just once, or using the background swatch color to replace the background color with the foreground color.

The Limits options include Discontiguous, which replaces any colors that you paint over; Contiguous, which only paints connected areas of color; and Find Edges, which also replaces only connected areas of color but keeps the edges sharp.

Using the Eraser tools

Photoshop includes three different eraser tools used to remove pixels. The Erase tool removes pixels revealing the background color underneath. The Mode options let you choose a smooth edged brush, a hard-edged pencil, or a square block, which is useful to get the sharp corner areas. You can also set the opacity and flow to use as you erase. The Erase to History option removes all changes applied to an image, leaving the base saved image when enabled.

The Background Eraser tool is used to replace the background of an image with transparency. When you drag with this tool, the color that is immediately under the center of the tool is sampled and removed from the areas where you paint, but the other colors and the edges of the images are retained.

The Magic Eraser tool works like the Magic Wand tool, letting you click on a background color that you want to erase. All connected pixels (if the Contiguous option is enabled) are erased, or all similar pixels in the entire image are deleted (if the Contiguous option is disabled).

Distorting images

Another useful way to edit images is to distort the pixels using the various distorting tools. These tools include the Smudge tool, the Blur tool, the Sharpen tool, the Dodge tool, the Burn tool, and the Sponge tool.

Cross-Reference   The effects of these pixel distortion tools may also be accomplished using the various Filters, which are covered in Chapter 10.

✦ **Smudge tool:** Used to smear the color of several pixels together like wiping wet paint across the canvas. This tool lets you choose from several different modes and a Strength value. The Finger Painting option uses the foreground color as you begin to smear the pixels.

✦ **The Blur and Sharpen tools:** Are the opposite of each other. The Blur tool softens hard edges and reduces details, and the Sharpen tool makes edges harder and more pronounced.

✦ **Dodge and Burn tools:** Used, respectively, to lighten and darken the pixels of an image. For each tool, you can set the Range to lighten or darken the highlights, the midtones, or the shadows.

✦ **Sponge tool:** Increase or decrease the saturation of pixels in the image. For this tool, you can select a brush tip, a Flow amount, and a Mode to be either Saturate or Desaturate.

✦ **History Brush and Art History tools:** As you make changes to an image, you may want to return to the original image, but only in one section. The History Brush lets you paint over pixels and replace the painted area with the pixel from the saved image file.

The Art History brush, like the History Brush tool, replaces the painted pixels with pixels from the original saved image file, but it paints them using a specialized Style simulating various famous artistic painting methods. These styles include Tight Short, Tight Medium, Tight Long, Loose Medium, Loose Long, Dab, Tight Curl, Tight Curl Long, Loose Curl, and Loose Curl Long.

Summary

✦ You can create and use objects in all the various CS applications. To create objects, tools and menu commands are used.

✦ Tools that create objects include the Pen, Type, Line Segment tools, and shape tools. You create freehand path objects with the Paintbrush and Pencil tools. The Paintbrush, Pencil, and Paint Bucket tools apply paint to the canvas in Photoshop.

✦ All CS applications include tools to select objects and images. These tools include shape tools like Photoshop's Marquee tools and freehand tools like the Lasso tool. Objects and images with similar areas are selected using the Magic Wand tool.

✦ Fills and strokes offer a way to add color to objects. Pixel selections may also be filled and stroked. Objects may also be filled with gradients and patterns as well as colors.

✦ Color is applied using the Color palette, the Color Picker, and color swatches.

✦ The CS applications deal with several different color models, including RGB, HSV, CMYK, Grayscale, and Web Safe colors.

✦ Illustrator can apply linear and radial gradients as fills and may be used to create custom patterns.

✦ Transparency is another common property that allows objects underneath overlapped objects to be partially visible.

✦ Often-used items are saved in libraries. Libraries include symbols, styles, swatches, and brushes.

✦ Symbols provide an efficient way to work with many duplicate objects.

✦ Each of the CS applications includes various tools and commands for editing objects and images, including tools and commands to combine objects and split and distort objects and images.

✦   ✦   ✦

Transforming Objects and Images

After you select objects, you can easily move them by clicking and dragging them to a new location. You can also moved selected images using Photoshop's Move tool, but there is much more to transforming than just dragging an object or image to a new location.

The CS applications include many different ways to transform objects and images. You can also use the bounding box that surrounds a selection to rotate and scale an object. Understanding the visual cursor cues allows you to transform objects without bothering with tools or menus.

Within the Photoshop, Illustrator, and InDesign toolboxes are several tools that are used to transform objects, such as the Rotate tool, the Scale tool, the Reflect tool, the Shear tool, and the Free Transform tool. If you choose Object ➪ Transform or go to the Transform palette in Illustrator and InDesign, you can find even more features that enable you to transform objects in multiple ways with a single action.

In addition to covering altering a selection's position and orientation, this chapter also discusses stacking order, alignment, and distribution, all of which are nothing more than special transformation cases.

Transforming Objects

Objects are found in all the CS applications. The various transformation methods let you place those objects into the precise location needed to create an appealing design. Acrobat is the oddball among the group. In Acrobat, you can rotate pages and you can move objects, but you have no options for transforming objects on a PDF page. The remaining CS applications offer you tools and methods for transforming objects.

A selected object or group is identified by a bounding box that surrounds the object. The color of this bounding box is the layer color. If multiple objects are selected, the bounding box encompasses all the selected objects, as shown in Figure 9-1.

Cross-Reference   Selecting objects is covered in Chapter 8.

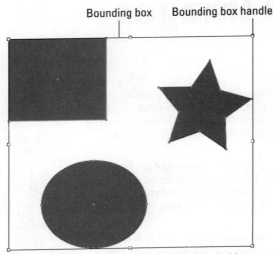

Bounding box   Bounding box handle

Figure 9-1: Selected objects are surrounded by a bounding box that is the same color as the layer where the object appears.

You can move and scale even the simplest objects in all the CS applications using the bounding box. Clicking inside the bounding box and dragging moves the selected object. Dragging on one of the handles that surrounds the object scales its size. But these actions are common features, and the bounding-box features covered next enable a wider range of transformations.

Using the bounding box

Perhaps the easiest and certainly the quickest way to transform objects is to use the selection's bounding box. You can use bounding-box transformations in Illustrator, Photoshop, and InDesign.

For all three of these applications, the bounding box is always rectangular and includes transformation handles at each corner and along each edge. By dragging these handles, you can scale or rotate an object using the Selection tool.

Note   In Illustrator, you can hide the bounding box by choosing View ➪ Show/Hide Bounding Box (Shift+Ctrl+B in Windows; Shift+⌘+B on the Mac), or in Photoshop, by disabling the Show Bounding Box option in the Option bar when the Move tool is selected. If the bounding box isn't visible when an object is selected, check these options.

Moving objects

To move selected objects, you simply need to click on the object's path or fill and drag it to its new position. If you drag an object with the Option/Alt key held down, then a duplicate copy of the original object is moved and the original copy stays in its place. Holding down the Shift key while dragging an object constrains it to move along regular 45-degree angles.

In addition to dragging with the mouse, you can also move objects using the arrow keys. The distance that the object moves when pressing each arrow key is determined by the Keyboard Increment value set in the General panel of the Preferences dialog box, shown in Figure 9-2. The default is set to 1 point. Holding down the Shift key while pressing an arrow key moves the selected object ten times the increment value.

Cross-Reference For more information on adjusting preferences, see Chapter 3.

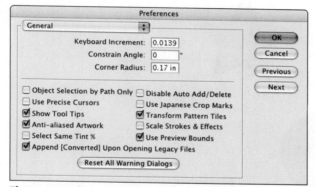

Figure 9-2: The amount an object is moved using the arrow keys is determined by the Keyboard Increment value found in the General panel of the Preferences dialog box.

Snapping objects

You can control where an object moves in Illustrator by choosing View ➪ Snap to Grid (Shift+Ctrl+" in Windows; Shift+⌘+" on the Mac) and View ➪ Snap to Point (Alt+Ctrl+" in Windows; Option+⌘+" on the Mac).

If the Snap to Grid option is enabled, then the corner points of objects that are moved snap to align with the grid intersection points. This enables you to precisely position objects relative to one another. Make grids visible by choosing View ➪ Show/Hide Grids. Set the grid size using the Guides & Grids panel in the Preferences dialog box.

The Snap to Point option aligns the point under the cursor when the selected object is clicked to the anchor point of another object or to a guideline. The cursor turns white when it's over a point to which it can snap.

Photoshop and InDesign also include snapping options. In Photoshop, you can select to snap to Guides, Grids, Slices, or Document Bounds using the View ➪ Snap To menu command. Snapping functionality may be turned on and off using the View ➪ Snap (Shift+⌘/Ctrl+;) menu command. InDesign includes commands in the View menu to Snap to Guides (Shift+⌘/Ctrl+;) and Snap to Document Grid (Shift+⌘/Ctrl+').

Rotating objects

When you move the Selection tool cursor near one of the bounding-box handles, the cursor changes. When the cursor looks like two small arrows and a curved line, you can drag the object to rotate it about its center point. Figure 9-3 shows three selected objects in Illustrator being rotated by dragging on its bounding box when the rotate cursor is visible.

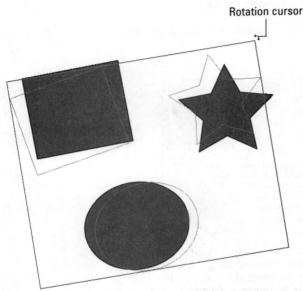

Rotation cursor

Figure 9-3: When the rotation cursor is displayed, you can rotate the selected object about its center point.

Rotating an object also rotates its bounding box. If you want to reset the bounding box in Illustrator, you can choose Object ➪ Transform ➪ Reset Bounding Box.

When objects are selected in Photoshop, a Reference Point is positioned within the center of the object. If the object is moved or scaled, the reference point remains in the center, but if you click and drag, you can reposition the reference point. This reference point is used to define the center about which the object is rotated. It can be positioned anywhere within the canvas.

Note   When an object is selected within InDesign, its bounding box doesn't enable rotation. InDesign objects can be rotated using the Object ➪ Transform ➪ Rotate menu command, but not using its bounding box.

Scaling and reflecting objects

Positioning the cursor directly over one of the bounding-box handles changes it to a double-headed arrow, and dragging the object with this cursor scales the object, as shown in Figure 9-4. If you drag a corner, the object scales horizontally and vertically; if you drag on one of the segment midpoint handles, the object scales in a single dimension.

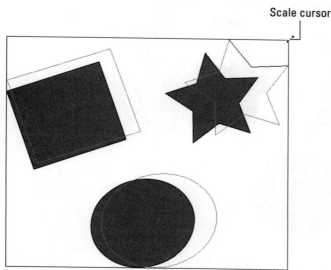

Figure 9-4: Dragging a selected object when the Scale cursor is displayed scales the object.

Holding down the Shift key while dragging one of the corner handles constrains the scaling to be uniform so that no distortion is introduced. Holding down the Option/Alt key while dragging scales the object about the center of the bounding box. Figure 9-5 shows an object that has been scaled with the Shift and Option/Alt keys held down. Notice how all objects have been scaled equally from the center outward.

If you drag one of the handles through the object to its opposite side, the object is reflected about the bounding-box sides through which it was dragged.

Using the transform tools

The third section of tools in both the Illustrator Toolbox and the InDesign Toolbox includes several tools that you can use to transform objects. These tools include the Rotate, Scale, Reflect, Shear, and Free Transform tools, as shown in Figure 9-6.

Note   The Shear tool in Illustrator is located as a flyout under the Scale tool and the Reflect tool is a flyout under the Rotate tool. InDesign doesn't include a Reflect tool.

Double-clicking on any of these tools opens a dialog box where you may enter precise values.

Using the Rotate tool

When the Rotate tool is selected, the rotation center for the selected object, called the reference point, is positioned in the center of the object as indicated by a small circle icon with four small lines extending from it, as shown in Figure 9-7. Dragging in the art board rotates the selected object, but if you click in the art board with the Rotate tool, you can position the rotation center. Any dragging then rotates about the new rotation center. Holding down the Shift key rotates the selected object using 45-degree increments.

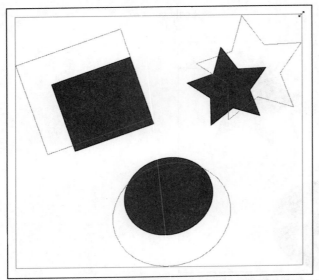

Figure 9-5: Scaling objects with the Shift key held down maintains the proportions of the object; with the Option/Alt key held down, it scales the objects about the selection center.

Illustrator
Toolbox

InDesign
Toolbox

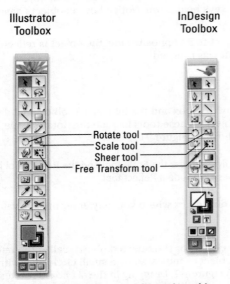

Rotate tool
Scale tool
Sheer tool
Free Transform tool

Figure 9-6: Transform tools are found in the Toolbox in Illustrator and in InDesign.

Rotation reference point

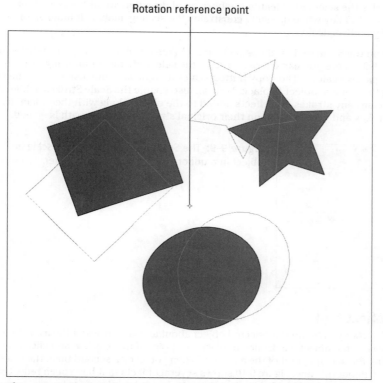

Figure 9-7: The rotation reference point marks the center about which the rotation takes place.

If you double-click on the Rotate tool or choose Object ➪ Transform ➪ Rotate command in Illustrator or InDesign, a simple dialog box opens, shown in Figure 9-8. Here, you can enter a precise Angle value. The Copy button rotates a duplicate copy of the object and leaves the original object in its place.

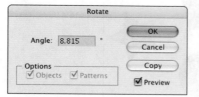

Figure 9-8: The Rotate dialog box

Using the Scale tool

The Scale tool works like the Rotate tool in that the scale point is positioned initially in the center of the selected object, but by clicking on the art board, you can place it in a different location. Dragging up and down scales the selected object in the vertical direction; dragging left and right scales the selected object in the horizontal direction about the scale point. Holding down the Shift key while dragging constrains the scaling, making it uniform or equal both horizontally and vertically.

Double-clicking on the Scale tool or choosing Object ➪ Transform ➪ Scale opens a dialog box, shown in Figure 9-9, where you can choose to scale the selected object uniformly or non-uniformly using precise values. The Copy button scales a duplicate copy using the scale values and leaving the original object in place. You can also enable the Scale Strokes & Effects option, which scales any strokes and effects added to the object along with the object. If disabled, the strokes and effects maintain their original size and only the path is scaled.

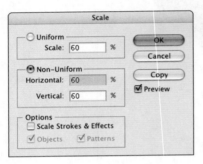

Figure 9-9: The Scale dialog box lets you scale an object in a uniform or non-uniform manner.

Using the Reflect tool

The Reflect tool allows you to flip the selected object about an axis. To select the axis about which to flip the selected object, click once to place one point of the axis line and click a second time to define the second point of the axis line. When you click a second time, the selected object is reflected about this line. Figure 9-10 shows several objects that have been reflected about an imaginary axis created by clicking two times in the art board.

Reflect axis

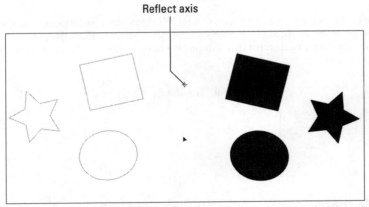

Figure 9-10: The Reflect tool mirrors the selected object on the opposite side of a designated axis.

If you hold down the Option/Alt key while clicking the second point, a copy of the original object is reflected. If you drag after clicking the second point, you can control the position of the reflected object; holding down the Shift key constrains the axis to 45-degree increments.

Note   The Reflect tool is only available in Illustrator, as a flyout under the Rotate tool, but you can flip objects in InDesign and Photoshop using menu commands.

The Reflect dialog box, shown in Figure 9-11, opened by double-clicking on the Reflect tool or by choosing Object ➪ Transform ➪ Reflect, lets you reflect the selected object horizontally, vertically, or about a specified angle. The dialog box also includes a Copy button.

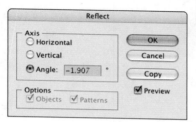

Figure 9-11: The Reflect dialog box lets you reflect the selected object horizontally, vertically, or about a designated angle.

Using the Shear tool

The Shear tool is a flyout under the Scale tool in Illustrator. It lets you distort the selected object by moving the opposite bounding-box edges in opposite directions. Dragging up and down shears the object vertically; dragging left and right shears the object horizontally. Clicking twice in the art board lets you place a shear axis, just like the Reflect tool. If the shear axis is located below an object, the entire object slants in the same direction with portions farther from the shear axis being sheared to a greater extent. Holding down the Shift key maintains the height or width of the object as it's sheared. Figure 9-12 shows several objects that have been sheared to the right. The square background was added to make the shear effect more obvious.

The Shear dialog box, shown in Figure 9-13, lets you specify a shear angle and the shear axis as horizontal, vertical, or a specified angle.

Using the Free Transform tool

The Free Transform tool enables you to perform all the transformations with a single tool. In many ways, it works just like the bounding box, but it has some additional features built in. Moving, rotating, scaling, and reflecting work just like with the bounding box, but you can also shear an object by holding down Ctrl+Alt (⌘+Option on the Mac) while dragging sideways on one of the side handles.

Note   In Photoshop, you can enable free transformation of paths using the Edit ➪ Free Transform Path (⌘/Ctrl+T) menu command.

Another unique feature of the Free Transform tool is that you can distort the selected object by moving a single bounding box corner without moving any of the other corner points. To do this, start dragging a corner handle and then press the ⌘/Ctrl key to move only the selected point. Figure 9-14 shows the selected objects in the process of being distorted in this way by dragging its upper-right corner handle.

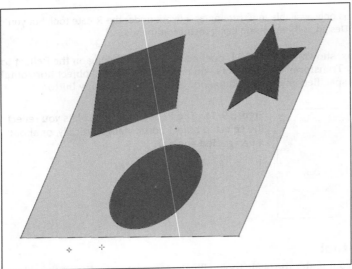

Figure 9-12: Placing the shear axis below the object causes the entire object to be sheared in one direction.

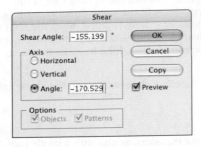

Figure 9-13: The Shear dialog box lets you specify the amount of shear with the shear angle and the axis about which the shear takes place.

You can also use the Free Transform tool to alter perspective by moving two corner points at the same time. You can accomplish this by dragging a corner point and then holding down Shift+Ctrl+Alt (Shift+⌘+Option on the Mac) at the same time. Figure 9-15 shows an object whose perspective has been altered using the Free Transform tool.

Note   The Free Transform tool has no dialog box that is opened when you double-click on the tool.

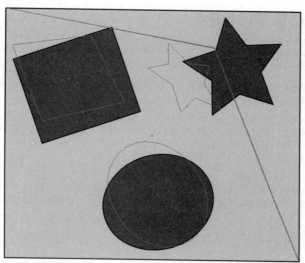

Figure 9-14: You can distort the bounding box by moving a single corner handle by holding down the ⌘/Ctrl key and dragging with the Free Transform tool.

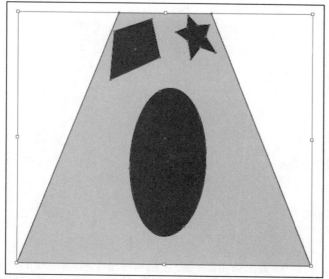

Figure 9-15: Dragging a bounding-box corner handle with the Free Transform tool while holding down Shift+Ctrl+Alt (Shift+⌘+Option on the Mac) alters an object's perspective.

STEPS: Transforming in Illustrator

1. **Create a symbol.** Create a sample object in Illustrator or drag an object from the Symbols palette. The symbol for these steps comes from the Logos Symbol Library accessed by choosing Window ➪ Symbol Libraries ➪ Logos.

2. **Select the object.** With the Selection tool, click on the symbol to select it. A bounding box surrounds the selected object.

3. **Create several duplicate copies.** Click on the symbol and begin to drag it downward. Then press and hold down the Shift and Option/Alt keys to create an aligned duplicate underneath the original. Repeat this step until six planets are aligned, as shown in Figure 9-16.

Figure 9-16: Dragging an object with the Option/Alt key held down moves a duplicate copy and keeps the original.

4. **Use the Rotate tool.** Select the second planet and double-click on the Rotate tool. In the Rotate dialog box, set the Angle value to 60 and click OK. The second planet is rotated so its rings are almost vertical.

5. **Use the Scale tool.** Select the third planet and double-click on the Scale tool. In the Scale dialog box, select the Non-Uniform option and set the Horizontal value to 60% and the Vertical value to 120%. Then click OK.

6. **Use the Reflect tool.** Select the fourth planet and click on the Scale tool. Click to the right of the planet and click again directly below the first click to form a vertical axis. Drag with the Option/Alt key held down to create a reflected duplicate of the planet to the right.

7. **Use the Shear tool.** Select the fifth planet and double-click on the Shear tool. In the Shear dialog box, enter **45** for the Shear Angle and choose the Horizontal axis. Then click OK. The planet is elongated by fitting it into a stretched bounding box.

8. **Use the Free Transform tool.** Select the sixth planet and choose the Free Transform tool. Drag the upper-right corner while holding down the Option/Alt key to scale the object about its center. Figure 9-17 shows all the resulting transformed planets.

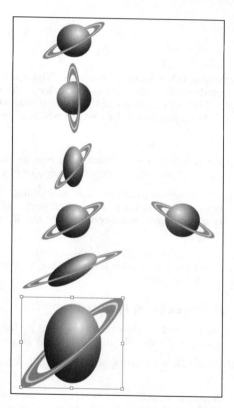

Figure 9-17: Each of these planets was transformed using a different transform tool.

Using the Transform menu

The Object ➪ Transform menu in Illustrator and InDesign includes several commands to open the dialog boxes for the various transform tools. You may access these same dialog boxes by double-clicking on the respective tool in the Toolbox, but the Transform menu in Illustrator also includes some additional commands such as Transform Again, Transform Each and Reset Bounding Box. In Illustrator, choosing Object ➪ Transform ➪ Move (Shift+Ctrl+M in Windows;

Shift+⌘+M on the Mac) opens the Move dialog box, shown in Figure 9-18, where you can enter precise values to move an object. You can also move objects by selecting an Angle and Distance values.

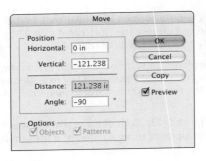

Figure 9-18: The Move dialog box lets you specify an object's horizontal and vertical position values or move an object a given distance along a specified angle.

Photoshop also includes several menu commands for transforming paths. These are located in the Edit ➪ Transform Path menu and include commands such as Again, Scale, Rotate, Skew, Distort, Perspective and several Rotate and Flip options. None of these menu commands open a dialog box, but they allow the path's bounding box to be transformed in a certain way.

Using Transform Again

Choosing Object ➪ Transform ➪ Transform Again (⌘/Ctrl+D) in Illustrator repeats the last transformation again. This enables you to quickly create multiple aligned copies of an object.

For example, if you select and move an object downward with the Shift and Option/Alt keys held down, the result is a duplicate copy of the object that is positioned directly under the first. After this is done, you can use the Transform Again menu command to quickly create a whole column of objects.

A similar command is found in Photoshop, Edit ➪ Transform ➪ Again (Shift+Ctrl+T in Windows; Shift+⌘+T on the Mac). This command repeats the last applied transformation, which may include multiple transformations, to the selected object.

STEPS: Creating an Array of Objects in Illustrator

1. **Create an object to duplicate.** Create or select an object that you want to duplicate many times in a repeating pattern. A simple symbol like this planet may be used.

2. **Select the object.** With the Selection tool, click on the symbol to select it. A bounding box surrounds the selected object.

3. **Create a single duplicate copy.** Click on the symbol and begin to drag the symbol downward, then press and hold down the Shift and Option/Alt keys to create an aligned duplicate underneath the original.

4. **Use the Transform Again command.** Choose Object ➪ Transform Again (⌘/Ctrl+D) to repeat the transformation. This creates a third planet object that is moved the same distance as the first duplicate. Hold down the ⌘/Ctrl key and press the D key six more times to create a column of planets that are equally spaced, as shown in Figure 9-19.

Figure 9-19: You can use the Object ➪ Transform ➪ Transform Each menu command to quickly and precisely repeat a transformation operation several times.

5. **Select the column of planets.** With the Selection tool, drag over the entire column of planets to select them all.

6. **Create a duplicate column.** Begin to drag the selected planets to the right, then press and hold down the Shift and Option/Alt keys to constrain the movements of the planets to the horizon, and the Option/Alt key creates a duplicate column of planets.

7. **Use the Transform Again command.** Choose Object ➪ Transform Again (⌘/Ctrl+D) and press the ⌘/Ctrl+D keyboard shortcut four more times. The resulting array of planets, shown in Figure 9-20, was created fairly quickly.

Using the Transform Each dialog box

In Illustrator, choosing Object ➪ Transform ➪ Transform Each (Alt+Shit+Ctrl+D in Windows; Option+Shift+⌘+D on the Mac) opens the Transform Each dialog box, shown in Figure 9-21. This dialog box combines several transformations into a single location and includes Scale, Move, and Rotate values. It also includes options to Reflect an object about the X or Y axis.

The small icon underneath the Reflect options lets you select the point about which the selected object is transformed. The selected transformation point is marked black. You can click on any of these points to specify the transformation point as the object center, any object corner, or side.

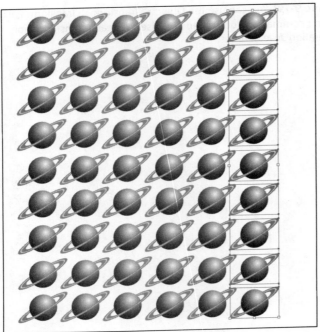

Figure 9-20: By duplicating and transforming objects and then using the Transform Again menu command, you can quickly and easily create an array of objects.

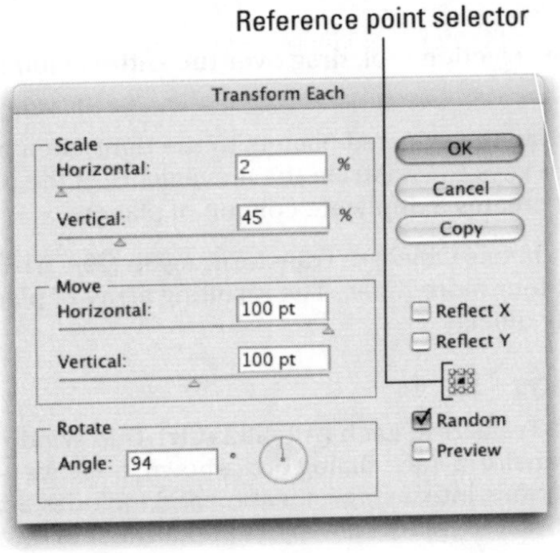

Reference point selector

Figure 9-21: The Transform Each dialog box combines the transformation values of several different transformations into a single dialog box.

The Random option chooses a random value between the default value and the specified value and applies the transformation using these random values. To see some of the random possibilities, enable and disable the Preview option multiple times to see some of the random transformations. Figure 9-22 shows many random stars created using the Random option in the Transform Each dialog box.

Figure 9-22: Enabling the Random option in the Transform Each dialog box produced a varied assortment of stars.

STEPS: Creating a Flower in Illustrator

1. **Create a simple path.** Click on the Paintbrush tool and drag in the art board to create a simple, mostly vertical line. In the Stroke palette, set the Weight to 3 pt, select the Round Cap button, and set the color to a dark red, as shown in Figure 9-23.

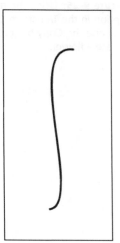

Figure 9-23: A simple path that may be randomly placed is created with the Paintbrush tool.

2. **Open the Transform Each dialog box.** Choose Object ⇨ Transform ⇨ Transform Each (Alt+Shift+Ctrl+D in Windows; Option+Shift+⌘+D on the Mac) to open the Transform Each dialog box. Set the Horizontal and Vertical Scale values to 100% and the Move values to 0. Then set the Rotate value to 360 degrees, select the center point as the reference point and enable the Random option. Then click the Copy button. Figure 9-24 shows the Transform Each dialog box after the values have been set.

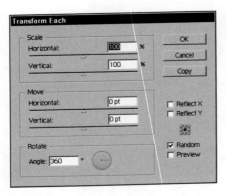

Figure 9-24: The Transform Each dialog box with the Random option enabled randomly rotates the selected object.

3. **Create duplicate objects.** Click the Copy button to close the dialog box and create a copy that is randomly rotated about its center point. With the duplicate selected, reopen the Transform Each dialog box using the Alt+Shift+Ctrl+D (Option+Shift+⌘+D keyboard shortcut, and click again on the Copy button. Repeat this step until enough copies are created to fill in the flower.

4. **Add a flower center.** Create a simple circle with the Ellipse tool and set its fill color to a bright yellow. Then drag the circle to the center of the flower. The resulting flower is shown in Figure 9-25.

Figure 9-25: Using the random option in the Transform Each dialog box and the Copy button, you can create a flower.

Rotating and flipping InDesign objects

You can quickly rotate and/or flip selected objects in InDesign using the popup up menu at the right end of the Options bar. The menu commands found there include Rotate 180 Degrees, Rotate 90 Degrees Clockwise, Rotate 90 Degrees Counterclockwise, Flip Horizontal, Flip Vertical, and Flip Both.

Rotating and flipping in Photoshop

Photoshop includes some menu commands found in the Edit @@ Transform Path menu to rotate and/or flip the selected object. The options include Rotate 180 Degrees, Rotate 90 Degrees CS, Rotate 90 Degrees CCW, Flip Horizontal and Flip Vertical.

Photoshop also includes commands to rotate and flip the entire Canvas. These commands are useful if you need to transform all objects. The commands are located in the Image ⇨ Rotate Canvas menu and include 180 Degrees, 90 Degrees CW, 90 Degrees CCW, Arbitrary (which lets you select an Angle value), Flip Canvas Horizontal, and Flip Canvas Vertical.

Using the Transform palette

In addition to the bounding box, tools and menus, several of the CS applications include a Transform palette including Illustrator, InDesign and GoLive.

Using the Transform palette in Illustrator and InDesign

Illustrator's Transform palette, shown in Figure 9-26 and which you can open by choosing Window ⇨ Transform, displays information about the object's position and size. By changing these values, you can transform the selected object. The Transform palette in InDesign looks and acts the same.

Figure 9-26: The Transform palette displays information about the position and dimensions of the selected object.

The X and Y values denote the horizontal and vertical positions of the reference point selected using the icon at the left of the Transform palette relative to the art board's lower-left corner. For example, if the object's center point is selected and the object is positioned on the page 100 points above the bottom of the art board and 50 points from the left edge, then the X and Y values in the Transform palette would be 100 pt and 50 pt. Changing the X and Y values in the Transform palette moves the selected object.

Note Most of the same values found in the Transform palette are also displayed in the Options bar in InDesign.

The W and H values denote the object's Width and Height. Clicking the link icon to the right of these values links the values together, so that changing one automatically changes the other. Changing the W and H values in the Transform palette scales the selected object. If the link icon is enabled, changing the values causes the selected object to be scaled uniformly.

At the bottom of the Transform palette are Rotate and Shear values. Changing these values causes the selected object to be rotated or sheared the given amount. InDesign's Transform palette also includes values for the Scale X and Scale Y Percentage values. These values can be linked to stay equal.

Illustrator's Transform palette may also be used to reflect the selected object using the Flip Horizontal or Flip Vertical palette menu commands. The palette menu also includes an option to Scale Strokes & Effects and options to Transform the object only, the pattern only, or both.

The palette menu options for the Transform palette in InDesign are different than the options in Illustrator. Within InDesign, you can select options to Scale Text Attributes, Transform Group Content and Reset Scaling to 100%. There are also options to Rotate and Flip the selected object.

At the bottom of InDesign's Transform palette menu are several toggle options that can be enabled including Transform Content, Dimensions Include Stroke Weight, Transformations are Totals, Show Content Offset and Scale Strokes. The Transform Content option causes the content within the selected frame to be transformed along with the frame when enabled. The Dimensions Include Stroke Weight option changes the Width and Height displayed values to include the stroke weight.

The Transformations are Totals option causes the displayed transformation values to be absolute relative to the document. For example, if a selected image inside a rotated frame is also rotated even further, then enabling the Transformation are Totals option would display the image's angle relative to the bottom of the document page and disabling the Transformations are Total option would display a rotation value that includes the rotation values of both the image and its frame.

The Show Content Offset option is used when content is selected within the frame. It displays the amount that the content is offset from the frame's reference point. When an offset value is displayed, two small plus signs appear next to the X and Y values, as shown in Figure 9-27.

Offset indicators

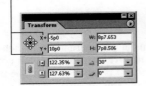

Figure 9-27: Two small plus signs appear in InDesign's Transform palette when the Show Content Offset option is enabled.

Using the GoLive Transform palette

GoLive also includes a Transform palette, shown in Figure 9-28, which displays the Position and Size values of the selected GoLive object, which may include a layer, objects on a Layout Grid, or image map hotspots. Using this palette, you can edit the position and size of the various elements relative to the upper-left corner of the Web page (for layers) or the upper-left corner of the Layout Grid.

GoLive layers are quite a bit different from the layers used in the other CS applications. The GoLive layers stem from HTML code and refer to areas that can hold text and images that may be stacked one on top of another.

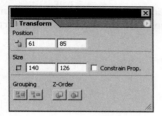

Figure 9-28: The Transform palette in GoLive displays Position and Size information for the selected object.

Cross-Reference

You can learn more about GoLive's layers in Chapter 11.

The stacking order for GoLive layers is determined by a Z-Index value, which is set in the Inspector palette when a layer object is selected.

Transforming Patterns and Fills

When an object is filled with a solid color, rotating the object has no affect on the fill color. However, if an object is filled with a gradient or a pattern, rotating an object may or may not impact the filled gradient or pattern depending on the setting in the Transform palette.

Transforming patterns in Illustrator

Using Illustrator's Transform palette menu, you can select to apply a transformation to the object only, the pattern only, or to both. When the Pattern Only option is selected, a small warning icon appears in the lower-left corner of the Transform palette, as shown in Figure 9-29, to remind you that any transformations are applied only to the pattern.

Note

Selecting the Pattern Only option in the Transform palette applies only to transformations that are done using the Transform palette. Transformations completed using the transform tools or by choosing Object ⇨ Transform are determined by the respective transformation dialog boxes.

Figure 9-29: A small warning icon appears in the lower-left corner of the Transform palette when the Pattern Only option is selected.

To transform a pattern or gradient using one of the transform tools or the Object ⇨ Transform menu, you need to enable the Patterns option in the dialog box for the selected transformation. Each transform dialog box includes options for selecting objects and patterns. Enabling the Patterns option applies the transformation to the pattern.

STEPS: Rotating a Pattern in Illustrator

1. **Create a filled object.** Select the Ellipse tool and drag in the art board to create a simple ellipse object. In the Swatches palette, select a striped pattern as the fill. The stripes run horizontally across the ellipse object, as shown in Figure 9-30.

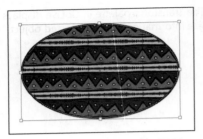

Figure 9-30: An ellipse object filled with a striped pattern that runs horizontally across the object

2. **Select and duplicate the object.** With the Selection tool, click on the ellipse object to select it. Then drag it downward with the Option/Alt key held down to create a duplicate copy.

3. **Create a single duplicate copy.** Click on the new ellipse and begin to drag it downward; then press and hold down the Shift and Option/Alt keys to create an aligned duplicate underneath the original. Then choose Object ➪ Transform ➪ Transform Again to duplicate another ellipse for a total of three.

4. **Enable the Transform Pattern Only option.** Choose Window ➪ Transform to open the Transform palette. In the palette menu, select the Transform Pattern Only option. A warning icon appears in the bottom-left corner of the Transform palette.

5. **Rotate the pattern.** Select the second ellipse object and type **45** in the Rotate field of the Transform palette. The pattern within the ellipse is rotated.

6. **Enable the Transform Both option.** In the Transform palette menu, select the Transform Both option.

7. **Rotate the pattern.** Select the third ellipse object and type **90** in the Rotate field of the Transform palette. The pattern and the ellipse are both rotated. Figure 9-31 shows the resulting rotations.

Transforming patterns in Photoshop

When a path or shape is created in Photoshop, it is automatically filled with the Foreground color. This color of the selected object may be changed to a pattern or a fill using the Layer ➪ Change Layer Content ➪ Pattern menu command. Applying this menu command opens a dialog box, shown in Figure 9-32, where you can select a pattern from the available presets and set the Scale of the pattern. The Snap to Origin button realigns the pattern so the upper-left corner of the pattern corresponds to the upper-left corner of the object.

Once a pattern or a gradient is applied to a path or shape, a fill thumbnail appears in the Layers palette next to the Vector Mask. Double clicking this fill thumbnail in the Layers palette opens the Pattern Fill dialog box again where you can change the Scale value.

Cross-Reference   More on working with layers is covered in Chapter 11.

A pixel selection may also be filled with a pattern using the Layer ➪ New Fill Layer ➪ Pattern menu command. This menu command creates a new layer and opens a dialog box where you can name the layer, choose a layer color, and set the blending mode and Opacity value. The Pattern Fill dialog box then opens letting you select a pattern and set a scale value.

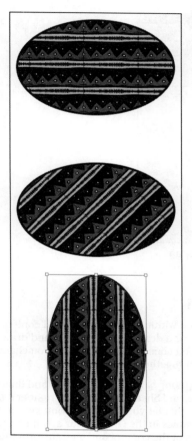

Figure 9-31: Using the options available in the Transform palette, you can rotate just the object, just the pattern, or both.

Figure 9-32: The Pattern Fill dialog box lets you scale the pattern used to fill an object. A similar scale setting is also available for Gradients.

Another way to apply a pattern to a layer is with the Pattern Overlay layer effect. To apply a layer effect, select a layer in the Layers palette and choose the Layer ⇨ Layer Style ⇨ Pattern Overlay menu command. Layer effects may be applied to any layer and all pixels or objects on that layer are covered with the selected pattern. Using the Layer Style dialog box, shown in Figure 9-33, you can set the pattern's blending mode, Opacity and Scale.

Note

Although patterns may be scaled and repositioned in Photoshop, there isn't any way to rotate a pattern once it is applied. Gradients, however, include both Angle and Scale controls that allow you to rotate and scale applied gradients.

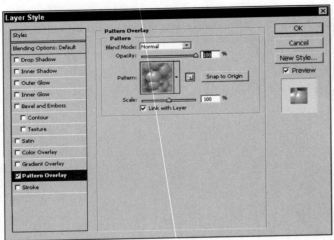

Figure 9-33: The Layer Style dialog box lets you overlay an object with a pattern. The pattern may also be scaled.

Transforming content in InDesign

InDesign is unique in how it handles content positioned within objects because all content in InDesign are placed within containers such as a frame or a drawn object. Images and drawings are added to a document using the File ➪ Place menu command. InDesign lets you change the move, rotate, and scale a container and its content together or independently.

With a frame that holds some content selected, the Options bar lists the position and dimensions of the selected frame, as well as its Scale, Rotate, and Shear values. At the right end of the Options bar, shown in Figure 9-34, are two buttons that let you select the container or select the content. If you select the content then the values in the Options bar are updated, a new bounding box appears that shows the dimensions of the content and all transform tools may be used to transform the content independent of the container. These buttons are also available as menu commands in the Object ➪ Select menu.

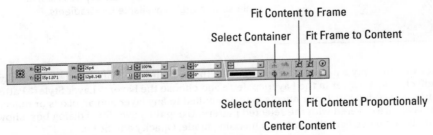

Figure 9-34: The Options bar includes buttons for selecting the frame or the content. Whichever is selected may be transformed using the Object ➪ Transform menu commands.

When a filled container is selected, the Options bar also includes several buttons for synching the size of the content with the container. These buttons include the following:

✦ **Fit Content to Frame:** Scales the placed image to fit the frame.

✦ **Fit Frame to Content:** Scales the frame to fit the placed image.

✦ **Center Content:** Moves the placed image so its center matches the frame without scaling the image.

✦ **Fit Content Proportionally:** Proportionally scales the placed image to fit within the frame.

These buttons are also found in the Object ⇨ Fitting menu. The keyboard shortcuts are Fit Content to Frame (Option/Alt+⌘/Ctrl+E), Fit Frame to Content (Option/Alt+⌘/Ctrl+C), Center Content (Shift+⌘/Ctrl+E), and Fit Content Proportionally (Option/Alt+Shift+⌘/Ctrl+E). Figure 9-35 shows each of these options applied to an image placed in a frame.

Each of the transform dialog boxes available from the Object ⇨ Transform menu, including Move, Rotate, Scale and Shear, includes a Transform Content option, such as the Shear Content option shown in Figure 9-36. If this option is enabled, then the specified transformation is applied to both the frame and the content. If this option is disabled, the transformation is applied only to the frame. If the content is selected, this option isn't available.

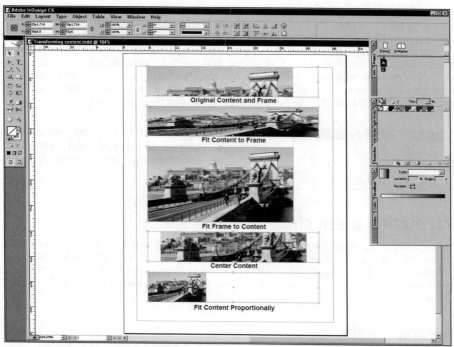

Figure 9-35: InDesign includes several methods for automatically scaling content and frames.

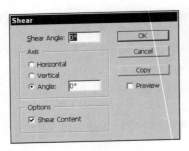

Figure 9-36: Each of the transform dialog boxes in InDesign includes an option to transform the content along with the frame.

Transforming Images in Photoshop

Images in Illustrator and InDesign are contained within objects and may not be selected or edited using pixel selections. But in Photoshop, pixel selections are very common, and they have several tricky aspects when dealing with transformations. One of the key differences between transforming objects and transforming images is that image selections are usually not rectangular, depending on the selection tool that was used. But if the Move tool is selected, a rectangular bounding box is placed about the selection. Using the bounding box, you can move, rotate and scale the selected pixels in a manner that is the same as that used for objects.

Another key aspect of transforming images is that every time you apply a transformation a pixel selection, you potentially alter the selection. Applying multiple successive transformations to a pixel selection distorts the pixels. To limit this effect, Photoshop keeps track of all the transformations that are made to a pixel selection at one time. Then when a different tool is selected, a confirmation dialog box, shown in Figure 9-37, appears asking if you want to apply the transformation with buttons for Apply, Cancel, and Don't Apply. By waiting until all the desired transformations are completed before applying them, the number of actual transformations is minimized and the fidelity of the pixel selection is maximized

Figure 9-37: This confirmation dialog appears after several transformation operations have been combined within Photoshop.

Translating a selection

When a selection is made, marching ants surround the selection and show the selected area. If you select the Select ⇨ Transform Selection menu command, then a bounding box surrounds the selection. Using this bounding box, the options in the Options bar or the Edit ⇨ Transform menu commands, you can transform the selection without altering the pixels within the selection.

Moving pixels

When an area of pixels is selected with one of the Marquee tools, dragging the selection with the Marquee tool has no impact on the pixels; instead, it moves only the selection. To move the selected pixels, you need to select the Move tool. With the Move tool selected, you can click within the selection and drag it to move the actual pixels. Figure 9-38 shows an image where a pixel selection has been moved using the Move tool.

Figure 9-38: Moving a pixel selection with the Move tool can abruptly alter the continuity of an image.

Holding down the Option/Alt key while dragging a pixel selection creates a duplicate copy of the pixels and leaves the original pixels in place. Holding down the Shift key while dragging a pixel selection constrains the movement to regular 45-degree angles.

Using Free Transform

Photoshop's Edit ⇨ Free Transform (⌘/Ctrl+T) menu command places a bounding box around the selection or encloses all objects on the current layer within a bounding box if there is no selection.

This bounding box works just like the bounding boxes used to transform objects. Clicking within the bounding box and dragging moves the selection. Dragging one of the corner or side handles scales the selection; moving the cursor near one of the handles until it changes to a rotation icon allows you to rotate the selection. You can also reflect an object by dragging it through its opposite side.

Holding down the Shift key while dragging a corner handle causes uniform scaling; holding down the Shift key while moving constrains the movements to 45-degree angles; and holding down the Shift key while rotating constrains the rotations to 15-degree increments. To scale opposite handles relative to the reference point, hold down the Option/Alt key while dragging. To move a corner handle independent of the other corner handles, hold down the ⌘/Ctrl key while dragging. To shear the selection, hold down the Shift+Ctrl keys (Shift+⌘ on the Mac) while dragging a side handle. Finally, to alter perspective, drag with the Shift+Alt+Ctrl keys (Shift+Option+⌘ on the Mac) held down.

With the Free Transform command selected, the values for the various transformations appear on the Options bar, as shown in Figure 9-39. The Reference Point icon lets you select the position about which the transformations take place. The X and Y values denote the position of the reference point relative to the upper-left corner of the image. The W and H values denote the Width and Height of the selection's bounding box. The final three values are the rotation, horizontal, and vertical shear values.

> **Note**   The link icon between the W and H values links the W and H values together so that altering one automatically alters the other. This causes all scaling to be uniform.

Figure 9-39: When the Free Transform command is selected, various transformation values appear in the Options bar.

Using the Transform menu

In Photoshop, choosing Edit ⇨ Transform ⇨ Again (Shift+Ctrl+T in Windows; Shift+⌘+T on the Mac) causes the last transformation to be repeated.

If remembering all the various keyboard keys to use for the various transformations is tricky, you can select the specific type of transformation that you want to apply to the object from the Edit ⇨ Transform menu. The options include Scale, Rotate, Skew, Distort, and Perspective.

The Edit ⇨ Transform menu also includes commands to rotate 180 degrees, rotate 90 degrees clockwise, rotate 90 degrees counterclockwise, flip horizontal, and flip vertical. The rotations and flipping takes place about the designated reference point.

Arranging Stacking Order

The order in which objects are displayed or printed is determined by the stacking order. This order places the object at the bottom of the stacking order on the document first and then stacks each additional object in order on the document up to the top object. If an object that is higher in the stacking order is placed on top of an existing object, and if the top object doesn't include any transparency, the lower object is obscured.

When objects are created, each new object is placed higher in the stacking order than those already created.

Controlling stacking order using layers

The easiest way to control stacking order is using layers. Layers at the top of the Layers palette have a higher stacking order and appear on top of all layers below it. By placing objects on a new higher layer, you may be assured that it appears above the objects on a lower layer.

> **Cross-Reference**   Layers and the Layers palette are covered in more detail in Chapter 11.

Layers provide a way to control stacking order, but within a single layer, objects may be stacked on top of one another. If you expand a layer in Illustrator by clicking on the arrow button to the left of the layer name, all objects within the layer are visible, as shown in Figure 9-40. The expanded objects in the Layers palette are listed in their stacking order with the top objects toward the top of the Layers palette.

If you select and drag an object in the Layers palette and drop it above another object, the stacking order is changed.

Figure 9-40: All the objects contained on a single layer are made visible by expanding the layer.

You can also reverse the order of several objects or layers using the Reverse Order palette menu command in the Layers palette. To use this command, select several adjacent objects or layers by selecting a layer and holding down the Shift key and clicking on the last sequential layer, then selecting the Reverse Order palette menu command.

Illustrator also includes the Object ➪ Arrange ➪ Send to Current Layer menu command, which moves the selected object to the current layer.

Changing stacking order with the Arrange menu

You can also control an object's position in the stacking order within a layer using the Object ➪ Arrange menu, found in Illustrator and InDesign.

The Object ➪ Arrange menu includes the following commands:

✦ Bring to Front (Shift+Ctrl+] in Windows; Shift+⌘+] on the Mac)

✦ Bring Forward (Ctrl+] in Windows; ⌘+] on the Mac)

✦ Send Backward (Ctrl+[in Windows; ⌘+[on the Mac)

✦ Send to Back (Shift+Ctrl+[in Windows; Shift+⌘+[on the Mac)

The Bring to Front and Send to Back menu commands move the selected object to the very top or very bottom of the stacking order, and the Bring Forward and Send Backward menu commands move the selected object forward or backward one place in the stacking order. With these commands you can quickly arrange the objects within a layer.

Changing stacking order with the Clipboard

Another way to change the stacking order of objects in Illustrator is to copy and paste them using the Edit ➪ Paste in Front (⌘/Ctrl+F) and the Edit ➪ Paste in Back (⌘/Ctrl+B) menu commands. These commands paste the object in front of or behind the selected object.

If no object is selected or if the Edit ➪ Paste (⌘/Ctrl+V) menu command is used, the object is pasted at the top of the stacking order for the selected layer.

Changing stacking order within a group

Objects within a group also have a stacking order. You can alter a group's stacking order by expanding the group in the Layers palette and dragging the one object above another, or by selecting an object within the group with the Group Selection tool and using the Object ➪ Arrange menu commands to alter its order.

Changing Z-Index in GoLive

Most objects on a web page cannot be stacked on top of one another. The exception to this rule is GoLive layers. The stacking order for GoLive layers is determined by a Z-Index value, which is set in the Inspector palette for the selected layer. Layers with a higher Z-Index value appear in front of layers with a lower value.

Aligning and Distributing Objects

To create aesthetic designs, there are times when you'll want to precisely orient two or more objects together. You can do this by recording the position values of the various objects and then changing those values for one of the objects to align it with the other one, but these can be time consuming if you have a lot of objects to align. Instead of a manual process, most of the CS applications include palettes and controls that make aligning and distributing objects easy.

Commands to align and distribute objects are contained on the Align palette (shown in Figure 9-41) for Illustrator, InDesign, and GoLive. You can access this palette by choosing Window ➪ Align (Shift+F7). The palette includes several icon buttons that align or distribute the selected objects to an edge or center.

Figure 9-41: The Align palette includes several rows of buttons that are used to align and distribute multiple objects.

Before you use an align or distribute icon button, you must select more than one object with the Selection tool. When you select one of the align or distribute icons, you can move all the selected objects to the match the edge or center of the selection boundary box. However, if you click on one of the objects after making the selection, that object becomes the Key Object and you must complete all alignment using the Key Object's center and edges.

If you select the wrong object as the Key Object, you can use the Cancel Key Object palette menu command to cancel the existing key object and select a new key object.

Note   The Align and Distribute buttons have no affect on objects that have been locked.

Aligning objects

To use the Align palette, select two or more objects that you want to align; then click on the align icon in the Align palette for the alignment that you want. The align options include Align Left Edges, Align Vertical Centers, Align Right Edges, Align Top Edges, Align Horizontal Center, Align Bottom Edges.

If you enable the Use Preview Bounds option in the Align palette menu, you can align the objects by their edges using the stroke width. If the Use Preview Bounds option is disabled, then the objects are aligned by the path edge, denoted by the bounding box.

To align objects to the art-board edges, enable the Align to Artboard option in the Align palette menu. This option works for aligning objects to the center of the art board as well as the art-board edges.

Note

The Align palette found in GoLive includes an additional row of buttons that are used to align a child object to its parent. You need only to select the child object to use these buttons. For example, several images within a Layout Grid may be selected and aligned to the top edge of the Layout Grid using the Align to Parent button. The images would be the children and the Layout Grid, the parent.

Distributing objects

Distributing objects is different from aligning objects in that the distribution icons in the Align palette position the selected objects so that the distance between the selected edges or centers of the selected objects is equal. For example, if three objects are selected and the Distribute Horizontal Centers button is clicked, then the middle object is moved so that the distance between the center of the bottom object and the middle object is equal to the distance between the center of the top object and the middle object.

The Distribution icons available in the Align palette include Distribute Top Edges, Distribute Vertical Centers, Distribute Bottom Edges, Distribute Left Edges, Distribute Horizontal Centers, and Distribute Right Edges.

Distributing spacing

If the Show Options palette menu command is selected, the Distribute Spacing buttons for Distribute Vertical Space and Distribute Horizontal Space appear. Using these buttons and the spacing value, you can space all the selected objects from the Key Object by the specified space amount.

The drop-down field at the bottom of the Align palette also includes an Auto option that automatically spaces the objects using an average of their current position. The Auto option also doesn't require that a Key Object be selected.

STEPS: Aligning Objects in InDesign

1. **Open an InDesign document.** Choose File ➪ Open and open an InDesign file that includes several misaligned objects like the images shown in Figure 9-42.

Figure 9-42: You can easily align randomly placed objects using the Align palette.

2. **Select all the objects to align.** With the Selection tool, drag over the top of all the objects that you want to align or hold down the Shift key and click on each one individually.

3. **Aligning objects with the Align palette.** With the objects selected, choose Window ➪ Align to open the Align palette. Click on the Align Bottom Edges button in the Align palette. The bottom edges of all the image objects are aligned, as shown in Figure 9-43.

4. **Distribute the image objects.** The alignment of the image objects looks good, but the spacing between the objects is still a problem. To fix this, use one of the Distribution buttons in the Align palette. With the image objects still selected, click the Distribute Right Edges button in the Align palette. This action evenly spaces the image objects, as shown in Figure 9-44.

5. **Move the final objects.** As a final step, you'll want to drag the image objects upward slightly with the Selection tool. With all the objects selected and aligned, they move together maintaining their alignment and spacing.

Cross-Reference   Once you've correctly aligned and positioned objects, you can lock them in place by clicking on the Lock icon in the Layers palette. More on locking layers is found in Chapter 11.

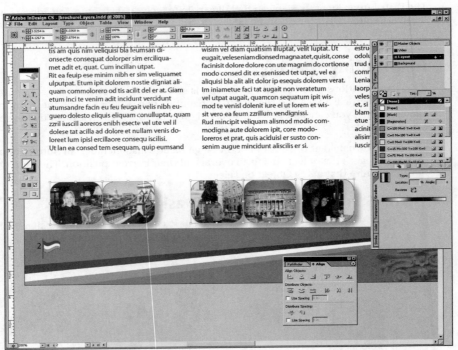

Figure 9-43: The Align palette enables you to align all these image objects using the Align Bottom Edges button in the Align palette.

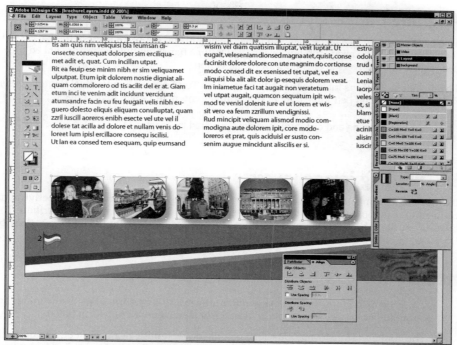

Figure 9-44: After distributing the image objects using their right edges, they line up perfectly spaced.

Aligning and Distributing Image Layers in Photoshop

Photoshop includes align buttons on the Options bar when the Move tool is selected. Using these buttons, you can align the current layer with the current selection. When the selected layer is linked to two or more layers, the distribution buttons become active on the Options bar.

Image selections may be aligned and distributed to a selected layer using the Move tool in Photoshop. With a selection made, click on the Move tool. Several align and distribute icon buttons appear on the Options bar, as shown in Figure 9-45.

Figure 9-45: When the Move tool is selected, several align and distribute buttons appear on the Options bar.

Aligning image layers

To align a selection to a layer, make an image selection and choose a layer in the Layers palette, then click one of the align icon buttons in the Options bar. If multiple layers are linked together, each of the linked layers is aligned with the selection.

The align icon buttons include the following: Align Top Edges, Align Vertical Centers, Align Bottom Edges, Align Left Edges, Align Horizontal Center, and Align Right Edges.

Cross-Reference More on aligning and distributing layers is covered in Chapter 11.

Distributing image layers

If three or more linked layers are selected, the distribute icon buttons become active and may be used to distribute the layer objects. The distribute icon buttons include Distribute Top Edges, Distribute Vertical Centers, Distribute Bottom Edges, Distribute Left Edges, Distribute Horizontal Centers, and Distribute Right Edges.

Summary

+ The CS applications include many different ways to transform objects including the bounding box, transform tools, a Transform menu, and a Transform palette.

+ The common transformation tools include Move, Rotate, Scale, Reflect, Shear, and Free Transform.

+ The Transform Each dialog box lets you combine several transformations into a single operation.

+ In addition to objects, patterns and gradients may also be transformed.

+ Images may be transformed in many of the same ways as objects using the Photoshop tools.

+ Stacking order determines which objects appear in front of other objects and is altered using layers and the commands in the Arrange menu.

+ Aligning and distributing objects is accomplished using the Align palette.

✦   ✦   ✦

Applying Effects to Objects and Images

When Adobe first introduced the concept of filters in Photoshop, it was a risky move. To allow other developers to access the inner workings of the Photoshop graphics engine and develop their own filters to alter images was brilliant or a huge mistake. History has now validated that the move was, indeed, brilliant.

Filters are found mainly in Photoshop and Illustrator, but Illustrator has taken the concept one step further with the introduction of effects. Effects are essentially filters applied in memory, allowing them to be edited or even removed at any time from the Appearance palette without affecting the rest of the attributes. Both Photoshop and Illustrator include filters and effects.

The variety of filters and effects found in both Photoshop and Illustrator are quite diverse, covering everything from unique brush strokes and object distortion to color adjustment and even 3D effects.

Many filters in Photoshop are moving into complex interfaces like the Filter Gallery that let you explore, preview, and apply many filters at once. Other common filter interfaces include the Extract, Liquify, and Pattern Maker interfaces.

Using Photoshop Filters

All the filters that may be applied to an image are contained within the Filter menu. Filters are applied to a selection or to the active layer if there is no selection. The top menu command in the Filter menu always lists the last filter command used. It includes a keyboard shortcut of ⌘/Ctrl+F, allowing it to be accessed quickly.

Note   Some filters may be applied only to images with the RGB color mode selected and some filters may only be applied to an 8-bit image. Filters that cannot be applied to the current image are disabled. In Photoshop, choosing Image ⇨ Mode lets you change these properties for the current image.

Accessing the Filter Gallery

The Filter Gallery lets you apply multiple filters at once or a single filter multiple times. To open the Filter Gallery, choose Filter ⇨ Filter Gallery. The Filter Gallery, shown in Figure 10-1, includes a preview pane that shows the results of the applied filters.

Note All the filters listed in the Filter Gallery also include their own menu commands in the Filter menu. Selecting a filter menu command for a filter that is part of the Filter Gallery opens the Filter Gallery with the selected filter highlighted.

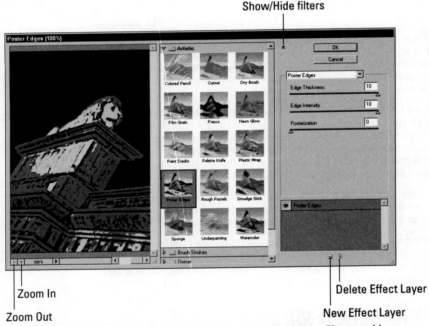

Figure 10-1: The Filter Gallery includes most of the Photoshop filters and lets you apply many filters at once.

The Filter Gallery interface is divided into three different panes. The left pane is the preview pane that displays the current layer or selection. The middle pane includes thumbnails of all the available filters. Clicking on a filter highlights it in gray and selects the filter. The right pane includes all the settings for the selected filter.

Note Although the Filter Gallery includes many filters, it doesn't include all filters available in Photoshop.

Using the Preview pane

Moving the mouse over the Preview pane changes the cursor to a hand. Dragging with this hand cursor pans the preview image within the pane. The buttons and popup menu at the bottom of the Preview pane are used to zoom in, zoom out, and select a specific zoom percentage.

The pop-up menu also includes an Actual Pixels option, which displays the image at its actual size of 100%; a Fit in View option, which zooms the image so the entire image is visible in the Preview pane; and a Fit on Screen option, which maximizes the Filter Gallery to fill the entire screen.

Clicking the Show/Hide button in the top-left corner of the Settings pane hides the filter thumbnails and uses that space to increase the size of the Preview pane, as shown in Figure 10-2.

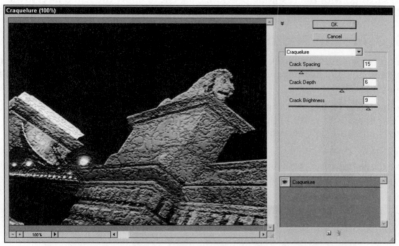

Figure 10-2: Clicking the Show/Hide button increases the size of the Preview pane by hiding all the filter thumbnails.

Using the Filter pane

The Filter pane is organized into several different categories of filters including Artistic, Brush Strokes, Distort, Sketch, Stylize, and Texture. Similar categories are found in the Filter menu. The category that includes the current selected filter is highlighted in bold.

Clicking on the small arrow to the left of the filter category name expands the category to reveal all the filters within that category. Clicking on a filter thumbnail selects the filter and displays all its settings in the Settings pane. The selected filter's name is displayed at the top of the interface along with the zoom percentage, and the background of its thumbnail is highlighted dark gray.

Using the Settings pane

The Settings pane includes a drop-down list of all the filters. Filters may be selected from this list when the filter thumbnails are hidden. Below this list the settings for the current selected filter are displayed. Changing any of these settings alters the effects of the filter, and the Preview pane shows the changes.

At the bottom of the Settings pane is a list of filters applied to the preview listed in the order in which they are applied to the image. If you click on a new filter, it replaces the currently selected filter. To apply an additional filter to the image, click on the New Effect Layer button at the bottom of the Settings pane. This freezes the current selection and adds a new filter layer to the interface. The name of this filter layer is that of the filter that was applied.

If you click on the Visibility icon to the left of the filter layer name to toggle it off, the Preview pane is updated to show the image without the filter. Selecting the filter layer and clicking the Delete Effect Layer button at the bottom of the Settings pane deletes filter layers.

If multiple filter layers exist in the Filter Galley, you can rearrange them by dragging one layer above or below another. Changing the order in which filters are applied, can drastically change the resulting image.

When you're satisfied with the resulting preview, click OK to apply the listed filter layers to the image. Click Cancel to exit the Filter Gallery without applying any filters.

STEPS: Using the Photoshop Filter Gallery

1. **Open an image in Photoshop.** Within Photoshop, choose File ➪ Open to open an image to which you want to apply some filters. To apply the filter to the entire image, do not select any portion.

2. **Open the Filter Gallery.** Choose Filter ➪ Filter Gallery to open the Filter Gallery interface. The image shows up in the Preview pane. Click and drag on the image in the Preview pane until an interesting portion of this image is visible.

3. **Select a filter.** Click on the Artistic category and select the Poster Edges filter. In the Settings pane, set the Edge Thickness to 0, the Edge Intensity to 1, and the Posterization to 2. Figure 10-3 shows the image with this single filter applied in the Filter Gallery.

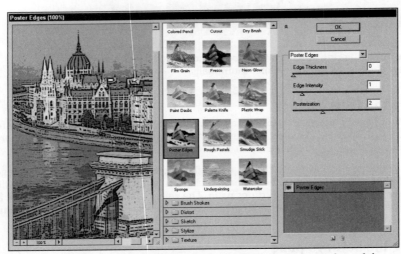

Figure 10-3: The Preview pane in the Filter Gallery shows a preview of the applied filter with its modified properties.

4. **Add another filter.** Click on the New Effect Layer button at the bottom of the Settings pane to add another filter to the image. Click on the Texture category and select the Texturizer filter. In the Settings pane, select the Canvas option from the Texture drop-down list. Set the Scaling value to 55%, the Relief value to 9 and the Light option to Top. Figure 10-4 shows the resulting image in the Preview pane.

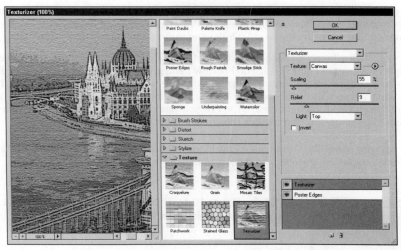

Figure 10-4: The Preview pane shows the resulting image after two filters are applied.

5. **Apply the selected filters.** Click the OK button to apply the two selected filters to the image. Figure 10-5 shows the resulting image with the filters applied.

Figure 10-5: Several filters may be applied to an image at one time using the Filter Gallery interface.

Using other filters

In addition to the filters included in the Filter Gallery interface, Photoshop has several other filters that are applied using the Filter menu.

Most of these filters have their own dialog boxes of settings that appear when the filter's menu command is selected. Some of the filters don't have any dialog boxes that open. The menu commands that have an ellipsis (. . .) following their menu command open a dialog box.

Most filter dialog boxes include a Preview option and a Preview pane, like the Gaussian Blur dialog box, shown in Figure 10-6. The Preview pane gives you an idea of what the filter effect is before it's applied to the entire image. By clicking and dragging on the image in the Preview pane, you can reposition the portion of the image that is displayed in the Preview pane. The plus and minus buttons underneath the Preview pane let you zoom in and out of the image. Enabling the Preview option applies the current filter settings to the entire image.

Caution   Applying some filters, even in Preview mode, can take some time depending on the calculations involved in the filter and the size of the image.

Figure 10-6: The Gaussian Blur dialog box, like most filter dialog boxes, includes a Preview pane.

Blurring an image

The Filter ➪ Blur menu includes several different filters that are used to blur an image or a selection by averaging local groups of pixels.

The first three Blur filters — Average, Blur, and Blur More — are applied without a dialog box. Average takes the average of all the selected colors and applies that average color to the entire selection. The Average filter is useful when used with the Magic Wand tool to create a single area with a single color.

The Blur filter removes any noise along hard edges by averaging the colors along these hard edges, resulting in a smoother overall image. The Blur More filter does the same, but to a greater extent.

The Gaussian Blur filter opens a dialog box where you can specify the amount of blur to add to the image. The Radius value determines the size of the groups of pixels that are averaged.

The Lens Blur filter opens a dialog box, shown in Figure 10-7, that lets you simulate a depth-of-field effect where the camera is focused on a particular point in the scene and all objects farther or nearer than that point are blurred in relationship to their distance from the focal point.

The Source field lets you base the focal point on the image's Transparency value or an included Depth Mask. The Iris Shape field lets you choose the shape of the defined averaged areas where the blur is applied as well as its Blade Curvature and Rotation. You can also specify values for Specular Highlights and Noise.

Figure 10-7: The Lens Blur dialog box includes a
Preview pane.

The Motion and Radial Blur filters let you control the direction of the blur lines. The Motion Blur filter specifies an Angle and a Distance value to blur the image linearly, as shown in Figure 10-8. The Radial Blur filter blurs the image in concentric circles about a point that you can select in the Radial Blur dialog box, also shown in Figure 10-8.

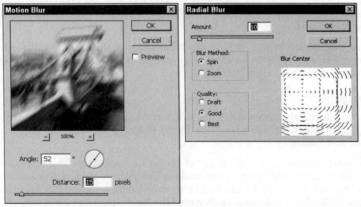

Figure 10-8: The Motion Blue and Radial Blur dialog boxes let you
blur the image using linear or radial lines.

The Smart Blur filter is unique in that it lets you blur areas of similar colored pixels based on the Threshold value. The Mode may be set to Normal, Edge Only, or Overlay Edge. The Edge Only and Overlay Edge options color the edges white based on the Threshold value. Figure 10-9 shows the Smart Blur dialog box. In the Preview pane, similar areas have been blended together.

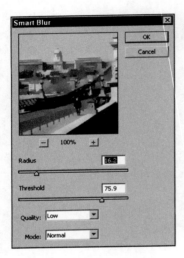

Figure 10-9: The Smart Blur dialog box is used to blur local areas of similar pixels.

STEPS: Blurring an Image's Background

1. **Open an image in Photoshop.** Within Photoshop, choose File ➪ Open and select an image that includes a background that you want to blur.

2. **Select the background.** Click on the Magnetic Lasso tool and drag around the foreground objects to roughly select the background. After making an initial selection, hold down the Shift key and select the additional areas with the Magic Wand tool. Figure 10-10 shows the selected background area.

3. **Apply the Lens Blur filter.** Choose Filter ➪ Blur ➪ Lens Blur. In the Lens Blur dialog box that opens, set the Radius value to 5 and zoom in on the Preview pane to see the applied blur, as shown in Figure 10-11. Then click OK.

Distorting an image

The Filter Gallery interface includes three filters in its Distort category, but the Filter ➪ Distort menu includes many more filters, including Displace, Pinch, Polar Coordinates, Ripple, Shear, Spherize, Twirl, Wave, and ZigZag.

The Displace filter distorts the image based on a loaded displacement map. The displacement map defines how the pixels move with black areas marking a negative displacement and white areas marking a positive displacement. Figure 10-12 shows an image with the Displace filter applied using the simple displacement map. Notice how the lion's head has been shifted along the line defined in the displacement map.

Note
Displacement maps must be saved using the PSD file format. Some sample displacement maps are found in the plug-ins\displacement maps directory.

Figure 10-10: With the background selected, the Lens Blur filter is used to make it blurry.

Figure 10-11: The Lens Blur dialog box lets you control how blurry the background becomes.

The remaining Distort filters all open a dialog box where you can enter the amount of distortion to apply. Most of these dialog boxes, like the Twirl dialog box shown in Figure 10-13, include a graphical representation of what the distortion looks like. In some cases, such as for the Shear filter, the graphical representation may be manipulated to define the distortion.

Of all the Distort filters, the Wave filter dialog box, shown in Figure 10-14, includes many unique settings for distorting the image such as selecting the Wave Type as Sine, Triangle, or Square, as well as a Randomize button.

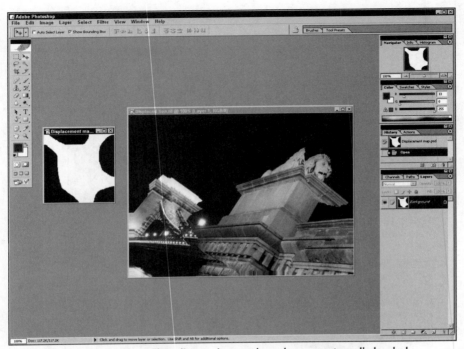

Figure 10-12: The Displace filter distorts images based on an externally loaded displacement map.

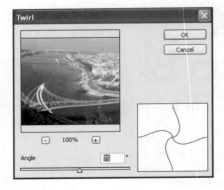

Figure 10-13: The Twirl dialog box includes a Preview pane and also a graphical representation of the distortion that is applied.

Adding noise to an image

When noise is added to an image, it randomly alters the colors of many of the surrounding pixels, making the image grainy. But it can also be used to blend areas that have been retouched, making them appear more realistic. The Filter ⇨ Noise menu includes several noise filters that are used to add and remove noise to an image or a selection.

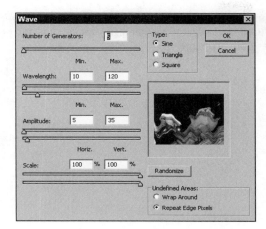

Figure 10-14: The Wave dialog box includes many settings for precisely controlling the distortion of an image.

The Add Noise filter opens a dialog box, shown in Figure 10-15, where you can specify the amount of noise to add to the image. The Uniform option randomly adds noise about the selected value, and the Gaussian option adds noise using a bell-shaped average curve. The Monochromatic option causes the noise to be black and white.

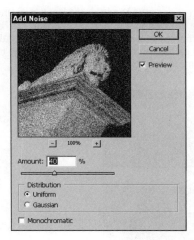

Figure 10-15: The Add Noise dialog box is used to specify the amount of noise added to the image.

The Despeckle filter doesn't open a dialog box, but it removes noise from the image. It also detects edges to maintain the details of the image. The Median filter also removes noise from the image by replacing the brightest and darkest pixels with a median-colored pixel.

Most scratches and dust irregularities are small enough that they may be removed using the Dust & Scratches filter. This filter looks for small abrupt changes that are as small as the designated Radius value and with a given threshold. This filter applies a general blurring of the entire image. Figure 10-16 shows the dialog box for this filter.

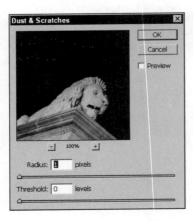

Figure 10-16: The Dust & Scratches dialog box may be used to eliminate irregular high-contrast dots and lines from an image.

Using the Pixelate filters

The Filter ➪ Pixelate filters are used to emphasize the pixel nature of an image by grouping several pixels together. The filters in this category include Color Halftone, Crystallize, Facet, Fragment, Mezzotint, Mosaic, and Pointillize. The Facet and Fragment filters apply the filter directly without opening a dialog box.

The shapes of the grouped pixels in each of these filters are slightly different, each creating a unique stylized look. For example, the Color Halftone filter changes each pixel group into a circle based on its brightness, the Crystallize filter changes groups of pixels into an irregular polygon shape, the Mosaic filter changes each grouping into a square, and the Pointillize filter groups pixels into solid dots. Figure 10-17 shows examples of several of these filters.

Figure 10-17: The Pixelate filters are used to alter an image by expanding the shape of specific pixel groups.

Using the Render filters

The process of rendering involves additional computations that alter the image in new and interesting ways. Using the filters in the Render category enables you to create clouds, fibers, and lighting effects like lens flares.

The Render filters include two filters for creating clouds — Clouds and Difference Clouds. The Clouds filter replaces the current image or selection with a random distribution of pixels using the Foreground and Background colors.

Tip Holding down the Option/Alt key while choosing Filter ⇨ Render ⇨ Clouds results in a cloud pattern that has a much higher contrast.

The Difference Clouds filter is similar, but instead of replacing the image, it blends the clouds with the image or the selection using a Difference blending mode, which inverts the colors of the image. Figure 10-18 shows an image where the Clouds filter has been applied to the left half, and the Difference Clouds filter has been applied to the right half.

Cross-Reference You can learn more about the various blending modes in Chapter 8.

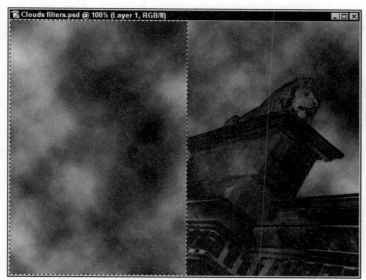

Figure 10-18: The Clouds filter has been applied to the selection on the left of this image, and the Difference Clouds filter has been applied to the right half of the image.

The Render ⇨ Fibers filter replaces the current selection or image with threads of fibers created using the Foreground and Background colors. The Variance value controls how long fibers of a single color are, and the Strength value defines how stringy the fibers are. The Randomize button mixes these two values; this filter is excellent for creating textures that are used as hair. Figure 10-19 shows the Fibers dialog box.

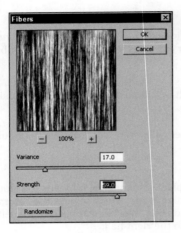

Figure 10-19: The Fibers dialog box is used to create long strands of fiber.

Lens flares are lighting anomalies that appear when you point a camera at a bright light. The Lens Flare filter opens a dialog box, shown in Figure 10-20, where you can click in the Preview pane to position the lens flare. You can also set the brightness of the lens flare and choose one of four lens types.

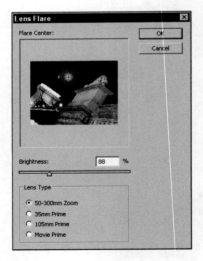

Figure 10-20: The Lens Flare dialog box lets you position the flare by dragging within the Preview pane.

Each of the various lens types creates a different pattern of streaks, rings, and glows. You can see results of each lens type in Figure 10-21.

Using the Lighting Effects filter

Of the various filters in the Render category, the Lighting Effects filter offers the most functionality. This filter may only be applied to RGB images using the Filter ➪ Render ➪ Lighting Effects menu command.

Figure 10-21: Each of the lens types creates a unique lens flare.

Caution   The Lighting Effects filter requires a substantial amount of memory, and if your system doesn't have enough memory available, a warning dialog box appears. You can make more memory available using the Edit ⇨ Purge menu command to free memory used by the Undo, Clipboard, and Histories features.

When the Lighting Effects filter is applied, the Lighting Effects dialog box, shown in Figure 10-22, is displayed. Using this dialog box, you can add multiple lights to shine upon the image shown in the Preview pane.

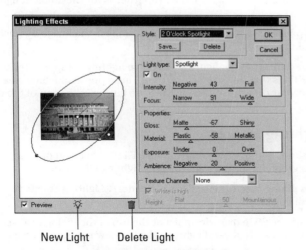

New Light   Delete Light

Figure 10-22: The Lighting Effects dialog box lets you position multiple lights around the image and change their settings.

To add a light to the image, click the Light icon at the bottom of the Preview pane and drag it into the Preview pane, or hold down the Option/Alt key and drag from an existing light to duplicate the light. All lights appear in the Preview pane as white dots. These lights may be repositioned by dragging the white dots to a new location.

When a light is selected in the Preview pane, an ellipse that represents the light's range is displayed. By dragging on its handles, you can change the light's range. Holding down the Shift key while dragging on these handles constrains the ellipse to change only a single dimension.

Lights are deleted by dragging their white dots to the Trash Can icon beneath the Preview pane.

The Light Type field lets you select from three different light types: Directional, Omni, and Spotlight. A Directional light shines light rays from a distant source, and all its rays are parallel much like the Sun. An ellipse represents a Spotlight and controls the Spotlight's angle and direction. A Spotlight decreases in intensity the further from its source it gets. An Omni light, represented by a circle, casts light equally in all directions, much like a light bulb.

Each light is enabled or disabled using the On option. Each light type also has an Intensity value, which may be positive or negative. A negative light value actually pulls light away from the image. Each light can also have a color, which is specified by the color swatch to the right of the Intensity setting. Click on the color swatch to open a Color Picker where you can change the light's color.

When the Spotlight type is selected, one end of the ellipse acts as the source and is the brightest point (or the darkest if the Intensity value is negative). The Focus value sets how much of the ellipse is filled with light.

The Properties values determine how the light interacts with the image surface. The Gloss value determines how shiny the surface is and how much the light reflects. The Material setting controls whether the light color (Plastic) or the image color (Metallic) gets reflected. The Exposure setting is a multiplier for the light, and the Ambience setting controls the background lighting in the image. The color swatch to the right of the Properties is for the ambient light color.

The Texture Channel field lets you select a channel and use it to emboss the image by raising the channel relative to the remaining pixels.

With all these controls, it may be difficult to configure an effective lighting setup. Photoshop includes several default Style settings that you can select from. These presets include a variety of settings, and you can save your own presets using the Save button at the top of the dialog box.

STEPS: Applying Lighting Effects

1. **Open an image in Photoshop.** Within Photoshop, choose File ➪ Open and open an image that includes a background that you want to apply lighting effects to.

2. **Open the Lighting Effects dialog box.** Choose Filter ➪ Render ➪ Lighting Effects to open the Lighting Effects dialog box.

3. **Select a lighting style.** From the Style drop-down list at the top of the dialog box, select the Five Lights Down style. This adds several lights to the Preview pane, as shown in Figure 10-23.

4. **Configure the lights.** Click on one of the white dots to select a light in the Preview pane. Notice that the Intensity value is already at maximum, but the lighting is still too dark. Drag the Ambience slider up to 25 to increase the overall light for the scene. Then click OK to apply the lighting to the image. Figure 10-24 shows the resulting image.

Sharpening an image

The Sharpen filters are used to enhance the details of blurry images by increasing the contrast of edges. Choose Filter ➪ Sharpen ➪ Sharpen to apply a general sharpening over the entire image without a dialog box. The Sharpen More filter increases the sharpening effect, and the Sharpen Edges focuses specifically on the image edges.

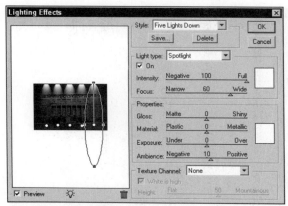

Figure 10-23: Selecting a lighting style automatically configures the Lighting Effects dialog box.

Figure 10-24: Applying a lighting effect to this image changes the image from a daytime image to a nighttime image.

The Unsharp Mask filter opens a dialog box, shown in Figure 10-25, that lets you adjust the amount of sharpness that is applied. This filter works by increasing the pixel contrast for areas where adjacent pixels have a value that is greater than the specified Threshold. The Radius value determines the size of the area where the pixel values are compared, and the Amount setting controls how much the contrast of adjacent pixels within the Threshold is increased.

Figure 10-25: The Unsharp Mask dialog box lets you control the amount of sharpening applied to an image.

Be warned that over-sharpening an image adds halos to the image edges. Images that include particularly bright colors may be over-saturated by setting the Amount setting too high. Figure 10-26 shows an image with the Unsharp Mask filter applied to different sections. The left end of the palace image has a large Radius value and a low Threshold causing the contrast to be increased for the entire section. The right end of the image has been sharpened with a high Amount and Radius settings and a low Threshold settings, causing the section to be over-saturated. The middle section is unchanged.

Figure 10-26: The Unsharp Mask filter has been applied to this image using different settings.

Using the Stylize filters

The Stylize filters apply a variety of unique effects that give an image a specific style. The filters in this category include the Diffuse, Emboss, Extrude, Find Edges, Glowing Edges, Solarize, Tiles, Trace Contour, and Wind.

The Diffuse filter moves pixels around to make the image appear unfocused. The options include Normal, Darken Only, Lighten Only, and Anisotropic. The Emboss filter colors the entire image gray and raises the image along its edges to form a relief. The Emboss dialog box lets you choose Angle, Height, and Amount values.

The Extrude filter divides the image into squares and colors each square to look like it is rising from the surface of the image. In the Extrude dialog box, you can select to use blocks or pyramids, set the size of the squares, and set the depth that they rise to.

The Find Edges and Solarize filters are applied without a dialog box. The Find Edges filter identifies all the edges in the image and displays them as dark borders on a white background. The Solarize filter combines the image with the image's negative to produce a darkened image with inverted colors.

The Tiles filter divides the entire image into square tiles and offsets each one slightly. In the Tiles dialog box, you can select the number of tiles and a maximum offset. The Trace Contour filter outlines the edges of the image, based on brightness, and displays them on a white background. The Wind filter spreads the edges of an image in different intensities as if something were dragged over the image when it was wet. Figure 10-27 shows a sampling of the Stylize filters applied to an image.

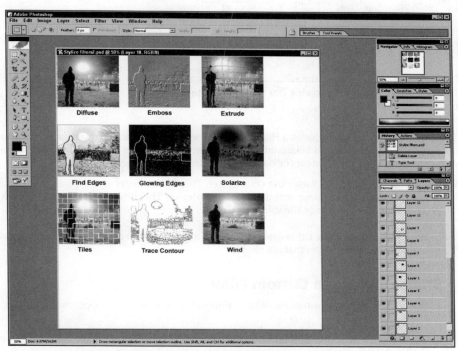

Figure 10-27: The Stylize filters may be used to create a number of unique effects.

Using the other filters

At the bottom of the Filter menu are two miscellaneous filter categories — Video and Other. The Video filters include De-Interlace, which is used to remove interlaced lines from images captured from a video source, and NTSC Colors, which limits the color palette to those used for broadcast television.

The Other category includes the Custom filter. This filter opens a dialog box, shown in Figure 10-28, that includes an array of value fields. Each text field represents the brightness value of the pixels that surround the pixel represented by the center text field. These brightness values can range from –999 to +999. The Scale value is used to divide the sum of all brightness values and the Offset value is added to the brightness values after scaling. By entering custom values into these text fields, you can create your own custom filter. These custom filters may be saved and reloaded as needed. The custom filters are saved with an ACF extension.

Figure 10-28: The Custom dialog box lets you create your own original filters.

The Other category also includes a High Pass filter, which highlights all the sharp color changing edges. The Minimum and Maximum filters look at a grouping of pixels defined by the Radius value and removes the brightest (or darkest) pixel from the group.

The Other category also includes the Offset filter. This filter offsets all the pixels in an image, making the image edges appear within the image interior. This filter is often used to mask the image edges to make an image tileable.

Note   Within Image Ready, the Other category includes a Tile Maker filter that may be used to create seamless background tiles that are tileable.

STEPS: Creating a Custom Filter

1. **Open an image in Photoshop.** Within Photoshop, choose File ➪ Open and open an image.

2. **Open the Custom dialog box.** Choose Filter ➪ Other ➪ Custom menu command to open the Custom dialog box.

3. **Enter filter values.** Enter a value of **5** in each cell in the top and bottom rows of the Custom dialog box. Then set the Scale value to **50**, as shown in Figure 10-29.

4. **Save the custom filter.** Click the Save button and save the custom filter with the name **Double exposure**. The resulting image is shown in Figure 10-30.

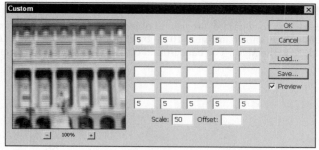

Figure 10-29: Entering values in these positions causes the image to blur.

Figure 10-30: This double-exposure image has a custom filter applied to it.

Using third-party filters

At the bottom of the Filter menu is a separator line. All third-party filters that are installed appear below this line. Photoshop, by default, includes one third-party filter category. The Digimarc filters enable you to embed a digital watermark into an image to secure copyright information.

Using the Filter interfaces

At the top of the Filter menu, along with the Filter Gallery, are three interfaces that let you interactively filter an image or a selection. These interfaces include the Extract interface, the Liquify interface, and the Pattern Maker interface.

Using the Extract interface

The Extract interface provides a way to separate foreground objects from the background of the image. Open the Extract interface, shown in Figure 10-31, by choosing Filter ➪ Extract (Alt+ Ctrl+X in Windows; Option+⌘+X on the Mac). The background objects are made transparent.

Eyedropper tool

Erser tool

Fill tool

Edge Highlighter tool

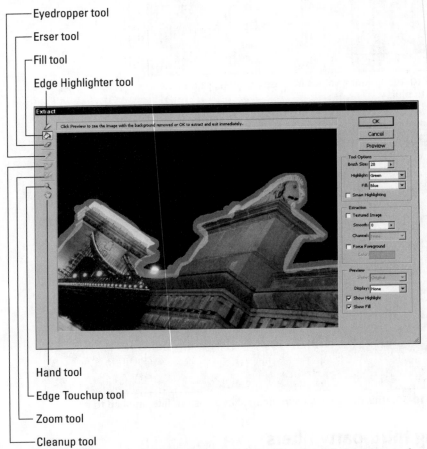

Hand tool

Edge Touchup tool

Zoom tool

Cleanup tool

Figure 10-31: The Extract interface lets you separate objects from their background.

The first step in extracting foreground objects is to highlight all the edges of the object that you want to extract with the Edge Highlight tool. By default, the edges are highlighted in green, but you may change this color along with the Brush Size in the Tool Options section. You can enable the Smart Highlighting option to have the Edge Highlight tool follow the edge boundary closely. The highlighted edges should follow the edges fairly closely, but they should overlap the background. The Eraser tool may be used to erase part of the highlighted edges if you need to correct a mistake.

Cross-Reference   Editing tools such as the Eraser tool are covered in Chapter 8.

After the edges are highlighted, you can fill the objects that you want to keep with the Fill tool. These areas appear in blue, but their color can also be changed.

When the object is highlighted and the area to keep is filled, you can select from two different extraction methods. The Textured Image option is used when the image contains a lot of texture. The Smooth value sets how smooth the highlighted edges are. If the image includes an alpha channel, then you can select the alpha channel as a way to define the edges.

The Force Foreground extraction option lets you select an interior color that closely matches the tones of the object that you want to extract. You can select a color from the image using the Eyedropper tool.

With an extraction area defined, click the Preview button to see the resulting extraction, as shown in Figure 10-32. With the extraction visible, the Cleanup tool and the Edge Touchup tool become active. The Cleanup tool is used to erase any background areas that were accidentally extracted. The Edge Touchup tool adds details back into the extracted image.

Figure 10-32: After an object is extracted, the background is made transparent.

In the Preview Show field, you can select to see the original image again and you can choose to display the extraction on a black, gray, or white matte, or on a custom color. Clicking OK in the Extract interface updates the selected layer with the extracted object on a transparent background.

STEPS: Extracting Foreground Objects

1. **Open an image in Photoshop.** Within Photoshop, choose File ⇨ Open and open an image that includes a well-defined object that you want to extract.

2. **Open the Extract interface.** Choose Filter ⇨ Extract to open the Extract interface. Click on the Zoom tool and zoom in on the object that you want to extract, as shown in Figure 10-33.

3. **Highlight the object.** Click on the Edge Highlighting tool. Then increase the Brush Size to 32 and drag around the object with the Edge Highlighting tool. Be sure to overlap the background as you highlight the edges.

Figure 10-33: The Extract interface includes Zoom and Hand tools to zoom in and focus on the object that you want to extract.

4. **Fill the object.** Click on the Fill tool and click within the object to fill the highlighted area. The filled area is shaded with a transparent blue, as shown in Figure 10-34.

Figure 10-34: The edges of the object to be extracted are highlighted in green and the object interior is highlighted in blue.

5. **Preview the extraction.** With the object filled, the Preview button becomes active. Select the Textured Image option and click on the Preview button. Photoshop calculates the extraction and displays it in the interface, as shown in Figure 10-35. After being extracted, the background becomes transparent and is shown as a checkerboard pattern, but this can make it difficult to see the extraction. You can change the background color using the

Display drop-down list in the lower-right corner of the interface. The Display options are None (checkerboard pattern), Black Matte, Gray Matte, White Matte or Other.

Figure 10-35: After an object is extracted, the background is transparent, but choosing to show the background as a Black Matte makes it easier to see the extraction.

6. **Clean the extraction edges.** Click on the Cleanup tool, set the Brush Size to 20, and erase those portions around the object that need to be deleted. Finally, click on the Edge Touchup tool and refill those edges that weren't included in the extraction. Figure 10-36 shows the object after it has been cleaned up.

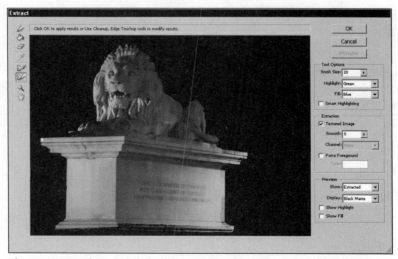

Figure 10-36: The extracted object may be cleaned up using the Cleanup and Edge Touchup tools.

Using the Liquify interface

The Liquify interface may be used to stretch and distort images and image selections as if they were placed on putty. To open the Liquify interface, shown in Figure 10-37, choose Filter ➪ Liquify (Shift+Ctrl+X in Windows; Shift+⌘+X on the Mac).

Moving the cursor over the Preview pane where the image is displayed reveals the outline of a brush. The brush options include its Size, Density, Pressure, Rate and Turbulence Jitter. Each of these options is set using the controls listed to the right.

Push Left tool

Bloat tool

Pucker tool

Twirl Clockwise tool

Reconstruct tool

Forward Warp tool

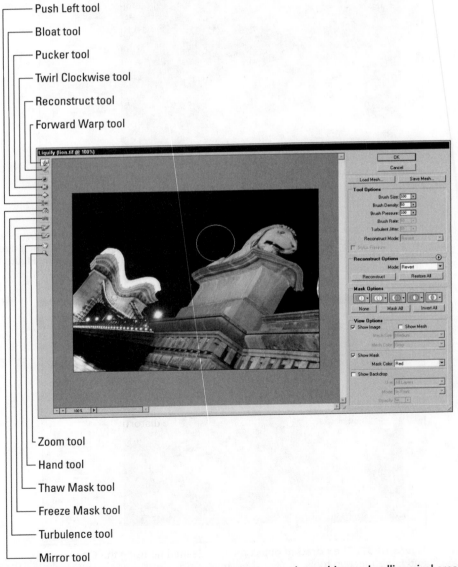

Zoom tool

Hand tool

Thaw Mask tool

Freeze Mask tool

Turbulence tool

Mirror tool

Figure 10-37: The Liquify interface lets you distort images by pushing and pulling pixel areas.

The various liquify tools are displayed in a toolbar to the left of the Preview pane and include the following:

✦ **Forward Warp tool:** This tool is used to push pixels in a forward direction as you drag the mouse. Holding down the Shift key while dragging moves the mouse in a straight line.

✦ **Reconstruct tool:** This tool is used to remove any liquify effects from the image and restore the brushed area to its original look.

✦ **Twirl Clockwise tool:** This tool is used to rotate the pixels about the center of the mouse in a clockwise direction. Holding down the Option/Alt key while dragging rotates the pixels in the counterclockwise direction.

✦ **Pucker tool:** This tool is used to move the pixels toward the center of the brush.

✦ **Bloat tool:** This tool is used to move the pixels away from the center of the brush.

✦ **Push Left tool:** This tool is used to move the pixels to the left when you drag upward. Dragging the mouse downward moves the pixels to the right. Rotating the mouse in a clockwise direction increases the areas. Rotating in a counterclockwise direction reduces the area. Holding down the Option/Alt key forces the mouse to drag straight up or down.

✦ **Mirror tool:** This tool is used to copy the pixels being dragged over to the opposite side of the brush. Holding down the Option/Alt key while dragging flips the effect to the other side.

✦ **Turbulence tool:** This tool is used to randomly move pixels underneath the brush area.

✦ **Freeze Mask tool:** This tool is used to paint a mask layer onto the Preview pane.

✦ **Thaw Mask tool:** This tool is used to erase a mask layer onto the Preview pane.

✦ **Hand tool:** This tool is used to drag the Preview pane to reposition the visible portion of the image. Double-click to fit in window.

✦ **Zoom tool:** This tool is used to zoom in on the image in the Preview pane. Holding down the Option/Alt key lets you zoom out. You can also zoom in on the image using the small plus and minus icon buttons in the lower-left corner. Double-click to see 100%.

Dragging with any of the Liquify tools in the Preview pane distorts the image. These distortions may be undone using the Reconstruct tool. The Reconstruct tool has several modes including Revert, Rigid, Stiff, Smooth, and Loose. Each of these modes reconstructs the image in a different manner. Pressing the Restore All button returns the image to its original state.

At any time during the modifications, you can use a mask to lock an area from any changes. The Mask Options dialog box includes buttons to replace, add, subtract, intersect, or invert the current mask selection, transparency, or layer mask.

The View Options let you toggle on and off the image, the distortion mesh, the mask, and the backdrop. The *backdrop* is the faded version of the original image.

STEPS: Using the Liquify Interface

1. **Open an image in Photoshop.** Within Photoshop, choose File ➪ New and create a new image.

2. **Set the Foreground color.** Click on the Fill box in the Toolbox and select a light blue color from the Color palette.

3. **Apply the Fiber filter.** Choose Filter ➪ Render ➪ Fibers to apply the Fibers filter to the blank canvas. In the Fibers dialog box, set the Variance to 16 and the Strength to 4. Then click OK. The fibers appear running vertical on the canvas, as shown in Figure 10-38.

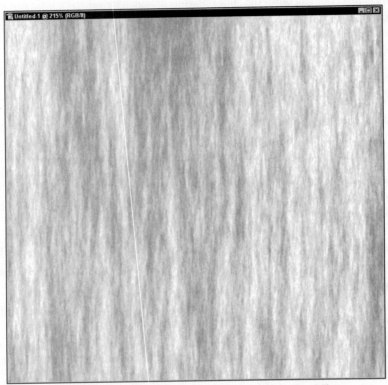

Figure 10-38: The Fibers filter is useful for creating strands of fiber.

4. **Rotate the canvas.** Choose Image ➪ Rotate Canvas ➪ 90 degrees CW to rotate the canvas so the fibers run horizontally, as shown in Figure 10-39.

5. **Use the Liquify interface.** Choose Filter ➪ Liquify to open the Liquify interface.

6. **Drag with the Liquify tools.** Select the Forward Warp tool and drag up and down throughout the image to create some ripples. Select the Bloat tool and drag small lines up and down to expand areas of the image. Finally, select the Turbulence tool and drag throughout the image to add some turbulence to the image. Figure 10-40 shows the final distorted image.

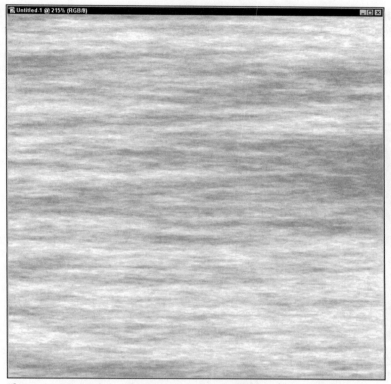

Figure 10-39: Rotating the canvas makes the fibers run horizontally.

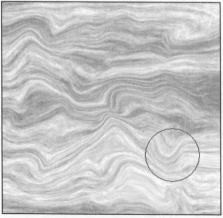

Figure 10-40: The Liquify interface allows you to add variety to the current image.

Creating patterns with Pattern Maker

Many designs make use of tileable background patterns. The opposite edges of the tileable patterns match perfectly so the background appears seamless. Creating seamless background patterns is manually possible with some help from the Filter ⇨ Other ⇨ Offset filter, but the Pattern Maker interface, shown in Figure 10-41, makes it quick and easy. Open the Pattern Maker interface by choosing Filter ⇨ Pattern Maker (Alt+Shift+Ctrl+X in Windows; Option+Shift+⌘+X on the Mac).

Figure 10-41: The Pattern Maker interface allows you to quickly create seamless patterns from a selected image.

Within the Pattern Maker interface, use the Rectangle Marquee tool to mark the area in the image that you want to use to create the pattern. Using the Width and Height fields, you can specify the size of the pattern tile, or you could click the Use Image Size button to create a pattern the same size as the current image. The Offset field lets you specify to offset the pattern either Vertically or Horizontally a specified amount.

After an area has been selected, click the Generate button to create a pattern. The Smoothness value defines how smooth the pattern is, and the Sample Detail defines the size of the sample used to create the pattern. Figure 10-42 shows a sample pattern.

When a pattern is generated, the pattern is saved in the Tile History section. To see the original image again, select the Original option from the Show field. Several patterns may be generated and viewed in the Pattern Maker interface and saved using the Saves Preset Pattern button.

Blending filters

Filters are applied with an Opacity value of 100%, making the filter take over the image completely. But you can make the applied filter effect transparent and even specify a blending mode by choosing Edit ⇨ Fade (Shift+Ctrl+F in Windows; Shift+⌘+F on the Mac).

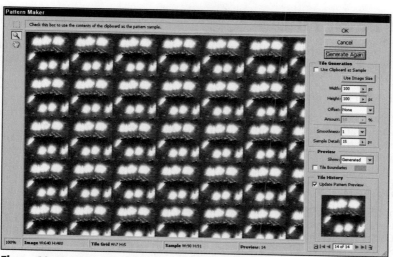

Figure 10-42: Generated patterns are displayed in the Preview pane and stored in the Tile History pane.

This command opens the Fade dialog box, shown in Figure 10-43, where you can specify an Opacity value and select a blending mode.

For more details on the various blending modes, see Chapter 8.

Figure 10-43: The Fade dialog box lets you blend the last applied filter by setting an Opacity value and selecting a blending mode.

Using Photoshop filters in Illustrator

Most of the default filters found in Photoshop are also available in Illustrator under the Filter menu. These filters are located at the bottom of the Filter menu underneath the Illustrator default filters.

These same Photoshop filters are also found in Illustrator in the Effect menu, allowing them to be applied as effects.

The Photoshop filters found in Illustrator may be applied only to raster images. If you select a vector object, these filters become disabled. However, but you can rasterize vector objects with the Edit ➪ Rasterize menu command. However, this command eliminates the vector nature of the object.

Most Photoshop filters work only in RGB mode, not in CMYK mode.

Using Illustrator Filters

In addition to the Photoshop filters, Illustrator also includes several filters that are unique to Illustrator. These filters are found in the Filter menu and include the Colors, Create, Distort, and Stylize submenus.

You can apply all of these default Illustrator filters to vector-based objects.

At the top of the Filter menu are two menu commands based on the last filter used. The top menu command re-applies the last applied filter using the same settings. The second menu command re-opens the filter dialog box for the most recently used filter, allowing you to change the filter settings.

Using the Colors filters

Because Photoshop deals with pixels, it includes many controls to adjust colors. Object colors may be adjusted and converted between color modes in Illustrator using the filters found in the Filter ➪ Colors menu. The filters included in this category include Adjust Colors, Blend Front to Back, Blend Horizontally, Blend Vertically, Convert to CMYK, Convert to RGB, Invert Colors, Overprint Black, and Saturate.

The Adjust Colors filter opens a dialog box where you can alter the color values for the fill and stroke colors. It also offers an option to convert between the various color modes. Another way to convert the selected object between color modes is with the several Convert filters found in this category.

The Blend filters are used to change the color of intermediate objects based on the colors of the two end objects. At least three objects must be selected to use any of these filters. If the Blend Front to Back filter is used, the middle object in the stacking order is changed. If the Blend Horizontally filter is used, the object between the leftmost and rightmost objects is changed. If the Blend Vertically filter is used, the middle object between the top and bottom objects is changed. Figure 10-44 shows a series of stacked rectangles before (on the left) and after (on the right) the Blend Front to Back filter was used.

Note   This same effect may be created using the Blend tool, but the filter doesn't maintain a link between the two end objects, so any updates to the end object's color has no impact on the intermediate object's color.

The Invert Colors filter replaces all the object colors with their negative counterparts. The Overprint Black filter lets you apply an overprint black to the selected object's fill or stroke. Finally, the Saturate filter opens a dialog box where you can adjust the Saturation Intensity for the selected object.

Using the Create filters

The Create category includes the Crop Marks filter to add crop marks to the current document based on the objects in the art board.

The Object Mosaic filter is only enabled when a raster image is selected. It lets you turn the image into a mosaic of small squares where each square is a selectable object, as shown in Figure 10-45.

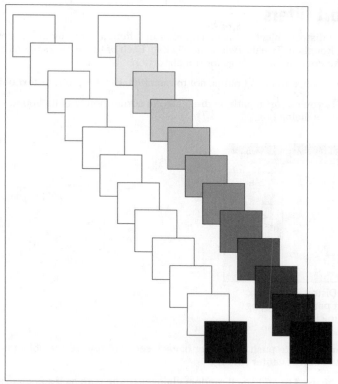

Figure 10-44: The Blend Front to Back filter changes the colors of all the intermediate objects.

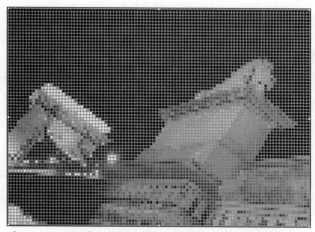

Figure 10-45: The Object Mosaic filter lets you change a raster image into many selectable square objects.

Using the Distort filters

The Distort filters let you distort object paths in a number of different ways, including Free Distort, Pucker & Bloat, Roughen, Tweak, Twist, and Zig Zag. Each of these filters opens a dialog box where you can control the settings for the distortion.

These filters may only be applied to object paths, not to raster images, symbols, or text objects.

The Free Distort filter lets you distort a path by dragging the corner points of its bounding box. Figure 10-46 shows this dialog box.

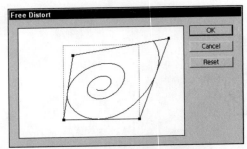

Figure 10-46: The Free Distort dialog box lets you distort an object path by dragging the corners of its bounding box.

The Pucker & Bloat filter is used to push the center of each segment toward the object center (Pucker) or away from the object center (Bloat).

The Roughen filter may be used to add small random changes to the path as if someone scribbled with a pen. The Tweak filter also applies randomness to a path by bending each segment inward or outward. The Twist filter lets you specify an Angle value that defines how much the path is twisted about its center. The Zig Zag causes the path to be angled back and forth in a regular pattern.

Figure 10-47 shows each of the Distort filters applied to a simple rectangle.

Using the Stylize filters

There are only three Illustrator Stylize filters — Add Arrowheads, Drop Shadow, and Round Corners.

The Add Arrowheads filter may only be applied to an open path. The Add Arrowheads dialog box, shown in Figure 10-48, lets you select from a library of arrowheads for the start and end of the path.

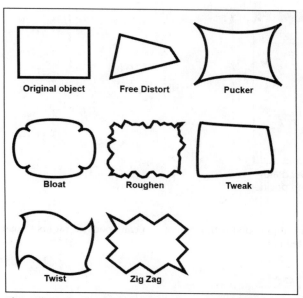

Figure 10-47: The Distort filters offer several unique ways to alter Illustrator paths.

Figure 10-48: The Add Arrowheads dialog box lets you select the arrow type to use for the Start and End of a path.

The Drop Shadow filter adds a simple drop shadow to the selected object using the Drop Shadow dialog box, shown in Figure 10-49. For the drop shadow, you can select a blending mode, an opacity, offset distances, a blur amount, and a color.

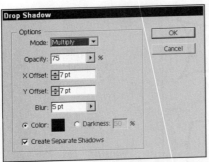

Figure 10-49: The Drop Shadow dialog box lets you control the look and position of the drop shadow.

The Round Corner filter opens a simple dialog box where you can specify a radius to use to round the corners of the selected path.

Using Illustrator Effects

If you compare the Filter and Effect menus in Illustrator, you'll see many of the same submenus. The key difference between applying a filter verses applying an effect is that effects show up in the Appearance palette, as shown in Figure 10-50, where they may be selected, edited, and removed at any time. Filters, on the hand, are permanently applied to an object and may only be removed using the Undo feature.

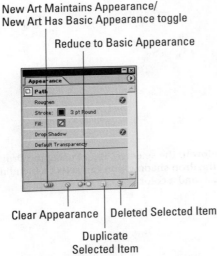

Figure 10-50: The Appearance palette lists all effects applied to the current selection.

Once an effect is applied to an object, the same effect is applied by default to all additional new objects that are created. To make new objects appear without these effects, click on the New Art Has Basic Appearance button at the bottom of the Appearance palette.

Effects can be removed from the selected object by selecting an effect in the Appearance palette and choosing the Remove Item menu command or by clicking on the Delete Selected Item button at the bottom of the Appearance palette. To remove all effects, click the Reduce to Basic Appearance button. This command causes all effects to be removed, but it doesn't change the stroke or fill settings. Clicking the Clear Appearance button removes all effects and sets the stroke and fill colors to None.

The drawback to using effects is that they take up valuable memory, and applying too many of them could significantly slow down the system, but if you have a lot of RAM, this shouldn't be a problem.

The Effect menu also includes many features that aren't found in the Filter menu. At the top of the Effect menu are two commands for instantly repeating the last applied effect and for recalling the dialog box used in the last applied effect.

Rasterizing effects

Many effects convert the object to a raster image before the effect is applied. Choose Effect ➪ Document Raster Effects Settings to open the dialog box shown in Figure 10-51. Here, you can set the global rasterization settings for all objects that are converted to raster images. The effects that require rasterization include all the SVG filters, all the Photoshop filters listed at the bottom of the Effect menu, and several of the Stylize effects.

Cross-Reference   SVG filters and the Document Raster Effects Settings dialog box are covered in more detail in Chapter 32.

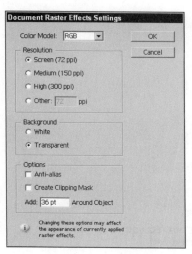

Figure 10-51: The Document Raster Effects Settings dialog box lets you specify the settings to use when an object is rasterized.

The Effect menu also includes a Rasterize menu command that opens up a dialog box with the same settings as the Document Raster Effects Settings dialog box. The settings in this dialog box are object-specific.

Creating 3D objects

The 3D category of effects lets you convert simple 2D paths into simple 3D objects. The 3D menu includes three different effects — Extrude & Bevel, Revolve, and Rotate. For example, a simple square path can be made into a cube with the Extrude effect, and a half circle path may be revolved to create a sphere. 3D objects in Illustrator created with these effects include shading using controllable lights.

Extruding objects

Extruding a 3D path is simply the process of adding depth to the path. This is accomplished using the 3D Extrude & Bevel Options dialog box, shown in Figure 10-52.

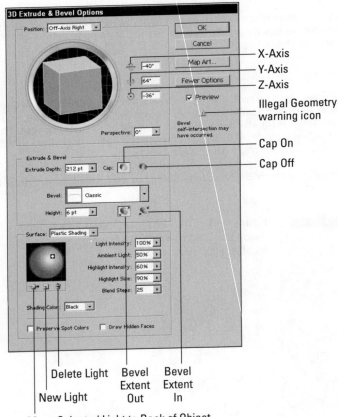

Figure 10-52: The 3D Extrude & Bevel Options dialog box lets you specify the direction and distance to extrude the selected path.

The Position field at the top of the dialog box lets you select one of the default preset positions. Selecting a position preset automatically updates the X-axis, Y-axis, Z-axis, and Perspective values. If any of these values are changed, then the Custom Rotation preset is used. The default position presets include positions such as Front, Left, Top, Off-Axis Front, Off-Axis

Top, Isometric Left, and so on. Isometric views are views where the Perspective value equals 0 and all parallel lines remain parallel.

Tip You can drag in the Preview pane, and the X-Axis, Y-Axis, and Z-Axis values are automatically updated.

The Extrude Depth value determines how far the path is moved to create depth. The Cap On and Cap Off buttons determine whether the extruded object is hollow or capped on either end.

The Bevel pop-up menu lets you choose the type of bevel to apply to the object. Each bevel type shows a profile curve. This curve matches the extruded portion of the object, and the Height value sets the maximum distance from the edge of the path. The bevel profile curve may be applied outward or inward using the Bevel Extent In and Bevel Extent Out buttons.

The Surface options define how the extruded object is shaded. The options include Wireframe, No Shading, Diffuse Shading, and Plastic Shading. If you click on the More Options button, several lighting controls appear. Figure 10-53 shows several extrude, bevel, and shading options applied to an object.

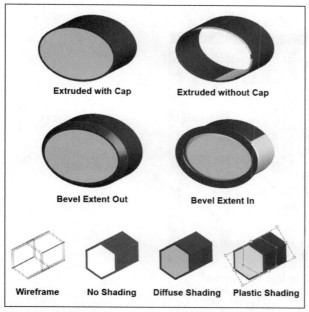

Figure 10-53: The Extrude & Bevel dialog box includes several different options for creating extruded 3D objects.

The Wireframe option only draws the lines that are used to make up the 3D object. The No Shading option colors each face of the object using the selected fill and stroke colors. Neither the Wireframe nor No Shading options have any lighting settings.

The Diffuse Shading option colors each face a different shade depending on how the light is cast upon the object. For this option, you can specify the Light Intensity, the Ambient Light percentage, the number of Blend Steps to use, and the Shading Color.

The Plastic Shading option colors the object as if the light were shining on an object with the surface made of plastic. Plastic objects are highly reflective and include specular highlights. For this option, you also have settings for the Highlight Intensity and Size.

When either the Diffuse or Plastic Shading options are selected, you can position the precise location of the lights used to illuminate the object by dragging in the Lighting Preview pane. Using the buttons underneath the pane, you can move the selected light to the back of the object so it shines from behind, create new lights, or delete a selected light. Lights are represented by the small white dots, and a single object can have many lights.

The Light Intensity value determines the strength of the light, which is at 100% at the center of its highlight. The Ambient Light value determines how much background light is used to light the object. The Blend Steps defines the number of different colors that are used to blend colors from the highlight to the shadows. The Shading Color is the color reflected off the object away from the highlight.

Mapping artwork

Within the Extrude & Bevel dialog box, the Map Art button opens another dialog box, shown in Figure 10-54, where you can select a Symbol to map onto the various surfaces of the extruded object.

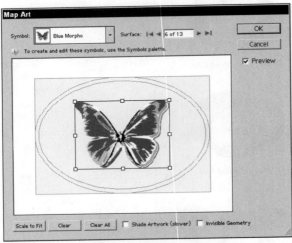

Figure 10-54: The Map Art dialog box lets you add symbols to the surfaces of the selected extruded object.

The Symbol pop-up menu lets you choose a Symbol from the active Symbol palette to apply to the selected surface. The Surface control includes arrows, which let you cycle through all the various surfaces that make up the extruded object. When a surface is selected, it is highlighted red in the art board.

Cross-Reference   Symbols and the Symbol palette are covered in Chapter 8.

The Scale to Fit button causes the selected symbol to be scaled to fit within the selected surface. The Clear button removes the mapped symbol from the selected surface and the Clear All button removes all mapped symbols from the entire object. The Shade Artwork option includes the mapped artwork as part of the shading calculations and the Invisible Geometry option may be selected to hide the geometry and show only the mapped artwork. Using the Invisible Geometry option is helpful to warp artwork along a 3D surface.

Revolving objects

The Effect ⇨ 3D ⇨ Revolve menu command opens a dialog box, shown in Figure 10-55, which is very similar to the Extrude & Bevel dialog box.

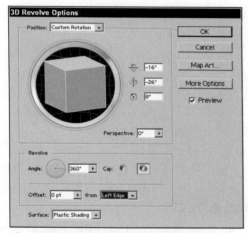

Figure 10-55: The 3D Revolve Options dialog box is similar to the dialog box for the Extrude & Bevel effect.

Using the Revolve effect, you can revolve a path about an axis to create a 3D object like the glass shown in Figure 10-56. The 3D Revolve Options dialog box lets you specify how much of an Angle to revolve about and whether the open ends are capped or not.

The Offset lets you specify the location of the center axis about which the selected path is revolved. The Surface options are the same as those for the Extrude & Bevel effect.

Rotating objects

The final effect in the 3D category is the Rotate effect. This effect lets you rotate and shade 2D and 3D objects and paths. The 3D Rotate Options dialog box includes the same position and shading controls as the other 3D effects.

Figure 10-56: Revolving an open path about its left edge creates a 3D revolved object.

Using the Convert to Shapes effects

The Convert to Shapes effects let you change the shape of an object into a Rectangle, a Rounded Rectangle, or an Ellipse. Each effect opens a dialog box, like the one shown in Figure 10-57, where you can specify the dimensions of the new shape.

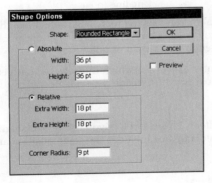

Figure 10-57: The Shape Options dialog box lets you convert shapes and bitmaps into a rectangle, a rounded rectangle, or an ellipse.

Applying standard Illustrator features as effects

Many of the effects found in the Effect menu offer the same functionality as features found elsewhere in Illustrator. For example, all the effects in the Distort & Transform category are exactly the same as those found in the Filter ➪ Distort menu, except for the Transform effect, which is identical to the Object ➪ Transform ➪ Transform Each dialog box.

Applying transforms as an effect causes the effect to appear in the Appearance palette where you have the ability to edit or remove them as needed at a later time without affecting the other attributes.

Cross-Reference   More details on the Appearance palette are covered in Chapter 8.

In addition to the Distort & Transform effects, the effects found in the Effect ➪ Path menu are identical to the features found in the Object ➪ Path menu. The Effect ➪ Pathfinder features are also found in the Pathfinder palette.

Using the Stylize effects

Most of the effects in the Effect ➪ Stylize menu are also found in the Filter ➪ Stylize menu, but several Stylize effects are unique to the Effect menu.

The Feather effect opens a simple dialog box where you can enter a Feather Radius amount. The Inner and Outer Glow effects open a dialog box like the one in Figure 10-58, where you can select a blending mode, a glow color, an opacity, and blur values, as well as whether the glow emanates from the center or from the edges of the object.

Figure 10-58: The Inner Glow dialog box lets you add a glow to the stroke of an object.

The Scribble effect opens a dialog box, shown in Figure 10-59, where you can make a path look like it was drawn using scribbled strokes. Although the resulting line looks like it was drawn freehand, the object is still a path and maintains it vector properties.

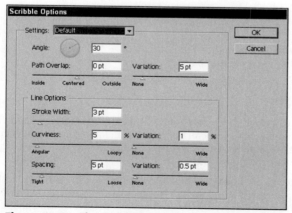

Figure 10-59: The Scribble Options dialog box lets you specify the options to create a rough scribbled look.

At the top of the Scribble Options dialog box is a drop-down list of presets. These presets lets you choose from several different setting configurations including Childlike, Dense, Loose, Moire, Sharp, Sketch, Snarl, Swash, Tight, and Zig Zag.

The Angle setting defines the angle at which the strokes are aligned, and the Path Overlap defines how often a drawn path crosses itself. Most settings include a Variation setting that is used to specify how random the attribute is. You can also define the Stroke Width, Curviness, and Spacing of the scribble marks.

Figure 10-60 shows examples of the Inner and Outer Glow effects and the Scribble effect.

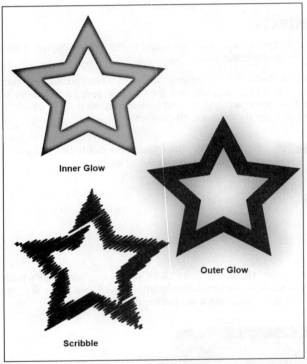

Figure 10-60: The Stylize effects offer some unique features that would be difficult or impossible to create manually.

Using the Warp effects

All the effects in the final category of the Effect menu open the same Warp Options dialog box, shown in Figure 10-61. Using this dialog box, you can deform the selected object into several different shapes including an Arc, Arc Lower, Arc Upper, Arch, Bulge, Shell Lower, Shell Upper, Flag, Wave, Fish, Rise, Fisheye, Inflate, Squeeze, and Twist.

The shape applied may be selected from the Style drop-down list at the top of the dialog box. For each shape, you can specify a Bend value, as well as Horizontal and Vertical Distortion values. The Bend value determines how closely the object matches the designated shape and the Distortion values skew the shape either vertically or horizontally.

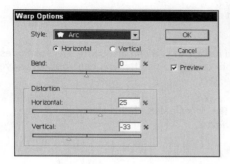

Figure 10-61: The Warp Options dialog box lets you choose the shape style to make the shape conform toward.

Figure 10-62 shows each of the Warp styles found in the Effect ➪ Warp menu applied to a simple rectangle.

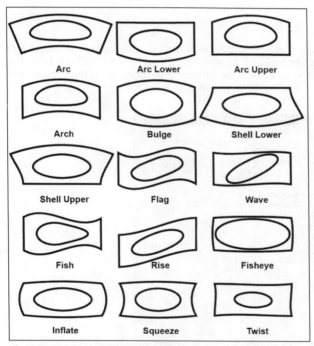

Figure 10-62: The Warp effects cause the selected object to warp to conform to the chosen shape.

Using Photoshop's Layer Effects and Styles

Although effects are typically found in Illustrator, Photoshop has a similar feature that may be applied to a layer called Layer Effects. A pop-up menu of Layer Effects is found at the bottom of the Layers palette.

Cross-Reference   Layers and the Layers palette are covered in detail in Chapter 12.

Not only can you apply these Layer Effects to a layer, but you can also store them as Styles in the Styles palette, shown in Figure 10-63. From the Styles palette, you can apply the Layer Effects to any image or selection.

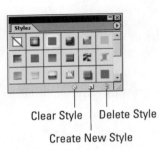

Figure 10-63: The Styles palette holds all styles, which include Layer Effects.

Clear Style | Delete Style

Create New Style

All the Layer Effects found in the Layers palette open the same dialog box, shown in Figure 10-64. This Layer Style dialog box includes a panel for each of the Layer Effects including Blending Options; Drop Shadow; Inner Shadow; Outer Glow; Inner Glow; Bevel and Emboss; Satin; Color Overlay; Gradient Overlay; Pattern Overlay; and Stroke.

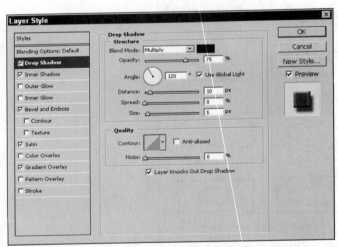

Figure 10-64: The Layer Style dialog box includes a separate panel for each Layer Effect.

Each Layer Effect may be turned on or off using the check box to the left of the effect name. To the right of the dialog box is a sample thumbnail of the defined style and a New Style button. Clicking the New Style button opens a dialog box where you can name the new style. Clicking OK adds the defined style to the Styles palette.

Each Layer Effect applied to a layer is listed in the Layers palette. Double-clicking on the effect in the Layers palette opens the Layer Style dialog box where you can edit the effects settings.

Applying Effects in InDesign

Although InDesign doesn't include support for graphic filters or effects, it does include several special effects that may be applied to objects including Drop Shadows, Feathering, and Corner Effects. Each of these features is found in the Object menu.

Adding drop shadows

Choosing Object ➪ Drop Shadow opens a dialog box, shown in Figure 10-65, where you can set the properties of the drop shadow including a blending mode, an opacity, an X and Y offset, a blur, and a color. The bottom of the dialog box includes several swatches that you can select from.

Note   For drop shadows, the default blending mode, Multiply, creates the most realistic shadow and is probably the most reliable blending mode for printing.

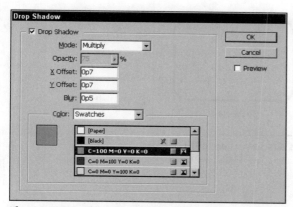

Figure 10-65: The Drop Shadow dialog box in InDesign lets you add drop shadows to any element.

Feathering objects

Choosing Object ➪ Feather opens a simple dialog box where you can set the Feather Width and choose whether the corners stay sharp, rounded, or diffused.

Creating corner effects

Choosing Object ➪ Corner Effects opens a simple dialog box where you can choose from the available effects. The options include None, Fancy, Bevel, Inset, Inverse Rounded, and Rounded. You can also set the size of the effect.

Figure 10-66 shows each of the corner effects available in InDesign.

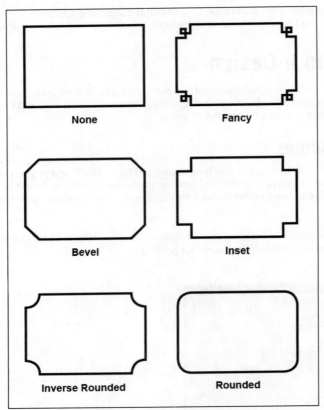

Figure 10-66: Using corner effects ads some flair to the rectangular frames.

Summary

✦ Most Photoshop filters are applied using the Filter Gallery interface. This interface includes a wide assortment of filters and allows you to preview and apply multiple filters at once.

✦ The Filter menu in Photoshop also includes many other filters that aren't part of the Filter Gallery. These filters are selected from the Filter menu.

✦ Photoshop includes three additional filter interfaces for working with images, including the Extract, Liquify, and Pattern Maker interfaces.

✦ Most of the Photoshop filters may also be applied to objects within Illustrator.

✦ In addition to the Photoshop filters, Illustrator also includes some filters that may only be used on vector objects. These filters are found at the top of the Filter menu.

✦ Effects used in Illustrator show up in the Appearance palette and may be edited or removed at any time.

✦ Layer Effects in Photoshop appear in the Layers palette and may be used to create a new style.

✦ InDesign includes a few effects in its Object menu.

✦   ✦   ✦

Working with Layers

The real benefit of layers is their ability to organize a project into several easy-to-select sections. Previously, this was done with groups, but groups can be tricky to work with, requiring the Group Selection tool to work within a group. Layers are a much more convenient way to organize all the images and objects in a document.

Another benefit of layers is that you can quickly turn them on and off. If a project is sluggish because of its size and content, you could place these large items on a layer and make them invisible so they don't slow down the rest of the project.

Layers may also be locked. You may want to lock parts of your completed project, so you don't accidentally select and move them.

You can also create several design ideas and keep them on several layers. Then you can quickly switch between the various designs using layers. This is a concept mastered by Photoshop with the Layer Comps feature.

Layers are available in Photoshop, Illustrator, InDesign, GoLive, and Acrobat, but the ways layers are used in each of these applications are very different. Layers in each of these applications include some basic concepts that are common for all applications:

+ **InDesign:** Layers in InDesign use the most basic layer features, but even InDesign includes some specialized layer features.

+ **Illustrator:** Illustrator expands on the layer basics with many additional layer features, including support for sublayers, layer templates, releasing items to layers, and clipping and opacity masks.

+ **Photoshop:** Photoshop takes layer functionality to a whole new level with support for layer sets, linked layers, transparency, adjustment and fill layers, layer effects, masks, and layer comps.

+ **Acrobat:** In Acrobat 6, you find support for Adobe PDF Layers. PDF documents containing layers must be authored in applications supporting layers and having the ability to export to the PDF 1.5 format. If you view a layered PDF document in earlier versions of Acrobat, the layers are flattened and viewed as a single layer document.

+ **GoLive:** The layers found in GoLive follow the Cascading Style Sheet (CSS) features for placing Web page content in stackable layers. This endows the GoLive layers with several unique features such as Web page placement, background colors and images, and animation capabilities.

In this chapter, we present these layer basics first, starting with InDesign. We then move on to the specific layer features for each individual application. In this chapter, we start by looking at the Layers palette's basic features found in InDesign. Finally, we show you how layered files exported to the PDF format can access layers in Acrobat.

Using the Layers Palette

Within the CS applications, layers for the current project and all the layer features are contained in the Layers palette, shown in Figure 11-1. Open this palette by choosing Window ➪ Layers (F7).

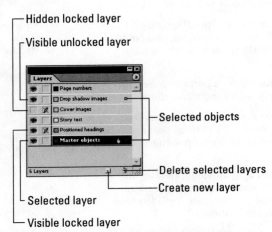

Figure 11-1: All layers for the current InDesign document display in the Layers palette.

All new projects created in Illustrator and InDesign include a default layer named Layer 1; a new layer added to the document is named Layer 2 by default. Double-clicking on a layer opens a dialog box where you can rename the layer and set the layer's properties.

Within the Layers palette are several visual icons that determine whether the selected layer is visible, locked, selected, or targeted. The eye icon in the first column to the left of the layer name determines layer visibility. The lock icon in the second column to the left of the layer name is used to show if a layer is locked.

Other icons appear to the right of the layer name and are used to denote the targeted layer and any selected objects on that layer. The selected layer(s) are highlighted and all menu commands that are selected are applied to all selected layers.

Creating layers

To create a new layer, select the New Layer palette menu command or click on the Create New Layer button at the bottom of the Layers palette. If you select the menu command, the Layer Options dialog box appears, shown in Figure 11-2. Here, you can name the new layer, select a layer color, and specify several layer properties. Clicking the Create New Layer button creates a new layer using default values without opening the Layer Options dialog box. To force the Layer Options dialog box to appear when you click on the Create New Layer button, hold down the Option/Alt key when clicking.

Figure 11-2: The Layer Options dialog box

The layer properties that appear in the Layer Options dialog box set options such as whether the layer is visible or locked.

Note   Other than layer name and color, the specific layer properties found in the Layer Options dialog box are unique for each CS application. For example, InDesign includes options to show guides, lock guides, and suppress text wrap when the layer is hidden; Illustrator includes options to make the layer a template, print, preview, and dim images to a percentage; and Photoshop includes options to use the previous layer to create a clipping mask, select a blending mode, and set an opacity.

If you double-click on a layer name or if you select a layer and choose the Layer Options palette menu command, the Layer Options dialog box reappears, letting you change the layer properties. Double-clicking the layer name in Photoshop or GoLive selects the name and lets you rename it within the Layers palette.

In InDesign, new layers always appear at the top of the Layers palette, but if you hold down the ⌘/Ctrl key while clicking on the Create New Layer button, the new layer appears directly above the selected layer. Creating a new layer in Illustrator or Photoshop places the new layer directly above the selected layer.

Selecting and targeting layers

Clicking on a layer name selects and targets a layer. To select multiple layers, hold down the ⌘/Ctrl key while clicking on each layer that you want to select, or hold down the Shift key and click on the first and last layers to select all layers between these two layers.

Note   Photoshop's Layer palette lets you select only a single layer at a time.

The targeted layer in InDesign is marked with a Pen icon to the right of the layer name. This icon denotes the targeted layer. Targeted layers in Illustrator are marked with a small triangle in the upper-right corner; the targeted layer in Photoshop is the selected layer. All new objects that you add to the project, including all newly created objects and any imported, copied, or placed files, are placed on the active layer.

Caution   If you lock the targeted layer, you can't create the new object, but a warning dialog box appears, informing you that the targeted layer is hidden or locked and asking if you want to unlock and show it.

Hiding and locking layers

The first column in the Layers palette holds the Visibility icon. If the eye icon is present, then the layer is visible, but if the eye icon isn't present, then the layer is hidden. You can toggle the eye icon by clicking on it. Hidden layers are not printed either, although you can print hidden layers in Illustrator if you select the Print option in the Layers Options dialog box.

The second column is the Lock icon. If the lock icon is present, then the layer is locked and cannot be selected or edited, but if the lock icon isn't present, then the layer is editable. You can also toggle the lock icon by clicking on it.

Note   Within InDesign, the lock icon looks like a pencil icon with a red line through it; in Illustrator, the lock icon looks like a lock. Photoshop uses the second column for other purposes and allows layers to be locked using the Lock properties at the top of the palette. Photoshop includes the option to lock specific items; the lock icon is displayed to the right of the layer name.

To hide or lock multiple layers at once, choose the Hide Others or Lock Others palette menu commands, and all layers that aren't selected are hidden or locked. If at least one layer is hidden or locked, these menu commands change to Show All Layers or Unlock All Layers.

Rearranging layers

The order in which the layers are listed in the Layers palette determines the stacking order of objects on the page, with the layer listed at the top of the Layers palette appearing in front of all other objects in the document.

You can rearrange layers by selecting and dragging one layer above or below another. A dark black line appears between the two layers where the dragged layer is positioned if dropped.

Copying objects between layers

The Selection tool may be used to select any object on any layer that is not locked. A small square icon appears to the right of the layer name of each layer that includes a selected object.

The bounding box of the selected object is colored using the layer color.

Tip   To select all objects on a single layer, hold down the Option/Alt key while clicking on the layer name in the Layers palette. If the layer doesn't contain any objects, then you can't select it with the Option/Alt key held down.

To move a selected object to another layer, click and drag the small square icon to the layer that you want to move the object to. If you hold down the Option/Alt key while dragging the small square icon, a copy of the selected object moves to the selected layer. If you hold down Ctrl+Alt (Windows) or ⌘+Option (Mac) while dragging the small square icon, the selected object may be moved onto a hidden or locked layer.

You can choose Edit ➪ Cut, Edit ➪ Copy, or Edit ➪ Paste to move objects between layers and between documents. If you enable the Paste Remembers Layers option (only available in Illustrator and InDesign) in the palette menu, then the pasted objects are pasted in the same layers from which you copied them. If you paste the copied objects into a document without the same layer names, the layer names for the selected objects are added to the new document and the copied objects are pasted on these new layers.

Duplicating layers

You can use the Duplicate palette menu command to duplicate a layer and all the objects on that layer. The duplicated layer appears directly above the original layer. You can also duplicate a layer by dragging a layer to the Create New Layer button at the bottom of the palette. The duplicated layer appears with the same layer name with the word, *copy* after it, so duplicating a layer named "Sword" results in a layer named "Sword copy." Duplicating this layer again results in a layer named "Sword copy 2."

Deleting layers

You can use the Delete palette menu command to delete the selected layers, or you can click on the Delete Selected Layers button at the bottom of the Layers palette. If the layer contains any objects, a warning dialog box appears confirming that you want to delete the objects on the layer.

To delete any empty layers in the current document, select the Delete Unused Layers palette menu command. This removes any layers that don't contain any objects.

Merging layers

You use the Merge Layers palette menu command to combine all objects on the selected layers. The objects all appear on the targeted layer, and the other selected layers are deleted. Selecting all layers and choosing this command offers a way to flatten all layers to a single layer.

STEPS: Creating a Layered Document

1. **Create a new document.** Within Photoshop, Illustrator, InDesign or GoLive, choose File ➪ New to create a new document.

2. **Open the Layers palette.** Choose Window ➪ Layers to open the Layers palette. The default layer is listed as Layer 1.

3. **Add content to the layer.** Using the tools in the Toolbox, add some content to the existing layer.

4. **Create a new layer.** Before you being to add a new type of content, click the Create New Layers button at the bottom of the Layers palette to create a new layer. In the New Layer dialog box that appears, name the layer appropriately.

5. **Hide and lock the first layer.** To hide the content on the first layer so it isn't accidentally edited, click on the eye icon to the left of the first layer's name. This icon hides the layer. If you need to see the content in the first layer, but you don't want it edited, click the eye icon again to make the layer visible; then click the lock icon in the second column to lock the layer.

6. **Rearrange the layers.** The new layer appears in front of the first layer. To change this order, click and the drag the first layer above the new layer in the Layers palette. Placing the first layer above the other layer makes its content come to the front of the stacking order.

STEPS: Dividing an Existing Document into Layers

1. **Open a document in InDesign.** Within InDesign, select a document that you want to divide into layers for better organization.

2. **Open the Layers palette.** Choose Window ➪ Layers to open the Layers palette.

3. **Create new layers.** Click on the Create New Layers button at the bottom of the Layers palette several times to create some new layers.

4. **Rename the layers.** Double-click on each of the new layers and, in the Layer Options dialog box that appears, type a new descriptive name for the layer.

5. **Move objects to their correct layer.** Move through each page in the document and select the objects on that page. Then drag the square selected icon in the Layers palette to the correct layer for that object. After an object is moved to its correct layer, its bounding box changes to the same color as its layer. Continue this step for all objects in the document. Figure 11-3 shows the layers created for this document.

Figure 11-3: After creating and naming the necessary layers, objects are easily placed on the correct layer.

Using Layers in InDesign

In addition to the basic features found in the Layers palette, InDesign also includes a couple of layer features that are unique to the application, including the ability to condense the layers list in the Layers palette, show and lock layer guides, suppress text wrap, and features for dealing with objects on Master pages.

Condensing the Layers palette

Within InDesign, the Layers palette may be condensed using the Small Palette Rows palette menu option. Figure 11-4 shows the Layers palette in InDesign with the Small Palette Rows option enabled.

Figure 11-4: The Small Palette Rows option condenses layer sizes.

Using guides

Guides in InDesign are especially useful for aligning and positioning elements; each layer may have its own set of guides. Guides are created for the selected layer by clicking on the Horizontal or Vertical rulers and dragging into the page. If the rulers aren't visible, you can choose View ➪ Show/Hide Rulers to make them visible.

Guides appear as straight lines in the document and the selected guide has the same color as the selected layer.

The View ➪ Show/Hide Guides menu command and the View ➪ Lock Guides menu command are used to show, hide, and lock all guides in the current document. But you can also select to show, hide, and lock guides on a specific layer using the Show Guides and Lock Guides options in the Layer Options dialog box. Double-clicking on a layer in the Layers palette opens this dialog box.

Suppressing text wrap on hidden layers

In an InDesign document, it's often helpful to separate text and graphics onto separate layers. By doing so, you can make the graphics hidden when you're proofreading the text, and you can hide the text when you're working on the graphics.

If the text object is set to wrap around a graphic, then making either layer hidden impacts the text wrapping. You can control whether the text is wrapped when the graphic layer is hidden using the Suppress Text Wrap When Hidden option in the Layer Options dialog box.

Figure 11-5 shows two similar documents that have separated the graphics and text onto two different layers. Although the text is set to wrap around the center graphic, the document on the left has the Suppress Text Wrap When Hidden option disabled in the Layer Options dialog box, so the text wrap is still visible; the document on the right has enabled this option, causing the text wrap to be suppressed.

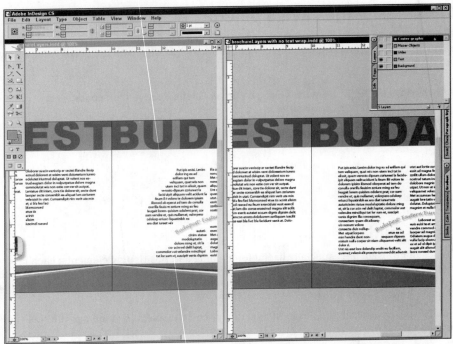

Figure 11-5: The Suppress Text Wrap When Hidden option controls whether the text wraps when the graphic layer is hidden.

Reordering Master objects above layers

By default, Master objects placed on the same layer as page objects appear behind those page objects. To make the Master object, such as auto page numbers, appear in front of the page objects, place the Master objects on a layer that is above the page object's layer.

STEPS: Making Page Numbers Appear in Front of Other Elements

1. **Open a document in InDesign.** Within InDesign, open a document that includes Master pages and auto page numbers.

2. **Add an element to the Master page.** In the Layers palette, select the Background layer. Then in the Pages palette, double-click on the SpreadMaster Master to select them. Then click on the Rectangle tool and drag a rectangle over the top of the flag and page number in the lower-left corner of the Master page. Change the rectangle's Fill color to white and its Stroke color to black with a Weight of 2 pt, as shown in Figure 11-6.

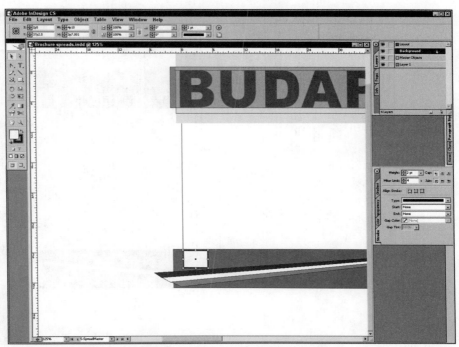

Figure 11-6: Adding an object onto the current layer places the object on top of the Master objects that appear on that page.

3. **Create a new layer for the Master page numbers.** In the Layers palette, click on the Create New Layer button at the bottom of the Layers palette. A new layer is added at the top of the Layers palette. Then double-click on the new layer, name the layer Master Page Numbers, and click OK.

4. **Move the Master Page Number element to the new layer.** Click the Visibility icon for the background layer to temporarily hide the background layer so you can see the page number and flag elements hidden behind the rectangle. Then select the page number and flag elements, as shown in Figure 11-7. In the Layers palette, drag the small rectangle to the right of the Master Objects palette to the Master Page Numbers layer to move the selected object to the new layer.

Figure 11-7: Clicking the eye icon makes a layer temporarily hidden so you can see the objects underneath.

5. **Make all layers visible.** As a final step, click the eye icon for the background layer to show all layers. The results are shown in Figure 11-8, where the page number and flag are positioned in front of the white rectangle.

Importing layered files

When layered files are placed within InDesign by choosing File ➪ Place, InDesign flattens all layers. This flattening only affects the image within InDesign and does not affect the original image file or its layers.

If you need to edit the original file, you can select the file in the Links palette and choose the Edit Original palette menu command. This opens the image file in the application that was used to originally create the image.

Cross-Reference

To learn more about working with the Links palette, see Chapter 24.

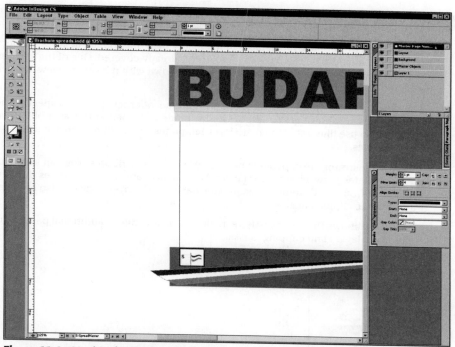

Figure 11-8: Moving the Master elements to a layer that is positioned above the layer with the obscuring object makes the Master elements visible.

Applying transparency and blending modes to a layer

You use blending modes to define how the colors of two overlapping transparent objects are blended. Although InDesign doesn't include a way to apply transparency or blending mode to a layer, you can quickly select all objects on a selected layer by holding down the Option/Alt key while clicking on the layer in the Layers palette. With all objects on a layer selected, you can set the layer's Opacity value and blending mode using the Transparency palette, shown in Figure 11-9.

Note Photoshop allows you to apply an Opacity value and blending mode to an entire layer.

Figure 11-9: The Transparency palette in InDesign

Cross-Reference Details on using transparency and the blending modes are found in Chapter 8.

Using Layers in Illustrator

Layers in Illustrator have much more functionality than those found in InDesign, but the Layers palette still includes all the basic layer features already covered. One of the key benefits is that the Illustrator's Layers palette lets you drill down within layers to view and select the each individual item included in a layer.

The Layer options within Illustrator are also unique, offering options to specify whether the layer objects are shown in Preview or Outline mode and whether the layer objects are printed. You can also use Illustrator to create layer templates that hold reference content such as traced images.

Layers in Illustrator are capable of holding appearance attributes. You can select and move these attributes between different layers. You can also apply graphic styles directly to a targeted layer from the Graphic Styles palette. Illustrator's Layers palette also includes a simple way to create clipping masks.

Figure 11-10 shows the Layers palette in Illustrator. It includes additional palette buttons for creating sublayers and clipping masks.

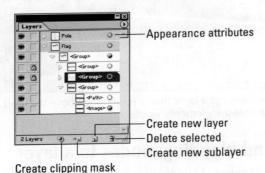

Figure 11-10: The Layers palette in Illustrator offers some additional features.

Changing the Layers palette view

Illustrator offers several different ways to view the Layers palette, as specified in the Layers Palette Options dialog box, shown in Figure 11-11. This dialog box is accessed using the Palette Options palette menu command.

The Show Layers Only option hides all sublayers and displays only the top-level layer names.

The Row Size section lets you choose the size of the layer rows in the Layers palette from Small, Medium, Large, or Other, where you can set the row size in pixels. The Small option displays the layers without any thumbnails, similar to the Layers palette in InDesign when the Small Palette Rows option is enabled. The Medium option displays smaller thumbnails, as shown in Figure 11-12, and the Large option is shown in Figure 11-11.

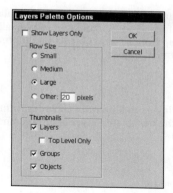

Figure 11-11: The Layers Palette Options dialog box

Figure 11-12: The Medium option decreases the size of the layer thumbnails.

The Thumbnails section lets you display the thumbnails for layers, the top level only, groups, and/or objects. Selecting the Top Level Only option only shows thumbnails for the top level and hides the thumbnails for all sublayers.

Using sublayers

All layers that contain objects have a small arrow to the left of the layer name. Clicking this arrow changes the arrow's direction and expands the layer to reveal all the layer's sublayers or objects. Clicking on an expanded arrow icon collapses the layer again. If you hold down the Option/Alt key while clicking on an arrow, all sublayers expand.

You can create new sublayers in Illustrator just as new layers by selecting the New Sublayer palette menu command or by clicking on the Create New Sublayer button at the bottom of the Layers palette. Selecting this command or holding down the Option/Alt key while clicking the Create New Sublayer button causes the Layer Options dialog box to appear.

Note   If you select the Top Layer Only option in the Palette Options dialog box, then thumbnails don't display for any sublayers.

As layers and/or sublayers are rearranged by dragging them in the Layers palette, if you drop a layer when a layer name is highlighted, the dropped layer becomes a sublayer under the selected layer.

With all the layers and sublayers, it can become difficult to find objects in the Layers palette. To locate an object's layer using the object, just select the object in the art board and choose the Locate Object palette menu command; the object's sublayer is selected in the Layers palette.

Object groups created by choosing Object ➪ Group show up in the Layers palette as a sublayer identified with the word *Group* listed in brackets. Expanding the Group sublayer reveals all the objects that are part of the group. If you create a group from several objects on different layers, all the objects move to the same layer as the frontmost object.

Printing and previewing layers

The Layer Options dialog box, shown in Figure 11-13, for layers in Illustrator includes Print and Preview options. These options determine whether the designated layer is printed and whether the layer is displayed in Preview or Outline mode.

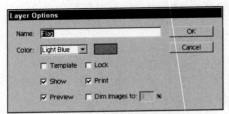

Figure 11-13: The Layer Options dialog box in Illustrator

Holding down the ⌘/Ctrl key while clicking on the Visibility icon toggles the selected layer between Preview and Outline mode. This changes the Visibility icon, as shown in Figure 11-14. Using the Outline Others palette menu command, or holding down Ctrl+Alt (Windows) or ⌘+Option (Mac) while clicking on the Visibility icon changes all layers except for the selected one to Outline mode.

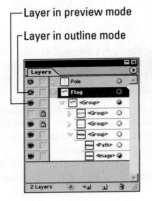

Figure 11-14: The eye icon shows what layers are in Outline mode.

The Layer Options dialog box also includes an option to dim images by a specific percentage. This is helpful if you're tracing images, as shown in Figure 11-15.

Disabling the Print option prevents the layer from printing when you choose File ➪ Print, even if the layer objects are visible. If you disable the Preview option, the layer objects are viewed in Outline mode. This is a useful option if you have a complex object that takes a long time to redraw.

Figure 11-15: The Dim Images By option makes tracing images easy.

Creating layer templates

The Layer Options dialog box also includes an option to make a layer into a template layer. You can also make a layer a template by selecting the Template palette menu command. The Visibility icon for templates changes as shown in Figure 11-16.

Note Layer templates are different from the Illustrator templates created by choosing File ➪ Save as Template. Illustrator templates have a different file extension (AIT), but layer templates may exist in any Illustrator document.

─ Normal layer

┌ Template layer

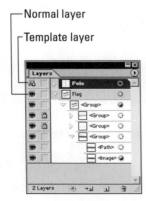

Figure 11-16: Template layers don't print or export with the rest of the layers.

Template layers are unique because you cannot print or export them. You can also hide them by choosing View ➪ Show/Hide Template (Shift+Ctrl+W in Windows; Shift+⌘+W on the Mac).

When you choose File ➪ Place, the Place dialog box includes a Template option. If this option is selected, the placed image is put on a new template layer. This new layer is positioned directly below the selected layer. By default, this template layer is locked and the layer dims to 50 percent.

You may change template layers back to normal layers by disabling the Template option in the Layer Options dialog box.

STEPS: Tracing Layers in Illustrator

1. **Open a new document in Illustrator.** Within Illustrator, open a new document by choosing File ➪ New.

2. **Open an image to trace from.** Choose File ➪ Place. In the file dialog box that opens, select an image that you want to trace from and enable the Template option, as shown in Figure 11-17. Then click on the Place button. The image is placed on a new template layer and the Dim Layer to 50% option is enabled in the Layer Options dialog box.

Figure 11-17: The Place dialog box includes a Template option.

3. **Trace the image.** Select a layer above the template layer and trace over the image with the Paintbrush tool, as shown in Figure 11-18.

4. **Hide the template layer.** After the sketch is complete, you can hide the template layer by clicking on the Visibility icon.

Figure 11-18: A dimmed image lets you easily trace an image.

Releasing items to layers

If a single layer has many different objects, you can use the Release to Layers palette menu commands to move (or copy) each successive object to its own layer.

Cross-Reference Illustrator's Release to Layers menu commands are useful in building animation sequences that you can then export to the SWF format. More information on this format and using the Release to Layers commands to create animations is covered in Chapter 32.

There are actually two different Release to Layers menu commands. The Release to Layers (Sequence) palette menu command moves each object to its own layer, but the Release to Layers (Build) menu command copies and accumulates the objects to new layers where first object gets copied to a new layer, the second object along with the first gets copied to the second layer, and so on until the final layer has all objects.

When objects with a layer are released to layers, the objects are added to layers starting with the object farthest back in the stacking order and moving forward, so the front-most object is placed on the highest layer.

With several layers selected, you can select to reverse their order in the Layers palette by using the Reverse Order palette menu command.

Collecting layers and flattening artwork

Illustrator includes palette menu commands for merging, collecting, and flattening layers. Collecting layers is similar to merging layers, but instead it collects the objects on several layers and moves them to a new layer. The Collect in New Layer palette menu command moves all objects on the selected layers to a new layer and deletes the old layers.

Illustrator also includes a Merge Selected menu command that merges the objects on all selected layers into the targeted layer.

The Layers palette only lets you select multiple layers within the same hierarchical level, so you cannot merge or collect layers at different levels within one another.

To merge all layers together, you could select all layers and use the Merge Selected palette menu command, or you could use the Flatten Artwork palette menu command. This merges all layers into one layer that includes all the objects in the file.

Caution The Flatten Artwork palette menu command cannot include layers that are hidden or locked. If you try to use the Flatten Artwork palette menu command with a hidden layer, a warning dialog box appears, asking if you want to discard the hidden art. Clicking the Yes button throws away all objects on the hidden layer and combines the rest of the objects into a single layer.

Importing Photoshop layers

When you choose File ➪ Open or you choose File ➪ Place to open or place a layered Photoshop image into the current document, the Photoshop Import Options dialog box appears, shown in Figure 11-19. The Photoshop Import Options dialog box gives you the option to convert the Photoshop layers to objects or flatten the Photoshop layers.

Note The Photoshop Import Options dialog box also gives you the option to import image maps and/or slices if they exist in the Photoshop image.

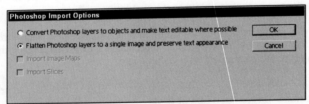

Figure 11-19: When you place layered Photoshop images in Illustrator, you can convert the layers to objects or flatten all the layers.

If you select to convert the layers to objects, Illustrator imports the Photoshop layers, as best it can, into the current selected layer. However, if the Photoshop layer includes features not supported in Illustrator such as Layer Effects, Adjustment or Fill layers are merged during the conversion process.

Any hidden layers included in the Photoshop image are imported as hidden layers, but if the hidden layer includes a feature that isn't supported, then the layer is simply ignored.

If the layered Photoshop image includes any text layers, the text layers are converted to text objects in Illustrator and may be edited in Illustrator using the Type tool.

Exporting CSS layers

When exporting Illustrator artwork to a Web-based format using the File ⇨ Save for Web menu command, you can choose to export the layers as Cascading Style Sheet (CSS) layers. These layers are recognized within GoLive and may be used to add animated effects on a Web page.

To export layers as CSS layers, select the Layers panel in the lower-right corner of the Save for Web dialog box, as shown in Figure 11-20, and enable the Export As CSS Layers option. The Layers panel also lets you select a specific layer and designate it as Visible, Hidden, or Do Not Export. If the Preview Only Selected Layer option is selected, only the layer selected in the Layer panel is visible in the Original panel.

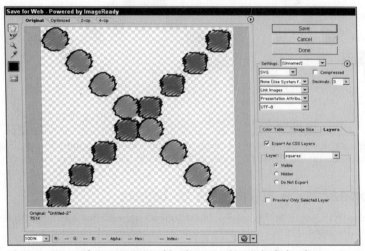

Figure 11-20: The Layers panel in the Save for Web dialog box

When you save the document, each layer is saved within a folder named images using the format designated in the Save for Web dialog box. The first layer is given the specified filename, and each additional layer has a sequential number following it. For example, if you save an Illustrator document with three layers as a GIF image with the name myFile, the first layer is named myFile.gif, the second layer becomes myFile01.gif, and the third layer becomes myFile02.gif.

If you select to have the Save for Web dialog box create an HTML page for you, then opening the HTML page in GoLive displays all layers as CSS layers in their same positions that were found in the Illustrator artwork, as shown in Figure 11-21. The layers are named Anonymous when opened within GoLive.

Note   CSS Layers are specified in the HTML page, so if you don't select to create an HTML page along with the graphics, the exported image won't include any layers.

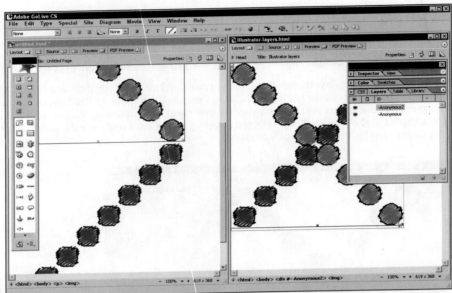

Figure 11-21: Opening the separated layers as images within a Web page (left) keeps all layer objects separate, but opening the HTML page places all layers in their original positions (right).

Applying appearance attributes to layers

The column of circles to the right in the Layers palette allows appearance attributes to be set for all objects on the targeted layer or sublayer.

Clicking on the circle once targets that layer to receive any appearance changes, such as fill or stroke color, an effect, or a style from the Graphic Styles palette. When a layer is targeted, an additional circle surrounds the existing circle, as shown in Figure 11-22. You can target multiple layers at the same time by holding down the Shift key while clicking on the circle icon for several layers.

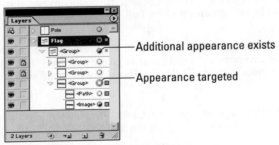

— Additional appearance exists

— Appearance targeted

Figure 11-22: The circle target is circled again when a layer is targeted.

With a layer (or several layers) targeted, change an attribute setting such as the fill color, a stroke setting, or a style in the Graphic Styles palette, or apply an effect from the Effect menu, and all the objects on the targeted layers are changed.

Note   If you move an object out of a layer that has certain appearance attributes applied, then the moved object no longer has those attributes. Attributes that you assign to a layer stay with that layer, not with the objects.

When a layer includes any appearance attributes other than standard fill and stroke attributes, the appearance attribute circle in the Layers palette appears shaded solid.

You can move appearance attributes between layers by dragging the appearance attributes circle from one layer to another. Holding down the Option/Alt key while dragging an appearance attribute copies the attribute to the other layer. Dragging the appearance attribute circle to the Delete Selection icon button at the bottom of the Layers palette deletes the attributes from the layer, except for the fill and stroke colors, which remain.

Cross-Reference   More on using effects and styles is covered in Chapter 10.

STEPS: Tracing Layers in Illustrator

1. **Open a new document in Illustrator.** Within Illustrator, open a new document by choosing File ➪ New. In the New Document dialog box, click OK.

2. **Create a circle.** Select the Ellipse tool and drag in the center of the art board with the Option/Alt and Shift keys held down to create a perfect circle in the center of the art board.

3. **Scale down the circle.** Choose Object ➪ Transform ➪ Scale. In the Scale dialog box, set the Uniform Scale value to 80% and click the Copy button.

4. **Duplicate the scaling command.** With the inner circle selected, choose Object ➪ Transform ➪ Transform Again or use the ⌘/Ctrl+D keyboard shortcut to apply this transformation eight more times. This creates nine centered circles in the center of the art board on a single layer, as shown in Figure 11-23.

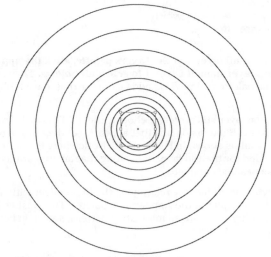

Figure 11-23: After scaling a duplicate object, you may use the Transform Again menu command to quickly create many additional copies.

5. **Release the objects to separate layers.** With the layer that holds all these objects selected in the Layers palette, choose the Release to Layers (Sequence) palette menu command. This moves each object to its own layer. Although each object was selectable as a sublayer previously, releasing the objects to layers makes them easier to reference and work with.

6. **Apply a fill color to every other circle.** Within the Layers palette, hold down the Shift key and select the appearance attribute targeting circle for every odd number layer starting with Layer 3. Then select a red color swatch from the Swatches palette. Every other circle is filled with this color, as shown in Figure 11-24.

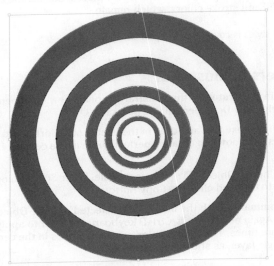

Figure 11-24: Using the target circle in the Layers palette, you can selectively choose exactly which layers get a certain appearance attribute.

7. **Change the stroke weight for all layers. In the Layers palette, click the appearance attribute target for the top layer named Layer 1 to select all objects.** Then set the Weight value in the Strokes palette to 4 pt. This adds a darker ring to each object, as shown in Figure 11-25.

8. **Apply an effect.** With the top layer still targeted, choose Effect ➪ Distort & Transform ➪ Pucker & Bloat. In the Pucker & Bloat dialog box that appears, set the Pucker/Bloat value to 50% and click OK. The result is shown in Figure 11-26. Notice how the appearance attribute target is now shaded for the top layer, indicating that an appearance attribute other than a fill and stroke has been applied.

9. **Increasing the Bloat effect.** Just for fun, try reapplying the Bloat effect with a value of 200% by double-clicking on the effect in the Appearance palette. This pushes the edges of the circles through each other to create an interesting pattern, shown in Figure 11-27.

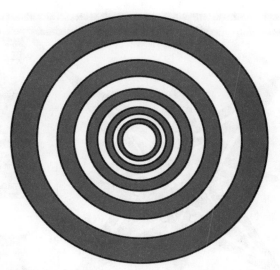

Figure 11-25: With all the sublayers conveniently located under a parent layer, you can easily target all layers.

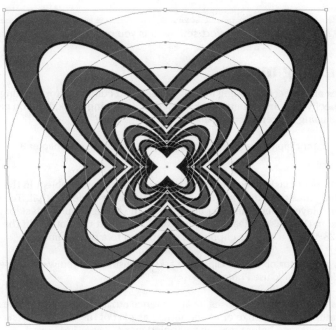

Figure 11-26: Even effects may be targeted and applied to specific layers.

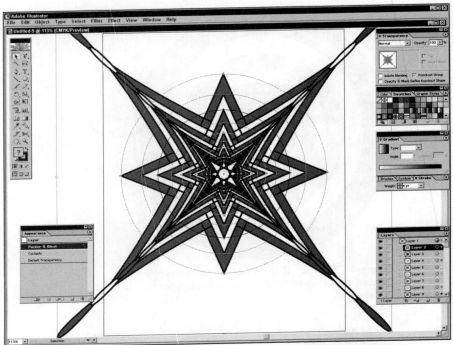

Figure 11-27: Manipulating the effect settings lets you create many unique shapes.

Creating clipping masks

Illustrator includes an Object ➪ Clipping Mask ➪ Make menu command for creating clipping masks. You can specify that an Opacity Mask is used as a clipping mask, but you can also create clipping masks using a layer or sublayer.

Cross-Reference

Standard Illustrator clipping masks and opacity masks are covered in Chapter 8.

When creating a clipping mask using a layer or sublayer, the topmost object in the layer becomes the clipping mask and it masks all objects in the layer underneath it. To create a clipping mask from a layer, select the layer and choose the Make Clipping Mask palette menu command, or click on the Make/Release Clipping Mask button at the bottom of the Layers palette. Figure 11-28 shows a sample clipping mask applied to a placed image.

Note

You can only use vector objects as clipping masks in Illustrator. If you want to use a raster image as a clipping mask, use Photoshop.

The object used as the clipping mask loses its appearance attributes, and its stroke is changed to none. If you want to use the stroke or effect outline as part of the clipping mask, choose Object ➪ Expand Appearance before making a clipping mask.

You can identify clipping masks in the Layers palette because they're separated from the objects that they mask by a dotted line. If you need to reposition the clipping mask or any of the objects that it masks, simply click on the target circle in the Layers palette and then click and drag the object or the mask to its new location. You can also choose Select ➪ Object ➪ Clipping Mask to select the clipping mask.

If you select a layer with a clipping mask, the palette menu changes to Release Clipping Mask, allowing you to remove a clipping mask.

Figure 11-28: By placing an object above the placed image, you can use the Make Clipping Mask palette menu command in the Layers palette.

STEPS: Creating a Clipping Mask

1. **Open a document in Illustrator.** Within Illustrator, choose File ➪ Place and open an image to which you want to apply a clipping mask. Figure 11-29 shows an image placed within an Illustrator document.

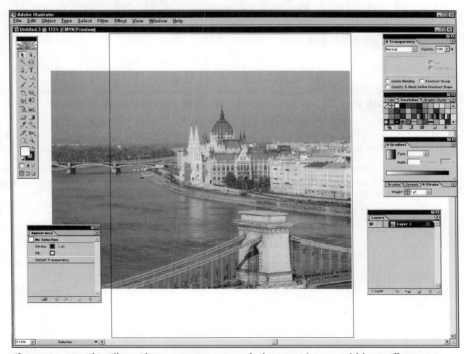

Figure 11-29: The File ➪ Place menu command places an image within an Illustrator document.

2. **Add some text to the image.** Select the Type tool and drag a text area on top of the image. Then type the word **DANUBE** (in all capitals). In the Character palette, change the Font to Cooper Black and the Size to 150 pt. The text, shown in Figure 11-30, doesn't cover much of the image, but this is easily fixed by stretching the text.

Figure 11-30: Use the Type tool to add text to an Illustrator document.

3. **Converting the text to outlines.** Before the text can be stretched, it needs to be converted to outlines. Choose Type ➪ Create Outlines to complete the conversion.

4. **Scale and position the text.** With the text converted to outlines, you can drag on its lower edge to stretch the text vertically. Then drag the text until it covers most of the relevant image areas, as shown in Figure 11-31.

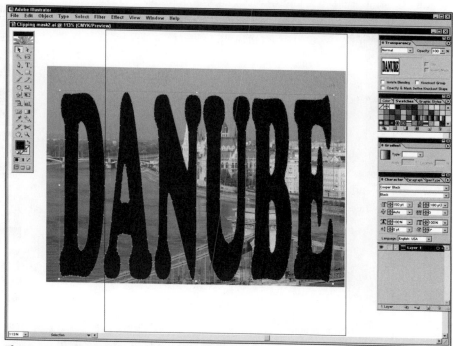

Figure 11-31: Converting text to outlines lets you stretch the text.

5. **Create a compound shape.** When the text is converted to outlines, all letters were grouped together and listed as a group in the Layers palette. This group contains compound paths, which confuses Illustrator when creating a clipping path. To get around this, select the text group and choose Object ➪ Ungroup. Then, with all the letters selected, choose Object ➪ Compound Path ➪ Make. This combines all the separate letters into a single object.

6. **Create a clipping mask.** In the Layers palette, click on the top layer and select the Make Clipping Mask palette menu command. The area beneath the text object is clipped, as shown in Figure 11-32.

Figure 11-32: When all letters are combined into a single compound path, the object is used as a clipping path to the image underneath.

Using Layers in Photoshop

Layers in Photoshop are more advanced than any other CS applications, enabling many additional features including layer sets, linked layers, specialized type and shape layers, property-specific locking, an opacity setting, layer effects, adjustment and fill layers, layer masking, and layer comps. Figure 11-33 shows the Layers palette found in Photoshop.

Like Illustrator, Photoshop also includes a Layers Palette Options dialog box, shown in Figure 11-34, which lets you change the size of the thumbnails viewed in the Layers palette.

Working with a Background layer

When you create a new document in Photoshop, Photoshop creates a single layer named Background. You set the color of this background layer using the New dialog box. The choices are White, Background Color, or Transparent. If you select either the White or Background Color option, a background layer appears in the Layers palette.

The background layer by default is locked and cannot be moved, but you can paint and draw on the background layer. You also cannot change its opacity or blending mode. It's always the lowest layer. By choosing Layer ➪ New ➪ Layer from Background or by choosing Layer ➪ New ➪ Background from Layer, you can convert a background layer to a normal layer or a normal layer to a background layer.

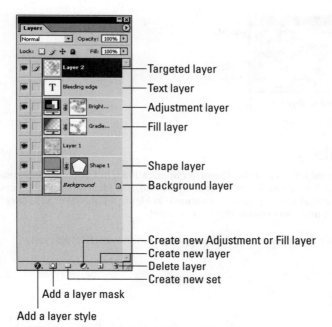

—Targeted layer
—Text layer
—Adjustment layer
—Fill layer

—Shape layer
—Background layer

—Create new Adjustment or Fill layer
—Create new layer
—Delete layer
—Create new set
Add a layer mask

Add a layer style

Figure 11-33: The Layers palette in Photoshop

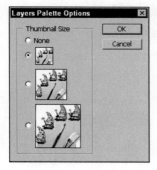

Figure 11-34: The Layers Palette Options dialog box

When you choose Layer ➪ New ➪ Layer from Background, the New Layer dialog box appears, shown in Figure 11-35. Here, you can set the layer's options, including the layer name, the layer color, the blending mode, and the opacity.

Tip   Double-clicking on the background layer opens the New Layer dialog box, allowing you to turn the background layer into a normal layer.

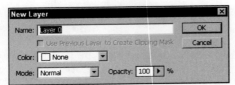

Figure 11-35: The New Layer dialog box
displays the layer options.

Creating layer sets

Photoshop lets you create new layers just like the other applications, but you can also create
layer sets. A layer set is a folder that includes several layers and, like Illustrator's sublayers, it
provides a way to bundle several layers together, as shown in Figure 11-36. Layer sets may be
nested up to five-levels deep and can contain any type of layer.

Note ImageReady allows you to organize layers into layer groups, which work like layer sets.

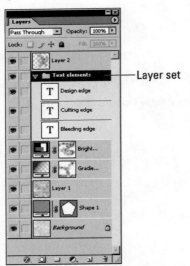— Layer set

Figure 11-36: Layer sets are used
to collect several layers together.

To create a layer set, select the New Layer Set palette menu command or click on the Create
New Set button at the bottom of the Layers palette. A layer set appears as a folder icon in the
Layers palette. Using the palette menu command or holding down the Option/Alt key while
clicking on the Create a New Set button opens the New Layer Set dialog box, where you can
name the layer set, select a color, a blending mode, and an opacity.

Tip Holding down the ⌘/Ctrl key while creating a new layer or a new set adds the layer below
the current selected layer.

To add layers to a layer set, drag them in the Layers palette and drop them when the layer set is selected, or select the layer set folder before creating a new layer.

Linking layers

Photoshop, unlike the other CS applications, allows you to select only a single layer at a time. This layer is marked with a Paintbrush icon in its second column.

However, you can move the contents of multiple layers together by linking the layers together. To link a layer, click the second column icon for the layer that you want to link. A small link icon appears in the column, and the bounding box in the canvas surrounds all objects in both layers.

Clicking on the link icon a second time unlinks the layer. Figure 11-37 shows both linked and unlinked layers.

Selected layer
Linked layer
Unlinked layer

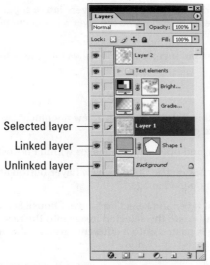

Figure 11-37: The link icon in the second column of the Layers palette determines whether a layer is linked or unlinked.

Aligning linked layers

With two or more layers linked together, you can align them by choosing Layer ➪ Align Linked. The align options include Top Edges, Vertical Centers, Bottom Edges, Left Edges, Horizontal Centers, and Right Edges.

When using the Align menu commands, the objects on the linked layers are aligned with the selected layer.

If the active layer includes a selection, then the Align Linked menu changes to Align to Selection, allowing you to align the current layer to the selection.

Distributing linked layers

When three or more layers are linked together, you can use the Layer ⇨ Distribute Linked menu command. The distribute options are the same as those for the align menu, including Top Edges, Vertical Centers, Bottom Edges, Left Edges, Horizontal Centers, and Right Edges.

Selecting one of these menu options moves the middle linked layers so that the space between the middle layer and the layers at either end are equal. For example, if you have five images that are horizontally aligned, you can equally space them by placing them on linked layers and choosing to distribute them using their vertical centers.

Deleting, combining to a set, and merging linked layers

When layers are linked, multiple Photoshop layers may be referenced at the same time and the palette menu includes some additional menu commands for working with the linked layers. The Delete Linked Layers palette menu command deletes all layers and their content marked as linked.

The New Set from Linked palette menu command combines all linked layers into a separate layer set. This command opens a dialog box where you can name the layer set and choose a layer color, blending mode, and opacity value.

The Merge Linked (⌘/Ctrl+E) palette menu command merges all linked files into the active selected layer.

STEPS: Distributing Images

1. **Open a new document in Photoshop.** Within Illustrator, open a new document by choosing File ⇨ New. In the New dialog box, click OK.

2. **Open several images.** Choose File ⇨ Open, and open several images within Photoshop.

3. **Create new layers.** In the Layers palette, click on the Create a New Layer button at the bottom of the Layers palette once for each opened image.

4. **Copy and paste the images.** Select the first layer and select an image. Choose Select ⇨ All to select the entire image; then copy and paste the selected image into the new document. Repeat this until every open image is pasted onto a different layer, as shown in Figure 11-38.

Tip   These steps are accomplished quickly using keyboard shortcuts with ⌘/Ctrl+A to select the entire image, ⌘/Ctrl+C to copy the selected image to the Clipboard, and ⌘/Ctrl+V to paste the image into the new document.

5. **Position the aligning image.** With the Move tool selected, move one of the images to its correct position.

6. **Align the images.** With the aligning image's layer selected, click on the second column for the other images that you want to align to link them to the selected layer. Then choose Layer ⇨ Align Linked ⇨ Left Edges. All the images are moved to align with the selected layer, as shown in Figure 11-39.

Figure 11-38: Placing each image on a separate layer makes it easy to align and distribute the images.

Figure 11-39: All the linked layers are aligned with the selected layer by using the Layer ⇨ Align Linked menu command.

7. **Position the two end images.** Before distributing the images, select the images that are to appear on either end of the row of images and place them in their correct positions.

8. **Distribute the images.** With the layers all still linked, choose Layer ⇨ Distribute Linked ⇨ Vertical Centers. This evenly spaces the aligned images, as shown in Figure 11-40.

Figure 11-40: When you distribute images, it makes the space between the linked layers equal.

Locking transparency, pixels, and position

You can lock each layer in Photoshop in a number of different ways using the Lock icon buttons at the top of the Layers palette, as shown in Figure 11-41. The Lock Transparent Pixels button prevents you from being able to paint on transparent areas. The Lock Image Pixels button won't let you paint on the image with any of the paint tools. The Lock Position button prevents the selection from being moved. The Lock All button prevents any edits to the layer objects.

If the Lock Image Pixels button is enabled, the Lock Transparent Pixels button becomes disabled. If the Lock All button is enabled, all other locks are disabled.

When the Lock All button is selected, a black lock icon appears to the right of the layer name; when any of the other locks are selected, a white lock appears to the right of the layer name.

Lock transparent pixels

Lock image pixels

Lock position   Lock all

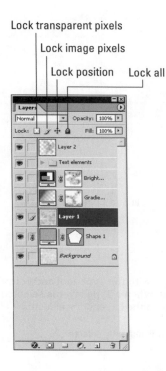

Figure 11-41: The Lock icon buttons are used to lock transparency, pixels, position, or all of these.

If the selected layer has a linked layer, the Lock All Linked Layers palette menu command may be used to open a dialog box, shown in Figure 11-42, where you select which locks to apply to the linked layers.

Figure 11-42: The Lock All Linked Layers dialog box

Working with Type and Shape layers

Type and Shape layers cannot be edited with any of the painting tools or filters because they hold vector-based data, but you can use the Layer ➪ Rasterize menu commands to convert these layers to pixel-based data. The options in the Rasterize menu include Type, Shape, Fill Content, Vector Mask, Layer, Linked Layer, and All Layers.

Creating a Type layer

When the Type tool is used to add type to an image, a Type layer is added to the Layers palette. Type layers are identified by a capital *T* in the thumbnail, as shown in Figure 11-43.

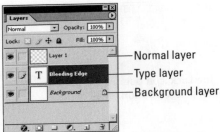

Figure 11-43: Type layers have a capital *T* in their thumbnail in the Layers palette.

Type layers automatically have both the Lock Transparent Pixels and Lock Image Pixels options disabled.

Cross-Reference   Working with Type is covered in detail in Part IV.

The key benefit of a Type layer is that you can select the text with the Type tool and edit, delete, and add new text even after it has been manipulated. When a Type layer is selected in the Layers palette, several menu commands are available in the Layer ⇨ Type menu.

Tip   If you double-click on the Type layer thumbnail, all the text is instantly selected.

Changing Type orientation and antialiasing

By default, text entered into a text layer appears horizontally from left to right, but you can change the text orientation so it runs vertically from top to bottom using the Layer ⇨ Type ⇨ Vertical menu command. You can use the Layer ⇨ Type ⇨ Horizontal menu command to reorient vertical text horizontally again.

Figure 11-44 shows two Type layers — one with a horizontal orientation and one with a vertical orientation.

The Layer ⇨ Type menu also includes several antialias options that are applied to the Type layer. The options include None, Sharp, Crisp, Strong, and Smooth.

Converting between paragraph and point text

If you click on the canvas with the Type tool, you create point text. Point text doesn't have a bounding box — the cursor just appears and lets you type without constraining the text flow to a certain area. Point text is typically used for headings or single lines of text.

If you click and drag on the canvas with the Type tool, you create Paragraph text. Paragraph text confines the text to the bounding box, so that any text that extends beyond the edge of the bounding box gets wrapped to the next line. This is useful for longer paragraphs of text, because the text is automatically wrapped to fit the designated area.

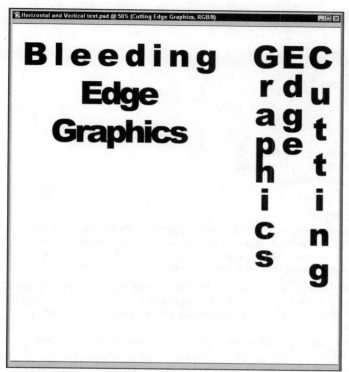

Figure 11-44: Type layers may be orientated horizontally or vertically.

The Layer ⇨ Type menu includes commands to switch between these two types. When a layer containing point text is selected, the Convert to Paragraph Text menu command is available, and vice versa.

Caution   When you convert paragraph text to point text, all characters that overflow outside the bounding box are deleted. To avoid this, resize the bounding box before performing the conversion.

Warping text

When Type layers are rasterized, you can distort and manipulate them using all the standard Photoshop tools, but doing so makes them uneditable as text objects. However, there are several distortions that you can do to text while keeping it editable, such as transforming and warping the text.

To warp a selected Type layer, choose Layer ⇨ Type ⇨ Warp Text. This opens a dialog box, shown in Figure 11-45, where you can select from several different warp types: Arc; Arc Lower; Arc Upper; Arch; Bulge; Shell Lower; Shell Upper; Flag; Wave; Fish; Rise; Fisheye; Inflate; Squeeze; and Twist.

Cross-Reference   These warp types are the same as those available within Illustrator and are covered in Chapter 10.

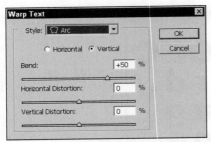

Figure 11-45: The Warp Text dialog box allows you to warp text objects in Photoshop the same way as text in Illustrator.

Creating a Shape layer

In addition to Type layers created with the Type tool, Photoshop's Toolbox also includes the Pen tool and several shape tools for creating rectangles, rounded rectangles, ellipses, polygons, straight lines, and custom shapes. When these tools are selected, the Options bar includes three different modes for applying these shapes as Shape Layers, Paths, and Fill Pixels.

The Shape Layers mode creates a shape layer in the Layers palette, as shown in Figure 11-46, the Paths mode creates a temporary work path that appears in the Paths palette, and the Fill Pixels mode lets you create a raster-based shape when a normal layer is selected.

Cross-Reference
The Paths and Fill Pixels modes, along with the Pen and Shape tools, are covered in more detail in Chapter 10.

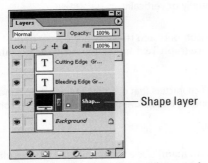

Shape layer

Figure 11-46: Shape layers show up in the Layers palette with two thumbnails — one for the fill and one for the layer mask.

Shape layers are displayed in the Layers palette with two thumbnails. The first thumbnail is the fill applied to the shape, and the second thumbnail shows the shape as a layer mask called a vector mask. When the Vector Mask thumbnail is selected, you can move the shape. The link icon between the fill and layer mask thumbnails binds the layer mask to the layer. If you click the link icon to unlink the layer mask, you can no longer reposition.

Cross-Reference
Layer masks are covered in more detail later in this chapter.

STEPS: Creating a simple logo

1. **Open a new document in Photoshop.** Within Photoshop, create a new document by choosing File ➪ New. In the New dialog box, click OK.

2. **Create a Type layer.** Select the Type tool, click and drag in the center of the canvas, and type the text within the bounding box. The Type layer appears in the Layers palette.

3. **Change the text style and size.** Choose Window ➪ Character to open the Character palette. Select the Type tool and drag over the text in the text layer to select it; then change the font to Croobie (or some other stylized font) and the size to 36 pt. In the Paragraph palette, select the Center Text button. The text should now look like Figure 11-47.

Figure 11-47: You can use the Type tool to select type, and the Character and Paragraph palettes to change the text settings.

4. **Warp the text.** With the Type layer selected, choose Layer ➪ Type ➪ Warp Text. In the Warp Text dialog box, select the Arc style and set the Bend value to 50%. Then click OK to apply the warp, as shown in Figure 11-48.

Figure 11-48: Using the Warp Text dialog box, you can distort text in a number of different ways.

5. **Add a background rectangle.** Click on the Rectangle tool and select the Shape Layer button in the Options box. Change the foreground color to red and drag to create a rectangle that covers the text. This adds a shape layer to the Shapes palette. With the shape layer selected, choose Layer ➪ Arrange ➪ Send to Back. This moves the shape layer below the Type layer and moves the red rectangle behind the text, as shown in Figure 11-49.

Figure 11-49: You can use the Rectangle tool to add shapes that you may move behind the text.

6. **Rasterize the Shape layer.** To add some details to the background rectangle with a filter, you'll need to rasterize the rectangle. With the Shape layer selected, choose Layer ⇨ Rasterize ⇨ Shape. This converts the Shape layer to a normal layer named Shape 1.

7. **Apply a filter to the background.** With the rectangle layer still selected, choose Filter ⇨ Distort ⇨ Ripple. This opens the Ripple dialog box. Set the amount to 150% and the size to Large; then click OK to ripple the edges of the background rectangle, as shown in Figure 11-50.

Figure 11-50: To add some details to the edges of the rectangle layer, the Ripple filter adds just what is needed.

Setting layer opacity and selecting a blending mode

Although you can set the opacity and blending mode when a layer is first created in the New Layer dialog box, the options may be changed at any time using the controls at the top of the Layers palette. The Opacity value and blending mode are applied to the entire layer.

Note You cannot change the opacity or blending mode for the Background layer or for any locked layer.

To change the blending options, choose Layer ⇨ Layer Style ⇨ Blending Options, or double-click on one of the normal layers. This command opens the Blending Options panel of the Layer Style dialog box, shown in Figure 11-51.

Cross-Reference   More on transparency and blending modes is covered in Chapter 8.

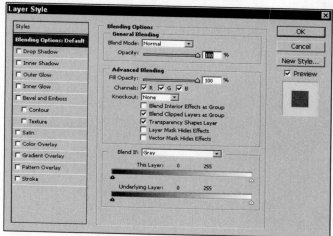

Figure 11-51: The Layer Style dialog box lets you set the blend mode for the layer.

Setting fill opacity

Directly beneath the Layer Opacity value is another value marked as Fill. This value is the Fill Opacity value. It is used to set the opacity for the layer pixels or shapes without affecting the opacity of any pixels added as layer effects, such as drop shadows or glows.

Creating a knockout

A knockout layer is used to remove, or knock out, a layer underneath it to reveal the Background layer or the bottom layer in a layer set. To create a knockout layer, simply place the knockout layer above the layer that you want to remove pixels from and choose one of the Knockout options in the Blending Options panel of the Layer Style dialog box.

The Knockout options include None, Shallow, and Deep. The Shallow option knocks out all layers to the bottom of the layer set that contains the knockout layer, but the Deep option knocks out all layers between the Knockout layer and the Background layer. If no Background layer exists, the knocked out area is made transparent.

You can control the amount of knockout using the Fill Opacity value. A Fill Opacity value of 0 knockouts all the in-between layers to reveal only the background and a Fill Opacity of 100 doesn't knockout any of the in-between layers. Figure 11-52 shows an arrow shape used as a Knockout layer, revealing a pattern in the Background layer.

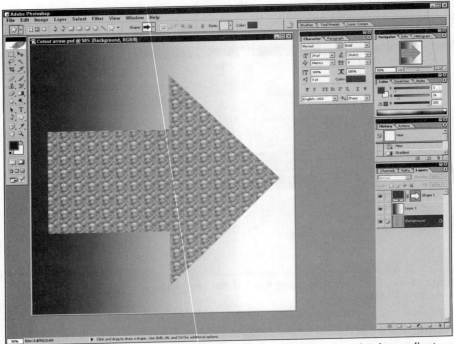

Figure 11-52: The arrow shape in the top layer is used as a knockout for the gradient layer, allowing the pattern on the Background layer to show through.

Using advanced blending options

In the Advanced Blending section of the Blending Options panel of the Layer Style dialog box are several additional options besides Fill Opacity and Knockout. The Channels check boxes let you apply the selected blending mode and options to specific channels only. Deselecting a channel causes it *not* to be included in the blending process. The availability of the channels depends on the color mode for the given image:

✦ **The Blend Interior Effects as Group option** treats any effects applied to the interior of the current layer as part of the layer and blends them with the layer pixels. Interior effects include Inner Glow, Satin, Color, and Gradient Overlay, but not Inner Shadow.

✦ **The Select Blend Clipped Layers as Group option** applies the blending mode to all layers that are part of a clipping mask. If this option is deselected, then each clipping mask retains its original blending mode and options. This option is enabled by default.

✦ **The Select Transparency Shapes Layers option** prevents knockouts and layer effects from interfering with the layer's pixels. This option is also selected by default.

✦ **The Select Layer Mask Hides Effects and Select Vector Mask Hides Effects options** are used to confine layer effects to the area defined by the Layer or Vector Mask.

You can use the sliders at the bottom of the Blending Options panel of the Layer Style dialog box to target only a certain range of pixels for blending. The Blend If field lets you choose which color channel to blend. Select Gray for all channels. The This Layer slider lets you specify the bright- and dark-colored pixels to blend for the current layer, and the Underlying Layer slider lets you specify the pixels to blend for a layer under the current one.

Tip If you hold down the Option/Alt key while dragging on the slider arrows, you can split the arrows in half to define a specific range of pixels.

Figure 11-53 shows a simple layer (top left) created with a stylized brush. The pixel-blending slider to the right has been moved to include all the bright pixels in the blending process, and the lower image shows the same document with all the dark pixels blended.

Figure 11-53: By manipulating the sliders in the Blending Options dialog box, you can select exactly which pixels are included in the blending operation.

STEPS: Creating a Knockout Border

1. **Open a document in Photoshop.** Within Photoshop, open a new document by choosing File ⇨ Open.

2. **Convert the image to a Background layer.** Select the Background layer and choose the Delete Layer palette menu command to remove the existing background. Then, with the image layer selected, choose Layer ⇨ New ⇨ Background From Layer. This converts the image layer to the Background layer.

3. **Create a new border layer.** Click on the Create a New Layer button at the bottom of the Layers palette. The new layer appears in the Layers palette. Change the Fill color to red, click the Paintbrush tool, and select the roses brush tip from the Brushes palette. Then drag over the entire layer to create a layer to use as a border, as shown in Figure 11-54.

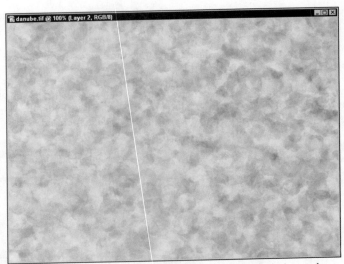

Figure 11-54: This layer, created with the roses brush, is used as a border for the image.

4. **Create a Shape layer.** Select the Rectangle tool and make sure the Shape Layer mode is selected in the Options bar. Then drag in the canvas to create a rectangle that leaves a border around the image, as shown in Figure 11-55. This creates a new Shape layer in the Layers palette.

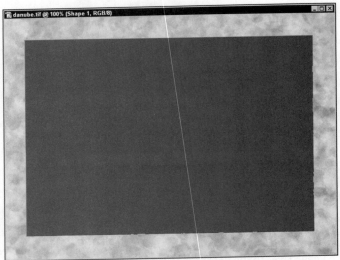

Figure 11-55: Shape layers are useful for selecting areas to be knocked out.

5. **Make the Shape layer a knockout**. Double-click on the Shape layer mask thumbnail to open the Blending Options panel of the Layer Style dialog box. Select the Deep option in the Knockout field and set the Fill Opacity value to 0%. Then click OK. Figure 11-56 shows the resulting image.

Figure 11-56: By knocking out the area defined in the Shape layer, the image has a nice border.

Using layer effects

You can add layer effects to the current layer by enabling an effect in the Layer Style dialog box. This dialog box is opened by selecting the Blending Options palette menu command, by selecting one of the Layer Effects from the Add a Layer Style button at the bottom of the Layers palette, or by double-clicking on the layer thumbnail. Figure 11-57 shows the Layer Style dialog box for the Drop Shadow effect.

Note   Layer effects may not be added to the Background layer or to a locked layer.

The available default Layer Effects include Drop Shadow, Inner Shadow, Outer Glow, Inner Glow, Bevel and Emboss, Satin, Color Overlay, Gradient Overlay, Pattern Overlay, and Stroke. Figure 11-58 shows each of these layer effects. Selecting any of these Layer Effects from the Add a Layer Style button opens the Layer Style dialog box and displays the settings for the selected effect.

Cross-Reference   Each of these layer effects is covered in Chapter 10.

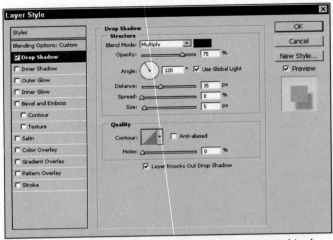

Figure 11-57: Each of the layer effects has its own panel in the Layer Style dialog box.

Figure 11-58: Photoshop's Layer Effects adds and controls effects.

When a Layer Effect has been applied to a layer, the Layer Effect icon appears to the right of the layer title. Clicking the arrow that appears next to this icon expands and displays the list of effects. Double-clicking on any of these listed effects opens the Layer Style dialog box again; here, you can edit the effect's settings.

To remove a layer effect, simply drag the effect to the Delete Selected button at the bottom of the Layers palette.

Adjusting global lighting

Several of the layer effects depend on a lighting effect to determine where the shadows are cast, including the Drop Shadow, Inner Shadow, and Bevel & Emboss layer effects. Although each of these effects has a setting that controls the light's Angle and Altitude, you can select the Use Global Light option. When this option is selected, the light settings are controlled using the Global Light settings.

To Access the Global Light settings, choose Layer ⇨ Layer Style ⇨ Global Light. This opens a dialog box, shown in Figure 11-59, where you can set the Angle and Altitude values. You can also drag the crosshairs within the light circle to reposition these values. Using the Global Light dialog box, you can ensure that all shadows within the document are consistent.

Figure 11-59: The Global Light dialog box

Scaling effects

Layer effects may be saved as styles and reapplied to other layers, but an effect that looks great on one layer may be too small or too big when applied to another layer. Instead of reconfiguring the settings for the effect, you can simply change its scale by choosing Layer ⇨ Layer Style ⇨ Scale Effect.

Cross-Reference

To learn more about working with styles and effects, see Chapter 8.

This command opens a simple dialog box with a slider for determining the scale of the effects applied to the current layer.

Turning effects into layers

You can separate effects from a layer by choosing Layer ⇨ Layer Style ⇨ Create Layers. This makes the layer effect an independent layer that you can manipulate and edit. Double-clicking on the new layer still opens the effect's settings in the Layer Style dialog box.

STEPS: Adding Layer Effects

1. **Open a document in Photoshop.** Within Photoshop, open a new document by choosing File ⇨ Open.

2. **Add a Type layer.** Click on the Type tool and click in the lower center of the image. Choose Window ⇨ Character to open the Character palette. Select the Myriad font with a bold face and set the size to 150 points with a color of white. Then type the word **BUDAPEST**, as shown in Figure 11-60, in all capitals.

Figure 11-60: Text helps identify the location, but the type is harsh against the image.

3. **Add an Inner Glow layer effect.** With the Type layer selected, click on the Add a Layer Style button at the bottom of the Layers palette and select the Inner Glow effect. In the Layer Style dialog box, set the blend mode to normal, the color to black, and the size to 25 pixels. Click OK. The text should now look blurred and the layer effect is added beneath the Type layer in the Layers palette, as shown in Figure 11-61.

Figure 11-61: Using the Inner Glow layer effect, the text is made to look somewhat blurred.

4. **Add an Outer Glow layer effect.** With the Type layer still selected, click on the Add a Layer Style button at the bottom of the Layers palette, and select the Outer Glow effect.

In the Layer Style dialog box, click on the color swatch to open the Color Picker, then click on the Eyedropper tool and click in the image to select a light yellow color. Set the size to 25 pixels and click OK. The layer effects offset the text so it isn't so harsh, as shown in Figure 11-62.

Figure 11-62: The Outer Glow layer effect smoothes the transition into the image using a color from the image.

Using adjustment and fill layers

Within Photoshop, the Image ⇨ Adjustment menu lets you adjust image properties such as contrast, color balance, and saturation, but applying the menu commands found in the Image ⇨ Adjustment menu permanently changes the image.

Using the Layers palette, you can apply an Adjustment layer to the image that holds the adjustment changes in a separate layer, so you can edit or even remove the adjustment changes at any time without affecting the image.

Fill layers are similar to adjustment layers. They're used to fill the canvas with a solid color, a gradient, or a pattern, but fill layers don't change the layers underneath them.

To add an adjustment layer, select one of the commands from the Layer ⇨ New Adjustment Layer menu or from the pop-up menu at the bottom of the Layers palette. The available adjustment layers include Levels, Curves, Color Balance, Brightness/Contrast, Hue/Saturation, Selection Color, Channel Mixer, Gradient Map, Photo Filter, Invert, Threshold, and Posterize. Figure 11-63 shows the Layers palette with an adjustment and a fill layer.

Cross-Reference You can learn more about these adjustment options in Chapter 8.

To add a fill layer, select one of the commands from the Layer ⇨ New Fill Layer menu or from the pop-up menu available at the bottom of the Layers palette. The available fill layers include Solid Color, Gradient, and Pattern.

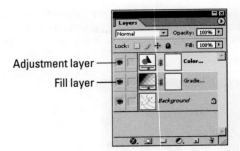

Figure 11-63: Adjustment and fill layers keep adjustments and fills separate from other layers.

Adjustment layer

Fill layer

Selecting any of these layers opens the appropriate dialog box for the layer type that was selected. Figure 11-64 shows the Color Balance dialog box.

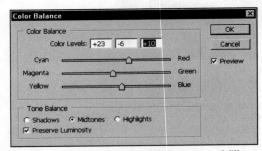

Figure 11-64: Each of the adjustment and fill layers opens a dialog box.

Masking with layers

Masks are used in Photoshop to hide areas of a layer. Photoshop creates masks out of pixel selections or shapes. When a mask is applied to a layer, it appears as an additional thumbnail in the Layers palette positioned to the right of the main thumbnail. The mask thumbnail shows all hidden areas as black, all visible areas as white, and all semitransparent areas as gray.

Creating a layer mask

To apply a mask to a layer, select the layer and choose Layer ➪ Add Layer Mask ➪ Reveal All to add a mask that displays the entire layer underneath, or click on the Add Layer Mask button at the bottom of the Layers palette. You can also choose Layer ➪ Add Layer Mask ➪ Hide All, or click on the Add Layer Mask button at the bottom of the Layers palette with the Option/Alt key held down to create a layer mask that hides the image underneath.

If a pixel selection exists, then that selection may be used as the basis for the mask. To make the interior of the selection a mask, choose Layer ➪ Add Layer Mask ➪ Hide Selection. To make all but the interior selection a mask, choose Layer ➪ Add Layer Mask ➪ Reveal Selection. The Add Layer Mask button at the bottom of the Layers palette may also be used with a selection.

The link icon that appears between the thumbnails in the Layers palette is used to make the layer move with its mask. Clicking on the link icon unlinks the two and allows the mask to move independently of the layer.

Editing a layer mask

To edit a mask, click on its thumbnail in the Layers palette and use the paint tools to color the canvas using black, white, and grayscale colors. A mask icon appears in the second column of the Layers palette, as shown in Figure 11-65, when a mask is selected and the foreground and background colors change to black and white.

Mask layer selected

Figure 11-65: The mask icon is displayed in the second column of the selected layer when the Mask layer is selected.

To see the mask in black and white while editing it, hold down the Option/Alt key while clicking on the mask thumbnail in the Layers palette.

If you click on the Layer Mask thumbnail with the Shift key held down, or if you choose Layer ➪ Disable Layer Mask, the layer mask is disabled and a red X appears through the thumbnail. Clicking the thumbnail again makes the mask active again.

Creating vector masks

Vector objects such as paths, shapes, and text may also be used as masks. The benefit of vector masks is that you can edit them after they've been applied. To create a vector mask, choose Layer ➪ Add Vector Mask ➪ Reveal All or choose Layer ➪ Add Vector Mask ➪ Hide All, just like the layer mask.

To use a vector object as a mask, select the layer that you want to mask and then select the Paths option in the Options bar. This allows you to create a path without creating a new layer. Then choose Layer ➪ Add Vector Mask ➪ Current Path.

Vector masks may be converted to a normal layer mask by choosing Layer ➪ Rasterize ➪ Vector Mask. However, layer masks cannot be converted to a vector mask.

Removing masks

To remove a layer mask, simply drag its thumbnail down to the Delete Selected button at the bottom of the Layers palette, or select the mask that you want to remove and choose Layer ➪ Delete Layer/Vector Mask. When a mask is removed, a warning dialog box appears, giving you the option to apply, cancel, or discard the mask. If you choose to apply the mask, the layer assumes the results of the mask.

STEPS: Painting a Layer Mask

1. **Open a document in Photoshop.** Within Photoshop, open a new document by choosing File ➪ Open.

2. **Add a layer mask.** With the image layer selected in the Layers palette, choose Layer ➪ Add Layer Mask ➪ Hide All. This command hides the entire layer under a white layer mask, and the entire layer mask appears black in the Layers palette.

3. **Paint on the layer mask.** Select the Paintbrush tool, select a wide stipple brush from the Brushes palette, and drag the paintbrush across the canvas to slowly reveal the image underneath. Figure 11-66 shows the results of painting on the layer mask with a stipple brush. It resembles looking through a foggy window.

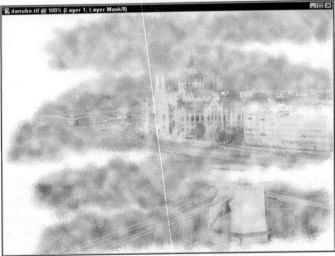

Figure 11-66: Painting on a layer mask with a stipple brush creates the effect of looking through a foggy window.

Using layer comps

Layer compositions (or *comps,* for short) offer a way to display multiple versions of a Photoshop file. Stored in the Layers Comp palette, shown in Figure 11-67, layer comps record a snapshot of the Layers palette by keeping track of each layer's Visibility, Position, and Appearance.

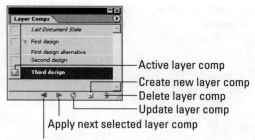

Figure 11-67: The Layer Comps palette holds snapshots of the visible layers.

To create a new layer comp, click the Create New Layer Comp button at the bottom of the Layer Comp palette. This opens a dialog box, shown in Figure 11-68, where you can name the new layer comp, specify which properties to record, and add a comment.

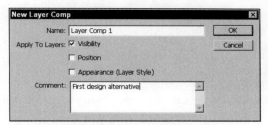

Figure 11-68: The New Layer Comp dialog box lets you name the layer comp and select which layer attributes to record.

If changes are made to a layer comp, you may update the comp by clicking on the Update Layer Comp button at the bottom of the Layer Comp palette.

The Apply Previous and Apply Next Layer Comp buttons at the bottom of the Layer Comps palette let you quickly cycle through the various layer comps.

To delete a layer comp, select it and click the Delete Layer Comp button at the bottom of the Layer Comps palette.

STEPS: Creating Several Layer Comps

1. **Open a document in Photoshop.** Within Photoshop, open a new document, such as the image with text and layer effects applied, by choosing File ➪ Open.

2. **Apply multiple layer effects.** Select the Type layer and apply each of the available layer effects to the Type layer. Figure 11-69 shows the image with the Pattern Overlay and Stroke layer effects applied.

Figure 11-69: Layer effects are displayed in the Layers palette where you can quickly hide or show them.

3. **Creating new layer comps.** Experiment with the applied layer effects by enabling and disabling certain combinations. When you come across a design that is appealing, choose Window ➪ Layer Comps to open the Layer Comps palette, and click the Create New Layer Comp button at the bottom of the palette. In the New Layer Comp dialog box that appears, name the layer comp appropriately, select the Visibility and Appearance options, and click OK. Figure 11-70 shows the Layer Comps palette with several options.

4. **Preview the layer comps.** When you've finished creating a number of layer comps, click on the Apply Next Selected Layer Comp several times to cycle through the available layer comps.

Figure 11-70: The Layer Comp palette lets you quickly cycle through a number of different design ideas.

Using Layers in GoLive

Layers in GoLive in some ways are similar to layers used in the other CS applications, but GoLive layers actually represent layers that are defined as part of the CSS specification, which makes them behave differently in many ways.

CSS layers work like the layers in the other CS applications in that they allow you to stack content on top of each other, but there are some differences that you need to be aware of including the following:

✦ CSS layers are always rectangular.

✦ CSS layers are positioned relative to the Web page's upper-left corner or relative to the upper-left corner of other layers.

✦ CSS layers may inherit attributes from a CSS.

✦ CSS layers are contained within the HTML code inside a `<DIV>` tag.

✦ CSS layers are not supported on all browsers and may not appear correctly if a user has disabled CSS features for his browser.

✦ CSS layers may be connected to execute actions when certain mouse events occur.

✦ CSS layers may be used to create simple animations by changing layers positioned in the same place.

Adding layers to a Web page

Layers are added to a Web page by dragging the Layer icon from the Objects palette, shown in Figure 11-71, to the Web page, or by clicking on the Create New Layer button at the bottom of the Layers palette. This button inserts a layer at the cursor position in the Web page. A small yellow marker marks the layer placeholder position.

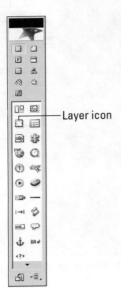

Layer icon

Figure 11-71: The GoLive Objects palette lets you add objects to a Web page by dragging the objects' icons.

When a layer is created, its name appears in the Layers palette, as shown in Figure 11-72. The Layers palette is opened by choosing Window ➪ Layers (⌘/Ctrl+4). The default names for new layers are simply layer1, layer2, and so on. To rename a layer, double-click on its name in the Layer palette and type a new name. A layer's name is known within the HTML code as its ID, and this ID is used in JavaScript to refer to the layer for interactive effects.

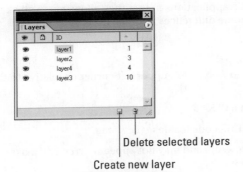

Delete selected layers

Create new layer

Figure 11-72: The Layers palette lets you sort layers by clicking on the column headings.

When a layer is created, its dimensions appear in the upper-left corner, and each layer is given a number based on the order in which they were created. This number is displayed in the lower-right corner, as shown in Figure 11-73. These lower-right-corner numbers are also used in the Timeline Editor to animate the layers.

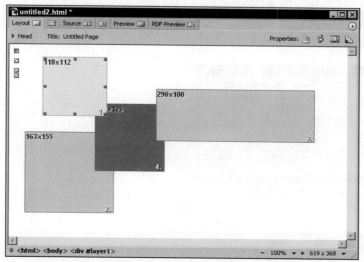

Figure 11-73: The dimensions of each layer are listed in the upper-left corner, and a sequential number is listed in the lower-right corner.

Layers are selected by clicking on their position marker, clicking the borders when the cursor changes to a hand icon or by clicking on its name in the Layers palette. When the hand icon appears when you click on a layer's border, you can move the layer by dragging it to a new position. Dragging on the layer handles lets you resize the layer.

Tip　When a layer is selected, you can move it by pressing the arrow keys. Holding down the Shift key while using the arrow keys lets you resize the layer; holding down the ⌘/Ctrl key lets you move the selected layer using grid spacing.

To delete a layer, just select it in the Layers palette and click the Remove Selected Layers button at the bottom of the Layers palette.

Using the Layers palette

The Layers palette includes some of the same layer features found in the other CS applications, including the eye and lock icons. Clicking on the first and second columns of the Layers palette, you can change the visibility of the selected layer or lock it in place.

To the right of the layer name is another column that lists the Z-Index value. Clicking on the Name or Z-Index column head lets you sort the layers by their name or Z-Index value.

Note　When a layer is selected, it's automatically brought to the front of the stacking order so the layer is visible. But when the layer is unselected, it returns to its correct position in the stacking order.

The palette menu includes two methods for viewing layers—hierarchic, which displays nested layers underneath their parents, and flat, which displays all layers at the same level.

Using layer grids

When working with layers, you can enable a grid to help position layers using the Layer Grid Settings palette menu command. This command opens a dialog box, shown in Figure 11-74, where you can set the horizontal and vertical spacing in pixels. You can also select to snap and make the grid visible while dragging.

Figure 11-74: The Layer Grid Settings dialog box lets you define the grid-spacing distance and whether objects snap to the grid.

The Prevent Overlapping option restricts objects from being positioned on top of other layers when enabled. When you disable this option, you can stack layers on top of one another.

Converting layers into layout grids

If you've gone to the effort to lay out a Web page using layers, only to discover that you need to abandon the layers design due to incompatible browser issues, you can use the Convert to Layout Grid palette menu command to create a new Web page where all layers and their content are converted to standard layout grids.

Caution   The Convert to Layout Grid palette menu command can only convert layers that aren't overlapped. If a Web page includes overlapped layers, the Convert to Layout Grid palette menu command is not available.

Editing layer attributes

When a layer is selected, its attributes display in the Inspector palette, shown in Figure 11-75. For layers, the Inspector palette includes three panels—Layer, Background, and Timeline.

Using the Layer panel

The Layer panel of the Inspector palette includes the Layer's Name in an editable field, its positions and/or dimensions, a Z-Index value, and a Visible check box. The layer's position values may be specified, or you can enter its Top and Left position values along with the Width and Height values. If all four position values and the Width and Height values are specified, the Width and Height values take precedence over the unneeded position values.

The correct values that are included in the HTML code are highlighted in blue, and if a value is invalid, it's highlighted in orange. The blue highlights don't indicate correct values; they merely indicate an entered or customized value. Unaltered fields stay black.

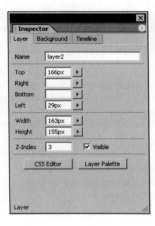

Figure 11-75: The Inspector palette changes depending on the selected object. When a layer is selected, the Inspector palette includes three different panels for Layer, Background, and Timeline.

The pop-up menu to the right of the Top, Right, Bottom, Left, Width, and Height fields lets you convert the current value between several different measurement systems including point, pica, pixel, em, ex, mm, cm, inch, and percentage of the total page.

The Z-Index value determines the stacking order of the layers with the higher values appearing on top of the lower values, so a layer with a Z-Index of 10 appears in front of a layer with a Z-Index of 2.

The Layer panel of the Inspector palette also includes buttons to open the CSS Editor and the Layer palette.

Using the Background panel

The Background panel, shown in Figure 11-76, lets you select a background color for the layer or load an image to be displayed within the layer. To change the background color, click on the lower-right corner of the color swatch and a pop-up color picker appears with Web-safe color swatches.

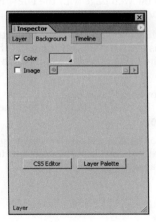

Figure 11-76: The Background panel of the Inspector palette lets you change the background color or image.

The Image option lets you fetch or browse for an image. If the image is larger than the available size, then only the portion of the image that fits in the layer is displayed. If the image is smaller than the layer, the image is placed in the upper-left corner of the layer.

Using the Timeline panel

The Timeline panel, shown in Figure 11-77, includes controls for enabling layer animations. From the Animation field, you can select the animation type from None, Linear, Curve, and Random. The Key Color changes the colors that are used to represent the layer in the Timeline Editor, and the Record button lets you create Timeline keyframes by moving and positioning the layers in the Layout Editor.

Figure 11-77: The Timeline panel of the Inspector palette includes several animation options and a Record button that lets you create animation keyframes.

Clicking the Open Timeline Editor button opens the Timeline Editor, where you can precisely control the animation.

STEPS: Creating Layers in GoLive

1. **Open a Web page in GoLive.** Within GoLive, open a new Web page with the File ➪ New Page menu command.

2. **Drag the Layer icon onto the page.** Select and drag the Layer icon from the Objects palette onto the blank Web page. The layer appears as a 100×100 pixel square at the top of the Web page, and the layer name appears in the Layers palette, as shown in Figure 11-78.

3. **Resizing and positioning the layer.** Drag the mouse over the layer edge, and click when the mouse icon changes to a hand icon. Resize the layer by dragging its corner handles, and drag the layer edges to reposition the layer.

4. **Change the layer's background color.** In the Inspector palette, select the Background tab and enable the Color option. Then drag the lower-right corner of the color swatch to open a color palette, where you can select a new background color. Figure 11-79 shows the new background color.

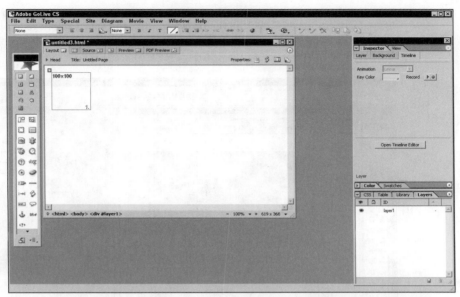

Figure 11-78: Layers are added to the Web page by dragging the Layer icon from the Objects palette to the Web page.

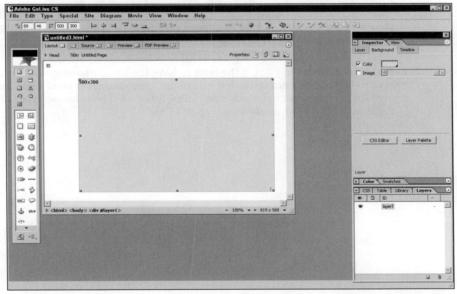

Figure 11-79: Using the Background panel of the Inspector palette lets you change the layer's background color.

5. **Add an image to the layer.** Drag the image icon from the Objects panel onto the layer. In the Inspector palette, click on the Browse button and select an image to open. Then click on the Align Center button in the Toolbar to center the image within the layer, as shown in Figure 11-80.

Figure 11-80: Content such as this image may be added to a layer by dragging items onto the layer from the Objects palette.

6. **Add text to the layer.** Click in the layer to have the text cursor appear. Use the arrow keys to move the cursor to the left side of the image and enter some text. Then drag over the text to select it, and choose Type ⇨ Size ⇨ +4. Then choose Type ⇨ Style ⇨ Bold to make the text bold, as shown in Figure 11-81.

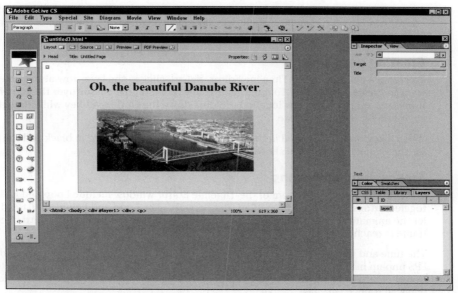

Figure 11-81: Clicking in the layer positions the text cursor within the layer. You can then use the arrows to move the mouse cursor to either side of the image.

Animating layers

Animating layers in GoLive is made possible with the Timeline Editor, shown in Figure 11-82. Within this editor, a number represents each layer. Corresponding numbers are listed in the lower-right corner of the layers in the Layout Editor.

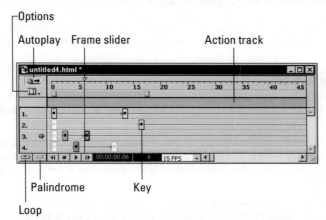

Figure 11-82: The Timeline Editor lets you place and position layer keyframes to define how the layer is animated.

Along the top are the frames of the animation; the position of each layer is denoted by color-coordinated small rectangles called *keys*. If a key is dimmed out, the layer is hidden for that frame.

Creating new keys

To create a new key in the Timeline Editor, ⌘/Ctrl+click in the layer row at the time that you want to create a keyframe. To move a keyframe, position the cursor over the top of the key-frame and drag it to its new location. Holding down the Option/Alt key while dragging a keyframe creates a duplicate.

When a keyframe is selected in the Timeline Editor, it's highlighted in black and the properties for the respective layer are shown in the Inspector palette.

Previewing animations

The buttons along the bottom of the Timeline Editor window include Loop and Palindrome toggle buttons, Backward, Stop, Play, and Forward. The Loop and Palindrome toggle buttons let the animation loop continuously through the total frames or play backward once the last frame is reached.

The time and frame number are also displayed along the bottom of the Timeline Editor. The FPS pop-up menu lets you specify the number of frames played per second. The options range from 1 FPS to 30 FPS. A setting of 1 FPS plays the frames very slowly, and a setting of 30 FPS plays all frames very fast.

Recording keyframes

Clicking the Record button in the Timeline panel of the Inspector palette causes all layer-position changes to automatically be recorded as keyframes that show up in the Timeline Editor. Depending on the Animation option selected in the Timeline panel, the dragged path is recorded as a straight line (Linear), a curved path (Curve), or as a random set of positions between the first and last spot (Random).

Creating a new animation scene

You can use the Timeline Editor to create several animation sequences called *scenes*. To create a new scene, click on the Option pop-up menu in the upper-left corner of the Timeline Editor and select the New Scene menu command. This opens a simple dialog box where you can name the new scene.

Add a Play Animation action

Actions are placed in the Action Track, which is positioned between the top timeline and layer tracks. To add an action to the current animation, hold down the ⌘/Ctrl key and click on the Action Track.

In the Timeline Editor, actions have a question mark inside of them. If you click on the Action icon in the Timeline Editor, a single button appears inside the Inspector palette titled Show Action Palette. Clicking this button makes the Actions panel in the Rollovers & Actions palette appear, as shown in Figure 11-83.

To add an action to play an animation scene, click the Action button and select the Multimedia ➪ Play Scene menu command in the pop-up menu. From the Scene field that appears, select the scene name that you want to play. After a specific action is selected, the question-mark icon in the Timeline Editor changes to a movie icon.

Figure 11-83: The Rollovers & Actions palette lets you define what action takes place when an event is triggered.

STEPS: Animating Layers

1. **Open a Web page in GoLive.** Within GoLive, open an existing Web page that includes a layer with the File ➪ Open menu command.

2. **Open the Timeline Editor.** Select the layer object in the Web page by clicking on its edge. Select the Timeline tab in the Inspector palette and click the Open Timeline Editor button. The Timeline Editor appears in the window.

3. **Create new keys.** Within the Timeline Editor, hold down the ⌘/Ctrl key and click on frame 15 and frame 30 for the first layer to add new keyframes, as shown in Figure 11-84.

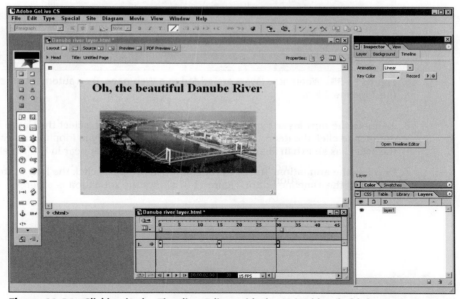

Figure 11-84: Clicking in the Timeline Editor with the ⌘/Ctrl key held down creates a new key for the selected layer.

4. **Set visibility.** With the keyframe at frame 1 selected, click the Layer tab in the Inspector palette and disable the Visible option. The keyframe turns white. This change causes the layer to be hidden until frame 15 and then to appear until frame 30.

5. **Add another layer.** Drag the Layer icon from the Objects palette and drop it on the Web page. Then drag the image icon onto the new layer. Click the Browse button in the Inspector palette, and add a new butterfly image to the layer. With the layer selected, in the Timeline panel of the Inspector palette, change the Key Color. Figure 11-85 shows the new layer.

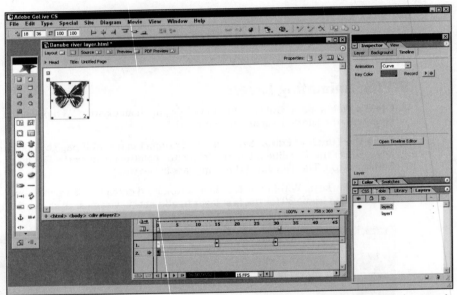

Figure 11-85: When new layers are added to a Web page, they automatically show up in the Timeline Editor.

6. **Animate the new layer by dragging.** In the Timeline panel, select the Curve Animation option and click the Record button. Then drag the butterfly in looping circles across the scene, as shown in Figure 11-86. Many new keyframes appear in the Timeline Editor.

7. **Preview the animation.** To see the animation in progress, click the Play button at the bottom of the Timeline Editor. Figure 11-87 shows the animation is progress.

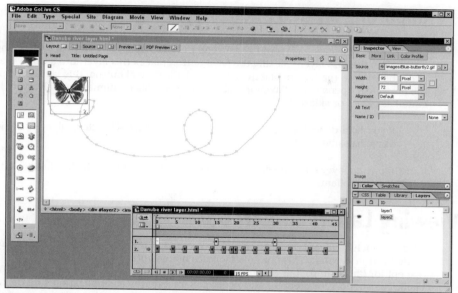

Figure 11-86: The Record button lets you create an animation path by dragging the layer object in the Web page.

Figure 11-87: You can preview animations in the Web page by clicking on the Play button.

Importing layered Photoshop images

You may import layered Photoshop images into GoLive by choosing File ⇨ Import ⇨ Photoshop Layers. After you select a layered Photoshop image to open, the Save for Web dialog box opens with the first layer. Clicking the Save button places this layer into a GoLive layer and adds the layer to the Layers palette. If you click the Cancel button, this layer is skipped and the next layer opens in the Save for Web dialog box. This continues until all layers have been added as layers or skipped.

Tip If you hold down the ⌘/Ctrl button and click the Save All button, all layers are imported using the same settings.

If the imported layer name begins with a number, GoLive automatically changes it to something Web-compliant.

Viewing Layers in Acrobat

Files that include layers that are saved or exported to the PDF file maintain their layers when loaded within Acrobat. This not only includes documents created in the CS applications (except for Photoshop), but also other applications that use layers such as AutoCAD and Visio. The support for creating Adobe PDF layers requires an application supporting layers and supporting exports to Acrobat 6 compatibility. If you use other programs supporting layers and those programs do not export to the Acrobat 6–compatible PDF 1.5 format, the layers are not retained in the PDF document. You can access Adobe PDF layers using the Layers tab located to the left of the interface, as shown in Figure 11-88.

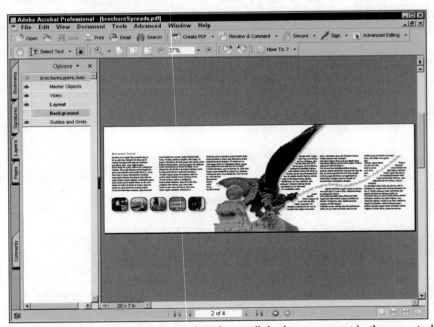

Figure 11-88: The Layers tab in Acrobat shows all the layers present in the exported PDF file.

Note

Viewing layers within Acrobat is available only for files that are exported using the PDF 1.5 (Acrobat 6.0–compatible) format. The layers of files that use previous format versions are flattened prior to being exported. When exporting documents to PDFs containing layers, the current layer view in the authoring document displays the same layer view in Acrobat. For example, if two layers are created and the background layer is hidden at the time of PDF export, the background layer is also hidden by default in the resultant PDF document.

If the Layers tab isn't visible, you can make it visible by choosing View ➪ Navigation Tabs ➪ Layers. Within the Layers tab, you can click on the Visibility icon to show or hide the selected layer.

When a PDF file that includes layers is opened in Acrobat, a small layered cake icon appears in the lower-left corner of the interface. This icon is a visual reminder that the current file has layers and that some of the layers may not be visible. If you click on the icon, the dialog box shown in Figure 11-89 opens with a reminder message visible.

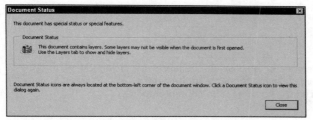

Figure 11-89: The Document Status dialog box opens when you click on the layered cake icon in the lower-left corner of the interface, reminding you that the current PDF file includes layers.

Layer options and properties

The Options pop-up menu at the top of the Layers tab includes the following options: List Layers for All Pages, List Layers for Current Page, Reset to Initial Visibility, Apply Print, Export and Layer Overrides, Merge Layers, Flatten Layers, and Layer Properties.

Listing layers

The list options let you choose to see all layers for the entire document or just the layers for the current page that is selected. If the latter option is selected, the layers listed in the Layers tab are updated when you switch among the different pages in the document.

Setting initial visibility

The initial visibility is determined by the layer's visibility when the document is exported to the PDF format. These initial states are remembered within the PDF file and may be recalled with the Reset to Initial Visibility option. The initial state of a layer is recorded as the Default State value in the Layer Properties dialog box. Changing this Default State value and saving the file with the File ➪ Save menu command lets you change the initial visibility of the PDF file.

Merging and flattening layers

Selecting the Merge Layers menu command from the Options pop-up menu opens the dialog box shown in Figure 11-90. Using this dialog box, you can select layers to be merged together. The pane on the left includes all layers both visible and hidden.

Select all the layers that you want to merge in the pane on the left, and click the Add button to move them to the center pane. Using the pane on the right, you may select the name of the layer that the layers are merged into. After clicking OK, all the layers listed in the center pane are deleted (except if one of these layers is selected in the right pane as the target layer) and all the content included on these layers is moved to the target layer.

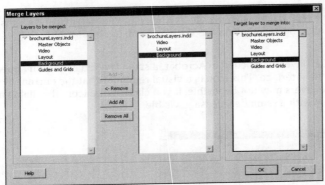

Figure 11-90: The Merge Layers dialog box lists all the layers in the left pane, lets you select which layers to merge in the center pane, and lets you select which layer to merge the content into in the right pane.

When the Flatten Layers menu command is selected in the Options pop-up menu, a warning dialog box opens explaining that this operation cannot be undone. The flattening operation merges the content on all visible layers together and deletes all layers. Any content contained on a hidden layer is deleted. Flattening a document reduces its file size.

Setting layer properties

The Layer Properties menu command opens a dialog box, shown in Figure 11-91, where you can change the layer's name, its default, and its initial states, as well as view information about the application from which it came. The Layer Properties dialog box applies to the selected layer only.

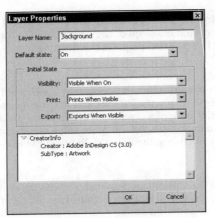

Figure 11-91: The Layer Properties dialog box lets you rename the layer and change its states.

Tip The Layers panel also lets you rename layers by double-clicking on the layer name and typing the new name.

The initial states may be set for a layer's visibility, print, and export options. The Visibility options include Visible When On, Never Visible, and Always Visible. The Visible When On option causes the layer's visibility to be determined by the eye icon in the Layers panel; the other two options cause the layer to never be visible or to always be visible.

You can also set states for when the PDF file is printed or exported. The Print and Export options include Prints (or Exports) When Visible, Never Prints (or Exports), and Always Prints (or Exports). Using these properties, you can control when a layer is printed with the document and when it's exported with the File ➪ Save As menu.

The Options pop-up menu in the Layers panel includes three options for overriding the Visibility, Print, and Export states set in the Layer Properties dialog box. So, if a layer is set to Never Print, selecting the Apply Print Overrides option causes the layer to be printed regardless of the setting in the Layer Properties dialog box.

Making the Layers tab appear when a document is opened

You open the Document Properties dialog box, shown in Figure 11-92, by choosing File ➪ Document Properties. If you click on the Initial View option in the pane on the left, you can set the Layers tab to appear when the document is first opened. In the Show field at the top of the dialog box, select the Layers Panel and Page option and save the PDF file. This option causes the Layers panel to appear when the PDF file is opened, revealing the available layers. Making the Layers panel visible when the PDF file opens is especially helpful for files that include hidden layers.

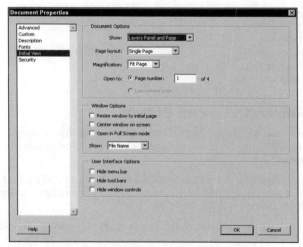

Figure 11-92: The Initial View pane of the Document Properties dialog box lets you set the Layers tab to appear when the document is opened.

Adding interactive layer buttons

When you choose Tools ➪ Advanced Editing ➪ Forms ➪ Button Tool, you can create a button and set its action to control the layer visibility. Before you create the button, click on the Visibility icons for the layers that you want visible when the button is clicked, and then create the button.

In the Button Properties dialog box, shown in Figure 11-93, select the Actions panel. In the Select Action field, choose the Set Layer Visibility option, and click the Add button. The action is added to the Action pane of the dialog box. After clicking the Close button, you can test the button by selecting the Hand tool and clicking on the button.

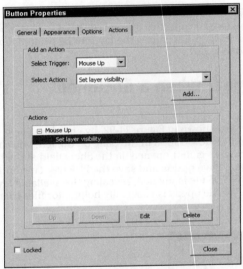

Figure 11-93: The Button Properties dialog box lets you create a button with an action that controls which layers are visible.

STEPS: Creating an Interactive Layer Button

1. **Open a document in Illustrator.** Within Illustrator, open a file that includes layers that have been exported as a PDF file. Some of the layers should be hidden and others should be visible before exporting.

2. **Open the Layers panel.** Click on the Layers tab to the left to open the Layers panel. All the available layers in the document are displayed and the visible layers have an eye icon to the left of their name, as shown in Figure 11-94.

3. **Set the viewable layers.** Click on the eye icon for the layers that you want to be visible when the button is clicked.

Figure 11-94: The Layers panel is opened by clicking on the Layers tab to the left of the interface.

4. **Create a button.** Choose Tools ⇨ Advanced Editing ⇨ Forms ⇨ Button Tool, and drag over the graphic in the lower-right corner of the last page. This opens the Button Properties dialog box.

5. **Set the button properties.** In the Button Properties dialog box, click on the General tab and name the button ShowVideo. This is the text that appears on top of the button. Then select the Actions panel, select the Mouse Up option in the Select Trigger field, set the Select Action field to Set Layer Visibility, and click the Add button. Then select the Play Media (Acrobat 6 Compatible) option in the Select Action field, and click the Add button again. Figure 11-95 shows the Button Properties dialog box after the actions have been set. Click the Close button to exit the dialog box.

6. **Reset layer visibility.** Click on the Options pop-up menu in the Layers panel and select the Reset to Initial Visibility menu command to restore the layer visibility to its initial state.

7. **Test the button.** Click on the Hand tool in the Acrobat toolbar and click on the newly created button. The selected layers should become visible and the video should begin to play, as shown in Figure 11-96.

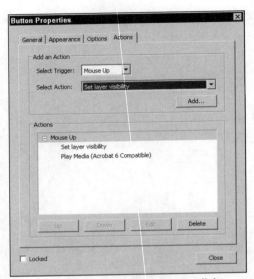

Figure 11-95: The Button Properties dialog box lets you add several actions to a single mouse event.

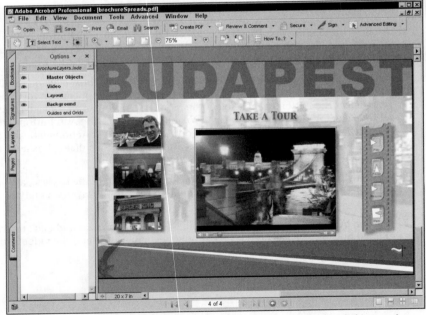

Figure 11-96: The Hand tool lets you test how a button works by clicking on it.

Summary

✦ Layers provide a way to organize objects into easy-to-select groups. These layers include properties such as visibility and locking that are enabled with a single click in the Layers palette.

✦ The Layers palette is used to create new layers, change the layer properties, move objects between layers, and manage layers.

✦ Layers may be used in all the CS applications, but the features available in each application are slightly different.

✦ Layers in Illustrator include the ability to work with sublayers, release layers, add styles to layers, and create clipping masks.

✦ Layers in Photoshop include layer sets, linked layers, transparency and blending modes, multiple locking attributes, adjustment and fill layers, type and shape layers, layer effects, and masks.

✦ The Layer Comps palette in Photoshop lets you take snapshots of different layer configurations and recall these snapshots quickly.

✦ Layers in GoLive enable you to place Web-page content on top of other layers. The GoLive layers follow the CSS specification.

✦ GoLive layers may be animated using the DHTML Timeline Editor.

✦ Individual layers may be selected for a file that includes layers within Acrobat using the Layers tab.

✦　　✦　　✦

Automating Tasks

Suppose you've been asked to alter all the images in a 1,000-page travel Web site by applying a simple Drop Shadow filter. Using the Actions palette, you could quickly record all the steps required to alter the images and apply these steps to the images, thereby eliminating this repetitive and boring task.

Many of the CS applications include features that automate mundane, repetitive tasks. Chief among these features is the Actions palette, found in Illustrator and Photoshop, which lets you record a series of commands and play them back with a single mouse-click.

In addition to playing back an action, you can also save actions for use on other projects and batch-processed against a large number of files and/or folders. Scripts are supported by Illustrator and Photoshop and provide a way to automate tasks that span several applications.

Photoshop includes many automated features that let you quickly perform such tasks as cropping and straightening scanned photos and create a page of thumbnails for printing. These features are found in Photoshop's File ⇨ Automate menu.

Illustrator and ImageReady include support for data-driven graphics. Data-driven graphics are document objects that are linked to variables and that an external program can read and alter to create numerous customized designs.

Finally, Acrobat includes an interface for batch-processing a series of commands called a *sequence*. Using the Batch Processing menu command, found in the Advanced menu, you may define your own sequences and execute them against a selection of files and/or folders.

If the goal is to get work done more quickly, automation is the name of the game and this chapter covers how to do it in the Creative Suite.

Using the Actions Palette

The Actions palette, shown in Figure 12-1, is used to create, manage, and execute actions within Illustrator and Photoshop. Access this palette by choosing Window ⇨ Actions. When the Actions palette is first opened, it contains several different default actions that you may select and use. These actions are all grouped in a folder called `Default Actions`.

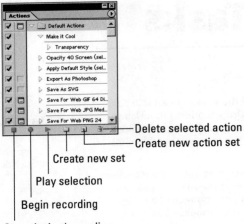

Delete selected action
Create new action set
Create new set
Play selection
Begin recording
Stop playing/recording

Figure 12-1: All created actions are stored and accessed from the Actions palette.

You can view the Actions palette in two different ways. The default view lists all sets, actions, and commands in hierarchical order. By expanding and collapsing the names in the Actions palette, you can view or hide the individual commands that make up each action. The second view is Button mode, which you enable using the Button mode palette menu command. This mode displays all actions as single buttons. Clicking on one of these buttons executes the action. Figure 12-2 shows the Actions palette in Button mode.

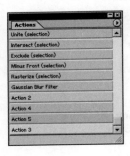

Figure 12-2: When the Actions palette is in Button mode, all actions appear as buttons.

Playing an action

Actions within the Actions palette may be executed by selecting an action, then select an object in the document to receive the action commands and choose the Play palette menu command or click on the Play Selection button at the bottom of the palette.

If you expand an action, the individual commands that are part of the action become visible. If you select a single command and press the Play Selection button, all commands from this selected command to the end of the action are executed. You can exclude any single command from an action by disabling the check box to its left.

Tip   Holding down the ⌘/Ctrl button while clicking the Play Selected button causes only the selected command within an action to execute.

By default, actions are set to be executed as quickly as possible, but you can slow them down using the Playback Options dialog box, shown in Figure 12-3. Open this dialog box with the Playback Options palette menu command.

Figure 12-3: The Playback Options dialog box lets you choose the speed at which actions are executed.

The Playback Options dialog box includes settings for Accelerated, Step by Step, and Pause. The Accelerated option plays the actions as quickly as possible; this is the default setting. The Step by Step option executes each command and then redraws the screen before continuing. The Pause option lets you set the amount of time in seconds to wait after each command is executed.

Creating and saving a new action set

Actions may be organized into sets making it easier to locate a given action. To create a new action set, select the New Set palette menu command or click on the Create New Set button at the bottom of the palette. This opens a simple dialog box where the set's name may be entered.

To add an existing action to the new set, select and drag the action and drop it when the new set's name is selected. The dropped action then appears as a child under the new set name.

You can save sets of actions using the Save Actions palette menu command. Action sets are saved using the AIA file extension in Illustrator and the ATN file extension in Photoshop.

Note   You can only save action sets. You cannot save individual actions.

You can reload saved action sets into the Actions palette with the Load Actions palette menu command. When new action sets are loaded into the Actions palette, they appear at the bottom of the Actions palette. To clear the Actions palette, select the Clear Actions palette menu command.

Creating new actions

New actions are created using the New Action palette menu command or by clicking on the Create New Action button at the bottom of the palette. This command opens the New Action dialog box, shown in Figure 12-4. You use this dialog box to give the new action a name, to add the action to an existing set, and to assign the action a Function Key and a color. The color is used to color the action button when the Actions palette is in Button mode. Clicking the Record button starts the recording process.

Holding down the Option/Alt key while clicking on the Create New Action button in the Actions palette instantly creates a new action named Action and a number and begins recording. To rename the action after recording has stopped, select the Action Options palette menu command.

Figure 12-4: The New Action dialog box lets you name the new action.

During the recording process, each new command is added underneath the action's name in the Actions palette. To stop the recording process, select the Stop Recording palette menu command or click on the Stop Playing/Recording button at the bottom of the palette.

Adding paths to an action

If a path is drawn as part of a recorded action, the path is typically not recorded as part of the action, but if you select the Insert Selected Path, the drawn path is included as part of the action and is redrawn in the same location when you execute the action.

Selecting objects as part of an action

When actions are executed, the commands are applied to any selected objects, but you may also select objects as part of the action using the Select Object palette menu command. This opens the Set Selection dialog box, shown in Figure 12-5, where you may enter the note text to search for and select. The Select Object command selects all objects that have a note with the same text as that entered in the Set Selection dialog box. The dialog box also includes options to match the whole word and to make the match case-sensitive.

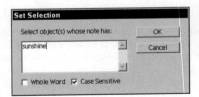

Figure 12-5: The Set Selection dialog box lets you select objects as part of an action by matching text to the text in the Note field of the Attributes palette.

To add text to an object's note, select the object and open the Attributes palette by choosing Window ➪ Attributes (F11). In the Attributes palette menu, select the Show Note palette menu command. This reveals a text area, shown in Figure 12-6, where you may enter text.

Figure 12-6: The Attributes panel includes a Note text area where you can enter a keyword that allows the object to be selected as part of an action.

Inserting menu items

Although actions are fairly robust in what they can record, you cannot record several commands, including drawing with the Pen, Paintbrush, and Pencil tools (although you may add a drawn path to an action); changing tool options; any commands in the Effects and View menus; and setting preferences.

Although you cannot record these commands, you may still add them to an action using the Insert Menu Item palette menu command. This command opens a simple dialog box, shown in Figure 12-7, where you may enter a command, type part of the command and press the Find button, or select a menu item to have it appear in the dialog box. Clicking OK adds this menu command to the action.

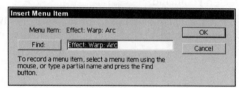

Figure 12-7: The Insert Menu Item dialog box lets you add unrecorded menu items to an action.

Adding a stop with comments

The Insert Stop palette menu command adds a stop to the action that suspends execution of the action allowing you to select new objects, check the progress of the action, or perform a task before continuing.

The Insert Stop palette menu command also opens a dialog box, shown in Figure 12-8, where you may type a message to appear when the stop point is reached. The Allow Continue option adds a Continue button to the stop point.

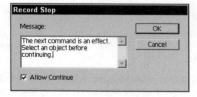

Figure 12-8: The Record Stop dialog box lets you enter a message that appears when execution of an action is halted.

Figure 12-9 shows the resulting message box that appears when the Stop command is encountered.

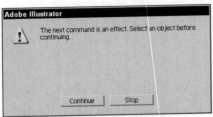

Figure 12-9: A dialog box like this one appears whenever a Stop command is encountered in an action.

Allowing dialog boxes to appear

The second column of the Actions palette, also shown in Figure 12-1, has several icons that represent a dialog box. If you disable this dialog box icon, then the command settings remain the same as when you recorded the command. But if you enable the dialog box, the action stops and displays the dialog box for the selected command.

If you enable the dialog box for a set or an action, then all dialog boxes for the entire set or the entire action are enabled. A red dialog box indicates that only some of the actions or commands have enabled dialog boxes.

Editing existing actions

You may change the options for a set using the Set or Action Options dialog boxes. These dialog boxes are opened for an existing set or action by double clicking on the item in the Actions palette or by selecting the Set Options or Action Option palette menu commands.

Rearranging actions and commands

Within the Actions palette, you can rearrange actions and commands by dragging the selected item above or below the other items. A line appears when dragging an action or a command to indicate where the dropped item is positioned. If an item is dropped on top of a selected set, then the item becomes a child of the selected item.

If you hold down the Option/Alt key while dropping a command or an action, the selected item is duplicated. You can also duplicate actions and commands using the Duplicate palette menu command.

Editing actions and commands

To add new commands to an existing action, select the action and press the Begin Recording button at the bottom of the Actions palette. Then complete the new commands. These new commands show up at the bottom of the current action.

If an action includes one command with a dialog box that isn't quite right, select the command in the Actions palette and choose the Record Again palette menu command. The command's dialog box, where you may change its values, opens. Double-clicking on a command also opens the dialog box.

Deleting actions and commands

You can delete actions and commands selected in the Action palette using the Delete palette menu command or by clicking on the Delete Selection button at the bottom of the palette.

Batch-processing actions

To execute an action on an entire folder of files, use the Batch palette menu command. This opens the Batch dialog box, shown in Figure 12-10.

Note   Open the Batch dialog box in Photoshop by choosing File ➪ Automate ➪ Batch. The Batch dialog box in Photoshop offers two additional Source options — Import and File Browser — and some additional options to suppress the File Open dialog boxes and Color Profile warnings.

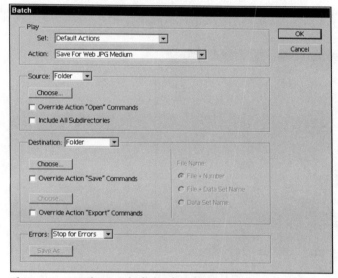

Figure 12-10: The Batch dialog box lets you select an action and execute it on all the files within a given folder.

The Batch dialog box lets you choose an action from all the sets and actions that are currently opened in the Actions palette:

✦ **Source options:** The Source field lets you choose to apply the selected action to all files in the folder or to apply the action to each data set in the current document. If the Folder option is selected, clicking the Choose button lets you select the folder to process. The Override Action Open Commands causes any commands in the action to open a file to be ignored because the folder and files are already designated. The Include All Subdirectories option causes all files in the folder and in its subsequence subdirectories to be processed.

✦ **Destination options.** These include None, Save and Close, and Folder. The None option leaves each document open in the application. The Save and Close option saves the files to the same folder after the changes are made. The Folder option lets you choose a new folder where the files are saved. If the action includes a save command, it can be disabled by enabling the Override Action Save Commands option. You may also select to export the altered file and select the Override Action Export Commands option.

✦ **FileName options.** If the Data Sets option is selected in the Source field, you may select to save the filename using the file and a number, the file and the data-set name, or just the data-set name.

✦ **Errors option.** The final option lets you define how to handle errors. The options include Stop for Errors and Log Errors to File. The Save As button lets you name and save the log file.

Creating a droplet

Photoshop includes an additional way to use actions called *droplets*. Droplets are created by choosing File ➪ Automate ➪ Create Droplet. This command opens a dialog box, shown in Figure 12-11. This dialog box looks similar to the Batch dialog box:

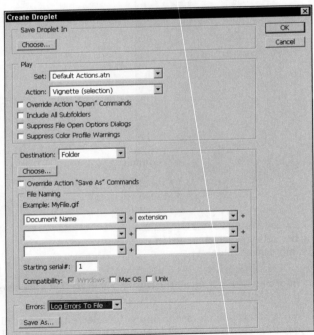

Figure 12-11: The Create Droplet dialog box lets you select where to save the droplet and which action to play to create the droplet.

✦ **Choose button.** The top Choose button opens a file dialog box where you may name and specify a location where the droplet is saved. Droplets are saved with an EXE extension on Windows.

✦ **Play section.** Lets you select an action to include in the droplet.

✦ **Destination section.** Lets you select where the altered images are saved.

The options in both of the Play and Destination sections work the same as those for the Batch dialog box.

After you create a droplet, you can place it anywhere that is convenient. Image files and folders that are dropped onto the droplet automatically open in Photoshop and process using the specified action.

STEPS: Creating an Action in Illustrator

1. **Open an Illustrator document.** With Illustrator open, choose File ➪ New to open a new Illustrator document. Within the document, create and select a simple rectangle object.

2. **Create a new action set.** Choose Window ➪ Actions to open the Actions palette. A set of default actions is listed. Select the New Set palette menu command. A simple dialog box opens. Type a name for the set and click OK. The new set is added to the Actions palette.

3. **Create a new action.** With the new set selected in the Actions palette, select the New Action palette menu command. In the New Action dialog box that appears, name the new action, "Random Shapes" and click the Record button. The new action is added to the Actions palette under the new set and the Record button at the bottom of the Actions palette turns red to indicate that the action is recording commands.

4. **Record commands.** With the Record button enabled, choose Object ➪ Transform ➪ Transform Each. The Transform Each dialog box opens. Drag the Horizontal and Vertical Scale sliders both to 0, drag the Horizontal and Vertical Move sliders both to 100, set the Angle value to 360, enable the Random option, and click Copy. The command appears in the Actions palette as part of the Random Shapes action. Click the Stop Playing/Recording button at the bottom of the palette.

5. **Add an object selection command.** Select the original rectangle object and, with the Transform Each command selected in the Actions palette, select the Insert Select Path palette menu command. This adds a Set Work Path command to the Actions palette.

6. **Rearrange the action commands.** Select and drag the Set Work Path command above the Transform Each menu command. Rearranging these commands causes the original object to be selected before the object is randomly transformed. Figure 12-12 shows the resulting Actions palette with the defined action expanded.

Figure 12-12: Each action and command may be expanded to reveal all its details.

7. **Duplicate commands.** Select all commands for the action just created in the Actions palette by holding down the Shift key while clicking on them. Then select the Duplicate palette menu command to duplicate the selected commands. Repeat this step nine more times until the commands appear ten times each.

8. **Disable the dialog boxes.** Locate the new action in the Actions palette and click on the dialog box icon in the column to the left of the action's name. This makes the action work without opening the Transform Each dialog box each time.

9. **Executing an action.** Select the new action in the Actions palette and click the Play Selected button at the bottom of the Actions palette. The selected object is duplicated ten times and randomly transformed, as shown in Figure 12-13.

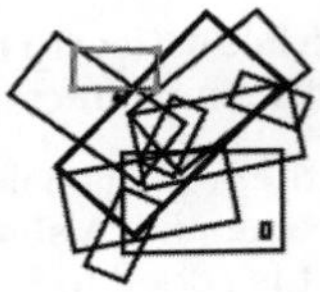

Figure 12-13: Using an action, all these random rectangles were created with a single button click.

Using Scripts

Another way to automate tasks in Photoshop and Illustrator is with scripts. These scripts are authored using Microsoft's Visual Basic, Apple's AppleScript, or JavaScript. A key advantage that scripts have over actions is that scripts can automate tasks across different applications.

Scripts are loaded and executed in Photoshop or Illustrator by choosing File ➪ Scripts ➪ Browse.

Both Photoshop and Illustrator include several default scripts. These scripts appear in the File ➪ Scripts menu. For Photoshop, the scripts include Export Layers to Files, Layer Comps to Files, Layer Comps to PDF, and Layer Comps to WPG. For Illustrator, the scripts include Add Watermark, Apply Style to Text Selection, Change Sizes of Text Selection, Export Docs as Flash, and Save Docs as PDF.

To add scripts to the File ➪ Scripts menu, simply copy the script file into the `Presets/Scripts` folder where Illustrator or Photoshop is installed.

Using Photoshop's Additional Automation Features

Photoshop includes support for actions, but it also includes several other valuable automation features available in the File ➪ Automate menu command. Using these features allows you to quickly perform complex Photoshop tasks using a simple dialog box.

The available automation tasks include the following:

✦ **Batch:** Lets you apply an action to an entire folder of image files in a single process.

✦ **PDF Presentation:** Lets you create a PDF slideshow using multiple selected files.

✦ **Create Droplet:** Lets you save an action as an executable file called a *droplet,* which processes files when they're dropped on top of it.

✦ **Conditional Mode Change:** Changes the color mode of the specified files.

✦ **Contact Sheet II:** Creates a page of thumbnail previews for the specified folder. This is useful for printing a catalog of images.

✦ **Crop and Straighten Photos:** Locates, crops, straightens, and separates several images from a scanned page.

✦ **Fit Image:** Resamples an image to a specified width and height.

✦ **Multi-Page PDF to PSD:** Converts each separate page of a PDF file to PSD files (one PSD file per PDF page).

✦ **Picture Package:** Creates and fits several copies of the selected image on a single page ready to be printed.

✦ **Web Photo Gallery:** Creates a Web page of thumbnail images with links to the full-sized images.

✦ **Photomerge:** Creates a panoramic image from several individual images that have overlapping sections.

Working with Data-Driven Graphics

Suppose it's Christmastime and you've designed a nice Christmas card to send to all your family and friends. Using data-driven graphics, you can set a variable that loads the family name into the design or swaps the images for your friends who celebrate Hanukkah.

By automating the production of multiple designs based on data contained in a list, an arduous task becomes simple. Data-driven graphic features are available in Illustrator and ImageReady.

Data-driven graphics work a bit differently in ImageReady from the way they work in Illustrator. Within ImageReady, the variables are defined in the Layers palette, and the commands for creating variables and data sets are located in the Images ⇨ Variables menu.

Defining variables

The first step in using data-driven graphics is to define variables. In Illustrator, variables are stored in the Variables palette, shown in Figure 12-14, which you can access by choosing Window ⇨ Variables. Every object in the document that changes needs to have a variable assigned to it.

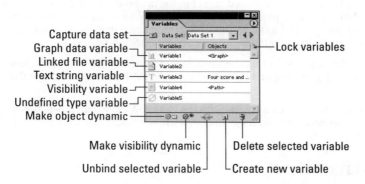

Figure 12-14: Variables are linked to the objects in the document that are changed.

Illustrator includes four different variable types. The type to select depends on the type of content that it represents. The four types are Graph Data, Linked File, Text String, and Visibility. Each variable type is identified by an icon to the left of the variable name in the Variables palette.

To create a new variable, select the New Variable palette menu command or click on the Create New Variable button at the bottom of the palette. Creating a new variable opens the Variable Options dialog box, shown in Figure 12-15. In this dialog box, you can give the variable a name and select the variable type. Clicking on the Create New Variable button or selecting the No Type option in the Variable Options dialog box creates an unbound variable.

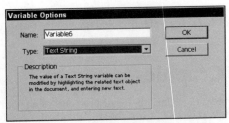

Figure 12-15: The Variable Options dialog box lets you name the variable and select a variable type.

Double-clicking on a variable in the Variables palette opens the Variable Option dialog box, where you can alter the variable's name and type.

When you have added all the variables to the Variables palette, clicking on the Lock Variables icon prevents variables from being deleted or changed.

Binding variables to objects

To link a variable to an object in the design, you should select the object when you create the variable. The selected object needs to match the variable type, except for the Visibility variable, which you can link to any type of object.

Unbound variables may be linked to a selected object in the art board using the Make Object Dynamic or Make Visibility Dynamic palette menu commands or by using one of the buttons at the bottom of the palette. The Make Object Dynamic button and palette menu command are only available if the selected object matches the selected variable's type.

Variables can also be unbound by selecting the variable and selecting the Unbind Variable palette menu command or by clicking on the Unbind Variable button at the bottom of the palette.

If you click on a variable in the Variables palette with the Option/Alt key held down, the linked object is selected in the art board or you may choose to use the Select Bound Object palette menu command.

Capturing a data set

Once a dynamic object has been added to the document, a data set is captured by selecting the Capture Data Set palette menu command or by clicking on the Capture Data Set button.

This saves all the attributes of the dynamic objects into a collection called a *data set*. Editing the dynamic objects and clicking the Capture Data Set button again creates a parallel set of data.

Each data set may have a different name and the various data sets may be selected from the list or by clicking on the arrow icons to the right of the data-set list.

Saving variables

Variables defined in the Variables palette may be saved to communicate the defined variables to a Web developer using the Save Variable Library palette menu command. This command opens a file dialog box where the variable library is named. The file is saved using the XML file format.

Cross-Reference   More information about the XML format is presented in Chapter 27.

XML variable libraries may also be loaded into the Variables palette using the Load Variable Library menu command. This command opens a dialog box where you can select an XML file to load. The loaded variables are then displayed in the Variables palette.

Batch-Processing PDF Files

Acrobat enables automation using its Batch Processing dialog box, shown in Figure 12-16. You can access the Batch Processing dialog box by choosing Advanced ⇨ Batch Processing. The dialog box includes several default batch-processing sequences, including Create Page Thumbnails, Fast Web View, Open All, Print 1st Page of All, Print All, Remove File Attachments, Save All as RTF, and Set Security to No Changes.

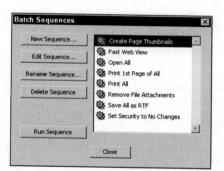

Figure 12-16: The Batch Processing dialog box lets you define new sequences, edit existing sequences, and run existing sequences.

Selecting one of these batch sequences, you can execute the sequence. This causes the steps of the sequence to run letting you select which files to apply the sequence steps to and where to save the changes. The dialog box also lets you edit the existing batch sequences and creating new sequences.

Executing sequences

To execute a sequence, simply select it from the list and click the Run Sequence button. A Confirmation dialog box, like the one in Figure 12-17, appears, listing where the input is coming from, what commands are to be executed, and where the output is saved.

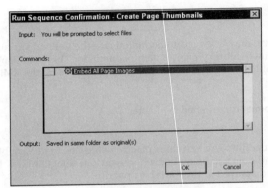

Figure 12-17: When you are executing a sequence, a confirmation dialog box appears explaining what is about to happen.

Editing sequences

You may edit existing sequences listed in the Batch Processing dialog box by selecting the sequence that you want to edit and clicking the Edit Sequence button. This button opens the Batch Edit Sequence dialog box, shown in Figure 12-18, where you can select new commands to add to the sequence, specify the files that the sequence is run against, and designate the output location.

Clicking the Select Commands button opens the Edit Sequence dialog box, shown in Figure 12-19, which lists all the available Acrobat commands in the pane on the left and lists all the commands included in the current sequence in the pane on the right. Selecting a command in the left pane and clicking the Add button adds the command to the sequence pane on the right. The Remove button is used to remove commands from the sequence pane.

If the command includes settings, you can expand the command to reveal the settings. Clicking the Edit button opens the appropriate dialog box of editable settings. The sequence commands may also be selected and moved up and down in order. If the selected command has a dialog box associated with it, click on the first column to the left of the command name in the right pane to enable the settings dialog box. When enabled, the dialog box of settings appears when the command is executed, allowing you to change the settings as the sequence is being run.

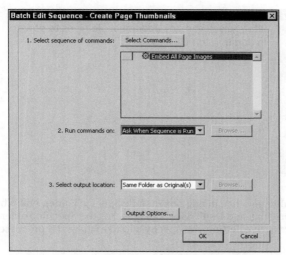

Figure 12-18: The Batch Edit Sequence dialog box lets you change the input, output, and commands for a sequence.

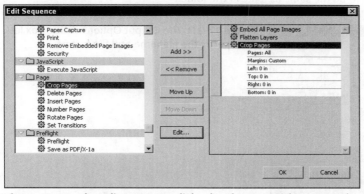

Figure 12-19: The Edit Sequence dialog box lets you pick commands to include in the sequence.

The input options for the sequence include Selected Files, Selected Folders, Ask When Sequence Is Run, and Files Open in Acrobat. These are the files that the sequence is executed on. If the Selected Files or Selected Folders options are selected, the Browse button becomes active. For the Selected Folders option, another button appears that opens a dialog box, shown in Figure 12-20, that lets you select which file types to include along with the PDF files.

Figure 12-20: The Source File Options dialog box lets you select many additional file types to process in addition to PDF files.

The Output options in the Batch Edit Sequence dialog box include Specific Folder, Ask When Sequence Is Run, Same Folder as Original, and Don't Save Changes. For the Specific Folder option, the Browse button becomes active, letting you specify a folder where the processed files are saved.

The Output Options button opens the Output Options dialog box, shown in Figure 12-21, which offers options for naming the processed files. You can save the file name with the same as the original or by appending a prefix or suffix to the filename with the Add to Original Base Name option. The Do Not Overwrite Existing Files option is a safeguard in case the new name of the file happens to be the same as a file in the folder.

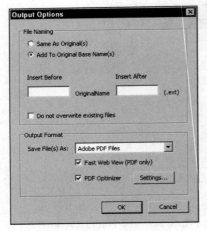

Figure 12-21: The Output Options dialog box lets you specify the filename and file format.

The Output Format selection list lets you select the format that is used to save the processed files. The options include Adobe PDF Files, Encapsulated PostScript, HTML 3.2, HTML 4.01 with CSS 1.00, JPEG, JPEG2000, Microsoft Word Document, PNG, PostScript, and Rich Text Format. For the PDF file format, you may select the Fast Web View option, which optimizes the PDF file by reducing its file size and optimizing its images. The PDF Optimizer makes the Settings button active, which opens the PDF Optimizer dialog box.

Cross-Reference   The PDF Optimizer is covered in Chapter 26.

Creating a new sequence

The New Sequence button opens a simple dialog box where the new sequence is given a name. After you name a sequence, the Batch Edit Sequence dialog box opens; here, you select the commands to add to the sequence, determine the files to process, and define the output settings.

After the sequence is defined, the new sequence is displayed in the Batch Sequences dialog box, where you can select and execute it. To rename a sequence, simply select it and press the Rename Sequence button. To delete a sequence, simply select it and press the Delete Sequence button.

Setting batch-processing preferences

Within the Preferences dialog box, shown in Figure 21-22, which you open by choosing Acrobat ➪ Preferences (on the Mac) or Edit ➪ Preferences (in Windows), is a panel of settings for the Batch Processing dialog box.

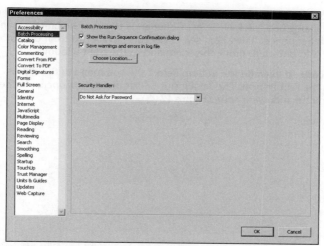

Figure 12-22: The Preferences dialog box includes some settings for the Batch Processing dialog box.

The Show the Run Sequence Confirmation dialog option causes the confirmation dialog box to appear when a sequence is executed. If you choose not to see this confirmation, disable this option. As a sequence is run, you can save all warning and errors to a log file. If this option is enabled, you may click the Choose Location button to define where the error log is saved.

The Security Handler offers options for controlling the security of the sequences. The options include Don Not Ask for Password, Password Security, and Certificate Security.

Creating batch sequences using JavaScripts

The CS applications probably offer no more automation possibilities than you'd find when using Acrobat and the Acrobat implementation of JavaScript. With JavaScripts, you can extend beyond preset options, menu commands, and keyboard shortcuts to an infinite number of actions that you can perform using custom batch sequences created with JavaScripts.

If you're not a programmer, you'll want to become a little familiar with JavaScripting by examining code written by other users. You can acquire PDF documents containing scripts from many Web sites and copy and paste code into your own documents after a short review of how JavaScript is handled in Acrobat. In addition, the *Acrobat JavaScript Scripting Reference* is a complete manual shipped with Acrobat; you can find it on the installer CD. After reviewing this guide and with a little practice writing simple code, you can add more automation for PDF processing in many ways. As an example, suppose you have a collection of PDF documents you want to stamp for not releasing information to the public. Instead of opening each document, adding a stamp comment, adding a comment note, and saving and closing the file, you can write a JavaScript for a custom batch sequence and Acrobat does all the work for you. To see how this is accomplished and learn the code to exercise such a task, follow these steps.

STEPS: Creating a JavaScript Batch Sequence

1. **Create a New Batch Sequence.** Choose Advanced ⇨ Batch Processing. In the Batch Sequences dialog box, select New Sequence. When the Name Sequence dialog box opens, type a name for the sequence. In this example, we use NotForDistribution. Click OK.

2. **Select Execute JavaScript and add it to the list of sequences to be executed.** In the Batch Edit Sequence dialog box, click on Select Commands to open the Edit Sequence dialog box. In the Edit Sequence dialog box, select Execute JavaScript from the list on the left and click the Add button to move the command to the right window.

3. **Add the JavaScript code to execute the action.** Select the command in the right window and click on the Edit button. The JavaScript Editor dialog box opens. In the JavaScript Editor, type the following code (Figure 12-23).

```
/* Add a Stamp comment to Page 1 in a PDF file */
var annot = this.addAnnot
({
   page:0,
   type: "Stamp",
   name: "NotForDistribution",
   strokeColor: color.blue,
   popupOpen: true,
   rect: [460, 450, 650, 500],
author: "Ted/Wendy/Kelly",
contents: "This document is not to be distributed publicly until
approved by management",
AP: "NotForPublicRelease"
})
```

4. **Save the JavaScript.** Click OK in the JavaScript Editor dialog box. Click OK in the Edit Sequence dialog box to return to the Batch Edit Sequence dialog box. The script is saved when you exit the JavaScript Editor dialog box.

5. **Set the output options.** Leave Run commands on at the default for Ask When Sequence Is Run. In the Select Output Location pull-down menu, select the option you want to use for the saved files location. If you want to be prompted at the time the sequence is run, select Ask When Sequence Is Run. Click OK in the Batch Edit Sequence dialog box, and the sequence is added to the list of Batch Sequences.

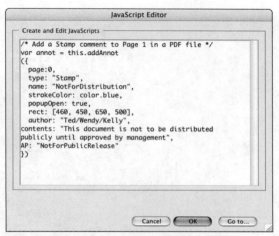

Figure 12-23: Type the code in the JavaScript Editor dialog box.

6. **Run the sequence.** Select the Add Stamp sequence in the Batch Sequences dialog box and click on Run Sequence.

 Note

If you closed the Batch Sequences dialog box after the last step, choose Advanced ➪ Batch Processing to reopen the dialog box.

7. **Examine the results.** Select a single file to process when the Select Files to Process dialog box opens. You should see a stamp comment in the top-right corner of the first page of the document page. The open pop-up note window displays the note contents, as shown in Figure 12-24.

The preceding steps create a stamp comment in line 2 (`var annot = this.addAnnot`) at the coordinates in line 9 (`rect: [460, 450, 650, 500],`). Note that the page size where the stamp is added is a custom landscape page measuring 10 by 7 inches. When using a Batch Sequence with multiple files, you need to run the sequence on PDF documents using the same page size to ensure the comment falls on the page. Note that JavaScript is zero based and line 4 (`page:0,`) targets the comment for page 1 in the file. In line 7 (`strokeColor: color.blue,`), the note pop-up window is set to blue and the pop-up window is opened after the Stamp is added to the page (`popupOpen: true,`). The content of the note pop-up is: *This document is not to be distributed publicly until approved by management* (line 11). Line 10 (`author: "Ted/ Wendy/Kelly",`) adds the author name (in this example, three author names were added). You can change the position of the note by editing the coordinates in line 9, changing the contents in line 11, or changing the stamp type in line 12 (`AP: "NotForPublicRelease"`). The code can be easily modified or you can copy and paste the code in the JavaScript Editor if you want to create other similar sequences.

Figure 12-24: The stamp comment is added to the first page of all documents processed with the Add Stamp routine created in the JavaScript Editor.

Summary

✦ Several of the CS applications include features for automating tasks.

✦ Repetitive tasks in Illustrator and Photoshop may be recorded and saved as an action in the Actions palette.

✦ Actions may be executed, edited, organized into sets, saved to a file, and run in a batch process against many selected files or folders.

✦ Additional automation is possible using scripts, which are run using the File ➪ Scripts menu command.

✦ Another way to automate the creation of many unique graphics based on a template is with data-driven graphics. By defining variables and linking those variables to objects, external programs can modify designs quickly and easily.

✦ Acrobat includes support for Batch Processing commands against selected files and folders.

✦   ✦   ✦

Working with Type

◆ ◆ ◆ ◆

◆ ◆ ◆ ◆

Working with Fonts

Understanding how to effectively manage and utilize fonts for CS applications is essential for creating an efficient workflow environment. This can be a daunting task, however, because it typically requires keeping track of hundreds or even thousands of fonts, which come in a variety of formats such as Type 1 or OpenType. In addition, fonts may have varying degrees of functionality depending on the kind of computer and software you use.

Understanding Fonts

Typesetting on desktop computers has been around for more than 20 years. During this evolutionary era of digital page layout and design, there have been phenomenal changes in the tools and methods we use to produce our work. As rapid advances have been made in software development, so also has font technology evolved. And just as software packages are available that aren't suitable for current operating systems and design needs, there are also different font formats that aren't suitable for layout and imaging.

Fonts have been developed over the years using different technologies and categorized as different formats. Some font formats are obsolete today and won't work properly in some of the CS applications and with newer printing devices. Knowing what fonts are acceptable for use with the CS programs will help you prevent problems associated with printing and font embedding.

Font formats

With literally thousands upon thousands of fonts to choose from, it's important to know the different formats and which ones are best suited for your individual working environment. Ideally, you should have a thorough knowledge of all the fonts currently installed on your system.

The various font types are covered in the following sections.

> ✦ **Type 1:** The most popular PostScript font today. These fonts are single-byte fonts handled well by Adobe Type Manager (Windows), Mac OS X, and all PostScript printers. Type 1 fonts use a specialized subset of the PostScript language that has been optimized for performance. Type 1 fonts are reliable, and present the fewest problems when embedding and printing to PostScript devices.

Type 1 fonts were designed to be used with the Compact Font Format (CFF). CFF was designed for font embedding and substitution with Acrobat PDFs. As is the case with all PostScript fonts, you must install two files to view and print fonts properly. Screen fonts display a font on your monitor; printer fonts carry the PostScript code necessary to download to your printer. Each font in your layout needs an accompanying printer font. For example, if you use Adobe Garamond Bold, you need an Adobe Garamond Bold printer font. If you attempt to bold a font by using the "B" in a type formatting palette, the font may display properly on the monitor and may even print properly on your laser printer. But if you don't have the matching printer font, it typically does not print properly when printing to commercial devices.

Note

When preparing files for output for commercial printing, Acrobat PDFs offer you an advantage, because the fonts used in a design piece can be embedded in the PDF file. (Be sure the font licensing agreement doesn't prohibit embedding.) This way, the fonts do not need to be supplied separately to your commercial printer.

✦ **Type 3:** Type 3 fonts are PostScript fonts that have often been used with type design and stylizing applications. These fonts can have special design attributes applied to them such as shading, patterns, exploding 3-D displays, and so on. Type 3 fonts can't be used with Adobe Type Manager (ATM), and they often present problems when printing to PostScript devices.

✦ **Type 4:** Type 4 was designed to create font characters from printer font cartridges for permanent storage on a printer's hard drive (usually attached by a SCSI port to the printer). PostScript Level 2 provided the same capability for Type 1 fonts and eventually made these font types obsolete.

✦ **Type 5:** This font type is similar to the Type 4 fonts but used the printer's ROM instead of the hard drive. PostScript Level 2 made this format obsolete.

✦ **Type 32:** Type 32 fonts are used for downloading bitmap fonts to a PostScript interpreter's font cache. By downloading directly to the printer cache, space is saved in the printer's memory.

✦ **Type 42:** Type 42 fonts are generated from the printer driver for TrueType fonts. A PostScript wrapper is created for the font, making the rasterization and interpretation more efficient and accurate. Type 42 fonts work well when printing to PostScript printers.

✦ **OpenType:** OpenType is a new standard for digital type fonts, developed jointly by Adobe and Microsoft. OpenType supersedes Microsoft's TrueType Open extensions to the TrueType format. OpenType fonts can contain either PostScript or TrueType outlines in a common wrapper. An OpenType font is a single file, which can be used on both Mac and Windows platforms without conversion. OpenType fonts have many advantages over previous font formats because they contain more glyphs, support more languages (OpenType uses the Unicode standard for character encoding), and support rich typographic features such as small caps, old style figures, and ligatures — all in a single font.

Beginning with Adobe InDesign and Adobe Photoshop 6.0, applications started supporting OpenType layout features. OpenType layout allows you to access features such as old style figures or true small caps by simply applying formatting to text. In most applications that don't actively support such features, OpenType fonts work just like other fonts, although the OpenType layout features are not accessible.

✦ **Compact Font Format:** Compact Font Format (CFF) is similar to the Type 1 format but offers much more compact encoding and optimization. It was designed to support Type 2 fonts but can be used with other types. CFF can be embedded in PDFs for all levels of PDF compatibility. Fonts supporting this format are converted by Acrobat Distiller during distillation to CFF/Type 2 fonts and embedded in the PDF. When viewed on-screen or printed, they're converted back to Type 1, which provides support for ATM and printing with integrity.

✦ **CID-keyed fonts:** This format was developed to take advantage of large character sets, particularly the Asian CJK (Chinese, Japanese, and Korean) fonts. The format is an extension of the Type 1 format and supports ATM and PostScript printing. Kerning and spacing for these character sets are better handled in the OpenType format.

✦ **TrueType:** TrueType is a standard for digital type fonts that was developed by Apple Computer and subsequently licensed to Microsoft Corporation. Each company has made independent extensions to TrueType, which is used in both Windows and Mac operating systems. Like Type 1, the TrueType format is available for development of new fonts.

Advantages of OpenType fonts

You can copy an OpenType font from Mac to Windows and vice versa. The OpenType format is supported for font embedding in Acrobat PDFs. Fonts produced with this technology are as reliable as you find with Type 1 and Type 42 fonts. In addition, OpenType offers a means for flagging the fonts for embedding permissions.

The OpenType format is an extension of the TrueType SFNT format that also can support Adobe PostScript font data and new typographic features. OpenType fonts containing PostScript data, such as those in the Adobe Type Library, have a filename extension of .otf, while TrueType-based OpenType fonts have a .ttf extension.

OpenType fonts can include an expanded character set and layout features, providing broader linguistic support and more precise typographic control. Feature-rich Adobe OpenType fonts can be identified by the word "Pro" in their name. OpenType fonts can be installed and used alongside PostScript Type 1 and TrueType fonts.

Cross-Reference

See Chapter 16 for more information on working with expanded character sets.

Creative Suite comes with 83 OpenType fonts that are installed as part of the Illustrator CS application. These fonts offer you an extended set of characters where you find more *ligatures* (character combinations) and special characters and symbols. Whereas PostScript fonts offer you a maximum of 256 glyphs (individual characters), OpenType fonts can contain more than 65,000 glyphs. Look for the OpenType "Pro" fonts and you'll find extended character sets.

As a standard of practice, you would be wise to replace your TrueType and PostScript fonts with OpenType. This is likely to be an expensive proposition, but if you gradually begin to convert your font library and acquire new fonts in OpenType format, you'll benefit by having access to more characters, enhanced typographic features, and increased printing reliability.

Font licenses

Fonts generally carry licensing restrictions, and you need to be sure to honor them. This can be a confusing issue, however, because different font manufacturers impose different restrictions, and many licensing agreements are difficult to interpret. In order to provide font files to your service center or printer, manufacturers often require you to get permission to distribute the font. Many manufacturers prohibit such distribution altogether. In addition, some manufacturers prohibit font embedding as you might do in programs like Acrobat. It's important to be aware of these limitations.

One possible way around font licensing issues is by converting any type not within your service provider's library to outlines in your documents before submitting them. In this way, the type becomes a graphic, and you don't need to copy your font files. This eliminates the transfer of the font's computer code, which is protected by copyright law. As a matter of practice, you should avoid converting large bodies of type to outlines, but in an emergency situation, it may mean the difference between getting the job out on time or not at all.

Managing Fonts

Font management has become more complicated for Mac OS X users. Prior to OS X, you could manage fonts easily using one of several different utilities, as well as by installing fonts in a single, logical location on your hard drive. With the introduction of Mac OS X, fonts are stored in several areas on your hard drive and, if not installed in the right folders, become inaccessible to your programs. In order to avoid complicated font installation procedures and ensure that fonts are accessible by CS applications, we highly recommend using a professional font-management utility. You'll find that this is a better solution than installing fonts in folders and letting your operating system handle the font management.

Installing fonts in Mac OS X

Just in case you haven't upgraded to Mac OS X Panther or you don't currently have a font-management utility, you need to know where fonts are installed on your computer to make them accessible by CS applications. Mac OS X allows you to create accounts (more accurate word and will be easier to find in the system prefes) for multiple users, and you can choose to install fonts at the system level so all users of the computer have access to the same fonts, or you can store the fonts in individual users' Home folders to make them accessible only to a specific user.

Fonts for the Mac are installed in these locations:

✦ **For fonts you want to be accessible to all users of the computer, store them on the hard drive in** Library/Fonts **(see Figure 13-1).** To install fonts in the system Library folder, open your hard drive and open the Library folder at the root level. Inside the Library folder, you'll find a Fonts folder. You can copy TrueType, PostScript, and OpenType fonts to this location.

✦ **For user-specific fonts, store them in** ~/Library/Fonts **(see Figure 13-2).** (The tilde represents a user's Home folder.) Fonts stored here are available only to the owner of the active Home folder, which means different users may have access t o different fonts. In case of font conflicts, fonts in this location take precedence over those in other folders.

Figure 13-1: Any user who logs onto the computer can access fonts stored in the system `Library` folder.

Figure 13-2: Fonts stored in the Home user's `Library` folder are only available to that specific user.

✦ **System fonts:** The Mac OS X System folder also contains a `Library` folder (see Figure 13-3). Once again, a `Font` folder resides inside the `Library` folder. As a default, Apple fonts required by the operating system are placed in this location. It's possible to add fonts here, but as a general rule, don't.

✦ **Mac OS 9:** For Classic applications, fonts are installed in the `System Folder/Fonts` location. In Figure 13-4, notice the folder is titled `System Folder` and not `System`. Because all the CS applications run in native mode on OS X, you don't need to bother loading fonts here.

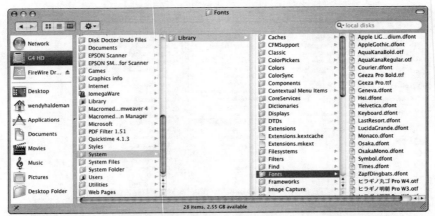

Figure 13-3: Fonts used by the Mac OS X operating system are stored in this folder. As a general rule, it's best not to add to or remove fonts from this location.

Figure 13-4: Fonts in the Classic System Folder are intended for Classic applications. These fonts are also available to OS X applications, but this location is the lowest priority level in case of conflicts.

Installing fonts in Windows

For Windows, like the Mac, you're best served by using a font utility. Follow these steps:

1. **Open the Settings menu from the Start menu.**

2. **From the Settings menu, select Control Panel and double-click on Fonts in the submenu. The Fonts folder opens.**

3. **From the File menu select Install New Font, as shown in Figure 13-5. A navigation dialog box opens where you can search your hard drive and locate a font to install.**

4. **Select the fonts you want to install and click OK.**

Figure 13-5: Open the Fonts dialog box and choose File ➪ Install New Font to install TrueType fonts in Windows.

Fonts are also located in the PSFonts folder. On your boot drive (usually drive C:), open the folder and copy PostScript and OpenType fonts to this folder.

Organizing your fonts

Fonts play a crucial role in any designer's work. Thus, it's important to take some time to learn how to best organize your fonts to ensure maximum productivity. The amount of time you invest up front in organizing your fonts will more than pay off down the road, especially if you face an eleventh-hour deadline and can't afford for anything to go wrong at the last minute.

Check your computer's fonts on a regular basis to be sure they organized properly. Whenever you add, move or delete fonts, there is a chance that something can go awry. Or, if you install a new operating system or font-management utility, you may need to reorganize your fonts, throw out obsolete formats, or replace existing formats to become more compatible with your current operating system and programs. If you continue to use old fonts that aren't optimized for current technology, you'll eventually experience problems.

On the other hand, if you use high-quality fonts designed to work with current software and output devices, you avoid annoying imaging problems. One of the more common font errors is the inability of the printing device to recognize the font information in the file. The printing device then automatically substitutes a default font for the one you specified, with the end result looking nothing like what you intended. Thus, choosing fonts that have a high degree of printing reliability may mean the difference between getting the job out on time and missing a critical deadline.

Using font-management tools

Font-management tools greatly facilitate font accessibility and usage. They also help prevent the installation of duplicate fonts, especially on the Mac. Mac OS X Panther users have a utility that ships with the operating system called Font Book. This is a good, basic utility that allows you to enable and disable fonts. It doesn't offer the convenience of auto-activation, however. You can also use third-party tools such as Extensis Font Reserve, Extensis Suitcase, or Adobe Type Manager (ATM) on Windows. (Because ATM for Mac was discontinued with the introduction of Mac OS X, it isn't available for Mac CS application users.)

If your workflow environment is cross-platform (that is, it includes both Mac and Windows computers), you should use a font-management utility that is also cross-platform. Among the most popular is Extensis Suitcase, which provides automatic font loading for programs like Illustrator and InDesign. This feature automatically loads needed fonts when you open a document in either program.

The Suitcase application launches automatically when you power up your computer and remains active in the background. When working in Suitcase, be careful only to minimize its window without actually quitting the program. If you quit, you'll need to relaunch the application to enable its functionality.

Open the Suitcase application by clicking on the program icon or alias. On the Mac, an alias appears in the dock. Click once on the program icon in the dock and the program opens as shown in Figure 13-6. Font sets are listed at the top, and open fonts are listed below.

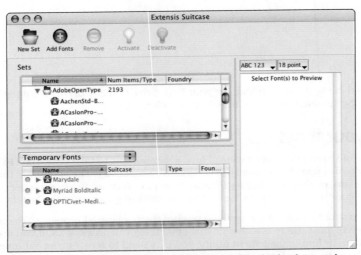

Figure 13-6: Although Suitcase remains active in the background, you must open it by double-clicking on the program icon or an alias. Or, click once when the program icon appears in the dock (Mac) or status bar (Windows).

In the Suitcase document window, you find icons at the top of the window for managing fonts. Click the New Set button to create a font set. A font set may include one font, a collection of fonts, or even all the fonts installed on your computer. After clicking New Set, an Untitled item appears in the top list. Click on Untitled and type a name for your new set. In essence, it's like creating a new folder. To add fonts to the new set, click on the Add Fonts button. A dialog box opens where you can browse your hard drive and select fonts to load in the set. The top-level list is merely the font sets you have created. You can open a set to see the fonts listed and double-click on the fonts you want to make accessible to the CS applications.

You can also load fonts temporarily if you need to activate fonts that aren't currently part of a set. Press ⌘/Ctrl+T and the Add Fonts dialog box opens. Double-click on the fonts you want to open. When you're finished, close the window by pressing ⌘/Ctrl+W. Once again, be certain not to quit the program.

Caution Be sure to keep your font-management utility upgraded to the most current version, especially on Mac OS X. There have been operating system changes, particularly between Mac OS X Jaguar and Panther. Earlier versions of Suitcase were problematic when running on the new, updated operating systems.

A nice benefit available from Extensis is that you can download a fully operational version of Suitcase from their Web site (www.extensis.com) and try it free for 30 days. This allows you to completely test the program before making a purchase. If you decide to purchase it after 30 days, you can do so online and your software will be permanently activated.

Creating Type Outlines and Special Effects

Creating outlines from type has long been a common practice by graphic artists and imaging technicians. If a stubborn font problem is encountered, a workaround solution is to convert the text to outlines so the type is transformed into an object. This way, the font information doesn't need to be downloaded to the output device in order for the document to be imaged properly. When word got out that converting text to outlines eliminated font imaging problems, many designers decided to convert text to outlines as a matter of practice.

One disadvantage in converting text to outlines is that the resulting file size can become quite large and thus take an inordinate amount of time to print. In some cases, the document is rendered unprintable. So, before you convert text to outlines, be certain that you use this option as a last resort.

Another disadvantage in converting text to outlines is that, unless you save a back-up copy of your document, you lose the ability to access and edit your file utilizing the original font information. Say, for example, you create a half a dozen logotype variations for a client using different fonts. You then convert the type to outlines in order to apply special effects, and resave the document. You won't be able to go back into the Character palette to see which fonts you used, nor will you be able to edit any text if there are copy changes. The caveat here is always to save a separate copy of the document that contains the original font information when you choose to convert text to outlines. Fortunately, when using the CS applications, you can use Version Cue to save a different version of the same document. When you want to return to the document containing the original font information, promote that version to the top level in Version Cue.

 Cross-Reference   For information on using Version Cue and promoting versions, see Chapter 7.

So, you may need to convert text to outlines either as a workaround for stubborn font printing issues, or when you want to apply certain type effects. The Create Outlines command is available in both Illustrator and InDesign. (Because Photoshop type can be rasterized when you flatten layers, there is no need to convert type to outlines in Photoshop.)

Converting type to outlines in Illustrator

To convert type to outlines in Illustrator, select the type with either of the selection tools in the Tools palette. (*Note:* You cannot use the Type tool here as you can in InDesign.) Next, Choose Type ➪ Create Outlines or press Shift+⌘+O or Shift+Ctrl+O. As you can see in Figure 13-7, after creating outlines each character becomes a compound path, editable with either the Selection tool or the Direct Selection tool. To edit or move individual characters with the Selection tool, you'll need to first ungroup the object. Choose Object ➪ Ungroup, or press Shift+⌘+G or Shift+Ctrl+G.

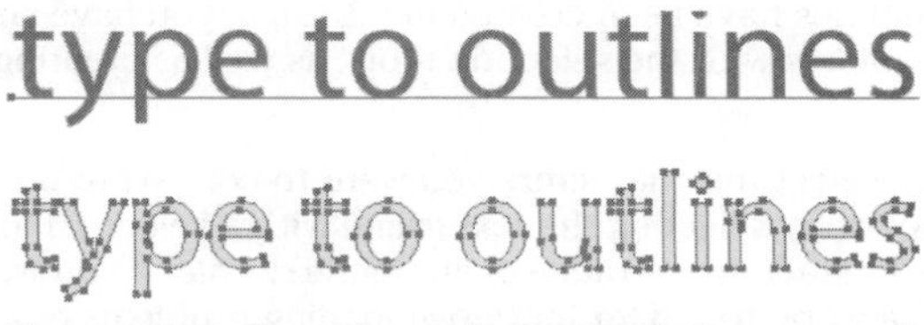

type to outlines

type to outlines

Figure 13-7: Type shown before and after converting to outlines. Each character becomes a compound path, which you can edit with the selection tools.

Creating type effects in Illustrator

The options are almost limitless when it comes to creating eye-catching type effects with Illustrator. You can apply custom gradients, transparency, meshes, shadows, lighting and shading, distortion, stylization, 3D effects, and more. Figure 13-8 shows an example of the 3D type effects you can achieve quickly in Illustrator. For a more in-depth look at the ways you can use Illustrator to enhance your type, see the *Illustrator CS Bible* by Ted Alspach and Jennifer Alspach (published by Wiley).

Figure 13-8: In Illustrator, this 3D effect was easily created using regular type (top) and then applying a stroke, gradient, extrude effect, warp effect, and drop shadow.

Creating type masks in Illustrator

Other interesting effects can be achieved by using type as a mask. Note that when creating type masks in Illustrator you can create a mask without converting the type to outlines.

Position the type in front of the artwork that will be masked. Select both the type and the item to be masked by shift-clicking if necessary (two objects must be selected for this command to work). Then choose Object ⇨ Clipping Mask ⇨ Make, or press ⌘+7 or Ctrl+7. Areas of the background artwork that are outside the type mask disappear, and your type now appears filled with the portion of the artwork directly behind it (see Figure 13-9). You can move the background image or the type around to experiment with different mask positions.

Converting type to outlines in InDesign

InDesign offers you the same option as Illustrator for converting type to outlines. With this feature, you can create many type effects directly in InDesign without having to create them in Illustrator and import them. After outlines have been created in InDesign, you have similar options as Illustrator for shaping text objects with the selection tools, as well as creating type masks.

To convert type to outlines in InDesign, select the characters you want to convert to outlines by highlighting them with the Type tool or by selecting the text frame with a selection tool. With the Type tool, you can select one character or a range of characters. *Note:* If you want to convert your entire page to outlines as a workaround for font downloading problems or licensing issues, select all by choosing either of the selection tools in the Tools palette and then pressing ⌘/Ctrl+A. Next, choose Type ⇨ Create Outlines or press ⌘+Shift+O or Ctrl+Shift+O.

Figure 13-9: You can create type masks in Illustrator without converting the text to outlines.

Creating type effects in InDesign

Many type effects can be achieved in InDesign without converting the type to outlines. As demonstrated in Figure 13-10, you can create sophisticated type treatments with strokes, fills, gradients, and drop shadows and still be able to edit the text. This is a difficult or impossible feat in most other page-layout programs.

Figure 13-10: InDesign CS allows you to create sophisticated type effects without converting the type to outlines. The text remains fully editable.

Note   A new feature of InDesign CS is the Stroke style editor. You can create and save striped, dotted, and dashed stroke styles and apply them to type, as well as underlines, strikethroughs, lines, and paragraph rules.

Creating type masks in InDesign

Type masks are created a little differently than they are in Illustrator. Instead of placing type over artwork to be masked, the type is essentially turned into a graphics frame. You can then paste or import an image into the frame.

After you've converted your type to outlines, simply select it and choose File ⇨ Place, or press ⌘/Ctrl+D, and navigate to the image you want to import. When selecting the type, you can use either the Selection tool or the Direct Selection tool. In Figure 13-11, type is converted to outlines and the text is selected with the Direct Selection tool.

BUDAPEST

Figure 13-11: After converting type to outlines, select the type with either the Selection tool or the Direct Selection tool.

When the Place dialog box opens, be certain to check the box for Replace Selected Item, as shown in Figure 13-12. If you don't check the box, the cursor is loaded with the graphic to be placed, and InDesign expects you to place the file somewhere on the document page. When you select Replace Selected Item, the file is placed within the outlined type, resulting in a mask shown in Figure 13-13.

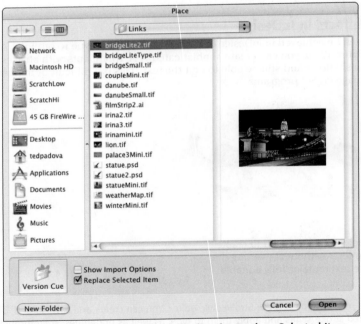

Figure 13-12: Be certain to check the box for Replace Selected Item in the Place dialog box.

Click OK or double-click on the image to place it into the selected outlines. If you need to move the image within the mask, select the Direct Selection tool. When the cursor approaches the text, the cursor changes to a Hand tool, thus informing you that the image can be moved within the mask.

BUDAPEST

Figure 13-13: When the Replace Selected Item check box is enabled, the image is placed within the selected object.

Working with Type in Photoshop

You can create similar effects for type masks in Photoshop as well as stylize type with shadows, embossing, filters, and brightness enhancements. Photoshop's array of editing tools allows you to apply effects to type in the same way you apply them to images. When you create type in Photoshop, type is added to a separate layer and remains as a vector object until you either flatten the layers or rasterize a layer by selecting Layer ➪ Rasterize ➪ Type.

If you import Photoshop files in InDesign or create PDF documents, you can keep your type in vector form by saving the Photoshop document with layers. Formats that can preserve layers include the native .psd, Photoshop PDF, and TIFF. Saving with layers keeps type as text and it remains editable. If you flatten the layers, the text is rasterized and you lose the ability to edit your text.

If you open a Photoshop PDF file in Acrobat with layers and vector data preserved, the text is searchable and editable. If you open the same file in Illustrator, Illustrator automatically converts the type to outlines. The same file saved as a native Photoshop (.psd) file opened in Illustrator preserves all type editing.

The type effects you can create in Photoshop are mind-boggling. For a comprehensive coverage see the *Photoshop CS Bible* by Deke McClelland (Wiley, 2004).

Cross-Reference   For more information on creating type effects in Photoshop, see Part III.

Summary

✦ The three main font formats in use today are PostScript Type 1, TrueType, and OpenType.

✦ OpenType fonts have two advantages: they work in cross-platform environments (Mac and Windows), and they support expanded character sets.

✦ Font-management utilities such as Extensis Suitcase help streamline your font-management tasks.

✦ Converting all type to outlines in your documents is a way to circumvent font downloading problems, but this approach should be used as a last option.

✦ Special type effects are easy to achieve in either Illustrator or InDesign. Illustrator offers a sophisticated array of transformation tools, including extrusion (3D) and lighting effects for type objects. InDesign allows certain type effects to be applied without first converting the type to outlines.

✦ Photoshop provides virtually unlimited options for creating type effects. If you want your text to remain editable, however, be sure to keep the type in vector form by preserving layers when saving your file.

✦   ✦   ✦

Working with Styles

Adding type to a page is one of the more common tasks performed by creative professionals. Long gone are the days when we ordered type from a professional typesetter. Today's graphic artists are both artists and typographers. Fortunately, the typographic tools in the CS applications make your job easier when setting type.

For anyone who has set type for manuals, books, and other long documents, style sheets should be familiar tools. It's hard to imagine working with large bodies of text without the use of style sheets. Without them, your labors would be tenfold. You would have to manually set the styles for each body of text throughout a document, and any style changes would require the same laborious process.

Illustrator CS now supports character and paragraph styles that make layouts much more flexible. In InDesign CS, you'll find impressive style sheet capabilities such as nested styles. In GoLive you have abundant opportunities for adding styles to Web page designs as we describe in Chapter 25.

Cross-Reference For information on working with styles in GoLive, see Chapter 25.

This chapter takes you through setting type in CS applications and creating character and paragraph styles in Illustrator and InDesign.

Setting Type

If you have type created in programs like Microsoft Word, you can import text into both Illustrator and InDesign, as described in Chapter 17. If you don't use a word-processing program to set type, you can add type in Illustrator, Photoshop, or InDesign with the Type tool. In Illustrator, setting type is a bit clumsy as compared to setting type in InDesign. Illustrator doesn't support the use of any special tools for typesetting such as InDesign's Story Editor. However, Illustrator adds some flexibility when setting type on irregular shapes and paths. Each program has its own strength in regard to typesetting, and it's worth your time to look at both programs so you know which one is best for a particular job.

Setting type in Illustrator

Illustrator has two kinds of type functions, both created with the Type tool. You create *point type* by clicking the cursor in the document window where you already have an anchor point. The primary limitation of point type is that the type doesn't wrap or conform to a specific area. If you keep typing, the characters eventually go off the page, unless you add a carriage return at the end of each line.

The other kind of type in Illustrator is *area type*. Area type conforms to a specific boundary and the type wraps to the outside boundary. The type boundary is created by clicking and dragging open a rectangle with the Type tool or by clicking the cursor inside an object. Doing so binds the type to the shape of the object. The object can be a simple geometric shape, a polygon, or an irregular shape.

You also have tools for creating vertical type. Click on the Type tool and keep the mouse button depressed to expand the toolbar. There are two vertical type tools — one for point type and one for area type. The results of creating type with the type tools are shown in Figure 14-1.

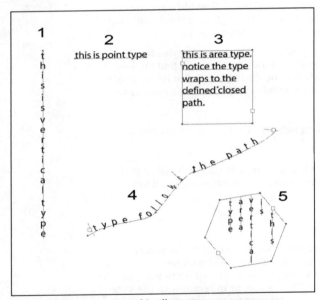

Figure 14-1: Type created in Illustrator can appear as (1) vertical point type, (2) point type, (3) area type, (4) type on a path, or (5) vertical area type.

Creating point type

To create point type, simply click on the Type tool in the Illustrator toolbox and click the cursor at the location where you want to begin typing. A blinking cursor appears.

After typing a line of text, you can use the Character palette or keyboard shortcuts to change type appearances. Choose Window ➪ Type ➪ Character or press ⌘/Ctrl+T to open the Character palette. The default view of the Character palette is collapsed. To expand the view and show more options, click on the right-pointing arrow to open the palette menu and select Show Options. In Figure 14-2 the palette view is shown with the options expanded.

Figure 14-2: The Character palette

The type control available in the Character palette includes the following:

A Font selection is made from the pull-down menu.

B Font style is selected from options in the pull-down menu.

C Type point size can be selected from fixed sixes in the pull-down menu or by typing values in the field box. The values range from 0.1 points to 1,296 points.

D Kerning type is handled by selecting from fixed sizes or by typing values in the field box.

E Horizontal scaling is defined from fixed values or by typing values in the field box.

F Baseline shifts move the baseline of the type up when positive values are entered and down when negative values are entered.

G Language selection is made from pull-down menu.

H Leading is controlled by selecting from fixed values or by typing values to ⅟₁₀₀th of a point.

I Tracking amounts are specified in whole numbers ranging from –1,000 to 10,000 points.

J Vertical scaling of type can be adjusted in increments ranging from 1% to 10,000%.

K Characters can be rotated in increments up to ⅟₁₀₀th of a point.

In addition to using the Character palette, you can perform several adjustments using keyboard shortcuts. To modify the type, use the following key combinations:

✦ **Alt+Right Arrow (Option+ Right Arrow on the Mac):** Increases tracking. Select type characters for the characters of which you want to change tracking amounts.

✦ **Alt+Left Arrow (Option+Left Arrow on the Mac):** Decreases tracking. Select type characters for the characters of which you want to change tracking amounts.

✦ **Alt+Up Arrow (Option+Up Arrow on the Mac):** Increases leading. Affects only selected characters.

✦ **Alt+Down Arrow (Option+Down Arrow on the Mac):** Decreases leading. Affects only selected characters.

✦ **Alt+ Shift+Up Arrow (Option+Shift+Up Arrow on the Mac):** Increases baseline shift. Affects only selected characters.

✦ **Alt+Shift+Down Arrow (Option+Shift+Down Arrow on the Mac):** Decreases baseline shift. Affects only selected characters.

✦ **Alt+Ctrl+Left Arrow (Option+⌘+Left Arrow on the Mac):** Tightens kerning on all selected characters. Clicking in a line of type tightens kerning between characters at the cursor position.

✦ **Alt+Ctrl+Right Arrow (Option+⌘+Right Arrow on the Mac):** Expands kerning. Clicking in a line of type expands kerning between characters at the cursor position.

Other options available in the Character palette are selected from the palette menu. Click the right-pointing arrow in the upper-right corner of the palette, and the palette menu opens as shown in Figure 14-3. The menu options include the following:

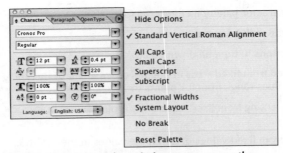

Figure 14-3: The right-pointing arrow opens the palette menu.

✦ **Standard Vertical Roman Alignment:** The direction of half-width characters such as Roman text or numbers changes in vertical alignment. When this option is checked, you can rotate selected individual characters within a block of text without affecting the rotation of the unselected characters.

✦ **All Caps:** Sets all selected characters to caps. (See Figure 14-4.)

✦ **Small Caps:** Sets all selected characters to small caps. (Refer to Figure 14-4.)

✦ **Superscript:** Selected characters appear as superscript above the baseline. (Refer to Figure 14-4.)

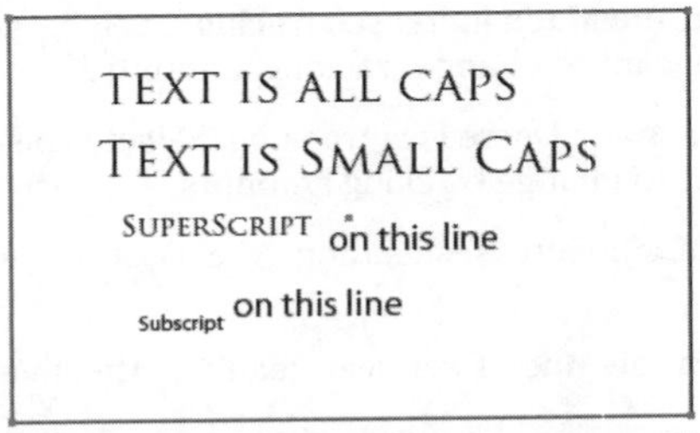

TEXT IS ALL CAPS
TEXT IS SMALL CAPS
SUPERSCRIPT on this line
Subscript on this line

Figure 14-4: Type styles: All caps, small caps, superscript, and subscript.

✦ **Subscript:** Selected characters are subscripted below the baseline. (Refer to Figure 14-4.)

✦ **Fractional Widths:** As a default, leave this item checked because the type is displayed in the best appearance. The spacing between characters varies. If disabled, the characters are monospaced.

✦ **System Layout:** Characters are previewed using the operating system's default text handling. This option is particularly helpful when designing user-interface designs where you might create dialog boxes, palettes, and menus.

✦ **No Break:** Prevents you from creating line breaks. If you enable the option while using either point type or area type, after pressing the Return key new type is set over the last line of type.

✦ **Reset Palette:** Restores the default character settings in the palette.

Creating area type

The Character palette by default is nested together with two other palettes. The Paragraph palette is used for paragraph formatting, and it makes sense to describe the options when discussing area type. The OpenType palette offers options for a number of different settings you can make when using OpenType fonts.

Cross-Reference   For more information on OpenType fonts, see Chapter 13.

Area type is created using the Type tool. Instead of clicking the cursor where point type is created, click the cursor and drag open a rectangle. By default, when you release the mouse button, a blinking I-beam cursor appears in the top-left corner of the rectangle. Area type can also be created within closed paths. Any object you draw in Illustrator can define the boundaries for area type. When adding area type to a closed path, simply click the cursor inside the path and the blinking I-beam informs you the object is ready to accept type. In Figure 14-5, you can see results of area type applied to different shapes.

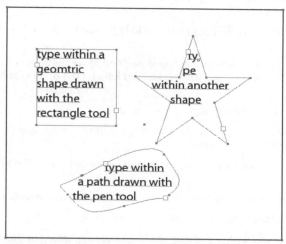

Figure 14-5: Area type added to different shapes

In the Paragraph palette, you'll find options for paragraph formatting. Some of the options, such as paragraph alignment, can also apply to point type. However, indents and paragraph spacing are more likely to be applied to area type.

When you create area type and want to change paragraph formatting, click on the Paragraph tab to show the options. If the palette is not in view, choose Window ➪ Type Paragraph, and the palette shown in Figure 14-6 opens.

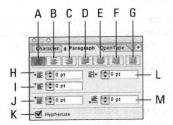

Figure 14-6: The paragraph palette has options for paragraph formatting.

As shown in Figure 14-6, the palette contains many options. These include the following:

A Align Left: Text alignment for the paragraph is aligned left.

B Align Center: Paragraph text is aligned centered.

C Align Right: Paragraph text is aligned right.

D Justify with Last Line Aligned Left: The paragraph is fully justified with the last line aligned left.

E Justify with Last Line Aligned Center: The paragraph is fully justified with the last line aligned center.

F Justify with Last Line Aligned Right: The paragraph is fully justified with the last line aligned right.

G Justify All Lines: All text is justified and the last line is justified. If you have only two words appearing in the last line of text, one word is aligned left and the other word is aligned right.

H Left Indent: Text is indented from the left edge of the text block.

I First Line Left Indent: The first line of text in the paragraph is indented left and the other lines are aligned left without indentation.

J Space Before Paragraph: Adds space above the paragraph in amounts specified in the field box.

K Hyphenation: When the check box is checked, hyphenation is applied to the paragraph.

L Right Indent: Text is indented from the right edge of the text block.

M Space After Paragraph: Adds space after a paragraph in amounts specified in the field box. Use the space after and space before paragraphs instead of using carriage returns.

The seven views of type formatted using the different paragraph formats are shown in Figure 14-7.

Figure 14-7: The seven different paragraph formats

Using OpenType

As detailed in Chapter 13, OpenType fonts offer you many more glyphs than TrueType or PostScript fonts. With more glyphs available in an OpenType Pro font, you have alternate choices for the way you want to display characters. Because the number of characters can vary between OpenType fonts, be aware that all options are not available with every font. As you open the Character palette and view the tabs, the final tab is the OpenType tab. Click this tab, and the options shown in Figure 14-8 appear.

Figure 14-8: The OpenType tab has options for OpenType fonts.

The palette displays two pull-down menus and a line of buttons. To have the menu commands and buttons active, you need to have an OpenType font selected. Not all options are available for all OpenType fonts. Depending on the number of characters and styles contained within an OpenType font, the options vary. From the Figure pull-down menu, the options include the following:

Note If using Asian OpenType fonts (Chinese, Japanese, and Korean), you may have more options available in the OpenType palette.

✦ **Default Figure:** Choose this option to use the default style for numbers appearing in the selected font.

✦ **Tabular Lining:** Only when the OpenType characters are available, the full-height figures line up proportionally. You might use this option when setting type in tables and charts.

✦ **Proportional Lining:** When characters are available, this option lines up characters with varying widths. You might use this option when setting type containing numbers and uppercase characters.

✦ **Proportional Oldstyle:** When characters are available, use this option when you want a classic type appearance. It creates a more sophisticated look when using lowercase characters.

✦ **Tabular Oldstyle:** Applies to varying height characters with fixed, equal widths. This option might be used when you want a classic appearance of old-style figures, but you want the characters to align in columns.

Another set of menu commands appears in the Position pull-down menu. The Position options offer choices for the placement of characters respective to the baseline. These options are particularly helpful when working with numbers and fractions. Again, these are available only if they are offered in the current OpenType font. The menu choices include the following:

✦ **Default Position:** Keeps the default position of characters for the selected font.

✦ **Superscript/Superior:** Raises characters above the baseline.

✦ **Subscript/Inferior:** Lowers characters below the baseline.

✦ **Numerator:** Applies to numerals designed as fractions. The fractional characters only are raised to appear as numerators.

✦ **Denominator:** Applies to numerals designed as fractions. The fractional characters only are lowered to appear as denominators.

Figure 14-9 displays the various options choices when using the Cronos Pro OpenType font and applying the different position options to alpha and numeric characters.

This is 1/2 of 1/4 of the work to be completed.	Default
This is $^1/^2$ of $^1/^4$ of the work to be completed.	Superscript/Superior
This is $_1/_2$ of $_1/_4$ of the work to be completed.	Subscript/Inferior
This is $^1/^2$ of $^1/^4$ of the work to be completed.	Numerator
This is ½ of ¼ of the work to be completed.	Denominator

Figure 14-9: The five different menu options for Position are applied to the OpenType font Cronos Pro.

Combining point type and area type

Many different types of documents can be opened and edited in Illustrator. Often, the objects appear to be translated without problems but you may find that a lot of the original paragraph formatting is lost. Files you may want to convert to Illustrator documents — CAD drawings, page layouts from other programs, charts and graphs, and so on — typically open in Illustrator with broken type blocks. To convert the point type segmented throughout a document, look over the following steps to see how you can fix such problems.

STEPS: Converting Point Type to Area Type

1. **Open an EPS file in Illustrator.** For this example, we use a QuarkXPress document saved from XPress using the Save Page as EPS menu command. Notice that in Figure 14-10, when all the type is selected in Illustrator, you see point type on each line of text and broken along the lines of type. This copy would be difficult to edit in its present form.

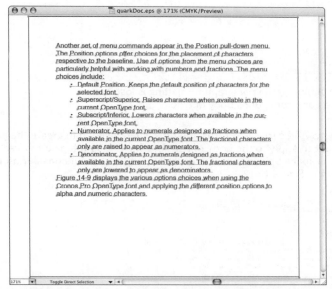

Figure 14-10: After selecting type, you can see where the type blocks are broken by observing the handles (small squares) on the baselines.

2. **Cut the text from the art board.** Choose Edit ➪ Select All or press ⌘/Ctrl+A to select all the type. Be certain to have either the Selection tool or the Direct Selection tool selected in the Toolbox before selecting the type. If the Type tool is selected and the cursor is blinking in a line of type, only that segment of type will be selected. After selecting the type, choose Edit ➪ Cut to cut the text to the Clipboard.

3. **Paste the type.** Select the Type tool and drag open a rectangle to define the boundaries for the area type. Choose Edit ➪ Paste. The type is pasted from the blinking cursor and fills the area type boundary. When the type is pasted, all paragraph formatting is lost, as shown in Figure 14-11. However, the type is one contiguous body of text.

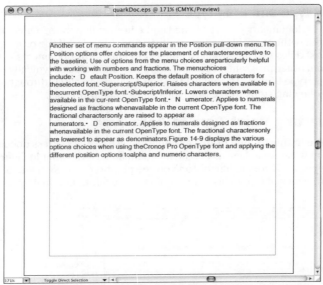

Figure 14-11: Although the paragraph formatting is lost, the text is pasted as one contiguous body of type.

4. **Format the type.** Add carriage returns and tabs where needed to create the paragraph format you want to apply to the body of text. Use the Paragraph palette to set type formats such as space before and after, as well as any alignment considerations you need, as shown in Figure 14-12.

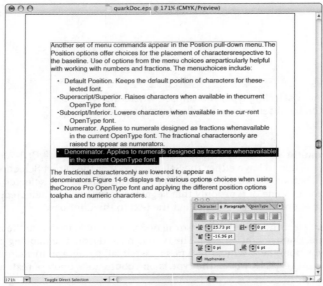

Figure 14-12: As a contiguous body of text, you can use the Paragraph palette to format the type.

For more-precise placement and sizing of the text block, you can use guides and create text frames according to guide positions. If you have legacy Illustrator files that were designed with point type where it makes more sense to use area type and paragraph formatting, you can cut the point type and paste it back into a type frame.

Updating type

The new additions to the type features in Illustrator CS required recoding the Illustrator type engine. The results of the update create some problems when opening legacy files in Illustrator CS. Any Illustrator document created from version 10 and prior uses a different type engine than Illustrator CS. When you open a legacy file in Illustrator CS, you first see an alert dialog box, as shown in Figure 14-13.

Figure 14-13: Opening legacy files in Illustrator CS prompts you to preserve the type appearance in the document or update the text.

If you click Update, the text is updated to conform to the new type engine. The text is editable, but you may experience shifts in type appearance and position. If you click OK, the text is not updated, and the type appearance and position remain intact. The type is not editable, however. The type blocks appear within rectangular bounding boxes, as shown in Figure 14-14.

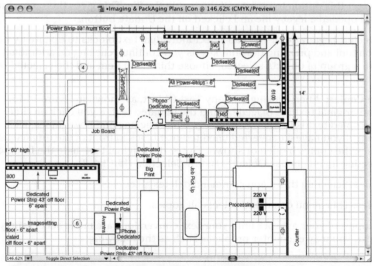

Figure 14-14: If you open legacy files without updating the text, text blocks appear within bounding boxes when the text is selected.

You can elect to update text on a block-by-block basis. If you click OK and don't update the type when opening a legacy file, you can individually update text blocks by clicking with the Type tool on a given body of text or by double-clicking on the type with the Selection tool. Illustrator then prompts you in another alert dialog box, offering you a few choices. In Figure 14-15, you can see the choices appearing for Copy Text Object and Update.

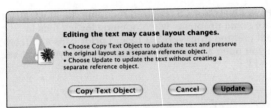

Figure 14-15: Clicking on any text block with the Type tool opens a dialog box where you can decide how the type is updated.

When you select Copy Text Object, a duplicate of the text block is placed behind the converted text. After copying the text, the foreground text is selected when you click with the Type tool. The other option for Updating the text accomplishes the same result as when you first open a legacy document and click on the Update button shown in Figure 14-13.

If you want to update multiple items, options are available in a menu command. Choose Type ➪ Legacy and a submenu offers options for handling legacy text. Note that the menu is grayed out unless you open a legacy file and do not update the text. If you click Update when opening a file, the Legacy submenu options are grayed out as they are when opening files originally authored in Illustrator CS.

In the Legacy submenu, the options include the following:

✦ **Update All Legacy Text:** If you open a legacy file and choose to not update the text, you can later select this option to update all the text in the file. This gives the same result as if you had opened a legacy file and clicked on the Update button.

✦ **Update Selected Legacy Text:** You can select individual text blocks to update by using the Selection tool and pressing the Shift key as you continue clicking on additional text blocks. With a group of objects selected, choose this menu item and the selected text is updated.

✦ **Show/Hide Copies:** When clicking on Copy Text Object, as shown in Figure 14-15, copies of the original text are placed behind the updated text. If you click on Hide Copies, the copied text is hidden. Conversely, when clicking on Show Copies, all hidden text is shown. If you have a converted unedited text block in front of the original text, you won't see the copies hidden or shown. To see the original text, hide the foreground text by selecting it and choose Object ➪ Hide ➪ Selection (⌘/Ctrl+3).

✦ **Delete Copies:** Selecting this menu command deletes all copies.

✦ **Select Copies:** This menu command selects all copies.

It's best to keep copies of your artwork until your text conversions are made successfully. When updating text, you may encounter problems such as the following:

✦ **Character position and attribute changes:** Updating text may shift characters and change attributes such as leading, tracking, and kerning.

✦ **Word shifts:** Words may shift to the next line. The text within a bounding box may scroll past the bottom of the text frame thereby hiding one or more lines of text. Hyphenation may be altered.

✦ **Word overflows:** In linked text frames, words may overflow to the next thread.

As a matter of practice, you should carefully check the type conversions on legacy files. Before deleting copies, be certain that the text attributes and word flow follow your design intent.

Setting type in Photoshop

Setting type in Photoshop is a task you optimally perform only on small bodies of text and when creating headlines and stylizing type. We say *optimally* because Photoshop is not as well suited for setting type as are Illustrator and InDesign. Therefore, we won't spend much time talking about typesetting in Photoshop.

You create type in Photoshop by clicking on the Type tool in the Toolbox and then clicking the cursor in the document window. A blinking I-beam appears, and you are now ready to type. The default type tool is Horizontal Type. If you click and hold down the mouse button in the Toolbox, you can also choose the Vertical Type tool, the Horizontal Type Mask tool, or the Vertical Type Mask tool. The latter two are used to create type masks that essentially are selections that can be filled, painted, or used to capture underlying pixels.

Type in Photoshop changed from raster-based to vector-based back in version 6. When you set type in Photoshop, it appears on a separate layer and remains fully editable as long as the Photoshop image is not flattened or the layer is not rasterized. If you want to preserve the type on a layer and keep it editable, you need to save the file with layers intact. Saving as a Photoshop PSD, TIF (with layers), or PDF (with layers) preserves the type on the layers and keeps it in vector form.

Tip   If you prepare files for PDF viewing, leave the type on a layer and save as Photoshop PDF. When the PDF is opened in Acrobat, all the type is searchable with Acrobat Search.

For typesetting in Photoshop, you have attribute choices you can make in the Options Bar as well as two palettes where character and paragraph options choices are made.

Using the Options Bar

When you click on the Type tool in the Photoshop Toolbox, the Options Bar displays options for setting type. As shown in Figure 14-16, the choices extend from character attributes to paragraph options. The individual settings include the following:

Figure 14-16: The Type tool changes its options to reflect attribute choices for setting type.

A **Change Text Orientation:** Click the icon to change from horizontal to vertical and vice versa. If a block of text has been created on a layer, you can change type orientation by simply selecting the layer and applying the change.

B **Font Family:** The pull-down menu lists all fonts available to your system. Photoshop reads installed fonts when you launch the program. Therefore, if you load a new font with a font-management tool, you need to quit Photoshop and relaunch it before the font is recognized in the menu.

C **Font Style:** You have choices for font style from pull-down menu commands. Choose from options such as Regular, Bold, Italic, and Bold Italic when the styles are available for a given font.

D **Font Size:** From the pull-down menu, you have choices for fixed point sizes, or you can enter a value in the field box. Sizes range from 0.01 to 1,296 points. Because the type is vector art, however, you can use the transformation tools to create any type size you want.

Cross-Reference   For more information on transforming objects, see Chapter 9.

E **Anti-Aliasing Method:** Anti-aliasing creates an illusion of smoothing objects. When you anti-alias objects, small gray pixels are added to objects, giving the appearance of smoother edges. Photoshop offers you several choices for anti-aliasing, including the following:

- **None:** Applies no anti-aliasing.

- **Sharp:** Adds a slight amount of anti-aliasing, keeping the type sharp in contrast.

- **Crisp:** Similar to Sharp but adds a little more anti-aliasing, making the appearance slightly less sharp.

- **Strong:** Creates a slightly bold appearance to the type. If you anti-alias type and it appears to lose the normal type weight, add Strong to thicken the characters.

- **Smooth:** Adds more anti-aliasing. A good choice for type that may appear with strong jagged edges.

F **Align Left:** Aligns text left.

G **Align Center:** Aligns text centered.

H **Align Right:** Aligns text right.

I **Text Color:** Click on the color swatch and the Photoshop Color Picker opens. You can make choices for the type color from the Color Picker, from the Color and Swatches palettes, or from the Foreground Color tool in the Photoshop Toolbox.

J **Create Warped Text:** Photoshop offers you many options for applying effects to type from the Create Warped Text tool. Select the type you want to use to apply a new style, and the Warp Text dialog box opens as shown in Figure 14-17. When warping text, you can apply changes by either selecting the text with the Type tool or selecting the layer containing the text.

K **Toggle the Character and Paragraph Palettes:** This toggles the Character and Paragraph palettes open and closed.

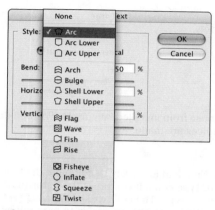

Figure 14-17: Selecting the type of warp effect you want

Using the Character palette

Some character attributes are the same in the Character palette as you find in the Options Bar. Choices for font family, font style, and anti-aliasing methods are duplicated in the Character palette. The palette also contains other options. When you open it, you'll notice the palette appears similar to the Character palette found in Illustrator. To open the palette, choose Window ➪ Character or click on the Toggle the Character and Paragraph Palettes icon in the Options Bar. The palette shown in Figure 14-18 opens.

Figure 14-18: The Photoshop Character palette

As you can see, the options are almost identical to those found in Illustrator. Notice that the horizontal and vertical scaling is flopped in the Photoshop Character palette, but the six attribute choices below the pull-down menus for font and style are identical to Illustrator.

Photoshop does offer additional choices that appear at the bottom of the palette. From the row of icons, reading left to right, you have the following choices:

✦ **Faux Bold:** Enables you to bold a font that does not have a bold equivalent with the chosen typeface

✦ **Faux Italic:** Enables you to italicize a font that does not have an italic equivalent

✦ **All Caps**

- ✦ **Small Caps**
- ✦ **Superscript**
- ✦ **Subscript**
- ✦ **Underline**
- ✦ **Strikethrough**

From the lower-left pull-down menu, you can choose from installed languages. The pull-down menu in the lower-right is where anti-aliasing choices are made.

Using the Paragraph palette

When creating type in Photoshop, you press the Num Pad Enter key to complete the typesetting and signal Photoshop that you've ended your type edits. If you press the Return/Enter key, Photoshop adds a carriage return to the body of type. The ability to add carriage returns means Photoshop supports paragraph type. The attributes you can assign to paragraphs are, in part, located in the Options Bar, where you can choose from three justification methods. The remaining choices are located in the Paragraph palette. When the Character palette is open, click on the Paragraph tab to open the palette shown in Figure 14-19.

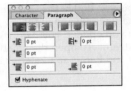

Figure 14-19: The Paragraph palette offers options for paragraph formatting.

As you can see in Figure 14-19, the Paragraph palette options in Photoshop are identical to those in Illustrator. As is the case with changing character attributes, you can select the text with the Type tool or simply click on the layer in the Layers palette. Changes you make in the Paragraph palette are applied to the text regardless of which selection you make.

Setting type in InDesign

In many design workflows, you're likely to be handed copy that has been composed in a word processing program. If you work with copywriters or obtain copy from clients, the files are usually Microsoft Word documents. And unless the author used style sheets you can import, you'll need to reformat the text in InDesign.

Cross-Reference   For more information on importing Microsoft Word Documents, see Chapter 17.

For some creative professionals, using word-processing programs may not be as appealing as setting type in InDesign. Certainly, for single-page ads and smaller pieces, you may use InDesign for both creating copy and performing the layout tasks. Fortunately, InDesign does have some impressive tools if you decide to use the program for creating copy.

Using the Story Editor

InDesign's Story Editor is like having your own word processor built into the program. In order to use the Story Editor, you need to have a text frame created on a document page. If no text frame exists, the Story Editor is not accessible.

To open the Story Editor, select a text frame and then choose Edit ➪ Edit in Story Editor (⌘/Ctrl+Y). The Story Editor opens and appears in front of the document window. The Story Editor is dynamic in many ways. As you type in the Story Editor, the text is updated on the document page within the selected text frame. As its own document window, the Story Editor does not prevent you from using other tools and menus in InDesign that are needed for setting type. Palettes used for styles and text formatting are accessible to you while working in the Story Editor. In Figure 14-20, the Story Editor is open where text is added in the editor and displayed on the document page. The Paragraph Styles palette is used to select styles and apply them in the Story Editor.

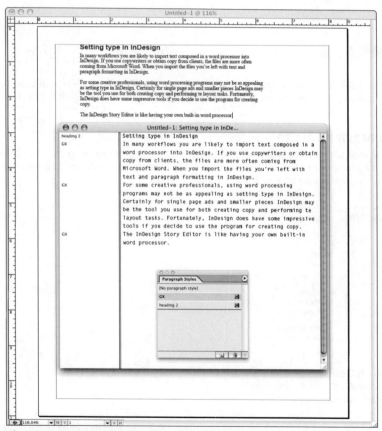

Figure 14-20: Text typed in the Story Editor

While working in the Story Editor, you can make choices from the Type menu and palettes where type attributes are selected, or you can make similar choices from a context menu. To open a context menu in the Story Editor, press the Control key and click (Mac) or right-click (Windows) and the context menu shown in Figure 14-21 opens.

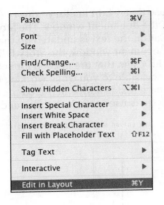

Figure 14-21: Context menus offer choices similar to the menu commands and palette options.

When you want to return to the InDesign document window, click the close box in the Story Editor window, or select Edit in Layout from the context menu (or choose Edit ⇨ Edit in Layout).

Using the Character palette

The Character palette in InDesign offers the same options as Illustrator, with the exception of the Skew option in place of the Rotate option. Below the Horizontal Scale setting, you see the Skew option (shown as a slanted *T*) as shown in Figure 14-22.

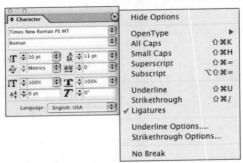

Figure 14-22: The InDesign Character palette offers almost identical options to those in the Illustrator Character palette.

From the palette menu, you can see some other options choices available only in InDesign. The underline and strikethrough options are listed in the palette, but each contains a companion Options menu where you can change attributes for underlines and strikethroughs, such as line weight, spacing, color, gaps, and so on. Select Underline Options and the dialog box opens as shown in Figure 14-23. The items in the dialog box should be self-explanatory. If you aren't certain what results are applied using a given setting, click the Preview button, and the changes you make to text are dynamically applied to the selected characters.

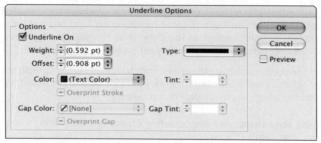

Figure 14-23: InDesign offers many options for setting underline attributes.

The options for strikethrough are similar to the options for underlining. Click on the Strikethrough Options menu command and a similar dialog box opens. Again, the options should be self-explanatory.

Another distinction you'll find between the Character palettes in Illustrator and InDesign are the options selections for OpenType fonts. In Illustrator, buttons appear in the bottom of the OpenType palette, and in InDesign you can see the submenu items in Figure 14-24 offering the same options.

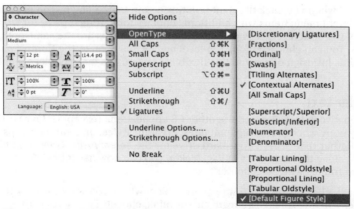

Figure 14-24: OpenType options in a submenu of the Character palette

Using the Control palette

Setting type in InDesign does not require you to access Character and Paragraph palettes to change attributes. The Control palette that appears by default at the top of the screen when you launch InDesign is one of the most frequently used tools favored by design professionals. Depending on the tool you select in the InDesign Toolbox, the palette changes to reflect options choices for the selected tool. In Figure 14-25, formatting options are shown for characters (top), paragraphs (middle), and objects (bottom).

With the type tool selected, you can toggle between character and paragraph options in the Control palette. Simply click on either the letter *A* or the paragraph symbol on the far left side of the palette. From there, you can make attribute choices by changing field box values and using pull-down menus. When using tools other than the Type tool, the palette displays options for applying attributes to objects, as shown in the last palette in Figure 14-25.

The Control palette is a handy place to select styles either for character or paragraph styles. From the pull-down menus, all the style sheets contained in your document are listed. When you add a new style, it's added to the appropriate pull-down menu.

Cross-Reference   For information on creating style sheets, see the "Creating Character Styles" and "Creating Paragraph Styles" sections later in this chapter.

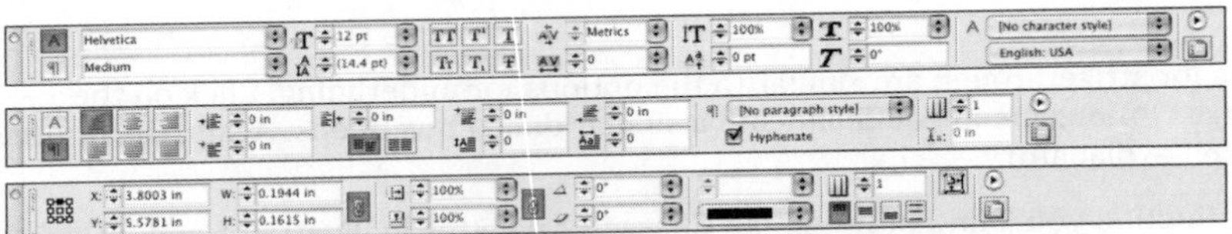

Figure 14-25: When the type tool is selected, you can toggle between formatting options for characters (top) and paragraphs (middle). When other tools are selected, options for transforming objects are displayed (bottom).

Another menu is found when you click the right-pointing arrow. Depending on the palette shown, you'll see different menu items with additional choices for setting type or for working with objects. Many of the options choices you see in pull-down menus are the same options found in the palettes. You can choose among top-level menus, palettes, or the Control palette to apply the same edits. InDesign offers you this flexibility so you can make choices quickly and easily.

Using placeholder text

One nice distinction between InDesign and the other CS applications (except GoLive) is the ability to use dummy copy when preparing templates, creating styles, or creating comps for a new design project. Rather than search your hard drive for the *Lorem Ipsum* Greek text file you've probably used since the early days of PageMaker, you can now use InDesign's built-in support for filling text frames with placeholder text.

To use placeholder text, click in any text frame or any object where you want to convert the object to a text frame. When you see the I-beam cursor blink, choose Type ➪ Fill with Placeholder Text. Greek text is added from the point of the blinking cursor to the end of the text thread, as shown in Figure 14-26.

If you create comps and layouts where Greek type is used frequently, you may want to create a keyboard shortcut to access the menu command. Look over the steps that follow to see how you can assign a keyboard shortcut to access the Fill with Placeholder Text menu command.

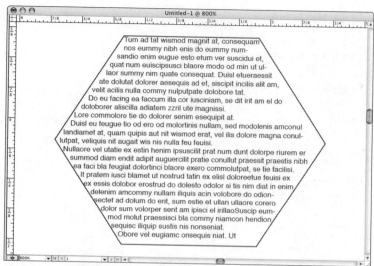

Figure 14-26: Filling a frame with Greek text

STEPS: Using Placeholder Text

1. **Assign a keyboard shortcut to the Fill with Placeholder Text menu command.** Choose Edit ⇨ Keyboard Shortcuts. The Keyboard Shortcuts dialog box opens. Select Type Menu from the Product Area pull-down menu and click on Fill with Placeholder Text, as shown in Figure 14-27. With the menu command selected, press the shortcut keys you want to use to assign to the menu command. A good choice is to use Shift+F12. This keyboard shortcut is easily accessible and doesn't conflict with any existing InDesign keyboard shortcuts.

2. **Create an object.** From the InDesign Toolbox, click on the Rectangle tool, the Ellipse tool, or the Polygon tool, and draw an object on the document page. For this example, we created an ellipse using the Ellipse tool, as shown in Figure 14-28.

3. **Convert the object to a text frame.** When you draw an object in InDesign, the object appears as an Unassigned object. You can convert the object to a text object or a graphic object via a menu command. For a quick and easy method, select the Type tool and position the cursor within the object. When the cursor shape changes to the Type tool, displayed with a marquee oval around the *T* character, click the mouse button. The I-beam cursor starts to blink, signifying the object is ready to accept type.

4. **Set the font attributes.** From the Control palette, select a font, point size, and other attributes you want displayed on the type. The type attributes you assign before filling the object with text are used when filling with placeholder text.

5. **Use your keyboard shortcut to fill with placeholder text.** Press the keyboard shortcut you assigned to the Fill with Placeholder Text command. The object is filled with text using the font attributes you selected in the Control palette. Figure 14-29 shows the results of filling an object with placeholder text.

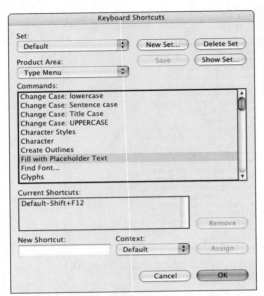

Figure 14-27: Assigning menu commands

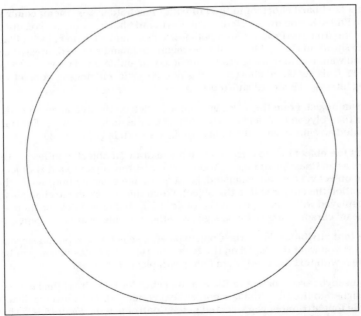

Figure 14-28: Create an object using any of the geometric object tools.

Figure 14-29: Use your new keyboard shortcut to fill the object text.

Using the Paragraph palette

The paragraph styles palette in InDesign offers many of the same options as found in Illustrator, with the exception of two icons used for defining drop caps in paragraphs. The last two icons, shown in Figure 14-30 as A and B at the bottom of the palette, contain an option for defining the height of a drop cap (A). Setting the value to 4, for example, creates a drop cap whose height is equivalent to the first four lines of the paragraph. On the lower-right side of the palette, you can specify the number of sequential characters you want to appear as drop caps (B).

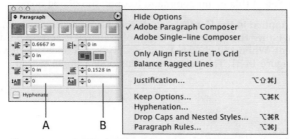

Figure 14-30: The last two field boxes offer options for choosing the number of lines a drop cap is applied to (A) and the number of characters to be used as drop caps (B).

You find more distinction between the Illustrator Paragraph palette and the InDesign Paragraph palette when opening the palette menus. InDesign offers some advanced formatting features not found in the other CS programs and some that are not found in any other layout and design program. When you open the palette menu, the options shown in Figure 14-30 appear. The menu commands include the following:

✦ **Adobe Paragraph Composer:** Break points are created to help prevent unattractive line breaks in paragraphs. Traditional methods for creating break points only handled one line at a time. The Adobe Paragraph Composer composes the breaks by taking into consideration the lines preceding and following the current line of text. This results in a more attractive paragraph. *(Available in InDesign, Illustrator, and Photoshop.)*

✦ **Adobe Single-Line Composer:** This option uses the more traditional method of creating break points, taking into consideration only single lines of text. *(Available in InDesign, Illustrator, and Photoshop.)*

✦ **Only Align First Line to Grid:** When aligning text to a grid, only the first line of text is aligned to the grid.

✦ **Balance Ragged Lines:** This option is helpful for headlines and pull quotes and when centering paragraphs. Multiple lines of type appear more balanced, as widow-type oversets at the end of the text block are eliminated. You must use Adobe Paragraph Composer to see any results with this menu command.

✦ **Keep Options:** Opens a dialog box where you can assign attributes to lines in paragraphs that you want to stay together when the paragraph flows to other frames and pages.

✦ **Hyphenation:** Offers similar options for controlling hyphenation as you find in Illustrator.

✦ **Drop Caps and Nested Styles:** One of the truly amazing features available for typesetting is the ability to create nested styles. When you are selecting the command, the Drop Caps and Nested Styles dialog box opens.

Cross-Reference   For more information on nested styles, see the "Creating Nested Styles" section later in this chapter.

✦ **Paragraph Rules:** The attributes for rules assigned to paragraphs are handled in the Paragraph Rules dialog box. Select this menu command to open the dialog box.

Paragraph formatting can also be applied in the Control palette and via menu commands. One particular option not found in either the Control or Paragraph palettes is setting paragraphs for Optical Margin Alignment. When you choose Window ➪ Type & Tables ➪ Story, the Story palette opens, as shown in Figure 14-31. The palette contains only a single option.

Figure 14-31: The Story palette

When you check the box for Optical Margin Alignment, paragraph alignment displays a different appearance. With traditional computer typesetting methods, paragraphs can appear misaligned, especially when punctuation marks and/or wide characters are used. In Figure 14-32, you can see where Optical Margin Alignment was applied to the bottom text block compared to the default margin alignment on the first text block. Because the punctuation hangs outside the text frame on the second block of text, the characters appear more aligned.

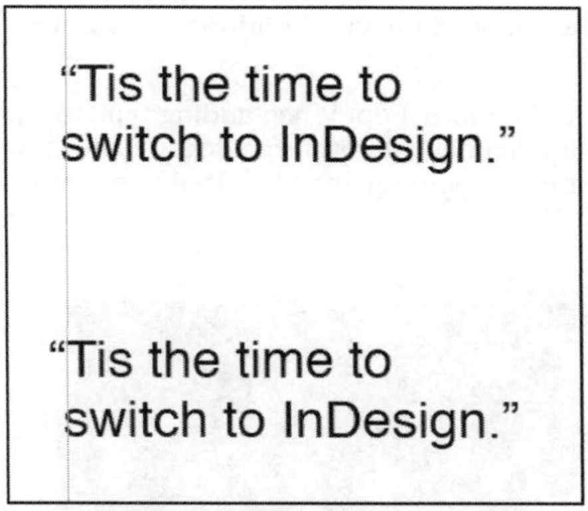

"Tis the time to
switch to InDesign."

"Tis the time to
switch to InDesign."

Figure 14-32: Optical Margin Alignment corrects misaligned characters.

InDesign has so many different options for setting character and paragraph attributes that a complete coverage would take the space occupied by all the chapters in this book. We've highlighted some of the main features here and discussed the options found in the menus and palettes. For a comprehensive view of setting type in InDesign, see the *Adobe InDesign CS Bible* by Galen Gruman (Wiley, 2003).

Creating type on paths

Once the job of Illustrator, applying type to paths is now available in Photoshop and InDesign. Applying type to paths opens up worlds of possibilities for each application. With the capability for adding type to paths in Photoshop, you can use familiar methods for stylizing type with shadows, embossing, filter effects, and so on, and you don't need to rely on rasterizing type in Photoshop that was originally created in Illustrator.

Adding type to paths is a simple process in any of the CS programs where this feature is available. Basically, you create a path either with the Pen tool or use segments from paths created with other tools used for drawing objects. In Photoshop, select the Type tool, click on a path and begin typing. In Illustrator and InDesign, use the Type on a Path tool. Access the Type on a Path tool by pressing the mouse button down on the Type tool and selecting it from the pop-up menu.

To add type to freeform paths, click the mouse button on the path and begin typing. For closed paths in either Illustrator or InDesign, the type is added to the outside edge of the path. The respective program knows the distinction between adding type to a path and creating type inside a closed path. This is determined with the proper selection of the Type tool. When the Type on a Path tool is selected, the type conforms only to the path and not to the inside of a closed path.

In Photoshop, the task is a little different. When you have a closed path, placing the cursor on the path and clicking the mouse button enables you to type on the path. If you move the cursor inside the path, the cursor shape changes to the oval marquee around the letter *T,* signifying that type is to be added inside the path. The shape of the cursor informs you where the type will be placed.

In Figure 14-33, you can see type added to a path in Photoshop. When adding type to a path, be certain to check the paragraph attributes for alignment. If your type doesn't show up on the path, you may need to adjust the alignment from center-aligned to left-aligned. After adding the type, you can change the alignment.

Figure 14-33: In Photoshop, create a path with the Pen tool and select the Type on a Path tool.

Both Illustrator and InDesign permit adjustments to type on paths in the same manner. When you add type to an open path, the type is added in a straightforward fashion. However, if you start with a closed object and then delete one side, type may be added to the shape flopped or upside-down. In each program, you can move type along a path or flop it by moving the centerline appearing within the type. In InDesign, the line is much less visible than in Illustrator, but it does exist. In Figures 14-34 and 14-35, you can see type added to a semicircle that began as an elliptical shape. The type is flopped. To move the type up where the type reads from left to right, drag the line at the center point upward.

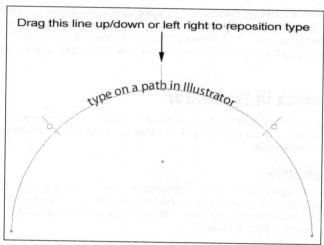

Figure 14-34: To align type on a path in Illustrator, drag the centerline left/right or upward.

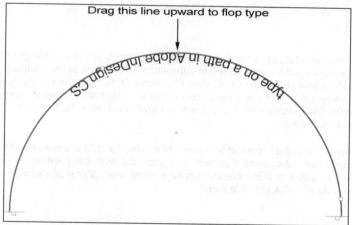

Figure 14-35: The same centerline appears in InDesign, but the line is less visible.

Creating Character Styles

In both InDesign and Illustrator, you have the ability to create style sheets at the character level. Using character styles allows you to specify formatting attributes for a selected range of text within your documents. For instance, you may want to use different character formatting for Web-site URLs and e-mail addresses that appear in your copy. Instead of changing type specs in the Character palette, or using tedious find-and-replace commands to alter attributes of single characters or a string of words within a document, you can apply global changes to characters quickly and easily by changing formatting options in the Character Styles palette. All text to which you've applied the specific style is changed automatically. Using both character and paragraph styles saves time and ensures that your documents have a consistent look.

Using character styles in Illustrator

In Illustrator, you can set up character styles from scratch or by designating preformatted text as the basis of the new style. You can also copy an existing style and make formatting variations in order to create a new style.

Creating new character styles

To create a new character style, open the Character Styles palette by choosing Window ➪ Type ➪ Character Styles. The palette lists all the styles that have been created for the document. If no custom styles have been created, the only style that appears is the default, Normal Character Style, as shown in Figure 14-36.

Figure 14-36: The Character Styles palette

To create a new style from scratch, click the Create New Style button in the lower-right portion of the palette. A new style with a default name automatically appears in the palette. An alternative way to create a new style is to select New Character Style from the palette menu. At this point, you're prompted to give the style a custom name. Either way, when the new style name appears in the list, double-click on it to edit its attributes with the Character Style Options box, shown in Figure 14-37.

Caution   Double-clicking on a style in the Character Styles palette applies the style to any text you currently have selected in your document. If no text is selected, the style is applied to any new text you type. To keep either of these events from happening, press Shift+Ctrl (Shift+⌘ on the Mac) when you double-click the style name.

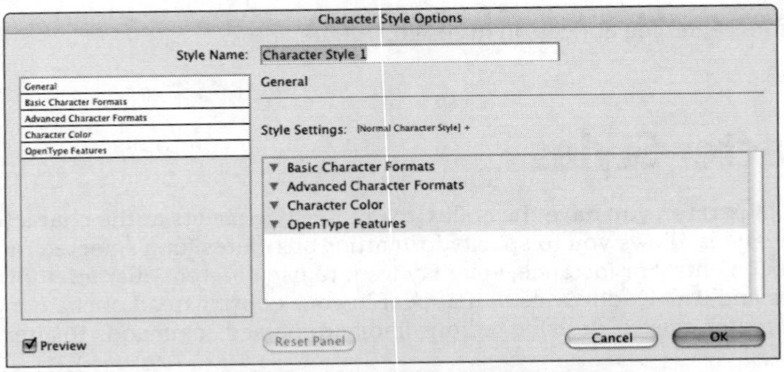

Figure 14-37: The Character Style Options dialog box

When the Character Style Options box opens, you see the name of the selected style at the top and five options to the left. The options include the following:

✦ **General:** This is the pane displayed when you first open the Character Style Options box. It's a summary of the remaining four settings, the style settings. You can view attributes of the separate style settings by toggling the gray arrows in the right side of the pane.

✦ **Basic Character Formats:** In this menu, you can specify font family, font style, size, leading, kerning, tracking, case, position (superscript or subscript), and whether or not you want Standard Vertical Roman Alignment.

✦ **Advanced Character Formats:** Here you can specify horizontal and vertical scale, baseline shift, character rotation, and desired language.

✦ **Character Color:** Choose your desired color, stroke, and overprint options here.

✦ **OpenType Features:** This panel allows you to set OpenType options just like those found in the OpenType palette (see the "Using OpenType" section, earlier in this chapter).

After you've set up your attributes the way you want them, simply click OK.

You can easily create copies of existing character styles by either dragging the style onto the Create New Style button, or by choosing Duplicate Character Style from the Character Styles palette menu. To delete styles, simply drag the style name to the trash icon, or select the style and choose Delete Character Style from the palette menu. You can also import styles from other Illustrator documents by using the Load Styles command.

Tip   You can easily create a new style sheet based on the formatting of existing text. This is handy if you're experimenting with different design options because it eliminates the need to manually type all the formatting details in the Character Style Options menus ahead of time. Simply select the text whose attributes you want to use, and click the Create New Style button.

Applying character styles

To apply character styles in Illustrator, first select the characters with the Type tool or a selection tool. If you're typing new characters, place the cursor where you want the style to begin. Then simply click the style name in the Character Styles palette. To designate a style to be used for any new type in the document, be sure to deselect all type objects first; then click the style name.

Using character styles in InDesign

The process of setting up and using character styles in InDesign is very similar to Illustrator. InDesign does offer a few additional options for refining your typesetting capabilities, however.

Creating new character styles

Open the Character Styles palette by choosing Type ➪ Character Styles, or Window ➪ Type &Tables ➪ Character Styles. As in Illustrator, the palette lists all the styles that have been created for the document. If no custom styles have been created, all you'll see is the default: No Character Style.

Creating a new style is the same procedure as in Illustrator: Click the Create New Style button in the lower-right portion of the palette or click the right arrow and select New Character Style. You can then specify attributes with the Character Style Options or New Character Style box.

The options here are pretty much like Illustrator's, with a few minor differences. As shown in Figure 14-38, with InDesign you have the added ability to base styles on existing styles and create shortcuts. There are also advanced options for underlining, strikethroughs, and ligatures, as well as a no-break option and a skew option in place of Illustrator's rotation option.

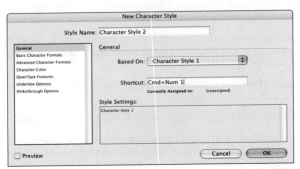

Figure 14-38: InDesign offers more character style options than Illustrator.

Duplicating, editing, and deleting Character Styles is the same as in Illustrator. InDesign can import character styles from other InDesign documents using the Load Character Styles command.

Applying character styles

There are three ways to apply a character style to selected text in InDesign. You can click the style name in the Character Styles palette, choose the style name from the pull-down menu in the Control palette, or use the keyboard shortcut you've assigned to the style.

Creating Paragraph Styles

Paragraph styles are especially helpful for managing large amounts of text in both InDesign and Illustrator. The one limitation you have with respect to both character and paragraph styles among the CS applications is that styles created in either Illustrator or InDesign cannot be imported across programs. You can import styles from application documents using the same application. For example, you can load character styles in Illustrator from another Illustrator document. However, you cannot load character styles in Illustrator from an InDesign document or vice versa. The same applies to paragraph styles. Furthermore, when you import Illustrator files containing style sheets in InDesign, or copy and paste text between programs, the style-sheet information is lost. In the next upgrade, maybe we'll see more interoperability between Illustrator and InDesign style-sheet usage.

Using paragraph styles in Illustrator

Just like with Character Styles, you can set up paragraph styles from scratch or by designating preformatted text as the basis of the new style. You can also copy an existing style and make formatting variations in order to create a new style.

Creating new paragraph styles

Open the Paragraph Styles palette by choosing Window ➪ Type ➪ Paragraph Styles (see Figure 14-39). You can change the display size of the palette items by choosing either Small List View or Large List View in the palette menu.

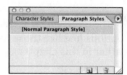

Figure 14-39: The Paragraph Styles palette

By default, every paragraph is assigned the Normal Paragraph Style. To create a new paragraph style, click the Create New Style button in the lower-right portion of the palette. A new style with a default name automatically appears in the palette. Or create a new style by selecting New Paragraph Style from the palette menu. At this point, you'll be prompted to give the style a custom name. Either way, when the new style name appears in the list, double-click on it to edit its attributes with the Paragraph Style Options box, shown in Figure 14-40.

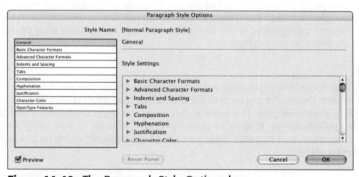

Figure 14-40: The Paragraph Style Options box

When the Paragraph Style Options box opens, you see the name of the selected style at the top and ten options to the left. These include the following:

✦ **General:** This pane is displayed when you first open the Paragraph Style Options box. It's a summary of the remaining nine settings, the style settings. You can view attributes of the separate style settings by toggling the gray arrows in the right side of the pane.

✦ **Basic Character Formats:** In this menu, you can specify font family, font style, size, leading, kerning, tracking, case, position (superscript or subscript), and whether or not you want Standard Vertical Roman Alignment.

✦ **Advanced Character Formats:** Here you can specify horizontal and vertical scale, baseline shift, character rotation, and desired language.

✦ **Indents and Spacing:** Specify alignment, left indent, first-line indent, right indent, space before, and space after.

- ✦ **Tabs:** Specify tab settings.

- ✦ **Composer:** Choose a composition method here.

- ✦ **Hyphenation:** Specify hyphenation preferences.

- ✦ **Justification:** Specify justification preferences.

- ✦ **Character Color:** Choose desired color, stroke, and overprint options.

- ✦ **OpenType Features:** This panel allows you to set OpenType options just like those found in the OpenType palette (see the "Using OpenType" section earlier in this chapter).

After you've set up your paragraph attributes the way you want them, click OK.

You can easily create copies of existing paragraph styles by either dragging the style onto the Create New Style button, or by choosing Duplicate Paragraph Style from the Paragraph Styles palette menu. To delete styles, simply drag the style name to the trash icon, or select Delete Paragraph Style from the palette. You can also import styles from other Illustrator documents by using the Load Paragraph Styles command.

Applying paragraph styles

To apply paragraph styles in Illustrator, insert the cursor in a single paragraph or select a range of paragraphs. Simply click the style name in the Paragraph Styles palette. To designate a style to be used for all new paragraphs in the document, be sure to deselect all type objects first; then click the style name in the palette.

About overrides

If you see a plus sign next to a paragraph style in the Paragraph Styles palette, it means the selected text has overrides. *Overrides* are formatting attributes that don't match the defined style. To clear overrides, simply reapply the same style or use the Clear Overrides command in the Paragraph Styles palette menu. Illustrator preserves overrides when you apply a different style to text with overrides, and to clear them you need to Option/Alt+click on the style name when you apply the style.

Using paragraph styles in InDesign

Just like with character styles, the process for setting up and using paragraph styles in InDesign is very similar to Illustrator. InDesign offers additional options here as well.

Creating new paragraph styles

Open the Character Styles palette by choosing Type ➪ Paragraph Styles, or Window ➪ Type &Tables ➪ Paragraph Styles. As in Illustrator, the palette lists all the styles that have been created for the document. If no custom styles have been created, all you see is the default — No Paragraph Style.

Creating a new style is the same procedure as in Illustrator: click the Create New Style button in the lower-right corner of the palette or select New Paragraph Style from the palette menu. You can then specify attributes with the Paragraph Style Options or New Paragraph Style box. The options here are similar to Illustrator, with the addition of keyboard shortcuts, basing styles on other styles, paragraph rules, keeping lines together, drop caps, nested styles, and underline and strikethrough options. As shown in Figure 14-41, the many options for paragraph-style formatting are selected in the left pane where individual options appear on the right side of the dialog box.

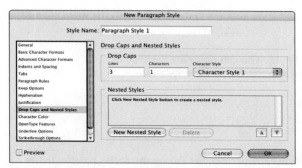

Figure 14-41: InDesign offers advanced features for creating paragraph styles.

Duplicating, editing, and deleting Paragraph Styles in InDesign is the same as in Illustrator. You can import Paragraph Styles from other InDesign documents using the Load Paragraph Styles command. This feature is particularly helpful in workflow environments where you can create layout templates with paragraph and character styles. All members of your workgroup can load styles from a master template and set type according to the styles defined for a particular project.

Applying paragraph styles

There are three ways to apply a paragraph style to selected text in InDesign. You can select the text and click the style name in the Paragraph Styles palette, choose the style name from the pull-down menu in the Control palette, or use the keyboard shortcut you've assigned to the style.

Note When you apply a paragraph style to text, it doesn't automatically remove any existing character formatting in the paragraph. A plus sign (+) appears next to the paragraph style in the Paragraph Styles palette if there is any formatting applied that doesn't match the current style. Even if you click No Paragraph Style, the formatting remains intact. If you want to remove all formatting, including the existing character styles, you must press Alt or Option and then click No Paragraph Style in the palette.

Creating Nested Styles

Nested styles enable you to apply complex formatting to text using two or more character styles. You may decide, for example, that multiple paragraphs in your layout need to include a custom drop cap, a special style treatment for the first sentence, and a third style for the remainder of the body copy. In this instance you would create three separate character styles, capture all three as a nested style, and apply the nested style to other paragraphs in your composition. Each time the nested style is applied to a new paragraph, the drop cap, first sentence characters, and remaining body copy styles are applied automatically.

The easiest way to create a nested style is to first create the individual character styles required. These individual styles need to be listed in the Character Styles palette. For the body copy, create a paragraph style and add it to the Paragraph Styles palette. Drag the paragraph style name to the Create New Style icon to create a duplicate style. Notice in Figure 14-42 the style named *Body* is selected. Drag the style name to the Create New Style icon, as shown in the figure. The duplicated style appears in the palette with the word *copy* after the style name.

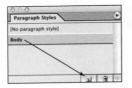

Figure 14-42: You can duplicate the style by dragging it to the Create New Style icon.

Double click on the paragraph style copy to open the Paragraph Styles palette. In the Paragraph Style Options dialog box, scroll down the list and select Drop Caps and Nested Styles in the left pane, as shown in Figure 14-43. The options change to settings used for creating nested styles. To make this process a little more comprehensible, work through the following steps to see how a nested style is created and then applied to a body of text.

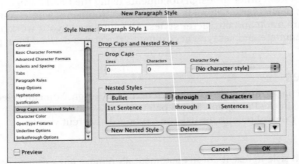

Figure 14-43: Select Drop Caps and Nested Styles on the left to access the attribute choices for creating nested styles.

STEPS: Creating and Applying Nested Styles

1. **Create a text passage in InDesign.** Import text from a text file or use placeholder text containing several paragraphs.

2. **Set type attributes for the body copy.** Select all the placed text and choose a font style and point size that represents the main body copy you intend to use.

3. **Define a new paragraph style.** Click the cursor anywhere in the placed text after setting the font attributes, and select New Paragraph Style from the Paragraph Styles palette menu. Provide a name for the style. In our example, we use *Body* for the style name. After creating the style, select all the text by placing the cursor anywhere in the text body and press ⌘/Control + A to select all. Click on the Body style name in the Paragraph Styles palette to apply the style to the selected text.

4. **Select the first two words in the first paragraph and change the font attributes.** Change the selected text point size to a larger point size than the body copy. Add points to the type in the Control palette and change the font. Open the Color palette and assign a new color to the character.

5. **Create a character style for the first two words.** Select the first two words you changed in Step 4, and select New Character Style from the Character Styles palette menu, shown in Figure 15-44. Name the style *1st two Words*.

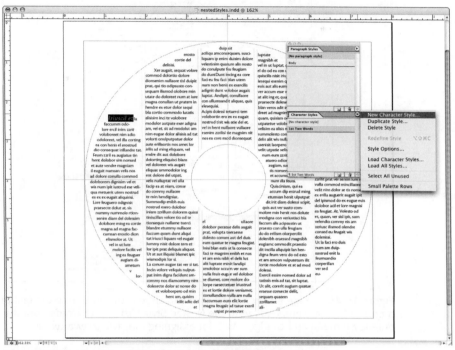

Figure 14-44: Create a character style for the first two words.

6. **Create another style for the first sentence**. Select the first character in the third word through the last character in the first sentence. Change type attributes to a different font style as the style used for the body copy. Open the Character Styles palette menu and select New Character Style. Be certain the cursor appears within the sentence where you just changed the font attributes before opening the New Character Style dialog box. Provide a name for the style, such as 1st Sentence, and click OK.

7. **Duplicate the Body text paragraph style.** Select Body in the Paragraph Styles palette and drag it to the Create New Paragraph Style icon. InDesign automatically names the new style *Body copy*.

8. **Create a nested style.** Double-click on the Body copy style you created in the Paragraph Styles palette to open the Paragraph Style Options dialog box. Click Drop Caps and Nested Styles in the left pane. Click the New Nested Style button. In the Nested Styles window, the highlighted item appears as No Character Style. When you click the item, a pull-down menu shows all the character styles you created in the Character Styles palette. Select *1st Two Words* from the menu items. Select Words on the right side of the new nested style entry in the Nested Styles window, as shown in Figure 14-45. Select the default number 1 and type 2 in the field box.

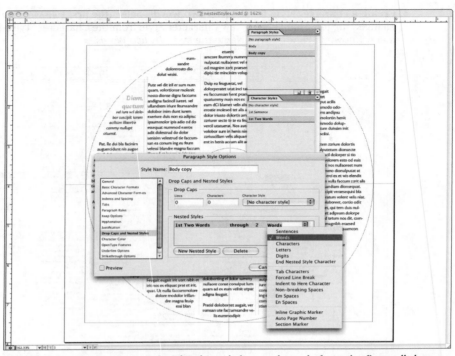

Figure 14-45: Create a new nested style and choose the style from the first pull-down menu. In the new entry added to the Nested Styles list, select Words from the last pull-down menu and change 1 to 2 for assigning the style to two words.

8. **Add a second character style to the nested style.** Click the New Nested Style button. From the Character Style pull-down menu on the left, select 1st Sentence (the second character style you created) as shown in Figure 14-46. Select Sentence in the last pull-down menu. Click OK when you're finished defining the style. Be certain to leave the value in the field box at the default 1 for one sentence.

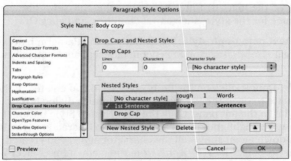

Figure 14-46: Add a second character style to the nested style.

9. **Apply the nested style to the copy.** Click the cursor in the text passage and press ⌘/Ctrl+A to select all the text. Click on the new nested style.

10. **Deselect the text.** Click the cursor anywhere on the page, and the text is deselected. The final copy edits appear as shown in Figure 14-47.

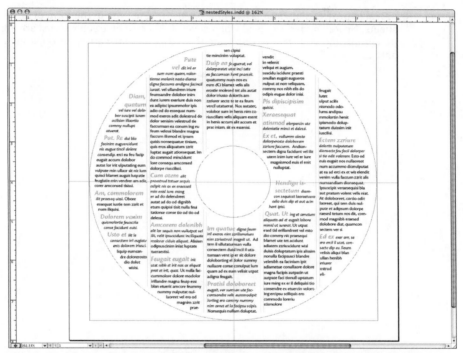

Figure 14-47: Deselect the text and examine the copy. All the paragraphs should appear with the assigned character styles.

Making changes to type attributes where nested styles have been assigned is easy. As is the case with paragraph styles, the nested style is based on the various character styles. You can revisit the Character Styles palette and make changes to type attributes. The type changes are dynamically updated in the nested style, which directly changes the type where the nested style was applied.

Summary

✦ Illustrator text is created as either point type or area type. When formatting paragraphs and working with larger bodies of text, click and drag the cursor to create area type.

✦ Legacy Illustrator files need to be updated to edit type. You can update type when opening a legacy file in Illustrator CS or at a later time after a document has been opened without updating the type.

- ✦ OpenType fonts offer you many more sophisticated typesetting features as compared to PostScript and TrueType fonts.

- ✦ Both Illustrator and InDesign offer options for creating character and paragraph style sheets. Style sheets are used to apply type formatting when repeating format designs throughout a layout.

- ✦ InDesign provides an impressive new typesetting feature in the form of nested style sheets. Nested styles are used when several different character styles are applied to a paragraph and you want to duplicate the paragraph formatting throughout a passage of text.

✦   ✦   ✦

Working with Text Frames

Photoshop, Illustrator, and InDesign allow you to create type within bounding boxes. In Photoshop you can create multiple paragraphs within a bounding box and choose justification options, but you have no ability to link multiple blocks of text (known as text threading). When you set type in a bounding box in Illustrator, the box is called a type area; in InDesign, it is referred to as a text frame. To make our discussion easier in this chapter, type bounding boxes in both InDesign and Illustrator will be referred to as text frames.

Both Illustrator and InDesign offer advanced options for handling text blocks, including the ability to thread text, apply attributes to text frames, and wrap text around objects. Text frames can assume many different shapes and can appear as graphic objects or flow around objects and images. In both Illustrator and InDesign, text frames give you great flexibility when working with type.

Creating Text Frames

Text frames are created in the same manner in both Illustrator and InDesign. Simply click the Type tool and drag open a rectangle. A blinking cursor tells you the program is ready to accept type within the frame you created.

To resize a text frame, click and drag any one of the handles on the bounding box and reshape as desired. Any text within the frame conforms to the new size. If you start typing in a text frame and you want to quickly reshape the frame, press the ⌘/Ctrl key and you temporarily gain access to the frame handles. Drag the handles to reshape the frame, and when you release the keyboard modifier the Type tool is left uninterrupted, and you're ready to continue typing.

Working with text threads

You can add text to a frame either by typing it in directly from the keyboard or by importing it from another document. If the text over-sets the frame (that is, the bounding box is not large enough to hold all the text) you will see a tiny red plus symbol (+) in a box at the bottom-right corner of the text frame. If you don't want the text to carry over to a new text frame, you need either to make the type smaller or the text frame larger, until the plus sign disappears. However, if you want to create a text thread (that is, carry the text over to a new frame), click on the plus symbol with the Selection tool. This action "loads" the cursor with all the overset text. Click and drag open a new text frame and the overset text automatically flows into the new frame.

In Illustrator, when you select threaded text frames, you see a visible link between them, as shown in Figure 15-1. You can hide the text threads by choosing View ⇨ Hide Text Threads.

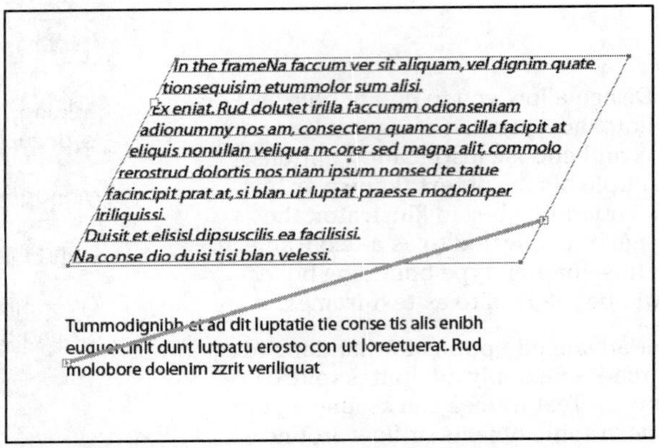

Figure 15-1: Visible text threads in Illustrator

InDesign's default setting hides the text threads, as shown in Figure 15-2. There is no visible indication that the text blocks are linked. If you want to view the text threads, choose View ⇨ Show Text Threads.

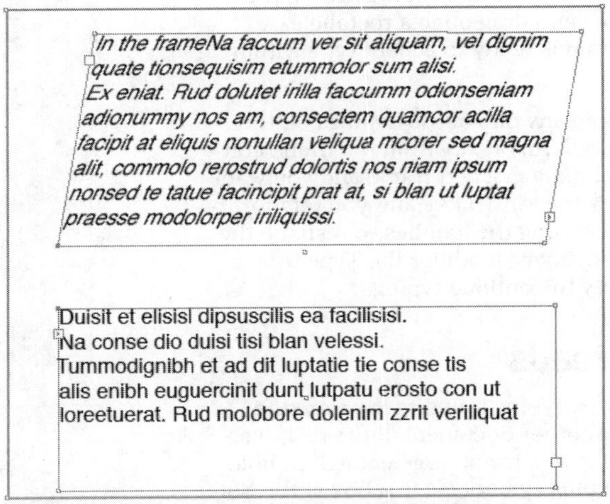

Figure 15-2: InDesign's default setting keeps text threads hidden.

Adding new frames to a text thread

Text frames in both Illustrator and InDesign have *in ports* and *out ports* that enable linking to other text frames for continuation of a thread. The in port is a small square located in the top-left area of the text frame and the out port is located at the bottom-right. An empty port indicates that no text precedes or follows the text frame. A port containing a right arrow indicates that text is threaded from one frame to another. An out port with a plus (+) symbol indicates that more text is contained within the frame but has not yet been threaded and remains hidden. In Figure 15-3, you can see a thread where the symbols are placed.

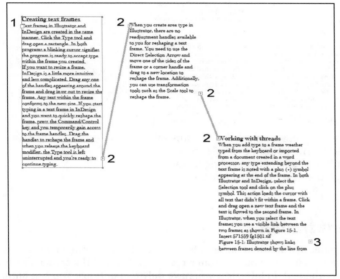

Figure 15-3: An empty port (1) indicates no text precedes the text in the frame. A port with a right arrow (2) indicates the thread flows from one frame to another. A plus (+) symbol in an out port (3) indicates there is overset text in the frame that has not yet flowed to another frame.

To flow overset text to a new text frame, simply click the plus symbol on the out port with the Selection tool. Click on a blank area of the document, or drag open a rectangle, and the overset text flows to the new frame.

If you need to add a new text frame between frames in an existing thread, use the Selection tool to click the out port preceding the frame where you want to add the new frame. Clicking on the out port loads the cursor with text following the selected frame. Click and drag open a new text frame, and the text is then threaded through it.

To make this process a little clearer, take a look at Figure 15-4. At the top you see two linked text frames with overset text as indicated by the plus symbol (+) in the out port of the second text frame. To eliminate this overset, we want to create a new text frame in the second column and thread the text through it. To do this, we click on the out port at the bottom-right of the text frame in column one. The cursor changes to indicate that it is loaded with all the text following that frame. Then we click and drag to create a new text frame in column two. As you can see in the bottom example in Figure 15-4, the text thread now runs through the newly created text frame, and is no longer overset in the third frame.

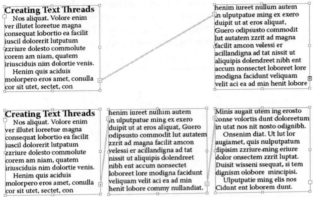

Figure 15-4: The top example shows an existing text thread with overset text in InDesign. The bottom example shows a new text frame added in the middle of the existing thread. The text now runs through the new frame, eliminating the overset text.

Unthreading text frames

Illustrator and InDesign differ a little when unthreading frames. In Illustrator, you can break a thread between two objects, release an object from a text thread, or cut the threads without changing the placement of the text. In InDesign, you have only two options: You can unthread frames that result in breaking the thread to all subsequent frames, or you can cut a frame from a thread. The methods for handling each of the three options in Illustrator and the two options in InDesign include the following:

✦ **Breaking a thread in Illustrator:** Using the Selection tool, double-click on an out port to break the thread to the current object, double-click on an in port to break the thread to a previous object, or use a single click on an in or out port and move the cursor to another in or out port and click the cursor.

✦ **Releasing an object from a text thread in Illustrator:** Click on the object you want to release from the thread with the Selection tool. Choose Type ➪ Threaded Text ➪ Release Selection.

✦ **Cutting threads in Illustrator:** Select a linked text object with the Selection tool and choose Type ➪ Threaded Text ➪ Remove Threading.

✦ **Breaking frames in InDesign:** To unthread or break frames in InDesign, start by clicking on an in or out port with the selection tool. The cursor loads with text. Move the cursor over an in or out port in another frame and double-click the mouse button. Note that when the cursor is loaded and positioned over an in or out port, the cursor shape changes to a broken-chain-link symbol informing you that the thread will be broken.

✦ **Cutting frames in InDesign:** To cut a frame in InDesign, start by selecting one or more frames in a thread with the Selection tool. For multiple frame selection where you want to cut several frames, use Shift+click. Choose Edit ➪ Cut. The frames are cut from the thread, but text is not lost — it flows from the frame preceding the cut frame(s) to the next frame in the thread order.

Setting Text Frame Attributes

Text frame attributes include options for creating columns, creating offsets, setting type, adjusting baselines, and so on. The ability to change text frame attributes is a time-saver because it allows you to make text formatting and/or layout changes quickly and easily. For example, if you need to change the type style and column width of multiple text frames, you can make these changes simply by selecting the text frames and applying the desired attributes. In both Illustrator and InDesign, dialog boxes offer options for setting attributes of text frames.

Creating columns and insets

When you create layouts in InDesign, you can specify the number of columns applied to pages. You can create threaded text frames within individual columns and flow the text through multi-columned pages. Likewise, in Illustrator, you can create several text frames and link the frames to create a single thread. As an alternative to creating multiple frames, you can create single text frames and divide the single frames into multiple columns. You can create multicolumn text frames in either Illustrator or InDesign.

In Illustrator, create an area type frame by selecting the Type tool and dragging open a rectangle. From the Type menu, select Area Type Options, and the Area Type Options dialog box opens, shown in Figure 15-5.

In Illustrator's Area Type Options dialog box, you can specify overall width and height, define rows, columns, and offset values, and select a text flow method. When experimenting with different attributes, place a check mark in the Preview box to dynamically preview the results.

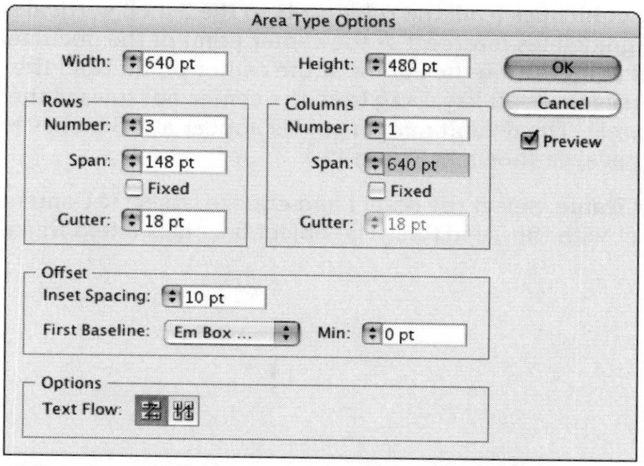

Figure 15-5: You can apply Area Type attributes in Illustrator.

InDesign has a similar dialog box for setting text frame attributes. In InDesign, choose Object ➪ Text Frame Options, and the Text Frame Options dialog box opens, as shown in Figure 15-6.

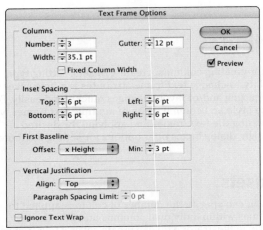

Figure 15-6: You can apply Text Frame attributes in InDesign.

The following steps show how you might apply options for text frame attributes using the Text Frame Options dialog box in InDesign.

STEPS: Setting Text Frame Options in InDesign

1. **Create a new document.** Open InDesign and choose File ➪ New Document. In the New Document dialog box, set the page size to 6 inches by 6 inches and uncheck Facing Pages.

2. **Create a frame object.** Drag guidelines from the ruler wells to the 3-inch vertical and horizontal ruler marks. The guidelines intersect at the center point of the document. Select the Ellipse Frame tool and position the cursor at the center point. Hold the Option/Alt key down, and press the Shift key. Drag from the center out toward the outside guidelines to create a circle. The default margin guides appear at 0.5 inches around the inside of the document page, as shown in Figure 15-7.

3. **Convert the object to a text frame.** Select the object and choose Object ➪ Content ➪ Text or click inside the object with the Type tool. The object becomes a text frame.

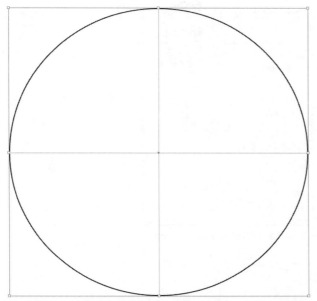

Figure 15-7: The Ellipse Frame tool creates a circle from the center point to the outside guidelines.

4. **Set the text frame options.** Select the text frame and choose Object ➪ Text Frame Options. The Text Frame Options dialog box opens. In the Columns section, set Number to 5, and Gutter to 6 points. If your unit of measure is currently set to inches and you want to specify point measurements instead, you can apply point units to the field boxes using 0*pn* — where 0 is picas, *p* stands for points, and *n* is the number of points. In the example shown in Figure 15-8, 0p6 is used in the Gutter field box. When you tab out of the field box, the value is translated to the defined unit of measure. In this example, 6 points translates to 0.0833 inches. In the Inset Spacing section, enter 0p8 for the inset. This will inset the text 8 points from the outer edge of the frame.

5. **View the text frame edges.** By default, you may not be able to see the column and inset spacing guidelines. If the guidelines are not shown, choose View ➪ Show Frame Edges. When the guidelines are visible, you should see an object similar to Figure 15-9.

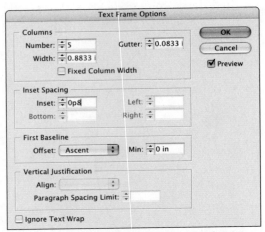

Figure 15-8: The Text Frame Options dialog box

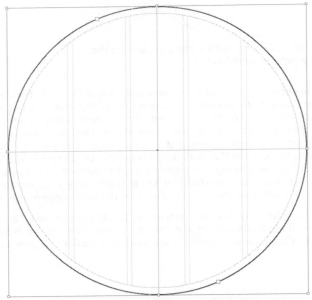

Figure 15-9: To view a text frame's guidelines for columns and inset spacing in InDesign, select Show Frame Edges the View menu.

6. **Set the text attributes.** From the Control palette, select the font and point size for your type. In the example, Kabel Book was selected from the Font drop-down list and the type size was set to 8 points.

7. **Fill with placeholder text.** If you created a keyboard shortcut for filling with place-holder text as discussed in Chapter 14, click the cursor in the first column and press Shift+F12. If you didn't create a keyboard shortcut, click the cursor in the first column and choose Type ⇨ Fill with Placeholder Text. The final result should appear similar to Figure 15-10.

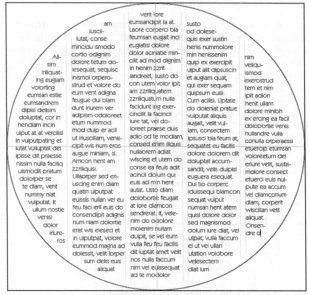

Figure 15-10: After setting font attributes, fill the columns with text.

Setting text attributes

You can set text attributes via the Control palette for options such as typeface, font size, lead-ing, kerning, and tracking. In addition, you have a couple of text formatting options in the Text Frame Options dialog box. They include First Baseline positioning and Vertical Justification options.

In the Text Frame Options dialog box (see Figure 15-8), the First Baseline section allows you to choose a first baseline offset method from a pull-down menu, and also lets you specify a minimum value for first baseline offset. The following explains these items in more detail:

✦ **Ascent:** With this setting, the first baseline is calculated so that the top edges of char-acters with ascenders (such as *d* and *b*) fall just below the top inset of the text frame.

✦ **Cap Height:** With this option, the top edges of uppercase letters touch the top inset of the text frame.

✦ **Leading:** This setting uses the text's leading value as the distance between the baseline of the first line of text and the top inset of the frame.

✦ **x Height:** Calculates the first baseline whereby the top of the *x* character falls just below the top inset of the text frame.

✦ **Fixed:** Allows you to specify the distance between the baseline of the first line of text and the top inset of the frame.

✦ **Minimum:** The field box to the right of the Offset pull-down menu is where you can specify a minimum value for the first baseline offset.

Vertical Justification allows you to specify how text is aligned vertically within a text frame. When you choose Top, Center, or Bottom vertical alignment, the text retains its specified paragraph leading and paragraph spacing values. When you choose Justify as the vertical alignment option, the lines are spaced evenly to fill the frame, regardless of the specified leading and paragraph spacing values. Figure 15-11 shows examples of the four vertical justification options available in InDesign.

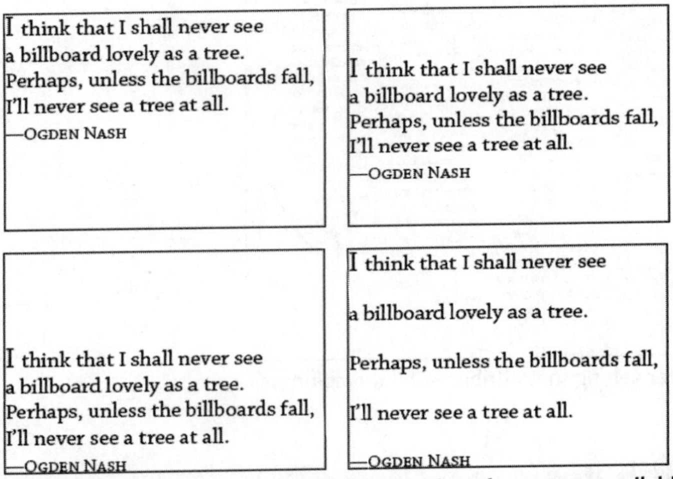

Figure 15-11: Four vertical justification options for text are available in InDesign. Shown clockwise from top, they are Top, Center, Bottom, and Justify.

Creating Text Frames on Master Pages

One big advantage of using layout programs is the ability to use *master pages*. Elements placed on the master page automatically appear on all subsequent pages where the master page is applied. The use of master pages eliminates repetitive keystrokes, ensures greater design consistency, speeds up the editing process, and conserves memory because objects are applied on a single page and referenced on all other pages. Master pages are only available in InDesign. Since Illustrator is limited to creating single-page designs, there is no need for master pages.

You can add a text frame on a master page and define the type attributes for the frame. On all subsequent pages where a given master page is applied, the text frame is positioned and ready for use. You can either type text in the frame or import text from another document. The text will automatically pick up the attributes you established on the master page.

Cross-Reference   For a more comprehensive view on creating master pages, see Chapter 23.

Creating manual text frames

You create text frames on master pages in the same way you create them on regular pages. Use either the Type tool or convert objects to text frames. To set text attributes, styles, and other options, click the cursor inside the frame. While the cursor is blinking, set the attributes using the various palettes and menu options used for type, such as the Control palette, the Type palette, and the Paragraph palette. In Figure 15-12, you can see a master page containing two separate text frames, a stroke below the second frame, and the folio. You set text attributes for the separate frames by clicking in each frame and then setting options.

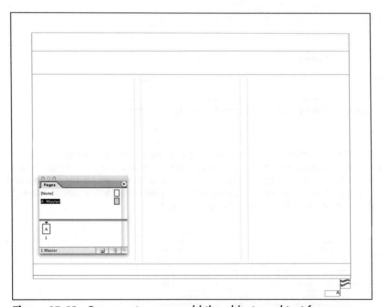

Figure 15-12: On a master page, add the objects and text frames.

When you have one or more frames created on a master page and you apply the master page to document pages, you can type in the frames or import text. Selecting the Type tool and clicking on a frame, however, does not access the frame. Neither the Type tool nor the selection tools alone can activate a text frame on a master page. You need to use ⌘/Ctrl+Shift and double-click on a frame. It doesn't matter what tool you select in the toolbox; pressing the ⌘/Ctrl key temporarily activates the Selection tool. Add the Shift key, double-click, and the I-beam cursor starts blinking in the text frame. At this point, you can type text or import text into the frame. In Figure 15-13, you can see two text frames with different text attributes. Both text frames were created on a master page.

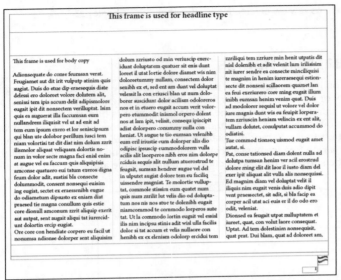

Figure 15-13: Assigning different type attributes to different frames on a master page

All the options you have for creating text threads, auto-flowing text, and assigning attributes are available to you when creating frames on master pages. If you create frame threads on master pages, you can flow text through the frames, as shown in Figure 15-14. The frames in Figure 15-14 were drawn on the master page, and text was placed on a document page. Notice that the frame threads show the direction of the text flow.

Figure 15-14: Frame threads on master pages can be applied to document pages keeping the thread order.

Creating master text frames

When you want to flow text through a document using InDesign's text autoflow feature, you need to create a master frame. Unlike manual frames, master frames are created at the time you set up your document. You add the master frame in the New Document dialog box, and InDesign automatically creates an indefinite thread when you place text within the frame using autoflow features. To understand more completely how this works, follow these steps.

STEPS: Autoflowing Text in Master Frames

1. **Create a new document.** Open InDesign and choose File ➪ New ➪ Document. In the New Document dialog box, check the box for Master Text Frame, as shown in Figure 15-15. Set attributes for the number of columns and margin distances.

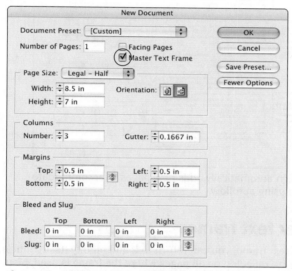

Figure 15-15: To add a master frame to the master page, check the box for Master Text Frame.

2. **Import text.** Choose File ➪ Place. The Place dialog box opens. Locate a text file you want to import, select the file, and then click Open. You can also double-click the file to be placed, but be certain not to triple-click the mouse button. The third click adds the text to the page.

3. **Autoflow the text.** When you double-click a filename or select a file in the Place dialog box and click Open, the cursor is loaded with text from the selected file. To place the text, you simply click the cursor to place text in an existing frame or click and drag the cursor to place text within a new frame. However, when placing text within a master frame, where you want to flow the text through many pages in your document, press the Shift key and you see the cursor change shape. Click the mouse button with the Shift key depressed, and the text flows through the master text frame. If more text is placed than can fit within the current frame, InDesign adds new pages with new master frames

and threads the text. More new pages are created with frames until the end of the passage of text is reached. In Figure 15-16, we added text to a master frame in a one-page document and InDesign created an additional nine pages to accommodate the text file.

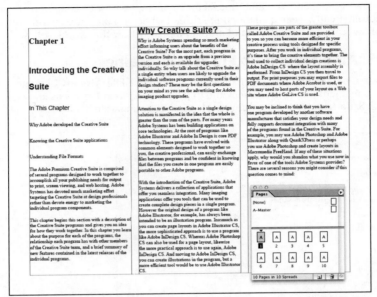

Figure 15-16: InDesign automatically adds new pages to accommodate text placement when using autoflow.

Modifying master text frames

When you create a master text frame, you can return to it and modify its attributes. Changes made on the master frame are reflected on all pages where the frame is used. Manual text frames placed on master pages, however, don't offer the same flexibility. If you create manual frames and link them on a master page, and then make changes to the frame attributes, the changes are not reflected on placed text within the frames in the document.

To modify a master frame, double-click on the master page where the frame is positioned. Select the frame with a Selection tool and either open a context menu and select Text Frame Options or select the Object menu and select Text Frame Options. The Text Frame Options dialog box opens. You can make changes to the number of columns, gutter spacing, inset spacing, baseline shifts, and vertical justification the same as when you make changes to frames drawn manually on individual pages. Likewise, you can also apply attribute choices for text styles and transformations to the master frames.

After making adjustments on the master frame, all text within a master frame thread is readjusted to the changes made to the frame on the master page. In Figure 15-17, text was placed on a page in a single column. The text was placed within a frame created from a master frame on the master page. By adjusting the Text Frame Options and changing the frame from one column to three columns, all the text in the document using the master frame adjusts automatically, as shown in Figure 15-18.

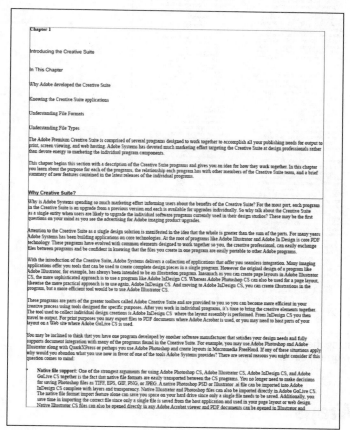

Figure 15-17: Text placed in a master frame where the frame attributes are set to one column

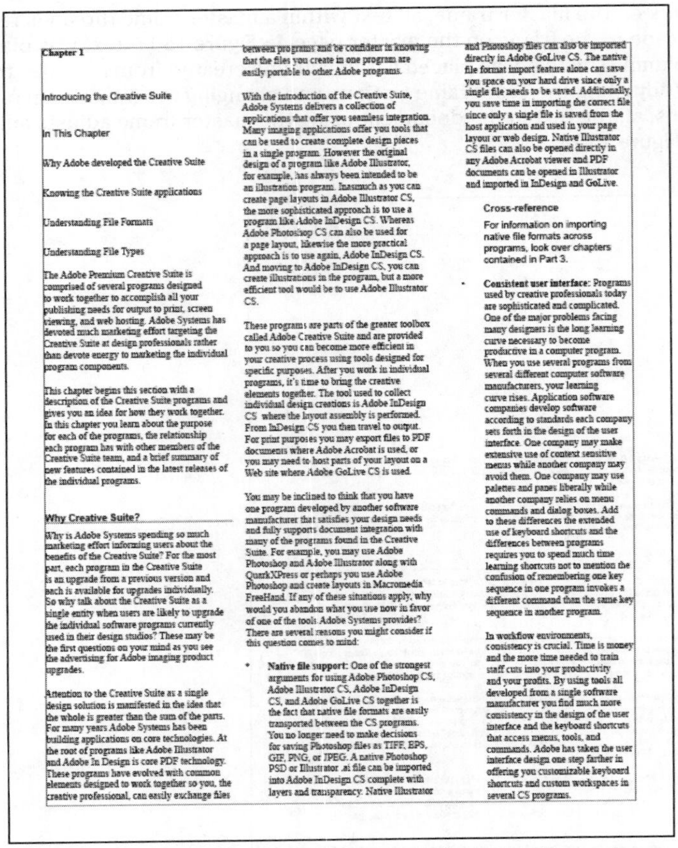

Chapter 1

Introducing the Creative Suite

In This Chapter

Why Adobe developed the Creative Suite

Knowing the Creative Suite applications

Understanding File Formats

Understanding File Types

The Adobe Premium Creative Suite is comprised of several programs designed to work together to accomplish all your publishing needs for output to print, screen viewing, and web hosting. Adobe Systems has devoted much marketing effort targeting the Creative Suite at design professionals rather than devote energy to marketing the individual program components.

This chapter begins this section with a description of the Creative Suite programs and gives you an idea for how they work together. In this chapter you learn about the purpose for each of the programs, the relationship each program has with other members of the Creative Suite team, and a brief summary of new features contained in the latest releases of the individual programs.

Why Creative Suite?

Why is Adobe Systems spending so much marketing effort informing users about the benefits of the Creative Suite? For the most part, each program in the Creative Suite is an upgrade from a previous version and each is available for upgrades individually. So why talk about the Creative Suite as a single entity when users are likely to upgrade the individual software programs currently used in their design studios? These may be the first questions on your mind as you see the advertising for Adobe imaging product upgrades.

Attention to the Creative Suite as a single design solution is manifested in the idea that the whole is greater than the sum of the parts. For many years Adobe Systems has been building applications on core technologies. At the root of programs like Adobe Illustrator and Adobe In Design is core PDF technology. These programs have evolved with common elements designed to work together so you, the creative professional, can easily exchange files between programs and be confident in knowing that the files you create in one program are easily portable to other Adobe programs.

With the introduction of the Creative Suite, Adobe Systems delivers a collection of applications that offer you seamless integration. Many imaging applications offer you tools that can be used to create complete design pieces in a single program. However the original design of a program like Adobe Illustrator, for example, has always been intended to be an illustration program. Inasmuch as you can create page layouts in Adobe Illustrator CS, the more sophisticated approach is to use a program like Adobe InDesign CS. Whereas Adobe Photoshop CS can also be used for a page layout, likewise the more practical approach is to use again, Adobe InDesign CS. And moving to Adobe InDesign CS, you can create illustrations in the program, but a more efficient tool would be to use Adobe Illustrator CS.

These programs are parts of the greater toolbox called Adobe Creative Suite and are provided to you so you can become more efficient in your creative process using tools designed for specific purposes. After you work in individual programs, it's time to bring the creative elements together. The tool used to collect individual design creations is Adobe InDesign CS where the layout assembly is performed. From InDesign CS you then travel to output. For print purposes you may export files to PDF documents where Adobe Acrobat is used, or you may need to host parts of your layout on a Web site where Adobe GoLive CS is used.

You may be inclined to think that you have one program developed by another software manufacturer that satisfies your design needs and fully supports document integration with many of the programs found in the Creative Suite. For example, you may use Adobe Photoshop and Adobe Illustrator along with QuarkXPress or perhaps you use Adobe Photoshop and create layouts in Macromedia FreeHand. If any of these situations apply, why would you abandon what you use now in favor of one of the tools Adobe Systems provides? There are several reasons you might consider if this question comes to mind:

- **Native file support:** One of the strongest arguments for using Adobe Photoshop CS, Adobe Illustrator CS, Adobe InDesign CS, and Adobe GoLive CS together is the fact that native file formats are easily transported between the CS programs. You no longer need to make decisions for saving Photoshop files as TIFF, EPS, GIF, PNG, or JPEG. A native Photoshop PSD or Illustrator .ai file can be imported into Adobe InDesign CS complete with layers and transparency. Native Illustrator and Photoshop files can also be imported directly in Adobe GoLive CS. The native file format import feature alone can save you space on your hard drive since only a single file needs to be saved. Additionally, you save time in importing the correct file since only a single file is saved from the host application and used in your page layout or web design. Native Illustrator CS files can also be opened directly in any Adobe Acrobat viewer and PDF documents can be opened in Illustrator and imported in InDesign and GoLive.

Cross-reference

For information on importing native file formats across programs, look over chapters contained in Part 3.

- **Consistent user interface:** Programs used by creative professionals today are sophisticated and complicated. One of the major problems facing many designers is the long learning curve necessary to become productive in a computer program. When you use several programs from several different computer software manufacturers, your learning curve rises. Application software companies develop software according to standards each company sets forth in the design of the user interface. One company may make extensive use of context sensitive menus while another company may avoid them. One company may use palettes and panes liberally while another company relies on menu commands and dialog boxes. Add to these differences the extended use of keyboard shortcuts and the differences between programs requires you to spend much time learning shortcuts not to mention the confusion of remembering one key sequence in one program invokes a different command than the same key sequence in another program.

In workflow environments, consistency is crucial. Time is money and the more time needed to train staff cuts into your productivity and your profits. By using tools all developed from a single software manufacturer you find much more consistency in the design of the user interface and the keyboard shortcuts that access menus, tools, and commands. Adobe has taken the user interface design one step farther in offering you customizable keyboard shortcuts and custom workspaces in several CS programs.

Figure 15-18: By changing the master text frame attributes from one column to three columns, all text using the frame is adjusted automatically.

Creating Text Wraps

Wrapping text around graphic elements in your design layouts can add greater visual appeal to your document. If you must manually set type around objects to create a text wrap, your job could become tedious and time-consuming. Fortunately, both Illustrator and InDesign offer you many different options for wrapping text around objects and images.

Wrapping text in Illustrator

You can wrap text around any placed object, around type objects, imported images, and objects you draw in Illustrator. If you save files as bitmaps from Photoshop with transparency, Illustrator can wrap text while ignoring transparent pixels. In Figure 15-19, you can see a text wrap around a Photoshop bitmap image with transparency.

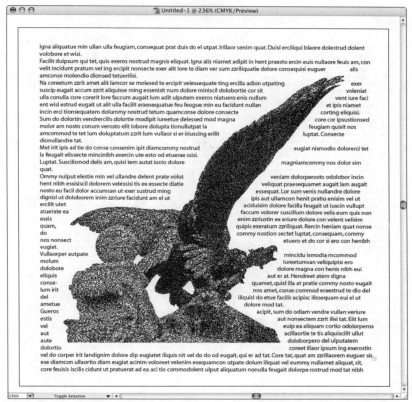

Figure 15-19: Illustrator can wrap type around objects as well as images with transparency, clipping paths, and transparent layers.

Wrapping graphic objects

To understand how to wrap text around graphic objects, look over the following steps.

STEPS: Applying Text Wraps to Objects in Illustrator

1. **Create area type.** Create a text block by selecting the Type tool and dragging open a rectangle where you want the text to appear. You can import text or type text in the text block.

Tip

If you want to use Greek text in Illustrator, open InDesign and use the Fill with Placeholder Text command to add Greek text to a text frame. Click the cursor inside the frame and choose Edit ⇨ Select All or press ⌘/Ctrl+A. Copy and paste the text in Illustrator.

2. **Place a graphic you want to use for the text wrap.** You can import an object created in another program or use objects created in Illustrator. If you don't have an object handy, use the Symbols palette and drag an object to the document window. Use the transformation tools to size the object as desired. In Figure 15-20, an object from the Symbols palette was sized and placed on top of the text. Be certain the object to be wrapped is on the same layer as the text and that it appears in front of the text.

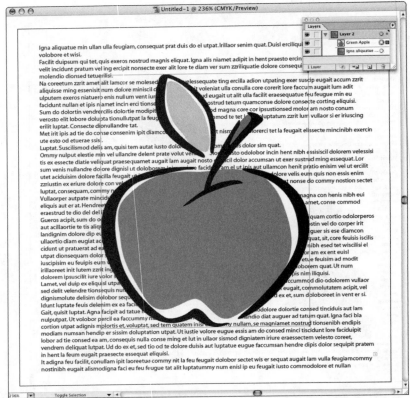

Figure 15-20: Objects to be wrapped need to be placed on the same layer as the text and appear in front of the text used for the wrap.

3. **Assign a text wrap to the object.** Objects are assigned attributes for a text wrap. Select the object with one of the selection tools and choose Object ➪ Text Wrap ➪ Make Text Wrap. The Text Wrap Options dialog box opens, as shown in Figure 15-21. Click the Preview check box and the text wraps in the document window, showing you the results of the wrap and offset. To adjust the offset amount, change the value in the Offset field box. Click OK when the wrap appears the way you want.

Figure 15-21: Click Preview in the Text Wrap Options dialog box, and the background document window displays the results of the text wrap. To change the distance between the object and the text, edit the value in the Offset field box.

In the Text Wrap Options dialog box, an option appears for inversing a wrap. Check the box and click Preview to see the results of an inverse wrap. This option is used for containing text within objects, as shown in Figure 15-22.

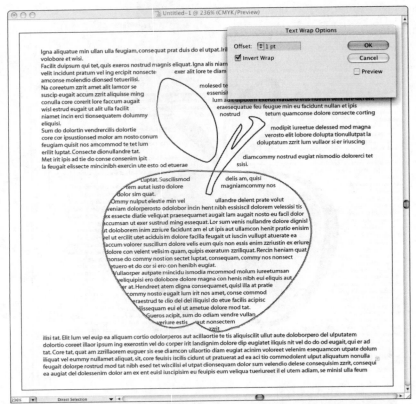

Figure 15-22: Check the box for Invert Wrap to contain text within an object.

Wrapping text objects

You can also wrap text around type objects. You can use the text frame as the object, or you can create outlines and wrap text around the outlined type. Be certain the type is within the same group on the same layer as your text and follow the same procedures for applying text wraps to graphic objects. In Figure 15-23, you can see the effects of wrapping text around a text frame (top) and text converted to outlines (bottom).

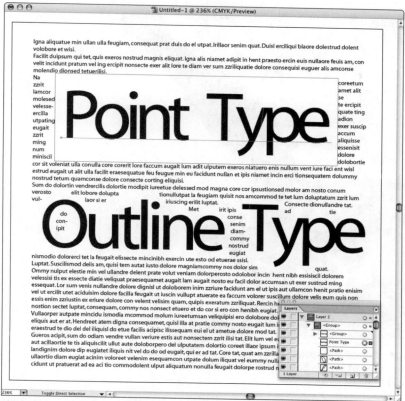

Figure 15-23: Text frames and type converted to outlines can be assigned text wrap attributes. All objects must be within the same group on the same layer.

Wrapping images

Images from Photoshop can be assigned text wraps. Follow the same steps as mentioned previously for applying text wraps to graphic objects. Be certain the placed Photoshop file is contained in the same group as the text that wraps the object. If a Photoshop file contains a mask or transparency, be certain to create a clipping path and save the file with the path in either Photoshop native format or EPS. In Figure 15-24, a clipping path is added to the image. Notice that the transparency is not enough to create the wrap around the object in Illustrator to properly designate the path. The clipping path is needed to mask the object so the text wrap falls around the image.

Figure 15-24: Create and save a clipping path in a Photoshop file when you want to mask an image. Save the document in Photoshop native format (PSD) or as an EPS.

When importing the Photoshop image in Illustrator, be certain to locate the placed image in the same group as the text wrapping the object, as shown in Figure 15-25. Notice that the text neatly wraps the image at the offset distance defined in the Text Wrap Options dialog box.

Wrapping text in InDesign

InDesign offers the same options for wrapping text that you find in Illustrator, as well as some additional options for setting the text-wrap and path attributes. You can adjust clipping paths and path tolerances in InDesign, as well as set the same options found in Illustrator's Text Wrap Options dialog box.

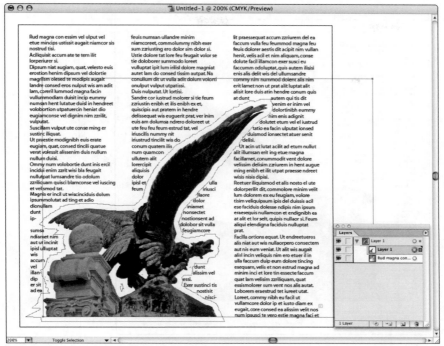

Figure 15-25: Text will wrap around the clipping path assigned in a Photoshop document when the image is positioned in the same group as the text.

Importing text wraps into InDesign

If you have an Illustrator document that needs to be imported into InDesign, you can create text wraps and complete the layout in Illustrator. When the file is imported into InDesign, the text wraps and layout appearance are preserved in InDesign when you place the file. In Figure 15-26, you can see the results of importing a native Illustrator document with a text wrap into InDesign.

Figure 15-26: Text wraps created in Illustrator are preserved when placed in InDesign. Save the Illustrator files in native Illustrator AI format and import directly by choosing File ➪ Place in InDesign.

InDesign offers you options for adjusting the clipping path on placed objects and also on objects placed in Illustrator and imported into InDesign. The path defined in Photoshop is the default path used in Illustrator and ultimately appears in the InDesign view.

You may have situations where artifacts appear around the edges of an image to which you have assigned a clipping path. If you need to adjust the tolerance so more of the path edge is cut off or the edge is pushed out to show more image and less mask, you can make the adjustments in InDesign. With the placed object selected, choose Object ➪ Clipping Path. The Clipping Path dialog box opens and here you can make adjustments to a path.

From the Type drop-down list, select Detect Edges. The Threshold and Tolerance sliders enable you to adjust the path. In Figure 15-27, you can see the results of changing the Tolerance and Threshold on the same image used in Figure 15-25.

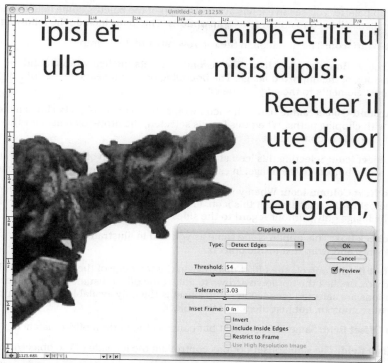

Figure 15-27: Open the Clipping Path dialog box to adjust the path edge. This dialog box lets you clip more of the image or reduce the mask to show more of the image.

Using InDesign text-wrap options

InDesign offers you a more elaborate set of options for wrapping text than you find in Illustrator. InDesign's Text Wrap palette lets you specify wrap options for a selected object in the foreground, as well as specify how the text behind the object is wrapped. In Figure 15-28, the Text Wrap palette is opened by choosing Window ➪ Type and Tables ➪ Text Wrap. As learn from viewing the Text Wrap palette, you have many different options for controlling the text-wrap attributes.

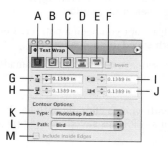

Figure 15-28: Choose Window ➪ Type and Tables ➪ Text Wrap to open the Text Wrap palette.

In the Text Wrap palette, you see five icons across the top of the palette, some field boxes, and drop-down lists, all used to adjust text-wrap options. The items include the following:

A **No Text Wrap icon:** The first icon in the top row turns off text wrap.

B **Wrap Around Bounding Box icon:** The second icon sets the text wrap around the bounding box of the imported image. The bounding box represents the periphery of the farthest elements to the edge of the object.

C **Wrap Around Object Shape icon:** This icon wraps the shape of objects and can include images with clipping paths. When this icon is selected, the drop-down lists for the Contour Options become active.

D **Jump Object icon:** Selecting this icon stops the wrap at the top of the image and starts it again at the bottom of the image. In essence, the wrap jumps over the object/image.

E **Jump to Next Column icon:** When you want the text to stop at the top of the image and continue below the image, select this icon. In essence, the wrap offset is used for the top of the image only, without regard to the sides or bottom of the image.

F **Invert check-box:** This option is the same as you find in Illustrator. It is used to invert the text wrap and wrap text inside objects.

G **Top Offset field:** Controls the offset distance on the top edge of the object/image. Edit the field box or click the up/down arrows to adjust the offset distance. Note: When contour options are selected (see below), Top Offset is the only available field and applies to the entire contour, not just the top of the object.

H **Bottom Offset field:** Same as Top Offset but controls the bottom offset distance.

I **Left Offset field:** The same offset options controlling the left side of the object/image.

J **Right Offset field:** Controls the offset for the right side of the object/image.

K **Contour Options Type drop-down list:** From the Contour Options Type drop-down list, you have options that are used when you select the Wrap Around Object Shape icon. The options in the menu include the following:

- **Bounding Box:** Choose this option when you want to place the wrap around the frame where the outside edges appear.

- **Detect Edges:** InDesign can automatically detect edges in objects and images with paths. To enable auto-detection of edges, use this option.

- **Alpha Channel:** Use this option when a Photoshop image contains an Alpha Channel or transparency and you want the image masked. InDesign interprets layered Photoshop files with transparency the same as when creating a clipping path. All the transparency is masked when you select this option.

- **Photoshop Path:** The same as Alpha Channel, except you need a path created in the image. InDesign clips the image to the path saved in Photoshop.

- **Graphic Frame:** The frame holding an object or image can be larger or smaller than the imported item. When you select this option, the wrap forms around the frame, ignoring the frame contents.

- **Same As Clipping:** The same as Photoshop Path when a clipping path has been saved. You can import native PSD files as well as EPS files saved with clipping paths.

L Contour Options Path/Alpha drop-down list: The second drop-down list is active only when either Photoshop Path or Alpha Channel is selected. When you choose Photoshop Path in the Contour Options Type pull-down menu, the menu options provide a selection of all named paths. If the image contains only a single path name, you can only select that name in the menu. When you select Alpha Channel in the Contour Options Type pull-down menu, all Alpha Channel names are listed in the menu. If you save only a single channel with the image, that channel is the only selection available.

M Include Inside Edges check-box: If you have an object with a cutout inside the object and want text to wrap around the outside and fill the inside cutout, select this option.

As is the case with Illustrator, you can adjust the text-frame options and change frames from single to multiple columns. In multiple-column frames, text wraps apply to all columns interacting with the object, as shown in Figure 15-29. If you create multiple frames on a page and either link the frames or keep them isolated as independent frames, the text wraps likewise occur for all text interacting with the object/image.

Figure 15-29: Text wraps are applied to multiple column frames and linked frames.

Summary

✦ Text is typed or imported into text frames in Illustrator and InDesign.

✦ When text is extended from one frame to another, the text follows a thread. Text frames in threads can be linked, unthreaded, or cut. New frames can be added between existing threaded frames.

✦ Text frames in Illustrator and InDesign can be assigned different properties. You can specify number of columns, inset spacing, column gutter widths, and font attributes.

✦ Frames created on master pages in InDesign can be used for autoflowing text.

✦ Text can be wrapped around graphic objects, text objects, and images in both Illustrator and InDesign.

✦ Text wraps can be applied to paths, transparencies, and clipping paths of Photoshop images placed in InDesign.

✦   ✦   ✦

Working with Special Characters

Both Illustrator and InDesign allow you to handle typography like a master, especially when working in conjunction with the new OpenType fonts that offer you thousands of character selections. InDesign, in particular, with its abundant set of menu commands and palette options, is the most powerful typesetting tool developed to date for desktop computers. With it, you have the ability to set high-quality type that rivals the output from professional typesetting machines used before the computer revolution.

Older PostScript fonts give you a maximum of 256 different characters, or glyphs. With the new OpenType fonts, however, you get as many as 65,0000 glyphs per font. (Eighty-three OpenType fonts are installed on your computer as part of the Illustrator CS installation.) These additional characters offer you many more options for pairing characters in ligatures, customizing fractions, accessing foreign language characters, and working with a wide variety of symbols and special characters that can be used as type or graphic elements.

Working with Glyphs Palettes

Both Illustrator and InDesign have a Glyphs palette that shows you, at a glance, the different characters available in any given font. It's much like the old Keycaps control panel available in earlier Mac operating systems. In addition to viewing glyphs in a scrollable palette, you can also create custom glyph sets in InDesign and you can view different special characters by selecting menu options in the palettes.

In Illustrator, choose Type ➪ Glyphs to open the Glyphs palette shown in Figure 16-1. The palette contains several menus, scrollbars to view any hidden characters, font selection menus, and zoom tools.

The default selection in the Show menu at the top is Entire Font. All characters in a given font are displayed in the scrollable palette. In the Show menu, you also have the option to show Alternates for Current Selection. Note in Figure 16-1 that when you press the mouse button on a particular character with a flag in the lower-right corner, a pop-up bar shows alternate characters. When you select the menu command, the alternate characters are displayed in the palette. Other options you have from the menu choices include many of the same options found in the Character palette.

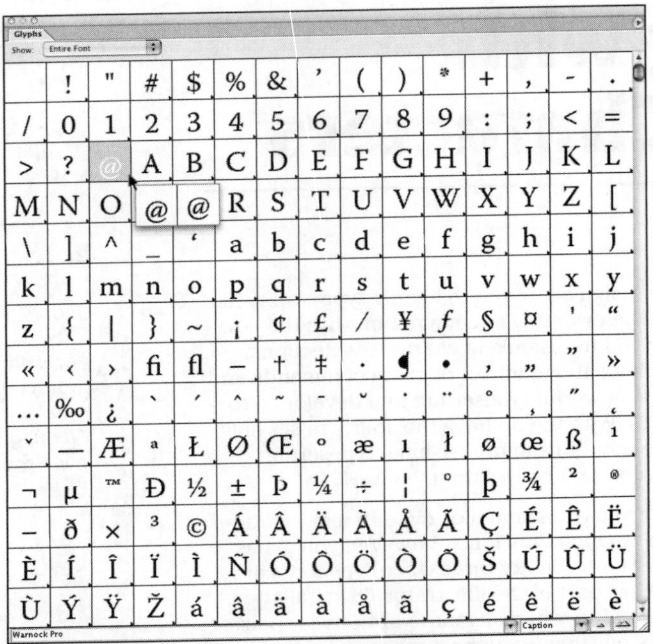

Figure 16-1: The Glyphs palette displays all characters in a given font.

Cross-Reference For more information on using the Character palette, see Chapter 14.

To use glyphs, and particularly to use alternate characters in Illustrator, you can easily access the palette and select characters for insertion in text as you type. For character insertions, follow these steps.

STEPS: Inserting Special Characters in Text Using the Glyphs Palette

1. **Begin by typing a body of text.** Add some area type to a page in Illustrator. Select the font you want to use by choosing Type ➪ Font. Next, drag open a rectangle with the Type tool, and begin to type.

2. **Open the Glyphs palette.** Choose Type ➪ Glyphs to open the Glyphs palette.

3. **Locate the character you want to insert.** The Glyphs palette opens with the current selected font displayed in the palette. Scroll the palette and find a character to insert. In our example, we use a ligature for combining the *f* and *l* characters into a single character.

4. **Insert the character.** When you find the character in the Glyphs palette, double-click on the character. The character is inserted at the cursor location. In Figure 16-2, the inserted character is highlighted.

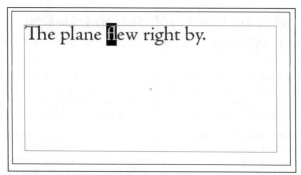

Figure 16-2: Double-clicking on a character inserts it at the cursor.

In addition to the different displays in the palette for showing various combinations of characters via the Show menu, you can make font selections from the pull-down menu at the bottom of the palette. If you're searching for a special character or want to view a specific font, use the menu to select fonts without disturbing your text editing. You can select a font family from the pull-down menu at the bottom-left side of the palette; you select the font style from the second pull-down menu at the bottom of the palette. In Figure 16-1, the selected font family is Warnock Pro and the selected style is Caption.

To the right of the Style pull-down menu, zoom buttons offer different zoom views. Click on the smaller mountain symbols to zoom out and click on the larger symbol to zoom in on the characters in the palette.

In InDesign, you have a few more style combinations that you can view in the Show menu, but the main distinction between Illustrator and InDesign exists with the fly-out menu commands accessible via the arrow at the top right of the Glyphs palette. In Illustrator, the only option available here is resetting the palette to the default view. But in InDesign there are options for working with glyph sets. Click on the right pointing arrow to open the fly-out menu and the options shown in Figure 16-3 appear.

Figure 16-3: InDesign supports several menu commands unavailable in Illustrator.

The menu commands available from the fly-out menu enable you to create and edit custom glyph sets. This feature can be a time-saver when you need to access special characters or alternatives while typesetting in InDesign. To understand how custom sets are created and used, follow these steps.

STEPS: Working with Custom Glyph Sets in InDesign

1. **Open the Glyphs palette in InDesign.** Choose Type ➪ Glyphs to open the Glyphs palette.

2. **Create a new glyph set.** You can use the Glyphs palette with or without a document open in the InDesign application window. You can temporarily ignore the current font selected. When you create a new set and add characters to your custom set, you can add characters from different fonts. From the fly-out menu select New Glyph Set.

3. **Name the new glyph set.** The New Glyph Set dialog box opens. Type a name in the field box for the name you want to use for your custom set. In our example, we use myGlyphs for the set name. You can view your new glyph set by choosing it from the Show menu or via View Glyph Set in the fly-out menu. Currently the palette includes no characters.

4. **Select a font family and font style.** Be sure the Show option is set to Entire Font. At this point, you can view all your installed fonts and available styles by making selections in the pull-down menus at the bottom of the Glyphs palette. Select a font family and the font style you want to view.

5. **Add a character to the custom glyph set.** When you find a character you want to add to the set, click on it to highlight it. Open the fly-out menu and choose Add to Glyph Set. A submenu opens where you should see your new custom set listed. If you create several sets, select the one you want to edit. In our case, we select myGlyphs from the submenu.

6. **Add additional characters to the custom glyph set.** Continue selecting and adding characters to the glyph set with the Add to Glyph Set command in the fly-out menu. When you want to use the custom set, select it from the Show menu at the top of the Glyphs palette or by choosing View Glyph Set in the fly-out menu. The characters you added to the set appear in the Glyphs palette, as shown in Figure 16-4. When you want to access a character from the set while you are typing in InDesign, simply open the set and double-click the desired character. It will automatically be inserted at the cursor location.

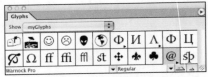

Figure 16-4: You can add a custom glyph set to the Glyphs palette.

7. **Delete a character from your custom glyph set.** If you want to delete a character from your glyph set, select the set in the Show menu. In the fly-out menu, select Edit Glyph Set. The Edit Glyph Set dialog box opens, as shown in Figure 16-5. Select the character you want to delete, and click the Delete from Set button. In addition to deleting characters, the Edit Glyph Set dialog box also enables you to change the font and style of individual characters included in the set.

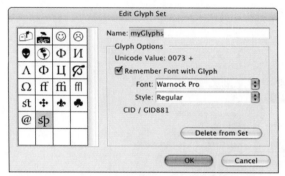

Figure 16-5: To delete a character, click the Delete from Set button.

Using Special Typographic Characters

A number of advanced typographic features are available to you in InDesign. By using simple menu commands, you can easily achieve special effects that are popular with layout artists and typographers. In the Type menu you will find several options for handling special characters. Three of these options provide an even wider selection of options in submenus. They include Insert Special Character, Insert White Space, and Insert Break Character.

Inserting special characters

When you choose Type ⇨ Insert Special Character, a submenu opens where a number of options provide you with features for handling special characters, as shown in Figure 16-6.

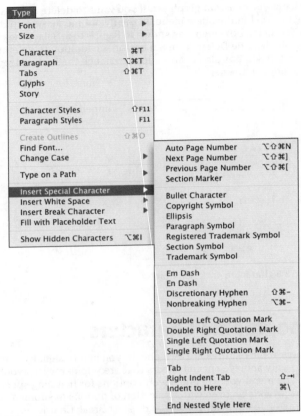

Figure 16-6: You find numerous special typographic features via the Type menu.

The submenu items available for Insert Special Character include the following:

✦ **Auto Page Number:** The keyboard shortcut for automatic page numbering is Alt+Shift+Ctrl+N (Windows) or Option+Shift+⌘+N (Mac). If you don't want to memorize the keyboard shortcut, you can use a menu command. To use the Auto Page Number command, open a master page, select a font and font style, and create a text frame. With the cursor blinking in the text frame, select the menu command. Automatic numbering is then applied to all pages associated with the master page. Although you often apply Auto Page Number to master pages, you aren't required to use it on master pages exclusively. You can also use it on regular document pages to number them individually.

✦ **Next Page Number:** The Next Page Number and Previous Page Number (see below) commands are helpful when you have blocks of text that start on one page and then continue on another page in your document (also known as "story jumps"). Where the text ends on one page, for example, you would want to inform the reader that it continues on another page with a "Continued on page X" notation (also known as a "jump line.") To do this, create a separate text frame that overlaps the text frame of the story you are jumping. Be sure to group these two text frames together so if you move the story, the jump line stays with it. Type **Continued on page**; then choose Type ⇨ Insert Special Character ⇨ Next Page Number. InDesign automatically inserts the "continued to" page number.

✦ **Previous Page Number:** This option works like Next Page Number, but instead of using a "continued to" page number, you use a "continued from" page number. Again, create a separate text frame that overlaps the text frame of the jumped part of the story. Type "Continued from page," then choose Type ⇨ Insert Special Character ⇨ Previous Page Number. InDesign automatically inserts the "continued from" page number. Again, you should group the text frames so the page reference stays with the story if you decide to move it.

✦ **Section Marker:** You can divide documents into sections using the Layout ⇨ Numbering and Section Options menu command. Once you create sections within a document, inserting the Section Marker inserts the number of the section at the cursor position.

✦ **Bullet Character:** The ability to insert special symbols with a menu command is particularly helpful to people who work in cross-platform environments and don't know the key combinations for certain characters. The bullet character inserts a bullet at the cursor insertion point.

✦ **Copyright Symbol (©):** Inserts the copyright symbol.

✦ **Ellipsis (. . .):** Inserts an ellipsis.

✦ **Paragraph Symbol (¶):** Inserts a paragraph symbol.

✦ **Registered Trademark Symbol (®):** Inserts a registered trademark symbol.

✦ **Section Symbol (§):** Inserts a symbol representing a new section.

✦ **Trademark Symbol (™):** Inserts a trademark symbol.

✦ **Em Dash (—):** Inserts an em dash.

✦ **En Dash (–):** Inserts an en dash.

✦ **Discretionary Hyphen:** Add a hyphen as desired by using this option.

✦ **Nonbreaking Hyphen:** Select this option when you don't want a hyphenated word to break to the next line.

✦ **Double Left Quotation Mark ("):** Inserts a double left quotation mark.

✦ **Double Right Quotation Mark ("):** Inserts a double right quotation mark.

✦ **Single Left Quotation Mark ('):** Inserts a single left quotation mark.

✦ **Single Right Quotation Mark ('):** Inserts a single right quotation mark.

✦ **Tab:** Has the same effect as pressing the Tab key.

✦ **Right Indent Tab:** Adds a tab indented from the right side of the text line.

✦ **Indent to Here:** Indents to the cursor position.

✦ **End Nested Style Here:** Ends a nested style at the cursor position.

Inserting white space characters

The next set of typographic controls you find in the Type menu are the spacing options. When you choose Type ➪ Insert White Space, a submenu offers commands for adding space between characters and words. The commands include the following:

✦ **Em Space:** Em spaces are equal in horizontal width to the vertical point size for a font. For example, in 18-point type, the em space is 18 points wide.

✦ **En Space:** En spaces are exactly one-half the width of an em space.

✦ **Flush Space:** You apply this option to fully justified paragraphs. A variable amount of space is added to the last line in a paragraph and justifies the last line of text.

✦ **Hair Space:** This option adds the smallest space between characters. It's ¼th the width of an em space.

✦ **Nonbreaking Space:** This option adds space equal to that of the Spacebar, but prevents the line from being broken at that point.

✦ **Thin Space:** One-eighth the width of an em space.

✦ **Figure Space:** The same space used for a numeric character in a font. This option is helpful when aligning numbers in columns.

✦ **Punctuation Space:** The same amount of space used for other punctuation marks such as commas, periods, colons, and exclamation marks.

Inserting break characters

Rounding out the options for using special typographic characters, you'll find a selection in the Type menu that controls line breaks. Choose Type ➪ Insert Break Character and the submenu items include the following:

✦ **Column Break:** When inserting a column break, text following the break flows to the next column in a multiple-column text frame. If text is set to a single-column frame, the text flows to the next frame in the thread.

✦ **Frame Break:** Flows text to the next frame in the text thread. If text is set to multiple columns and you insert a frame break in column 1, the text is flowed to the next frame thread, ignoring columns 2 and 3.

✦ **Page Break:** Flows text to the next page when text is threaded across pages.

✦ **Odd Page Break:** Flows text to the next odd-numbered page when following a thread.

✦ **Even Page Break:** Flows text to the next even-numbered page when following a thread.

✦ **Forced Line Break:** Forces a line break (same as pressing Shift+Enter/Return).

✦ **Paragraph Return:** Inserts a paragraph return (same as pressing Enter/Return).

Inserting Inline Graphics

You can automatically scroll text to separate columns, threads, and pages. Graphics placed in your layout in image frames do not follow the threading behavior of the text. This is a problem if you reformat your text and you need the graphics to stay connected to specific parts of the copy. Normally, you would have to move the graphic elements separately each time your text reflowed. However, if you use inline graphics, then the graphic is interpreted similar to the way text is interpreted and maintains its respective position within a given line of text.

Creating an inline graphic is easy. You simply select an object or image, cut it from a page, and paste the graphic back into a text frame with the cursor blinking at the spot where you want the object to appear. To see an example of this process, look over the following steps.

STEPS: Creating an Inline Graphic

1. **Place type within a frame.** Either place a body of text from a file or type a few lines of text.

2. **Cut a graphic from the document page.** Use an object imported from Illustrator, use the Glyphs palette, select a character, and convert the character to outlines, or draw an object in InDesign. Select the object and choose Edit ➪ Cut.

3. **Identify the insertion point in the text.** Place the cursor at the point where you want to insert the inline graphic in the text frame. Use the Type tool and wait for the blinking I-beam cursor to appear.

4. **Paste the graphic.** Choose Edit ➪ Paste. The graphic is now part of the text block and follows the same scrolling behavior as the line of text where it resides. Figure 16-7 shows the results of pasting a graphic in a line of text.

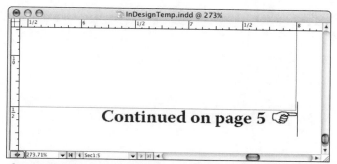

Figure 16-7: To place a graphic as an inline object, cut the object and click in a text block. Choose Edit ➪ Paste and the object is pasted at the cursor position.

Summary

✦ OpenType fonts support more than 65,000 glyphs in a given font. Opening the Glyphs palette in Illustrator or InDesign displays examples of all the glyphs contained within a selected font.

✦ InDesign allows you to create custom glyph sets where you can access frequently used characters in a single palette.

✦ InDesign has numerous options for accessing special typographic characters and functions. These include symbols, punctuation, white space options, line breaks, automatic page numbering, tab settings, and more.

✦ Inline graphics are inserted in text frames and scroll with the text as it is flowed through a frame or frame thread.

✦   ✦   ✦

Using Creative Suite and Microsoft

Importing Microsoft Word Documents

Whether it is copy for an InDesign layout, product descriptions for a GoLive Web page, or a marketing line you want to manipulate in Illustrator, you create most text on a word processor like Microsoft Word and import it into the CS applications. Although the CS applications handle type very well, they aren't designed to handle type from a design standpoint.

This chapter covers the crucial workflow step of importing text. Although there are several different word processors available, Microsoft Word is the most popular word processor available today, and it is used for all the examples in this chapter.

There are essentially two methods for importing text from Microsoft Word. One method uses the Clipboard and the Cut, Copy, and Paste features. The other method exports (or saves the Word document) in a format that you can easily import into the CS applications. Both Illustrator and InDesign open Word documents saved in the Word (DOC) format. After you import the text, you can easily move among any of the CS applications using the PDF format.

Importing a Word document into InDesign or Illustrator, not only moves text, but can also import the text styles.

Using the Clipboard

In Microsoft Word, you copy selected text to the Clipboard by choosing Edit ➪ Cut (⌘/Ctrl+X) or Edit ➪ Copy (⌘/Ctrl+C). You can then paste the text into the various CS applications by choosing Edit ➪ Paste (⌘/Ctrl+V). Text pasted into Illustrator and InDesign appears within a newly created text object, like that shown in Figure 17-1.

In addition to the standard Edit ➪ Paste menu command, Illustrator also includes Paste in Front (⌘/Ctrl+F) and Paste in Back (⌘/Ctrl+B) commands. These commands place the pasted text on top of (or behind) the currently selected object.

Figure 17-1: Text pasted into Illustrator from Microsoft Word

InDesign includes Paste Into (Alt+Ctrl+V on Windows; Option+⌘+V on the Mac) and Paste in Place (Alt+Shift+Ctrl+V on Windows; Option+Shift+⌘+V on the Mac) commands. You use the Paste Into command to mask an image by pasting into a converted outline. You cannot use this command on imported text. The Paste in Place command pastes the text in the same place as the original text object.

Cross-Reference   Masking images in InDesign using a converted outline is covered in Part III.

Text pasted into Illustrator and InDesign appears within a newly created text object unless you previously selected some text using the Type tool. If you selected text, then the pasted text replaces the selected text.

In addition to transporting text using the Clipboard, text that you select in Word and drag and drop in an Illustrator or InDesign document moves the text into the target application.

Maintaining formatting

Although text pasted into Illustrator maintains formatting, text pasted into InDesign, by default, does not maintain any formatting. However, InDesign includes a Preference setting that causes pasted text to maintain its formatting. You find this setting in the General panel of the Preferences dialog box, which you open by choosing InDesign/Edit ➪ Preferences ➪ General. The option is Preserve Text Attributes When Pasting, as shown in Figure 17-2.

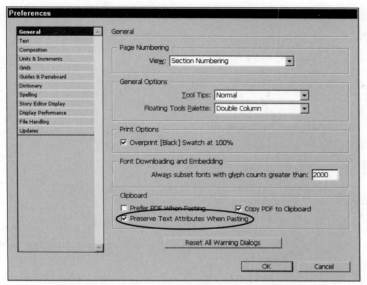

Figure 17-2: This option maintains formatting you paste from Microsoft Word.

Text pasted into GoLive from Microsoft Word also maintains formatting.

Missing fonts

If the text that you paste into Illustrator or InDesign from Microsoft Word is missing a font, a warning dialog box, like the one in Figure 17-3, appears listing the offending font. In addition to the warning dialog box, both applications list the missing font in brackets in the Control palette, and highlight the text that uses this font in pink, as shown in Figure 17-4.

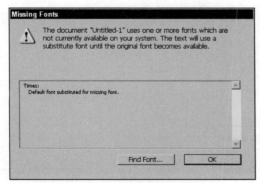

Figure 17-3: The Missing Fonts dialog box

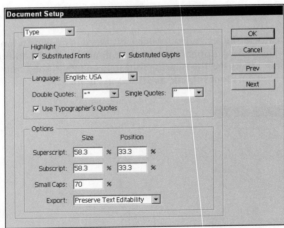

Figure 17-4: Pink highlighting identifies missing fonts.

If you choose Type ➪ Font, you'll find a Missing category that lists all the missing font faces and styles.

You enable the highlighting missing fonts in Illustrator in the Type panel of the Document Setup dialog box, shown in Figure 17-5. You open this dialog box by choosing File ➪ Document Setup (Alt+Ctrl+P on Windows; Option+⌘+P on the Mac). The Highlight Substituted Fonts and Highlight Substituted Glyphs options cause all text that uses a missing font to be highlighted pink.

Figure 17-5: Illustrator's Document Setup dialog box

Cross-Reference For more information on glyphs, see Chapter 16. Installing and locating missing fonts is covered in Chapter 13.

Exporting Text from Word

Part IV covers in-depth how to create text in the CS applications, but if you already have the text available in a Word documents, the easy workflow path is to export it from Word and import it into the CS applications.

Word doesn't include a File ➪ Export menu command, but you use the File ➪ Save As menu command to save the file into one of several different formats, including Rich Text Format (RTF) and Plain Text (TXT). In addition to these formats that are imported into most CS applications, Illustrator and InDesign can open and place native Word (DOC) files.

Caution   Although Word includes a File ➪ Save as Web Page menu command, Word adds some markup to the Web page content that might confuse GoLive and some Web browsers. The best approach is to import the Web-page text into GoLive using the Rich Text Format or the Plain Text format and let GoLive add the Web-page markup.

The difference between the Rich Text Format and Plain Text is that the former maintains any formatting within the text and the latter strips all formatting out.

Importing Text

Importing text into the various CS applications happens by opening a file saved from within Word into a CS application. The two most useful CS applications for doing this are Illustrator and InDesign. Both can open native Word documents (DOC), as well as files saved using the Rich Text Format (RTF) and Plain Text (TXT) formats.

Cross-Reference   Working with fonts and text is covered in Part IV.

Opening Word documents in Illustrator

You open Word documents natively within Illustrator by choosing File ➪ Open (⌘/Ctrl+O). In the file dialog box that appears, select the Microsoft Word (DOC) file type. This format includes support for files created using Word 97, 98, 2000, and 2002. All formatting in the Word document is maintained as the file is imported into Illustrator.

After you select and open a file, another dialog box of options opens, as shown in Figure 17-6. This dialog box lets you specify whether to import the Table of Contents Text, Footnotes/ Endnotes, and Index Text. You can also select Remove Text Formatting.

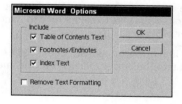

Figure 17-6: The Microsoft Word Options dialog box

If the fonts used in the Word document are not available to Illustrator, a Font Problems dialog box opens, shown in Figure 17-7, listing the fonts in question.

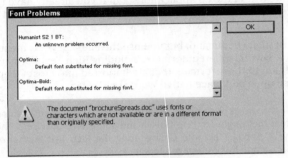

Figure 17-7: The Font Problems dialog box

Opening and placing text documents in Illustrator

Text files saved using the Rich Text Format (RTF) and Plain Text (TXT) formats are also opened in Illustrator with the File ⇨ Open menu command. Rich Text Format files use the same Options dialog box as the Word (DOC) files, but Plain Text files present a different dialog box of Options, as shown in Figure 17-8.

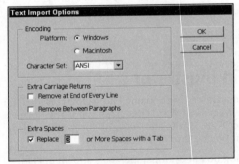

Figure 17-8: The Text Import Options dialog box

The Text Import Options dialog box lets you specify the encoding platform as Windows or Mac and which Character Set to use. The dialog box also has options to select how to handle extra carriage returns and to replace a specified number of spaces with a tab.

If you want to import a Word document into an existing Illustrator document, choose File ⇨ Place. This command opens the Word or text document into the current Illustrator document.

Placing Word documents into InDesign

The File ➪ Place (⌘/Ctrl+D) menu command in InDesign opens a file dialog box where you select Microsoft Word and Excel files that you want to open and place into the current document. Once you select a file and click the Place button, the mouse cursor changes to indicate that it is holding the imported text. To place the imported text, you need to click the location in the document where you want to place the upper-left corner of the imported text.

Cross-Reference
Importing Excel data as tables is covered in Chapter 19.

The Place dialog box, shown in Figure 17-9, includes a Show Import Options check box and a Replace Selected Item check box. Holding down the Shift key while clicking the Open button forces the Options dialog box to appear.

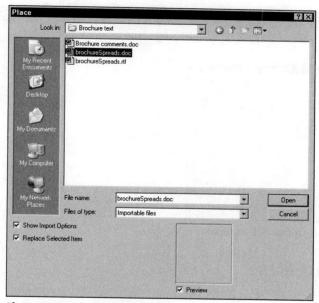

Figure 17-9: The Place dialog box

Note
You use only the Preview option to show previews of images and PDF files. You cannot preview text files with this option.

The Microsoft Word Import Options dialog box, shown in Figure 17-10, includes the same features as mentioned previously for Illustrator including the ability to specify the inclusion of table of contents text, footnotes and endnotes, and index text. It also offers several formatting options — you can select the Use Typographer's Quotes check box and the Remove Text and Table Formatting check box, as well as select from the Convert Tables To drop-down list and the Manual Page Breaks drop-down list. For RTF files, the same options are available.

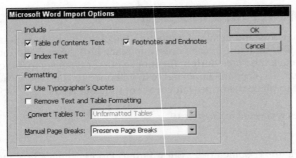

Figure 17-10: The Microsoft Word Import Options dialog box

Plain Text files open the Text Import Options dialog box, shown in Figure 17-11. This dialog box lets you select a character set, platform, and dictionary. It also offers options for handling extra carriage returns, replacing spaces with tabs, and using typographer's quotes.

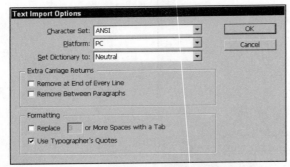

Figure 17-11: The Text Import Options dialog box

Drag-and-drop text files

Dragging and dropping Word files from the Finder (Mac) or from Windows Explorer also opens text into Illustrator, InDesign, or GoLive.

Importing Word documents in Photoshop

Of all the Creative Suite applications, Photoshop is one of the more popular. Many designers are so comfortable with Photoshop that they choose to create layouts including the extensive use of text in Photoshop rather than InDesign or Illustrator. For these designers, this section covers importing Microsoft Word into Photoshop.

If you copy and paste text from Word into Photoshop, it appears as a graphic image with all its formatting in place. This is fine, but it requires that you make all the edits in Word, which leaves you with only Word's design features.

A better way to handle the import process is to create a text layer in Photoshop by dragging a bounding box with the Type tool before pasting the Word text. With the text bounding box selected, the pasted text appears as editable text in the text bounding box. The drawback to this approach is that all the formatting is stripped from the Word text, but you can still use Photoshop's type formatting tools. Figure 17-12 shows some text that has been imported into a Photoshop text object from Word.

Tip If you hold down the Option/Alt key while dragging with the Type tool, a dialog box appears where you can enter exact width and height values for the paragraph.

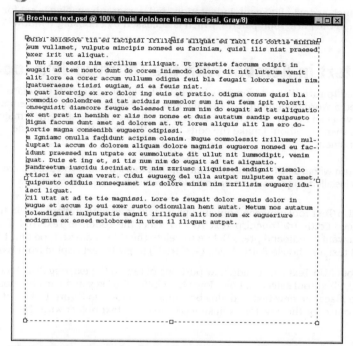

Figure 17-12: You can edit text from Word in a text object in Photoshop.

You can also import Word text into a Point text object. You create Point text objects by simply clicking in the document rather than dragging an area. Be warned that importing text into a Point text object won't limit the text within an area but places an entire line of text (up to a paragraph return) on a single line. All paragraph returns in the pasted text wraps the text to a new line.

Cross-Reference More details on creating text layers and Point text objects are in Part IV.

Formatting imported text in Photoshop

When you import text into a Photoshop text layer, you use the Type tool to select and edit the text. Clicking once on the text object text with the Type tool selects the text layer. When the text layer is selected, you can drag with the mouse over the text to select words or characters. The selected text is highlighted. Clicking twice selects a word, clicking three times selects an entire line of text, clicking four times selects an entire paragraph, and clicking five times selects all the text in the text layer.

Pressing the Delete key deletes any selected text, and typing new text replaces the selected text with the newly typed text. Any characters that you add to the text use the same formatting as the existing text area.

Selected text is formatted using the Character palette, which is opened by choosing Window ➪ Character. With this palette, you can change the text font, style, size, leading, kerning, scale, color, and anti-aliasing.

Paragraph formatting such as text alignment, indentation, and paragraph spacing is set for the selected paragraph in the Paragraph palette, which is accessed by choosing Window ➪ Paragraph.

Pasting Word text in Acrobat with the TouchUp Text tool

Acrobat is typically used to turn Word documents into PDF files by choosing File ➪ Create PDF. If you've converted a Word document to a PDF file and then found some minimal edits that need to be made, you can use the TouchUp Text tool to edit the PDF document. If major text edits are required, then you should make the edits within Word and then you should regenerate the PDF document.

Caution   You can only edit text within a PDF file with the TouchUp Text tool if the font you used to create the PDF file is installed on your system or embedded within the PDF document.

When using the TouchUp Text tool, you can copy and paste text from within Word. To do this, choose Tools ➪ Advanced Editing ➪ TouchUp Text Tool to select the TouchUp Text tool. Then select the text that you want to edit and press Delete to delete the selected text, type new text to replace the selected text, or choose Edit ➪ Paste (⌘/Ctrl+V) to paste text copied from Word.

You can also use the TouchUp Text tool to add new portions of text to the existing PDF document. With the TouchUp Text tool selected, hold down the Option/Ctrl key and click the position where you want to place the new text. A dialog box appears, shown in Figure 17-13, letting you select a font face to use for the new text. Clicking OK creates a text object with "New Text" selected in it.

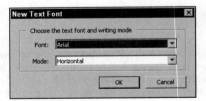

Figure 17-13: The New Text Font dialog box lets you select a font face.

With the new text object selected, you can type new text to replace this text or paste text from Word by choosing Edit ➪ Paste. Text pasted from Word loses its formatting and uses the selected font face. The pasted text also loses all its line returns, but you can easily place these back in with the TouchUp Text tool. The line returns are easy to identify because they're replaced with a character (often just a simple square). Selecting each square character with the TouchUp Text tool and pressing the Enter key re-formats the pasted text.

If you need to move the newly created text object, you can select the TouchUp Object tool by choosing Tools ➪ Advanced Editing. This tool lets you select and move text objects by clicking and dragging with the mouse.

This process requires some additional work, but if you don't have the original document, then it's worth the trouble if you need to add some text. Figure 17-14 shows a PDF file where some new text has been pasted from Word using the Option/Ctrl+TouchUp Text tool. When the text was pasted, it all appeared on a single line. Some paragraph returns have been added using the TouchUp Text tool to show more of the text.

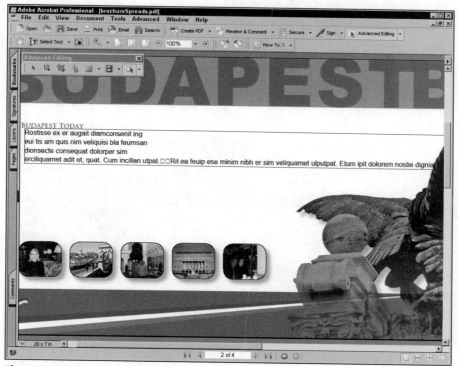

Figure 17-14: You can paste new text into an existing PDF file using the TouchUp Text tool.

Pasting Word text into Acrobat notes and form fields

When reviewing and commenting a PDF file, you can create notes with the Note tool. Choose Tools ➪ Commenting ➪ Note Tool to select this tool and then click and drag at the location in the PDF document where you want to place a note. A note box appears that includes the creator's name and the time and date. Figure 17-15 shows several commenting notes. Typing enters the text for these note boxes, or you may paste the note text from Word by choosing Edit ➪ Paste.

In addition to pasting text in note boxes, you can also paste Word text into form fields that appear within the PDF document. You can use Tab and Shift+Tab to move forward and backward between form fields on a page. When a form field is selected, you may type the text or paste text from Word.

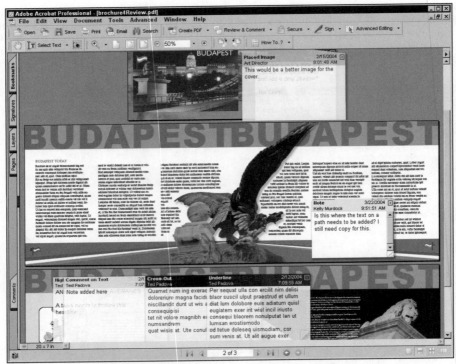

Figure 17-15: You can add Note boxes to a PDF document with the Note tool.

Importing Styles

When importing text files into InDesign, the styles are also imported. All imported styles from Microsoft Word appear in the Paragraph Styles palette using the same style name. The imported styles are also identified by a small disk icon to the right of the style's name, as shown in Figure 17-16.

Cross-Reference

Using text styles in Illustrator and InDesign is covered in Chapter 14.

You can prevent the styles from being imported by enabling the Remove Text and Table Formatting option in the Microsoft Word Import Options dialog box. If the Preserve Text Attributes When Pasting option in the General panel of the Preferences dialog box is enabled, styles are also imported when text is pasted from Word.

Note

If the imported style has the same name as an existing InDesign style, the style is not imported from Word, and the text is formatted using the InDesign style.

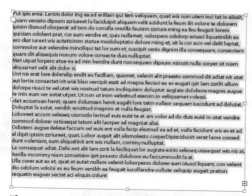

Figure 17-16: A Word document is imported into InDesign with all its styles.

Editing imported styles

In the Paragraph Styles palette, click on a style to select it. Then choose Style Options from the palette menu (or you could right-click on the style and choose Edit from the pop-up menu). This action opens the Paragraph Style Options dialog box, shown in Figure 17-17. Using these options, you set the paragraph formatting style options.

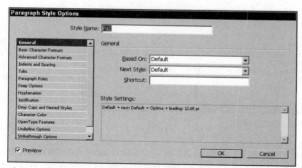

Figure 17-17: The Paragraph Style Options dialog box

Deleting imported styles

The Paragraph Styles palette menu includes several useful commands. When a layout is complete, use the Select All Unused menu command to instantly select all the styles that aren't referenced in the document. These styles, whether native or imported, are then deleted with the Delete Style menu command. Deleting unused styles is an easy way to clean up a document, especially if text has been imported from Word.

Working with Imported Text

As a final working example of the process of importing and using Microsoft Word documents, we'll walk you through the steps involved. These steps are similar for both Illustrator and InDesign, with only slight differences between the two.

STEPS: Importing Microsoft Word Text into InDesign

1. **Open the DOC document in Word.** Figure 17-18 shows a Word document that includes all the text for the brochure. Each section of text is separated by a section break. Styles have been applied to each. Using the features of Word, the document has been spell-checked and grammar-checked, and all edits are ready to be moved to InDesign.

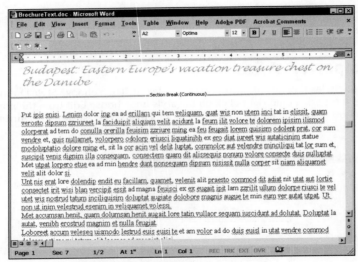

Figure 17-18: Open a Word document.

2. **Save the Word document.** Choose File ➪ Save As in Word and save the file using the default DOC file format. This format includes all the referenced styles. After you save the file, close the Word file by choosing File ➪ Close. If you forget to close the Word document, InDesign opens an alert dialog box stating "This file is already in use by another application," when you try to place the Word document in InDesign.

3. **Open the current InDesign file.** If you already have a start on the layout, open the existing file in InDesign by choosing File ➪ Open.

4. **Place the text file in InDesign.** Choose File ➪ Place (⌘/Ctrl+D) to open the Place dialog box, shown in Figure 17-19. Make sure Show Import Options is enabled; then select the Word document and click the Open button.

5. **Set the import options.** In the Microsoft Word Import Options dialog box, shown in Figure 17-20, you can disable the Table of Contents Text, Footnotes and Endnotes, and Index Text options because none of these elements are included in the original document. Also, make sure the Remove Text and Table Formatting option remains disabled, or the text styles aren't imported. Click OK to proceed.

Figure 17-19: The Place dialog box

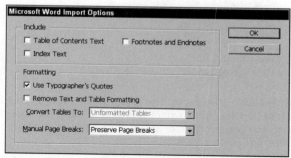

Figure 17-20: Several of the Include options are disabled because they aren't included in the original document.

6. **Locate the missing fonts.** When the import options are set, the import process proceeds and a Missing Fonts dialog box appears, as shown in Figure 17-21. The dialog box lists all the fonts used in the Word document that aren't available to InDesign. Click the Find Font button to open the Find Font dialog box, shown in Figure 17-22. Using this dialog box, locate and change the missing fonts. The Find Next button locates the first instance of text in the InDesign document that uses the specified font. Click Done when you're finished.

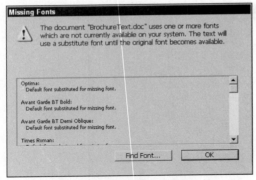

Figure 17-21: The Missing Fonts dialog box

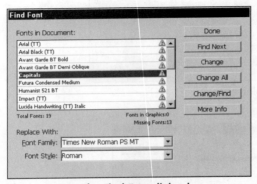

Figure 17-22: The Find Font dialog box

7. **Place the text into the InDesign document.** The cursor holds the imported text. Click at the location in the InDesign document where you want to place the imported text. Notice how the Word styles have been imported into InDesign and now appear in the Paragraph Styles palette, as shown in Figure 17-23.

Figure 17-23: Imported text and styles used within InDesign

Summary

✦ A word processor like Microsoft Word makes a good workflow piece for creating importable text.

✦ Text in Word may be easily copied and pasted into most of the CS applications.

✦ Illustrator and InDesign can open and place existing Word documents using Word's native DOC file format. The Rich Text Format (RTF) and Plain Text (TXT) file formats are also available.

✦ Text styles defined in Microsoft Word are also imported and show up in the Paragraph Styles palette in InDesign.

✦   ✦   ✦

Exporting Text to Microsoft Word

Although Creative Suite includes many programs that can work with text (which you can learn about in Part IV), a word processor is not included as part of the suite. Text for design purposes is very different from text produced with a word processor, but there are times in your design workflow when you want to export text from CS applications into a word processor.

Writing copy is often much easier in a word processor because its features focus on manipulating text rather than design. For example, Microsoft Word includes a grammar checker that benefits longer sections of text. You can take advantage of this feature by exporting text to a word processor, checking its grammar, and then importing it again.

Of the available word processors, Microsoft Word is the most popular. Most word processors available today have similar features, so we focus only on Word in this chapter. We also cover the text-export features found in the Creative Suite applications that enable you to move text to Microsoft Word.

Exporting Text

The chapters in Part IV focused on creating text within the Creative Suite applications, and the last chapter covered importing text created in Microsoft Word. This chapter completes the topic by discussing how to export text from the various CS applications to Microsoft Word.

Cross-Reference   Part IV covers creating text within the CS applications. Importing text from Word is covered in Chapter 17.

Before we discuss the techniques used in exporting text, we need to discuss the purpose behind exporting text. The first question to ask yourself is this: With all the power found in Creative Suite, why would you want to export text to an application like Microsoft Word? The answer lies in Word's ability to do what it does best — create text documents.

Recognizing the advantages of Word

Many of the features found in Word are out of place in the Creative Suite applications. Here is a list of some of the Microsoft Word features of which you can take advantage when working with large portions of text:

✦ **Outline mode:** Word can view documents in several different modes including Normal, Web Layout, Print Layout, and Outline. The layout modes are a far cry from the features found in Illustrator, Photoshop, and InDesign, but the Outline mode is very helpful for organizing a table of contents or a large structured list of items. In Word's Outline mode, you can quickly promote and demote headings and rearrange entire structures by dragging.

✦ **Headers, footers, and footnotes:** Word's ability to automatically create and adjust headers, footers, and footnotes is much easier to use than anything you find in Creative Suite.

✦ **AutoCorrect:** Word's AutoCorrect feature is very helpful as you type long sections of text. Because this feature can automatically capitalize the first letter of a sentence makes it worth the trouble to export the text into Word. With some fine-tuning, the AutoCorrect feature saves many keystrokes, allowing you to finish a document in less time.

✦ **Interactive spelling and grammar check:** Word underlines all misspelled words in red and all grammatical errors in green as you type. This immediate feedback lets you fix the problems as you type, which offers a benefit over the spell-check features found in the CS applications.

✦ **Multi-language support:** Word's ability to create documents with co-mingled languages makes doing translation work a joy.

This short list isn't exhaustive, nor does it do justice to the plethora of features found in Word, but it gives you a brief idea of the types of features that you can take advantage of by exporting to Word.

Identifying exporting methods

All the CS applications deal with text, and all can export text to Word. There are essentially three different methods for exporting text from the various CS applications:

✦ **Copy and paste to the Clipboard:** Most CS applications can take advantage of this feature. By selecting text objects or portions of text, you can cut (⌘/Ctrl+X) or copy (⌘/Ctrl+C) them to the system Clipboard and then paste (⌘/Ctrl+V) them into the Word document.

✦ **Using an export command:** Several applications include a File ➪ Export command that you can use to export the text from the source application to Word.

✦ **Save to an importable file:** The final method is to save the text using a text-file format (such as TXT or RTF) that you can import into Word.

Each of these methods has its advantages and disadvantages.

Selecting text

Before exporting any text to Word, you need to locate and select the text that you want to move. For most CS applications, you select text using the Type tool. To select text, just click the Type tool and drag over the text that you want to select. The selected text is highlighted.

Illustrator and InDesign use text objects. If a text object is selected with the Selection tool, the borders that make up the text object are highlighted in blue and all text contained within the text object is selected. If multiple text objects are selected, all text contained within the selected text objects is selected.

Exporting formatting

Through the exporting process, the text formatting is often lost. Some techniques maintain formatting and others do not. Copy and pasting via the Clipboard typically discards formatting. Exporting text using the TXT file format also discards formatting. If you need to keep the formatting intact, look to export the text using the Rich Text Format (RTF), which maintains the formatting during export.

Tip   If you lose your formatting during an export, keep track of the changes that you make to the text in Word, and manually enter those changes into the formatted text in the CS application.

In some cases, the export command offers you the chance to specify the font standard. If you have a choice, use the OpenType font standard, which has the same font file for both Windows and Mac computers. This lets you maintain your fonts as you export them, regardless of the system to which you export them.

Cross-Reference   You can learn more about the OpenType font standard in Chapter 13.

Using the Clipboard

The easiest way to export smaller pieces of text from the CS applications is to use the Clipboard. Although the Clipboard can handle large sections of text, it relies on the amount of available memory.

The Office Clipboard can copy many pieces of text to the Clipboard at a time (up to 24 by default). You can then select these different pieces from the Office Clipboard and paste them into the current Word document. You can make the Office Clipboard, shown at the right in Figure 18-1, appear by choosing Edit ➪ Office Clipboard or by pressing ⌘/Ctrl+C twice. After you select text, simply click on it to paste it into the current document. Right-click on the text to reveal a pop-up menu with a Delete option.

Note   The Office Clipboard menu is a Windows-only feature.

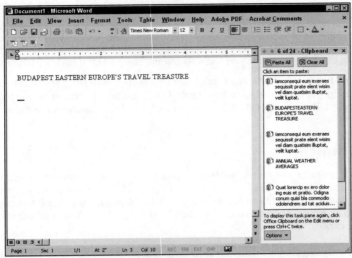

Figure 18-1: Items on the Office Clipboard are placed within Word simply by clicking on them.

Moving Illustrator, Photoshop, and GoLive text into Word

Selected text within Illustrator is copied to the Clipboard by choosing Edit ➪ Cut (⌘/Ctrl+X) or Edit ➪ Copy (⌘/Ctrl+X). This moves the selected text to the Clipboard. From the Clipboard, text is pasted into Word by choosing Edit ➪ Paste (⌘/Ctrl+V).

Caution   You can only paste text that you cut or copy from an Illustrator document into Word as unformatted text. Text you copy from InDesign and Acrobat maintains its formatting.

Word also includes an Edit ➪ Paste Special menu command that opens the dialog box shown in Figure 18-2. This dialog box identifies the source application and allows you to paste the Clipboard contents as unformatted text, several image formats, or unformatted Unicode text. Text that you save on the Clipboard cannot be saved as an image using the Paste Special command.

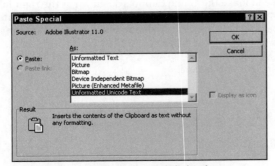

Figure 18-2: The Paste Special dialog box identifies the source application and offers several paste choices based on that application.

Object Linking and Embedding (Windows only)

Another exporting option is to create a link between the content created in a CS application and Microsoft Word using a technology known as Object Linking and Embedding (OLE). However, object linking works only with image content, not with text.

CS applications—including Photoshop, Illustrator, and InDesign—can act as an OLE 2.0 server. This allows you to copy and paste a piece of content into Word using the Paste Special menu command. This action causes the Paste Special dialog box to appear with a Paste Link option, which lets you paste an object as a recognized CS object. After you paste the object, you can double-click on the object in the Word document to load it within the native CS application for more editing. Changes made to the object are automatically forwarded back to the object in the Word document, thereby keeping the two in sync. You can force the documents to update by choosing File ⇨ Update.

 Caution Be aware that any text that you export to Word loses its positional constraints, such as wrapping around images or type on a path.

You move text in Photoshop to Word using the same Clipboard technique discussed for Illustrator in this section. The only exception is that you must select the text using Photoshop's Type tool. You also move text in GoLive using the Clipboard without formatting.

Moving InDesign text to Word

You move formatted text in InDesign to Microsoft Word using the Copy and Paste features. The standard Copy and Paste features retain the formatting created in InDesign.

 Caution In order to copy text in InDesign to the Clipboard, you need to select the Type tool and drag over the text. You can't just select the text object as you can in Illustrator.

Within Word, you can also choose Edit ⇨ Paste Special. This action opens the Paste Special dialog box, shown in Figure 18-3, which includes the same options as those for Illustrator, except it can handle RTF text.

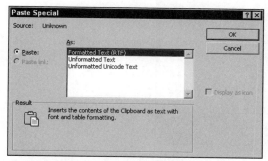

Figure 18-3: The Paste Special dialog box offers several options for pasting text as formatted text, unformatted text, or unformatted Unicode text.

Moving Acrobat text to Word

You select text in Acrobat using the Select Text tool. You can then cut or copy the selected text to the Clipboard by choosing Edit ➪ Cut (⌘/Ctrl+X) or Edit ➪ Copy (⌘/Ctrl+C). Acrobat also offers an option to copy an entire file to the Clipboard (also in the Edit menu).

The Edit ➪ Paste Special command in Word opens the same dialog box as the one shown in Figure 18-3, including the option to paste as formatted text.

Using Export Menu Commands

When it comes to moving entire documents, the Clipboard isn't the best choice. Instead, you should rely on the export menu commands, typically found in the File menu. These export commands let you save CS documents to a format that is easily imported into Word.

Caution   Be aware that text in Photoshop is exported via the Clipboard only.

Exporting Illustrator text

You export text from Illustrator by choosing File ➪ Export and using the TXT format, but be aware that you lose all formatting applied to the text in Illustrator. All text included in an Illustrator document is exported to a single text file by choosing File ➪ Export. If you select a text object, multiple text objects, or text within a text object, only the selected text exports.

The File ➪ Export menu command opens an Export dialog box, like the one shown in Figure 18-4. The Save as Type pull-down menu includes many different file formats that you can use to export the existing document, but only the TXT format makes the text editable within Word.

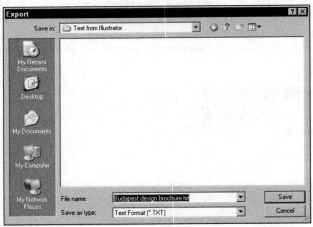

Figure 18-4: The Export dialog box

After clicking the Export (Mac) or Save (Windows) button, another dialog box, shown in Figure 18-5, opens. This dialog box lets you specify the Platform as PC or Mac, as well as the Encoding standard to use. The Encoding options are Default Platform and Unicode. If the text you're exporting includes any foreign text or any special glyphs, use the Unicode Encoding option.

Note

The File ➪ Export command exports all visible text objects, even if the text within those text areas isn't visible. However, if hidden text object, are not exported.

Figure 18-5: The Text Export Options dialog box

When the exported text file is opened in Word, the File Conversion dialog box appears, shown in Figure 18-6, if an encoding standard other than the default platform is used. This dialog box includes a Preview window that shows the text before you open it.

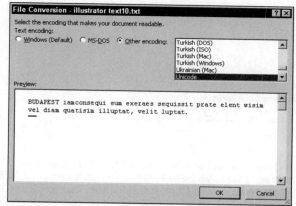

Figure 18-6: The File Conversion dialog box

Caution

Illustrator includes tight integration with Microsoft Office using the File ➪ Save for Microsoft Office menu command. Be aware that this command saves the Illustrator document as a PNG image file that you can import into Word, but you can't edit any of the text.

Exporting text from InDesign

InDesign includes an Export command under the File menu that exports formatted text to a number of different formats. To export text, you must first select the text within a text object using the Type tool. If you don't select specific text, the Rich Text Format and Text Only options are not available as file types in the Export dialog box.

Note

When exporting from InDesign, each story exports as a separate document.

Batch-converting files in Word

If you have a large number of documents that you've exported to Rich Text Format and that you want to convert to Word documents, you can use Word's Batch Conversion Wizard. To access this wizard in Word, choose File ➪ New (⌘/Ctrl+N), and click on the General Templates link. In the Templates dialog box that opens, select the Other Documents tab and double-click on the Batch Conversion Wizard icon.

This action launches the Conversion Wizard, shown in the figure. Following the wizard steps, you can select the format to convert from and the format to convert to along with Source and Destination directories. The following figure shows the Conversion Wizard dialog box, which walks you through the batch-conversion process.

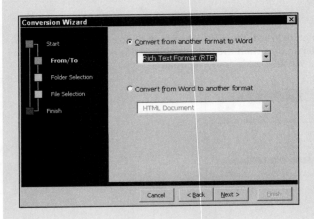

Choosing File ➪ Export in InDesign gives you the options to export the current file using the following formats: Adobe InDesign Tagged Text, Adobe PDF, EPS, InDesign Interchange, JPEG, Rich Text Format (RTF), SVG, SVG Compressed, Text Only, and XML. Note that only the RTF format and the Text Only format are used to import text into Word

If you export text from InDesign using a format other than RTF or Text Only, the file includes a lot of additional mark-up information that you probably don't want to see. For example, Figure 18-7 shows the File Conversion dialog box that opens in Word when an InDesign document exported using the SVG format is opened. Notice in the Preview pane how the XML syntax is visible. If you scroll down further in the document, you'll find a lot of gibberish that Word was unsuccessful in converting.

Exporting text from Acrobat

Choosing File ➪ Save As from within Acrobat lets you save the current PDF file using a number of different formats, many of which are suitable for moving text to Word including Word's default format (DOC). The Rich Text Format (RTF) and Text Only (TXT) formats are options also.

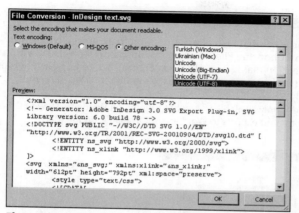

Figure 18-7: You can use Word to see the raw XML exported from InDesign.

Note

By default, any images contained within a PDF file that you save as a Word document is saved using the JPEG format. However, you can select the PNG format in the Settings dialog box if you prefer.

In Acrobat's file dialog box, you can click the Settings button, which opens the Save As Settings dialog box. The Save As DOC Settings dialog box is shown in Figure 18-8. The Settings dialog box for RTF is the same as that for the DOC format.

Figure 18-8: The Save As DOC Settings dialog box

In the Settings dialog box, you can choose to include comments and/or images. You can also downsample the image resolutions, which is a good idea if you're exporting to Word to check just the text. You may also want to keep the text files small by specifying Grayscale as the Colorspace. PDF files that were saved in Acrobat using the RTF format that are subsequently imported into Word are easy to identify because each piece of content is separated from the others by a section break.

Exporting comments from Acrobat

In addition to moving text to Word, Acrobat also offers an option to export all comments in the Acrobat document to Word. Choosing File ➪ Export Comments to Word from within Acrobat causes a warning/information dialog box, shown in Figure 18-9, to appear. The same menu command is also available in the Document ➪ Export Comments to Word menu.

Note   Exporting comments to Word is only available in Acrobat running on Windows XP with Office 2002 or greater installed. Comment exports to Word are not available on the Mac.

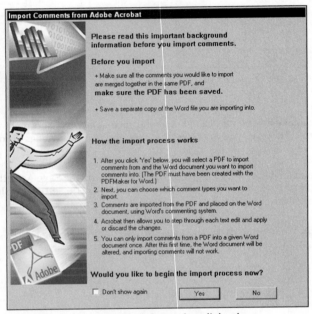

Figure18-9: This warning/information dialog box

    Before you can export comments to Word, you must be certain to use the proper comment tools. The Text Edit tools are designed to mark text for insertions, deletions, underlines, strikethroughs, and so on that are exported to Word. If you know that you're going to export your comments to Word, be certain to inform all users in your workflow to use these tools. Inasmuch as Mac users can't export comments to Word, the Text Edit tools are available in Acrobat on the Mac and comments you make with these tools can be exported to Word from Acrobat running on Windows XP.

Cross-Reference   For more information on using commenting tools, including the Text Edit tools, see Chapter 22.

Using this menu command opens Word and presents the Import Comments from Adobe Acrobat dialog box, shown in Figure 18-10. Selecting a source PDF file and a destination DOC file and clicking Continue moves all the comments from the Acrobat file to the Word file. This dialog box also gives you options to export All Comments, All Comments with Checkmarks, or the Text Edits Only. The Text Edits Only option includes only the text that has been edited with the Commenting toolbar. You can also select to turn on Word's Track Changes feature.

Note　The Exporting Comments to Word command can also be initiated from within Word using the Adobe Comments ⇨ Import Comments from Acrobat menu command. This command uses the same dialog boxes as the command in Acrobat.

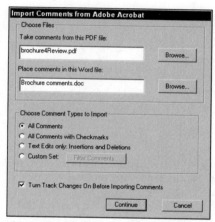

Figure 18-10: The Import Comments from Adobe Acrobat dialog box

Batch-converting files in Acrobat

You can also use Acrobat to convert a large number of Acrobat files to Word or RTF files using the Batch Sequences dialog box. You can access this dialog box (which is available only within Acrobat Professional) by choosing Advanced ⇨ Batch Processing.

The Batch Sequences dialog box, shown in the figure, includes a predefined batch command called Save All as RTF. Selecting this command and clicking the Run Sequence button executes the command, allowing you to select the files you want to convert. The Batch Sequence dialog box includes a number of predefined commands, but you can also create a new sequence of commands or edit an existing one.

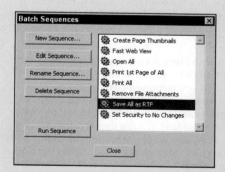

Clicking the New Sequence or Edit Sequence buttons lets you create a different set of commands for execution. For more information on using the Batch Sequence commands, see Chapter 28.

The dialog box shown in Figure 18-11 opens if the import has been successful. It tells you the number of placed comments.

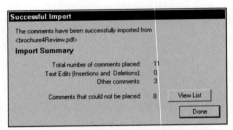

Figure 18-11: The Successful Import dialog box shows the results of the import.

After you move the comments to Word, you can use the Acrobat Comments menu to review the changes, accept or delete all changes, and enable the Reviewing toolbar.

Dynamic Text Editing

Exporting text from one of the CS programs is typically an exercise where you need to get copy back to Microsoft Word, create changes in the copy, and import the text back to your original design. The most likely candidates for this activity are Illustrator and InDesign. Unless you want to burden yourself with clumsy typesetting tools and extraordinary file sizes, you'll stay away from Photoshop.

Reintroducing type in an existing design can mean quite a bit of work. If the edits are extensive, you may need to delete long passages of text and then reformat pages in InDesign after importing the edited text. For Illustrator files, you only have to deal with single pages, but the complexity of the design could be quite complicated and take some time to rework the text.

Ideally, you're best bet is to recompose a layout when you need to make major edits. However, in some circumstances, you may have moderate to light modifications to make in layouts. If you exported documents to PDF and need to make text changes, you need to return to the original authoring program, make your edits, and re-create the PDF document. In some workflows, this is a simple task, especially if all the native files are easily accessible. However, if you only have a PDF document and don't have access to the native application document, you may want to use another method by editing text and let the text edits dynamically change the PDF file.

Dynamic text editing is handled in Adobe Illustrator when text is targeted for editing from within Acrobat. You start in Acrobat and select the body of text you want to edit with the TouchUp Object tool. Click on the text line to be edited or marquee a paragraph, multiple paragraphs, or an entire page. When the text is selected, open a context menu and choose Edit Object. Alternately, you can press Option/Alt and double-click on the selected objects. This action launches Illustrator CS and opens the selected text in a document window. Unfortunately, the text is broken up in Illustrator and all paragraph formatting including word wrap is lost. To reform the paragraphs, select all the text and click the Type tool in the document page at the same location where the first character in the first line of text was before you cut it. When the I-beam cursor starts blinking, choose Edit ➪ Paste. The text may need a little tweaking, but the paragraph formatting including word wrap is regained.

To update a PDF document after making such edits in Illustrator, choose File ➪ Save. Be certain you don't use Save As and write the file using a new filename. The current document has a link to the PDF file. When you choose Save and return to Acrobat, the text is dynamically updated.

Caution Be certain you have all the type fonts used in the original document loaded on your system before attempting to edit text externally in Illustrator. Also, check your work very carefully. Some edits may not be accurate, especially when you attempt to edit text with transparency and other forms of stylized fonts.

This process seems a little complicated, but after you've made a few text edits, you won't find it difficult to repeat. To illustrate the process further, look over the following steps where text is edited in Illustrator and dynamically updated in Acrobat.

STEPS: Dynamically Updating Text in PDF Documents

1. **Open a PDF document in Acrobat.** In Figure 18-12, a document is opened in Acrobat. The type on a path needs to be edited for text changes, eliminating the drop shadow, and changing the text color. You could try to edit the text in Acrobat, but with text on a path, the results can often be unsatisfactory. Furthermore, eliminating the drop shadow can't be accomplished using the TouchUp Text tool. A document like this needs to have the text edited in an external editor.

Figure 18-12: Open a document in Acrobat where you want to edit text.

2. **Select the text needing editing.** Selecting the text you want to edit can at times be a challenge. You can edit the entire page, but often you'll find it best to select just the text you want to edit. In this example, it makes sense to select the text columns and the

text on a path together because it makes the task of selecting the text on a path much easier. To select the text shown in Figure 18-13, marquee through the text with the TouchUp Object tool. If you select other objects not needed for the edits, press the Shift key and click on selected objects to deselect them.

Figure 18-13: You select multiple objects with the TouchUp Object tool.

3. **Open the text in Illustrator.** From a context menu, open the selected text. Choose Edit Objects from the menu commands, as shown in Figure 18-14. Alternately, you can press Option/Alt and double-click the selected text. (Be certain the TouchUp Object tool is used with either the context menu or the double mouse click.) Acrobat initiates the Illustrator CS launch and the selected text is opened in a new document window.

Note   Depending on how your text was formatted, you may see some warning dialog boxes open, informing you that tags must be eliminated and the appearance of the page may appear different. Click Yes in the dialog boxes and the file eventually opens in Illustrator.

4. **Select all the text.** Press ⌘/Ctrl+A to select all. Notice the selected objects in Figure 18-15. For the text columns, the selected text is broken and Illustrator interprets each line of text as a separate paragraph. For the text on a path, the text is broken at each character, making the line of text very difficult to edit.

5. **Hide the text that won't be edited.** In this example, the text columns won't be edited. To eliminate the text from view so you can easily work with only the text you want to edit, click the text and press ⌘/Ctrl+3. The keyboard shortcut hides selected text. Continue selecting and hiding text until only the text to be edited remains in view.

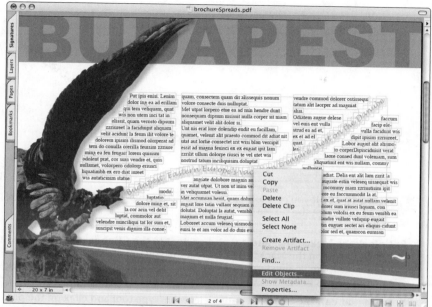

Figure 18-14: Choose Edit Objects to launch Illustrator.

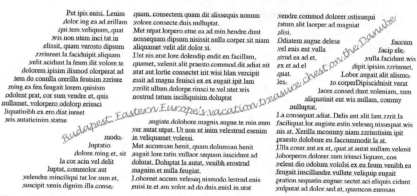

Figure 18-15: Select all objects and you can easily see where text is broken up.

6. **Lock the text in view.** Press ⌘/Ctrl+A to select all text and press ⌘/Ctrl+2 to lock the selected text. The text is temporarily locked so you won't disturb it while creating a path.

7. **Draw a new path to match the path of the existing text.** Select the Pen tool and draw a path following the same general path shape as the text along the path you want to edit. In Figure 18-16, you can see a path drawn while the view in Illustrator is set to Outline view.

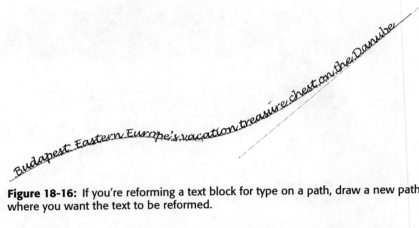

Figure 18-16: If you're reforming a text block for type on a path, draw a new path where you want the text to be reformed.

8. **Unlock the locked text and cut and paste it to the Clipboard.** Press Ctrl+Alt+2 (⌘+Option+2 on the Mac) to unlock text. As you unlock the text, the text is selected, while the stroke you just created is deselected. Choose Edit ➪ Copy or press ⌘/Ctrl+X to cut the selected text to the Clipboard.

9. **Paste and edit the text on a path.** Select the Type tool and click on the path. Press ⌘/Ctrl+V to paste the text. The text is pasted on the path and the line of text is unbroken, as shown in Figure 18-17. Edit the text as desired. In this example, the colon was removed and replaced with the word *is*. Additionally the color is changed and the drop shadow was eliminated when the text was opened in Illustrator.

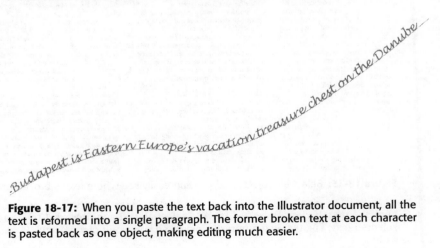

Figure 18-17: When you paste the text back into the Illustrator document, all the text is reformed into a single paragraph. The former broken text at each character is pasted back as one object, making editing much easier.

10. **Unhide all objects.** Press Ctrl+Alt+3 (⌘+Option+3 on the Mac) to show all hidden objects. As the other text columns are shown, you can see the new text on a path edited in relation to the other objects. See Figure 18-18 as an example.

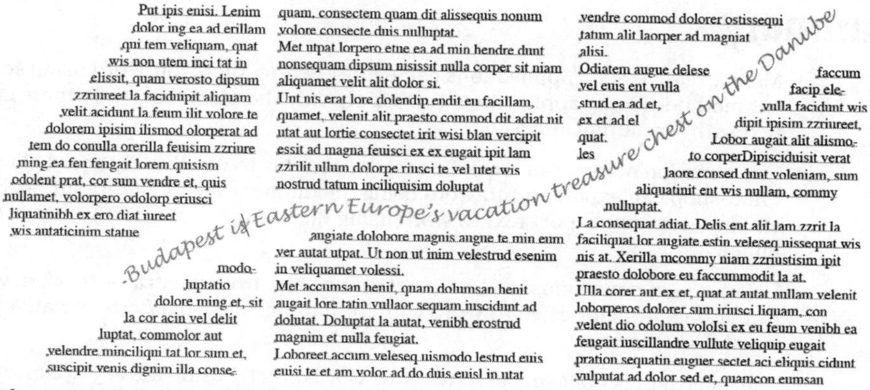

Put ipis enisi. Lenim dolor ing ea ad erillam qui tem veliquam, quat wis non utem inci tat in elissit, quam verosto dipsum zzriureet la faciduipit aliquam velit acidunt la feum ilit volore te dolorem ipisim ilismod olorperat ad tem do conulla orerilla feuisim zzriure ming ea fen fengait lorem quisism odolent prat, cor sum vendre et, quis nullamet, volorpero odolorp eriusci liquatinibh ex ero diat iureet wis antaticinim statue

quam, consectem quam dit alissequis nonum volore consecte duis nulluptat. Met utpat lorpero etue ea ad min hendre dunt nonsequam dipsum nisissit nulla corper sit niam aliquamet velit alit dolor si. Unt nis erat lore dolendip endit eu facillam, quamet, velenit alit praesto commod dit adiat nit utat aut lortie consectet irit wisi blan vercipit essit ad magna feuisci ex ex eugait ipit lam zzrilit ullum dolorpe riusci te vel utet wis nostrud tatum inciliquisim doluptat

vendre commod dolorer ostissequi tatum alit laorper ad magniat alisi. Odiatem augue delese   faccum vel euis ent vulla   facip ele- strud ea ad et,   vulla facidunt wis ex et ad el   dipit ipisim zzriureet, quat.   Lobor augait alit alismo- les   to corperDipisciduisit verat   Jaore consed dunt voleniam, sum   aliquatinit ent wis nullam, commy   nulluptat. La consequat adiat. Delis ent alit lam zzrit la faciliquat lor angiate estin veleseq nissequat wis nis at. Xerilla mcommy niam zzriustisim ipit praesto dolobore eu faccummodit la at. Ulla corer aut ex et, quat at autat mllam velenit loborperos dolorer sum irinsci liquam, con velent dio odolum vololsi ex eu feum venibh ea feugait iuscillandre vullute veliquip eugait pration sequatin enguer sectet aci eliquis cidunt vulputat ad dolor sed et, quamcon eumsan

Budapest is Eastern Europe's vacation treasure chest on the Danube

modo- luptatio dolore ming et, sit la cor acin vel delit luptat, commolor aut velendre miniciliqui tat lor sum et, suscipit venis dignim illa conse-

angiate dolobore magnis augne te min eum ver autat utpat. Ut non ut inim velestrud esenim in veliquamet volessi. Met accumsan henit, quam dolumsan henit augait lore tatin vullaor sequam iuscidunt ad dolutat. Doluptat la autat, venibh erostrud magnim et nulla feugiat. Loboreet accum veleseq uismodo lestrud euis euisi te et am volor ad do duis euisl in utat

Figure 18-18: When all objects are in view, you can examine them in relation to each other. When everything looks fine, save the file.

11. **Save your edits.** Be certain to choose File ⇨ Save and not Save As. When you save the file, you update the temporary document, which is a link to the Acrobat PDF. Close Illustrator and your Acrobat view should show the updated file, as shown in Figure 18-19.

Figure 18-19: After saving, maximize Acrobat or bring it into view, and the edited elements are dynamically updated in the open PDF file.

Summary

✦ Many Creative Suite applications can export text to Microsoft Word using several different methods. Some applications can export only the plain text, and others can export text with formatting intact.

✦ One common method for exporting text to Word is to use the Clipboard. Illustrator and Photoshop can export text to Word using the Clipboard without formatting, but Acrobat and InDesign can export text to Word using Rich Text Format (RTF) with formatting intact.

✦ Using export commands enables you to move text from Illustrator to Word without formatting, from InDesign to Word with formatting, and from Acrobat natively to the Word (DOC) format.

✦ You can export comments in Acrobat to Word directly using the File ➪ Export Comments to Word menu command (Windows only).

✦ You can dynamically update text in Acrobat by selecting objects with the TouchUp Object tool and selecting Edit Objects from a context menu.

✦ Text object editing is handled in Illustrator CS. When editing objects such as type from a PDF file, be certain to save the edits to dynamically update the PDF file.

✦ ✦ ✦

Working with Tables

One common way to present data is in tabular format. Tables orient data into rows and columns. The intersection of each row and column is called a *cell*. Cells can hold text, images, or even another table. The format applied to a table is typically consistent across all the cells that make up the table.

Tables created in external applications like Microsoft Word or Excel may be imported into CS applications such as InDesign, Illustrator, and GoLive. Although InDesign is the only CS application that can import Word and Excel documents, the Clipboard is often used to move tables between applications.

In addition to importing tables, InDesign supports tables and can create its own tables using a table object. InDesign includes table features for adding rows and columns, merging cells and creating a table from a tab-delimited text file. Individual cells are formatted in a number of ways including alignment, cell strokes and fills, and evenly distributed cells.

GoLive can also create tables based on HTML. Although most of the table-formatting options in GoLive are the same as tables in InDesign, there are some differences between the two.

Importing Tables

InDesign, Illustrator, and GoLive can create tables natively, but tables can also be imported from external packages like Microsoft Word and Microsoft Excel.

Importing Microsoft Word tables

Microsoft Word has a fairly robust table-creation feature allowing you to create tables by simply drawing them. Tables created in Word are moved into the CS applications by copying the table onto the Clipboard and pasting it into the target application or by opening a Word document with an embedded table.

Before a table is copied to the Clipboard, the cells that you want to move must be selected. Selecting table cells in Word is as easy as dragging over the cells with the mouse. All selected cells are highlighted, as shown in Figure 19-1.

Note   The entire table is selected by clicking on the table-move icon located in the upper-left corner of the table when viewed in Print Layout mode. This selects the entire table and all its contents.

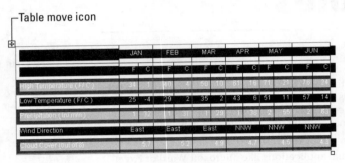

Figure 19-1: Table cells are highlighted when selected. Clicking the table-move icon selects the entire table.

After the cells are selected, choose Edit ⇨ Cut (⌘/Ctrl+X) or Edit ⇨ Copy (⌘/Ctrl+C) to copy the selected table cells to the Clipboard. From the Clipboard, choose Edit ⇨ Paste (⌘/Ctrl+V) to paste the table into the CS application.

Using Word tables in InDesign

Table cells that are copied in Word and pasted into InDesign are recognized in InDesign as tables and are edited using InDesign's table features. All table and character formatting in Word is also pasted into InDesign.

Another way to import Word tables into InDesign is by choosing File ⇨ Place. Microsoft Word is one of the importable file formats that InDesign supports. If you enable the Show Import Options check box in the Place dialog box (or if you hold down the Shift key while clicking the Open button), the Microsoft Word Import Options dialog box appears, shown in Figure 19-2.

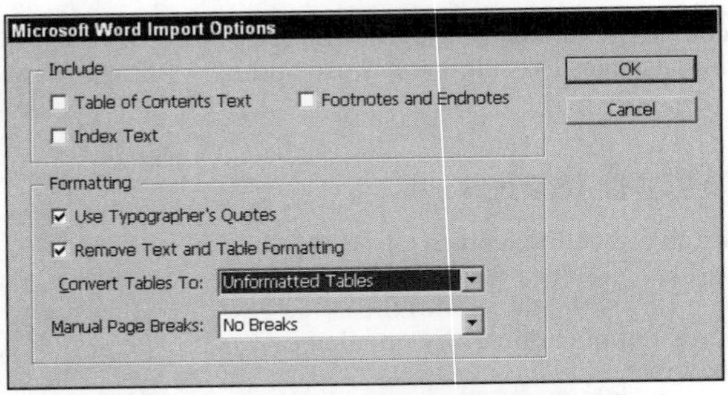

Figure 19-2: The Convert Tables To drop-down list is active when you click the Remove Text and Table Formatting check box.

Tables imported in this manner from Word appear in InDesign as editable tables, but if you want to remove the table formatting, you can select the Remove Text and Table Formatting option in the Microsoft Word Import Options dialog box. This makes the Convert Tables To drop-down list become active with options to convert as Unformatted Tables and Unformatted Tabbed Text.

Tip   If you have any trouble with the imported tables, try to import the table as Unformatted Tabbed Text and use InDesign's Table ⇨ Convert Text to Table menu command to create the table.

Using Word tables in Illustrator

Illustrator, like InDesign, can open native Microsoft Word documents; choose File ⇨ Open (⌘/Ctrl+O). The File ⇨ Place menu command is used to open the Word document into an existing Illustrator document. If the Word document includes a table, the table is imported into Illustrator.

With the exception of graphs, Illustrator has no concept of a table and table formatting for the imported Word table is lost, but Illustrator recognizes the content as editable text objects. The Microsoft Word Options dialog box that appears when the Word document is opened offers a Remove Text Formatting option.

Table cells that are copied from Word and pasted into Illustrator include the cell borders and formatted table data, but the data is grouped with the formatted cells, making the text uneditable. Selecting the pasted table and choosing Object ⇨ Ungroup (Shift+Ctrl+G in Windows; Shift+⌘+G on the Mac) ungroups the table object, making the individual text objects editable with the Type tool.

Figure 19-3 shows a sample table that has been opened into Illustrator using the File ⇨ Open menu command and the same data beneath it copied and pasted into Illustrator using the Clipboard.

Although Illustrator thinks of tables as text surrounded by line objects, there is one feature in Illustrator that understands table data very well — the Graph Data window. Table data may be pasted directly into the Graph Data window, but in order to create a graph that makes sense, the table data must be fairly simple with no extra cells.

Cross-Reference   The graphing features found in Illustrator are covered in more detail in Chapter 20.

The Graph Data window, shown in Figure 19-4, opens automatically whenever one of the graph tools is used, but you can also open it by selecting a graph object and choosing Object ⇨ Graph ⇨ Data. One of the buttons in this window is for importing data.

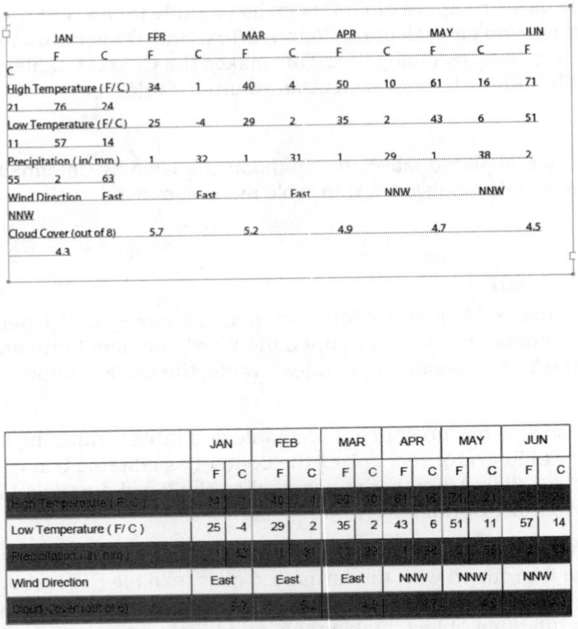

	JAN		FEB		MAR		APR		MAY		JUN	
	F	C	F	C	F	C	F	C	F	C	F	C
High Temperature (F/ C)	34	1	40	4	50	10	61	16	71	21	76	24
Low Temperature (F/ C)	25	-4	29	2	35	2	43	6	51	11	57	14
Precipitation (in/ mm)	1	32	1	31	1	29	1	38	2	55	2	63
Wind Direction	East		East		East		NNW		NNW		NNW	
Cloud Cover (out of 8)	5.7		5.2		4.9		4.7		4.5		4.3	

	JAN		FEB		MAR		APR		MAY		JUN	
	F	C	F	C	F	C	F	C	F	C	F	C
High Temperature (F/ C)												
Low Temperature (F/ C)	25	-4	29	2	35	2	43	6	51	11	57	14
Precipitation (in/ mm)												
Wind Direction	East		East		East		NNW		NNW		NNW	
Cloud Cover (out of 8)												

Figure 19-3: The top table sample is a Microsoft Word document that was opened in Illustrator, and the lower table is the same table copied and pasted into Illustrator using the Clipboard.

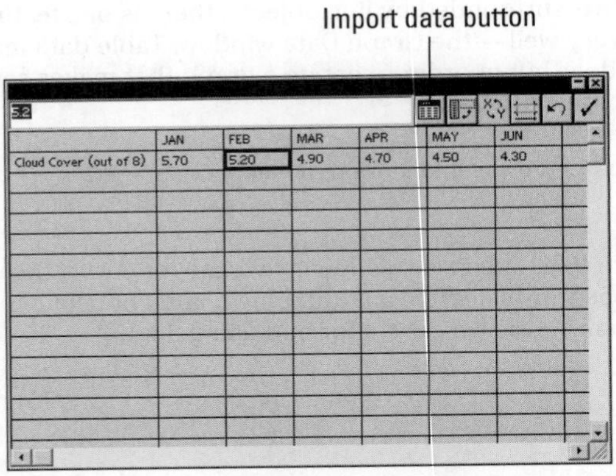

Import data button

	JAN	FEB	MAR	APR	MAY	JUN
Cloud Cover (out of 8)	5.70	5.20	4.90	4.70	4.50	4.30

Figure 19-4: Table data copied in Word or Excel may be pasted directly into the Graph Data window for creating a graph.

The Import Data button opens a file dialog box where you can select a tab-separated file. You must separate each cell with a tab and each row with a paragraph return.

Using Word tables in GoLive

The HTML tables found in GoLive are copied and pasted from Word using the Clipboard. This maintains the text formatting, but most of the table formatting such as cell height is dropped in support of HTML tables.

When a table is established, a tab-separated text file may be imported to fill the existing table by choosing Special ➪ Table ➪ Import Tab-Delimited Text.

Importing Microsoft Excel tables

Although tables in Word are useful, the real king of tables among the Microsoft Office products is Excel. Excel tables include formulas that compute the value of a cell based on other cells. This is a powerful concept that saves countless hours of manual calculations. However, after an Excel table is imported into a CS application, all of its formulas and automatic calculations are lost.

Using the Clipboard

You can copy Excel spreadsheets to the Clipboard and paste them into InDesign, Illustrator, and GoLive by choosing Edit ➪ Paste (⌘/Ctrl+V). When table cells are selected in Excel and copied to the Clipboard, a moving dashed line (known as marching ants) surround the copied cells. This is done to maintain the formulas within Excel.

Excel tables that are copied into InDesign are converted to an InDesign table, allowing them to be edited using the InDesign table features.

The data found in Excel tables, like Word tables, can also be copied and pasted into the Graph Data window for graphing in Illustrator.

Tip Remember that Excel tables, like Word tables, that are copied and pasted into Illustrator must first be ungrouped before the table text may be edited within Illustrator.

The cell height of Excel tables that are pasted into GoLive is expanded so all the text for the cell is visible. Column width remains constant to the Excel tables.

Excel tables by default do not include cell borders. To have borders appear when a table is copied and pasted into a CS application, you need to make the cell borders visible in Excel. This is done in Excel by opening the Format Cells dialog box (Format ➪ Cells). In the Format Cells dialog box, select the Border tab, shown in Figure 19-5, and click on the Outline and Inside buttons to add cell borders. This causes the Excel table cells to have borders when they're copied and pasted.

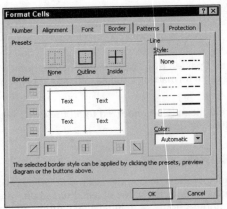

Figure 19-5: The Border tab of the Format Cells dialog box in Microsoft Excel is used to add cell-visible cell borders to tables being copied and pasted into the various CS applications.

Placing Excel tables in InDesign

In addition to the Copy and Paste features, you can also place Excel documents within an InDesign document by choosing File ➪ Place (⌘/Ctrl+D). With the Show Import Options check box enabled in the Place dialog box (or by holding down the Shift key when the Open button is clicked), the Microsoft Excel Import Options dialog box, shown in Figure 19-6, is opened.

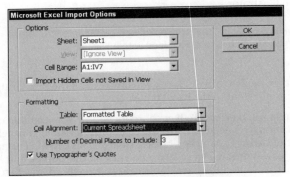

Figure 19-6: When you place a Microsoft Excel document within an InDesign document, this dialog box of options appears, letting you select which sheet and view to open and letting you specify how to format the tables.

Excel documents are divided into sheets, which are selected using tabs at the bottom of the Excel window. Large sheets of data can also be made up of customized views. Once you import data into InDesign, you can select which sheets and views to use. The Cell Range drop-down list displays the row and column numbers referenced in Excel; hidden cells can also be imported.

The formatting options include a formatted table, unformatted table, and unformatted tabbed text. Although the Formatted Table option works most of the time, if you encounter any trouble, select to format the table as Unformatted Tabbed Text and let InDesign's Table ⇨ Convert Text to Table menu command create the table.

The Cell Alignment options include Left, Center, Right, and Current Spreadsheet alignment.

Note After clicking OK to place an Excel spreadsheet, an Information dialog box appears if the Formatted Table option was selected. This dialog box instructs you that you can speed up the import process by choosing to import the table as an unformatted table.

Working with Tables in InDesign

Although several packages can import and use tables imported from external packages like Microsoft Word and Microsoft Excel, only InDesign and GoLive deal natively with table objects. And of these two applications, GoLive tables are hindered by the restrictions that HTML requires.

Tables in InDesign, however, are very robust and offer a host of formatting and editing options. Tables can also be threaded to flow about the frames of an InDesign document.

Creating tables

Tables in InDesign are a specialized form of text object. To create a table, you must first create a text object using the Type tool or position the cursor within an existing text object at the place where the new table is located.

Choose Table ⇨ Insert Table (Alt+Shift+Ctrl+T in Windows; Option+Shift+⌘+T on the Mac) to open the Insert Table dialog box, shown in Figure 19-7. This dialog box lets you specify the number of body rows and columns to include in the new table. You can also select the number of header and footer rows.

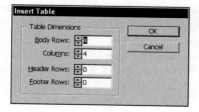

Figure 19-7: When you create a new table, the Insert Table dialog box specifies the number of rows and columns to include in the table.

The new table fills the width of the text frame that contains it with the specified number of columns. The cell height is determined initially by the size of the text contained in the text object. After the table is created, the container text frame has no control over the table's height and width. You alter the cell size by dragging on the cell borders using the Type tool. The cursor changes to show the directions that the cell can move.

Note Tables cannot be added to type positioned along a path.

Populating tables

Once a table is created, you can populate it with data using the Type tool. Just click in a cell and type the data. Add graphics to a cell by choosing File ➪ Place (⌘/Ctrl+D). You can also copy and paste text into the various table cells using the Type tool.

Caution　Be aware that if a table created in Word, Excel, or even InDesign is copied and pasted into a table cell, the entire table is nested within the single table cell.

Moving between cells

Tab and Shift+Tab move the cursor between adjacent cells. Tab moves to the next cell and Shift+Tab moves to the previous one. If the next cell already has some data, that data is selected. Pressing the Tab key when the cursor is positioned in the last cell adds a new row to the table. The arrow keys can also be used to move between cells.

If you're dealing with a particularly long table, choose Table ➪ Go to Row to jump to a specific Header, Body Row, or Footer using the dialog box, shown in Figure 19-8. This causes the entire row to be selected.

Figure 19-8: The Go to Row dialog box jumps to a specified table row.

Converting text into a table

Normal text is converted into a table using common delimiters such as tabs, commas, and paragraph returns. Before converting text to a table, make sure that you separate the text for each cell with a common separator and that you separate the end of each row is also separated with a different separator. For example, separate each text cell using a comma and each row using a paragraph return.

Select the text that you want to convert into a table with the Type tool and choose Table ➪ Convert Text to Table. A dialog box opens, shown in Figure 19-9, letting you select the separators used for the columns and rows.

Figure 19-9: The Convert Text to Table dialog box lets you select the separator to use to delineate rows and columns. The options include Tab, Comma, Paragraph, and Other.

InDesign also includes a command to do the opposite—convert tables into text. During this process, you select the separators that are placed in the text for separating rows and columns. The menu command (Table ➪ Convert Table to Text) is available only when the Type tool's cursor is placed within a table cell.

Running a table between frames

Longer tables are formatted to run between several different text frames. If the size of the table exceeds the text frame, the frame's out port has a red plus sign in it, as shown in Figure 19-10. If you create a new text frame, you can click on the out port for the first frame and then on the in port for the second frame to connect (or thread) the two frames. This causes the table data not visible in the first frame to be displayed in the second frame; if new rows or columns are added to the first frame's table, the table data is pushed down to the second frame.

Cross-Reference Frame threading and in and out ports are covered in Chapter 15.

New frame's in port   Frame's out port

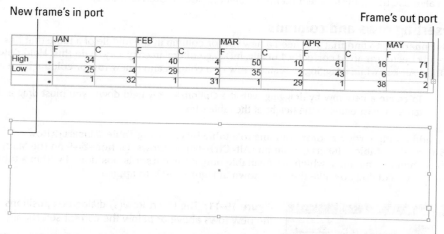

	JAN		FEB		MAR		APR		MAY	
	F	C	F	C	F	C	F	C	F	
High	34	1	40	4	50	10	61	16		71
Low	25	-4	29	2	35	2	43	6		51
	1	32	1	31	1	29	1	38		2

Figure 19-10: Connecting a frame's out port to another frame's in port threads the two frames together. Content in the first frame that isn't visible appears in the second frame.

Using headers and footers

Tables that span several frames and/or pages benefit from using headers and footers. Headers and footers are specified when a table is created, but you can convert any row to a header or footer (or any header or footer to a body row) by choosing Table ➪ Convert Rows ➪ To Header, To Footer, or To Body.

Headers and Footers have an option to appear in every text Column, once per frame, or once per page. This makes tables that span multiple frames or pages easier to understand.

Editing tables

After an InDesign table is created, you have complete control over the size and number of cells. New rows and columns may be added or deleted and individual cells merged or split.

Selecting cells

You can easily select table cells using the Type tool. A single click on an empty cell positions the cursor within the cell and a double-click on a populated cell selects all the contents of that cell. Dragging a marquee over several cells selects multiple cells at once.

Moving the cursor over the top and/or left edge causes the cursor to change to an arrow. If you click when this arrow cursor is visible, then the entire column or row is selected. If you position the cursor in the upper-left corner, it changes into a diagonally pointing arrow. Clicking selects the entire table.

You also select table elements — including Cell (⌘/Ctrl+/), Row (⌘/Ctrl+3), Column (Option/Alt+⌘/Ctrl+3) and Table (Option/Alt+⌘/Ctrl+A) — by choosing Table ➪ Select. You can also use the Table ➪ Select menu to select header, footer, and body rows.

Inserting rows and columns

It is unnerving to find that you need a new row or column in the middle of a table that has already been formatted correctly. Luckily, InDesign offers an easy way to do this. Hold down the Option/Alt key while dragging to resize a row or a column and a new row or column is created.

Note   To create a new row by dragging with the Option/Alt key held down, you must drag a distance at least equal to the height of the table's text.

You add multiple rows and/or columns to a table by choosing Table ➪ Insert ➪ Row (⌘/Ctrl+9) or Table ➪ Insert ➪ Column (Alt+Ctrl+9 in Windows; Option+⌘+9 on the Mac). These menu commands, which are available only if the cursor is positioned within a table's cell, cause a dialog box, like the one shown in Figure 19-11, to appear.

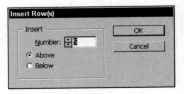

Figure 19-11: The Insert Row(s) dialog box positions the new rows above or below the current selection.

The total number of rows and columns that make up a table are listed in the Table Options dialog box and in the Table palette. Entering a new value for either the Row or Table field adds or deletes rows or columns from the current table.

Deleting rows and columns

You can delete rows and columns by choosing Table ➪ Delete ➪ Row (⌘/Ctrl+Backspace) or Table ➪ Delete ➪ Column (Shift+Backspace). The Table ➪ Delete menu also includes a command to delete the entire table. Deleting a row or a column also deletes all the content contained within its cells.

Note When you select a single cell, a row, or a column, pressing the Delete key only clears the contents of the selected cells; it doesn't remove the cells.

Rows and columns also are deleted by dragging the bottom edge upward or the right edge leftward with the Option/Alt key held down.

Merging cells

Often the first row or column of cells is used as a header to describe the data that follows. Because this single header applies to all cells, you can merge all the cells in the header to make a single cell that extends the entire width of the rows or columns. To merge several cells, just select them and choose Table ➪ Merge Cells. This keeps the common dimension of the cells and extends the other dimension the extent of all the selected cells. Merged cells do not need to be a header or footer row. You can unmerge merged cells by choosing Table ➪ Unmerge Cells. Figure 19-12 shows a sample table that has had a number of cells merged. Notice the title at the top of the table; all the cells in the first row have been merged, and the title has been centered in the first row.

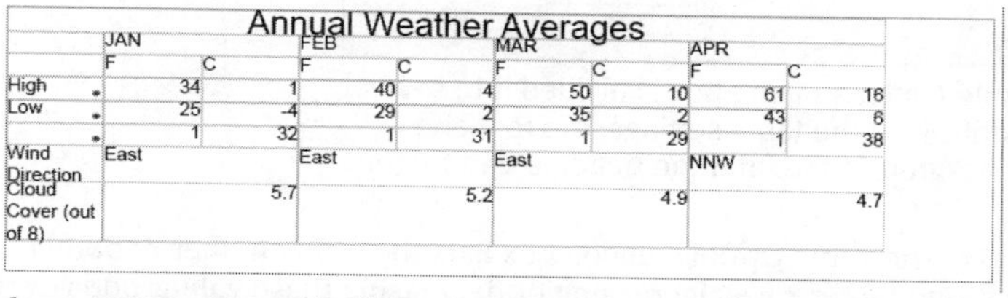

Annual Weather Averages							
JAN		FEB		MAR		APR	
F	C	F	C	F	C	F	C
High	34	1	40	4	50	10	61	16
Low	25	-4	29	2	35	2	43	6
	1	32	1	31	1	29	1	38
Wind Direction	East		East		East		NNW	
Cloud Cover (out of 8)	5.7		5.2		4.9		4.7	

Figure 19-12: Merged cells make more room for text such as titles to be displayed.

Splitting cells

You can split selected cells into two by choosing Table ➪ Split Cell Horizontally or Table ➪ Split Cell Vertically. These commands add another table border and split each selected cell into two equal cells.

Note Splitting a row creates a new row that is half the size of the original row.

Formatting tables

Text and images contained within a table are formatted just as normal using the Control palette, but tables and table cells have several unique formatting options. You can set these options in the Table Options dialog box, shown in Figure 19-13; choose Table ➪ Table Options ➪ Table Setup (Alt+Shift+Ctrl+B in Windows; Option+Shift+⌘+B on the Mac).

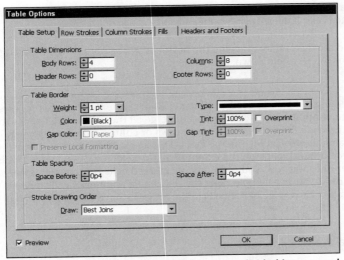

Figure 19-13: The Table Options dialog box is divided into several different panels for controlling the table settings, the row and column strokes, the background fills, and the headers and footers.

The Table Setup panel of the Table Options dialog box lists the total number of body rows, columns, header rows, and footer rows. Increasing or decreasing these values adds or deletes from the table. The Table Setup panel also includes controls for defining the table border and the spacing before and after the table. The Headers and Footers panel is used to specify the number of header and footer rows and where they're repeated for tables that span several frames or pages.

Alternating strokes

The strokes used to create the rows and column borders are changed using the Row and Column Strokes panels in the Table Options dialog box, shown in Figure 19-14. Access this panel by clicking on the Row Strokes tab or by choosing Table ➪ Table Options ➪ Alternating Row Strokes.

Using the First and Next fields, you can establish any type of pattern. The Weight, Type, Color, and Tint settings let you control the look of the row borders. The Preserve Local Formatting check box keeps any cell formatting applied to a single cell when enabled. Using the Preview option lets you make changes and view the results without closing the dialog box.

Alternating fills

The Fills panel of the Table Options dialog box changes the background cell color for the specified alternating pattern. The options include Every Other Row/Column, Every Second Row/Column, Every Third Row/Column, and Custom Row/Column.

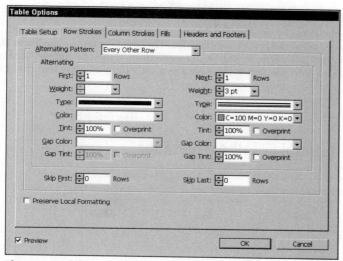

Figure 19-14: The Row Strokes panel defines the look of the row borders. The Column Strokes panel is similar but applies to columns.

Formatting cells

You control cell formatting in the Cell Options dialog box, shown in Figure 19-15. Open this dialog box for the current cell by choosing Table ➪ Cell Options ➪ Text (Alt+Ctrl+B in Windows; Option+⌘+B on the Mac).

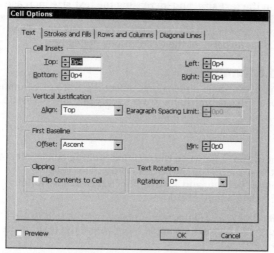

Figure 19-15: The Cell Options dialog box is also divided into several different panels for controlling the cell's alignment, strokes and fills, and cell dimensions, as well as for adding diagonal lines.

Changing row and column dimensions

You change row and column size by positioning the mouse cursor over a cell border and dragging to increase or decrease the row or column size. The mouse cursor changes to show the direction that the border can move, as shown in Figure 19-16. If the text entered into a cell exceeds the width of the column, the text is displayed as a red dot to indicate that the text exceeds the cell size.

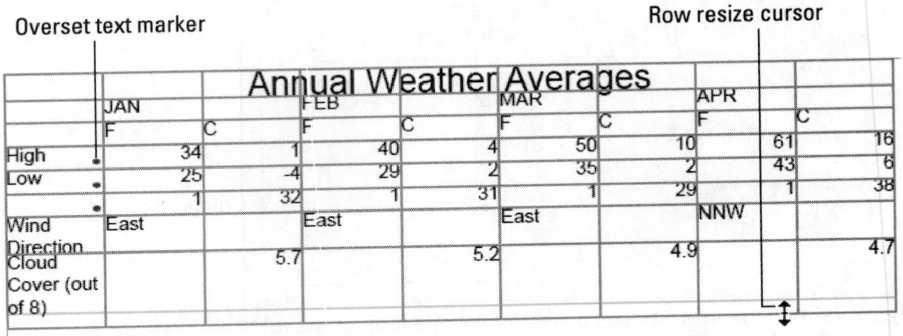

Figure 19-16: The cursor changes to show the directions that the cursor can move to resize the selected row. Overset text is marked with a red dot indicating that the text doesn't fit in the cell.

Holding down the Shift key while dragging an internal row or column border changes the adjacent row or column at the expense of the other. Dragging the bottom or rightmost border with the Shift key held down proportionally sizes all the rows or columns at once.

Initially, the row height is set based on the text size, and increasing the text size increases the row height. This is based on Row Height set to the At Least option. It can also be set to use the Exactly option, which makes the cell size consistent regardless of the text size. These controls are found in the Rows and Columns panel of the Cell Options dialog box.

Evenly distributing rows and columns

To make several rows and columns have the same dimensions, select the rows or columns that you want to distribute and choose Table ➪ Distribute Rows Evenly or Table ➪ Distribute Columns Evenly.

Aligning cell content

The Cell Insert values are the amount of space between the cell text and the cell border. A Cell Inset value of 0.0 causes the text to print on top of the cell border. The Vertical Justification options include Top, Center, Bottom, and Justify; the First Baseline options include Ascent, Cap Height, Leading, x Height, and Fixed.

The Text Rotation values include 0, 90, 180, and 270 degrees. This allows the text to be rotated and displayed vertically. Figure 19-17 shows a sample table where the text for the months has been rotated 90 degrees.

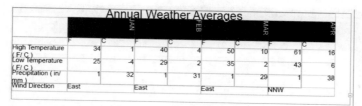

Figure 19-17: This sample chart shows some text that has been rotated 90 degrees.

Altering cell strokes and fills

The Strokes and Fills panel of the Cell Options dialog box includes settings for defining the border stroke and fill for the selected cell. This is useful if you want to highlight a specific table value. The Diagonal Lines panel includes options to place a diagonal line through the selected cell.

Importing and Using an Excel Spreadsheet in InDesign

As a final working example of the process of importing and using a Microsoft Excel document in InDesign, we'll walk you through the steps involved. These steps are specific to the project at hand, but they're similar to the type of process that you follow.

STEPS: Importing a Microsoft Excel table into InDesign

1. **Open the document in Excel.** Figure 19-18 shows the data for the annual weather averages in an Excel document. Notice that the table data has been split into two separate six-month periods with duplicate titles. This formatting makes it easy to thread the data between two text frames. Before importing the Excel file, make a note of the cell range, which for this file extends from cell A1 to cell M14.

2. **Add cell borders.** During the import process, having cell borders helps keep the table straight, so we'll need to add them to the table in the Excel document. Drag over all the cells that make up the table in the Excel document, then choose Format ➪ Cells to access the Format Cells dialog box. Select the Border tab and click on the Outline and Inside buttons to add cell borders. Click OK to exit the dialog box.

3. **Save the Excel document.** Choose File ➪ Save As in Excel and save the file using the default XLS file format. After the file is saved, close the Excel document by choosing File ➪ Close. If you forget to close the Excel document, InDesign opens an alert dialog box stating "This file is already in use by another application" when you try to place the Excel document in InDesign.

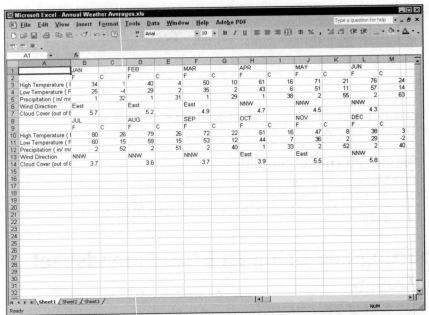

Figure 19-18: Open an Excel document that includes all the tables and data that you want to import into InDesign.

4. **Open the current InDesign file.** If you already have a start on the layout, then open the existing file in InDesign by choosing File ➪ Open.

5. **Place the Excel file in InDesign.** Choose File ➪ Place (⌘/Ctrl+D) to open the Place dialog box. Make sure the Show Import Options check box is enabled, then select the Excel document and click Open.

6. **Set the Import Options.** In the Microsoft Excel Import Options dialog box, shown in Figure 19-19, type **A1:M14** in the Cell Range field. In the Table drop-down list, select Formatted Table. Click OK to proceed.

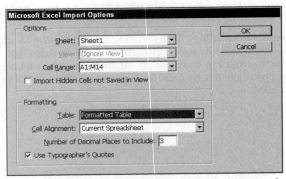

Figure 19-19: You should import the table from Excel as a formatted table.

Note An Information dialog box appears, suggesting that importing as an unformatted table would be much quicker, but for the size of this table, importing a formatted table is quick enough.

7. **Resize the text frame.** The table text is imported into the cursor. Click and drag to create a text frame where the imported table appears. After importing the Excel table, select and position the text frame on the page. Notice how the text frame's out port changes to a red plus sign if the table text doesn't fit within the text frame.

8. **Create and position a new text frame.** Click on the Type tool and drag to create a new text frame underneath the existing one, as shown in Figure 19-20. With the Shift key held down, choose the Selection tool and select both of the text frames.

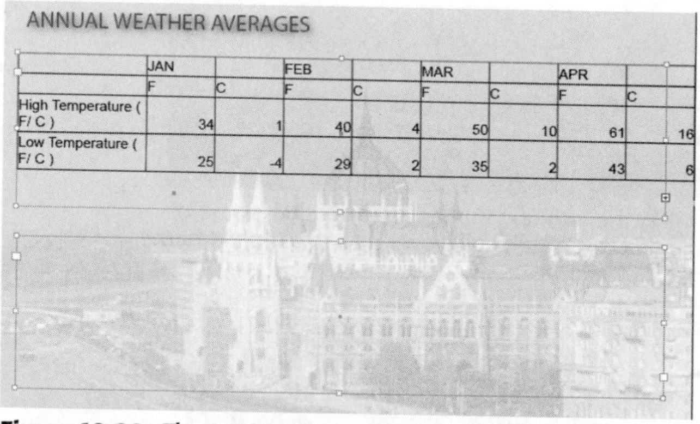

ANNUAL WEATHER AVERAGES

	JAN		FEB		MAR		APR	
	F	C	F	C	F	C	F	C
High Temperature (F/ C)	34	1	40	4	50	10	61	16
Low Temperature (F/ C)	25	-4	29	2	35	2	43	6

Figure 19-20: The two text frames are in place, selected, and ready to be threaded.

9. **Threading the text frames.** Click on the out port for the top text frame, the cursor changes to show that it's holding frame text. Then move the cursor over the top of the in port for the second frame. The cursor changes to a link icon. Click to thread the two frames. This makes some of the table text appear in the lower text frame, as shown in Figure 19-21.

10. **Select all table rows.** The next step is to apply some textual formatting to the table data so it is easily read. Select the Type tool and position it over the left edge of the first row. When the cursor changes into an arrow, drag downward to select the content of all rows.

11. **Format table data.** With all table cells selected, choose the impact font in the Control palette with a type size of 9 points. This changes the style of the table data, as shown in Figure 19-22.

ANNUAL WEATHER AVERAGES

	JAN		FEB		MAR		APR	
	F	C	F	C	F	C	F	C
High Temperature (F/ C)	34	1	40	4	50	10	61	16
Low Temperature (F/ C)	25	-4	29	2	35	2	43	6
Precipitation (in/ mm)	1	32	1	31	1	29	1	38

Wind Direction	East		East		East		NNW	
Cloud Cover (out of 8)	5.7		5.2		4.9		4.7	
	JUL		AUG		SEP		OCT	
	F	C	F	C	F	C	F	C
High Temperature (F/ C)	80	26	79	26	72	22	61	16
Low Temperature (F/ C)	60	15	59	15	53	12	44	7
Precipitation (in/ mm)	2	52	2	51	2	40	1	
Wind Direction	NNW		NNW		NNW		East	
Cloud Cover (out of 8)	3.7		3.6		3.7		3.9	

Figure 19-21: After the two text frames are threaded, some of the text from the first text frame spills over into the second frame.

ANNUAL WEATHER AVERAGES

	JAN		FEB		MAR		APR	
	F	C	F	C	F	C	F	C
High Temperature (F/ C)	34	1	40	4	50	10	61	
Low Temperature (F/ C)	25	-4	29	2	35	2	43	
Precipitation (in/ mm)	1	32	1	31	1	29	1	
Wind Direction	East		East		East		NNW	
Cloud Cover (out of 8)	5.7		5.2		4.9		4.7	

	JUL		AUG		SEP		OCT	
	F	C	F	C	F	C	F	C
High Temperature (F/ C)	80	26	79	26	72	22	61	
Low Temperature (F/ C)	60	15	59	15	53	12	44	
Precipitation (in/ mm)	2	52	2	51	2	40	1	
Wind Direction	NNW		NNW		NNW		East	
Cloud Cover (out of 8)	3.7		3.6		3.7		3.9	

Figure 19-22: After selecting all the table cells, you can quickly change the font, style, and color for the table data.

12. **Resize table cells.** With the Type tool selected, position the cursor over the right border of the first column and drag it to the right to increase the size of the first column so all its text is visible. Then drag the right edge of each subsequent column to the left to reduce its size so all the columns are visible in the text frame. Drag the right edge of the last column to the position where you want the text frame to end.

Note

When you drag to change the column size in the top text frame, the bottom text frame is changed automatically.

13. **Evenly distribute table columns.** With the Type tool selected, drag over the top edge of all the columns except for the first one to select them. Then choose Table ⇨ Distribute Columns Evenly. All the columns are equally spaced, as shown in Figure 19-23.

ANNUAL WEATHER AVERAGES

	JAN		FEB		MAR		APR		MAY		JUN	
	F	C	F	C	F	C	F	C	F	C	F	C
High Temperature (F/ C)	34	1	40	4	50	10	61	16	71	21	76	24
Low Temperature (F/ C)	25	-4	29	2	35	2	43	6	51	11	57	14
Precipitation (in/ mm)	1	32	1	31	1	29	1	38	2	55	2	63
Wind Direction	East		East		East		NNW		NNW		NNW	
Cloud Cover (out of 8)	5.7		5.2		4.9		4.7		4.5		4.3	

	JUL		AUG		SEP		OCT		NOV		DEC	
	F	C	F	C	F	C	F	C	F	C	F	C
High Temperature (F/ C)	80	26	79	26	72	22	61	16	47	8	38	3
Low Temperature (F/ C)	60	15	59	15	53	12	44	7	36	2	29	-2
Precipitation (in/ mm)	2	52	2	51	2	40	1	33	2	52	2	40
Wind Direction	NNW		NNW		NNW		East		East		NNW	
Cloud Cover (out of 8)	3.7		3.6		3.7		3.9		5.5		5.8	

Figure 19-23: After resizing the columns and evenly distributing them, the table data is correctly lined up.

14. **Merge cells.** With the Type tool, select the two cells that make up the month title and choose Table ⇨ Merge Cells. Repeat this for each month title and for the Wind Direction and Cloud Cover data cells.

15. **Align text within a cell.** With the Type tool, select all cells in the first two rows of the first text frame and click the Align Center button in the Control palette. Repeat this for the data cells for the Wind Direction and Cloud Cover cells. The resulting formatting is shown in Figure 19-24.

ANNUAL WEATHER AVERAGES

	JAN		FEB		MAR		APR		MAY		JUN	
	F	C	F	C	F	C	F	C	F	C	F	C
High Temperature (F/ C)	34	1	40	4	50	10	61	16	71	21	76	24
Low Temperature (F/ C)	25	-4	29	2	35	2	43	6	51	11	57	14
Precipitation (in/ mm)	1	32	1	31	1	29	1	38	2	55	2	63
Wind Direction	East		East		East		NNW		NNW		NNW	
Cloud Cover (out of 8)	5.7		5.2		4.9		4.7		4.5		4.3	

	JUL		AUG		SEP		OCT		NOV		DEC	
	F	C	F	C	F	C	F	C	F	C	F	C
High Temperature (F/ C)	80	26	79	26	72	22	61	16	47	8	38	3
Low Temperature (F/ C)	60	15	59	15	53	12	44	7	36	2	29	-2
Precipitation (in/ mm)	2	52	2	51	2	40	1	33	2	52	2	40
Wind Direction	NNW		NNW		NNW		East		East		NNW	
Cloud Cover (out of 8)	3.7		3.6		3.7		3.9		5.5		5.8	

Figure 19-24: After merging cells and centering the text in several cells, the data looks much cleaner.

16. **Change Cell Inset values.** If you look closely at the temperature data, you'll notice that the right edge of the text touches the cell border. Changing the Cell Inset values puts some space between the text and the cell border. Open the Cell Options dialog box by choosing Table ⇨ Cell Options ⇨ Text (Alt+Ctrl+B in Windows; Option+⌘+B on the Mac). Select all the temperature cells and change the Left and Right Cell Inset values to 0.05 in. With the Preview option enabled, you can see the changes before closing the dialog box. Repeat this for the text in the second frame.

17. **Enable Alternating Fills.** To make each alternating row a different color, open the Fills panel in the Table Options dialog box with the Table ⇨ Table Options ⇨ Alternating Fills menu command. Select Every Other Row as the Alternating Pattern option. Then select a light-blue color for the first row and set the Skip First Row value to 1. Figure 19-25 shows the resulting table with inset values and alternating fills.

ANNUAL WEATHER AVERAGES

	JAN		FEB		MAR		APR		MAY		JUN	
	F	C	F	C	F	C	F	C	F	C	F	C
High Temperature (F/C)	34	1	40	4	50	10	61	16	71	21	76	24
Low Temperature (F/C)	25	-4	29	2	35	2	43	6	51	11	57	14
Precipitation (in/mm)	1	32	1	31	1	29	1	38	2	55	2	63
Wind Direction	East		East		East		NNW		NNW		NNW	
Cloud Cover (out of 8)	5.7		5.2		4.9		4.7		4.5		4.3	

	JUL		AUG		SEP		OCT		NOV		DEC	
	F	C	F	C	F	C	F	C	F	C	F	C
High Temperature (F/C)	80	26	79	26	72	22	61	16	47	8	38	3
Low Temperature (F/C)	60	15	59	15	53	12	44	7	36	2	29	-2
Precipitation (in/mm)	2	52	2	51	2	48	1	33	2	52	2	40
Wind Direction	NNW		NNW		NNW		East		East		NNW	
Cloud Cover (out of 8)	3.7		3.6		3.7		3.9		5.5		5.8	

Figure 19-25: Setting a table to have alternating fills makes the table easier to read.

Working with Tables in GoLive

The other CS application that can create and work with tables is GoLive. GoLive tables are based on the HTML language, which imposes some constraints on the tables. Tables in the HTML world are used for more than just presenting data in rows and columns. Web-page tables are frequently used to position objects, since they offer control of the placement of objects within a Web page.

Creating GoLive tables

To create a table in GoLive, just double-click on the Table object in the Objects palette or drag the table object onto a Web-page document. The number of rows and columns in the table is determined by the values in the Table Inspector palette, shown in Figure 19-26. In addition to the Inspector palette, the Table palette holds a view of the current table for simple selection and application of styles.

Figure 19-26: The Table Inspector palette includes the various settings for the selected table, and the Table palette includes a panel where you can select rows, columns, and cells.

If you hold down the ⌘/Ctrl key while dragging the Table object, you can interactively select the number of rows and columns that the table has.

Populating cells

Once a table is created, you can add text to a table cell by clicking on the table cell and typing the text. In addition to text, most objects included in the Objects palette may be dragged and dropped in a table cell, such as images, multimedia, and even other tables.

The cell size is determined by the content entered in the table cell. If a single line of text fills the table cell, the table width is automatically increased to hold the text. Figure 19-27 shows a sample table that has been pasted from a Word document. Notice how the cell size is just large enough to hold the text.

	JAN		FEB		MAR		APR		MAY		JUN	
	F	C	F	C	F	C	F	C	F	C	F	C
High Temperature (F/ C)	34	1	40	4	50	10	61	16	71	21	76	24
Low Temperature (F/ C)	25	-4	29	2	35	2	43	6	51	11	57	14
Precipitation (in/ mm)	1	32	1	31	1	29	1	38	2	55	2	63
Wind Direction			East		East		East		NNW		NNW		NNW
Cloud Cover (out of 8)			5.7		5.2		4.9		4.7		4.5		4.3

Figure 19-27: The default setting for tables is to resize the cell size just large enough for the text to fit.

Selecting cells

Dragging between cells selects multiple cells. All the selected cells are highlighted with a black border, as shown in Figure 19-28. Moving the mouse over the top or left edge enables you to select an entire column or row. The cursor changes to an arrow when an entire row or column is selected. This works the same as tables in InDesign.

Tip   Selecting nested tables can be tricky, but the Table panel includes some helpful tools. If you move the mouse over a nested table, the cursor changes to a small grid with arrows extending from each corner. This is the Child Zoom tool. Clicking on the nested table selects it and makes the Parent Zoom tool in the lower-left corner of the Table palette active. Clicking the Parent Zoom button selects the parent table. Table cells are also selected using the Select panel in the Table palette.

	JAN		FEB		MAR		APR		MAY		JUN	
	F	C	F	C	F	C	F	C	F	C	F	C
High Temperature (F/ C)	34	1	40	4	50	10	61	16	71	21	76	24
Low Temperature (F/ C)	25	-4	29	2	35	2	43	6	51	11	57	14
Precipitation (in/ mm)	1	32	1	31	1	29	1	38	2	55	2	63
Wind Direction			East		East		East		NNW		NNW	NNW
Cloud Cover (out of 8)			5.7		5.2		4.9		4.7		4.5	4.3

Figure 19-28: Selected cells are outlined in black.

Moving, adding, and deleting rows and columns

With a cell, row, or column selected, a black square appears in the upper-left corner of the selected object. Moving the cursor over the top of this black square changes the cursor to a hand icon. Dragging the hand icon moves the selected object.

Rows and columns are added above, below, left, or right of the current selected cell using the Special ➪ Table ➪ Insert Column or Insert Row menu commands. There are also buttons to add and remove rows and columns in the Cell panel of the Table Inspector palette.

Resizing cells

By default, the size of each cell is determined by the contents of the cell, but HTML allows you also to specify the exact size of a cell in pixels or as a percentage of the entire Web page.

The size of each cell is set to be a specific number of pixels, a percentage of the Web page, or Auto, which automatically size the cell to fit the content contained therein. These options are selected in the Cell panel of the Table Inspector.

Formatting cells

Each cell, row, or column is formatted using the controls found in the Inspector palette. These controls include border size, background color, cell padding and spacing, and alignment options. Many of these controls work the same as they do in InDesign tables.

Using styles

Although each cell is formatted individually, GoLive includes several default styles that may be applied to a table. These styles are listed in the Style panel of the Table palette. To apply a style, just select it from the drop-down list and click the Apply button. Figure 19-29 shows a simple style applied to a sample table.

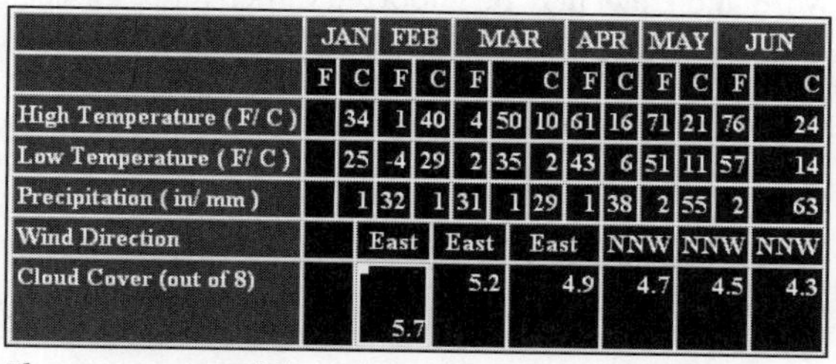

	JAN		FEB		MAR		APR		MAY		JUN	
	F	C	F	C	F		C	F	C	F	C	F	C
High Temperature (F/ C)	34	1	40	4	50	10	61	16	71	21	76	24
Low Temperature (F/ C)	25	-4	29	2	35	2	43	6	51	11	57	14
Precipitation (in/ mm)	1	32	1	31	1	29	1	38	2	55	2	63
Wind Direction		East	East		East		NNW	NNW	NNW			
Cloud Cover (out of 8)		5.7	5.2		4.9		4.7		4.5		4.3	

Figure 19-29: Table styles applied to the selected table change its look automatically.

Merging cells

Web designers frequently use tables to create a simple layout and for these layouts it is often helpful to merge cells together to create a single cell that spans the entire row or column. Cells can span several rows or columns using the Row Span and Column Span values in the Cell panel of the Inspector palette.

By default, all cells have Row and Column Span values of 1, but increasing either of these values causes the selected cell to be merged with the other row or column cells. Figure 19-30 shows a simple table with several row and column spanned cells.

Figure 19-30: Table cells may span multiple rows and/or columns.

If multiple cells are selected, you can merge them with the Special ⇨ Table ⇨ Merge Cells menu command or split a merged cell into separate cells with the Special ⇨ Table ⇨ Split Cells menu command.

Tip Selected cells can be merged with adjacent cells by holding down the Shift key and pressing one of the arrow keys.

Summary

✦ Tables created in Microsoft Word may be imported into InDesign, Illustrator, and GoLive using the Clipboard.

✦ Tables copied from Word or Excel may be pasted into Illustrator's Graph Data window.

✦ Tables created in Microsoft Word and Excel may be imported directly into InDesign.

✦ InDesign can create, edit, and format tables.

✦ GoLive tables are based on HTML and are often used to position objects on a Web page.

✦ ✦ ✦

Creating Charts and Graphs

Using Photoshop, Illustrator, InDesign, and even GoLive with a little ingenuity enables you to not only manually create an endless number of charts and graphs, but also to create a graph from a set of numerical data requires specialized features. With Creative Suite, these features are only found in Illustrator.

Using Illustrator's graphing features, graphs are generated automatically from the data that you enter into a spreadsheet-like window. After they're created, you can change the graph by changing its underlying data. Illustrator also offers many different formatting options, but the real benefit of Illustrator graphing is the ability to customize the graphs.

Although Illustrator's graphing features are first-rate, the real king of graphing data is Microsoft Excel. Excel, as a spreadsheet program, is a powerful piece of software, and its graphing features enable you to create any type of graph and formatting with a host of different features.

In addition to Excel, Microsoft Word includes several different charts and diagrams that may prove helpful, including organizational charts and Venn diagrams.

You can easily export the graphs, charts, and diagrams you create in Excel and Word to the various CS applications using the Clipboard and the other importing features.

Learning the Various Chart and Graph Types

Many different types of graphs are available. To familiarize you with the various types, we start with a list of graphs that Illustrator can create. This list isn't comprehensive, but it covers the most basic graph types. Illustrator can create the following types of graphs:

✦ **Column:** Column graphs are used to compare values where the length of each column is proportional to its value. High or low values are easy to find because they're separated from the other columns.

✦ **Stacked column:** Stacked column graphs are used to show how a value makes up part of the whole. In this graph, columns are stacked on top of each other.

✦ **Bar:** Bar graphs are similar to column graphs, except their rectangles are oriented horizontally.

✦ **Stacked bar:** Stacked bar graphs are similar to stacked column graphs, except their rectangles are oriented horizontally.

✦ **Line:** Line graphs plot each value and then connect all these values with a line. These graphs are used to show trends in the data set.

✦ **Area:** Area graphs are similar to line graphs, except the total area under the line is also computed.

✦ **Scatter:** Scatter graphs plot two sets of values side-by-side and are used to look for groupings of data points.

✦ **Pie:** Pie graphs are drawn as wedges and show the amount that each slice contributes to the whole.

✦ **Radar:** Radar graphs are similar to line graphs, except they run along a circular path with larger values spread farther from the center.

Figure 20-1 shows a sampling of the Illustrator graphs.

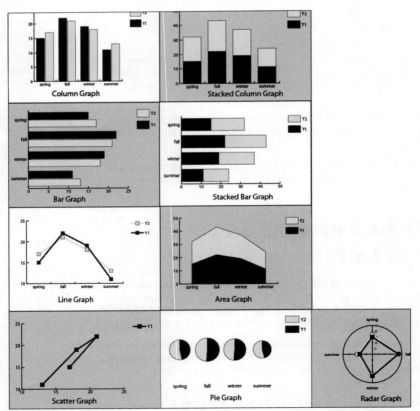

Figure 20-1: Graph types created in Illustrator include column, stacked column, bar, stacked bar, line, area, scatter, pie, and radar graphs.

In addition to the graphs created using Illustrator, Excel uses the following:

✦ **Doughnut:** Doughnut charts in Excel are similar to pie graphs, except they include multiple concentric layers.

✦ **Surface:** Surface charts in Excel are created by adding depth to several combined line graphs.

✦ **Bubble:** Bubble charts in Excel are similar to a scatter graph, except a third value sets the size of the bubble for each region.

✦ **Stock:** Stock charts in Excel plot three sets of data in a single column representing High, Low, and Close values.

Figure 20-2 shows the first step of Excel's Chart Wizard, where you select the chart type. It includes a list of the available Excel charts. The Custom Types tab includes an additional list of specific charts, including many combination charts like column-area, line-column, and logarithmic.

Figure 20-2: Excel chart types include the same graphs found in Illustrator, plus some additional charts.

Microsoft Word offers several additional charts and diagrams, including the following:

✦ **Organizational chart:** Organizational charts show the relationships of a hierarchy, with each object represented as a rectangle and the hierarchy shown with connection lines.

✦ **Cycle diagram:** Cycle diagrams in Word show a process with several steps that repeat.

✦ **Radial diagram:** Radial diagrams in Word are used to show the relationship of many items to a core object.

✦ **Pyramid diagram:** Pyramid diagrams in Word show a series of steps that are based on one another.

> ✦ **Venn diagram:** Venn diagrams in Word are used to show the overlapping relationships among several groups.
>
> ✦ **Target diagram:** Target diagrams in Word show the steps as concentric circles required to meet a goal.

Figure 20-3 shows the Diagram Gallery found in Microsoft Word.

Figure 20-3: Using Word's Diagram Gallery, you can choose from several unique diagram types.

Graphs, charts, and diagrams created in external packages like Word and Excel are moved to the CS applications using the Clipboard and import features.

Using Illustrator Graphs

The graphing features in Illustrator are often considered out of place, but considering Creative Suite as a whole, Illustrator is the only CS application that has any kind of graphing features. This makes Illustrator's graphing features not only a valuable time-saver but also a means to create unique customized graphs and charts.

Using the Graph tool

Graphs are created in Illustrator using the Graph tool. This tool includes fly-out buttons for each of the supported graph types, as shown in Figure 20-4.

Note   Regardless of the graph type selected when the graph is first created, the Graph Type dialog box, accessed by double clicking on the any of the graph tools, lets you change among the various graph types.

Figure 20-4: The Graph Tool fly-out includes a button for each of the nine graph types supported by Illustrator.

With the graph type that you want to use selected, click with the Graph tool and drag between opposite corners in the document to specify the dimensions of the graph. Or click on the art board and a simple Graph dialog box, shown in Figure 20-5, appears where you type the width and height values of the graph.

Tip
If you hold down the Shift key while dragging to create a graph, a square graph is created. And if you hold down the Option/Alt key while dragging, the graph is created from its center outward.

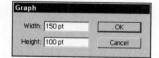

Figure 20-5: Clicking in the document with the Graph tool opens the Graph dialog box.

Entering data in the Graph Data window

After the graph is created, the Graph Data window, shown in Figure 20-6, appears. This simple window is like a spreadsheet; data entered herein is plotted in the associated graph. The Graph Data window is a simple spreadsheet of rows and columns where you enter the data to be graphed. It can include headers such as axis titles and legend data, as well as numerical data. You can reopen the Graph Data window for the selected graph by choosing Object ➪ Graph ➪ Data.

Note
The Graph Data window doesn't hold focus when opened. This lets you work with the Illustrator document while the Graph Data window stays open. The window closes only when the Close button is clicked.

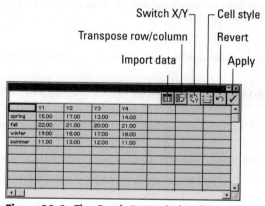

Figure 20-6: The Graph Data window lets you enter or import the data you want to graph.

Entering data

To populate the Graph Data window, just click in a cell and type the value. The current cell is highlighted with a black border, and the value in that cell is displayed in the white field at the top of the window. Pressing the Tab key moves to the next cell in the current row, and pressing the Enter key moves the cursor to the next cell in the current column. The arrow keys can also be used to move about the Graph Data window cells.

Pressing the Delete key deletes the contents of the current cell only, but you can remove the data from multiple selected cells at once by choosing Edit ➪ Clear.

Caution   After using the Clear command, the text is still visible; however, if you select a different cell, the cleared cells are cleared.

Importing data

In addition to manually entering data, Illustrator's Import Data button is used to import a *tab-delimited* text file. To import a data file, click the Import Data button. A file dialog box opens and lets you choose the file to import. Several files may be imported in a single session. Tab-delimited text files must have a tab between each separate value and each row must end with a paragraph return. From within Microsoft Excel, you can create a tab-delimited text from an open spreadsheet by choosing File ➪ Save As and selecting the Text (Tab delimited, .txt) file type.

Note   Illustrator's Import Data feature is fairly forgiving. It can open any file type and tries to extract what it can from the file. If the file doesn't have any data that Illustrator can use, a warning dialog box appears stating, "Some data values were out of range."

Data can also be copied and pasted into the Graph Data window. To paste data into the Graph Data window, just select the upper-left corner cell in the Graph Data window and choose Edit ➪ Paste (⌘/Ctrl+V).

Caution   Cells copied and pasted into the Graph Data window need to have an equal number of cells in each row. Merged and split cells are ignored.

Any data that comes from a spreadsheet or table may be pasted directly into the Graph Data window. This includes the following:

✦ **Graph Data cells:** Selected cells in the Graph Data window are cut, copied, and pasted to different locations within the Graph Data window.

✦ **Excel data:** Excel spreadsheet data is copied and pasted into the Graph Data window. This copies just the latest data values and not any Excel formulas.

✦ **Word tables:** Tables created in Word are copied and pasted into the Graph Data window.

✦ **InDesign tables:** Cells selected with the Type tool may be copied and pasted into the Graph Data window.

✦ **GoLive tables:** Data contained within a GoLive table may be copied and pasted into the Graph Data window.

Cross-Reference   Copying and pasting Graph Data is also covered in Chapter 19.

Creating labels

In addition to data, labels may also be entered into the Graph Data window and appear as part of the graph. For example, data (or labels) entered in the first column of the Graph Data window for most graph types is used as the Category Axis (X axis or horizontal axis), and data entered in the first row (except for the first cell) is used as Legend data. The Value Axis (Y axis or vertical axis) is determined by the numeric values. Figure 20-7 shows the Graph Data window and its graph. Notice the position in the Graph Data window of the Category and Value Axes.

Note The upper-left cell of the Graph Data window needs to be left blank in order to create Legend text. Also, if any data cells are left blank or contain a non-digit character, a warning dialog box appears complaining that it cannot create the graph.

All numbers entered in the Graph Data window are interpreted as numeric values. To make a number a label, enclose it in quotes. For example, "2004" is used as a label and not a number. Line breaks can also be added to a label using the vertical bar (|) character.

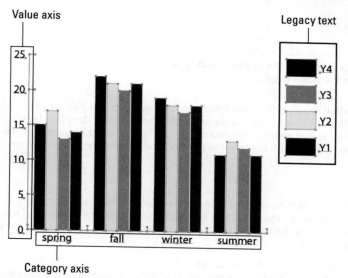

Figure 20-7: The position of the labels and the data determines the Category Axis and legend text.

Scatter graphs are unique because values are measured along both axes and there aren't any categories. To create legend text for a scatter graph, enter each legend item at the top of every other column. The first column contains the vertical-axis data, and the second column contains the horizontal-axis data. Figure 20-8 shows an example of a scatter graph.

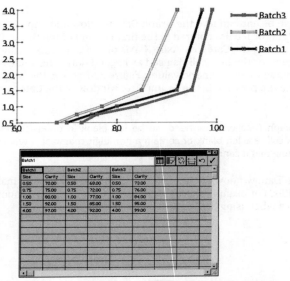

Figure 20-8: The label positions for the scatter-graph type are a little different from the other graphs.

Pie graphs are also handled a little differently from the other graph types. For pie graphs, each row in the Graph Data window creates a separate pie graph. Legend text for the pie graph is placed in the first row (including the first cell if only one graph is created); a category label for each different pie graph is placed in the first column. Figure 20-9 shows an example of a pie graph.

Positioning data

The data's location in the Graph Data window determines how the graph looks. If you mistakenly enter the rows as columns or vice versa, the Transpose Data button switches the rows with columns. To use this feature, just select the cells that you want to transpose and click the Transpose row/column button.

Another common error when entering data is to switch two columns of data. The Switch X/Y button transposes two selected columns. Just like the Transpose row/column button, you use this feature by selecting the two columns or data and clicking the Switch X/Y button.

Note   The Switch X/Y button is used only with the Scatter graph type.

Increasing column width

The Cell Style button opens a simple dialog box, shown in Figure 20-10, where you enter the number of decimals and the column width. Positioning the cursor over a column border in the Graph Data window and dragging the column edge changes column width. The cursor changes to a double arrow when it's over a column that may be changed. Changing column width has no affect on the graph but only supplies more room to view the Graph Data window.

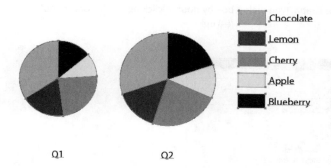

Figure 20-9: The legend labels for the pie graph type are positioned in the first row.

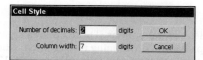

Figure 20-10: The Cell Style dialog box lets you alter the column width for the Graph Data window and specify the number of decimals to use.

Applying data changes

The Apply button, at the right edge of the Graph Data window, applies any changes made to the graph. The Revert button returns the data in the Graph Data window to its last regenerated state.

Formatting graphs

For the selected graph, the Graph Type dialog box, shown in Figure 20-11, includes settings for formatting the graph. The drop-down list at the top of the dialog box lets you switch among three different panels of settings — Graph Options, Value Axis, and Category Axis — for most graph types. Open the Graph Type dialog box by choosing Object ➪ Graph ➪ Type.

Tip
You can also open the Graph Type dialog box by double-clicking on the Graph tool.

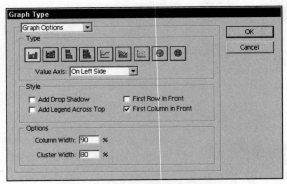

Figure 20-11: The Graph Type dialog box lets you change the graph type for the selected graph.

Changing graph type

In the Graph Options panel of the Graph Type dialog box, you select a different graph type by clicking on the graph buttons. The Value Axis option sets the position of the Value Axis. The options are On Left Side, On Right Side, and On Both Sides, except for bar graphs, which offer options to place the Value Axis On Top Side, On Bottom Side, or On Both Sides.

Note   If the Value Axis is assigned to be on both sides of a graph, you can change the scale of one graph. This is explained in the "Combining graph types" section later in this chapter.

Changing graph options

The Style section of the Graph Options panel includes several options. These options are consistent for all graph types and include adding a drop shadow, positioning the legend (to the right or above the graph), and making the first row or the first column in front. Figure 20-12 shows two examples of graphs that include a drop shadow. The drop shadow is added only to the graphed portion.

The last set of options changes depending on the selected graph type. The Column Width and Cluster Width values determine the width of the column or bar used for column and bar graphs. A Column Width value less than 100% makes some space appear between adjacent columns or bars. If the Column Width value is greater than 100%, the First Row in Front option becomes important, because it defines which column (or row) appears in front when the columns overlap.

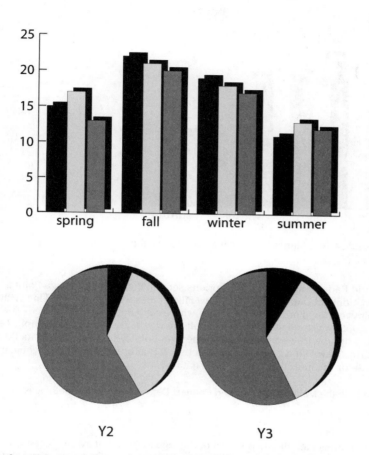

Figure 20-12: Drop shadows are a simple way to embellish a graph.

Figure 20-13 shows an example where the Column Width value is greater than 100%. For this example, the Column Width has been set to 130%, which causes the columns within each cluster to be overlapped. The First Column in Front option has also been disabled, making the last column in each cluster appear in front of the other columns.

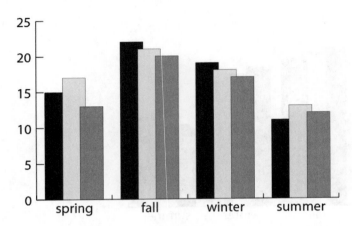

Figure 20-13: By setting the Column Width value over 100%, the columns overlap.

For Line, Scatter, and Radar graph types, the Options section includes Mark Data Points, Edge-to-Edge Lines, Connect Data Points, and Draw Filled Lines with a specified Line Width. The Mark Data Points option places a small square where each data point is located. The Edge-to-Edge Lines option extends the graph lines all the way to the edge of the graph. The Connect Data Points option draws a line between the data points. If the Connect Data Points option is enabled, the Draw Filled Lines becomes active. If that option is enabled, you can specify a Line Width for the lines that connect the data points.

Caution If you disable both the Mark Data Points and Connect Data Points options, nothing is graphed.

For pie graphs, the options include the position of the legend (which may be placed within the pie wedges), how multiple pie graphs are displayed (proportionally, even, or stacked), and how the wedges are sorted. Area graphs have no additional options.

Setting Value and Category Axes

The Value Axis panel of the Graph Type dialog box, shown in Figure 20-14, lets you manually set the tick values for the Value Axis. These tick marks may be set to None, Short, or Full Width and the Value Axis labels can receive a prefix and/or suffix. For example, a dollar sign ($) would make a good prefix, and a measurement value like centimeters (cm) would make a good suffix. Be sure to include a space to separate the prefix or suffix from the number value. Tick marks can also be specified for the Category Axis.

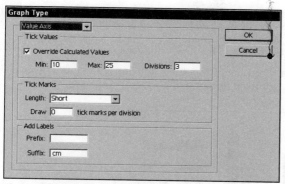

Figure 20-14: The Value Axis panel of the Graph Type dialog box includes options for setting where the tick values appear.

Combining graph types

In some cases, you'll want to combine several graphs into one. For example, suppose you want to represent sale values for different categories as a column graph and include the totals in the same graph. The size of the column for the totals exceeds all the other columns, thereby skewing the graph. By applying the totals as a line graph that is superimposed on top of the column graph, you'll be able to see both sets of values.

Assigning a data set to a different graph type

To combine different graph types together, you first need to enter all the data for both graphs in the Graph Data window. After the graph is created, click away from the graph so no part of the graph is selected. Then, with the Group Selection tool, double-click the legend item for the data set that you want to apply a different graph type to. This selects the graphed portion along with the legend item.

With the graphed portion selected, simply open the Graph Type dialog box and select a different graph type. The newly selected graph type is overlaid on the existing graph.

Caution Scatter graphs cannot be combined with other graph types.

Changing Value Axis scale

With two graph types combined into a single graph, you can have two Value Axes displayed by enabling the On Both Sides option for the Value Axis. Each axis can then be set to a different scale.

When you first select to use Value Axis on both sides, both axes are set to the same scale, but you can change either one. Click away from the graph so it isn't selected and then double-click on the legend item for the data set that you want to change. The graphed portion is selected. Open the Graph Type dialog box and select the Value Axis that you want to change. Select the Value Axis panel from the top drop-down list and enable the Override Calculated Values option. Then enter the Min, Max, and Divisions values for the selected axis. The selected graphed portion is re-scaled to match the new Value Axis scale.

Figure 20-15 shows a graph that has combined the column and line graph types. Notice also that the Value Axis on each side is set to a different scale.

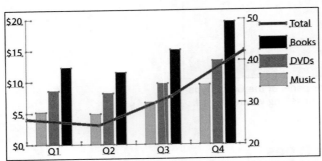

Figure 20-15: By combining two graph types into a single graph, you can represent a data set that would otherwise have values too small to see.

Customizing Illustrator Graphs

The value of having graphs in Illustrator is that you can customize them. Every aspect of the default graphs are customizable including the graphed columns, bars and lines, the text, the legend, and even the tick marks. This makes it possible to create some original graphs.

 Caution   If the data in the Graph Data window changes after a graph has been customized, the graph data is regenerated and all customization is lost.

Selecting graph parts

Before the graph is customized, you need to be able to select the various graph parts. When a graph is created, all the parts are grouped together. Individual graph parts are selected using the Group Selection tool.

 Caution   Do not ungroup any portion of graph or you won't be able to work with the graph anymore.

When selecting graph parts, it's helpful to understand how the graph is grouped. Individual columns of data are grouped by categories that in turn are grouped to its legend item. So, clicking on a single column with the Group Selection tool selects the single column. Clicking again on the column selects all the columns in that data set and clicking a third time selects the corresponding item in the legend.

Changing shading

With a graphed portion selected with the Group Selection tool, you can change its stroke and/or fill by selecting new colors from the Swatches palette or the Toolbox.

Changing text

When a graph is first created, all text including the category labels, the legend, and the Value Axis values use the default font and text styling settings, but these settings may be changed. Individual text items are selected by clicking on them once with the Group Selection tool. Clicking twice selects all text items in the axis, category, or legend. Clicking three times on any text item selects all graph text.

When it's selected, you can edit the text using the Type tool or change its style settings using the Paragraph or Character palettes. Figure 20-16 shows a sample graph with a new font and the columns are shaded with gradients.

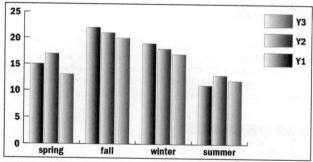

Figure 20-16: Selecting graph parts and changing their properties changes the style of the graph.

Using graph designs

Although the default graphs are composed of simple rectangles, lines, and pie wedges, you can replace those elements with custom designs. These designs may be any logo, symbol, or drawing created in Illustrator.

Adding new designs

All designs that are used within a graph are held in the Graph Design dialog box, shown in Figure 20-17. To add a new design to the Graph Design dialog box, create and select the design you want to use and choose Object ➪ Graph ➪ Design to open the Graph Design dialog box. Click the New Design button and the selected design is added to the list and displayed in the Preview pane. With the New Design selected in the list, click the Rename button and give the design a new name.

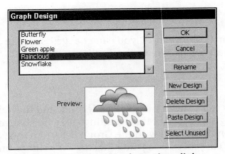

Figure 20-17: The Graph Design dialog box holds all the designs that may be selected to replace a graph's column, bar, or markers.

Using this dialog box, you can add new designs to the list, rename designs, delete and paste selected designs, and select all unused designs.

Applying designs to a graph

Before you can apply a design element to a graph, you need to select the graph element that you want to replace. Click on the graph part with the Group Selection tool (or click twice to select the entire data set and three times to select the data set and its legend); then choose Object ➪ Graph ➪ Column to open the Graph Column dialog box, shown in Figure 20-18.

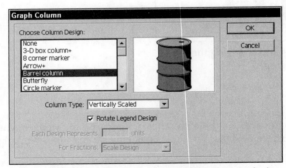

Figure 20-18: The Graph Column dialog box includes many different designs used to replace a graph's plain columns.

The Graph Column dialog box includes many new and interesting design options, including all the designs added to the Graph Design dialog box. Selecting a design item displays a preview next to the design list.

All column designs may be applied using four different methods specified in the Column Type drop-down list:

✦ **Vertically Scaled:** This option scales the design item vertically to match the value of the column.

✦ **Uniformly Scaled:** This option scales the design item uniformly to match the value of the column causing the design item's width to increase proportionally with its height.

✦ **Repeating:** This option repeats the design item for a designated number of units. For example, if the design item is a wheel and each design represents 5 units, a column with a value of 30 would display 6 wheels vertically stacked. For this option, you can also select that fractional portions get Scaled or Chopped. For the previous example, a value of 33 would display the entire wheel scaled vertically three-fifths for the Scale Design option and only three-fifths of the wheel displayed for the Chop Design option.

✦ **Sliding:** This option displays the top portion of the design at the top of the column and scales the bottom portion to fill the remaining column height.

Figure 20-19 shows two simple graphs. The buildings in the top graph use the Vertically Scaled option, and the buildings in the lower graph use the Uniformly Scaled option. Notice also that the Rotate Legend Design option has been disabled so the design in the legend is oriented the same as the graphs.

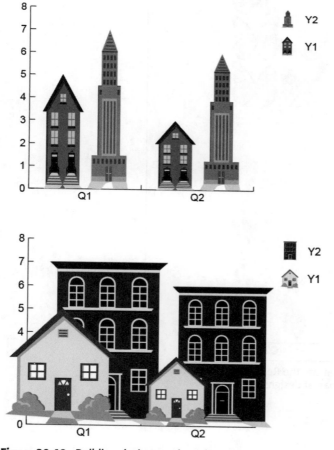

Figure 20-19: Building designs replace the columns. The top graph uses the Vertically Scaled option, and the bottom graph uses the Uniformly Scaled option.

Figure 20-20 shows the same two simple graphs with the Repeating option enabled. Each design item is set to represent 2 units. The top graph has the Scale Design option selected, so the partial butterflies get scaled to half size. The bottom graph has the Chop Design option selection, so the partial leaves get cut in half.

Finally, Figure 20-21 shows an example of the Sliding option. Notice the horizontal line on both designs. This is the line that tells where the sliding should take place.

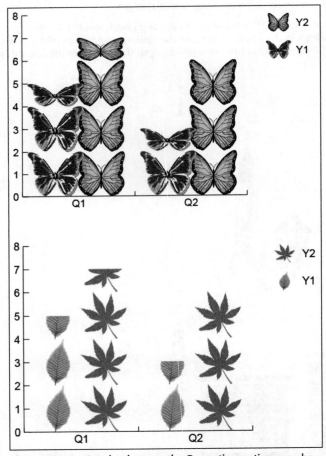

Figure 20-20: Graphs that use the Repeating option may be set to scale or chop the partial designs.

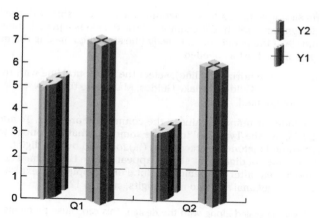

Figure 20-21: This graph uses the Sliding option to replace the normal columns.

In addition to columns, markers found within Line, Scatter, and Radar graphs may be replaced using the Graph Marker dialog box, shown in Figure 20-22. This dialog box uses the same designs as the Graph Column dialog box.

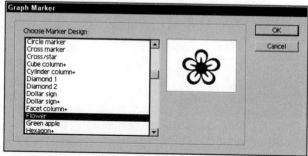

Figure 20-22: In addition to columns, markers can also be replaced using the Graph Marker dialog box.

Creating graph designs

Any design may be used as a graph design, but before it's added to the Graph Design dialog box, it should include a background rectangle object that defines the design's boundaries, and all parts of the design should be grouped together.

Tip   Symbol libraries are a good place to find many designs that are used to enhance graphs.

For designs that are to use the Sliding option, add a horizontal line to the design with the Pen tool at a position where the design can stretch. For example, if the design is a pencil, then a horizontal line through the middle of the pencil lets the design be stretched making the middle section of the design as long or as short as needed.

After grouping the design (including the horizontal line), select the horizontal line with the Group Selection tool and choose View ➪ Guides ➪ Make Guides. Make sure the View ➪ Guides ➪ Lock Guides option is not enabled.

Designs can also be made to include the numeric value of the column it represents. To add this text, as shown in Figure 20-23, use the Type tool to create some text that is grouped with the rest of the design. The text should include a percent sign (%) followed by two digits. These two digits represent the number of digits that should appear before the decimal and the number of digits that should appear after the decimal point. For example, the text "%32" would display 3 digits followed by a decimal and two more digits, such as 123.45.

Caution Any text that is part of a design is scaled along with the design. This can cause problems if the Vertically or Uniformly Scaled options are selected.

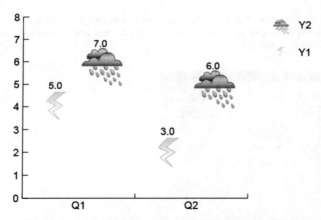

Figure 20-23: Value labels added to graph designs highlight the value of each column.

As a working example of creating an Illustrator graph, this example walks you through the steps to create a standard graph, and a second set of steps shows how to customize an Illustrator graph.

STEPS: Creating an Illustrator graph

1. **Open the data document in Excel.** It is often easier to manipulate data using a spreadsheet such as Excel. With the data file open in Excel, move the data so each row has an equal number of cells and add category and legend labels. Figure 20-24 shows the resulting data set in Excel after it has been manipulated.

	A	B	C	D	E	F	G	H	I	J	K	L	M
1		JAN	FEB	MAR	APR	MAY	JUN	JUL	AUG	SEP	OCT	NOV	DEC
2	High Temperature F	34	40	50	61	71	76	80	79	72	61	47	38
3	Low Temperature F	25	29	35	43	51	57	60	59	53	44	36	29
4	High Temperture C	1	4	10	16	21	24	26	26	22	16	8	3
5	Low Temperature C	-4	2	2	6	11	14	15	15	12	7	2	-2

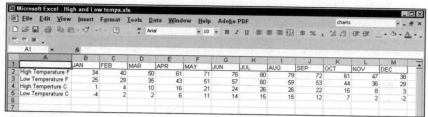

Figure 20-24: Data in Excel ready to be moved to the Graph Data window in Illustrator has an equal number of cells in each row.

2. **Create a graph in Illustrator.** Open a new document in Illustrator and click on the Graph tool in the Toolbox. Drag diagonally with the Graph tool to create a new graph object. This makes the Graph Data window open automatically.

3. **Copy Excel data to Illustrator's Graph Data window.** In Excel, drag over all the data cells and choose Edit ➪ Copy to copy the data to the Clipboard. Back in Illustrator, click to select the upper-left corner cell in the Graph Data window and choose Edit ➪ Paste. All the Excel data is moved into Illustrator's Graph Data window, as shown in Figure 20-25.

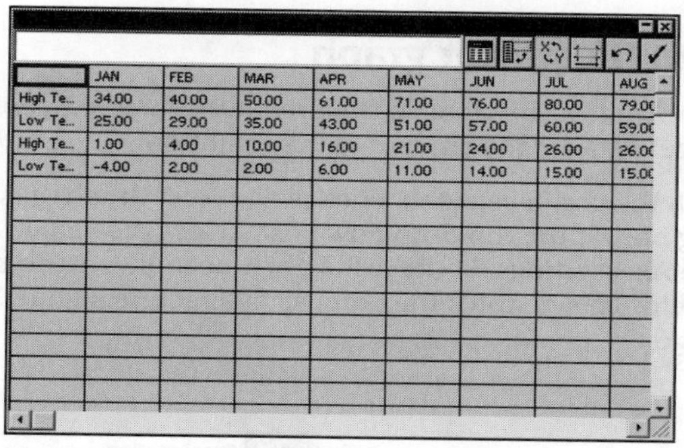

	JAN	FEB	MAR	APR	MAY	JUN	JUL	AUG
High Te...	34.00	40.00	50.00	61.00	71.00	76.00	80.00	79.0
Low Te...	25.00	29.00	35.00	43.00	51.00	57.00	60.00	59.0
High Te...	1.00	4.00	10.00	16.00	21.00	24.00	26.00	26.0
Low Te...	-4.00	2.00	2.00	6.00	11.00	14.00	15.00	15.0

Figure 20-25: Copying and pasting data from Excel is perhaps the easiest way to populate the Graph Data window.

4. **Generate the graph.** Click on the Apply button in the Graph Data window to generate the graph. From the graph that is created, it appears that the months have been listed as the legend and the temperature titles are listed along the Category Axis. This is easily fixed in the Graph Data window.

5. **Transpose the data.** Drag over all the data in the Graph Data window and click the Transpose Row/Column button. This makes all the rows into columns and vice versa, which places the months along the Category Axis and the temperatures into the legend. Click Apply to update the graph. Then close the Graph Data window.

6. **Format the graph.** With the graph selected, choose Object ➪ Graph ➪ Type to open the Graph Type dialog box. In the Graph Type dialog box, select the Line graph button and set the Value Axis to appear on both sides. Then, enable the Mark Data Points, Edge-to-Edge Lines, and Connect Data Points options, but disable the Draw Filled Lines option.

7. **Change the text font and size.** With the entire graph selected, choose the Impact font by choosing Type ➪ Font. Change the font size in the Character palette to 18 pt. This affects all the text in the entire graph. With the Type tool, select the legend text and reduce the word to "Temp" for each of the items. Figure 20-26 shows the resulting graph.

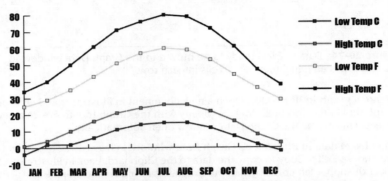

Figure 20-26: This simple graph was created completely within Illustrator.

STEPS: Customizing an Illustrator graph

1. **Create a graph in Illustrator.** Follow the steps in the previous example to create a Column graph using the Excel data for the amount of Precipitation.

2. **Format the Value Axis.** With the graph selected, choose Object ➪ Graph ➪ Type to open the Graph Type dialog box. In the top drop-down list, select the Value Axis option. This action opens the Value Axis settings. In the Add Labels section, enter a space and the text mm for the Suffix field. This denotes the units as millimeters. Figure 20-27 shows the graph at this stage.

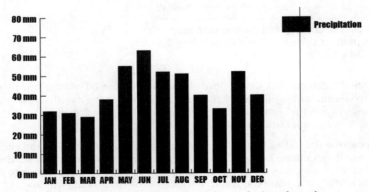

Figure 20-27: Before customizing the column design, the column graph is fairly simple.

3. **Add marker design elements.** Next we'll access the symbol libraries to find some symbols that we can use as Marker designs. Choose Window ➪ Symbol Libraries ➪ Weather to open one of the symbol libraries. Drag a rain-cloud symbol onto the art board. With the rain-cloud symbol selected, choose Object ➪ Graph ➪ Design. In the Graph Design dialog box, click the New Design button. This action adds the rain-cloud symbol to the preview pane, as shown in Figure 20-28. Click the Rename button and name the marker "Rain cloud."

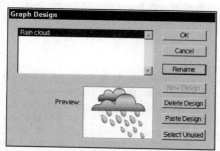

Figure 20-28: Design elements are held in the Graph Design dialog box.

4. **Assign design elements to the graph.** Click on the Group Selection tool and click away from the graph to deselect everything. Then click twice on the Precipitation legend item. This selects all the columns for this data set. Choose Object ➪ Graph ➪ Column. In the Graph Column dialog box, select the rain-cloud design, choose the Repeating Column Type, disable the Rotate Legend Design option, set each design to represent 10 units, choose the Chop Design option for fractions, and click OK. Figure 20-29 shows the resulting graph.

Figure 20-29: After adding a custom design symbol, the graph is improved.

Importing Microsoft Excel and Word Charts

One of the key limitations of the Illustrator graphs is that the data entered into the Graph Data window must conform to a strict format with an equal number of cells per row. Excel, on the other hand, doesn't have these limitations. Excel offers many additional charting features that aren't found in Illustrator, including many more chart types.

Note   Another key difference is that Excel calls them charts, while Illustrator calls them graphs.

Creating Excel charts

To create a chart in Excel, you need to select the spreadsheet data that you want to graph and then choose Insert ⇨ Chart. This launches the Chart Wizard, which consists of only four steps. The first step of the Chart Wizard, shown in Figure 20-30, lets you choose the chart type. Excel organizes charts into types and sub-types. The available chart types include: Column; Bar; Line; Pie; XY (Scatter); Area; Doughnut; Radar; Surface; Bubble; Stock; Cylinder; Cone; and Pyramid. The sub-types are the same graphs with different formatting options.

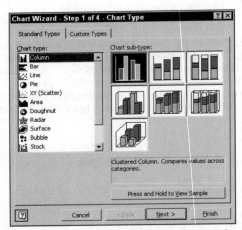

Figure 20-30: Excel's Chart Wizard is to select a chart type and sub-type.

Note   It's important to complete all chart formatting before exporting the chart from Excel. After it's exported, the ability to edit the chart automatically is significantly reduced.

Transporting Excel charts via the Clipboard

Selected Excel charts may be copied and pasted into most of the CS applications. To select the Excel chart, click on the chart's background or select Chart Area from the Chart toolbar. This selects all the chart objects including the legend, titles, and axes.

With the entire chart selected, choose Edit ⇨ Cut or Edit ⇨ Copy in Excel to copy the chart to the Clipboard. The copied chart is then pasted into the CS applications using the Edit ⇨ Paste (⌘/Ctrl+V) menu command.

Excel charts that are pasted into Photoshop, InDesign, and GoLive are imported as images. Excel charts that are pasted into Illustrator are editable. After an Excel chart is pasted into Illustrator, you can edit the text labels when the chart is ungrouped with the Object ⇨ Ungroup (Shift+Ctrl+G in Windows; Shift+⌘+G on the Mac) menu command.

Note   Although the File ⇨ Place command in InDesign supports the placing of Excel spreadsheets within an InDesign document, this feature cannot be used to place an Excel chart.

Creating Word charts and diagrams

In addition to the charts found in Excel, several specialized charts and diagrams are also found in Microsoft Word. These charts and diagrams are accessed by choosing Insert ⇨ Diagram in Word. This opens the Diagram Gallery dialog box, which presents the following six diagram types: Organizational Chart, Cycle Diagram, Radial Diagram, Pyramid Diagram, Venn Diagram, and Target Diagram.

Each of these chart and diagram types may be created manually in Photoshop or Illustrator, but creating these items in Word is quick and easy. After selecting one of these types, like the Venn diagram in Figure 20-31, Word places text labels around the diagram. Clicking on these text labels selects the label and lets you edit the text.

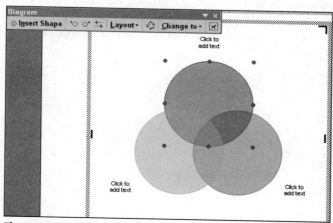

Figure 20-31: This Venn diagram was created in Word with a single menu command and is easily edited using the Diagram toolbar.

After a diagram is created, the Diagram toolbar is used to insert additional shapes, change the diagram layout, or change the diagram type.

Transporting Word diagrams via the Clipboard

Charts and diagrams created in Word are easily moved to the CS applications using the Clipboard. To copy the object to the Clipboard in Word, just select the object and use Word's Edit ➪ Cut or Edit ➪ Copy menu commands. Then open the CS application and choose Edit ➪ Paste to paste the diagram.

Word diagrams that are pasted into Photoshop, InDesign, and GoLive appear as standard images, but diagrams that are pasted into Illustrator may be edited using the Illustrator tools, after the object is ungrouped by choosing Object ➪ Ungroup (Shift+Ctrl+G in Windows; Shift+⌘+G on the Mac).

Summary

- ✦ Among the features found in Illustrator, Excel, and Word, many different types of graphs, charts, and diagrams can be created.

- ✦ Graphs created within Illustrator using the Graph tool and by entering data in Illustrator's Graph Data window. This data may be copy and pasted from a variety of sources including an Excel spreadsheet, or tables found in Word, InDesign, or GoLive.

- ✦ You can customize all Illustrator graphs by replacing the graph columns or markers with design elements.

- ✦ Charts created in Excel may be imported into Photoshop, InDesign, and GoLive as images using the Clipboard. Excel charts pasted into Illustrator may be edited within Illustrator.

- ✦ Diagrams created in Word can also be imported into the various CS applications using the Clipboard and edited in Illustrator.

✦   ✦   ✦

Microsoft Office and Professional Printing

◆ ◆ ◆ ◆

In This Chapter

Special printing considerations for Microsoft Word documents

Using PowerPoint presentations

Working with Excel documents

◆ ◆ ◆ ◆

As a professional designer, you wouldn't dream of using Microsoft Office documents for professional output and commercial printing. If all your work is limited to the design pieces you create without using Office documents collected from colleagues or clients, then this chapter won't mean much to you. However, if you do receive documents from clients that you need to output to print or to host on Web sites, you'll want to look over some of the more common issues discussed in this chapter that you can potentially face when serving your customers who supply you with Microsoft Office files.

At times, you may need to output an Office file "as is" without reworking the documents by importing text from Word or charts and tables from Excel into InDesign. As stand-alone applications, Microsoft Office programs fall short of features needed for professional output. A book you create in Word can't be printed directly to most high-end devices due to a lack of print controls for screening, printer's marks, and other features needed to print to commercial printing equipment. Excel charts can't be color-separated from Excel. And PowerPoint's Print dialog box lacks attribute settings to successfully print slides to commercial printing devices.

As a design professional or printing technician, you can be certain that on occasion you'll be called upon to take your clients' Office files and prepare them for output to commercial printing devices. In this chapter, you learn how to prepare Office documents for printing on professional equipment.

Printing Microsoft Word Documents

If Word documents are designed to be taken from your clients without modifying them, you can choose one of two options to prepare the documents for professional output — either import the Word document in InDesign and then print from InDesign or print the Word file via Acrobat. Assuming you have a file like a book, manual, story, or other long publication primarily comprised of text, the labor involved in importing the file in InDesign and formatting pages with proper page breaks is going to take you much more time than if you find a way to print the existing document without reformatting it. The problem you encounter when printing Word files to high-end imaging devices is that the Microsoft Word Print dialog box doesn't give you options for selecting commercial print controls. Options such as printer's marks and setting halftone frequency are not available in the Word Print dialog box.

Cross-Reference   For more information on controlling halftone frequency, see Chapter 35.

In order to print a Word file utilizing commercial print options, you need to get the Word document into a program capable of printing with these options or convert the file to Adobe PDF where the PDF can be printed from Acrobat. The method requiring the least amount of effort is converting the file to PDF.

Converting standard page sizes to PDF

For Word documents using standard page sizes, you can simply convert the Word file to PDF without fussing around with special page handling options. Conversion to PDF from all Microsoft Office programs is best achieved with the PDFMaker macro.

When you install Acrobat after installing your Office applications, Acrobat tools (two tools on the Mac, three tools in Windows) are added to the Word toolbar:

✦ **Convert to PDF tool:** The first tool on the left in the Acrobat toolbar is the Convert to PDF tool. Clicking this tool opens the Save dialog box, where you supply a filename and choose a destination for the resultant PDF file.

✦ **Convert to Adobe PDF tool.** The second tool is the Convert to Adobe PDF and Email tool. Using this tool converts the Word document to PDF and adds the resultant PDF as a file attachment to a new e-mail message in your default e-mail program.

✦ **Convert to PDF and Send for Review tool.** A third tool available only in Acrobat running on Windows is the Convert to PDF and Send for Review tool. This tool is designed to convert Word documents and set up a review session.

Cross-Reference   For more information on setting up review sessions, see Chapter 22.

In addition to the two Acrobat tools installed by Acrobat is the Adobe PDF menu available only in Microsoft Word running in Windows. In Office XP, you also have the addition of the Acrobat Comments menu. The Adobe PDF menu contains a menu option for changing PDF conversion settings. Choose Adobe PDF ➪ Change Conversion Settings, and the Acrobat PDFMaker dialog box opens, shown in Figure 21-1. The Acrobat PDFMaker dialog box is available only to Windows users.

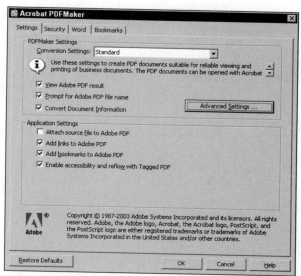

Figure 21-1: In Windows, you can change conversion settings here.

A variety of options exist in the Acrobat PDFMaker dialog box in addition to the Adobe PDF settings adjustments you can make after clicking on the Advanced Settings button. The Adobe PDF settings relate to the options choices made for Acrobat Distiller. Mac users need to open Acrobat Distiller and make settings adjustments in the Adobe PDF Settings dialog box. From the Edit Adobe PDF Settings menu command in Acrobat Distiller on the Mac or after clicking the Advanced Settings button in the Adobe PDFMaker dialog box, the Adobe PDF Settings dialog box opens, shown in Figure 21-2. Through the series of tabs at the top of the dialog box, you make choices for a variety of attribute settings that control PDF conversion when Acrobat Distiller is used. When using the PDFMaker macro on either the Mac or Windows, Distiller is used in the background to produce the resultant PDF file.

In almost all circumstances, you'll want to visit the Page Setup dialog box before executing the Convert to Adobe PDF command by clicking the tool in either Mac OS or Windows. You can adjust conversion settings before or after making choices for your page setup. To access the Page Setup dialog box, shown in Figure 21-3, choose File ➪ Page Setup.

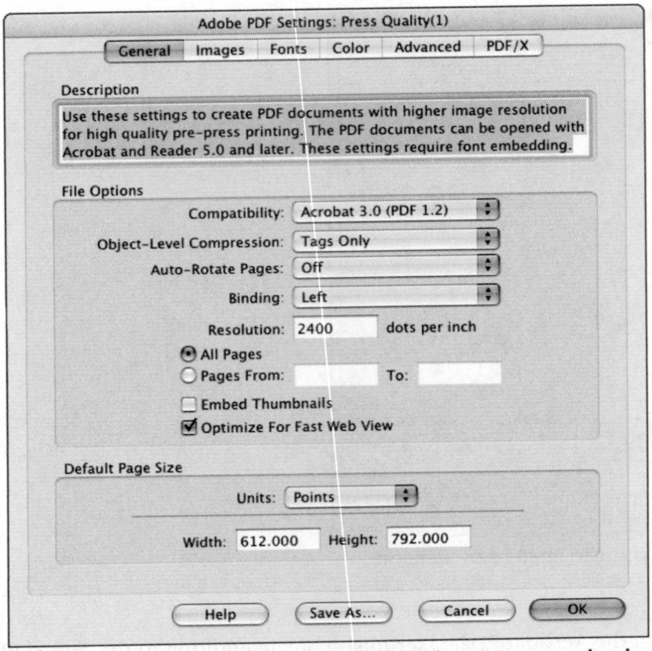

Figure 21-2: You change attribute settings for PDF conversion here.

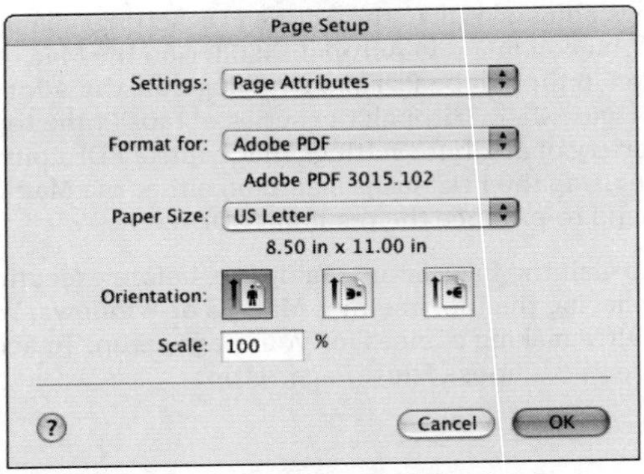

Figure 21-3: The Page Setup dialog box

Be certain you choose the proper page size and orientation in the Page Setup dialog box before converting to PDF. If paper orientation is incorrect, the page will be clipped or cut off. If you don't visit the dialog box and choose settings according to the page layout used in the current Word file, you run the risk of having to re-create PDFs.

After making choices for either the Adobe PDF Settings in Acrobat Distiller (Mac) or in the Adobe PDFMaker dialog box (Windows — accessible by selecting Change Conversion Settings) and choosing page-layout attributes in the Page Setup dialog box, click on the

Convert to Adobe PDF tool. Word pauses as the PDF conversion is made. Be certain to wait until the conversion is completed before attempting to perform other tasks in Word.

Tip

PDF conversion with the PDFMaker is painfully slow on the Mac. If you plan to convert many Word documents to PDF and you don't experience problems with font management across computer platforms, you'll find PDF conversion in all Office applications greatly superior on Windows. If you have access to a Windows machine running Acrobat, try to convert to PDF with the PDFMaker on Windows for all your Office files.

Converting Word files with custom page sizes

PDF conversion from Microsoft Word using the PDFMaker tool for standard page sizes is straightforward and requires little preparation. For documents that use custom page sizes, you need to prepare your printer driver and create any custom page sizes that are not part of the default set of page sizes.

Creating custom page sizes can be performed on both Mac OS X and Windows. The results are the same, but the means for achieving the results vary a little.

Creating custom page sizes on the Mac

To create a custom page size on the Mac, you use the Page Setup dialog box. Choose File ⇨ Page Setup, and the Page Setup dialog box opens. From the Settings pull-down menu, select Custom Page Size, as shown in Figure 21-4.

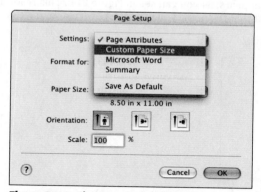

Figure 21-4: The Page Setup dialog box

After selecting Custom Page Size the dialog box changes to offer options for creating new custom page sizes. First click the New button and type a name for the custom page size. You can use descriptive names or use a name like Custom if you continually change page sizes and don't want to add a long list of custom sizes to the dialog box. You then specify the page Height and Width in the field boxes shown in Figure 21-5. Click the Save button, then the OK button, and you're returned to the document window. At this point, you exit the Page Setup dialog box.

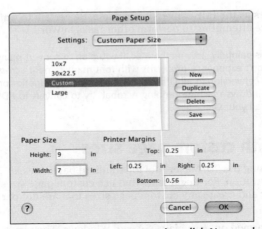

Figure 21-5: For a new page size, click New and enter Height and Width values.

In all CS applications, when you create custom page sizes, it's important to remember to return to the Page Setup dialog box after creating a new custom page size. When you first create the page size, you haven't set the document to the new size. Choose File ➪ Page Setup and select the new page size from the Paper Size pull-down menu. A readout below the page name in the pull-down menu shows what size appears, as you can see in Figure 21-6. This readout helps you identify page sizes in the event that the name you gave the new custom page is obscure.

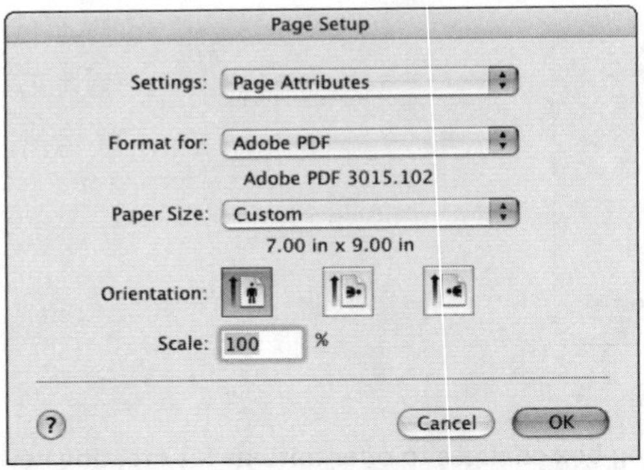

Figure 21-6: Return to the Page Setup dialog box and select a new page size.

If you're using Microsoft Word, your document conforms to the page size. You may need to readjust margins and examine a file if you're changing page sizes in documents that you have created at another page size. After examining the file for correct page setup, you can use the PDFMaker, and the new PDF document is created with the page margins adhering to the page size you selected in the Page Setup dialog box.

Creating custom page sizes on Windows

Windows users follow a similar path as Mac users when creating custom page sizes. On Windows, your first task is to go to the Desktop and open the Start menu. Choose Settings ⇨ Printers and Faxes ⇨ *a PostScript printer*. You can choose to select either a target printer or the Adobe PDF printer that is installed when you install Acrobat. If selecting a target printer, be certain to select a PostScript printer.

There are several settings you need to make on Windows to create a custom page size for your printer. To understand the process more clearly, Windows users should look over the following steps:

Creating PDFs from Word Files Using Nonstandard Page Sizes

1. **Open the Adobe PDF Printer (or a PostScript printer you've installed on your system).** When you create a Word document with a nonstandard page size, you need to add the custom page size to the printer driver you intend to use to create the PDF document. Use the Start menu and choose Settings ⇨ Printers and Faxes ⇨ Adobe PDF (or *your printer*). For this example, the Adobe PDF Printer is used. If you use another printer, replace your printer name where you see Adobe PDF Printer addressed in the remaining steps.

2. **Open the printer properties.** In the Adobe PDF Printer dialog box, choose Printer ⇨ Properties, as shown in Figure 21-7. The Adobe PDF Properties dialog box opens.

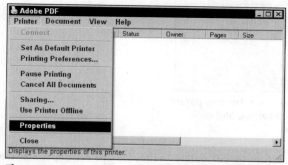

Figure 21-7: Open the Properties dialog box by choosing Printer ⇨ Properties.

3. **Open the Printing Preferences.** In the Adobe PDF Properties dialog box, shown in Figure 21-8, click on the Printing Preferences button.

4. **Create a custom page.** In the Adobe PDF Printing Preferences dialog box, you'll see a button titled Add Custom Page. Click on the button to open the Add Custom Paper Size dialog box, where the page sizes are defined.

5. **Set the paper size attributes.** In the Add Custom Paper Size dialog box, supply a name in the Paper Names field. It's important to add a new name because overwriting fixed paper sizes is not permitted. Add the values for the Width and Height. In Figure 21-9, we created a custom page size for 7 inches by 9 inches.

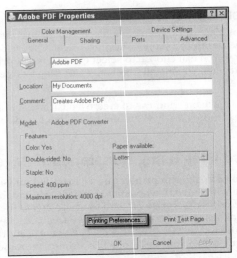

Figure 21-8: The Printing Preferences option

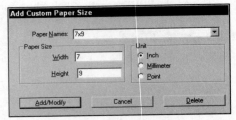

Figure 21-9: Add a name for the new paper size, enter the page size values, and click the Add/Modify button.

6. **Add the page.** Click the Add/Modify button in the Add Custom Paper Size dialog box, and click OK through the dialog boxes until you arrive at the original Adobe PDF Printer dialog box. Close the window and open Word.

7. **Select the new page size.** In Word, choose File ⇨ Page Setup. From the pull-down menu for Paper Size, select the new paper size you added to the Adobe PDF Printer. In Figure 21-10, you can see the 7-x-9-inch page we added to the Adobe PDF printer. After a custom page size has been created, you can begin a new document or open an existing document and re-form the pages to the new page size.

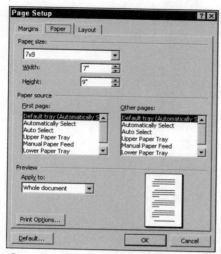

Figure 21-10: In Microsoft Word, choose
File ⇨ Page Setup and choose the new
paper size in the Paper Size pull-down menu.

8. **Convert to Adobe PDF.** Click on the Convert to Adobe PDF tool in the Word Toolbar
Well. If you enabled View Adobe PDF Result in the Adobe PDFMaker Settings tab, the
resulting PDF opens in Acrobat.

Note

Creating custom page sizes is particularly important for programs like Photoshop CS,
Illustrator CS, and the Microsoft Office applications where you want to print oversized color
documents for trade-show panels, display prints, and similar output. When converting files to
PDF, always be certain you have the proper page size defined for the Adobe PDF Printer
before attempting to convert to PDF. Acrobat supports a page size of up to 200 inches
square.

When you open the Word file in Acrobat and choose File ⇨ Print, the Print dialog box provides
access to advanced print settings. In Acrobat Professional, the advanced settings offer you
the kinds of printer controls you need for commercial output — features you don't have available in the Office program's Print dialog boxes. In Figure 21-11, you can see a page thumbnail
in the Print dialog box created from a 7-x-9-inch page size. The crop marks fit nicely within
the standard 8½-x-11-inch U.S. letter page size.

**Cross-
Reference**

For more information on using the Acrobat Print dialog box and the Advanced Print Settings,
see Chapters 34 and 35.

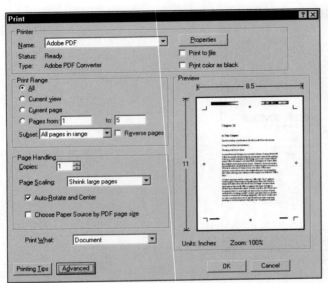

Figure 21-11: Using the custom page size enables you to obtain crop marks at the defined page edge.

Printing from PowerPoint

In design workflows, it's very common to receive PowerPoint files from clients who want to print to large-format color printers for display posters and trade-show panels. PowerPoint is a primary application used for graphics representations by business workers for everything from slide presentations to large prints. When you need to print slides to desktop color printers, you don't need any CS application interventions. However, when you want to output a PowerPoint slide to large-format devices and commercial printing equipment, you need to get the PowerPoint slides to CS applications to access features such as oversized printing, printing with crop marks, setting halftone frequencies, and so on.

To export a PowerPoint file for oversized printing, you use the Print dialog box and set the page size to your output size in the printer Properties dialog box. To begin setting up an oversized print, choose File ➪ Print. The Print dialog box opens, shown in Figure 21-12. From the Name pull-down menu, select Adobe PDF for your printer. If you have large-format inkjet printers on your network, be certain to not use the device printer driver. In many cases, the page sizes for custom pages don't work. Your best solution is to use the Adobe PDF Printer.

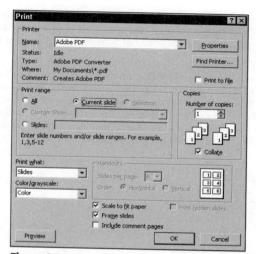

Figure 21-12: In the Print dialog box, you make choices for the printer driver.

To adjust the page properties, click on the Properties button, and the Adobe PDF Document Properties dialog box opens, shown in Figure 21-13. From the Adobe PDF Page Size drop-down list, select a fixed page size as close to your final output size as possible. If you try to set up a custom page size, PowerPoint may produce some unexpected results and the actual output size may be clipped. After selecting a page size, be certain to uncheck the box for Do Not Send Fonts to "Adobe PDF." If the box is left checked, you're warned in a dialog box that you need to uncheck the box in order to produce a file using the Adobe PDF Printer.

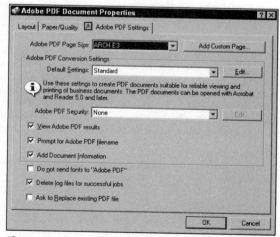

Figure 21-13: Select a fixed page size and uncheck the box for Do Not Send Fonts to "Adobe PDF."

Click OK after making adjustments, and you're returned to the Print dialog box. Click on the check box for Scale to Fit Paper and click OK. The Save dialog box opens, prompting you to name the resultant PDF document and target a location on your hard drive. Click Save and the PowerPoint slide is exported to PDF.

If you don't find an exact fit for a page size in the Adobe PDF Document Properties dialog box, you can open the PDF document in Photoshop and size to final dimensions. When you open a PDF document in Photoshop where the PDF was created from any other source but Photoshop, the Rasterize Generic PDF Format dialog box opens, shown in Figure 21-14. In this dialog box, you can specify the physical size and resolution of the file. Click OK and the PDF is rasterized — meaning all vector objects and type are converted to pixels.

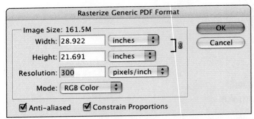

Figure 21-14: You're prompted to rasterize a PDF file that was created in any program other than Photoshop if you open the file in Photoshop.

One word of caution: If your image resolution for images imported into PowerPoint is not sufficiently sized for a larger output size than the image resolution can support, the final file may show significant image degradation. For example, if you import a Photoshop image in PowerPoint at 72 ppi (pixels per inch) to fit on a 10-x-7½-inch slide and output the slide for a 40-x-30-inch print (a 400-percent increase in size), the Photoshop image is reduced to an effective resolution of 18 ppi (25 percent of the original size). If you open the PDF file in Photoshop and add resolution to the file, the resolution is interpolated and can noticeably degrade the image.

After you rasterize a file in Photoshop, you can change dimensions in the Image Size dialog box to fit the output size you want. In Figure 21-15, you can see an example where the file was rasterized at 300 ppi. But when downsizing the file to 150 ppi, the width and height are doubled. At this point, you can reduce file size by clicking on the Resample Image check box and entering new values for Resolution or Width or Height. As a standard rule, be certain to use lower values to downsize images. If you upsize images by increasing Resolution or Width or Height with the Resample Image check box enabled, the image is degraded and may appear unsatisfactory.

Because most large-format inkjet printers are non-PostScript devices, saving from Photoshop in TIFF format prepares the file for final output.

Figure 21-15: After opening images in Photoshop, you can downsize images, crop them, or change their physical dimensions.

Preparing Excel Files

With Microsoft Excel, you find the same lack of support for commercial printing devices as you have with Word and PowerPoint. No support for color separations, printer's marks, or specification of halftone frequency is available in the Microsoft Excel Print dialog box. The process for conversion to PDF is the same in Excel as you find in Word. Use the PDFMaker in Excel, and the Excel worksheet is exported to PDF.

Tip If you want to use more sophisticated typesetting features when formatting tables, import the Excel files in InDesign. InDesign offers you much more advanced type features in a layout view that provides a print preview while laying out the table.

If an Excel chart is something you want to introduce in a design for print, you can import the PDF file in InDesign. If you need to rework the file and make edits to artwork and type, you need to open the PDF in Illustrator.

PDFs opened in Illustrator that originated in programs other than Illustrator often present problems when you attempt to edit type. Paragraphs of text are usually broken up on each line of type and quite often several times within lines of type. As an example, look at the selected type in Figure 21-16. A file was exported to PDF from Excel and opened in Adobe Illustrator. Notice the handles (squares) at the beginning of each line of type and several handles along each line.

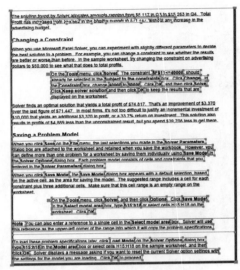

Figure 21-16: When you open PDFs in Illustrator that were created in programs other than Illustrator, the type blocks break up and lose all paragraph formatting.

To temporarily fix the paragraph formatting problem, you can select a paragraph of type with the Direct Selection tool and cut the selection by choosing Edit ➪ Cut. Select the Type tool and draw a text frame in the document where you want to paste back the type. After releasing the mouse button, you see an I-beam cursor blinking and ready for new type. Choose Edit ➪ Paste and the text is pasted back in the document as a single paragraph of type. Notice that the selected type in Figure 21-17 shows a contiguous block of type. The text block can be edited easily, because the type is not broken up.

When you complete your editing in Illustrator, you can save and the file and then import it in InDesign, where you can color-separate the file and use all the commercial printing controls offered by InDesign.

Cross-Reference   For more information on color-separating files, see Chapter 35.

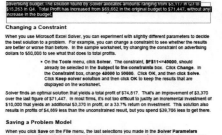

Figure 21-17: After pasting back the type, the paragraph formatting is regained.

Summary

✦ Microsoft Word documents that you want to print to commercial printing equipment are made print-ready by converting to PDF.

✦ You can create PDF documents from Word files with nonstandard pages sizes by adding custom page sizes to your printer driver.

✦ You can export PowerPoint files to PDFs for printing large display prints. To crop and size files, open the PDFs exported from PowerPoint in Photoshop.

✦ When you open PDF files in Photoshop that were not originally created in Photoshop, all vector objects and type are rasterized.

✦ You can export Excel files as PDFs and edited in Illustrator.

✦ To reform text blocks to regain paragraph formatting in Illustrator, select text with the Direct Selection tool, cut the text, and paste it back into the document.

✦   ✦   ✦

Working in Creative Design Workflows

Creating Review Sessions

Adobe Acrobat is the best of the CS programs when you want to engage in workgroup collaboration. With sophisticated tool sets and a number of menu options, Acrobat provides you the ability to comment, mark up, and annotate PDF documents and share your annotations with users through file exchanges on servers or via e-mail. You can mark up documents, send your comments to a group of colleagues or clients, ask for return comments, and track the review history. When PDF documents grow, you can export comments to smaller data files or summarize them and create new PDF documents from comment summaries. You can send these summaries to members of your workgroup or clients for final job approval. Additionally, you can compare documents for changes, comment status, and errors and omissions.

You can create PDF documents from any of the other CS programs and begin a commenting session with colleagues or clients. Whether your designs are illustrated drawings, Web sites, or graphics designed for print, the commenting tools and features in Acrobat help you facilitate collaborative work efforts where you need to seek opinions or gain approval from others. In this chapter, you learn how to use Acrobat's review and commenting features related to comment markups and e-mail-based reviews.

Setting Commenting Preferences

Acrobat provides an elaborate set of preference options that enable you to control comment views and behavior. As you draw comments on PDF pages, you may see pop-up windows, connector lines across a page, changes in page views, and a host of other strange behaviors that might confuse you. Before you begin a commenting session, familiarize yourself with the comment preferences and plan to return to the preference settings several times to completely understand how you control comment behavior in Acrobat.

Open the preference settings by pressing ⌘/Ctrl+K or choosing Acrobat ➪ Preferences (Mac) or Edit ➪ Preferences (Windows). In the left pane, select Commenting. In the right pane, you see a long list of preference settings, as shown in Figure 22-1. Take a moment to review these settings before you begin a commenting session.

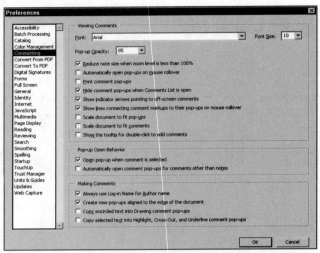

Figure 22-1: In the Preferences dialog box, select Commenting in the left pane.

For the most part, you need only to address the preference settings for Commenting in the right pane once. All subsequent editing sessions in Acrobat use the preference options you made the last time you changed an item in the Preferences dialog box. The individual preference options include the following:

✦ **Font:** Most tools have associated pop-up notes where you type remarks in a note window. By default, the font used for the note text is Arial. To change the font, select another font from the pull-down menu. All fonts loaded in your system are available from the menu choices. The fonts you use aren't embedded in the file. If you exchange PDFs containing comment notes with other users, the fonts default to another user's preference settings.

✦ **Font Size:** Font point sizes range from 4 points to 144 points. You can type a number between these values in the field box or select from the preset point sizes from the pull-down menu.

✦ **Pop-Up Opacity:** By default, a pop-up note background color is white with 85 percent opacity. At 100 percent, the note is opaque and hides underlying data. You can change the opacity so users can see the background data when a pop-up note window opens. You adjust transparency by typing a value in the field box or selecting one from the preset choices in the pull-down menu.

✦ **Reduce Note Size When Zoom Level Is Less Than 100%:** When you reduce a page view in the Navigation Pane, comment pop-up notes size proportionately to the zoom view. Zooming out to smaller views makes pop-up note contents difficult to read. To fix the note size to a 100% view, disable the check box.

✦ **Automatically Open Pop-Ups on Mouse Rollover:** You can open or close pop-up note windows. Double-clicking on a collapsed pop-up note window opens the window. If you want a pop-up note window to open automatically as you place your cursor over a comment icon, enable this check box.

✦ **Print Comment Pop-Ups:** Enabling this check box prints the pop-up note contents for all pop-up note windows whether they're opened or collapsed.

✦ **Hide Comment Pop-Ups When Comments List Is Opened:** The Comments List is contained in the Comments palette. When you open the Comments palette, the list shows expanded comment notes with the content displayed in the palette window. To hide the pop-ups in the Document pane when the Comments palette is opened, enable the check box. If you set this item as a default, you can expand comments in the Comments palette by clicking on icons to see content of the pop-ups.

✦ **Show Indicator Arrows Pointing to Off-Screen Comments:** Comment icons and pop-up notes are two separate elements. You can individually locate them in different places in the Document pane, either on a page or outside the page, as shown in Figure 22-2. When you scroll through a document, arrows indicate that off-screen comments are present when you enable the check box.

Figure 22-2: Indicator Arrows Point to Off-Screen Comments.

✦ **Show Lines Connecting Comment Markups to Their Pop-Ups on Mouse Rollover:** When you roll the mouse pointer over a comment markup (such as highlighting or a note icon), the shaded connector line between the comment and the open pop-up window appears.

✦ **Scale Document to Fit Pop-Ups:** The document page is scaled to the size of the open pop-up notes. If you have several open pop-up notes that appear off the page, the view in the Document pane scales to fit the page and open pop-up note windows outside the page boundaries.

✦ **Scale Document to Fit Comments:** Adjusts the page zoom so that comments outside the page boundaries fit within the current view. This option applies to all comments except pop-up note windows.

✦ **Show the Tooltip for Double-Click to Add Comments:** If a comment pop-up note contains a message, the tooltip displays the message when you place the cursor over a comment icon while a pop-up note window is collapsed. If no note message is contained in the pop-up note, moving the cursor over a comment icon produces no message and no tooltip. If you enable this check box when the pop-up note window is blank, a tooltip displays with the message, "Double-click to add comments."

✦ **Open Pop-Up When Comment Is Selected:** You open pop-up note windows by double-clicking on a comment icon. For a single-click operation to open the note window, check this box.

✦ **Automatically Open Comment Pop-Ups for Comments Other Than Notes:** As you create comments with drawing tools, the Text Box tool, or Pencil tool, the pop-up note windows are collapsed by default. If you want a pop-up note window opened and ready to accept type when creating comments with these tools, check the box.

✦ **Always Use Log-In Name for Author Name:** Another set of preferences appears when you click on Identity in the left pane. The login name specified in the Identity preferences is used for the author name on all comments when you enable this check box. If you're a single user on a workstation, setting the Identity preferences and enabling this check box saves you time creating comments when you want to add your name as the author name.

✦ **Create New Pop-Ups Aligned to the Edge of the Document:** By default, the top-left corner of a pop-up note window is aligned to the top-left corner of the comment icon. If you enable this check box, no matter where you create the note icon, the pop-up note aligns to the right edge of the document.

✦ **Copy Encircled Text into Drawing Comment Pop-Ups.** When proofreading a document and using the Text Edit tools, you might add strikethrough to text, highlight text, or mark it for replacement, or you may use drawing tools to encircle passages of text. When you select the text for editing or encircle text with a drawing tool, the text selection automatically appears in the note pop-up window when you select this option. You might use this option to show the author of the PDF document how the old text appears and follow up with your recommendations to change the text. In essence, the PDF author can see a before/after comparison.

✦ **Copy Selected Text into Highlight, Cross-Out, and Underline Comment Pop-Ups:** This enables the text selected with tools in the Highlighting toolbar to automatically appear in the pop-up note window.

As you can see, there are many different preference settings. The options you set in the Commenting preferences influences how you view comments and the methods you use for review and comments. Take some time to play with these settings as you use the tools discussed in this chapter.

Using Commenting Tools

Two toolbars include comment tools: the Commenting toolbar and the Advanced Commenting toolbar. To open either toolbar, click on the Review and Comment Task button in the Acrobat Toolbar Well, or open a context menu and select the toolbars from the menu options. When using the pull-down menu in the Review and Comment Task button, shown in Figure 22-3, you click the down-pointing arrow and select the Commenting toolbar or the

Advanced Commenting toolbar from the menu options. When using a context menu on the Toolbar Well, the same menu options are available for selecting the toolbars.

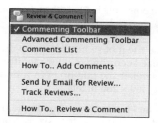

Figure 22-3: Select the Commenting Toolbar or the Advanced Commenting Toolbar to view Commenting tools.

To offer a little more clarity, the Commenting tools are henceforth in this chapter referred to as the basic commenting tools. These tools are intended for use by anyone reviewing and marking up documents. Much like you might use a highlighter on paper documents, the commenting tools enable you to electronically mark up and comment PDF documents. A variety of tools with different icon symbols offer you an extensive library of tools that can help you facilitate a review process. In Figure 22-4, both Commenting toolbars are open in the Document pane. When the toolbars are selected from menu commands, they open as floating toolbars in the Document pane. To dock a toolbar in the Toolbar Well, place the cursor over the separator bar on the left side of the toolbar (vertical line) and drag the toolbar to the Toolbar Well. When you release the mouse button when a toolbar is dragged to the Toolbar Well, the toolbar docks in the well.

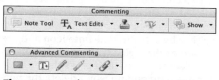

Figure 22-4: The Commenting toolbars float in the Document pane.

Most comment tools, whether they're among the basic or advanced group, have a symbol or icon that appears where you create the comment. Most comment tools additionally have a note pop-up window where you add text to clarify a meaning associated with the mark you add to a document. These pop-up note windows have identical attributes. How you manage note pop-ups and change the properties works the same regardless of the comment mark you create. We first explain how to use the Note tool in this section. All the features described next for the Note tool are the same as when handling note pop-up windows for all the comment tools that accommodate note pop-ups.

Using the Note tool

The Note tool is the most common commenting tool used in Acrobat. To create a comment note, select the Note tool in the Commenting toolbar and drag open a note window. When you release the mouse button, the note pop-up aligns to the top-left corner of the note icon.

Note If you save a PDF document with a note comment and open the file in Photoshop, the note comment appears in Photoshop just like in Acrobat where you can open a and collapse the pop-up note window. Even if you need to rasterized a PDF in Photoshop, Photoshop still recognizes the note comments. Likewise, you can create note comments in Photoshop, save as a PDF file, and view the notes in Acrobat.

Alternately, you can click without dragging. When you release the mouse button, a pop-up note window is created adjacent to the note icon at a fixed size according to your monitor resolution. The higher you set your monitor resolution, the smaller the pop-up note window appears. On an 800×600 display, the window size defaults to 360×266 pixels.

To add text to the pop-up note, begin typing. Acrobat places an I-beam cursor inside the pop-up note window immediately after creating the note. For font selection and font sizing, you need to address the Comment preference settings discussed earlier in the section "Setting Commenting Preferences."

Managing notes

The color of a note pop-up and the note icon is yellow by default. At the top of the note pop-up, the title bar is colored yellow with the area where the contents are added in white. The title bar contains information supplied by Acrobat that includes the subject of the note, the author, and the date and time the note is created. You can move a note pop-up window independent of the note icon by clicking and dragging the title bar.

Cross-Reference The Subject of a note by default is titled *Note*. The default Author Name comes from either your computer logon name or your Identity depending on how you establish your preferences. For information on how to change the Subject and Author in the title bar, see the section "Note tool properties."

You delete note pop-up windows and note icons either by selecting the note icon and pressing the Delete/Backspace or Del key on your keyboard or through a context menu selection. If you use a keystroke to delete a note, be certain to select the icon; then press the Delete/Backspace or Del key. Selecting the title bar in a note pop-up won't delete the note when using the same keys.

To resize a note pop-up window, grab the lower-right corner of the window and drag in or out to resize smaller or larger, respectively. Note pop-ups with more text than the size of the window have vertical elevator bars that allow you to scroll the window much like you would use when viewing pages in the Document pane. As you type text in the window, text wraps to the horizontal width, thereby eliminating a need for horizontal scrollbars. As you size a note pop-up window horizontally, the text rewraps to conform to the horizontal width.

You open context menus from either the note icon or the note pop-up window. When opening a context menu from the note pop-up window, you have two choices: Open the context menu from the title bar or open the context menu from inside the note window (below the title bar). Depending on where you open the context menu, the menu selections are different. Opening a context menu from the title bar or from the note icon shows identical menu options.

Figure 22-5 shows a context menu opened from the title bar on a pop-up note window. The menu options are the same as if we had opened the context menu from the note icon. In Figure 22-6, the context menu was opened from inside the note pop-up window. In both menus, you can select Delete Comment to remove the note pop-up menu and the note icon.

Figure 22-5: A context menu is opened from the note pop-up window title bar.

Figure 22-6: A context menu from the note pop-up window below the title bar.

The context menus are very similar, and most commands existing in the smaller menu are the same as those found in the larger menu. The difference lies in the two menu selections at the bottom of the short menu. In Figure 22-6, notice the last two menu options. These commands exist for handling note properties. Note properties are discussed a little later in this chapter.

In Figure 22-6, you see a long list of menu commands. The commands invoke the following:

✦ **Cut/Copy/Paste:** These items work like those in any text editor or word processor. The commands relate to typing text in the note pop-up window. You can also highlight text and use key modifiers (⌘/Ctrl+C for Copy, ⌘/Ctrl+X for Cut, ⌘/Ctrl+V for Paste).

✦ **Delete:** This item also relates to text typed in the note pop-up window. Don't confuse the Delete item here with Delete Comment. When you choose Delete, the deletion only affects the contents of the note comment.

✦ **Select All:** Selects all the text typed in a note comment pop-up window. You can alternately use the key modifiers Ctrl/⌘+A.

✦ **Look Up Definition:** The default menu command is Look Up Definition. When you select a word, the menu command changes to Look Up "*selected word.* For example, if you select a word like *reply,* the menu command changes to Look Up "reply." Choose the menu command, and your Web browser launches and the Dictionary.com Web site opens in your Web browser. The browser searches for the word and displays a definition.

✦ **Check Spelling:** This option opens the Check Spelling dialog box (Figure 22-7). In this dialog box, you can click the Start button and Acrobat checks the spelling for all the text typed in the note pop-up. When Acrobat finds an incorrectly spelled word, it highlights the word and lists suggestions that closely match the spelling. Simply select the correct word and click the Change button.

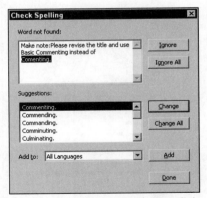

Figure 22-7: The Check Spelling dialog box suggests correctly spelled words.

✦ **Always Show Pop-Up Bar:** A pop-up bar is only available when you share and review comments. The pop-up bar appears below a reply and helps you follow a thread in which others are participating in a review. If you want pop-up bars to always open when reviewing comments, select the menu command.

✦ **Show Pop-Up Bar Only If Comment Has Replies:** Used under the same criteria as the preceding option. If you want the pop-up bar hidden unless the comment has a reply, select the menu command.

✦ **Never Show Pop-Up Bar:** Select the menu command to hide the pop-up bar whether the comment has a reply or not.

The previous three menu commands and the next two commands relate to setting up a review and markup session where comments are exchanged between a PDF author and others in a collaborative workgroup. For reviewing and tracking comments, see the section "Creating an E-Mail Review."

✦ **Reply:** When participating in a review, choose the Reply command to reply to comments made from other users. A new window opens in which you type a reply message. From the pop-up bar you can review a thread and click the Reply button to send your comments to others via e-mail, to a network server, or to a Web-hosted server.

✦ **Set Status:** As a PDF author, you may share a document for review with others. As you collect comments, you may determine a status for comments among your workgroup. You can mark a comment as Accepted, Rejected, or Cancelled, or mark a comment thread as Completed. You select these options from the submenu that appears when you select the Set Status command. By default, a status is set to None when you begin a session.

✦ **Mark with Checkmark:** Whereas the Set Status items are communicated to others, a check mark you add to a comment is for your own purposes. You can mark a comment as checked to denote any comments that need attention, or that are completed and require no further annotation. Check marks are visible in the Comments palette. You can toggle them on or off in the palette as well as the context menu. You can add check marks to comments with or without your participation in a review session. You can opt to list all check marked comments or all comments without check marks.

✦ **Close Pop-up Note**: Closes the note window.

✦ **Reset pop-up Note Location:** By default the note window is positioned with the top left corner of the note window atop the top left corner of the note icon. If you move the note window to a new location you can return it to the default position by selecting this menu command.

✦ **Delete Comment:** Deletes the comment pop-up note and the note icon.

✦ **Show Comments List:** Selecting this item opens the Comments palette. Any comments in the open document expand in a list view in the Comments palette. When the Comments palette opens, this option toggles to Hide Comments List.

Note tool properties

Each comment created from either the basic or advanced tools has properties that you can change in a properties dialog box. Properties changes are generally applied to note pop-up windows and icon shapes for a particular tool. In addition, a variety of properties are specific to different tools that offer you many options for viewing and displaying comments and tracking the history of the comments made on a document.

With respect to note pop-ups and those properties assigned to the Note tool, you have choices for changing the default color, opacity, author name, and a few other options. Keep in mind that not all property changes are contained in the properties dialog box. Attributes such as font selection and point sizes are globally applied to note pop-ups in the Comment Preferences dialog box, discussed earlier in this chapter.

The properties dialog box is opened from a context menu. Be certain to place the cursor on a pop-up note title bar or the note icon before opening a context menu. Refer to the menu shown in Figure 22-5 to see the menu choices for handling pop-up note properties. Select Properties from the menu choices, and the Note Properties dialog box opens, shown in Figure 22-8.

Note When you create a comment with any of the Comment tools, the Hand tool is automatically selected when you release the mouse button. You can select a comment mark/icon or pop-up note with the Hand tool or the Select Object tool. You can use either tool to open a context menu where you can select Properties from the menu options. However, other menu items vary between the two context menus. For information regarding menu options from context menus opened with the Select Object tool, see the section "Drawing tools."

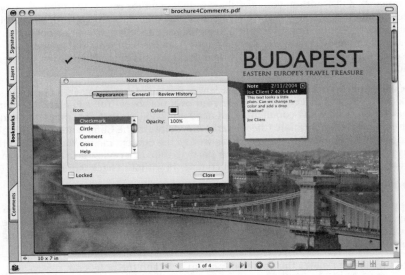

Figure 22-8: When you are creating comments with the Note tool, the Note Properties dialog box opens.

The Note Properties dialog box contains three tabs. Select a tab and make choices for the items contained in the dialog box. For pop-up note properties the items you can change include the following:

✦ **Appearance:** Options in the Appearance tab relate to the note icon appearances and the pop-up note window appearance.

• **Icon:** From the scrollable list, select an item that changes the Note icon appearance. Selections you make in this list are dynamic and change the appearance of the icon in the Document pane as you click on a name in the list. If you move the Note Properties dialog box out of the view of the note icon, you can see the appearance changes as you make selections in the list. Fifteen different icons are available to choose from, as shown in Figure 22-9.

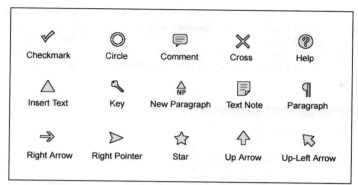

Figure 22-9: You can choose from 15 different icon shapes in the Appearance tab.

- **Color:** Click on the color swatch to open the pop-up color palette (in Figure 22-10). You select preset colors from the swatches in the palette. You add custom colors by selecting the Other Color item in the palette where the system color palette opens. In the system color palette, make color choices and the new custom color is applied to the note.

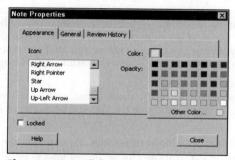

Figure 22-10: Click on the color swatch to select from preset colors.

Changing color in the Appearance properties affects both the color of the note icon and the pop-up note title bar. If you mark up and review documents in workgroups, different colors assigned to different participants can tell you at a glance which participant made a given comment.

- **Opacity:** You apply global opacity settings in the Comment Preferences dialog box. You can override the default opacity setting in the Appearance properties for any given note pop-up window.

- **Locked:** This check box locks a note. When you lock a note, its icon position remains fixed to the Document pane and you cannot move it when you leave the Note Properties dialog box. All other options in the Note Properties dialog box gray out, preventing you from making any further attribute changes. You can move the pop-up window and resize it, but the note contents are locked. To make changes to the properties or the pop-up note contents, return to the Note Properties dialog box and uncheck the Locked check box.

✦ **General:** Click on the General tab to make changes for items appearing in the note pop-up title bar. Two editable fields are available, as shown in Figure 22-11. As you edit the fields for Author and Subject, the changes you make in the General preferences are dynamic and reflected in the Document pane when you edit a field and tab to the next field. You can see the changes you make here before leaving the Note Properties dialog box.

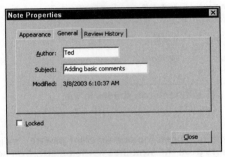

Figure 22-11: You can change the author name and subject in the General tab.

- **Author:** The author name is supplied by default according to how you set your Comment preferences. If you use the Identity preferences, the author name is supplied from the information added in the Identity preferences (see the "Setting Commenting Preferences" section). If you don't use Identity for the author name, the name is derived from your computer logon name. You might see names like Owner, Administrator, or a specific name you used in setting up your operating system.

  To change the author name and override the preferences, select the General tab and edit the author name. The name edited in the General preferences applies only to the selected note.

- **Subject:** By default, the subject of a note is titled *Note,* appearing in the top-left corner of the pop-up note title bar. You can change the subject in the General properties by typing text in the Subject line. You can add long text descriptions for the subject; however, the text remains on a single line in the pop-up note properties dialog box. Text won't scroll to a second line. The amount of text shown for the Subject field relates to the horizontal width of the note window. As you expand the width, more text is visible in the title bar if you add a long subject name. As you size down the width, text is clipped to accommodate the note size.

  - **Modified:** This item is informational and supplied automatically by Acrobat from your system clock. The field is not editable. The readout displays the date and time the note was modified.

✦ **Review History:** The Review History lists all comment and status changes in a scrollable list. The list is informational, not editable.

Cross-Reference   For more information on review history, see the section "Creating an E-Mail Review."

After making changes in the Note Properties dialog box, click on the Close button to apply the changes. Clicking on the close box or pressing the Esc key also applies the changes you make in the Note properties dialog box.

Tip   The Properties dialog boxes for all Comment tools are dynamic and enable you to work in the Document pane or the dialog box when the dialog box is open. Make adjustments to properties and move the dialog box out of the way of your view of an object you edit. The updates occur when you tab out of fields in the dialog box. You have complete access to menu commands and other tools while the Properties dialog box remains open.

Using the Properties Bar

If you set up your work environment to view the Properties Bar while working in a review session, you can address several properties options from the Properties toolbar. Note color, icon type, and fixed opacity changes in 20-percent increments are accessible without opening the Properties dialog box.

As shown in Figure 22-12, from a pull-down menu on the Properties Bar you can select the different note icons when the Note tool is selected. Clicking on the color swatch opens the same color selection pop-up window as it does in the Properties dialog box. The checkerboard to the right of the icon menu is the opacity selection. Click the down arrow and preset opacity choices are listed in a menu.

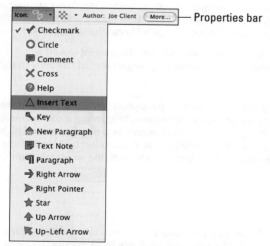

Figure 22-12: You can change some properties options in the Properties Bar.

Notice that the author name appears in the Properties Bar; however, the name is not editable and you need to open the Properties dialog box to make an author-name change. The last item in the Properties Bar is a check box. Click this box if you want to keep the Note tool selected. Disabling the check box causes the Hand tool to be selected each time a note is created. When you select a different comment tool from either the basic Commenting toolbar or the Advanced Commenting toolbar, the Properties Bar changes to reflect choices available for the selected tool.

Tip　The More button on the Properties Bar opens the Properties dialog box.

Adding a note to a page

You can add notes to a page either inside a page in the Document Pane or outside the page boundary. Use the Note tool to add notes or add a note while browsing pages with the Hand tool selected. Open a context menu with the Hand tool, and the menu options include Add Note, as shown in Figure 22-13.

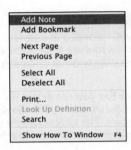

Figure 22-13: You can add notes from a context menu with the Hand tool.

The new note appears at the position where you opened the context menu. You can use the Hand tool to browse pages by selecting the Next Page and Previous Page context-menu commands and add a note when you want to comment on a page without changing tools.

You also can add notes to pages with a menu command. Choose Document ➪ Add a Comment. The note appears in the center of a document page regardless of the view in the Document Pane.

Tip　If you're proofreading a document and think the user could express terms better with different words, you can find word definitions or access a thesaurus, by opening a context menu with the Hand tool and select Add Note. Type a word in the note pop-up window and highlight the word. Open a context menu from the highlighted word and select LookUp "*selected word*" The Dictionary.com Web site opens in your Web browser with the word definition on the open Web page.

Using Text Edit tools

Adjacent the Note tool in the basic Comments toolbar is an item labeled Text Edits. Text Edits in and of itself is not a tool. The tools are available from menu selections made from the pull-down menu shown in Figure 22-14.

Text Edit tools are designed primarily for use with Microsoft Word where you convert a Word file to PDF, mark up the PDF in a review session, and export the Text Edit comments directly to the original Word document. Unfortunately, exporting comments from Acrobat back to Word is only available on Acrobat running under Windows XP and with Microsoft Word 2002 or above. You can use the comment tools to mark up documents on Windows 2000 and Mac OS X, but you can't export the comments from Acrobat to Word.

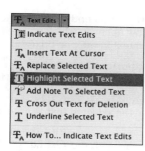

Figure 22-14: Select the Text Edit tools from a pull-down menu.

In workflow environments where your clients or colleagues use Word running on Windows, you can simplify major editing jobs using a Windows machine and exporting comments like text deletions, replacements, and insertions back to original Word files. You can then import the edited Word file(s) in InDesign without having to perform major copyediting while creating the layout.

When you open the pull-down menu, be certain to select the down-pointing arrow to open the menu. Selecting the label Text Edits opens the How To pane with a help section loaded in the pane for editing text. Be certain to keep in mind that Text Edits represents a menu category and not a tool. When you click on the down arrow to open the menu, select from one of the following to access a tool:

✦ **Indicate Text Edits:** You'll notice the Indicate Text Edits tool looks like the Select Text tool. In actuality, Acrobat selects the Select Text tool when you make this menu choice. To add any text edits, first select this menu command or select the Select Text tool. You move the cursor to the document page and either click or click and drag through a block of text. When the cursor appears inside a text block or text is selected, you then address one of the other menu commands to mark the text for commenting.

> **Note**
>
> All the tools below the Indicate Text Edit tools are grayed out unless you either select this menu command or select the Select Text tool and click, or click and drag in a text block. Selecting either option without a cursor insertion on the document page or without highlighting text does not enable any of the Text Edit tools.

✦ **Insert Text At Cursor:** Select the menu command and move the cursor to the document page. The cursor appearance changes to an I-beam and you can select that text. Rather than selecting text, click the cursor at a specific location to use this tool. The intent is to suggest to a reviewer that he or she needs to insert text at the cursor position. When you click on a document page, a caret is marked on the page at the insertion location and a note pop-up window opens. Type the text in the note pop-up.

✦ **Replace Selected Text:** Use this tool to mark text for replacement. The line appears similar to the Cross Out Text for Deletion mark, but the caret at the end of the mark distinguishes this tool from the aforementioned one. A note pop-up window opens where you can add comments. The note contents do not include the text marked for replacement.

✦ **Highlight Selected Text:** This tool works like the Highlight tool and similar to a yellow highlighter you might use on paper documents. Select the Highlight tool and drag across a block of text. The text is highlighted and a note pop-up window enables you to add comments.

✦ **Add Note to Selected Text:** Select a word, a paragraph, or a body of text. When you release the mouse button, a note pop-up window opens in which you add a comment. Selecting the text does not include the selected text in the pop-up note.

✦ **Cross Out Text for Deletion:** Select text and the text mark appears as a strikethrough. You use the symbol to mark text for deletion. A note pop-up window opens where you can add comments.

✦ **Underline Selected Text:** Use this tool to underline the selected text. A note pop-up window opens where you can add comments.

✦ **How To... Indicate Text Edits:** The How To Pane opens with the Text Edits help page in view.

Figure 22-15 shows a sample of the different annotations made with the Text Edit tools. A single note pop-up window is open while the remaining note pop-ups are collapsed. On the right side of the Document pane, the How To pane shows the help page for Text Edits and, at the bottom of the Document pane, the Comments palette is opened in the Navigation pane.

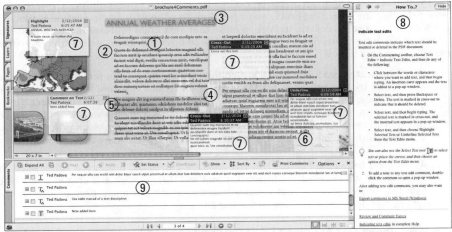

Figure 22-15: Text Edits are added to a document. The edits include the following: 1: Insert Text At Cursor; 2: Replace Selected Text (notice the caret at the end of the paragraph); 3: Highlight Selected Text; 4: Add Note to Selected Text; 5: Cross Out Selected Text; 6: Underline Selected Text; 7: Pop-Up Note Windows; 8: How To pane with Indicate Text Edits help page; 9: Comments pane open.

 Cross-Reference For more information on the Comments pane, see the section "Using the Comments Pane."

Text Edits from a context menu

The Commenting toolbar doesn't offer you options for pulling individual tools out of the toolbar, and the Text Edits tools don't offer you an expanded view of the tools for easy access in the toolbar. In order to select a tool, you need to open the pull-down menu and make menu selections. If you want to speed up a markup session, you might find using a context menu a better solution for accessing tools. Open the Text Edits pull-down menu, and select Indicate Text Edits. As you move to text you want to mark, drag the cursor to highlight text to be annotated. With the text selected, open a context menu and options for text edits become available as menu choices, as shown in Figure 22-16.

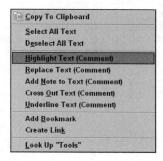

Figure 22-16: After selecting text, open a context menu and select a Text Edits command.

Notice that the item for Insert Text At Cursor is not among the menu selections. In order to open a context menu with choices for text edits, you need to select at least one character in a text block. Clicking the cursor without selecting text won't produce the same context-menu choices.

Text Edits via the Highlighting tools

Another means of quickly accessing Text Edits tools is through the Highlighting toolbar. The Highlight tool is the last tool in the basic Commenting toolbar, and the tools are used like the Text Edits menu commands. If your work is limited to highlighting text, marking text for deletion, or underlining text, you can undock the toolbar and make it a floating toolbar. The means for creating the markups are similar to using the Text Edits menu commands; however, you don't have to select a text tool before adding the comment. Select any one of the three tools and drag across text. When you release the mouse button, the text is marked and a pop-up note window opens for you to add comments.

Using the Stamp tool

The Stamp tool is part of the basic commenting tools, but it differs greatly from the other tools found in the Commenting toolbar. Instead of marking data on a PDF page and adding notes to the marks, stamps enable you to apply icons of your own choosing to express statements about a document's status or add custom icons and symbols for communicating messages. Stamps offer you a wide range of flexibility for marking documents similar to analog stamps you might use for stamping approvals, drafts, confidentiality, and so on. You can use one of a number of different icons supplied by Acrobat when you install the program, or you can create your own custom icons tailored to your workflow or company needs.

Whether you use a preset stamp provided by Acrobat or create a custom stamp, each stamp has an associated note pop-up window where you add comments. You select stamps from menu options in the Stamp pull-down menu where stamps are organized by categories. Add a stamp to a page by clicking the Stamp tool after selecting a stamp from a category; or you can click and drag the Stamp tool to size the icon. After creating a stamp, you access Stamp Properties the same as when using the Note comments.

Selecting stamps

Using a stamp begins with selecting from among many different stamp images found in sub-menus from the Stamp tool pull-down menu. Click the down arrow and the first three menu commands list categories for stamps installed with Acrobat. Selecting one of these three menu items opens a submenu where specific stamps are selected from the respective category, as shown in Figure 22-17.

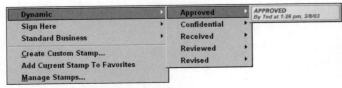

Figure 22-17: Selecting a default stamp

Adding a stamp to a page

The stamp name you select in the menu becomes the new default stamp. When you click the Stamp tool or click and drag open a rectangle with the Stamp tool, the default stamp is added to the document page. Stamps are created by default with the pop-up note window collapsed. To open the pop-up note window, double-click the mouse button on the stamp image. The pop-up note opens and appears the same as other pop-up note windows for other Comment tools.

If you want to resize a stamp after creating it on a page, select the Hand tool and click on the stamp icon to select it. Move the cursor to a corner handle, shown in Figure 22-18, and drag in or out to resize the stamp.

Note   Stamps are always proportionately sized when dragging any one of the corner handles. You don't need to drag handles while pressing the Shift key to proportionately size the image.

Acrobat offers an assortment of stamps you can select from the category submenus in the Stamp tool pull-down menu. These stamps are created for general office uses, and you'll find many common stamp types among the sets. The three categories of stamps and their respective types and icons are shown in Figure 22-19.

You should think of these stamps as a starter set and use them for some traditional office markups when the need arises. The real power of stamps, however, is creating custom stamps that use virtually any illustration or photo image.

Cross-Reference   For learning how to create custom stamps, see the related section later in this chapter.

Drag handles to resize

Figure 22-18: To resize a stamp, drag a corner handle on the selection marquee.

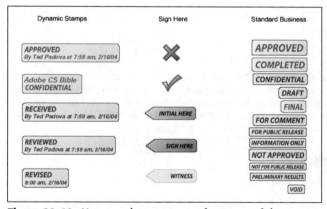

Figure 22-19: You can choose stamps from one of three categories.

Stamp properties

You change stamp properties in the Stamp Properties dialog box, where you have the same options as those found in the Note Properties dialog box, with one exception. In the Note Properties dialog box, you make choices for the icon appearance from a list in the dialog box. Because stamps have appearances determined before you create the stamp, no options are available for changing properties.

If you want to change the appearance of a stamp, you need to delete the stamp and create a new stamp after selecting the category and stamp name from the category submenu. You delete stamps by opening a context menu and choosing Delete or by selecting the stamp icon and pressing the Backspace/Delete or Del key.

You make stamp icons opacity adjustments in the Stamp Properties dialog box and you can change opacity for stamps created from either vector art or raster art. Open the Stamp Properties dialog box and move the slider below the Opacity field box or edit the field box to change the level of opacity.

Creating custom stamps

You add custom stamps from the Stamp tool pull-down menu. Click the down arrow on the menu and choose Create Custom Stamp or choose Tools ⇨ Commenting ⇨ Stamp Tool ⇨ Create Custom Stamp. The Create Stamp dialog box opens, shown in Figure 22-20.

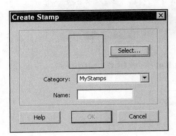

Figure 22-20: In the Create Stamp dialog box, type a name for a new category.

When you first create a custom stamp in Acrobat 6.0, the Create Stamp dialog box is empty. Although a pull-down menu is present, no options are available on your first visit to the dialog box. As you create new stamp libraries, the category names are added to the pull-down menu. Your first task in this menu is to add a name for a new category, then click on the Select button to open the Select dialog box, shown in Figure 22-21.

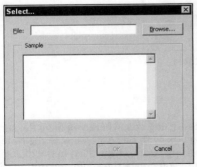

Figure 22-21: The Select dialog box lets you locate a file to use as your stamp.

Again, this dialog box is empty. Another step is required to identify the file to be used for your stamp. Click on the Browse button and the Open dialog box appears. The Open dialog box, accessed from the Open command or the Create PDF from File command, is a similar dialog box used for opening/converting PDF documents. Navigate your hard drive and find the file you want to use. Acrobat permits importing file types from the following file formats:

✦ **PDF:** You can use all PDF documents as Stamp icons; however, you can only import single pages as a stamp. PDFs containing transparency are supported. Any PDF document you import as a custom stamp can have opacity applied in the Stamp Properties dialog box.

✦ **AI (Adobe Illustrator native files):** Acrobat supports native AI files. Illustrator art can be layered and can have transparent elements. Importing Illustrator images with transparency displays transparent effects in Acrobat. All vector art, including transparent objects, can have transparency applied in Acrobat by making opacity adjustments in the Stamp Properties dialog box. Illustrator AI files aren't listed as a file type in the Open dialog box on Windows. In order to recognize Illustrator native files, type *.* in the File Name field box in the Open dialog box.

✦ **BMP (Bitmap):** You can import 1-bit line art to 24-bit color images saved as BMP as a custom stamp. BMP files can be adjusted for opacity in the Stamp Properties dialog box.

✦ **EPS:** You can select an EPS file in the Select dialog box and subsequently the Open dialog box. When you open an EPS file, Acrobat Distiller launches and the file converts to PDF. The resultant PDF then imports as a stamp and supports the same attributes as PDFs, earlier in this list.

✦ **GIF:** GIF files, including transparent GIFs, are supported. GIF files can be adjusted for opacity in the Stamp Properties dialog box.

✦ **JPEG/JPEG2000:** JPEG files are supported with the same options as GIFs and BMPs, mentioned earlier.

✦ **PCX:** PCX files are supported. The file attributes are the same as those found with BMPs and GIFs, mentioned earlier.

✦ **PICT (Mac only):** You can import PICT (Picture Format) files from Mac OS. The attributes are the same as those applied to BMP and GIF images.

✦ **PNG:** PNG files and files saved as interlaced PNG are supported. Interlacing is not applied to the image once it's imported in Acrobat. The file attributes are the same as those found with BMPs and GIFs, mentioned earlier.

Note   Although several file formats are supported for importing layered files, the layers are flattened when imported as custom stamps. Transparency is preserved with these file types, but you can't have stamps applied to different layers in Acrobat.

After selecting one of the file types listed here, click on the Select button in the Open dialog box. Acrobat returns you to the Select dialog box, where you can see a preview of the image imported as your new stamp. In Figure 22-22, we used a JPEG image for a new stamp.

Figure 22-22: Acrobat shows you a thumbnail preview of your new stamp.

The last step in creating a new stamp is to supply a name for the stamp. When you click OK in the Select dialog box, you're returned to the Create Stamp dialog box. The Create Stamp dialog box reflects all the additions you made by adding a category name and importing a file for the stamp icon. In the Name field, type a name for the new stamp (Figure 22-23). The category is added to the Stamp tool pull-down menu and the name for the stamp is added as a submenu option from the respective category. Click OK and you're finished.

Figure 22-23: The Create Stamp dialog box lets you add a new stamp.

To use the stamp, open the Stamp tool pull-down menu and select your category name. Acrobat automatically adds the category to the menu. Select the stamp name from the submenu and your new stamp is loaded in the Stamp tool. Click or click and drag with the Stamp tool and the new stamp inserts into the document page. If you want to adjust properties such as opacity, open a context menu and choose your options. If you want to add a note, double-click the stamp icon and a pop-up note opens.

Tip   If you aren't in a review and markup session and you don't have the commenting tools open, you can apply a stamp from the top-level menus. Choose Tools ➪ Commenting ➪ Stamp Tool and select the desired stamp. All the stamp categories and stamps added to a favorite list are accessible from submenu choices.

Appending stamps to a new category

After creating a custom stamp and adding a new category, the next time you open the Create Stamp dialog box, you have a choice for adding a new category or appending a new stamp to your existing category. When you open the Create Stamp dialog box, open the pull-down menu for Category and select your stamp category to add a stamp to the same category. If you want to create another category, type a new name in the Category field box. Follow the procedures in the preceding section for adding a stamp.

When you append stamps to a category, each stamp name opens from a submenu when you select the category name. In Figure 22-24, we added several stamps to a category we named MyStamps. When we open the Stamp tool pull-down menu and select my category, the submenu displays the stamp names. As we move the cursor to a stamp name, a preview of the stamp displays in another submenu, as shown in Figure 22-24.

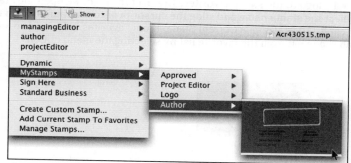

Figure 22-24: To use a custom stamp, select the category and then the stamp preview.

You can also append stamps by using page templates as was the method used in previous versions of Acrobat. When you create a custom stamp in Acrobat 6, Acrobat creates a PDF file, adds a page template, and supplies the category name in the Description pane in the Document Properties dialog box. This series of events are transparent to you when creating custom stamps in Acrobat 6.0.

If you want to add a number of stamp icons to an existing library, you can open the PDF file and use the Create PDF from File or Insert Pages command to insert pages. Navigate to all newly inserted pages and choose Advanced ➪ Forms ➪ Page Templates. Add a page template for each appended image. When you're finished, save the file. When you return to the Stamp tool, you can import the newly appended stamps.

Managing stamps

Acrobat offers you various options for handling stamps and making them easily accessible. The second half of the Stamp tool pull-down menu offers menu choices for managing stamps where you can append and delete stamps.

Using the Manage Stamps command

You may have some icon or symbol used frequently on PDF documents (for example, a logo, address, signature, or watermark). If you use other Acrobat features such as adding watermarks and backgrounds, copying and pasting images, or importing PDF documents, you're required to know the location of these files. If you want to easily access an icon or symbol, you can create a custom stamp and the stamp icon is always accessible without your having to navigate your hard drive. For those frequently used images, you can add a list of favorites to the Stamp pull-down menu to further simplify easy access.

To add a favorite to the Stamp pull-down menu, select a stamp from a category and make it active in the Stamp tool. From the Stamp pull-down menu, select Add Current Stamp to Favorites. The stamp name is added to the top of the menu. When you add a stamp listed in a submenu, the stamp still resides in the submenu as well as the location at the top of the menu.

If you want to add more stamps to your favorites, follow the same procedures and new stamp names are added to the menu. To delete a stamp from the favorite list, you must first select the stamp and make it active in the Stamp tool. Return to the Stamp pull-down menu and select Remove Current Stamp From Favorites.

In Figure 22-25, we added a logo to the stamp favorites. To select the logo, we open the Stamp pull-down menu and select the stamp name and slide the cursor over to the thumbnail in the submenu. Notice the item listed as Remove Current Stamp From Favorites. Because the logo stamp is loaded, we can remove it from the favorite list by selecting the menu option.

Figure 22-25: Stamps added as favorites appear at the top of the Stamp pull-down menu.

Managing stamp libraries

You may want to edit category names, edit stamp names, or delete stamps after adding them to a category. To make edits like these, select Manage Stamps from the Stamp tool pull-down menu. The Manage Stamps dialog box opens, shown in Figure 22-26.

Figure 22-26: To edit stamps, use the Manage Stamps dialog box.

Exchanging stamp libraries

If you work in an environment where you want to share custom stamp libraries, you can copy files created on any computer and export them across computers of the same or different platforms. The stamp files must be located in a folder where Acrobat can recognize the documents as stamps.

On Windows XP, stamp files are saved to the My Documents/Adobe/Acrobat/Stamps folder. On Mac OS X, stamps are located in the Library/Acrobat User Data/Stamps folder. Locate the file you want to send to other computer users and copy the file across your network or e-mail the file to a colleague. The user on the other end needs to copy the file to the same folder.

When you add a stamp file to the Stamps folder on either platform, or you append the file using page templates, you may need to quit Acrobat and relaunch the program. If at first you don't see new stamps, be certain to relaunch Acrobat.

Creating custom dynamic stamps

You'll notice that several stamps listed in the Dynamic submenu have duplicate counterparts in the Standard Business submenu. For example, you find Approved listed in the Dynamic submenu, and Approved is also listed in the Standard Business Stamps submenu. You both stamps when you want to stamp a document as approved. The difference is that the Approved dynamic stamp adds the time and date when you stamp a document. The date and time is dynamic, because the values are retrieved from the current time on your computer clock in a text field using a JavaScript calculation. Additionally, some of the dynamic stamps retrieve identifying information you supply in the Identity preferences also displayed in text fields with JavaScript calculations. Figure 22-27 shows the appearance of the dynamic stamps with date and time and identity information added from JavaScript calculations in text fields.

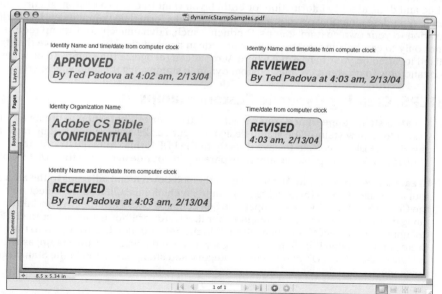

Figure 22-27: The dynamic stamps use JavaScript to retrieve time information.

Before using a dynamic stamp, be certain to add identifying information in the Identity preference settings. Open the Preferences dialog box by pressing ⌘/Ctrl+K and click on Identity in the left pane. Type your identifying information in the field boxes in the right pane, as shown in Figure 22-28.

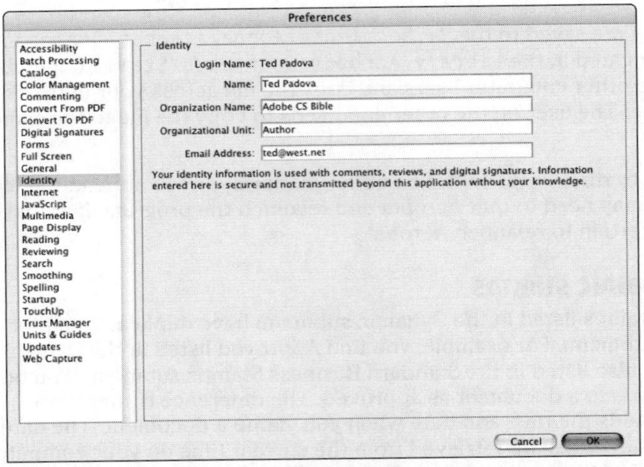

Figure 22-28: To use dynamic stamps, supply your identifying information here.

Each of the dynamic stamps contains a form field with a JavaScript calculation that changes the time and date, identity information, or both. If you want to create a custom stamp using dynamic time/date stamping or your name, you can add a form field containing a JavaScript calculation to your own custom stamps. Producing such a dynamic custom stamp requires you not only to carefully create the JavaScript code in a form field, but also to save the stamp in a fixed location on your hard drive where Acrobat can recognize the stamp. To completely understand how to go about creating custom dynamic stamps, try the following exercise.

STEPS: Creating Dynamic Custom Stamps

1. **Create a stamp appearance.** You can either Illustrator or Photoshop to create a custom design for a new stamp. The stamp design in Figure 22-29 was created in Illustrator and saved as a PDF. Be certain to save directly to the PDF format from Illustrator or Photoshop. You can preserve any transparency in your design using the PDF format.

2. **Create a custom stamp in Acrobat.** Open the pull-down menu adjacent to the Stamp tool and select Create Custom Stamp from the menu items. Click on the Select button in the Create Stamp dialog box to open the Select dialog box. Click the Browse button and navigate to the stamp you created in either Illustrator or Photoshop. Select the PDF document, click Select, and then click OK in the Select dialog box to return to the Create Stamp dialog box. Supply a category name and a name for the stamp, as shown in Figure 22-30. Click OK and the new category and stamp are listed in the Stamp pull-down menu.

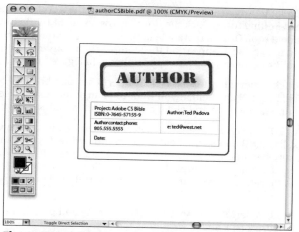

Figure 22-29: Design a stamp appearance in either Illustrator or Photoshop and save it as a PDF document.

Note

When you first create a custom stamp using the Create Stamp dialog box, you can add a stamp located anywhere on your hard drive. As a stamp is added to your custom stamp list, Acrobat saves the stamp to a separate file Acrobat creates.

The stamp you created resides on your hard drive in a file and a location Acrobat decided for you. On both the Mac and Windows, your custom stamp filename is a crazy name and appears something like: GaOI1MXmLLcZqn90q3uC.pdf. The location for the file on the Mac is: UserLogonName\Library\Acrobat User Data\Stamps. In Windows, the file location is found at one of two locations: [install directory]\plug-ins\Annotations\Stamps\[language] or [user directory]\Application Data\Adobe\Acrobat\6.0\Stamps.

Figure 22-30: Type a category name and a name for the stamp.

3. **Open the custom stamp file.** It's important to add your form field and JavaScript on the file located in the directory mentioned in Step 2 and not in the PDF document you created for your stamp appearance. Navigate to the directory where your custom stamps are located, and open the file located in the folder (remember this file has an unusual name provided by Acrobat and not the filename you used when you saved it from Illustrator or Photoshop).

4. **Add a form field.** Click the Advanced Editing Task button in the Acrobat Toolbar Well to open the Advanced Editing tools. Click the down arrow adjacent to the Button tool, and select the Text Field tool. Draw a rectangle in the area where you want to have the time and date, your name, or both appear on the stamp. When you release the mouse button, the Text Field Properties dialog box opens, shown in Figure 22-31.

5. **Add a field name.** Click General in the Text Field Properties dialog box and type a name for the text field in the Name field. If you want to change the text and text attributes, click the Appearance tab and change text attributes as desired.

6. **Open the JavaScript Editor.** So far, the text field is empty and ready to receive text you type in the field box. Rather than use the field for a user to add text, you want to automatically have text supplied in the field box for the time and date, identity, or both. For this to occur, you need to add a JavaScript. To add a JavaScript, click Calculate and click the Edit button adjacent to the Create Custom JavaScript field box, as shown in Figure 22-32.

7. **Add a JavaScript.** The JavaScript code that calculates a date and places the results in the field is shown in Figure 22-33, and is written as follows:

```
event.value = (new Date()).toString();
AFDate_FormatEx("h:MM tt, m/d/yy");
```

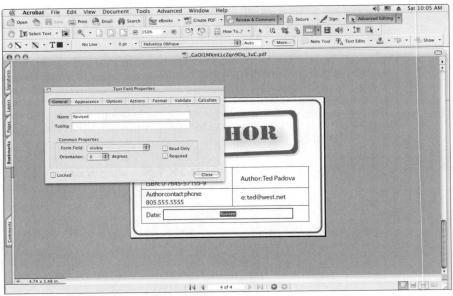

Figure 22-31: The Text Field Properties dialog box

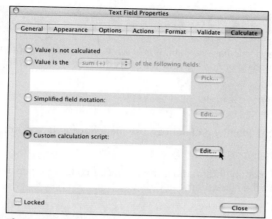

Figure 22-32: You can add JavaScript code via the Custom calculation script option.

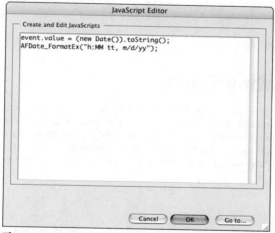

Figure 22-33: Type the code in the JavaScript Editor dialog box.

8. **Save the file.** Click OK in the JavaScript Editor and click Close in the Text Field Properties dialog box. Click File ➪ Save to update your edits. Be certain to not use Save As and change the filename or location. The next time you use your custom stamp, the date appears in the text field as supplied by the custom JavaScript.

Adding identities to text fields

The code used in the preceding steps calculates a date. If you want to use identity information, you need to change the JavaScript code. For adding your name as defined in the Identity preferences, use the following:

```
event.value = "By " + (identity.name || identity.loginName);
event.value = "By " + (identity.name || identity.loginName);
```

To add the organization field from the Identity preferences, use the following JavaScript:

```
event.value = (identity.corporation || identity.loginName);
```

If you want to combine dates and identity information, the following code produces the name used in the Identity preferences and the current time and date:

```
event.value = (new Date()).toString();
AFDate_FormatEx("h:MM tt, m/d/yy");
event.value = "By " + (identity.name || identity.loginName) + " at " +
event.value;
```

Windows users can open the dynamic stamps file from the Acrobat folder and copy and paste fields from the PDFs used for the dynamic stamps. Mac users need to code the fields as described here.

Advanced Commenting Tools

The Advanced Commenting tools offer you more options for marking up documents, attaching files, importing sound comments, and copying/pasting data to add as a comment. The Advanced Commenting tools are an extension of the basic Commenting tools but they're only available to Acrobat Professional users. Many of these tools also have associated note pop-up windows where you can use descriptions for markups, and they all have various options in a properties dialog box.

Drawing tools

Drawing tools comprise a set of instruments that enable you to create geometric and freeform shapes. Each tool has a variety of options for appearance settings, and they all support an associated pop-up note window. When you open the Advanced Commenting toolbar, select the pull-down menu beside the Rectangle tool and choose Show Drawing Toolbar. A set of seven different tools opens in a separate toolbar. An example of the markings made from these tools is shown in Figure 22-34.

The drawing tools can be placed in two groups: lines and shapes. The options for applying property changes are the same among common tools in a group. That is to say, all the line tools have common properties and all the shape tools have common properties.

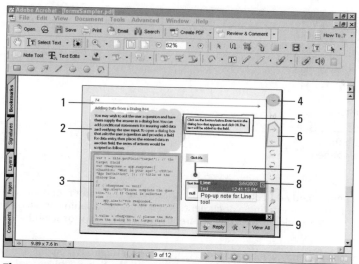

Figure 22-34: Examples of the drawing tools' marks include: 1: Arrow tool; 2: Cloud tool; 3: Rectangle tool; 4: Oval tool; 5: Polygon Line tool; 6: Polygon tool; 7: Line tool. In addition to the Drawing tools, 8: Pop-up note window and 9: Review Status Bar are shown.

Line tools

The line tools are used for creating straight lines. You might use line tools with or without arrowheads to illustrate points of interest, where background elements need to be moved, pointing to an object, or similar kinds of notations. These tools include

 Arrow tool: Creates lines for arrowheads, although applying arrowheads is a matter of user preference. You can draw straight lines on a 360-degree axis.

 Line tool: The Line tool can have the same attributes as the Arrow tool, making them indistinguishable from each other. However, the line tool does not have arrowheads. When marking up a document with both line tools, you don't need to keep addressing the Line Properties dialog box each time you want to toggle on or off arrowheads. It's a matter of user preference, though; you can choose to add or eliminate arrowheads from either tool.

 Polygon Line tool: The Polygon Line tool also creates straight lines, but the lines are connected as you click the cursor to move in another direction. When you finish drawing a shape or lines with angles, double-click the mouse button to complete the line.

Line tools and context menus

When you use any of the Drawing tools to create a mark on a page, releasing the mouse button automatically selects the Hand tool. You can use either the Hand tool or the Select Object tool to open a context menu. Depending on which tool you use, the context-menu options appear different depending on what tool you use to select the comment. In Figure 22-35, a context menu is opened on a line with the Hand tool.

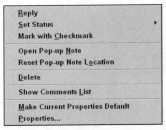

Figure 22-35: Menu options from a context menu opened with the Hand tool.

When you create comments and add comment notes, notice that the Hand tool context-menu options are suited for initially annotating a document. You'll find that opening and closing notes, deleting notes, and accessing properties are frequent tasks you perform while reviewing a document.

After creating comments, you may want to manage comments for alignment, sizing, cutting, copying, and pasting. These options are available when you use the Select Object tool, shown in Figure 22-36. When you use the Hand tool, you can select only a single comment. When using the Select Object tool, you can select all the comments on a page or select a group of objects. Open a context menu and you can apply changes to all selected objects. This feature is particularly helpful for aligning Drawing tool comments.

Figure 22-36: You can manage multiple comments with a context menu.

When comments share common properties options, you can use the Select Object tool to select the Properties dialog box for multiple comments. If you attempt to select objects where the properties options are different for the comments — for example the Line tool and the Cloud tool — the Properties dialog box offers only property changes that are common between the comments.

Line tools properties

With either the Hand tool or the Select Object tool, click on a line tool comment and open a context menu. Alternatively, you can open the Line Properties dialog box by selecting a comment with the Select Object tool and clicking on the More button in the Properties dialog box or double-clicking with the Select Object tool on a line. From the menu options, select Properties. If you have more than one comment selected when using the Select Object tool, the Line Properties dialog box opens, shown in Figure 22-37.

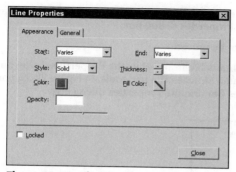

Figure 22-37: The Line Properties dialog box displays two tabs.

The Line Properties dialog box opens with two tabs accessible for changing line attributes. If you use the Hand tool or select a single comment with the Select Object tool, the third tab, Review History, is accessible. Review History is displayed only for individual comments. The Appearance tab includes the following options:

✦ **Start:** From the pull-down menu you select an arrowhead for the beginning of a line, as shown in Figure 22-38. The default is None for no arrowhead.

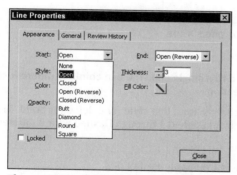

Figure 22-38: Select an arrowhead from the Start or End menu options.

✦ **End:** Same as the preceding option but applied to the end of the line. The pull-down menu choices are the same as for Start.

✦ **Thickness:** Line weights are selected from 0 to 12 points. Click the arrows or type a value in the field box.

✦ **Color:** Represents the stroke color. Color choices are made from the pop-up swatches palette the same as with note tools.

✦ **Fill Color:** Represents the Fill color. For drawing tools where a fill can be applied, the color choices are made from the color swatch pop-up menu.

✦ **Opacity:** Opacity is applied to both the stroke and fill colors. Move the slider the same as when adjusting opacity in the Note Properties dialog box.

✦ **Locked:** When checked, the line cannot be moved.

The choices you make for arrowheads are obtainable from either the Properties dialog box or the Properties Bar. Not all choices are the same between the two tools. In Figure 22-39, you see the results of choices from the Properties Bar and the Properties dialog box.

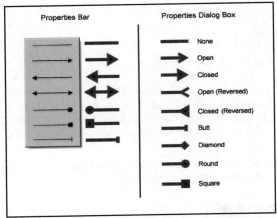

Figure 22-39: The Properties dialog box offers more selections for arrowheads.

Figure 22-39 shows arrowheads applied to a single end. You can combine different shapes in the same line with a start and end selection.

The Style pull-down menu offers you choices for a line style. The default is Solid. The remaining line styles are dashed lines. Select from Dashed 1 through Dashed 6 for a different style, as shown in Figure 22-40.

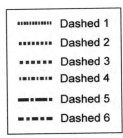

Figure 22-40: Six different dashed-line styles display in the Style menu.

The other two tabs in the Properties dialog box are the same as those found when using the Note tool. A Subject line is included in the General properties tab like the Note tool. The default name for the Subject is Line when using the Line tool. The default name changes according to the tool used to create the shape.

Managing line comments

To move drawing objects, align them, or reshape them, you need to select an object with the Hand tool. If you experience difficulty selecting a line, it may be due to the preference option where you Enable text selection for the Hand tool. If selecting drawing tool objects is awkward, open the Preferences dialog box (⌘/Ctrl+K) and select General in the left pane. Disable the check box for Enable Text Selection for the Hand tool.

Click on an object and you see handles appearing either at the ends of lines or at each end of line segments around polygon objects (see Figure 22-41). You can drag any handle in or out to resize or reshape objects. To move an object click on a line or a fill color and drag the shape.

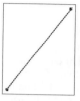

Figure 22-41: To reshape objects, click and drag a handle.

You can copy, cut, paste, delete, align, distribute, and size Drawing tools. Use the Select Object tool and open a context menu while one or more objects are selected. Choose a menu command for the operation desired.

 Tip When selecting with the Select Object tool, you can draw a marquee through objects to select them. You don't need to completely surround comments within a marquee to select them.

Shape tools

You use the remaining Drawing tools to draw shapes as opposed to lines. You can fill as well as stroke the objects. You can use different colors for the fills and strokes. Also found in the Drawing toolbar, these tools include the following:

 Rectangle tool: Draw rectangle or square shapes. To keep the object constrained to a square, hold down the Shift key as you click and drag.

 Oval tool: Same process as the preceding for constraining objects to circles. Oval shapes are drawn without adding the Shift key.

 Cloud tool: You use this tool like the Polygon Line tool. You click, release the mouse button, and move the cursor, click, and move the cursor again, and continue until you draw a polygon shape. Return to the point of origin, release the mouse button, and Acrobat closes the path. The paths appear as a cloud shape that you can fill and stroke. (Refer to Figure 22-35.)

 Polygon tool: Use the same sequence of clicking and moving as described in the preceding Cloud tool bullet. When you release the mouse button back at the point of origin, the shape closes with flat edges instead of semicircles like the Cloud tool.

Drawing shapes properties

The Properties dialog box and the Properties Bar offer options similar to the styles available with the Line tools. A solid line and six dashed lines are among the menu choices in either pull-down menu. Two additional options are added to these tools. The last two menu choices are Cloudy 1 and Cloudy 2. By default the Cloud tool uses a Cloudy line style. However the cloud effect can be applied to the other three tools in this group by selecting either Cloudy 1 or Cloudy 2 from the menu choices. Cloudy 1 renders smaller semicircles along the edge of shapes. Cloudy 2 renders larger semicircles.

Opacity settings made from either the Properties Bar or the tool's Properties dialog box applies equal levels of transparency to the strokes and the fills. Acrobat offers no option for rendering a stroke with a different level of transparency than the fill.

Text Box tool

The Text Box tool is used for creating text when more than a single line is created with the TouchUp Text tool or when adding messages in large blocks of text. You have more control over fonts, text attributes, and flexibility with the Text Box tool than when using a Note comment. Using the Text Box tool as a comment tool, you can track review history and see comments in the Comments list.

The Text Box tool offers you much more control over type than the type controls used with pop-up notes. As shown in Figure 22-42, you can bold, italicize, underline, strikethrough, superscript, subscript, and justify text left, right, and center. You can change fonts and point sizes in the same text block and Acrobat checks spelling on-the-fly as you type.

Figure 22-42: The Text Box tool enables you to add text on a page.

In the Text Box Properties dialog box, you can change opacity for text boxes, background colors, and line styles for borders. The remaining options are similar to properties for other comment tools.

Pencil tool

You use the Pencil tool to draw freeform lines. Whereas all the line tools draw straight lines, you use the Pencil tool for marking a page by drawing with a pencil, as you would with pencil and paper. The properties for pencil markings include choices for line weights, line colors, and line opacity settings.

Pencil comments are one contiguous line. If you stop drawing by releasing the mouse button, click, and drag again, a new comment is added to the document. After drawing a Pencil comment you can reshape the comment by selecting the line and dragging corner handles.

Pencil Eraser tool

The Pencil Eraser tool erases lines drawn with the Pencil tool. You cannot erase lines drawn with other tools. When you draw a line with the Pencil tool and erase part of the line, the remaining portion of a Pencil comment is interpreted as a single comment. Broken lines where you may have several smaller lines remaining after erasing part of a Pencil comment are considered part of the same comment. A note pop-up is associated with the entire group of line segments. In Figure 22-43, we drew an oval shape with the Pencil tool and later used the Pencil Eraser tool to erase parts of the shape. The remaining line segments are grouped. When clicking on any segment, the comment is selected as a single group.

Figure 22-43: The Pencil Eraser tool erases lines drawn with the Pencil tool.

Comment properties are associated with the Pencil comment. The Pencil Eraser tool itself has no properties.

Attach File tool

File attachments enable you to attach any document file on your hard drive to an open PDF file. Once attached, the file is embedded in the PDF document. Embedding a file provides other users the capability to view attachments on other computers and across platforms. At first it may appear as though the attachment is a link. However, if you transport the

PDF document to another computer and open the attachment, the embedded file opens in the host application. Users on other computers need the original authoring application to view the embedded file.

To use the Attach File tool, select the tool and click in the document window. The Select File to Attach dialog box opens, in which you navigate to a file and select it for the attachment. You can attach any file on your computer. Select a file and click Select. The File Attachment Properties dialog box opens with the Appearance tab in view, as shown in Figure 22-44.

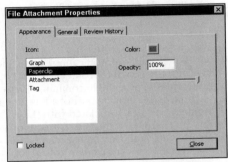

Figure 22-44: The Description field contains the name of the file attachment.

The Appearance properties for file attachments offer you choices for icon appearances to represent file attachments. Choose from one of the four icon choices shown in Figure 22-44. By default, the Paperclip icon is used.

By default the name of the file attachment is placed in the Description field box. You can edit the Description field, but leaving it at the default keeps you informed of what file is attached to the document. Figure 22-45 shows the General tab with the description noted as the name of the attached file.

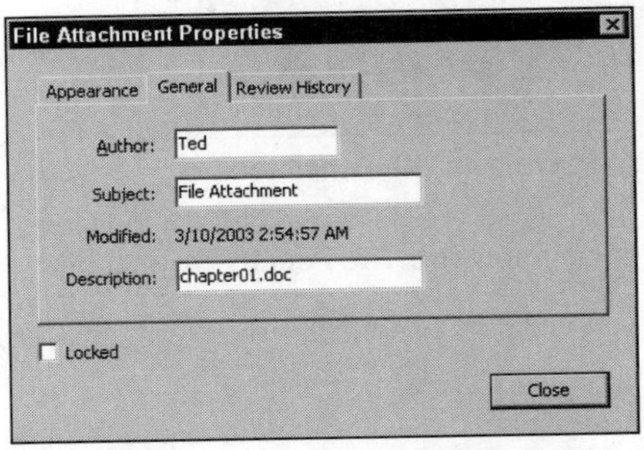

Figure 22-45: You enter the author, subject and description in the General tab.

If you place the cursor over a file attachment icon, a tooltip displays the attached filename. The name shown in the tooltip is related to the Description field in the General properties. As a matter of practice, it's best to leave the descriptions at the default, in order to be clear about what files are attached to documents.

The Attach File comment does not support an associated pop-up note. Double-clicking on an Attach File comment icon opens a dialog box where you're asked whether you want to open the file. Click Open in the dialog box. If the file is a file type other than PDF, the authoring application is launched and the program that created the file opens the file.

You can use PDF documents like a security wrapper for any file you want to exchange with colleagues and coworkers. Use the Attach File tool and attach one or more files to a PDF document. Secure the PDF with Password Security and use the Email tool to send the file to members of your workgroup. You can protect the document with password security and prevent unauthorized users from opening your PDF or extracting attached files. In this regard, you can use Acrobat to secure any document you create from any authoring program.

Cross-Reference For more information on using Password Security, see Chapter 28.

File attachments are embedded in PDFs and double-clicking on the Attach File icon unembeds the file. If you want to save an embedded file to disk without opening the file, open a context menu and select Save Embedded File to Disk. Acrobat opens a dialog box where you can navigate your hard drive and designate a location for the file save.

Attach Sound tool

Sound comments are recorded from within the PDF document or from prerecorded sounds saved in WAV (Windows or Mac) or AIFF (Mac). For recording a sound, you must have a microphone connected to your computer. The resulting sound file is embedded in the PDF when you use the Attach Sound tool.

Attaching prerecorded sounds

Select the Attach Sound tool and click on a PDF page. The Sound Recorder dialog box in Windows (see Figure 22-46) or Record Sound dialog box on the Mac (see Figure 22-47) opens. Click on Browse (Windows) or Choose (Mac).

Figure 22-46: In Windows, to select a sound file for attachment, click Browse.

Figure 22-47: On the Mac, to select a sound file for attachment, click Choose.

The Select Sound File dialog box opens after selecting Browse (Windows) or Choose (Mac). Navigate your hard drive and find a sound file to attach to the document. Select the sound file and click on the Select button. Acrobat returns you to the Sound Recorder dialog box

(Windows) or Record Sound dialog box (Mac). At this point, you can play the sound or click OK to embed the sound in the PDF. Click on the right-pointing arrow (Windows) or Play (Mac) and you can verify the sound before importing it. After you click OK, the Sound Attachment Properties dialog box opens.

After embedding the sound file in the PDF document, you can play the sound by opening a context menu on the Attach Sound icon and selecting Play File.

Recording sounds

Click the mouse button with the Attach Sound tool to open the Sound Recorder dialog box (Windows) or Record Sound dialog box (Mac). Click the Record button and speak into the microphone connected to your computer. When you've finished recording the sound, click the OK button (Windows) or Stop button (Mac). The Sound Attachment Properties dialog box opens immediately after stopping the recording. In Windows, the General properties are shown (see Figure 22-48); on the Mac, the Appearance properties are shown (see Figure 22-49).

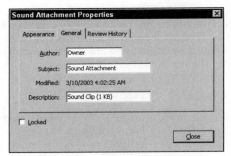

Figure 22-48: In Windows, after stopping a recording, the Sound Attachment Properties dialog box opens.

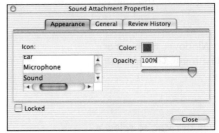

Figure 22-49: On the Mac, after stopping a recording, the Sound Attachment Properties dialog box opens.

When you close the Sound Attachment Properties dialog box, you can play the sound like imported sounds. Open a context menu and select Play Sound (or double-click the Attach Sound icon). Because the sound becomes part of the PDF document, you can transport the

PDF across platforms without having to include a sound-file link. All sound files are audible on either platform after they're imported into PDFs.

Sound attachment properties

Properties for sound comments are made available in the same manner as with other comments. Open a context menu and select Properties to open the Sound Attachment Properties dialog box. The Sound Properties dialog box (refer to Figure 22-48), offers selections for adding a text description and editing the author name. By default, the Description field shows the file size of the sound clip. You can change the description by typing in the field box. All descriptions are also viewed in the Comments palette. (See "Using the Comments palette" later in this chapter).

The Appearance properties offer you options for three different icon appearances. The color swatch and opacity adjustment are used to change the color of the icon.

Paste Clipboard Image tool

Paste Clipboard Image is a great new addition to the comment tools in Acrobat 6.0. To use this tool, you copy an image in another authoring application like Adobe Photoshop or Adobe Illustrator and paste the image in a PDF as a comment. As a comment, you have all the options for properties changes and review tracking. Keep in mind that pasting with this tool is much different than pasting data using menu and context-menu commands.

In Figure 22-50, a PDF page was copied to the Clipboard using the Snapshot tool. The Paste Clipboard tool was used to bring the Clipboard data into the document as a comment. When you double-click on the image with the Hand tool, a pop-up note window opens where a text description is added.

Figure 22-50: Pasted Clipboard data becomes a comment.

Pasting data with the Paste Clipboard Image tool requires you to copy image data. If you copy a passage of text, Acrobat doesn't recognize the text on the Clipboard for use with the Clipboard tool. The tool is grayed out unless an image is copied to the Clipboard.

Tip   If the Paste Clipboard Image tool is grayed out, you don't have an image copied to the Clipboard. To verify content on the Clipboard, open the Create PDF Task Button pull-down menu. If you see the From Clipboard menu item grayed out, you've verified that no image data exists on the Clipboard.

Using the Comments Pane

The Comments palette conveniently contains many tools and options for managing comments. By default, the Comments palette opens horizontally across the bottom of the Acrobat window and lists all the comments created in a PDF document. If you toggle views between several PDF files, the Comments palette dynamically updates the list of Comments to reflect comments on the file active in the Document pane.

Depending on the size of your monitor, you'll find that viewing the palette occupies substantial space in the Acrobat window. If you're working on a small monitor, the amount of room left over for viewing pages, after loading toolbars in the Toolbar Well and expanding the Comment palette, can be very skimpy. Fortunately, you can view the palette docked in the Navigation pane and control the size of the palette by dragging the horizontal bar at the top of the palette down to reduce the size, as shown in Figure 22-51.

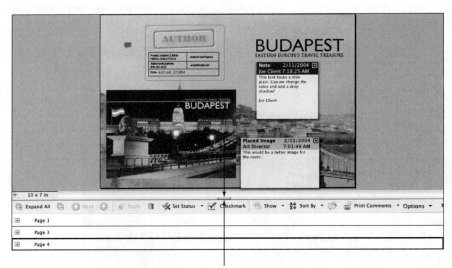

Move bar to resize palette

Figure 22-51: You can resize the Comments palette using the horizontal bar.

You also have a choice for floating the palette by undocking it from the Navigation pane and resizing the palette. To undock the Comments palette, click on the tab and drag the tab to the Document pane, as shown in Figure 22-52. You can resize the palette by dragging the lower-right corner in or out to reduce or expand the size.

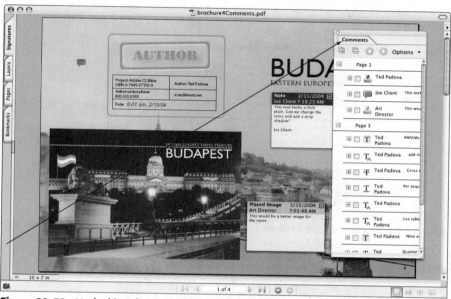

Figure 22-52: Undocking the Comments palette from the Navigation pane.

Whichever way you choose to view the Comments palette, you'll find using it to be a great asset when reviewing documents and participating in review sessions. At first, it may be a struggle to find the right size and location for the palette, but with a little practice you'll find the many tools contained in the palette much easier to access than using menu commands.

Viewing comments

The Comments palette lists all the comments contained in the active document. By default, the comments are listed by page. In a multi-page document, you'll see Page 1, Page 2, Page 3, and so on displayed in the list on the left side of the palette.

You can view the list of comments expanded or collapsed. In Figure 22-51, the list is collapsed. In Figure 22-52, you see the list expanded. Expanded lists show comments in a hierarchy like bookmarks are shown in the Bookmarks palette. You can expand individual pages where comments are contained by clicking on the plus (+) symbol (Windows) or the right-pointing arrow (Mac). To expand all comments, click on the Expand All button in the Comments palette toolbar (refer to Figure 22-51). Conversely, you can collapse all comments by clicking on the Collapse All button.

Comments are listed in a hierarchical order. If you have several comments on a page and you click on the icon to the left of the comment to expand the page comments, you see the Comment icon, author, and content of a note pop-up. You can further expand each comment in the expanded list by clicking on the plus (+) symbol (Windows) or right-pointing arrow (Mac). When further expanded, the comment subject and the creation date display in the palette. Figure 22-53 shows Page 1 and Page 2 expanded. On Page 1, the first two comments are expanded and the second two comments are collapsed. Pages 3 and 4 are collapsed.

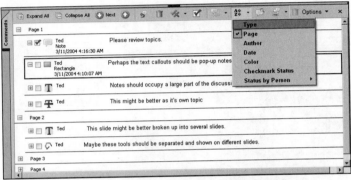

Figure 22-53: Comments are ordered in a hierarchical list.

Sorting comments

Also shown in Figure 22-53 is the pull-down menu that allows you to change how comments are sorted. You can change the default-page sorting to any of the following:

✦ **Type:** Comments are sorted together by the type of comment contained on pages. All note comments appear together, highlight comments together, stamps together, and so on.

✦ **Page:** The default. Comments are listed together successively by page.

✦ **Author:** If a document has comments from several different authors, the comments are listed by author and sorted in alphabetical order by author name.

✦ **Date:** The creation date is the sort order with the most recent date appearing first in the list.

✦ **Color:** Comments are sorted according to the color settings made in the comment properties dialog box.

✦ **Checkmark Status:** You can check a comment for your own personal method of flagging a comment. You may create checking comments to alert yourself to review comments, perhaps mark them for deletion, or to spend more time in a later editing session reviewing the comments made by others. The choice for what the check mark signals is a personal choice. When you view comments according to Checkmark Status, all unchecked Comments (Unmarked) are listed first, followed by comments marked with a check mark.

✦ **Status by Person:** The menu option includes a submenu where you can select an author. Select an author name from the submenu and comments are sorted with the comments for the selected author appearing first. The unchecked comments are listed next by author name. You must have Status set on at least one comment to activate this command.

Navigating comments

The up and down arrows in the Comments toolbar enable you to move back and forth between comments. Click the down-pointing arrow to move to the next comment in the list. Click the up-pointing arrow to navigate to a previous comment. The arrow tools are grayed out when comments are collapsed. In order to use the tools, you need to have one or more groups of comments expanded and have a comment selected.

Double-clicking on a comment in the list takes you to the page where the comment appears. When you double-click on the comment in the Comments palette, an associated pop-up note also opens.

Searching comments

The contents of comment pop-up notes can be searched. To find a word in a pop-up note, click on the Search Comments tool. Enter the search criteria and click Search Comments. You can also open the Search pane and select the Search in Comments check box. The Search pane offers you the same search options used for searching open PDF documents. You can match case, search for whole words only, and use other search criteria. The results of your search, however, return words found in the document as well as words found in comment pop-up notes.

When a word is found in a comment pop-up note, the page where the note appears opens and the pop-up note opens with the found word highlighted.

Printing comments

The Print Comments tool does more than print the comments in a document to your printer. When you select the Print Comments tool, a pull-down menu opens where you can choose from three menu options. These menu commands include the following:

✦ **Print Comments Summary:** Use this command to create a summary page as a new PDF file and print the summarized comments to your default printer. The comment summary is a temporary file that Acrobat creates while you print the summarized comments. After printing, Acrobat deletes the summary.

✦ **Create PDF of Comments Summary:** Use this command to create a new PDF document that summarizes the comments in your document, instead of printing a file to your printer. You can save this file and keep it around to review a summary of the comments. This document is created with a Continuous-Facing page layout.

✦ **More Options:** This option opens a dialog box where you can choose from a number of different attributes for the way the comment summary is created. After making options choices in the Summarize Options dialog box, click OK. A PDF file is created according to the options you select in the dialog box.

From each of the menu commands, Acrobat handles comments with summarized pages. If you want to print pages with comments, choose File ➪ Print with Comments.

Deleting comments

In addition to the context menus used when creating comments, you can delete them from within the Comments palette. Select a comment in the palette and click on the Trash icon to delete the selected comment. After deleting a comment, you have one level of undo available to you. If you change your mind after deleting a comment, choose Edit ⇨ Undo. Selecting multiple comments and clicking on the Trash icon can also be undone. Choose Edit ⇨ Undo Multiple Deletes if you change your mind after deleting multiple comments. In the event you lose the Undo command, you need to choose File ⇨ Revert to bring back the comment. The Revert command reverts back to the last saved version of the file.

Marking comments

You use the Mark the Current Comment with a Checkmark tool to flag comments for a special purpose. You can select a comment in the Comments list in the palette and click on the tool to checkmark the current selection. Check marks are also applied to comments by clicking in the open check-mark box when a comment is expanded (see Figure 22-53 to see a check mark applied to the first comment in Page 1). Between the expand/collapse icon and the comment icon is a check box. Click the box to checkmark a comment. Comments do not need to be selected to mark the check boxes when viewing an expanded list.

Setting comment status

Marking a comment with a check mark, described in the preceding section, is a method for you to keep track of comments for your own purposes. The Set the Comment Status tool is used to mark a comment's current status; it's intended for use in comment reviews and in sharing comments with other users. From the tool pull-down menu, you have several options for marking the status of a comment.

When you mark comments for status and view the comments sorted according to Status by Person, the comments are sorted according to the status groups. Beginning with Rejected, comments are listed for an author for all rejected comments appearing first in the list. Next, the same author's completed comments are listed, followed by the cancelled comments. Comments marked as None are listed last for each author. (The order is: Rejected, Completed, Cancelled, Accepted, None.)

Editing comment pop-up notes

A very handy feature available to you when viewing comments in an expanded list is the ability to edit note pop-up text. Instead of navigating to each page containing a comment and opening the associated note pop-up window to make your edits, you can delete, change, or modify text listed in the Comments palette.

When you select the note pop-up text in the Comments palette, the note pop-up window opens in the Document pane. As you make changes in the Comments palette, changes are reflected in the pop-up note window. If you edit text in the pop-up note window, the text edits are reflected in the Comments palette. To enable the dynamic viewing between the pop-up notes and the Comments palette, be certain to disable the check box in the Comment preferences for Hide Comment Pop-Ups when Comments List Is Open.

Creating an E-Mail Review

The abundant number of comment tools, properties, and menu commands would be nothing more than overkill if all you wanted to do was add some comments on PDF pages for your own use. Acrobat is designed with much more sophistication when it comes to commenting, and the tools provided are intended to help you share comments in workgroups. You'll notice we skipped a few tools in the Comments palette and we haven't yet covered the Options menu. These remaining features are used for community reviews and summarizing comments. We first address setting up a review session; later in this chapter, we cover comment summaries and filtering.

Comment and review among workgroups is handled in two ways:

✦ You can set up an e-mail review and exchange comments between your coworkers and colleagues where PDFs and data are exchanged through e-mail.

✦ You can set up a browser-based review where comments are uploaded and downloaded by participants to a Web server in the review process.

In Acrobat 5, you were limited to collaboration with commenting on Web-hosted documents. If you didn't have the right Web server or server-side programming set up, there was no easy way to set up an online collaboration event.

Adobe engineers realized the problems for users configuring Web servers for online commenting and created this new feature for setting up e-mail reviews where virtually anyone with an e-mail account can start a review session and invite users to participate. What the e-mail review is intended for is when you want to distribute a document to reviewers for feedback sessions. You receive feedback from reviewers and make corrections on a document. At that point you either finalize the PDF or send a revised copy back to reviewers for another feedback session. E-mail review is not intended for use as a communication thread where users exchange comments back and forth. You can exchange comments back and forth between you and your reviewers, but the intent for e-mail-based reviews is for reviewers to comment once where you make document corrections based on the single one-time responses. This was the intent of engineers when they developed Acrobat 6; however, many users may use the e-mail-based review for exchanging comments in multiple review sessions. There's nothing preventing you from doing so, but realize that there is another method available to you in the form of browser-based reviews for Windows users.

Browser-based reviews are designed for users to exchange comments back and forth, where all participants comment and review each other's comments. The users start comment threads and exchange messages back and forth until the commenting event is completed. Unfortunately, online commenting is not available to Mac users. In version 6.0 of Acrobat, no support for online commenting was made available. Therefore, the discussion in this chapter covers only e-mail-based reviews, because this form of commenting is available to both Mac and Windows users.

Initiating an e-mail review

An e-mail review is a method for you, the PDF author, to share a document with other users and ask them to make comments for feedback on a proposal or draft document that needs input from other users. As comments are submitted from other users, you can track comments from others and make decisions about how the comments are treated. Decisions like accepting or rejecting comments are part of this process. The comment exchanges between you and your workgroup members are handled through e-mail exchanges.

When you send a file for review, a modified FDF (Forms Data Format) and a copy of your original PDF as one file is sent to users in an e-mail list. When a recipient receives the document, it arrives as an FDF packaged with the PDF document. The recipients open the e-mail attachment in Acrobat and make comments. When a reviewer finishes commenting, the reviewer sends the data back to the PDF author. The data sent from the reviewers are also sent as FDF files, but the PDF document is not sent along with the comment data. If you start with a large PDF file, the comment exchanges require much smaller data transfers, because the comment data are typically much smaller than original PDF files.

Note   Before initiating a review, be certain to add your e-mail address in the Identity preferences. Open the Preferences dialog box and select Identity. Add your personal identity information including your e-mail address. The e-mail address you supply in the Identity preferences is used when e-mailing PDFs from within Acrobat. If the Identity preferences are not completed, Acrobat prompts you in a dialog box to type your e-mail address each time you start a review.

To begin a review session, open a PDF you want to use for the session and choose File ⇨ Send by Email for Review. After selecting Send by Email for Review, the Send by Email for Review dialog box opens, shown in Figure 22-54. The dialog box offers you detailed instructions for starting a review session.

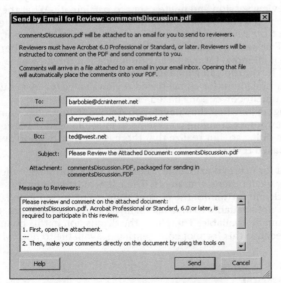

Figure 22-54: The Send by Email for Review dialog box gives you instructions for starting a review.

Avoiding problems with e-mail reviews

Understanding what data is exchanged during an e-mail review is critical. When you begin a review and choose the Send by Email for Review command, an FDF (Form Data File) *wrapper* embeds a PDF document in the e-mail attachment. Other participants receive the PDF document, and add comments to the document.

When the review participants send responses back to the PDF author, only FDF data is sent without an embedded PDF document. If a participant wants to add a reviewer, and the participant sends the FDF data to a user who is not invited to participate in a review, the new participant can't open the FDF file.

If recipients want to invite additional users, the *unwrapped* PDF needs to be distributed to other users. If you want to send the FDF data, you need to send the FDF file *and* the PDF document to users who have not been invited for participation from the PDF author.

If you receive additional comments during a review, an FDF data file is sent to you. Double-clicking on the FDF data file opens the PDF document you originally sent (or started with) if you haven't deleted the file or changed the directory path. When working with e-mail reviews, remember that two files exist. If you experience problems trying to open an FDF file in Acrobat, you either don't have the PDF on your hard drive or Acrobat lost the connection to the file.

When the author wants to invite new users to participate in a review, it's important to make the invitation with the proper menu command. You add additional users to a review by opening the Review Tracker and selecting Invite More Reviewers from the Manage pull-down menu. When you select this command, the PDF is contained in the FDF wrapper and sent to new users.

Fill in the To and Cc field boxes with e-mail addresses of the reviewers you want to use. The message each recipient receives is displayed in the Message to Reviewers window of the Send by Email for Reviewers dialog box. If you want to add your own message, or modify the default message, insert the cursor in the window and type your message. Click Send and the file is attached to a message in your e-mail application. If your e-mail program is configured to send e-mail automatically, an outgoing mail message dialog box opens. Click Send and the file is sent to all recipients. If your e-mail program is not configured for auto-sending mail, you may need to first launch the e-mail application and later click the Send button.

Note   You can also initiate e-mail reviews from within Microsoft Word and Microsoft Excel. The PDFMaker macro includes a menu option for converting to PDF and e-mailing the converted document for a review. Use the Convert to Adobe PDF and Send for Review tool or menu command in Word or Excel to initiate a review.

Participating in a review

Participants in a review include you, the PDF author and review initiator, and the people you select as reviewers. In your role, you field all comments from reviewers. If you use the e-mail-based review to send comments back to users, Acrobat does permit you to reply to users' comments. A review session is designed for a single set of responses; however, if you want, you can exchange comments back and forth between you and the reviews.

Before you begin a review, be certain to save any edits made on the PDF. If you insert pages, delete pages, or perform a number of other edits without saving, the comments retrieved from others will appear out of place and make it difficult to understand. Also, be certain to keep the original PDF in the same folder. If you decide to move the PDF to another folder, keep track of the location where the PDF resides. As you update comments, Acrobat needs to keep track of the directory path where the original PDF can be found. If Acrobat can't find the PDF, you'll be prompted to search for it.

During a review period, you and your recipients use tools in Acrobat designed for use with e-mail reviews. When starting an e-mail review, the first time you access the Send File for Email Review menu command, the FDF file and the PDF copy are sent to recipients. All subsequent comment exchanges between you and reviewers are handled with other tools. Don't return to the command if you decide to respond to user comments. Doing so sends another FDF wrapper with the embedded PDF. If PDF files are large in file size, the redundancy in sending the original PDF burdens users by having to download larger files when retrieving their e-mails.

Recipient participation

A recipient receiving your e-mail with the FDF attachment can open the attachment from the attachment folder or from directly within the e-mail message. Double-clicking on the file attachment launches Acrobat and loads the PDF in the Document Pane.

Note   When a recipient sees the file attachment in an e-mail message, the file appears as an FDF file. Although instructions are provided in the e-mail message on how to open the file, some users may become confused about the file when they see the FDF extension on the filename. You may need to explain that, although the file reads as an FDF file, the user can double-click on the file attachment to open the wrapped PDF document.

Reviewers make comments with any of the comment tools discussed earlier in this chapter. After a reviewer completes a review session, the reviewer clicks on the Send Comments button in the basic Commenting toolbar, shown in Figure 22-55. The tool appears in the Commenting toolbar when a recipient receives a file for review.

Figure 22-55: A reviewer clicks on Send Comments and the comment data is sent back to the PDF author.

When the reviewer sends a response back to the PDF author, the PDF author's e-mail address is automatically supplied in the To field in the e-mail program. The reviewer clicks Send and the FDF data is sent back to the PDF author.

Author participation

As comments are submitted from reviewers, you'll want to track reviews and decide to mark them for a status. If you want to reply to the recipients, you can send a reply to recipient comments; however, in most cases you'll want to make corrections and start a new review session. If you send a reply, each comment is treated like a separate thread in Acrobat. Rather than having to select different tools to make responses scattered around a document page, Acrobat keeps each thread nested together in the Comments tab to make following a thread easier.

To review comments added from recipients along a particular comment thread, select a comment with the Hand tool. The Review Status Bar opens where you can navigate through a comment thread, as shown in Figure 22-56. You click on the left and right arrows to navigate through comments added by you or other recipients. If you want to set the status of a comment, open the pull-down menu from the Status tool and select from the menu options.

Figure 22-56: If you want to mark a comment's status, select from the status states in the pull-down menu.

Updating comments

You send a file to recipients for review. The reviewers then send comments back to you. Your original document needs updating to reflect the reviewer's new additions. When you receive an e-mail attachment, the data are submitted to you in FDF format, containing all the comment information. Only a single PDF resides on your computer. If you want to merge the data sent by other reviewers with your existing PDF document, double-click the file attachment sent back to you. Acrobat updates your PDF document with the new comments.

Asking new reviewers to participate

You may begin a review and later decide you want to add new users to participate in the review. You can add new reviewers to a review at any time. To add a reviewer, open the PDF and open the Review Tracker by selecting the Review & Comment task button and choosing Track Reviews from the menu options. The Review Tracker opens in the How To pane. From the Manage pull-down menu, select Invite More Reviewers. The same dialog box opens as when you initiate a review. Add the recipient's e-mail address, as well as any additional message in the Message to Reviewers window; then click OK.

Cross-Reference For a detailed description of the Review Tracker, see the section "Using the Review Tracker."

Replying to comments

[Reply] The PDF author and the reviewers can reply to a comment that becomes part of a thread. The reply you create is the same comment type fixed to the same location on a page. For example, if a reviewer created a note comment on a page, you can reply to the note with another note placed exactly on top of the original reviewer's note. Instead of selecting the Note tool, you click on the Reply tool in the Review Status Bar.

When you click on Reply, a new comment pop-up note appears on top of the pop-up note you reply to. Type your message in the pop-up note. The new note is associated with the same note icon. As more reviewers reply, new notes are added to the same thread. If you click and drag a note pop-up window, no underlying note pop-ups are visible. The only way to see other notes is to navigate through notes in the Review Status Bar or open the Comments palette and review the comments list.

Likewise, if you move the comment icon, only a single icon appears on the document page for the respective note pop-up. All note pop-ups in a thread are associated with a single icon. You can move both icons and notes to a different location on the page, but you can only select a single icon and a single note pop-up. Although Acrobat provides you a means for creating a comment thread in an e-mail-based review, these tasks are better handled in browser-based reviews.

Using the Review Tracker

The Review Tracker is a pane in the How To window where you find menu commands to help manage e-mail-based reviews and browser-based reviews. To open the Review Tracker, select Track Reviews from the Review & Comments Task Button pull-down menu or select Open Review Tracker from the Comments palette Options menu. The Review Tracker opens in the How To pane, as shown in Figure 22-57.

Viewing documents in the Review Tracker

The pane contains two scrollable windows. You may have several reviews in progress at the same time and want to toggle between documents where a review is in progress. The top window lists current documents where reviews have been initiated. The list contains two groups that you can expand and collapse like comments listed in the Comments palette. One group contains all the e-mail-based reviews and the other group contains all browser-based reviews. To expand or collapse the list, click on the icon adjacent to the heading for Email-based or Browser-based.

To open a file currently under review, select the filename in an expanded list and click on the Open button. As you select filenames and click Open, each document opens in the Document pane, with the last file brought forward in the pane. To close a file, click the Close button in the Document pane or choose File ➪ Close like you would with any other PDF document.

The lower scrollable window contains information specific to the document selected in the upper window. Filename, type of review (e-mail-based or browser-based), status, and creation date are listed as informational items. Below this information is a list of all recipients by e-mail address. If you need a reminder for who was included in your review invitation, scroll the list and observe the e-mail addresses.

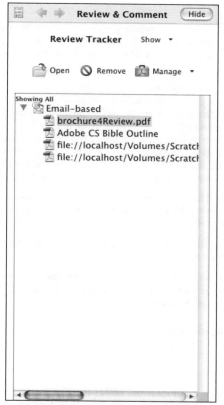

Figure 22-57: The Review Tracker helps you manage e-mail- and browser-based reviews.

Showing status

From the Show pull-down menu, you have several options for displaying the status of your reviews. These status options are different from the status options found with the Set Comment Status tool in the Comments palette. The Show commands include the following:

✦ **All:** Shows the status for all other menu options in the Show pull-down menu.

✦ **Active:** Until you mark a thread for completion, comments are active. When you enable the check box and disable the other options, only the active comments appear.

✦ **Completed:** If you disable Active and enable Completed, all comments you marked for completion are shown.

✦ **Sent:** Comments sent back to reviewers are shown. The responses from reviewers are hidden when the following option is disabled.

✦ **Received:** The opposite of the Sent menu command. All comments received from reviewers are shown, whereas the comments *you* send are hidden when the preceding option is disabled.

Managing comments

The Manage pull-down menu offers you options for communicating with reviewers. In order to activate the menu commands, you need to select a document name in the first scrollable window where your list of active documents appears. Select a file and open the pull-down menu to choose from these options:

✦ **Email All Reviewers (Windows only):** Selecting the menu command opens your e-mail program with all reviewers listed in the To, Cc, and Bcc fields. The position of the recipient's name corresponds to how you sent the original invitation to participate in the review. For example, if you supply one name in the To field and three names in the Cc field, the names are placed in the respective fields in the original order you supplied them. The Subject line defaults to Follow-up to *<filename*.pdf>. Where *filename* is the name of the PDF document you sent to the reviewers. You can change the Subject field to any subject you want. Add a note and send the e-mail message to all your recipients.

✦ **Send Review Reminder (Windows only):** The same action occurs as when selecting the preceding menu command. The difference is that the Send Review Reminder command creates a message reminding reviewers to comment.

✦ **Invite More Reviewers:** This opens the Send by Email for Review dialog box, where the PDF document automatically attaches to an e-mail message.

✦ **Go Back Online:** For browser-based reviews, you can comment offline; then you can reconnect to the server where the online commenting has been initiated. Select the command to reconnect to the server and upload your comments.

For more information on online commenting, see Chapter 20.

Removing links to PDF documents

If you end a session or no longer want to continue collaboration, select the PDF in the list window and click on the Remove button in the Review Tracker pane. The PDF document is removed only from the Review Tracker window, and the link from Acrobat to the PDF document is broken. The file remains on your hard drive and you can open it by choosing File ➪ Open or by using the Open tool.

Access to the menu commands is also available from context-menu commands. To open a context menu, place the cursor in the first information window where the filenames are listed. Open a context menu, and the same options for managing comments are listed in the menu.

Exporting and Importing Comments

If you ask a colleague to comment on a document, you can bypass the e-mail-based and browser-based reviews by having a reviewer export comments and e-mail the exported file to you. When you export comments from a PDF document, the data is exported as an FDF file. The data file results in much smaller file sizes than PDF documents and you can easily import it into the original PDF or copy of the original PDF document.

To export comments from a PDF document, choose Document ➪ Export Comments. The Export Comments dialog box opens. The dialog box behaves similarly to a Save As dialog box, where you select a destination folder, provide a filename, and click a Save button.

Acrobat provides a default name by using the PDF filename with an FDF extension. You can use the default name or change the name in the File Name field box. From the Save as Type pull-down menu (Windows) or the Format pull-down menu (Mac), you can select between FDFs and XFDFs (XML-based FDF file). The default is FDF.

Click Save in the Export Comments dialog box. You can export the resulting file to a user who has the same PDF document from which the FDF file was created. If you receive an FDF file and want to load the comments, choose Document ⇨ Import Comments. The Import Comments dialog box opens. Navigate to the location where the data file is located and select it. Click the Select button and the comments are imported into the open PDF document.

When you import comments in a PDF document, all the comments are imported in the exact location where they were originally created. If you delete a page in a PDF file and import comments, Acrobat ignores comments where it can't find matching pages. Note pop-ups and icons are matched with the way they appear in the file from which the comments were exported.

Exporting selected comments

You can select comments and choose to export only the selected comments to an FDF file. Open the Comments palette and select comments according to the sort order listed in the Comments palette. The default is by page. Select a page in the list and open the Options pull-down menu from the Comments palette toolbar. Select Export Selected Comments from the menu options, as shown in Figure 22-58.

Figure 22-58: Selecting the Export Selected Comments option.

The Export Comments dialog box opens. Navigate your hard drive to find the folder where you want to save the FDF file. Provide a name for the file, and click the Save button.

Tip When exporting all comments, leave the filename for the FDF-exported file at the default that Acrobat provides. When exporting Selected Comments, be certain to edit the filename. By default, Acrobat uses the same name. If you export all comments and then want to export selected comments, you might mistakenly overwrite files with the same filename. If you make a habit of being consistent when naming files, you'll prevent potential mistakes.

Exporting comments to Microsoft Word

If you create PDFs from Microsoft Word and use comments in Word and Acrobat, it may be easier to export comments directly back to your Word document. In order to take advantage of this feature you must be running Windows XP Service Pak 1 or above and you must be using Word 2002 or above. The feature is not supported on Mac OS X or Windows 2000.

Be certain to use the Export Comments to Word feature on files that are not changed while importing or exporting comments. If you edit a Word document after creating the PDF file, or you edit the PDF document by inserting, deleting, or performing other page-editing functions, the import/export operations may not work properly.

Comments that are exported from Acrobat to a Word document appear as comment bubbles in Word. Marking text for deletion and insertion is also supported in Word.

You can either start this process from within Acrobat with Export Comments to Word, or you can start this process from within Microsoft Word with Import Comments from Acrobat. In both cases, the Import Comments from Adobe Acrobat dialog box is launched.

To export comments to a Word document from Acrobat, choose from one of several menu commands — such as File ⇨ Export Comments to Word or Document ⇨ Export Comments to Word — or use the Comments palette Options pull-down menu and choose Export Comments to Word.

To import the exported comments in a Word document, in Word 2002 on Windows XP open the Word file that you converted to PDF. In Word, choose Acrobat Comments ⇨ Import Comments from Acrobat. The Import Comments from Adobe Acrobat dialog box opens. You can select the comments you want to import and choose from All Comments, All Comments with Checkmarks, and Text Edits Only: Insertions and Deletions. For a specific set of comments, select Custom Set and choose the filter options to filter the comments.

Cross-Reference   For information on comment filtering, see the next section in this chapter.

If you import text-edit comments, Word prompts you for confirmation as each comment is imported. Be certain to track changes in Word, or you won't see the dialog box appear. As you're prompted to accept changes, you can choose to apply changes or discard them as the comments are imported.

Filtering Comments

You can further enhance the features available to you for review and markup, exporting and importing comments, and viewing comments in the Comments palette, by filtering comments in groups. Filtering comments temporarily hides comments you don't want to use at the moment. You can choose to display all comments by an author, a date, a reviewer, selected types of comments, and a range of other criteria. When you filter comments, Acrobat only applies exporting comments or creating comment summaries (explained in the next section) to those comments currently in view and excludes any hidden comments.

You manage the comment filter via the pull-down-menu selections under the Filter the Comments Displayed tool in the Comments palette, as shown in Figure 22-59. The assortment of options available to you includes the following:

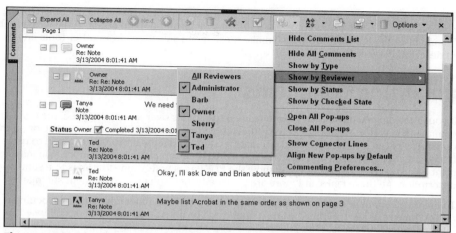

Figure 22-59: The Filter the Comments Displayed tool has options for filtering comments.

✦ **Hide Comments List:** Hides the Comments palette. The command works the same as clicking on the Palette tab. To reopen the list, choose View ➪ Show Comments List.

✦ **Hide/Show All Comments:** Enables you to hide comments while leaving the Comments palette open. By default, you may have all options for filtering comments enabled. If you want to view comments contributed by a single author, you might first select this menu item, then choose the author comments you want to see listed in the Comments List.

✦ **Show by Type:** Presume you want to export all Text Edit comments. You make the selection for the comment type from the submenu. Among the comment types that you can select for filtering are All, Notes, Drawing Markups, Text Editing Markups, Stamps, and Attachments. When you select All, all comment types are used. You can select one or more comment types from the other choices.

✦ **Show by Reviewer:** If you want to select comment notes from three different reviewers and export the comments, you select the comment type, then open the submenu for Reviewers and select those reviewers you want to export. Each reviewer is listed as a separate name in the submenu. All Reviewers selects all reviewers that are subsequently shown in the Comments palette.

✦ **Show by Status:** The Status items you check during a review are applied to comments where you make the edits. To filter comments for status, you can choose from the submenu options All Status, None, Accepted, Rejected, Cancelled, and Completed.

✦ **Show by Checked State:** The check mark you use for your own purposes includes either checked or unchecked states. From the submenu items, choose from Checked and Unchecked, Checked, or Unchecked.

Tip

If you know ahead of time that you want to export edits back to Microsoft Word, you can mark only those comments received from reviewers that you intend to export to Word. After the review session, choose View ➪ Comments ➪ Hide All Comments. Open the menu again and choose Show by Type ➪ Text Editing Markups. Return to the menu and choose Show by Checked State ➪ Checked. Export the comments and only the Text Edit comments with the items you checked during the review export to Word.

The remaining menu options include non-filtering menu choices such as opening/closing note pop-ups, showing connector lines, aligning icons and pop-up notes, and accessing the Comment preferences. You can also make these menu selections from other tools and menus, as described earlier in this chapter.

Summarizing Comments

If you create an extensive review from many participants over a period of time, the number of comments may become too great to comfortably manage in the Comments palette or on the document pages. Or you may need to create a comment summary for distribution to users that filters out comments that you don't want included in a summary. Furthermore, you may want to print a hard copy of comments that show the PDF pages with connector lines to a summary description. All these tasks and more are provided when you create comment summaries.

To create a comment summary, you need to have a PDF document open in the Document pane and comments in view in the Comments palette. The palette can be open or collapsed. You can filter comments according to the sorts and filtering you want to apply, but at least one comment with the criteria must exist for a summary report to contain comment information.

If the Comments palette is collapsed, you create a comment summary by choosing Document ➪ Summarize Comments. If the Comments Pane is open, you can choose the menu command from the Options menu.

When you choose Summarize Comments from either menu command, the Summarize Options dialog box, shown in Figure 22-60, opens. Users of earlier versions of Acrobat can appreciate the greater number of options you have in Acrobat 6.0 for displaying comment summaries.

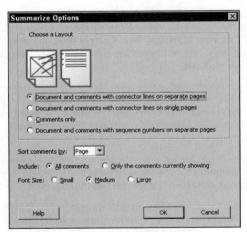

Figure 22-60: The Summarize Options dialog box

The first four radio buttons in the dialog box offer you choices for the way the summary pages are created and the page-layout view that may contain single-page views or page-layout views in Continuous — Facing Pages. The resulting summaries are created as separate PDF documents.

Choices for creating a comment summary in the Summarize Options dialog box include the following:

✦ **Document and Comments with Connector Lines on Separate Pages:** The first choice is a comment summary created with each summary page aside the respective document page, with connector lines from each comment on a page to the summarized item in a new summary. When the summary is created, Acrobat automatically switches to a Continuous – Facing Pages layout, as shown in Figure 22-61.

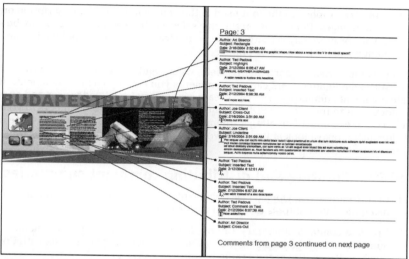

Figure 22-61: Summarized comments are shown with connector lines.

✦ **Document and Comments with Connector Lines on Single Pages:** The summary is similar to the preceding option; however, the PDF document and the summary are created together on a single standard U.S. letter landscape page. One advantage of this summary view is that the comments, connector lines, and summary data require a little less room on your monitor to view the original file and the summary information. Furthermore, if you export summaries for other users, the summarized information and original file are assembled together in a single document.

✦ **Comments Only:** This summary option is similar to summaries created in earlier versions of Acrobat. Only the summarized data is assembled together on single pages. The comment summaries are shown in a hierarchy according to the sort order you select in this dialog box. The page layout is a single-page view.

✦ **Document and Comments with Sequence Numbers on Separate Pages:** Summaries are created similarly to the method described in the preceding bullet, but with the addition of sequence numbers assigned to each comment according to the sort order and the order in which the comments were created. The page-layout view is Continuous — Facing Pages, which shows the comments with sequence numbers and the resulting summary in the opposing page view.

✦ **Sort Comments By:** From the pull-down menu, you can choose from four different options. The default is Page. If you want another sort order, choose from Author, Type, or Date from the pull-down menu options. The sort order selected in the Summarize Options dialog box supersedes the sort order selected in the Comments palette.

✦ **Include:** Selecting the All Comments radio button summarizes all comments on the PDF pages regardless of whether the comments are in view or hidden. Selecting the Only the Comments Currently Showing radio button creates a comment summary from the comments visible in the Comments palette.

✦ **Font Size:** Applies to the font used in the comment summary description on the newly created pages. Depending on the size selected, the summary pages may be fewer (Small) or more pages (Large). The point size for small is 7.5 points; for medium, 10 points; and for large, 13.33 points.

Comment summaries are particularly useful when sending PDF documents to Adobe Reader users. Although Reader users can see comments you create in a PDF document, they cannot create comment summaries. You can create a summary for a Reader user and append the new document to the existing PDF file, then send the file to other members in your workgroup. For an example of creating a summary, appending pages, and ultimately e-mailing a PDF document, take a look at how this workflow might be performed by following these steps:

STEPS: Creating and distributing comment summaries

1. **Create comments.** Open a PDF document. Get creative and add a number of comments using the different tools discussed in this chapter.

2. **Create a comment summary.** Choose Document ⇨ Summarize Comments. In the Summarize Comments dialog box, select Document and Comments with Connector Lines on Pages (the second radio button).

3. **Save the comment summary.** The summary is created as a new PDF document, but the file isn't. Choosing File ⇨ Save As saves the file to disk.

4. **View documents in a Tiled view.** The summary opens as a new PDF document. Your original PDF and the summary are open together in the Document pane. To see both documents in the Document pane, choose Window ⇨ Tile ⇨ Vertically.

5. **Append pages.** Click on the Pages tab in each document to open the palette and view page thumbnails. Select all the summary pages in the PDF file created as the comment summary, and drag them to the pages palette in the original PDF document. As you drag to the original PDF document, move the cursor below the last page, as shown in Figure 22-62.

6. **Save the PDF document.** Update the original PDF document by choosing File ⇨ Save As. Rewrite the file to optimize it and overwrite the original file. If you want to create a copy of the original file, use another filename in the Save As dialog box. Close the summarized file.

7. **E-mail the modified PDF document.** With your updated PDF in view in the Document pane, click the Email tool or choose File ⇨ Email. Your default e-mail program is launched and the PDF document is attached to a new message, as shown in Figure 22-63. Enter your own e-mail address so you can receive the PDF and review it in Acrobat.

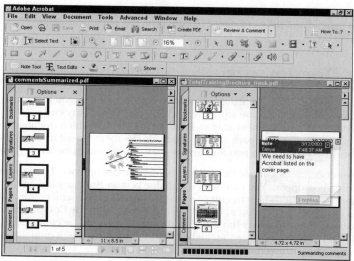

Figure 22-62: Drag the page thumbnails in the summarized document to the Pages palette in the original PDF document.

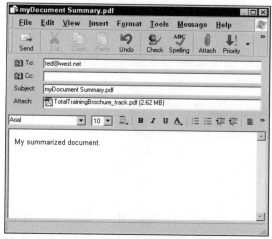

Figure 22-63: Sending your modified PDF document by e-mail

8. **Open your mail and retrieve the file.** In your e-mail program, double-click the file attachment. You should see the appended pages at the end of the document.

If you want to send just a comment summary instead of the appended PDF document, save the summary file and e-mail the file as described in the preceding steps. You can often use comment summaries with members of your workgroup who use the Adobe Reader software, to keep them abreast of progress in a review process. Because Reader users can't import comments and take advantage of smaller FDF files, you can trim file sizes by sending comment summaries.

Comparing Documents

If you set up a review for users to provide feedback on a document, you can incorporate recommended changes in a file. As you work on modifying files, you may end up with several documents in different development stages. If you aren't certain which document contains your finished edits, you can compare files to check for the most recent updates. Acrobat's Compare feature lets you analyze two files and report all differences between them.

To compare two documents choose Document ➪ Compare Documents. The Compare Documents dialog box opens. You can open the dialog box without any file open in the Document pane or open both files to compare and then select the menu command. In Figure 22-64, two files — graph.pdf and grapha.pdf — are identified in the Compare Documents dialog box. Because these two files have similar names, it's easy to be confused about which document is intended to contain for the final artwork. Therefore, the documents are selected for comparison to check the differences.

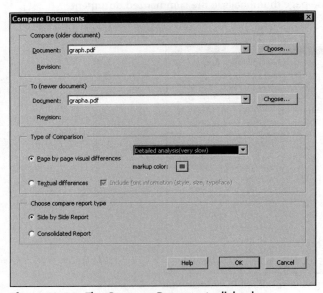

Figure 22-64: The Compare Documents dialog box

The Compare Documents dialog box contains the following options:

✦ **Document:** The first two items identify the documents for comparison. If no files are open in the Document Pane, click the Choose button and select a file in the Open dialog box that appears. Click the second Choose button and open a second file. If you have the two documents to be compared open in the Document pane before opening the Compare Documents dialog box, the pull-down menus show you both open files. Select one file in the top pull-down menu and the second file in the next pull-down menu.

✦ **Page by Page Visual Differences:** Three options are available from pull-down-menu choices. Depending on which item you choose, the reports are more or less detailed, and the speed in which the documents are compared relates to how much detail you want to analyze. A detailed analysis takes more time than the other two options. Choose from Detailed Analysis, Normal Analysis, and Coarse Analysis. Small visual differences between documents are reported when choosing the Detailed Analysis (Very Slow) option. The resulting report shows differences in very small graphics. The Coarse Analysis ignores small graphics that may appear on one document or another, and the Normal Analysis option falls somewhere between the other two.

✦ **Textual Differences:** Selecting this radio button deselects the preceding radio button. Use this option lets you compare text in the document while ignoring graphics. If you want to compare fonts between documents, select the Include Font Information (Style, Size, Typeface) check box.

✦ **Markup Color:** A report is created with markups. You can choose what color is used for the markups by clicking on the color swatch and selecting a preset color or a custom color.

✦ **Choose Compare Report Type:** After comparing two files, Acrobat creates a report. The type of report can be either a Side by Side Report with the two documents displayed in a Continuous – Facing Page layout and comparison marks showing the differences, or a Consolidated Report, where differences are marked with comment notes in a single PDF document. Choose the report type and click OK.

Acrobat compares the documents according to the attributes selected in the Compare Documents dialog box. When the comparison is finished, the report is created according to the report type selected in the Compare Documents dialog box.

Summary

✦ Acrobat provides an extensive set of Comment preferences. Before beginning any review session, you should review the preference settings by choosing Edit ⇨ Preferences and clicking on Commenting in the left pane.

✦ Two toolbars exist with commenting tools in Acrobat Professional — the Commenting toolbar and the Advanced Commenting toolbar.

✦ Most comments created in Acrobat have associated note pop-up windows where you can type comments.

✦ You access comment properties by opening context menus from a note icon or pop-up note title bar.

✦ You can create custom stamps in Acrobat from a variety of different file formats.

✦ The new Paste Clipboard Image comment tool enables you to copy images to the Clipboard and use the pasted image as a comment with an associated comment note.

✦ The Comments palette lists all comments in a PDF document. Additional tools are available in the Comments palette, where you can mark status changes in comments, check comment status, and filter comments.

✦ The Review Tracker opens in the How To window. All active documents under review are listed in the Review Tracker pane. You can select from a number of ways to communicate with reviewers from menu options in the Review Tracker.

✦ Anyone with an e-mail address can participate in an e-mail review. A PDF author sends a PDF document to selected members of a review team who comment on the document and send the comment data back to the PDF author.

✦ Comment threads are viewed by navigating comments in the Review Status Bar. A Comment thread contains a single note icon and pop-up window. Reviewer comments in a thread are viewed by clicking on arrows in the Review Status Bar.

✦ Comments can be filtered and sorted to isolate authors, types, dates, and other criteria. When exporting comments, only the sorted comments in view in the Comments palette are exported.

✦ Comments exported from a document can be imported in a matching PDF file. The comment data is saved as an FDF and results in smaller file sizes.

✦ Comments can be exported directly to Microsoft Word files on Windows XP with Word 2002.

✦ Comment summaries are displayed in one of four different report styles. When a summary is created, it can be sorted upon creation and saved as a separate PDF file.

✦ The Compare Documents command enables you to locate differences in text and images between two PDF documents. Reports are generated with comments describing the found differences.

✦   ✦   ✦

Designing Layouts

Imagine the process of creating a sidewalk. The first step is to create the forms that define the edges of the sidewalk. If you create these before you mix the cement, the cement easily flows into the right location and the job is completed rather quickly. However, if the forms are not straight or secure, the cement flows outside the bounds and finished work won't be smooth and straight. Similarly, if you complete the layout design is completed beforehand, the text and images flow easily into the document in the correct positions.

This chapter covers the basics of creating a useful layout in InDesign. The initial settings for a layout document are set when you create a new document. You can use the Pages palette to add and delete pages, rearrange pages, and create spreads and Master pages. Master pages provide a convenient way to update similar content on many pages at once. Several other useful layout objects include rulers, grids, guides, and frames. Using these objects, you can quickly lay out all the objects that are included in a page before the content is ready. The content can then be easily placed within these frames when it's ready.

Establishing an InDesign Layout

You establish layouts in InDesign when you create a new document. The New Document dialog box that opens when you create a new document includes settings for defining the number of pages, the page size, the orientation, the margins and columns, and the bleed and stub areas. You can save these settings and reuse them to create other new documents. You can also change settings at any time using the Document Setup dialog box.

Creating new documents

You initially specify basic layout design in InDesign when you first create a new document. Choose File ➪ New (⌘/Ctrl+N) and the New Document dialog box opens, shown in Figure 23-1. The settings specified in this dialog box determine the initial document layout.

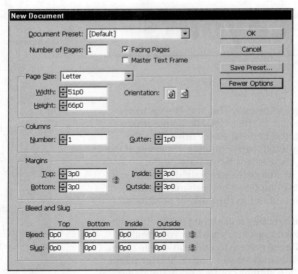

Figure 23-1: The New Document dialog box includes settings for initial layout.

Using the New Document dialog box, you can specify the total number of pages that make up the layout. The Facing Pages option causes left and right pages to face one another. If this option is disabled, each page stands alone, which is common if you plan on printing on both sides of a sheet. The Master Text Frame option causes a text frame to be added to the Master.

The following options on the New Document dialog box control the page layout of your new document:

✦ **Page Size options:** The Page Size drop-down list includes several common paper-size options including Letter, Legal, Tabloid, Letter – Half, Legal – Half, A4, A3, A5, B5, Compact Disc, and Custom. Selecting any of these sizes automatically adjusts the Width and Height settings. The Custom option lets you manually set the Width and Height values.

Tip   You can add your own options to the Page Size menu by editing the New Doc Sizes.txt file located in the InDesign\Presets folder. Just follow the same format used by the other entries in this text file.

The Orientation icon buttons include Portrait and Landscape options. A Portrait orientation has a height that is greater than its width, and a Landscape orientation has a larger width than height. Clicking the unselected icon button swaps the Width and Height values. Figure 23-2 shows two new Letter-sized documents. The left one has a Portrait orientation, and the right one has a Landscape orientation.

Pages versus spreads

The seemingly simple Facing Pages option in the New Document dialog box defines the differences between pages and spreads. If the Facing Pages option is disabled, then each page is separate from the others and displays on its own art board. If you enable the Facing Pages option, then adjacent pages are combined together to create a spread.

To understand a spread, open a book or a magazine and notice how two pages are viewed at once with one page on each side. Together these pages make up a spread. Spreads in InDesign are displayed together on a single art board.

When you create a spread, you always place odd-numbered pages on the right (the *recto*) and even-numbered pages on the left (the *verso*). The first page (numbered page 1 by default) appears by itself. Each successive even-and-odd-page pair is a spread.

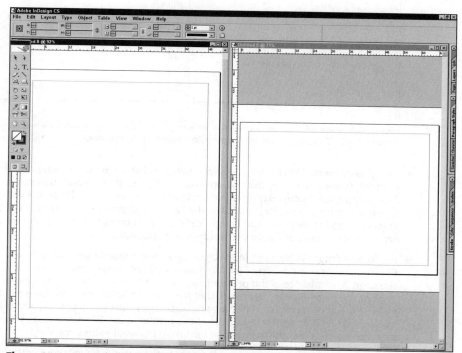

Figure 23-2: You orient new documents with a Portrait (left) or a Landscape setting (right).

✦ **Column options:** The Columns section of the New Document dialog box lets you specify the number of text columns on all pages in the layout. The gutter is the space between each column. Figure 23-3 shows two new layouts. The left layout has two columns and the right layout has three columns with a wider gutter.

Figure 23-3: Columns split the page into several different areas.

✦ **Margins options:** *Margins* are the space between the edge of the paper and the page content. Guides, which appear where you specify margins, denote this space. You have four margin values correlating to each edge of the page—Top, Bottom, Left, and Right. If you select the Facing Pages option, the Left and Right margins become the Inside and Outside margins. Between the margin values is an icon button with an image of a link on it. Clicking this button sets all settings to equal values.

✦ **Bleed and Slug:** Clicking the More Options button expands the dialog box to reveal Bleed and Slug settings. The Bleed and Slug areas of a page extend beyond the edges of the page. The *Bleed* tells the printer how far to extend a color or image beyond the edge of the page in order to ensure that the color or image runs all the way to the paper edge after trimming. The *Slug* area displays printer instructions and other information that isn't intended to be part of the printed page. Bleed and Slug values include settings for each margin and an icon button to make all values equal.

When you create a new page, several guides denote the various page-layout settings. These guides are color-coordinated, with the margins represented by pink-colored guides, the columns and gutters represented by purple guides, the Bleed areas represented by red guides, and the Slug area represented by light-blue guides. The page edges are displayed as black guides. Figure 23-4 shows the various guides.

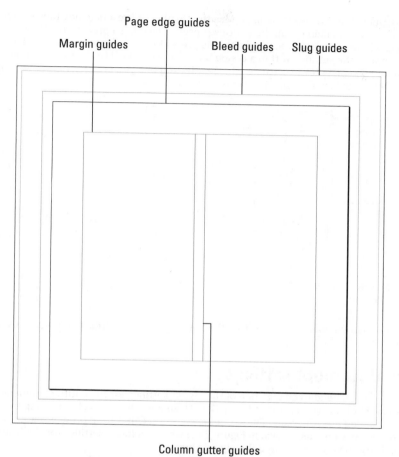

Figure 23-4: The layout of each new document is denoted with color-coded guides.

Creating a document preset

If you find yourself changing the default layout options every time you create a new document, you may benefit from a document preset. When you make the setting changes, click the Save Preset button and a simple dialog box appears where you can name the new preset.

After it's saved, the new preset is available for selection from the Document Preset list at the top of the dialog box. Selecting the preset name changes all the settings automatically. Saved presets are also available by choosing File ➪ Document Presets.

Tip Holding down the Shift key while selecting a preset from the File ➪ Document Presets menu command creates a new document without opening the New Document dialog box.

Choosing File ⇨ Document Presets ⇨ Define opens the Document Presets dialog box, shown in Figure 23-5, where you can manage all the various presets. Selecting a preset from the list of presets displays all the settings associated with this preset in the lower text pane. Clicking the Edit button opens the settings within a dialog box that is identical to the New Document dialog box, where you can edit the settings. The New button lets you create a new document preset, and the Delete button deletes the selected preset.

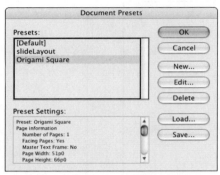

Figure 23-5: You can create and manage document presets here.

You can save and load document presets from the hard drive. These presets are saved using the DCST extension.

Changing document settings

If you discover that you need to change one of the layout settings for the entire document, you can revisit most of the same settings in the New Document dialog box by opening the Document Setup dialog box. Choosing File ⇨ Document Setup (Alt+Ctrl+P on Windows; Option+⌘+P on the Mac) opens, shown in Figure 23-6, which includes settings for the Number of Pages, Page Size and Orientation, and Bleed and Slug.

Changing the default layout settings

When you first create a new document, the default layout settings are used. You can alter these default settings by changing the settings in the Document Setup dialog (choose File ⇨ Document Setup) and/or the Margins and Columns dialog box (choose Layout ⇨ Margins and Columns) when you have no documents open.

If you don't have any other documents opened when you make changes to these dialog boxes, and you create a new document, the default layout updates.

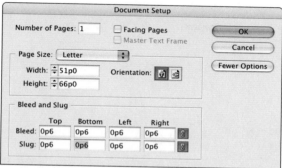

Figure 23-6: The Document Setup dialog box resets most of New Document dialog box options.

You use the Margins and Columns dialog box to change the margins and columns settings, shown in Figure 23-7. You open this dialog box by choosing Layout ⇨ Margins and Columns. However, any changes entered into this dialog box affect only the current page or spread.

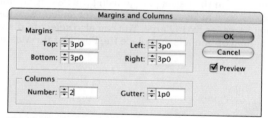

Figure 23-7: The Margins and Columns dialog box changes only the current page or spread.

To change the margin and column settings for all pages in the document, select all pages in the Pages palette before opening the Margins and Columns dialog box.

Working with Pages and Spreads

After establishing a layout, you use the Pages palette to work with the different pages and/or spreads. Using this palette, you can select, target, rearrange, delete or add pages and/or spreads. The Pages palette also provides access to Master pages.

Using the Pages palette

The Pages palette, shown in Figure 23-8, provides a high-level view of all the pages in the current document. It displays each page and spread as an icon. You use it to quickly select, add and delete pages as well as to apply a Master document to specific pages. You can open the Pages palette by choosing Window ⇨ Pages (or by pressing F12).

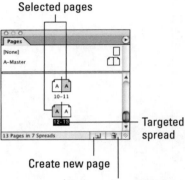

Figure 23-8: The Pages palette shows
icons for all pages, spreads, and
Masters in the current document.

You can change the size and position of icons in the Pages palette using the Palette Options palette menu command. This dialog box, shown in Figure 23-9, lets you set an icon size for Pages and Masters to be Small, Medium, Large, or Extra Large. You can also select to display the icons Vertically or Horizontally. The final option lets you place the Pages or the Masters at the top of the palette.

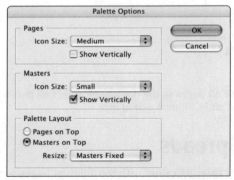

Figure 23-9: The Palette Options dialog box
changes the icon size and placement within
the Pages palette.

Selecting and targeting pages and spreads

You can easily select and target pages and spreads by using the following actions in the Pages palette:

✦ **Click.** Selects the page or spread icon.

✦ **Double-click.** This *targets* the page or spread or moves it to the center of the interface.

✦ **Holding down the Shift key while clicking on the page icons.** This selects multiple pages or spreads.

The Pages palette icons are highlighted for all selected pages. When you apply certain actions, such as applying a master or adding page numbers, they affect all selected pages.

Targeted pages are the pages that are currently active, and they're the pages that receive any newly created objects or any object that is pasted from the Clipboard. You can also identify the targeted page because it is the page whose ruler is not dimmed. You can target only one page or spread at a time. The targeted page in the Pages palette has its page numbers highlighted.

Tip You can also select and target pages using the Page Number drop-down list located at the bottom-left corner of the interface.

The Layout menu includes several commands for select pages and spreads:

✦ **Layout ⇨ First Page** selects the first page.

✦ **Layout ⇨ Last Page** selects the last page.

✦ **Layout ⇨ Previous Page/Next Page** moves between adjacent pages.

✦ **Layout ⇨ Previous Spread/Next Spread** moves between adjacent spreads

✦ **Layout ⇨ Go Back/Go Forward** moves you back and forth through pages.

Inserting and deleting and rearranging pages

You add pages to a new document using the Insert Pages palette menu command, which opens the Insert Pages dialog box, shown in Figure 23-10. This dialog box lets you add a specified number of pages to the current document. The Insert options include After Page Number, Before Page Number, At Start of Document, and At End of Document. You can also select a Master page to use.

Note You can also add pages to the current document by entering a high value in the Number of Pages field for the Document Setup dialog box. The new pages are added onto the end of the current pages.

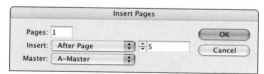

Figure 23-10: The Insert Pages dialog box places new pages exactly where you want them.

You can add pages to the current document by clicking on the Create New Page icon button at the bottom of the Pages palette.

In addition to inserting pages, the palette menu includes several other menu commands that are applied to the selected pages. The Duplicate Page (or Duplicate Spread, if a spread is selected) palette menu command creates a duplicate of the selected page (or spread). This duplicate also includes a duplicate of the page contents.

The Delete Page (or Spread) palette menu command removes the selected pages from the current document. If these pages contain any content, a warning dialog box appears, asking if you're sure about the deletion. You can also delete selected pages by clicking on the Delete Selected Pages icon button at the bottom of the Pages palette.

In addition to the palette menu, the Pages palette is also used to rearrange pages and spreads. By selecting and dragging the page icons in the Pages palette, you can rearrange the page order.

Creating and Using Masters

A Master is a page that holds all the elements that are common for several pages. It can include items such as page numbers, headers and footers, logos, and so on. All the items placed on the Master show up on the pages that the Master is applied to.

Each new document includes a single Master called the A-Master. This Master is selected from the top of the Pages palette, shown in Figure 23-11, or by using the Page Number drop-down list located at the bottom-left corner of the interface. You create and apply new Master pages to selected pages, so a document may have several master pages applied to different pages. Each page may only have a single master applied to it.

Master pages

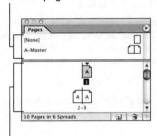

Normal pages

Figure 23-11: The top of the Pages palette holds the Master pages

Creating a Master

To create a new Master page, select the New Master palette menu command. This opens the dialog box shown in Figure 23-12, which allows you to give the Master document a Prefix and a Name and to select another Master to base it on. You can also select the number of pages in the Master spread.

Tip   By basing all newly created masters on a single main Master page, you can make changes to the main Master page, and all other Masters that are based on this main Master inherits the changes also.

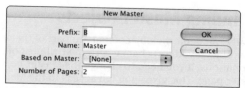

Figure 23-12: You name a new Master
document with the New Master dialog box.

New Masters are also created by dragging a page or spread from the Pages palette to the
Masters section at the top of the Pages palette. If the dragged page contains any objects,
those objects become part of the Master page. If the dragged page has a Master applied to it,
the new Master is based on the applied Master.

You can change the Master options by selecting the Master and choosing the Master Options
palette menu command. This opens the Master Options dialog box again.

You can delete Master pages, like normal pages, by dragging them to the trash icon button
at the bottom of the Pages palette or by selecting the Delete Master Spread palette menu
command.

Applying Masters

The Pages palette makes it easy to apply Masters to different pages and spreads. Simply drag
the Master that you want to apply and drop it on the icon in the Pages palette of the page or
spread that you want to apply it to. Masters should only be applied to spreads with the same
number of pages. The Pages palette displays the prefix for the Master that is applied to it, as
shown in Figure 23-13.

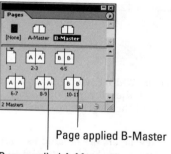

Figure 23-13: The letter on the page icon shows
which Master has been applied to it.

Page applied B-Master

Page applied A-Master

If you select multiple pages and Option/Alt+click on a master page, that master page is
applied to all the selected pages. You can also select the Apply Master to Pages palette menu
command. This action opens a simple dialog box where you can select a Master and type in
the page numbers of the pages that you want to apply the Master to. To include multiple contiguous pages, use a dash symbol.

Overriding, detaching and hiding Master objects

If a page or a spread is selected, you typically can't edit the objects that are part of the Master. However, if you override the Master object, you can change certain attributes of the objects such as its stroke, fill, and transformations. If you need to change the Master object even more, you can detach it from the Master page. This gives you full access to the Master object on the selected page and breaks its association with the Master page.

Overriding all the Master objects on the selected page is accomplished using the Override All Master Page Items (Alt+Shift+Ctrl+L on Windows, Option+Shift+⌘+L on the Mac) palette menu command. This command lets you edit all the Master objects for the selected page without changing the Master.

If you want to edit only a single Master object on the selected page or spread, you can hold down the Shift+⌘/Ctrl keys while clicking on the item to change only the single Master item for the selected page without altering the other Master objects.

All Master page objects are detached using the Detach All Objects from Master palette menu command. You can also click on a single Master item with the Shift+⌘/Ctrl keys held down to detach a single object.

All page objects that are provided by a Master may be hidden or shown by choosing View ⇨ Show/Hide Master Items.

Using Layers

Document pages as well as Master pages have layers. Layers are used to organize pages objects and also to control which objects appear above other objects. Objects placed on a higher layer appear on top of objects placed on a lower layer.

Cross-Reference   More details on working with layers can be found in Chapter 12.

Creating new layers

All layers are displayed in the Layers palette, shown in Figure 23-14. Each layer has a name and a color associated with it. All objects are highlighted with their layer color when selected. Using the columns in the Layers palette to the left of the layer name, you can make a layer Visible or Locked.

All new documents include a single layer named Layer 1. New layers are created using the New Layer palette menu command or by clicking on the Create New Layer button at the bottom of the palette. The New Layer menu command opens a dialog box, shown in Figure 23-15, where you can enter a name, choose a color, and select other options.

Current layer

Visible layer   Selected objects

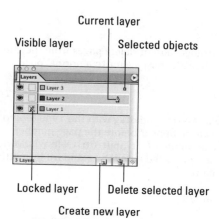

Locked layer   Delete selected layer

Create new layer

Figure 23-14: The Layers palette lists all the available layers.

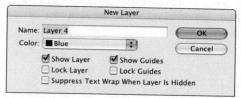

Figure 23-15: The New Layer dialog box lets you name the new layer, choose its color, and set other options such as visibility and locking.

Positioning Master objects on top of document objects

Be default, all Master page objects appear behind the document objects, but you can force objects on a Master page to appear on top of the document objects by assigning a higher layer to the Master objects.

If you've already created an object on a Master page that has a lower layer number than the document object that you want to place it on top of, you can create a higher layer in the Layer palette by selecting the New Layer palette menu command or by clicking on the Create New Layer button at the bottom of the Layer palette. Then select the objects that you want to move to the new layer and drag the small square icon to the right of the layer name to the new layer. The highlight of the object changes colors to match the new layer.

Note   You can also move objects between layers by choosing Edit ➪ Cut, Edit ➪ Copy, or Edit ➪ Paste, but if you enable the Paste Remembers Layers option in the Layer palette menu, pasting an object on a new layer won't change its layer.

Adding Numbering

Page numbering automatically updates as you rearrange, add or delete pages from the current document. Auto page numbers may be added to a Master page or to a normal page.

Adding auto page numbering

To add auto numbering to a page, select the page or Master and drag with the Type tool to create a text object. Then type any text that you want to appear before the page number. Choose Type ➪ Insert Special Character ➪ Auto Page Number (Alt+Shift+Ctrl+N in Windows, Option+Shift+⌘+N on the Mac). The text objects are formatted using the standard formatting features found in the Character and Paragraph palettes.

For more information on formatting text, see Part IV.

By default, auto numbering calls the first page "page 1," the second page "page 2," and so on, but you can change the number formatting to Roman numerals or letters and also start with a number other than 1 using the Numbering & Section Options dialog box, shown in Figure 23-16. Open this dialog box by choosing Layout ➪ Numbering & Section Options.

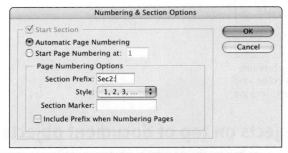

Figure 23-16: Use the Numbering & Section Options dialog box to add sections.

Defining sections

To define a section, choose the first page for the section in the Pages palette; then open the Numbering & Section Options dialog box and choose the numbering options. Enabling the Start Section option creates a new section. You can also specify a Section Prefix and a Section Marker. The Section Prefix displays along with the page number when you enable the Include Prefix When Numbering Pages option. You can add the Section Marker to the numbering text object by choosing Type ➪ Insert Special Character ➪ Section Marker.

You can also use the specified numbering style in the table of contents and the index pages.

When the dialog box is closed, the Pages palette displays the page numbers using the selected numbering style and a small down-arrow icon appears above the first page of each section. Double-clicking on the section arrow icon in the Pages palette opens the Numbering & Sections dialog box. You can add several sections to the current document.

Note You can set InDesign to display absolute page numbers or section page numbers in the Pages palette using the Page Numbering option in the General panel of the Preferences dialog box.

Enhancing Layouts

Once you create a layout, you can enhance various elements that you want to appear consistently throughout the document. For example, you can quickly add a sidebar element to designated pages by creating a guide that identifies the placement of the element. Using rulers, grids, and guides provide an effective way to enhance a layout.

Using rulers

Rulers are positioned on the left side and above the art board and are consistent to the page regardless of the amount of zooming. If you right-click on the ruler, you can change its measurement units using the pop-up menu shown in Figure 23-17. The options include Points, Picas, Inches, Inches Decimal, Millimeters, Centimeters, Ciceros, and Custom.

Tip If the rulers aren't visible, you can make them appear by choosing View ➪ Show/Hide Rulers (⌘/Ctrl+R).

Figure 23-17: Right-clicking on a ruler presents a pop-up menu of measurement units.

Using grids

InDesign has two different types of grids that can overlay the document. The Baseline Grid, shown in Figure 23-18, includes horizontal lines used to mark text baselines. It's confined to the page.

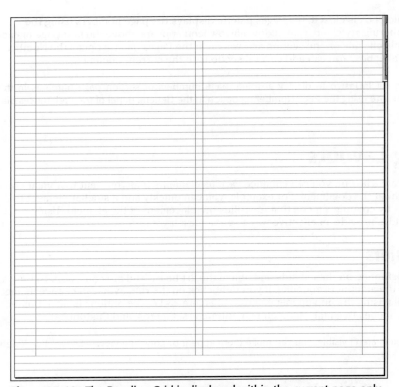

Figure 23-18: The Baseline Grid is displayed within the current page only.

The Document Grid type, shown in Figure 23-19, is made up of small grid squares and overlays the entire art board.

Both of these grids are made visible by choosing View ⇨ Show/Hide Baseline Grid (Alt+Ctrl+' in Windows, Option+⌘+' on the Mac) or View ⇨ Show/Hide Document Grid (Ctrl+' in Windows, ⌘+' on the Mac). You can also cause objects to snap to the Document Grid lines by enabling the View ⇨ Snap to Document Grid (Shift+Ctrl+' in Windows, Shift+⌘+' on the Mac) menu command. You configure both the Baseline Grid and the Document Grid using the Preferences ⇨ Grids panel.

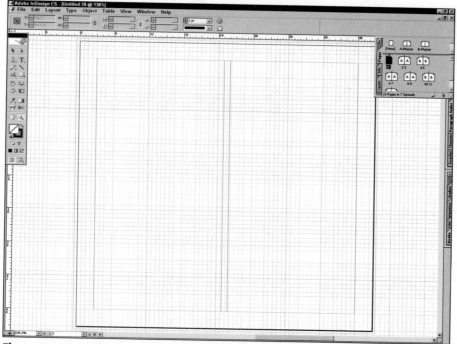

Figure 23-19: Items snap in place when you overlay a Document Grid.

Using guides

Guides are simply lines that extend from the ruler, providing a visual boundary for page objects. InDesign uses two different types of guides. Page guides are only seen within the page, and Spread guides run across the entire spread including the art board.

You create a Page guide by clicking on a ruler and dragging onto the page. Holding down the ⌘/Ctrl key while dragging from the ruler onto a page creates a Spread guide. Figure 23-20 shows each of these guide types. Choosing Layout ➪ Ruler Guides opens a simple dialog box where you can set the View Threshold and Color for these guides.

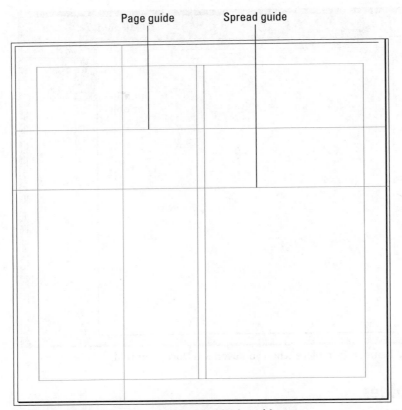

Page guide   Spread guide

Figure 23-20: Guides are useful for positioning objects.

You create a series of consistent guides using the Create Guides dialog box, shown in Figure 23-21, which you accessed by choosing Layout ➪ Create Guides. This dialog box lets you specify the number of rows and columns and the gutter between each.

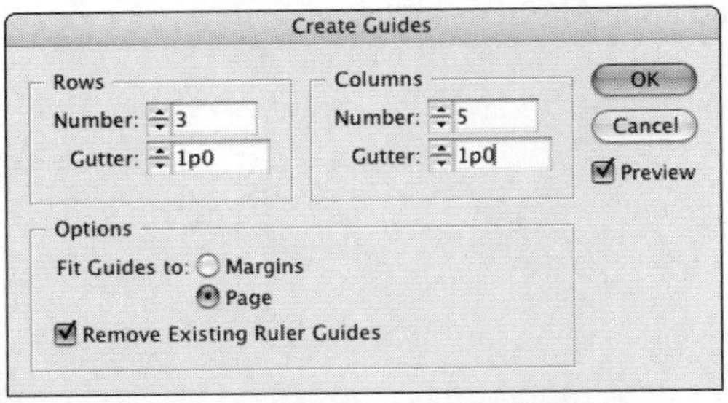

Figure 23-21: The Create Guides dialog box creates a series of evenly spaced guides.

You can select and move guides after they're created. To lock all guides so they can't be moved accidentally, choose View ➪ Lock Guides (Option/Alt+;). All guides are hidden by choosing View ➪ Show/Hide Guides (⌘/Ctrl+;).

Using frames

With grids and guides in place, another helpful object is a layout frame. You create frames, which act as placeholders for graphics or text, using any path or object in the Toolbox including Rectangles, Ellipses, Polygons, or any freehand drawn shape.

To create a frame, select a drawing tool in the Toolbox, such as the Rectangle Frame tool (F) and drag in the page to create a frame. With the frame selected, you can specify what type of content the frame holds by choosing Object ➪ Content ➪ Graphic, Object ➪ Content ➪ Text, or Object ➪ Content ➪ Unassigned.

Note You can also create text-assigned frames with the Type tool.

Graphic frames have an X through their center, and text-assigned frames have ports that thread multiple frames, as shown in Figure 23-22.

Graph assigned frame

Text assigned frame   Unassigned frame

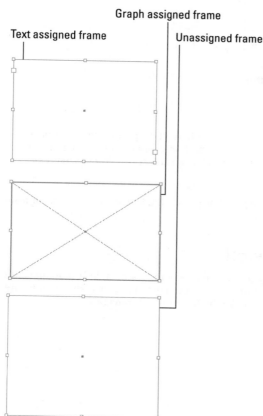

Figure 23-22: Frames create placeholders for different content types.

Importing Images

As you create a layout with frames, it's often helpful to import a stub image, which acts as a placeholder for final artwork, with the correct dimensions from Photoshop and Illustrator. After importing stub images, you can create the artwork using either Photoshop or Illustrator, and if you establish links between the two packages, the artwork can update dynamically.

Importing Photoshop artwork

You can import Photoshop artwork into a selected frame by choosing File ⇨ Place (⌘/Ctrl+D). If you enable the Show Import Options, then the Image Import Options dialog box, shown in Figure 23-23, appears after you select the image file in the file dialog box.

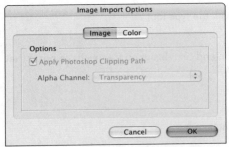

Figure 23-23: The Image Import Options dialog box includes panels for selecting the Alpha Channel and Color Management profiles.

The Apply Photoshop Clipping Path and the Alpha Channel drop-down list options are enabled if the imported object includes a clipping path and/or an Alpha Channel. For imported images that include an Alpha Channel, you can select the Transparency or Graduated Transparency option.

Note   InDesign offers the option of importing an image with Graduated Transparency — a feature that isn't offered in Quark XPress.

Importing Illustrator artwork

Artwork created in Illustrator that is placed within a selected frame in InDesign opens the Place PDF dialog box if Show Import Options is enabled. This dialog box, shown in Figure 23-24, lets you set a cropping option and make the background transparent.

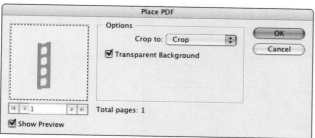

Figure 23-24: You import Illustrator's AI files into InDesign with the Place PDF dialog box options.

Dynamically updating content

You may open and edit artwork created using Photoshop and/or Illustrator in their original application by right-clicking the image and choosing Graphics ➪ Edit Original. This causes the image to open within the original application. Any saved edits you make to the image in the original application are automatically updated within InDesign.

Creating a Layout

This chapter concludes with an example that takes you through the steps to create a sample layout in InDesign.

STEPS: Creating an InDesign layout

1. **Create a new document.** Within InDesign, choose File ➪ New ➪ Document (⌘/Ctrl+N). In the New Document dialog box, set the Number of Pages to 7 and enable the Facing Pages option. Select the Custom Page Size and set the Width to 10 in. and the Height to 7 in. with a Landscape orientation. In the Margins and Columns section, set the Top margin to 0.5 in. and click the Make All Settings the Same button. Then set the number of Columns to 1 with a Gutter of 0.1667 in.

2. **Set the Bleed and Slug settings.** If the Bleed and Slug sections aren't visible, click the More Options button. Set the Bleed values to 0.125 in. and click the Make All Settings the Same button. Set all Slug values to 0.0, except for the Bottom value, which is 0.75 in. Figure 23-25 shows the New Document dialog box with the appropriate settings. Click OK to create the new document. Figure 23-26 shows the resulting new document with its guides.

3. **Edit the Master spread.** In the Pages palette, select and target the A-Master spread by double-clicking its title. The spread icons are highlighted in the Pages palette, and the spread is centered in the interface. Select the Master Options for the A-Master palette menu command. This opens the Master Options dialog box for the A-Master spread. Change the Prefix to S and the Name to SpreadMaster. Click OK to close the dialog box.

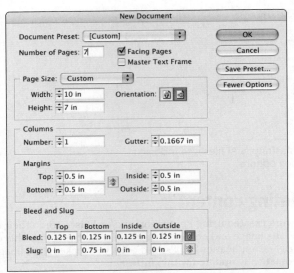

Figure 23-25: The New Document dialog box includes many initial settings for creating a layout document.

Figure 23-26: Color-coded guides in the new document show the position of the various layout settings.

4. **Create a New Master spread.** In the Pages palette, select the New Master palette menu command. The New Master dialog box opens, shown in Figure 23-27. Enter a Prefix value of C, enter a Name of CenterOpen, and set the spread to Based on the S-SpreadMaster Master. Click OK to close the dialog box.

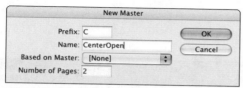

Figure 23-27: The New Master dialog box lets you name the Master spread and give it a prefix.

5. **Apply the Master spreads to the pages.** In the Pages palette, drag the Master page named None to the first page. Then drag the C-CenterOpen Master to the spread in pages 2 and 3. The remaining spreads already have the S-SpreadMaster Master applied to them.

6. **Adding content to the Master spreads.** Double-click the S-SpreadMaster to select and target it. Create the objects and position them within the Master spread. Figure 23-28 shows the Master spread with several content items added to it.

Figure 23-28: Content added to the Master spread appears on every page that the Master is applied to.

7. **Place artwork.** With the Master spread still selected and targeted, choose File ➪ Place. In the file dialog box that opens, select the artwork pieces that you want to place within the Master spread and click OK. The artwork is added to the Master spread. Select them and position them within the Master spread document. Figure 23-29 shows the Master spread with some artwork added to it.

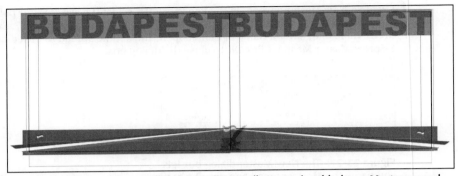

Figure 23-29: Artwork created in Photoshop or Illustrator is added to a Master spread using the File ⇨ Place menu command.

8. **Add Auto Page Numbering.** With the Type tool, drag to create a small text object in the lower-left and lower-right corners of the Master spread. With the text object selected, choose Type ⇨ Insert Special Character ⇨ Auto Page Number. A letter *S* appears in each text object, which is the prefix for the Master spread. Click on several of the pages in the Pages palette and see the numbering updated.

9. **Alter the secondary Master.** Double-click the title for the C-CenterOpen Master in the Pages palette. This selects and targets the second Master spread. For this spread, hold down the Shift+⌘/Ctrl keys and click on the artwork located at the center of the bottom edge. Then press the Delete key to delete these objects. Figure 23-30 shows this secondary Master spread with these elements missing.

Figure 23-30: Clicking on an object with the Shift+⌘/Ctrl keys held down selects objects included on the Master spread.

Summary

✦ You create Layout documents using File ➪ New ➪ Document to open a dialog box of settings including the number of pages, the page size and orientation, the margins, and the columns.

✦ You use document presets to save layout settings for reused.

✦ You change layout settings for an existing document via the Document Setup and the Margins and Columns dialog box.

✦ Icons of all pages and spreads are viewed from within the Pages palette.

✦ The Pages palette helps you create Master pages, which hold objects that appear on all pages to which you apply the Master.

✦ The Layers palette is used to place objects on different layers.

✦ You enable Auto page numbering by adding the Auto Page Number object to a text object. When placed on a Master page, all pages show the page number. The document may also be divided into sections, each with a different numbering scheme.

✦ Rulers, grids, guides, and frames are useful in establishing layouts.

✦ You can import artwork created in Photoshop and Illustrator into InDesign.

✦   ✦   ✦

Modifying Layouts

Once you create a layout, you may need to modify it. For example, including all the images you use in your layout in an InDesign document may result in a large, difficult-to-handle file size. However, you can places links to the larger original artwork elements within InDesign to make your file more manageable and embed smaller elements.

This chapter shows you how to access links via the Links palette to see what links you need to relink, move, update or embed as well how to update edited image files. It also illustrates how to manage files with Adobe's Version Cue, which provides a file-management solution for a multiple-users environment. Finally, this chapter shows how you can edit and dynamically update images and objects within Acrobat using the original authoring software with the TouchUp Object tool.

Using Artwork Versions

When you place images in an InDesign document, the image file isn't copied into InDesign. Instead, a lower-resolution version of the image displays allowing you to position the image in the layout while maintaining a link to the original image. Using links to the original image helps keep the size of the InDesign document manageable. When you print or export the document, all the links are followed and the original images are used.

You place images using the File ⇨ Place (⌘/Ctrl+D) menu command All images that you import into InDesign show up in the Links palette where the image filename and the page it appears.

Note   Files that are smaller than 48K are actually embedded within the InDesign document, but they're still listed in the Links palette for version control.

Using the Links palette

The Links palette, shown in Figure 24-1, lists all imported images in an InDesign document. It also lists the image's location in the document. You open the Links palette by choosing Window ⇨ Links (Shift +Ctrl+D in Windows; Shift+⌘+D on the Mac).

Figure 24-1: The Links palette lists all the image files.

Depending on the state of the image file, one of the three icons may appear to the right of the image name:

✦ **Circular red question-mark.** Indicates that the image file is missing. This means that the defined link is incorrect and that the file has been moved, renamed, or is on a network or CD-ROM that can no longer be found.

✦ **Yellow triangle with an exclamation point.** Denotes that a more up-to-date version of the image file is available and that you need to update the link.

✦ **Gray square.** Marks any embedded image files within the current document.

You can sort the image files listed within the Links palette by Name, Page, or Status using the commands found in the palette menu.

Editing and locating original artwork

All image files in the Links palette have links, which point to the original image-file location. The Links palette also shows which application was used to create the original image.

If you double-click on a placed image in the layout with the Option/Alt key held down, the original image opens within the application originally used to create it.

You can also open an image in its original application by selecting the Edit Original palette menu command in the Links palette or by selecting an item in the Links palette and clicking the Edit Original button at the bottom of the palette.

The Links palette is also helpful in locating images placed within InDesign. Selecting an image file in the Links palette and choosing the Go to Link palette menu command displays the page upon which the placed image is located. Alternatively, you can retrieve information by clicking the Go to Link button at the bottom of the Links palette.

Viewing link information and relinking

Double-clicking on an image name in the Links palette opens the Link Information dialog box. This dialog box, shown in Figure 24-2, shows information about the linked image file including its name, the last date it was modified, size, color space, file type, and so on. It also lists the link to the original object with a Relink button.

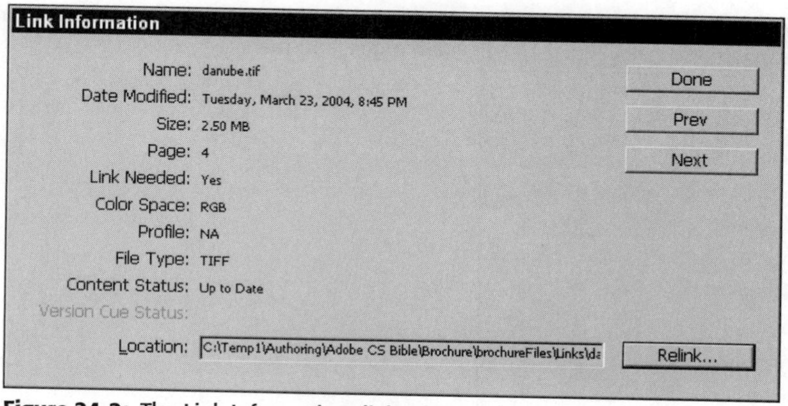

Figure 24-2: The Link Information dialog box

Clicking the Relink button in the Link Information dialog box, opens a file dialog that points to the selected image file. If the image file displays the Missing Image icon, you can use this button to locate the original image and reestablish the link.

If you do not select objects in the Links palette, selecting the Relink palette menu option or clicking the Relink button at the bottom of the palette, causes InDesign to scan for any missing image files. When a missing image file is found, a Relink dialog box (Figure 24-3) opens, allowing you to locate the missing file. When the image file is found or when you click the Skip button, the list is scanned again until all the missing files have been relinked.

Figure 24-3: The relink dialog box opens when a missing image file is found.

Any out-of-date image files may be manually updated using the Update Link palette menu command or by selecting the image link in the Links palette and clicking on the Update Links button at the bottom of the palette.

STEPS: Relinking placed image files

1. **Open an InDesign document.** Choose File ➪ Open and locate an InDesign document that includes placed images.

2. **Open the Links palette.** Choose Window ➪ Links to make the Links palette appear, as shown in Figure 24-4. If the links are broken for any of the placed images, a circular red question-mark icon appears next to the image file name in the Links palette.

3. **Relink missing files.** From the palette menu, select the Relink menu command. InDesign scans the Links palette and presents a Relink dialog box, shown in Figure 24-5, for each image file that is missing. Click the Browse button to open a file dialog box where you can locate the missing image file. Repeat this step for all missing files.

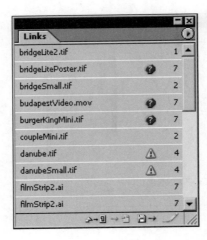

Figure 24-4: Files you need to relink are marked with a question-mark.

Figure 24-5: The Relink dialog box shows the current linked path.

Embedding linked images

To ensure that an image doesn't end up missing, you can embed them within the InDesign document using the Embed File palette menu command from the Links palette. This action places a small gray square icon next to the image's name in the Links palette and disables the link to the original file. Any future changes made to the original image file do not update in InDesign. In addition, the InDesign file size increases to accommodate the embedded file.

You unembed embedded files using the Unembed File palette menu command or by relinking the file to its original.

Setting the display quality

For placed images, you can set the display quality of raster images, vector images, and images that include transparency. The three display options available for placed images include Optimized, Typical, and High Quality. Figure 24-6 shows an example of each of these options.

You set the Display Performance level for the selected object by choosing Object ➪ Display Performance. The options include each of the levels along with Use View Setting. If you select the Use View Setting option, the level set in the View menu determines the Display Performance level.

For the current view, you can select each of the following settings by choosing View ➪ Display Performance:

✦ **Optimized**: Alt+Ctrl+O in Windows; Option+⌘+O on the Mac.

✦ **Typical**: Alt+Ctrl+Z in Windows; Option+⌘+Z on the Mac.

✦ **High Quality:** Alt+Ctrl+H in Windows; Option+⌘+H on the Mac.

Figure 24-6: Display-quality options are Optimized (left), Typical (middle), and High Quality (right).

The Preserve Object-Level Display Settings option causes all placed images to use the selected Display Performance setting, except for the objects that have their own specified display level. These settings are configurable using the InDesign/Edit ➪ Preferences ➪ Display Performance menu command. The Display Performance panel of the Preferences dialog box, shown in Figure 24-7 lets you adjust the view settings for each of these levels. You can also enable anti-aliasing and Greek type below a certain point size.

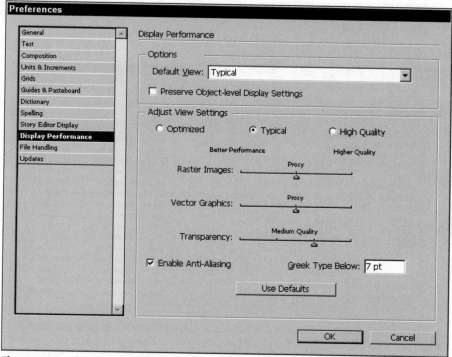

Figure 24-7: The Display Performance panel of the Preferences dialog box

Updating artwork with Version Cue

Another way to update artwork in an InDesign layout is to use Version Cue. Version Cue is a workflow management feature available only in CS version applications. Version Cue includes features for managing file versions, maintaining security, backing up projects, and granting access to resources. This chapter focuses on using Version Cue to manage and update image resources within InDesign.

Cross-Reference   For more details on Version Cue, see Chapter 7.

Adding files to the project

Once a project is created, you can add files to it either one by one, using the Save As dialog box, or by moving all project files to the Documents/Version Cue folder (Mac) or the My Documents/My Projects folder (Windows). Then select the Synchronize option from the Project Tools popup menu. Figure 24-8 shows the Version Cue dialog box—which lists the status and version of the file—after several files have been synchronized.

Note   Before InDesign images may be saved within Version Cue, Version Cue must be enabled and a new project must be created. Chapter 7 includes details on enabling Version Cue and creating a new project.

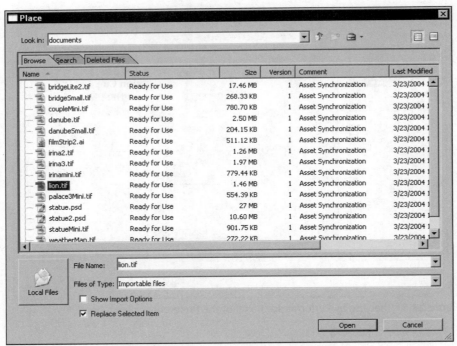

Figure 24-8: The Version Cue dialog box lists information about the file.

Saving file versions

You can open files added to a project and save them again using the Version Cue dialog box included in the Open and Save file dialog boxes. When you make edits to a project file, choose File ➪ Save to save the local file. To save a new version of a file, choose File ➪ Save a Version. This opens a dialog box, shown in Figure 24-9, where you may enter a comment describing the changes to this version. Clicking the Continue button saves this version to Version Cue, where the file's version number is updated.

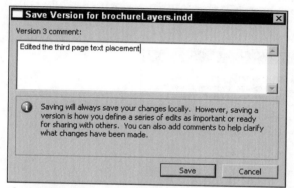

Figure 24-9: The Save Version dialog box lets you add a comment to the saved version.

STEPS: Updating Files with Version Cue

1. **Add an InDesign file to the project.** With Version Cue enabled and a new project created, choose File ➪ New ➪ Document to create a new InDesign document. Enter the layout settings and click OK. Choose File ➪ Save. In the Version Cue dialog box, locate the new project name and double-click it, then double-click on the Documents folder. Give the file a name, add some version comments, and click Save.

2. **Add placed image files to the Version Cue project.** If all the linked image files are already part of a Version Cue project, you can use the Place dialog box to select the files and place them in the InDesign document. If the image files are not part of a Version Cue project, you can locate the local files in the Finder (Mac) or in Windows Explorer, then move them to the Version Cue project located in the Documents/Version Cue folder (Mac) or in the My Documents/My Projects folder (Windows).

3. **Synchronize project files.** After you move the files to the correct directory, choose File ➪ Open to open a file dialog box and click the Version Cue button. Select Synchronize in the Project Tools pop-up menu. All moved files appear in the Version Cue project.

4. **Place image files.** When you synchronize the image files with the Version Cue project, you may place them within the InDesign file using the File ➪ Place menu command.

5. **Saving a version.** After making changes to the InDesign project, choose File ➪ Save a Version. Enter some version comments in the dialog box that appears, and click the Continue button.

Dynamically Updating Acrobat Images

InDesign isn't the only application that benefits from dynamically updated images. You can also dynamically update images included within Acrobat files using the TouchUp Object tool.

With an Acrobat file open, choose Tools ➪ Advanced Editing ➪ TouchUp Object Tool. With this tool, you can click and drag objects within the document to reposition them. If you hold down the Option/Ctrl key while double-clicking on them (or select Edit Image from the right-click contextual menu), the selected object opens within its original authoring package for more editing. A warning dialog box, shown in Figure 24-10, appears if the image includes transparency.

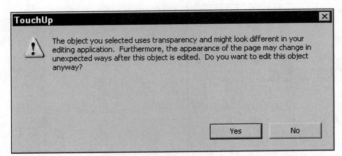

Figure 24-10: A warning dialog box for images that include transparency.

Images that you edit and save automatically update back in the Acrobat document as long as you still have the object.

Note   Images that you edit in Photoshop need to be flattened before they are saved and dynamically updated back in Acrobat.

If you select a different object in the Acrobat document while editing an object using the TouchUp Object tool, then the link between the object and its authoring application breaks and the image does not dynamically updated when you save the image file.

You can select which software package to use to edit images and objects with the TouchUp Object tool in the TouchUp panel of the Preferences dialog box, shown in Figure 24-11. Choose Acrobat/Edit ➪ Preferences (⌘/Ctrl+K) and select the TouchUp panel. Click on the Choose Image Editor or the Choose Page/Object Editor buttons to locate the software package that you want to use to edit images and objects. For Creative Suite users, Photoshop and Illustrator are enabled by default.

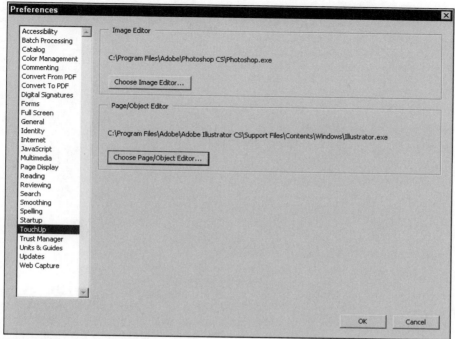

Figure 24-11: The TouchUp panel of the Preferences dialog box

Summary

✦ All images placed within an InDesign document appear in the Links palette.

✦ The Links palette may be used to relink missing image files, to update changed image files, and to locate placed images within the layout.

✦ You can enable Adobe's Version Cue features to manage files in a central location for multiple users.

✦ The TouchUp Object tool in Acrobat may be used to edit images and objects using their original authoring package.

✦ ✦ ✦

Document
Repurposing

Exporting Designs for Web Hosting

Document repurposing deals with reusing designs for different media. In today's business climate, designs created for print are frequently reused to produce Web sites, CD-ROMs, PDF files, and video products. Repurposing designs can save a lot of time and it presents a consistent look across several products.

This chapter presents one repurposing example among many. Documents created for print in InDesign may be packaged and exported for use in GoLive.

Cross-Reference For more information on document repurposing, see Chapter 26.

Packaging for GoLive

One common design repurposing path is to move layouts created in InDesign to the Web. To facilitate this process, InDesign includes a feature that enables you to quickly move a print design to GoLive and the Web. Choose File ➪ Package for GoLive. This compiles all graphics and text in the current document and places them in a neat little folder where you can open and manipulate them in GoLive.

The packaging process converts each InDesign story to a separate XML file. The formatting for this text is converted to a Cascading Style Sheet (CSS). All other images and objects are converted to either the JPEG or GIF formats or packaged in their native format for more controlled optimization later in GoLive.

Note Graphics created in InDesign, such as rectangles, freehand lines, and buttons, are not packaged.

Packaging an InDesign document

To package an InDesign document for use in GoLive, open the document in InDesign and choose File ➪ Package for GoLive. This opens a file dialog box where you can give the package a name and specify a location. After clicking the Package button, the Package for GoLive dialog box, shown in Figure 25-1, displays.

Note If any linked image files are missing from the InDesign document, a warning dialog box appears, informing you that if you continue, the missing images are packaged with low-resolution versions of themselves.

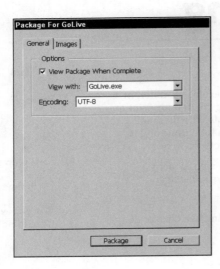

Figure 25-1: The Package for GoLive dialog box lets you open the package in GoLive or in a Web browser.

The Package for GoLive dialog box includes two tabs — the General tab and the Images tab. The General tab (refer to Figure 25-1) lets you open the package in GoLive or in a Web browser when complete. You can also select Other to choose a separate application to view the package. The Encoding field lets you choose the encoding type for the package.

 Note If you make changes to the InDesign document after creating a package, you can choose File ⇨ Package for GoLive again to re-package the InDesign document using the same package folder.

Copying images

The Images tab, shown in Figure 25-2, lets you specify which images are copied to the package folder and the settings for all images that are optimized.

All images contained within the InDesign document are copied to a separate Images folder located within the Package folder. The Copy to Images Sub-Folder options in the Images tab can copy the original images, optimized original images, and/or optimized formatted images. Checking the Original Images check box moves a copy of the original images to the Images folder. Checking the Optimized Original Images check box converts the image to a JPEG or GIF image that is suitable for the Web. These images have _opt added to their filenames inside the package. Optimized formatted images are images that have been cropped or scaled within InDesign. These images have _for added to their filenames.

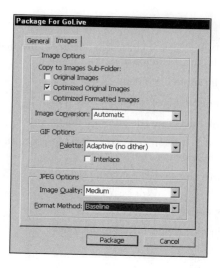

Figure 25-2: The Images controls settings for optimized images.

The Image Conversion drop-down list lets you select to optimize all images using either the GIF or JPEG image format. The Automatic option lets InDesign decide which format to use. For GIF images, you can select which color palette to use. The options include Adaptive (No Dither), Web, System (Mac), and System (Win). You can also enable interlacing. The JPEG Options section lets you set the image quality (to Low, Medium, High, or Maximum) and the format method to Baseline or Progressive.

JPEG versus GIF images

The two most common image formats on the Web are JPEG and GIF. Each of these formats has its advantages and disadvantages:

JPEG images support 16.4 million colors and are used with photographs and images with gradients. GIF images support a 256-color palette, making this format useful for logos and images with large sections of similar color such as buttons and banners.

Because GIF images use a small palette of colors, they have considerably reduced their file sizes. JPEG images use a compression algorithm that throws away image information in an effort to reduce its file size. Therefore, JPEG images include a setting to determine the amount of compression to apply. A Low image-quality setting aggressively compromises the image quality to decrease the file size and a Maximum image-quality setting maintains image quality but requires a larger file size.

You can set both GIF and JPEG formats to slowly appear line-by-line as they're downloaded onto a Web page. For the GIF format, this feature is called *interlacing*. For JPEG images, these images are called *progressive JPEGs*. Progressive JPEGs appear block by block as the image is downloaded. Progressive JPEGs require a larger file size and more memory to be viewed than *baseline JPEGs,* which appear on a Web page only after the entire image downloads.

Examining package contents

If you look into the package folder created by InDesign after an InDesign document has been packaged for GoLive, you'll find several files, including the following:

✦ A PDF file that is used as a preview of the InDesign document

✦ A TOC.html file (Figure 25-3) listing all details and files in the package folder

✦ An XML file that begins with "story" with all the text in the InDesign document

✦ Several other XML files, including root, links, layout, geometry, tags, idmap, and glprefs, which provide details about the InDesign document

✦ A CSS file named Glstyles with the text formatting styles that the InDesign document uses

✦ All images files, each within its own folder and all in a folder named Images

✦ Any other movie or sound files included in the original InDesign document

<table>
<tr><td colspan="3" align="center">**Master spreads for Brochure**</td></tr>
<tr><td>Package Name:</td><td colspan="2" align="center">Master spreads for Brochure</td></tr>
<tr><td>Package Location:</td><td colspan="2" align="center">file:///C:/Temp1/Authoring/Adobe%20CS%20Bible/scratch/Master%20spreads%20for%20Brochure</td></tr>
<tr><td>Creation Date:</td><td colspan="2" align="center">Wednesday, March 24, 2004, 1:57 PM</td></tr>
<tr><td>Modification Date:</td><td colspan="2" align="center">Wednesday, March 24, 2004, 1:57 PM</td></tr>
<tr><td>InDesign Version:</td><td colspan="2" align="center">3.0 (build 424, change list 225054)</td></tr>
<tr><td>PACKAGE FOR GOLIVE.APLN Version</td><td colspan="2" align="center">3.0</td></tr>
</table>

File	Type	Source
Master spreads for Brochure.pdf	pdf	Master spreads for Brochure.indd
root.xml	doc_root	Master spreads for Brochure
statue_opt.gif	optimize_image	statue.psd
links.xml	link	Master spreads for Brochure.indd
statue_frmt.gif	format_image	statue.psd
story_226.incd	incopy_story	Master spreads for Brochure.indd
story_260.incd	incopy_story	Master spreads for Brochure.indd
layout.xml	layout	Master spreads for Brochure.indd
geometry.xml	geometry	Master spreads for Brochure.indd
tags.xml	tags	Master spreads for Brochure.indd
idmap.xml	idmap	Master spreads for Brochure
glprefs.xml	glprefs	Master spreads for Brochure.indd
glstyles.css	glstyles	Master spreads for Brochure.indd
toc.html	doc_toc	Master spreads for Brochure

Figure 25-3: The TOC.html file located in the Packaged folder.

Viewing the package in GoLive

If the View Package When Complete option in the Package for GoLive dialog box is selected, then the package opens automatically within GoLive. Figure 25-4 shows a package that has been opened in GoLive. The most noticeable aspect of an exported package is the PDF preview that appears in its own window within GoLive.

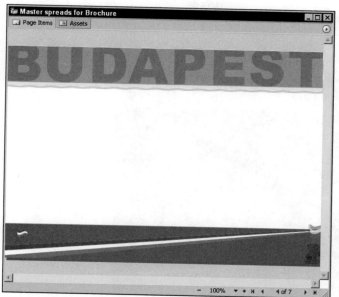

Figure 25-4: Packages opened within GoLive show the PDF preview page.

If you enable the View Package When Complete option, you can open the package in GoLive by opening the `TOC.html` file or by choosing File ➪ Import ➪ From InDesign within GoLive.

STEPS: Packaging an InDesign document for GoLive

1. **Open the print document within InDesign.** Open InDesign and choose File ➪ Open to access a file dialog box. Select the file to open and click the Open button. The file opens within InDesign.

2. **Package the document for GoLive.** Choose File ➪ Package for GoLive. This opens the Package Publication for GoLive dialog box. Type a name for the package folder and click the Package button, which opens the Package for GoLive dialog box. In the General tab, enable the View Package When Complete option and open the Images tab. In the Images tab, enable the Optimized Original Images option and disable the Original Images option. Then click the Package button.

   After the packing process is complete, the packaged document is opened in GoLive, as shown in Figure 25-5.

Figure 25-5: Packaged InDesign documents automatically open in GoLive.

Creating Web Pages in GoLive

Each of the applications included in the Creative Suite has its own purpose, and the purpose of GoLive is to create Web pages and manage Web sites. Web pages are much different than the layout designs found in any of the other CS applications, because they're constrained to conform to the Hypertext Markup Language known as HTML.

HTML is the language that Web browsers read that defines the placement of text and images on a Web page. HTML is very linear in its layout approach, with objects positioned on top of one another from the upper-left corner of the page to the bottom of the page following the left edge of the page.

Text isn't placed within frames, but pushes surrounding objects to fit all the text in the designated size. Images, likewise, aren't cropped or sized, but appear at their actual resolution where they rest between any text on the page.

All of these idiosyncratic rules are understood by GoLive, but be aware that if objects don't seem to stay where you put them, HTML, not GoLive, is to blame.

Building Web pages and using views

The first place to start building Web pages is the package that you exported from InDesign. You can drag and drop Items displayed on the PDF Preview window directly on a blank Web page.

You add Web pages to a site project by choosing File ➪ New Page (⌘/Ctrl+N). Each Web page displays in its own window (Figure 25-6). You have several ways to view each page using the tabs at the top of the window:

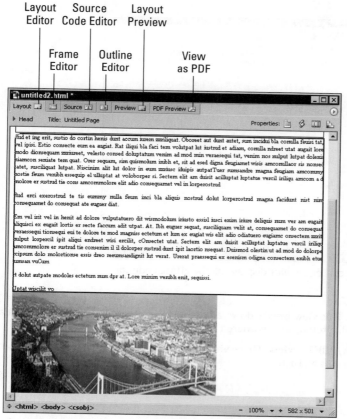

Figure 25-6: Each Web page displays in its own window.

✦ **Layout Editor.** The default view, which displays laid out Web-page objects, allows you to easily select and reposition objects.

✦ **Frame Editor.** Divides the Web page into frames.

✦ **Source Code Editor.** Displays the HTML code that generates the Web page, as shown in Figure 25-7.

Figure 25-7: The Source Code Editor displays all the HTML code for the Web page.

✦ **Outline Editor.** This view breaks down all the HTML code into logical blocks that are easily expanded, altered, and reordered (see Figure 25-8).

✦ **Layout Preview/PDF Preview.** These views show the Web page as it would appear in a browser or saved as a PDF file.

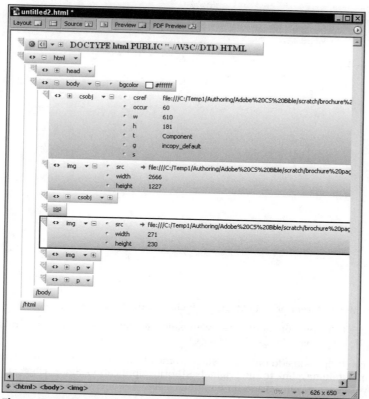

Figure 25-8: The Outline Editor offers another way to work with the HTML code in easy-to-manipulate blocks.

Adding objects to Web pages

All the objects you insert on a Web page are available as icons in the Objects palette (Figure 25-9), which displays categories at the top and objects at the bottom.

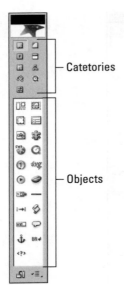

Figure 25-9: The Objects palette holds all the various Web-page objects.

— Catetories

— Objects

The Toolbox holds nine different object categories including the following:

✦ **Basic:** Includes the most commonly used Web-page elements, such as Layout Grids, Layout Text Boxes, Tables, Images, and Lines.

✦ **Smart Objects:** Helps you add objects created in the other CS applications to a Web page while maintaining a link to the original authoring application. Smart Objects include easy-to-use prebuilt JavaScript functions called Actions.

✦ **Form Elements:** Includes objects found on form pages, such as buttons, labels, popups, and text fields.

✦ **Head Elements:** Includes objects found in the head section of an HTML page, such as meta tags and keywords.

✦ **Frames and Framesets:** Creates frames with different formatted options.

✦ **Site Items:** Includes items that affect the entire site, such as the e-mail addresses, colors, and fonts.

✦ **Diagrams:** Includes dozens of different objects for creating site maps and wireframe walkthroughs.

✦ **QuickTime Elements:** This category of QuickTime-related technologies includes items like movies and sounds that you can combine into interactive multimedia presentations.

✦ **SMIL Elements:** Includes SMIL-related items for creating time-based media presentations using the SMIL language.

After you locate the correct object in the Toolbox, you can add it to a Web page window by dragging it from the Toolbox and dropping it on the Web page or by double clicking on an object to add it at the cursor's location.

Changing object properties

You select objects on a Web page in the Layout Editor by clicking on them. A border around the object appears and the properties for the selected object appear in the Inspector palette. Figure 25-10 shows the Inspector palette when an image is selected in the Web page.

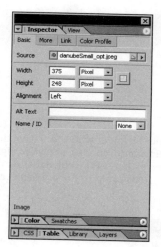

Figure 25-10: Properties for the selected Web-page object are displayed in the Inspector palette.

Setting Up a Site Design with the Site Wizard

Web sites are a collection of Web pages that you publish to the Web. The typical workflow for Web sites is to design the site first and then to flesh out the individual Web pages. GoLive includes a Site Wizard that steps you through the process of creating a Web site. The Site Wizard creates a `project` folder that includes the project file (identified with the `.site` extension) and three folders — `web-content`, `web-data`, and `web-settings`. All the Web pages, images, and content loaded on the server are saved in the `web-content` folder. The other two folders hold configuration settings.

STEPS: Using the Site Wizard

1. **Choose File ➪ New Site (Alt+Shift+Ctrl+N in Windows; Option+Shift+⌘+N on the Mac) to start the Site Wizard.** The first step lets you select to create a single-user or a Version Cue project. Single-user projects are saved on your local hard drive.

2. **Select the appropriate options for your site.** The second step lets you create a blank site, a site based on imported local files, a site based on imported server files, or a site based on a GoLive template (Figure 25-11).

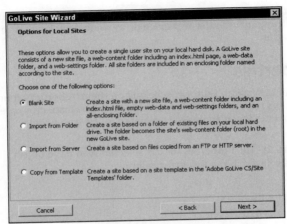

Figure 25-11: The Site Wizard lets you create sites based on imported files or on a site template.

3. **Select a name and location.** The name is used to name the folder where you save the site content. When the Site Wizard is finished, a project window opens, shown in Figure 25-12. This window displays all the Web pages included as part of the current site in the left side of the window and all the files that have been transferred to the publish server on the right side of the window.

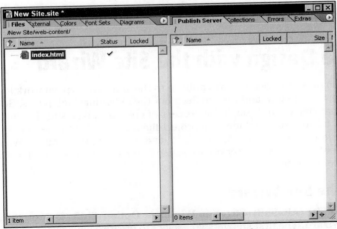

Figure 25-12: The Site Wizard displays the site's home page (index.html).

Adding pages to a site

You can add Web pages that you created before creating the site using several different methods. Right-clicking in the site window and choosing New ➪ New Page from the pop-up menu adds a Web page to the site. You can also import an existing page with the File ➪ Import ➪ Files to Site menu command. Finally, you can drag files from the Finder (or from Windows Explorer) and drop them in the Site window to add them to the site.

From the site window, you open Web pages by simply double-clicking them in the Files section.

Linking Web pages

You can add links, which open another Web page within a browser, to text or images within a Web page. To create a link, select the text or image you want for a link. The selected object's properties appear in the Inspector palette (Figure 25-13). In the Inspector palette, you can click the Browse button and select the Web page or image to which you want to link. The Web-page name appears in the link field. Be aware that the Browse button is tedious and error-prone. The recommended method is to interactively link to pages or objects within the site with the Fetch URL icon (also known as the Point and Shoot Tool). To use this tool, drag the icon to the site window, and select the Web page, image, or resource to link to.

Once you create links between Web pages, the Preview view lets you test the links.

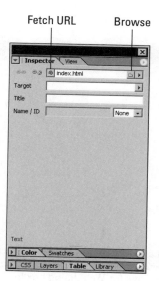

Fetch URL   Browse

Figure 25-13: You specify the Web page or object to which you want to link at the top of the Inspector palette.

Using Smart Objects

Smart Objects are unique to GoLive. They let you work with images created in Photoshop, Illustrator, and Acrobat without having to worry about the larger file sizes common to those applications. Smart Objects are available for Photoshop, Illustrator, Acrobat, and generic image formats such as TIFF, EPS, and BMP.

You add Smart Objects to a Web page by dragging them over from the Toolbox. They appear initially in the Web page as simple icons. After you add them to a Web page, you can click on the Browse button in the Inspector palette (Figure 25-14) to identify the source image file.

A smarter way to work with Smart Objects is to place the source files into the SmartObjects folder in the Extras tab of the Site Window. From this location, you can drag and drop the source files directly into the Layout Editor. This action causes the Save for Web dialog box to open where you can specify the optimization settings.

Note   All images that are part of an exported InDesign package and that you drag to a Web page are Smart Objects.

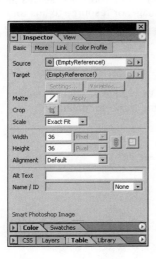

Figure 25-14: The Inspector palette for Smart Objects offers several settings.

Using the Save for Web dialog box

When you drag and drop a native source file into GoLive's Layout Editor as a Smart Object, the image file loaded in the Save For Web dialog box (Figure 25-15). You use this dialog box to configure an optimized version of the source image file. The Save for Web dialog box in GoLive is identical to the one found in Photoshop and Illustrator.

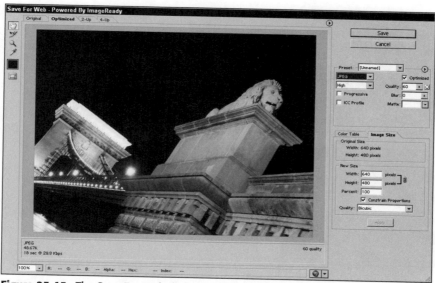

Figure 25-15: The Save For Web dialog box lets you specify how to compress a source image for viewing on a Web page.

Using this dialog box, you can select the image format, quality setting, image dimensions, and other settings. You use the tabs at the top-left corner of the dialog box to compare the selected settings between the original and optimized images. The 2-Up and 4-Up view options offer an interface where you can specify and visually compare two or four different settings before saving the Web image. Figure 25-16 shows the 4-Up display option. The settings and file size for each pane are listed under each pane.

Cross-Reference   Each of the various Web graphic formats is briefly explained in Chapter 8.

When you're comfortable with the settings, click the Save button and a file dialog box appears where you may save the optimized image in the site folder. This file is called the target image file and although it's linked to the original source file, it's a separate file.

Note   After you save and add a target image to a Web page, you can revisit the Save for Web dialog box by selecting the target image and clicking the Settings button in the Inspector palette.

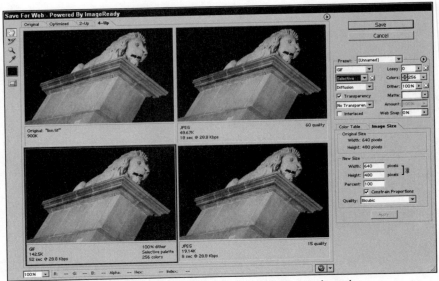

Figure 25-16: You use the 4-Up view to compare different Web settings.

Editing the Smart Objects image

To edit a source image, simply double-click on a target image within GoLive. This opens the source image in the application used to create it (for example, Photoshop, Illustrator, or Acrobat). After completing your edits, save the source file, and GoLive automatically updates the target file using the same target filename, same target file location, and same optimization settings from the Save for Web dialog box.

If you open and edit a source image in its native application, you can have GoLive check for updated images by choosing Site ➪ Update Files Dependent On ➪ Library. This automatically updates all Smart Objects and packages exported from InDesign.

Cropping Smart Objects

Another advantage of Smart Objects is that you can resize and crop them without affecting the native source files using tools in GoLive. To resize a Smart Object, just drag its borders and hold the Shift key to constrain proportions.

To crop a Smart Object, select the target image in the Layout Editor, click the Crop Image button in the Inspector palette, then drag to outline the crop area in the Layout Editor. After you draw the outline, you can drag on the outline borders to resize the crop area. Double-click inside the outline area to complete the crop action. Figure 25-17 shows an image cropped within GoLive.

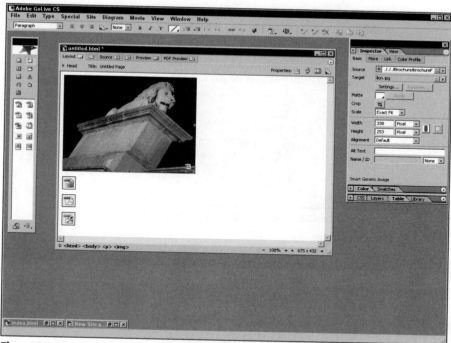

Figure 25-17: You can easily crop Smart Objects in GoLive.

Cascading Style Sheets

All text within a Web page can have formatting applied to it. These formatting styles are saved in a style sheet and may be applied to several sections of text within the Web page. If you need to change the style of text in the Web page, you can make the change to the style sheet and all text sections that use that style automatically update.

A single Web page may have several style sheets applied to it. For example, a single Web page may have an internal style sheet defined within its header that affects only the text within that Web page, but Web pages may also reference an external style sheet that governs the text styles for all the Web pages within a site. When this happens, the style that you apply to a specific text section is cascaded down according to a defined precedence.

Tip   An external style sheet makes the text styles for a whole Web site consistent, controlled, and easy to update.

Using the CSS Editor

You create Cascading Style Sheets (CSS) within GoLive using the CSS Editor. You can open this editor by choosing View ➪ CSS Editor (Alt+Shift+Ctrl+C in Windows; Option+Shift+⌘+C on the Mac) or by clicking on the stair-looking icon in the upper-right corner of the Web-page window. Figure 25-18 shows the CSS Editor when it's first opened.

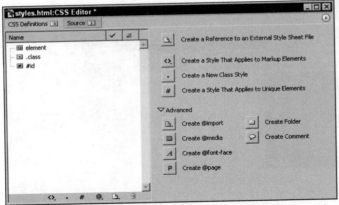

Figure 25-18: You use the CSS Editor to create style sheets and define styles.

The CSS Editor can list all the default styles along with examples. To see these examples, choose New Style ⇨ Edit Style Examples. Clicking on a style in the left pane shows an example of the style in the right pane (see Figure 25-19).

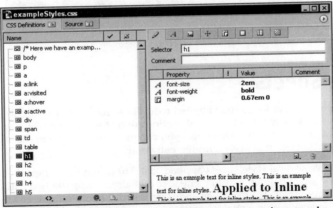

Figure 25-19: You can use the CSS Editor to view style examples.

Defining styles

You may define styles for standard HTML elements, such as h1, h2, body, p, and so on. You can also define styles using a `.class` definition and styles that are applied to all objects that have a specified ID. The CSS Editor includes a button for each of these style types at the bottom of the window. Clicking on these buttons adds a style rule to the left pane of the CSS Editor.

Selecting a style in the left pane displays its properties in the panels on the right (see Figure 25-20). Using these panels, you may set many different properties, including Font, Text, Block, Margin, and so on. An example of the text style is displayed in the text area under the property panels as you edit the various properties.

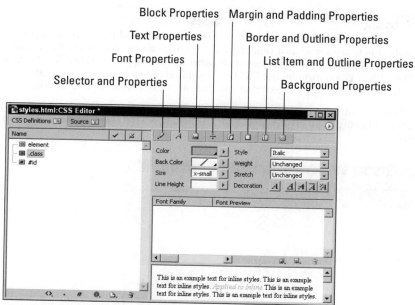

Figure 25-20: You define style properties with the property panels on the CSS Editor.

Applying styles

Element styles (h1, p, a, and so on) are applied automatically whenever you use the HTML element. To defined class styles, you can select the text in the Layout Editor and select the type of style to use in the CSS palette, shown in Figure 25-21, by placing check marks in the appropriate column. You can apply class styles to an inline section of text, an entire block of text, a spanned section, or selected element.

Figure 25-21: You use the CSS palette to apply styles to selected text using the CSS palette.

You apply ID styles by adding `ID="id_name"` to the HTML tag for the text item to which you want to apply the style. This is done in the Source Code Editor or the Visual Tag Editor (Shift-⌘/Control-E).

Creating an external style sheet

When you define and apply styles to text, they're automatically added to the Web page. External style sheets are saved as a separate file. To create an external style sheet, you first need to create a reference to the external style sheet by clicking the Create a Reference to an External Style Sheet File button on the CSS Editor's initial panel. You can also create a reference using the Create New Link to external CSS button at the bottom of the CSS Editor.

Select the Reference item in the left panel and a Create button appears on the right, as shown in Figure 25-22. Clicking this button opens a file dialog box where you can name and save the external style sheet.

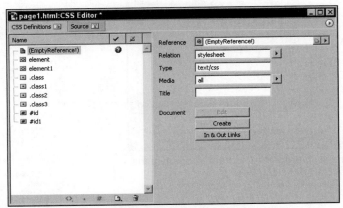

Figure 25-22: The CSS Editor lets you define styles and save them as a style sheet.

Summary

✦ You can repurpose documents created in InDesign for use on the Web by creating a package for GoLive. This process bundles all the necessary files into a folder that GoLive can use.

✦ GoLive is a robust editor for creating and designing Web pages. These Web pages can include a myriad of objects. You edit object properties using the Inspector palette.

✦ A site project includes many Web pages. You can create site projects using GoLive's Site Wizard.

✦ Smart Objects allow you to place Photoshop, Illustrator, and Acrobat source files within GoLive Web pages as target images that are optimized for viewing on the Web.

✦ Cascading style sheets are an efficient way to apply text styles to a section of text within a Web page.

✦   ✦   ✦

Preparing Documents for Distribution

Electronic documents are often created for one purpose and eventually modified to suit another purpose. You may initially create
a design piece for print where images are optimized for high-resolution output and later want to modify the design piece for screen viewing, where image-resolution requirements are significantly less than
for print. Taking a document designed for one purpose and modifying
it for another purpose is known as *document repurposing*.

To prepare files for distribution electronically, via the Web, or on
CD-ROMs, you may need to resample files for image resolutions
appropriate for viewing, set viewing attributes suited for on-screen
viewing, and create search indexes for easy access to selected files.
In this chapter, we discuss preparing files for a variety of output
purposes and how to optimize files for viewing.

Repurposing Documents

One of the more common needs for repurposing documents is taking
a file originally designed for print and modifying it for downloading
from a Web site. For high-resolution output, image files can be 300 ppi
(pixels per inch) or more. For Web viewing and viewing documents
on your computer monitor, you need file sizes of 72 ppi when viewing
in a 100% view. Files with lower resolutions are smaller; when you are
downloading documents from a Web server, smaller file sizes mean
shorter download times.

Native files created in Illustrator, Photoshop and InDesign require
much more work to modify documents originally designed for print
to a file suited for Web hosting. Furthermore, you must convert files
hosted on the Web to either PDF or HTML to make them easily accessible to other users.

Fortunately, if files are converted to PDF for any kind of output,
you can easily repurpose a file for other types of output. There is
one caveat in this notion: You can repurpose files for downward
optimization only. In other words, you can take a document with
high-resolution images designed for print and downsize the images to

make it suitable for Web viewing, but you cannot upsize a Web-designed document and make it suitable for print.

The ideal file format for documents you want to repurpose is PDF. You can convert a page layout in InDesign to PDF while keeping all images at high resolution and send off the document to a commercial printer for high-end prepress and printing. You can then take the same PDF and *downsample* images (reduce the file sizes) for a piece to be hosted on a Web site or electronically exchanged with other users. When you're using PDFs for your output needs, you have several ways to repurpose files through Acrobat menus and commands.

Reducing file size

Reduce File Size is a menu command found in the File menu in both Acrobat Standard and Acrobat Professional. Choose File ➪ Reduce File Size and the Reduce File Size dialog box opens, shown in Figure 26-1.

Figure 26-1: The Reduce File Size dialog box

From the pull-down menu in the Reduce File Size dialog box, you have three options for Acrobat PDF compatibility. The more recent the Acrobat compatibility, the more file-size reduction you can expect. Therefore, using Acrobat 6 compatibility reduces a PDF document size more than using either Acrobat 4 or Acrobat 5 compatibility.

The Reduce File Size command offers you a simple tool for reducing file size and offers no options choices for how much image sampling you can apply to the file-size reduction. If you're using Acrobat Standard, the Reduce File Size command is the only tool you have available in Acrobat to reduce file sizes.

After choosing Acrobat compatibility, click OK and the Save As dialog box opens. Find a folder location on your hard drive, supply a filename, and click Save. Acrobat uses an internal algorithm to downsample images and adds compression, thereby reducing file size.

If you want to examine file size after exercising the command and saving a new file, choose File ➪ Document Properties or press ⌘/Ctrl+D. The Document Properties dialog box, shown in Figure 26-2, opens. Click on Description in the left pane, and you can see the file size noted on the right side of the dialog box.

Using PDF Optimizer

A much more sophisticated approach to optimizing files and reducing their size is to use the PDF Optimizer found only in Acrobat Professional. The PDF Optimizer reduces file sizes through downsampling images according to user-specified amounts and a variety of other settings that offer options for eliminating unnecessary data. With the Reduce File Size command in the last section, you don't have user-definable settings to determine how file reduction affects data. With PDF Optimizer, you can choose different settings to determine what data is affected during optimization. The PDF Optimizer also offers you an option for analyzing a file so you can see what part of the PDF document occupies higher percentages of memory.

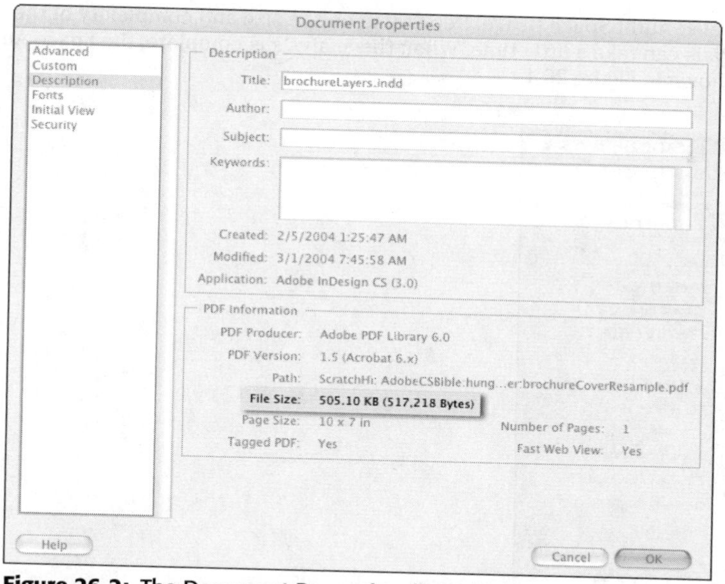

Figure 26-2: The Document Properties dialog box

Auditing space usage

The first step in optimizing files with the PDF Optimizer is to analyze a file so you can see what content occupies the larger amounts of memory. You analyze a document and use the PDF Optimizer in the PDF Optimizer dialog box (Figure 26-3), which opens when you choose Advanced ➪ PDF Optimizer.

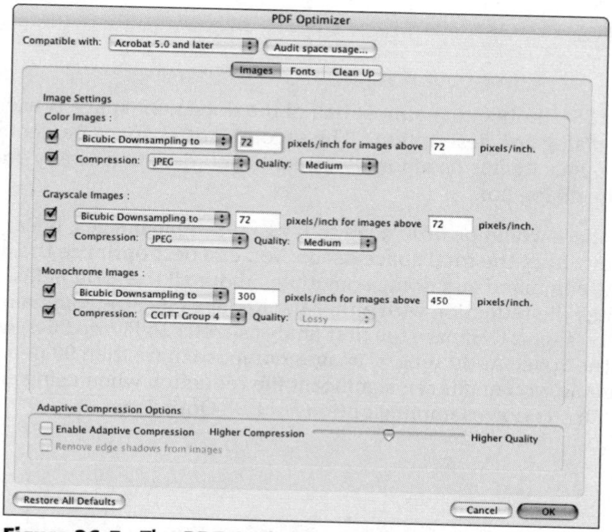

Figure 26-3: The PDF Optimizer dialog box

Click the button labeled Audit Space Usage. Depending on the size and complexity of the document, the analysis can take a little time. When the analysis is complete, the Space Audit dialog box opens, shown in Figure 26-4.

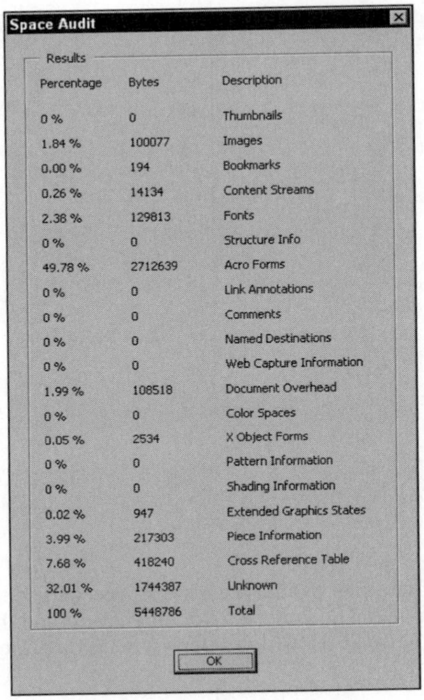

Percentage	Bytes	Description
0 %	0	Thumbnails
1.84 %	100077	Images
0.00 %	194	Bookmarks
0.26 %	14134	Content Streams
2.38 %	129813	Fonts
0 %	0	Structure Info
49.78 %	2712639	Acro Forms
0 %	0	Link Annotations
0 %	0	Comments
0 %	0	Named Destinations
0 %	0	Web Capture Information
1.99 %	108518	Document Overhead
0 %	0	Color Spaces
0.05 %	2534	X Object Forms
0 %	0	Pattern Information
0 %	0	Shading Information
0.02 %	947	Extended Graphics States
3.99 %	217303	Piece Information
7.68 %	418240	Cross Reference Table
32.01 %	1744387	Unknown
100 %	5448786	Total

Figure 26-4: After the analysis is completed, the Space Audit dialog box opens.

In the example shown in Figure 26-4, notice that almost half of the document space is used for form fields (Acro Forms in the dialog box description). The second largest space percentage is an item denoted as *Unknown*. This item is used for all elements not identified as any one of the other items described in the dialog box.

The analysis informs you that there would be little need to try to resample images, because the image space is only 1.84 percent of the total space usage. You can best optimize the file by resaving it using the Save As command and doing something about all the form fields. If all the form fields are essential, then file reduction with either the Reduce File Size command or the PDF Optimizer might only be slight. Compare the first analysis (refer to Figure 26-3) with Figure 26-5. As you can see in the Space Audit report, images compose more than 90 percent of the space usage. In this example, you might see significant file reduction when using either the Reduce File Size command or the downsampling options of PDF Optimizer.

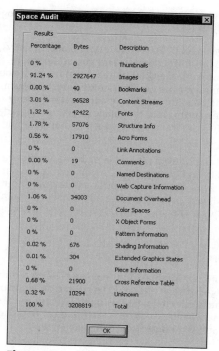

Figure 26-5: This shows that this document has a high percentage of images.

Optimizing files

The file analyzed in Figure 26-5 was originally created for professional printing, and the images are all sampled at 300 ppi. To repurpose the document and reduce the file size for Web hosting, the images need to be resampled at 72 ppi. Using the PDF Optimizer, you can specify image-size reductions as well as perform cleanup of content that occupies space for unnecessary items like comments, bookmarks, destinations, or other items that add to overhead in the file.

Image settings

To reduce file size with the PDF Optimizer, use the first set of options that opens in the Images tab, as shown in Figure 26-3. You can make choices for downsampling color, grayscale, and bitmap images by typing values in the field boxes for the sampling amounts desired. In our example, we edited the field boxes for color and grayscale images and chose 72 ppi as the amount of downsampling. To the right of the downsampling amount, another field box is used to identify images that are downsampled. In this box, we added 72 ppi, which instructs Acrobat to look for any image above 72 ppi and downsample the file to the amount supplied in the first field box—in this example, to 72 ppi. Other options in the PDF Optimizer dialog box include the following:

✦ **Compression pull-down menu:** Offers choices for JPEG2000 (Acrobat 6 setting only), JPEG, and Zip compression. For either form of JPEG compression, you additionally have choices for the amount of compression from the Quality pull-down menu. If you choose a JPEG compression and use Minimum for the Quality choice, your images may appear severely degraded. As a general rule, Medium quality results in satisfactory image quality for Web hosting. If you try one setting and the images look too degraded, you can return to the original file and apply a different Quality setting, then examine the results.

✦ **Adaptive Compression Options:** This is at the bottom of the dialog box and offers a means of adjusting the ratio between quality and compression. If you enable the check box for Enable Adaptive Compression, all other compression options are grayed out. This compression method uses advanced image processing like edge-shadow elimination and other effects not available with the downsampling models listed in the Image Settings area of the dialog box.

✦ **Remove edge shadow from images:** If you enable this option, shadows that may appear with scanned images are removed.

If you elect to choose Adaptive Compression Options, you may find that the file-size reduction is not as compact as choosing from the Image Settings options. Everything depends on the files and whether the images contain data that's affected when using the Adaptive Compression Options. The best way to determine what settings result in the most compact suitable files is to test compression with Image Settings controls and then again with Adaptive Compression.

Fonts settings

When you click the Fonts tab in the PDF Optimizer, only fonts available for unembedding are listed. On the left side of the dialog box, fonts are listed that can be unembedded. If no fonts appear in the list, you can move on to the next tab. If fonts are listed in the left window, select the fonts to unembed and click the Move button adjacent to the right chevron.

On the right side of the dialog box are fonts listed for unembedding. If you want to keep the font embedded, select it in the right window and click the Move button adjacent to left chevron. To select multiple fonts in either window, Shift+click to select a list in a contiguous group, or ⌘/Ctrl+click to select fonts in a noncontiguous group.

Clean Up settings

Click on the Clean Up tab and you find a list of items checked by default that you can safely use without affecting the functionality of your document. You can enable all other items that appear unchecked, but you should have an idea of what will happen to the PDF, in terms of functionality, if you optimize the file with any additional items checked. If you check one or more of the items and return to the PDF Optimizer, the new checked items become a new set of default settings. To restore the dialog box to original defaults, click on the Restore All Defaults button at the bottom of the dialog box; the check boxes return to original defaults, as shown in Figure 26-6.

Discarding items like comments, form actions, JavaScript actions, cross-references, and thumbnails affect document functionality as you might suspect. If the respective items are eliminated, any PDF interactivity created with these items is also eliminated. If you know that one or any group of these items won't have an effect on the way the repurposed document is viewed or printed, enable the check boxes for the items you want to remove.

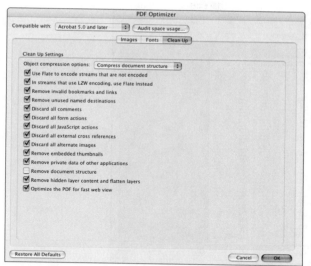

Figure 26-6: By default, a partial list of Clean Up settings is checked.

Removing private data of other applications doesn't affect the PDF functionality. When the check box is enabled, the data removed affects only data useful to the original authoring application. For example, saving to PDF from Adobe Illustrator while preserving Illustrator editing capabilities contains data in the PDF file useful only to Adobe Illustrator. Removing document structure eliminates tags and structure and can affect accessibility and also can present problems with the document functionality. Removing hidden layers and flattening the layers results in a file where all hidden layers are discarded and the visible layers are flattened.

After you make your preferred settings in the PDF Optimizer, click OK and wait for the processing to finish. As a comparison between using Reduce File Size and the PDF Optimizer, using the same file with an original file size of 3.06MB, we reduced the file size with the Reduce File Size command and produced a PDF that was resampled to 454KB. The same file processed with PDF Optimizer was reduced to 285KB. The increased file reduction from PDF Optimizer was due to eliminating some document overhead and structural information.

Redistilling files

Creating a PostScript file from a PDF document and redistilling with Acrobat Distiller with different Adobe PDF options is something that may not always work. Everything depends on the fonts embedded in the file and whether you have fonts installed on your system that aren't embedded in a PDF. In other words, it doesn't always work, but in many cases, it's usually best to try if using the Reduce File Size or PDF Optimizer doesn't produce a sufficiently smaller file for your output consideration.

Using the file analyzed earlier in this chapter (refer to Figure 26-4), where almost half the space is taken up by form fields, both the Reduce File Size command and the PDF Optimizer had little effect in reducing the file size. If the Clean Up item for Discard All Form Actions is selected in the PDF Optimizer dialog box, the file size is significantly smaller, but all the form-field data is lost. Figure 26-7 shows one of 13 pages in the original 5.2MB file.

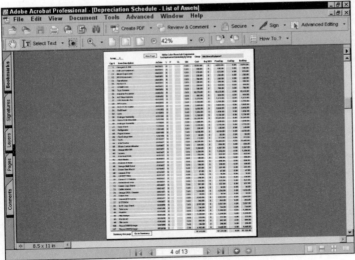

Figure 26-7: One of the 13 pages in a file at 5.2MB

Before we discuss downsizing a file, there are a few assumptions to be made when redistilling a file containing form fields:

✦ After the data is added to the document, the form fields are no longer needed.

✦ The final document, complete with the data, is then used for e-mailing, hosting on a hard drive or network server, or hosting on a Web site for users to review.

✦ If changes are to be made, the original file is kept stored on a drive for editing purposes.

With these assumptions in mind, the task at hand is to keep the data in the file while finding the most efficient means for downsizing the original 5.2MB file.

Because neither the Reduce File Size command nor the PDF Optimizer does the job, the next option is to choose File ➪ Save As and save the file as a PostScript file. After it's in PostScript, open Acrobat Distiller and select an Adobe PDF setting for the output desired.

The reason the PDF Optimizer doesn't do the job when downsizing PDF forms is the form fields and data are lost if you elect to remove form fields during optimization. When the fields are eliminated, they toss the data contained in the fields. When you print a PostScript file to disk and redistill the file, the form fields are eliminated from the document; however, the form-field data is stamped down on the background and all data originally supplied in form fields remains part of the newly created PDF. In the earlier example, where the original file size was 5.2MB, the file optimized with the PDF Optimizer reduced the file size to 3.45MB. The file printed to disk and redistilled in Acrobat Distiller produced a file of 63KB.

Tip

If you have interactive elements in a document such as bookmarks, form fields, destinations, and so on, and you want to preserve the interactive elements when redistilling PDFs, understand that these items are lost with Acrobat Distiller. To regain bookmarks, form fields, and so on, open the original file in Acrobat. Choose Document ➪ Pages ➪ Replace. Locate the new file created with Acrobat Distiller in the Select File with New Pages dialog box and replace all pages in the file. Choose File ➪ Save As to write a new optimized file to disk. The new file uses the optimized pages and the old file's interactive elements. You'll see a little increase in the file size due to the interactive elements, but the overall file size is much smaller in your new file compared to the original file.

Once again, be aware that redistilling files is not always successful; however, in more circumstances than not, we've found the procedure described in this section to be successful when file reduction cannot be successfully accomplished via other means.

Note You can also eliminate form fields while retaining the form data to reduce file sizes by using one of several different plug-ins you can purchase from third-party manufacturers. For a comprehensive list of third-party plug-ins working with Acrobat, demonstration versions of the software, and a description for each third-party product, log on to `www.pdfstore.com` and visit the Planet PDF store.

Setting Document Open Preferences

When users acquire your PDF documents from CD-ROMs, from Web downloads, from network servers, or from documents you send via e-mail, one double-click on the file opens the PDF in a user's default Acrobat viewer. The initial view of the PDF in the Document pane is the opening view. Depending on what user preferences are set up on a given computer, the initial view conforms to the preference settings unless you specifically assign open view preferences and save them within a document.

To understand viewing preferences, choose Acrobat ➪ Preferences (Mac) or Edit ➪ Preferences (Windows) or press ⌘/Ctrl+K to open the Preferences dialog box. Click Page Display in the left pane, and the options choices for initial views appear in the right pane. From the pull-down menu options at the top of the dialog box, you have choices for Default page layout where you can choose what additional panes you want to display when the file is opened—items such as Page Only, Bookmarks and Page, Layers and Page, and so on are available. The Default zoom pull-down menu offers choices for several zoom magnifications as you can see in Figure 26-8.

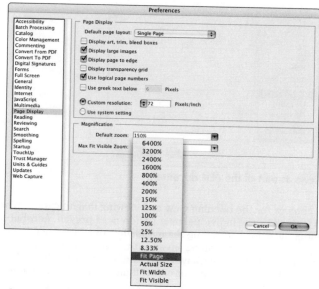

Figure 26-8: Choices for various viewing options when you first open a PDF

The preferences choices made here affect all PDF documents you open in Acrobat on your computer where no initial view has been saved inside a PDF file. For example, you can view a PDF document at a 100% view as long as Default was selected for the initial view when the file was last saved. Typically, all PDF documents exported from the CS applications save PDFs with default selections unless you specifically assign an initial view when creating the PDF.

Setting initial views

If you distribute a collection of PDF documents and use interactive buttons to open and close files for users to browse different documents, you may want to embed initial views in all your PDF documents. Because the Default view depends on settings assigned by each user, your files could conceivably be shown at different sizes depending on how a given user sets the Page Display preferences.

You can keep the viewing of your files consistent by embedding initial views in files. To set a view and save that opening view as part of the PDF, choose File ➪ Document Properties or ⌘/Ctrl+D. In the Document Properties dialog box, click on Initial View in the left pane, and the choices available for setting initial views appear in the right pane, as shown in Figure 26-9.

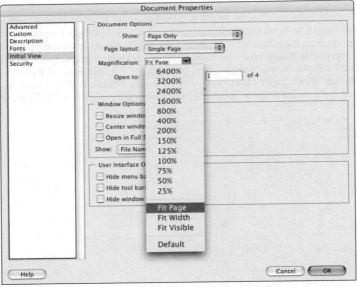

Figure 26-9: Setting initial views as part of the PDF document

In this dialog box, you make choices for the opening view and viewing magnification. When no settings have been saved with a file, the individual user preferences prevail. Acrobat provides you with many different choices for controlling the initial view of a PDF when opened in any Acrobat viewer. Settings you make here can be saved with your document. When you establish settings other than defaults, the settings saved with the file override the end user's default settings. The options available to you for controlling the initial view include the following:

✦ **Document Options:** The default opening page is the first page of a PDF document. You can change the opening page to another page, and you can control the page-layout views and magnification by selecting choices from the Document Options section. The choices include

- **Show:** Four choices are available from the pull-down menu. Select Page Only to open the page with the Navigation Pane collapsed. Use Bookmarks Panel and Page to open the Bookmarks tab when the file opens. Use Pages Panel and Page to open the Pages tab where the thumbnails of pages are viewed. Use Layers Panel and Page to open the Layers tab when the file opens.

- **Page Layout:** The default for Page Layout is noted in the pull-down menu as Default. When you save a PDF file with the Default selection, the PDF opens according to the default value a user has set for page viewing on the user's computer. To override the user's default, you can set a page layout in the opening view from one of four choices. Choose Single Page to open the PDF in a single-page layout. Choose Continuous to open in a continuous page view. Choose Facing to open with facing pages or use Continuous – Facing to open with continuous facing pages.

- **Magnification:** Choose from preset magnification views from the pull-down menu. If you want the PDF document to open in a fit-in-window view, select Fit Page. Choose from other magnification options in the pull-down menu or edit the field box for a custom zoom level.

- **Open To:** You can change the opening page to another page by entering a number in the field for Page Number. You might use this setting if you wanted a user to see a contents page instead of a title page.

✦ **Last-viewed page:** This is another option for the opening page. When enabled, the most recently viewed page viewed opens. This setting is intended for eBooks, where you might begin reading a novel and want to mark the page like a bookmark and later return to the page where you left off.

✦ **Window Options:** The default window for Acrobat is a full screen where the viewing area is maximized to occupy your monitor surface area. You can change the window view to size down the window to the initial page size, center a smaller window on-screen, and open a file in Full Screen mode. If you enable all three check boxes, the Full Screen mode prevails.

✦ **Show:** From the pull-down menu choose either File Name or Document Title. If File Name is selected, the title bar at the top of the Acrobat window shows the filename. If Document Title is used, the information you supply in the Document Properties dialog box for Document Title is shown in the title bar.

✦ **User Interface Options:** The Interface Options in the Initial View Document Properties dialog box have to do with user-interface items in Acrobat viewers such as menu bars, toolbars, and scrollbars. You can elect to hide these items when the PDF document opens in any Acrobat viewer. You can hide any one or a combination of the three items listed under the User Interface Options. When all three are enabled, the PDF is viewed as shown in Figure 26-10. If you elect to save files without any of the user-interface items in view, it's a good idea to create navigational buttons so users can move around your document.

The window controls you see in Figure 26-11 include the scrollbars, the status bar, and the Navigation pane. If you hide the toolbars and menu bar but elect to leave the window controls visible, users can access tools for page navigation.

Figure 26-10: Here, toolbars, the menu bar, and window controls are hidden.

Figure 26-11: With window controls visible, users can navigate with tools.

Caution If you elect to eliminate the toolbars and menu bar from view and later want to go back and edit your file, you need to use shortcut keys to get the menu bars and toolbars back. Be certain to remember the F8 and F9 keys — F8 shows/hides the toolbars and F9 shows/hides the menu bar.

Saving the initial view

When you decide what view attributes you want assigned to your document, you can choose between one of two save options. The first option updates the file. Click on the Save tool in the Acrobat File toolbar or choose File ⇨ Save. Any edits you make in the Initial View properties activates the Save command. The Save command is inactive and grayed out by default until you make any changes to your file or reset any kind of preferences that can be saved with the document.

The second method for updating your file uses the Save As command. When you choose File ⇨ Save As, the Save As dialog box opens. The default filename is the same name as the file you opened. If you elect to save the file to the same folder where it resides, Acrobat prompts you with a warning dialog box asking whether you want to overwrite the file. Click Yes and the file is rewritten. There are many times during your Acrobat sessions that using Save As will be a benefit. As you work on documents, they retain more information than necessary to view and print the file. By using Save As and overwriting the file, you optimize it for a smaller file size. In some cases, the differences between Save and Save As can be extraordinary in terms of the file sizes. As a matter of habit, try to use the Save As command after eight to ten different saves and completely rewrite the file. If you need a backup copy of a document, you can also use Save As and supply a new name in the Save As dialog box. When you click Save, a copy of your PDF is written to disk with the new name.

Note After editing a file and using the Save command ten times, Acrobat asks you if you want to use the Save As command to rewrite the file and optimize it.

Using Acrobat Catalog

Regardless of whether you create PDF documents for clients for wide distribution or you use PDF documents to catalog your own files in your studio, searching through archives is a task you frequently repeat. Acrobat 6 does offer you the capability of searching collections of PDFs on CD-ROMs, on network servers, and on local hard drives without the use of a search-index file. However, the internal search capabilities in Acrobat are painfully slow and limiting compared to searching an index. As a matter of common practice, you'll want to create a search-index file when archiving or distributing large quantities of documents.

To search an index file, you must have one present on your computer, network server, or some media-storage device. Index files are files containing all the words among PDF documents that were catalogued with Acrobat Catalog. You create index files by launching Catalog from within Acrobat. Note that in earlier versions of Acrobat, Catalog was a separate executable program. In Acrobat 6, Catalog is a plug-in and requires you to first launch Acrobat before you can access Catalog.

Note Acrobat Catalog is available only in Acrobat Professional. All Acrobat viewers, including Adobe Reader, can use search indexes. A search index is not usable in Acrobat when hosted on Web sites.

To launch Acrobat Catalog from within Acrobat Professional, choose Tools ⇨ Catalog. Catalog is robust and provides many options for creating and modifying indexes. After a search index is created, any user can access the search index from any Acrobat viewer to find words using search criteria in the search pane. However, before you begin to work with Acrobat Catalog, you need to take some preliminary steps to be certain all your files are properly prepared and ready to be indexed.

Preparing PDFs for indexing

Preparation involves creating PDFs with all the necessary information to facilitate searches. All searchable document description information needs to be supplied in the PDF documents at the time of PDF creation or by modifying PDFs in Acrobat before you begin working with Catalog. For workgroups and multiple-user access to search indexes, this information needs to be clear and consistent. Other factors, such as naming conventions, location of files, and performance optimization should all be planned prior to creating an index file.

Note   Adding document descriptions is not a requirement for creating search indexes. You can index files without any information in the document-description fields. Adding document descriptions merely adds relevant information to your PDF documents and aids users in finding search results faster.

Document descriptions

You should supply all PDF files with document description information, which expands your search capability. Creating document descriptions and defining the field types for consistent organization allows multiple users to searches documents quickly.

You supply document-summary information in the Document Properties dialog box, shown in Figure 26-12. Choose File ⇨ Document Properties or press ⌘/Ctrl+D and click on Description in the left pane. The document summary data is contained in the Title, Subject, Author, and Keywords fields. The data should be consistent and it should also follow a hierarchy consistent with a company's organizational structure and workflow.

The document-summary items should be mapped out and defined. When adding data to the Description fields, consider the following:

✦ **Title:** Title information is an outline — the parent statement, if you will. Use descriptive titles to help users narrow searches within specific categories. You can also use the Title field to display the title name at the top of the Acrobat window when you select viewing titles in the Initial View properties.

✦ **Author:** Avoid using proper names for the Author field. Personnel changes in companies and roles among employees change. Identify the author of PDF documents according to departments, workgroups, facilities, and so on.

✦ **Subject:** If the Title field is the parent item in an outline format, the Subject is a child item nested directly below the title. Consider subjects subsets of titles. When creating document summaries, be consistent. Don't use subject and title or subject and keyword information back and forth with different documents. If an item, such as *corporate identity,* is listed as a subject in some PDFs and then listed as titles in other documents, users will become confused with the order and searches become unnecessarily complicated.

✦ **Keywords:** If you have a forms identification system in place, be certain to use form numbers and identity as part of the Keywords field. You might start the Keywords field with a form number and then add additional keywords to help narrow searches. Be consistent and always start the Keywords field with forms or document numbers. If you need to have PDF author names, add them here in the Keywords field. If employees change roles or leave the company, the Author field still provides the information relative to a department.

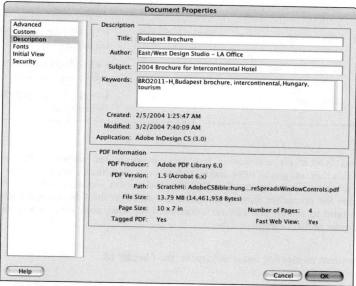

Figure 26-12: Document-summary information

To illustrate some examples, take a look at Table 26-1.

Table 26-1: Document Summary Examples

Title	Author	Subject	Keywords
Descriptive titles. Titles may be considered specific to workgroup tasks.	Department names. Don't use employee names in organizations; employees change, departments usually remain.	Subsection of Title. Subjects may be thought of as child outline items nested below the parent Title items — a subset of the Titles.	Document numbers and random identifiers Forms ID numbers, internal filing numbers, and so on can be supplied in the Keyword fields. If employee names are a must for your company, add employee names in the Keywords field box. List any related words to help find the topic.

Continued

Table 26-1 *(continued)*

Title	Author	Subject	Keywords
Corporate brochure	Seattle office	2004 Spring product line	CB-101, Spring brochure
FDA compliance	Quality assurance	Software validation	SOP-114, QA-182, J. Wilson, regulations, citations, eye-implant device
County fair campaign	Copy writing	1995 fair celebrity show	F-3709G, fairgrounds, talent, fair board
Receivables	Accounting	Collection policy	F-8102, M-5433, finance, collections, payments
eCommerce	Marketing	Products	M-1051, e-117A, golf clubs, sports, leisure

Tip

Legacy PDF files used in an organization may have been created without a document description, or you may reorganize PDFs and want to change document summaries. You can create a batch sequence to change multiple PDF files and run the sequence. Organize PDFs in a folder where the document summaries are to be edited. In the Edit Sequence dialog box, select the items to change and edit each document summary item. Run the sequence, and an entire folder of PDFs can be updated.

Cross-Reference

For more information on creating batch sequences, see Chapter 28.

File structure

The content, filenames, and location of PDFs to be cataloged contribute to file structure items. All the issues related to file structure must be thought out and appropriately designed for the audience that you intend to support. Among the important considerations are the following:

✦ **File-naming conventions:** Names provided for the PDF files are critical for distributing documents among users. If filenames get truncated, then either Acrobat Search or the end user will have difficulty finding a document when performing a search. This is of special concern to Mac users who want to distribute documents across platforms. As a matter of safeguard, the best precaution to take is always use standard DOS file-naming conventions. The standard eight-character maximum filename with no more than three-character file extensions (`filename.ext`) will always work regardless of platform.

✦ **Folder names:** Folder names should follow the same conventions as filenames. Mac users who want to keep filenames longer than standard DOS names must limit folder names to eight characters and no more than a three-character file extension for cross-platform compliance.

✦ **File- and folder-name identity:** Avoid using ASCII characters from 133 to 159 for any filename or folder name. Acrobat Catalog does support some extended characters in this range, but you may experience problems when using files across platforms. (Figure 26-13 lists the characters to avoid.)

133	à	139	ï	144	É	149	ò	154	Ü
134	å	140	î	145	æ	150	û	156	£
135	ç	141	ì	146	Æ	151	ù	157	¥
136	ê	142	Ä	147	ô	152	_	158	_
137	ë	143	Å	148	ö	153	Ö	159	ƒ
138	è								

Figure 26-13: When providing names for files and folders to be cataloged, avoid using extended characters from ASCII 133 to ASCII 159.

✦ **Folder organization:** Folders should have a logical hierarchy. Copy all files to a single folder or a single folder with nested folders in the same path. When nesting folders, keep the number of nested folders to a minimum. Deeply nested folders slow down searches, and path names longer than 256 characters create problems.

✦ **Folder locations:** For Windows users, location of folders must be contained on a local hard drive or a network server volume. Although Macintosh users can catalog information across computer workstations, creating separate indexes for files contained on separate drives would be advisable. Any files moved to different locations make searches inoperable.

✦ **PDF structure:** File and folder naming should be handled before creating links and attaching files. If filenames are changed after the PDF structure has been developed, many links become inoperable. Be certain to complete all editing in the PDF documents before cataloging files.

Optimizing performance

You can quickly perform searches if you take a little time in creating the proper structure and organization. You can avoid pitfalls, and thus slow searches, by organizing files. Consider the following:

✦ **Optimize PDF files:** Perform optimization on all PDF files as one of the last steps in your workflow. Use the Save As Optimizes for Fast Web View in the General category in the Preferences dialog box and run the PDF Optimizer located in the Advanced menu. Optimization is especially important for searches you performed from CD-ROM files.

Cross-Reference

For information on PDF Optimizer, see the section "Repurposing Documents."

✦ **Break up long PDF files:** You should break books, reports, essays, and other documents containing numerous pages into multiple PDF files. If you have books to be cataloged, break up the books into separate chapters. Acrobat Search runs much faster when finding information from several small files. It slows down when searching through long documents.

Managing multiple PDF documents

Books, reports, and manuals can be broken up into separate files and structured in a way that still appears to the end user as a single document. Assuming a user reads through a file in a linear fashion, you can create links to open and close pages without user intervention. Create navigational buttons to move forward and back through document pages. On the last page of each chapter, use the navigation button to open the next chapter. Also on the last page of each chapter, create a Page Action that closes the current document when the page is closed. You can link all the chapters from a table of contents where users can open any chapter. With careful thought, your user will find browsing the contents of multiple files no different from reading a book in the analog world.

Cross-Reference   For more information on PDF interactivity and creating link buttons to open and close files, see Chapter 29.

Creating a new index file

After your files are optimized and saved in final form, it's time to create the search index. Choose Advanced ⇨ Catalog to open the Catalog dialog box, shown in Figure 26-14. In the dialog box, you make choices for creating a new index file or opening an existing index file. Click on the New Index button to create a new index file.

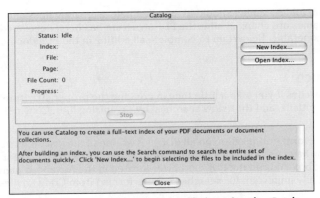

Figure 26-14: You create an index file by using the Catalog dialog box.

The New Index Definition dialog box, shown in Figure 26-15, opens where you set specific attributes for your index and determine what folder(s) are to be indexed.

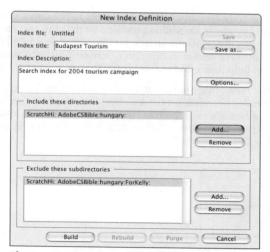

Figure 26-15: Set attributes for index files in the New Index Definition dialog box.

✦ **Index title:** The title that you place in this field is a title for the index, but not necessarily the name of the file you ultimately save. The name you enter here does not need to conform to any naming conventions because in most cases it won't be the saved filename. When you open an index file, you search your hard drive, server, or external media for a filename that ends with a PDX extension. When you visit the Search Pane and select the menu option for Select Index, the Index Selection dialog box (Figure 26-16) opens. The Index Selection dialog box lists indexes by their Index Title names. These names are derived from what you type in the Index Title field in Acrobat Catalog.

Note
When you get ready to build a file, Acrobat prompts you for the index filename. By default, the text you type in the Index Title field is listed in the File Name field in the Save Index File dialog box. This dialog box opens when you click on the Build button in the Catalog dialog box (see the section "Building the index" later in this chapter). In most cases where you supply a name as a description in the Index Title, you'll want to change the filename to a name consistent with standard DOS conventions (that is, an eight-character maximum with a three-character-maximum extension). Make this change when you're prompted to save the file.

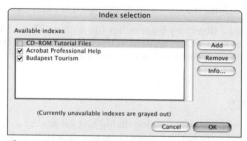

Figure 26-16: The Index selection dialog box lists all loaded indexes.

✦ **Index description:** You can supply as many as 256 characters in the Index Description field. Descriptive names and keywords should be provided so that the end user knows what each index contains. Index descriptions should be thought of as adding more information to the items mentioned earlier in this chapter regarding document descriptions. Index descriptions can help users find the index file that addresses their needs.

When an index is loaded, the index title appears in the Select Indexes dialog box. To get more information about an index file, click on the Info button (refer to Figure 26-16). The Index Information dialog box opens, shown in Figure 26-17. The Index Information dialog box shows you the title from the Index Title field and the description added in Acrobat Catalog in the Index Description field.

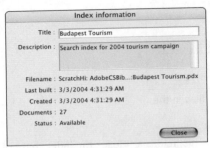

Figure 26-17: The Index information dialog box

✦ **Include these directories:** If you add nothing in this field, Catalog won't build an index because it won't know where to look for the PDF files to be included in the index. Adding the directory path(s) is essential before you begin to build the index. Notice the first Add button on the right side of the dialog box in Figure 26-15. After you click Add, a navigation dialog box opens, enabling you to identify the directory where the PDFs to be indexed are located. Many directories can be added to the Include These Directories list. These directories can be in different locations on your hard drive. When you select a given directory, all subfolders are also indexed for all directory locations unless you choose to exclude certain folders. When the directories have been identified, the directory path and folder name appear in the Include These Directories field.

✦ **Exclude these subdirectories:** If you have files in a subdirectory within the directory you're indexing and want to exclude the subdirectory, you can do so in the Exclude These Subdirectories field. The folder names and directory paths of excluded directories appear in the Exclude These Subdirectories field, as shown in Figure 26-15.

✦ **Remove:** If you decide to remove a directory from either the Include These Directories or Exclude These Subdirectories lists, select an item in the list and click on the Remove button. You can add or delete directories in either list prior to building an index or when modifying an index.

Saving index definitions

Two buttons appear at the top-right corner of the Catalog dialog box for saving a definition. If you begin to develop an index file and supply the index title and a description and want to come back to Catalog later, you can save what you type in the Index Definition dialog box using the Save As button. The Save button does not appear active until you've saved a file with the Save As option or you're working on a file that has been built. Saving the file only saves the definition for the index. It doesn't create an index file. The Save As option enables you to prepare files for indexing and interrupt your session if you need to return later. For example, suppose you add an index title and you write an index description. If you need to quit Acrobat at this point, click Save As and save the definition to disk. You can then return later and resume creating the index by adding the directories and building the index.

After you've saved a file, you can update the file with the Save button. After a definition is saved, when you return to Acrobat Catalog, you can click on the Open button in the Catalog dialog box and resume editing the definition file. When all the options for your search index have been determined, you click on the Build button to actually create the index file.

Using Save As or Save is not required to create an index file. If you set all your attributes for the index and click on the Build button, Acrobat Catalog prompts you in the Save Index File dialog box to supply a name for the index and save the definition. Essentially, Catalog is invoking the Save As command for you.

If, at any time, you click on the Cancel button in the lower-right corner of the Index Definition dialog box, all edits are lost for the current session. If you add definition items without saving, you'll need to start over when you open the Index Definition dialog box again. If you start to work on a saved file and click Cancel without saving new edits, your file reverts to the previously saved version.

Options

To the right of the Index Description field in the New Index Definition dialog box (Figure 26-15) is a button labeled Options. Click this button and the Options dialog box appears, allowing you to choose from a number of different attributes for your index file, as shown in Figure 26-18. Some of these options are similar to Preference settings for Acrobat Catalog made in the Preferences dialog box. Any edits you make here supersede preference settings. The options in this box include the following:

For information on setting catalog preferences, see the section "Setting preferences."

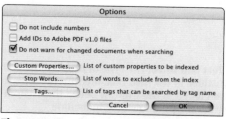

Figure 26-18: The Options dialog box assigns attributes to the index file.

✦ **Do not include numbers:** By selecting this option, you can reduce the file size, especially if data containing many numbers is part of the PDF file(s) to be indexed. Keep in mind, though, that if numbers are excluded, Search won't find numeric values.

✦ **Add IDs to Acrobat 1.0 PDF files:** Because Acrobat is now in version 6.0, it may be rare to find old PDF 1.0 files that you need to updated with IDs for Acrobat 1.0 files. If you do have legacy files saved as PDF 1.0 format, it's best to batch-process the older PDFs by saving them out of Acrobat 6.0. As software changes, many previous formats may not be supported with recent updates. To avoid this, update older documents to newer file formats.

Cross-Reference   For more information on batch processing, see Chapter 28.

If you have legacy files that haven't been updated and you want to include them in your search index, check the box. If you're not certain whether the PDFs were created with Acrobat 1.0 compatibility, check it anyway just to be safe.

✦ **Do not warn for changed documents when searching:** If you create an index file, then return to the index in Acrobat Catalog and perform some maintenance functions, save the index, and start searching the index, Acrobat notifies you in a dialog box that changes have been made and asks whether you want to proceed. To sidestep the opening of the warning dialog box, check the Do Not Warn for Changed Documents When Searching option.

✦ **Custom Properties:** This button opens a dialog box (Figure 26-19) which helps you customize Acrobat with the Acrobat Software Development Kit (SDK). This item is intended for programmers who want to add special features to Acrobat. To add a Custom Property to be indexed, you should have knowledge in programming and the PDF format.

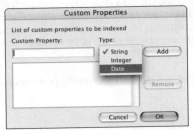

Figure 26-19: You can add custom data fields to Acrobat.

You add Custom Properties to the field box and select the type of property from the pull-down menu. You type the property values in the field box, identify the type, and click the Add button. The property is then listed in the window below the Custom Property field box. The types available from the pull-down menu include

- **String:** This is any text string. If numbers are included with this option, they are treated as text.

- **Integer:** The integer field can accept values between 0 and 65,535.

- **Date:** This is a date value.

Support for programmers writing extensions, plug-ins, and working with the SDK is provided by Adobe Systems. For developers who want to use the support program, you need to become a member of the Adobe Solutions Network (ASN) Developer Program. For more information about ASN and SDK, log on to the Adobe Web site at `http://partners.adobe.com/asn/developer`.

✦ **Stop Words:** To optimize an index file that produces faster search results, you can add stop words. You may have words, such as *the, a, an, of,* and so on that you would typically not use in a search. You can exclude such words by typing the word in the Word field box and clicking the Add button in the Stop Words dialog box. Click on Stop Words in the Options dialog box to open the Stop Words dialog box (Figure 26-20). To eliminate a word after it has been added, select the word and click the Remove button. Keep in mind every time you *add* a word, you're actually adding it to a list of words to be excluded.

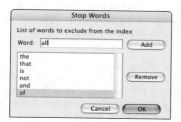

Figure 26-20: You can eliminate words from an index file.

Tip

You can create an elaborate list of stop words and may want to apply the list to several index files, but Acrobat (as of this writing) does not include an ability to import or swap a list of words to be excluded from an index file. For a workaround, you can open any existing Index Definition field and change all attributes except the stop words. Add a new index title, a new index description, and select a new directory for indexing. Save the definition to a new filename and click on the Build button. A new index is built using stop words created in another index. In workgroups, you can save an index definition file without adding directories and use it as a template so all index files have consistent settings for the stop words.

✦ **Tags:** If you have a Tagged PDF, you can search document tags when the tags are included in the search index. Click on Tags in the Options dialog box to open the Tags dialog box (Figure 26-21). Tagged PDFs with a tagged root and elements can have any item in the tagged logical tree marked for searching. To observe the tags in a PDF file, open the Tags palette and expand the tree. All the tags nest like a bookmark list. To mark tags for searching, type the tag name in the Tags dialog box and click the Add button. You remove tags from the list window by selecting a tag and clicking the Remove button.

Cross-Reference

For more information on creating tagged PDF documents and the use of tags, see the *Adobe Acrobat 6 PDF Bible* (Wiley Publishing).

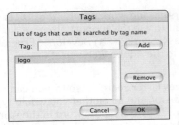

Figure 26-21: You can mark tags for searches in index files.

Building the index

After you set all the attributes for the index definition, you're ready to create the index file. Clicking the Build button in the New Index Definition dialog box (Figure 26-15) creates indexes. When you click this button, Acrobat Catalog opens the Save Index File dialog box, where you supply a filename and target a destination on your hard drive. The default file extension is PDX. Don't modify the file extension name. Acrobat recognizes these files when loading search indexes.

The location where you instruct Catalog to save your index file can be any location on your hard drive regardless of where the files being indexed reside. You can save the index file inside or outside the folder that Catalog created during the indexing. Therefore, you have an index file and a folder containing index resources. The relationship between the index file and resource folder locations is critical to the usability of the index. If you move the index file to a different location without moving the supporting folder, the index is rendered unusable. To avoid problems, create a folder either when you're in the Save Index File dialog box or before you open Catalog and save your index file to your new folder. Make the name descriptive and keep the index file together in this folder. When you want to move the index to another directory, to another computer, or to an external media cartridge or CD-ROM, copy the folder containing the index and supporting files.

Click the Save button in the Save Index File dialog box and Catalog closes the Index Definition dialog box, returns you to the Catalog dialog box, and begins to process all the files in the target folder(s). Depending on how many files are indexed, the time to complete the build may be considerable. Don't interrupt the processing if you want to complete the index generation. When Catalog finishes, the progress bar stops and the last line of text in the Catalog dialog box reads, "Index build successful." If for some reason the build is not successful, you can scroll the window in the Catalog dialog box and view errors reported in the list.

The structure of index files

When you produce an index file in Acrobat Professional, Catalog creates a single resource folder where files with an IDX and INFO extensions reside. You need to copy the index file and the folder together and maintain the same directory path. If the index file doesn't find the folder, the index won't work.

The PDX file you load as your search-index file is a small file that creates the information in the IDX and INFO files. The IDX files contain the actual index entries the end user accesses during a search. When you build an index, rebuild an index, or purge data from an index, the maintenance operation may or may not affect the PDX file and/or IDX files depending on which option you choose. For specific information related to how these files are affected during index creation and maintenance, see the following pages for building, rebuilding, and purging index files.

Stopping builds

If you want to interrupt a build, you can click on the Stop button while a build is in progress. When building an index, Catalog opens a file where all the words and markers to the PDF pages are written. When you click on the Stop button, Catalog saves the open file to disk and closes it with the indexed items up to the point you stopped the build. Therefore, the index is usable after stopping a build and you can search for words in the partial index. When you want to resume, you can open the file in Catalog and click on the Rebuild button in Catalog.

Building existing indexes

When files are deleted from indexed folders and new files are added to the indexed folders, you'll want to maintain the index file and update to reflect any changes. You can open an index file and click on Build for a quick update. New files are scanned and added to the index, but the deleted files are marked for deletion without actually deleting the data. To delete data no longer valid, you need to use the Purge button. Purging can take a considerable amount of time even on small index files. Therefore, your routine maintenance might be to consistently build a file and only periodically purge data.

Building legacy index files

When you open an index file created with an Acrobat Catalog version earlier than version 6.0, a dialog box opens, as shown in Figure 26-22, informing you the index is not compatible with the current version of Acrobat. In the dialog box, you have three options: Create Copy, Overwrite Old Index, and Cancel. Click on the Create Copy button to make a copy of the index file. A new index file is created leaving the original index file undisturbed. You can click on the Overwrite Old Index button and the file rewrites, replacing the old index. If you choose this option, your new index file won't be compatible with Acrobat viewers earlier than version 6.0. Clicking on Cancel in the dialog box returns you to the Index Selection dialog box, leaving the index file undisturbed.

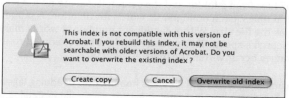

This index is not compatible with this version of Acrobat. If you rebuild this index, it may not be searchable with older versions of Acrobat. Do you want to overwrite the existing index ?

Create copy   Cancel   Overwrite old index

Figure 26-22: With Acrobat Catalog version earlier than 6.0, you're informed that your index won't work with Acrobat 6.0.

If you know some users won't be working with the new Acrobat viewers, be certain to make copies of your index files. Until all users have upgraded to a viewer 6.0 or higher, you may need to organize your indexes according to viewer versions.

Tip   If your workflow requires having different versions of Acrobat viewers, then keeping a complete installation of Acrobat 5.05 installed on a separate computer on your network is to your advantage. If you inadvertently overwrite index files or need to perform some task specifically related to Acrobat versions less than 6.0, you can use the older version to keep compatibility with other users. In addition, you can test many new files you edit in version 6.0 or higher to ensure they work with viewer versions less than 6.0. Ideally, all your colleagues, coworkers, and clients should upgrade to Acrobat 6.0. However, in a real world, we know some users are reluctant to let go of the familiar, and convincing some of your clients that upgrading Acrobat is the best solution may take some time.

Building index files from secure documents

In all earlier versions of Acrobat, you could not create index files from secure PDFs encrypted with either Acrobat Standard Security or Acrobat Self-Sign Security. Now in version 6.0 of Acrobat, you have complete access to secure files with Acrobat Catalog. Any form of encrypted file using the Acrobat-supported security features can be included in your index files. Creating an index does not compromise your security and won't affect the permissions you set forth when the files were saved.

If you have legacy files that have been secured, you can index them like other files saved in earlier PDF format compatibilities. You can only use these files, or any other files you create with Acrobat Professional, with Acrobat viewers 6.0 and later.

 Cross-Reference   For more information on encryption and security, see Chapter 28.

Rebuilding an index

Rebuilding index files completely re-creates a new index. You can open an Acrobat 6.0–compatible index file and click on Rebuild. The file rewrites the file you opened much like you would use a Save As menu command to rewrite a PDF document. If a substantial number of PDF documents have been deleted and new files added to the indexed folders, rebuilding the index could take less time than purging data.

Purging data

As indexes are maintained and rebuilt, you'll need to perform periodic maintenance and purge old data. A purge does not delete the index file, nor does it completely rewrite the file; it simply recovers the space used in the index for outdated information. Purging is particularly useful when you remove PDF files from a folder and the search items are no longer needed. If you've built a file several times, each build marks words for deletion. A purge eliminates the marked data and reduces the file size. With a significant number of words marked for deletion, a purge improves a search's speed. This operation might be scheduled routinely in environments where many changes occur within the indexed folders.

 Tip   When changing options for eliminating words and numbers from indexes or adding tags and custom properties in the Options dialog box, first open the index.pdx file in Catalog and purge the data. Set your new criteria in the Options dialog box and rebuild the index. Any items deleted will now be added to the index, or any items you want to eliminate will subsequently be eliminated from the index.

Setting preferences

Preference settings are contained in the Preferences dialog box. Choose Edit ⇨ Preferences and click on the Catalog item in the left Pane as shown in Figure 26-23. Notice that the Index Defaults items use the same settings as found in the Options dialog box from the New Index Selection dialog box. The top three options under Indexing in Catalog Preferences are obtained only here in these preference settings.

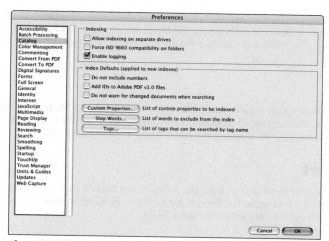

Figure 26-23: Open the Preferences dialog box and click on Catalog.

✦ **Indexing:** The three options found in the Indexing section of the Catalog preferences include

- **Allow indexing on separate drives:** When creating index files where you want to include folders on network servers and/or computers on your network, select this item. The indexing option only includes indexing files on local networks. Unfortunately, you can't index files on Web servers and use indexes from within Web browsers.

- **Force ISO 9660 compatibility on folders:** This setting tells Catalog to look for any folders that aren't compliant with standard DOS conventions (eight-character maximum with three-character-maximum extensions) for folder/directory names. If Catalog encounters An unacceptable folder name, it stops the process and reports an error in the Catalog dialog box. Folder names and directory paths are listed for all incompatible names. You can review the list and manually rename folders. After changing folder names, try to create the index again.

- **Enable logging:** A log file, created during an index build, describes the processing for each indexed file. You can open the file, which is ASCII text, in any text editor or word processor. Any errors are noted in the log file, along with all documents and directory paths. If you don't want to generate a log file at the time of indexing, deselect the check box, but realize that you're prevented from analyzing problems.

✦ **Index Defaults:** These options are identical to the options you have available in the New Index Definition Options dialog box (see Figure 26-18). These default/options settings exist in two locations for different reasons:

- When you set the options in the Preferences dialog box, the options are used for all index files you create. When you elect to use the options from the New Index Selection Options dialog box, the settings are specific to the index file you create. When you create a new index file, the options return to defaults.

- If you set a preference in the Catalog Preferences and disable the option in the New Index Selection Options dialog box, the latter supersedes the former. That is to say, the New Index Selection Options dialog box settings always prevail.

Using Index Files

As stated earlier, the main reason you create index files is for speed. When you search hundreds or thousands of pages, the amount of time to return found instances for searched words is a matter of seconds compared to using the Search tool in the Search pane.

Loading index files

To search using an index file, you need to first load the index in the Search pane. Click on the Search tool or press ⌘/Control + F to open the Search pane. From the Look In pull-down menu, choose the Select Index menu option, as shown in Figure 26-24.

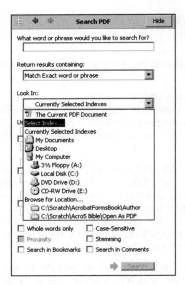

Figure 26-24: Your first step in using indexes is to load the index file(s)

The Index Selection dialog box opens after making the menu selection. Click on the Add button and the Open Index File dialog box opens, as shown in Figure 26-25. In this dialog box, navigate your hard drive to find the folder where your index file is located. Click on the index filename and click on the Open button.

After selecting the index to load, you're returned to the Index Selection dialog box. A list of all loaded indexes appears in the dialog box. To the left of each filename is a check box. When a check mark is in view, the index file is active and can be searched. Disabled check boxes have the index file loaded, but the file remains inactive. Search will not return results from the inactive index files. If an index file is grayed out, as shown in Figure 26-26, the file path has been disrupted and Acrobat can't find the index file or the support files associated with the index. If you see a filename grayed out, select the file in the list and click on the Remove button. Click on the Add button and relocate the index. If the support files aren't found, an error is reported in a dialog box, indicating the index file could not be opened.

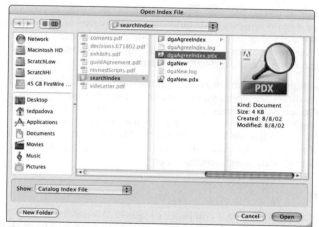

Figure 26-25: Select an index to load and click on the Open button.

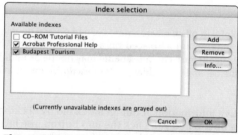

Figure 26-26: If a file is grayed out, the index is not accessible.

If you can't open a file, you need to return to the Catalog dialog box by selecting Advanced ➪ Catalog and click on the Open button. Find the index file that you want to make active and rebuild the index. After rebuilding, you need to return to the Index Selection dialog box and reload it.

Note   If you load an index file from a CD-ROM and the CD is not inserted in your CD-ROM drive, the index-file name is grayed out in the Index Selection dialog box. After inserting the CD-ROM containing the index, the index-file name becomes active. If you know index files are loaded from CDs, don't delete them from the Index Selection dialog box. Doing so requires you to reload the index file each time you insert a CD.

Disabling indexes

If you want to eliminate an index from searches, you can deactivate the index by disabling its check box. In a later Acrobat session, you can go back and enable indexes listed in the Index Selection dialog box (open the Search pane as described in the previous section and choose Select Index from the Look In pull-down menu to open the Index Selection dialog box). You should always use this method rather than deleting an index if you intend to use it again in a later Acrobat session. However, at times, you may want to delete an index file. If you no longer intend to use the index, or you relocate your index to another drive or server, you may want to completely remove the old index. If this is the case, select the index file you want to delete and click the Remove button. You can enable or disable indexes before you select Remove. In either case, the index file is removed without warning.

If you inadvertently delete an index, you can always reload the index by clicking the Add button. Placing index files in a directory where you can easily access them is a good idea. To avoid confusion, try to keep indexes in a common directory or a directory together with the indexed PDF files. Acrobat doesn't care where the index file is located on your hard drive or server — it just needs to know where the file is located and the file needs to keep the relative path with the support files. If you move the index file to a different directory, be certain to reestablish the connection in the Index Selection dialog box.

Index information

When a number of index files are installed on a computer or server, the names for the files may not be descriptive enough to determine which index you want to search. If more-detailed information is desired, the information provided by the Index Information dialog box may help identify the index needed for a given search. To open the Index selection dialog box click Select Index in the Look In pull-down menu. Click the Info button in the Index selection dialog box to display the index information.

Note   Index information may be particularly helpful in office environments where several people in different departments create PDFs and indexes are all placed on a common server. What may be intuitive to the author of an index file in terms of index name may not be as intuitive to other users. Index information offers the capability of adding more-descriptive information that can be understood by many users.

Fortunately, you can explore more-descriptive information about an index file by clicking the Info button in the Index Selection dialog box. When you click the Info button, the Index Information dialog box opens, displaying information about the index file, as shown in Figure 26-27. Some of the information displayed requires user entry at the time the index is built. Acrobat Catalog automatically creates other information in the dialog box when the index is built. The Index information dialog box provides a description of the following:

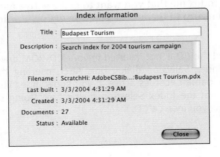

Figure 26-27: The Index information dialog

✦ **Title:** The user supplies title information at the time the index is created. Titles usually consist of several words describing the index contents. Titles can be searched so the title keywords should reflect the index content.

✦ **Description:** Description can be a few words or several sentences containing information about the index. (In Figure 26-27, the description was supplied in Acrobat Catalog when the index was created.)

✦ **Filename:** The directory path for the index file's location on a drive or server displays with the last item appearing as the index filename.

✦ **Last built:** If the index file is updated, the date of the last build is supplied here. If no updates have occurred, the date is the same as the date of creation.

✦ **Created:** This date reflects the time and date the index file was originally created and is, therefore, a fixed date.

✦ **Documents:** Indexes are created from one or more PDF documents. The total number of PDF files from which the index file was created appears here.

✦ **Status:** If the index file has been identified and added to the list in the Index Selection dialog box, it will be Available. Unavailable indexes appear grayed out in the list and are described as Unavailable.

Searching an index

After your index file is prepared and loaded in the Index Selection dialog box, it's ready for use. You search index files in the Advanced Search pane. From the Look In pull-down menu, select Currently Selected Indexes, as shown in Figure 26-28.

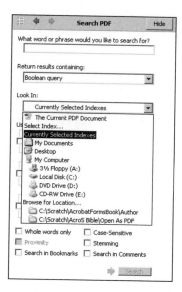

Figure 26-28: To search all active index files, select Currently Selected Indexes.

All the options discussed earlier for advanced searches are available to you. Select from the Return Results Containing pull-down menu, enter your search criteria, and select the options you want. Click on the Search button and you'll find the search results reported much faster than using other search methods.

Index files can be created from PDF collections contained on external media where the index file can remain on your computer without the need for copying the PDF documents to your hard drive. When you insert a media disc like a CD-ROM, your search index is ready to use to search the media. To understand a little more about creating search indexes and using them with external media, follow these steps.

STEPS: Creating Index Files from Media Storage

1. **Set preferences.** Choose Edit ➪ Preferences. Click on Catalog in the left pane. Check Allow Indexing on Separate Drives. In order to create an index file from a device other than your local hard drive(s), this preference setting must be enabled. Click OK to exit the Preferences dialog box.

2. **Open Catalog.** Choose Advanced ➪ Catalog.

3. **Open the New Index Definition dialog box.** Click on New Index in the Catalog dialog box and the New Index Definition dialog box opens in the foreground.

4. **Add an Index title.** Click in the first field box and type a title for your index file. The example in Figure 26-29 uses "Budapest Tourist" for the title.

5. **Add an Index Description.** Type a description for the index. You can use any text you want to help remind you later what this index file is used for. An example description appears in Figure 26-29.

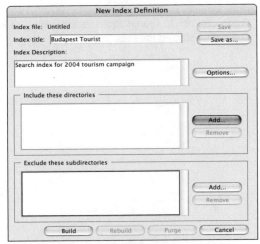

Figure 26-29: Add an index title and an index description.

6. **Change Options.** Click on the Options button to open the Options dialog box, shown in Figure 26-30, where you can make options choices. Check Do Not Warn for Changed Documents When Searching. Click OK.

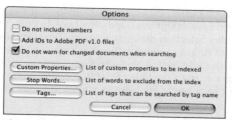

Figure 26-30: The Option dialog box

7. **Add a folder to the Include These Directories list.** Click the first Add button adjacent to the list for Include These Directories. The Browse for Folder dialog box opens. If you have a folder you want to catalog, select the folder in the Browse for Folder dialog box. If you have a CD where your files are stored, click on the CD drive where the CD containing the files is located. Click OK in the Browse for Folder dialog box.

8. **Build the index.** Click on the Build button in the Catalog dialog box. Acrobat prompts you with the Save Index File dialog box for the location to save your index file. Select the location on your hard drive where you want to save your file. Type a name in the File Name field. Use a short name for the file. The extension defaults to PDX. Leave the default extension and click the Save button.

   Acrobat Professional reads all the files on the CD-ROM and writes the Index file. Let your computer continue writing the index until it finishes the build.

9. **Examine the build results.** When Acrobat completes the build, the Catalog dialog box reports the results of the build. The last line in the results list reports the index build as successful, as shown in Figure 26-31.

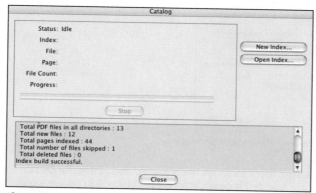

Figure 26-31: Examine the results to verify that the build was successful.

10. **Quit Catalog.** Click on the Close button to quit Catalog.

11. **Load the index file.** Click the Search button in the Acrobat File toolbar or press ⌘/Ctrl+F and select Use Advanced Search Options. Open the Look In pull-down menu and click on Select Index. The Index Selection dialog box opens. Deselect any active index files by clicking on the check boxes to remove the check mark adjacent to the index names in the list. Click the Add button and select your new index in the Open Index File dialog box. Click OK to return to the Index Selection dialog box. Verify that your new index is listed and the check box is enabled, as shown in Figure 26-32.

Index selection
Available indexes
Acrobat Professional Help
Budapest Tourism
Add
Remove
Info...
(Currently unavailable indexes are grayed out)
Cancel
OK

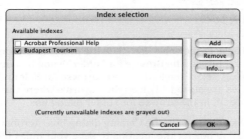

Figure 26-32: Be certain your new index file is loaded and enabled.

12. **Review the index information.** Select the index file in the Index Selection dialog box. Click on the Info button to open the Index Information dialog box, as shown in Figure 26-33. Review the contents and notice the description appears as you added it in the Index Description dialog box. Click Close to return to the Index Selection dialog box. Click OK in the Index Selection dialog box to return to the Acrobat Document Pane.

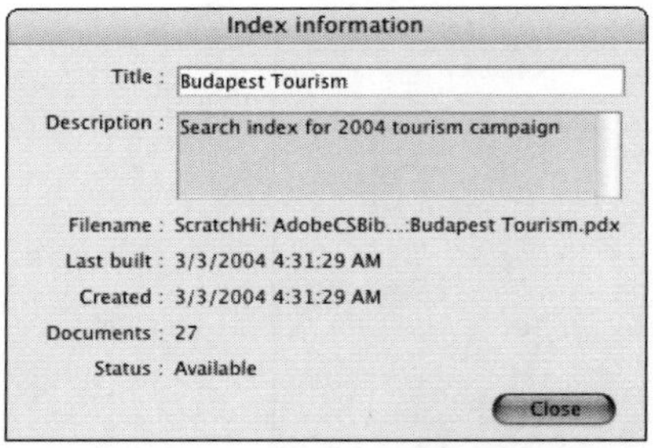

Index information
Title : Budapest Tourism
Description : Search index for 2004 tourism campaign
Filename : ScratchHi: AdobeCSBib...:Budapest Tourism.pdx
Last built : 3/3/2004 4:31:29 AM
Created : 3/3/2004 4:31:29 AM
Documents : 27
Status : Available
Close

Figure 26-33: Examine the Index information.

13. **Search the new index file.** The index file is loaded and active. Be certain the menu option for Currently Selected Indexes is active in the Look In pull-down menu. Enter **Search AND Index Description** in the first field box. Select Boolean Query from the Return Results Containing pull-down menu. Click on Search in Bookmarks at the bottom of the Search pane, as shown in Figure 26-34.

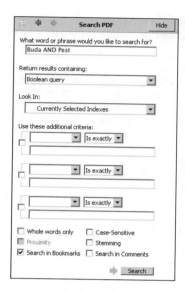

Figure 26-34: Type the words that you want to search for.

14. ![binoculars icon] **Invoke the Search.** Click the Search button at the bottom of the Search pane. The results are reported in the list within the Search pane. Click on any text highlighted in blue to open the file and page where the results are found.

Practice searching your new index file using different options and search criteria. To compare the difference between using a search index file and using the advanced search options, you can choose the Browse for Location menu item and search the CD-ROM for the same criteria. Go back and forth to see the differences between searching folders and searching an index file. It should be obvious that when using an index file your search results are reported much faster.

Searching external devices

A computer network server, another computer on your network, a CD-ROM, a DVD-ROM, an external hard drive, or a removable media cartridge is considered external to your local computer hard drive(s). Any of these devices can be indexed and the index file can be located on any of the devices you index. If you want to save an index file on a device different from where the PDF collection is stored, be certain to open the Preferences dialog box for the Catalog Preferences and enable the check box for Allow Indexing on Separate Drives. This preference setting enables you to index across media devices.

Note   When you want to write index files to read only media such as CD-ROMs and DVDs, you need to create the index file from PDFs stored on your hard drive. After the index file is created, copy the index file, the supporting files, and the PDFs to your media and burn the disk.

When you want to search an index, you can activate the index in the Index Selection dialog box and invoke a search, whether your external media is mounted and accessible or not. The search index returns results from the index PDX file and the IDX files without looking at the

PDFs that were indexed. You can examine the results of the search in the Search pane and find the files where the search criteria match the PDF documents in the index collection.

If you want to open the link to the PDF document where a result is reported, you need to have the media mounted and accessible. If a network server or other computer contains the related files, the server/computer must be shared with appropriate permissions and visible on your desktop. If you use external media-storage devices, the media must be mounted and visible on your desktop in order to view the PDFs linked to the search results. If you attempt to view a document when the device is not mounted, Acrobat opens an error dialog box, as shown in Figure 26-35.

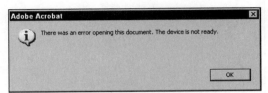

Figure 26-35: An error dialog box informs you that the device is not ready.

If you see an error dialog box like the one shown in Figure 26-35, click OK in the dialog box and insert your media, connect an external hard drive, or access a computer or network server. Wait until the media is mounted, and click on a search result. Acrobat opens the linked page and you're ready to continue your search.

A search-index file created on one computer can be moved or copied to another computer. To copy an index file to another computer, be certain you copy the index file (PDX) and all supporting files in the folder created by Catalog.

You can load the index file and external media on another computer and perform the same searches as were performed where the index file was created. When you're distributing CD-ROMs and DVDs, you can copy these index files to your media and all users can access the index files. If you access an index file on a network server and the PDF collection is stored on an external device such as a CD-ROM, you cannot open files from another computer unless the CD-ROM is mounted. You may see your network server, but the associated devices with the server need to be individually mounted in order to open PDF files remotely.

Summary

✦ You can reduce file sizes with the Reduce File Size menu command.

✦ You use the PDF Optimizer, available with Acrobat Professional, to reduce file sizes and eliminate unnecessary data in PDF files. PDF Optimizer can often reduce file sizes more than when using the Reduce File Size command.

✦ Selecting options in the Clean Up tab in the PDF Optimizer other than the default options can interfere with the PDF functionality.

✦ In some cases, saving a PDF file to disk and redistilling with Acrobat Distiller can reduce file sizes.

✦ Users determine initial views when setting preferences for all files saved with default views. When you save initial views in PDF files, they override user preferences.

✦ Search index files are created in Acrobat Catalog. Searching index files returns results much faster than Acrobat built-in search tools.

✦ You can search document descriptions with advanced searches and via index file searches.

✦ Index files can be built, rebuilt, and purged with Acrobat Catalog. Old index files created with PDF formats earlier than version 6.0 need to be rebuilt with Acrobat Catalog.

✦ Tags and XML data can be searched with advanced searches and from index searches.

✦ You can copy index files to other computers, network servers, and external media-storage units.

✦   ✦   ✦

Working with XML

XML, or *Extensible Markup Language*, is often used as a data-transport media. As a popular format for exchanging data on the Web, many of the CS applications support XML.

InDesign, in particular, includes broad support for XML that lets you mark InDesign elements with XML tags. Exporting an InDesign document to the XML format with these tags produces an XML document that holds the content of the InDesign document. InDesign also allows you to export XML documents into the current document. Importing an XML document displays all tagged elements in the Structure pane where you can drag them into framed placeholders in the document. If you must further edit an XML document, you can use GoLive to view, edit, and create XML documents using its Outline and Source Code Editors. Acrobat also includes features to save PDF files as XML documents.

Understanding XML

To easily understand XML, consider starting with its sister technology, HTML, or *Hypertext Markup Language*. HTML is a set of syntax commands that display Web pages within a browser. If you choose View ➪ Source in a Web browser, the HTML code for the Web page displays.

If you examine some HTML code, you'll find that it is text-based and may be created using any standard text editor. HTML code is also simplistic and fairly readable, as shown in Figure 27-1. It isn't too difficult to figure out, but the language is rigid and requires that you follow the syntax exactly in order to get the desired results.

HTML has a limiting problem: It describes how to place text and images on Web pages, but it doesn't know anything about the type of data it's displaying. XML addresses this concern, allowing a developer to customize the tags that are used in order to describe it. The extensible portion of XML doesn't make it stick to one particular set of tags.

For example, you use the `<img>` tag in HTML to display an image on a Web page, but in XML, you could create a `<circle>` tag with attributes such as radius and color. By endowing XML documents with tags that define different types of objects, the XML document becomes a great way to save data. Applications may then be written that use the XML document to process the data in different ways.

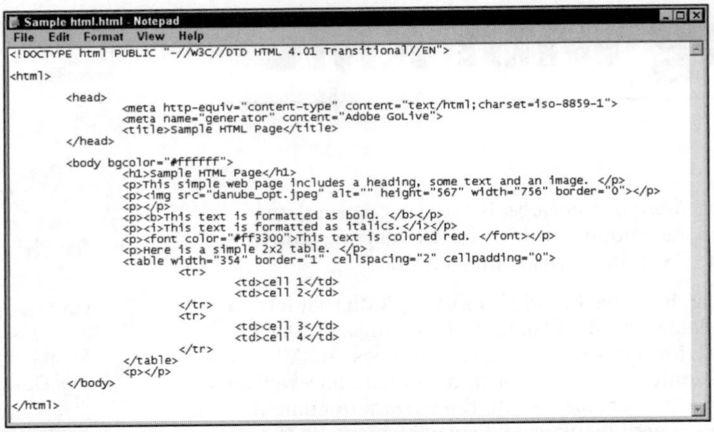

```
<!DOCTYPE html PUBLIC "-//W3C//DTD HTML 4.01 Transitional//EN">

<html>

	<head>
		<meta http-equiv="content-type" content="text/html;charset=iso-8859-1">
		<meta name="generator" content="Adobe GoLive">
		<title>Sample HTML Page</title>
	</head>

	<body bgcolor="#ffffff">
		<h1>Sample HTML Page</h1>
		<p>This simple web page includes a heading, some text and an image. </p>
		<p><img src="danube_opt.jpeg" alt="" height="567" width="756" border="0"></p>
		<p></p>
		<p><b>This text is formatted as bold. </b></p>
		<p><i>This text is formatted as italics.</i></p>
		<p><font color="#ff3300">This text is colored red. </font></p>
		<p>Here is a simple 2x2 table. </p>
		<table width="354" border="1" cellspacing="2" cellpadding="0">
			<tr>
				<td>cell 1</td>
				<td>cell 2</td>
			</tr>
			<tr>
				<td>cell 3</td>
				<td>cell 4</td>
			</tr>
		</table>
		<p></p>
	</body>

</html>
```

Figure 27-1: The source code for any HTML Web page is readable within a text editor.

XML tags may also include attributes. *Attributes* are additional properties embedded within the tag, further defining the tag object. Attributes are just keywords that are assigned a value.

To keep track of all the tags used in an XML document, you can create a controlling document called the *Document Type Definition* (DTD). This document lists all the different tags that are possible for the XML document that it's applied to and defines the tags, the attributes of those tags, and the overall structure of the XML.

XML and Creative Suite

So what does XML have to do with the Creative Suite applications? Several of the Creative Suite applications include support for XML and use it as a data-transport format. For example, InDesign can tag content with XML tags and import them into other documents where they may be reused. InDesign can also export XML documents. GoLive is also used to actually create and view XML documents.

XML and SVG

Although you can create custom XML tags to define a specific object, it would become pretty confusing if each company defined its own tags a little differently from everyone else. For example, you may need to share data sets with other companies. Several standard DTDs with broad appeal have been defined using working groups that include participants and input from many different companies.

One such DTD is used to define vector data for use on the Web called *Scalable Vector Graphic* (SVG). The SVG DTD includes all the tags to define vector graphics; using a plug-in, a Web browser is able to parse the XML document and display the vector graphics in a Web page.

If you were to open an SVG file in a text editor, you would see tags that are similar to HTML, like the file shown in Figure 27-2.

Cross-Reference The SVG format is covered in Chapter 32.

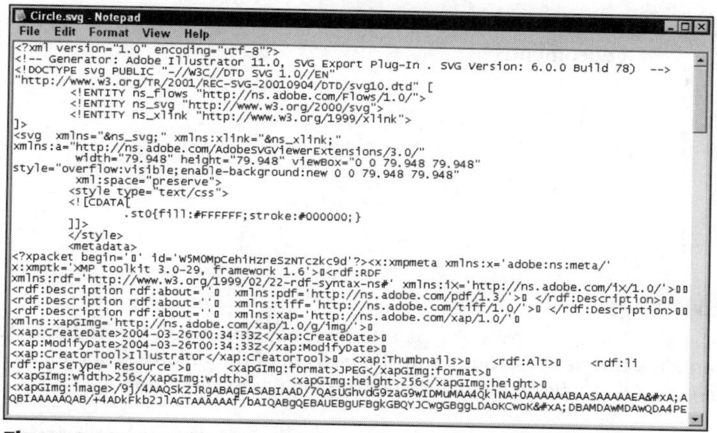

```
Circle.svg - Notepad
File Edit Format View Help
<?xml version="1.0" encoding="utf-8"?>
<!-- Generator: Adobe Illustrator 11.0, SVG Export Plug-In . SVG Version: 6.0.0 Build 78)  -->
<!DOCTYPE svg PUBLIC "-//W3C//DTD SVG 1.0//EN"
"http://www.w3.org/TR/2001/REC-SVG-20010904/DTD/svg10.dtd" [
	<!ENTITY ns_flows "http://ns.adobe.com/Flows/1.0/">
	<!ENTITY ns_svg "http://www.w3.org/2000/svg">
	<!ENTITY ns_xlink "http://www.w3.org/1999/xlink">
]>
<svg  xmlns="&ns_svg;" xmlns:xlink="&ns_xlink;"
xmlns:a="http://ns.adobe.com/AdobeSVGViewerExtensions/3.0/"
	 width="79.948" height="79.948" viewBox="0 0 79.948 79.948"
style="overflow:visible;enable-background:new 0 0 79.948 79.948"
	 xml:space="preserve">
	<style type="text/css">
	<![CDATA[
		.st0{fill:#FFFFFF;stroke:#000000;}
	]]>
	</style>
	<metadata>
<?xpacket begin='□' id='W5M0MpCehiHzreSzNTczkc9d'?><x:xmpmeta xmlns:x='adobe:ns:meta/'
x:xmptk='XMP toolkit 3.0-29, framework 1.6'>□<rdf:RDF
xmlns:rdf='http://www.w3.org/1999/02/22-rdf-syntax-ns#' xmlns:iX='http://ns.adobe.com/iX/1.0/'>□□
<rdf:Description rdf:about=''□  xmlns:pdf='http://ns.adobe.com/pdf/1.3/'>□ </rdf:Description>□□
<rdf:Description rdf:about=''□  xmlns:tiff='http://ns.adobe.com/tiff/1.0/'>□ </rdf:Description>□□
<rdf:Description rdf:about=''□  xmlns:xap='http://ns.adobe.com/xap/1.0/'□
xmlns:xapGImg='http://ns.adobe.com/xap/1.0/g/img/'>□
<xap:CreateDate>2004-03-26T00:34:33Z</xap:CreateDate>□
<xap:ModifyDate>2004-03-26T00:34:33Z</xap:ModifyDate>□
<xap:CreatorTool>Illustrator</xap:CreatorTool>□  <xap:Thumbnails>□  <rdf:Alt>□  <rdf:li
rdf:parseType='Resource'>□   <xapGImg:format>JPEG</xapGImg:format>□
<xapGImg:width>256</xapGImg:width>□    <xapGImg:height>256</xapGImg:height>□
<xapGImg:image>/9j/4AAQSkZJRgABAgEASABIAAD/7QAsUGhvdG9zaG9wIDMuMAA4QklNA+0AAAAAABAASAAAAAEA&#xA;A
QBIAAAAAQAB/+4ADkFkb2JlAGTAAAAAAf/bAIQABgQEBAUEBgUFBgkGBQYJCwgGBggLDAoKCwoK&#xA;DBAMDAwMDAwQDA4PE
```

Figure 27-2: SVG files are XML-based and, like HTML files, are also readable in a standard text editor.

Using XML in InDesign

InDesign content can be exported using the XML format. InDesign also includes features that let you mark page content with tags. Content that is exported as an XML file may be imported into the current InDesign document where all the tagged content is loaded and displayed in the Structure pane. By dragging the content from the Structure pane into the layout, you can quickly reuse any XML exported content within the new layout.

Content can be tagged using custom XML tags, but you can also import a Document Type Definition (DTD) document. When a DTD is imported, all the tags that are defined in the DTD become available for tagging content. The DTD may also be used to validate all tags before exporting the tagged content as an XML file.

Note InDesign tagged text is different from applying XML tags.

For more editing, exported XML files may also be opened and viewed within GoLive.

Marking elements with XML tags

You can apply XML tags to design elements using the Tags palette, shown in Figure 27-3, which you open by choosing Window ➪ Tags. To apply a tag to the selected layout element, just click on the tag name in the Tags palette. This causes the tagged element's bounding box to assume the tag's color.

To remove a tag from an element, simply select the element and click the Untag button in the Tags palette. Untagging an element doesn't change the content or formatting of the element.

Figure 27-3: The Tags palette has all the tags that you can apply to a document.

Creating new XML tags

You can create new tags selecting the New Tag palette menu command on the Tag palette. Alternatively, you can click the New Tag button at the bottom of the palette. This opens a simple dialog box (Figure 27-4), where you can select the tag name and color.

Caution   Because tag names need to adhere to the XML syntax standards, they cannot contain any spaces, tabs, or special characters. Replacing spaces with the underscore (_) character is common.

Figure 27-4: New tags are given a name and a color.

You can also do the following:

✦ **Delete the tag** using the Delete Tag palette menu command, which opens a simple dialog box where a replacement tag is selected.

✦ **Rename or change a tag's color** by double-clicking on the tag in the Tags palette or select Tag Options from the palette menu.

✦ **Select all tags that aren't used in the current document** by choosing the Select All Unused Tags palette menu command.

Creating tags from styles

If you've already gone to the trouble of defining and using custom character or paragraph styles, you can map these styles to specific tags. The Tags palette includes two palette menu commands to do this.

The Map Tags to Styles palette menu command opens a dialog box, shown in Figure 27-5. This palette lists all the available tags and allows you to select a style to map to each tag. The Map Styles to Tags palette menu command does just the opposite. It opens a dialog box that lists all the available styles and where you can select and map each tag to a style.

If the tag names match the style names, use the Map by Name button to automatically map styles and tags with the same name. You use the Load button to load tag definitions from another InDesign document.

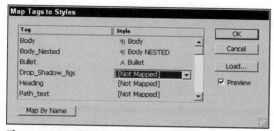

Figure 27-5: The Map Tags to Styles dialog box

Importing and viewing XML tags

You can load tags that you define in one InDesign document into the current document using the Load Tags palette menu command. This command opens a file dialog box where you may choose any InDesign or XML document. Clicking the Open button imports all the defined tags in the selected file into the Tags palette.

The color specified in the Tags palette for each tag appears as the frame color that surrounds and shades the element. These frame colors for tagged elements are hidden by choosing View ➪ Structure ➪ Show/Hide Tagged Frames.

You can mark individual characters within an element with a separate tag. This text is surrounded with brackets that are the same color as the tag. These tags may also be hidden by choosing View ➪ Structure ➪ Show/Hide Tag Markers.

Using the Structure pane

You can view all the tags that you've applied to a document according to their hierarchal order in the Structure pane. This pane appears to the left of the document, as shown in Figure 27-6, when you choose View ➪ Structure ➪ Show/Hide Structure (Alt+Ctrl+1 in Windows; Option+⌘+1 on the Mac).

Tags displayed in the Structure pane also include small icons that match the type of element it is. If a tagged element isn't visible, click on the expand arrow to see all the objects underneath it in the hierarchy. All elements are under the root element, which always appears at the top of the Structure pane.

Selecting, adding, and deleting elements

The Structure pane lets you quickly select a tagged element by double-clicking its tag or by selecting the tag in the Structure pane and choosing the Go to Item pane menu command. The tag in the Structure pane that corresponds to the element that is selected in the layout is underlined in Structure pane.

If you add a new element to the layout, it doesn't appear in the Structure pane until it's tagged. After it's tagged, it appears at the bottom of the Structure pane.

Although most elements within the Structure pane are associated with some content in the layout, new elements may be created that act as containers for other tags. These container elements, like the root element, are identified with an icon that has brackets on it.

Validate Structure using current DTD

Add an Attribute

Add an Element

Remove Selected Elements

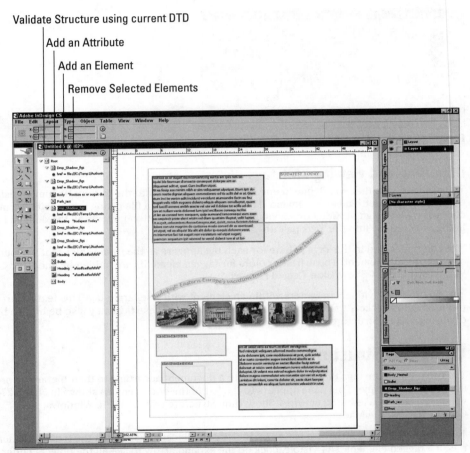

Figure 27-6: The Structure pane lists all the tagged elements.

To create a new element, select the New Element pane menu command or click on the New Element button at the top of the Structure pane. This causes a simple dialog box to open, where the tag type to use for this element is selected.

To delete an element from the Structure panel, click to select it and then choose Delete from the pane menu or click on the Delete Selected Elements button at the top of the pane. A dialog box, shown in Figure 27-7, appears, explaining that deleting the element also deletes the content in the layout. It also gives you a change to simply untag the content, which eliminates the tag element but keeps the content.

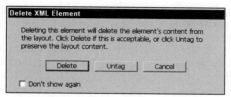

Figure 27-7: You can delete the element with its content or untag the content.

Rearranging tags

The order in which the tags are listed in the Structure pane is the same order in which the tags are listed in the exported XML file. You rearrange tags by dragging and dropping them above or below another tag. If a tag becomes highlighted when you drop a tag, the dropped tag becomes a child under the highlighted tag.

You can also reorder tags in the Structure pane by choosing Edit ⇨ Cut, Edit ⇨ Copy, or Edit ⇨ Paste. Simply select the element to move and cut or copy it to the Clipboard; then select the tag in the Structure pane just above where you want the tag to appear and use the Paste command.

Adding information to a tag

You can add additional information including attributes, comments, and processing information to the selected element using the pane menu commands. This information is exported with the element tag to the XML document.

Attributes are properties and values that carry additional information about the element. A good example of this is the href attribute. This attribute is added to every image that is tagged and holds the location where the image is found. Attributes are identified in the Structure pane by a black circular bullet under the tag that it defines.

To add an attribute to an element, select the element and choose New Attribute from the pane menu or click on the Add an Attribute button at the top of the pane. A dialog box, shown in Figure 27-8, appears; here, an attribute name and its value are added. To edit an attribute after its creation, simply double-click on it and a dialog box appears where you may edit its name and value.

Tip   Selecting the Hide Attributes menu command from the pane menu clears much of the Structure pane by hiding all attributes.

Figure 27-8: You name and assign values in the New Attribute dialog box.

In addition to attributes, you can also add comments and processing instructions to elements using similar pane menu commands. Comments are simple text statements that have no affect on the XML document but make it more understandable to the developer who may be reading it. Processing instructions are used by applications written to parse and use the XML document. The New Processing Instructions dialog box includes fields for entering target and data information.

Importing a DTD

The Structure pane also includes an Import a DTD menu command. Importing a DTD is another way to add XML-specific tags to the Tags palette. All tags imported from a DTD file are locked in the Tags palette and cannot be changed. Figure 27-9 shows some locked tags that were imported from a DTD.

Figure 27-9 Tags imported from a DTD file are locked.

An imported DTD is identified in the Structure pane by the presence of a DOCTYPE element that appears above the root. The DOCTYPE statement is one of the first statements that appear in an XML document. It identifies the DTD that the tags in the document adhere to. Double-clicking on the DOCTYPE element in the Structure pane opens the DTD document in a text window, shown in Figure 27-10, where you can view it.

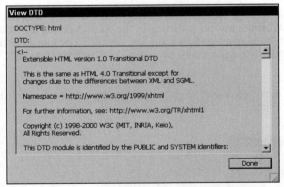

Figure 27-10: Double-clicking the DOCTYPE element opens the DTD document.

Validating structure

If a DTD is imported, clicking the Validate Structure Using Current DTD button at the top of the Structure pane compares the tagged elements to the DTD definitions and flags any elements that don't adhere to the DTD specifications. All elements with errors are marked with a yellow warning icon and the errors are then listed in a pane below the Structure pane, as shown in Figure 27-11.

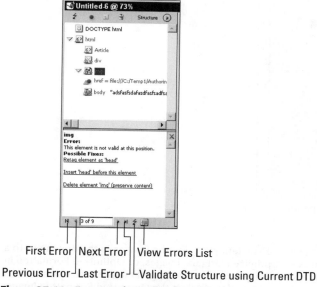

First Error | Next Error | View Errors List

Previous Error ┘ Last Error ┘ └ Validate Structure using Current DTD

Figure 27-11: Errors and possible fixes are reported for any invalid elements.

Clicking on the warning icon displays the error for that element and also lists any possible fixes. The arrow buttons at the bottom of the Structure panel move back and forth between the errors and let you open a list of errors.

Exporting XML

You can export InDesign files to the XML format by choosing File ➪ Export (⌘/Ctrl+E). In the Save as Type field, select the XML option and name the file. After you click Save, an Export XML dialog box appears, which includes two panels — the General panel and the Images panel.

The General panel, shown in Figure 27-12, has options to include the DTD declaration; view XML using GoLive, Internet Explorer, or another selected application; export from the selected element; and specify the encoding method. The Include DTD Declaration option places a statement at the top of the XML document that lists the DTD that the document adheres to. To view the exported XML document, you may select GoLive or Internet Explorer, or you can choose the Other option to open a file dialog box where you may select a separate application to view the XML document. If you select the Export from Selected Element, the exported XML document only includes the elements from the selected element in the Structure pane to the end of the document. The Encoding options include UTF-8, UTF-16, and Shift-JIS. Shift-JLS is used for Japanese characters.

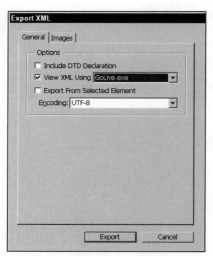

Figure 27-12: The General panel of
the Export XML dialog box

The Images panel, shown in Figure 27-13, lets you copy the images in the document to a separate subfolder as Original Images, Optimized Original Images, or Optimized Formatted Images. If you select the Optimized Original Images option, the original images are optimized using the settings in the Images panel. However, if you select the Optimized Formatted Images option, the image retains any formatting applied in InDesign before it's optimized. This may include scaling or cropping the image.

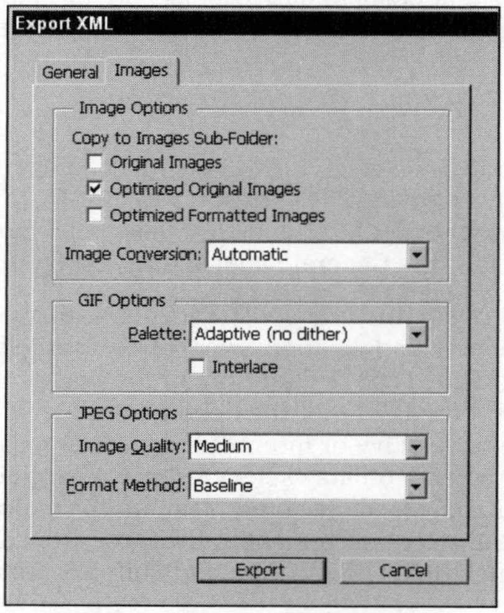

Figure 27-13: The Images panel of
the Export XML dialog box

Optimized images are copied into the subfolder with _opt appended to the end of the file-name. Optimized formatted images are copied into the subfolder with _for appended to the end of the filename.

The Image Conversion option lets you select to convert the images to the GIF and JPEG formats. The Automatic option lets InDesign decide which format to use.

Cross-Reference More information on exporting layouts is covered in Chapter 24.

Importing XML tagged content

The typical workflow for importing XML documents is to create an InDesign document with tagged elements that match the tags used in the XML document that you want to import. Then choose File ➪ Import XML and select a file to import. The Import XML dialog box, shown in Figure 27-14, includes options to have the imported content replace the existing content or append to the existing content. If you select an element in the Structure pane, you may also select to import into the selected element.

Figure 27-14: The Import XML dialog box lets you replace or append the contents of the XML file to the current document.

If you enable the Replace Content option, the content within the XML document loads into those tagged elements with matching tag names, but if you select the Append Content option, all the imported tags appear at the bottom of the Structure pane, where you can drag and drop them onto elements in the current document.

Note The XML document only contains content and no formatting. You apply formatting to the element placeholders in the layout using styles.

STEPS: Tagging and Exporting an InDesign Layout to XML

1. **Open an InDesign document.** Open a layout document within InDesign by choosing File ➪ Open.

2. **Create tags from styles.** Choose Window ➪ Tags to open the Tags palette. Open the Character Styles and Paragraph Styles palettes to see the defined styles. Select the New Tag palette menu command from the Tags palette and name the new tag to match the defined styles. Select the Map Styles to Tags palette menu command and in the dialog box that opens, shown in Figure 27-15, click the Map by Name button. For the styles that aren't mapped, select the matching tag from the drop-down list to the right. Click OK button when you're finished.

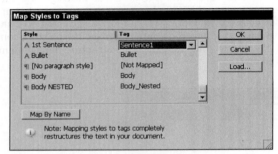

Figure 27-15: The Map by Name button matches all the custom styles with the tag names that are the same.

3. **Create other tags.** Select the New Tag palette menu command and create new tags for all additional elements that don't have styles, including headers and figures. Figure 27-16 shows the Tags palette with these other tags added.

Figure 27-16: The Tag palette contains all tags.

4. **Tag page elements.** Select an item in the layout and click on the appropriate tag for each element. To see all the tagged elements, choose View ➪ Structure ➪ Show Structure. The Structure pane appears to the left of the document. Click on the arrow to the left of the Root element to see all the tagged elements, as shown in Figure 27-17.

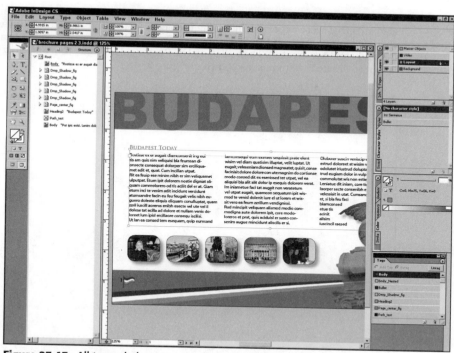

Figure 27-17: All tagged elements are displayed in the Structure pane.

5. **Export to the XML format.** Choose File ➪ Export. In the Export dialog box that appears, type a filename and select XML in the Save as Type drop-down list. Then click the Save button. In the Export XML dialog box, select the General and Images options and click the Export button.

STEPS: Importing an XML Document

1. **Create a new InDesign document.** Create a new layout document within InDesign by choosing File ➪ New ➪ Document.

2. **Import the necessary tags.** Select the Load Tags palette menu command from the Tags palette and, in the file dialog box that opens, select the exported file from the last example. All the previous tags created for the exported XML document are loaded into the Tags palette.

Note

Only the tags used in the exported document are saved and imported.

3. **Create the content placeholders.** For the new layout, we want to use only certain elements that were exported, including the heading, the body text, and the five drop-shadow figures. Click on the Type tool and drag it in the layout where the heading and the body text are located. Then click on the Rectangular Frame tool and drag in the layout to create five frames, as shown in Figure 27-18.

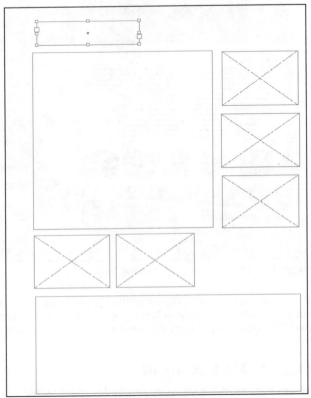

Figure 27-18: Placeholders for the new layout are positioned and ready for tagging.

4. **Tag the placeholders.** Select each layout placeholder and click on its appropriate tag in the Tags palette. Each placeholder becomes the color of its tag and the elements appear in the Structure pane, as shown in Figure 27-19.

Note

The order in which the placeholders are tagged becomes the order in which the XML elements appear, so the first drop_shadow_fig element in the XML document becomes the first placeholder that is tagged, which is the first element in the Structure pane.

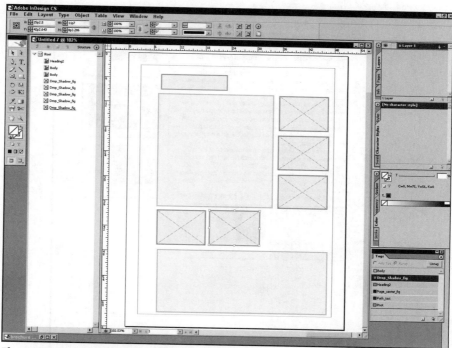

Figure 27-19: Tagged elements appear in the Structure.

5. **Import an XML document.** Choose File ➪ Import XML and, in the file dialog box that appears, select the exported XML file from the previous example. Then enable the Replace Content option and click Open. Figure 27-20 shows the results of importing the XML document.

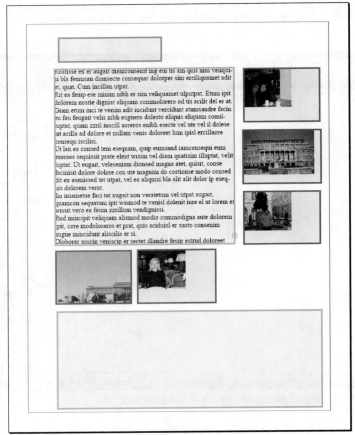

Figure 27-20: Importing an XML document fills all tagged placeholders.

6. **Drag unmatched elements into their placeholders.** All elements in the XML document that don't have a matching placeholder appear in the Structure pane. You can add these elements to the layout by dragging the element name from the Structure pane to the placeholder. You can also delete unneeded elements using the Delete pane menu command. Figure 27-21 shows the final layout after adding the unmatched elements and deleting the unneeded elements.

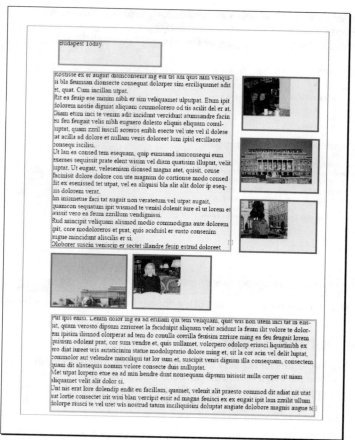

Figure 27-21: The layout has all its content and is ready for formatting.

Viewing and Editing XML Data in GoLive

You may open and edit XML documents within GoLive by choosing File ➪ Open (⌘/Ctrl+O). Opened XML documents appear within GoLive's Outline Editor, as shown in Figure 27-22.

Note

Although XML is not one of the file types in the Open Document dialog box, you can open XML documents when you select the All Documents option.

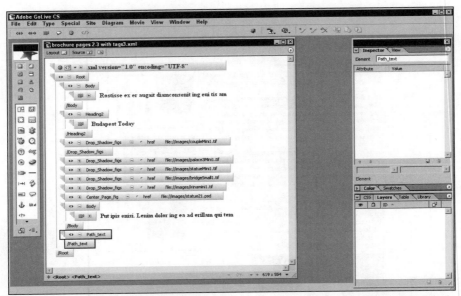

Figure 27-22: XML documents opened in GoLive appear in the Outline Editor by default.

Using the Outline Editor

The Outline Editor separates all tag sets into individual bars. You can expand each of these bars by clicking on the plus-sign icon. You can select each bar by clicking on the bar. The selected tag bar is highlighted with a black outline. The tag bars are also listed according to their hierarchy. You can move tag bars within the document by dragging on the tag-bar handle to the left of the tag bar. To edit and add new code:

✦ **Editing code:** The attributes and content for each tag appear when you click on the plus sign positioned to the right of the bar. Clicking on any of the attributes, content, or tag names opens a text field where you can edit the item. Existing tags may also be cut, copied, and pasted to a different location using the commands in the Edit menu.

Note The Layout Editor also displays the document in expandable bars, but it lets you edit only the content, not the tags.

✦ **Adding new code:** When the Outline Editor is selected, several icon buttons appear in the top toolbar, as shown in Figure 27-23. You can use these buttons to add new items to the XML document. Clicking on any of these buttons adds the selected item to the Outline Editor directly below the current selection where it may be edited. The Toggle Binary button is used to add or remove the closing tag from certain tags that don't need them.

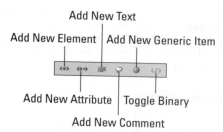

Add New Text

Add New Element | Add New Generic Item

Add New Attribute | Toggle Binary

Add New Comment

Figure 27-23: Use these toolbar buttons to add new items to the XML document.

Using the Source Code Editor

In addition to the Outline Editor, clicking on the Source Code Editor tab at the top of the document window lets you view and edit the actual text contained in the XML document. The Source Code Editor is shown in Figure 27-24.

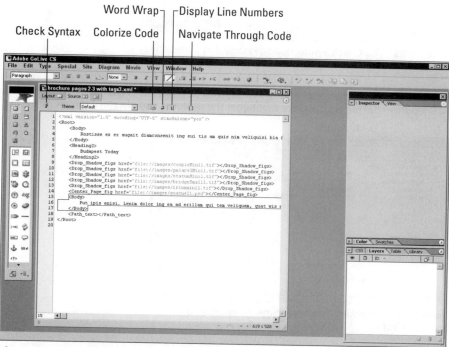

Word Wrap ┐ ┌Display Line Numbers

Check Syntax   Colorize Code   Navigate Through Code

Figure 27-24: The Source Code Editor displays the actual XML text file.

Along the top of the Source Code Editor window are some icon buttons. The Check Syntax button opens a dialog box, shown in Figure 27-25, where the type of check to execute is selected. The Well-Formedness Only check looks for matching starting and end tags, correct attribute formatting, and syntax-related problems. The !DOCTYPE check validates the XML file according to the DTD listed in the DOCTYPE statement.

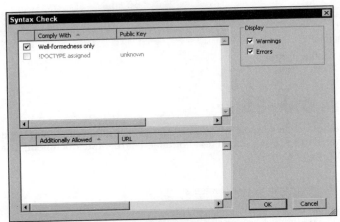

Figure 27-25: The Check Syntax option is useful in eliminating potential errors.

If any errors are found after checking syntax, they're reported in a dialog box, shown in Figure 27-26. Double-clicking on the error highlights the problem code in the Source Code Editor.

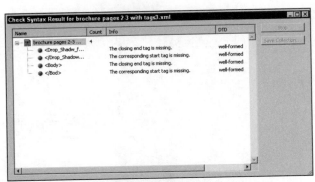

Figure 27-26: Checking syntax displays all errors in a separate window.

The Theme drop-down list at the top of the Source Code Editor window, shown in Figure 27-27, lets you select from several text-display options. Each of these options highlights the text differently. The Colorize Code button causes different sections to be highlighted different colors. For example, the default settings color all tags dark blue, all attributes light blue, all values dark red, and all content black. This makes it easy to find different parts of the file.

The Word Wrap button causes all text to wrap so it's visible in the window. The Display Line Numbers button causes line numbers to appear to the left of the text file. These line numbers are references in the Syntax Error window if errors are found.

The Navigate Through Code button lets you name and place markers within the code. The marker's name then appears in a pop-up menu when the Navigate Through Code button is clicked, allowing you to quickly locate a marked section of code again.

Splitting the editors

When the Outline or Layout editors are selected, a small double-arrow icon appears at the bottom-left corner of the window. This button is the Show/Hide Split Source button. Clicking this button displays the Outline Editor (or Layout Editor) in the top half of the window and the Source Code Editor in the lower half of the window, as shown in Figure 27-27.

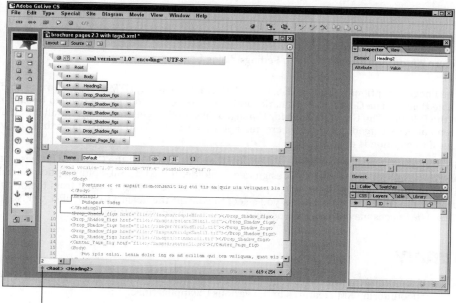

Show/Hide Split Source

Figure 27-27: Splitting the window lets you view the Outline Editor and the Source Code Editor at the same time.

Saving Acrobat Files as XML Documents

You may save Acrobat PDF files as XML documents by choosing File ➪ Save As. In the file dialog box, name the file, select XML 1.0 as the Save as Type, and click the Save button.

Note   Exporting a PDF file to XML exports only its content. All formatting associated with the content is lost during the conversion process.

The Settings button at the bottom of the file dialog box opens the Save As XML 1.0 Settings dialog box, shown in Figure 27-28.

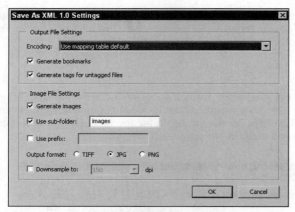

Figure 27-28: The Save As XML 1.0 Settings dialog box

The Encoding options include UTF-8, UTF-16, UCS-4, ISO-Latin-1, HTML/ASCII, and Use Mapping Table Default. The Generate Bookmarks option creates links from all the defined bookmarks in the PDF file. The Generate Tags for Untagged Files option generates tags for all files that aren't already tagged. All PDF files created before Acrobat 4.0 did not use tags; they're given tags if this option is enabled.

To have the PDF image files saved along with the XML file, select the Generate Images option and these images are placed in a designated subfolder if the Use Sub-Folder option is enabled. The Use Prefix option lets you add a prefix to the filename to distinguish it from the original image files. The Output format lets you select to convert the images to TIFF, JPG, or PNG image files. The images may also be downsampled to a specified dpi setting.

Summary

✦ Understanding what XML documents are and how they may be used is helpful when encountering XML features in the various CS applications.

✦ InDesign documents can use XML as a transport media to tag and export layout content.

✦ You can import XML documents into an InDesign document.

✦ GoLive is useful for viewing, editing, and creating XML documents from scratch.

✦　　✦　　✦

Creative Suite Document Delivery Workflows

Understanding Digital Rights Management

Digital Rights Management (DRM) is a term used to describe protecting intellectual property against unauthorized viewing, editing, reproduction, and/or distribution. As a member of a creative-design workflow, you may have needs for restricting document viewing to selected individuals; or you may want to share design concepts with clients so they can view your designs, but you don't want the documents printed or edited.

All the CS programs offer you a vehicle for protecting documents via export to PDF. Document security is applied to PDF files and not directly in the CS application documents. Therefore, you first need to know how to generate a PDF from the other CS applications and then apply security either at the time of PDF creation or from within Acrobat. In this chapter, you learn how to export CS application documents to PDF and secure the files against unauthorized viewing, editing, and printing.

Understanding Document Security

Securing documents created with CS applications means you ultimately get a document to PDF and apply Acrobat security either at the time of exporting a file to PDF or later, after you open a PDF in Acrobat. In either case, Acrobat security is used.

Methods of security available in Acrobat include two primary types of encryption. You can secure a file against opening and editing by applying Acrobat security at different levels of encryption, or you can secure files using certificates acquired from users when they create digital IDs. The first method should be thought of as security you might apply globally to PDFs either from within the CS programs at the time of exporting to PDF or later in Acrobat. Security added at the time of export to PDF is generally when you want the public to have a password to open your PDFs or you want to restrict editing features. This type of security is referred to as *unknown users*.

The second method of security is restrictions you want to apply for a selected group of people in your workgroup (coworkers, colleagues, or individuals with whom you have direct communication), or among your client base. This is referred to as *known users*. This method requires the use of digital IDs and Trusted Certificates.

Permissions

Permissions relate to the access you grant end users. You may restrict printing a document and, as such, you grant permission for users to view and possibly edit a file but prevent users from printing. When using the second method of security for known users, you can grant different permissions for different users all in the same document. This form of security uses digital ID identities and is discussed later in the "Securing Files with Identities" section.

Levels of encryption

Depending on the form of Acrobat compatibility you use (for example, Acrobat 4-, 5-, or 6-compatible files), the level of encryption changes according to each compatible file format. Acrobat 4 compatibility uses 40-bit encryption, Acrobat 5 uses 128-bit encryption, and Acrobat 6 uses 256-bit encryption. The level of encryption is not as important for you to understand as just realizing that, with each level of encryption, Acrobat offers you additional permissions. For example, with Acrobat 4 compatibility, you can grant permissions to print a document or prevent a user from printing a document. With Acrobat 5 and 6 compatibility, where you use 128-bit or greater encryption, you can add to the printing permissions a restriction to only print files as low-resolution prints. This feature and others are added to encryption methods above 40-bit encryption.

Signature handlers

When you use digital IDs to encrypt files for restricting permissions, Acrobat offers you a choice for using Acrobat Certificate Authority or a signature handler you acquire from a third-party supplier. Acrobat warns you that files secured with Acrobat Certificate Authority carry no guarantee that the security cannot be compromised. For more critical Digital Rights Management, warning dialog boxes point you in the direction of third-party vendors offering signature handlers.

In normal production workflows, you're not concerned with sophisticated signature handlers from third-party vendors. When sending clients drafts of your artwork, the turnaround time is relatively short and the likelihood of a client exerting the energy and taking the time to break password security is incredibly far-fetched. Some algorithms running on powerful computers can take years to break a password.

As a matter of practice, use a minimum of 10 to 12 characters when supplying passwords to protect a file. The more characters you use, the more difficult a software routine has in trying to break the code.

If you work with sensitive material that requires sophisticated security measures offered by third-party vendors, you can find a list of vendors offering various solutions on Adobe's Web site (www.adobe.com/security).

Securing Documents

If you create an Illustration or a layout, or you have some photos that you need to secure, you can save or export your files as PDF documents and add security at the time you create the PDF. You can also add security in Acrobat for all PDFs created without setting permissions at the time of PDF creation. Regardless of where you add permissions, the options available to you for securing PDFs are the same in all the CS programs except GoLive. You must export GoLive files to PDF and then add the security in Acrobat.

Although the options are all the same, you still might get a little confused over the nomenclature that identifies attributes for permissions restrictions. The results are the same, but the language that describes the options changes a bit between Acrobat and the other CS programs. Because all the permissions are Acrobat-related, the first order of business is to understand how security is applied in Acrobat.

Adding security in Acrobat

For documents converted to PDF to which you want to add security later, you add permissions in Acrobat. The options you choose are contained in the Password Security – Settings dialog box. To open the dialog box with a document currently open in the Document pane, choose File ⇨ Document Properties. When the Document Properties dialog box opens, click Security in the left pane. By default, the security is turned off if you added no security when you exported the PDF or distilled it in Acrobat Distiller. From the Security pull-down menu in the Document Properties dialog box, select Password Security and the Password Security – Settings dialog box opens, shown in Figure 28-1. You can also open the same dialog box by clicking the down arrow in the Secure Task button to open the pull-down menu and select Restrict Opening and Editing.

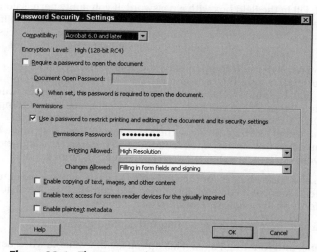

Figure 28-1: The Password Security – Settings dialog box

Note The same options for adding security exist in the PDFMaker for Microsoft Office files and in the Acrobat Distiller for PostScript files. For more information on using Distiller and applying security during distillation, refer to the *Acrobat 6 PDF Bible* (published by Wiley).

The security you add in this dialog box restricts a user from opening or changing a file's content. Users must know the password you assigned this dialog box to open a file and/or make changes. Realize that you can restrict a file from opening unless a password is supplied or you can omit a password for opening a file but limit permissions for printing and editing. You can add two passwords — one for opening a file and another for restricting editing or printing features. The options in the Password Security – Settings dialog box are:

✦ **Compatibility:** Options include Acrobat 3, Acrobat 5, and Acrobat 6 compatibility. If you select Acrobat 6 compatibility and save the PDF document, users need an Acrobat viewer of version 6 or greater to open the file. The same holds true when saving with Acrobat 5 compatibility for users who have Acrobat viewers lower than version 5.

✦ **Encryption Level:** Acrobat informs you what level of encryption is applied to the document based on the compatibility choice made in the pull-down menu. If you select Acrobat 3 and Later from the compatibility, the encryption level is 40-bit encryption. Acrobat 5 and Acrobat 6 compatibility are encrypted at 128-bit encryption. The higher encryption levels offer you more options for restricting printing and editing.

✦ **Require a password to open the document:** Enable this option if you want a user to supply a password to open the PDF document. Once enabled, the field box for Document Open Password becomes active and you can add a password. Before you exit the dialog box, Acrobat prompts you in another dialog box to confirm the password.

✦ **Use a password to restrict printing and editing of the document and its security settings:** You can add a password for opening the PDF document and also restrict permissions from the items active in the Permissions area of the dialog box. You can also eliminate the option for using a password to open the PDF document and make permissions choices for printing and editing. Either way, you check this box to make choices in the Permissions options. If the check box is disabled, no permissions options are available to you.

✦ **Permissions Password:** Fill in the field box with a password. If you apply permissions options for opening the PDF and restricting permissions, the passwords must be different. Acrobat opens a dialog box and informs you to make different password choices if you attempt to use the same password for opening the file and setting permissions.

✦ **Printing Allowed:** If you use Acrobat 3 compatibility, the options are available to either enable printing or disallow printing. The choices are None and High Resolution. Although choice reads High Resolution, the result simply enables users to print your file. With Acrobat 5 and 6 compatibility you have a third choice for enabling printing at a lower resolution (150 dpi). If you select Low Resolution (150 dpi) from the menu options, users are restricted to printing the file at the lower resolution. This choice is typically something you might use for files intended for digital prepress and high-end printing or to protect your content from being printed and then re-scanned.

✦ **Changes Allowed:** You can make choices for the kinds of changes you allow users to perform on the document. Acrobat 3 compatibility offers you four choices; Acrobat 5 and 6 compatibility offers you five choices. These options include

  • **None:** Prevents a user from any kind of editing and content extraction.

  • **Inserting, Deleting, and Rotating Pages:** This option is not available when using Acrobat 3 compatibility. Users are permitted to insert, delete, and rotate pages. If you create PDFs for eBooks, allowing users to rotate pages is helpful when they view PDFs on tablets and portable devices. *(Acrobat 5 and Acrobat 6 compatibility only)*

  • **Filling in Form Fields and Signing:** If you create Acrobat Forms and want users to digitally sign documents, enable this check box. Forms are useless to users without the ability to fill in the form fields.

  • **Commenting, Fill-In Form Fields, and Signing:** You might use this option in a review process where you want to have users comment on a design, but you don't want them to make changes in your file. You can secure the document against editing, but allow commenting and form-field fill-in and signing.

  • **Any Except Extracting Pages:** All the permissions are available to users except extracting pages from the document and creating separate PDFs from selected pages.

✦ **Enable copying of text, images, and other content and access for the visually impaired (Acrobat 3 only) and access for the visually impaired:** If you restrict permissions for any of the previous pull-down menu options, users aren't allowed to copy data. You can add permission for content copying by enabling this check box. This option is available to users of all Acrobat viewers version 3 and greater. *(Acrobat 3 only)*

✦ **Enable text access for screen reader devices for the visually impaired:** As a matter of practice, enabling this option is always a good idea because you can restrict all editing features while permitting users with screen-reading devices to read your files. If the option is disabled, screen readers cannot read the PDF document and all the options for using the View ➪ Read Out Loud menu command are grayed out. Furthermore, users can index your files with Acrobat Professional using Acrobat Catalog when this check box is enabled, regardless of the other items you prevent users from accessing. *(Acrobat 5 and 6 compatibility only)*

✦ **Enable plaintext metadata:** If selected, users can create search indexes from encrypted files. The document's metadata is made accessible to other applications. *(Acrobat 6 only)*

After making decisions for the permissions you want to restrict, you need to save the file. Choose either File ➪ Save or File ➪ Save As after making choices in the Password Security – Settings dialog box.

Setting permissions in the Password Security – Settings dialog box works fine for a single PDF document you want to secure, but it's a bit tedious when you want to secure a number of files. For automating the task where a common password is used in all files that need to be secured, you can use the Acrobat Batch Processing command. For a firsthand view of creating a batch sequence and applying steps in the sequence to a collection of PDF documents, follow these steps:

STEPS: Creating and Running Batch Sequences

1. **Open Batch Sequences.** Select Advanced ➪ Batch Processing. The Batch Sequences dialog box opens, shown in Figure 28-2.

Note   You can only create and run batch sequences in Acrobat Professional.

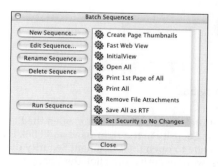

Figure 28-2: The Batch Sequences dialog box creates a new sequence.

2. **Create a new sequence.** Click New in the Batch Sequences dialog box. The Name Sequence dialog box opens. Type a name for your sequence and click OK to open the Batch Edit Sequence – *[name of your sequence]* dialog box shown in Figure 28-3. Note that the name for the dialog box in the figure is Batch Edit Sequence – Add Security.

We created a new sequence and named the sequence *Add Security,* thus the name is reflected in the dialog box name. For the purposes of clarity, this dialog box is henceforth referred to as the Batch Edit Sequence dialog box.

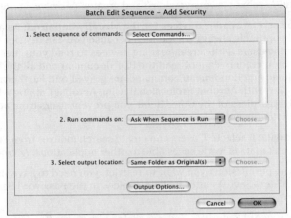

Figure 28-3: The Batch Edit Sequence dialog box

3. **Add Security to the sequence.** Click the Select Commands button in the Batch Edit Sequence dialog box. The Edit Sequence dialog box opens, shown in Figure 22-4. In the left pane, scroll down the window until you see Security appear at the end of the Document options. Select Security in the left pane and click the Add button to move Security to the right pane.

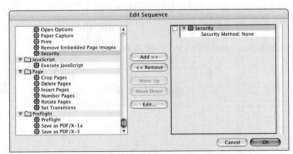

Figure 28-4: The Edit Sequences dialog box

4. **Edit the security permissions.** To set the security permissions, open the Password Security – Settings dialog box. Click on Security in the right pane and click Edit or double-click on Security in the right pane to open the Document Security dialog box. From the pull-down menu, select Password Security and click the Change Settings button to open the Password Security – Settings dialog box, shown in Figure 28-5.

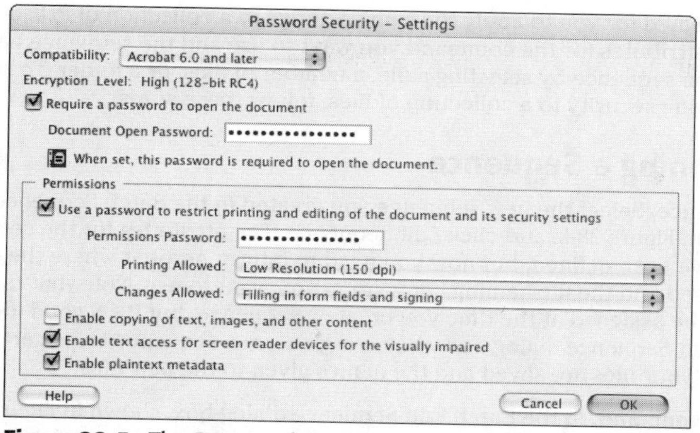

Password Security - Settings
Compatibility: Acrobat 6.0 and later
Encryption Level: High (128-bit RC4)
Require a password to open the document
Document Open Password:
When set, this password is required to open the document.
Permissions
Use a password to restrict printing and editing of the document and its security settings
Permissions Password:
Printing Allowed: Low Resolution (150 dpi)
Changes Allowed: Filling in form fields and signing
Enable copying of text, images, and other content
Enable text access for screen reader devices for the visually impaired
Enable plaintext metadata
Help
Cancel
OK

Figure 28-5: The Password Security – Settings dialog box

Edit the security items you want to use, and be certain to use passwords of ten or more characters. Click OK and a warning dialog box opens. Click OK again and the Confirm Permissions Password dialog box opens. Retype your password using the same letter case and click OK. You're returned to the Document Security dialog box. Click Close and you're returned to the Edit Sequence dialog box. Click OK and you arrive at the Batch Edit Sequence dialog box. Click OK again and you see your new sequence added to the Batch Sequences dialog box.

Note that the number of dialog boxes is extraordinary. Just keep in mind that, after editing the security options, you return to the Batch Sequences by clicking OK through all the dialog boxes. When the sequence is added to the Batch Sequences dialog box, shown in Figure 28-6, you're ready to run the sequence. You can run a sequence immediately after creating it or at a later time in another Acrobat editing session. After the new sequence is added to the batch Sequences dialog box, the sequence remains there until you physically remove it. If you want to dismiss the dialog box without running a sequence, click the Close button.

Batch Sequences
New Sequence...
Edit Sequence...
Rename Sequence...
Delete Sequence
Run Sequence
Add Security
Create Page Thumbnails
Fast Web View
InitialView
Open All
Print 1st Page of All
Print All
Remove File Attachments
Save All as RTF
Set Security to No Changes
Close

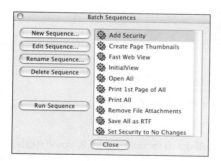

Figure 28-6: You change permissions attributes in the Password Security Settings dialog box.

Sequences are designed for you to apply the same settings to a collection of PDF documents. When you set the attributes for the command you want to use and the sequence has been created, you run the sequence by selecting a file, a number of files, or a folder. To run a sequence for applying security to a collection of files, follow these steps:

STEPS: Running a Sequence

1. **Edit a sequence.** Select the new sequence you created in the Batch Sequence dialog box, shown in Figure 28-6, and click Edit Sequence. The attributes for the security permissions have been defined, but now you need to inform Acrobat where the edited files are to be saved and the file-naming convention you want to use. Note that these options can be assigned at the time you create a sequence, but it's a good idea to visit the Batch Edit Sequence dialog box whenever you run a sequence to be certain you know where your files are saved and the names given to the new files.

2. **Running a command.** In the Batch Edit Sequence dialog box, shown in Figure 28-7, open the pull-down menu for item 2. You have several options from which to choose for when a command is run. The default is Ask When Sequence is Run. When selected, this option instructs Acrobat to prompt you for what files to run a sequence. Other choices enable you to identify a specific folder location, specific files, or currently opened files. The default is set to run a sequence by asking where a navigation dialog box opens and permits you to search through your hard drive to find files you want to add to the sequence. Unless you want to run the sequence on a specific folder, leave the setting at the default.

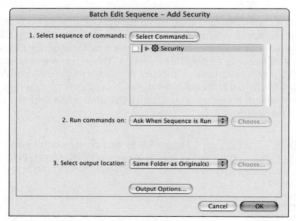

Figure 28-7: The Batch Edit Sequence – Add Security dialog box

3. **Select an output location.** From the pull-down menu for item 3, you determine where the edited files are saved. The default is set to save files in the same folder as the original files. You also have choices for saving to a specific folder (prompting you for a

folder location) or not saving changes. If you save files to the same folder, be careful about already overwriting existing files. If you leave the default at Same Folder as Originals, edit the filenames in the Output Options so new files are saved with new names as opposed to overwriting files. If you make mistakes when assigning attributes in your batch sequence, you can always return to the original files.

4. **Set output options.** Click the Output Options button and the Output Options dialog box, shown in Figure 28-8, opens. In this dialog box, you assign filenames. You can choose to use the default name for saving files with the same name that ultimately overwrites your existing files, or you can add to an existing name either a prefix or a suffix. If you click Add to Original Base Name(s), the field boxes for Insert Before and Insert After become active. Enter a prefix or suffix extension by typing characters in the field boxes. If you leave the default at Same As Original(s) and check the box for Do Not Overwrite Existing Files, Acrobat automatically adds to the filenames to prevent the new files from overwriting the old files. Make your choices in this dialog box and click OK to return to the Batch Edit Sequence dialog box. Click OK and you return to the original Batch Sequences dialog box.

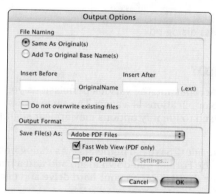

Figure 28-8: The Output Options
dialog box

5. **Run a sequence.** In the Batch Sequence dialog box, click on your new sequence and click Run Sequence. If you elected to be prompted for files to select, the Select Files to Process dialog box, shown in Figure 28-9, opens. Navigate your hard drive and open the folder where the files you want to process are located. To select files individually, ⌘/Ctrl+click to select files in a noncontiguous order. For a contiguous selection, select a file and press the Shift key to select the last file in a list. All files between the two you clicked are selected.

Click the Select button and Acrobat adds security to all the files you selected for processing. After completing the task, be certain to verify files and note the password used to protect the files.

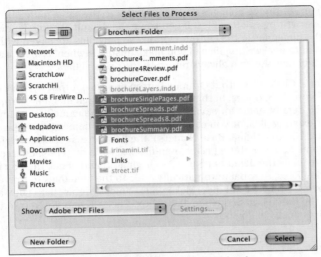

Figure 28-9: The Select files to Process dialog box

Adding security in Illustrator

When you understand adding security in Acrobat and the various permissions you can assign to PDF files, adding security in all other CS applications is a snap. The same options exist when exporting to PDF but the language used to identify options may appear slightly different from what you see in Acrobat.

To add security to an Illustrator file choose File ➪ Save As. In the Save As dialog box, shown in Figure 28-10, select Adobe PDF (pdf) from the Format pull-down menu and add a name for your file in the Save As field box. Locate the destination on your hard drive and click Save. The Adobe PDF Options dialog box opens.

In the Adobe PDF Options dialog box, click General in the left pane. From the Compatibility pull-down menu, choose the Acrobat compatibility you want to use (for example, 4-, 5-, or 6-compatible PDF files). Whatever you select in this dialog box has an effect on the available options in the Security settings, and the options available are identical to those found in Acrobat.

Click on Security in the left pane, and the right pane changes to provide you attribute choices like those shown in Figure 28-11. Once again, these choices are the same as you find with Adobe Acrobat. Make your choices for the permissions, supply the password(s), and click Save PDF. Illustrator prompts you in another dialog box to confirm your password. Retype the password and click OK. The file is saved with the permissions identified in the Adobe PDF Options dialog box.

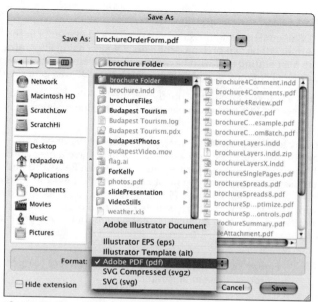

Figure 28-10: Select Adobe PDF (pdf) for the format, supply a filename, and click Save to open the Adobe PDF Options dialog box.

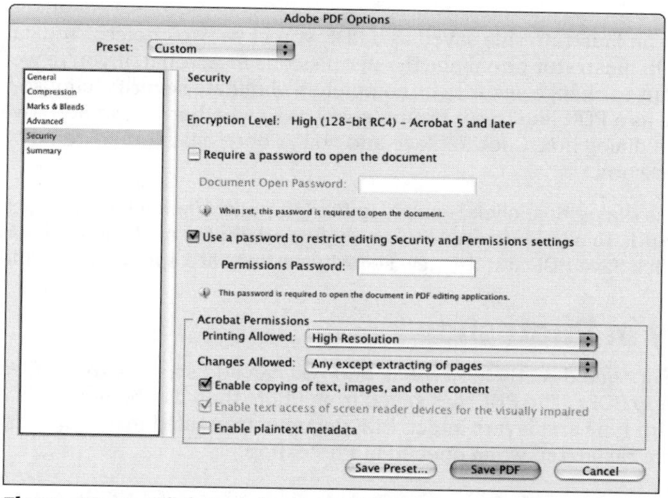

Figure 28-11: Click Security in the left pane to open the security options.

Opening secure files

Adobe Illustrator can open PDF documents and directly access type and elements in the PDF file. PDFs created with other applications can present problems if you're using Illustrator to edit the files. But you have the best editing tool with Illustrator if you need to perform edits on a PDF and don't have the original source document from which the PDF was generated.

You may wonder what happens when you attempt to open a secure PDF document. You know that in Acrobat you can open a secure PDF without a password if a Document Open Password was not assigned.

Illustrator is another matter. Any level of security—whether it be security added as a Document Open Password or Permissions Password—requires you to have a password to open the PDF in Illustrator. If you add a password for the Document Open Password and another password for the Permissions Password, you must supply the Permissions Password to open the file in Illustrator. When you open a secure PDF in Illustrator, the Password dialog box (shown in Figure 28-12) opens first. Type the Permissions Password in the dialog box and click OK. If the password is not typed correctly, Illustrator informs you that password is not correct and you need to try again.

Figure 28-12: Type the permissions password to open a protected file in Illustrator.

Removing security

To remove security from an Illustrator file saved as a PDF, you have two choices. You can change the permissions in Illustrator or change the permissions in Acrobat. If you're working in Illustrator and you want to change security or completely eliminate security, choose File ⇨ Save As and save the file as a PDF. Illustrator prompts you as to whether you want to overwrite the existing file in a dialog box. Click Replace and you're once again presented with the Adobe PDF Options dialog box.

In the Adobe PDF Options dialog box, click Security in the left pane. Uncheck both check marks for adding passwords to eliminate security, or change attributes as desired to make permissions changes. Click Save PDF and the new security settings are applied to the file.

Adding security in Photoshop

Photoshop PDFs can be opened directly in Acrobat, and you can add security to the files when saving as Photoshop PDFs. The PDF files saved from Photoshop can be reopened in Photoshop, complete with type and layers intact. PDF documents created in all applications other than Photoshop are rasterized when opened in Photoshop.

Note   Rasterizing documents in Photoshop coverts vector objects, such as those objects you might create in Illustrator, to bitmaps or pixels. Type, because type fonts are also vector objects, is also converted to pixels.

To save Photoshop documents with password security, select File ⇨ Save As and select Photoshop PDF from the Format pull-down menu in the Save As dialog box. If you have layers in the Photoshop file and want to preserve all layers, transparency, and type fonts, check the box for Layers and click the Save button. The PDF Options dialog box opens, shown in Figure 28-13.

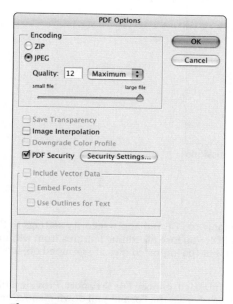

Figure 28-13: The PDF Options dialog box opens.

In the PDF Options dialog box, check the box for PDF Security and click the Security Settings button. The PDF Security dialog box opens, shown in Figure 28-14. As you can see, this dialog box offers the same permissions choices as you find in the Adobe Illustrator Adobe PDF Options dialog box. The difference between Illustrator and Photoshop is that Photoshop offers choices for compatibility settings in the same pane as you find the permissions options.

Make your choices for the permissions you want and click the OK button. The file is saved with security and, thus, users cannot open it in Photoshop unless They supply the Permissions Password. Note that limiting permissions when you check Password Required to Change Permission and Passwords has no effect in Photoshop. You need to supply a password when you open a secure PDF in Photoshop, but after it's open you can change the image. Permissions limiting high-resolution printing, copying data, and so on cannot be protected after the file is opened in Photoshop. These restrictions are only available in Acrobat where a PDF can be opened and viewed yet various permissions can restrict printing, editing, and so on.

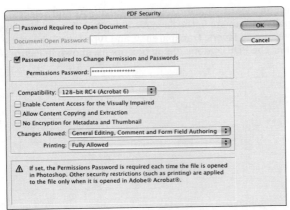

Figure 28-14: You make compatibility and permissions choices in the PDF Security dialog box.

Adding security in InDesign

Securing files from InDesign requires you to export to PDF and apply security settings to the PDF document. After you convert the file to a PDF, you lose all editing features from within InDesign. InDesign can import PDF documents, but the imported files are grouped objects and cannot be edited.

To secure a PDF document during export from InDesign, choose File ➪ Export. Provide a file-name in the Save As field box and select Adobe PDF from the Format pull-down menu. Click Save and the Export PDF dialog box opens, shown in Figure 28-15. Click on Security in the left pane and the permissions settings options are shown in the right pane.

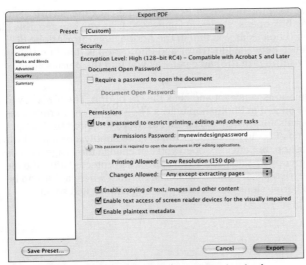

Figure 28-15: You secure PDFs from InDesign in the Export PDF dialog box.

The same options are available in InDesign as you have in the other CS programs. One slight difference you'll notice is that InDesign displays the text characters as you type them in the field boxes where passwords are supplied. In all other CS programs, the text appears as bullets as you type your password names. This metaphor is used in other programs to prevent onlookers from seeing passwords as you type them. In a way, InDesign is a bit easier when it comes to adding passwords, because you can easily see a typo in the password name before you're asked to confirm the password. In other programs, you may become confused when you try to confirm a password if the original password contains a typo. Because bullets are used in other programs, you don't know if a password was typed correctly. The only solution for you when passwords don't match is to start over. Notice that in Figure 28-16 you can easily move the Password dialog box aside to see an original password used in the security settings. In other CS programs, passwords are displayed as bullets in dialog boxes.

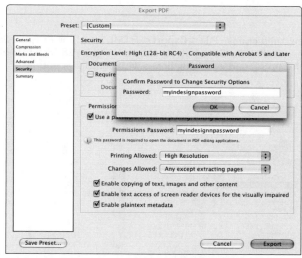

Figure 28-16: When confirming passwords in InDesign, move the Password dialog box aside so you can see the original password

After you export a PDF with security, you need to supply the correct password if you want to introduce the PDF as a placed graphic back in InDesign. Likewise, passwords are necessary when viewing and/or editing in Illustrator, Photoshop, or Acrobat.

Adding security in GoLive

GoLive is the only CS application that doesn't offer you options for securing PDF documents from within the program exporting to PDF. When you click PDF Preview while viewing an HTML page in GoLive, the Inspector palette, shown in Figure 28-17, doesn't offer you options for adding security.

Figure 28-17: The GoLive Inspector palette has no options for securing PDFs.

When you first click PDF Preview, then choose File ➪ Export ➪ HTML as Adobe PDF, the Save: GoLive dialog box opens. When you click the Save button, shown in Figure 28-18, a PDF of the HTML is created. GoLive provides no secondary dialog boxes with additional options for adding security.

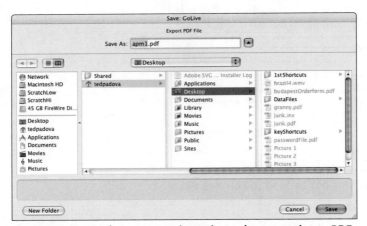

Figure 28-18: You have no security options when exporting to PDF from GoLive.

To secure files exported from GoLive, you need to perform two steps. First, create the PDF from GoLive; then apply the security in Acrobat. If you have a complete Web site to convert to PDF or several pages, you might want to use a Batch Sequence as explained earlier in this chapter, in the "Adding security in Acrobat" section.

Securing Files with Identities

Digital IDs are used to electronically sign documents. You can use Acrobat to create a digital ID, or you can use a third party to create and manage your digital IDs. From an ID, you can create a Trusted Certificate. This certificate is a file unique to you and is derived from the digital ID you either create in Acrobat or acquire from a third-party vendor.

A Trusted Certificate is a public file you exchange with other users for the purpose of authenticating your signature on documents you electronically sign in Acrobat. Trusted Certificates are also used for the purpose of securing documents. This form of security is unique to your personal digital ID and the password you chose when you first set up your ID. Therefore, when a PDF author uses your Public Certificate to encrypt a file, only the user who knows your personal password can open the file.

The advantage of using encryption through Trusted Certificates is that you can secure a single PDF document for multiple users while granting different permissions to each user. When a user tries to open an encrypted file, he or she must supply his or her unique password to view the document. When a document is in view in Acrobat, the user is restricted to those permissions set by the PDF author.

When using encryption through Trusted Certificates, you need to know how to create and manage digital IDs and how to encrypt files using Public Certificates. This form of encryption is unique to Acrobat and not available in the other CS applications. However, if you want to secure CS native files or documents created in other applications, you can use file attachments in PDF documents and secure the PDFs with either Acrobat security or encryption using trusted certificates.

Cross-Reference For more information on using file attachments, see "Securing Files with Attachments," later in this chapter.

Creating and managing digital IDs

Acrobat offers you two different menu options for creating a digital ID and another menu option for customizing the appearance of digital IDs. The menu commands are selected from different task buttons and different menus. In essence, you can arrive at the same dialog box from different menus and task buttons. When you first create a new identity, you may be a little confused because different options are available in different menu commands and appearances are added in a separate menu. Access to dialog boxes for Digital ID creation, appearance settings, and ID profile management are located in the following areas:

✦ **Security Preferences:** Use these preferences to add appearances to digital IDs you create from different menu commands. If you want to add a logo, analog signature, symbol, or some text to an ID, you can handle the appearance settings by choosing Edit ⇨ Preferences. Click on Digital Signatures in the left pane, and the window on the right side of the dialog box lists all your currently configured signatures. You can select a signature profile and add a new appearance in this dialog box by clicking on the New button shown in Figure 28-19.

✦ **Secure Task button:** Open the pull-down menu from the Secure Task button and select Encrypt for Certain Identities Using Certificates. If no ID has been created, the Document Security – Digital ID Selection dialog box opens with no certificates listed, as shown in Figure 28-20. Click on the Add Digital ID button to open the Add Digital ID dialog box, shown in Figure 28-21. Here you can create a new ID or click on a button to open a Web page hosted by Adobe, where you can obtain information on third-party signature handlers.

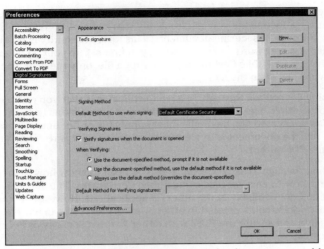

Figure 28-19: On the right side of the dialog box, you can add an appearance to a digital ID. Adding appearances require you to first create a digital ID.

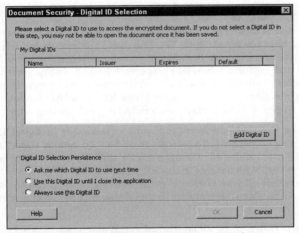

Figure 28-20: The Document Security – Digital ID Selection dialog box

✦ **Sign Task button:** Menu commands appear in the pull-down menu accessed from the Sign Task button. You can sign a document and also validate signed documents from menu commands in the Sign Task button. If you haven't created a digital ID, navigation through several dialog boxes eventually takes you to the same dialog box, shown in Figure 28-20, where you create your digital ID.

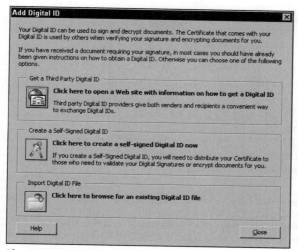

Figure 28-21: The Add Digital ID dialog box opens

✦ **Document menu:** The Document menu contains the same menu options found in the Secure Task button pull-down menu.

✦ **Advanced menu:** Under the Advanced menu, the Manage Digital IDs menu command opens a submenu where commands are used to manage your digital IDs, as shown in Figure 28-22. Select My Digital ID from the submenu and the Manage My Digital IDs dialog box opens, shown in Figure 28-23. By default, no IDs are listed in the dialog box. Click the Add button and the Add Digital ID dialog box opens, shown in Figure 28-21.

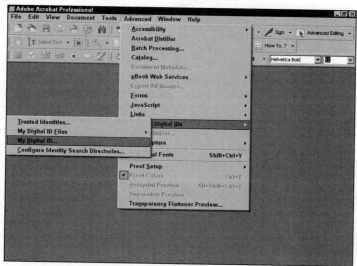

Figure 28-22: Select Advanced ➪ Manage My Digital IDs ➪ Manage Digital ID to open the Manage My Digital IDs dialog box.

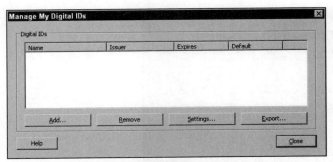

Figure 28-23: The Manage My Digital IDs dialog box

As you can see from all the dialog boxes shown in Figures 28-19 through 28-23, the creation and management of digital IDs can be accessed via many menu commands and through the use of task buttons. Where you arrive to create a digital ID is at the Add Digital ID dialog box. However, the path you use to arrive at the dialog box can be through many different menu commands.

Creating a digital ID

Choose Advanced ➪ Manage Digital IDs ➪ My Digital ID Files ➪ Select My Digital ID File. The Select My Digital ID File dialog box opens, shown in Figure 28-24. By default, if you haven't created any digital IDs, the field boxes are empty.

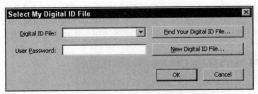

Figure 28-24: The Select My Digital ID File
dialog box

To create your first ID, click on the New Digital ID File button. The Self-Signed Digital ID Disclaimer dialog box opens, shown in Figure 28-25. This dialog box displays disclaimer information informing you that, if you want to have another individual validate your signature, the profile you create may not work if other users are using third-party products for signature validation. If other users work with Default Certificate Security, you should experience no problem as long as you send the authenticators your Public Certificate.

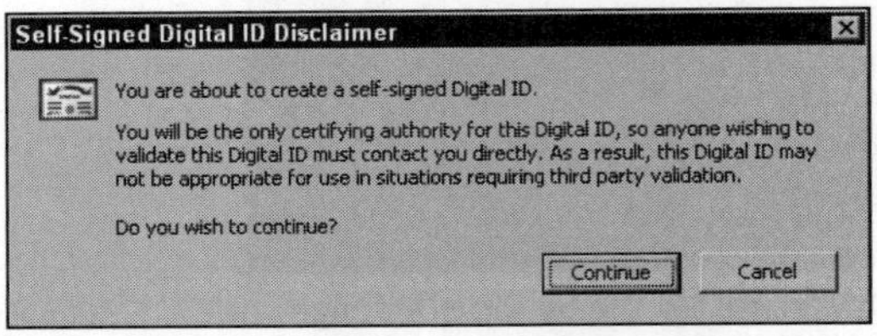

Figure 28-25: The Self-Signed Digital ID Disclaimer
dialog box

Click Continue in the disclaimer dialog box and the Create Self-Signed Digital ID dialog box opens, shown in Figure 28-26. In this dialog box, you select options for creating your profile. The options include the following:

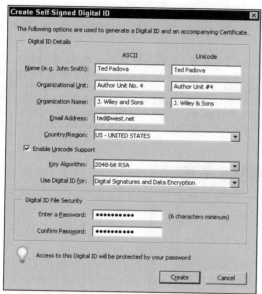

Figure 28-26: The Create Self-Signed Digital ID dialog box offers options for attributes assigned to your new profile.

✦ **ASCII:** Two columns are visible when you click on the check box for Enable Unicode Support. The left column is used for ASCII-only characters and doesn't support high ASCII values for special characters like #, /, *, and so on. If you want to use non-ASCII characters, enter them in the field boxes under the right column, Unicode. The first three field boxes identify your name, organization unit, and organization name. To eliminate the organization items, leave the field boxes blank.

✦ **Unicode:** Listed in previous paragraphs where you want to use non-ASCII characters. You must have Enable Unicode Support selected to use this option.

✦ **Email Address:** Add your e-mail address to this field box.

✦ **Country/Region:** There is an option for none if don't want to identify a country. The field box is not editable, so you can't add a new country name to specify a country not listed in the pull-down menu.

✦ **Enable Unicode Support:** If this check box is disabled, the Unicode field boxes are hidden. Enable this check box only if you want to use Unicode characters.

✦ **Key Algorithm:** Two choices are available from the pull-down menu. If you use the higher bit encryption of 2,048-bit the files are encrypted with a more reliable method; using 2,048-bit encryption enables Acrobat 5 and 6 users to open the files, but Acrobat 5 users won't be able to verify signatures when 2,048-bit encryption is used.

✦ **Use Digital ID For:** Three choices are available in this pull-down menu. Choose to use your profile with Digital Signatures, for Data Encryption, or for both (Digital Signatures and Data Encryption). You can create multiple profiles and choose from among your list of profiles what kinds of uses you want to apply to them.

✦ **Password:** Two fields are listed for supplying a password. Enter a password in the Enter a Password field box, and confirm your password by retyping it in the Confirm Password field box.

Set the attributes for your new digital ID and click on the Create button in the Create Self-Signed Digital ID dialog box. The New Self-Signed Digital ID File dialog box opens, shown in Figure 28-27. By default, the name for your file is the name you used in the Create Self-Signed Digital ID dialog box with a PFX extension. You can change the name for the file in the File Name field, but be certain to leave the PFX extension as the default. You can save your IDs to any directory on your hard drive. As a matter of practice, saving IDs to a common directory so you can easily back them up is a good idea.

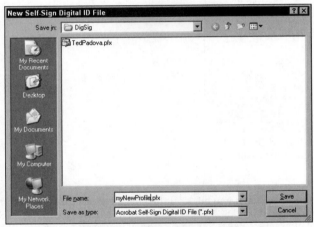

Figure 28-27: Provide a name and locate a directory for storing your digital ID. Click Save and the ID is ready for use.

After you click Save, you're logged in with the new digital ID. You can sign documents or secure them with data encryption according to the option selected for Use Digital ID For in the Create Self-Signed Digital ID dialog box. If you create multiple IDs, your list of IDs appears in the Select My Digital ID File dialog box in the Digital ID File pull-down menu, as shown in Figure 28-28. In this example, three digital IDs were created and all are displayed in the pull-down menu. You can select and use Either ID and use the ID within the use limitations in the Create Self-Signed Digital ID dialog box.

Figure 28-28: For multiple IDs, select from a list in the Digital ID File menu.

Users of earlier versions of Acrobat will notice that there is no menu option in Acrobat 6 for logging in as a user. When you want to log in as a new user, choose Advanced ⇨ Manage Digital IDs ⇨ Select My Digital ID File to open the Select My Digital ID File dialog box. Select the ID you want to use and you're logged in as a user. To log in, choose Advanced ⇨ Manage Digital IDs ⇨ My Digital IDs menu command and select Close My Digital ID File: *name of current open ID*. In Figure 28-29, the menu is opened displaying options for opening and closing IDs.

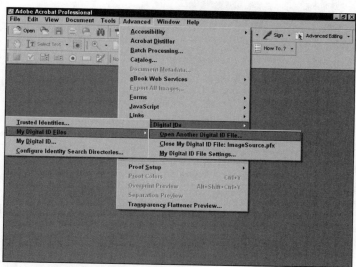

Figure 28-29: To open or close a digital ID file, choose Advanced ⇨ Manage Digital IDs ⇨ My Digital ID.

Deleting IDs

If you add several digital IDs, and the pull-down menu shown in Figure 28-28 displays a list of current IDs you created, you may want to edit an ID or delete one from your list. As you work through the dialog boxes for managing IDs, notice there is no option for deleting an ID from the Select My Digital ID File pull-down menu. If you want to delete an ID from this list, open the directory from the Desktop view where your digital IDs are stored. Select the file you want to delete and move it to the Trash. When you return to the Select My Digital ID File dialog box and open the pull-down menu, the menu lists only those IDs contained in the folder where the IDs are stored.

Managing multiple IDs

In Figure 28-29, the menu option for opening another ID is listed in the Manage Digital ID Files submenu. If you have several IDs and want to open a second ID file, the next file you open doesn't necessarily become a default for signing digital signature fields or encrypting documents. Priorities are assigned to IDs in the Set Digital ID Usage dialog box where priority options are defined for each ID.

Assume for a moment you have a digital signature field and you want to sign a document by clicking on the signature field. Further assume you have multiple digital IDs used for different signing purposes. You can use any one of your signatures or you can always use a default signature depending on how your digital ID usage Selection Persistence is configured. The options for Selection Persistence are established in the Set Digital ID Usage dialog box. The first step in addressing the settings is to choose Advanced ⇨ Manage Digital IDs ⇨ My Digital ID. The first dialog box that opens is the Manage My Digital IDs dialog box, shown in Figure 28-30.

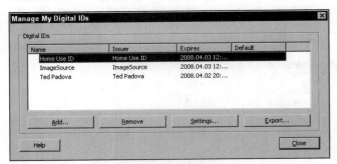

Figure 28-30: The Manage My Digital IDs dialog box

Figure 28-30 shows three IDs added to the list window. By default, the window is empty and you need to manually add IDs you create in Acrobat or IDs you acquire from third-party providers. Click on the Add button, and the Add Digital ID dialog box opens. Click on the button listed below Import Digital ID File, and the Locate Digital ID File dialog box opens. Navigate to the folder where your IDs are stored and select an ID. By default, PFX, P12, and APF files are listed in the dialog box. Click Open and Acrobat prompts you for a password. The password you enter is the same password used when you created your ID. Type the password and click OK. The ID is then added to the list window in the Manage My Digital IDs dialog box.

Note Users of earlier versions of Acrobat who saved IDs with an APF extension can import those IDs in Acrobat 6.

In the list window, select an ID and click on the Settings button. The Set Digital ID Usage dialog box opens. By default the Digital ID Selection Persistence is set to the first option, Ask Me Which Digital ID to Use Next Time, as shown in Figure 28-31.

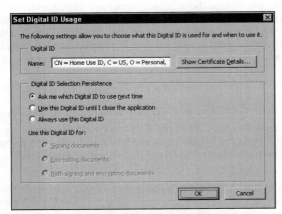

Figure 28-31: The Set Digital ID Usage dialog box offers you options for the Digital ID Selection Persistence. By default, the first radio button is selected.

When you use the default setting, each time you digitally sign a document or encrypt a file with Default Certificate Security, the Data Exchange File – Digital ID Selection dialog box, shown in Figure 28-32, opens.

Note

When you sign or encrypt a document, an alert dialog box opens asking you whether you want to certify the document with a certificate from an Adobe Partner or continue signing the document. If you click on the Continue Signing button, the dialog box shown in Figure 28-32 opens.

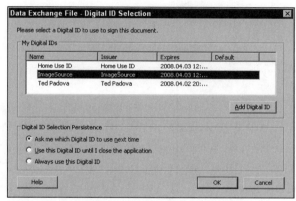

Figure 28-32: The Data Exchange File – Digital ID Selection dialog box

The three options in the Data Exchange File – Digital ID Selection dialog box are self-explanatory. Use the default when you want to be prompted to select an ID as you sign or encrypt documents with Default Certificate Security. The Use This Digital ID Until I Close the Application option waives the subsequent opening of the Data Exchange File – Digital ID Selection dialog box and uses the ID for all signing and encryption until you quit Acrobat. The Always Use This Digital ID option sets a new default and the ID is used whenever you sign or encrypt a document with Default Certificate Security. When you quit Acrobat and re-launch the program, it remains the default until you change the settings in the Set Digital ID Usage dialog box.

The Set Digital ID Usage dialog box contains options for how your digital ID is used. These options are the same choices you made when you created your digital ID. If you want to edit the choices for using the ID for signing only, data encryption only, or both, you can make an option selection in this dialog box. Any options you chose when you originally created the ID are overridden by the choice made in this dialog box.

Also contained in the Set Digital ID Usage dialog box is a button that opens the Certificate Attributes dialog box, shown in Figure 28-33. Click on the Show Certificate Details button in the Set Digital ID Usage dialog box, and you can examine the attributes assigned to the ID and review items such as level of encryption (that is, 1,024-bit or 2,048-bit), the certificate serial number, the fingerprint, and the usage key. If you need to edit the certificate attributes — for example, changing the encryption level — you need to create a new profile with the desired attributes.

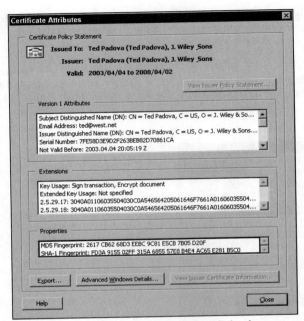

Figure 28-33: The Certificate Attributes dialog box

At first glance, all these dialog boxes may be confusing to you. Realize that creating multiple IDs is not necessary in many workflows where Default Certificate Security is used. You may find that using Default Certificate Security is adequate for your needs, and using a single ID is all you require. In this regard, you won't need to manage multiple IDs. If you do need multiple digital IDs, a few practice runs through the dialog boxes will help you get up to speed and understand better how to manage your IDs.

Adding an appearance to a digital ID

You can assign different appearances to a signature. You might want to use an analog signature (your handwritten signature) that you scan in, so your analog signature is added each time you digitally sign a document, or you may want to use a logo or icon that's added as an appearance item to your signature certificate. As you review all the dialog boxes discussed thus far, you'll notice that no options exist for importing images or defining text for a signature. Signature appearance configuration requires you to access another dialog box.

> **Note**   Appearances set in earlier versions of Acrobat required you to apply an appearance setting to each signature individually. If you used several signatures, you needed to define an appearance for each signature even if the appearance was identical for all your signatures. In Acrobat 6, you can use a single appearance and apply that appearance to all your signatures or a selected group of signatures. If you import signatures created in Acrobat versions lower than 6, all your appearances are lost. You need to reassign appearances in Acrobat 6 for all imported IDs created in earlier versions of Acrobat.

Open the Preferences dialog box (refer to Figure 28-19) by choosing Edit ➪ Preferences. In the left pane, select Digital Signatures. On the right side of the dialog box, you make some choices for the default method and the signature verification.

To add a new appearance, click on the New button in the top-right corner of the dialog box. The Configure Signature Appearance dialog box opens, shown in Figure 28-34. At the top of the dialog box, add a name for your appearance setting. In the dialog box, you have choices for no graphic, importing a graphic, or adding a name to the appearance under the Configure Graphic title.

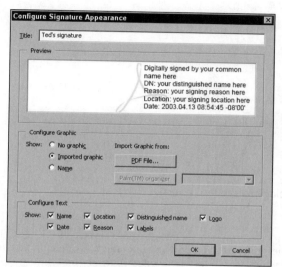

Figure 28-34: Adding a name for your appearance setting

> **Note** The name you supply in the Title field at the top of the Configure Signature Appearance dialog box applies only to the name you associate with the signature appearance. This name has nothing to do with the name you use for profiles. Many different profiles can use the same or different appearances.

If you want to add a graphic such as a logo or an analog signature, you can use any file type compatible with the Create PDF from File menu command. To select a file for the appearance, click on the Imported Graphic radio button and click the PDF File button. Notice that the button suggests that a PDF file must be used, but importing TIFF images, JPEG images, and a host of other formats are also options.

After you click on the PDF File button the Select Picture dialog box opens. Click on the Browse button, and you can search your hard drive to find the file to import. By default the Adobe PDF Files (*.pdf) format is selected in the Open dialog box that appears after you click on the Browse button. If you want to select another file type, open the Files of Type (Windows) or Show (Mac) pull-down menu. Select the file format you used to save your appearance item, and click the Select button.

The Select Picture dialog box displays a thumbnail view of the file selected for the appearance, as shown in Figure 28-35. If you change your mind or you inadvertently selected the wrong item, click on Browse again and you can replace the current figure with a new image. When the right image is selected, click on the OK button to return to the Configure Signature Appearance dialog box.

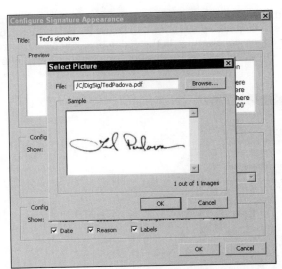

Figure 28-35: The Select Picture dialog box shows a thumbnail of your image.

At the bottom of the Configure Signature Appearance dialog box are several check boxes for configuring the text displayed on the signatures you add to a document. By default, all check boxes are enabled. You can choose which text items you want to include or omit from signature appearances by enabling or disabling the check boxes. In Figure 28-34, all the check boxes are enabled and the text items are displayed on the right side of the Preview window. As you disable various check boxes in the Configure Text area of the Digital Signatures Preferences dialog box, the respective items disappear.

Click OK in the Configure Signature Appearance dialog box and you're ready to apply the appearance settings to any signature(s) you use.

Encryption Using Trusted Certificates

Encryption using Trusted Certificates is a means for you to add security for a select group of users. The beauty of using Trusted Certificates is that you can control the permissions settings individually for each user in the same PDF document. For example, you may want to allow a user to view your document, but restrict printing. For another user, you may want to disallow editing, but enable printing. For a third user, you may want to allow editing and printing. All these permissions can be set for each user in the same PDF document using Trusted Certificates.

To encrypt a file using Trusted Certificates, you need to collect the public identities for each user and load them in a recipient's list. After loading all the trusted certificates, you specify permissions settings individually for each user. To handle this means of securing PDF files, you need to understand creating Public Certificates, gathering them from users, managing the certificates, and loading them for use in a recipient's list.

Exporting Public Certificates

Public certificates are used for validating signatures and encrypting files with trusted certificates. For another user to validate your signature or encrypt a file unique to your profile, you need to export your Public Certificate and share it with other users. Your Public Certificate does not compromise your password settings or ability to secure your own files. Public certificates are generated from your profile, but do not send along your password to other users.

To export a Public Certificate, you need to start with a digital ID you've already configured. Choose Advanced ➪ Manage Digital IDs ➪ My Digital ID to open the Manage My Digital IDs dialog box. The same dialog box shown in Figure 28-23 opens. If you have more than one ID listed in the dialog box, select the ID you want to use and click the Export button. The Data Exchange File – Export Options dialog box opens, shown in Figure 28-36.

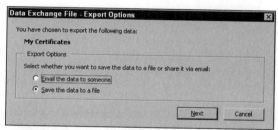

Figure 28-36: You can save the Public Certificate as a file or e-mail it.

In this dialog box, you make a choice for saving your Public Certificate to disk or e-mailing the certificate to another user. If you elect to save the file to disk, you can later attach it to an e-mail and send it to users as needed. If you select the radio button for Email the Data to Someone and click the Next button, the Compose Email dialog box opens, where the recipient(s) e-mail address is added. Enter an e-mail address and click the Email button; the data file is attached to a new e-mail message. Acrobat supplies a default message in the e-mail note for you, providing instructions for the recipient, but you can edit the message if you want.

Whether you save the file to disk or send the file to another user, the file type is saved as a Form Data Format (FDF), Certificate Message Syntax – PKCS#7 (P7C), or Certificate File (CER) depending on which pull-down menu item you select in the Export Data As dialog box. This data file is used for signature validation and encrypting PDF documents using Trusted Certificates.

Trusted identity preferences

At some time before or after compiling a list of recipients from other users, you'll want to visit the Trust Manager Preferences. The permissions settings you assign to individual users don't cover handling file extractions or multimedia. For determining how these items are handled, you need to choose options in the Trust Manager Preferences. Choose Edit ➪ Preferences (Windows) or Acrobat ➪ Preferences (Mac). Select Trust Manager in the left pane when the Preferences dialog box opens, as shown in Figure 28-37.

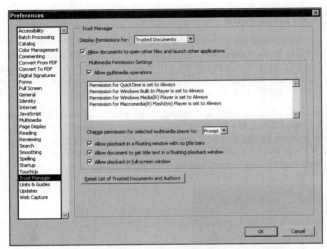

Figure 28-37: The Trust Manager option displays settings for Trusted Certificates.

In this dialog box, you determine whether users can open file attachments and how multimedia operations are handled. In the list of multimedia operations, select the items individually and choose the permission setting from the pull-down menu. For example, if you wanted to restrict users to only using QuickTime, you would select all permissions lines except QuickTime and select Never from the pull-down menu. If you want users to have permission to use any of the listed applications to view multimedia, be certain either Always or Prompt is selected for each item. By default, all four applications are handled via a user prompt.

Note   The list of multimedia players is derived from installed players on your system. If you don't see one of the options listed in Figure 28-37, you don't have the player installed or you may have a version not compatible with Acrobat 6. If you want to restrict viewing to additional players, install them and verify that the player you want to use appears in the Preferences dialog box.

The three check-box options at the bottom of the dialog box determine how media clips are viewed on-screen. You can choose from displaying in floating windows, displaying the title text in floating windows, and allowing the playback in a full-screen window. The settings in the Trusted Manager Preferences are intended more for the restrictions you want to employ to correspond with the way you intend media files to be viewed.

Click OK in the Preferences dialog box and you're ready to move on to loading recipients for either validating signatures or encrypting files for certain identities.

Encrypting files

After you collect Public Certificates, you need to load the certificates and assign permissions individually when encrypting files for certain identities. To load certificates, click the Secure Task button and open the pull-down menu (or choose Document ➪ Security ➪ Encrypt for Certain Identities Using Certificates). From the menu items, select Encrypt for Certain

Identities Using Certificates. If you haven't set a default for security handling, you're prompted for which method is to be used in the Certificate Security – Choose Method dialog box. Select the method — either the Default Certificate Security or Windows Certificate Security (Windows only) or Third Party. Click OK and the Document Security – Digital ID Selection dialog box opens (if you've selected Default Certificate Security). Supply your password to log on and click OK. If you have more than one ID, select the ID to be used and click OK in the Document Security – Digital ID Selection dialog box. After logging on and clicking OK, the Restrict Opening and Editing to Certain Identities dialog box opens, shown in Figure 28-38.

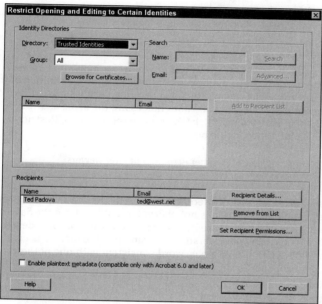

Figure 28-38: The Restrict Opening and Editing to Certain Identities dialog box

By default, the directory for your identities is selected for you and appears as Trusted Identities. Groups are added when you manage trusted identities in another dialog box, discussed later in this chapter. By default, All is selected in the dialog box under Group. To add a recipient, click on the Browse for Certificates button. A dialog box opens where you can browse your hard drive or network server to locate certificates collected from other users. Select a certificate and click Open. The certificate loads into the first window. Select the name in the top window and click on the Add to Recipient List button. The certificate is then moved to the lower window list of recipients.

Add a certificate and return to the Browse for Certificates button. Continue adding new certificates to your list of recipients. After all recipients have been added to the list, you apply individual permissions settings by selecting a recipient in the list and clicking on the Set Recipient Permissions button. The Recipient Permission Settings dialog box opens, shown in Figure 28-39.

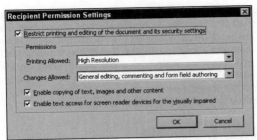

Figure 28-39: The Recipient Permission Settings dialog box

Make the restriction choices according to what you want to allow for individual users. To change permissions from the default, check the box for Restrict Printing and Editing of the Document and Its Security Settings. Printing and document editing permissions are set from menu selections made from the pull-down menus. Your choices are the same as when securing files with 1,028-bit or 2,048-bit encryption. Click OK and you return to the Restrict Opening and Editing to Certain Identities dialog box.

Note The encryption settings are compliant with either Acrobat 5 or later viewers.

After you establish permissions for a group of users, click OK in the Restrict Opening and Editing to Certain Identities dialog box. The file is not encrypted until you use the Save or Save As command to save the file, and then close it. After you close the PDF, only designated recipients using their IDs and you (using your personal ID) can open the file. If a user attempts to open the file and does not supply a password consistent with one of the recipients, a warning dialog box opens, as shown in Figure 28-40.

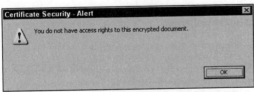

Figure 28-40: A warning dialog box informs you that you don't have access to the file.

By default, your personal identity is added to the recipient list. It's important to not remove your name from the list. If you delete your profile and encrypt the PDF for other users, all other users can open the file, but you can't.

Managing identities

You manage trusted identities in the Manage Trusted Identities dialog box that opens when you choose Advanced ➪ Manage Digital IDs ➪ Trusted Identities. In the Manage Trusted Identities dialog box, you can create different groups where you add individual recipients to one of the groups. After adding a new group, you can import collected certificates or request a certificate from users. Click on the Request Contact button and the Email a Request dialog box opens, much like the e-mail you send when exporting certificates to other users.

When you request a contact and the user responds to you, your e-mail message from the other user contains an FDF file of the Public Certificate as an e-mail attachment. Double-click on the file in your e-mail program and the recipient is automatically added to your list of recipients according to the group you selected when the request was submitted.

When you return to the Restrict Opening and Editing to Certain Identities dialog box, shown in Figure 28-38, you select the group from the Group pull-down menu and all your recipients for that group are listed. Add them to the recipient list, and you're ready to individually assign permissions.

Securing Files with Attachments

If your workflow requires you to exchange original documents that need to be secured, obviously converting to PDF isn't a solution. The CS programs don't offer you options for securing files unless you convert to PDF. However, you can use PDF to protect native documents against unauthorized opening and viewing and you can attach any file to a PDF. If the need arises for protecting word-processing files, spreadsheets, financial documents, layouts, images, and so on, you can use PDF as the container for native files and password-protect the contents.

By using file attachments in Acrobat, you use the PDF as a wrapper and secure the PDF document with open permissions. If a user doesn't have a password to open the PDF document, the attached file is inaccessible.

There are restrictions when using file attachments compared to using PDF security. For example, if you want to secure an InDesign file against unauthorized viewing, you can embed the InDesign document in a PDF and use an open password to protect the file. However, you can't restrict editing and printing the InDesign file. When using file attachments, you prevent users from viewing the documents or grant all permissions — there are no other options for securing native documents.

In terms of the kind of security you want to employ with PDFs containing file attachments, you can use either Acrobat Certificate Authority or Trusted Certificates. In either case, users need to have a password to gain access to the embedded file attachment(s).

Acrobat is a handy tool for exchanging files that need to be protected against unauthorized viewing, and you can easily secure any kind of document by attaching the file to a PDF. In order for users to extract a file from a secured PDF, they need to have the open password and the original application that created the file attachment. For example, embedding a Microsoft Word file in a PDF document requires you to have MS Word installed on your computer in order to extract the file.

To understand more about attaching files to PDF documents and securing them against unauthorized viewing, follow these steps:

Securing PDFs with File Attachments

1. **Open the JavaScript Editor in Acrobat.** If you want to exchange a file with other users and you don't have a PDF document handy, you can easily create a new blank PDF document with a JavaScript. To create a JavaScript, launch Acrobat and press ⌘/Ctrl+J or choose Advanced ➪ JavaScript ➪ Debugger. (*Note:* This command is accessible only in Acrobat Professional.) The JavaScript Editor window opens after using the keyboard shortcut.

2. **Create a new blank PDF document.** Acrobat does not have a command to create a new blank document. In order to create a new file, you need to write a JavaScript. In the JavaScript Editor, type the following code in the window below the Type pull-down menu:

```
app.newDoc(640,480);
```

Press the Num Pad Enter key with the cursor in the line of code you typed. A new blank document 640 by 480 pixels appears in the Document pane. Close the JavaScript Editor by clicking on the close box at the top of the window.

Note You can specify page sizes when creating new documents with JavaScript by typing the horizontal and vertical dimensions within the parentheses. If you want to create a standard U.S. Letter page, don't add any values within the parentheses [`app.newDoc();`]. The default is a U.S. Letter page in Portrait view.

3. **Attach a file.** Select the Attach File tool and click on the new document. The Select File to Attach dialog box opens, shown in Figure 28-41. From the Show pull-down menu, select All Files. Navigate to the folder location where your file to be attached is located and select it. Click Select and the File Attachment Properties dialog box opens.

Figure 28-41: Select All Files from the Show pull-down menu if you attach a file type other than PDF.

Note that you can attach any type of file to a PDF document. In this example, a compressed archive containing many different files is attached to the open document.

4. **Select the Attachment properties.** In the File Attachment Properties Appearance settings, select the type of icon you want to use to display the file attachment and click the color swatch to select a color for the attachment icon. For Icon, you have four items from which to choose, as shown in Figure 28-42. When you click on the color swatch, other preset or custom colors are accessible.

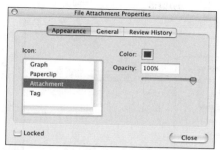

Figure 28-42: The File Attachment Properties dialog box

5. **Edit the file attachment General properties.** Click on the General tab and add a subject and description as desired. In Figure 28-43, descriptive information was added to the Subject and Description fields. Click Close after editing the File Attachment properties.

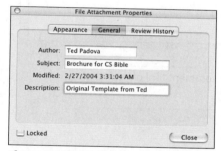

Figure 28-43: Click General to add descriptive information for author, subject, and description.

6. **Add comments.** The Attach File comment does not support an associated pop-up note window. If you want to add comments, you need to use another comment tool. Depending on the length of your comment and the kind of note you want to add, choose a comment type. In this example, we use the Stamp comment, as shown in Figure 28-44.

7. **Secure the file.** Open the Secure Task button pull-down menu and select Restrict Opening and Editing. The Password Security – Settings dialog box opens, shown in Figure 28-45. Check the box for Require a Password to Open the Document and type the password you want to use in the field box. Select from the Compatibility pull-down menu the level of Acrobat compatibility you desire. This option is not so critical when you're securing a document against opening it, because permissions options only change according to compatibility when adding a permissions password. Click OK after making your password choice, and retype the password in the Password dialog box. Click OK and save the file.

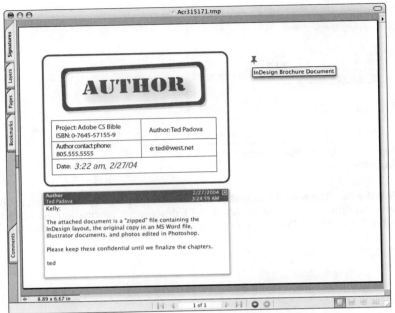

Figure 28-44: Add a note using the comment tool of your choice.

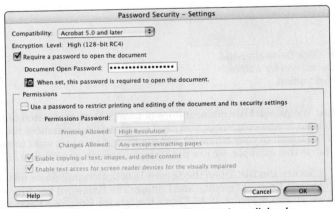

Figure 28-45: The Password Security – Settings dialog box

When you save the document and exchange the file with other users, the end user needs the open password in order to access the file attachment. As a file is opened with an open password in Acrobat, the first item appearing is the Password dialog box, shown in Figure 28-46. Type the password and the PDF opens in the Document pane.

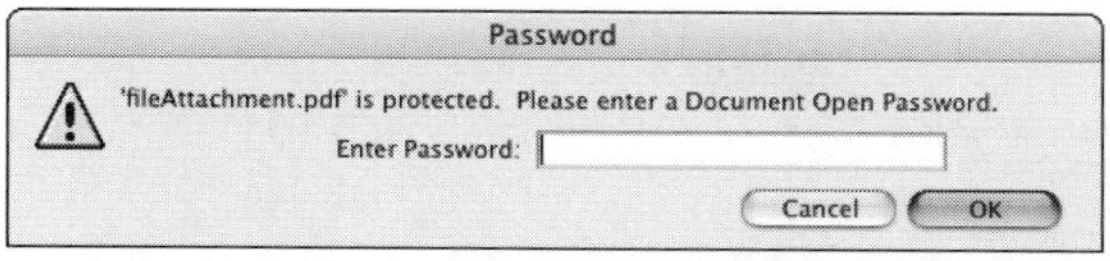

Password

⚠ 'fileAttachment.pdf' is protected. Please enter a Document Open Password.

Enter Password: [   ]

⸨ Cancel ⸩ ⸨ OK ⸩

Figure 28-46: Typing the correct password prevents you from opening the file.

To access the attached document, double-click on the file-attachment icon with the Hand tool or open a context menu, like the one shown in Figure 28-47, and select Open File.

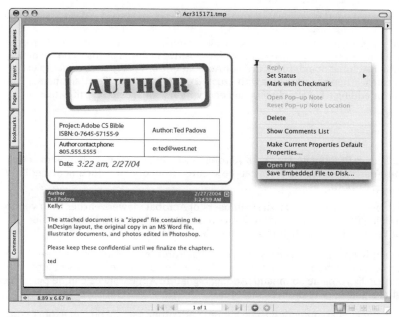

Figure 28-47: To extract a file attachment, double-click on the file-attachment icon or open a context menu and select Open File.

If the file you open is an application document, you need to have the corresponding application on your hard drive. When the file is extracted, it launches the host application where the file is displayed. Before you actually open the attachment, a warning dialog box opens to inform you that the file may contain macros or viruses. This warning is intended to alert you if you receive files from unknown sources where a potential virus may be contained in the file attachment. If you're receiving documents from trusted sources, click Open and the dialog box shown in Figure 28-48 appears.

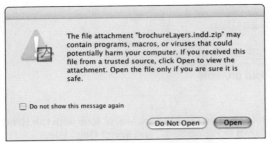

Figure 28-48: Click Open to extract the file attachment.

As you can see, by using Acrobat you can secure all documents created in all the CS programs or any other application used in your workflow. When sensitive material needs to be exchanged, you can use either Acrobat Standard Security or Acrobat or third-party security handlers with Trusted Certificates. When securing files with Trusted Certificates and file attachments, follow the same steps for adding a file attachment and encryption with Trusted Certificates.

Summary

✦ You can secure PDF documents with Acrobat Security and security handlers acquired from third-party developers. Files can be secured from opening documents, editing documents, or both.

✦ Different levels of security can prevent users of Acrobat viewers earlier than version 6 from opening files. It's important to know your user audience and what version of Acrobat viewers they use before securing files.

✦ You can apply appearance settings to your signatures in the form of scanned documents, icons, and symbols from files saved as PDF or other file formats compatible with the Create PDF from File command. Adding Signature Appearances can be performed in the Digital Signature Preferences dialog box.

✦ Public certificates are intended to be shared with other users. You can export your Public Certificate to a file or attach your Public Certificate to an e-mail message from within Acrobat.

✦ You can encrypt files for a group of users using other user identities you collect from the users. A single PDF document can be secured for different users and with different permissions for each user.

✦ Any kind of document can be attached to a PDF. When you password-secure a PDF document with a file attachment, a user needs the password to gain access to the attached file.

✦   ✦   ✦

Adding Interactivity in InDesign

InDesign includes support for several interactive elements including hyperlinks, bookmarks, buttons, movies, and sound. Hyperlinks and bookmarks enable you to select objects that link to other sources. You can make the destination another page within the document, a text anchor or an online URL. You can configure buttons to take a certain action when a user interacts with them. You can also add movie and sound files to an InDesign document. All of these elements add functionality to the design when used as a Web page.

After you create these elements in InDesign, you can export them to Acrobat or GoLive where the elements remain interactive. When you export movie and sound files to the PDF format, you can make them active. Exporting an InDesign document to the PDF format lets you take advantage of more-elaborate interactive tools and coding JavaScripts in Acrobat.

Within InDesign, you can create several interactive elements that are useful as the InDesign document is saved and used in other CS applications. The interactive elements that InDesign can create include the following:

- ✦ **Hyperlinks:** Hyperlinks are simple text selections that are linked to an external source such as a Web page or another location within a PDF file.

- ✦ **Bookmarks:** Bookmarks mark a location within the PDF file. These bookmarks are listed in the Bookmark pane in Acrobat.

- ✦ **Buttons:** Buttons have actions associated with them. When clicked, they can open an external file, start a movie, or play a sound. Other action types offer options for creating dynamic document viewing.

- ✦ **Movies and sound clips:** You can add movies and sound clips to a document and have them play within a PDF file or on a Web page.

Cross-Reference

Interactive elements in an InDesign document may also be exported to a Web page. By choosing File ➪ Package for GoLive, you can create a package that GoLive can open, which includes all the various interactive elements and their referenced files. Using the Package for GoLive menu command is covered in detail in Chapter 25.

Creating hyperlinks

InDesign hyperlinks are created using the Hyperlink palette, shown in Figure 29-1. Open this palette by choosing Window ➪ Interactive ➪ Hyperlinks. Each hyperlink has a source consisting of a section of selected text, a text object or a graphic frame, and a destination, which is where the hyperlink connects to when it's clicked.

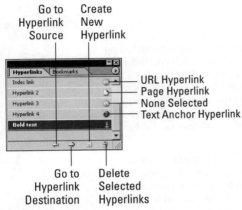

Figure 29-1: The Hyperlinks palette lists all hyperlinks for a document.

Specifying a hyperlink destination

Before creating a hyperlink, it's easiest if you first to create a *destination*. This is the target location for the hyperlink. To create a new destination, select the New Hyperlink Destination palette menu command. This opens the dialog box shown in Figure 29-2 and presents three different destination types — Page, Text Anchor, and URL:

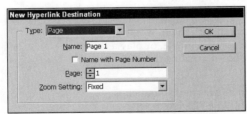

Figure 29-2: The New Hyperlink Destination dialog box helps you create destinations.

A Page destination lets you create a hyperlink that jumps to a specified page, like what you'd find in a table of contents or an index. The Name field lets you enter a name that you can select when you create the hyperlink, or you can enable the Name with Page Number option to automatically set the name to the selected page number. The Zoom Setting option lets you specify the zoom level when the page is displayed. The options include Fixed, Fit View, Fit in Window, Fit Width, Fit Height, Fit Visible, and Inherit Zoom.

The Text Anchor option makes the selected text an anchor that the hyperlink jumps to. For this anchor, you may give it a name that is used to select the anchor in the Create Hyperlink dialog box. The URL option lets you name and specify the Web address of a site on the Web.

Creating a new hyperlink

After you create and name a destination, you can select an item in the current document for use as a new hyperlink. You then create the hyperlink using the New Hyperlink palette menu command or by clicking on the Create New Hyperlink button at the bottom of the Hyperlinks palette.

This opens the New Hyperlink dialog box (Figure 29-3) where you can give the hyperlink a name, specify a destination, and determine its appearance. In the Destination section, select a document from the open documents or browse to another local document using the Browse option. The Type list includes the Page, Text Anchor, URL and All Types options, and the Name drop-down list lets you choose from the named destinations already created. There is also a None option that you may select if you have not yet created or named the destination.

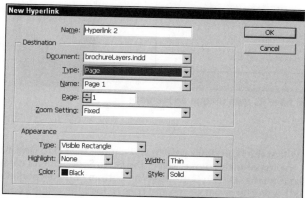

Figure 29-3: The New Hyperlink dialog box lets you specify link properties.

The Appearance section lets you define how the hyperlink looks. The Type could be Visible Rectangle or Invisible Rectangle; the Highlight could be None, Invert, Outline, or Inset; the Color could be one of many default named colors; the Width could be Thin, Medium, or Thick; and the Style could be Solid or Dashed. The Highlight appearance shows up only when the document is exported to Acrobat. Figure 29-4 shows each of these options.

After the Create Hyperlink dialog box is closed, the new hyperlink appears in the Hyperlinks palette and the hyperlink content in the document is highlighted using the designated appearance settings. An icon denoting the type of hyperlink appears to the right of the hyperlink name in the Hyperlinks palette. Choose View ➪ Show/Hide Hyperlinks to hide all the hyperlinks. To edit an existing hyperlink, double-click on it in the Hyperlinks palette or select the Hyperlink Options menu command.

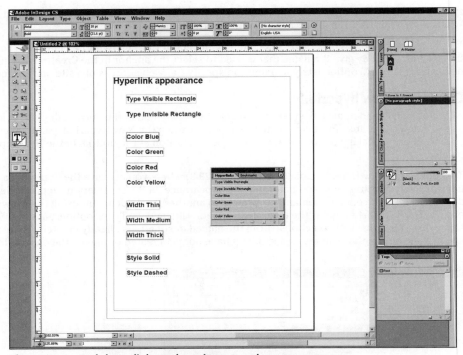

Figure 29-4: Each hyperlink can have its own unique appearance.

Testing hyperlinks

To test a hyperlink, simply select it in the Hyperlinks palette and choose the Go to Destination palette menu command. To see the hyperlink's source, select the Go to Source menu command. These commands are also available as icon buttons at the bottom of the Hyperlinks palette. If the destination is a URL, a Web browser opens and tries to load the requested URL.

STEPS: Creating a hyperlink

1. **Open an InDesign document.** Within InDesign, choose File ⇨ Open and open a document to which you want to add a hyperlink.

2. **Open the Hyperlinks palette.** Choose Window ⇨ Interactive ⇨ Hyperlinks to open the Hyperlinks palette.

3. **Select a destination.** Within the InDesign document, select the destination item for the hyperlink and choose the New Hyperlink Destination palette menu command from the Hyperlinks palette. Select the hyperlink type and give the destination a name, then click OK. Figure 29-5 shows this text-anchor destination.

4. **Select the source item.** Locate and select the item that is the hyperlink source. Select the New Hyperlink palette menu command to open the New Hyperlink dialog box. In the dialog box, enter a name for the hyperlink, and select Text Anchor as the type. The Name is set to the only created destination. Set the Appearance Type to Invisible Rectangle and the Highlight to None. Then click OK.

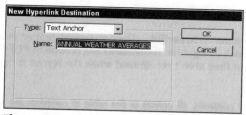

Figure 29-5: You can use the New Hyperlink Destination to create a destination.

5. **Test the hyperlink.** After its creation, the link's name appears in the Hyperlinks palette. Click on the Go to Hyperlink Destination button at the bottom of the Hyperlinks palette. InDesign should jump to the destination location. Select the hyperlink and click the Go to Hyperlink Source button at the bottom of the Hyperlinks palette to return to the hyperlink's source item. Figure 29-6 shows the source item selected.

Figure 29-6: Jumping to a destination or a source item (upper left corner) automatically selects it.

Adding bookmarks

Bookmarks in many ways are very similar to hyperlinks. They also mark text or images that link to places with the PDF file for quick navigation. Bookmarks are unique to PDF files and appear in the left Bookmark pane, but they aren't recognized when the layout is converted to a Web page.

 Note When InDesign creates a table of contents, all entries in the table of contents are automatically added to the document as bookmarks.

You create and manage bookmarks using the Bookmarks palette, shown in Figure 29-7, which is accessed by choosing Window ➪ Interactive ➪ Bookmarks.

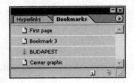 **Figure 29-7:** The Bookmarks palette manages all bookmarks for the document.

You add new bookmarks to the document by selecting the bookmark item and choosing the New Bookmark palette menu command or by clicking on the Create New Bookmark button at the bottom of the Bookmark palette. If no bookmarks are selected in the palette, the new bookmark is added to the bottom of the list of bookmarks. But if a bookmark is selected, the new bookmark is added as a child bookmark under the selected bookmark.

After creation, a book mark's name appears as highlighted text, which you can edit. The bookmark's name appears in Acrobat's Bookmark pane. If some selected text is the bookmark, the selected text appears as the bookmark's name unless you change it.

The order of bookmarks within the Bookmarks palette also determines the order that the bookmarks appear in Acrobat's bookmark pane. You can rearrange the listed bookmarks by dragging the bookmarks within the Bookmarks palette. As you're dragging a bookmark, a line appears defining where the bookmark appears when you release the mouse. If you drop a bookmark on top of an existing bookmark, the bookmark becomes a child to the highlighted bookmark.

Creating interactive buttons

You can create buttons in InDesign to jump to a page, or perform a certain action like playing a movie or sound. When you export an InDesign document containing buttons to Acrobat, the defined button and its function remain active.

 Note Buttons created in InDesign and exported to a PDF document are different from buttons created in Acrobat.

You create simple buttons in InDesign using the Button tool. You drag the tool in the layout where you want to locate the button, or you click in the document to open a simple dialog box (Figure 29-8), where you enter the Width and Height of the button. Holding down the Shift key while dragging constrains the button to a square shape. Holding down the Option/Alt key while dragging lets you drag from the button's center. If you hold down the Spacebar while dragging, you can move the button's location. Buttons are identifiable by a button icon and name that displays in the upper-left corner of the button.

Figure 29-8: The Button dialog box dialog box lets you enter precise dimensions.

In addition to regular rectangular objects created with the Button tool, you can also convert any selectable object including text objects and images to buttons by choosing Object ➪ Interactive ➪ Convert to Button.

Button objects may also be converted to normal objects by choosing Object ➪ Interactive ➪ Convert from Button.

Setting button options and behavior

You set button options using the Button Options dialog box (Figure 29-9), which appears when you choose Object ➪ Interactive ➪ Button Options or when you double-clicking on the button. The Button Options dialog box consists of two panels — General and Behaviors.

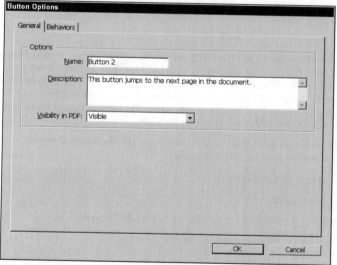

Figure 29-9: The General panel defines how a button looks and acts.

The General panel of the Button Options dialog box includes fields for naming and entering a button description. The text in the Description field appears in Acrobat when you move the mouse cursor over the button. The Visibility of the button in an exported PDF may be set to Visible, Hidden, Visible But Doesn't Print, or Hidden But Printable.

The Behavior panel of the Button Options dialog box, shown in Figure 29-10, lets you define what happens when you interact with a button. The pane on the left holds all the defined behaviors for the selected button.

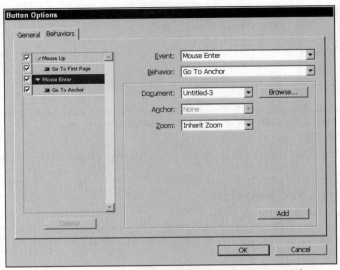

Figure 29-10: The Behaviors panel defined the events and behaviors of a button.

The Event options are different ways to interact with a button. The options include Mouse Up, Move Down, Mouse Enter, Mouse Exit, On Focus, and On Blur. The Mouse Down and Mouse Up events occur when the mouse button is pressed and released. The Mouse Enter and Mouse Exit events occur when the mouse moves over and away from the button's bounding box. The On Focus and On Blur events occur when the button has or loses focus. A button has focus when it's selected with the mouse or Tab key.

The Behavior options are all the actions that may be set when the designated event happens. The available behaviors include the following:

✦ **Close:** Closes the current PDF document.

✦ **Exit:** Causes the application to exit.

✦ **Go to Anchor:** Jumps to a specified hyperlink anchor or bookmark.

✦ **Go to First Page:** Jumps to the first page in the document.

✦ **Go to Last Page:** Jumps to the last page in the document.

✦ **Go to Next Page:** Jumps to the next page in the document.

✦ **Go to Next View:** Jumps to the next page in the view history. This behavior only becomes active after the Go to Previous View behavior is used.

✦ **Go to Previous Page:** Humps to the previous page in the document.

✦ **Go to Previous View:** Jumps to the last viewed page in the view history.

✦ **Go to URL:** Opens a Web browser with the designated URL address loaded.

✦ **Movie:** Lets you play, pause, stop, and resume a movie.

✦ **Open File:** Opens another selected PDF file or opens another file type in its default application.

✦ **Show/Hide Fields:** Show or hide a specified form field.

✦ **Sound:** Lets you play, pause, stop, and resume a sound.

✦ **View Zoom:** Lets you designate how the current page zooms. The options include Full Screen, Zoom In, Zoom Out, Fit in Window, Actual Size, Fit Width, Fit Visible, Reflow, Single Page, Continuous, Continuous-Facing, Rotate Clockwise, and Rotate Counterclockwise.

Various settings appear under the Behavior field depending on the Behavior that you select. For example, selecting the Go to Anchor behavior displays settings for choosing the Document from the active documents, a Browse button for locating a local document, and a field for selecting an Anchor by name. The Go to URL behavior lets you type in a URL. The Movie and Sound behaviors display a field where you can select a movie or sound added to the document, as well as an option to Play, Pause, Stop, or Resume. The Open File behavior lets you browse and select a file to open. All the go to page options, plus the Go to Anchor and the View Zoom behaviors, offer a list of zoom options to use when the user jumps to the page. The Show/Hide Fields behavior presents a list of fields in the current document along with check boxes to mark which ones are visible.

After you select and define an event and a behavior, you must click the Add button to add the behavior to the pane on the right.

Setting button states

Although you can create various button states for rollovers using behaviors, button states are more easily defined using the States palette, shown in Figure 29-11. To access this palette, choose Window ⇨ Interactive ⇨ States. Each button maintains three different states — Up, Rollover, and Down:

✦ **Up:** The button's default state.

✦ **Rollover:** Occurs when the mouse cursor moves over the top of the button.

✦ **Down:** Occurs when a user clicks the button.

You can use the States palette to change the button's look for each of these states.

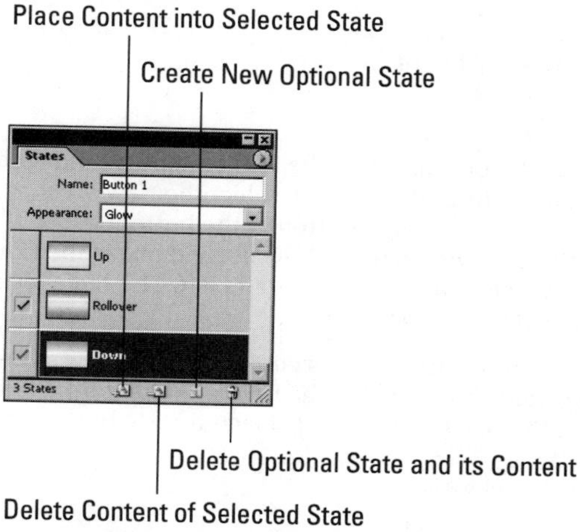

Place Content into Selected State

Create New Optional State

Delete Optional State and its Content

Delete Content of Selected State

Figure 29-11: The States palette changes the button's appearance for different states.

When you first open the States palette, the name of the selected button displays in the Name field; from the Appearance field, you may select an appearance style for the selected button. Options include Bevel, Drop Shadow, Glow, Custom, and None.

The three available appearance presets automatically create new Rollover and Down states and apply a modified appearance to the button. These modified states and their appearances are visible in the States palette. Selecting one of the states in the States palette causes the document button to show the appearance for that state.

The Bevel option adds a shaded border to the edge of the button and changes the color of each button state. The Drop Shadow option adds a gradient across the face of the button along with a drop shadow. The Glow option adds a glowing gradient vertically down the face of the button, which is inverted for the Rollover state. Figure 29-12 shows each of the default states for the preset appearances.

Note

Changing between the default appearance presets presents a dialog box warning you that adding the new preset will delete the appearance of any existing buttons that use the appearance preset that is being replaced.

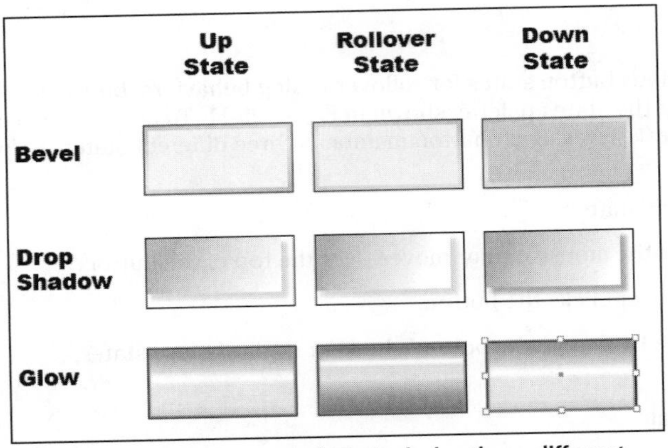

	Up State	Rollover State	Down State
Bevel			
Drop Shadow			
Glow			

Figure 29-12: The States palette includes three different preset appearance options.

In addition to the default appearance presets, you can select the Custom option and create your own state buttons. To add a new state to the States palette, select the New State palette menu command or click on the Create New Optional State button at the bottom of the palette. The first state that is created is the Rollover state, and the second one is the Down state. You can disable either of these states using the check box to its left. The red check mark highlights the state currently displayed in the document.

When a new state is created, the original button appearance is copied into the new state. You can remove this content by selecting the state and choosing the Delete Content from State palette menu command, or by clicking on the Delete Content of Selected State button at the bottom of the palette.

To replace the graphic of the selected state with another graphic file, choose the Place Content into State palette menu command or click on the Place Content into Selected State button at the bottom of the palette. This opens a file dialog box where you may select a file to place in the state.

Objects created within InDesign may be grouped and added to a button state by positioning them as they would fit in the button and then by cutting them with the Edit ➪ Cut menu command. Select the button state and choose Edit ➪ Paste Into.

To change the text within a button state, simply select the state in the States palette, click on the button frame with the Type tool, and start typing. To change the fill and stroke for a button state, simply select the button state and change the fill and stroke properties.

Setting tab order

One common way to navigate about documents is using the Tab key. This key moves the focus from one element to another. You can execute the element with the focus by pressing the Return/Enter key.

For InDesign documents that include several buttons, the order in which the Tab key moves between these buttons is defined using the Tab Order dialog box, shown in Figure 29-13. Open this dialog box by choosing Object ➪ Interactive ➪ Set Tab Order.

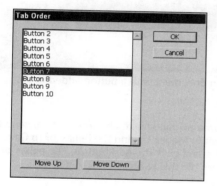

Figure 29-13: The Tab Order dialog box

STEPS: Creating a button

1. **Open an InDesign document.** Within InDesign, choose File ➪ Open and open a document that you want to add a button to.

2. **Create a button with the Button tool.** Select the Button tool and drag in the lower-right corner of the document to create a small button, as shown in Figure 29-14. The button object is named Button 1. With the button selected, change the Fill color to white and the stroke color to black. Then change the stroke width to 3 pt.

3. **Enable the button's states.** With the button selected, choose Window ➪ Interactive ➪ States to open the States palette. Select the Glow option in the Appearance field. This adds two states to the States palette.

4. **Set the button options.** Choose Object ➪ Interactive ➪ Button Options. This opens the Button Options dialog box. In the Description field, type the words, **Next Page**. This is the text that appears when a user moves the mouse cursor over the top of the button in Acrobat. Then select the button to be Visible in the PDF.

Figure 29-14: The first page of the InDesign document with a button added to the lower-right corner

5. **Set the button's behavior.** In the Button Options dialog box, click on the Behaviors tab to access the Behaviors panel. Set the Event to Mouse Up and the Behavior to Go to Next Page. Then set the Zoom to Actual Size and click the Add button. The behavior is added to the list at the left. Click OK to close the dialog box.

Adding movies and sound clips

The final interactive element supported by InDesign includes movies and sound files. Although InDesign supports the placing of these files within its document, they cannot actually be played until the document is exported to the PDF format or the document is packaged for use in GoLive. However, the media files may be previewed in InDesign by holding down the Option/Alt key while double-clicking on the media file's frame.

The movie formats supported by InDesign include QuickTime, AVI, MPEG, and SWF movies and WAV, AIF, and AU sound files.

Note   The MPEG and SWF movie formats are only playable in Acrobat version 6 or Adobe Reader version 6. QuickTime and AVI movie formats are only playable in Acrobat version 5 or later.

Placing media files

You add movie and sound files to the current document by choosing File ➪ Place. The placed media file appears within a frame. Selecting the object and choosing Object ➪ Interactive ➪

Movie Options or Object ⇨ Interactive ⇨ Sound Options opens a dialog box where the settings for the movie or sound file are specified. If you create an empty frame, you may access either Options dialog box and select a file at a later time.

Setting movie options

The Movie Options dialog box, shown in Figure 29-15, includes Name and a Description field. The Name appears in the object's frame; the Description appears in Acrobat when the mouse cursor is moved over the top of the object.

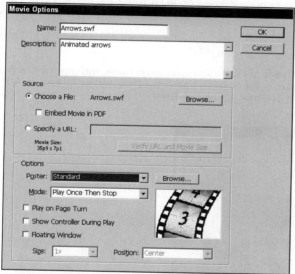

Figure 29-15: The Movie Options dialog box defines which movie file plays and when it plays.

The Move Options dialog box lets you either choose a file or specify a URL. Although you cannot embed movies within the InDesign document, you can embed the movie in the PDF. If you enable the Embed Movie in PDF option, the movie file embeds within the PDF file when it's exported. If you disable this option, you must move movie file needs along with the exported PDF file that references it. The Specify URL option lets you type in the address to a media file on the Web. If a connection to the Internet is established when the media file is viewed, the movie file is downloaded into the PDF document. The Verify URL and Movie Size button checks the URL to make sure it's valid and points to a movie file.

A Poster is an image that represents the movie. This image appears when the movie isn't being played. There are several Poster options including the following:

✦ **None:** Hides the movie file when it isn't being played.

✦ **Standard:** Displays the image contained in the `StandardMoviePoster.jpg` image file. This generic image displays to the right in Figure 29-16.

✦ **Default Poster:** Presents the poster image that is bundled with the movie file. If the movie doesn't include a poster image, the first frame of the movie is used.

   ✦ **Choose Image as Poster:** Lets you browse and load an image and display it as the movie poster.

   ✦ **Choose Movie Frame as Poster:** Lets you view the movie using the pane to the right, where you may select a single frame of the movie to use as a poster.

The Mode options define how many times the movie file plays. The options include Play Once Then Stop, Play Once Stay Open, and Repeat Play. The Play on Page Turn option causes the movie to start playing when the page that includes the movie is displayed. The Show Controller During Play option shows controls along with the movie file. These controls let the viewer play, pause, and stop the movie file. The Floating Window option displays the movie within a floating window. The size and position of the floating window are set using the fields at the bottom of the dialog box.

Setting sound options

The Sound Options dialog box, shown in Figure 29-16, includes Name and Description fields. The Name is the name that appears in the object's frame; the Description appears in Acrobat when the mouse cursor is moved over the top of the object.

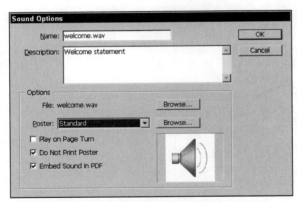

Figure 29-16: The Sound Options dialog box

The Sound Options dialog box, like the Movie Options dialog box, also lets you Browse for a new sound file. The Poster options are limited to None, Standard, and Choose Image as Poster. The Play on Page Turn option causes the sound file to play when the page that contains it is displayed. The Do Not Print Poster option ensures that the sound frame isn't printed with the rest of the document when the document is printed. The Embed Sound in PDF causes the sound file to be embedded within the PDF, which frees you from the concern of copying the sound file along with the exported PDF but increases the PDF file size.

Exporting Interactive Elements to Acrobat

When you export an InDesign document that contains interactive elements to the PDF file format using the File ➪ Export menu command, an Export PDF dialog box appears, shown in Figure 29-17. In this dialog box, you can select the interactive elements to include in the conversion.

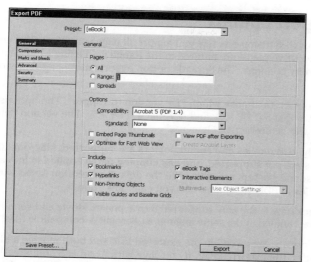

Figure 29-17: The Export PDF dialog box includes many different panels.

 Cross-Reference Other PDF export options are covered in Chapter 35.

Using export presets

At the top of the Export PDF dialog box is the Presets drop-down list. These presets include many default setting configurations that you have saved for easy recall. The default presets include Custom, eBook, Screen, Print, Press, PDF/X-1a, PDF/X-3, and Acrobat 6 Layered.

You save new presets using the Save Preset button in the lower-left corner. All export presets are also available by choosing File ➪ PDF Export Presets, which opens a dialog box, shown in Figure 29-18, where all the available export presets are managed. You save all export presets using the PDF file extension.

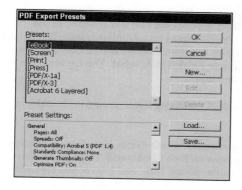

Figure 29-18: The Save PDF Export Presets dialog box

Setting general export options

The General panel of the Export PDF dialog box lets you export all pages or only a number of pages in the Range field. Consecutive pages are entered in the Range field using a hyphen; individual pages are separated by commas. The Spreads option exports multi-page spreads as a single page.

The dialog box also offers an option to choose which PDF version to support. The options include Acrobat 4 (PDF 1.3), Acrobat 5 (PDF 1.4), and Acrobat 6 (PDF 1.5). The version determines the availability of the various interactive elements.

For the Acrobat 4 version, only RGB movies and sound posters are supported. Macromedia Flash (SWF) and MPEG movies are not supported, and any clipping paths applied in InDesign are ignored. The movies and sound posters are resized to the default resolution saved with the file. You can't embed movies in PDF document, and you can't link sounds.

For the Acrobat 5 version, QuickTime is the only supported movie player. Movie and sound files regarding links and imports are handled in the same manner as Acrobat 4–compatible files.

For the Acrobat 6 version, layers are preserved in the exported PDF and both movies and sounds may be embedded within the exported PDF. If you save with Acrobat 6 compatibility, users need an Acrobat 6 or greater viewer. Embedded movies and sounds won't play when viewing PDFs in viewers earlier than version 6.

The Standard option lets you choose to convert the document to a Portable Document Format Exchange (PDF/X) compliant format. The options include None, PDF/X-1a, and PDF/x-3.

Cross-Reference   For more information on PDF/X files, see Chapter 35.

The Embed Page Thumbnails option creates and embeds thumbnail previews of each page. These thumbnails display in the Pages pane in Acrobat. Including embedded thumbnails increases the file size, but makes the various pages easier to find. With Acrobat viewers version 5 and greater, thumbnails are created on-the-fly in Acrobat. Therefore, embedding thumbnails is not needed when these viewers are used.

The View PDF after Exporting option opens the exported PDF file in Acrobat after the exporting process is finished.

The Optimize for Fast Web View option takes steps to reduce the overall file size by optimizing all images to be viewed faster in a Web browser.

The Create Acrobat Layers option is only active if Acrobat version 6 is selected in the Compatibility field. This option converts all InDesign layers into Acrobat layers. The default layer view in InDesign becomes the default view in Acrobat. If layers are hidden in InDesign, they're converted to Adobe PDF Layers and appear hidden in Acrobat. The Layers pane in Acrobat provides options for showing and hiding layers.

Note   You can also export Adobe Illustrator files to PDF preserving layers created in Illustrator.

The Include section of the General panel lets you select which items, including interactive items, to include in the exported PDF. Your options include Bookmarks, Hyperlinks, Non-Printing Objects, Visible Guides and Baseline Grids, eBook Tags, and Interactive Elements. The Interactive Elements option includes all movies, sounds, and buttons that have been added to the InDesign document.

The Multimedia field lets you choose to embed or link to the movie and sound files. The options include Use Object Settings, Link All, and Embed All. With all the settings selected, click the Export button to complete the export process. Figure 29-19 shows a sample exported PDF file opened and viewed in Acrobat.

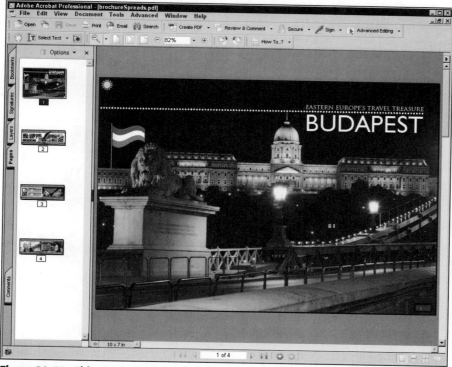

Figure 29-19: This exported PDF includes a hyperlink and button interactive elements.

Summary

✦ You can add various interactive elements including hyperlinks, bookmarks, buttons, and media files to InDesign documents.

✦ Hyperlinks can link to pages or text anchors within the document or to a URL.

✦ Bookmarks in an InDesign document may link to pages, text anchors, or URLs. These bookmarks show up in the Bookmarks tab within Acrobat.

✦ You can endow buttons with events and behaviors that define a resulting action. This action occurs when a user performs an event such as a mouse-click or a mouse-rollover.

✦ You can add media files, including movies and sounds, to an InDesign document and select options for playing them.

✦ During the PDF export process, you can include or exclude interactive elements.

✦ ✦ ✦

Hosting Documents on the Web

After you've completed the design for your Web site, the final step in the repurposing workflow is uploading Web content to an online server. But you must first obtain some server space from a hosting company and enter the server information within GoLive. You can then upload, download, or synchronize with the server. In addition, you can use GoLive to export the site to a local Web folder that an external Web program can use to upload the files.

PDF files offer another common way to present designs on the Web. PDF files may include links to other Web resources and if hosted using Adobe's Content Server can be made secure. eBooks provide yet another way to distribute designs.

Preparing to Publish a Web Site

One of the key advantages of GoLive is that it's a complete Web-authoring and Web-publishing solution: It's used to design and create Web sites and also to publish those sites to a Web server. The first step in publishing Web sites is to configure GoLive so that it can access to the Internet and locate the Web servers. GoLive actually provides two ways to upload files to a Web server:

✦ You can use the Publish Server tab of the site window.

✦ You can use a File Browser opened with the File ➪ Connect to FTP/WebDAV menu command.

Setting up Internet access

The steps to configure GoLive so that it can publish to a Web site are simple, but much of the information required to configure the system comes from the Internet Service Provider (ISP) that you're using to host your site. Each ISP has different required settings, but you must follow some general guidelines.

The ISP settings within GoLive are located within the Internet panel of the Preferences dialog box, which is accessed by choosing GoLive/Edit ➪ Preferences (⌘/Ctrl+K). This panel, shown in Figure 30-1, lets you specify an FTP proxy or an HTTP proxy.

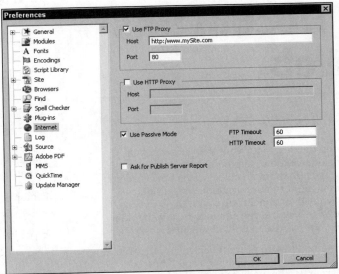

Figure 30-1: The Internet panel of the Preferences dialog box

Select the Use FTP Proxy or the Use HTTP Proxy option, and enter the host URL and its port number. Your ISP can provide you with this information.

Note   Internet connections use the TCP/IP network protocols. Before you can connect to the Internet, you need to set up this networking protocol for your system.

FTP versus HTTP

Two different protocols are commonly used to transferring files on the Internet—File Transfer Protocol (FTP) and Hypertext Transfer Protocol (HTTP). FTP sites are structured like a file system with subfolders within subfolders. Understanding this directory structure helps you place files in the correct location. Web browsers use HTTP to retrieve Web pages. HTTP uses a Universal Resource Locator (URL) to specify the location of files. The URLs are the Web addresses that request Web pages and resources.

Another key difference between the FTP and HTTP protocols is that FTP is a connection-oriented protocol and HTTP is a connectionless protocol. When you establish a connection to an FTP, the connection remains open until you send a command to disconnect it. This limits the number of concurrent connections that you make to a server (typically to 250). When you make any requests using HTTP, the request is fulfilled and the connection is immediately released. By not holding the connection open, many HTTP requests are handled simultaneously. This can make uploading a large number of files much slower on HTTP than on FTP, because connections need to be reestablished for every file.

Another difference is the port numbers that the two protocols typically use. The Web server uses port numbers to identify the different protocols. The default port number for HTTP requests is typically 80, and the default port number for FTP requests is typically 21, but check with your ISP to confirm these port numbers.

Some Web servers require that you connect using Passive mode, especially if the Web server uses a firewall. If your ISP specifies this, enable the Use Passive Mode option. The Timeout values are the amount of time in seconds that GoLive keeps trying to connect before canceling the connection.

Note If you're having trouble connecting to a server, the server may be offline.

The Publish Server Report option causes a text report to be generated every time you connect to the server. This report includes information about every file uploaded or modified.

Specifying a publish server

Once you connect to the Internet, you can browse Web pages and get e-mail using your system. The next step in the publishing workflow for GoLive is locating the Web server to which you want to publish. GoLive can keep track of several different Web servers using its Edit Publish Server dialog box, shown in Figure 30-2. Open this dialog box by choosing GoLive ➪ Server for Macintosh or Edit ➪ Server for Windows.

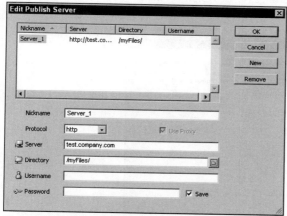

Figure 30-2: The Edit Publish Server dialog box holds Web server information.

To enter the information for a new server, click the New button. You need to provide the following information:

✦ **Nickname:** This is the common name that appears in the Publish Server tab. The available protocols for transferring the files are File, FTP, and HTTP. The File option let you publish your Web pages to a local directory. For Web servers, whether you should select FTP or HTTP depends on the type of Web server to which you're uploading the files. Some Web servers require a specific transfer protocol. Check with your ISP to find out which one is required in your situation.

✦ **Server:** You type the URL for the Web server here.

✦ **Directory:** This field lets you specify a directory on the Web server that is opened when the connection is made. If you're connected to the Internet, you can click the browse button (to the right of the Directory field) to see the Web server's directory structure.

✦ **Username:** Most servers also require a username and password.

✦ **Save option:** You click this check box to save the password along with the server information so you don't need to type it every time you connect to the server.

Caution

If you enable the Save option, then anyone who sits at your computer has access to your hosted Web files. For security reasons, it's best *not* to enable the Save option and, instead, type in your password every time. Also, as an additional security feature, you should regularly change Web server passwords.

Adding and configuring sites

With several Web servers added to the Publish Server dialog box, you can select which one to use for a given site using the Site Settings dialog box, shown in Figure 30-3. With the site window selected, choose Site ➪ Settings (⌘/Ctrl+Shift+Y) menu command to open the Site Settings dialog box.

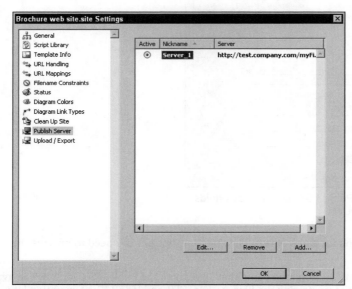

Figure 30-3: The Site Settings dialog box has all the site settings.

Click on the Publish Server option in the left pane, and then click on the Add button. The Publish Server dialog box opens; here, you can select the Web server that you want to use. Clicking OK adds the server to the Site Settings dialog box.

The Site Settings dialog box allows you to add several different servers for a single site. However, you can only select one as the active Web server.

The Site Settings dialog box also includes a panel of options for specifying how files are uploaded or exported. In the Site Settings dialog box, opened by choosing Site ⇨ Settings, select the Upload/Export panel from the list on the right. The Upload/Export panel, shown in Figure 30-4, appears. By enabling the Site Specific Settings, you can configure the upload options for the selected site.

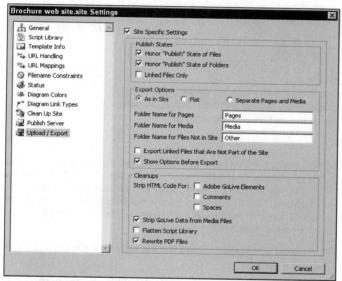

Figure 30-4: The Site Settings dialog box allows you to configure upload options.

If you want to configure the upload and export options for all sites, you find the same settings in the Preferences dialog box (Figure 30-5), which you access by choosing GoLive ⇨ Preferences (Mac) or GoLive ⇨ Edit ⇨ Preferences (Windows). Both the Site Setting dialog box and the Preference dialog box have the following configuration options.

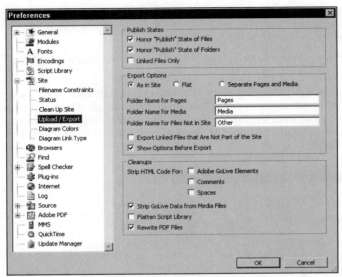

Figure 30-5: The Preferences dialog box also includes an Upload/Export panel.

✦ **Publish States:** Each file and/or folder can have an assigned publish state. You can designate this state as Always, Never, or If Referenced in the Inspector palette when you select a file or folder in the site window. These states are used in the Upload/Export panel with the Honor Publish State of Files and Honor Publish State of Folders options. With these options, you can select the designated states when uploading files. There is also an option to include linked files only.

✦ **Export Options:** This section lets you configure the file structure for the site as it's exported with the following options:

   • **As in Site:** Copies the exact file structure in the local file system to the Web server.

   • **Flat:** Copies all files in the site to a single root directory on the Web server.

   • **Separate Pages and Media:** Copies the pages and media files into separate subfolders as indicated by the Folder Name for Pages and Folder Name for Media fields.

   • **Folder options:** You can also create a separate folder for other files that are uploaded — files that aren't pages or media.

   • **Export Linked Files that Are Not Part of the Site:** Linked files that aren't part of the site typically aren't uploaded with the site, but you can export these files along with the site by enabling this option.

   • **Show Options Before Export:** Displays these settings every time you choose File ➪ Export, so you can change the folder names as needed.

Cross-Reference

Linking Web pages is handled in the HTML code. However, file linking between PDF documents is handled within the PDFs. For information on how to link PDF documents, see the "Hosting PDF Documents" section, later in this chapter.

✦ **Cleanups:** This section optimizes your Web pages:

  • **Strip HTML Code:** By stripping HTML code for Adobe GoLive elements, comments, and spaces, you reduce your Web page's the file size. This makes decreases download time.

  • **Strip GoLive Data from Media Files:** This strips GoLive data from media files to reduce their file size. This mainly applies to Smart Objects that include references to open the media files in Photoshop, Illustrator, or Acrobat.

Caution

Stripping the GoLive elements out of Web pages makes your pages uneditable in GoLive; stripping comments and spaces makes it difficult to understand the HTML code when viewed on the Web server. If you select any of these cleanup options, be careful not to download the file over the top of the local file, or it hinders your ability to make changes in GoLive.

  • **Flatten Script Library:** Removes all GoLive information from any scripts that are part of the site.

  • **Rewrite PDF Files:** This likewise optimizes any PDF files.

Publishing a Web Site Using GoLive

After you configure your system to connect to a Web server, the actions involved in publishing a site are rather simple. GoLive provides two methods for actually uploading the Web-site files to the Web server. One method uses the Publish Server tab and the other uses a File Browser.

Connecting to a server

Before you can view a Web site on the Internet, you must transfer all the files that make up the site to the Web server. The Web server then presents the files to the user's browser upon request. You accomplish the action of moving these files using the Publish Server tab. With the site window opened in GoLive, choose Site ➪ Publish Server ➪ Connect. Once connected, the server URL or file path displays at the top of the right pane of the site window and all the uploaded files are listed, as shown in Figure 30-6.

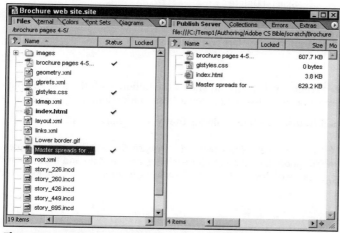

Figure 30-6: When you establish a connection to the server, files display.

If GoLive has any trouble connecting to the server, a warning dialog box appears with information on the problems that were encountered.

Uploading, downloading, and synchronizing files

After connecting, you can upload, download, or synchronize files, depending on your situation. You upload and download files using the Upload dialog box. You synchronize files using the Synchronize dialog box. With both boxes, if you select a file in the Site column, information about the file is displayed. Icons to the right of the site filenames indicate whether a file is to be skipped, uploaded, downloaded, or deleted.

✦ **Uploading files:** You can upload all the files that are part of a site by choosing Site ➪ Publish Server ➪ Upload All. This opens the Upload dialog box (Figure 30-7), where you can confirm all the files you want to upload. When you click OK, a dialog box appears and lists the number of items to upload. The upload dialog box as two check boxes:

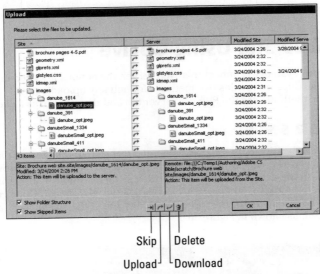

Figure 30-7: The Upload dialog box lets you confirm which files to upload.

- **Show Folder Structure:** This option shows the folders with the files to upload. When disabled, you see a list of files regardless of location.

- **Show Skipped Items:** This hides all files that you've marked as Skip.

Note   When you upload files to the Web server using the Publish Server tab, GoLive copies to the server the last modification date and time for each file, not the date and time when the files were uploaded. Because of this, the local files may be synchronized with the files on the Web server.

Once you upload an entire site, you can selectively upload certain files by choosing Site ➪ Publish Server ➪ Upload Selection. Alternatively, you can upload only those items that you've modified since the upload by choosing Site ➪ Publish Server ➪ Upload Modified Files. This command causes the Upload dialog box to appear, but the Upload Selection menu command does not. You may also manually copy files to the Web server from the site window by dragging and dropping them from the left pane to the right pane.

✦ **Downloading Files:** Choosing Site ➪ Publish Server also offers several commands for download files from the Web server to your local file system. These menu commands include Download All, Download Selection, and Download Newer. Using both the Download All and Download Newer menu commands opens the Download dialog box, which is identical to the Upload dialog box, except all files or those files with a newer modification date on the Web server are marked for download.

✦ **Synchronizing Files:** Choose Site ➪ Publish Server ➪ Synchronize uploads and downloads files at the same time. The Synchronization dialog box — another version of the Upload and Download dialog box opens. All local files with a newer modification date and time are marked for upload, and all Web server files with a newer modification date and time are marked for download. If you've changed a file on both the local file system and the Web server, a yellow triangular Synchronization Conflict icon appears, as shown in Figure 30-8, allowing you to mark these files for upload or download. If you want to simply synch the modification dates instead of moving files, you can choose Site ➪ Publish Server ➪ Sync Modification Times All or Sync Modification Times Selected.

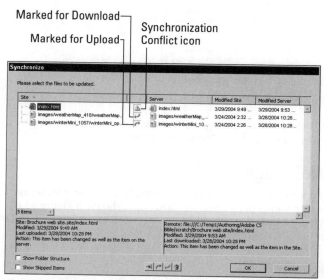

Figure 30-8: The Synchronize dialog box lets you upload and download files simultaneously.

Using the File Browser to transfer files

If you don't need to transfer the entire site or just need to transfer files that have changed, you can open a File Browser within GoLive to view all the files on the Web server. Then using drag and drop, you can upload or download files.

To open the File Browser window, shown in Figure 30-9, choose File ➪ Connect to FTP/WebDAV. From the Servers field at the top of the window, you can select the server to which that you want to connect. To open the Publish Servers dialog box, click the Edit Servers button. You may also browse the local file system with the Browse Local button. This opens a simple file dialog box where you can browse to a local directory. The Connect button connects to the selected server.

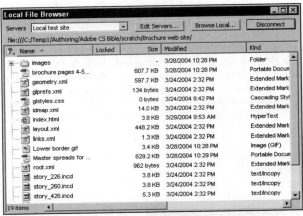

Figure 30-9: The File Browser dialog box lets you view files on the Web server.

After you're connected to a Web server or to a local directory, you can transfer files by dragging them from the File Browser to the site window or vice versa.

Downloading a Web page

Choosing File ➪ Download Page (Shift+⌘/Ctrl+O), you can specify a URL for a Web page to download into GoLive. This command opens a simple dialog box, shown in Figure 30-10, where you can specify a Web page URL. If your system is connected to the Internet, GoLive then retrieves the Web page.

Figure 30-10: The Download Page dialog box lets you enter a Web page's URL.

STEPS: Publishing a Web Site

1. **Open a Web site in GoLive.** Within GoLive, choose File ➪ Open and open a Web site. With the Web site open, select the site window.

2. **Adding a Publish Server.** Choose Site ➪ Settings to open the Settings dialog box for this site, as shown in Figure 30-11. Click on the Publish Server panel in the right pane. Then click Add.

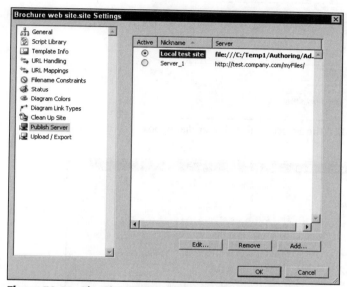

Figure 30-11: The Site Settings dialog box lets you select a server.

3. **Specifying the Publish Server settings.** In the Publish Server dialog box that opens, shown in Figure 30-12, click New. Type a nickname for the server, select a protocol, and enter the server's URL and directory. Next, enter the username and password for the server. Uncheck the Save option for added security and click OK. Then select the server in the Site Settings dialog box.

4. **Enable the Upload options.** In the Site Settings dialog box, select the Upload/Export panel in the right pane to display the Upload/Export panel, shown in Figure 30-13. Enable the Site Specific Settings option. Select the Honor Publish State of Files and Honor Publish State of Folders options. Then in the Cleanups section, enable all the Strip HTML Code options to reduce the file sizes of the uploaded files. Click OK to close the Site Settings dialog box.

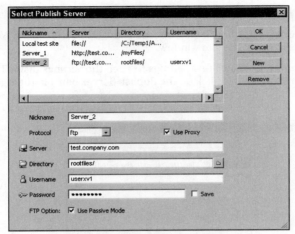

Figure 30-12: The Select Publish Server dialog box

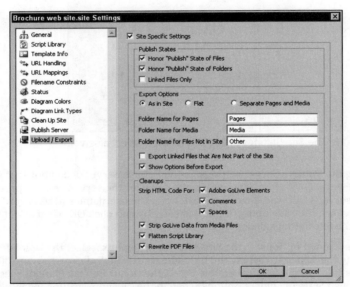

Figure 30-13: The Upload/Export panel of the Site Settings dialog box

5. **Connect to the Web server.** Make sure you're connected to the Internet and choose Site ➪ Publish Server ➪ Connect. GoLive connects to the Web server using the settings you specified. Because the Save Password option was disabled, a Connect to Server dialog box (Figure 30-14) appears; here, you can enter the username and password needed to log on to the Web server.

Figure 30-14: The Connect to Server dialog box

6. **Upload site files.** After connecting to the Web server, the files on the Web server display in the right pane of the site window. Choose Site ➪ Publish Server ➪ Upload All. The Upload dialog box (Figure 30-15) appears with all files marked from upload. Click OK to begin the uploading. A dialog box appears listing a count of the number of items that were uploaded.

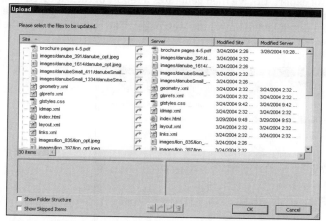

Figure 30-15: The Upload dialog box lists files you want to upload.

7. **Verify the site online.** After the files upload, you can check the Web site online by entering the URL for the Web server in a browser.

Exporting a Web Site

If you have difficulty connecting or uploading files to a Web server using GoLive, you can always export the files to a local directory and then upload the directory using an external file-transfer program. To export a site, select the site windows and choose File ➪ Export ➪ Site (⌘/Ctrl+E). If you enable the Show Options before Export option in the Upload/Export panel of the Preferences dialog box, the Export Site Options dialog box appears, shown in Figure 30-16.

Figure 30-16: The Export Site Options dialog box

After confirming the export options, a file dialog box opens where you can specify a folder name to which files will export. GoLive then generates a report of the exported site, as shown in Figure 30-17. This report lists all files that it couldn't find, that weren't part of the site, and that were exported but not linked to any of the Web pages. The report also lists the options you selected for the export process.

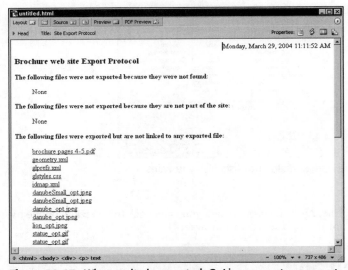

Figure 30-17: When a site is exported, GoLive generates a report.

Hosting PDF Documents

In the real world, many creative professionals do not handle Web-site designs and uploading files. Your work may involve the design of content that you ultimately deliver to your client; the client's own Web administration personnel may be responsible for uploading files and maintaining the Web site. If this is your workflow, you must provide documents to Web administration personnel complete with file links that are needed outside normal HTML coding.

Web pages are linked using HTML code, but PDF documents require file linking instructions within the PDF documents. For example, if you have a contents page viewed as a PDF document that you want to link to other PDF documents, you must create file links within the contents PDF page that link to other PDF documents. This process requires you to use Acrobat for file linking.

Another variable when viewing PDFs on the Web is how the browser and your operating system handle PDF documents. On Windows, you have more flexibility than you have on the Mac. Therefore, it is important to understand PDF Web viewing before you go about setting up file links.

Viewing PDFs in Web browsers

You have several ways to configure a Web browser for handling PDFs on Web servers. You can opt to view a PDF directly in an HTML file where the PDF appears as if it were actually created as HTML. You can save a PDF file to disk rather than view it from a Web connection, then later view it in an Acrobat viewer. You can view file outside the Web browser in an Acrobat viewer window, and you can also view a PDF file through the use of an Acrobat viewer directly inside a Web browser, which is called *inline viewing*. You'll immediately notice an inline view in your Web browser when the Acrobat tools appear below the browser tools. This form of PDF viewing unfortunately is only available on Windows in Acrobat Professional. Earlier versions of Acrobat viewers supported inline viewing on both the Mac and Windows.

You open a PDF in a Web browser the same way you would a file to view an HTML document. You specify a URL and filename to view the PDF directly in the browser or click on a Web link to open a URL where a PDF is hosted. For example, going to `www.client.com/file.pdf` displays the PDF page inside the browser window on Windows. The same URL link on the Mac opens the PDF document in the default Acrobat viewer.

Note   If you use Apple's Safari on the Mac, you may experience problems viewing PDF documents immediately in your Acrobat viewer. Safari can display a blank page in the Web browser, but the PDF downloads to your disk. You can view the PDF by opening it in Acrobat by choose File ➪ Open.

Inline viewing requires the proper configuration of components provided with the Acrobat installer CD and configuration of your Web browser. By default, viewer plug-ins are installed for Web browsers. Be certain to install your Web browser before you install Acrobat. If inline viewing is not the default when you view PDF files in your Web browser, you may need to configure the browser's helper applications. Be certain to review the applications in the browser preferences and select the viewer plug-in for handling PDFs.

PDF viewing on Windows

Adobe's first release of Acrobat Professional is much more compatible with Microsoft Internet Explorer running under Microsoft Windows when Web viewing. On Windows, you have tools and features not accessible to Mac users. On Windows, you can create PDF documents directly from within Explorer and open files in Internet Explorer easily with the Adobe PDF Explorer Bar.

To take advantage of the plug-ins that make inline viewing possible, you need to use Microsoft Internet Explorer version 5.0 or greater, Netscape Navigator version 7.0 or greater, or America Online 6.0 or greater. Users of earlier versions of Web browsers will find PDF viewing problematic, so be certain to upgrade your browser to one of the preceding versions and install Acrobat after your browser installation.

If your favorite browser is one other than Explorer, you may want to dedicate Explorer to PDF viewing and use your other browser for all other Web viewing. This is not a personal preference, but simply a reflection of the fact that Adobe has added much more functionality with Explorer than with other browsers.

PDF viewing on the Macintosh

As of this writing, support for Web viewing on the Macintosh is much more limited than viewing PDFs in Web browsers on Windows. If you use Apple's Safari and PDFs appear to download but don't display properly in an Acrobat viewer, click the Save Task button and save the downloaded file to disk. If you cannot find the PDF that downloads to disk or for some reason the download did not occur, you can often open the PDF directly in an Acrobat viewer after saving the file.

Microsoft Internet Explorer users can view PDFs only in Acrobat viewers. When you navigate to a URL and open a PDF document, the PDF opens in the current open Acrobat viewer or your default viewer launches. If, for example, you have Adobe Reader and Acrobat Professional on your computer and you open Adobe Reader, you view PDFs Reader when you navigate to a PDF from within Internet Explorer. If no Acrobat viewer opens and your default viewer is Acrobat Professional, Acrobat Professional launches when you navigate to a PDF. In essence, both your Web browser and your Acrobat viewer open simultaneously.

Regardless of whether you use Safari or Microsoft Internet Explorer, the first release of Acrobat 6.0 does not support inline viewing for either browser. This is a disadvantage for Mac users who want to create seamless file links that take the user between PDFs and HTML documents.

Users of earlier versions of Acrobat may attempt to adjust Internet Explorer preferences for viewing PDFs. If you open the Edit File Helper dialog box in Internet Explorer and try to change the viewing options for how to handle a PDF document, as shown in Figure 30-18, PDFs open in your Acrobat viewer regardless of what setting you choose. Don't bother trying to adjust the preferences, because the only option you have is to view a PDF in an Acrobat viewer.

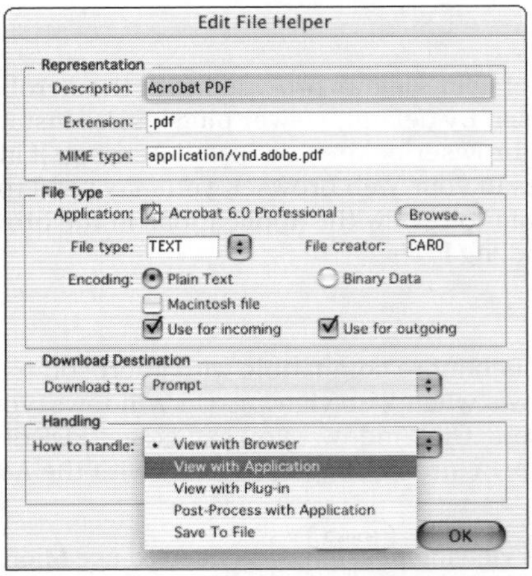

Figure 30-18: PDFs are opened only in Acrobat viewers on the Mac.

If you are a Mac user, visit the Adobe Web site regularly to see if a maintenance upgrade is available for download. Web-viewing PDFs is a limitation in the first release of Acrobat Professional for Mac users, so you can expect more support with future upgrades. If, at the time you purchase this book, you find that inline viewing is supported on the Mac, you should be able to take advantage of the features we discuss in this chapter related to viewing PDFs inside Web browsers.

Setting Web-viewing preferences (Windows)

On Windows, rather than setting preferences in your Web browser, you make preference choices for Web-viewing PDFs from within Acrobat viewers; to change preferences, choose Edit ⇨ Preferences. In the Preferences dialog box, select Internet in the left pane. The viewing preferences appear in the right pane, as shown in Figure 30-19.

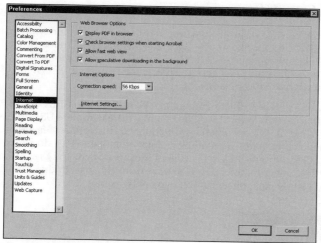

Figure 30-19: The Internet panel in the Preferences dialog box

Options for handling PDFs on Web sites with Acrobat viewers include the following:

✦ **Display PDF in Browser:** When enabled, PDFs viewed on Web sites display as inline views in browser applications. If disabled, PDFs display in Acrobat viewers. The default Acrobat viewer installed on your computer opens if you have no viewer currently open. The target document appears in the Acrobat viewer Document pane.

✦ **Check Browser Settings When Starting Acrobat:** Each time you launch an Acrobat viewer, your default browser settings are checked against the viewer application. If you did not configure your default browser to use the Acrobat viewer, a dialog box opens asking whether you want to set the configuration to use Acrobat with the default Web browser.

✦ **Allow Fast Web View:** This option speeds up viewing PDFs on Web servers. When enabled, a single page downloads to your computer and shows how you set your preferences — in the browser window or in an Acrobat viewer window. As you scroll pages in a PDF document, each new page downloads when the page is loaded in the Document pane. If disabled, the entire PDF document downloads to your computer before the first page appears in the browser window or the Acrobat Document pane.

✦ **Allow Speculative Downloading in the Background:** If you select the preceding Allow Fast Web View option, and want to continue downloading multiple-page PDF documents, check this box. As you view a page, the remaining pages continue to download until the complete PDF downloads from a Web site.

✦ **Connection Speed:** Select the speed of your Internet connection from the pull-down menu choices. This setting applies to viewing Web pages, but it also influences the speed selection for viewing multimedia.

✦ **Internet Settings:** If you click on the Internet Settings button, the Internet Properties dialog box opens. In the Internet Properties dialog box, you can make choices for configuring your Internet connection, choosing default applications for e-mail, making security-settings choices, setting privacy attributes, and other such system-level configurations.

Working with Web links

Web links to PDFs hosted on Web sites occur from within HTML documents and from within PDF files. If you're using an HTML editor like Adobe GoLive or writing HTML code, you create Web links the same as you link to Web pages. A PDF Web link in HTML might look like `http://www.client.com/brochure.pdf` — where the link is made to the PDF instead of a document that ends with an `.htm` or `.html` extension.

Web addresses contained in the text of a PDF document can be hot links to URLs where PDFs are hosted. To make a link from text functional, you must supply the complete URL address in the text, including `http://`. Text in PDF documents with complete URL addresses are converted to Web links via a menu command. To create Web links from text in PDF documents, choose Advanced ➪ Links ➪ Create from URLs in Document. Acrobat opens the Create Web Links dialog box (Figure 30-20). Select All to create Web links from all pages in the PDF. The From button enables you to supply page ranges in the two field boxes.

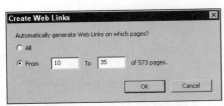

Figure 30-20: The Create Web Links dialog box

Acrobat can also globally remove Web links from all pages or a specified page range. To remove Web links, choose Advanced ➪ Links ➪ Remove All Links from Document. The same options are available in the Remove Web Links dialog box as those found in the Create Web Links dialog box.

Tip You can only create Web links from text that you have properly identified in the text of the PDF file. To add a Web link, you can easily create the text in Acrobat without returning to the authoring program. Select the TouchUp Text tool from the Advanced Editing toolbar. Hold down the Option/Ctrl key and click. The text cursor blinks where you click and is ready for you to add new text on the page. Type the URL for the Web link and deselect the text by selecting the Hand tool, and then click in the Document pane. Choose Advanced ➪ Links ➪ Create from URLs in Document. Acrobat creates the Web link from the URL you added to the document.

Adding Web links to multiple pages

You may have documents where you need to create Web links across multiple pages. An example of this is a repurposed document whose original design was created for output to prepress, then later downsampled and hosted on a Web site. In the original design, you might have a Web link on the cover page. But for the Web-hosted document, you may want to create a Web link to an order form or your home page on each page in the brochure document. Where the same URL is specified on each page and the location of the Web link is the same on every page, you can create the Web links in Acrobat after the PDF has been sampled for Web display. The following steps outline a procedure for creating Web links on multiple pages for similar designs or legacy files that don't have Web addresses added in the original authoring application document before a PDF has been created:

STEPS: Creating Web Links on Multiple PDF Pages

1. **Add a header/footer to a multipage PDF document.** Open the file where you want to add the Web links and choose Document ➪ Add Headers & Footers. In the Add Headers & Footers dialog box, create a header or footer and set the type size, the alignment, and the offset distance desired. In this example, we added a header, center aligned, used Arial 8-point text, and set the bottom offset to 0.1 inch, as shown in Figure 30-21. *Note:* Be sure to add the complete URL in the Insert Custom Text field box.

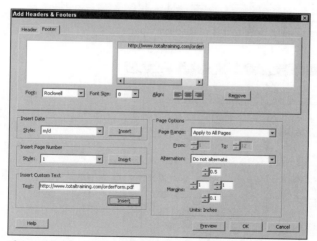

Figure 30-21: Adding the URL text in the Insert Custom Text field box

2. **Preview the header/footer.** Click Preview in the Add Headers & Footers dialog box. A preview of the text placement appears in the Preview dialog box, as shown in Figure 30-22.

3. **Embed the font.** Click OK in the Add Headers & Footers dialog box. Select the TouchUp Text tool in the Toolbar Well and select the text added as a header or footer on the first page in the PDF document. Open a context menu and select Properties. In the TouchUp Properties dialog box, check the boxes for Embed and Subset (Figure 30-23). Click Close after checking the boxes.

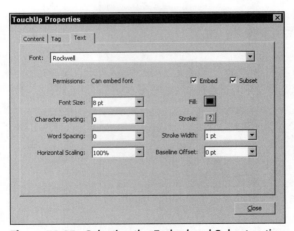

Text added
in Headers
and Footers

Figure 30-22: Previewing how text is placed on a page

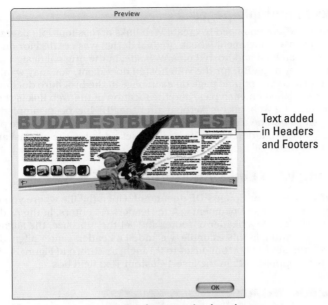

Figure 30-23: Selecting the Embed and Subset options

4. **Create URL links.** Choose Advanced ➪ Links ➪ Create from URLs in Document. Select the All radio button in the Create Web Links dialog box and click OK. When you return to the Document pane and place the Hand tool cursor over a Web link, a tooltip shows the URL, as shown in Figure 30-24.

Figure 30-24: The Hand cursor displays the URL in a tooltip.

Tip
If you want Web links to appear rotated along the left or right side of your PDF document, choose Document ⇨ Pages ⇨ Rotate Pages. Add a header or footer as described in the preceding steps, and create the Web links described in Step 4. Choose Document ⇨ Pages ⇨ Rotate Pages and select the rotation option that turns the pages back to the original view. Save the document, and the Web links are positioned vertically on each page.

Adding Web links from form fields

The Add Headers & Footers dialog box gives you limited control of font attributes for type. For example, to make your Web links appear in a color that users can easily see, you can't specify font colors for headers and footers. However, when assigning font attributes, you can use form fields and set the font attributes in the form-field appearance properties.

To create Web links from form fields:

1. **Select the Text Field tool in the Forms toolbar.** Create a form field rectangle at the location on a page where you want the link to appear. By default, the Text Field Properties dialog box opens.

2. **Click on the Appearance tab.** Select the font type, size, and color, as shown in Figure 30-25.

3. **Click on the General tab.** Check the box for Read Only. Click Close to close the Text Field Properties dialog box. You return to the Document Pane.

4. **Select the Hand tool and add the URL text to the field.** To duplicate the field on the remaining pages in your document, select the Select Object tool or the Text Field tool and click on the field to select it. Open a context menu and select Duplicate. In the Duplicate dialog box, enter the page range by clicking the From radio button and supplying the From and To page ranges. If you create the field on page 1 in the document and want to duplicate the field on the remaining pages, enter **2** in the From field box and the last page number in the To field box. In Figure 30-26, we duplicated a field from page 2 to page 12.

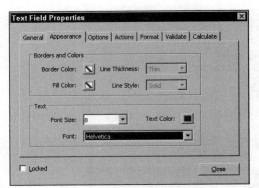

Figure 30-25: Setting the Appearance properties

Figure 30-26: Enter the page range in the Duplicate Field dialog box.

5. **Choose Advanced ➪ Links ➪ Create from URLs in Document.** Add the page range for all form fields including the first field you created. A link rectangle is placed over the form field rectangle with a link to the URL specified within the text field.

Viewing Web links

Depending on how you have your Internet preferences set for Web browser options, clicking on a URL link in Acrobat or in your Web browser either displays the PDF in the browser window or in an Acrobat viewer window. If the link is made to an HTML page, and the preferences are set to view the Web link in an Acrobat viewer, the Web page is converted to PDF with Web Capture. If you're using Adobe Reader, the PDF displays in the Web browser regardless of how you set your viewing preferences because Adobe Reader cannot convert Web pages to PDF.

For an alternate view of where URL links are viewed, you can press the Option/Ctrl key down when clicking on a link. If the preference settings are enabled for viewing links in a Web browser, using the modifier key displays the link in your Acrobat viewer and vice versa.

Controlling links to view behavior

By default, when you click on a URL link to a PDF document, whether from within your Web browser or from within Acrobat, the resulting view takes you to the same view established in your Initial View properties. Therefore, if your Initial View properties are set to Page Only, Single Page, Fit Page, and Page Number 1, the PDF document opens in the Web browser according to these settings as you would view the file in Acrobat.

Cross-Reference

For more information on setting initial views in PDF documents, see Chapter 26.

When you create links to open different documents and different pages in a PDF file, the links are often unusable when you're viewing PDFs in Web browsers. A link, for example, that opens a secondary PDF won't work in a Web browser unless you modify the link properties and link to the URL where the destination document resides. The Web browser needs URL links to open secondary files. Inasmuch as you may have all links working well for CD-ROM distribution, you need to make some adjustments before you can host the PDF documents with useable links on Web servers.

As an example, if you want to open page 2 in a PDF file on a Web server, you create a link in one document, direct the link to the URL where the PDF is hosted, and instruct the Web browser or Acrobat viewer to open page 2. To create the link, use either the Link tool or a form-field button and enter the following code in an Open Web Link action:

```
http://www.budapesttourism.com/travelbrochure.pdf#page=2
```

In this example, the #page=2 text following the PDF filename is the trigger to open page 2. In addition to accessing user-specified pages, you can also control viewing behavior for page layouts, page views, zooms, linking to destinations, and a host of other attributes you assign to the Open Web Link action. Some examples of the code to use following the PDF document name in URL links include the following:

- ✦ **Zoom changes:** #zoom=50, #zoom=125, #zoom=200
- ✦ **Fit Page view:** #view=Fit
- ✦ **Destinations:** #nameddest=Section1
- ✦ **Open Bookmarks palette:** #pagemode:bookmarks
- ✦ **Open Pages palette:** #pagemode=thumbs
- ✦ **Collapsing palettes:** #pagemode=none
- ✦ **Combining viewing options:** #page=3&pagemode=bookmarks&zoom=125

The preceding are some examples for controlling view options when opening PDFs in Web browsers. As a creative professional, you may be responsible for PDF file linking when designing or repurposing documents for Web hosting. For each item, be aware that you need to use the complete URL address and add one of these options following the location where the PDF document is hosted. Using the pagemode example, the complete open action URL might look like this: http://www.clinet.com/file.pdf#pagemode=bookmarks.

Securing File Content on Web Servers

You may serve clients who want to create additional revenue streams by selling content on Web servers. Institutions, organizations, and business organizations may have protected content that they want to include as part of their product offerings. Your job may be to create the content and also offer your clients alternatives to generate additional revenue through the sale of the content you help them create.

The Adobe Creative Suite offers you a collection of tools that, in part, provides you the necessary means for creating content that your clients can protect and distribute. You use tools like Illustrator, Photoshop, and InDesign for file creation; GoLive for managing Web sites for eCommerce; and Acrobat as your distribution vehicle. In addition to the Creative Suite, Adobe offers other products to help you further protect content from unauthorized distribution.

Suppose you create content in the form of manuals, books, articles, or guides that your client wants to sell on an eCommerce Web site. You can create the document using the CS applications, convert to PDF, and protect the PDF from being edited. However, none of the CS applications alone can prevent the end user from distributing PDFs. Any other user with a password to open a document or open a nonsecure PDF can view the file.

Through the use of Adobe's Content Server 3 software, you can add more security and prevent unauthorized distribution. The result is in the form of eBooks downloaded from a Web site and encrypted to the hardware device downloading the content. When an end user sends a copy of the content to another user, the other user cannot open the file. However, the recipient receives information related to the URL where the content can be purchased.

To guide your clients to the possibilities available with eBook creation and distribution, you should become familiar with the eBook tools in Acrobat. The Adobe Content Server 3 software is something you'll want to leave to the Web-administration people; point them to www.adobe.com/products/contentserver on Adobe's Web site where more information is available.

Getting started with eBooks

To become familiar with eBook acquisition and how eBooks are used with Acrobat, you can test the tools and eBook features with public-domain content on the Internet. Your first step is to set up an activation account. When you install Acrobat, you have an option for setting up an Activator Account for handling eBook borrowing and purchasing. If you elect to postpone activation, you can set up an account at any time by choosing Advanced ➪ eBook Web Services ➪ Adobe DRM Activator. In Adobe Reader, choose Tools ➪ eBook Web Services ➪ Adobe DRM Activator.

Your default Web browser launches and the activation page on Adobe's Web site appears in your browser window. If you have an existing account, you can click on a button for Activate and your account updates to include the eBook activation. If you haven't set up an account, you receive options for activating an account with Adobe Systems or with Microsoft.NET. Supply a username and password and you're taken to the activation page, where you click Activate to create your account with your new username and password. Activating an account either with Adobe Systems or Microsoft.NET is free.

Activating multiple devices

If you have an account on one computer and want to open eBooks on another computer, you must activate all devices. After setting up an account and logging on to Adobe's Web site, follow the on-screen information for activating your second device, and you're ready to view and manage eBooks on your other computer(s).

If you have a handheld device such as a Palm Pilot, you need to activate your account on it. To activate a Palm device, place the unit in its synchronization cradle and choose Advanced ➪ eBook Web Services ➪ Adobe DRM Activator. On the Adobe Web site, click on the Activate Palm OS Device button. You must activate the device before you can download eBooks designed to be used with Acrobat viewers. If you attempt to download an eBook without activation, Adobe's Web site and activation page opens in your Web browser where you can create an account. You can receive eBooks from other users who send you content via e-mails or downloads. If the file is encrypted with Adobe DRM (Digital Rights Management), again you're required to create an account and comply with the purchase requirements before gaining access to the content.

Adobe Content Server 3

The default Digital Rights Management (DRM) for eBooks viewed with Acrobat viewers is handled with Adobe's server-side software. The Adobe Content Server 3 enterprise solution is designed for content providers to encrypt and manage electronic content with the highest levels of security. You may not be concerned with the product, but you may want to point your client's Web-administration people to where more information can be found about the product.

Note Adobe partners such as FileOpen Systems, Authentica, SealMedia, and Docurights offer third-party solutions that legally use the Adobe Reader technology.

For enterprises, however, the mission is to protect against unauthorized distribution of products. With the Adobe Content Server 3 product or other third-party solutions you can protect documents and distribute them to users meeting requirements for distribution. If a user exchanges content with another user who has not obtained permission to access the content, the user is directed to the Web site where purchases are made.

Acquiring eBooks

After setting up your activation account, you're ready to download eBooks and store them on your Bookshelf—a feature built into all Acrobat viewers. You can test the activation and eBook download procedures by downloading sample eBooks free of charge from Adobe's Web site.

 To download an eBook, select the pull-down menu for the eBook Task button and select Get eBooks Online. Your Web browser launches and takes you to the Adobe eBook Mall. On the Web page, you find helpful information about purchasing eBooks and some sample books you can download without purchasing the content. From a pull-down menu, you can select the country where you live and download eBooks in other languages. The default location is for USA and Canadian users.

Click on a book to download, and a progress bar displays the download progress. When the download completes, you're prompted in a dialog box whether you want to read the downloaded book. Click OK and the book opens in your Acrobat viewer, as shown in Figure 30-27.

If you select No when asked whether you want to read an eBook, the downloaded material is stored on your Bookshelf. Depending on the borrowing timeframe, you can read the book at any time by opening your Bookshelf and double-clicking on the book you want to read. The Bookshelf is used to store all downloaded eBooks and any other PDF documents you want to organize and store in an easily accessible and organized manner. To open your Bookshelf, open the eBook Task button pull-down menu and select My Bookshelf or choose File ⇨ My Bookshelf. The Bookshelf opens as a floating window on top of the Document pane, as shown in Figure 30-28.

Obviously, acquiring eBooks in PDF format is not limited to downloads from the Adobe Systems Web site. The real value for you and your clients is to use the Adobe Content Server 3 software and create a site that distributes content.

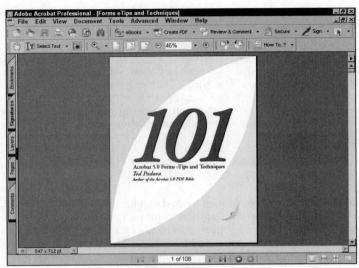

Figure 30-27: Selecting to open an eBook makes the eBook appear in the Document pane.

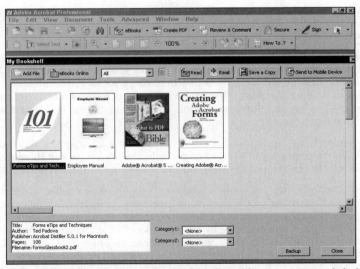

Figure 30-28: To view, organize, and read eBooks, open My Bookshelf.

Managing eBooks

You manage eBooks in the My Bookshelf window (refer to Figure 30-28). Downloading an eBook automatically adds the eBook to My Bookshelf with the most recent download appearing first in the default thumbnail list. In the Bookshelf window, you have several tools and commands to help you organize books, acquire new content, and create category listings for storing books according to preset or custom topics. The options contained in the My Bookshelf window include:

✦ **Add File:** The first button at the top-left corner of the My Bookshelf window enables you to add any PDF document to the Bookshelf. Click on Add and a dialog box opens where you navigate your hard drive and select a document to add to the list. Click Add File and the new acquisition is placed at the first position on the left side of the current thumbnail.

✦ **eBooks Online:** Click on the eBooks Online button and you're returned to the Adobe Web site eBook Mall in your Web browser.

✦ **Category Views:** The default is All. From the pull-down menu, you select which category you want to view on the Bookshelf. You can categorize each eBook with one of the preset categories created when you installed Acrobat or a custom category you create in the My Bookshelf window.

✦ **Views:** The two icons adjacent to the pull-down menu offer viewing options in the Bookshelf. By default, thumbnail views are shown in the list. Thumbnails are created from the first page in a document. If you select the second icon, the books are listed alphabetically by eBook titles.

✦ **Read:** To read a book, you can double-click on one of the books in the list or select an eBook and click on the Read button. When you read books, they open in the Acrobat Document pane hiding the Bookshelf window. To reopen the Bookshelf, select the pull-down menu command from the eBook Task button or choose File ➪ My Bookshelf.

✦ **Save a Copy:** Click Save a Copy and save a duplicate of a selected eBook. Be certain to click on the book you want to copy before clicking the Save button.

✦ **Send to Mobile Device:** This button is only installed when you install Adobe software for handheld devices. By default, the button is not installed with Acrobat. Click on the button if you install software to read PDFs on handheld devices and want to copy a document to your handheld device. Before copying an eBook to the device, you must activate your device for eBooks, as described earlier in this chapter.

✦ **Summary Window:** The window in the lower-left corner of the Bookshelf lists information relative to a selected document. Some information is derived from the Document Summary of the PDF file, and other information may include total pages in the book, filename, ISBN number, publisher, and so on.

✦ **Category:** There are two category lists. You apply a category by selecting a document and opening the pull-down menu for one of the categories. The document is assigned to one or two different categories. If you make selections from both pull-down menus, the book is categorized for two categories and appears when books are sorted for either category. When you return to the category views at the top of the window and select a category, only those documents specified for the respective category are shown in either the thumbnail list or the alpha list.

✦ **Time-Out:** If a book is borrowed, you see a tiny clock icon in the top-right corner on books in the Bookshelf. The books may be borrowed for limited time use. After reading a borrowed book, click on the clock icon and the Document Expiration dialog box opens, shown in Figure 30-29. You can view the information about the lending period or choose to return the book. If you select Return to Lender, the book is eliminated from your Bookshelf. If you click OK, the book remains on your Bookshelf until you return it, delete it, or refresh the Bookshelf.

Figure 30-29: The Document Expiration dialog box opens.

You have other options available to you in the My Bookshelf window. You can categorize books and view them in sorted categories. For many user purposes the acquisition of material from your clients may not be so abundant that there would be a need to categorize the books. However, if your client is a publisher and a given user's acquisitions are many, you'll want to become familiar with the various organization tools contained in My Bookshelf.

Keep in mind that the eBook features in Acrobat are not necessarily related to eBooks in a traditional sense. Your clients may distribute any kind of content that can ultimately be converted to PDF including documents with multimedia. By guiding your clients to some of the Web hosting tools available from Adobe Systems, you may find alternatives not available with any other kind of solution.

Summary

✦ To upload a Web site, you must configure GoLive by entering the server information in the Site Settings dialog box, which includes settings for uploading, exporting, and cleaning up files.

✦ After configure and connect to the Web server, you can see the files on the Web server in the site window.

✦ You can use the Publish Server tab in the site window to upload, download, or synchronize files between the local file system and the Web server.

✦ You can also use the File Browser to transfer files between the local file system and the Web server.

✦ Choose File ➪ Export ➪ Site to export to a local folder all the files that make up a site.

✦ Creating links between Acrobat PDF documents requires editing in PDF files and not through HTML programming.

✦ On Windows, you view PDFs as inline views where documents appear within the browser window. On the Mac, all PDF viewing from Web-hosted documents is handled in Acrobat viewers.

✦ Adobe Content Server 3 software and the eBook tools in Acrobat protect content against unauthorized distribution. For clients who sell content on the Web, Adobe Systems offer one solution for creating new revenue streams.

✦   ✦   ✦

Replicating CD-ROMs

Publishing creative works was once entirely dominated by print publishing. Today, you have a number of choices for publishing design works. Print is still a large market, but your clients may want files posted on Web sites or distributed on CDs. Not only is CD-ROM distribution much less expensive than distribution of printed documents, but with CD-ROMs you can also include multimedia clips as part of your distributed collection. The content for your CD-ROM documents may include designs originally created for print, multimedia documents, Web documents, or other kinds of files where you can effectively display artwork.

Within the Creative Suite, you have tools that provide a simple but sophisticated means of creating files for distribution. When you need to organize files on your CDs, you can choose the Acrobat PDF file format and guarantee that anyone working on either Windows or Mac can see your files with complete document integrity, such as proper font displays and embedded images. In this chapter, you learn how to prepare PDF files for distribution on CD-ROMs.

Preparing PDF Documents

PDF is an ideal format for distributing files because you can freely distribute the Adobe Reader installer software on the CD-ROM and make the most recent version easily accessible to your client's customers. As long as you distribute the licensing information for Acrobat, Adobe Systems grants you permission to distribute the Adobe Reader installer for Windows and Mac.

The PDF format is further beneficial in that the PDFs you produce can have all the type fonts, images, and links contained in the PDFs and displayed as you want the end user to view the files.

Cross-Reference Font embedding presumes you're using fonts that have licensing permissions granted for embedding fonts. For more information on fonts and font embedding, see Chapter 13.

Obviously your first step is to produce PDF documents from designs you create in other CS applications. If you designed pieces for print, you'll want to repurpose the print documents to a more suitable file for viewing from CD-ROM sources. If you include non–Adobe CS documents, you'll need to produce PDFs from other applications.

Cross-Reference
There are many different ways to create PDFs from other programs, depending on the program and the level of support within Acrobat Professional for PDF creation. A description of the number of different programs and the ways PDFs are created from typical authoring applications is beyond the scope of this book. For a detailed look at PDF creation from the most popular computer programs, look at the *Adobe Acrobat 6 PDF Bible* (published by Wiley).

Creating PDFs from Adobe Illustrator

Adobe Illustrator, like other Adobe programs, is built on core PDF technology. In past years, the Adobe Illustrator development team has traditionally developed the PDF specification. You find more compatibility between PDF documents and Adobe Illustrator than any other program. Illustrator can open PDFs and often edit all the objects and type. PDFs imported in any other program always come in to the program as grouped objects, preventing you from editing the file.

When creating PDF files from Adobe Illustrator, you have three options:

✦ **You can save the Illustrator document as a PDF file from the Save or Save As dialog box**. As a rule, you'll always want to use the Save or Save As command and save as a PDF document when creating PDF files from Adobe Illustrator.

✦ **You can save the file in Illustrator's native format (AI) with PDF compatibility.** When you do this, format, you can open the file in Acrobat, but any layers contained in the PDF are flattened. If you're saving as a PDF from Illustrator, you can preserve the Illustrator layer views by creating Adobe PDF layers.

✦ **You can save as an EPS (Encapsulated PostScript) and use the Acrobat Distiller software to convert the EPS to PDF.** This is the least advantageous method for converting Illustrator documents to PDF. When distilling EPS files, you flatten layers and lose native Illustrator editing capabilities. Files saved as PDF can be more easily edited back in Illustrator when you save them preserving Illustrator editing capabilities.

Documents you may create from Illustrator that don't get imported into InDesign might be files like forms, single-page product sheets, single-page flyers and newsletters, corporate identity documents, or other similar designs.

To export PDF files from Adobe Illustrator, choose File ➪ Save or File ➪ Save As. The available format options include Adobe Illustrator Document, Illustrator EPS, Illustrator Template (AIT), Adobe PDF, SVG Compressed (SVGZ), and SVG. In Illustrator, choose File ➪ Save from a new document window. A Save dialog box opens that enables you to name the file, choose the destination, and select one of the formats just noted. When you select Acrobat PDF and click the Save button, the Adobe PDF Options dialog box opens; here, you can set various PDF options before saving the file as a PDF. Six general categories are listed in the left pane of the Adobe PDF Options dialog box — General, Compression, Marks and Bleeds, Advanced, Security, and Summary — covered in the following sections.

Note
You use the Save As command when a file has been saved as a native Illustrator file or an EPS file and you want to save a copy to the PDF format. You might have an Illustrator native file imported into an InDesign document and want to add the Illustrator document as a PDF to a CD-ROM. In this case, you open the native document and use the Save As command to generate a PDF.

General

The General options offer settings to describe the general format attributes for the PDF document. At the top of the dialog box is the Preset pull-down menu, shown in Figure 31-1, accessible regardless of which category is selected in the left pane. From the Preset menu, you can choose Illustrator Default, Press, or Acrobat 6 Layered. Certain fixed attributes related to PDF compatibility and the amount of file compression are fixed when using one of the presets. If none of the presets suit your output needs, you can make choices for changing attributes in each category.

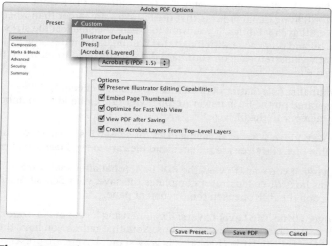

Figure 31-1: When saving to PDF, choose a preset or make changes in the various categories to create a custom preset.

Options choices for General settings include:

✦ **Compatibility:** Three choices are available in the File Compatibility section of the Options dialog box. Here you can set the file compatibility for the Acrobat viewers that ultimately display your PDFs. In most cases, you can open PDFs in all viewers back to Acrobat 3. However, there are some aspects of newer PDFs that won't properly display in older viewers. For example, Adobe PDF layers and embedded multimedia clips cannot be seen in viewers earlier than version 6.0.

  • **Acrobat 4.0:** If files are to be printed to high-end devices, you may want to use Acrobat 4 compatibility. Also, if your client's files need to be delivered to the largest range of users who are still using older viewers, then you might want to use this compatibility.

  • **Acrobat 5.0:** Acrobat 5 compatibility offers you some additional security options over Acrobat 4 compatibility and more features related to Adobe PDF forms — especially forms containing JavaScript. Generally, most documents converted to PDF as Acrobat 5 compatible can be seen in Acrobat 4 viewers.

- **Acrobat 6.0:** Unless there is some unique reason for not including the Adobe Reader 6 installer on the CD-ROM and asking users to use the latest viewer, you'll want to use Acrobat 6 compatibility where you can be assured your files are seen by all users who install the Adobe Reader 6 viewer.

✦ **Preserve Illustrator Editing Capabilities:** If you've ever tried to edit PDF files in Illustrator, you know there are many problems with nested grouped objects, masking, and handling text. When this option is checked, PDF files are preserved in terms of their editing capabilities after they're saved as PDFs and reopened in Illustrator. Check this box as a matter of default so you can easily return to Illustrator and make updates and edits on your files. The downside of saving Illustrator files as PDFs while Preserving Illustrator Editing Capabilities is that the file sizes are larger than when saving without the editing capabilities. If you want to create the smallest file sizes, keep the checkbox off and don't save with Illustrator Editing Capabilities. You can keep a duplicate copy native Illustrator file on your hard drive if you need to return to the document and edit the file.

✦ **Embed Page Thumbnails:** As a matter of default, keep this box unchecked. Page thumbnails are generated on-the-fly in newer Acrobat viewers; embedding thumbnails adds unnecessary memory to the file size.

✦ **Optimize for Fast Web View:** Whenever saving PDFs for screen displays or Web hosting, always check this box. File sizes are reduced and files are viewed faster on-screen.

✦ **View PDF after Saving:** If you want to view the PDF in Acrobat after saving from Illustrator, check this box. When Illustrator completes the save, your default Acrobat viewer is launched, and the PDF opens in the Document pane.

✦ **Create Acrobat Layers from Top-Level Layers:** If you're using layers in Illustrator and you want to preserve the layer view, check this box. Note that unless you have the Acrobat 6 compatibility selected, the check box is grayed out. Layers are preserved only in Acrobat 6–compatible PDFs.

Tip

The default view in Illustrator is the view that displays in Acrobat when you save PDFs with layers. If you want to view certain layers and to hide other layers in the resultant PDF, create the view you want in Illustrator before saving to PDF. All hidden layers can be turned on in Acrobat.

✦ **Save Preset:** This button is accessible from any options group. When you click the button, you can save all the changes you make to the attributes as a new preset. The preset you name and save is added to the Preset pull-down menu at the top of the Adobe PDF Options dialog box.

Compression

Click the Compression item in the left pane, and the options in the right pane change, as shown in Figure 31-2. The Compression settings enable you to reduce file sizes by lowering resolution in raster images and compressing vector objects.

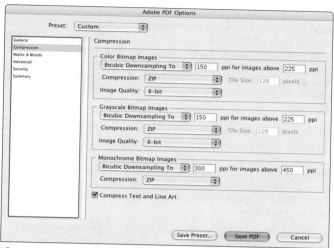

Figure 31-2: Compression options enable you to change image resolution.

✦ **Color Bitmap Images/Grayscale Bitmap Images:** Options for raster-based images, either color or grayscale, are the same. These images are imports from Photoshop or scans. If you're designing documents for print and then distributing them on CD, you might want to change the resolution of your photo images. When creating PDFs from Illustrator, you can reduce image file sizes by making choices for downsampling and compressing files. The options you have for both color and grayscale images include the following:

Cross-Reference

For a complete understanding of file compression and the differences in file compression methods, see the Illustrator Online Help document attained by selecting Help ⇨ Illustrator Help or press the F1 key.

- **Color/Bitmap Images:** The first setting for both color and bitmap images is made from the pull-down menu below each section head. The default is Bicubic Downsampling, which typically is the best method to use and takes the longest time to save the file. You can also choose to not downsample by selecting Do Not Downsample from the pull-down menu. Other choices include Average Downsampling and Subsampling, both of which are methods for reducing file sizes.

  To the right of the pull-down menu are two field boxes. The rightmost box is used to identify what images are to be downsampled in terms of file sizes. If you have files above 300 ppi (pixels per inch) and enter 300 in the field box, all files above 300 ppi are downsampled. The first box adjacent to the pull-down menu determines the amount of downsampling employed with the file save. If you want to sample all files above 300 ppi to 72 ppi, add 72 in the first field box.

- **Compression:** The compression method is selected from the Compression pull-down menu. Choices are None, Automatic JPEG, Automatic JPEG 2000, JPEG, JPEG 2000, and Zip. Both the automatic choices assess each imported image and make a determination based on an image's content whether JPEG compression or Zip compression is used. For the JPEG 2000 options compression is highest without data loss. Zip is a lossless compression. Typically, if you're repurposing or creating files for CD-ROM replication, use JPEG compression to create smaller file sizes.

Caution   Saving files with JPEG2000 is compatible with Acrobat 6 and the PDF 1.5 format only. If you need to save files with Acrobat compatibility lower than version 6, do not use this option.

- **Image Quality:** Five choices exist from the pull-down menu, ranging from Minimum to Maximum. The higher the quality, the larger the file size becomes. As a rule, it's a good idea to test results and pick the lowest quality that doesn't visibly demonstrate any image degradation.

✦ **Monochrome Bitmap Images:** Monochrome bitmap images are images that might be line art created in Photoshop. A scanned black-and-white logo saved as a bitmap from Photoshop would qualify. The general rule for these kinds of images is that image resolution should equal device resolution. Therefore, if you're printing to a 600 dpi laser printer, the image resolution of bitmap images should be 600 ppi. If your files were designed to print on office printers, choosing 600 ppi is sufficient. So downsample all files above 600 ppi (in the far-right field box) to 600 ppi (the left field box).

The Compression pull-down menu offers the same options you have for color and grayscale images.

✦ **Compress Text and Line Art:** Check this box as a matter of default. When checked, all type and objects drawn in Illustrator are compressed. The compression doesn't produce a loss in image quality, and you can use this setting confidently for all file saves from Illustrator.

Marks and bleeds

Unless you want to distribute PDFs for printing purposes, leave all the marks and bleed settings unchecked, as shown in Figure 31-3. If CDs are written to take a large volume of files to a print shop, you may want to submit PDFs for printing and use the marks and bleeds. If this is the case, see how these items are used in Chapter 35.

Advanced

Advanced settings offer options for color management and transparency flattening. Settings in the dialog box shown in Figure 31-4 relate to documents destined for high-end prepress. Don't be concerned about making choices here for PDFs designed for screen viewing.

Cross-Reference   For more information on color management, see Chapter 6. For more information on transparency flattening, see Chapter 35.

The Advanced settings also include an option for subsetting fonts. By default, the field box is set to 100% where fonts are subset when the percentage of characters in a given font set is less than 100%. This makes editing the PDF possible if you need to make a quick text edit. If you have volumes of text documents you want to write to CDs, lower the value to 35%, and the file sizes will be a little smaller.

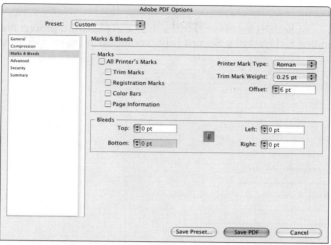

Figure 31-3: For screen viewing, be certain to disable all marks and bleeds.

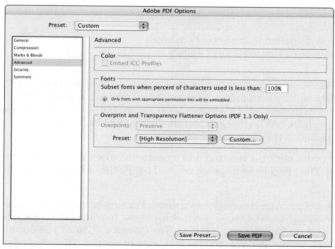

Figure 31-4: Color-profile embedding and transparency flattening don't need adjustments for files viewed on-screen.

Note that fonts are embedded automatically when you save to PDF from Illustrator. There is no option to toggle on and off font embedding.

Cross-Reference   For more information on fonts and font embedding, see Chapter 13.

Security

The Security settings offer you options for file encryption. You can password-protect files against opening and/or editing and changing. Security options shown in Figure 31-5 include the following:

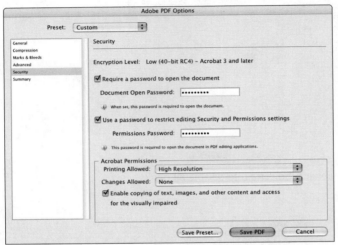

Figure 31-5: File encryption is applied in the Security options, where you can secure files against viewing and/or editing.

✦ **Document Open Password:** The check box is used when you want users to supply a password to access your PDF documents. Check this box and add a password in the field box. If you want to protect your files from being edited but don't care who views your PDFs, leave the check box unchecked and the field box blank. Securing files against editing is applied in the Permissions settings.

✦ **Permissions Password:** Check the box and add a password when you want to protect files against editing. The specific settings are applied below the field box in the Acrobat Permissions area.

✦ **Acrobat Permissions:** You make choices for two items: Printing Allowed and Changes Allowed. From the Printing Allowed pull-down menu, choose to allow printing at low resolution, printing at high resolution, or no printing. The Changes Allowed pull-down menu offers different options for the kinds of changes you want to restrict. These include

- **None:** No edits are permitted. Users won't be able to copy any content, extract pages, add comments, or digitally sign documents.

- **Inserting, Deleting, Rotating Pages:** Permits users to edit pages by inserting other PDF pages, deleting pages, and rotating pages. However, all the other editing options are not permitted.

- **Filling In Forms and Signing:** Enables users to fill in PDF forms and sign documents with digital signatures.

- **Commenting, Filling In Forms, and Signing:** Adds to form fill-in and signing the ability to add comment notes and use all the comment tools.

- **Any Except Extracting Pages:** Enables users to edit PDFs with all the tools except extracting pages.

✦ **Enable Copying of Text, Images, and Other Content.** When enabled, this setting also affects the next item for enabling PDFs to be read by screen readers for the visually challenged. Content can be copied but you can disable all other editing by selecting None from the pull-down menu for Changes Allowed.

✦ **Enable Text Access of Screen Reader Devices for the Visually Impaired:** You can check this box and uncheck the box for enabling copying of text. When this item is checked, it ensures that assistive devices can read your PDFs for vision- and motion-challenged persons.

✦ **Enable Plaintext Metadata:** One advantage to checking this box is that, when it's checked, you can create a search index file even though the PDF is protected against all other changes.

Note

All the preceding options are available when Acrobat 6 Compatibility is selected in the General options. Changing compatibility settings offers fewer or more options for Acrobat Permissions, depending on the compatibility you choose.

Summary

When you click Summary in the left pane, the right pane shows you a list of the options choices you made for all the other panes. A single option exists for the Summary with the Save Summary button. Click this button and the summary information listed in the scrollable window shown in Figure 31-6 is saved to a text file.

If you want to keep a record or if you want to share your options choices in a workgroup with other users, click the Save Summary button. The Save Summary dialog box opens; here, you can provide a filename and choose a destination.

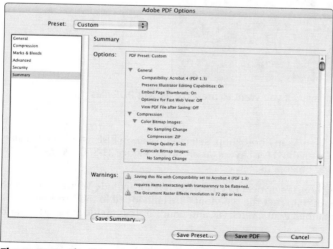

Figure 31-6: The Summary shows you a list of all the options choices you made for creating the PDF file.

Creating PDFs from Adobe Photoshop

Photoshop offers several different tools for presenting and archiving images that can be saved to the PDF format. You can use the standard-vanilla flavor of just saving a Photoshop document to the PDF format, or you can use a little creativity in Photoshop to suit various needs before saving to Photoshop PDF.

Saving to Photoshop PDF format

Photoshop saves direct to the PDF format. The file you save from Photoshop has a slightly different flavor than PDF documents you create from other programs. You'll find this most noticeable when you try to open PDFs in Photoshop that were generated from other programs. When opening such files, Photoshop wants to rasterize the data — converting all vector objects and type fonts to pixels. However, when you're saving to PDF from Photoshop, you can preserve vector data and type fonts. As a matter of fact, PDF is the only file format other than Photoshop's native PSD format that preserves vector data and type when saving. When you save Photoshop files containing type as PDFs, you can search a CD-ROM's contents for PDFs containing text meeting your search criteria.

When saving files containing type as PDFs from Photoshop, be certain to keep the layers intact, as shown in the example in Figure 31-7. Don't flatten the layers, because all the type attributes are lost and all type and vectors convert to pixels.

Figure 31-7: Don't flatten layers if you want to preserve type in PDF files saved from Photoshop.

When you select Save or Save As in Photoshop, select Photoshop PDF as the file Format and be certain the check box is enabled for Layers, as shown in Figure 31-8. Click the Save button and the PDF Options dialog box opens.

In the PDF Options dialog box, it's critical to check the box for Include Vector Data, as shown in Figure 31-9. Also, to be certain that the type fonts are embedded in the resultant PDF document. Check the box for Embed Fonts. Click OK and your Photoshop file is saved as a PDF.

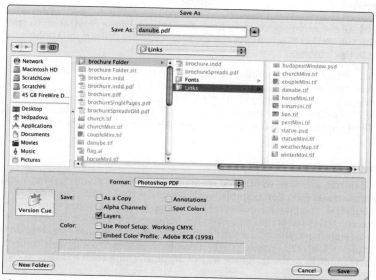

Figure 31-8: Select Photoshop PDF as the format and check the Layers option.

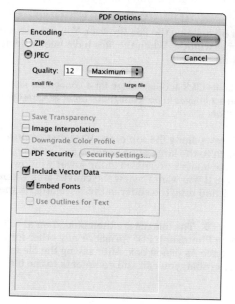

Figure 31-9: Check the box for Include Vector Data to preserve the type, and click Embed Fonts to embed fonts in the PDF file.

Notice the PDF Options dialog box in Photoshop offers you an option for adding security. You can secure files with all the same options you have available in Adobe Illustrator. To review the options, see the subsection "Security" in the section "Creating PDFs from Adobe Illustrator" earlier in this chapter.

A final note on saving PDFs from Photoshop has to do with the Encoding area of the PDF Options. You can choose between Zip and JPEG compression. Zip is lossless, while JPEG loses data in amounts according to the quality setting. As the quality is reduced, more data is eliminated from the file. Be certain to view the resultant PDFs in Acrobat to test the compression amounts you apply to images. Try to test a few images before writing folders of images to PDF format.

Using Photomerge

Depending on your needs, you may want to do something other than simply saving a collection of images to individual PDFs. For example, suppose you want to write files to CD-ROM as a means of archiving jobs. You may have several Photoshop images that you want to view together and add some notes to remind you what the images were used for or perhaps some specific attributes pertaining to the job or the files used on the job. Rather than rely on the File Browser to display a folder of images, you can combine images in a single document, save as PDF, and add notes in Acrobat. A nice way of accomplishing such a task is using Photoshop's Photomerge command.

Photomerge was not designed to create a single-page document from random files. The true intent for Photomerge is to combine images taken in a panoramic view and merge them into a single file. However, Photomerge is not limited to using the command for just panoramic photos.

To merge photos into a single document, start by opening the File Browser. You can use a folder of images or select files in the File Browser window. When the files have been selected or the folder identified, choose Automate ➪ Photomerge.

Tip   Click on an image in the File Browser and Shift+Click another image for a contiguous selection between the two selected images. To select images in noncontiguous order ⌘/Ctrl+Click each image you want to include in the selection.

Photomerge places your images as thumbnail views along the top of the Photomerge dialog box. You can click and drag the thumbnails down to the large open window and arrange the images to your liking. In Figure 31-10, you can see images organized in the lower window while the last image is dragged down to position. If you want to view the canvas area where the images are arranged in a zoomed view, click and drag the slider in the Navigator on the right side of the dialog box.

When the files are arranged on the canvas, click OK. The images are then placed on a Photoshop canvas where you can save the file in Photoshop PDF format or any other format available from the Format menu in the Save or Save As dialog box. After saving the file in PDF, open the document in Adobe Acrobat. In Acrobat, you can add comments to the file using the commenting tools.

Figure 31-10: Drag the thumbnails down and position the images around the Photomerge canvas area.

Saving multi-page PDFs

Yet another way to display Photoshop images in a PDF file is to convert each image to a separate PDF page. Whereas the Photomerge feature in the File Browser creates a single-page document, the PDF Presentation option, also available in the File Browser, takes selected files and converts each file to separate PDF pages. A single PDF document is created with pages sized to the size of the original images saved as PDF. In other words, you can have page sizes of 3-x-5, 4-x-6, and 8-x-10 inches all in the same file.

To create a multi-page document from a collection of photo images, start by opening the File Browser. Use your shortcut to open the File Browser; otherwise, choose Window ➪ File Browser. In the File Browser window, navigate your folders to find the folder containing images you want to convert to PDFs. If all the photos in a given folder are to be converted, press ⌘/Ctrl+A to select all; otherwise, press ⌘/Ctrl+click to select individual files.

Although you can select files in different folders when you open the PDF Presentation dialog box, it's much easier to drag all the files you plan to convert to a single folder. When you select the files in the File Browser, choose Automate ➪ PDF Presentation in the File Browser window.

The PDF Presentation dialog box opens, as shown in Figure 31-11. The Browse button enables you to search other folders and identify images you can add to the list of files targeted for conversion. Under Output options you have two options for the way the converted files are viewed in Acrobat. Click the radio button for Multi-Page Document. The other button, Presentation, is used for a self-running presentation.

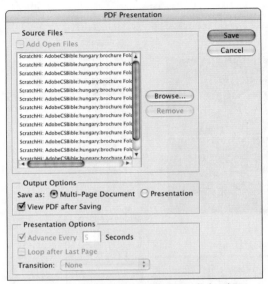

Figure 31-11: The PDF Presentation dialog box

Cross-Reference For information on creating Presentations and setting presentation attributes, see Chapter 33.

Check the box to View PDF after Saving if you want to see the PDF document immediately after conversion. The presentation options only apply when you click the radio button for Presentation in the Output Options. Click Save and the Save dialog box opens. Supply a name, locate a folder, and click Save in the Save dialog box; the PDF Options dialog box opens.

The PDF Options are the same as the ones you have available when saving individual files as Photoshop PDF. You can include vector data, add PDF Security, and choose from different compression options. After making choices in the PDF Options dialog box, click OK and the file opens in Acrobat if you checked the box to View PDF after Saving. If you have images of different sizes, you'll note the thumbnails in the Pages pane are all the same size, whereas the pages in the Document pane appear at different sizes, as shown in Figure 31-12.

Creating PDFs from Adobe InDesign

Adobe InDesign exports direct to PDF format. You can export a file to PDF for the purposes of printing and prepress or use other export options for exporting files that are intended for screen views. If you create design pieces for clients and want to catalog files, exporting to PDF is an easy method for indexing and filing your documents. If you want to create CD-ROMs for your client to distribute to customers, creating PDFs can save huge amounts of money compared to printed material.

To export a file to PDF from InDesign, choose File ➪ Export. The Export dialog box opens, shown in Figure 31-13. From the Format pull-down menu, be certain to select Adobe PDF. Target a location, add a name to the Save As field box, and click the Save button.

Figure 31-12: Click on the Pages tab in the Navigation pane to view page thumbnails.

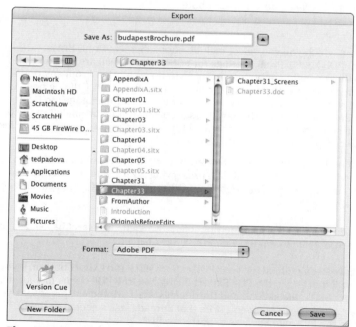

Figure 31-13: Be sure to select Adobe PDF from the Format pull-down menu in the Export dialog box.

After clicking Save in the Export dialog box, the Export PDF dialog box opens, shown in Figure 31-14. Notice there are several category topics in the left pane and options settings respective to the selected category in the right pane. The default options are the General settings. At the top of the dialog box is a pull-down menu for Presets.

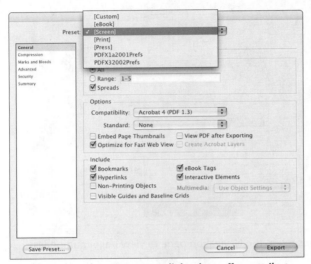

Figure 31-14: The Export PDF dialog box offers attribute options.

The default presets from which you can select include eBook, Screen, Print, Press, PDF/X1a2001Prefs, and PDF/X32002Prefs. Settings for eBook and Screen are optimized for viewing on-screen; all the remaining options have more to do with print. From any option set, you can select a preset; then you can edit attributes in the Export PDF dialog box. As soon as you change an option in any category, the Preset menu option changes to Custom. After changes have been made, click on the Save Preset button at the bottom-left of the dialog box to save the custom settings. In future InDesign editing sessions, you can open the Preset pull-down menu and access all the custom sets you saved.

Depending on the kind of document you want to view in Acrobat, you can make choices in the General export settings for Acrobat compatibility, preserving layers, interactivity, various viewing items, and optimizing files for Fast Web View. Other options exist when clicking on the different categories in the left pane.

Cross-Reference   To embed tags, see Chapter 27. For preserving interactive elements, see Chapter 29. For printing presets, see Chapter 34. For more on PDF/X, see Chapter 35.

When the attributes have been defined for your PDF export, click the Export button. If you selected View PDF after Exporting in the PDF Export dialog box, the PDF opens in your default Acrobat viewer. In Figure 31-15, the second and third pages were printed as spreads, as you see in the Pages palette in the PDF document. Note that Spreads was selected in the PDF Export dialog box when the InDesign File was exported to PDF.

Note

Spreads are set up in InDesign when you have facing pages. Although each page is an individual page, you can print the document in spreads where two facing pages print as a single page. In Figure 31-15, the InDesign document had five pages, yet when exported to PDF, three pages were created. Page 1 was a single page, while pages 2, 3, 4, and 5 were facing pages.

Figure 31-15: In the Pages pane, you can see the single page and the two pages created as spreads.

Creating PDFs from Adobe GoLive

As a matter of rule, you may want to leave HTML files in native format when copying files to CD-ROMs. Users are even more likely to view pages in a Web browser than in an Acrobat viewer. However, if there is a need to archive files, you may want to add notes and comments to files created in GoLive. If this is the case, you do have an opportunity to create PDF pages from GoLive.

Tip

You can export an entire site to PDF by selecting File ➪ Export ➪ HTML as Adobe PDF. For more information on using the Export command and setting export attributes, see the GoLive Help document acquired by selecting Help ➪ GoLive Help.

Be aware that you don't have to use GoLive to convert Web pages to PDF. Windows users can use the PDFMaker in Microsoft Internet Explorer (MSIE); Mac users can create Web pages from files viewed in Web browsers via the Print dialog box. On Windows, the PDFMaker is installed when you install Adobe Acrobat. You access the command by clicking on the Create PDF tool. You see in the MSIE toolbar after the PDFMaker is installed. On the Mac, open a Web page and choose File ⇨ Print. In the Print dialog box, click Save as PDF.

Caution   Macintosh users who create PDF documents via the Print dialog box wind up with files much larger than PDFs created with Acrobat's Web Capture command. If you convert Web pages to PDF on the Macintosh, open the Create task button pull-down menu and select From Web Page.

If you want to convert GoLive pages to PDF, click on the PDF Preview tab at the top of the document window in GoLive, as shown in Figure 31-16. The open HTML document in GoLive displays as a PDF preview.

Figure 31-16: Click on the PDF Preview tool to show the page as a PDF in GoLive.

If the Preview looks good, you can export the page to a PDF document, and you view the created file exactly like the preview in GoLive. To export to PDF, choose File ⇨ Export ⇨ HTML as Adobe PDF. The Save: GoLive dialog box opens. Navigate your hard drive and find the folder where you want to save the file. Supply a name and click Save. Any other editing you want to do can then be performed in Acrobat.

Acquiring images in Acrobat

Another way to create PDFs from image files is to use Adobe Acrobat rather than Photoshop for the file conversions. You can convert images to separate PDF documents or convert a folder of images to a single PDF file. A variety of different file formats are supported, including TIFF, PNG, JPEG, and GIF. Unfortunately, native PSD files are not supported, but you can always convert those in Photoshop as described earlier.

The advantage you have in converting image files to PDF from within Acrobat is the opportunity to use the Acrobat Picture Tasks feature where you can print image files to a variety of different print sizes. Picture tasks also work on PDF presentations created with Photoshop CS. For example, you can take a collection of digital-camera images or TIFF images used in a client advertising campaign and use Acrobat to convert the images to a single PDF document. After they're converted to PDF, the Picture Tasks task button appears in the Tasks toolbar in any Acrobat viewer including Adobe Reader. You open the pull-down menu from the Picture Tasks task button and select Print Pictures, as shown in Figure 31-17.

Note   The Picture Tasks task button is not available as a default tool in Acrobat. There is no way to select the tool to show it in the Tasks toolbar. The Picture Tasks task button opens automatically when you convert image files to PDF or you open files created by certain programs such as Adobe Photoshop Album. When you close a file where the Picture Tasks task button is visible, the tool disappears from the Tasks toolbar.

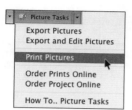

Figure 31-17: Select Print Pictures to open the Select Pictures dialog box.

After selecting the Print Pictures menu command from the Picture Tasks pull-down menu, the Select Pictures dialog box opens, shown in Figure 31-18. In this dialog box, you select pictures by Shift+clicking the thumbnails for a contiguous selection, by ⌘/Ctrl+clicking to individually select images in a noncontiguous group, or by clicking the Select All button to select all pages.

Figure 31-18: If you want to print all pictures, click Select All; then click Next.

After you click Next, the Print Pictures dialog box opens, shown in Figure 31-19; here, you select the output size for final prints. To print index prints that print a thumbnail image you can insert in a jewel case for a CD, click on the Index button. Click Next and you see a preview of the file to be printed and the Acrobat Print dialog box.

Using Acrobat to print image files offers you a nice way to print index prints that can easily be inserted in CD jewel cases and help you quickly locate files on archived CDs.

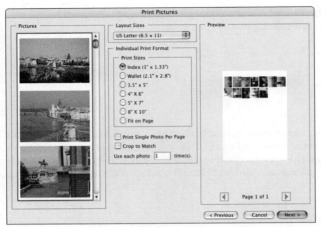

Figure 31-19: Select the size for your prints and click Next.

Writing PDFs to CD-ROMs

The advantage in hosting PDFs on the Web is that you can keep them updated as they're changed. With CD-ROMs, you lose this advantage. However, CD-ROMs have their own advantages that you can't duplicate with Web-hosted documents. For example, you can eliminate any problems for users accessing your PDFs, and you can create search indexes for faster searches. You can eliminate long download times for large files and you can minimize confusion when several PDFs are interactive and need to be housed in the same directory to work properly. With some of these advantages, you may find replicating CD-ROMs a viable solution for distributing your PDFs.

If you replicate CD-ROMs for distributing documents, you'll want to exercise some care in creating a master CD that works properly and provides a user with all the features you want them to enjoy.

Organizing a CD-ROM collection of PDFs

When organizing your documents for CD-ROM replication, you must consider two important measures. First, you must preserve the directory path for all actions that open and close files. If you use a button, a page action, a bookmark, a link, a JavaScript, or any interactive element that opens another file, the path that Acrobat searches is absolute. If you relocate files after creating links and copy them to a CD-ROM, Acrobat won't find the linked files. The best way to prevent a potential problem is to create a single folder on your hard drive, then nest subfolders below the main folder. Create the links and test them thoroughly before creating a master used to replicate the CD-ROMs. You can copy all the files and subfolders from the main folder on your hard drive to the root location on the CD-ROM, but don't move any files from the subfolders. The folders and folder names need to be preserved.

Cross-Reference   For information on linking PDF documents, see Chapter 29.

The second precaution is to ensure all filenames are preserved when copying PDFs to a CD-ROM. This issue is related to the software used to write the CD. You must use naming conventions that preserve long names. Writing CDs for a cross-platform audience is always best. Therefore, if you use a Mac, be sure the filenames aren't disturbed when files are viewed on a Windows machine and vice versa. As a matter of practice, using standard DOS naming conventions (an eight-character-maximum name with a three-character-maximum extension) is always successful. As a final step, you should test a CD-ROM before replication on both platforms.

Replicating CD-ROMs

If you have a limited number of CD-ROMs to copy, a personal CD-R device can satisfy your needs. These devices come with different interfaces where the write speed varies greatly according to the interface type. USB devices are extremely slow whereas FireWire drives are the top of the line. Even if your CD-ROM write needs are occasional, you'll appreciate the much faster completion time of a FireWire drive.

If your CD-ROM replication involves writing many CDs, then use a replication center. You can reduce the cost of replicating CD-ROMs to less than $1 apiece, depending on the number of CDs you order. For a replication source, search the Internet and compare the costs of the services. When you find a service, send them a CD-ROM of the PDF files you want replicated. In order to ensure the filenames and directory paths are properly specified on the destination media, thoroughly test your own CD to be certain everything works properly before submitting the files to the replication center.

Adding a Web page for updates

After you distribute a CD-ROM to clients or employees, you have no idea how long people may use the files. You might go through several updates of the same files before someone updates your CD to the latest version. To guard against obsolescence, create a folder with an HTML file to be included on the CD. For all the button and text links, make the hypertext references to the pages on your Web site where updates are routinely reported. You can add a README file or a PDF to instruct users they should frequent your Web site for updated forms. Be certain to keep the directory paths fixed on your Web site so even a user with an antiquated CD can easily access the pages without having to search your site.

Tip   README files are text-only documents. On Windows use Windows WordPad or Notepad and type your help information. Save the file as text-only. On the Mac, type your help information in TextEdit and save the file as text-only.

Creating a welcome file

You can make a file that describes the CD, its contents, and a general statement about visiting your Web site into a text-only file or a PDF document. If you create a PDF file, then the user needs to have an Acrobat viewer installed on his/her computer. Any computer user can read a text file, so you may want to add both.

Unfortunately, everyone won't view the README files. Some users avoid them and jump right into your documents. If you want to ensure that every user sees your welcome file at least one time, you can add an autoplay file that automatically launches your welcome file when the CD-ROM is inserted in a CD drive. Windows users can add an autoplay to a CD by writing a few lines of code and saving text as INI. Macintosh users need to use a commercial CD-writing utility.

Cross-Reference
Because authoring programs change so fast, rather than guide you to programs used for creating autoplay CDs, let me point you to the Internet, where you can search for the most recent programs that help you create autoplays. In a search engine, search for *autoplay* and you'll see many links to sites where public domain and commercial sites provide products for creating autoplay files.

Adding Adobe Reader

You should always check with Adobe's Web site for the current rules and licensing restrictions before distributing software like Adobe Reader. The distribution policy can change at any time, so what is said today may not be true tomorrow.

As of this writing, Adobe permits you to copy the Adobe Reader software installer to a media source for distribution. You must comply with the licensing policy and include all licensing information with the installer application. For specifics related to the distribution of the Acrobat Reader software, visit Adobe's Web site at `www.adobe.com/products/acrobat/distribute.html` for the most recent copy of Adobe Reader and the current distribution policy.

If you include the Adobe Reader installer on a CD-ROM, also create a Web page that links to the download page of the current Reader software. If your CD is out for a long time, Reader may go through several versions before a user updates to your latest CD-ROM version.

Adding Security to CD-ROMs

Securing PDF documents, whether it be Acrobat Certificate Authority or third-party signature handlers, works great for protecting content in PDF documents and protecting files from being opened when a user doesn't have access to a password. But what if you want to encrypt files against content copying, and changing, and don't want the encrypted documents circulated? Providing a user with a password to open the PDF doesn't guarantee that your documents won't be distributed along with the password to open them. eBooks are a good example of a situation in which you want to license a single copy of your content to a single user.

Note
Contact StarForce at: `www.star-force.com` in San Francisco or `www.star-force.ru` in Moscow, Russia for a Windows utility used for protecting CD-ROMs.

PDF Pro 1.1 is a marvelous tool for anyone who wants to license a single copy of PDF documents contained on CD-ROMs. The product was designed especially for publishers, governments, corporations, and small-business users who want to distribute eBooks, eZines, reports, statistical data, scientific, and any type of sensitive material that needs to be protected against copying, extraction, modification, and distribution.

The protection of each PDF document incorporates a unique algorithm with encryption. The end user installs the Protection plug-in that initiates the StarForce PDF protection module each time the user's Adobe Reader application is launched. Another user cannot use the plug-in module, and anyone who attempts to view any of the protected CD-ROM content is denied access. The behind-the-scenes encryption actually uses the physical parameters of the CD-ROM drive and a unique 24-byte key on each batch of licensed CD-ROMs. StarForce claims that CD-ROMs duplicated from individual users or through plant manufacturing are completely unusable.

If a user tries to access PDF files with other Acrobat viewers or applications supporting imports of PDF documents, the user is likewise denied access. The manufacturer claims the product is effective against any kind of workaround where a user may attempt to extract the content from an encrypted CD-ROM and circulate the data. If your needs include mass copy protection, this product is worth examining.

Summary

✦ All the Creative Suite applications export or save to the PDF format. PDF documents are a good means of hosting files on CD-ROM, because the file integrity is preserved with font and image embedding.

✦ Picture Tasks enable you to print PDF pages to different page sizes. Among the page sizes are index prints where you can create thumbnail prints that you can insert in CD jewel cases for easy referencing.

✦ You can copy the Adobe Reader installer to CD-ROMs as long as you comply with Adobe licensing restrictions.

✦ Autoplay files help you direct a user to a central navigation page. Autoplay routines are developed with CD-ROM authoring programs, script writing, or applications designed for the specific purpose of creating autoplays.

✦ Through the use of a third-party application, you can secure CD-ROMs against copying and distributing PDF documents.

✦   ✦   ✦

Creating SWF and SVG Files

The Web's popularity has seen the appearance of several new technologies that add interactivity and portability within Web pages. Of these, Flash (SWF) files and Scale Vector Graphic (SVG) files, both vector-based image formats, create files a fraction of the size of their raster-based counterparts, making them useful for creating animations. You can also use these formats to scale images to any size without sacrificing image quality.

You can create both Flash (SWF) files and Scalable Vector Graphics (SVG) from within Illustrator and use them in GoLive and Acrobat. You create SWF animation in Illustrator by placing the graphics for each frame of the animation on a separate layer, which you then convert to animation frames. You can apply XML-based filters to SVG graphics and still maintains the vector nature of the SVG file. You can also make SVG files interactive.

Creating SWF Files in Illustrator

Although you typically create SWF files using the Macromedia Flash program, Flash isn't the only application that works with vector-based images. Adobe Illustrator also creates vector-based designs, so converting a native Illustrator graphic to the SWF format is a simple conversion. You can save any Illustrator graphic as an SWF file for use on the Web. You can also use Illustrator to create SWF animations by placing each frame of the animation in a separate layer.

Creating SWF animations with layers

You can create simple animations in Illustrator using layers. By placing each frame of an animation on a separate layer, you can then cycle through the layers to create an animated sequence. The Layers palette includes a feature that automatically creates a layer for each object in the current file and places each object in its own layer.

Before using this feature, you must create and position each object that appears in the animation. If the animation features a single moving object, you must duplicate that object for each frame of the animation. An easy way to do this is to create the object; choose Edit ⇨ Copy (⌘/Ctrl+C), then choose Edit ⇨ Paste in Front (⌘/Ctrl+F). After pasting a copy of the object, move it to its correct position.

Tip   You can also duplicate the selected object by holding down the Option/Alt key while dragging the object to a new location.

After you have copied and positioned all the objects, you can select the Release to Layers (Sequence) palette menu command from the Layers palette (Figure 32-1). This command creates a new layer for each object, placing each in its own layer.

Figure 32-1: Each frame of the animation is placed on a separate layer.

You may now export the file to the SWF format by choosing File ➪ Export. If you select the AI Layers to SWF Frames option in the Macromedia Flash (SWF) Format Options dialog box, the animation sequence exports to the SWF file where it's viewed on a Web page.

The Layers palette also includes a Release to Layers (Build) menu command. This command is similar in that it also creates a new layer for each object, but each new object is cumulatively added to the existing objects. For example, if the original layer includes five objects, the first layer includes a single object, the second layer two objects, and the fifth layer all objects.

Using symbols

If a simple animation sequence requires a separate object for every frame of an animation, file sizes could potentially grow progressively larger as an animation sequence gets longer. However, there is a solution that keeps file sizes small — using symbols.

When you use a symbol in an SWF file, the symbol is included only once and simply referenced every other time it is used within the file. So a simple animation that includes a symbol moving across the screen would require that you duplicate the symbol multiple times and place a copy of the symbol on a separate layer for each frame of the animation, but the SWF file would only include the symbol once.

You can either use a symbol from Illustrator's Symbol palette, or create your own symbol:

✦ **Using the Symbol palette:** Illustrator includes many symbols in the Symbols palette (Figure 32-2). You can access additional symbols using the symbol libraries, which you open by choosing Window ➪ Symbol Libraries. To use a symbol contained in the Symbols palette or in a symbol library, simply drag it onto the art board.

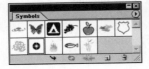

Figure 32-2: The Symbol palette holds all the symbols you need in Illustrator.

✦ **Creating your symbols:** Draw and select the artwork that you want to use as a symbol, then select the New Symbol palette menu command or drag the artwork to the Symbols palette. If you double-click on a symbol in the Symbol palette, a dialog box appears where you can rename the symbol.

Illustrator and SWF differences

Several objects behave differently between Illustrator and Flash, which could impact the file when it's exported:

✦ **Gradients and meshes:** Gradients and mesh objects that use more than eight stops convert to a raster image during export. Gradients with less than eight stops export as gradients. To keep file sizes low, only use gradients with less than eight stops for artwork exported to the SWF format.

✦ **Patterns:** All patterns are rasterized and tiled when exported to the SWF format.

✦ **Caps and joins:** The SWF format only supports rounded type caps and joins. Butt and Project caps and Miter and Bevel joins are converted to round caps and joins during the export process.

✦ **Text and strokes:** Text and strokes that are filled with a pattern are converted to paths and then filled with a rasterized pattern during export.

✦ **Text kerning, leading, and tracking**: These are not supported in exported SWF files. Instead, the text is exported as a separate text object positioned to simulate the kerning, leading, and tracking. To maintain text as a single object, covert the text to outlines prior to exporting.

✦ **Transparency:** SWF files use a basic transparency model that doesn't include support for many of Illustrator's blending modes. For artwork that uses the various blending modes, export a text graphic to see the result as an SWF file.

Saving SWF files

There are two different paths for exporting Illustrator graphics to the SWF file format. The first is choosing File ➪ Export, and the second is choosing File ➪ Save for Web. Both of these options offer the same options, but the Save for Web dialog box lets you preview and change options before saving the file.

Note   Keep in mind that SWF files require that you install the Flash Player browser plug-in to view files on the Web.

Exporting SWF files

Choose File ➪ Export to open the Export dialog box. Within this dialog box, you can select Macromedia Flash (SWF) as the Save as Type. Click Save, and the Macromedia Flash (SWF) Format Options dialog box appears, shown in Figure 32-3. The options in this dialog box include the following:

✦ **The Export As:** Includes three options — AI File to SWF File, AI Layers to SWF Frames, and AI Layers to SWF Files. The AI File to SWF File option exports the Illustrator document to a single frame. The other two options convert the artwork contained on each layer to either an SWF frame or to a separate SWF file.

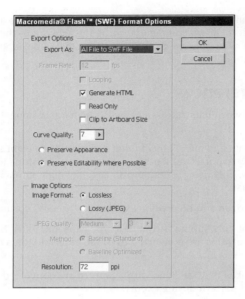

Figure 32-3: The Macromedia Flash (SWF) Format Options dialog box

✦ **Frame Rate:** If you select the AI Layers to SWF Frames option, you can choose a *frame rate,* which is the rate at which the animation frames play. Most animations on the Web are fine at 12 frames per second (fps), but if your animation includes a lot of fast-changing details, you may want to increase this value to 24 fps.

✦ **Looping:** Lets the animation play continuously. If disabled, the animation plays through only once.

✦ **Generate HTML:** For an SWF file to be visible on a Web page, the Web page must include some HTML code that references the Flash plug-in. The Generate HTML option causes the export process to write this HTML code for you. You save the code to the same directory as the SWF file using the same name with an HTML extension. Figure 32-4 shows the HTML code that was generated for a simple example.

Tip Double-clicking on the generated HTML file in the Finder or in Windows Explorer causes the exported SWF artwork to open and display within the default Web browser.

✦ **Read Only:** This option allows viewers to download SWF files without allowing them to open or edit them, thus safeguarding your designs.

✦ **Clip to Artboard Size:** This option exports the entire art board document, excluding any artwork outside of the art board. If disabled, only the document objects exported.

✦ **Curve Quality:** Sets the accuracy of the Bezier curves for the artwork. Lower Curve Quality values reduce the file size by decreasing the number of points as well as the curve's quality. Higher values maintain the curve quality but increase the overall file size.

Tip Most standard curves are adequately maintained with a Curve Quality setting of 7.

Figure 32-4: The Generate HTML option generates a separate HTML file.

✦ **Preserve Appearance:** For lower Curve Quality settings, you can select this option to reduce the curve quality while maintaining the appearance attributes.

✦ **Preserve Editability Where Possible:** This sacrifices the appearance of the curve to keep the most number of points. Preserving all points isn't always possible with a Curve Quality setting of 0.

✦ **Lossless:** This keeps all the image data, resulting in large file sizes.

✦ **Lossy:** Compresses the images using a JPEG format, which throws away image data depending on the JPEG Quality setting. If you select Lossy, you can specify the amount quality as Low, Medium, High, or Maximum. The Low setting results in the smallest file sizes at the expense of image quality, and the High setting yields a large file size but maintains the image quality. You can also select to use the Baseline or Baseline Optimized compression method. The Baseline Optimized method provides an additional level of compression.

✦ **Resolution:** Lets you specify the resolution value for the SWF artwork. For SWF files that are viewed online, a setting of 72 ppi is sufficient, but if you plan to print your artwork, select a higher ppi setting. Higher resolution settings result in larger file sizes.

Using the Save for Web window

Another way to save Illustrator artwork using the SWF format is with the Save for Web window. Open this interface by choosing File ➪ Save for Web (Alt+Shift+Ctrl+S in Windows; Option+Shift+ ⌘+S). The Save for Web window displays a preview of the artwork to be exported, as shown in Figure 32-5.

Tip   The preview pane in the Save for Web window is convenient for viewing the changes to the artwork as a result of lowering the Curve Quality setting.

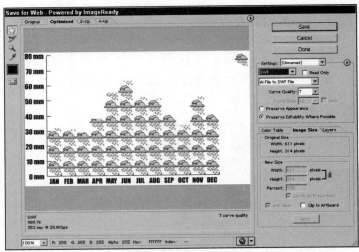

Figure 32-5: You can save Illustrator artwork by using the Save for Web window.

To save the artwork to the SWF format, you must select SWF from the format drop-down list located to the right. All the settings for this format type appear, including many of the same settings mentioned for the File ➪ Export process.

Cross-Reference For more on the File ➪ Export process, see the section "Exporting SWF Files."

Note When using the Save for Web window, all image files are exported to a separate images folder when you select to save both the HTML and Image files.

With the SWF format selected, the Read Only and Loop settings are selected and the Curve Quality and Frame Rate settings appears as value fields. You can still select Preserve Appearance or Preserve Editability Where Possible, but the drop-down list under the Format list only includes options to save the AI file to an SWF file or to save the AI layers to SWF frames.

In the Save for Web window, you cannot choose to save each layer as a different SWF file. The window doesn't include options for setting how you save raster images, nor does it include an option to generate HTML. However, when the file dialog box appears, you can save the images only, the HTML only, or both. The Clip to Artboard option is found within the Image Size panel.

Note Although the Save for Web window doesn't include any options for setting how raster images are saved, any raster images included within the artwork are saved using the last used settings specified in the Export SWF Options dialog box.

The Save for Web window does offer an option to export the layers as CSS Layers. The Export As CSS Layers option is found in the Layers panel (Figure 32-6). After the Export As CSS Layers options is enabled, you can select each layer and set it as Visible, Hidden, or Do Not Export. Layers set to Visible or Hidden are included within the HTML file where JavaScript controls which layers are visible and which are hidden.

Figure 32-6: The Layers panel in the Save for Web window.

STEPS: Creating a Simple Animation Sequence and Exporting It as an SWF File

1. **Open a new file in Illustrator.** Within Illustrator, choose File ⇨ New to create a new document.

2. **Add a symbol to the document.** Choose Window ⇨ Symbol Library ⇨ 3D Symbols to open a symbol library of 3D objects. Drag a 3D arrow symbol to the art board. The symbol displays (Figure 32-7).

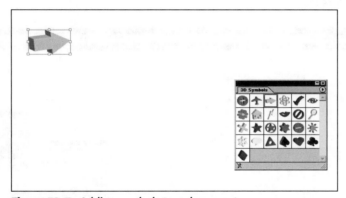

Figure 32-7: Adding symbols to a document

3. **Duplicate and position the symbol.** Hold down the Option/Alt key and drag the arrow symbol to the right. Repeat this action four times until a row of arrow symbols is positioned as shown in Figure 32-8.

4. **Releasing objects to layers.** Choose Window ⇨ Layers to open the Layers palette. Then choose the Release to Layers (Sequence) palette menu command. This creates five new sublayers under Layer 1, as shown in Figure 32-9. Each sublayer includes a single symbol object.

5. **Export to SWF.** Choose File ⇨ Export. This opens a file dialog box, shown in Figure 32-10. In the Save as Type drop-down list, select Macromedia Flash (*.SWF). Then type a name in the File Name field and click Save.

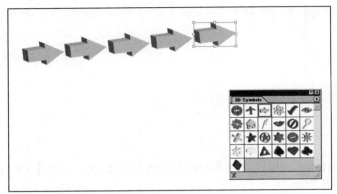

Figure 32-8: Creating duplicate copies of the object

6. **Setting export options.** Clicking Save opens the Macromedia Flash (SWF) Format Options dialog box (Figure 32-11). Within this dialog box, set the Export As option to AI Layers to SWF Frames. This makes each layer a separate SWF frame. Also enable the Looping, Generate HTML, and Read Only options. Finally, set the Image Format to Lossless with a Resolution of 72 ppi. Then click OK.

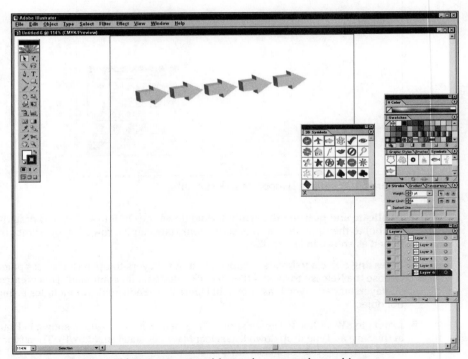

Figure 32-9: New sublayers are created for each separate layer object.

Figure 32-10: The Export dialog box lets you select the file type to save.

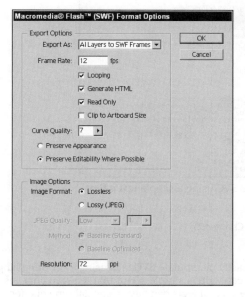

Figure 32-11: Selecting the AI Layers to SWF Frames option

7. Viewing the animated SWF file. Locate the saved `Arrows.html` file in the Finder (Mac) or in Explorer (Windows) and double-click on it. This launches the default Web browser for your system and displays the animated SWF file.

Note   To import the SWF file in a Acrobat PDF document, use the Movie tool and double-click in the Document pane. The Add Movie dialog box opens. Click the Choose button in the Add Movie dialog box and locate the SWF file. Click on the filename and click Select. The SWF document is added as a movie clip.

Creating SVG Files in Illustrator

Macromedia Flash (SWF) files are popular on the Web, but they aren't the only Web technology for displaying vector-based images. Another Web technology that is growing in popularity is Scalable Vector Graphics (SVG).

SVG files have many advantages over Flash files. For one, SVG files are XML-based, meaning they're created using their own unique set of markup tags just like HTML. Thus, you can create and edit them using a standard text editor instead of a complex application. Figure 32-12 shows a simple SVG file of a circle within a text editor.

```
Circle.svg - Notepad
File  Edit  Format  View  Help
<?xml version="1.0" encoding="utf-8"?>
<!-- Generator: Adobe Illustrator 11.0, SVG Export Plug-In . SVG Version:
6.0.0 Build 78)  -->
<!DOCTYPE svg PUBLIC "-//W3C//DTD SVG 1.0//EN"
"http://www.w3.org/TR/2001/REC-SVG-20010904/DTD/svg10.dtd" [
        <!ENTITY ns_flows "http://ns.adobe.com/Flows/1.0/">
        <!ENTITY ns_svg "http://www.w3.org/2000/svg">
        <!ENTITY ns_xlink "http://www.w3.org/1999/xlink">
]>
<svg  xmlns="&ns_svg;" xmlns:xlink="&ns_xlink;"
xmlns:a="http://ns.adobe.com/AdobeSVGViewerExtensions/3.0/"
        width="79.948" height="79.948" viewBox="0 0 79.948 79.948"
style="overflow:visible;enable-background:new 0 0 79.948 79.948"
        xml:space="preserve">
        <style type="text/css">
        <![CDATA[
                .st0{fill:#FFFFFF;stroke:#000000;}
        ]]>
        </style>
        <metadata>
<?xpacket begin='' id='W5M0MpCehiHzreSzNTczkc9d'?><x:xmpmeta
xmlns:x='adobe:ns:meta/' x:xmptk='XMP toolkit 3.0-29, framework 1.6'>
<rdf:RDF xmlns:rdf='http://www.w3.org/1999/02/22-rdf-syntax-ns#'
xmlns:iX='http://ns.adobe.com/iX/1.0/'> <rdf:Description rdf:about=''
xmlns:pdf='http://ns.adobe.com/pdf/1.3/'> </rdf:Description>
<rdf:Description rdf:about=''  xmlns:tiff='http://ns.adobe.com/tiff/1.0/'>
</rdf:Description> <rdf:Description rdf:about=''
xmlns:xap='http://ns.adobe.com/xap/1.0/'
xmlns:xapGImg='http://ns.adobe.com/xap/1.0/g/img/'>
<xap:CreateDate>2004-03-26T00:34:33Z</xap:CreateDate>
<xap:ModifyDate>2004-03-26T00:34:33Z</xap:ModifyDate>
```

Figure 32-12: You can edit XML-based SVG using a simple text editor.

Cross-Reference   An overview of XML is covered in Chapter 27.

Being XML-based also allows you to easily manipulate SVG files using a scripting language such as JavaScript. For example, you can write a simple script that lets you changes the size of a circle SVG element on a Web page. SVG objects can have a special type of effects called SVG effects in Illustrator applied to them. These effects are resolution-independent and are XML-based just like the SVG file. Illustrator can enhance SVG elements with Web page interactivity in response to certain actions like clicking and rollover of a button using the SVG Interactivity palette. All interactivity added to SVG graphics are saved along with the graphics in the SVG file. Finally, the SVG format has broad industry support from many companies involved in both Web and print.

Many Illustrator effects cause the object to which they're applied to rasterize when they're saved to the SVG format. These effects include Rasterize, Artistic, Blur, Brush Strokes, Distort, Pixelate, Sharpen, Sketch, Stylize, Texture, and Video. Avoid these effects for artwork that you intend to save to the SVG format. You can duplicate several of these effects using SVG filters.

Using SVG effects

SVG filters are specialized XML-based filters that perform mathematically operations on SVG objects. Illustrator includes many filters in its Effect ⇨ SVG Filters menu, including several variations of the following:

✦ **AI_Alpha:** Randomly overlays alpha channel transparency.

✦ **AI_BevelShadow:** Adds a smooth beveled drop shadow.

✦ **AI_CoolBreeze:** Inverts the object color and moves the pixels toward the top of the document.

✦ **AI_Dilate:** Gradually expands all lines outwards from the object center.

✦ **AI_Erode:** Gradually pulls all lines inward toward the object center.

✦ **AI_GaussianBlur:** Adds a Gaussian blur to the entire object.

✦ **AI_PixelPlay:** Converts all lines to anti-aliased pixilated lines.

✦ **AI_Shadow:** Adds a simple drop shadow.

✦ **AI_Static:** Fills the object and strokes with static noise.

✦ **AI_Turbulence:** Adds static and random transparent lines.

✦ **AI_Woodgrain:** Fills the object with random wood-grain colors.

> **Note**
>
> Although the SVG filters are special types of filters, they're applied in Illustrator as effects, making it possible to modify and even remove the effect using the Appearance palette.

Figure 32-13 shows samples of each of these SVG filters applied to an object.

To apply one of the default SVG filters to the selected object, select the filter from the Effect ⇨ SVG Filters menu. Alternatively, you can apply these SVG filters using the Apply SVG Filter dialog box (Figure 32-14), which you access via the Effect ⇨ SVG Filters ⇨ Apply SVG Filter menu command. You can import additional default SVG filters by choosing Effect ⇨ SVG Filters ⇨ Import SVG Filter.

The Apply SVG Filter dialog box list all the default SVG filters. To apply a filter, select it from the list and click OK. You can also preview the filter before applying it by enabling the Preview option.

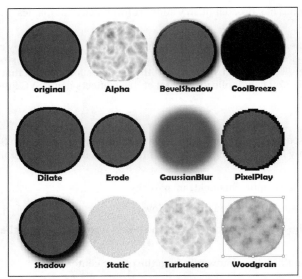

Figure 32-13: The properties for each of the default SVG filters are configurable.

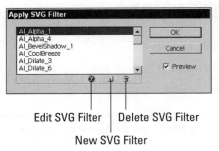

Edit SVG Filter | Delete SVG Filter

New SVG Filter

Figure 32-14: The Apply SVG Filter dialog box lists all the default SVG filters.

Note　After you apply an SVG filter to an object, a rasterized version of the artwork displays in Illustrator, but the SVG file displays as a vector image on a Web page.

A single object may have multiple SVG filters applied to it. All SVG filters that are applied to an object show up in the Appearance palette, shown in Figure 32-15, when you select the object. You can delete applied filters from an object using the Remove Item palette menu command, or by selecting the item and clicking on the trash-can icon at the bottom of the palette.

Caution　Although an object may have several filters applied to it, for SVG files, the final filter in the Appearance palette must be an SVG filter or the entire object is rasterized.

You can edit the default SVG filters by clicking Edit SVG Filter in the Apply SVG Filter dialog box or by double-clicking on the filter you want to edit. The Edit SVG Filter dialog box (Figure 32-16) opens, listing all the XML filter commands. To edit the filter, just type the new commands or change the values within quotes.

Figure 32-15: The Appearance palette holds all SVG filters.

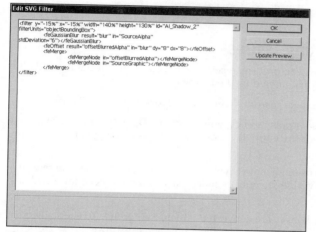

Figure 32-16: The Edit SVG Filter dialog box lets you edit XML code.

The Apply SVG Filter dialog box also includes a New SVG Filter icon button at the bottom of the dialog box that opens a blank Edit SVG Filter dialog box where you can compose new filters.

Adding interactivity

Within a Web page, you can use JavaScript to modify SVG objects. You can also use Illustrator to add some basic interactivity to objects that you want to make SVG files. The code for this interactivity is added to the SVG file automatically when you save the file. You add SVG interactivity to Illustrator objects using the SVG Interactivity palette (Figure 32-17):

✦ **Event:** These are actions that take place in a Web page including onclick, onmouseover, onkeydown, onload, and so on.

✦ **JavaScript:** With an event selected, you can enter a JavaScript command to execute when this event takes place in the JavaScript field. Press the Enter key to confirm the command, and the line of JavaScript is added to the palette.

You can also load a JavaScript file that executes when the event occurs. You do this by selecting the JavaScript Files palette menu command or by clicking on the Link JavaScript Files button at the bottom of the palette. All JavaScript statements listed in the palette are saved in the SVG file when you save the file.

Figure 32-17: The SVG Interactivity palette adds JavaScript commands.

Note   You may open SVG files in the default browser by double-clicking on the file in the Finder (Mac) or in Explorer (Windows). An SVG Viewer is required to view SVG files within a browser. The Adobe SVG Viewer is installed automatically on systems where Illustrator is installed.

Addressing exporting issues

Although SVG is a fairly robust vector format, several aspects of the format are still different from Illustrator's native AI format, including the following:

✦ **Mesh objects:** These objects rasterize when you export them to SVG format.

✦ **Opacity:** To correctly see transparency, you adjust the Opacity for each layer object. Changing the Opacity for the entire layer causes all objects to appear opaque when saved as an SVG file.

✦ **Symbols:** Symbols are used effectively within SVG files. Symbols that are reused several times within a single SVG file are only included once and referenced for all other instances.

✦ **Objects:** Objects in each layer are converted into an SVG group. To keep objects easy to select within the SVG file, place each object on a separate layer.

Saving SVG files

There are also two different ways to save SVG files in Illustrator. One method is to select the SVG file type in the Save As dialog box; the other is to use the Save for Web window. If you look at the file types available in the Save As dialog box, you'll find two different SVG options — SVG and SVG Compressed with the SVGZ file extension. SVG Compressed (SVGZ) files lose their ability to be edited in a text editor. If you know you won't need to edit an SVG file, you can reduce its size even further by saving it using the SVG Compressed format.

Including font glyphs

After you click the Save button in the Save As dialog box, the SVG Options dialog box opens, shown in Figure 32-18. Within this dialog box, you can select a number of options:

✦ **Font Subsetting:** The options include None, which causes a user's system fonts to be used; Only Glyphs Used, which includes only those glyphs contained within the current document; Common English, which includes a set of English characters; Common Roman, which includes a set of Roman characters; and All Glyphs, which includes both English and Roman characters. There are also options to include Common English & Glyphs Used and Common Roman & Glyphs Used. These options include the given set of characters along with any characters contained in the document that aren't included in the given set.

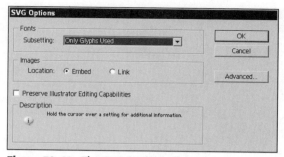

Figure 32-18: The SVG Options dialog box

Including All Glyphs increases the file size much more than including only the glyphs used. If you're certain that the text contained within the SVG file won't change, then you can substantially reduce the file size by selecting the Only Glyphs Used option. If the graphic that you want to save as an SVG file includes only a small bit of text (or no text at all), you can keep the file size small by converting the text to outlines and selecting the None option for the Font Subsetting setting.

✦ **Images Location:** You can embed any raster images that are part of the artwork within the SVG file or link them externally. Embedding images increases the file size, but it makes the image available. If you link the image, the SVG file includes a reference to the image file.

Caution   If the Illustrator document includes a Photoshop (PSD) image file (or any file type that isn't a JPEG or PNG file) and the Link option is selected as the Image Location in the SVG Options dialog box, then the image file is saved using a cryptic filename consisting of random numbers and letters, such as EA5865421.jpg.

✦ **Preserving editing information:** When you select this option, certain information about Illustrator is included within the SVG file. This information allows you to edit the objects in Illustrator.Enabling the Preserve Illustrator Editing Capabilities option adds around 450KB of data to your SVG file. If you save an SVG file for use on the Web, make sure this option is disabled. If you plan on editing the SVG within Illustrator in the future, save another copy of the SVG file with this option enabled or save the file using the AI format.

Saving advanced SVG options

More SVG file options are available in the SVG Advanced Options dialog box, which you access by clicking on the Advanced button in the SVG Options dialog (Figure 32-19).

✦ **CSS Properties:** Lets you select the method to save the CSS properties within the SVG file. The options are Presentation Attributes, Style Attributes, Style Attributes (Entity References), and Style Elements. The first option applies the styles at the presentation level, which embeds the style within the actual objects. The Style Attributes options add CSS code to the top of the SVG file where it is easily extracted or manipulated using JavaScript. The Style Elements option applies the styles as elements that may be reused and applied to HTML elements.

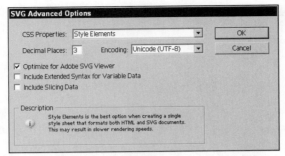

Figure 32-19: The Advanced button opens a dialog box of additional options.

+ **Decimal Places:** Allows you to set the number of decimals to include for all data saved in the SVG file. Although values for this option can range from 1 to 7, anything over 3 is really overkill and simply increases the file size.

+ **Encoding:** Lets you specify the encoding standard used for data saved to the SVG file. The options include ISO 8859-1, Unicode (UTF-8), and Unicode (UTF-16). The UTF-8 encoding standard includes a broad character set with Chinese, Arabic, and all European languages and is generally sufficient for most browsers.

+ **Optimize for Adobe SVG Viewer:** Includes additional information in the SVG file that makes the SVG file render more quickly when viewed in Adobe's SVG Viewer plug-in. The extra data isn't significant enough to drastically alter the file size.

+ **Include Extended Syntax for Variable Data:** Saves all variable data entered in the Variables palette within Illustrator. These variables are used to create data-driven templates.

+ **Include Slicing Data:** Saves all slicing data in the SVG file.

Using the Save for Web window

Another way to save SVG files is with the Save for Web window. Choosing File ⇨ Save for Web (Alt+Shift+Ctrl+S in Windows; Option+Shift+⌘+S on the Mac) opens this interface, shown in Figure 32-20.

After you select the SVG file format, many of the same options discussed in the SVG Advanced Options dialog box appear, including Font Subsetting, Embedding or Linking raster images, CSS Properties, Encoding, and Decimal Places. You can also select the Compressed option to save the SVG file as an SVGZ file.

STEPS: Saving an SVG File

1. **Open a new file in Illustrator.** Within Illustrator, choose File ⇨ New to create a new document.

2. **Create the graph to export.** Using the Illustrator tools, create a design to save as an SVG file. For easier manipulation, place each separate object on a separate layer.

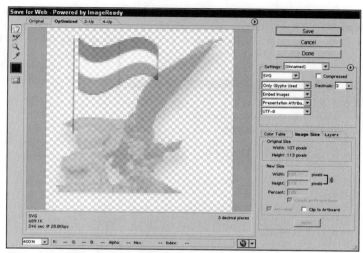

Figure 32-20: You can use the Save for Web window to save Illustrator designs as SVG files.

3. **Add a Shadow SVG filter.** Select the flag objects and choose Effect ⇨ SVG Filter ⇨ Apply SVG Filter. The Apply SVG Filter dialog box appears. Click the Preview option and choose the Al_Shadow_1 filter from the list. Click OK to apply the filter. Figure 32-21 shows the object with the shadow filter applied.

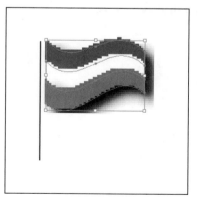

Figure 32-21: A simple drop shadow applied using an SVG filter

Note After the SVG filter is applied, the object is displayed as a raster object instead of as a vector object.

4. **Editing an SVG filter.** Select one of the flag ribbons and choose Window ⇨ Appearance to open the Appearance palette. Notice that the SVG filter appears toward the bottom of the Appearance palette. Double-click on the SVG filter in the Appearance palette. This re-opens the Apply SVG Filter dialog box with the Al_Shadow_1 filter selected.

Click on the Edit SVG Filter button at the bottom of the dialog box. The Edit SVG Filter dialog box opens. Change the dy and dx values within the quote marks to 2, as shown in Figure 32-22. Then click OK to close the dialog box. Figure 32-23 shows the flag with the updated SVG filter applied.

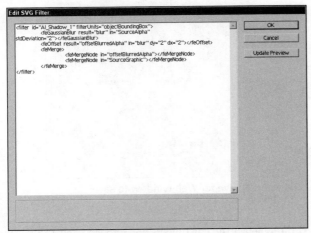

Figure 32-22: The Edit SVG Filter dialog box allows you to edit syntax.

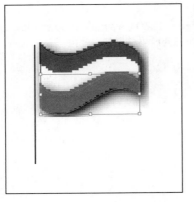

Figure 32-23: After editing the SVG filter, a smaller drop shadow appears.

5. **Save the SVG file.** Select the File ➪ Save As menu command. Type a name for the SVG file and click the Save button. The SVG Options dialog box opens. Because this file doesn't include any text, select None as the Font Subsetting option. Disable the Preserve Illustrator Editing Capabilities option and click OK. The SVG file is saved to the hard drive.

6. **Viewing the saved SVG file.** Locate the saved SVG file on your system and double-click on it to open it within the system's default Web browser. Figure 32-24 shows the resulting flag in a Web browser.

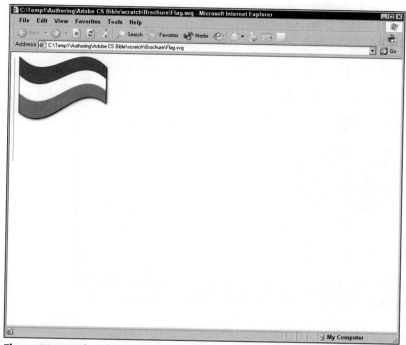

Figure 32-24: The object appears as a vector image when viewed in a Web browser.

Using SWF and SVG Files in GoLive

After you create an SWF or SVG file, you can use it to enhance a Web page in GoLive. You add SWF and SVG files to a Web page as objects by dragging them from the Basic category in the Toolbox. Alternatively, you can convert them from an Illustrator Smart Object.

Adding SWF and SVG objects to a Web page in GoLive

After you have an SWF or SVG file saved on your hard drive, you can add either to a GoLive Web page by dragging the respective SWF or SVG object icon from the Toolbox and dropping it on a Web page at the position where you want the SWF or SVG file to appear. Both SWF and SVG objects are found in the Basic Elements category in the Toolbox.

Dropping either an SWF of SVG object onto a Web page displays an object icon. These object icons are placeholders for the file and you can resize them by dragging on their borders. The properties for the selected object also display in the Inspector palette. Figure 32-25 shows a blank Web page with an SWF and an SVG object dropped onto it.

To load an SWF or SVG file into the respective object, click on the Browse button in the Inspector palette. This opens a file dialog box where you can select the file to use. The filename then appears in the Inspector palette, and the file loads into the Web page within the Layout Editor. The filename is also listed at the top of the object. Figure 25-26 shows a Web page with SWF and SVG files loaded.

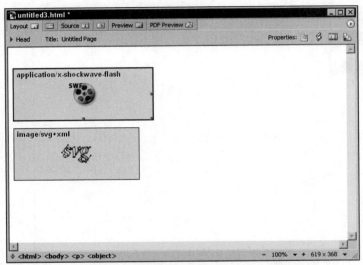

Figure 32-25: The SWF object appears as an icon on the Web page.

When either an SWF or an SVG object is selected in the Web page, the Inspector palette includes four tabs:

✦ **Basic tab:** Lists the File, MIME, and Class for the object. The File field holds the path and name for the file that is loaded into the object. It includes a Fetch URL button, which lets you select files by dragging the icon to the filename in the site window, and a Browse button, which opens a file dialog box where you can select a file to open. The MIME field includes code that identifies the file type to the browser. The Class field identifies the plug-in used to view the file. For SWF and SVG files, the MIME and Class fields are filled in automatically as needed.

The Basic panel also lets you specify the dimensions and alignment for the object. When a file is specified, the dimensions specified in the file are loaded automatically into the Width and Height fields, but you can change these values by typing new values or by dragging the object borders in the Layout Editor. Clicking the button to the right of the Width and Height fields resets the object to the dimensions specified in the file.

✦ **More tab:** Includes several additional properties. The Name field lets you name the element. This is the name that is used within the Web page and with JavaScript to identify the object. The Page and Code fields are used to specify a location where the information about the needed plug-in is located and the location of that plug-in. For SWF files, these fields are populated automatically. The Palette options are used to make the plug-in appear in the foreground or background. The HSpace and VSpace values define the amount of padded white space that vertically and horizontally surround the object. Finally, the Is Hidden option hides the object on the Web page. If the object is only used to play sound for instance, you'll want to hide the object but not its action.

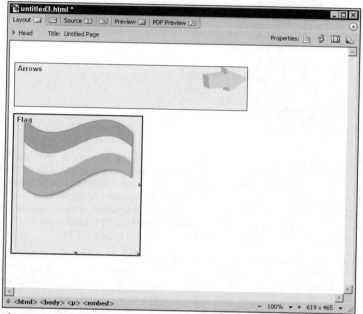

Figure 32-26: The files appear within the Web page.

✦ **Attribs tab:** Lists all the settings for the specific object as set in the final panel.

✦ **SWF tab:** With the SWF object selected in the Web page, the Inspector palette lists the SWF-specific settings in the SWF panel, shown in Figure 32-27.

• **Autoplay:** Causes any animation associated with the SWF file to begin as soon as the Web page is loaded in a browser.

• **Loop:** Causes the animation sequence to repeat again after it's finished.

• **Quality:** You can set this to Default, Best, High, Auto High, Auto Low, and Low. These settings correspond to the appearance of the animation versus the play-back speed. The Default setting lets the browser player determine this setting. The Best setting shows all the details of each frame regardless of how it impacts the playback speed, and a Low setting sacrifices the quality of the animation frames in order to play back the animation at the target frame rate. The Autohigh and Autolow settings work to maintain image appearance and playback speed, respectively, while improving the other when it can.

Figure 32-27: The SWF panel in the Inspector palette

- **Scale:** This setting determines how to handle the display of SWF files where there is a difference in the size specified on the Web page and the size of the actual SWF file. The Default setting maintains the aspect ratio of the original file within the designated Web-page area. This causes borders to appear on two sides of the SWF object. The No Border option also maintains the aspect ratio of the SWF file but crops the file so no borders appear. The Exact Fit option stretches the SWF file to fit within the given area. This may distort the SWF file.

The SVG-specific options are listed in the SVG panel of the Inspector palette when an SVG object is selected in the Layout Editor. The only option on the SVG panel is Use Compressed SVG. With this option enabled, the SVG file is saved using the SVGZ extension.

Using Illustrator Smart Objects

Another way to add SWF and SVG objects to a Web page is using the Illustrator Smart Object. Dragging the Illustrator Smart Object from the Toolbox to the Layout Editor places an icon and loads the object's properties in the Inspector palette. Clicking on the Browse button opens a file dialog box where you can select the Illustrator (AI) file to open.

Selecting an Illustrator file to open makes the Conversion Settings dialog box appear, shown in Figure 32-28. From this dialog box, you can convert the selected Illustrator file to a bitmap format, an SVG, a compressed SVG, or an SWF file.

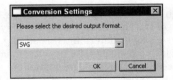

Figure 32-28: The Conversion Settings dialog box

Selecting the Bitmap Formats option opens the Save for Web window where you can select to save the Illustrator file as an optimized GIF, JPEG, PNG, or WBMP file. The SVG, Compressed SVG, and SWF options load the file in Illustrator and open the SVG Options dialog box or the Macromedia Flash (SWF) Format Options dialog box, where you can specify the options to use to convert the file.

STEPS: Adding SWF and SVG Files to a Web Page

1. **Open a Web page in GoLive.** Within GoLive, choose File ➪ Open to open a Web page where you want to add the SWF and SVG files, or locate and double-click on the Web page in the site window.

2. **Add SWF and SVG objects to the Web page.** With the Web page open, click on the Basic Elements category button in the Toolbox and drag both an SWF and an SVG object from the Toolbox to the Web page. The objects appear as icons, as shown in Figure 32-29.

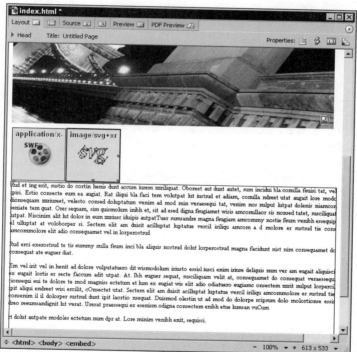

Figure 32-29: Objects initially dragged from the Toolbox display as icons.

3. **Specify the SWF and SVG files.** Select the SWF object in the Layout Editor and click on the Browse button in the Inspector palette. In the file dialog box that opens, locate an SWF file and click the Open button. Repeat for the SVG object. The selected files are loaded into the Web page. Figure 32-30 shows the Web page with the file loaded.

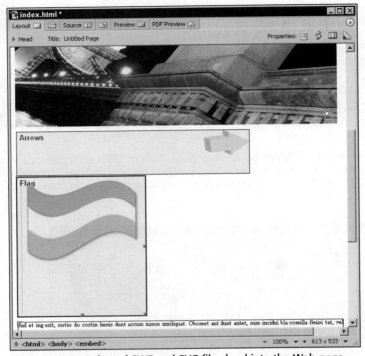

Figure 32-30: Selected SWF and SVG files load into the Web page.

4. **Resizing the SVG object.** Select the SVG flag object and drag on its lower-right corner while holding down the Shift key to reduce its size until its height is equal to the SWF file. Holding down the Shift key constrains the aspect ratio of the object. Figure 32-31 shows the Web page after the SVG flag has been resized.

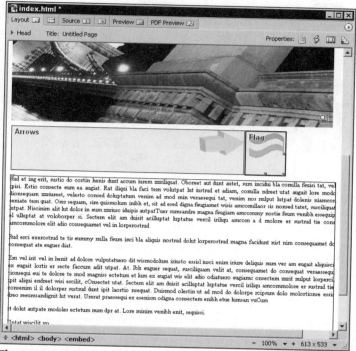

Figure 32-31: GoLive lets you change the width and height of objects.

5. **Setting the SWF properties.** With the SWF object selected, click on the SWF tab in the Inspector palette. Enable the Autoplay and Loop options and set the Quality setting to Autolow. This ensures that the playback speed stays constant.

6. **Previewing the Web page.** To see a preview of the SWF and SVG objects added to the Web page, select the Preview tab above the Web-page window. In this view, you can see the animation sequence for the SWF file, as shown in Figure 32-32.

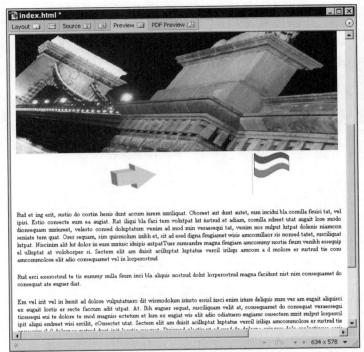

Figure 32-32: The Preview panel shows the Web page, as it would appear in a Web browser.

Using SWF Files in Acrobat

Acrobat offers you two interesting ways to import SWF files in PDF documents. One method is to convert animated Web pages containing SWF files to PDF documents. The other use for SWF with PDFs is to import the motion graphics directly in a PDF file as a movie-file import. Depending on your source files and the content you want to create in Acrobat, you'll find benefits using both of these methods.

Converting Web pages to PDF

You can convert Web pages to PDF using the File ➪ Create PDF ➪ From Web Page menu command in Acrobat on either the Mac or Windows. Windows users have an extra benefit when using Microsoft Internet Explorer, because a task button appears in the Explorer window that enables you to convert Web pages in view to PDF. When you create PDF documents from Web pages, all the page content is converted and the page is viewed in Acrobat viewers much like you see the page viewed in a Web browser, including Flash animations.

Acrobat 6 and greater viewers support two different media compatibilities. You can import a variety of media files using either the Acrobat 5 compatibility or Acrobat 6 compatibility. A few differences between the two compatibility levels are that you can embed Acrobat 6–

compatible media in the PDF document and the number of media formats supported are much greater. When you convert Web pages or import SWF files, the files are imported as Acrobat 6–compatible media and either embedded or linked to a PDF file. You have no option for importing SWF files as Acrobat 5–compatible media.

To convert a Web page to a PDF document, choose File ➪ Create PDF ➪ From Web Page (Shift+ Ctrl+O in Windows; Shift+⌘+O on the Mac). This opens the Create PDF from Web Page dialog box, shown in Figure 32-33. Note that Windows users can use the PDF Maker task button installed in Microsoft Internet Explorer. By default, this task button is installed in Explorer at the time of your CS Premium or Acrobat 6 installation.

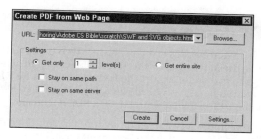

Figure 32-33: The Create PDF from Web Page dialog box

The Create PDF from Web Page dialog box has the following options:

✦ **URL:** To select a Web site, type the URL in the URL field box or click on the Browse button to select a Web site stored locally on your hard drive or network server.

✦ **Settings section:** You have the following options:

• **Get only/Get entire site:** You can select linked pages according to the number of levels contained on a Web site or you can convert the entire site to PDF. Note that if you convert more than one level or use the Get Entire Site option, you can convert an extraordinary number of pages. When converting Web sites with which you aren't familiar, be certain to gradually convert pages rather than the entire site to avoid creating PDFs of extraordinary size.

• **Stay on same path/Stay on same server:** These options choices prevent linked Web pages from other sites and servers being converted to PDF, thereby keeping your resultant PDF smaller in size with less clutter. Obviously, if you need linked pages to be converted to PDF then you'll want to reach out to other servers and levels. You can always return to the PDF file and append more pages if needed.

Any SWF files included in the converted Web pages are added to the final PDF document. You can embed the SWF files in the PDF document or link the files to the PDF. Either way, you can select, copy and paste them between PDF files.

Note

You can embed or link multimedia files, including SWF, to a PDF file. By default, the media is embedded in the PDF during HTML-to-PDF conversion. If you want to link the files, click on Settings in the Create PDF from Web Page dialog box. In the Web Capture dialog box, scroll the list and select HTML. Click on the Settings button, and the HTML Conversion Settings dialog box opens. From the Multimedia pull-down menu, select Reference Multimedia Content by URL. The file is then linked to the PDF.

If you want to convert a Web site containing an animated page using an SWF file, convert the file and use either the Movie tool or the Select Object tool in Acrobat to select the movie frame. Copy the file by choosing Edit ➪ Copy and paste the file into another PDF document. These steps might be helpful when working in a workflow where you want to use animated graphics from your client's Web site and don't have immediate access to the Web-site source files or a password to retrieve files from the client's Web site. In such a case, simply convert Web pages to PDF and copy and paste the movie frames as needed.

Note   SWF files can be viewed in PDF documents, but SVG files are not supported in Acrobat. As of this writing, you cannot convert SVG files to PDF nor import them in existing PDFs.

Importing SWF files in PDF documents

You use the Movie tool to import SWF files in Acrobat PDFs. If you convert Web pages to PDF, you need to copy and paste SWF files using the Movie tool or the Select Object tool to select the movie frame and copy the file. However, you cannot export the frame back to an SWF file for use in HTML documents or for viewing in stand-alone SWF viewers. If you create an SWF file in either Flash or Illustrator, you can import the SWF file directly in a PDF document.

To import an SWF file, click on the Movie tool in the Advanced Editing toolbar. You can either drag open a rectangle frame or double-click the Movie tool in the Document pane. Either action opens the Add Movie dialog box, shown in Figure 32-34.

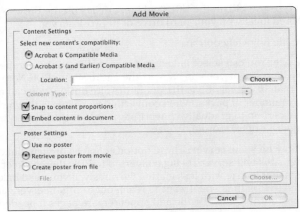

Figure 32-34: The Add Movie dialog box offers options for importing.

The options you have in this dialog box include the following:

✦ **Adobe Compatibility options:** The first two option choices offer you selections for choosing either Acrobat 5 or Acrobat 6 compatibility. If you select Acrobat 5 (and Earlier) Compatible Media, Acrobat won't recognize the SWF files on your computer as you try to import them in the open PDF document. You need to select Acrobat 6 Compatible Media then click on the Choose/Browse button to open the Select Movie File dialog box where movie files are identified for importing. You select the file and click on the Select button; the file is imported into the PDF document. After importing the movie file (including SWF files), you're returned to the Add Movie dialog box.

✦ **Snap to content proportions:** Keeps the movie frame proportional as you size it, thereby preventing distortion when playing the movie.

✦ **Embed content in document:** Offers an option to either embed the content (when the check box is enabled) or create a link to the file (when the check box is disabled). If you uncheck this box, the movie file needs to travel along with the PDF document as you send the file to other users.

✦ **Poster Settings:** These have to do with the visual contained within the movie frame known as the movie poster. You can choose to use no poster, create a poster from the first frame in the movie, or create a poster from a file. When creating posters from files, you click the Choose/Browse button to navigate your hard drive to locate the image you want to use as the poster. All files compatible with Create PDF from File can be used as a poster image. Select the file you want to use and it's converted to PDF and placed as the contents for the movie frame. As the movie plays, the poster disappears; it returns after the movie stops playing.

After using the Movie tool and importing an SWF file or other type of movie file, you can adjust various properties for the movie and the playback in Acrobat. To open the Properties dialog box, select either the Movie tool or the Select Object tool and open a context menu on the movie frame. Select Properties from the menu options, and the Multimedia Properties dialog box opens, shown in Figure 32-35.

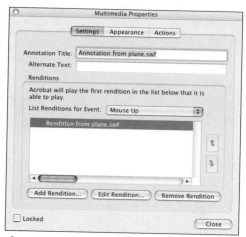

Figure 32-35: The Multimedia Properties dialog box

The default pane that appears when opening the Multimedia Properties dialog box is the Settings pane. To edit various options for the movie play, click on the Edit Rendition button. The Rendition Settings dialog box, shown in Figure 32-36, opens. In this dialog box, you have a considerable number of choices to describe attributes for playing media files.

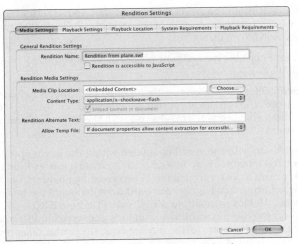

Figure 32-36: The Rendition Settings dialog box

Of particular importance to many users are the settings found in the Playback Settings pane. Click on Playback Settings at the top of the Rendition Settings dialog box, and the pane shown in Figure 32-37 opens.

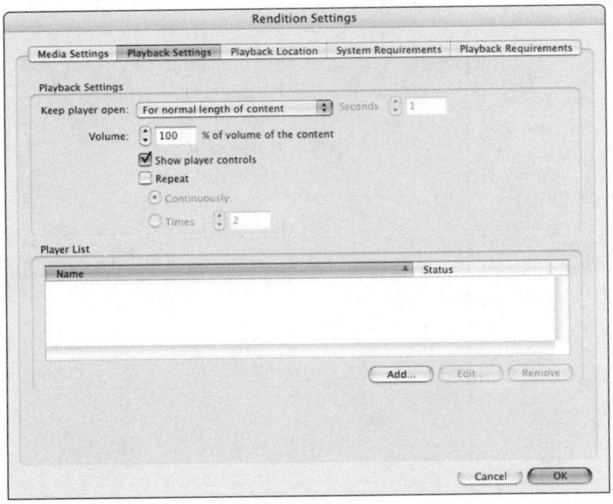

Figure 32-37: The Playback Settings pane

If you want to show player controls where a media clip can be stopped, paused, restarted, and so on, check the box for Show Player Controls. After exiting the Renditions Settings, you'll see a player control appear at the bottom of the movie frame, as shown in Figure 32-38.

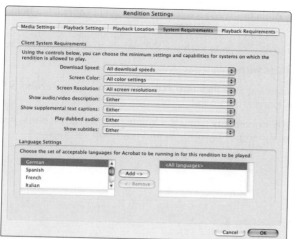

Figure 32-38: Player controls appear at the bottom of a media clip.

The rendition settings offer you much more than controlling the media play with player controls. You can create several renditions in the same PDF document and identify what rendition is played according to download speeds for different users. For example, users who have modem connections at 28.8 baud can receive and view a small media file, while users with DSL and cable-modem connections can view media clips of larger sizes. You can create renditions that play according to user download speeds, where Acrobat analyzes a user's connection and delivers the media defined for the respective speed. Other options in the rendition settings offer choices for where media is played within the document, embedding or linking options, associating JavaScripts with media plays, timing movie plays for a given length of time, foreign-language selections, showing subtitles, and much more.

Cross-Reference
For a detailed review of multimedia and PDF files, refer to the *Adobe Acrobat 6 PDF Bible* (published by Wiley).

Keep in mind that the SWF files you create in Illustrator are ultimately media clips. They're handled in Acrobat and assigned properties, as any movie file would be.

Summary

✦ You use Illustrator to export graphics to SWF files.

✦ You create SWF animation sequences in Illustrator by placing the objects for each frame on a separate layer. These layers convert to frames during export.

✦ You can separate several objects included on a single layer in layers using the Layers palette's Release to Layers command.

✦ You can save objects as an SVG or as a Compressed SVG file using Illustrator's File ➪ Save As menu command.

✦ You can apply SVG filters to objects saved as SVG files to prevent them from being rasterized.

✦ You attach JavaScript code to SVG objects with the SVG Interactivity palette.

✦ You place SWF and SVG objects within Web pages using GoLive.

✦ You convert Web pages containing SWF files into PDF documents using Acrobat's File ⇨ Create PDF ⇨ From Web Page menu command.

✦ You import SWF files into PDF documents using the Movie tool. As movie clips, you can assign SWF files a number of different play options and rendition settings.

✦   ✦   ✦

Creating Slide Presentations

Slide presentations may be something you want to use in client meetings when proposing new concepts or campaigns, or your clients may ask you to create presentations they want to use at trade shows, meetings, and conferences. Whether for your own needs or your clients' needs, at one time or another design professionals periodically find a need to create slide presentations. If creating slide presentations is not something you usually do, the last thing you'll want to do is try to learn a new program to quickly assemble a presentation for yourself or your client.

Dedicated slide-creation programs like Microsoft PowerPoint and Apple's Keynote are designed specifically for creating presentations. However, if you're not up to speed with these programs and need to design a presentation quickly, you'll find working in programs you know to be much less frustrating. In this chapter, you learn how to use the CS programs for creating slide presentations and converting presentations from the dedicated slide-presentation applications to file formats usable with the CS programs.

Converting Presentation Documents to PDF

Because slide presentations may exist in a variety of different formats, you may need to convert an existing file that was created by your client to something workable with the CS programs. The most-popular presentation documents you'll find are Microsoft PowerPoint files — but you're not necessarily limited to PowerPoint. You may find old layouts in QuarkXPress, Adobe PageMaker, or other application documents that were once used as a presentation and now need to be updated or refined for current presentations.

In addition to converting existing documents to a format workable with the CS programs, you may need to integrate current files created in Illustrator, Photoshop, InDesign, and/or GoLive with older presentation documents. Assuming you're not up to speed in a program designed to create presentations, you need to convert files to a format usable as a display tool for presentations. Fortunately, you can convert all files from any authoring program to PDF, and you can use Adobe Acrobat as a presentation tool.

Acrobat is not a mere substitute for presentation programs. Acrobat can stand alone as a sophisticated presentation tool where you can add transitions, create links to documents, show multimedia film clips, display presentations in self-running modes for kiosks, add animation, and take advantage of all the other features one would expect from a presentation program. If you've begun to master the CS programs, you'll find creating PDF files for presentations a better solution in your workflow if you aren't familiar with creating slides in a presentation program.

Converting PowerPoint slides to PDF

The de facto standard presentation program on Windows is Microsoft PowerPoint. Microsoft Office users are so familiar with PowerPoint that they tend to create documents ranging from slide presentations to large-format display prints. If you work with corporate clients who supply files to you, you'll definitely see many PowerPoint files.

You can convert PowerPoint slides to PDF and add slide pages to an InDesign document for further development of a presentation, or convert PowerPoint slides to PDF while preserving animation effects created in PowerPoint. Any Acrobat viewer can see the animation exported with the PowerPoint slides.

Note   Knowing you can view the files you convert to PDF in any Acrobat viewer is an important issue. You may author files in Acrobat Professional, yet you may deliver PDF documents to coworkers or clients who use either Acrobat Standard or Adobe Reader. File conversions from PowerPoint can be viewed in any Acrobat viewer, complete with transition effects.

To convert PowerPoint slides to PDF you can use the Convert to PDF from File command in Acrobat (this works only on Windows for Office file formats) or the PDFMaker in PowerPoint. Using either method requires you to have PowerPoint installed on your computer. Therefore, if you receive PowerPoint files from your clients, be certain you own a copy of Microsoft Office, or have your clients send you a PostScript file or have them convert the PowerPoint PPT files to PDF.

Note   The PDFMaker macro is installed automatically in Microsoft Office applications (Word, Excel, and PowerPoint) when you first install Microsoft Office and then install either Adobe Acrobat or the CS applications that include the Acrobat installation. The order of installation is critical. If you install Office *after* Adobe Acrobat, the PDFMaker won't be accessible in any Office application. When Acrobat is installed properly, you can access the PDFMaker by clicking the Acrobat tool in the Office application toolbar.

Cross-Reference   For more information on using PDFMaker, see Part V.

Setting up the page

When exporting to PDF via PDFMaker in PowerPoint or using the Create PDF from File menu command, the correct page size is defined in the Page Setup dialog box. Select File ➪ Page Setup and check the page size. By default, the slides in PowerPoint default to 10 x 7.5 inches in a landscape view. Be certain the page size matches the slide pages. If you don't have the page size available as a choice, you must create a custom page size and add it to your Page Setup dialog box.

On the Mac, select File ➪ Page Setup. In the Page Setup dialog box, click on the Options button to open the second Page Setup dialog box, shown in Figure 33-1. If you don't have a paper size equivalent to current slide sizes, select the Adobe PDF Printer in the Format For pull-down menu and open the Settings pull-down menu. From the menu choices, select Custom Paper Size. The Page Setup dialog box changes where custom page sizes can be added and defined for new custom page choices. After you click through the dialog boxes, select File ➪ Print to open the Print dialog box.

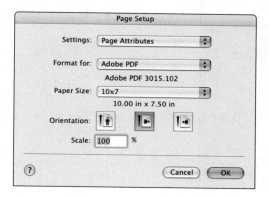

Figure 33-1: Begin the PowerPoint to PDF conversion by opening the Page Setup dialog box.

In the Print dialog box shown in Figure 33-2, be certain to select Microsoft PowerPoint from the pull-down menu just below the Presets pull-down menu. The Print dialog box changes so you can select what you want to convert to PDF. If animation is included in the slideshow, select Slides (with Animation) from the Print What pull-down menu.

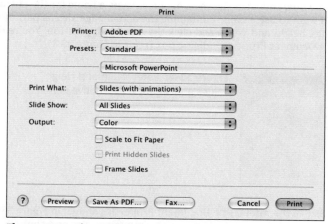

Figure 33-2: The Print dialog box

Instead of clicking Print, click the Preview button and you see a preview for how the PDF pages are displayed in the resultant PDF document. If all looks well, close the Preview and click on the Create Adobe PDF tool in the PowerPoint toolbar.

On Windows, you set up custom pages in the Print dialog box. Select File ➪ Print to open the Print dialog box and check the printer in the Name field box. To be safe, select the Adobe PDF Printer from the Name pull-down menu, and you're assured of using a color PostScript printer driver. Click Properties in the Print dialog box to open the Adobe PDF Document Properties dialog box, shown in Figure 33-3.

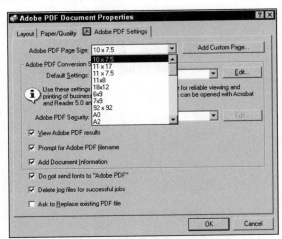

Figure 33-3: The Adobe PDF Document Properties dialog box

Click on the Custom Page button in the Adobe PDF Document Properties dialog box and the Add Custom Paper Size dialog box, shown in Figure 33-4, opens. Type a name for the custom page size — generally, you'll want to use a name containing the actual page size as part of the name. Enter the values for the height and Width and click the Add/Modify button. You're then returned to the Adobe PDF Document Properties dialog box (refer to Figure 33-3).

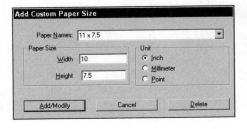

Figure 33-4: Enter Width and Height values and supply a descriptive name.

From the Adobe PDF Page Size in the Adobe PDF Document Properties shown in Figure 33-3, you find the new page size added to the pull-down menu. Click the page size and click OK.

Because you're working in the Print dialog box and you don't really want to print the file, you need to register your new settings without printing the file. When you return to the Print dialog box, shown in Figure 33-5, click the Preview button. You're provided a preview of the slides that will eventually show up in Acrobat. If the page size is not right or the orientation is wrong, you need to go back to the Print dialog box and click the Properties button again to make adjustments in the Adobe PDF Document Properties dialog box.

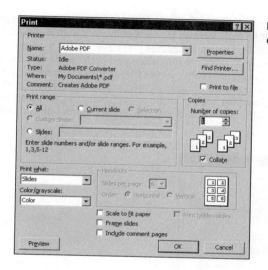

Figure 33-5: In the Print dialog box, click the Preview button to preview.

Close the document-preview window and you're returned to the PowerPoint application window. If everything looks okay in the preview window, you're ready to convert to PDF using the PDFMaker.

Caution   PowerPoint enables you to print slides, handouts, notes pages, or an outline view of the pages. What is printed is determined in the Print dialog box. Be certain you have Slides selected in the Print What pull-down menu before converting your slides to PDF.

Using PDFMaker

If you have the luxury of using both platforms and can work on a Windows machine, by all means use Windows when exporting to PDF from PowerPoint. The PDFMaker on the Mac works painfully slow and, if you struggle with page sizes and need to re-create the PDF a few times just to get it right, generating the final PDF document of an eight-page slide presentation could take you hours on the Mac. On Windows, the same file takes a matter of minutes.

On Windows, you have the advantage of editing Conversion Settings from a menu command in the PowerPoint application menu. Conversion Settings offer you choices for how the PDF is created in terms of file compression, preserving various settings made in PowerPoint including transitions and effects, converting multimedia, and a host of options you have available by editing the Adobe PDF settings. To open the Adobe PDF Maker dialog box where Conversion Settings are adjusted, click on the Adobe PDF menu in PowerPoint, as shown in Figure 33-6. Select Conversion Settings from the menu options.

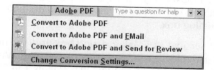

Figure 33-6: Select Conversion Settings from the Adobe PDF menu.

In the Adobe PDFMaker dialog box, shown in Figure 33-7, check the boxes for the items you want to enable or disable. To edit the Adobe PDF Settings that are employed with Acrobat Distiller, click the Adobe PDF Settings button. The same options you have available when adjusting the Distiller Adobe PDF Settings are available to you when you click on the Advanced Settings button. In most cases, you won't need to create custom PDF settings. Therefore, just select the conversion settings you want to use from choices in the Conversion Settings pull-down menu. By default, you should see Standard appear in the menu. Using the Standard settings generally does the job for creating slide presentations shown on-screen but not printed on commercial printing devices.

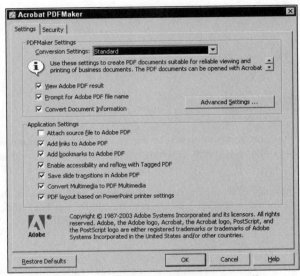

Figure 33-7: The Adobe PDFMaker dialog box offer options for creating a PDF.

Cross-Reference   Understanding the Adobe PDF Settings (called *job options* in earlier versions of Acrobat) is an elaborate and complicated process. For almost all the PDF creation you perform with the CS programs, you won't need to adjust conversion settings and won't find a need to create custom Adobe PDF Settings. If you do find that you need to understand more and want to create your own custom settings files, see the *Adobe Acrobat 6 PDF Bible* (published by Wiley).

Leave the default check boxes checked in the Adobe PDFMaker dialog box, and click OK to return to the PowerPoint application window. To create the PDF file, you need to select Convert to Adobe PDF from the Adobe PDF menu (Windows only) or click the Convert to Adobe PDF tool in the toolbar (Mac and Windows). PowerPoint begins to convert the open document to PDF using all the settings you made in the Print dialog box.

If you're working on a Mac, be certain to leave the Acrobat PDFMaker dialog box undisturbed until you see the View File button highlighted. After the PDF creation is completed, click View File or open the PDF from within Acrobat. If you checked the box to View PDF Result, the PDF opens automatically in your default Acrobat viewer.

Converting Apple Keynote slides to PDF (Mac)

Apple Keynote is a dedicated slide-presentation authoring application that offers a robust authoring environment with simplicity and ease in creating slideshows. The charting features in Keynote are easy to use, with intuitive palettes for editing chart types and data, as shown in Figure 33-8.

Keynote supports file imports for many image formats, video and sound, and PDF imports that can be sized and scaled. The templates installed with the program are attractive and well designed. After creating a slideshow in Keynote, choose File ⇨ Export. A dialog box drops down from the application menu bar where format options offer you exporting to QuickTime, PowerPoint, or PDF formats, as shown in Figure 33-9. To export directly to PDF format, select the PDF radio button and click Next. Locate the folder where you want the PDF file saved, and click on the Export button.

If you want to create a PDF for handout notes, choose File ⇨ Print Slides. From the pull-down menu below the Presets pull-down menus, select Keynote. Select Adobe PDF to create the PDF file using the Adobe PDF settings options. Select Slides with Notes, as shown in Figure 33-10.

As is the case with any application on Mac OS X, you also have an option to create a PDF document by clicking on the Save As PDF button. For PDF creation, you'll find writing PDFs to the Adobe PDF Printer to be a better choice. When using the Adobe PDF Printer, you have choices for selecting the Adobe PDF settings. Using the Save As PDF option in the Mac OS X Print dialog box uses a fixed set of options to create PDF files.

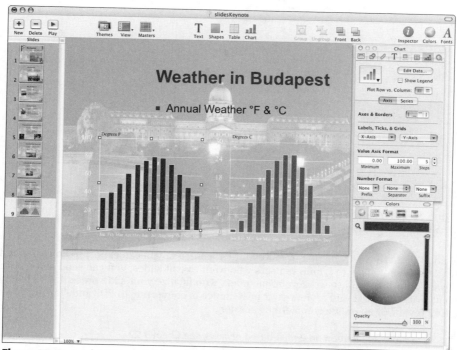

Figure 33-8: Apple's Keynote is a robust slide-creation program with sophisticated graphing features.

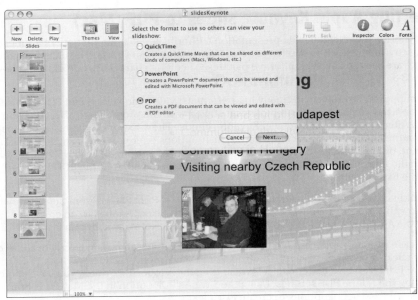

Figure 33-9: To convert Keynote slides to PDF, click the PDF option.

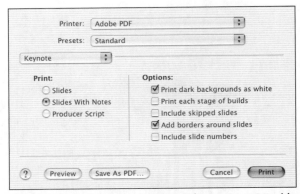

Figure 33-10: You convert slides with notes to PDF with the Slides with Notes option.

In addition to the PDF creation from Keynote documents, you can export to PowerPoint. If sending Keynote files to Windows users who want to edit slides, you can send an exported PowerPoint document to workgroup members who finalize your slide presentation in Power-Point. For comments and review, your best choice is converting to PDF and starting an e-mail-based review or an online commenting session.

Cross-Reference   For more information on e-mail-based reviews, see Chapter 22.

Caution

If you exchange files with users on different platforms, be certain the fonts installed on Windows and Mac systems are compatible.

Creating Presentations in CS programs

If your comfort zone is strictly limited to the CS applications, you may not want to learn either PowerPoint or Keynote. If so, then you can use some of the CS programs as presentation-authoring tools. All the CS programs except Adobe Acrobat can be used as the authoring tool, while Acrobat is used as the display tool for showing presentations. In practicality, using Adobe GoLive is more cumbersome (unless, of course, the presentation format will be HTML), while the most likely candidate to help you create a presentation project is Adobe InDesign.

Using InDesign as a presentation-authoring tool

Creating slides in InDesign has its advantages and disadvantages. In terms of disadvantages, InDesign does not offer you dynamic outlining where you add text in an outline format that is automatically applied to individual slides. The actual creation of text on slides is much faster in a dedicated slide-creation tool. Additionally, you have no options for printing notes or handouts, adding animation to text and objects, editing charts and graphs, and a few other specific slide-creation features.

On the advantage side of using InDesign, you have much more design freedom than using dedicated slide-creation programs, including the ability to import native CS application documents; the ability to import files saved from a wider range of formats; better typographic control; more-sophisticated editing of graphic elements such as applying drop shadows, adding transparency, and feathering objects; and all the options InDesign offers you for creating sophisticated layouts. In Figure 33-11, you can see a native Photoshop image in the lower-left corner of the slide with transparency and a graduated transparent edge at the bottom of the image. In addition, drop shadows were applied to both the image with transparency and the photo in the center of the slide. The soft shadow and same transparency in the native Photoshop document could not be created in either PowerPoint or Keynote.

Creating bookmarks

As a final editing task, you may want to add bookmarks to your presentation. Bookmarks can help you easily return to areas of discussion when answering questions or adding information on topics as you make a presentation. You have a choice for adding bookmarks directly in InDesign and having those bookmarks exported in the PDF document or creating bookmarks in Acrobat. In some workflows, you may find a benefit in creating bookmarks in InDesign if a layout specialist is unfamiliar with Acrobat and doesn't have the full version installed on a computer.

To create bookmarks in InDesign, select Window ➪ Interactive ➪ Bookmarks to open the Bookmarks palette. Creating bookmarks is easy in both InDesign and Acrobat. Find text on a page you want to use as a bookmark title and select the text. Click on the right-pointing arrow in the palette to open the fly-away menu, and select New Bookmark, as shown in Figure 33-12. In Acrobat, the menu command to create a new bookmark is found in the Bookmark pane Options menu.

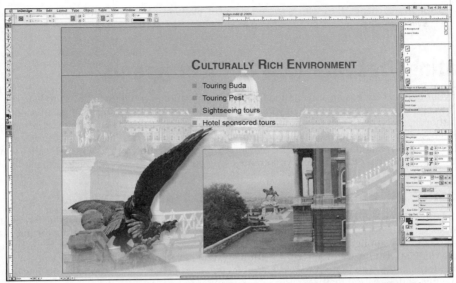

Figure 33-11: Using InDesign to create slides allows you to import native files with transparency.

Creating bookmarks: Acrobat or InDesign?

There's a big difference between bookmarks created in InDesign and bookmarks created in Acrobat. When you create bookmarks in Acrobat, the bookmark captures the view of the bookmarked page. When zooming in 400 percent and creating a bookmark, you capture the page and the zoom view. Therefore, if you are in a 100-percent view and click on a bookmark that was bookmarked at a 400-percent view, Acrobat takes you to the page bookmarked and zooms in to a 400-percent view. When you create a bookmark in InDesign, the zoom is derived from the current view. Therefore, if you zoom to 400 percent to view pages, and then click a bookmark, the bookmarked page opens at 400 percent even though the bookmark may have been created at 100-percent view. If you zoom out to a Fit Page view in the same document and continue clicking on bookmarks, the bookmark zooms inherit the current view (for example, Fit Page). Note that if the bookmarks are created in InDesign and the file is exported to PDF, viewing the bookmarked pages in Acrobat treat the zoom levels with the same inherited page views.

At first blush, you may think it more of an advantage to create bookmarks in InDesign so that all page links go to inherited zoom levels. However, there's a price to pay for having the feature. When you create bookmarks in InDesign, you add more overhead to your file because inDesign creates not only bookmarks but also Destinations. In Acrobat Destinations are similar to bookmarks where you can click on Destinations to navigate pages. However, adding Destinations to a PDF file significantly adds to the file size. For small to moderate-size presentations that are viewed from files stored on your hard drive, it shouldn't be an issue. However if you post files on the Web or use very large PDF documents, you'll want to avoid using Destinations. The added file sizes can slow down performance in Acrobat and add to the download time with Web-hosted documents.

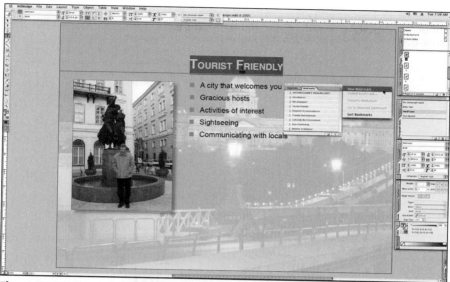

Figure 33-12: To capture the page view, select New Bookmark.

If you want to create a bookmark without capturing highlighted text as the bookmark name, don't select any text, but select New Bookmark from the fly-away palette. InDesign automatically names the bookmark simply as Bookmark. To edit the name, select Rename Bookmark in the fly-away palette. A dialog box opens where you edit the name.

After creating bookmarks, scroll the Bookmark palette and review the bookmark names. To check the bookmark links, double-click on a name and InDesign opens the page associated with the bookmark. Note that InDesign requires you to double click a bookmark name to view the destination, while Acrobat requires only a single mouse click.

Exporting to PDF

After you've created your slides, added bookmarks, and reviewed the document, you need to export the file as a PDF for a more-suitable file format for viewing slides. Don't attempt to use InDesign as a slide viewer, especially when you need to exchange files with clients or across platforms. Obviously, one advantage to creating PDF documents is that any user can display the slide presentation with the free Adobe Reader software. If you distribute InDesign files, every user who wants to view the presentation needs a licensed copy of InDesign.

To export the file to PDF, choose File ➪ Export and the Export dialog box opens, shown in Figure 33-13. Supply a filename in the Save As field box and navigate your hard drive for a destination. Be certain Adobe PDF is selected in the Format pull-down menu and click Save.

The next dialog box that opens is the Export PDF dialog box, shown in Figure 33-14. Here, you make choices for the PDF attributes. First, select the preset you want to use from the Preset pull-down menu. If you make a change from the standard presets, the preset changes to Custom. For slide presentations, you can use the Screen preset, but if you change something like the format compatibility, the preset changes to Custom. You might, for example, want to use the compression and file sizes consistent with screen viewing; yet you want to use

Acrobat 6 compatibility and preserve layers in the PDF. In this case, the preset changes to Custom, because the compatibility for the Screen preset is Acrobat 4 compatibility. When you change the compatibility to Acrobat 6, you essentially use a custom preset.

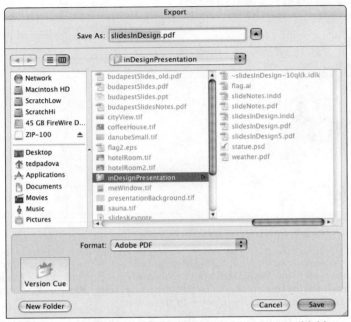

Figure 33-13: In the Export dialog box, supply a name and folder destination.

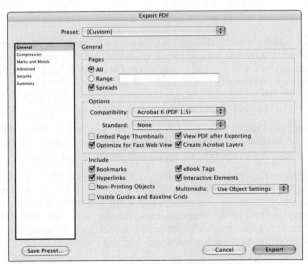

Figure 33-14: Choose a preset and make attribute choices.

If you created bookmarks, check the box for bookmarks and any other interactive elements you may have included in the InDesign file. When you're finished with the attribute choices, click Export and the file is exported to PDF. If you selected View PDF after Exporting, the file opens in your default Acrobat viewer. In Figure 33-15, you can see a PDF exported from InDesign with bookmarks.

Figure 33-15: The exported bookmarks should be visible in the open pane.

Cross-Reference

Note that there are several categories from which to choose in the left pane in the PDF Export dialog box. The options below the General category are discussed in Chapters 28 and 35.

Creating notes and handouts

All the InDesign editing features you learned in Parts III, IV, and V are available to you when creating slide presentations just like other kinds of layouts. Using master pages, character and paragraph styles, tables, and so on is helpful in creating any kind of layout. Creating notes and handouts, however, is another matter. If you want to create note pages with slides on each page like you can with the slide-presentation programs, you need to export slide pages from InDesign and import them back into a template designed for creating note pages. Assuming you have a PDF document you want to use as a slide presentation, the following steps demonstrate how you can use InDesign to create note handouts:

Creating Note Handouts in InDesign

1. **Create a new document in Adobe InDesign.** Launch Adobe InDesign and select File ➪ New to create a new document. Set the page attributes to a letter-page size (8½ x 11 inches) and a portrait orientation. Set the margin distance to 0.5 inches for all sides, and click OK in the New Document dialog box.

Note   If you know ahead of time the number of slides in the presentation, enter the value in the Number of Pages field box. If you don't remember the exact number of pages in your PDF document, enter an approximate value and you can add or delete pages when working in the InDesign document.

2. **Create a master page.** Open the Pages palette and double-click the default A-Master master page. On the master page, draw lines for note comments, and add any graphic objects, an auto page number, a title, and other items you want to display on each note page.

 Cross-Reference   For information on working with master pages and adding auto page numbers, see Chapter 23.

3. **Add a graphic frame placeholder to the master page.** Select the Rectangle Frame tool in the InDesign toolbox, and click the cursor anywhere on the document page. The Rectangle dialog box opens. Enter the width and height you used in your slide presentation and click OK. Drag the frame rectangle so the top-left corner resets at the top and left guidelines. Press ⌘/Ctrl+Shift to constrain the frame size, and drag the lower-right corner to rest on the right guideline, as shown in Figure 33-16.

Figure 33-16: Set up the master page with the text and graphics.

Tip

You can use a note template for not only slides created in InDesign, but also slides you may have created in PowerPoint or Keynote. After they're exported to PDF, you have the same opportunities to design note handouts in InDesign. If you want more freedom for the way your handouts are designed, import them into an InDesign layout. If you use the standard 10-x-7½-inch slide format, enter those values in the Rectangle dialog box that opens when clicking on the Rectangle Frame tool.

Cross-Reference

For more information on sizing frame rectangles, see Part III.

4. **Select the PDF file to import.** Navigate to the first page in your InDesign file and select File ➪ Place. In the Place dialog box, navigate your hard drive and locate the PDF document to be imported. At the bottom of the Place dialog box, check the box for Show Import Options, as shown in Figure 33-17. When the Show Import Options check box is checked, the Place PDF dialog box opens, where you have options for selecting pages in the PDF document to be placed in the InDesign file.

Figure 33-17: Be certain to check Show Import Options.

5. **Select the page to place.** Click Open in the Place dialog box, and the Place PDF dialog box opens, as shown in Figure 33-18. Select page 1 in the dialog box by either typing in the field box or clicking on the first-page tool below the thumbnail image (the first-page tool is denoted by a vertical line and left-pointing arrow).

6. **Place the first page in the rectangle frame.** Click Open in the Place PDF dialog box, and the cursor loads the graphic. Be certain to move anywhere atop the rectangle frame location and click the cursor. Inasmuch as the frame is not visible on the current page, clicking in the frame location accepts the placed graphic. The first page in the PDF file is placed inside the rectangle frame, as shown in Figure 33-19.

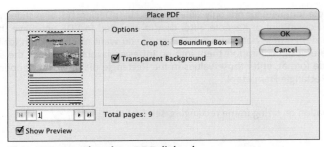

Figure 33-18: The Place PDF dialog box

 Note

The Rectangle Frame from the master page is not selectable on the document pages. There is no indication as to where the frame is located. Click anywhere in the general area where you know the frame is located on the master page, and the graphic drops into the invisible frame.

Figure 33-19: The first page in the PDF document is placed in the frame.

7. **Size the graphic to the frame size.** Press Shift+Ctrl+Alt+E (Shift+⌘+Option+E on the Mac) and the graphic image is proportionally sized to fit inside the rectangle frame. Continue to place pages from the PDF to additional pages in the InDesign document. As you arrive at the Place PDF dialog box, change the PDF page to the next page for each subsequent page placed in InDesign.

Note A nice feature in the Place PDF dialog box is that InDesign remembers your last placed page. As you place new pages, the last page is in view in the page thumbnail. Just click the next-page tool and you know that the next PDF page belongs after the last page placed in InDesign.

8. **Export to PDF.** If you want to send your file off to a copy shop for printing or host the note handouts on a Web site for attendees to download, convert the file to PDF. The copy shop won't need links, fonts, or a copy of InDesign CS to print the file, and those downloading your file from a Web site can use the free Adobe Reader software to view the document.

If you want to make edits in your note handouts, you can easily return to the master page and edit any text or images, or modify the rectangle frame. The rectangle frame in Figure 33-20 was edited by adding a keyline border and drop shadow after all the PDF pages were placed in the document. The file was then exported as a PDF. Simple edits on master pages save you much time over editing each page individually.

Using Photoshop as an authoring tool

Obviously, using Photoshop to create slides is not the most practical solution. Having only one page to edit in a file at one time is certain to slow your progress, not to mention that it results in much larger files than you have using any other application. However, Photoshop does have one nice feature for creating slide presentations when creating a presentation from a collection of photos or design comps you want to display as slides: You can easily create a self-running slideshow complete with transitions and add sound to the presentation if desired.

To create a slide presentation in Photoshop, start by opening the File Browser (File ➪ Browse also works Window ➪ File Browser or use Shift+F12 if you added a custom keyboard shortcut as was explained in Chapter 4). In the File Browser, click on the Folders tab and locate the folder where the images you want to convert to a presentation are located. Select the thumbnails of the images you want to convert to PDF or press ⌘/Ctrl+A to select all images in the folder.

Tip If you have a digital camera and want to select files from your digital camera, you can open the File Browser and navigate to a camera attached to a USB or FireWire port on your computer (if such ports exist on your camera). Thumbnail images of the photos on your camera's memory card display in the File Browser window.

From the Automate pull-down menu in the File Browser, select PDF Presentation, as shown in Figure 33-21. Selecting this command opens the PDF Presentation dialog box.

In the PDF Presentation dialog box, shown in Figure 33-22, you have several options for setting attributes of the resultant PDF file. If you click the check box for Add Open Files, any files open in Photoshop are added to the file exported to PDF. In the Save As area under Output Options, click the radio button for Presentation. If you want to view the PDF file after converting to PDF, click View PDF after Saving. From the Transition pull-down menu, you can choose from a variety of different transitions applied to slide wipes.

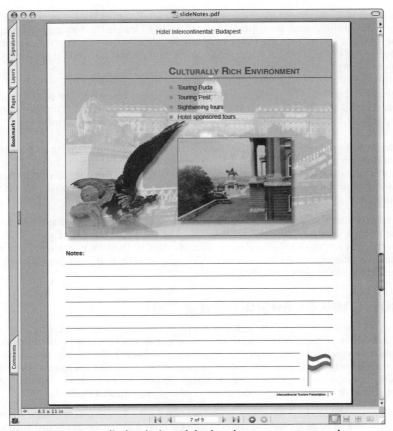

Figure 33-20: To edit the design of the handout page, return to the master page.

Figure 33-21: Select Automate ⇨ PDF Presentation.

When you click Save, the image files selected in the File Browser convert to PDF and combine together in a single PDF document. The file opens in Acrobat in Full Screen mode complete with transitions as slide pages scroll automatically at the interval specified in the PDF Presentation dialog box. By default, the transition interval is 5 seconds. To bail out of Full Screen mode, press Esc or press ⌘/Ctrl+L. In Figure 33-23, a presentation is shown in Acrobat with the Pages palette open.

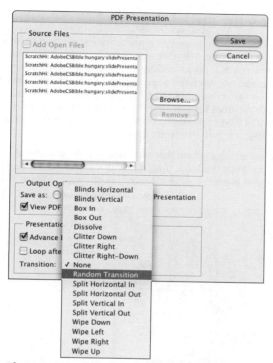

Figure 33-22: Select the attributes for the presentation document.

Figure 33-23: A presentation created from Photoshop

Using Adobe Illustrator as an authoring tool

Illustrator has the same obvious disadvantage when used as a presentation authoring program as Photoshop in regard to single-page editing. What's more likely to happen in your workflow is integrating Illustrator documents in a presentation. You may use Illustrator for an illustration or drawing, a chart, or a form and not have the page as part of a layout in InDesign. If you want to integrate a single-page Illustrator document in a PDF file, you have several options. You can use menu commands in Acrobat for opening files and inserting pages, and you can tile two PDF documents in Acrobat and copy pages from the Pages pane from one file to another. The easiest method is just dragging and dropping files.

To copy an Illustrator page to a slide presentation, open the presentation file in Acrobat and click Pages to open the Pages panel. From your desktop, drag a PDF document to the Pages panel below the page thumbnail where you want the page inserted, as shown in Figure 33-24.

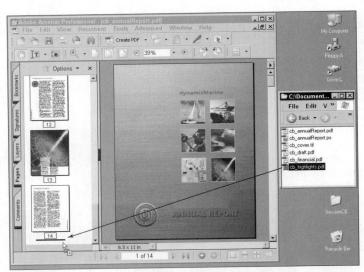

Figure 33-24: Select a PDF on the Desktop and drag it to the Pages panel.

Inserting pages in this manner is not restricted to single-page PDF documents created from Adobe Illustrator. You can likewise insert any PDF file and files with multiple pages in PDF documents in the same manner.

Using Layers with Presentations

Layers offer you another dimension when creating slide presentations. Text can pop up as you cover topics in a presentation when you use layers and toggle on and off layer views. You can also use layers when you need to toggle back and forth between two slide views. Think of a slide where you want to use text and images, then move to a video, return to the text, and move to another video. Layers can handle some of these switching-back-and-forth routines as opposed to creating different slides. In many cases, changing layer views results in faster screen refreshes than changing slide pages.

To create presentations using layers, the authoring program you use needs to support two essential ingredients:

✦ Layers

✦ Writing to the PDF 1.5 format and exporting Adobe PDF Layers

Although Photoshop and GoLive support layers, they don't export Adobe PDF Layers. InDesign and Illustrator both export layers that you can view in Acrobat with layers intact.

For an example of using layers and changing layer visibility in the Acrobat PDF, look at Figure 33-25. The default layer view is shown when the user moves to this page. You can see the Layers pane showing the Layout layer in view while the Video layer is hidden. A button in the lower-right corner has a link action that changes layer visibility to hide the Layout layer and show the Video layer. In addition, the button action plays a video that was originally imported in InDesign before exporting to PDF.

Figure 33-25: The default layer view changes when a user clicks a button.

The button and button actions to show and hide layer visibility were added in Acrobat. When the user clicks the button on the default layer, the visibility changes to show the hidden layer. Notice as you look at Figure 33-26 that the background data assigned to the Background layer does not change. The elements assigned to the background are the banners at the top and bottom of the page. When you're creating layers, you can place text and images on layers common to different layer views and keep these layers visible. This eliminates a need to show/hide data that remains constant while other data is hidden and shown with different layer visibility. The result is faster screen refreshes, because some data remains in view.

Cross-Reference For more information on creating layers in CS programs and exporting Adobe PDF Layers, see Chapter 12. For information on creating buttons and interactive actions, see Chapter 29.

Figure 33-26: Clicking the button on the default layer changes the layer visibility.

Adding Page Transitions

Page transitions are available in both Edit mode and Full Screen mode in Acrobat 6. A *page transition* is an effect such as a fade-out and fade-in applied to pages as they're turned. You can set page transitions for all pages in a file or among selected pages in the Pages palette. You might add page transitions to PDF documents for trade-show displays where you want to show slides in self-running kiosks.

To set transitions on all pages in a document, or a specified range of pages while remaining in Edit mode (as opposed to Full Screen mode), choose Document ⇨ Pages ⇨ Set Page Transitions. If you want to set transitions for pages in a noncontiguous order, open the Pages palette and ⌘/Ctrl+click on the individual pages where you want page transitions. After making the page selections, choose Document ⇨ Pages ⇨ Set Page Transitions. The Set Transitions dialog box opens, shown in Figure 33-27.

From the Effect pull-down menu, you select the transition you want to apply to the selected pages, either from pages you selected in the Pages palette or a range of pages you specify in the Pages Range field boxes. Acrobat offers you a total of 50 different choices for different effects. One choice is to set no transition, with the remaining 49 choices being different effects.

If you check the Auto Flip check box, pages scroll at an interval automatically according to the number of seconds you select from the pull-down menu below the Auto Flip check box. Choices for the interval are between 1 and 32,767 seconds. You can select fixed interval options or type a value within the acceptable range. If you want to manually scroll pages, leave the check box disabled.

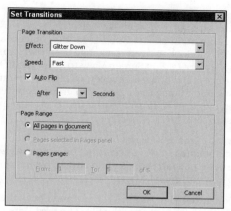

Figure 33-27: In this dialog box, select a page transition from the Effect menu.

If you don't select pages in the Pages palette, you make choices for applying transitions to all pages or specify a page range in a contiguous order by clicking on the Pages range and typing in the page From and To field boxes. When you select pages in the Pages palette, the Pages Selected in the Pages Panel check box becomes active by default and the transitions are applied to the selected pages.

After setting the effects and page range, click OK and transitions apply to the pages when you scroll pages in Edit mode.

Although it isn't necessary in Acrobat 6, you can apply page transitions in authoring applications prior to PDF conversion. If you happen to have an old Acrobat 3 installer CD, you'll find a folder on the CD titled `Transitions`. The `Transitions` folder contains EPS files with PostScript code to create transitions when pages are scrolled in Edit mode. If you use InDesign to create your slide presentations, place one of the EPS transition effects on a master page and convert to PDF. The transitions are applied to all the pages as you scroll through the document. If you elect to use this method, you don't have the flexibility of quickly changing transition effects. Users of the Creative Suite Standard Edition who don't have Acrobat 6 might use this method for creating transitions. Because the Adobe Reader software can't save PDF documents, CS Standard Users can create some workarounds when exporting PDFs from InDesign.

Using Full Screen Views

The Full Screen view shows PDF pages without the presence of the Acrobat tools, title bar, or palettes. Not only do Full Screen views offer you a different appearance for displaying PDF pages, but also the mode is also necessary if you want to view certain effects. PowerPoint presentations with animation, for example, can only display effects created in the original PowerPoint file while viewing a PDF in Full Screen mode.

Cross-Reference

For more information on creating PDF documents from PowerPoint files, see the "Converting Presentation Documents to PDF" section, earlier in this chapter.

Viewing slides in Acrobat

If you converted PowerPoint slides containing animation effects, such as motion objects and transitions, the animation is not viewable in Edit mode. You need to change the viewing mode to Full Screen mode. Press ⌘/Ctrl+L or choose Window ➪ Full Screen View to show the PDF in Full Screen mode. Press the Page Down key, press the down-arrow key, or click the mouse button to scroll pages. As you scroll pages, any animations associated with graphics or text are visible as long as you remain in Full Screen mode. In Figure 33-28, the text is moving from left to right for each line of text as pages are scrolled.

If you prepare presentations for clients and want to make it easier for them to launch Full Screen mode, you can save the PDF file so the document always opens in Full Screen view. Choose File ➪ Document Properties while the slide presentation is open and active in the Document pane. The Document Properties dialog box opens, shown in Figure 33-29.

In the Document Properties dialog box, click on Initial View in the left pane and check the box for Open in Full Screen mode in the right pane. Click OK and save the file. The next time you open the PDF file either by double-clicking the document icon or by choosing File ➪ Open inside Acrobat, the file opens in Full Screen mode.

Setting Full Screen preferences

If you want to set up a kiosk or workstation for viewing documents in Full Screen mode, start by making some choices in the Full Screen preferences. In the preference settings, you can control some of the viewing options. Choose Edit ➪ Preferences on Windows or Acrobat ➪ Preferences on the Mac. In the left pane select Full Screen; the preference choices appear, as shown in Figure 33-30.

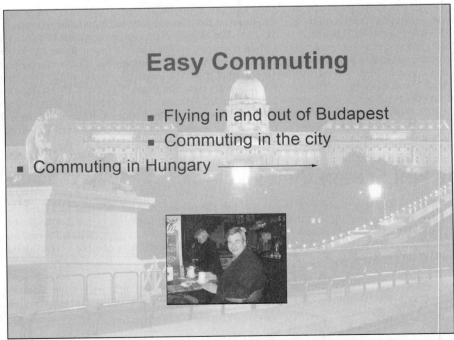

Figure 33-28: Animated text is visible when viewing files in Full Screen mode.

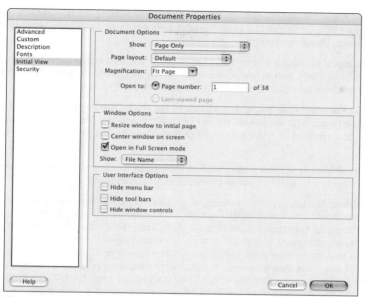

Figure 33-29: You activate Full Screen mode in the Document Properties dialog box.

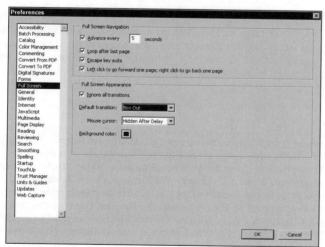

Figure 33-30: To open Full Screen preferences, press ⌘/Ctrl+K and click Full Screen in the left pane.

The preference choices include the following:

✦ **Advance Every:** The slide presentation automatically scrolls pages at the interval specified in the field box adjacent to the check box. The values permitted for the interval are between 1 and 60 seconds.

✦ **Loop after Last Page:** Using this option and the preceding setting for auto-advancing, you can set up a kiosk and have the slide presentation continue with auto repetition. After the last page, the presentation starts again.

✦ **Escape Key Exists:** If you want to exit Full Screen view, you can strike the Esc key when you enable this check box. Be certain to leave the check box at the default switch. If you disable the check box, remember to use ⌘/Ctrl+L to exit Full Screen view.

✦ **Left-Click to Go Forward One Page, Right-Click to Go Back One Page.** With this option, you can navigate pages with mouse clicks. For both Windows and Mac users who use a two-button mouse, clicking on the left or right button navigates pages in the respective direction.

✦ **Ignore All Transitions:** If you set transitions while in Edit mode and want to eliminate the transition effects while in Full Screen view, enable this option.

✦ **Default Transition:** From the pull-down menu, you have choices for one of the same 49 different transition effects. If you apply a transition in the Full Screen preferences, then all pages use the same transition. Selecting Random from the menu choices offers you effects that change randomly as you move through slide pages. If you want to use specific transitions that change for selected pages, set the transitions from the Document ➪ Pages ➪ Page Transitions menu command before opening the Preferences dialog box. Disable Ignore All Transitions and the effects you choose for page transitions applied to selected pages in the Pages palette are used when you enter Full Screen mode.

✦ **Mouse Cursor:** There are three choices from the pull-down menu for the mouse-cursor display while viewing slides in Full Screen mode. You can choose from Always Visible, Always Hidden, or Hidden After Delay. The Hidden After Delay menu choice shows the cursor position when you scroll pages, and then hides it after a short delay.

✦ **Background Color:** Click on the color swatch, and the preset color palette opens; here, you can make choices for the background color. The background color appears outside the slide pages on all pages that don't fit precisely within the monitor frame. If you want to use a custom color, click on Other Color at the bottom of the palette and select a custom color from your system palette.

Scrolling pages

To advance through slides when in Full Screen mode, you can use the preference setting and scroll pages with mouse clicks. If the preference choice for Left-Click to Go Forward One Page; Right-Click to Go Back One Page is disabled, you scroll pages with keystrokes. Strike the Page Down or Page Up keys to move forward and backward through slides. Additionally, you can use the up- or left-arrow keys to move backward and the down- or right-arrow keys to move forward. Use the Home key to move to the first page and the End key to move to the last page. If you want to move to a specific page without leaving Full Screen mode, press Shift+⌘/Ctrl+N and the Go to Page dialog box opens. Enter the page number to open in the field box and click OK.

Creating interactivity in Full Screen mode

You may have a slide presentation that doesn't require access to Acrobat menus and tools, but you want to show cross-document links. Perhaps you design a presentation about a company's financial status, economic growth, or projected growth, and your client wants to show a financial spreadsheet, another PDF document, or a scanned image of a memo or report. The slideshow created in PowerPoint with the motion objects and viewing in Full Screen mode is what you want, but you also want the flexibility for opening other files without leaving the Full Screen mode.

Creating links and buttons for cross-document linking

If you want to open a secondary document while in Full Screen mode, you can create links or form-field buttons to secondary files. When you click on the link, the link action is invoked. If opening a secondary file, the file link opens in Full Screen mode. After viewing the file, press ⌘/Ctrl+W to close the file and you're returned to the last slide view also in Full Screen mode.

To set up a file link, create a link or form-field button and create a link to open a file. Acrobat offers you options for opening a linked document in the existing window or a new window. You can create the kind of file linking and views to make things easy on your clients, and they won't need to struggle finding files located on a hard drive or launching external applications. All the file linking and activation can be created with buttons in Acrobat.

 Cross-Reference For information on creating interactive links and buttons, see Chapter 29.

You can also create URL links to display a Web site while in Full Screen mode by using the Open a Web Link action. Click on the link and your Web browser opens at the specified URL. When you quit the Web browser, you're retuned to the slide presentation in Full Screen mode. If you use PowerPoint effects, the effects aren't disturbed.

 Cross-Reference To learn more about setting link actions to URLs, see Chapter 30.

Using interactive devices

Another interactivity tool that you can use with Full Screen view is a remote-control device. For about $50 to $75 you can purchase a handheld remote control. The control comes in two parts. The control device has two buttons used for moving forward and backward in the slide presentation. The companion unit is plugged into a USB port on a laptop or desktop computer. You open the slide presentation in Full Screen view and click the left or right button to navigate slides while you walk across a stage. Some devices also have a button for cursor control. You can remotely move the cursor on a slide and click on a button that opens a secondary file, Web link, or other action associated with the button or link.

When using remote devices, be certain to set your Full Screen preferences to Left-Click to Go Forward One Page; Right-Click to Go Back One Page.

Summary

✦ You convert PowerPoint slides to PDF with the PDFMaker macro.

✦ To create note handouts from PowerPoint, use the Print dialog box and print the file to the Adobe PDF Printer after making the attribute choices in the Print dialog box for the type of handouts you want to create.

✦ You can export Apple Keynote slides to PDF and PowerPoint formats. Keynote offers Macintosh users a robust slide-creation program with easy, intuitive palettes and tools.

✦ You can use layout programs such as InDesign to create slide presentations. For creating handout notes, set up a master page with objects and elements to be added to each page. Import the PDF slide presentation and convert to PDF.

✦ Layered PDFs add additional viewing options in slide presentations. To create layered PDFs use programs, such as InDesigns CS and Illustrator CS, supporting layers and exporting to the PDF 1.5 format.

✦ Page transitions are applied to pages individually using the Document ➪ Pages ➪ Set Page Transitions command in Acrobat. To apply different transitions to different pages, select pages in the Pages palette and adjust the transitions in the Set Transitions dialog box.

✦ When using Full Screen mode, open the Preferences dialog box and select Full Screen.

✦ Full Screen views support file-linking with link and button actions, Microsoft PowerPoint animation, and transitions applied to pages with either the Full Screen preferences or the Set Page Transitions command.

✦   ✦   ✦

Printing and Digital Prepress

Choosing Print Setups

Files created for print fall into two categories — designs for composite prints and designs for color separations or commercial printing. When you design documents for composite printing, your output device might be a laser printer, a desktop inkjet printer, a large-format inkjet printer, a color copier, a film recorder, or a high-end commercial color printer. Files designed for commercial printing are typically color-separated and printed to film or direct to plate.

This chapter is concerned with setting print attributes for composite color that may print to your office desktop printers as well as advanced settings for commercial devices designed for printing prepress.

Selecting Desktop Printers

The first step in printing files is to select the target printer and the print attributes associated with the printer, such as paper size, paper feed, paper tray, and so on. If you work as an independent designer in a small shop, you may have only one printer on your network. After you assign your printer as the default printing device, you don't need to worry about printer selection. However, if you work in production workflows in larger shops, you may have a variety of printers attached to your network. In these environments, it's essential you make the proper printer selection before sending off a job for print. Selecting printers varies between Mac OS and Windows.

Printer selection on the Mac

One of the clear disadvantages of using the CS programs when you print a document is the inconsistency between what you see in an application document window versus what prints. The programs vary in what dialog boxes you access, whether you have access to a printing device PPD, how to set up custom pages, and what print attributes to use. To fully comprehend printer selection, we need to look at the CS programs individually.

InDesign

In InDesign on Mac OS, you make printer selections in the Print dialog box. Notice that you don't have a command under the File menu for Page Setup. If you choose File ➪ Document Setup, the Document Setup dialog box opens; here, the options choices are restricted to page sizes and defining bleeds and slugs. No options for printer choices or print attributes are made in the Document Setup dialog box.

Cross-Reference   For more information on bleeds and slugs, see Chapter 23.

To make a printer choice, choose File ➪ Print. In the Print dialog box, shown in Figure 34-1, you choose your target printer from the Printer pull-down menu. You select a printer from the menu choices and then make various print-attribute choices by clicking on the items listed in the left pane and respective choices on the right side of the dialog box.

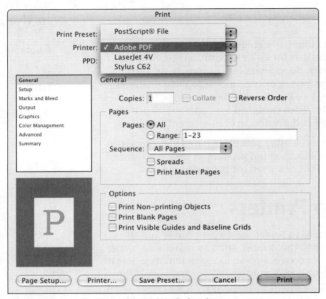

Figure 34-1: The InDesign Print dialog box on a Mac

Notice that you have a choice for accessing the Page Setup dialog box in the Print dialog box. Click on Page Setup and a warning dialog box opens, as shown in Figure 34-2. The warning informs you that settings can be made in InDesign's Print dialog box without opening the Page Setup dialog box. Be certain to use the InDesign option rather than the Page Setup dialog box. Conflicts can persist if you make choices in the Page Setup dialog box.

Figure 34-2: Clicking Page Setup opens a warning dialog box.

Illustrator

Also in the Print dialog box is a Printer pull-down menu where you select your target printer in Illustrator. Like InDesign, Illustrator has a Document Setup dialog box where no print options are selected. Additionally, no Page Setup dialog box is available in Illustrator.

To select a target printer in Illustrator, choose File ⇨ Print. The Print dialog box opens, shown in Figure 34-3. From the Printer pull-down menu, select the printer you want to use.

Note   Adobe PDF is a printer option in all applications, because it's installed with Adobe Acrobat. For device output, you typically won't use the Adobe PDF printer. However, when preparing PostScript files, the Adobe PDF printer is often your best choice when a device PPD is not available.

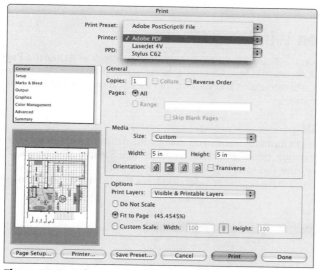

Figure 34-3: Select a printer from the Printer menu in the Print dialog box.

Photoshop, GoLive, and Acrobat

Photoshop, GoLive, and Acrobat all make use of a Page Setup dialog box. Rather than use the Print dialog box to access a printer, your first choice in these programs is the Page Setup dialog box, shown in Figure 34-4. From the Format For pull-down menu, select the printer you want to use.

If you need to define custom page sizes for your output, set up the custom page by selecting Custom Paper Size in the Settings pull-down menu. After you create a custom page size return to the Page Setup dialog box and select the new page size before moving to the Print dialog box.

Cross-Reference   For more information on creating custom page sizes, see Chapter 21.

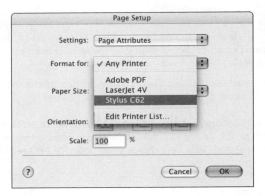

Figure 34-4: Photoshop, GoLive, and Acrobat use the Page Setup dialog box.

Printer selection on Windows

Similar to printer selections on the Mac, Windows users access printers in either the Page Setup or Print dialog boxes. Also like the Mac CS applications, some programs don't have a Page Setup dialog box, while others require you to first visit a Page Setup dialog box when selecting a printer and paper size.

InDesign and Illustrator

When using Windows in InDesign and Illustrator, you make your printer selections in the Print dialog boxes. Like the Mac versions, these programs have no Page Setup dialog boxes. The Document Setup dialog boxes offer the same options as you find in the Mac counterparts. In InDesign, choose File ➪ Print and make a printer selection from the Printer drop-down list, shown in Figure 34-5.

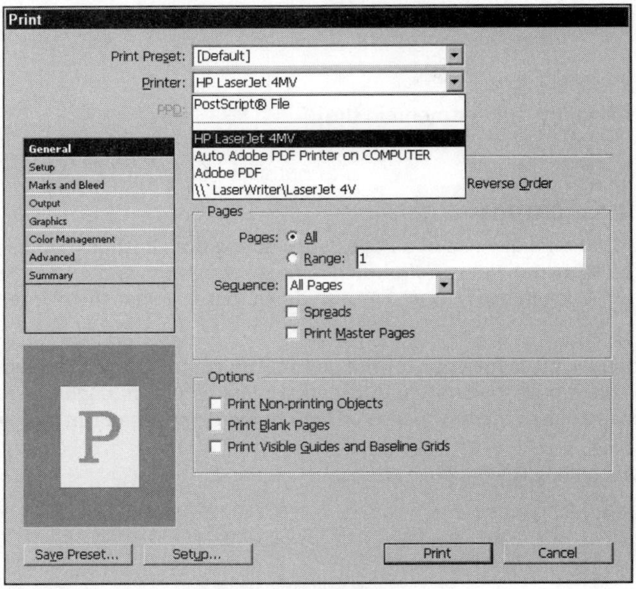

Figure 34-5: In InDesign on Windows.

Likewise, in Illustrator choose File ➪ Print and select your target printer from the Printer drop-down list shown in Figure 34-6. Notice the print options available in the InDesign and Illustrator Print dialog boxes match the same options found on the Mac.

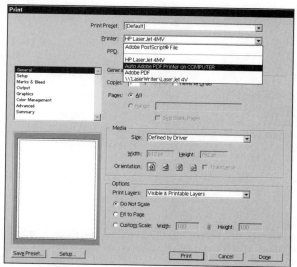

Figure 34-6: Like InDesign, Illustrator uses a similar drop-down list.

Photoshop and GoLive

Photoshop, GoLive, and Acrobat all use different dialog boxes for printer selection than you the dialog box you use for printing. In Photoshop and GoLive, you use the Page Setup dialog box; in Acrobat, you use the Printer Setup dialog box. From either Photoshop or GoLive, choose File ➪ Page Setup and the Page Setup dialog box opens, shown in Figure 34-7. This is the first of two dialog boxes you use in these programs to make a printer selection.

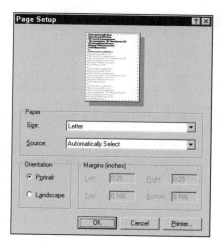

Figure 34-7: In Photoshop and GoLive, you use the Page Setup dialog box.

Printer selection is made in a second dialog box you open by clicking on the Printer button in the Page Setup dialog box. Click on Printer and another Page Setup dialog box opens, shown in Figure 34-8. From the Name drop-down list, select your target printer.

Figure 34-8: Selecting your target printer in the second Page Setup dialog box

After selecting your target printer, click OK and make a choice for the paper size in the first Page Setup dialog box (refer to Figure 34-7).

Acrobat

Acrobat treats printer selection similar to Photoshop and GoLive, but the Page Setup dialog box in Acrobat is called the Print Setup dialog box and the printer selection and paper size are both selected in the same dialog box. In Acrobat, choose File ➪ Print Setup, and the Print Setup dialog box opens, shown in Figure 34-9.

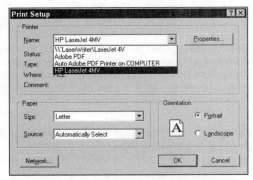

Figure 34-9: In Acrobat, select a printer in the Print Setup dialog box.

From the Name drop-down list, you make a choice for your target printer, and subsequently you make a choice for paper size in the same dialog box.

After making a printer selection, you then make choices for print attributes in the Print dialog boxes. If paper selection is handled in Page or Print Setup dialog boxes, be certain to make the proper paper choice before opening the Print dialog box.

Setting Print Options

If your task is to print composite color to desktop or large-format commercial printers, you don't need to manage many of the print attributes in the print dialog boxes. Items such as emulsion, screening, separations, and so on are used most often for prepress and commercial printing. In some circumstances, you must use an option designed for commercial printing when printing composite color. For example, when printing on Mylar on your desktop color printer, you must print emulsion down so the image is reversed on the back of the *substrate* (printing material). Special conditions like this require you to know all the print features in the print dialog boxes.

Although you may not use all the options available to you when printing CS application documents, an elaborate description is offered here for both composite and commercial printing. Use this information in conjunction with the material in Chapter 35 when printing to commercial printing devices. Because each program has some different attribute settings, look over the settings descriptions according to the program you use for final output.

Setting print options in Illustrator

In Illustrator, choose File ⇨ Print to open the Print dialog box, where you select your printing device. As a matter of rule, you first want to select the printing device. Items such as page sizes and PPDs (PostScript Printer Description files) are accessed after making the printer choice. A PPD contains information related to your printer when printing to PostScript devices. Such information relates to a series of fixed page sizes, color handling, screening, and similar characteristics. When you open the Print dialog box, a list of categories appear in the left pane (Figure 35-10). Clicking an item in the left pane changes options on the right side of the dialog box.

> **Tip** PPD files are text documents. If you need to install a PPD from a Mac to a Windows machine or vice versa, you can copy the file to either platform. As text-only documents, they're completely cross-platform compliant.

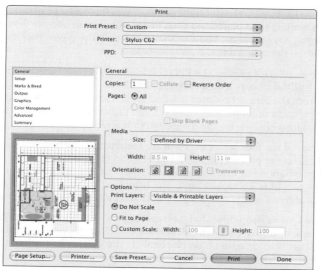

Figure 34-10: Choose File ⇨ Print to open the Print dialog box.

General settings

The default series of settings are the General print options. When you select General in the left pane, the options choices include the following:

✦ **Print Preset:** At the bottom of the dialog box, notice the Save Preset button. You can change options in all the settings related to selections in the left pane and as a last option setting, click Save Preset. Illustrator opens a dialog box where you supply a name for the preset and the new preset appears in the Print Preset drop-down list. When you want to use the same print options, choose the preset name from the drop-down list, and all the settings associated with the preset are applied. The file prints according to the preset options.

✦ **Printer:** As discussed in the previous "Printer selection on Windows" and "Printer selection on the Mac" sections, you select the target printer from the drop-down list. You also have a selection for Adobe PostScript File. Use this option if you want to create a PostScript file that ultimately downloads to a printing device. You might use a PostScript file if you have a printer driver and PPD for a commercial printing device at your service center, but you don't have the printer online at your studio. You can create a PostScript file that your service center can download to its printer using all the attribute choices made from the PPD file.

✦ **PPD:** You select PostScript Printer Description file from the drop-down list. In Figure 34-10, an Epson Stylus C62 printer is selected in the Printer drop-down list. Like most desktop color printers, the Epson Stylus C62 is a non-PostScript printer and, therefore, does not support a PPD file. Unless your printer is a PostScript printer, you won't have an option for PPD selection. If you're using a PostScript printer, choose the associated PPD for your printer.

✦ **Copies:** If you're printing more than one copy, change the value in the field box to the desired number of copies. By default, 1 appears in the field box.

✦ **Reverse Order:** This item works when you print Illustrator documents as tiled pages. Because you don't have options for creating multiple pages with Illustrator files, the item is grayed out unless you tile pages whereby multiple pages are printed.

✦ **Pages:** This also only works when you print tiled pages. If you have a large drawing, you can print the document as tiled pages and then make a change in one portion of the document by selecting a page range. You can then print only the pages that have been altered since printing the original file.

✦ **Media:** If you're using a PostScript printer, the PPD contains all the page sizes supported by the printer and generally supports a custom page size. If the PPD supports custom pages, select Custom from the Size drop-down list and enter values in the Width and Height field boxes. If you use a non-PostScript printer, the Printer driver contains the fixed page sizes and you lose options for creating custom pages.

✦ **Orientation:** Click on one of the four icons for Portrait, Landscape, Portrait Rotated, or Landscape Rotated. Transverse rotates pages 90 degrees and is typically used on roll-fed machines to conserve paper. For example, you can rotate a portrait letter page 11 inches high so the page height is 8.5 inches high. The print is still a portrait view, but the image is rotated 90 degrees so the roll of paper uses 8.5 inches instead of 11 inches.

✦ **Options:** From the Print Layers drop-down list, you can print all visible and printable layers, only visible layers, or all layers — where layers marked for not printing are also printed. You also have controls for scaling. Do Not Scale is the default and prints the document at 100 percent. Fit to Page reduces or enlarges the illustration to the page size you print. The Custom Scale option enables you to type scaling values in the Width and Height field boxes. The chain link between Width and Height is activated by default, ensuring proportional scaling. If you click on the chain link, you can distort the drawing by typing values independently for width and height, without regard to proportional sizing.

Setup

Click the Setup category in the left pane and the Setup options appear, as shown in Figure 34-11.

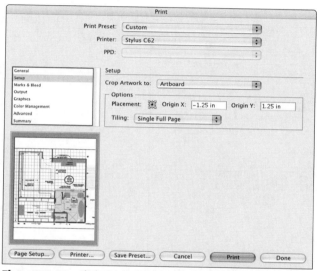

Figure 34-11: Click Setup in the left pane to open the Setup options.

✦ **Crop Artwork To:** Choices from the drop-down list include Artboard for the artwork contained within the page setup; Artboard Bounding Box, which includes all the space defined by the artwork edges, even artwork off the art board space; and Crop Area, which relates to a specific area you define as a crop region. You create a rectangle and, with the rectangle selected, choose Object ➪ Crop Area ➪ Make to define a crop area. When you select Crop Area in the Setup options, the area within the defined crop area prints.

✦ **Placement:** You can move artwork in the thumbnail image around the page area and you can target a section of a large drawing for printing on your selected page size. Click and drag in the thumbnail image on the left and the X,Y origins change values. You can also type new values in the field boxes to change the artwork position on the page and use the small Placement rectangle to select points of origin on the center, four corners, or midpoints on each side.

✦ **Tiling:** This is helpful when you print composite color on small desktop devices where you design a piece for a large display print. If you need to proof the artwork on your printer before sending it off to an imaging center, use the Tiling options for Tile Full Pages or Tile Imageable Areas. The artwork prints on several pages in sections, which you can piece together to see the full print.

Marks and bleeds

Printer's marks are essential when printing files to commercial equipment especially when printing color separations. Items such as color names, registration marks, and crop marks are needed when preparing printing plates and trimming paper. On composite color prints, you may print an image on a larger-size paper to accommodate a bleed and, therefore, need to add crop marks so you know where to trim the paper. Click on Marks and Bleed, and the options for adding printer's marks appear in the Print dialog box, as shown in Figure 34-12.

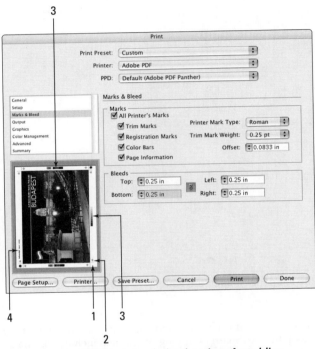

Figure 34-12: The Marks and Bleed options for adding printer's marks

✦ **All Printer's Marks:** When you check All Printer's Marks, the marks for (1) Trim, (2) Registration, (3) Color Bars, (4) and Page Information appear in the output and are visible in the thumbnail proof (Figure 34-12). If you want some of the available printer's marks to print, individually check those items.

✦ **Printer Mark Type:** Choices are Roman or Japanese. Select the type of mark from the drop-down list. To see the differences between the two marks, toggle the view by selecting from the two options in the drop-down list.

✦ **Trim Mark Weight:** You have choices for the stroke weight of the trim marks at 0.125, 0.25, and 0.5 stroke weights. Select the desired weight from the drop-down list.

✦ **Offset:** Specifying an offset amount offsets the bleed and trim marks from the artwork.

✦ **Bleeds:** You can specify the bleed amount uniformly on all sides or in individual distances by typing values in the Bleeds field boxes. Click the chain-link icon to toggle between uniform distances and nonuniform distances.

Output

Output settings offer options for printing composite or separations, controlling emulsion, and screening and setting halftone frequencies. For composite color, you probably won't need separations or screening. For some composite color printers, several options are grayed out, as shown in Figure 34-13.

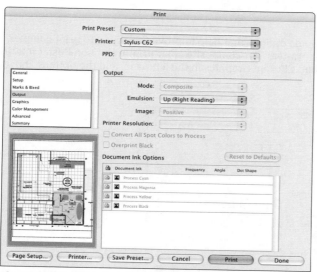

Figure 34-13: Click Output to open options for color and screening.

✦ **Mode:** Three choices appear for Composite, Separations (Host-Based), and In-RIP Separations. Host-based separations separate the file before it is delivered to the PostScript RIP (Raster Image Processor). In-RIP separations deliver the composite file to a PostScript 3 RIP, where the RIP separates the file.

✦ **Emulsion:** Choices are for Up (Right Reading) or Down (Wrong Reading). Typically, composite prints are printed positive emulsion up, while film separations are printed negative emulsion down. Upon occasion, you may need to print emulsion down for such items as iron transfers, Mylar, LexJet, and so on. The option is available from the Emulsion drop-down list.

✦ **Printer Resolution:** For imagesetting and platesetting equipment at commercial print shops, you find resolution and halftone settings in the Printer Resolution drop-down list. These options are related to the PPD used for PostScript printers but are not accessible for non-PostScript printers such as desktop color printers. For printing composite color, you won't need to access any resolution/screening options.

✦ **Convert All Spot Colors to Process:** If your file contains spot color and the prints appear best when printing CMYK, click the check box for converting spot color to process color. Note that the option is used for spot color only and does not apply to RGB color. Also note that the conversion takes place at the printing device RIP and does not change the color in the file.

✦ **Overprint Black:** For files where you have black type against color backgrounds, you may want to globally overprint the black.

✦ **Document Ink Options:** A list of all used colors appears at the bottom of the Output settings. You can change Frequency, Angle, and/or Dot Shape by clicking in the respective column according to color and editing the value. After clicking, a field box appears where you can type new values.

Graphics

The Graphics settings offer some options that help improve the ability to print complex Illustrator files on PostScript printers. For composite color printing on non-PostScript printers, the options are grayed out. Click on Graphics in the left pane, and the options shown in Figure 34-14 are available.

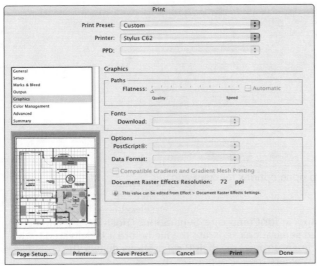

Figure 34-14: Click Graphics to open options for simplifying printing.

✦ **Paths:** Move the slider to the right to increase the flatness. Flatness breaks up complex paths to more simplified paths that make the entire drawing easier to print. If you increase the amount of flatness to the maximum, you can run the risk of distorting shapes where circles appear as polygons. In Figure 34-15, you can see how the flatness amount is measured. The original circle with an exaggerated flatness setting appears as a polygon. The flatness amount is measured by the distance between the original circle and a midpoint on a chord created with the flatness adjustment.

✦ **Fonts:** For PostScript printing, you can download fonts to the printer's RIP at the time a file is printed. Select None to download no fonts. Select Subset to download only font characters within font sets that are contained in the file. Select Complete to download the entire font character set.

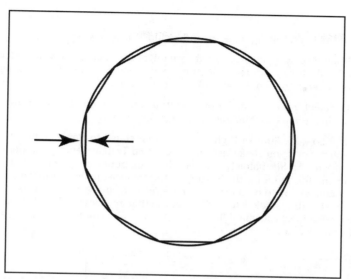

Figure 34-15: If you greatly increase flatness, circular shapes become polygons.

✦ **PostScript:** Select a Language level for the PostScript printer used. In some cases, the drop-down list is grayed out and Illustrator makes an automatic selection between PostScript Level 2 and PostScript 3 depending on the printer used.

✦ **Data Format:** When printing a PostScript file, you have choices for selecting Binary or ASCII encoding. For almost all purposes, use binary encoding and the file sizes become much smaller than selecting ASCII. For other printer selections, Illustrator makes the choice for you for ASCII or Binary and grays out the drop-down list preventing you from changing the option.

✦ **Compatible Gradient and Gradient Mesh Printing.** Unless you experience problems printing gradients or gradient meshes on a PostScript RIP, don't select this check box. This option resolves problems when these gradients don't print.

Color management

For color-managed workflows, you can use ICC profiles and select your profiles from the Profile drop-down list. Select an Intent from the drop-down list options for Perceptual, Saturation, Relative Colormetric, or Absolute Colormetric. The choices you make in the Color Management settings should be consistent with the color-managed workflow in your environment.

Cross-Reference

For more information on ICC profiles, managing color, and understanding the print space intent, see Chapter 6.

Advanced

Advanced options are shown in Figure 34-16 and include the following:

✦ **Print as Bitmap:** For a quick proof print, you might use this option where all the vector art in your illustration is printed as a bitmapped image. Selecting this option prints the file as a rasterized bitmap but does not rasterize the file.

✦ **Overprints:** Select from options for overprinting items identified in your drawing for overprints. The options are Simulate, Preserve, or Discard.

✦ **Preset:** Select Low, Medium, or High for resolution related to transparency flattening and bitmap conversion. If you click Custom, the Custom Transparency Flattener Options dialog box opens. In this dialog box, select the amount of transparency flattening you want by moving the slider for the Raster/Vector Balance and adjust resolution for line art and text conversion to bitmaps as well as gradients and gradient meshes. If you want to convert text and/or strokes to outlines at the time of printing, select those options. Clip Complex Regions also simplifies printing; if you have difficulty printing a file, enable this check box.

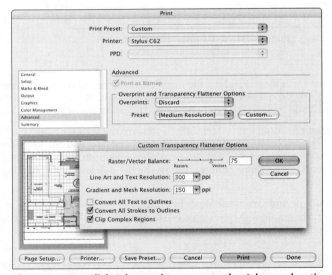

Figure 34-16: Click Advanced to move to the Advanced options.

Summary

Click on Summary and the summary options are displayed in the Print dialog box, as shown in Figure 34-17. The Options list displays a list of the settings you made from all the other categories. If your document contains items that won't print correctly or if you made options choices that prevent printing with optimum results, the Warnings box lists potential problems you may encounter. Read the warnings and return to either your document or the other categories and make corrections as needed.

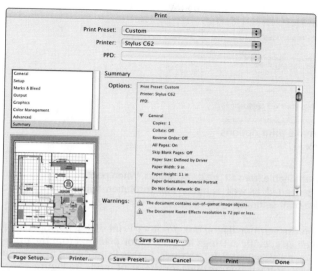

Figure 34-17: Summary summarizes the choices made in the Print dialog box.

Printing Illustrator files to non-PostScript printers

Depending on your printer and the complexity of your design, you may find rasterizing your Illustrator file in Adobe Photoshop to be the only way you can print the document. Some desktop printers do well with printing directly from Illustrator while some printers may have some difficulties for properly printing a file. In addition, some older PostScript printers may likewise have problems printing your Illustrator artwork. If you experience such problems, open the Illustrator file in Photoshop. The first dialog box you encounter is the Photoshop Rasterize Generic dialog box. Depending on whether the file saved from Illustrator was a native file, an EPS, or a PDF, the dialog box reads Rasterize Generic PDF Format (or another formatted file type used for the name of the dialog box). In this dialog box you specify the width and height of the file. By default the original size is automatically supplied in the dialog box for you. You also specify the resolution and color mode. Click OK and the file opens in Photoshop, where all the vector objects are converted to pixels, thus rasterizing the file.

As a Photoshop file, you can print directly from Photoshop or save the file in a format that can be downloaded directly to printers supporting direct file downloads. For example, many large-format inkjet printers support downloading TIFF files. In such cases, you would save the file from Photoshop in TIFF format.

Using device print settings

Color printers have unique attributes you select from the device printer driver. On the Mac, when you choose File ➪ Print and make your choices for the print options you want to use, your next series of options are selected in another Print dialog box. Click on Printer in the Print dialog box, and a warning dialog box opens, as shown in Figure 34-18.

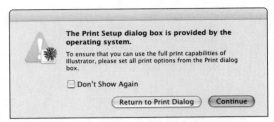

Figure 34-18: A warning to make print options choices in the Print dialog box

Note

Device print settings are attainable from all the CS programs. When printing to devices where special paper handling is needed, as well as options for resolution output and color-mode selections, use the device print settings.

Click Continue to pass through the warning dialog box. Another Print dialog box opens offering a range of print options as well as specific settings for your color printer. From the drop-down list below the Presets drop-down list, select Print Settings. In this Print dialog box, you make choices for the media type, inks, and various settings for the print mode. In Figure 34-19, the options for a low-end Epson color printer are shown.

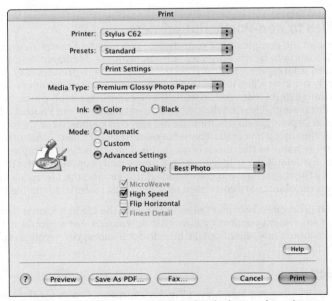

Figure 34-19: Specific print options for desktop color printers.

On Windows, you make the same kinds of choices from the Page Setup dialog box. Click Printer in the Page Setup dialog box to open the Print dialog box. Select your printer from the Name drop-down list and click the Properties button. Advanced print settings are made in subsequent dialog boxes and offer options similar to those found on the Mac.

Because the range of printers is so great, discussing all the options for all printers isn't possible. For specific information related to the options choices you need to make for media type, inks, color profiles, and mode settings, consult your printer's user manual.

Setting print options in Photoshop

Printing from Photoshop is usually performed when you print composite color. For prepress and color separations, Photoshop files usually find their way into Illustrator or InDesign documents. You can print to commercial equipment from Photoshop, but most imaging technicians generally import the Photoshop files into a layout program for printing.

If you're printing composite color, you first visit the Page Setup dialog box and set the page size for the output on your printer. Be certain that when you create a custom page size in the Page Setup dialog box you return to the Page Setup dialog box and select the new custom page as was described in Chapter 21.

After selecting the Page Setup, choose File ➪ Print with Preview. You'll notice that Photoshop has two menu commands for selecting a Print dialog box. If you select Print from the File menu, the print options are much more limited and don't provide you a thumbnail preview for how the document will lay down on the printed page. The Print with Preview command offers many more options with a thumbnail preview, as shown in Figure 34-20.

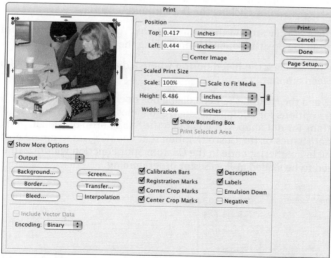

Figure 34-20: Choosing Print with Preview shows a thumbnail of your artwork.

In the Print dialog box that opens when you select Print with Preview, the following options appear:

✦ **Position:** If you uncheck Center Image, you can move the artwork around the page where a dynamic preview displays in the thumbnail. You can type coordinate values in the field boxes or click and drag the image in the preview box.

✦ **Scaled Print Size:** Use the field boxes to scale the image up or down. Be aware that, when scaling images up, you need to consider the relationship between scaling size and resolution. As a 150 ppi (pixels per inch) image is scaled up 200 percent (or twice the size) the resolution drops to 75 ppi (or one-half the resolution). You can scale by editing the Scale field box, by checking the box to scale the image to fit the media, by typing values for the height and width, or by dragging handles at one of the four corners of the bounding box.

✦ **Show Bounding Box:** You may have white space at one or more sides of your image or around the entire image. When you check the box for Show Bounding Box, a rectangle is displayed at the image size including the white space.

✦ **Print Selected Area:** Prints a selection in the image.

✦ **Output:** If you check the Show More Options check box, the dialog box expands to show the options below the Show More Options check box. The first of the more-options settings is the Output. Output shows the options choices shown in Figure 34-20. If you select Color Management from the drop-down list, the options choices change where you can select a color profile and the Intent.

✦ **Background:** By default, the background or area outside the image area is white. You can change the color by clicking on Background and selecting a new color in the Color Picker dialog box that opens after clicking the Background button.

✦ **Border:** Border prints a border around the bounding box. You specify point size for the border in the Border dialog box that opens after clicking the Border button.

✦ **Bleed:** If you want a bleed, click the Bleed button where a dialog box opens enabling you to specify the bleed amount.

✦ **Screen:** Click Screen, and the Halftone Screens dialog box opens, as shown in Figure 34-21. The dialog box offers options for adding custom frequencies and screen angles, including a number of options for dot shapes. If you open the Shape drop-down list, you can choose from fixed dot shapes or the Custom option that enables you to create custom dot shapes by typing in PostScript code in the Custom Spot Function window. To use this feature, you need to be skilled at PostScript programming.

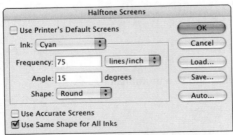

Figure 34-21: The Halftone Screens dialog box

If you edit a Photoshop file and import the image in InDesign, any custom frequencies are only preserved when you save your Photoshop file as EPS. Essentially, you embed screening attributes in the Photoshop image and preserve them whether printing directly or importing in other programs. If the need arises, you can embed one frequency in a Photoshop image that you may use as a background in an InDesign layout. You can print your InDesign file with one frequency — say, 150-line screen — while your Photoshop image has an embedded screen of something like 85 lines. In this example, the image prints at one frequency while the other document elements print at another frequency, all on the same page.

Another use for embedding frequencies is when printing spot color separations for screen printing. You may have a document with 6, 8, or more colors that need to be color-separated for a silk screener. If you want to print directly from Photoshop, visit the Halftone Screens dialog box and be certain to set the screen angles apart from each other to avoid printing a moiré.

When you add custom frequencies in the Halftone Screens dialog box, you must save the settings if you want to export the file to InDesign or some other program. Click Done in the Print dialog box, and the settings apply to the document. Save the file as an EPS from Photoshop, and you can import the image in any program supporting the EPS format.

✦ **Transfer:** Click Transfer to open the Transfer Functions dialog box, shown in Figure 34-22. Transfer functions enable you to remap shades of gray on your final output. If an output device prints lighter or darker than the brightness values you see on your monitor, you can remap the grays to result in printing a lighter or darker image. Messing around with the transfer functions is not something you want to do before sending off a file for final print. As a creative professional, you're more likely to receive a set of transfer functions or guidelines for using them from your printer. Make adjustments according to your printer's recommendations and save the file as EPS.

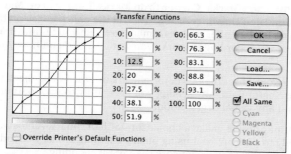

Figure 34-22: The Transfer Functions dialog box remaps the grays in your file.

Note that when you make adjustments to either the screens or transfer functions, choose File ➪ Save As, and choose the Photoshop EPS format, the EPS Options dialog box opens after you click Save. In the EPS Options dialog box, shown in Figure 34-23, you have options for Include Halftone Screen and Include Transfer Function. Check these boxes when you want to preserve any settings made for either screens or transfer functions. When you click OK and save the file, the settings are embedded in the document and cannot be overridden when printing from most other programs. Some programs such as Acrobat do enable you to override the settings.

Caution   Unless you want to embed screening or transfer functions, always keep the check boxes unchecked when saving Photoshop files as EPS.

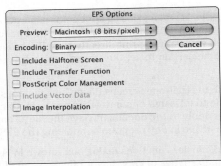

Figure 34-23: The EPS Options dialog box

✦ **Interpolation:** For use only with PostScript Level 2 and greater RIPs. When you check the box, the output device up sizes the image 200%, then reduces the image to its original size using bicubic interpolation. The result is low-resolution images with a less jagged appearance.

✦ **Calibration Bars, Registration Marks, Corner Crop Marks, Center Crop Marks, Description, Labels, Emulsion Down, and Negative:** All the check boxes on the right side of the Print dialog box offer options similar to those you find with Adobe Illustrator. Check the boxes according to marks you want printed and how you want emulsion handled.

✦ **Include Vector Data:** If your file contains vector objects or type fonts, check this box and the data is sent as vector data. Any scaling you may apply to your output scales the vector data without any visual degradation.

✦ **Encoding:** For PostScript printers, make a choice for ASCII or Binary. Almost all printers you use today are likely to perform best using binary encoding. Binary encoding prints faster and sends less data across your network than ASCII encoding.

Setting print options in InDesign

When you print from InDesign, all the print controls are contained in the Print dialog box. Unlike Photoshop the page setup and paper size selections are made in the same dialog box where you set all the other print attributes. Select File ➪ Print and the default General print options open, as shown in Figure 34-24.

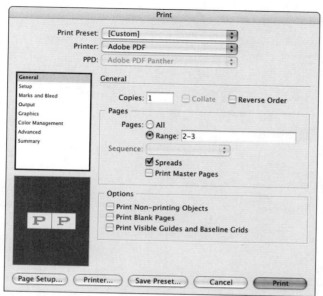

Figure 34-24: All the print options, including page size and page setup, are contained in the Print dialog box.

General print options

Items such as printer selection, page range, collating are the same in InDesign as you find in the other CS applications. As you look over the settings below, realize that what is noted here are those items *not* found in either the Illustrator or Photoshop Print dialog boxes.

✦ **Spreads:** Printer spreads can be output from InDesign. Spreads take two facing pages and prints them on the same page. When you set up the page size for printing spreads, be certain to add the width dimension to accommodate both pages. Two letter portrait pages for example would be set up for 17 by 11 (2 times 8.5 inches by 11 inches high).

✦ **Print Master Pages:** Check this box to print the master pages.

✦ **Print Non-Printing Objects:** You can identify some objects and layers for non printing. When this option is selected, all objects targeted for nonprinting are printed.

✦ **Print Blank Pages:** Just as the name suggests, any blank pages contained in the file are printed.

✦ **Print Visible Guides and Baseline Grids:** Something that can help you in the design of a piece is to print the pages with guides and baseline grids. You can see the guide and grid lines on the printed pages and carefully look them over for alignment and formatting.

Setup print options

Click Setup in the left pane to show options for selecting paper size, scaling and tiling as shown in Figure 34-25.

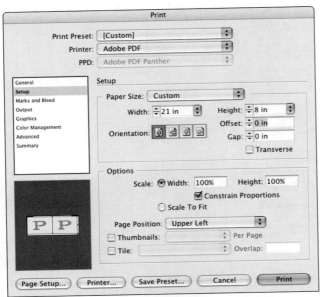

Figure 34-25: Click Setup to open options settings for selecting paper size and scaling choices.

✦ **Setup:** The Setup options include choices for selecting paper sizes. In InDesign you have choices for choosing fixed paper sizes from the Paper Size pull-down menu or by adding a Custom paper size and typing values in the Width and Height field boxes. The fixed sizes are derived from the PPD selected in the PPD pull-down menu. Custom sizes can be added in InDesign without going to a Page Setup dialog box and defining a custom page size. As you tab out of the Width and Height fields the thumbnail preview shows you how the page sizes appear on selected or custom page sizes.

✦ **Offset:** For roll fed imaging equipment, the offset offsets the printed image from the paper edge.

✦ **Gap:** Also on roll fed machines, the gap is the distance between printed pages.

✦ **Orientation and Transverse:** Same options are available in InDesign as you find in Illustrator.

✦ **Options:** Options settings include scaling output, page position in one of four locations, printing thumbnail images of a layout, tiling large pages that can't fit on a single paper size, and setting the overlap gap for tiled pages.

Marks and Bleeds

Marks and bleeds are similar to options you find in Illustrator and Photoshop. The items in the Marks area of the Marks and Bleeds section of the Print dialog box shown in Figure 34-26 are self-descriptive. InDesign has an additional item not found in either Illustrator or Photoshop in the Bleed and Slug area of the dialog box.

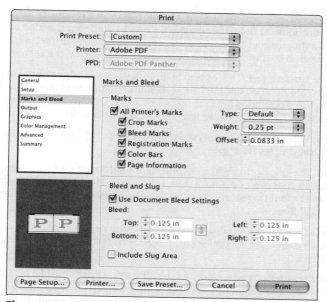

Figure 34-26: Options for setting marks, bleeds, and slugs

Output

Output options include specific settings for printing composites or separations. Color control and ink management are included in the options shown in Figure 34-27.

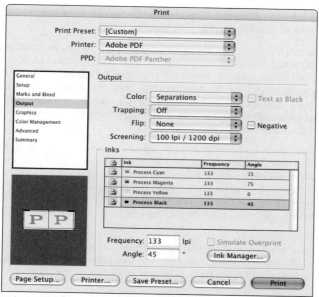

Figure 34-27: Option settings that control inks and emulsion

✦ **Color:** Choices are Composite Leave Unchanged, Composite Gray, Composite RGB, Composite CMYK, Separations, or In-RIP Separations. Choices made for the kind of composite print you want can affect the color, so be certain to choose the setting appropriate for your desired output. The Color choices defined include the following:

- **Composite Leave Unchanged:** This option is intended for use where you print to color printers that are Pantone-certified and can simulate spot-color inks. Very few printers are capable of rendering accurate spot colors, so this option is one you won't use unless working with a printer that can accurately reproduce spot colors.

- **Composite Gray:** When printing to grayscale printers, use this option. All colors are printed with varying levels of gray.

- **Composite RGB:** Use this option when outputting for screen or when printing to inkjet color printers that prefer printing from RGB mode. Most inkjets typically use CMYK color inks, but large-format inkjets like the Colorspan DisplayMakers prefer printing RGB files.

- **Composite CMYK:** For most composite color prints, you're likely to use this option. When your inkjet printer prefers printing CMYK color, select this option from the drop-down list.

- **Separations:** Use separations when printing to RIPs using PostScript Level 2 and below or when printing to PostScript RIPs not supporting In-RIP separations. Also, if you aren't certain of the RIP PostScript level or whether In-RIP separations are supported and you're preparing PostScript files for your service center, use Separations.

- **In-RIP Separations:** A composite image is sent to the printer's RIP where the RIP separates the file. Many PostScript 3 RIPs support In-RIP separations, but not all PostScript 3 RIPs. If preparing files for imaging centers, be certain to inquire about their capabilities for printing before sending PostScript files.

✦ **Text as Black:** Check this box to print text as pure black color as opposed to printing a mix of RGB or CMYK color to produce black.

✦ **Trapping:** The drop-down list commands are made available only when Separations or In-RIP Separations are selected. Options include one of three choices. You can turn trapping off, use InDesign built-in trapping, or use In-RIP trapping. InDesign has a sophisticated built-in trapping technology, and the Adobe In-RIP Trapping engine is even more powerful. If you don't have more-powerful dedicated trapping software, either option provides you with some impressive results. Note that In-RIP Trapping is available only on PostScript 3 RIPs that support In-RIP Trapping.

✦ **Flip:** Flipping a page is available for separations as well as composite printing. If you print to Mylar, LexJet, and other substrates necessitating printing documents flipped, InDesign CS offers new options over previous versions of the program and can accommodate separation and composite printing when page flipping is needed. For printing to imagesetters and platesetters, reading and emulsion are typically handled at the writing engine or the RIP. Therefore, you most often print files emulsion up and without flipping a page.

✦ **Screening:** Derived from the selected PPD, you make fixed halftone screen selections from the drop-down list. To add a custom frequency not available from the drop-down list, you can manually adjust the inks for frequency and angle below the Inks table.

✦ **Frequency:** You can adjust the halftone frequency manually by selecting inks in the Inks table and typing values in the Frequency field box.

✦ **Angle:** The default angles for process color includes Cyan at 15°, Magenta at 75°, Yellow at 0° and Black at 45°. Spot colors all default to 45° — the same angle used for black. If you introduce spot colors, be certain that the color angles are set apart from the other color angles. For example, on a two-color job containing Black and a spot color, change the spot color to either the Cyan or Magenta angle of 15° or 75°. If you have process color and a spot color, set the spot color angle 22° apart from the other process colors — something like 22° or 37°.

Graphics

The Graphics pane includes options for how image files are printed, font handling, and PostScript level. These options are generally used for proofing when printing for high-end prepress and commercial printing. The options shown in Figure 34-28 include:

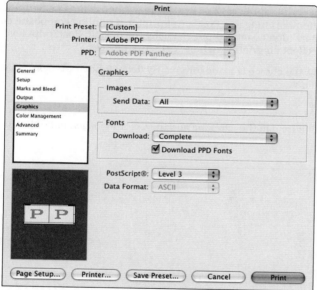

Figure 34-28: The Graphics pane has options for image and font handling as well as PostScript level.

✦ **Images:** From the drop-down list you have choices for what data is sent to your printer:

- **All**: Sends all the image data to the printer and is the choice you want to use for composite color printing.

- **Optimized Subsampling:** Sends enough data to the printer for an optimized print but downsamples images if the resolution is more than needed to output a satisfactory print.

- **Proxy:** Sends a 72 ppi image to the printer, resulting in a faster print for proofing purposes.

- **None:** Sends no image data for a quick printer where you can examine type and layout without printing the images.

✦ **Fonts:** From the drop-down list you have three choices:

- **None:** Downloads no fonts. Use this option only when you know that all the fonts in your document reside in your printer's memory or on a hard drive attached to your printer.

- **Complete:** Downloads all fonts to your printer's memory.

- **Subset:** Only sends the characters in a font to your printer's memory.

✦ **Download PPD Fonts:** Font lists contained in your printer's PPD are downloaded to your printer's memory. The PPD fonts are generally the fonts contained in your printer's memory. Most laser printers have the fonts Courier, Helvetica, Times, and Symbol burned into the ROM chips in the printer. The PPD for the printers list these fonts where the printer retrieves them when files containing the fonts are printed.

✦ **PostScript:** Choices are PostScript Level 2 or PostScript 3. Choose the PostScript level according to your printer if printing to a PostScript printer. If printing composite color to non-PostScript printers, don't worry about changing the default. PostScript-level choices won't have an effect on printing to non-PostScript devices.

✦ **Data Format:** Generally, the choice is made for you. By default, Binary is selected and you'll see ASCII grayed out.

Color management

Click on the Color Management item in the left pane and the Color Management options open, as shown in Figure 34-29.

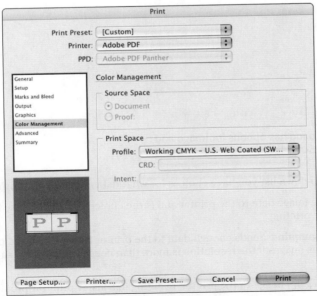

Figure 34-29: Options settings for managing color

✦ **Source Space:** Choose either Document, which uses the document's color space, or Proof, which uses the color space provided by the printer.

✦ **Print Space:** From the Profile drop-down list, select a color space that InDesign uses to map the color from the document's color space to the printer. If you select PostScript Color Management, you use a profile based on the CRD (color rendering dictionary) available for PostScript 3 devices that have built-in color management. Choose Default to use the color space provided by the printer, or choose from other options to override the device profile.

✦ **Intent:** From the drop-down list, you select from one of four rendering intents that are the same as those found in Illustrator.

Advanced

Click Advanced in the left page to open options for the Advanced settings, as shown in Figure 34-30. Options such as OPI (open press interface) management and transparency flattening are contained in this pane.

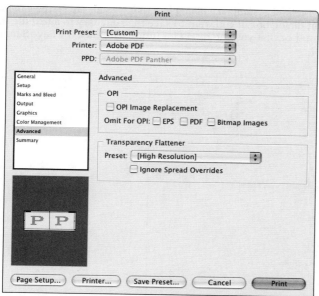

Figure 34-30: Options settings for OPI management and transparency flattening

✦ **OPI Image Replacement:** This option and the check boxes for EPS, PDF, and bitmap images relate to replacing FPO (for-position-only) low-resolution images with high-resolution images during lay out. When computers were less powerful and had less memory, OPI was used when service centers archived high-resolution images while designers used low-resolution images to create layouts. Today, with powerful computers that have plentiful RAM and hard-drive space, most people use high-resolution images for lay out. For composite color printing, you're likely to never use the OPI settings.

✦ **Transparency Flattener:** On most PostScript RIPs, you need to flatten transparency to successfully print your document. Any use of the Transparency palette, applying drop shadows to objects in InDesign, applying a feather, using blending modes, or using transparency in imported images requires you to flatten the transparency. From the presets use:

- Low Resolution for quick proof prints on desktop printers

- Medium Resolution for desktop proofs on desktop color printers and copy machines, on-demand printers, and so on

- High Resolution for all files printed as separations and on high-end commercial PostScript devices

✦ **Ignore Spread Overrides:** You can flatten transparency on spreads by viewing a spread in the Document window and choosing Spread Flattening on the Pages menu. You can override Spreads flattened by enabling this check box at the time of printing or export.

Summary

As in other CS applications, you have a summary dialog box that lists all the settings made through the panes in the Print dialog box. If you want to save the summary to a text file that you can send to a service center or that you can retain for future use, click the Save Summary button, shown in Figure 34-31.

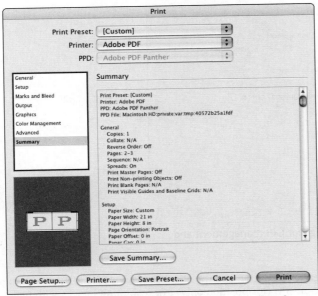

Figure 34-31: The Save Summary button saves a list of printer settings.

Setting print options in Acrobat

One of the new additions to Acrobat 6 is the introduction of professional printing tools now contained within the program. In previous versions of Acrobat, you needed to acquire third-party plug-ins to print PDF documents to commercial printing devices. Acrobat contains all the print controls needed for high-end prepress as well as all the settings you need for print-ing composite color. Additionally, you can use Acrobat to print files originating in the other CS applications after converting documents to PDF. Using Acrobat as your printing tool sim-plifies the printing process because you need to learn only those print options from a single set of dialog boxes.

The first place to start when printing files from Acrobat is to visit the Page Setup dialog box. After selecting the proper page size and orientation or defining a custom page size, choose File ➪ Print to open the print dialog box shown in Figure 34-32.

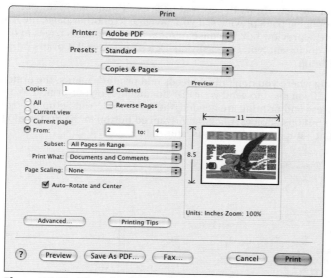

Figure 34-32: The Print dialog box in Acrobat

There are two sets of print dialog boxes in Acrobat. The default opening view is the Print dialog box. The second print dialog box is the Advanced Print Setup dialog box that opens after you click on the Advanced button; this is the place where options typically used for commercial printing are found. The Print dialog box includes the following options:

✦ **Copies/Collated:** Use the field box to enter the number of copies you want to print. The Collated check box collates pages when printing multiple copies.

✦ **All:** Prints all pages in the document.

✦ **Current View:** This option enables you to print a portion of a page. Zoom in to the document page and select Current View to print the page as you see it displayed on your monitor.

✦ **Current Page:** Navigate to the page you want to print and select Current Page. The result is a print of the page currently viewed in the Document pane.

✦ **Subset:** Subset contains several options in the drop-down list. Choose to print all pages in a range, odd pages only, or even pages only. Click on the Reversed check box to print pages in back-to-front order.

✦ **Print What:** From the drop-down list, you have choices for printing the document as you might print any file. Acrobat offers additional options not available in other

CS applications, such as comment notes and form fields. The Document and Comments option prints the document and the contents of the comment notes. When you select the item, the comments on the first page, if they exist, display in the Preview area. The Form Fields Only option prints only the form fields from an Acrobat form.

✦ **Page Scaling:** Page Scaling offers options for None, Fit to Paper, Shrink Large Pages, Tile Large Pages, and Tile All Pages. Select the option you want from the drop-down list choices.

✦ **Auto-Rotate and Center:** When enabled, pages are auto-rotated and centered.

✦ **Preview:** A document preview shows the current page as a thumbnail in the preview box. By default, the opening page previews. If you navigate to another page, the respective page displays in the preview box. Because Acrobat accommodates pages of different sizes in the same document, you can easily check a page to see if it prints properly on the current page setup.

For composite color printing where you don't need bleeds and printer's marks, the options in the Print dialog box are all you need to send your PDF documents to your printer. When high-end commercial prepress and printing are needed, the Advanced Print Setup dialog box is where you need to make options choices. Click the Advanced button in the Print dialog box, and the Advanced Print Setup dialog box opens, shown in Figure 34-33.

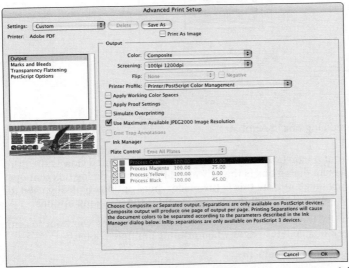

Figure 34-33: The Advanced Print Setup dialog box has commercial printing options.

On the left side of the Advanced Print Setup dialog box, you make choices for options associated with output, marks and bleeds, transparency flattening, and PostScript. The first item available for selection is **Print as Image.**

Print as Image: For composite color printing when you have difficulty printing a document to your desktop printer, use as a last resort the Print as Image option. When you check the box, all vector objects and type convert to bitmaps. The results are often less than optimum, but can mean the difference between printing the page or not. For proofing purposes, where PostScript errors generate at the time of printing, check the box.

Output

Output options offer choices for handling color and screening. In the Options pane, you find settings for the following:

✦ **Color:** The same options for composite and separations are available in Acrobat as you find in InDesign and Illustrator. See Setting print options in Illustrator and Setting print options in InDesign earlier in this chapter.

✦ **Screening:** Fixed values are derived from the PPD for PostScript printers. You select custom frequencies and screen angles in the Ink Manager at the bottom of the Output pane.

✦ **Apply Working Color Spaces:** This setting, in effect, applies the profile you select in the Color Management Preferences dialog box as the source space to the PDF document. If the PDF is calibrated, it uses the calibrated color spaces in the PDF document as the source.

✦ **Apply Proof Settings:** This setting is available for composite printing only. If you want to apply settings made in the Proof Setup for a simulated print, enable the check box.

✦ **Simulate Overprinting:** This option, also available for composite, prints a proof showing the effects of overprints assigned in the document. This feature emulates the overprinting previews of high-end color proofers that display overprints in composite proofs.

✦ **Use Maximum Available JPEG2000 Image Resolution:** When enabled, the maximum usable resolution contained in JPEG2000 images is used.

✦ **Emit Trap Annotations:** Only applies to documents where trap annotations are included in the file. The trap annotations are sent to RIPs when In-Rip separations are used on PostScript 3 devices.

✦ **Ink Manager:** If your file contains spot colors or RGB colors, you can convert spot or RGB to CMYK color by clicking on the check box. The spot color converts to CMYK color when the X in the check box turns to a fill with CMYK color. To edit the frequency and angle for each plate, double-click on a color and the Edit Frequency and Angle dialog box opens. Supply the desired frequency and angle for each color by successively opening the dialog box for each color.

Marks and bleeds

Click on the Marks and Bleeds option in the left pane and the marks and bleeds options appear, shown in Figure 34-34. Acrobat behaves a little differently from the other CS applications because you don't have a document setup to define page size like the other applications. You need to be certain that the Page Setup page size is large enough to accommodate printer's marks. However, you need to define the bleeds in the document you convert to PDF. If bleeds were not included (say, from an InDesign file), the PDF won't set a bleed outside the printer's marks. Be certain you include bleed amounts in your Illustrator and InDesign files before exporting to PDF.

Check All Marks or individually click on the check boxes below the Marks Style drop-down list. From the drop-down list options, you can choose Western Style or Eastern Style. Use Eastern Style for printing files in Far Eastern countries.

The Emit Printer Marks check box is active when printer marks were exported when the document was converted to PDF. Checking this box applies the bleed settings contained in the exported document.

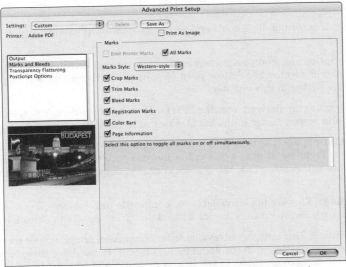

Figure 34-34: Click Marks and Bleeds to apply printer's marks.

Transparency flattening

Click on Transparency Flattening in the left pane to apply settings. Acrobat has a Transparency Flattener Preview where you can examine the results of applying transparency before you open the Print dialog box. The amount of flattening you determined from the Flattener Preview dialog box is applied here. As you move the slider toward Rasters, you'll notice the preview doesn't change. The flattening of the transparency occurs only when you print the file, or save it as PostScript.

For more information on using the Flattener Preview, see Chapter 35.

Rasterizing Resolutions are similar to the options found in InDesign. For high-end printing, use 1,200 ppi (pixels per inch) when flattening the transparency.

The Options choices offer you settings for converting type and strokes to outlines. As a last resort for printing stubborn fonts that you know are embedded in the PDF document, you can convert the type to outlines. As a general rule, try to avoid converting type to outlines, because the file takes longer to RIP and print than when downloading fonts to the RIP. Clicking the check box for Clip Complex Regions can reduce the amount of memory required to print a file. This can assist you in printing difficult files to PostScript devices.

PostScript options

The PostScript Options section includes a variety of settings used for preserving embedded halftone frequencies, transferring functions, handling color, and some other miscellaneous settings. Click PostScript to open the options choices for the PostScript settings, as shown in Figure 34-35.

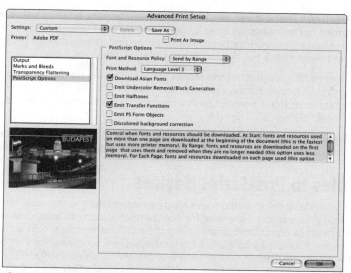

Figure 34-35: The PostScript pane has various settings for PostScript printing.

✦ **Font and Resource Policy:** Three options are available from the drop-down list:

- **Send at Start:** Sends all fonts to the printer as the print job starts.

- **Send by Range:** Sends fonts encountered on the pages as new pages print and where the fonts stay in memory until the job finishes printing.

- **Send for Each Page:** Conserves memory where the fonts are flushed after each page prints. This option takes more time to print but can overcome problems when experiencing difficulty in printing a job.

✦ **Print Method:** Choose from PostScript Level 2 or PostScript 3 depending on the level of PostScript used by the RIP.

✦ **Download Asian Fonts:** Check the box if Asian characters are in the document and not available at the RIP.

✦ **Emit Undercolor Removal/Black Generation:** GCR/UCR removal is only necessary if the original file contain embedded settings. Deselect the box to remove any embedded settings that you might have inadvertently added and saved in Photoshop. If you want to apply any embedded settings, checking the box to emit the settings applies them as they were embedded in the authoring program.

✦ **Emit Halftones:** If the PostScript file contained embedded halftones, you can preserve them here, and the frequency assigned in the Output options are used to print the file. Check the box to apply the frequency embedded in a file. You preserve halftones when you want an embedded halftone frequency in an image to print at a different frequency than the rest of the job.

✦ **Emit Transfer Functions:** Deselect the box to eliminate any transfer functions that might have been embedded in Photoshop images. If you know you want images to print with embedded transfer functions you may have applied according to instructions provided from a publication house, check the box to preserve the transfer functions.

✦ **Emit PS Form Objects:** PostScript XObjects store common information in a document — things like backgrounds, headers, footers, and so on. When PostScript XObjects are used, the printing is faster, but it requires more memory. To speed up the printing, check the box to emit PostScript XObjects.

✦ **Discolored Background Correction:** Enable this option only when printing composite proofs where backgrounds print darker or with a discolored appearance like a yellow tint.

Printing PDF files to PostScript devices

For composite printing to desktop PostScript devices, you can successfully print using the Print and Advanced Print Setup dialog boxes. However, for commercial printing to imagesetters, platesetters, and direct-to-press equipment, printing direct from Acrobat can produce some unexpected results. A better option is to generate a PostScript file and download the PostScript file to your printer. When printing directly to high-end devices, you can experience problems with color handling, black type printing with tints, and PostScript errors that prevent the job from being printed.

For commercial output, choose File ➪ Save As and select PostScript as the output format. Click the Settings button where options choices identical to the Advanced Print Setup dialog box are contained. Make your options choices and save the file as PostScript. The resultant PostScript file is then downloaded to your printer. This method generally produces more-reliable output.

Cross-Reference For more information on saving files as PostScript for printing purposes, see Chapter 35.

Summary

✦ Some CS applications require you to use the Page Setup dialog box before opening the Print dialog box.

✦ Print options for screening, color handling, separations, printer's marks, and so on are found in advanced print options dialog boxes generally available through the Print dialog box.

✦ Desktop color printers often have special print options where choices for paper types and color handling are accessed via the printer's print driver.

✦ InDesign and Acrobat are the most commonly used applications for commercial printing.

✦   ✦   ✦

Commercial Printing

In This Chapter

Proofing documents on your monitor

Checking jobs for potential imaging problems

Preparing files for prepress and printing

Printing on commercial devices

As a production artist, you participate in workflows with production workers and technicians at prepress houses and print shops. Your role extends beyond the creative work you do to include proper file preparation, proofing your work, checking files for potential problems, and delivering a product that has an excellent chance for successful output. The Creative Suite applications offer you many tools for diagnosing documents and reporting back to you potential imaging problems. In addition, some CS applications offer you options for creating file formats optimized for high-end prepress and printing.

This chapter begins with soft-proofing color and separations on your monitor before files are sent to an imaging center, and continues with file checking known as *preflighting*. The last part of the chapter covers packaging jobs for imaging centers. You should consider the contents of this chapter as covering one of the most important aspects of your production workflow when creating documents designed for commercial printing.

Soft-Proofing Documents

Soft-proofing a document is viewing the file on your monitor and checking various conditions for potential printing problems. You can check issues such as overprints, proper color assignment, transparency flattening, and font problems using some of the CS applications. Your two best sources for soft-proofing documents are InDesign and Acrobat. Although InDesign has some impressive tools for soft-proofing documents, Acrobat is a more likely tool for examining files because it offers many more soft-proofing options and is a better choice for packaging documents.

For more information on packaging documents, see the section "Packaging Documents for Commercial Printing" at the end of this chapter.

Soft-proofing files in InDesign

In InDesign, you can check files for transparency flattening and color separations. Open the Window menu and you see menu commands for Transparency Flattener and Separation Preview. Select one of the menu commands and the respective palette opens as a floating palette.

Transparency flattening

As described in Chapter 34, transparency flattener previews show you the results of applying flattening amounts. The actual flattening of transparency only occurs at the time of printing or exporting your InDesign document. To open the Transparency Flattener, choose Window ⇨ Output Preview ⇨ Flattener. The Flattener Preview palette opens, shown in Figure 35-1.

Figure 35-1: The Flattener Preview palette

The Flattener Preview palette offers you various options for previewing the results of flattening transparency. You navigate to pages and see results on the page in the Document window as you apply settings and refresh the screen to update different settings options. The following options are available in the palette:

✦ **Rasterize Complex Regions:** From the drop-down list, the first choice is this option. From the Flattener Preview fly-away menu, opened when you click on the right-pointing arrow, you can show Transparency Flattener Presets in a dialog box. The dialog box contains buttons for creating new presets or editing presets you load or create. When you create or edit a preset, the Transparency Flattener Preset Options dialog box opens; here, you control the amount of transparency by moving the Raster/Vector Balance slider. The slider position in the Transparency Flattener Preset Options dialog box determines the amount of rasterizing complex regions.

✦ **Transparent Objects:** When you select this option from the drop-down list, transparent objects are highlighted on the page, including alpha channels in Photoshop images, objects with blending modes, and objects with opacity marks such as drop shadows applied in InDesign.

✦ **All Affected Objects:** Next in the drop-down list is this setting, which highlights overlapping objects where at least one of the objects contains transparency. All the highlighted objects are flattened according to the amount specified in the Transparency Flattener Preset Options dialog box.

✦ **Affected Graphics:** This setting highlights placed objects where transparency effects are involved.

✦ **Outline Strokes:** Following along in the drop-down list, this option highlights all strokes that have been marked for outlines.

✦ **Outline Text:** Highlights all text that has been converted to outlines when involved with transparency.

✦ **Raster-Fill Text and Strokes:** Object fills and strokes can be rasterized during transparency flattening. This option previews the results of rasterizing.

✦ **All Rasterized Regions:** Objects and intersections throughout the document are highlighted to show the results of rasterization. Photoshop files are also previewed for the results of rasterization, as are all effects that involve transparency, such as drop shadows and feathering.

✦ **Auto Refresh Highlight:** When the check box is checked, the highlighted preview refreshes as you toggle menu commands and adjust settings.

✦ **Refresh:** If you want to manually refresh the preview, uncheck the Auto Refresh Highlight check box and click the Refresh button as you want the preview updated.

✦ **Preset:** InDesign is installed with three presets for transparency adjustments. You can add custom presets and the new presets are added to the drop-down list. Select from the menu the preset you want to use.

✦ **Ignore Spread Overrides:** For individual spreads where you want to ignore flattener presets, check the check box.

✦ **Apply Settings to Print:** When the preview results look appropriate for your output, click the Apply Settings to Print button to apply the transparency flattening settings to your document. When you open the Print dialog box, the results of the transparency flattening appear.

The Transparency Flattener Presets dialog box provides options for managing presets. You open the dialog box shown in Figure 35-2 by selecting Transparency Flattener Presets from the fly-away menu in the Flattener Preview palette. Options for managing presets include the following:

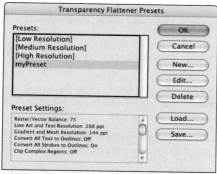

Figure 35-2: The Transparency Flattener Presets dialog box manages presets.

✦ **New:** Opens the Transparency Flattener to open the Transparency Flattener Preset Options dialog box where you assign attributes for new presets.

✦ **Edit:** You can return to a given preset and edit it in the Transparency Flattener Presets dialog box (Figure 35-3). Select the preset to edit, then click Edit. Note that you cannot edit or delete the default presets installed with InDesign.

✦ **Delete:** Click a preset you want to remove and click Delete.

✦ **Load:** You can save a preset as a file and load it back into the Transparency Flattener Presets dialog box. In workflow environments, you can save presets and share them with colleagues so all designers use the same transparency flattening for all files for a given campaign.

✦ **Save:** To load a preset, you must first have a file resident on your hard drive or network server (or external media). Click Save to open the Save Transparency Flattener Presets dialog box where you can type a name for the preset and save to a folder on your hard drive.

Defining options for a transparency flattening preset are established in the Transparency Flattener Preset Options dialog box. When you click either the New button or the Edit button, the dialog box shown in Figure 35-3 opens. Make your adjustments in this dialog box and the collective settings are captured to the preset you create or edit.

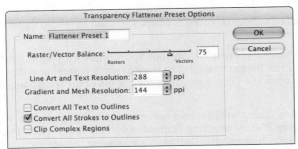

Figure 35-3: The Transparency Flattener Preset Options dialog box

The options choices you have for defining attributes for a preset include the following:

✦ **Name:** Type a name in the field box and the name is reflected in the Transparency Flattener Presets dialog box. Try to use descriptive names so you can easily recall a particular preset used for a given job.

✦ **Raster/Vector Balance:** Move the slider to apply varying amounts of flattening. As you move the slider and target a particular amount, you can return to the Flattener Preview palette and preview the transparency settings.

✦ **Line Art and Text Resolution:** You adjust resolution for rasterizing line art and text in the field box or by clicking on the up and down arrows to change the value.

✦ **Gradient and Mesh Resolution:** A separate field box is used for rasterizing gradients and meshes.

✦ **Convert All Text to Outlines:** When checking the box, you can preview the results in the Flatten Transparency dialog box by selecting Outline Text from the drop-down list.

✦ **Convert All Strokes to Outlines:** The same applies to this option as the Convert All Text to Outlines. Use the Raster-Fill and Strokes Menu command in the Flattener Preview palette to preview the flattening.

✦ **Clip Complex Regions:** Once again, the same applies to this option. Use the Flattener Transparency dialog box and choose Rasterize Complex Regions to preview the results.

Previewing separations

A nice addition to InDesign CS is being able to preview separations and color modes before you send a file off to the printer. If you inadvertently specify spot colors where you intend to print a process color job, the Separations Preview palette immediately shows you all process and spot color in a document to help you avoid costly errors. To open the Separations Preview palette (Figure 35-4), choose Window ➪ Separations Preview.

Figure 35-4: The Separations Preview palette displays all document colors.

While the Separation Preview palette is open, you can move the cursor around the document page, and ink percentages are reported in the palette for the cursor position. You can toggle each color on and off by clicking on the eye icon. Therefore, single inks or combinations of inks can be displayed in the palette and reflected in the Document window.

From the View drop-down list, you have a menu command to display ink limits. Select the menu command and the Separation Preview palette changes to the view shown in Figure 35-5. You can alter the ink coverage by selecting from fixed values in the drop-down list or typing values in the field box. Ink limit coverage should be assigned according to advice obtained from your printer. The ink limit is designed to keep ink limits within the capabilities of a press.

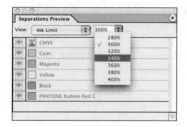

Figure 35-5: To alter ink coverage, select Ink Limit and a fixed ink-limit value.

From the fly-away palette, you can access the Ink Manager where individual ink densities are assigned and spot color to process conversions can be applied. Open the fly-away palette by clicking on the right-pointing arrow and selecting Ink Manager. The Ink Manager dialog box opens, shown in Figure 35-6.

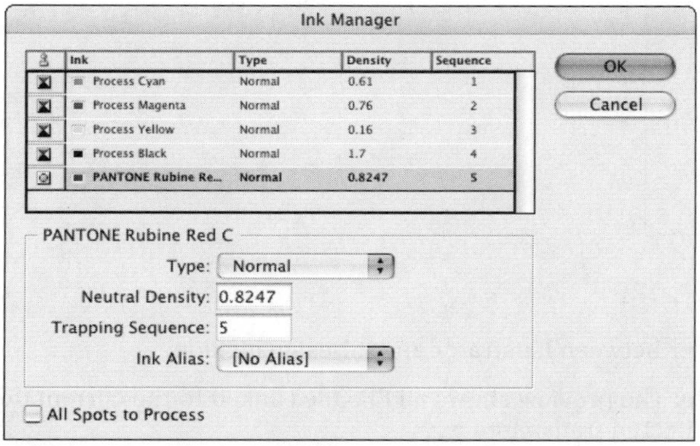

Figure 35-6: The Ink Manager dialog box

You make any settings dialog box according to recommendations from your commercial printer. The neutral densities established as the default values when you install InDesign are defined according to the language version used during your installation. As you use printers from other parts of the world, you might find changes in standards for neutral densities. Neutral densities are important because the trapping engine uses the values to determine precise placement of traps. You don't want to mess around with the values until you receive precise guidelines for adjustments from your printer.

The check box for All Spots to Process is the item in this dialog box you're likely to use often. If you specify spot-color inks during a design stage, you can convert the spot colors to process values with this option.

In the Separations Preview fly-away palette, you have a menu option for displaying spot colors as black. Select Show Single Plates in Black and, when previewing the spot colors in the file without the CMYK colors previewed, each spot color is displayed in the Document window as black. Note that you need to turn off all the process colors to see the spot colors appear as black. When the menu command is deselected, all spot colors display in their color values when viewing single plates as well as when viewing all plates.

Soft-proofing files in Illustrator

Many of the transparency flattening preview options found in Illustrator are the same as the ones in InDesign. Open the Window menu and select Flattener Preview to open the Flattener Preview dialog box, shown in Figure 35-7.

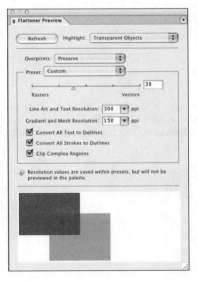

Figure 35-7: The Flattener Preview palette has options similar to InDesign.

Transparency flattening

Those options choices that differ between Illustrator and InDesign include:

✦ **Affected linked EPS Files:** The preview shows all EPS files linked to the current document as they related to affected transparency.

✦ **Expanded Patterns:** The highlights show all patterns that will expand because they involve transparency.

From the Overprints drop-down list, you have additional options not found in InDesign. The default choice is to preserve all overprints. You have other options to eliminate all overprints or to simulate overprints:

✦ **Discard:** Obviously discards all overprints. You might use this option when sending files to print shops that perform all the trapping on your files.

✦ **Simulate:** Maintains the appearance of overprinting in composite proofs. Use this when printing to composite color printers that can display the overprints.

The Presets drop-down list offers you choices for different presets installed as defaults in Illustrator and a list of all presets you save by selecting Save Transparency Flattener Preset from the fly-away menu. Illustrator handles saving presets differently than InDesign. When you select the menu command, the preset is automatically saved without prompting you in a Save dialog box. You can return to the Presets drop-down list, and the saved preset is listed.

Editing a preset works a bit differently in Illustrator than it does in InDesign. To change options on a preset you saved, select the preset in the Presets drop-down list. Make your new options choices, open the fly-away palette, and select Redefine Preset. The new attributes are assigned to the saved preset.

Managing presets

If you need to delete a preset, you won't find an option in the Flattener Preview dialog box. Instead, you must open the Edit menu and select Transparency Flattener Presets. The transparency Flattener Presets dialog box opens. Figure 35-8 shows you a dialog box with the exact same options choices as you have in InDesign. Notice that you can edit a preset in this dialog box as well as when redefining a preset as mentioned earlier, in the "Preview transparency flattening" section.

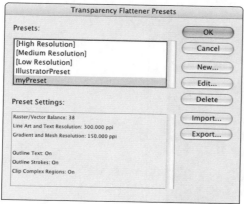

Figure 35-8: You manage presets in the Transparency Flattener Presets dialog box.

Soft-proofing documents in Acrobat

Acrobat PDF is the best form of document format for submitting files to print shops. The ability to embed graphic images and type fonts is one of the advantages you have with PDF files. In addition to being a desirable format for delivering documents for press, Acrobat Professional also offers an abundance of soft-proofing and preflighting tools.

Swapping presets

As is the case with many presets and palette exports among the CS applications, you cannot swap the transparency flattening presets between programs. This is to say that you cannot create a preset in InDesign, export the preset as a file, and import the preset in Illustrator or vice versa. Likewise, you cannot export color swatches, libraries, and other such settings from one application into other CS applications. This is one of the current limitations of the continuity between the CS programs and somewhat of a minor detriment to workflow environments. As the CS programs evolve, we think the ability to swap exported files between programs will be greatly enhanced. Keep your eye on maintenance upgrades and future versions of the CS product for newer implementations where settings files can be swapped back and forth between the programs.

Transparency flattening

Acrobat also contains a transparency flattener preview. Choose Advanced ➪ Transparency Flattener Preview to open the Flattener Preview window (Figure 35-9). Notice that the options are the same as those available in InDesign and Illustrator.

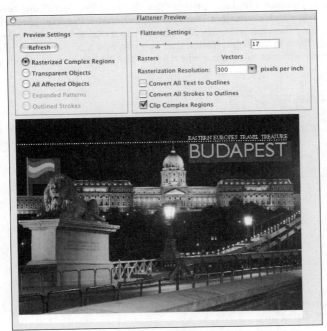

Figure 35-9: The Transparency Flattener Preview window in Acrobat

Keep in mind that, as you adjust settings, you need to click the Refresh button to display the preview with new settings. Acrobat has one limitation that InDesign and Illustrator don't have: You don't have options for saving and loading presets. Otherwise, the options are identical to the options in the other CS applications.

Proof setup

Acrobat offers you more options for soft-proofing color than you'll find in either InDesign or Illustrator. The soft-proofing commands in Acrobat are contained in the Advanced menu. Select Advanced and choose from options for Custom, Proof Colors, or Overprint Preview.

Custom

Custom enables you to select from a list of International Color Consortium (ICC) profiles. A number of preset profiles are available from which to choose, and you can also create your own custom profiles and add them to the list. You create custom profiles with either software applications like Adobe Gamma (Windows), Apple Color Sync (Mac), or hardware/software devices that are designed specifically for calibrating monitors and creating ICC profiles. As a profile is created, it's saved as a file to your hard drive.

 Cross-Reference   For information and definitions of ICC profiles, see Chapter 6.

For Acrobat to recognize the ICC profiles you create, you must store profiles in the proper directory. By default, utilities and commercial devices used for calibrating color save profiles to a directory that makes them accessible to Acrobat. If you want to remove ICC profiles so fewer profiles show up in the Proof Colors dialog box or you have problems getting a profile to the right directory, open the folder where the profiles are stored. On Windows the path is `System32\Spool\Drivers\Color`. On Mac OS X, look in `Macintosh HD:Library:ColorSync: Profiles:Displays`. When new profiles are added to the folder according to your operating system, you can access the profiles in Acrobat after you quit the program and relaunch it if the profile was added while Acrobat was open.

Choose Advanced ➪ Proof Setup ➪ Custom to open the Custom Proof Setup dialog box, shown in Figure 35-10. In the drop-down list, you'll see a number of different profiles. If you have an ICC profile developed for your system as the result of calibrating your monitor, select the profile in the list. If you haven't created a profile, you can choose from one of the preinstalled profiles. As a general rule, select a CMYK proofing profile such as U.S. Web Coated (SWOP) 2 for files you intend to print as process (CMYK) color. For Web and screen uses, select sRGB IEC61966-2.1. You can make a number of other selections, but be certain to test results of selecting one profile over another. If you select profiles like Apple RGB or Wide Gamut RGB, you may find the color works well for your screen viewing, but other Acrobat users may see different color if they're using a different profile.

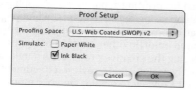

Figure 35-10: The Proof Setup dialog box

If you want to preview the PDF document as it theoretically is printed on paper, choose from either an ICC profile you created or from the preset profiles such as Euroscale, SWOP, and so on. For printing on offset press on coated stock, use U.S. Web Coated (SWOP) v2. When you select one of the presets for soft-proofing prints, the two check boxes for simulating ink and paper become accessible.

Tip

To ensure your color proofing uses the same profile each time you view a file on-screen, open a document in Acrobat. Choose Advanced ➪ Proof Setup ➪ Custom and choose the profile that works best in your workflow. Quit Acrobat and relaunch the program. Your last choice becomes the new default. You don't need to quit the program to make the profile choice a new default, but if the program crashes during a session, you lose preferences applied in that session. Quitting after making a preference choice ensures you that the preference is held in all subsequent Acrobat sessions.

Paper White

If you enable the check box for Paper White in the Proof Setup dialog box, the preview shows you a particular shade of gray as simulated for the paper color by the profile you choose. You may find that the preview looks too gray or has too much black. This result may not be the profile used, but rather the brightness adjustment on your monitor. If your monitor is calibrated properly and the profile accurately displays the paper color, the preview should show you an accurate representation of the document as it is printed on paper.

Ink Black

When you enable this check box, the preview shows you the dynamic range of the document's profile. Dynamic range is measured in values usually between 0 and 4, although some scanner manufacturers claim dynamic ranges of 4.1, 4.2, or higher. A dynamic range of something like 3.8 yields a wide range of grays between the white point and the black point in a scanned image. If the dynamic range is high, you see details in shadows and highlights. If the dynamic range is low, highlights can get blown out and shadows lose detail. When you enable the Ink Black check box, look for the distinct tonal differences in the preview and detail in shadows and highlights.

Proof colors

Choose Advanced ➪ Proof Colors to preview the document using a profile you selected in the Proof Setup submenu. If you select the Proof Colors dialog box and choose a profile, the Proof Colors menu command is selected for you. You can turn off proofing without affecting your profile choice by returning to the Advanced menu and selecting Proof Colors again to turn the proofing off.

Overprint preview

You often use overprints to *trap* colors in files intended for printing separations. Trapping a color creates a color overlap that prevents gaps from appearing between colors, when paper moves during the printing process. You might assign an overprint to text to avoid any trapping problems where black text prints on top of a background color. In other cases, a designer might unintentionally assign an overprint to a color during the creative process. As a measure of checking overprints for those colors that you properly assign and to review a document for potential problems, you can use Acrobat's Overprint Preview to display on your monitor all the overprints created in a file. To view overprints in a PDF document, choose Advanced ➪ Overprint Preview.

Note

Overprint Preview is available in both Acrobat Standard and Acrobat Professional. The remaining preflighting and soft-proofing tools are available only in Acrobat Professional.

To understand what happens with overprints and knockouts, look at Figure 35-11. The composite image is created for printing two colors. These colors are printed on separate plates for two different inks. When the file is separated, the type is *knocked out* of the background, leaving holes in the background, as shown in Figure 35-12. Because the two colors butt up against each other, any slight movement of the paper creates a gap where one ink color ends and the other begins. To prevent the problem, a slight bit of overprinting is added to the type. In an exaggerated view, in Figure 35-13, you can see the stroke around the type characters. The stroke is assigned an overprint so its color, which is the foreground color, prints on top of the background color without a knockout.

Figure 35-11: Color-separation makes each color appear on a separate printing plate.

Figure 35-12: The background appears with the foreground type knocked out.

Figure 35-13: The overprint area of the type color prints on top of the background color.

Designers can apply overprints in programs like Illustrator and InDesign. If a designer inadvertently makes a mistake and selects the fill color to overprint, the color of the foreground image results in a different color created by the mix of the two colors. In Figure 35-14, you view a file in Acrobat without an overprint preview. The figure shows the document as it should print. When you choose Advanced ⇨ Overprint Preview, the overprints shown in Figure 35-15 appear. As you can see, the assigned overprints in the file were a mistake. Using Acrobat's Overprint Preview command, you can check for any overprint errors in illustrations.

Tip   To carefully examine overprints assigned to type characters, select the Loupe tool in the Zoom toolbar. Move the cursor around the document to preview overprints on small type.

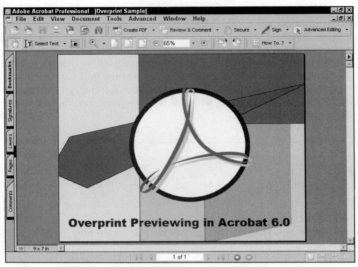

Figure 35-14: The file appears as it is intended to be printed.

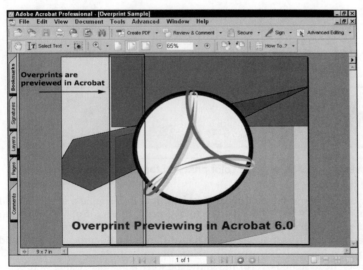

Figure 35-15: Viewing all colors in an overprint shows erroneous overprint assignments.

Separation preview

One of the great new features for soft-proofing color in Acrobat Professional is the addition of the separation preview, similar to the same preview offered in InDesign. To preview a color separation, choose Advanced ⇨ Separation Preview. The Separation Preview dialog box appears, shown in Figure 35-16.

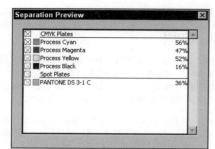

Figure 35-16: Separation Preview shows all colors contained in a file.

Assessing ink values

As you move the cursor around a document, the values for each colorant are reported according to the profile you select in the Color Management Preferences. To open the Color Management Preferences, choose Edit ⇨ Preferences. Click on Color Management and make choices for your working spaces from the profiles you select from drop-down lists, as shown in the figure. The profiles available to you are the same as those you choose in the Proof Setup dialog box discussed in the section "Proof setup."

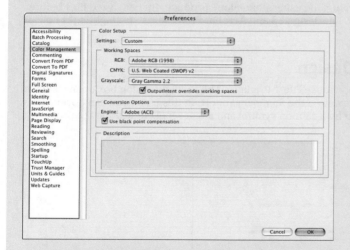

Although assessing colors in the Separation Preview dialog box is fine in most cases, there are situations where you might assess a color and the printed result is different from the value reported in the Separation Preview dialog box. Achieving accurate proofing all depends on the proper creation of the PDF file, selecting the proper profile in the Color Management Setup preferences, and the output space you select when you print the file.

For more information on color management among the CS applications, see Chapter 6.

For color proofing multiple files, open them in Acrobat Professional and choose Window ⇨ Tile ⇨ Vertically (or Horizontally). Open the Separation Preview dialog box. Move the cursor from one document to another. As the cursor enters a page in the tiled view, the separation preview displays the colors relative to the cursor position. As you move the cursor to a different document with different colors, the colors are dynamically reflected in the Separation Preview dialog box.

If you intend to print a file in four-color process, the Separation Preview dialog box identifies any potential problems if you have spot colors in the file. Likewise, if a spot-color job contains colors that you don't intend to print, they also show up.

You can selectively view individual colors by disabling the check boxes adjacent to each color name, view selected colors only, and view spot colors converted to CMYK. When you click on the X in a check box for a spot color, the first preview is a process equivalent. Click again and the color is hidden in the document. Click a third time and the color returns as a spot color.

You evaluate color values by moving the cursor around the document with the Separation Preview dialog box open. Notice the percentage values on the far right side of Figure 35-16. These values represent the percent of ink at the cursor position.

Preflighting Documents

Preflighting is a term used by creative professionals and service technicians to analyze a file for suitability in printing. A preflight assessment examines a file for the proper color mode of images, whether images are compressed, whether fonts are accessible, or any number of other conditions that might interfere with successfully printing a job.

The tools used to preflight files might be stand-alone applications or features built into programs used for printing to commercial printing equipment. Prior to upgrades to the CS applications, you needed to preflight a file using stand-alone products that analyzed files before sending them to your printer. InInDesign CS and Acrobat Professional, preflighting is now built into the programs.

Preflighting in InDesign

To preflight a file in InDesign, choose File ➪ Preflight. The Preflight dialog box opens, shown in Figure 35-17. The default review is the Summary report. In this pane, you can observe any immediate problems denoted by a caution symbol and a text report indicating the problem(s).

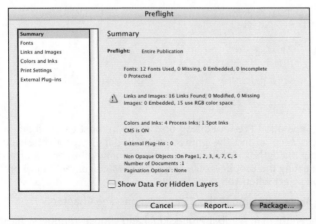

Figure 35-17: The Preflight dialog box reports any printing problems.

On the left side of the dialog box are several categories specific to issues related to printing that you'll want to examine. These options include:

✦ **Summary:** All problems are reported in summary form to show you at a glance if the file will encounter potential printing problems.

✦ **Fonts:** All fonts used in the system are listed in a scrollable window. The type of font (TrueType, Type 1, OpenType, and so on) is listed, as is the current status in terms of the font available to your system. This is helpful if you intend to export to PDF and want to ensure that all fonts are loaded.

✦ **Links and Images:** Links are listed in a scrollable window according to file type, page where the link is placed, status (linked or unlinked), and any ICC profiles embedded in the images.

✦ **Colors and Inks:** All colors used in the file are listed in a scrollable window, as shown in Figure 35-18. If you have spot colors in the file, the list window reports the colors. If printing a process-color job, you'll know when to convert colors from spot to process.

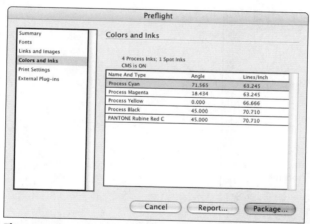

Figure 35-18: The Colors and Inks pane lists all colors in the open document.

✦ **Print Settings:** A summary of the settings in the Print dialog box is listed.

✦ **External Plug-Ins:** If any third-party plug-ins are used to create the layout, they're listed in a scrollable window.

If problems exist in the document, you need to remedy all problems before packaging your file for output. If you have no problems and you want to send the native InDesign document to your printer, click the Package button and the InDesign document, links, and fonts are packaged collectively to a folder. If exporting to PDF, you Cancel the Preflight dialog box after checking your file and use the Export command to create a PDF file.

Cross-Reference For information on converting to PDF and packaging files for press, see the "Packaging documents for commercial printing" section, at the end of this chapter.

Preflighting in Acrobat

Acrobat offers you preflight controls to analyze files for commercial printing that are much more impressive than the controls offered in InDesign. You can perform detailed analyses of files, create preflight profiles specific to your needs, acquire profiles from your printer and load them for use in Acrobat to check your documents for conditions set forth by your printer, create validation reports, and create PDF/X files.

Cross-Reference For information on PDF/X, see the "Packaging documents for commercial printing" section at the end of this chapter.

To preflight a PDF document in Acrobat, choose Document ➪ Preflight. Notice the preflight option is contained in the Document menu and not in the Advanced menu. Preflighting is only available in Acrobat Professional. When you select the menu command, Acrobat pauses momentarily to load profiles already created as presets from your initial Acrobat installation. After the profiles are loaded, the Preflight: Profiles dialog box opens, shown in Figure 35-19.

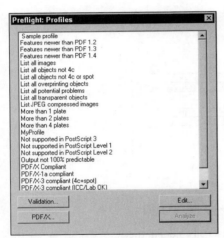

Figure 35-19: The Preflight: Profiles dialog box opens.

Preflight profiles

A preflight profile contains one or more *conditions* that are contained within *rules*. A condition might be something like *is not a spot color*. A rule may contain a single condition or multiple conditions. For example, a rule like *ProcessColor* might contain conditions like *is not spot color, is not grayscale, is not RGB color*. The profile is created from a single or several rules. For example a profile might contain *ProcessColor, Not Compressed, Fonts not Embedded*. A profile containing rules and conditions is listed in the opening dialog box when you select the Preflight menu command.

When you install Acrobat Professional, a list of preset profiles appears in the Preflight: Profile dialog box. You can use one of these profiles to preflight a job, you can create your own custom profile and add it to the list, or you can acquire a profile developed by a service center or print shop and add it to the list. After a profile appears in the list, you use all the rules and conditions contained in the profile to analyze the current open document in Acrobat Professional. If problems are found, Acrobat reports all conditions not met as measured against the conditions in the profile.

Creating a new profile

Before moving on to actually preflighting a document, start by looking at how profiles are created. Click the Edit button in the Preflight: Profiles dialog box. After you click Edit, the Preflight: Edit Profiles dialog box opens, shown in Figure 35-20.

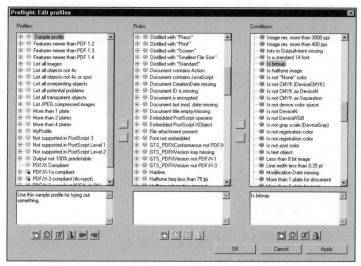

Figure 35-20: The Preflight: Edit Profiles dialog box

At the top of the dialog box, you see three column headings for Profiles, Rules, and Conditions. In this dialog box, you work from right to left. In the column at the right, you create a new condition or select an existing condition from the list. In the Rules column, you create a new rule or select a rule from the list. When an item in a list is selected, it moves to the selected item in the column to the left. For example, if you select a rule, then select a condition, you click on the left-pointing chevron and your condition is added to the selected rule. You then select a profile and select a rule to add to the profile. You can add multiple conditions to a single rule and add multiple rules to a single profile. However, you add conditions and rules one at a time. Repeat the steps to add one to the other with successive selections and clicks on the left chevrons.

You can modify any one of the existing profiles or rules. You can choose from presets in the columns and move items from one column to selected items in the other columns. If none of the existing presets work for you, you can create new rules, conditions, and profiles. The icons at the bottom of the dialog box enable you to manage the conditions, rules, and profiles. The icons include the following:

✦  **New (condition, rule, profile):** Click this icon in the respective column to create a new condition, rule, or profile.

✦  **Duplicate (condition, rule, profile):** Select an item in the respective list and the condition, rule, or profile is duplicated.

✦  **Edit (condition, rule, profile):** Select an item in the respective list and the condition, rule, or profile edit dialog box opens.

✦  **Delete (condition, rule, profile):** Select an item in the respective list and the condition, rule, or profile is deleted.

For profiles only, two other buttons appear at the bottom of the column. The tools are

✦  **Import:** Select a profile and click this button. A profile created by a print shop or service center can be e-mailed to you, and you can load profiles from vendors who send you their recommended conditions for preflighting jobs.

✦  **Export:** If you're responsible for creating profiles at a service center or in a company where you want to implement a set of standards, click on the Export button. The profile selected when you click on the button is exported to a file that you can send to other users who, in turn, import the profile.

Creating conditions

Click on the New Condition button at the bottom of the Conditions column in the Preflight: Edit profiles dialog box. The Preflight: Edit This Condition dialog box opens, shown in Figure 35-21. In this dialog box, you can add descriptive information in field boxes, select a group, and select a property as it applies to conditions.

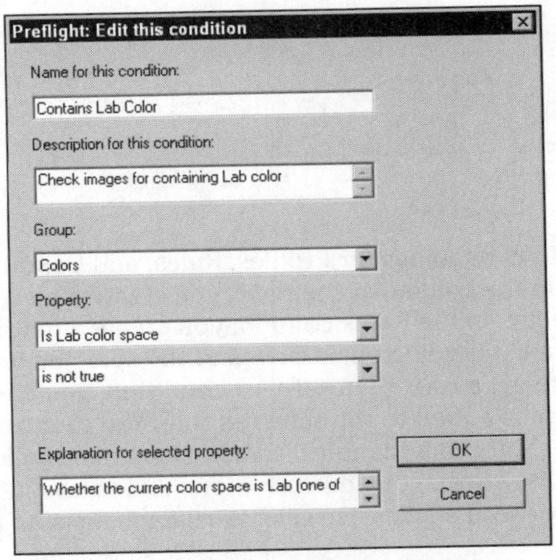

Figure 35-21: The Preflight: Edit This Condition dialog box.

The options include

✦ **Name for this Condition:** Type any name you want. Try to add a name that describes the condition so it's clear to you what condition you're selecting when you return to the Conditions list.

✦ **Description for This Condition:** The text you type in this field box is visible only when you return to the Edit dialog box. Add a description for what the condition does or why you're using it.

✦ **Group:** Conditions are made up of selections from the Group drop-down list and the Properties drop-down list. The Group drop-down list contains categorical items that are further defined in the Properties drop-down list. Select a group by opening the drop-down list and making a menu selection.

✦ **Property:** After selecting the Group item, open the Property drop-down list and select an item. In the example, Is Lab Color Space is selected. The second drop-down list is the conditional item. For your Lab color analysis, you want the preflight to pass if there are no Lab color images in the file. Therefore, you select Is Not True from the drop-down list. When the condition is checked, a problem is reported if the condition is true. If all images are not Lab color, the preflight reports no problems.

✦ **Explanation for Selected Property:** The message at the bottom of the dialog box is informational. A help message reports any condition you select. Before creating a new condition, you can check the definition to be certain what you selected checks the condition you want.

After choosing the options, click OK to add the new condition to the Conditions list.

Creating rules

You create rules by either duplicating an existing rule or creating a new rule. The composition of a rule is the addition of one or more conditions. When you click on the New Rule button at the bottom of the Rules column in the Preflight: Edit Profiles dialog box, the Preflight: Edit Rule dialog box opens, shown in Figure 35-22.

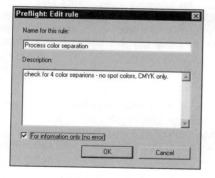

Figure 35-22: Click on New Rule and the Preflight: Edit Rule dialog box opens.

Notice that no preflight conditions are added in the Edit dialog box. You add a name for the rule in the dialog box and supply a description. After you click OK, the rule is empty. To add conditions to the rule, you select it in the Rules column and select one or more conditions to move to the rule by clicking on the left chevron. The rule must be selected to receive the conditions you move from the Conditions column.

Also in the Preflight: Edit Rule dialog box is a check box titled For Information Only (No Error). If you want the report to show if a condition was not met but still pass the preflight without reporting problems, check the box.

Creating profiles

After adding all the conditions to one or more rules, the last step is to create a profile to use for preflighting a job. Click on the New Profile button at the bottom of the Profiles column in the Preflight: Edit Profiles dialog box, and a dialog box similar to the dialog box used when creating rules opens. Add the name for the profile and a description, as shown in Figure 35-23.

Figure 35-23: The New Profile button opens the Preflight: Edit Profile dialog box.

After naming the profile and adding a description, click OK and the profile is added to the Profiles column in the Preflight: Edit Profiles dialog box. Select the profile and select a rule to add to the profile. Click on the left chevron between the columns, and the rule is added to the profile. Note that only a single profile is moved at one time. To add additional rules to the same profile, click on the next rule to add and click the left chevron.

Note   Preflighting PDF documents is intended primarily for assessing a document's reliability in printing properly. The number of rules and conditions, however, go beyond print conditions and may be used for checking files suitable for other output modes such as distributing files on Web servers or CD-ROMs. Be certain to check the conditions available to you for preflight options other than printing.

Importing/exporting profiles

After creating a profile, you may want to send the profile to another user. Select the profile you want to export from the list of profiles in the Preflight: Edit Profiles dialog box and click on the Export button. The Export Profile as Package dialog box opens. Find a location on your hard drive where you want to save the file, and click Save. The file is saved with a default extension of KFP.

Importing profiles is handled similarly. Click on the Import button and locate a file to import. Only KFP files are listed in the Import Profile from Package dialog box. Select the file to import and click Open. The imported profile is added to the list of profiles in the Preflight: Profiles dialog box.

Tip   If you want to e-mail a profile to another user, create a PDF document with a description of the profile and how to load it. Adding help information can make it easier for other users. In the PDF file, select the Attach tool from the Advanced Commenting toolbar and attach the KFP file to the PDF document. Click on the Email tool in the Toolbar Well to attach the PDF with the file attachment to a new e-mail message. Note that the recipients of your document need either Acrobat Standard or Acrobat Professional to open the attached file. Adobe Reader is not capable of extracting data from a PDF.

Analyzing a file

To see the profiles you've created for preflighting jobs you want to send off to a commercial printer, choose Document ➪ Preflight. To check a document against the conditions and rules specified in the profile, select the profile from the list in the Preflight: Profiles dialog box and click on the Analyze button. After a few moments, Acrobat opens the Preflight: Results dialog box, shown in Figure 35-24.

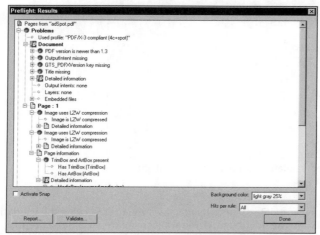

Figure 35-24: The Preflight: Results dialog box shows any problems.

A report shows you a list of items described as problems if the conditions in the profile were not met during preflight. Click on any + (plus) shown in the list to expand an item and review the detail associated with the item. If more than one page exists in the document, problems are reported according to each page.

If problems are reported that prevent successful printing, you need to return to the authoring program, resolve the problems, and create a new PDF document. For example, if images are RGB color and you analyze a file for four-color process printing, you need to go back to the original images and convert them to CMYK color, update the links, and create a new PDF document.

Validating a file

When you preflight a file and the report shows No Problems Found, you can create a validation stamp that can be viewed by a service center printing your file. The validation stamp is embedded in the PDF document and won't interfere with printing the file. While still in the Preflight: Results dialog box, click on the Validate button. A dialog box opens asking whether you want to append a validation stamp to the file. In Figure 35-25, the Do You Want to Continue dialog box is shown.

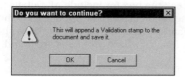

Figure 35-25: A dialog box confirms the addition of a validation stamp to a file.

Click OK in the dialog box to add the validation stamp to the document. You can view the validation stamp by clicking Validation in the Preflight: Profiles dialog box. You need to return to the original dialog box where you began the preflight. When you click Validation, the Preflight: Validations dialog box opens, shown in Figure 35-26.

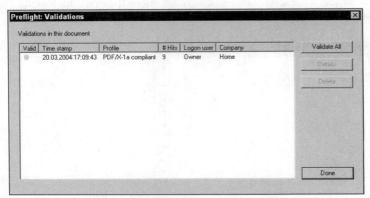

Figure 35-26: The embedded validation appears in the Preflight: Validations dialog box.

The validation is time-stamped and date-stamped and shows the user viewing the validation what profile was used to validate the document. If you want to create a validation report, you have another option. In the Preflight: Results dialog box, click on the Report button. The Preflight: Report dialog box opens, shown in Figure 35-27.

Note   To see the Report button, you need to preflight the job again. You don't have an option for returning to the Preflight: Results dialog box. Return to the Preflight: Profiles dialog box, click on Analyze, and click on Report in the Preflight: Results dialog box.

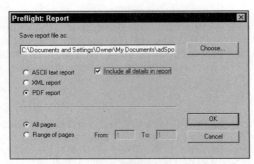

Figure 35-27: The Preflight: Reports dialog box

In the Preflight: Reports dialog box, select the file format you want to use for the report from among ASCII text report, XML report, or PDF report. Check the box for Include All Details in Report if you want a detailed report. Select the page range and click OK to produce the report. The report lists all problems and descriptions as bookmarks. Expand the bookmarks to show detail for items listed in the Bookmarks tab. If you have images where problems are found, the images are converted to separate document pages.

Packaging Documents for Commercial Printing

Packaging a file for printing involves collecting all the assets required for printing and gathering them on a disk, CD-ROM, or a compressed archive you intend to e-mail or FTP to your service center. With Photoshop documents, you don't need to package for printing; all assets are contained within the Photoshop document. Flatten the image and send the file off to your printer. With Illustrator and InDesign, you have issues needing attention, such as font usage and links. When you package these files, you must include all links with the active file to send to your printer.

With fonts, you're faced with some potential problems related to font licensing. Many font-manufacturer licensing restrictions prevent you from legally distributing fonts to your service provider. If your provider does not have a given font, the provider must purchase the font or you need to search for a different provider.

The complex issues related to packaging native files together with legal restrictions is reason enough to search for a better solution than sending your native files to service providers. Fortunately, the CS applications offer you a much better alternative. Quite simply, your package utility is Acrobat PDF. When you send PDF documents to your printer, you have advantages such as the following:

✦ **Font embedding:** Not all fonts are licensed for font embedding in PDF documents. However, the more popular Adobe fonts, OpenType fonts, and many TrueType fonts carry no licensing restrictions for embedding the fonts in PDF documents. When the fonts are embedded, you don't have to worry about whether your service provider has the fonts contained in your document.

✦ **Image embedding:** All images are embedded in PDF documents. You don't need to worry about missing links when sending PDF files to your printer.

✦ **Smaller file sizes:** PDF documents occupy the least amount of space on your hard drive and are most often smaller in size than compressed native files. The results of smaller file sizes provide you with faster electronic transfer times via e-mail and FTP.

✦ **Optimized file types for printing:** With PDF documents, you can create PDF/X files that are optimized for commercial printing. Developing PDF/X-compliant files provides a much more reliable format for correctly imaging your documents.

Because PDF is the best file format for sending files to prepress and commercial printing, we'll skip the packaging features for bundling native documents and focus on creating PDF documents optimized for professional printing.

PDF creation in Illustrator

If you intend to print Illustrator files rather than introduce them into an InDesign layout, you can save directly to PDF from Illustrator. Choose File ➪ Save As and select Adobe PDF as the file format. After you name the file and click Save in the Save As dialog box, the Adobe PDF Options dialog box (Figure 35-28) opens.

What you do in Illustrator is rather simple. Just select Press from the Preset drop-down list and save the file. After you save the file as a PDF, you can handle preflighting and final packaging in Acrobat.

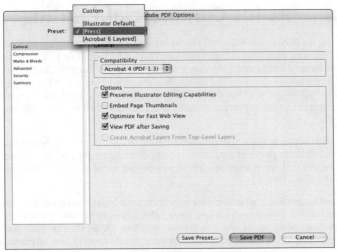

Figure 35-28: To print commercially, select Press from the Preset list.

PDF creation in InDesign

In InDesign you might use the preflight check built into the program before exporting to PDF. InDesign enables you to completely package the file for press via an export to PDF. After pre-flighting, choose File ⇨ Export. Provide a name for your file and be certain that you select the PDF in the Format drop-down list. Click Save, and the Export PDF dialog box opens, shown in Figure 35-29.

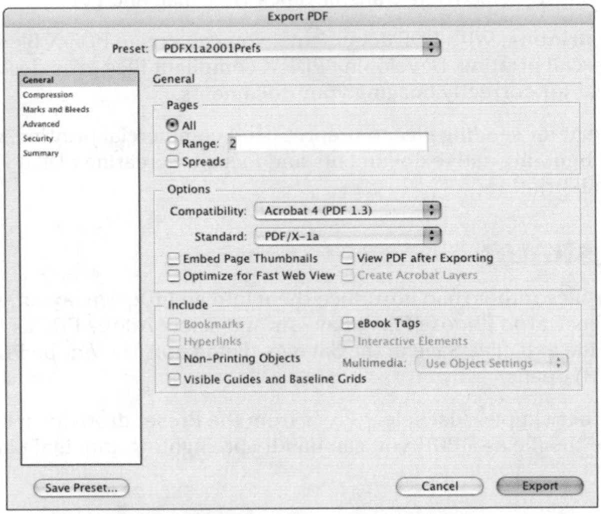

Figure 35-29: The Export PDF dialog box has options for PDF.

When exporting for prepress and printing, you have two options for the PDF format. From the Preset drop-down list, select PDFX1a2001Prefs or PDFX32002Prefs. Depending on the content of your InDesign document, one of the two PDF/X formats is ideal for commercial printing.

Understanding PDF/X

PDF/X is a subset of the PDF format developed by an International Organization for Standardization (ISO) standards committee outside Adobe Systems. Adobe is a participant on the committee and supports the development and advances in PDF/X standards.

PDF/X has gained much acceptance among commercial printing companies for the purposes of creating files suitable for printing. PDF is a reliable format for any kind of electronic file exchange. However, files developed for viewing in Acrobat viewers, Acrobat PDF forms, Web-hosted documents, and so on carry a lot of overhead not necessary for printing on commercial printing devices. The PDF/X compliance standard was developed to streamline documents by eliminating unnecessary data and optimizing files for print. The process of tailoring a PDF document for print by creating a PDF/X-compliant file does not necessarily reduce file size. In many cases, file sizes grow from a standard PDF to a PDF/X file. Because PDF/X is optimized for printing, you benefit in converting your Illustrator and InDesign documents to PDF/X. In almost all cases, if a file meets PDF/X compliance standards, it's likely to print on almost any device. Native files can't give you that kind of confidence.

The PDF/X options are available to you in InDesign and through preflighting in Acrobat either a PDF/X-1a-compliant file or a PDF/X-3-compliant file. These file types are different versions of the PDF/X format. PDF/X-1a is designed to work well with both process and spot color, but no support is provided for color management or profile embedding. PDF/X-3 supports process and spot color, as well as color-managed workflows and International Color Consortium (ICC) profile embedding. Therefore, when you're exporting to PDF from InDesign, use PDF/X3 when working in a color-managed workflow. When you're not using color-profile embedding in your images or InDesign files, use the PDF/X1-a format.

When you export PDF/X from InDesign, you're checking the file for PDF/X compliance. If the file does not meet the PDF/X standard you select (that is, PDF/X-1a or PDF/X-3), the file ultimately fails to export and you know there may be potential problems printing the file. If a file meets PDF/X compliance, you have much greater assurance that your PDF document will print on almost any kind of commercial printing device.

Producing a PDF/X-compliant file in Acrobat

You may have legacy PDF documents or files from programs that don't export to PDF/X, and need to convert the PDF file to a PDF/X-compliant file. In Acrobat, after successfully passing a preflight for suitable printing, you can produce a PDF/X-compliant file. After running the preflight, return again to the Preflight: Profiles dialog box. Click on the PDF/X button and the Preflight: PDF/X dialog box opens, shown in Figure 35-30.

From the top of the dialog box, select either Use PDF/X-3 Specification or Use PDF/X-1a Specification. For each button on the right side of the dialog box, you'll see a description of the results of clicking on the button. If you click on the button for PDF/X (1a or 3) Sets, another dialog box opens where you can add a new set based on an ICC profile calibrated for your system, as shown in Figure 35-31.

Cross-Reference For more information on ICC profiles, see Chapter 6.

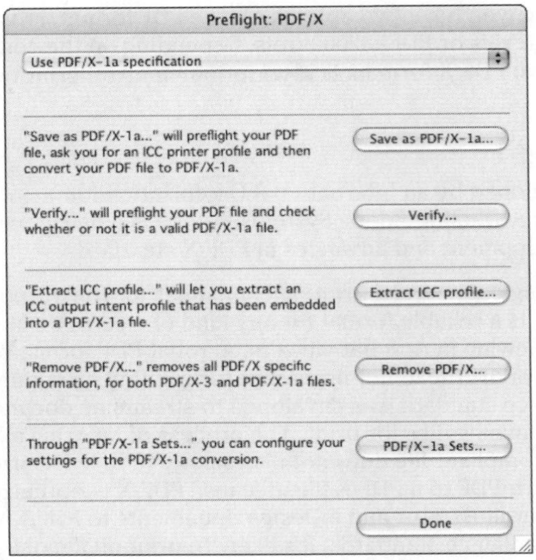

Figure 35-30: The Preflight: PDF/X dialog box

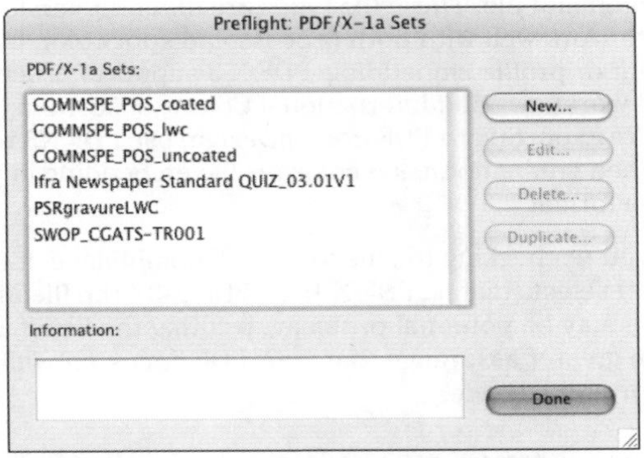

Figure 35-31: You can add a custom set based on the ICC profile you use.

To gain further understanding for converting PDF documents to PDF/X compliant files, look over the steps below and try to produce your own PDF/X file.

STEPS: Creating PDF/X Files

1. **Open a PDF document to convert to PDF/X.** Use a file converted to PDF from InDesign or Illustrator that was intended for print output. Be certain to use a file with transparency flattened and originally created for printing conditions.

2. **Open the Preflight: PDF/X dialog box.** Select Document ⇨ Preflight. The Preflight: Profiles dialog box opens. In the Preflight Profiles dialog box, click the PDF/X button. The Preflight: PDF/X dialog box shown in Figure 35-30 opens.

3. **Select the appropriate PDF/X compliant specification.** For 4 color separations and printing when not using color profile embedding, select Use PDF/X-1a specification from the pull-down menu at the top of the dialog box. If you use color profiles, select Use PDF/X-3 specification from the pull-down menu.

4. **Save the file as PDF/X.** Click the button labeled Save as PDF/X-1a (or PDF/X-3) at the top of the dialog box. The Preflight: Save as PDF/X-1a dialog box opens as shown in Figure 35-32.

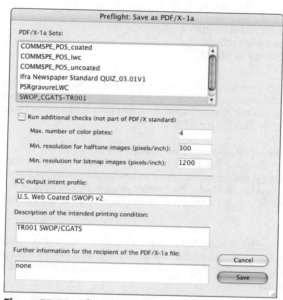

Figure 35-32: After clicking the Save PDF/X-1a button, the Preflight Save as PDF/X-1a dialog box opens.

5. **Select a Profile.** In the Preflight:Save as PDF/X-1a dialog box, a list of PDF/X-1a Sets appear in a scrollable window. (If using PDF/X-3, the sets appear as PDF/X-3 Sets). Select the profile you want to use from the list by clicking on the profile name. If printing for standard SWOP (Standard Web Offset Printing) printing, select the SWOP_CGATS-TR001 profile. If you have a profile created for your use, by all means use your custom profile.

6. **Save the file.** Click the Save button in the Preflight: Save as PDF/X-1a dialog box after selecting the profile from the list shown in Figure 35-32. The Acrobat Save dialog box opens where you can navigate your hard drive and locate a folder to save the file. Click the Save button in the Save dialog box to the desired folder destination. After saving the file, Acrobat displays a confirmation dialog box as shown in Figure 35-33.

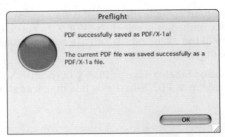

Figure 35-33: After saving the file as PDF/X, a confirmation dialog box opens indicating the file was successfully saved as PDF/X.

If the file is not PDF/X-compliant, you won't be able to save the file. You need to return to the Preflight: Profiles dialog box and begin again by either viewing the validation report or analyzing the file. Locate the problems in the file and make changes in the authoring program. When you fix the problems, return again and create a PDF/X file.

Note   You may preflight a file with a profile you created or obtained from a service center that fails PDF/X compliance. After preflighting the job with your profile, run a preflight using a PDF/X profile and review problems in the report. You need to resolve the problems before you can save the file with PDF/X compliance. Ideally, the profiles you use should include the rules for the PDF/X version you use so a single preflight is all you have to do when preflighting your files.

The files you create from saving PDF/X-compliant files are optimum for digital prepress and printing. If you follow the steps and produce files that pass the preflights with no problems and you create PDF/X-compliant files, you'll rarely experience any problems when placing orders at commercial print shops.

Printing PDF/X Files

All the attributes set in the Page Setup and Print dialog boxes discussed in Chapter 34 are used when printing PDF/X documents. However, rather than output from the Print dialog box and make options choices in the Advanced Print Setup dialog box, most commercial printing is best achieved by exporting your PDF/X document back to PostScript and downloading the PostScript file.

To prepare a PostScript file for downloading to a commercial printing device, choose File ➪ Save As in Acrobat. From the Format drop-down list, select PostScript. When you select PostScript, the Settings button becomes active. Click on the Settings button and the Save As Settings dialog box opens, shown in Figure 35-34. This dialog box contains all the print options found in the Advanced Print Setup dialog box.

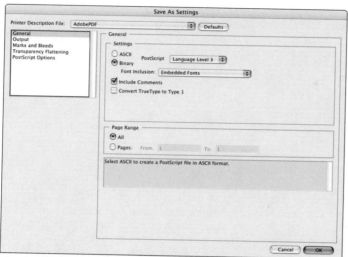

Figure 35-34: The Save As Settings dialog box

In the left pane, you make choices for the four different categories that offer the same options as the Advanced Print Setup dialog box. Use the same set of options choices as was discussed in Chapter 34, and click OK. You're returned to the Save As dialog box. Provide a name for the file, and click Save. The resultant document is a file that you can download directly to a PostScript device.

Tip   The only limitation in the Settings dialog box is the absence of a page preview. To verify that your document fits on the output, open the Print dialog box and check the thumbnail preview against the page size when printer's marks are included. If all looks fine, cancel out of the Print dialog box and return to the Save As Settings dialog box.

Summary

✦ InDesign, Illustrator, and Acrobat provide tools for flattening transparency.

✦ InDesign and Acrobat offer you tools for preflighting documents against potential printing problems and for soft-proofing files for proper color assignment.

✦ Acrobat offers the most sophisticated tools for preflighting and soft-proofing color. You can create or acquire preflight profiles suited to specific output equipment.

✦ For packaging files for prepress and printing, Acrobat PDF format offers many benefits, including font embedding, image embedding, and smaller file sizes.

✦ PDF/X is a subset of the PDF format and is the most desirable format for commercial prepress and printing.

✦ When printing PDF documents to commercial equipment, the preferable method for printing is to save the PDF to PostScript and download the PostScript file to a printer.

✦   ✦   ✦

Keyboard Shortcuts in the Adobe CS Programs

Keyboard shortcuts can save a lot of time and help speed your design time by helping you quickly access tools, menus, and palette menus. Obviously, with all the programs at hand and the extended number of options available for invoking commands and features resulting from keystroke combinations, you're not likely to remember all the shortcuts available to you. In this appendix, you'll find an exhaustive list of keyboard shortcuts that you can use as a reference. As you perform frequent edits where you can use a keyboard shortcut, try to begin using the shortcuts as you work. Use this appendix as a guide to help you learn more shortcuts over time.

Tip   This appendix shows you information taken from the individual program help menus. If you're working on a project and don't have the *Adobe Creative Suite Bible* at hand, open the help menu for your program and search for Shortcuts. The help documents can assist you in finding keyboard shortcuts quickly.

Cross-Reference   More information on accessing Help menus is contained in Chapter 4.

Adobe Illustrator

Keyboard shortcuts in Illustrator are used for accessing tools and menu commands and specific functions in palettes. In many cases, you need to select an object before using a keyboard shortcut.

Selecting Tools

Tool	Windows	Mac
Selection tool	V	V
Direct Selection tool	A	A
Magic Wand tool	Y	Y
Lasso tool	Q	Q
Pen tool	P	P
Add Anchor Point tool	+ (plus)	+ (plus)
Delete Anchor Point tool	- (minus)	- (minus)
Convert Anchor Point tool	Shift+C	Shift+C
Type tool	T	T
Line Segment tool	\ (backslash)	\ (backslash)
Rectangle tool	M	M
Ellipse tool	L	L
Paintbrush tool	B	B
Pencil tool	N	N
Rotate tool	R	R
Reflect tool	O	O
Scale tool	S	S
Warp tool	Shift+R	Shift+R
Free Transform tool	E	E
Symbol Sprayer tool	Shift+S	Shift+S
Column Graph tool	J	J

Viewing Tools

Action	Windows	Mac
Toggle among Standard Screen mode, Full Screen mode, and Full Screen mode with Menu Bar	F	F
Fit imageable area in window	Double-click Hand tool	Double-click Hand tool
Magnify 100%	Double-click Zoom tool	Double-click Zoom tool
Switch to Hand tool (when not in Text Edit mode)	Spacebar	Spacebar

Action	Windows	Mac
Switch to Zoom tool in Magnify mode	Ctrl+Spacebar	⌘+Spacebar
Switch to Zoom tool in Reduce mode	Ctrl+Alt+Spacebar	⌘+Option+Spacebar
Move Zoom marquee while dragging with the Zoom tool	Spacebar	Spacebar
Hide unselected artwork	Ctrl+Alt+Shift+3	⌘+Option+Shift+3
Convert between horizontal and vertical guide	Alt+drag guide	Option+drag guide
Release guide	Ctrl+Shift+double-click guide	⌘+Shift+double-click guide

Selecting and Moving Objects

Action	Windows	Mac
Switch to last-used selection tool (Selection tool, Direct Selection tool, or Group Selection tool)	Ctrl	⌘
Switch between Selection tool and Direct/Group selection tool (last used)	Ctrl+Tab	⌘+Tab
Switch between Direct Selection tool and Group Selection tool	Alt	Option
Add to a selection with Selection tool, Direct Selection tool, Group Selection tool, or Magic Wand tool	Shift+click	Shift+click
Subtract a selection with Selection tool, Direct Selection tool, Group Selection tool, or Magic Wand tool	Shift+click	Shift+click
Add to selection with Lasso tool	Shift+drag	Shift+drag
Subtract from selection with Lasso tool	Alt+drag	Option+drag
Move selection in user-defined increments	Right Arrow, Left Arrow, Up Arrow, or Down Arrow	Right Arrow, Left Arrow, Up Arrow, or Down Arrow
Move selection in 10x user-defined increments	Shift+Right Arrow, Left Arrow, Up Arrow, or Down Arrow	Shift+Right Arrow, Left Arrow, Up Arrow, or Down Arrow
Lock all deselected artwork	Ctrl+Alt+Shift+2	⌘+Option+Shift+2
Constrain movement to 45° angle (except for when using Reflect tool)	Hold down Shift	Hold down Shift
Change pointer to crosshair for selected tools	Caps Lock	Caps Lock

* Set keyboard increments in General Preferences

Function Keys

Action	Windows	Mac
Invoke Help	F1	F1
Cut	F2	F2
Copy	F3	F3
Paste	F4	F4
Show/hide Brushes palette	F5	F5
Show/hide Color palette	F6	F6
Show/hide Layers palette	F7	F7
Show/hide Info palette	F8	F8
Show/hide Gradient palette	F9	F9
Show/hide Stroke palette	F10	F10
Show/hide Attributes palette	F11	F11
Revert	F12	F12
Show/hide Styles palette	Shift+F5	Shift+F5
Show/hide Appearance palette	Shift+F6	Shift+F6
Show/hide Align palette	Shift+F7	Shift+F7
Show/hide Transform palette	Shift+F8	Shift+F8
Show/hide Pathfinder palette	Shift+F9	Shift+F9
Show/hide Transparency palette	Shift+F10	Shift+F10
Show/hide Symbols palette	Shift+F11	Shift+F11

Illustrator: Editing Paths

Action	Windows	Mac
Switch Pen tool to Convert Anchor Point tool	Alt	Option
Switch between Add Anchor Point tool and Delete Anchor Point tool	Alt	Option
Switch Scissors tool to Add Anchor Point tool	Alt	Option
Switch Pencil tool to Smooth tool	Alt	Option
Move current anchor point while drawing with Pen tool	Spacebar+drag	Spacebar+drag
Cut a straight line with Knife tool	Alt+drag	Option+drag
Cut at 45° or 90° angle with Knife tool	Shift+Alt+drag	Shift+Option+drag
Turn shape mode buttons in Pathfinder palette into Pathfinder commands	Alt+Shape mode	Option+Shape mode

Painting Objects

Action	Windows	Mac
Toggle between fill and stroke	X	X
Set fill and stroke to default	D	D
Swap fill and stroke	Shift+X	Shift+X
Select Gradient Fill mode	>	>
Select Color Fill mode	<	<
Select No Stroke mode	/ (forward slash)	/ (forward slash)
Switch between Paint Bucket tool and Eyedropper tool	Alt	Option
Sample color from an image or intermediate color from a gradient	Shift+Eyedropper tool	Shift+Eyedropper tool
Sample style and append appearance of currently selected item	Alt+Shift+click+ Eyedropper tool	Option+Shift+click+ Eyedropper tool
Add new fill	Ctrl+/ (forward slash)	⌘+/ (forward slash)
Add new stroke	Ctrl+Alt+/ (forward slash)	⌘+Option+/ (forward slash)
Reset gradient to black and white	Ctrl+click Gradient button in Toolbox	⌘+click Gradient button in Toolbox

Transforming Objects

Action	Windows	Mac
Set origin point and open dialog box when using Rotate tool, Scale tool, Reflect tool, or Shear tool	Alt+click	Option+click
Duplicate and transform selection when using Selection tool, Scale tool, Reflect tool, or Shear tool	Alt+drag	Option+drag
Transform pattern (independent of object) when using Selection tool, Scale tool, Reflect tool, or Shear tool	~ (tilde)+drag	~ (tilde)+drag

Illustrator: Navigating Selected Text

Action	Windows	Mac
Move one character right or left	Right Arrow or Left Arrow	Right Arrow or Left Arrow
Move up or down one line	Up Arrow or Down Arrow	Up Arrow or Down Arrow
Move one word right or left	Ctrl+Right Arrow or Left Arrow	⌘+Right Arrow or Left Arrow

Continued

Illustrator: Navigating Selected Text *(continued)*

Action	Windows	Mac
Move up or down one paragraph	Ctrl+Up Arrow or Down Arrow	⌘+Up Arrow or Down Arrow
Select one word right or left	Shift+Ctrl+Right Arrow or Left Arrow	Shift+⌘+Right Arrow or Left Arrow
Select one paragraph before or after	Shift+Ctrl+Up Arrow or Down Arrow	Shift+⌘+Up Arrow or Down Arrow

Formatting Type

Action	Windows	Mac
Align paragraph left, right, or center	Ctrl+Shift+L, R, or C	⌘+Shift+L, R, or C
Justify paragraph	Ctrl+Shift+J	⌘+Shift+J
Insert soft return	Shift+Enter	Shift+Return
Highlight kerning	Ctrl+Alt+K	⌘+Option+K
Reset horizontal scale to 100%	Ctrl+Shift+X	⌘+Shift+X
Increase or decrease point size*	Ctrl+Shift+> or <	⌘+Shift+> or <
Increase or decrease leading*	Alt+Up Arrow or Down Arrow	Option+Up Arrow or Down Arrow
Set leading to the font size	Double-click leading icon in the Character palette	Double-click leading icon in the Character palette
Reset tracking/kerning to 0	Ctrl+Alt+Q	⌘+Option+Q
Add or remove space (kerning) between two characters*	Alt+Right Arrow or Left Arrow	Option+Right Arrow or Left Arrow
Add or remove space (kerning) between characters by five times the increment value*	Ctrl+Alt+Right Arrow or Left Arrow	⌘+Option+Right Arrow or Left Arrow
Add or remove space (kerning) between selected words*	Alt+Ctrl+\ or Backspace	Option+⌘+\ or Backspace
Add or remove space (kerning) between words by five times the increment value*	Shift+Alt+Ctrl+\ or Backspace	Shift+Option+⌘+\ or Backspace
Increase or Decrease baseline shift*	Alt+Shift+Up Arrow or Down Arrow	Option+Shift+Up Arrow or Down Arrow
Switch among Type and Vertical Type, Area Type and Vertical Area Type, and Path Type and Vertical Path Type tools	Shift	Shift
Switch between Area Type and Point Type, Path Type and Area Type.	Alt+click Type tool	Option+click Type tool

Paragraph and Character Palette Keys

Action	Windows	Mac
Increase/decrease the selected value by a small increment	Up Arrow or Down Arrow	Up Arrow or Down Arrow
Increase/decrease the selected value by a large increment	Shift+Up Arrow or Down Arrow	Shift+Up Arrow or Down Arrow
Highlight the Font Name field in the Character palette	Ctrl+Alt+Shift+F	⌘+Option+Shift+F

Using Palettes

Action	Windows	Mac
Set options (except for Action and Brush palettes)	Alt+click New button	Option+click New button
Delete without confirmation (except for Variable palette)	Alt+click Delete button	Option+click Delete button
Apply value and keep text box active	Shift+Enter	Shift+Return
Highlight last-used text box in palette	Ctrl+~ (tilde)	⌘+~ (tilde)
Select range of actions, brushes, layers, links, styles, or swatches	Shift+click	Shift+click
Select noncontiguous actions, brushes, layers (same level only), links, styles, or swatches	Ctrl+click	⌘+click
Show/Hide all palettes	Tab	Tab
Show/Hide all palettes except the Toolbox	Shift+Tab	Shift+Tab

Using Actions Palette

Action	Windows	Mac
Expand/Collapse entire hierarchy for action set	Alt+click expansion triangle	Option+click expansion triangle
Set options for action set	Double-click folder icon	Double-click folder icon
Play a single command	Alt+click Play button	Option+click Play button
Play the current action	Ctrl+double-click Play button	⌘+double-click Play button
Begin recording actions without confirmation	Alt+click New Action button	Option+click New Action button

Using Brushes Palette

Action	Windows	Mac
Open Brush Options dialog box	Double-click brush	Double-click brush
Duplicate brush	Drag brush to New Brush button	Drag brush to New Brush button

Using Color Palette

Action	Windows	Mac
Select the complement for the current color fill/stroke	Ctrl+click color bar	⌘+click color bar
Change the nonactive fill/stroke	Alt+click color bar	Option+click color bar
Select the complement for the nonactive fill/stroke	Ctrl+Alt+click color bar	⌘+Option+click color bar
Select the inverse for the current fill/stroke	Ctrl+Shift+click color bar	⌘+Shift+click color bar
Select the inverse for the nonactive fill/stroke	Ctrl+Shift+Alt+click color bar	⌘+Shift+Option+click color bar
Change the color mode	Shift+click color bar	Shift+click color bar
Move color sliders in tandem	Shift+drag color slider	Shift+drag color slider
Switch between percentage and 0–255 values for RGB	Double-click to right of a numerical field	Double-click to right of a numerical field

Using Gradient Palette

Action	Windows	Mac
Duplicate color stops	Alt+drag	Option+drag
Swap color stops	Alt+drag color stop onto another stop	Option+drag color stop onto another color stop
Apply swatch color to active (or selected) color stop	Alt+click swatch in the Swatches palette	Option+click swatch in the Swatches palette

Using Layers Palette

Action	Windows	Mac
Select all objects on the layer	Alt+click layer name	Option+click layer name
Show/hide all layers but the selected one	Alt+click eye icon	Option+click eye icon
Select Outline/Preview view for the selected layer	Ctrl+click eye icon	⌘+click eye icon
Select Outline/Preview view for all other layers	Ctrl+Alt+click eye icon	⌘+Option+click eye icon
Lock/unlock all other layers	Alt+click lock icon	Option+click lock icon
Expand all sublayers to display entire hierarchy	Alt+click expansion triangle	Option+click expansion triangle
Place new sublayer at bottom of layer list	Ctrl+Alt+click New Sublayer button	⌘+Option+click New Sublayer button
Place layer at top of layer list	Ctrl+click New Layer button	⌘+click New Layer button
Place layer below selected layer	Ctrl+Alt+click New Layer button	⌘+Option+click New Layer button
Copy the selection to a new layer, sublayer, or group	Alt+drag selection	Option+drag selection

Using Swatches Palette

Action	Windows	Mac
Create new spot color	Ctrl+click New Swatch button	⌘+click New Swatch button
Create new global process color	Ctrl+Shift+click New Swatch button	⌘+Shift+click New Swatch button
Replace swatch with another	Alt+drag a swatch over another	Option+drag a swatch over another
Select swatch by name (using keyboard)	Ctrl+Alt+click in the swatch color list	⌘+Option+click in the swatch color list

Using Transform Palette

Action	Windows	Mac
Apply a value and keep focus in edit field	Shift+Enter	Shift+Return
Apply a value and copy object	Alt+Enter	Option+Return
Apply a value and scale option proportionately for width or height	Ctrl+Enter	⌘+Return

Using Transparency Palette

Action	Windows	Mac
Change mask to grayscale image for editing	Alt+click on mask thumbnail	Option+click on mask thumbnail
Disable opacity mask	Shift+click on mask thumbnail	Shift+click on mask thumbnail
Re-enable opacity mask	Shift+click on disabled mask thumbnail	Shift+click on disabled mask thumbnail
Increase/decrease opacity in 1% increments	Click opacity field+Up Arrow or Down Arrow	Click opacity field+Up Arrow or Down Arrow
Increase/decrease opacity in 10% increments	Shift+click opacity field+Up Arrow or Down Arrow	Shift+click opacity field+Up Arrow or Down Arrow

Adobe Photoshop

Keyboard shortcuts in Photoshop work similarly to the ones you find in Adobe Illustrator. Quite a few palettes are available to you in Photoshop and many keyboard shortcuts are used with different palettes. Any tool that is an identical match in Adobe ImageReady as well as identical menu commands are accessed using the same keyboard shortcuts in ImageReady as used in Photoshop.

Selection Tools

Tool	Windows	Mac
Rectangle/Elliptical Marquee tool		
Shift+M toggles only these two tools	M	M
Move tool	V	V
Lasso/Polygonal/Magnetic tool		
Shift+L toggles tools	L	L
Magic Wand tool	W	W
Crop tool	C	C
Slice/Slice Select tool		
Shift+K toggles tools	K	K
Healing Brush/Patch/Color Replacement tool		
Shift+J toggles tools	J	J
Brush/Pencil tool		
Shift+B toggles tools	B	B
Clone Stamp/Pattern Stamp tool		
Shift+S toggles tools	S	S

Tool	Windows	Mac
History Brush/Art History Brush tool		
Shift+Y toggles tools	Y	Y
Eraser/Background Eraser/Magic Eraser tool		
Shift+E toggles tools	E	E
Gradient/Paint Bucket tool		
Shift+G toggles tools	G	G
Blur/Sharpen/Smudge tool		
Shift+R toggles tools	R	R
Dodge/Burn/Sponge tools		
Shift+O toggles tools	O	O
Path Selection/Direct Selection tool		
Shift+A toggles tools	A	A
Horizontal Type tool/Vertical Type tool/ Horizontal Type Mask tool/Vertical Type Mask tool		
Shift+T toggles all tools	T	T
Pen/Freeform Pen tool		
Shift+P toggles only two tools	P	P
Rectangle/Rounded Rectangle/Ellipse/ Polygon/Line/Custom Shape tools		
Shift+U toggles all tools	U	U
Notes/Audio Annotation tool		
Shift N toggles tools	N	N
Eyedropper/Color Sampler/Measure tool		
Shift+I toggles tools	I	I
Hand tool	H	H
Zoom tool	Z	Z
Foreground/Background Color Defaults (Black foreground/white background)	D	D
Switch Foreground/Background Color	X	X
Cycle through tools with the same shortcut key	Shift+press shortcut key (*when Use Shift Key for Tool Switch preference is disabled)	Shift+press shortcut key (*when Use Shift Key for Tool Switch preference is disabled)
Cycle through hidden tools	Alt+click+tool (*except Add Anchor Point, Delete Anchor Point, and Convert Point tools)	Option+click+tool (*except Add Anchor Point, Delete Anchor Point, and Convert Point tools)

Selecting Tools in the Extract Toolbox

Action	Windows	Mac
Edge Highlighter tool	B	B
Fill tool	G	G
Eyedropper tool	I	I
Cleanup tool	C	C
Edge Touchup tool	T	T

Selecting Tools in the Liquefy Toolbox

Tool	Windows	Mac
Action	Windows	Mac
Forward Warp tool	W	W
Reconstruct tool	R	R
Twirl Clockwise tool	C	C
Pucker tool	S	S
Bloat tool	B	B
Push Left tool	O	O
Mirror tool	M	M
Turbulence tool	T	T
Freeze Mask tool	F	F
Thaw Mask tool	D	D

Working with Extract*, Liquefy, and Pattern Maker*

Action	Windows	Mac
Cycle through controls on right from top	Tab	Tab
Cycle through controls on right from bottom	Shift+Tab	Shift+Tab
Temporarily activate Hand tool	Spacebar	Spacebar
Change Cancel to Reset	Alt	Option

Action (Extract* and Liquefy)	Windows	Mac
Decrease or increase brush size	[or]	[or]

Action (Extract* and Pattern Maker*)	Windows	Mac
Fit in window	Ctrl+0 (zero)	⌘+0 (zero)
Temporarily selects Zoom In tool	Ctrl+Spacebar	⌘+Spacebar
Select Zoom Out tool	Alt+Spacebar	Option+Spacebar

Action (Extract* only)	Windows	Mac OS
Toggle between Edge Highlighter tool and Eraser tool	Alt	Option
Toggle Smart Highlighting	Ctrl with Edge Highlighter tool selected	⌘ with Edge Highlighter tool selected
Remove current highlight	Alt+Delete	Option+Delete
Highlight entire image	Ctrl+Delete	⌘+Delete
Fill foreground area and preview extraction	Shift+click with Fill tool selected	Shift+click with Fill tool selected

* Not available in ImageReady

Viewing Images

Action	Windows	Mac
Cycles through open documents	Ctrl+Tab	Control+Tab
Toggle between Standard mode and Quick Mask mode*	Q	Q
Toggle among Standard Screen mode, Full Screen mode, and Full Screen mode with menu bar	F	F
Toggle image maps visibility	A	A
Toggle slices visibility	Q	Q
Preview document	Y	Y
Preview in default browser	Ctrl+Alt+P	⌘+Option+P
Edit in ImageReady*		
Edit in Photoshop	Ctrl+Shift+M	⌘+Shift+M
Fit image in window	Double-click Hand tool	Double-click Hand tool
Magnify 100%	Double-click Zoom tool	Double-click Zoom tool
Switch to Hand tool (when not in Text Edit mode)	Spacebar	Spacebar

Continued

Viewing Images *(continued)*

Action	Windows	Mac
Switch to Zoom In tool	Ctrl+Spacebar	⌘+Spacebar
Switch to Zoom Out tool	Alt+Spacebar	Option+Spacebar
Move zoom marquee while dragging with the Zoom tool*	Spacebar+drag	Spacebar+drag
Apply zoom percentage, and keep zoom percentage box active*	Shift+Enter in Navigator palette	Shift+Return in Navigator palette
Zoom in on specified area of an image*	Ctrl+drag over preview in Navigator palette	⌘+drag over preview in Navigator palette

Used in File Browser

Action	Windows	Mac
Open File Browser	Ctrl+Shift+O	⌘+Shift+O
Move up a folder (in folder view) or a row	Up Arrow	Up Arrow
Move down a folder (in folder view) or a row	Down Arrow	Down Arrow
Move up a level (in folder view)	Ctrl+Up Arrow	⌘+Up Arrow
Move left one item	Left Arrow	Left Arrow
Move right one item	Right Arrow	Right Arrow
Move to the first item	Home	Home
Move to the last item	End	End
Commit an inline renaming	Enter	Return
Add to selection	Ctrl+click	⌘+click
Refresh tree and thumbnail panes	F5	F5
Add an item to the selection	Shift+Right Arrow, Left Arrow, Up Arrow, or Down Arrow	Shift+Right Arrow, Left Arrow, Up Arrow, or Down Arrow
Rotate clockwise	Ctrl+]	⌘+]
Rotate counter-clockwise	Ctrl+[	⌘+[
Open a file and close the File Browser	Alt+Enter or Alt+double-click file	Option+Return or Option+double-click file
Launch File Browser palette in maximized state and auto-hide palettes	Ctrl+click the Toggle File Browser icon in the options bar	⌘+click the Toggle File Browser icon in the options bar
Open a file and suppress open option and color warning dialog boxes	Shift+Enter or Shift+double-click File Browser thumbnail	Shift+Enter or Shift+double-click File Browser thumbnail

Used in Filter Gallery

Action	Windows	Mac
Apply a new filter on top of selected	Alt+click on a filter	Option+click on a filter
Open/close all disclosure triangles	Alt+click on a disclosure triangle	Option+click on a disclosure triangle
Change Cancel button to Default	Ctrl	⌘
Change Cancel button to Reset	Alt	Option
Undo/Redo	Ctrl+Z	⌘+Z
Step forward	Ctrl+Shift+Z	⌘+Shift+Z
Step backward	Ctrl+Alt+Z	⌘+Option+Z

Used in Camera Raw dialog box

Action	Windows	Mac
Display highlights that will be clipped in Preview	Alt+drag Exposure or Shadows sliders	Option+drag Exposure or Shadows sliders
Skip file conversion when selecting multiple files (turn OK button to Skip)	Shift	Shift
Update raw settings without opening file (turn OK button to Update)	Alt	Option

Keys used with Photomerge

Action	Windows	Mac
Select Image tool	A	A
Rotate Image tool	R	R
Set Vanishing Point tool	V	V
Zoom tool	Z	Z
Hand tool	H	H
Switch to Hand tool	Spacebar	Spacebar
Step backward	Ctrl+Z	⌘+Z
Step forward	Ctrl+Shift+Z	⌘+Shift+Z
Move selected image 1 pixel	Right Arrow, Left Arrow, Up Arrow, or Down Arrow	Right Arrow, Left Arrow, Up Arrow, or Down Arrow
Change Cancel to Reset	Alt	Option
Show individual image border	Alt+move pointer over image	Option+move pointer over image

Keys used with Blending Modes

Action	Windows	Mac
Cycle through blending modes	Shift+Alt++ (plus) or - (minus)	Shift+Option++ (plus) or - (minus)
Normal	Shift+Alt+N	Shift+Option+N
Dissolve	Shift+Alt+I	Shift+Option+I
Behind	Shift+Alt+Q	Shift+Option+Q
Clear	Shift+Alt+R	Shift+Option+R
Darken	Shift+Alt+K	Shift+Option+K
Multiply	Shift+Alt+M	Shift+Option+M
Color Burn	Shift+Alt+B	Shift+Option+B
Linear Burn	Shift+Alt+A	Shift+Option+A
Lighten	Shift+Alt+G	Shift+Option+G
Screen	Shift+Alt+S	Shift+Option+S
Color Dodge	Shift+Alt+D	Shift+Option+D
Linear Dodge	Shift+Alt+W	Shift+Option+W
Overlay	Shift+Alt+O	Shift+Option+O
Soft Light	Shift+Alt+F	Shift+Option+F
Hard Light	Shift+Alt+H	Shift+Option+H
Vivid Light	Shift+Alt+V	Shift+Option+V
Linear Light	Shift+Alt+J	Shift+Option+J
Pin Light	Shift+Alt+Z	Shift+Option+Z
Hard Mix	Shift+Alt+L	Shift+Option+L

Selecting and Moving Objects

Action	Windows	Mac
Reposition marquee while selecting‡	Any marquee tool (except single column and single row)+spacebar+drag	Any marquee tool (except single column and single row)+spacebar+drag
Add to, subtract from, or intersect a selection	Any selection tool+Shift or Alt+drag	Any selection tool+Shift or Option+drag
Constrain marquee to square or circle (if no other selections are active)‡	Shift+drag	Shift+drag
Draw marquee from center (if no other selections are active)‡	Alt+drag	Option+drag

Action	Windows	Mac
Constrain shape and draw marquee from center‡	Shift+Alt+drag	Shift+Option+drag
Switch to Move tool	⌘ (except when Hand, Slice, Path*, Shape*, Rectangle Image map, Circle Image Map, Polygon Image Map, or any Pen* tool is selected)	⌘ (except when Hand, Slice, Path*, Shape*, Rectangle Image map, Circle Image Map§, Polygon Image Map, or any Pen* tool is selected)
Switch from Magnetic Lasso tool to Lasso tool*	Alt+drag	Option+drag
Switch from Magnetic Lasso tool to polygonal Lasso tool*	Alt+click	Option+click
Apply/cancel an operation of the Magnetic Lasso*	Enter/Esc	Return/Esc or ⌘+period
Move copy of selection	Move tool+Alt+drag selection‡	Move tool+Option+drag selection‡
Move selection area 1 pixel	Any selection+Right Arrow, Left Arrow, Up Arrow, or Down Arrow†	Any selection+Right Arrow, Left Arrow, Up Arrow, or Down Arrow†

Editing Paths

Action	Windows	Mac
Select multiple anchor points	Direction selection tool+Shift+click	Direction selection tool+Shift+click
Select entire path	Direction selection tool+Alt+click	Direction selection tool+Option+click
Duplicate a path	Pen (any pen tool), Path Selection, or Direct Selection tool+Ctrl+Alt+drag	Pen tool+⌘+Option+drag
Switch from Path Selection, Pen, Add Anchor Point, Delete Anchor Point, or Convert Point tools, to Direct Selection tool	Ctrl	⌘
Switch from Pen tool or Freeform Pen tool to Convert Point tool when pointer is over anchor or direction point	Alt	Option
Close path	Magnetic Pen tool+double-click	Magnetic Pen tool+double-click
Close path with straight-line segment	Magnetic Pen tool+ Alt+double-click	Magnetic Pen tool+ Option+double-click

Painting Objects

Action	Windows	Mac
Eyedropper tool	Any painting tool+Alt or any shape tool+Alt (*except when Paths option is selected)	Any painting tool+Option or any shape tool+Option (*except when Paths option is selected)
Select background color	Eyedropper tool+Alt+click	Eyedropper tool+Option+click
Color sampler tool*	Eyedropper tool+Shift	Eyedropper tool+Shift
Deletes color sampler*	Color sampler tool+Alt+click	Color sampler tool+Option+click
Sets opacity, tolerance, strength, or exposure for painting mode	Any painting or editing tool+number keys (for example, 0 = 100%, 1 = 10%, 4 then 5 in quick succession = 45%) (*When Airbrush option is enabled, use Shift+number keys)	Any painting or editing tool+number keys (for example, 0 = 100%, 1 = 10%, 4 then 5 in quick succession = 45%) (*When Airbrush option is enabled, use Shift+number keys)
Sets flow for painting mode*	Any painting or editing tool+Shift+number keys (for example, 0 = 100%, 1 = 10%,4 then 5 in quick succession = 45%) (*When Airbrush option is enabled, omit Shift)	Any painting or editing tool+Shift+number keys (for example, 0 = 100%, 1 = 10%, 4 then 5 in quick succession = 45%) (*When Airbrush option is enabled, omit Shift)
Cycles through blending modes	Shift++ (plus) or - (minus)	Shift++ (plus) or - (minus)
Fills selection/layer with foreground or background color	Alt+Backspace, or Ctrl+Backspace†	Option+Delete, or ⌘+Delete†
Fills from history*	Ctrl+Alt+Backspace†	⌘+Option+Delete†
Displays Fill dialog box	Shift+Backspace	Shift+Delete
Lock transparent pixels on/off	/ (forward slash)	/ (forward slash)
Connects points with a straight line	Any painting tool+Shift+click	Any painting tool+Shift+click

Transforming Selections and Paths

Action	Windows	Mac
Transform from center or reflect	Alt	Option
Constrain	Shift	Shift
Distort	Ctrl	⌘

Action	Windows	Mac
Apply	Enter	Return
Cancel	Ctrl+. (period) or Esc	⌘+. (period) or Esc
Free transform with duplicate data	Ctrl+Alt+T	⌘+Option+T
Transform again with duplicate data	Ctrl+Shift+Alt+T	⌘+Shift+Option+T

Selecting, Editing, and Navigating text

Action	Windows	Mac
Move type in image	Ctrl+drag type when Type layer is selected	⌘+drag type when Type layer is selected
Select 1 character left/right or 1 line down/up, or 1 word left/right	Shift+Left Arrow/Right Arrow or Down Arrow/Up Arrow, or Ctrl+Shift+Left Arrow/Right Arrow	Shift+Left Arrow/Right Arrow or Down Arrow/Up Arrow, or ⌘+Shift+Left Arrow/Right Arrow
Select characters from insertion point to mouse click point	Shift+click	Shift+click
Move 1 character left/right, 1 line down/up, or 1 word left/right	Left Arrow/Right Arrow, Down Arrow/Up Arrow, or Ctrl+Left Arrow/Right Arrow	Left Arrow/Right Arrow, Down Arrow/Up Arrow, or ⌘+Left Arrow/Right Arrow
Create a new text layer, when editing text	Shift+click	Shift+click
Select word, line, paragraph, or story	Double-click, triple-click, quadruple-click, or quintuple-click	Double-click, triple-click, quadruple-click, or quintuple-click
Show/Hide selection on selected type	Ctrl+H	⌘+H
Display the bounding box for transforming text when editing text, or activate Move tool if cursor is inside the bounding box*	Ctrl	⌘
Scale text within a bounding box when resizing the bounding box*	Ctrl+drag a bounding box handle	⌘+drag a bounding box handle
Move text box while creating text box	Spacebar+drag	Spacebar+drag

Formatting Type

Action	Windows	Mac
Align left, center, or right*	Horizontal type tool+Ctrl+Shift+L, C, or R	Horizontal type tool+⌘+Shift+L, C, or R
Align top, center, or bottom*	Vertical type tool+Ctrl+Shift+L, C, or R	Vertical type tool+⌘+Shift+L, C, or R
Return to default font style	Ctrl+Shift+Y	⌘+Shift+Y
Choose 100% horizontal scale*	Ctrl+Shift+X	⌘+Shift+X
Choose 100% vertical scale*	Ctrl+Shift+Alt+X	⌘+Shift+Option+X
Choose Auto Leading*	Ctrl+Shift+Alt+A	⌘+Shift+Option+A
Choose 0 for Tracking*	Ctrl+Shift+Q	⌘+Control+Shift+Q
Justify paragraph, left aligns last line*	Ctrl+Shift+J	⌘+Shift+J
Justify paragraph, forces last line*	Ctrl+Shift+F	⌘+Shift+F
Toggle paragraph hyphenation on/off*	Ctrl+Shift+Alt+H	⌘+Control+Shift+Option+H
Toggle single/every-line composer on/off*	Ctrl+Shift+Alt+T	⌘+Shift+Option+T
Decrease or increase type size of selected text 2 pts/px	Ctrl+Shift+< or >†	⌘+Shift+< or >†
Decrease or increase leading 2 pts/px	Alt+Down Arrow or Up Arrow††	Option+Down Arrow or Up Arrow††
Decrease or increase baseline shift 2 pts/px	Shift+Alt+Down Arrow or Up Arrow††	Shift+Option+Down Arrow or Up Arrow††
Decrease or increase kerning/tracking 20/1000 ems	Alt+Left Arrow or Right Arrow††	Option+Left Arrow or Right Arrow††

Slicing and Optimizing

Action	Windows	Mac
Toggle browser dither for selected image pane in Optimized view	Ctrl+Shift+Y	⌘+Shift+Y
Toggle through gamma previews in selected image pane	Ctrl+Alt+Y	⌘+Option+Y
Toggle through Optimized/2up/4up/Original window	Ctrl+Y	⌘+Y
Toggle between Slice tool and Slice Selection tool	Ctrl	⌘

Action	Windows	Mac
Draw square slice	Shift+drag	Shift+drag
Draw from center outward	Alt+drag	Option+drag
Draw square slice from center outward	Shift+Alt+drag	Shift+Option+drag
Reposition slice while creating slice	Spacebar+drag	Spacebar+drag
Open context-sensitive menu	Right-click on slice	Control+click on slice

Using Palettes

Action	Windows	Mac
Set options (except for Actions, Styles, Brushes*, Tool Presets*, and Layer Comps palettes)	Alt+click New button	Option+click New button
Delete without confirmation (except for the Brushes* palette)	Alt+click Trash button	Option+click Trash button
Apply value and keep text box active*	Shift+Enter	Shift+Return
Load as a selection	Ctrl+click channel, layer, or path thumbnail	⌘+click channel, layer, or path thumbnail
	Ctrl+Alt+click layer in ImageReady	⌘+Option+click layer in ImageReady
Add to current selection	Ctrl+Shift+click channel, layer, or path thumbnail	⌘+Shift+click channel, layer, or path thumbnail
	Ctrl+Shift+Alt+click layer in ImageReady	⌘+Shift+Option+click layer in ImageReady
Subtract from current selection*	Ctrl+Alt+click channel, layer, or path thumbnail	⌘+Option+click channel, layer, or path thumbnail
Intersect with current selection*	Ctrl+Shift+Alt+click channel, layer, or path thumbnail	⌘+Shift+Option+click channel, layer, or path thumbnail
Show/Hide all palettes	Tab	Tab
Show/Hide all palettes except the toolbox and options bar	Shift+Tab	Shift+Tab
Highlight options bar	Select tool and press Enter	Select tool and press Return
Increase/decrease units by 10 in a pop-up menu	Shift+Up Arrow/Down Arrow	Shift+Up Arrow/Down Arrow

Using Actions

Action	Windows	Mac
Turn command on and all others off, or turns all commands on*	Alt+click the check mark next to a command	Option+click the check mark next to a command
Turn current modal control on and toggle all other modal controls*	Alt+click	Option+click
Change action set options	Alt+double-click action set	Option+double-click action set
Display Options dialog box	Double-click set or actions	Double-click set or actions
	Alt+double-click set or action in ImageReady	Alt+double-click set or action in ImageReady
Play entire action	Ctrl+double-click an action	⌘+double-click an action
Collapse/expand all components of an action	Alt+click the triangle	Option+click the triangle
Play a command	Ctrl+click the Play button	⌘+click the Play button
Create new action and begin recording without confirmation	Alt+click the New Action button	Option+click the New Action button
Select contiguous items of the same kind*	Shift+click the action/command	Shift+click the action/command
Select noncontiguous items of the same kind*	Ctrl+click the action/command	⌘+click the action/command

Brushes Palette

Action	Windows	Mac
Delete brush*	Alt+click brush	Option+click brush
Rename brush*	Double-click brush	Double-click brush
Decrease/increase brush size*	[or]	[or]
Decrease/increase brush softness/hardness in 25% increments*	Shift+[or]	Shift+[or]
Select previous/next brush size*	, (comma) or . (period)	, (comma) or . (period)
Select previous/next brush size	[or]	[or]
Select first/last brush*	Shift+, (comma) or . (period)	Shift+, (comma) or . (period)
Select first/last brush	Shift+[or]	Shift+[or]
Display precise crosshair for brushes	Caps Lock	Caps Lock
Toggle airbrush option*	Shift+Alt+P	Shift+Option+P

Channels Palette

Action	Windows	Mac
Set options for Save Selection as Channel button	Alt+click button	Option+click button
Create a new spot channel	Ctrl+click Create New Channel button	⌘+click Create New Channel button
Select/deselect multiple color-channel selection	Shift+click color channel	Shift+click color channel
Select/deselect alpha channel and show/hide as a rubylith overlay	Shift+click alpha channel	Shift+click alpha channel
Display channel options	Double-click alpha or spot channel thumbnail	Double-click alpha or spot channel thumbnail
Display composite	~ (tilde)	~ (tilde)

Color Palette

Action	Windows	Mac
Select background color	Alt+click color in color bar	Option+click color in color bar
Display Color Bar menu	Right-click color bar	Control+click color bar
Cycle through color choices	Shift+click color bar	Shift+click color bar

History Palette

Action	Windows	Mac
Rename snapshot*	Double-click snapshot name	Double-click snapshot name
Step forward through image states	Ctrl+Shift+Z	⌘+Shift+Z
Step backward through image states*	Alt+Shift+Z	Option+Shift+Z
Duplicate any image state, except the current state*	Alt+click the image state	Option+click the image state
Permanently clear history (no Undo)*	Alt+Clear History (in History palette pop-up menu)	Option+Clear History (in History palette pop-up menu)

Info Palette

Action	Windows	Mac
Change color readout modes*	Click eyedropper icon	Click eyedropper icon
Change measurement units*	Click crosshair icon	Click crosshair icon

Layers Palette

Action	Windows	Mac
Load layer transparency as a selection	Ctrl+click layer thumbnail	⌘+click layer thumbnail
Merge visible layers	Ctrl+Shift+E	⌘+Shift+E
Create new empty layer with dialog box	Alt+click New Layer button	Option+click New Layer button
Create new layer below target layer	Ctrl+click New Layer button	⌘+click New Layer button
Activate bottom/top layer	Shift+Alt+[or] (left/right bracket)	Shift+Option+[or] (left/right bracket)
Select next layer down/up	Alt+[or] (left/right bracket)	Option+[or] (left/right bracket)
Move target layer down/up	Ctrl+[or] (left/right bracket)	⌘+[or] (left/right bracket)
Merge a copy of all visible layers into target layer	Ctrl+Shift+Alt+E	⌘+Shift+Option+E
Merge down	Ctrl+E	⌘+E
Bring target layer to back/front (or back/front) of set	Ctrl+Shift+[or] (left/right bracket)	⌘+Shift+[or] (left/right bracket)
Pass through blending mode for layer set	Shift+Alt+P	Shift+Option+P
Copy current layer to layer below	Alt+Merge Down command from the palette pop-up menu	Option+Merge Down command from the palette pop-up menu
Copy all visible layers to active layer	Alt+Merge Visible command from the palette pop-up menu	Option+Merge Visible command from the palette pop-up menu
Copy visible linked layers to active layer	Alt+Merge Linked command from the palette pop-up menu	Option+Merge Linked command from the palette pop-up menu
Show/hide this layer/layer set only or all layers/layer sets	Right-click the eye icon	Control+click the eye icon
Show/hide all other currently visible layers	Alt+click the eye icon	Option+click the eye icon

Layer Comps Palette

Action	Windows	Mac
Create new layer comp without dialog box	Alt+click Create New Layer Comp button	Option+click Create New Layer Comp button
Open Layer Comp Options dialog box	Double-click layer comp	Double-click layer comp
Rename inline	Double-click layer comp name	Double-click layer comp name
Select/deselect multiple contiguous layer comps	Shift+click	Shift+click
Select/deselect multiple noncontiguous layer comps	Ctrl+click	⌘+click

Paths Palette

Action	Windows	Mac
Add path to selection	Ctrl+Shift+click path name	⌘+Shift+click path name
Subtract the path from selection	Ctrl+Alt+click path name	⌘+Option+click path name
Retain intersection of path as a selection	Ctrl+Shift+Alt+click path name	⌘+Shift+Option+click path name
Hide path	Ctrl+Shift+H	⌘+Shift+H
Set options for Fill Path with Foreground Color button, Stroke Path with Brush button, Load Path as a Selection button, Make Work Path from Selection button, and Create New Path button	Alt+click button	Option+click button

Swatches Palette

Action	Windows	Mac
Create new swatch from foreground color*	Click in empty area of palette	Click in empty area of palette
Select background color	Ctrl+click swatch	⌘+click swatch
Delete color	Alt+click swatch	Option+click swatch
Select multiple contiguous colors	Shift+click on a second color	Shift+click on a second color
Select multiple noncontiguous colors	Ctrl+click on multiple colors	⌘+click on multiple colors

Web Content Palette

Action	Windows	Mac
Edit image map name and show Image Map palette	Double-click image map thumbnail	Double-click image map thumbnail
Edit mouse action for rollover state	Double-click rollover state thumbnail	Double-click rollover state thumbnail
Edit image slice name and show Slice palette	Double-click image slice thumbnail	Double-click image slice thumbnail
Toggle visibility of animation frames	Right-click state with an animated frame icon and select new state from context menu	Control+click state with an animated frame icon and select new state from context menu
Create an image map rollover	Ctrl+click Create Layer-Based Rollover button	⌘+click Create Layer-Based Rollover button

Function Keys

Action	Windows	Mac
Invoke Help	F1	
Undo/Redo*		F1
Cut*	F2	F2
Copy*	F3	F3
Paste*	F4	F4
Show/Hide Brushes palette*, Show/Hide Slice palette	F5	F5
Show/Hide Color palette	F6	F6
Show/Hide Layers palette	F7	F7
Show/Hide Info palette	F8	F8
Show/Hide Actions palette*	F9	Option+F9*, Control+F9
Show/Hide Optimize palette	F10	Control+F10
Show/Hide Animation palette	F11	Control+F11
Revert	F12	F12
Fill*	Shift+F5	Shift+F5
Feather Selection*	Shift+F6	Shift+F6
Inverse Selection*	Shift+F7	Shift+F7

ImageReady Only

Those tools common to Photoshop and ImageReady use the same keyboard shortcuts in both programs. Many tools contained in Photoshop don't appear in ImageReady; hence, you won't find keyboard shortcuts for tools or functions not available. ImageReady also contains tools you won't find in Photoshop. Those keyboard shortcuts unique to ImageReady are listed in the following two tables.

Color Table Palette

Action	Windows	Mac
Select background color	Alt+click swatch	Option+click swatch
Select multiple contiguous colors; last color clicked becomes foreground color	Shift+click a second swatch	Shift+click a second swatch
Select noncontiguous colors; last color clicked becomes foreground color	Ctrl+click multiple swatches	⌘+click multiple swatches
Add current background color	Alt+click New Color button or drag color proxy from Tools palette onto color table	Option+click New Color button or drag color proxy from Tools palette onto color table
Add current foreground color	Click New Color button or drag color proxy from Tools palette to New Color button	Click New Color button or drag color proxy from Tools palette to New Color button

Animation in Image Ready

Action	Windows	Mac
Select/deselect multiple contiguous frames	Shift+click on second frame	Shift+click on second frame
Select/deselect multiple noncontiguous frames	Ctrl+click on multiple frames	⌘+click multiple frames
Replace destination frame with copied frames	Shift+Alt+Paste Frames command from the palette pop-up menu	Shift+Option+Paste Frames command from the palette pop-up menu
Paste using previous settings without displaying the dialog box	Alt+Paste Frames command from the palette pop-up menu	Option+Paste Frames command from the palette pop-up menu

Adobe InDesign

InDesign has a toolbox and a Control palette that is similar to a toolbox. The Control palette changes options depending on tools selected in the toolbox or in palettes. When learning keyboard shortcuts for tools in InDesign, be certain to review the Control palette tools as well as the tools in the toolbox.

InDesign makes use of a number of different palettes. You'll notice that many keyboard shortcuts are used with various palette functions. As when using Illustrator, you often need to have objects or type selected in order to invoke a key command.

Selecting Tools

Tool	Windows	Mac
Selection tool	V	V
Direct Selection tool	A	A
Toggle Selection and Direct Selection tool	Ctrl+Tab	⌘+Control+Tab
Pen tool	P	P
Add Anchor Point tool	=	=
Delete Anchor Point tool	-	-
Convert Direction Point tool	Shift+C	Shift+C
Type tool	T	T
Type on a Path tool	Shift+T	Shift+T
Pencil tool	N	N
Line tool	\	\
Rectangle Frame tool	F	F
Rectangle tool	M	M
Ellipse tool	L	L
Rotate tool	R	R
Scale tool	S	S
Shear tool	O	O
Free Transform tool	E	E
Eyedropper tool	I	I
Measure tool	K	K
Gradient tool	G	G

Using the Control Palette

Action	Windows	Mac
Enable/Disable controls	Spacebar	Spacebar
Toggle focus to/from Control palette	Ctrl+6	⌘+6
Toggle Character/Paragraph text attributes mode	Ctrl+Alt+7	⌘+Option+7
Change reference point when proxy has focus	Any key on the numeric keypad or keyboard numbers	Any key on the numeric keypad or keyboard numbers
Display the pop-up menu that has focus	Alt+Down Arrow	
Open the Units & Increments panel of the Preferences dialog box	Alt+click Kerning icon	Option+click Kerning icon
Open the Character Style Options dialog box	Alt+click Character Style icon	Option+click Character Style icon
Open the New Character Style Options dialog box	Double-click Character Style icon	Double-click Character Style icon
Open the Text Frame Options dialog box	Alt+click Number of Columns icon	Option+click Number of Columns icon
Open the Move dialog box	Alt+click X or Y icon	Option+click X or Y icon
Open the Rotate dialog box	Alt+click Angle icon	Option+click Angle icon
Open the Paragraph Style Options dialog box	Alt+click Paragraph Style icon	Option+click Paragraph Style icon
Open the Scale dialog box	Alt+click X or Y Scale icon	Option+click X or Y Scale icon
Open the Shear dialog box	Alt+click Shear icon	Option+click Shear icon
Open the Text panel of the Preferences dialog box	Alt+click Superscript, Subscript, or Small Caps button	Option+click Superscript, Subscript, or Small Caps button
Open the Underline Options dialog box	Alt+click Underline button	Option+click Underline button
Open the Strikethrough Options dialog box	Alt+click Strikethrough button	Option+click Strikethrough button

Selecting/Moving Objects

Action	Windows	Mac
Temporarily select Selection or Direct Selection tool (last used)	Any tool (except selection tools)+Ctrl	Any tool (except selection tools)+ ⌘
Temporarily select Group Selection tool	Direct Selection tool+Alt; or Pen, Add Anchor Point, or Delete Anchor Point tool+Alt+Ctrl	Direct Selection tool+Option; or Pen, Add Anchor Point, or Delete Anchor Point tool+Option+⌘
Add to or subtract from a selection of multiple objects	Selection, Direct Selection, or Group Selection tool+ Shift+click (to deselect, click center point)	Selection, Direct Selection, or Group Selection tool+ Shift+click (to deselect, click center point)
Duplicate selection	Selection, Direct Selection, or Group Selection tool+Alt+drag*	Selection, Direct Selection, or Group Selection tool+Option+drag*
Duplicate and offset selection	Alt+Left Arrow, Right Arrow, Up Arrow, or Down Arrow key	Option+Left Arrow, Right Arrow, Up Arrow, or Down Arrow key
Duplicate and offset selection by ten times**	Alt+Shift+Left Arrow, Right Arrow, Up Arrow, Down Arrow key	Option+Shift+Left Arrow, Right Arrow, Up Arrow, Down Arrow key
Move selection**	Left Arrow, Right Arrow, Up Arrow, Down Arrow key	Left Arrow, Right Arrow, Up Arrow, Down Arrow key
Move selection by ten times**	Shift+Left Arrow, Right Arrow, Up Arrow, Down Arrow key	Shift+Left Arrow, Right Arrow, Up Arrow, Down Arrow key
Select master page item from document page	Selection or Direct Selection tool+Ctrl+Shift+click	Selection or Direct Selection tool+⌘+Shift+click
Select next object behind or in front	Selection tool+Ctrl+click, or Selection tool+Alt+Ctrl+click	Selection tool+⌘+click or Selection tool+Option+ ⌘+click
Select next or previous frame in story	Alt+Ctrl+Page Down/Page Up	Option+⌘+Page Down/Page Up
Select first or last frame in story	Shift+Alt+Ctrl+Page Down/Page Up	Shift+Option+⌘+Page Down/Page Up

*Press Shift to constrain movement to 45° angles.

**Amount is set in Edit ➪ Preferences ➪ Units & Increments (Windows) or InDesign ➪ Preferences ➪ Units & Increments (Mac).

Editing Paths and Frames

Action	Windows	Mac
Temporarily select Convert Direction Point tool	Direct Selection tool+Alt+Ctrl, or Pen tool+Alt	Direct Selection tool+Option+ ⌘, or Pen tool+Option
Temporarily switch between Add Anchor Point and Delete Anchor Point tool	Alt	Option
Temporarily select Add Anchor Point tool	Scissors tool+Alt	Scissors tool+Option
Keep Pen tool selected when pointer is over path or anchor point	Pen tool+Shift	Pen tool+Shift
Move anchor point and handles while drawing	Pen tool+spacebar	Pen tool+spacebar

Keys for Using Tables

Action	Windows	Mac
Insert or delete rows or columns while dragging	Begin dragging row or column border, and then hold down Alt as you drag	Begin dragging row or column border, and then hold down Option as you drag
Resize rows or columns without changing the size of the table	Shift+drag interior row or column border	Shift+drag interior row or column border
Resize rows or columns proportionally	Shift+drag right or bottom table border	Shift+drag right or bottom table border
Move to next/previous cell	Tab/Shift+Tab	Tab/Shift+Tab
Move to first/last cell in column	Alt+Page Up/Page Down	Option+Page Up/Page Down
Move to first/last cell in row	Alt+Home/End key	Option+Home/End key
Move to first/last row in frame	Page Up/Page Down key	Page Up/Page Down key
Move up/down one cell	Up Arrow/Down Arrow key	Up Arrow/Down Arrow key
Move left/right one cell	Left Arrow/Right Arrow key	Left Arrow/Right Arrow key
Select cell above/below the current cell	Shift+Up Arrow/Down Arrow key	Shift+Up Arrow/Down Arrow key
Select cell to the right/left of the current cell	Shift+Right Arrow/Left Arrow key	Shift+Right Arrow/Left Arrow key
Start row on next column	Enter (numeric keypad)	Enter (numeric keypad)
Start row on next frame	Shift+Enter (numeric keypad)	Shift+Enter (numeric keypad)
Toggle between text selection and cell selection	Esc	Esc

Transforming Objects

Action	Windows	Mac
Duplicate and transform selection	Transformation tool+Alt+drag*	Transformation tool+Option+drag*
Display Transform Tool dialog box	Select object+double-click Scale tool, Rotate tool, or Shear tool in Toolbox	Select object+double-click Scale tool, Rotate tool, or Shear tool in Toolbox
Decrease size by 1%**	Ctrl+<	⌘+<
Resize frame and content	Selection tool+Ctrl+drag	Selection tool+⌘+drag
Resize frame and content proportionately	Selection tool+Shift	Selection tool+Shift
Constrain proportion	Ellipse tool, Polygon tool, or Rectangle tool+Shift+drag	Ellipse tool, Polygon tool, or Rectangle tool+Shift+drag

*After you select a transformation tool, hold down the mouse button, and then hold down Alt (Windows) or Option (Mac) and drag. Press Shift to constrain movement to 45° angles.

**Press Alt (Windows) or Option (Mac) to increase or decrease size by 5%.

Finding and Changing Text

Action	Windows	Mac
Insert selected text into Find What box	Ctrl+F1	⌘+F1
Insert selected text into Find What box and finds next	Shift+F1	Shift+F1
Find next occurrence of Find What text	Shift+F2 or Alt+Ctrl+F	Shift+F2 or Option+⌘+F
Insert selected text into Change To box	Ctrl+F2	⌘+F2
Replace selection with Change To text	Ctrl+F3	⌘+F3

Working with Type

Action	Windows	Mac
Bold	Shift+Ctrl+B	Shift+⌘+B
Italic	Shift+Ctrl+I	Shift+⌘+I
Normal	Shift+Ctrl+Y	Shift+⌘+Y
Underline	Shift+Ctrl+U	Shift+⌘+U
Strikethrough	Shift+Ctrl+/	Shift+⌘+/
All Caps (on/off)	Shift+Ctrl+K	Shift+⌘+K
Small Caps (on/off)	Shift+Ctrl+H	Shift+⌘+H
Superscript	Shift+Ctrl++ (plus)	Shift+⌘++ (plus)

Action	Windows	Mac
Subscript	Shift+Alt+Ctrl++ (plus)	Shift+Option+⌘++ (plus)
Reset horizontal or vertical scale to 100%	Shift+Ctrl+X or Shift+Alt+Ctrl+X	Shift+⌘+X or Shift+Option+⌘+X
Align left, right, or center	Shift+Ctrl+L, R, or C	Shift+⌘+L, R, or C
Justify all lines	Shift+Ctrl+F (all lines) or J (all but last line)	Shift+⌘+F (all lines) or J (all but last line)
Increase or decrease point size*	Shift+Ctrl+> or <	Shift+⌘+> or <
Increase or decrease point size by five times*	Shift+Ctrl+Alt+> or <	Shift+⌘+ Option+> or <
Increase or decrease leading*	Alt+Up Arrow/Down Arrow key (horizontal text) or Right Arrow/Left Arrow key (vertical text)	Option+Up Arrow/Down Arrow key (horizontal text) or Right Arrow/Left Arrow key (vertical text)
Increase or decrease leading by five times*	Alt+Ctrl+Up Arrow/Down Arrow key (horizontal text) or Right Arrow/Left Arrow key (vertical text)	Option+⌘+Up Arrow/Down Arrow key (horizontal text) or Right Arrow/Left Arrow key (vertical text)
Select or deselect preferences setting for typographer's marks	Shift+Alt+Ctrl+" (quote)	Shift+Option+⌘+" (quote)

Navigating through and Selecting Text

Action	Windows	Mac
Move to right or left one character	Right Arrow/Left Arrow key	Right Arrow/Left Arrow key
Move up or down one line	Up Arrow/Down Arrow key	Up Arrow/Down Arrow key
Move to right or left one word	Ctrl+Right Arrow/Left Arrow key	⌘+Right Arrow/Left Arrow key
Move to start or end of line	Home/End key	Home/End key
Move to previous or next paragraph	Ctrl+Up Arrow/Down Arrow key	⌘+Up Arrow/Down Arrow key
Move to start or end of story	Ctrl+Home/End key	⌘+Home/End key
Select one word	Double-click word	Double-click word
Select one character right or left	Shift+Right Arrow/Left Arrow key	Shift+Right Arrow/Left Arrow key
Select one line above or below	Shift+Up Arrow/Down Arrow key	Shift+Up Arrow/Down Arrow key
Select start or end of line	Shift+Home/End key	Shift+Home/End key

Continued

Navigating through and Selecting Text *(continued)*

Action	Windows	Mac
Select one paragraph	Triple-click or quadruple-click paragraph, depending on Text Preferences setting	Triple-click or quadruple-click paragraph, depending on Text Preferences setting
Select one paragraph before or after	Shift+Ctrl+Up Arrow/Down Arrow key	Shift+⌘+Up Arrow/Down Arrow key
Select current line	Shift+Ctrl+\	Shift+⌘+\
Select characters from insertion point	Shift+click	Shift+click
Select start or end of story	Shift+Ctrl+Home/End key	Shift+⌘+Home/End key
Select all in story	Ctrl+A	⌘+A

Viewing Documents and Document Workspaces

Action	Windows	Mac
Temporarily select Hand tool	Spacebar (with no text insertion point), Alt+drag (with text insertion point), or Alt+spacebar (in both text and nontext modes)	Spacebar (with no text insertion point), Option+drag (with text insertion point), or Option+spacebar (in both text and nontext modes)
Temporarily select Zoom In tool	Ctrl+spacebar	⌘+spacebar
Temporarily select Zoom Out tool	Alt+Ctrl+spacebar or Alt+Zoom In tool	Option+⌘+spacebar or Option+Zoom In tool
Zoom to 50%, 200%, or 400%	Ctrl+5, 2, or 4	⌘+5, 2, or 4
Access Zoom Percent field	Ctrl+Alt+5	⌘+Option+5
Redraw screen	Shift+F5	Shift+F5
Open new default document	Ctrl+Alt+N	⌘+Option+N
Optimize screen redraw	Ctrl+. (period)	⌘+. (period)
Switch between current and previous zoom levels	Alt+Ctrl+2	Option+⌘+2
Switch to next/previous document window	Ctrl+F6 or Ctrl+~ (tilde)/ Shift+Ctrl+F6 or Ctrl+Shift+~ (tilde)	⌘+F6 or ⌘+~ (tilde)/ ⌘+Shift+~ (tilde)
Scroll up/down one screen	Page Up/Page Down key	Page Up/Page Down key
Go back/forward to last-viewed page	Ctrl+Page Up/Page Down key	⌘+Page Up/Page Down key
Go to previous/next spread	Alt+Page Up/Page Down key	Option+Page Up/Page Down key
Select page number in page box	Ctrl+J	⌘+J
Fit selection in window	Ctrl+Alt++ (plus)	⌘+Option++ (plus)

Navigating XML

Action	Windows	Mac
Expand/Collapse element	Right Arrow/Left Arrow key	Right Arrow/Left Arrow key
Expand/Collapse element and child elements	Alt+Right Arrow/Left Arrow key	Option+Right Arrow/Left Arrow key
Extend XML selection up/down	Shift+Up Arrow/Down Arrow key	Shift+Up Arrow/Down Arrow key
Move XML selection up/down	Up Arrow/Down Arrow key	Up Arrow/Down Arrow key
Scroll structure pane up/down one screen	Page Up/Page Down key	Page Up/Page Down key
Select first/last XML node	Home/End key	Home/End key
Extend selection to first/last XML node	Shift+Home/End key	Shift+Home/End key
Go to previous/next validation error	Ctrl+Left Arrow/Right Arrow key	⌘+Left Arrow/Right Arrow key

Keys for Indexing

Action	Windows	Mac
Create index entry without dialog box	Ctrl+Alt+U	⌘+Option+U
Open Index Entry dialog box	Ctrl+U	⌘+U
Create proper name index entry (last name, first name)	Shift+Ctrl+F8	Shift+⌘+F8

Using Palettes

Action	Windows	Mac
Delete without confirmation	Alt+click Trash button	Option+click Trash button
Create item and set options	Alt+click New button	Option+click New button
Apply value and keep focus on option	Shift+Enter	Shift+Enter
Activate last-used option in last-used palette	Ctrl+Alt+~ (tilde)	⌘+Option+~ (tilde)
Select range of styles, layers, links, swatches, or library objects in a palette	Shift+click	Shift+click

Continued

Using Palettes *(continued)*

Action	Windows	Mac
Select nonadjacent styles, layers, links, swatches, or library objects in a palette	Ctrl+click	⌘+click
Apply value and select next value	Tab	Tab
Move focus to selected object, text, or window	Esc	Esc
Show/Hide all palettes, Toolbox, and Control palette (with no insertion point)	Tab	Tab
Show/Hide all palettes except the Toolbox and Control palette (docked or not)	Shift+Tab	Shift+Tab
Open or close all stashed palettes	Ctrl+Alt+Tab	⌘+Option+Tab
Stash a palette group	Alt+drag any palette tab (in the group) to edge of screen	Option+drag any palette tab (in the group) to edge of window
Select item by name	Alt+Ctrl+click in list, and then use keyboard to select item by name	Option+⌘+click in list and then use keyboard to select item by name

Character and Paragraph Palettes

Action	Windows	Mac
Open Justification dialog box	Alt+Ctrl+Shift+J	Option+⌘+Shift+J
Open Paragraph Rules dialog box	Alt+Ctrl+J	Option+⌘+J
Open Keep Options dialog box	Alt+Ctrl+K	Option+⌘+K
Activate Character palette	Ctrl+T	⌘+T
Activate Paragraph palette	Ctrl+Alt+T	⌘+Option+T

Character and Paragraph Styles Palettes

Action	Windows	Mac
Make character style definition match text	Select text and press Shift+Alt+Ctrl+C	Select text and press Shift+Option+⌘+C
Make paragraph style definition match text	Select text and press Shift+Alt+Ctrl+R	Select text and press Shift+Option+⌘+R

Action	Windows	Mac
Change options without applying style	Shift+Alt+Ctrl+ double-click style	Shift+Option+⌘+ double-click style
Remove style and local formatting	Alt+click paragraph style name	Option+click paragraph style name
Clear overrides from paragraph style	Alt+Shift+click paragraph style name	Option+Shift+click paragraph style name
Show/hide Paragraph and Character Styles palettes, respectively	F11 or Shift+F11	F11 or Shift+F11

Tabs Palette

Action	Windows	Mac
Activate Tabs palette	Shift+Ctrl+T	Shift+⌘+T
Switch between alignment options	Alt+click tab	Option+click tab

Layers Palette

Action	Windows	Mac
Select all objects on layer	Alt+click layer	Option+click layer
Copy selection to new layer	Alt+drag small square to new layer	Option+drag small square to new layer

Pages Palette

Action	Windows	Mac
Apply master to selected page	Alt+click master	Option+click master
Base another master page on selected master	Alt+click the master you want to base the selected maser on	Option+click the master you want to base the selected maser on
Create master page	Ctrl+click Create New Page button	⌘+click Create New page button
Display Insert Pages dialog box	Alt+click New Page button	Option+click New Page button
Override all master page items for current spread	Ctrl+Alt+Shift+L	⌘+Option+Shift+L
Add new page after last page	Shift+Ctrl+P	Shift+⌘+P

Links Palette

Action	Windows	Mac
Go to the linked item	Alt+double-click link filename	Option+double-click link filename
Select all filenames	Ctrl+double-click link filename	⌘+double-click link filename

Color Palette

Action	Windows	Mac
Move color sliders in tandem	Shift+drag slider	Shift+drag slider
Select a color for the nonactive fill or stroke	Alt+click color bar	Option+click color bar
Switch among color modes (CMYK, RGB, LAB)	Shift+click color bar	Shift+click color bar

Separation and Preview Palette

Action	Windows	Mac
Turn on Overprint preview	Ctrl+Alt+Shift+Y	⌘+Option+Shift+Y
Show all plates	Ctrl+Alt+Shift+~ (tilde)	⌘+Option+Shift+~ (tilde)
Show Cyan plate	Ctrl+Alt+Shift+1	⌘+Option+Shift+1
Show Magenta plate	Ctrl+Alt+Shift+2	⌘+Option+Shift+2
Show Yellow plate	Ctrl+Alt+Shift+3	⌘+Option+Shift+3
Show Black plate	Ctrl+Alt+Shift+4	⌘+Option+Shift+4
Show 1st Spot plate	Ctrl+Alt+Shift+5	⌘+Option+Shift+5
Show 2nd Spot plate	Ctrl+Alt+Shift+6	⌘+Option+Shift+6
Show 3rd Spot plate	Ctrl+Alt+Shift+7	⌘+Option+Shift+7
Show 4th Spot plate	Ctrl+Alt+Shift+8	⌘+Option+Shift+8
Show 5th Spot plate	Ctrl+Alt+Shift+9	⌘+Option+Shift+9

Swatches Palette

Action	Windows	Mac
Create new swatch based on the current swatch	Alt+click New Swatch button	Option+click New Swatch button
Create spot color swatch based on the current swatch	Alt+Ctrl+click New Swatch button	Option+⌘+click New Swatch button
Change options without applying swatch	Shift+Alt+Ctrl+double-click swatch	Shift+Option+⌘+double-click swatch

InDesign: Transform Palette

Action	Windows	Mac
Apply value and copy object	Alt+Enter	Option+Enter
Apply width, height, or scale value proportionally	Ctrl+Enter	⌘+Enter

Adobe GoLive

GoLive doesn't actually have a toolbox. The palette on the left looks like a toolbar, but it's actually an Objects palette used via drag and drop. Keyboard shortcuts are used to access various palette options.

Working in Document Windows

Action	Windows	Mac
Close a window without saving		⌘+D
Duplicate selected object	Ctrl+drag	Option+drag
Move boxes in Layout Grid (by pixel)	Ctrl+Alt+Left Arrow, Right Arrow, Up Arrow, or Down Arrow	Option+Left Arrow, Right Arrow, Up Arrow, or Down Arrow
Move boxes based on Snap-to-Grid setting	Left Arrow, Right Arrow, Up Arrow, or Down Arrow	Left Arrow, Right Arrow, Up Arrow, or Down Arrow
Show next window in workspace	Ctrl+Tab	No Mac equivalent
Show previous window in workspace	Shift+Ctrl+Tab	No Mac equivalent
Change focus to Text Inspector Link field	No Windows equivalent	With cursor in Document window, ⌘+, (comma)
Change focus to Document window	No Windows equivalent	With cursor in Text Inspector, ⌘+; (semicolon)

Handling Text

Action	Windows	Mac
Cursor to beginning of current word	Ctrl+Left Arrow	Option+Left Arrow
Cursor to next word	Ctrl+Right Arrow	Option+Right Arrow
Cursor to beginning/end of line	Home	⌘+Left Arrow
Cursor to end of line	End	⌘+Right Arrow
Select a word	Double-click	Double-click

Continued

Handling Text *(continued)*

Action	Windows	Mac
Select a line	Triple-click	Triple-click
Select a paragraph	Quadruple-click	Quadruple-click
Increase selection	Shift+Left Arrow, Right Arrow, Up Arrow, or Down Arrow	Shift+Left Arrow, Right Arrow, Up Arrow, or Down Arrow
Select to beginning of line	Shift+Home	⌘+Shift+Left Arrow
Select to end of line	Shift+End	⌘+Shift+ Right Arrow
New line instead of paragraph	Shift+Enter	Shift+Return
Nonbreaking space	Shift+Spacebar	Option+Spacebar
Insert word break tag `<WBR>`, enabling the browser to hyphenate the work at the point of insertion	Ctrl+dash	

Handling Source Code

Action	Windows	Mac
Cursor to next word	Ctrl+Right Arrow	Option+Right Arrow
Cursor to preceding word	Ctrl+Left Arrow	Option+Left Arrow
Cursor to beginning of line	Home	⌘+Left Arrow
Cursor to end of line	End	⌘+Right Arrow
Select a word	Double-click	Double-click
Select a line	Triple-click	Triple-click
Decrease selection one character	Shift+Left Arrow	Shift+Left Arrow
Increase selection one character	Shift+Right Arrow	Shift+Right Arrow
Decrease selection one word	Ctrl+Shift+Left Arrow	Option+Shift+Left Arrow
Increase selection one word	Ctrl+Shift+Right Arrow	Option+Shift+Right Arrow
Decrease selection one line	Shift+Up Arrow	Shift+Up Arrow
Increase selection one line	Shift+Down Arrow	Shift+Down Arrow
Decrease selection to beginning of source code	Home+Shift+Up Arrow	⌘+Shift+Up Arrow
Decrease selection to end of source code	Home+Shift+Down Arrow	⌘+Shift+Down Arrow
Increase selection to beginning of source code	End+Shift+Up Arrow	⌘+Shift+Up Arrow
Increase selection to end of source code	End+Shift+Down Arrow	⌘ +Shift+Down Arrow

Using Site Window

Action	Windows	Mac
Activate tab on drag and drop	Move over tab while dragging	Move over tab while dragging
Locate file in Explorer	Right-click file, choose Open/Reveal in Explorer in the context menu	@@Control+click > Open > Reveal in Finder.
Show properties information for object	Right-click file, choose Open/Show Properties	Ctrl+click file, choose Open/Show Properties

GoLive: Links/Navigation View in Site Window

Action	Windows	Mac OS
Select next file in x-direction	Left Arrow, Right Arrow, Up Arrow, or Down Arrow	Left Arrow, Right Arrow, Up Arrow, or Down Arrow
Start a partial tree from selection	Ctrl+Up Arrow	⌘+Up Arrow
Toggle Expand button (hide/show children)	Ctrl+Down Arrow	⌘+Down Arrow
Add parent to selection	Shift+Up Arrow	Shift+Up Arrow
Add children to selection	Shift+Down Arrow	Shift+Down Arrow
Select previous sibling or jump to nearest item to the left of selection	Ctrl+Left Arrow	Option+Left Arrow
Select next sibling or jump to nearest item to the right of selection	Ctrl+Right Arrow	Option+Right Arrow
Select the closest item above selection	Ctrl+Up Arrow	Option+Up Arrow
Select the closest item below selection	Ctrl+Down Arrow	Option+Down Arrow
Toggle partial tree from selection and move to center	Esc	Esc
Select top-level references	Ctrl+Home	⌘+Home
Select first sibling	Home	Home
Select last sibling	End	End
Open the selected references	Enter or double-click	Return or double-click
Hand tool for scrolling	Spacebar	Spacebar
Select the reference with matching text	Type any characters	Type any characters
Zoom toggle (between 100% and 200%)	Shift+click	Option+click
Create a "zoom box" (when the mouse is released, the selected region zooms to fit the screen)	Shift+drag	Option+drag

Handling Tags in the Outline Editor

Action	Windows	Mac
Expand or collapse the selected tag	Enter (numerical keypad)	Return
Recursively expand or collapse the selected tag	Shift+Enter (numerical keypad)	Option+Return
Show or hide the tag attribute list	Enter (numerical keypad)	Enter
Recursively show or hide the tag attribute list	Shift+Enter (numerical keypad)	Option+Enter
Activate the next text box	Tab	Tab
Activate the preceding text box	Shift+Tab	Shift+Tab
Activate the Tag Selection pop-up menu	Ctrl+click tag name	⌘+click tag name

Timeline DHTML

Action	Windows	Mac
Select next keyframe	Right Arrow	Right Arrow
Select previous keyframe	Left Arrow	Left Arrow
Select next track	Down Arrow	Down Arrow
Select previous track	Up Arrow	Up Arrow
Play a scene beginning at the current time cursor location	Enter (numerical keypad)	Enter (numerical keypad)
Stop scene playback	0 (numerical keypad)	0 (numerical keypad)
Create a new keyframe	Ctrl+click a time track	⌘+click a time track
Duplicate a keyframe	Alt+drag keyframe	Option+drag keyframe
Create an action placeholder	Ctrl+click action on action track	⌘+click action on action track
Scale an animation while maintaining the relative time positions of all keyframes on the same time track	Ctrl+Shift+drag	Control+drag

Using Tables in Layout View

Action	Windows	Mac
Change height and width of a row or column	Alt+resize	Option+resize
Select cells	Click cell border	Click cell border
Select multiple adjacent cells	Click+drag	Click+drag
Select multiple nonadjacent cells	Shift+click additional cells	Shift+click additional cells
Select all cells in column	Click top edge of column	Click top edge of column
Select all cells in row	Click left edge of row	Click left edge of row
Add row above	*	*
Add columns to the left	+	+
Add columns to the right	-	-
Interactively add cells and rows	Ctrl+Shift+drag bottom/right edge of table	⌘+drag bottom/right edge of table
Delete current column	Ctrl+Del	Backspace
Delete current row	Shift+Ctrl+Del	Shift+Backspace
Span columns, joining current cell with cell to the right	Shift+Right Arrow	Shift+Right Arrow
Reduce column span, splitting the current cell	Shift+Left Arrow	Shift+Left Arrow
Span rows, joining current cell with cell below	Shift+Down Arrow	Shift+Down Arrow
Reduce row span, splitting the current cell	Shift+Up Arrow	Shift+Up Arrow
Move text cursor to next cell to the right	Tab	Tab
Move text cursor to next cell to the left	Shift+Tab	Shift+Tab
Switch from Text Entry to Cell Selection mode	Ctrl+Enter	Ctrl+Return

Using QuickTime Editor

Action	Windows	Mac
Select keyframe of the upper or lower tracks and samples displayed in the Timeline window	Up Arrow or Down Arrow	Up Arrow or Down Arrow
In the Track Content area, select previous or next sample	Left Arrow or Right Arrow	Left Arrow or Right Arrow
In the Track Content area, select upper or lower sample or track	Up Arrow or Down Arrow	Up Arrow or Down Arrow
In the Track List area, select upper or lower track	Up Arrow or Down Arrow	Up Arrow or Down Arrow
In the Track Ruler area, step forward or backward	Right Arrow or Left Arrow	Right Arrow or Left Arrow
Drag and copy track	Ctrl+drag in the Content or List area	Option+drag in the List area
Create keyframe sample of a sprite	Ctrl+click	⌘+click
Drag and copy keyframe sample of a sprite		Option+drag in Content area
Select next time marker	Shift+Right Arrow or Left Arrow	Shift+Right Arrow or Left Arrow
Open or close tracks, subtracks	Ctrl+Up Arrow or Down Arrow	⌘+Up Arrow or Down Arrow
Scale sample time	Shift+drag	Shift+drag
Jump to start or end of movie in timeline	Ctrl+Left Arrow or Right Arrow	⌘+Left Arrow or Right Arrow

Working with Links

Action	Windows	Mac
Create new link (works only for linking text, not linking images).	Select item+Alt+drag to desired destination. Release mouse when the object highlights.	Select item+⌘+drag to desired destination. Release mouse when the object highlights.
Link text with desired content file.	Ctrl+drag to desired page in site window	⌘+drag to desired page in site window

Adobe Acrobat

Acrobat by default doesn't permit you to use keyboard shortcuts for tool access unless you adjust a preference setting. When first launching Acrobat and adjusting your work environment, open the Preferences dialog box (Adobe Acrobat ➪ Preferences on the Mac or Edit ➪ Preferences on Windows or Ctrl/⌘+F). Select General in the left pane and select the Use Single Key Accelerators to Access Tools check box. Only when the check box is checked are you able to use keyboard shortcuts to access tools.

Basic Commands

Action	Windows	Mac
Close	Ctrl+W	⌘+W
Close all open documents	Ctrl+Alt+W	⌘+Option+W
Close dialog box (Cancel)	Esc	Esc or ⌘+. (period)
Compress PDF file size	Ctrl+Shift+C	⌘+Shift+C
Create PDF from file	Ctrl+N	⌘+N
Open	Ctrl+O	⌘+O
Open Context menu	Right-click or Shift+F10	Control+click
Open Document Properties dialog box	Ctrl+D	⌘+D
Open Help document	F1	F1
Open/Close How To menu	F4	F4
Open Preferences dialog box	Ctrl+K	⌘+K
Open Web page	Ctrl+Shift+O	⌘+Shift+O
Print Setup	Ctrl+Shift+P	⌘+Shift+P
Print	Ctrl+P	⌘+P
Print with comments	Ctrl+T	⌘+T
PrintMe Internet Printing	Alt+Ctrl+P	⌘+Option+P
Quit	Ctrl+Q	⌘+Q
Save	Ctrl+S	⌘+S
Save As	Ctrl+Shift+S	⌘+Shift+S
Spell Checker	F7	F7
Undo	Ctrl+Z	⌘+Z

Selecting Tools

Tool	Windows	Mac
Article tool	A	A
Attachment tool	J	J
Cycle through Attachment tools (when an Attachment tool is active)	Shift+J	Shift+J
Form tool	F	F
Cycle through Form tools	Shift+F	Shift+F
Graphics Markup tool	U	U
Cycle through Graphics Markup tools (when a Graphic Markup tool is active)	Shift+U	Shift+U
Snapshot tool	G	G
Hand tool	H	H
Hand tool temporary select when another tool is active	Spacebar	Spacebar
Link tool	L	L
Movie tool	M	M
Note tool	S	S
Cycle through Note tools (when a Note tool is active)	Shift+S	Shift+S
Pencil tool	N	N
Cycle through Comment tools	Shift+N	Shift+N
Select Object tool	O	O
Sound tool	Shift+ M	Shift+M
Highlight Text tool	U	U
Cycle through Highlight tools		
Select Text tool	V	V
Cycle through Selection tools	Shift+V	Shift+V
TouchUp Text tool	T	T
Cycle through TouchUp tools	Shift+T	Shift+T
Zoom In tool	Z	Z
Zoom Out tool	Shift+Z	Shift+Z

Editing Tools

Action	Windows	Mac
Cut	Ctrl+X	⌘+X
Copy	Ctrl+C	⌘+C
Create Bookmark	Ctrl+B	⌘+B
Delete Pages	Ctrl+Shift+D	⌘+Shift+D
Deselect All	Ctrl+Shift+A	⌘+Shift+A
Insert Pages	Ctrl+Shift+I	⌘+Shift+I
JavaScript Debugger (Console)	Ctrl+J	⌘+J
Paste	Ctrl+V	⌘+V
Rotate Clockwise	Ctrl+Shift++ (plus)	⌘+Shift++ (plus)
Rotate Counterclockwise	Ctrl+Shift+− (minus)	⌘+Shift+− (minus)
Rotate Pages	Ctrl+Shift+R	⌘+R
Select All	Ctrl+A	⌘+A
Crop Pages	Ctrl+Shift+T	

Search Tools

Action	Windows	Mac
Find	Ctrl+F	⌘+F
Find Again	Ctrl+G or F3	⌘+G
Query (Search)	Ctrl+Shift+F	⌘+Shift+F
Find Again Going Backwards	Ctrl+Shift+G	⌘+Shift+G
Select Indexes	Ctrl+Shift+X	⌘+Shift+X
Next Search Action (Document)	Ctrl+]	⌘+Shift+]
Previous Search Action (Document)	Ctrl+[	⌘+Shift+[
Word Assistant	Ctrl+Shift+W	⌘+Shift+W

Viewing and Navigation Tools

Action	Windows	Mac
Accessibility Quick Check	Ctrl+Alt+Q	⌘+Option+Q
Actual Size	Ctrl+1	⌘+1
Auto Scrolling	Ctrl+Alt+A	⌘+Option+A
Cascade Windows	Ctrl+Shift+J	⌘+Shift+J
Display Restrictions and Security	Ctrl+Alt+S	⌘+Option+S
Grid Show/Hide	Ctrl+U	⌘+U
Grid Snap To	Ctrl+Shift+U	⌘+Shift+U
First Page	Home or Ctrl+Shift+Page Up	Home or Ctrl+Shift+Page Up
Fit Page in Document Pane	Ctrl+0	⌘+0
Fit Width	Ctrl+2	⌘+2
Fit Visible	Ctrl+3	⌘+3
Full Screen Show	Ctrl+L	⌘+L
Full Screen Hide/Off	Esc or Ctrl+L	Esc or ⌘+L
Go to Page	Alt+Ctrl+N	⌘+N
Last Page	End or Ctrl+Shift+ Page Down	End or Control+Shift+ Page Down
Move Focus to Menus	F10, Arrow Keys	
Move Focus to Toolbar	Alt, Ctrl+Tab	
Navigation Pane/Document Pane Toggle View	F6	Shift+F6
Next Document	Alt+Shift+Right Arrow	⌘+Shift+Right Arrow
Next Document	Alt+Shift+Right Arrow	⌘+Shift+Right Arrow
Next Floating Window	Alt+F6	
Next Field	Tab	Tab
Next Page	Page Down or Right Arrow	Page Down or Right Arrow
Next Tab in Navigation Pane	Ctrl+Tab	⌘+Tab
Next View	Alt+Right Arrow	⌘+Right Arrow
Next Window	Ctrl+F6	
Overprint Preview	Ctrl+Alt+Shift+Y	⌘+Option+Shift+Y
Previous Document	Alt+Shift+Left Arrow	⌘+Shift+Left Arrow
Previous Field	Shift+Tab	Shift+Tab
Previous Page	Page Up or Left Arrow	Page Up or Left Arrow

Action	Windows	Mac
Previous View	Alt+Left Arrow	⌘+Left Arrow
Proof Colors	Ctrl+Y	⌘+Y
Reflow Text	Ctrl+4	⌘+4
Rulers Show/Hide	Ctrl+R	⌘+R
Scroll Up	Up Arrow	Up Arrow
Scroll Down	Down Arrow	Down Arrow
Show/Hide Pages Tab when Pages tab is selected	F6	F6
Show/Hide Bookmarks by default	F6	F6
Show/Hide Toolbars	F8	F8
Show/Hide Menu Bar	F9	F9
Show/Hide Navigation Pane	F6	F6
Split Vertical	Shift+F12	Shift+F12
Split Off	Shift+F12	Shift+F12
Tile Horizontally	Ctrl+Shift+K	⌘+Shift+K
Tile Vertically	Ctrl+Shift+L	⌘+Shift+L
Toggle Toolbars	Ctrl+Tab	
Use Local Fonts	Ctrl+Shift+Y	⌘+Shift+Y
Zoom In	Ctrl++ (plus)	⌘++ (plus)
Zoom Out	Ctrl+- (minus)	⌘+- (minus)
Zoom To	Ctrl+M	⌘+M
Zoom In temporary access to Zoom in tool	Ctrl+Spacebar	⌘+Spacebar
Zoom Out temporary access to Zoom Out tool	Ctrl+Alt+Spacebar	⌘+Option+Spacebar

✦　　✦　　✦

Index

Symbols and Numerics

Continued

Continued

Continued

Continued

Continued

Continued

Continued